Handbook of the
Psychology of
Women and Gender

Handbook of the Psychology of Women and Gender

Edited by Rhoda K. Unger

John Wiley & Sons, Inc.

New York • Chichester • Weinheim • Brisbane • Singapore • Toronto

Library of Congress Cataloging-in-Publication Data:

Handbook of the psychology of women and gender / edited by Rhoda K. Unger.

    p.   cm.
  ISBN 0-471-33332-8 (cloth : alk. paper)
  1. Women—Psychology. 2. Gender identity. I. Unger, Rhoda Kesler.
HQ1206.H36 2001
155.3'3—dc21   00-039277

Printed in the United States of America.

10 9 8 7 6 5 4 3 2 1

Preface

When I was a graduate student there was no area identified as the "psychology of women and gender." Women were not studied except as a deficient group who deviated from norms developed from the study of men. Sex, when it was not considered a nuisance variable, was consigned (along with race and, occasionally, social class) to the realm of individual differences—a subfield with little theoretical justification. "Gender" as a descriptor of the non-biological aspects of human females and males had not yet entered the psychological vocabulary.

The area has become increasingly visible in recent years. For example, the most recent edition of the *Handbook of Social Psychology* included an extensive chapter on gender. A special issue of the *Journal of Social Issues* on the significance of gender was also published recently. Researchers and scholars who were involved in these projects have also contributed to the present volume.

Besides the material published in traditional areas such as social, personality, and developmental psychology, there are three major journals that focus on women and gender. Despite the budget crunch for purchasing new media, the *Psychology of Women Quarterly, Sex Roles,* and *Feminism & Psychology* (an international journal) may be found in many university libraries. Many citations to these journals are included in chapters of this handbook.

More than half the universities in the United States currently offer psychology courses with women in the title, and many are adding courses on gender to their curriculum as well. The area is also a favored one for research by graduate students who often need citations which are not available from faculty at their own institutions. Most universities have only one senior professor who specializes in this area.

Although a number of textbooks, primarily for undergraduates, and several recent books of readings exist, what has been missing from the field is a book that could serve as a current and authoritative source of reference materials for graduate students, faculty in the field, and faculty in more traditional areas whose research and teaching impinge on this area. This handbook was developed to present recent theory in those areas where the most exciting new developments are to be found. However, the construction of a handbook in our subdiscipline is challenging because a wide range of theoretical perspectives coexists within it which influences both the kind of questions asked and the terminology used to ask them. For example, one can look at belief systems based on gender in terms of stereotypes, images, or representations. Researchers who use one of these terms are also making a statement about the context with which they deal (ranging from the laboratory to the culture as whole) as well as the kind of research methodology they prefer (the quantitative/qualitative distinction is important here). Similarly, there is no consensus in the field about the extent of differences between the sexes or, even, whether or not this is a useful question to ask.

This first handbook takes into account the wide variety of perspectives within the field. It takes a synthetic approach—drawing on scholars who are both knowledgeable about an area and who are willing to offer a balanced view of current theory and research without sacrificing their own viewpoint. Readers should not, therefore, be surprised that a number of the chapter titles include the word "feminist." Their authors, like myself, are committed to a reflexive stance that acknowledges one's own viewpoint and recognizes that all scholarship stems from a particular standpoint. This position is set out fully in several chapters of the handbook.

A more difficult gap to bridge is that between empiricist and postmodern perspectives that often dictate what kind of methodology one uses as well as how one talks about one's findings. I have tried to include experts who are knowledgeable about the wide range of perspectives within each content area. I did not, however, limit contributors' preferred style and language. Readers will find chapters that are traditionally empirical in tone and others that utilize postmodern language and methodology. In part, these differences reflect the preferred mode of inquiry in particular content areas, but they also illustrate how scholarship is enhanced when all theoretical positions are taken into account. In keeping with this theme of communication across boundaries, scholars from Canada and the United Kingdom have contributed chapters. They bring with them resources and insights that are new to many U.S. readers.

One of the most important insights of this new psychology is the recognition that sex and gender do not influence women's and men's behavior in isolation from other socially constructed categories. Each contributor to this handbook was asked to be sensitive to both multicultural and cross-cultural perspectives. They drew on the newer scholarship of sexual orientation, race/ethnicity, and social class to illustrate how these variables braid with each other as well as with gender. In other words, the chapters examine women and girls (and, sometimes, men and boys) in their particular social milieu. This inclusivity provides a rich portrait of lives in context.

As it has grown, the field has become more sophisticated. We now recognize that biological as well as social factors may influence some gendered behaviors. Thus, chapters on biological influence and evolutionary perspectives have been included in the handbook. We also recognize that sex and gender should be studied on many levels of analysis including intrapsychic, interpersonal, socio-structural, and cultural domains. Processes that unfold at each of these levels also interact with each other. There is nothing simple about sex and gender.

As much as possible, the handbook is organized around levels of analysis. The first section is on historical, theoretical, and methodological issues. It includes chapters that explore the disciplinary origin of our current study of women and gender and its relationship to the history of women psychologists, current important theoretical perspectives within the field and how these perspectives lead to different questions, and how choices about both quantitative and qualitative methodologies affect the strengths and weaknesses of our research. Other chapters in this section provide both a critique and positive alternatives to current thinking about women and gender. They explore feminist alternatives to evolutionary psychology, a balanced view of questions about gender similarities and differences; and a synthesis of various sources of personal and social identity in a rich historical context.

The second section of this handbook explores developmental issues throughout the lifespan. One chapter looks at biological factors that may predispose (but not predetermine) gender-characteristic behaviors in boys and girls. Another chapter explores the many kinds of information about gender that children learn and how such learning is assisted by parents and peers. A third chapter explores adolescence as a locus of gender intensification and as a problematic area for girls. Still other chapters examine family and work roles for women and the uniquely female role of mother and mothering. A final chapter in this section looks at gender and old age. These chapters make it clear that there is no period in human development that is gender neutral.

The third section of this handbook examines social roles and social systems. The first chapter in this section shows that gender is not just about women. The authors demonstrate how traditionally masculine roles are harmful to men as well as to women. Other chapters explore changing perceptions about what we want women and men to be and how people communicate their views in language, nonverbal behaviors, and gendered social interactions and relationships. The final chapter in this section integrates the literature on sexual orientation and gender.

The next section of this handbook is on gender and physical and mental health. The first chapter focuses on physical illnesses that are more common to women than to men and explores the societal factors that may produce sex-related differences. The following three chapters in the section look at various aspects of mental health. One explores the current framework of psychological diagnosis, one explores feminist therapy, and one looks at sociocultural issues that are particularly salient in the treatment of women of color. These chapters should be particularly useful to clinical and counseling psychologists as well as researchers interested in the negative impact of racism and sexism on individuals.

The final section of the handbook looks at gender as a systemic phenomenon. The first chapter in this section focuses on power and gender. Using sophisticated social psychological experiments, the authors unveil U.S. men's ambivalence about women. The next chapter looks at all facets of sexual harassment. Its authors review the large number of factors that influence harassment ranging from individual beliefs, through the structure of organizations, to aspects of the law. Similarly, the next chapter explores other forms of violence against women using a developmental perspective. The fourth chapter in this section delineates a richly textured analysis of responsibility, showing how it is gendered in ways that victimize women in their personal and social roles and in their interactions with the law. A final chapter explores the historical/developmental context of personal change and social activism. All of these chapters combine to provide a detailed look at individual behavior in sociocultural context.

This volume seems to me to be more exciting than the usual handbook. The contributors—all noted scholars and researchers—responded to the opportunity to be part of the first handbook in the area by developing theoretically sophisticated analyses in addition to extensive reviews of the current literature. Many of these reviews span several disciplines and are particularly timely because all of the contributors are active researchers in the field. I want to thank all of them for their hard work and the rich insights they have provided for experienced as well as new readers. I also want to thank my editor, Jennifer Simon, for her encouragement and enthusiasm about the project. It would not have been done without her.

This book transcends traditional distinctions in the field and brings together a group of contributors with great expertise and eclectic perspectives. They provide depth and breadth of knowledge in a large number of content areas, as well as the ability to communicate and the willingness to take into account work from different theoretical perspectives and methodologies than their own. These researchers are also able to communicate clearly with those who may be unfamiliar with scholarly work in this area. They offer readers current and detailed coverage of an exciting and evolving field.

I hope this handbook will facilitate a more complete understanding of the complex issues and concerns of psychologists interested in women and gender. The dynamic tension produced by competing methodologies and theoretical understandings makes this field exciting and contributes to its strength. I expect that you will learn a great deal from these chapters, as I have.

RHODA UNGER

About the Contributors

Barrie Bondurant is assistant professor of psychology at Lyon College. She received her PhD in social psychology from the University of North Carolina at Greensboro where she worked with Jacqueline White. She has been actively involved in scholarly, campus, and community efforts to understand and prevent violence against women for the past fifteen years. Her research and writing center on interpersonal aggression including sexual assault, physical violence, and sexual harassment.

Lyn Mikel Brown is associate professor of education, human development, and women's studies at Colby College. She is currently working on a book about adolescent girls' friendships. She is author of *Meeting at the Crossroads: Women's Psychology and Girls' Development* (with Carol Gilligan, 1992) and *Raising Their Voices: The Politics of Girls' Anger* (1998) as well as numerous articles on girls' development and education and feminist research methods.

Silvia Sara Canetto is an associate professor of psychology at Colorado State University. She has graduate degrees from the University of Padova (Italy) and the Hebrew University (Jerusalem, Israel). She also has a PhD in clinical psychology from the older adult program at Northwestern University. She is the author of over 60 articles and chapters, mostly on gender and suicidal behavior. She is the coeditor of the first and second volumes of the *Review of Suicidology* and of the book *Women and Suicidal Behavior* (1995). Her contributions to suicide research were recognized by the Shneidman Award of the American Association of Suicidology in 1997.

Sarah Carney is a graduate student in the social-personality subprogram at the City University of New York, Graduate Center. Her doctoral research is on the construction of legal narratives.

Joan C. Chrisler is professor of psychology at Connecticut College. She has published extensively on the psychology of women and gender and is best known for her work on women's health, especially for her work on menstruation, menopause, weight and eating disorders, and coping with chronic illness. She is coeditor of several books including: *Arming Athena: Career Strategies for Women in Academe* (1998) and *Lectures on the Psychology of Women* (2000).

Elizabeth R. Cole is an associate professor of psychology, women's studies, and African American studies at the University of Michigan. She received her PhD in personality psychology from the University of Michigan. She is the coauthor of *Speaking of Abortion: Television and Authority in the Lives of Women* (1998). Her research is concerned with the relationship between social identity and political thought and action, particularly among women and African Americans.

Mary Crawford is professor of psychology and director of women's studies at the University of Connecticut. She has spoken and written about women's issues for audiences as diverse as the British Psychological Society and the Oprah Winfrey Show. She has authored or coedited a number of books including: *Gender and Thought: Psychological Perspectives* (1989), *Talking Difference: On Gender and Language* (1995), *Gender Differences in Human Cognition* (1997), *In Our Own Words* (1997), *Coming into her Own: Educational Success in Girls and Women* (1999), *Women and Gender: A Feminist Psychology* (2000), and the recently published *Innovative Methods for Feminist Psychological Work* (2000).

Kay Deaux is distinguished professor of psychology and women's studies at the Graduate Center of the City University of New York. Her areas of research interest include stereotypes and discrimination, gender-related behaviors, and social identification. She has served as president of the American Psychological Society and has been active in a variety of professional organizations. Professor Deaux received her BA from Northwestern University and her PhD from the University of Texas at Austin.

Karen K. Dion, after receiving her PhD from the University of Minnesota, joined the faculty at the University of Toronto where she is now a professor of psychology. In addition to the topic of relationships and interpersonal processes, she also has current research interests in stereotyping and attribution processes, gender and ethnocultural identity, and adult development.

Kenneth L. Dion completed his PhD in psychology at the University of Minnesota and then joined the faculty of the University of Toronto where he is currently a professor of psychology. In addition to the topic of gender and relationships, his research interests include the social psychology of prejudice and discrimination, ethnicity, language, stereotyping, group and intergroup processes, acculturation, and immigration. He is also interested in research methodology and quantitative approaches in social research.

Patricia N.L. Donat is assistant professor of psychology at Mississippi University for Women. Her research and scholarly writing have focused on the area of gender and aggression. She has taught psychology of women for over five years and has received awards for her innovation in teaching and inclusion of diversity.

Robert S. Done received his PhD from the University of Arizona in 2000. His current research examines personality characteristics of those who engage in deviant behavior in organizations.

Lauren E. Duncan is an assistant professor of psychology at Smith College. She received her PhD in personality psychology and a graduate certificate in women's studies from the University of Michigan in 1995. Her research focuses on the effects of social events on women's lives and on the development of feminist consciousness and women's rights activism.

Julia A. Eichstedt received her BS in psychology in 1995 from the University of Toronto and her MA in 1997 from Concordia University in Montreal. She is currently completing her doctoral studies at Concordia under the supervision of Dr. Lisa Serbin. Her current research focuses on the development of gender concepts in infancy.

Michelle Fine is a professor of social psychology and women's studies at the Graduate Center of the City University of New York. Her most recent books include: *The Unknown City,* 1998 (with Lois Weis), *Off-White,* 1997 (with Linda Powell, Lois Weis, and Mun Wong), and *Becoming Gentlemen,* 1997 (with Lani Guinier and Jane Balin). Her most recent research is with incarcerated women, studying the impact of college on the women, their children, and the prison environment.

Susan T. Fiske, is a professor of psychology at Princeton University. She has taught at the University of Massachusetts, Amherst and at Carnegie-Mellon University. A Harvard BS and PhD, she has authored over 100 journal articles and book chapters. Her edited books include: *The Handbook of Social Psychology,* 1998 (with Gilbert and Lindzey) and *The Annual Review of Psychology* (with Schachter and Zahn-Waxler). Her graduate text with Shelley Taylor, *Social Cognition* (1984, 2nd ed., 1991), defined the subfield of how people think about and make sense of other people. Her federally funded social cognition research focuses on social structure, motivation, and stereotyping, which led to expert testimony cited by the U.S. Supreme Court in the first sex discrimination case to use social science research.

Lucia Albino Gilbert is vice provost, former director of the Center for Women's Studies, and professor of educational psychology at the University of Texas at Austin. She studies two-earner families, women's career development, and gender processes in adolescence. She is the author of four books and numerous articles and the recipient of awards for teaching and research excellence, including the Carolyn Wood Sherif Award recognizing her contributions to the field of the psychology of women as a scholar, teacher, and mentor.

Glenn E. Good is associate professor and director of the APA-accredited Counseling Psychology program at the University of Missouri-Columbia. He has provided more than 100 presentations at national and international conferences and has authored more than 50 scholarly articles and books. He is coeditor (with Gary Brooks) of *The Handbook of Counseling and Psychotherapy Approaches for Men* (in press) and coeditor of *The Handbook of Counseling and Psychotherapy with Men* (1987). His research has documented the detrimental consequences of masculine gender roles on men's mental health. He has served as president of the Society for the Psychological Study of Men and Masculinity and has been a recipient of that organization's Researcher of the Year Award as well as the Kathryn Hopwood Award for meritorious contributions to counseling psychology.

Stephanie A. Goodwin, visiting research fellow, Yale University, has taught at Boston College. A 1997 graduate of the University of Massachusetts, Amherst doctoral program in social and personality psychology, she received the American Psychological Association Doctoral Dissertation Award and the Association of Women in Science's National Merit Award for her dissertation research investigating the role of power in stereotyping. She currently holds a National Science Foundation grant to investigate the effects of social power on implicit cognitive processes.

Patricia Adair Gowaty is a professor of ecology at the Institute of Ecology, University of Georgia. She is a behavioral ecologist who studies fitness dynamics of individuals to understand social behavior evolution of birds and flies. She has had a long-term interest in the intellectual interaction between feminism and evolutionary biology. She is first president-elect of the Animal Behavior Society and past associate editor of *Evolution, American Naturalist,* and *Animal Behaviour.*

Barbara Gutek is McClelland professor in the University of Arizona's Department of Management and Policy, where she served as head from 1993–1999. Gutek had published over 90 articles and chapters and 12 books including *Sex and the Workplace* (1985) and *Demographic Differences in Organizations* (1999). She was president of the Society for the Psychological Study of Social Issues (1997–1998) and served on the Board of Governors of the Academy of Management. In 1994, she received two awards from APA: the Division 35 Heritage Award and the Committee on Women in Psychology Award as a "Distinguished Leader for Women in Psychology."

Dawn Johnson is a doctoral candidate in counseling psychology at the University of Kentucky. She has specialized in feminist therapy, trauma therapy, and evidence-based interventions with women. She is currently working on her dissertation research which investigates the reliability and validity of a measure of personal empowerment and well-being in women as an outcome of therapy.

Meredith M. Kimball is a professor in the Departments of Women's Studies and Psychology at Simon Fraser University and chair of Women's Studies. Her research interests include theories of gender, the history of women in psychology and psychoanalysis, and women in science. Her book *Feminist Visions of Gender Similarities and Differences* (1995) received a Distinguished Publication Award from the Association for Women in Psychology. She has recently published two articles exploring the early history of women and psychoanalysis: one on Freud's seduction theory and another on the life and work of Bertha Pappenheim ('Anna O').

Mary E. Kite is professor of psychological science at Ball State University. Her research interests include gender-associated stereotyping and prejudice, particularly as it relates to antigay prejudice and ageism. She is also interested in the factors that promote and hinder women's success especially in academia and recently explored this question as a member of the American Psychological Association's Task Force on the Status of Women.

Celia Kitzinger is chair in conversational analysis, gender, and sexuality and professor of sociology at the University of York in England. She has published 8 books and over 80 articles and book chapters on issues related to sexualities and gender. She is the recipient of a Distinguished Publication Award from the Association for Women in Psychology for her book, *The Social Construction of Lesbianis* (1987), and a Distinguished Scientific Contribution Award from APA Division 44 for her contributions to lesbian psychology. She is currently the inaugural chair of the British Psychological Society's Lesbian and Gay Psychology Section. Her current research interests are in conversational analysis and on issues involving intersex individuals.

Marianne LaFrance is a professor of psychology and women's studies at Yale University. She formerly taught at Boston College and has written many articles and book chapters on gender and power, nonverbal behavior, and interpersonal perception. With Kay Deaux she contributed the chapter on gender to the most recent edition of the *Handbook of Social and Personality Psychology* (1998).

Jeanne Marecek is a professor of psychology and head of women's studies at Swarthmore College. She is the coauthor (with (Rachel Hare-Mustin) of *Making a Difference: Psychology and the Construction of Gender* (Yale University Press, 1990). She works on theory and meta-theory in psychology, especially the intersections of feminist theory, postmodern thought, and psychology. Trained as a clinical psychologist, she has worked in Sri Lanka for over a decade, studying suicide, gender, and the cultural practices of emotion. Recently, she has been engaged in a discursive study of feminist-identified therapists in collaboration with Diane Kravetz.

Harriette Marshall is professor of critical and feminist psychology at Staffordshire University, Stoke-on-Trent, United Kingdom. Her research interests include identities and identifications; issues around "race," culture, and gender; and the role of psychology in relation to inequalities. Her recent research includes a project on transitions to adulthood, which is examining young people's accounts and visual representations.

Daniela Martin is a doctoral candidate in social-personality psychology at the Graduate Center of the City University of New York. Her research interests focus on identity, culture, and immigration. Among her works are the examinations of identity and motivation in second-language learning, immigrant group perceptions, and the effects of group membership and experiences of discrimination on immigrant assimilation strategies. She is interested in innovative theories and methods to explore issues related to subject positioning within diverse social contexts and the conditions leading to the establishment of positive images of difference.

Diane Poulin-Dubois is an associate professor in the Department of Psychology and a member of the Centre for Research in Human Development at Concordia University. She received her PhD from the Universite de Montreal and completed her postdoctoral training at Harvard and McGill. She has been a visiting professor at Cornell University and Oxford University. She has published numerous articles and book chapters on infants' categorization, social cognition, and lexical development.

Kimberly K. Powlishta received her PhD from Stanford University, working with Eleanor Maccoby, and completed her postdoctoral training at Concordia University. She has been an assistant professor at Northern Illinois University and the University of Massachusetts, Dartmouth and is now a research associate at Washington University in St. Louis. She has published many articles on gender development, intergroup processes, and stereotyping in children. Currently, she is expanding her area of expertise to include adult development and aging, focusing on Alzheimer's Disease.

Vita Carulli Rabinowitz is professor and chairperson of psychology at Hunter College of the City University of New York. She received her doctorate in social psychology from Northwestern University, where she developed a lifelong love of research methodology from Donald Campbell and Thomas Cook. She writes about methodological issues, with a particular focus on gender issues in health and coping research. Her current project is an examination, using qualitative and quantitative methods, of how gender is represented in biomedical research. She is coauthor, with Florence Denmark and Jeri Sechzer, of the recently issued text, *Engendering Psychology* (1999).

Jill Rader is a student in the doctoral program in counseling psychology at the University of Texas at Austin. Her research interests include therapy and gender and sexuality issues in counseling. She was a journalist for a number of years before she returned to graduate school.

Maya G. Sen received her BS from Lewis and Clark College in Portland, Oregon in 1991 and her PhD at the Institute of Child Development at the University of Minnesota under the supervision of Patricia Bauer. She is currently a postdoctoral fellow at the Centre for Research in Human Development at Concordia University, working with Lisa Serbin and Diane Poulin-Dubois.

Lisa A. Serbin completed her PhD at the State University of New York at Stony Brook working with Daniel O'Leary. She is currently the director of the Centre for Research in Human Development and professor of psychology at Concordia University in Montreal. She is the author of numerous research articles on the subjects of gender development in children. She also codirects a longitudinal intergenerational project on psycho-social risk.

Nancy B. Sherrod is currently an advanced doctoral student in the APA-accredited Counseling Psychology program of the Department of Educational and Counseling Psychology at the University of Missouri, Columbia. She majored in psychology at the University of Colorado from which she received her BA summa cum laude. She conducts research in the areas of gender, sexual assault, trauma, stress, and psycho-oncology. She has coauthored articles, book chapters, and presentations at national conferences and has worked for two years as coordinator of the University of Missouri's Rape Education office.

Abigail J. Stewart is professor of psychology and women's studies at the University of Michigan and the former director of the Institute for Research on Women and Gender. Her research has focused on the intersection of gender, individual personality development, and social history and social structure. Along with sociologist Mary Romero, she has published a collection of *Women's Untold Stories* in 1999.

Deborah L. Tolman is senior research scientist and director of the Adolescent Sexuality Project at the Center for Research on Women at Wellesley College. She is currently completing *Dilemmas of Desire: Adolescent Girls' Struggle with/for Sexual Subjectivity*. She is coeditor of *Women, Girls, and Psychotherapy: Reframing Resistance,* 1991 (with Carol Gilligan and Annie Rogers) and *From Subjects to Subjectivities: A Handbook of Interpretive and Participatory Methods* (with Mary Bryden-Miller), and she is the author of numerous articles and book chapters on female adolescents, adolescent sexuality, and research methods.

Rhoda Unger received her PhD in experimental psychology from Harvard University, but quickly became involved in the burgeoning field of the psychology of women and gender. She is the author/editor of eight books in this area including: *Woman: Dependent or Independent Variable?* (with Florence Denmark and published in 1975), *Women, Gender, and Social Psychology* (coedited with Virginia O'Leary and Barbara Wallston), *Representations: Social Constructions of Gender, Women and Gender,* and *In Our Own Words* (both collaborations with Mary Crawford). Her most recent book, *Resisting Gender: Twenty-five Years of Feminist Psychology,* was published in 1998. She has been the recipient of a number of awards including the first Carolyn Wood Sherif Lectureship from Division 35 of APA and two distinguished publication awards and a distinguished career award from the Association for Women in Psychology. She has been president of both Division 35 and the Society for the Psychological Study of Social Issues and currently is the inaugural editor of ASAP—a new electronic journal sponsored by the latter organization. She is professor emerita of psychology at Montclair State University and a resident scholar in women's studies at Brandeis University.

Jacquelyn W. White, professor of psychology at the University of North Carolina at Greensboro, has published numerous articles and book chapters in the area of gender and aggression. Her special research area is violence against women. She is coeditor, with Cheryl Travis, of *Sexuality, Society, and Feminism: Psychological Perspectives on Women* (2000) recently published by the American Psychological Association. She is the editor of the *Psychology of Women Quarterly* and an associate editor for *Aggressive Behavior.* She recently completed a term as director of women's studies at her university and was UNCG's 1996 Senior Research Excellence Award recipient.

Sue Wilkinson is reader in feminism and social psychology in the Department of Social Sciences at Loughborough University, United Kingdom. She is the founding and current editor of the international journal *Feminism & Psychology* and her books include *Feminist Social Psychologies: International Perspectives* (1996), *Feminism and Discourse* (with Celia Kitzinger, 1995), and *Representing the Other* (1996).

Anne Woollett is a professor in the Department of Psychology at the University of East London, United Kingdom, where she teaches developmental and family psychology. She has written on motherhood, mothering, infertility, and women's reproductive health. With Ann Phoenix and Eva Lloyd she edited *Motherhood: Meanings, Practices, and Ideologies* (1991). She is currently engaged in researching young people's ideas about families and family transitions.

Judith Worell is a licensed clinical psychologist and professor emerita at the University of Kentucky. She is a past editor of the *Psychology of Women Quarterly* and has recently coauthored books on feminist therapy, adolescent girls, and the future of feminist psychology. Her current research explores processes and outcomes in feminist therapy, and assessment strategies to support a theoretical model of resilience and positive well-being in women.

Karen Fraser Wyche is an associate professor at the Ehrenkrank School of Social Work, New York University. She received her MSW from the University of Maryland and her PhD in clinical psychology from the University of Missouri, Columbia. Her research, writing, and clinical work focus on culturally appropriate mental health interventions; ethnic and gender identity; resilience and strength in minority women living in stressful life circumstances; and research and training in community based agencies. Currently she is conducting a study of coping among foster parents who are caring for HIV/AIDS diagnosed children.

Alyssa N. Zucker graduated from the University of Michigan in 1998, earning both a doctorate in personality psychology and a graduate certificate in women's studies. She is currently a postdoctoral scholar in the Gender and Mental Health program at the University of Michigan. Her research concerns social identity development and the relationship of feminist identity to political participation and health behaviors.

Kenneth J. Zucker is head of the Child and Adolescent Identity Clinic and senior psychologist in the Child Psychiatry program, Centre for Addiction and Mental Health—Clarke Division, Toronto, Ontario, and associate professor, Departments of Psychology and Psychiatry, University of Toronto.

Contents

Handbook of the
Psychology of
Women and Gender

PART I

HISTORICAL, THEORETICAL, AND METHODOLOGICAL ISSUES

CHAPTER 1

Women as Subjects, Actors, and Agents in the History of Psychology

RHODA K. UNGER

The purpose of this chapter is to provide readers with a brief overview of the history of the psychology of women. This is not as simple as it seems. There are a number of different lenses through which one can examine the history of women and psychology. These include (1) the history of women in psychology (e.g., women as the agents of psychological research), (2) the history of psychology about women (e.g., women as the subjects of theory and research), and (3) the history of organizations concerned with the psychology of women. The definition of the field has also differed, so that even within the English-speaking world (the United Kingdom, Canada, Australia, New Zealand, and the United States) some organizations have defined themselves as being interested in feminist research rather than the psychology of women. Feminist scholarship is not necessarily conducted by women and often examines both women and men. Feminist psychologies exist in a variety of forms as well. Their focus has changed and developed over time (M. Crawford & Marecek, 1989b; Unger, 1998).

Research by and about women is also influenced by the organizational and intellectual climate of the time. This context influences what questions are asked as well as how they are answered. Different questions were posed when women existed as an isolated and invisible minority within psychology than are asked today. Some questions, moreover, "fit" better into the theoretical and disciplinary structure of psychology at a particular time. Some of the questions that were asked by women psychologists in a previous feminist era were erased by official histories of the field (cf. Bohan, 1992a). Yet, some of these questions appear to be surprisingly modern and are still relevant today.

An important question for those interested in history is: Why are some issues seen as vital and compelling and others ignored? At this point, one may move from the history of psychology to critical psychology, which is concerned with the role of values and politics in the creation of knowledge (see D. Fox & Prilleltensky, 1997; Ibanez & Iniguez, 1997). These are issues that feminist psychologists have been concerned with for a long time (cf. C. Sherif, 1979; Unger, 1983; Wallston, 1981). As outsiders, women psychologists looking at psychology looking at women have had much to offer this emerging field.

THE CONSTRUCTION OF WOMEN IN EARLY PSYCHOLOGICAL RESEARCH

Although the study of the psychology of women has been an established subdiscipline within psychology for only 27 years (dating from the establishment of a division of the American Psychological Association devoted to this area in 1973), females have, of course, been studied by psychologists far longer. Most of the early studies were conducted from an individual difference perspective derived from Sir Francis Galton's work in the 19th century. This work had a weak theoretical framework and can justly be called both sexist and racist (cf. S.A. Shields, 1975a;

3

S.J. Gould, 1981; Lewin, 1984). For example, Galton concluded that "women tend in all their capacities to be inferior to men" (cited in Lewin & Wild, 1991, p. 582). He also concluded that people of color were inferior to White English men (sic!), and he measured larger psychological "deficiencies" the more his subjects deviated from his Anglo-Saxon norm (S.J. Gould, 1981).

Women were also the "favored" subjects of psychoanalytic work by Freud and his followers. There have been many excellent critiques of Freud's views of women that I will not repeat here (see Chesler, 1972; Griscom, 1992, Hare-Mustin, 1983; Lakoff, 1990; Lerman, 1986). Most of these critiques focus on Freud's confusion between biological and sociocultural forces and the power he had to force his definitions of reality on his patients. It is noteworthy, however, that one of his female students, Helene Deutsch, wrote the first book titled *The Psychology of Women,* which was published in 1944. In this book, Deutsch focused on the important role of eroticism and motherhood in the lives of women. But, like her mentor, she saw women as narcissistic and as having more vulnerable psyches than men and stressed the idea that masochism was a major source of problems for women.

Early Pioneers in Psychology for Women

It is certainly no accident that critiques of theories of women's inferiority began to emerge early in the 20th century. This was the period of the first wave of political and social feminism in the United States and Great Britain and focused on the demand for voting rights for women. There were, however, few women psychologists who had been trained to make such critiques.

Laurel Furumoto and Elizabeth Scarborough (1986; Scarborough & Furumoto, 1987) have done a great deal of work toward replacing women in psychology's history. They have focused on the first generation of women psychologists in the United States. These include such well-known women as Mary Calkins, who became the first woman president of the American Psychological Association in 1905, and Margaret Floy Washburn, who was elected as that organization's second woman president in 1921. Nevertheless, "They were the only women to serve as president of the APA during its first seventy-nine years. Following Washburn, it was to be fifty years—a full half century—before another woman was elected to that honored office" (Scarborough & Furumoto, 1987, p. 173).

Another illustrious member of this cohort was Christine Ladd-Franklin, whose name is still associated with an important theory of color vision. Ladd-Franklin was 20 years older than Calkins and Washburn and was the only one of the three women who objected to the exclusion of women from collegial networks, especially from an influential group known as The Experimentalists founded by Titchener in 1904. Women were explicitly banned from this group until 1929, when it was reorganized a few years after Titchener's death. Almost no important male psychologists objected to the exclusion of women, even those women who had been their doctoral students (see Scarborough & Furumoto, 1987, for the full story of this shameful episode).

This exclusion from what became known as the Society of Experimental Psychology appears to have had an impact on women psychologists for a long period after it officially ended. Few women were elected to membership in the society and the percentage of women psychologists who became experimentalists remained low. Until the 1980s, there were few women experimental psychologists on the faculty of large research institutions. Both Calkins and Washburn continued their careers as faculty members at exclusively female institutions that focused on undergraduate education. Ladd-Franklin was able to teach an occasional graduate course at Columbia University (where her husband was on the faculty) but was awarded only part-time lectureships and occasionally taught without pay (Scarborough & Furumoto, 1987).

Although these careers may seem lackluster for women psychologists today, other women in this cohort have been even more invisible in histories of psychology. Furomoto and Scarborough (1986) found differences in women's career trajectories to be dependent on whether they had married. Women who married were no longer considered to be professionals and were denied academic appointments of any kind. Women who married other psychologists or men employed in other academic fields were more likely to retain ties to the profession, although they, too, were unlikely to receive university appointments because of nepotism rules. This pattern persisted in later cohorts of women psychologists who were married to prominent men in the field. Such women, many of whom have made impressive contributions to the field, include Leta Hollingworth, Georgene

Seward, Carolyn Sherif, Janet Spence, Helen Astin, and Jeanne Block. Until recently, their work was often attributed to their more well-known husbands (M.D. Bernstein & Russo, 1974).

WOMEN AND THE STUDY OF SEX DIFFERENCES

Because their differences from men were used to exclude them, it is not surprising that those women who continued to conduct experiments were attracted to questions about sex differences. For example, Leta Hollingworth and Helen Montagu examined the hospital weight and length records of 2,000 newborn boys and girls to test the Darwinian hypothesis that males were innately more variable than females. They did not confirm this hypothesis (S.A. Shields, 1975b). Helen Wooley Thompson examined the mental abilities of adult males and females in her doctoral research and repeatedly found more similarities than differences between them (R. Rosenberg, 1982; Scarborough & Furumoto, 1987). These studies remained largely invisible to later generations of researchers. Studies that failed to confirm dominant theories were unlikely to remain part of psychology's official history (Unger, 1979b)

An interest in sex differences continued to engage successful generations of women psychologists. For example, Georgene Seward, an activist on behalf of women in psychology during the period around World War II, later coauthored a little-known book in this area (J.P. Seward & Seward, 1980). Both Anne Anastasi and Leona Tyler, the third and fourth women presidents of APA, who were elected in the early 1970s, were interested in individual differences, although neither appeared to be concerned with gender equality. Only in 1979 did APA elect a woman president, Florence Denmark, with an explicitly feminist agenda. She provocatively titled her presidential address "Psyche: From Rocking the Cradle to Rocking the Boat" (1980).

Even modern work demonstrating sex similarities rather than differences tends to be altered as it becomes part of psychology's official record. For example, Eleanor Maccoby and Carol Jacklin (1974) found few confirmed sex differences and many sex similarities in their landmark survey of sex differences studies. Although this survey is discussed in virtually every introductory psychology textbook, the few sex differences are much more apt to be mentioned than the much more numerous sex similarities (Unger, 1998). A similar bias in favor of sex differences has also been found in textbook discussions of Gilligan's studies on the ethic of care (Hurd & Brabeck, 1997).

THE DEPRESSION, WORLD WAR II, AND DISCRIMINATION AGAINST WOMEN IN PSYCHOLOGY

Although the percentage of female members of APA rose to 18% by 1923, women continued to be excluded from professional roles similar to those of men. Under the guise of maintaining "quality control," APA (prompted by E.G. Boring who had been Titchener's most important doctoral student) instituted a two-tiered membership arrangement in 1926. All the current membership became fellows, but new members became associates who had to be elected to fellow status by the usually all-male council. By the early 1940s, women psychologists recognized that this system had restricted their position within APA. "The statistical evidence was indisputable: while the percentage of women in the society had risen from 18 to 30% between 1923 and 1938, the number of women fellows rose only 1%, from 18 to 19%" (Capshew & Lazlo, 1986, p. 160).

Women psychologists had little opportunity to do the kind of research that was rewarded by their predominantly male professional organization. Few held academic positions. By 1938, 76.3% of the male members of APA held academic positions, compared to only 37.6% of the female members (M.R. Walsh, 1985). Those women who did obtain jobs in academia were concentrated in two areas: educational and child psychology (Rossiter, 1982).

The Great Depression reduced career opportunities for male and female psychologists alike. In fact, one reason for the formation of the Society for the Psychological Study of Social Issues (SPSSI) in 1936 was to find ways to deal with the high unemployment among young psychologists (Stagner, 1986). Although this organization had many progressive views about contemporary political and economic issues (cf. B. Harris, Unger, & Stagner, 1986), it also excluded women from positions of leadership. During its first 25 years, only four women served as officers of SPSSI, and the organization's first woman president, Marie Jahoda, served from 1955 to 1956—almost 20 years after SPSSI's founding (Capshew, 1986; Unger, 1986). A second woman president, Marcia Guttentag, was not elected until 1971.

World War II offered many job opportunities to male psychologists, including testing of recruits, training for special duties such as aviation, and the development of user-friendly wartime technology. Women of course, were, excluded from these activities. They formed an organization called the National Council of Women Psychologists to explore ways that their training and experience could help the war effort. By 1943, the organization had 261 members: 19% of the qualified women psychologists in the United States (M.R. Walsh, 1985). Although the organization was able to gain representation for women on various wartime committees, it was unable to effect any meaningful social change. By the end of the war, fewer than 40 women psychologists had served in the U.S. Armed Forces compared to more than 1,000 of their male counterparts (Capshew & Lazlo, 1986).

Work in and for the armed forces provided men with collegial networks that proved to be very valuable in their later careers. Wartime professional activities, moreover, produced a shift toward more applied and service activities—previously seen as feminine areas of psychology. Women became marginalized in these areas as well, and the war produced a relative erosion in the status of women psychologists. (See Capshew & Lazlo, 1986, for a detailed analysis of gender politics during and after World War II.)

The autobiographical recollections of women in psychology during these years also attest to their marginalization. Several women were employed, for example, as university teachers during World War II and let go once male psychologists were again available (see O'Connell & Russo, 1983). Like the pioneering cohort, many of these women found permanent employment at women's colleges.

A few women continued to explore the reasons for women's low status relative to that of men. Many eminent men in the field agreed that there was indeed a "woman problem," as shown by the underemployment of women psychologists following World War II, but denied that there was any systematic discrimination against women. They believed that women were biologically and culturally unsuited for high-status careers and blamed women themselves for their lack of progress. During the war, however, E.G. Boring (who considered himself the self-appointed gadfly of the APA) collaborated on a series of articles with Alice Bryan, a psychologist who had been unusually successful in having an impact on wartime decision making (Capshew & Lazlo, 1986; M.R. Walsh, 1985).

This collaboration was problematic because Bryan was a feminist and Boring was a conservative in a variety of areas, including the role of women. He believed, however, that their biases would cancel each other out and produce an objective account of the issues involved (Boring, 1961). But although he was able to water down Bryan's assertions in their published articles, Boring felt compelled to write his own view of the "woman problem" a few years later (Boring, 1951). In this article, Boring explained the continuing low status of women in the profession as due to their lack of productivity and unwillingness to work long hours in the laboratory. He considered this to be not sexism but "realism." He recommended that women who sought prestige write books (preferably with general, not specific, themes) and to consider the effect of marriage. Privately, he was more blunt about the impact of marriage: "If married, they have more divided allegiance than the man. If unmarried, they have conflict about being unmarried. Although I did not say that. It seemed too infuriating to say" (Boring, 1951, cited in Capshew & Lazlo, 1986, p. 174). Boring's article marked the end of the public discussion about the role of women psychologists. Feminist protest did not reappear in organized psychology until the late 1960s, when the social climate was more supportive of efforts for social change.

One might ask why more women did not protest their exclusion and why the organizations formed by women psychologists during World War II did not produce meaningful change and ceased to exist shortly afterwards. It seems to me that one of the major problems at this time was the lack of a structural analysis of "the woman problem." Many of the women involved in psychology at this time had internalized societal norms about women's roles and were unable to differentiate between their own problems as individuals and those produced by their membership in a socially marginalized group. For example, Ruth Tolman (who, as the wife of a prominent faculty member at

Berkeley and the sister-in-law of Edward Tolman, was less marginalized than many women psychologists of her time) wrote in a letter to Boring: "I always find it hard to abstract 'being a woman' from being a particular woman and tend to hold responsible my particular idiosyncrasies rather than my sex for the particular arrangements of my life" (1946, cited in Capshew & Lazlo, 1986, p. 177). Mary Henle, another prominent psychologist of this era, also made an explicit statement about this kind of confusion in her autobiography when she discussed the sexism and anti-Semitism that were prevalent in psychology during the depression of the 1930s and later: "It is hard to say whether, as a woman, I had special difficulty in finding employment, though I suppose I did. In addition to the scarcity of positions, anti-Semitism was prevalent and often explicit. Thus, if I did not get a job for which I applied, I could not know for sure whether I lacked the qualifications, or whether it was because I was a woman or Jewish" (1983, p. 227).

One of the major differences between the 1940s and the 1960s was the lack of a network of women who could share stories of injustices and recognize them as general rather than particular problems. One of the few women who recognized the structural nature of sexism was Georgene Seward, who wrote a number of articles and books with such titles as *Sex and the Social Order* (1946) and "Race, Sex, and Democratic Living" (G.H. Seward & Clark, 1945). Seward's understanding of the generic nature of prejudice may have been facilitated by the fact that she had been a student of Leta Hollingworth. However, because few women were involved in graduate training, there was little opportunity for similar "female dynasties" to emerge. There was no one left to inform younger women of this history that had largely been written out of formal histories of the field.

In the United States at least, there have been many efforts to recover women in the history of psychology (see, e.g., Bohan, 1992a; O'Connell & Russo, 1991). Of necessity, this chapter sketches only the general outline of the role of women psychologists in the field as a whole. However, a number of more specialized histories of women in particular subdisciplines of psychology also exist. These include the history of women in social psychology (compare, e.g., Berscheid, 1992, and Lott, 1991b, for nonfeminist and feminist versions of this history), clinical psychology (Marecek & Hare-Mustin, 1991), experimental and cognitive psychology (Morawski & Agronick, 1991), and the history of women doing social issues research (P.A. Katz, 1991).

THE SECOND WAVE OF FEMINISM AND THE DEVELOPMENT OF WOMEN'S NETWORKS

Throughout the 1950s and early 1960s, women were largely absent from professional psychology. Only about 11% of women psychologists participated in APA's annual convention in 1956 and the figure had risen to only 14% in 1966 (Mednick, 1978). These numbers only partially convey the isolation of women psychologists both within the university environment and, especially, when we ventured into the "outside world" of conferences and conventions.

One reason for this absence was the persistent sexual harassment reported by women who attended professional meetings during this period: "Women graduate students were courted, ogled in elevators, invited to the bar and to parties, and pursued by the most eminent of men within our discipline. . . . These contacts were sexist and shallow" (Lott, 1995b, p. 315). Similar "war stories" have been told by a number of women who were active conference attendees during this period (cf. Chesler, 1995; M. Crawford, 1997b; Unger, 1998; Weisstein, 1977).

Another indicator of the scarcity of women at these meetings is the small number involved in APA convention programming during this period. In 1965, for example, 12 women chaired symposia or delivered invited addresses at APA. Presumably, somewhat more women appeared in symposia or gave papers, but these figures are minuscule when one considers that over 1,700 participants were listed in the program. Only two presentations were on the psychology of women: a symposium chaired by Jessie Bernard (a sociologist) on low-income family patterns and a presentation on need achievement in women (Unger, 1998).

In 1966, there were two symposia on the psychology of women, none in 1967, and two again in 1968. The number of convention presentations was growing during this period, but only 14 women chaired symposia or made invited presentations in 1966, 17 did so in 1967, and 23 in 1968. Nineteen women appeared in featured positions in the 1969 APA program, but this program contained the first harbinger of change—a symposium chaired by JoAnn Evans Gardner with what must be the longest title in APA history: "What Can the Behavioral Sciences Do to Modify the World So That Women Who Want to Participate Meaningfully Are Not Regarded as and Are Not in Fact Deviant?"

The APA convention in 1970 was strikingly different in terms of the presence of feminism in its program. Eleven symposia were presented that included such titles as "Women Psychologists: Psychologists? Militants?"; "A Monkey on the Psychologist's Back: The Evolution of Women"; "The Fall and Rise of Feminism"; and "Social Psychology and Women's Liberation." Names that would become familiar to those interested in the psychology of women began to appear on the program. These included Martha Mednick, Sandra Tangri, Matina Horner (all of whom knew each other at the University of Michigan), Judith Long Laws and Naomi Weisstein (who were involved in feminist activist politics in Chicago), and Nancy Henley, another founding member of the Association for Women in Psychology (AWP).

The surge of feminism could not have been predicted from earlier APA programs. In fact, the women who had been active in the earlier APA conventions were not the women who sponsored these feminist symposia. Instead, feminist activity within APA was provoked by AWP, whose behind-the-scenes activities during this period have been recounted by Leonore Tiefer (1991).

Most of these programs were sponsored by Division 9 of APA (also known as SPSSI), although several other APA divisions had a greater number of women members. There was no connection between the proportion of women members, or even women's contributions to the programs of particular divisions, and feminist programming. For example, although Divisions 12 and 16 (Clinical and School Psychology) had 54 female symposia chairs or invited speakers during the years 1965 to 1973, they sponsored only four symposia on the psychology of women. In contrast, SPSSI had 40 female chairs or speakers but sponsored 20 feminist symposia during these years.

SPSSI's support in this area was due to the organizational involvement of AWP activists such as JoAnn Gardner (who was a member of SPSSI's executive committee during this period) as well as more mainstream feminists. The latter were part of APA's ad hoc Task Force on the Status of Women, which was responsible for the formation of Division 35. This task force was chaired first by Helen Astin and later by Martha Mednick (Women's Program Office, 1993).

By 1971, the task force was cosponsoring APA symposia such as one entitled "Clinical Psychology and Theories of Feminine Personality." In 1971, there were 8 symposia on the psychology of women, 17 in 1972, and 14 in 1973. By 1974, a division on the psychology of women (Division 35) had been formed and its programs became an official part of APA. The division sponsored 11 symposia in its first year (Unger, 1998).

What does this history tell us? Programs on the psychology of women did not ignite spontaneously under the influence of the burgeoning feminist movement. Organizational activism both inside and outside of APA was necessary for networks to develop, programmatic themes to coalesce, sympathetic divisions to be identified, and symposia to be proposed. These things are not easily done in ignorance. The women who were involved in the early feminist programs had also been involved in other APA programs over time. (Their involvement can be documented in programs from 1965 through 1970—not always on topics related to women, but almost always with some social issues theme.) Once the new division was formed, however, new names also began to appear in these programs (Unger, 1998).

THE ORGANIZATIONAL HISTORY OF THE FIELD

Continuing sexism, both personal and professional, led to renewed attempts at organization on behalf of women. Details about the climate of the times may be found in Leonore Tiefer's (1991) history of the founding of AWP. For example, book titles were unabashedly sexist and heterosexist, positions were advertised for men only, and if women were interviewed for positions, they were routinely asked about their marital and childbearing plans.

AWP began from informal conversations at meetings of graduate students and younger academic women who had been influenced by popular feminism (the National Organization for Women [NOW] was founded in 1966). It was an enormous relief to share experiences with other women who were having difficulty getting positions, were underemployed, and, somewhat later, were encountering difficulties obtaining tenure. The women also shared stories about the difficulties of finding mentors, juggling roles, sexual harassment, and the alienation we felt from being in a virtually all-male environment (Unger, 1998).

This younger cadre of conference attendees were the foremothers of AWP. AWP virtually high-jacked the official business meeting at the APA convention in 1969, demanding that APA make restitution for its contributions to the devaluation of women (Tiefer, 1991). Their demands and "unladylike behavior" forced APA to appoint an ad hoc Task Force on the Status of Women in 1970 (Mednick, 1978). This task force became the Committee on Women in Psychology (CWP) in 1972 (Russo & Dumont, 1997).

Unlike AWP, CWP was formed to work from within rather than outside the organizational structure of the APA. As one might expect, CWP was initially less radical and activist than AWP; it comprised more established academic women as well. CWP decided that an important step in legitimizing women in psychology would be to create a division of APA on the psychology of women. Accordingly, they engaged in a petition campaign within the APA membership and acquired enough signatures and commitments to induce the APA Council of Representatives to accept the division (Mednick & Urbanski, 1991).

The goals of the division, as first stated, were not particularly activist in nature: "To promote the research and study of women, including both biological and socio-cultural determinants of behavior. To encourage the integration of this information about women with the current psychological knowledge and beliefs in order to apply the gained knowledge to the society and its institutions" (excerpted from Article 1.2, Division 35 By-Laws). Instead, the organizers stressed the scientific value of scholarship on women. Of course, this was partly a strategy to obtain legitimacy from the male establishment, but it also reflected the professional commitments of many of the senior women who organized the campaign.

Most, if not all, of these women were unaware of the existence of AWP, a group mostly comprising graduate students, new Ph.D.s, and clinicians who had no academic affiliation. AWP, in turn, was not involved in the efforts of CWP in organizing a division on the psychology of women because most of its members were either not members of APA or uninterested in or hostile to the formal professional organization.

In spite of a rather contentious beginning (see Unger, 1998), the division quickly became a force within APA. Over 350 people applied for membership applications during its first year. The early membership was, as it remains, 93% female. During the 1970s, a majority of the membership held academic positions, although this has changed (as has APA) in the direction of a larger percentage of clinicians in private practice. The membership came from virtually every subdiscipline of psychology, though primarily from clinical and counseling psychology, with a surprisingly small 8% from social and an even smaller percentage from experimental psychology (Unger, O'Leary, & Fabian, 1977). Of course, no one was trained in the psychology of women. We had the joys and the challenge of helping to develop the field.

Since 1973, the division has grown enormously in size and influence (see Russo & Dumont, 1997). For example, it established the journal the *Psychology of Women Quarterly,* whose first issue appeared in 1976. It sponsored an increasing number of convention programs at the annual convention of the APA (reaching a high of 51 hours in 1996). It sponsors a number of research awards, both for senior scholars and for graduate students in various subfields of the psychology of women, such as clinical psychology and research on women of color. It sponsors workshops on developing curricula in the field as well as on the development of feminist approaches to clinical training, theory, and practice. One of the division's most recent activities is a book series on specific issues in the area. The first book in this series, *Bringing Cultural Diversity to Feminist Psychology,* was edited by Hope Landrine and published in 1995.

Division 35 has also played an important role in the political life of its parent organization, APA. It sends several representatives to the governing council of that organization, was instrumental in organizing a women's caucus, and has been a champion of minority rights issues throughout its existence (Russo & Dumont, 1997). Two presidents of the division have subsequently been elected president of APA: Florence Denmark and Norine Johnson. Several other female presidents of APA have been active members of the division.

SOME COMPARISONS AMONG FEMINIST PSYCHOLOGICAL ORGANIZATIONS IN THE ENGLISH-SPEAKING WORLD

From the vantage point of a strong presence of women in U.S. psychology's organizational hierarchy, it might appear that expanding psychology's knowledge base and increasing the power of individual women psychologists were inevitable developments once the "woman problem" was explained and understood. It is important, therefore, to explore the history of feminist organizing in other parts of the English-speaking world (space limitations preclude the inclusion of non-English-speaking national organizations).

In Canada, the United Kingdom, Australia, and New Zealand, as in the United States, women psychologists responded to the second wave of societal feminism by developing organized groups devoted to both political action and change in the intellectual content and methodology of their field (Getz, 1997; Pyke & Greenglass, 1997; S. Wilkinson, 1990a, 1990b). These attempts took somewhat different forms, aroused varying levels of opposition from the primarily male psychological establishment in each country, and had different outcomes.

As in the United States, organizational efforts were preceded by attempts to restructure the field's knowledge about women. However, proposals involving this new knowledge had difficulty being accepted by established disciplinary structures. For example, a session on the psychology of women was rejected by the program committee of the Canadian Psychological Association in 1972 because "it didn't fit in anywhere" (Greenglass, 1973, p. 11). After repeated and futile attempts to pass the screening, six women psychologists organized an underground independent symposium held in conjunction with the official meeting of the Canadian Psychological Association. Although CPA actively opposed this action, the symposium was well attended (Pyke & Stark-Adamec, 1981). A symposium on sex roles was accepted as an official part of the program for the annual meeting the following year (Getz, 1997). The creation of the Task Force on the Status of Women followed quickly and became the basis for the foundation of the Section on Women and Psychology (SWAP), which was recognized as an official section of the CPA in 1976.

The establishment of an official section on the psychology of women was much more problematic in the United Kingdom. Although a session on sex-role stereotyping and psychology was presented at the annual meeting of the British Psychological Society (BPS) in 1975 and an international conference on this subject was held in Cardiff in 1977, official recognition of a section on the psychology of women came only after a considerable amount of conflict (S. Wilkinson, 1990b). In fact, the Council of BPS rejected the request for such a section when it was first proposed in 1985.

The governing body had three major objections to the proposal: (1) The section was seen as neither fitting the scientific concerns of the BPS nor meshing well with other sections of the organization (such as social and developmental psychology) that purportedly dealt with the psychology of women; (2) the name of the new section, Women in Psychology, was mistakenly seen as separatist; and (3) the organization was seen as a quasi-political pressure group concerned with feminist causes. The organizers were asked to make clear the conceptual distinction between scientific responsibility and the promotion of causes based on moral conviction alone (BPS to section proposers, July 1985, cited by S. Wilkinson, 1990b). After a two-year campaign by the members of the Women in Psychology organization and a change in the name to the Psychology of Women, the section became an official part of the BPS in 1987. A very similar pattern has been found in Australia, where an initial proposal for a Women in Psychology interest group was first rejected by the Professional Board and accepted two years later in 1984 (S. Wilkinson, 1990a).

Of the English-speaking countries surveyed, only New Zealand has no organization on the psychology of women. Feminist psychologists attempted to establish one in the 1970s, but unlike feminist psychologists in other countries, opted for a women-only division. The male leaders of the New Zealand Psychological Society rejected this proposal because it violated rules of the Human Rights Commission, which upheld their decision (S. Wilkinson, 1990a). The movement lost its momentum and a formal organization still does not exist (Lapsley, personal communication, December 10, 1999).

What do these various patterns tell us? In every country surveyed, attempts to form organizations of, for, and about women produced conflict with established authorities. Sue Wilkinson

(1990a) has suggested that opposition took three forms, all of which involve the use of institutional power to control deviance. The first mechanism is control by definitions or rules; for example, organizations that focused on women were seen as not fitting into the current taxonomy of psychology. A second mechanism is more informal, ignoring the deviant organization or failing to provide it with information necessary for effective functioning. For example, although the militant activities of AWP pressured the APA to set up its Task Force on Women, AWP was not officially informed about its proposal to set up a Division on the Psychology of Women (Unger, 1998). A third mechanism involves the use of rhetoric to justify formal and informal methods of exclusion; here, the most frequently evoked argument is the incompatibility of science and advocacy (Unger, 1982).

Those who study the psychology of women are themselves ambivalent about the relationship between scholarship and advocacy. In the United States, this dilemma has been partially resolved by the continued existence of two groups, one inside (Division 35) and one outside of (AWP) official psychological structures. Although this frees AWP to be an advocate for women, it also remains less legitimate than Division 35. At times, their different status has created friction between the two groups, although they also work together on a variety of projects (Russo & Dumont, 1997; Tiefer, 1991; Unger, 1998).

INSIDE/OUTSIDE? COMPETING TRENDS IN THE NEW PSYCHOLOGY OF WOMEN

Does the structure and legitimacy of women's organization within psychology influence scholarship? Certainly, some of the scholarly work produced in the late 1960s and early 1970s was more activist than most of what is published in the psychology of women today. It questioned the status quo in both society and the discipline. For example, Naomi Weisstein (1968a) began what is considered to be the first important paper of the second wave of feminist psychology with the challenging statement that psychology had nothing to say about what women are really like, what they need, and what they want because psychology did not know. Weisstein was part of a feminist group in Chicago and this paper was first given as a talk and later published as a monograph by a feminist press (cf. Weisstein, 1993a, for some details about the circumstances that led to the paper). This paper (which has been reprinted over 25 times) was a radical, polemical piece that foreshadowed later feminist theoretical concerns with social construction.

Weisstein's ideas appear to have had more impact on feminists outside of psychology than within it. As noted earlier, Division 35 chose to emphasize the scientific nature of the subdiscipline, and in the United States, the psychology of women remains more empirical and less theoretical than feminist scholarship in most other disciplines. The strong positivist, empiricist orientation of psychology has had a great influence on the study of women and gender. Many of the women in the field had internalized its norms and, even when we began to reject them, it was difficult to find publication outlets for work that was "deviant" in both method and content (Unger, 1998).

THE CONTENT OF EARLY U.S. TEXTS IN THE PSYCHOLOGY OF WOMEN

Because mainstream scholarship in psychology tends to be both individualistic and conservative, it is not surprising that early U.S. textbooks on the psychology of women also focused on intrapersonal forces. For example, the content of the first two textbooks on the psychology of women, authored by Judith Bardwick (1971) and Julia Sherman (1971), indicates the important early influence of theories stressing intrapsychic differences between the sexes. These books reflected both the training and the interests of their authors (both clinical/personality psychologists) and what materials were available. But they also reflected the state of the art of the psychology of women at its inception.

The chapters in Bardwick's (1971) book emphasized psychoanalytic theory, sexuality and the female body (with particular emphasis on psychosomatic dysfunctions involving the reproductive system), and differences between male and female brains. The text also included chapters on identification, self-esteem, achievement, and changes in motives and roles during different life stages. One chapter is entitled "Dependence, Passivity, and Aggression." This rather brief book (218 pages) illustrated the intrapsychic bias of psychology. This bias is retained even within the psychology of women today and contributes to its conservatism relative to feminist scholarship in other disciplines (A.S. Kahn & Yoder, 1989). The book also assumed the existence of major sex differences in personality and behavior and stressed the negative correlates of female reproductive phenomena such as menstruation, pregnancy, and menopause.

Bardwick (1971) was, at best, ambivalent about feminism. Consider, for example, this passage from her book:

> Feminism is not and actually never has been a widespread movement among American women, and the goals and values held by most women are gratified primarily in the traditional feminine activities. Given the extent of the preference in the culture for masculine activities, one must ask why this is so, why so few women are motivated to perform professionally. Most women may never have developed a strong achievement motivation as children and adolescents, they may fear failure because they fear competition and the implications of public failure, and they may fear that success will make them less feminine. (p. 145)

These comments clearly blame the victim, giving little consideration to external barriers, although Bardwick did acknowledge restrictions on women due to lack of institutionalized child care arrangements.

The chapters in J.A. Sherman's (1971) book also indicated a preoccupation with biological and psychodynamic issues. The book contained chapters on biological and psychological sex differences, several chapters on female development with an emphasis on Freudian theory, and chapters focusing on particular life stages such as adolescence, pregnancy, and motherhood. This text had, however, a more feminist flavor than Bardwick's (1971). For example, although Sherman extensively discussed reproductive events and their relationship to women's psyches, she also acknowledged the important role of societal values and socialization on women's behavior. The book was also more inclusive: An examination of the subject index shows 4 page references to Black women, 4 to homosexuality, and 19 to social class (there are 246 pages in the book). Although "feminism" was not a category in her subject index, Sherman's commitment to egalitarianism is evidenced by five page references to "equality" and five to the "double standard."

Later texts were more social psychological in tone. For example, Rhoda Unger and Florence Denmark (1975) put together a composite text and reader titled *Woman: Dependent or Independent Variable?* that explicitly challenged intrapsychic explanations for sexual inequality. This text began with a section on sex-role stereotypes, examined how therapists viewed women, and examined the development of sex differences and sex roles before moving to explanations of sex differences in cognitive function: whether there is psychosexual neutrality at birth, unique female conditions such as menstruation and pregnancy, and concluding with a chapter on internal versus external barriers to female achievement. Other early textbooks used a more developmental framework (e.g., Hyde & Rosenberg, 1974). All of their authors believed, however, that good science would explain societal sexism and eventually do away with the need for a separate psychology of women (Unger, 1979a, p. 487).

EARLY RESEARCH ON THE PSYCHOLOGY OF WOMEN

Relatively little of the research and scholarship on the psychology of women that began to be published in the late 1960s and early 1970s focused on societal sexism. Exceptions were Weisstein's (1968a) scathing critique of psychological methodology and content, an important chapter by Sandra Bem and Darryl Bem (1970) titled "Training the Woman to Know Her Place: The Power of an Unconscious Ideology," and Nancy Henley's (1973) groundbreaking work on the "politics of touch."

Instead, consistent with the individualistic focus of U.S. psychology, feminist psychologists began to explore sexism in interpersonal attitudes and behavior. For example, a group of psychologists began a series of studies on sex-role stereotypes (Broverman, Broverman, Clarkson, Rosenkrantz, & Vogel, 1970; Broverman, Vogel, Broverman, Clarkson, & Rosenkrantz, 1972; Rosenkrantz, Vogel, Bee, Broverman, & Broverman, 1968). They documented the existence of stereotypes in college students, their parents, and mental health practitioners. They found that sex-role stereotypes had changed little from the last time anyone had looked for them (C. Kirkpatrick, 1936; McKee & Sheriffs, 1957). Other researchers looked at the effect of sex on evaluative judgments as well as more overt behaviors. Philip Goldberg (1968), for example, conducted an early study showing that women were more likely to evaluate essays purportedly written by women more negatively than identical essays purportedly written by men. Other researchers looked at the effect of a driver's sex on other drivers' horn honking behavior (Deaux, 1971; Unger, Raymond, & Levine, 1974).

Many of these studies were atheoretical in nature. They were designed to show that discrimination against women existed in a variety of circumstances, in minor as well as major arenas. They formed a counterpoint to studies of discrimination at an institutional level such as that by Helen Astin (1969) on the woman doctorate in America. Funded by the Russell Sage Foundation and using "real" rather than analogue data, she was able to document discrimination against women in academia. She found that even when women had academic qualifications equivalent to those of men and had contributed equally to their disciplines in terms of scholarly publications, they were promoted more slowly and received fewer rewards.

Linda Fidell (1970) provided a dramatic example of such discrimination in psychology in a study that probably could not be replicated in today's more suspicious climate. She sent department "chairmen" (used advisedly, in terms of the time period) a collection of resumes of junior faculty with the justification that she was trying to find out what criteria determined whether they would be hired and the rank and salary that would be offered them. The chairs received different versions of the same resumes, with male or female names attached. She found that men were more likely to be hired than women with the same qualifications and offered higher rank with fewer qualifications. Her study was considered important enough to be published in the *American Psychologist*, the journal of record of the APA.

This study was an empirical verification of what those of us in the job market during this period already knew. It was, however, the kind of evidence that psychologists were more willing to listen to and accept. It showed how empirical information could be used as an argument for social action.

Surprisingly, many of these studies were conducted by clinical rather than social psychologists (Unger, 1998). A major exception to this trend was the publication in 1972 of a special issue of the *Journal of Social Issues* entitled "New Perspectives on Women." This collection was edited by Martha Mednick and Sandra Tangri. It was an extraordinarily useful resource that provided powerful scholarly material for the new courses on the psychology of women. Many of the articles were reprinted in the 1970s and early 1980s but may not be as familiar to today's generation of feminist psychologists as they are to those of us whom they energized when we were the younger generation.

The issue focused on the theme of achievement, an early focus in the psychology of women as high-achieving feminists tried to figure out why women were not as successful as men. This issue included articles such as Matina Horner's (1972) classic work on "fear of success," an important article summarizing their work on sex-role stereotypes by Inge Broverman and her associates, and a paper on personality by Rae Carlson, who had been one of the earliest psychologists to criticize psychology for its differential treatment of women and men (E.R. Carlson & Carlson, 1961).

Despite its theme of achievement, the issue focused more on internal variables such as attitudes and motives than on external barriers to success. The psychology of women seems to have begun to turn inward at this point. Having demonstrated that prejudice and discrimination against women were pervasive, researchers began to ask questions that were generated by more disciplinary concerns, such as What are the characteristics of people who stereotype? Do sex-role stereotypes have any basis in fact? Do stereotypes influence behavior?

In other words, researchers in the psychology of women began to move away from exploring the cues for prejudice to the examination of the psychology of prejudice. This was a move from behavior to attitudes. It helped make the psychology of women more legitimate within the discipline, but at some cost to activist research. For example, behavior can be changed by rules and laws, whereas attitudes require much more long-term solutions, such as changes in familial socialization or educational strategies. Internal or intrapsychic explanations for social inequalities are very popular with society as a whole as well as within the discipline. Nevertheless, they continue to be seen as problematic by more activist feminists in the field. As Mednick (1989) has pointed out, "The focus on personal change diverts scholarship and action away from questions that could be directed toward an understanding of the social foundations of power alignments and inequity" (p. 1122).

FEMINIST SCHOLARSHIP OUTSIDE THE UNITED STATES

Because of the smaller numbers involved, feminist psychologists in other parts of the English-speaking world have not separated into insider/outsider groupings. I also know of no studies that have looked at the comparative legitimacy of the field in each country. It appears, however, that Canadian and British feminist psychologists are more aware than those in the United States of structural constraints on feminist scholarship. Celia Kitzinger (1990b) has pointed out, for example, "When I write as a feminist, I am defined out of the category of 'psychologist.' When I speak of social structure, of power and politics, when I use language and concepts rooted in my understanding of oppression, I am told what I say does not qualify as 'psychology'" (p. 124). Like feminist organizations in earlier times, explicitly feminist work is ignored or marginalized. This exclusion makes it difficult for feminist psychologists to achieve professional success, and indeed, there are fewer women fellows of the BPS and fewer women in important gatekeeping positions than their numbers warrant (S. Wilkinson, 1991).

One response to the exclusion of particular categories of scholarship was to establish a journal, as Division 35 did some years earlier. The contents of *Feminism and Psychology,* the international journal founded by British psychologists in 1991, support the view that the British version of the psychology of women is more radical than the U.S. version (S. Wilkinson, 1997b). This journal publishes much more qualitative and theoretical work than its U.S. counterpart, which is more quantitative and empirical in focus. Indeed, several content analyses comparing U.S. feminist journals in psychology with their mainstream counterparts have found little difference between them in terms of either method or content (Fine & Gordon, 1989; Lykes & Stewart, 1986). Recently, however, there has been more communication between U.S. and British feminist psychologists (probably because of the new journal), and the *Psychology of Women Quarterly* recently published two issues on innovative methods for feminist research (M. Crawford & Kimmel, 1999a).

STAGE THEORIES OF PROGRESS IN THE PSYCHOLOGY OF WOMEN

Mary Crawford and Jeanne Marecek (1989b) have argued that development during the first 20 years (from 1968 to 1988) of the psychology of women can be characterized in terms of four major themes: "exceptional women," in which empirical work focused on the correlates of high achievement in women and the reevaluation of women's history; "woman as problem," in which research emphasized explanations for "female deficiencies" such as fear of success and the deficits of females compared to males; "psychology of gender," in which research shifts from its focus on individual women and moves to a consideration of gender as a form of social organization that structures relations between women and men; and "transformation," which challenges the values, assumptions, and normative practices of the discipline.

Similarly, I have suggested that feminist scholarship in the United States can be traced through a series of stages (Unger, 1998). The first stage of such scholarship (discussed earlier in this chapter) challenged the bases for discrimination against women (with the rather naïve assumption that if cues of femaleness and maleness could be shown to be inaccurate predictors of attitudinal and behavioral differences between the sexes, they would disappear from use). A second stage involved the examination of power at the individual, interpersonal, and sociostructural level (see Henley & Freeman, 1975; J.B. Miller, 1976; C. Sherif, 1979). A third stage involved feminist critique of method and content (e.g., see Grady, 1981; McKenna & Kessler, 1977; Parlee, 1981; Wallston & Grady, 1985). Finally, feminist psychologists have begun to concern themselves with epistemology (see Riger, 1992; Unger, 1983; Wittig, 1985); this stage is probably analogous to the transformational stage suggested by M. Crawford and Marecek (1989b).

These stages may not be inevitable. British feminists, in particular, seem to have been aware of systemic processes earlier than feminists in the United States. For example, although they too did early work on sex-role stereotyping (Hartnett, Boden, & Fuller, 1979), books with such titles as *The Sex Role System* (Chetwynd & Hartnett, 1978) appeared at the same time. British psychologists also appear to have been less interested in reevaluating their history or examining female achievement than were feminists in the United States. These differences may reflect their greater familiarity with French feminist theory. For example, terms such as "standpoint," "subjectivity," and "positionality" are more apt to be found in British than in U.S. work (see Henwood, Griffin, & Phoenix, 1998; Hollway, 1989).

USING THE PAST TO LOOK AT THE FUTURE

Until recently, the psychology of women in the English-speaking world has suffered from in-group bias. With few exceptions, the unit of analysis has been White, middle-class women and girls. As women from more diverse backgrounds have entered the field, however, it has paid more attention to issues involving race/ethnicity (see Comas-Diaz, 1991; B.A. Greene & Sanchez-Hucles, 1997; Landrine, 1995; P.T. Reid, 1993), class (see Walkerdine, 1996a), and sexuality (see L.W. Brown, 1989; C. Kitzinger, 1996). More important, feminist psychologists have recognized that marginal categories are not just the responsibility of members of marginalized groups. Thus, feminist scholars have begun to interrogate "Whiteness" (Fine, Weis, Powell, & Wong, 1997) and heterosexuality (S. Wilkinson & Kitzinger, 1993a) as sites of privilege.

Recognition of the existence of many kinds of women makes generalizations about women as a group more difficult. It is possible, therefore, that this proliferation of groups studied may finally eliminate the study of sex differences as a major area of research (Unger, 1992). But this area of research has not yet disappeared and has, in fact, been fueled by the development of meta-analytic techniques that permit researchers to examine large numbers of studies in particular areas and compare the results. Feminist psychologists are on both sides of the debate in this area, arguing both that sex-related differences in traits and cognitions are substantial and meaningful (Eagly, 1995) and that they are trivial and transient (Hyde & Plant, 1995).

Other arguments from the past have also not disappeared. For example, evolutionary psychology has supplanted sociobiology as an important theoretical framework that views sex differences as caused primarily by genes and sees sex differences as adaptive in nature. As in earlier times, differences between women and men are used to explain societal inequalities.

Unlike in earlier periods, the psychology of women has become a legitimate part of psychology in the United States at least. There are many examples of female lineages, among them some influential feminist psychologists (mentioned in this chapter) who have been mentored by other feminists. They include, for example, Stephanie Shields, who was mentored by Carolyn Sherif, and Sandra Tangri, who was mentored by Martha Mednick. The development of feminist organizations within psychology also facilitated more informal collegial networks among women similar to those fostered for men by World War II. Thus, a number of younger feminist researchers at various U.S. institutions were tutored in social construction by Carolyn Sherif (cf. Unger & Kahn, 1998); some of the early leaders of Division 35 received a political education from Florence Denmark (Unger, 1998); and after she received her Ph.D., Kay Deaux's scholarly interest in gender was facilitated by Janet Spence (Deaux, personal communication, December 16, 1999). Courses on the psychology of women are taught in more than 50% of all undergraduate and graduate programs in the United States (Women's Program Office, 1991). And the number of textbooks on the psychology of women that have been published since 1971 is too large to enumerate here.

This degree of legitimacy would seem to suggest that women and their accomplishments will never again disappear from psychology's history. However, there are some disturbing trends. Courses and textbooks with the title *Psychology of Gender* are beginning to replace courses and texts on the psychology of women. At first glance, this appears to be a positive step, but it is positive only if gender is used as a "verb" rather than a "noun" (Unger, 1988).

Because of psychology's individualistic focus, gender as a social construction is easily confused with the socialization of gendered traits: "Rather, the constructionist argument is that gender is not a trait of individuals at all, but simply a construct that identifies particular transactions that are understood to be appropriate to one sex" (Bohan, 1993, p. 7). These transactions both construct and maintain gender and may be independent of the individual's actual biological sex.

Texts that focus on gender appear to be more interested in comparisons between females and males than are those that identify themselves as women-centered. It is possible, therefore, that the study of women will be subsumed under the study of gender, which would further distance the field from its activist roots.

In another disturbing development, feminist critique has largely disappeared into the critiques of critical psychology, which has global concerns about the impact of values on psychology's questions, methods, and knowledge claims. The insights of feminist pioneers in these areas are used, but not necessarily attributed to them This is how history is re-created. Critical psychologists and historians have taught us that there is no one "true" version of history. Therefore, it is well to be vigilant when we write histories of our own.

CHAPTER 2

Theoretical Perspectives on Women and Gender

SUE WILKINSON

Very few psychology of women textbooks include a chapter on theoretical perspectives. A focus on theory is often considered to be uninteresting, unnecessary, or irrelevant—an abstract academic exercise, far removed from the realities of women's lives. Theory is commonly treated as an optional extra to the real business of feminist research and activism. In this chapter, by contrast, I hope to demonstrate that theory is an integral part of feminist scholarship by focusing on *theory as method.* Particular theoretical perspectives underpin the kinds of research questions feminist psychologists ask, the kinds of methods we use to pursue these questions, the kinds of analyses we undertake, and the kinds of answers we obtain. I will introduce three key theoretical perspectives—feminist positivist empiricism, feminist experiential research, and feminist social constructionism—and illustrate the main types of scholarship typically informed by each. To make clearer the relevance of theory to everyday research practice, I will present a data extract from my current research on breast cancer; and I will analyse this extract in three different ways—from within a positivist empiricist framework, from within an experiential framework, and from a social constructionist framework. These parallel analyses not only exemplify the type of data analysis that might be performed by a feminist psychologist working within each of these theoretical perspectives (see also S. Wilkinson, 2000c), but also highlight the crucial importance of the researcher's theoretical perspective for the type of conclusions she is able to draw.

My current research involves a series of focus group discussions between women with breast cancer (see S. Wilkinson, 1998a, 1998b). These women were recruited through a symptomatic breast clinic at a general hospital in a city in the north of England: most were working class and middle-aged or older, and the majority were within five years of diagnosis. The (relatively unstructured) discussions ranged across the women's feelings at first diagnosis, treatments, coping and support systems, and the effects of their cancer on their lives and relationships (see S. Wilkinson, 2000a). One of the issues that interests me is what these women say about the possible causes of breast cancer (see S. Wilkinson, 2000c). The data extract presented in Box 2.1 is an example of a discussion about causes between three women—Gertie, Doreen, and Freda—that occurs toward the end of one of the focus groups. The extract is typical of qualitative data collected by researchers working in the area of "lay aetiology," that is, commonsense, lay, or folk understandings of the causes of health and illness (e.g., Blaxter, 1983; S. Payne, 1990; Pill & Stott, 1982).

In the sections that follow, I look at the kinds of sense we can make of Gertie, Doreen, and Freda's discussion from within positivist empiricist, experiential, and social constructionist theoretical frameworks, respectively.

Box 2.1
Data Extract from a Focus Group Discussion

Three women with breast cancer respond to the moderator's question, "D'you have any idea what *caused* your breast cancer?"

Gertie: I can't think off hand, I knew, I knew a lot that I've heard over the years from people who've passed on, "Oh yeah well, that causes cancer"

Doreen: Mm

Gertie: but I don't know, but-

Doreen: [cuts in] I mean, erm-

Gertie: Now *I've* no views on this, [To Doreen] have you?

Doreen: No - The only thing is, I mean from my point of view, I don't know, they say that, they say that breast feeding is supposed to, erm [tch], give you some *protection,* well I breast fed and I mean [laughs], it obviously didn't work with me, did it? Erm, what's the other thing? Then they say that taking the pill, it's not proved to be . . . [pause] have I got this right?, it's not proved that it's only, it's not caused an increase in breast cancer, so that, I mean I did t-, you know, obviously I took the pill at a younger age, I mean, I don't know whether the age at which you have children makes a difference as well because I had my [pause] eight year old relatively *late,* I was an old mum when I got, I mean, [pause] yeah, I was thirty two when I-, just nearly thirty two when I had John, so I was a relatively *old mum,* so whether it's-, so whether the age at which you have children has got anything to do with it I don't know, I mean there's no family *history*

Freda: [cuts in] They say that if you've only had *one* that you're more likely to get it than if you had a *big* family [indistinct]

FEMINIST POSITIVIST EMPIRICISM

Feminist positivist empiricism is by far the most widely used theoretical perspective in the psychology of women, particularly in the United States. Positivist empiricist research uses conventional scientific methods—particularly experiments, tests, and scales—to produce "factual" knowledge about an objectively present, and so observable and measurable, external world. Key criteria for "good" positivist empiricist research include the objectivity of the researcher, the standardization of measures, and the replicability and generalizability of findings. Although often equated with quantitative methods, a positivist empiricist framework also frequently underpins qualitative research, especially that in which qualitative data are transformed into quantitative indices: see, for example, Tolman and Szalacha's (1999) quantification of young women's narratives of sexual desire or Peel's (1999) statistical analysis of a questionnaire on reasons for reporting violence against lesbians and gay men (with items originally derived from a series of in-depth interviews). Typically, when open-ended qualitative data—such as those from interviews or focus groups—are collected within a positivist empiricist framework, these data are coded and classified into closed categories as a preliminary to quantitative analysis. An example of this can be seen in the content analysis of my breast cancer data extract in Box 2.2, in which the causes of breast cancer identified by the participants are classified into three categories derived from the previous literature on "lay aetiology" ("heredity/familial tendencies," "drugs or the contraceptive pill," and "caused by childbearing/menopause")—and a frequency count is undertaken on responses within each category. Content analysis is a very common way of analyzing qualitative data within a positivist empiricist framework.

Studies using the standard techniques of positivist empiricism (e.g., random sampling, quantification of questionnaire data, statistical testing) have been responsible for some of the "classic" findings of feminist research: for example, that 50% of North American female college students have submitted to unwanted sexual intercourse because of male pressure, social status, or physical force (Koss, Gidysz, & Wisniewsi, 1987); and that 14% of married women in the United States have been raped by their husbands (D.E. Russell, 1990). Documenting the facts of women's

---

Box 2.2
A Positivist Empiricist Analysis of the Data Extract: Content Analysis

Key Assumptions:

Participants have beliefs or opinions about the causes of breast cancer, and these can reliably be inferred from an analysis of what they say (i.e., talk reflects cognitive content).

Key Additional Information:

Sample details: The participants are working-class women from the north of England.

Method of Analysis:

All mentions of the causes of breast cancer are coded into categories derived from the lay aetiology literature—specifically, Blaxter (1983). These categories summarize and systematize the content of the data, and afford ready comparison with other similar studies.

Analysis:

Category 1: Heredity/familial tendencies: 2 instances
Category 2: Drugs or the contraceptive pill: 1 instance
Category 3: Caused by childbearing/menopause: 5 instances

(Intercoder reliability: 0.95)

Conclusion:

These women most frequently mention reproductive factors as possible causes of breast cancer. This finding supports that of Blaxter's (1983) study with working-class Scottish women, and suggests that, among working-class women at least, certain beliefs about the cause of illness may be relatively common and stable over time.

---

oppression is often an important first step in campaigning for social change—and data presented within the evidential framework of science (especially statistical data) may be particularly persuasive to funding bodies and policy makers (see, e.g., Love, 1995; Kaufert, 1998, in relation to feminist activism around breast cancer).

A positivist empiricist perspective also provides feminist psychologists with a valuable tool for critiquing mainstream psychology. Using positivist empiricist criteria for "good science," feminists have been able to expose mainstream psychology as "bad science" (e.g., as unrepresentative, unreplicable, or ideologically biased); and also to conduct their own "better science." This tactic dates back to the beginnings of psychology of women in the late 19th and early 20th century, when Mary Putnam Jacobi completed a dissertation challenging the (male) medical orthodoxy that women are debilitated by their menstrual periods (cf. C. Sherif, 1979), and Leta Stetter Hollingworth conducted extensive laboratory experiments to demonstrate empirically that this is not the case, using a range of performance measures (cf. S.A. Shields, 1975a)—a tradition of work that continues today (e.g., Sommer, 1992). In 1910, pioneer feminist psychologist (and experimentalist) Helen Thompson Wooley published a swingeing criticism of mainstream psychological research on sex differences as characterized by "flagrant personal bias, logic martyred in the cause of supporting a prejudice, unfounded assertions, and even sentimental rot and drivel" (Wooley, 1910, p. 340), that is, as thoroughly "bad science."

A major feminist criticism of the sex differences in literature has been its bias in favor of men. In this literature (as in psychology more generally), male characteristics and behavior typically provide the benchmark—when women are compared with men, any differences found are interpreted as female deficits. For example, there is a fairly consistent sex difference in self-confidence: on tasks such as estimating how many points they think they earned on an exam before the actual grades are known, women estimate fewer points (on average) than do men. This finding has often been interpreted as indicating that women lack self-confidence. In fact, when estimated scores are compared with *actual* scores, feminist psychologists have shown that men *overestimate* their performance by about as much as women *underestimate* theirs (Hyde, 1994b). Compared with *men,* women supposedly have lower self-esteem; undervalue their own efforts; are less self-confident; have more difficulty developing a separate sense of self; and are more likely to say they are "hurt" than to admit they are "angry." But feminists have offered, as critique, an alternative—and equally valid—reading of these findings, based on a female benchmark. Compared with *women,* men may be seen as more conceited; overvaluing the work they do; less realistic in assessing their abilities; having more difficulty in forming and maintaining attachments; and as more likely to accuse and attack others when unhappy, rather than stating that they feel hurt and inviting sympathy (Tavris, 1992, 1993). In other words, feminists have shown, from a positivist empiricist perspective, that these are not "objective" findings of sex differences—rather, they depend on an (implicit) assumption of male-as-norm.

In 1968, Naomi Weisstein used positivist empiricist principles in castigating clinical psychologists and psychiatrists for promulgating "theory without evidence":

> [They] simply refuse to look at the evidence against their theory and practice. And they support their theory and practice with stuff so transparently biased as to have no standing as empirical evidence. (Weisstein, 1968/1993b, p. 197)

Such early critiques paved the way for feminist psychologists to mount a successful institutional challenge to the *Diagnostic and Statistical Manual* (*DSM*) of the American Psychiatric Association (the handbook on which many mental health practitioners base their clinical judgments). This challenge was based on positivist empiricist criteria for "good science." Feminist psychologists took issue with two particular categories in the *DSM,* both predominantly applied to women: Self-Defeating Personality Disorder (SDPD, or masochistic personality); and Late Luteal Phase Dysphoric Disorder (LLPDD, or premenstrual syndrome). Reviewing the evidence for SDPD, they suggested that (1) the existence of the category is not supported by empirical data, (2) research in the field is seriously flawed methodologically, and (3) the category has poor diagnostic power (Caplan, 1991). Paula Caplan and her colleagues have argued that the category is not the result of objective scientific investigation, but rather stems from the ideological bias of white male psychiatrists—that it is a "way to call psychopathological the woman who had conformed to societal norms for a feminine woman" (p. 171), while there is no parallel category for the man who has conformed to social norms for a masculine man (Delusional Dominating Personality Disorder, or macho personality: cf. Caplan, 1991). Feminist psychologists have used similar arguments about "bad science" and "ideological bias" to challenge the LLPDD category, highlighting the scientific inadequacies of premenstrual syndrome research (e.g., Parlee, 1973), describing it as "plagued with methodological errors" and as "deeply flawed" (Caplan, McCurdy-Myers, & Gans, 1992, p. 27).

In sum, then, a positivist empiricist perspective allows feminist psychologists to critique mainstream psychology on its own (scientific) terms—as biased and as methodologically flawed. Feminists have exposed the bias in classic psychological theories derived from all-male samples and inappropriately generalized to women (e.g., Kohlberg's theory of moral reasoning; Erikson's theory of life-span development); and they have challenged the findings of many mainstream empirical studies, criticizing these studies as riddled with technical flaws, such as experimental biases, inadequate sampling techniques, lack of control groups, insufficiently sensitive measurement techniques, unreplicated findings, and unspecified effect sizes (e.g., Eagly, 1994; Hyde, 1994b; Tavris, 1992). A positivist empiricist perspective also offers feminist psychologists the possibility of doing "better science" within this traditional framework. It is therefore perhaps not surprising that positivist empiricism is such a pervasive approach in the psychology of women, and that it has been dubbed by feminist researchers as "one of the most powerful tools at our disposal" (Unger, 1996, p. 166; see also Eagly, 1995; S.A. Shields & Crowley, 1996).

However, positivist empiricism has also been extensively criticized—on methodological grounds—as artificial, decontextualizing, and exploitative, and as unable to address the complexity and diversity of women's lives in a sufficiently sensitive and respectful way (see S. Wilkinson, 1999 for a recent review; also Peplau & Conrad, 1989; Worell & Etaugh, 1994). Feminist psychologists' use of tests, scales, and experiments (indeed, reliance on quantitative research more generally) is out of step with contemporary feminist research in other disciplines, which is predominantly qualitative (cf. Maynard & Purvis, 1994; Reinharz, 1992). In addition, critics have argued—on epistemological and political grounds—that, in challenging the scientific objectivity of mainstream psychology, feminist psychologists simply reinforce the notion that objectivity is potentially attainable; and also obscure the extent to which the practice of science is deeply enmeshed in the social and political practices of which it is a part (C. Kitzinger, 1990c). I will return to epistemological critiques of positivist empiricism later, in discussing feminist social constructionism (see also Bohan, 1992b; Hare-Mustin & Marecek, 1990a; Riger, 1992; Unger, 1989c).

FEMINIST EXPERIENTIAL RESEARCH

Critics of positivist empiricism have often argued for a more experiential approach to women's lives. The key feature of a feminist experiential perspective is an emphasis on individual *experience:* individuals are regarded as "experts" on their own lives, and as "authorities" on their own experience. Emphasizing that, historically, women's experience has systematically been ignored, trivialized, or distorted, a feminist experiential approach reclaims women's experience as central—and aims to listen to women speaking in their own voices, expressing their own meanings and concerns. In contrast to positivist empiricist research, which limits and constrains responses by means of standardized questions, scales, and measures, and "loses" the individual in statistical summaries, experiential research generates vivid, personal accounts of experience and analyses grounded in the specificities of women's lives. Within this theoretical framework, qualitative methods of data collection—including, for example, interviews, focus groups, ethnography, memory work, and the elicitation of (auto)biographical accounts—are *always* used. Experiential research *cannot* be undertaken using experiments, tests, and scales (indeed, its adherents have long been critical of the "triviality" and "contextual sterility" of such methods: e.g., Parlee, 1979; Reinharz, 1983).

Feminist experiential research derives from a variety of feminist theory often called "standpoint theory" (cf. S. Harding, 1993; Hartsock, 1983), which—broadly speaking—holds that women see the world from a particular perspective, or standpoint, because of the experience of being a woman in a patriarchal world. It also recognizes the specificities of knowledge deriving from other standpoints/experiences—for example, those based on sexual identity, social class, or ethnicity—and the interrelationships between standpoints (e.g., R.M. Brewer, 1993; Henwood, Griffin, & Phoenix, 1998). An experiential perspective challenges the positivist empiricist notion of a single, external reality, which can best be apprehended by objective scientific enquiry. Rather, knowledge is seen as contingent upon the standpoint of the knower, and as dependent upon the specificities of her experience. Feminist experiential researchers offer a variety of different ways of analyzing qualitative data, including grounded theory (Henwood & Pigeon, 1995); narrative analysis (Reissman, 1993); and interpretive biography (Gluck & Patai, 1991). Central to these are notions of empathy, intuition, and sensitive "listening" (DeVault, 1990; Kasper, 1994; Mauthner & Doucet, 1998), although exact analytic techniques are rarely specified—indeed, data analysis within an experiential framework appears more akin to art than science. An example of such an analysis, again using the extract from my breast cancer data, but this time drawing on the techniques of interpretive biography, can be seen in Box 2.3. Here, one participant's (Doreen) contribution to the discussion is interpreted within the context of her personal biography—and also within the context of the researcher's understanding of experiential research on "women's voices."

Within the field of feminist psychology, the theoretical perspective of experiential research has been an influential counterpoint to positivist empiricism. Perhaps the best-known work to use this perspective is the Harvard Project on Women's Psychology and Girls' Development. Feminist psychologists working within, or influenced by, the Harvard Project, have argued that psychology, with its male voice, has described the world from its own male standpoint which it has confused with absolute truth. The task of feminist psychology, then, is to listen to the voices of women and girls who speak in a "different voice" (L.M. Brown & Gilligan, 1992, 1993; Gilligan, 1982) and have distinctive "ways of knowing" (Belenky, Clinchy, Goldberger, & Tarule, 1986). Lyn Mikel Brown and Carol Gilligan (1992) have developed a "voice-centered relational

---

Box 2.3
An Experiential Analysis of the Data Extract: Interpretive Biographical Analysis

Key Assumptions:

Each participant experiences herself as a unique individual, with a sense of continuity across time. She therefore strives to make sense of the "biographical disruption" (Bury, 1982) produced by a breast cancer diagnosis in relation to the broader circumstances of her lifeworld and experienced identity. (Some commonalities can, however, be seen in the way in which individuals do this.)

Key Additional Information:

Individual biographical details: Doreen is the youngest participant in the group—she is aged 40 and has an 8-year-old son (her only child). She also works (part-time) outside the home.

Method of Analysis:

Doreen's exploration of what may have caused her breast cancer is considered in relation to her biographical details. (Note: The individual's story may be taken at face value, but is more commonly subjected to further analysis by the researcher.) The way in which she tells her story is also examined carefully—in relation to experiential research on "women's voices."

Analysis:

Unlike the other group members, Doreen is relatively young to have developed breast cancer, while still of childbearing age. In addition, the birth of her son is a relatively recent key life event, and childcare arrangements currently structure her working day. She therefore explores possible explanations of her breast cancer in relation to reproductive factors, particularly the age at which she had her son (which she sees as relatively late in life, compared to other women). This exploration is very tentative: Doreen invokes the views of experts ("they say"); emphasizes her lack of knowledge ("I don't know"); and expresses uncertainty ("what's the other thing?"; "have I got this right?"). This shows a lack of confidence in expressing her own opinion and a lack of certainty as to its validity and acceptability.

Conclusion:

Doreen favors late childbearing as the explanation for her breast cancer. This reflects the extent to which her role as a mother is central to her identity. However, the hesitancy and lack of confidence with which she produces this explanation is typical of women's "uncertainty talk" (cf. Brown & Gilligan, 1992). It appears that, like many women, Doreen's own voice has been "silenced" (or at least muted) by the voice of recognized (medical) authorities.

---

method" to enable them to listen responsively to the voices of women and girls (see also Tolman and Brown, this volume). They emphasize the radical potential of starting from these voices:

> What we have learned most of all . . . is the power of beginning with girls' voices. From listening to girls at the edge of adolescence and observing our own and other women's responses, we begin to see the outlines of new pathways in women's development and also to see new possibilities for women's involvement in the process of political change. (p. 32)

According to these researchers, describing the world from a female standpoint may offer a different version of the world, a different kind of truth.

This work has been enormously influential; and the Harvard Project's approach (and underlying theoretical perspective) has been enthusiastically embraced in a range of applied areas, especially counseling, youth work, and secondary education. The importance of this perspective lies in its assertion of "an alternative voice in the culture," its insistence that "there is more than one way of looking at the world" (Haste, 1994, pp. 399–403), and its prioritizing of women's *own* expressed concerns. However, it has also been criticized for its assumption that women, simply by virtue of being women, can utter truths about the world and thereby reveal their authentic selves (e.g., M. Crawford, 1997a). A key discovery from listening to women's voices is that women inhabit a more "relational" world than do men: women are more "connected with" and "caring" about other people (see also Jordan, Kaplan, Miller, Stiver, & Surrey, 1991)—yet this feeds back into traditional ideas about women's roles, and reinforces the social structures that impose on women the burdens of caring for small children and elderly relatives (Faludi, 1991). Other critics have suggested that work influenced by the Harvard Project often imposes a false homogeneity on the diversity of women's voices across many dimensions of difference (K. Davis, 1994), although this is perhaps less the case with more recent publications (e.g., J.M. Taylor, Gilligan, & Sullivan, 1995).

Another important body of research informed by a feminist experiential perspective is that which draws on narrative and autobiography—relying on women's own tellings and their own understandings of their stories. Some of this work uses case studies of single individuals to illuminate personal understandings and social processes (e.g., Fine, 1989; Hurtado, 1999), while some of it uses particular groups or communities of women to explore a broader shared consciousness or sociopolitical context (e.g., Espin, 1995; Lykes, 1989). Some of it focuses on discrete events in women's lives, such as health care encounters (e.g., P.E. Stevens, 1998), while some of it treats whole lives as units of analysis, taking a biographical perspective (e.g., Franz & Stewart, 1994; Lieblich & Josselson, 1994). Diversity is often a key concern: narrative and autobiographical anthologies of women's lives typically seek to make visible the experience of a wider range of women than has traditionally been the case. The task of the researcher is often to act as a conduit for hitherto "unheard voices" or "untold stories" (e.g., Romero & Stewart, 1999a)—and, of course, it is no accident that it is often the voices of minorities (e.g., lesbians and women of color) which have been silent or silenced, and their stories which are now being told (e.g., Rothblum & Weinstock, 1996; Wyche & Crosby, 1996).

Women of color, and non-Western women, have provided powerful critiques of the "false essentialism" of white, Western feminist theory—challenging not only the predominant theoretical perspectives of feminism but also its predominant methods of enquiry and modes of expression (e.g., Anzaldua, 1987; Christian, 1985; L.T. Smith, 1999; Trinh, 1989). These researchers and writers have sought to develop theory grounded within their own particular standpoints and experiences of oppression, particularly black/African-American standpoints (e.g., Guy-Sheftall, 1995; P.H. Collins, 1990; hooks, 1990; Lorde, 1984b) and postcolonial perspectives (e.g., Mama, 1995; Mohanty, 1988; Mohanty, Russo, & Torres, 1991; Spivak, 1987).

In sum, experiential research has often been seen as corrective or complement to positivist empiricist research. Rather than providing objective knowledge in the form of broad, general findings drawn from tightly controlled experiments or large-scale surveys, it offers a detailed, in-depth understanding of women's own subjective experiences of their lives. Its main advantages are the richness and complexity/subtlety of its data and its prioritizing of women's own particular concerns. Challenging the male monopoly on truth has enabled women to name—and understand—their own experience (e.g., sexism, sexual harassment, marital rape, and date rape). Challenging the white, Western monopoly on truth has enabled black and non-Western women to assert the specificities of their oppressions. Challenging the heterosexual monopoly on truth has made visible the experience of lesbian, gay, bisexual, intersexed, and transgendered persons (see also Kitzinger, this volume). However, experiential research is often criticized on methodological grounds (particularly by positivist empiricists) because it does not use the standard framework of scientific enquiry and is rarely generalizable or replicable. It is also criticized on epistemological grounds (particularly by social constructionists), regarding the status of experience. The typical argument here is that experience does not exist in a "pure" form, independent of the telling of it, but is highly contingent on context (i.e., stories are told for particular purposes, and researcher and participant "co-construct" reality). Such critics have raised issues about what the feminist researcher is doing when she "represents" another's experience (S. Wilkinson & Kitzinger, 1996); and what she should do when her participants' stories do not fit her own theoretical/political framework (C. Kitzinger & Wilkinson, 1997). Such criticisms prefigure the theoretical basis of social constructionism.

FEMINIST SOCIAL CONSTRUCTIONISM

The theoretical perspective of feminist social constructionism (cf. Bohan, 1993; M.M. Gergen & Davis, 1997; Hare-Mustin & Marecek, 1990a; S.J. Kessler & McKenna, 1978; C. Kitzinger, 1987; Unger, 1989a, 1990) provides major challenges to both positivist empiricist and experiential perspectives, particularly in relation to epistemology. It is part of the "turn to language" in social science and feminist research more generally (S. Wilkinson & Kitzinger, 1995), often seen as having intellectual roots in the sociological traditions of ethnomethodology, symbolic interactionism, phenomenology, and labeling theory. Central to social constructionism is the view that "facts" are always dependent on the particular forms of language and the particular language communities which have created and maintained them. Social constructionists argue that we cannot "know" the external world through observation and measurement (as positivist empiricists contend) or the internal world through reflective introspection or careful listening (as experiential researchers contend) because all knowledge is mediated by—indeed, constructed through—the specificities of language. For instance, changing conceptions of "homosexuality" are both reflected through and mediated by language: sin, sickness, and sexual perversion have given way to gay pride, lesbian chic, and queerdom. The acknowledgment that social/cultural/historical contexts influence what we know about the world and who we are as people is sometimes referred to as "weak" social constructionism (C. Kitzinger, 1995b), and such a theoretical perspective is (relatively) acceptable to many feminist researchers.

In its "strong" form, however, social constructionism entails a much more radical epistemology. Strong social constructionism encompasses the view that *all* ways of speaking, *all* forms of naming, and *all* familiar category systems are themselves social constructions. A strong social constructionist perspective challenges even our most taken-for-granted, and seemingly immutable, categories, such as "biological sex"—the distinction between "women" and "men" (cf. J. Butler, 1990). This distinction is such a fundamental organizing principle within our world that it is not easy to imagine that it is arbitrary, or that we could eliminate it from our vocabularies and ways of thinking—the argument that people do not "naturally" come in two sexes seems counterintuitive. Feminist social constructionists have argued that this is because our "intuitions" are formed under male supremacy, making it very difficult to see how the construction of men and women as separate categories is an ideological (rather than biological) distinction, and a political necessity for sexist oppression. Instead, then, of asking questions about the real differences between men and women, feminist psychologists in this tradition ask questions about how men and women are *constructed* as different (cf. Hare-Mustin & Marecek, 1994; Hollway, 1994). Sometimes these differences are constructed physically (as in surgery on transsexuals to change the biological markers of their sex to those of the other sex). More often, though, they are constructed socially and psychologically, through repeated assertions (in talk and texts) about what men and women are "really" like—these come to constitute the dominant discourses of masculinity and femininity. Such discourses construct our notions of the world and our identities.

Feminist social constructionism encompasses work drawing on the theoretical frameworks of poststructuralism (e.g., Gavey, 1989; Hollway, 1995; Walkerdine, 1996b) and postmodernism (e.g., Flax, 1987; M.M. Gergen, 1990a; Lather, 1991), although the theoretical distinctions are not always clear. Any type of data may be collected and analyzed from a social constructionist perspective: The key criterion is not the type of data, nor the specific type of analysis undertaken but, rather, the central theoretical assumption that category systems are constructed, rather than fixed. Examples of quantitative feminist social constructionist work include the use of attitude scales (e.g., The Attitudes Toward Reality Scale: Unger, 1984–1985; Unger, Draper, & Pendergrass, 1986); Q-methodology (C. Kitzinger, 1987; Snelling, 1999); and the semantic differential technique (M. Crawford, Stark, & Renner, 1998). More commonly, however, feminist social constructionists use qualitative methods of data collection (particularly interviews, focus groups, and naturally occurring conversations) and the most frequently used type of data analysis—particularly in the United Kingdom—is (some form of) discourse analysis (cf. S. Wilkinson & Kitzinger, 1995).

There are three broad strands of discourse analytic work (although these are not rigidly separable): critical discourse analysis, conversation analysis, and discursive psychology. Critical discourse analysis is based on poststructuralist theory, especially Foucauldian, and affords a central role to power and social structure (cf. Burman et al., 1996; Burman & Parker, 1993; Fairclough, 1995; van Dijk, 1993). Conversation analysis derives from the sociological tradition of ethnomethodology, and prioritizes the fine-grained analysis of naturally occurring conversation, or talk-in-interaction (cf. Atkinson & Heritage, 1984; M.H. Goodwin, 1990; Sacks, 1992; Schegloff, 1997). Discursive psychology originates primarily in the sociology of scientific knowledge and combines elements of critical discourse analysis and conversation analysis to study a broad range of materials, and to reconstruct central psychological concepts (cf. D. Edwards, 1997; D. Edwards & Potter, 1992; Potter, 1996; Potter & Wetherell, 1987). For a discussion of the relationship between critical discourse analysis and conversation analysis, from the perspective of discursive psychology, see Wetherell (1998).

Perhaps not surprisingly, given its emphasis on power and social structure, critical discourse analysis has—to date—been the discourse analytic approach favored by feminist researchers. Researchers using critical discourse analysis typically seek to identify (preexisting) discourses in talk (or texts), and to consider how these discourses structure both the material conditions of women's lives, and their subjective experiences. Critical discourse analysts often invoke factors outside talk itself (e.g., social-structural or intrapsychic factors) to explain how discourses operate and produce "real" effects (in the world or in the psyche). For example, Hollway (1989) has identified three dominant discourses of heterosexual sex (the male sexual drive, have and hold, and permissive discourses), which, she says, "position" women as sexually subservient and submissive, and ensure that it is very difficult to develop an "emancipatory" discourse of women's heterosexual desire. Further, Hollway argues (adding a psychodynamic explanation), women become emotionally dependent on these discourses—a process which ensures that they continue to reproduce gendered power relations in their sexual practices. Building on this work, in analyzing women's accounts of unwanted sex with men, Gavey (1992) has shown how dominant discourses of heterosexual sex operate as "technologies of coercion"—and how women attempt to resist and subvert the coercive power of these discourses (Gavey, 1996). Critical discourse analysis is also widely used by feminist researchers in the field of health psychology—in relation to, for example, anorexia, PMS, smoking, pregnancy/childbirth, and screening for cervical cancer—see the anthologies edited by Ussher (1997), Yardley (1997), and Willig (1999); also Braun and Gavey (1999), and M. Morgan (1999).

By contrast, conversation analytic approaches have been relatively little used in feminist research. Feminist researchers working in this tradition do not see discourses as preexisting (either in the external world or inside people's heads), but see talk as constructed by participants in and through the course of conversation. These researchers typically focus on the fine details of talk, paying particular attention to the immediate local context of a given utterance (its specific place within an interview, focus group, medical consultation, or courtroom exchange, for example; and what happens in the talk immediately before and after it). Conversation analytic researchers do not study the thoughts, emotions, attitudes, beliefs, or life experiences presumed to lie behind (and to be expressed through) talk. Rather, they treat talk—including talk about thoughts and emotions—as a form of action in its own right, as doing specific things (e.g., disagreement with another speaker, supporting a point of view, or presenting a particular identity); and they focus, in particular, on how the people actually talking to each other understand what their talk is doing, as those understandings are displayed in the talk itself. In their study of young women's talk about sexual negotiation, for example, Frith and Kitzinger (1998) demonstrate how participants' talk about doing "emotion work" (e.g., soothing the hurt feelings and massaging the egos of their male partners) can be analyzed as a resource through which young women construct consensual versions of men as emotional weaklings and portray themselves as active agents who are knowledgeable about heterosexual relationships. For other examples of feminist psychological research drawing on conversation analysis, see C. Kitzinger (2000a), C. Kitzinger and Frith (1999), Speer (2000), Stokoe (1998), and S. Wilkinson and Kitzinger (2000).

Discursive psychology (a somewhat hybrid approach) has been rather more widely used by feminists than has conversation analysis. Although it shares a number of key features with conversation analysis (e.g., an emphasis on talk as a form of action, constructed for particular purposes), discursive psychology typically looks at the broader construction of talk and text by means of a range of styles, linguistic resources, and rhetorical devices (D. Edwards & Potter, 1992). It also attempts to rework some of the (traditionally cognitive) psychological categories such as attitudes, beliefs, and memory; and to analyse how key social processes—such as sexism, racism, and heterosexism—are played out in talk. For example, one of discursive psychology's explanatory devices for understanding the content and organization of discourse is the "interpretative repertoire" (cf. Wetherell,

1998). This device has been used, for example, to analyze racist discourse—differentiating between use of the term "culture" as indicating "heritage" and its use as indicating "therapy"—two interpretative repertoires typically used in different contexts, and with very different implications for social policy (Wetherell & Potter, 1992). Discursive psychologists also study the "discursive practices" through which personal and social identities are constructed: the "imaginary positions" invoked in young men's negotiation of masculinity, for example (Wetherell & Edley, 1999).

One key device in identity construction is the management of "stake and interest" (Potter, 1996). Speakers are typically alert to others' potential constructions of them as *accountable*—as having an ingrained set of prejudices, something important to gain or lose, or a particular axe to grind, for example—and there are various ways in which this accountability may be managed by the speaker, so as to demonstrate a lack of stake or interest in the topic under discussion. One way is conspicuously to "display" ignorance or uncertainty (e.g., repeatedly to assert "I don't know" or "I'm not sure"); another is to appear to be groping for a (partially or perhaps inaccurately remembered) piece of information (e.g., to use expressions like "let me see now" or "what is it?")—in other words, to display disinterestedness and/or lack of commitment precisely at a point where

---

Box 2.4
A Social Constructionist Analysis of the Data Extract: Discursive Psychological Analysis

Key Assumptions:

Participants' talk is a form of action, constructed in the course of interaction. Talk is designed by speakers for its specific conversational context (i.e., that particular point in the focus group discussion)—and each bit of talk is doing something relevant to, and occasioned by, that context. (Note: Talk is not seen as reflecting *either* cognitive content, *or* the search for meaning and continuity in identity/the lifeworld.)

Key Additional Information:

Transcription conventions: Underlining marks emphasis; a dash (-) indicates that a word or syllable is cut off abruptly; and square parentheses enclose transcriber's notes. (Note: This is much simpler than the version typically used in conversation analysis.)

Method of Analysis:

Doreen's long "turn" is considered in relation in its interactional context (i.e., what happens immediately before and after it in the conversational sequence); in relation to the sorts of concerns that typically structure talk (e.g., accountability, the presentation of identity); and in relation to the sorts of conversational devices people typically use to manage such concerns (e.g., demonstrating a lack of stake or interest via expressions of uncertainty or vagueness).

Analysis:

In this extract, Doreen can be seen to be managing issues of accountability, in relation to the interactional context of the moderator's question. If she provides a direct answer to the question, she could be open to challenge, disagreement, or even ridicule (as Gertie has been just before this extract begins). So she distances herself from the possible causes she puts forward, formulating her response with some care (three times she breaks off abruptly and starts again); and attributing her suggestions to unspecified others ("they say")—as does Freda, in the following turn. Doreen also demonstrates her lack of investment in the suggestions she puts forward, by offering a conspicuous display of ignorance or uncertainty ("I don't know," three times), and by apparently groping for imperfectly remembered information ("what's the other thing?"; "have I got this right?").

Conclusion:

Doreen's careful presentation of some of the possible causes of her breast cancer is designed to protect herself against challenge or disagreement. Specifically, she takes care to demonstrate to her co-conversationalists that she has no particular stake or interest in the causes she puts forward (cf. Potter, 1996)—she is simply repeating others' views, in an apparently half-remembered way, and with protestations of her own ignorance/uncertainty.

accountability (i.e., one's stake or interest in a topic) could be an issue (cf. Potter, 1996, pp. 124–132). In Box 2.4 Doreen's management of accountability is part of a discursive psychological analysis of the breast cancer data extract. Note, in particular, that this (social constructionist) analysis offers a completely different interpretation of Doreen's hesitancy and vagueness from that provided within an experiential theoretical framework—and one which is theoretically incompatible with it.

In sum, social constructionist research is the most demanding of these three theoretical perspectives: Indeed, it is often counterintuitive. Its radical potential lies in the recognition that if the categories through which we understand our social world are constructions, then these categories are potentially open to reconstruction in the service of emancipatory goals. A social constructionist perspective has been criticized, however, for the difficulty of its theoretical concepts, the (sometimes seemingly willful) abstruseness of its writing, and for the difficulty of translating its theoretical challenge into a clear political program (e.g., Weisstein, 1993b). In particular, it has been argued that if we deconstruct the very categories upon which our oppression is based (e.g., woman, lesbian) then we have no principled basis upon which to organize against it (e.g., Gill, 1995). Proponents of the various forms of discourse analysis are also critical of each others' approaches. For example, critical discourse analysis has been criticized for its failure to specify clear criteria for the identification of discourses in talk (C. Kitzinger & Wilkinson, 1997) and for its privileging of particular, politically motivated analyses (Widdicombe, 1995). Most recently, conversation analysis has come under attack as antifeminist (Billig, 1999a, 1999b)—the argument here is that in privileging the fine detail of talk over individual people or structural oppression, conversation analysis risks reducing lived experience and material suffering to mere discursive productions. Conversation analysis is said to occlude the exercise of power in talk and to discount the analysis of broader social variables, such as gender (see C. Kitzinger (2000a); Schegloff (1999a, 1999b) for counterarguments).

CONCLUSION

In this chapter, positivist empiricism, experiential research, and social constructionism are presented as three contrasting theoretical perspectives for feminist psychology. No attempt has been made to adjudicate between these theoretical perspectives in terms of their value for feminist scholars because *all* are useful, albeit for different kinds of research purposes, and in different research contexts. However, some of the main strengths and weaknesses of each have been indicated.

Three different analyses of the breast cancer data extract illustrate just how different—in terms of underlying assumptions, methods, and types of findings—research conducted within each of these theoretical traditions is likely to be. The content analysis (as an example of a positivist empiricist approach) provides a systematized summary of (some of) these working-class women's beliefs about the causes of breast cancer. As such, its findings are readily comparable with those of other similar studies. The interpretive biographical analysis (as an example of an experiential approach) offers a richer and more contextualized focus on one woman's preferred explanation of her breast cancer, in relation to the particular circumstances of her life. It also examines the way in which she tells her life story, as typical of women's narratives. The discursive psychological analysis (as an example of a social constructionist approach) provides a sophisticated analysis of the specific actions performed by this piece of talk about the causes of breast cancer in the context of this focus group discussion. As such, it also offers the researcher an example of the more general phenomenon of identity management in interaction.

To influence policy makers, it may be useful to draw on the "evidential" framework of science, and—particularly—to be able to present the kind of statistical summary that typically accrues from positivist empiricist research. By contrast, experiential approaches are often seen as honoring participants' realities, by remaining more faithful to lived experience; and as providing an opportunity to represent hitherto "unheard" or "silenced" voices. By contrast again, social constructionist approaches have the potential to destabilize radically what we take for granted; if we can understand the world we know as just one version, constructed via specific practices for specific (social and political) purposes, then we open up the possibility of constructing a different—and better—kind of world.

I have argued elsewhere against "a unified field with a single 'politically correct' line," and in favor of the diversity offered by "a potentially dazzling variety of approaches" (S. Wilkinson, 1996a, p. 2). It is my view that theoretical eclecticism (and the epistemological and methodological diversity it sustains) is crucial both to the academic field of psychology of women and to the broader feminist project of better understanding—and improving—women's lives.

CHAPTER 3

Choices and Consequences: Methodological Issues in the Study of Gender

VITA CARULLI RABINOWITZ and DANIELLA MARTIN

In traditional psychology, gender functions as a construct or a research variable with which we study women, or women and men. In more recent formulations, the study of gender extends to a perspective or research framework within which we study other constructs, and social relations more generally. In this view, gender is placed as a locus of understanding the terms of inclusion and exclusion that support divisions between the sexes or other groups constructed on the basis of difference (Unger, 1989b). With regard to methodology, the redefinition of the study of gender, born of the critical consciousness of the women's movement of the 1970s, established for future scholars that the choice of problems under study, the definition of data, and the ultimate objectives of research would become subject to scrutiny (M. Gould, 1985; Lott, 1981). As a lasting legacy of this spirit, gender studies today is one of the sites in the discipline where we can most clearly see the lack of agreement about methodological and epistemological assumptions of mainstream psychology.

At the same time that feminism has been the defining force in transforming the study of gender, other approaches have appeared in and around psychology that have identified similar issues in areas other than gender. Critical frameworks are being erected throughout the social sciences to address the inadequacies of traditional research methods, particularly as they define and attempt to solve social problems (D. Fox & Prilleltensky, 1997). They reveal that the dilemmas faced by feminist psychologists and psychologists studying gender are not unique. The marginalization of critical approaches within the discipline of psychology has ensured that their common dilemmas and achievements remain obscure. With regard to research methods, this points to the need to look outside—and, critically, within—the discipline for innovative research strategies that would place the "gendered" perspective, as a fundamentally critical and inclusive perspective, into a broader academic and intellectual context.

In this chapter, we first discuss different frameworks for studying gender in psychological research. We briefly review the common frameworks in the study of gender, from gender as individual difference to gender as viewed and studied in levels of analysis from the individual to the cultural levels. Our points in this section are that research is a process that profits from understanding and acknowledging the assumptive framework from which one works, and that the choice of framework, like all subsequent methodological choices, has consequences for what questions are asked, what methods are selected, and what findings will be obtained. Next we discuss

Correspondence concerning this article should be addressed to Vita C. Rabinowitz, Department of Psychology, Hunter College of the City University of New York, 695 Park Ave., New York, NY 10021. Electronic mail may be sent to vrabinowitz@gc.cuny.edu. Do not quote without permission.

enduring and emerging issues in research methods as they apply to the study of gender or the taking of a gendered perspective. The stalwarts of evaluating research—validity and reliability/replicability—are examined with respect to gender, alongside of alternative ways of evaluating research, including trustworthiness, reflexivity, and voice. More specific issues that emerge in common and not-so-common research methods, spanning experiments, quasi-experiments, survey methods, interviews, focus groups, and archival methods, are discussed in detail, as are issues concerning the combination of different approaches in a program of research or even a single study. Throughout, our approach to research methods is descriptive, analytic, and critical, promoting an understanding of the multiple and often competing research concerns over simplistic prescriptive judgments. Our theme is that methodological choices have consequences. Our hope is to be useful.

CONCEPTUALIZING RESEARCH QUESTIONS

The first step in the research process, one that is more often implicit than explicit, is the conceptualization of the research question or problem. When we set out to study persons, we start with a certain set of epistemological assumptions about personhood, the self, and how the self relates to others. Similarly, when gender is the object of study, the research questions we ask follow from a preformed understanding of gender and how gender operates to create a set of meanings in society. It is important that the assumptions we carry about the nature of gender (or any other categories and identities) enter into the discussion of the research process, for, as we will show, they directly affect the methodological choices we make throughout that process.

GENDER AS INDIVIDUAL DIFFERENCE

Among many other things, gender is a seemingly natural and meaningful way of dividing people. The term "natural" equates gender with sex, a biological category, whereas "difference" represents the notion that gender is a property of individuals, distinguishing one group of people from another. In psychological research, the notion of gender as individual difference has been alternatively suppressed (folded under the larger concept of "people") and exaggerated, as in studies that claim essential differences in the abilities of women and men (Hare-Mustin & Marecek, 1990b; Kimball, this volume). Comparing men and women on various psychological traits and behaviors has been a popular and often useful framework for studying gender and other constructs. Historically, it helped to debunk some untruths about women's inferiority. More recently, this framework has resurfaced in evolutionary explanations of differences in men's and women's behaviors, with emphasis on psychological mechanisms originating over the long expanse of human history to solve specific adaptive problems entailed in social experience (Buss, 1996; Gowaty, this volume).

However, as is now well understood, the sexes differ not only physically and biologically, but psychologically, socially, economically, and politically. It should not be surprising that the routine testing for sex differences in many areas will "find" them, sometimes reliably enough to foster the thinking that such differences are basic, static, immutable—essential. Most notably, some research in psychology of gender has critically examined predominant research practices and assumptions to discover that many previously established sex differences disappeared when contextual factors were examined rather than controlled through the research design (Deaux, 1984; Deaux & Major, 1987). Following these and similar findings, feminist research called for de-essentializing gender differences (J.R. Martin, 1994). By pointing to the role of social context, and specifically the effects of hierarchical relationships in the production of "gender differences," many researchers questioned the conceptualization of sex or gender as a biologically determined and immutable category.

The awareness that sex difference is at least partially a product of research design has important implications for arguments about the nature of gender and its role in social and individual experience. Despite important problems with the construal of gender as difference and the study of sex differences, such research is not likely to cease any time soon; indeed, the evidence is that it will flourish in psychology and related fields, and, due to statistical advances like meta-analysis and structural equation modeling, become more sophisticated, precise, and powerful. In many fields, including biomedicine, health, and education, the study of gender is regarded as critical to the improved circumstances of all people, but especially girls and women. Indeed, the study of gender as difference is now federally mandated by such important funding agencies as the National Institutes of Health (Mizrahi & Rabinowitz, 1996). Such mandates recognize that the long-standing neglect of the study of gender in areas like health has led to a false equation of the experiences and conditions of men and women, and diminished opportunities for institutional and social change (Hare-Mustin & Marecek, 1990b). Studying gender as difference can be important in illuminating the consequences of social practices on different groups of people as well as the sites where these effects are routinely re-created and challenged (Parlee, 1981; Thorne, 1993). At the same time, this approach to gender remains problematic for all the reasons discussed.

CONTEXTS OF GENDER AT DIFFERENT LEVELS OF ANALYSIS

A common conceptual framework that organizes contextual effects in gender research takes the approach of examining gender at multiple levels of analysis (Deaux & LaFrance, 1998). Originally developed in social psychology (Doise, 1997) and social ecological psychology (Bronfenbrenner, 1979), this perspective guides research by expanding the frame of analysis from individual difference to interpersonal, social, and cultural levels of explanation. Thus, gender effects can be viewed through multiple, embedded lenses of social and cultural contexts, providing a dynamic interplay of factors that constrain and reinforce the operation of gender in society. This approach recognizes that an individual's gendered behaviors are part of interactions among men and women, structured by cultural norms and channeled and supported through organizational systems that reward individuals for engaging in behaviors deemed culturally appropriate.

In research practice, adopting the levels of analysis approach to study gender invites several questions: At what levels does one enter the system (Deaux & LaFrance, 1998)? And, though it is difficult to study individual, social, and cultural phenomena simultaneously, what do we gain or lose by selecting the study of one level over another? One answer to these questions is that the study of gender on any level is useful, for it can be combined with insights from the study of other levels in a meta-analytical fashion, simply fitting multiple pieces to create a complete picture. However, it is also important to consider that the results obtained at any one level of analysis will be of necessity reductionistic and may, in themselves, seriously misinform our understanding of gender. For example, analyses focused on the effects of institutions or cultural norms on gender may create an overly deterministic picture that leaves little space for individual choice and agency. Similarly, when individual and interpersonal gender transactions are examined, individuals are portrayed as primarily responsible for their choices as well as their failures, without an acknowledgment of the constraints of ideological/institutional contexts on individual behavior (I. Prilleltensky & Nelson, 1997).

Although the study of gender advances by taking a look at any one or two levels of analysis, it is becoming increasingly desirable to approach research in a fashion that investigates the dynamic interplay of individual and contextual factors. We need to examine how different levels of context interact, creating ever new human environments, and how these environmental contexts interact with individual factors. Current research in organizational psychology and group dynamics has addressed this problem by developing a typology of composition models (Chan, 1998), based on a critique of common shortcomings in single-level research (Moritz & Watson, 1998). The typologies provide answers as to what kind of functional relationships exist among constructs on different levels of analysis (e.g., individual and organizational) to serve as a basis for analyzing data either in an additive or an integrative fashion. The term "additive" refers to a strategy that treats group response as equivalent to the sum (average) of individual perceptions. For example, a measure of organizational climate may be created by averaging individual employees' perceptions of the organization, assuming an additive relationship between the lower-level and the higher-level construct. In contrast, nonadditive (transformative) composition types take into account the variability within the group, such as the degree of consensus manifested by individual employees of the organization. By modeling the degree of agreement among individual responses (based on analyses of within-group variance), the properties of the group level such as group size, gender composition, and style of leadership may be linked to individual perceptions as they are structured within a particular group system.

Observing the emergence of shared social perceptions by using multilevel research design is particularly relevant to the study of gender. An important research tradition in European social psychology, the study of social representations (Moscovici, 1988), took a multilevel approach to the study of social cognition long before such thinking came into vogue. Current work in social representations relies, with equal facility, on qualitative and quantitative studies that examine individual opinions, attitudes, or stereotypes to find their common organizing principles, and then links these with people's psychological characteristics and social positions, such as gender. In one example, Lorenzi-Cioldi (cited in Doise, Clemence, & Lorenzi-Cioldi, 1993) studied how sex-stereotypical descriptions of the self emerge as a function of gender composition of a group (either male or female) and information provided to respondents about their personal characteristics (either consistent or inconsistent with sex stereotypes). Using correspondence factor analysis of the responses obtained from girls and boys, he found that the experimental manipulation supplying information about the self interacted with the "natural" condition of the respondents' sex. When girls and boys were placed into groups labeled consistently with stereotypes about their sex (autonomous for boys and dependent for girls), their responses were highly sex-stereotypical. However, when respondents were placed into groups characterized by attributes of the other sex, their responses approached the patterns characteristic of the other sex (Doise, Clemence, & Lorenzi-Cioldi, 1993). These results showed how sex differences emerge as a function of group relationships in addition to cognitive principles that typically guide the symbolic relationships between sex groups, and that the representations of individuals are far less rigid than is attributed to them by a research tradition that treats sex as a natural category. As this example illustrates, the multilevel perspective, by focusing on the interdependent nature of social psychological processes, underlines the socially constructive nature of various effects that may sometimes be incorrectly attributed to sex as a biological and individual category (see also Daiute, Jones, Rawlins, & Stern, 1999, on boys' and girls' nonstereotypical development). Moreover, multilevel research may provide valuable insights into locations most suitable for social change (Toro, Trickett, Wall, & Salem, 1991).

Approaching the study of gender through single-level (sex comparison) versus multilevel perspectives requires the use of different analytical methods. The sex comparison framework is best served by adopting experimental or quasi-experimental methodologies to analyze group differences. This approach is less suitable to the study of higher-level contextual factors, such as societal beliefs, norms, and other culturally shared psychological phenomena. Today, new statistical developments in systems analysis allow for representation of hierarchically structured data embedded in different levels of a system (Moritz & Watson, 1998). Qualitative approaches have importantly filled the need for development of research tools at the sociocultural levels of analysis. Narrative approaches, such as discourse analysis (I. Parker, 1997), focus on the role of communication as a mediator of social and individual processes, bridging across levels of analyses by depicting multiple positions of speakers and their audiences in a complex system of social meanings. However, some authors point out that discursive approaches may pay excessive attention to language at the expense of an attention to the materiality of power (I. Parker & Burman, 1993). With this in mind, we later discuss mixed model research—various combinations of qualitative and quantitative methods—as a particularly promising approach to the complex contextual meanings of social constructs such as gender.

In our view, research that appreciates and, where possible, incorporates multiple levels of analysis, from the biological to the cultural, represents one of the most exciting developments in psychology, and yet it has been widely overlooked by scholars in the study of gender. Many topics highly relevant to gender, such as intimate relationships and group processes, are now being studied more by our colleagues in sociology, communications, family studies, and organizational behavior. If we continue to conceptualize our research in terms of individual-level variables, we will further narrow the scope and impact of gender studies in psychology.

ENDURING AND EMERGING ISSUES IN RESEARCH DESIGN

In this section, we discuss key general concerns in choosing and evaluating research methods as they pertain to the study of gender. We begin with the classical issues of validity and reliability and end with the more recent concerns of trustworthiness, voice, and reflexivity. Throughout this section, our guiding question is: What constitutes good research?

VALIDITY

Validity is an overall evaluative judgment of the degree to which empirical evidence supports the adequacy and appropriateness of interpretations and actions based on the results of a study or assessment (Messick, 1995). Notions of validity are based on paradigms or philosophical positions about reality and our ability to apprehend it, with internally consistent axioms concerning ontology (the nature of reality), epistemology (the relationship of the knower to the known), and axiology (the role of values in inquiry). The most influential views of validity in the social sciences today are rooted in the postpositivist paradigm (Popper, 1959; D.T. Campbell & Stanley, 1966), which is a revision of the untenable axioms of positivism. There are variations among adherents, but postpositivists generally hold that, although an external reality exists, it can be understood only imperfectly and probabilistically, and that our understanding of reality is constructed (if constrained by external reality). Postpositivists express appreciation for the "theory-ladenness of facts" and the "value-ladeness of inquiry," but also act as if some findings are "objectively true" and some truths are transhistorical and transcontextual. They hold that values can be controlled or neutralized (Tashakkori & Teddlie, 1998). The postpositive paradigm characterizes most quantitative and even much qualitative inquiry today, at least those studies that rely on the hypothetico-deductive model of scientific inquiry that follows an iterative process of theory development to data collection.

D.T. Campbell and Stanley (1966) and later T.D. Cook and Campbell (1979) offered influential validity typologies, which, in their most basic and memorable form, established for generations of scholars that there are two separate types of validity, internal validity and external validity, and that these are especially relevant to particular kinds of studies: those making causal claims. The focus on evaluating studies making causal claims reflects the conviction that there are reasonably stable, lawful causal relationships among social phenomena, that there is a hierarchy of questions worth asking, and that causal questions—questions probing causal relationships among variables—are at the top of that hierarchy.

Internal validity is relevant to the quality of causal inference: whether the independent variable in fact caused a change in the dependent variable, whereas external validity is relevant to the generalizability of the results, that is, whether the findings of a study can be applied to people, times, and settings not sampled. The assumption underlying the typology is that internal validity is to a study what health is to the body or justice to a system of government: its first virtue. Consequently, a study that is not internally valid is without merit, useless, or worse: mischievous, misleading, pernicious. In contrast to internal validity, external validity is widely seen as less central to a study and is often merely assumed, questioned only when the research involves women, ethnic minorities, people from countries outside the United States, and other "specialized groups," or when the research is explicitly about culture, which is rare in psychology (S. Sue, 1999).

These kinds of typologies can be meaningfully applied to the study of gender, yet the application reveals how troublesome gender is to study using conventional methods. We first review what conventional internal and external validity analyses reveal about gender, then consider the limits of such analyses, and conclude with the consideration of newer criteria for evaluating research on and with gender.

As an internal validity matter, when gender is a "subject variable"—that is, when male and female subjects are compared in a gender-as-difference framework—causal statements about sex and gender cannot be made because people are not randomly assigned to gender. Gender of respondents is not manipulated, but merely measured. The males and females in any given study may differ in age, height, weight, muscle mass, distribution of hormones, experience with throwing a baseball, disclosure patterns, empathy, grade-point average, expectations for success, verbal fluency, number of close friends, and style of dress—all or none of which may be the active ingredient in a response pattern.

In the parlance of traditional validity analyses, males and females are "inherently nonequivalent groups," and studies that treat gender as a variable and compare males and females must explicitly rule out the threat of selection, which operates when an effect may be due to the differences between the kinds of people in various groups. Besides elevating the preexisting difference into a variable in the study, other ways of dealing with nuisance variables is to control them—restrict the study to one level, in this case, one gender, or let the variable vary at random and randomly assign both males and females to different treatments so that the pesky—if profound—differences between them can be distributed equally among treatment groups and neutralized, thus permitting generalizations across gender.

Sex and gender can be manipulated and studied experimentally as a causal variable when sex-of-stimuli is studied (Unger, 1979b), as when respondents are asked to read and evaluate identical essays, some ostensibly written by women and some by men. In fact, the sex of the essayists is manipulated by the investigator. When gender is studied in this manner, we often find that identical male and female behaviors are rarely evaluated identically, because sex and role are highly confounded or confused in our society (Unger, 1998). When this insight is the point of the study, the findings can be informative and important theoretically and socially. For instance, men and women observing an interaction between a smiling man and woman see the "same" exchange differently, with men more likely than women to see flirtatiousness and sexual intent on the part of the female stimulus person (Abbey, 1982). The external world presents two smiling individuals of different sexes, but the meaning of the events is reliably different depending on who is observing it.

External validity gets to the issue of whether findings obtained on one population, in one setting, at one point in time are likely to hold over variations in people, settings, and times. Gender differences that are reasonably consistent (reliable) across populations, settings, and times have been quite successfully used to support essentialist views of gender, such as evolutionary explanations of how men and women behave in romantic and sexual relationships (Buss, 1989). Across many cultures and times, men are more likely than women to express desire for young and physically attractive mates, and women are more likely than men to express interest in a partner's resources. There are some striking consistencies in gender-related differences, including cross-cultural similarities in schemas and stereotypes about males and females. But most gender-related effects, with their "now you see them, now you don't" quality, are particularly poor candidates for generalization.

A central problem with conventional validity analyses is that they assume that the social world is a wholly external world and that there is a single truth that captures it. In our view, a more sophisticated and useful validity analysis recognizes that social phenomena exist in objective and subjective worlds, that there are "social facts" such as inequality and power differences as well as differing interpretations of and meanings attached to such facts. External reality likely *constrains* the numbers and kinds of interpretations people can meaningfully make, but it also *allows* others, depending on various features of the event, including ambiguity, and of the observer, including standpoint (Clinchy & Norem, 1998). As Rhoda Unger (1998) has posed it, a central challenge to psychology is how to deal with the subjective without losing the objective.

In classical treatments of validity, validity questions are treated more or less as technical ones, rather than as the interpretive and social questions they are. Moreover, conventional treatments assume that all research is conducted primarily to advance knowledge rather than to advance an agenda, whether personal or social, and that validity criteria and concerns are shared by a universal yet unnamed community of truth-seekers. Yet, we must always ask: Valid for what purpose, and valid to whom? We find a useful guide to validity in one of Donald Campbell's (1999a) lesser known provocations: "If I am wrong, who would know?" Today, this issue resonates even more deeply, as many of us question the notions of a single social truth and of communities converging on it.

REPLICABILITY

Validity is rarely discussed in social science without reference to replicability of studies (or, in measurement terms, reliability), the extent to which independent investigations of a phenomena produce similar results. It is a truism in science that if findings are not reproducible, they cannot be valid. The positivist ideal of empirical investigation since the 17th century has been that "each member of the scientific community could replicate a demonstration for himself [*sic*]. . . . Each scientist was to be allowed to inspect the apparatus and try out the shared recipe" (D.T. Campbell, 1999b, p. 193). In social science, where samples and settings could never be duplicated exactly and contextual factors outside of the experimental setting (such as social climate and economic conditions) as well as within it were always in flux, exact or explicit replications were never the norm, or even the ideal. Implicit or conceptual replications, where alternative samples, settings, and, more important, operational definitions or measures were used, were considered desirable. But in fact, as Campbell notes, explicit and even implicit replications have always been uncommon in areas such as social psychology because they are usually unpublishable, always of low prestige, and do not justify their effort and cost. Social psychology more often relies on the single dramatic study or demonstration as a basis for future work. Without the "threat of replication," fields suffer from a proliferation and opportunistic overreliance on monomethod, small-sample studies, and "overediting" of data to achieve publishability. In this view, the absence of the norms and practices of replication makes it "theoretically predictable that the social disciplines will make little progress" (p. 194).

Postpositivist views rest on the assumption that although the historical date and particular location of the research cannot be disregarded, transtemporal and transcontextual knowledge is possible and important to gain. D.T. Campbell (1999b) notes that fields far more interpretive than psychology, for example, hermeneutics and history, have achieved impressive replicability at the level of facts (though theories remain in dispute). But in gender areas, even so-called facts, such as gender differences in preference for characteristics of a partner, or in some cognitive abilities, such as visual/spatial ones, need constant revisiting and revising as societies and social structures evolve and conditions for women change, so that new qualifiers or moderator variables are constantly revealed.

Critical psychologists have raised numerous challenges to the ideal of replicability. Replicability rests on the notion that what is measured is stable and consistent: There are stable selves, identities, and subjectivities. With some exceptions—moods and other affective states—most of what has been deemed worthy of study in psychology is presumed to be stable and consistent over time, persons, and settings. But if a stable self does not exist, if people have multiple and conflicting identities and if the meanings that people attach to things are transient, if demographic characteristics sometimes function as psychological variables and other times do not, then the notion of replicability becomes problematic and all claims are contingent. If people's responses in interviews differ over time, we cannot be sure that this is because the method is unreliable or because people's opinions, feelings, memories, or behaviors have changed. If different focus groups yield different insights, we cannot be sure that this is because the method is unreliable or because of differences in group dynamics.

Despite these difficulties, most critical scholars, whatever their epistemology, believe that research and inquiry are desirable, and that the insight that research is historically and contextually singular does not preclude the possibility of understanding, shared meaning, or theory development. The question remains: Can we reconcile the views that replicability is the cornerstone of empirical research, the necessary precursor to validity, with the understanding that the complex and dynamic nature of self and situational, structural, and cultural contexts renders replicability less meaningful and less attainable? Should we even try?

TRUSTWORTHINESS

To some qualitative or nonexperimental researchers, validity is "owned" by positivism/postpositivism, and, along with the discredited assumptions on which positivism rests, the notion of validity should be abandoned entirely or drastically qualified (Altheide & Johnson, 1994; Guba & Lincoln, 1989). If traditional validity criteria are set aside, the question of how (else) research might be evaluated comes to the fore, and several answers have been put forth, one of the most prominent being trustworthiness (Lincoln & Guba, 1985; Mishler, 1990). Trustworthiness, introduced by Lincoln and Guba, was defined in terms of persuasiveness to an audience: "The basic issue in relation to trustworthiness is simple: How can an inquirer persuade his or her audiences (including self) that the findings of an inquiry are worth paying attention to, worth taking account of? What arguments can be mounted, what criteria invoked, what questions asked, that would be persuasive on this issue?" (p. 290). Mishler added, "If our overall assessment of a study's trustworthiness is high enough for us to act on it, we are granting the findings a sufficient degree of validity to invest our own time and energy, and to put at risk our reputations as competent investigators. As more and more investigators act on this assumption and find that it 'works,' the findings take on the aura of objective fact; they become 'well-entrenched'" (cited in N. Goodman, 1983, p. 419).

The key shift from validity to trustworthiness in some quarters highlights the significance of the transaction between the researcher and the communities of readers of the work. Central to the notion of trustworthiness is the idea that research is argument. All studies stake some claim and attempt to persuade some audience that their claim is supported and that their research findings are "solid" enough so that others can base their own work on them. Research presented for publication is—or certainly should be—written with a community of readers in mind, readers who are more or less joined by their agreement about what are worthy questions or claims, what counts as evidence for those claims (i.e., warrants), and what constitutes good evidence (i.e., sufficiency, reliability, accuracy of evidence) (Booth, Colomb, & Williams, 1995). There is no useful discussion of trustworthiness without considering the readers of the work. In our view, this is also true of validity, yet the writer-reader relationship is obscured in traditional discussions of validity.

Lincoln and Guba (1985) have introduced a number of strong criteria for evaluating the trustworthiness of interpretive work: credibility, transferability, dependability, and confirmability. Many of them—prolonged engagement with participants, persistent observation, reanalysis of raw data, and checking analytic categories with respondents—can conceivably be cast as translatable to replicability or reliability; others, such as use of multiple methods and triangulation, "exposing" oneself to a disinterested peer, and identifying cases that contradict one's analysis (negative case analysis), seem similar to classical validity concerns. This suggests that good arguments have characteristic logical structures linking claims to warrants to evidence, and such structures speak to the best habits of scholarship in all communities.

VOICE

Carol Gilligan (1982) inspired a generation of feminists within psychology and far beyond the borders of the discipline when she published her critique of classical psychological theories of moral development, *In a Different Voice*. In this landmark volume, she identified psychology as speaking with a male voice, as she states in this interview: "I picked up what you're not supposed to pick up in psychology—that there was a voice, and I asked, 'Who's speaking?', 'Whose voice is this?,' 'Whose body and where's it coming from?' If you listen to the imagery of sexuality and separation . . . you realize that this is a man's body. This is a man's voice speaking as if from nowhere" (Gilligan, cited in S. Wilkinson, 1997a, p. 258).

Gilligan's research and theoretical positions have been criticized on several fronts by feminist and mainstream scholars for nearly 20 years, but her insistence on the importance of standpoint or social location in psychological analyses and her remarkable sensitivity to the missing voices of women and girls in the discipline are enduring contributions. Today, many scholars who care about women and gender in psychology find it necessary—and wonderful!—to listen and give voice to participants. What does it mean to give or hear voice, and why is it important?

Giving voice to participants implicitly recognizes that some people are denied a voice and a place in psychology, and the field, as well as groups of people, suffer for it. Listening to people's voices means hearing what they have to say on their own terms rather than testing preconceived hypotheses using preformed categories and the idiom of the researcher. It means taking seriously life experiences and conditions and people's attempts to make meaning from them, elevating and examining everyday practices as well as everyday language and thinking. Giving participants voice means sharing the right to name categories and codirect the process of data collection. As G.M. Russell and Bohan (1999a) say, it is talking *with* people and not *about* them. Social inequalities are produced and perpetuated through talk (S. Wilkinson & Kitzinger, 1995). As such, there are moral as well as conceptual dimensions to the importance of giving voice in research.

Attention to voice has many implications for research methods. It disposes the researcher to use particular methods, generally qualitative methods, but, specifically, measures with open and unrestricted opportunity to respond, and to forgo measures that impose severe restrictions on responses. It compels the researcher to take seriously as data the words of the researched, whether they emerge in conversation, dialogue, or narrative, in semistructured or unstructured interviews, focus groups, Q-sorts, or other activities. It also commits the researcher to find means of analyzing discourse in ways that are not reductionistic (Marecek, 1999a).

There are complex issues in voice: Some scholars have noted that attention to voice comes from a tradition that maximizes and celebrates the differences among people and minimizes the differences within groups such as gender groups (K. Davis, 1994; S. Wilkinson, 1997a). Feminist psychologists have long noted that listening to voices does not mean that researchers are hearing truths, or that women's voices or voices of poor people are more "truthful" than more frequently heard voices. There is, of course, no simple relation between the discursive and material aspects of experience; rather, these relationships must be explored—theorized, problematized, reconciled, and validated—but not taken for granted. Psychology has a long tradition of suspecting and dismissing the words of research participants. Several large bodies of literature in the discipline suggest how difficult it is to identify what is in people's minds, that people cannot accurately reconstruct their pasts, predict how they will behave in the future, or explain why they do what they do. Some of the most celebrated theories in the history of social psychology present people as irrational self-justifiers, defensive self-servers, or mindless evaluators. Lay theories of how and why we behave as we do are often portrayed as hopelessly naïve, despite evidence suggesting that commonsense knowledge, with its departures from expert knowledge, adequately serves most practical purposes in ways undocumented by science (Fiske, 1992). These theoretical assumptions are some of the factors that have suppressed voice in psychology and to this day affect the perception and acceptance of qualitative research in the field (Sechrest & Sidani, 1995).

REFLEXIVITY

There is a large and growing literature in critical, feminist, and other psychologies about the importance of reflexivity, defined as consciousness of the relationship of the researcher to the researched. G.M. Russell and Bohan (1999a) proposed this definition:

> The term "reflexivity" refers to two intertwined issues. First, it points to the need for researchers to reflect on the ways in which our own and our informants' location in the world shapes our work. This includes the fact that in research we enter into relationships with our informants, and those relationships become part of the context that frames the research process. Second, reflexivity refers to the fact that when we study human beings we cannot stand apart from our own humanity; our vision is unavoidably influenced by the fact that what we see in our informants is also true of ourselves. Embedded in both meanings of reflexivity lies the recognition that research is not an objective rendering of reality but a form of participation in the phenomenon under study. (p. 404)

Consideration of the relationship of the researcher to the researched has an interesting history in the social and behavioral sciences and was not always as unspoken and stylized as it appears in most contemporary research (Morawski, 1988). It has been an uncomfortable topic for some, reminding us not only of the value-laden nature of inquiry and of the limitations of researchers and research, but also of our moral responsibilities to participants and other, often multiple stakeholders in our research (Fine, Weis, Weseen, & Wong, 2000). Reflexive research recognizes the importance of social position, power, and control in research practice. At least sometimes, and especially in field or applied settings, researchers are seen by themselves and their participants as outsiders who, at least on the surface, have little in common with participants (race, social class, conditions of life). This leads reflexive researchers to question who they are to do this research, and how they can possibly comment meaningfully on the lives of people different from themselves. Elizabeth Merrick (1999) has written movingly of her experiences researching childbearing with several poor, pregnant African American adolescents. She was challenged to consider that the "important questions" that came from members of her qualitative research group and colleagues were not meaningful to her participants, even though they dutifully answered them. She notes: "Through this reanalysis, I also realized that my original categories themselves were oriented to an outsider and were not reflective of the participants' view of the phenomenon or their world. For example, my original focus on topics like birth control, abortion, and marriage were not relevant to understanding their pregnancies. Although I asked about participants' birth control histories, and they had responded, the amount and quality of data suggested this was not an important issue in their perspective and should not be construed as a major category or theme" (p. 52).

Sandra Harding (1991) has encouraged scholars to do good research about people whose lives are different from their own. In her view, this begins with taking responsibility for researchers' own locations and standpoint, dealing as honestly and explicitly as possible about their likely influence on the research, and reinventing themselves as "other," so that they "begin thinking from [participants'] lives." Merrick took to heart Harding's challenge to reinvent herself by reimmersing herself in the data: reading and rereading transcripts after periods of time and relistening to audiotaped interviews to hear the participants, as the question shifted from "What am I hearing?" to "What are they really saying?" Merrick also sought exposure to the participants' world through other media: literature, her research group, Black American colleagues and friends. These sources helped her deal with issues of representation of material that is socially and politically charged. This is particularly important—and challenging—when the respondents' circumstances, perspectives, and responses are "other" than those of the White middle class, from whom most researchers and readerships are drawn. For example, Merrick reports her initial hesitancy to discuss the participants' limited relationships with their babies' fathers, in part because she did not wish to risk supporting a societal stereotype of unwed Black adolescent mothers. Further, reflexive researchers attempt to understand how they are viewed by participants and how those views affect the extent and nature of research participation.

Decision making about disclosure is always complex, as research is always embedded in social relations. N. Porter (1999) writes about her experiences as a White, middle-aged professional woman counseling adolescents in a high school for pregnant teens and teen mothers: "They had their survival to consider and needed to make sure that I did not screw up their family life, friendships, relationships with boyfriends, friends, or teachers, ability to attend school, financial wellbeing, or even their residency in the United States. They often began by telling me what they thought I wanted to hear to avoid further negative judgment about their lives" (pp. 60–61). Less frequently, scholars have written about the complex issues involved with interviewing respondents who are friends (M. Franklin, 1997). The outsider/insider perspective is a continually shifting one as different characteristics and experiences become salient or recede.

Researchers are more powerful than participants by virtue of their education and degrees, their status as scientists and professors, their university affiliations, and the means they have to procure participation. Researchers also have more power than participants to frame the questions and control the collection, interpretation, and dissemination of data. Finally, researchers are more powerful by virtue of the fact that their respondents and not they are interrogated and are asked to disclose. Reflexive researchers are aware of and uncomfortable with these power inequities and have sought a variety of innovative ways of sharing power, including disclosing one's position and negotiating with participants, with greater and lesser degrees of success (Lykes, 1989).

To whom is the research useful, and how can it be used? Can the work harm the participants or others? Taking to heart the relationship between researcher and researched means taking responsibility for considering how the results of the study may be used by multiple stakeholders in the research, and for acting to empower participants with the results, especially those in marginal social positions. It is often noted that those most likely to be affected by the research are the participants whose behaviors and conditions are exposed. But, of course, the other likely stakeholders are the researchers themselves, whose work serves as the basis for their employment, tenure, and promotion, not to mention respect, admiration, even celebrity. Speaking for oppressed people or speaking against oppression are ways of establishing one's credentials as a "good person" to some audiences. More crucially, the arguments presented in research serve to establish the social legitimacy of researchers to publicly tell their stories (Fine et al., 2000; L.T. Smith, 1999). Some feminist scholars have written about how to give the research back to participants and other lay communities, for example, by entering into collaborative arrangements that engage them in the collection, analysis, interpretation, and evaluation of data (Fonow & Cook 1991; Morawski, 1997), or by means of media presentations such as documentary videos (G.M. Russell & Bohan, 1999a).

FORMS OF RESEARCH IN THE STUDY OF GENDER

In this section, we discuss just a few key research frameworks across the large spectrum of possibilities available to scholars of gender. We briefly present methodological concerns specific to the study of gender in the use of experiments and quasi-experiments, survey methods, interviews and focus groups, and archival methods. Each of these methods is uniquely and differently important for the study of gender. We offer this selection because it samples the available methods from a range of what are often called experimental to nonexperimental, traditional to transformative, or quantitative to qualitative methods. We find none of these distinctions particularly compelling—indeed, they are inherently polarizing—and on close examination, the boundaries between categories and the methods within them often dissolve. Of the qualitative/quantitative divide, it is hard to conceive of quantitative studies that do not rely profoundly on qualitative knowing, and qualitative studies that do not offer some sense of extent, amount, frequency, or intensity of variables (Rabinowitz & Weseen, 1997, in press). We conclude this section with a call to methodological pluralism and the use of mixed or multiple methods, and a review of recent work on integrating methods.

EXPERIMENTS AND QUASI-EXPERIMENTS

There is no research method more emblematic of psychology as a discipline than the experiment, and none more often maligned by critical psychologists, including feminists, and psychologists who study gender. The experiment, particularly the laboratory experiment, poses a fundamental problem for those who study gender, in that it actively seeks to limit or obliterate the very set of factors that many gender scholars view as essential to a gendered perspective: the social and cultural contexts, by which is meant the norms, beliefs, representations, and expectations that come with being female or male in different societies, along with the structural and situational cues that make gender more or less salient (Deaux & LaFrance, 1998; Deaux & Major, 1987). If gender is the "air we breathe," then it is present in the psychological laboratory or field setting no less than in social institutions and social roles and interpersonal relations. But social realities go unremarked and unaccounted for in the experiment. Indeed, in experiments, the critical importance of context is implied mainly through the elaborate arrangements that are made to simplify and control it, and in the obligatory, if unheeded, exhortations to repeat experiments under different conditions. This is not to say that experiments cannot be useful for studying the effects of social context—they can be, as we will discuss, especially for studying small, systematic variations in social and environmental factors. Because of their historic and continuing prominence and power in the field, our review of experiments begins with a brief critique of them, ending with a focus on how experiments have been and can be used in a more thoughtful study of gender.

Experiments are conducted for one reason: to test causal relationships among variables by ruling out plausible rival hypotheses to the one that the treatment of interest caused the effect. There are two defining characteristics of (true) experiments: manipulating the independent variable while holding constant (controlling) all other factors, and randomly assigning participants to conditions. Quasi-experiments are generally similar to experiments in the manipulation of the independent variable and control over factors and differ only in that there is not random assignment to conditions. The absence of random assignment to groups means that the groups are not equivalent at the start of the study and renders causal inference far more problematic than in cases where random assignment is successfully implemented.

The privileging of causal questions and experiments has not gone uncriticized in psychology: Many have noted that experimentation can be premature, as when phenomena are poorly understood and research programs are not sufficiently advanced for relevant variables and possible causal paths to be identified. Beyond that, not all questions of interest are causal questions. Causal questions are largely irrelevant to describing the lives and activities of people; for documenting the nature or extent of a phenomenon, event, or practice; for understanding such processes as development; for apprehending people's experience in their own voice or from their point of view; or for taking into account the larger historical and cultural influences.

Even when causal questions are appropriate or useful, experiments are problematic vehicles for understanding them. Because they involve uninvited intrusions into and manipulations of people's lives, experiments are—and need to be—massively constrained ethically and practically, with profound consequences for what can be studied and how things can be studied. It has been noted, for example, that the possible and permissible range of such manipulated variables as fear, anger, grief, or guilt is restricted to very low levels in an experiment. Treatments that are larger in intensity or duration or meaningfulness, or complicated theoretically or practically so that they cannot be broken down into constituent elements are far harder to study experimentally. On the dependent variable side, experiments study the easily observable or accessible: small, decontextualized behaviors, most often verbal responses on rating scales, but also relatively superficial, mechanistic, nonverbal behaviors such as donating small amounts of money or signing up for a course. These behaviors are labeled the same regardless of characteristics of the setting, context, or respondents (Landrine, 1995). Conceptualizing and defining behaviors in standardized ways as we do in experiments purposefully removes them from their sociocultural and historic contexts, and possibly from their meanings as well.

Some of the most trenchant critiques of experiments have come from psychologists interested in gender, particularly feminist empiricists, who are well versed in experimental methodology and focus on how sexist biases enter into every stage of the research process, from choosing a topic to formulating a question and reviewing the literature, selecting a design, operationalizing the variables, recruiting "subjects," analyzing and interpreting the results, and writing up the report. These biases are numerous and weighty enough to have inspired many articles over the past few decades (cf. E.R. Carlson & Carlson, 1960; Denmark, Russo, Frieze, & Sechzer, 1988; McHugh, Koeske, & Frieze, 1986; Rabinowitz & Sechzer, 1993; C.W. Sherif, 1987). We take the example of sexuality—an area still hampered by concern over its legitimacy as a topic of study in science—to illustrate some of these biases. Many of the questions asked by researchers interested in sexuality are rife with sexist and ethnocentric assumptions, for example, that only women have fluctuating hormones, or that sexual desire and functioning are more important for men and boys than for women and girls. Topics and questions of primary interest to women and questions about women that women want answered, for example, about women's desires and sexual capacities, have been understudied. Atheoretical experimental studies of mechanistic bodily responses and behaviors still predominate. Women's sexuality has long taken a back seat to men's, in part because, compared to the "experimentally accessible penis," female sexual response is not easily observed or measured (Ussher, 1999, p. 41). Girls' sexuality has until recently been narrowly construed as problematic and negative and studied almost exclusively in terms of age at first intercourse, contraceptive use, and teenage pregnancy (but see Tolman & Szalacha, 1999).

More fundamentally, others have argued that the detached and disinterested orientation and manipulation and control of variables inherent in experiments are themselves androcentric, representing a male, agentic style of research (cf. R. Carlson, 1972; Keller, 1982). Morawski's (1997) review of the literature suggests that seemingly basic experimental design and mundane technologies reproduce sexist social relations, for example, that the inequalities in the relationship of the researcher and the researched reenact dominance hierarchies in the larger society.

Experiments can be criticized on these and other grounds, but it remains the case that science and society bestow on the experiment a power and prestige unmatched by any other research method. Aside from their scientific standing, experiments are demonstrations, and share with demonstrations an arc and drama that are quite compelling. This is in part because they tend to yield results in the form of "take-home points": The groups differed, they did not differ, one treatment is better or worse than another for some purpose, and so on. They permit (and are permitted to make) strong, usually quantified conclusions that are easily conveyed and meaningful to stakeholders in the research. Their power and prestige render them particularly problematic, but uniquely useful.

We find the view of experiments as inherently sexist unfortunate, as it removes from the toolbox a critical item. Causal questions and the experiments that probe them are vital because they suggest—to large audiences and in dramatic fashion—what can be changed and what might result. This is obviously critical to those, like feminists and other social activists, who seek to improve circumstances for women and other oppressed people. The exciting research on stereotype vulnerability exemplifies the power of experimental evidence and its potential for contributing to the social good (Steele, 1997). In one demonstration of this program, women were exposed to difficult math exams under two instructional sets, one that suggested that there were reliable gender differences in math exam performance and one that did not. Women performed worse than men when told that the test reflected gender differences, but performed equal to men when the test was represented as neutral with respect to gender. Steele makes the point that the gender difference condition—the "normal" social condition under which people take such tests—affected performance not by triggering internalized anxieties that women have about their abilities, but rather through situational pressure, setting up an interpretative frame that signals well-known stereotypes about men, women, and science. More important, by locating the source of achievement, and underachievement, in the interaction between a group's social identity and its social psychological context, Steele suggests how alternative social practices can reduce underachievement of women in certain academic domains, namely, those that carry social prestige and have been historically dominated by men.

Recently, social psychological analyses of gender offer gender-in-context models that suggest likely proximal determinants of gender-related behaviors (Deaux & LaFrance, 1998; Deaux & Major, 1987). These models, which grant a significant role to current structural and situational factors, are useful guides for experimental studies of gender. For example, social roles, social status, and power all vary with gender in the natural world but can be manipulated in the laboratory (see Goodman & Fiske, this volume). Research also suggests that gender-related behavior depends on the sex composition of groups and situational demands to facilitate communality or competence (see LaFrance, this volume). Gendered characteristics of stimuli and tasks in experiments can be critical in determining performance, judgments, evaluations, and attributions (Eagly, 1987).

Although critical of much of empirical work on gender in psychology, Unger (1979b, 1996) is a feminist psychologist who has long noted the rich potential of the psychological laboratory as a particular kind of social context that can reduce or exaggerate gender differences and of experimentation as one form of rhetorical argument against the status quo. She has elaborated on some of the contextual variables that are likely to be particularly important in experimental work on gender (Unger, 1990). She suggests a comparison of behaviors in public and private contexts, noting that the presence of others causes an "invasion" of social norms that enhances gender differentiation. (But, intriguingly, some of the largest gender differences we know are in intensely private behaviors, for example, masturbation [Oliver & Hyde, 1993], and the content and frequency of sexual fantasies [Leitenberg & Henning, 1995]). Because people appear to perceive themselves as less gender-typed than they perceive others, comparisons of what gender-related things people say about themselves and what they say about others may be informative. Unger also points to such variables as the sex ratios of groups as well as the transience and permanence of groups as producing gender assimilation and distinctiveness.

We conclude this section by noting that certain limiting features common to experiments are not inherent in them, and that the study of gender might profit from being more experimental about experiments. For example, the vast majority of experiments feature constrained response formats and quantitative measures, but these are not necessary features of experiments. It is certainly possible to manipulate certain features of more naturalistic settings to further our understanding. For example, a researcher may experimentally vary the nature and extent of a disclosure about a stigmatized identity to a group, and observe the verbal and nonverbal responses of the group (see Dion & Dion, this volume, for an example of how this process can operate in the "real world"). Unger (1999) has proposed that the gender or ethnic composition of focus groups might be systematically varied. The presence of individuals with different status, viewpoints, styles, or levels and types of disclosure may well affect the negotiation of meaning in different groups, though, of course, we could not generalize from such settings to the generation of meaning in more natural settings. In any case, experiments, particularly field experiments on real groups, remain potentially rich ways of investigating how the presence of women and men elicit different possibilities and how gender resides in context, more a complex phenomenon than a simple difference.

SURVEY METHODS USING QUESTIONNAIRES

The term "survey" refers to systematic data collection about a sample drawn from a specified larger population. Surveys may use face-to-face or telephone interviews, but in this section, we consider issues specific to written (or computerized) responses, as in questionnaires. Survey methodology is more often associated with sociology than psychology, but psychologists interested in gender are both major consumers of survey research and, increasingly, regular contributors to such research, especially with regard to questionnaire construction. Most often, the survey is a questionnaire, a data collection tool with which psychologists are very familiar, and one that has many important psychological aspects to its use. Moreover, many of the most prominent lines of research in the history of gender study in psychology rely heavily on the use of standardized questionnaires or surveys, for example, the groundbreaking work of Inge Broverman and her colleagues on sex-role stereotypes (Broverman, Broverman, Clarkson, Rosenkrantz, & Vogel, 1970); Sandra Bem (1974) on psychological androgyny; and Janet Spence and her colleagues on masculinity and femininity, expressiveness, and instrumentality (Spence, Helmreich, & Stapp, 1974). To this day, psychologists interested in gender issues are often involved in standardized questionnaire construction and the conduct of surveys in areas as diverse as personal epistemology (Unger, 1996), emotion (S.A. Shields & Crowley, 1996), rape (Koss, 1998), sexual harassment (Fitzgerald, 1996), and ambivalent sexism (P. Glick & Fiske, 1996; see Kite, this volume). Indeed, it may be the case that the most common study of gender-related issues today takes the form of several variables—attitudes, beliefs, affect, expectations, attributions, values—measured by means of a battery of questionnaires. Questionnaires are, of course, often used as dependent variables in experiments when effecting a change in attitudes, beliefs, affect, and so on, is the point of the study.

Many of our comments in this section are specific to questionnaires in the study of gender, as a data collection tool rather than a research method, but a few comments about survey research are in order. The relative scarcity of surveys in psychology undoubtedly reflects structural factors such as the technical expertise and cost involved in drawing appropriate samples, coordinating sampling design and questionnaire construction, and collecting and analyzing these kinds and amounts of data. But it also reflects psychology's methodological biases in regarding nonexperimental methods as inferior to experimental ones and external validity based on random or representative samples as less sacred than internal validity based on random assignment to group, and in its historic mistrust of what people say about themselves—or anything else. It also reflects deep conceptual biases such as seeing social processes as distinct from and less central to people's concerns and behaviors than individual processes.

Research on gender does not appear to share these biases to the same extent as the field as a whole. We believe that survey research is vital to the study of gender and will flourish within because it is one of the best methods of determining the nature and extent of certain gendered phenomena that cannot otherwise be estimated at all (e.g., the content and prevalence of sexual fantasizing and the division of household labor) or that is estimated otherwise only with severe bias (e.g., using crime statistics or emergency room admissions to gauge the prevalence of rape or partner abuse, and using formal complaints to gauge the prevalence of sexual harassment). Survey research can also help identify differences among groups and changes over time. Obviously, this kind of information is critical in documenting inequalities and other problems and suggesting where change is needed (Reinharz, 1992).

This said, there is little evidence that survey research is any more gender-conscious than experimental research generally is. In the recent (fourth) edition of the *Handbook of Social Psychology* (D.T. Gilbert, Fiske, & Lindzey,1998), there is an entire chapter on survey methods, but issues relating to sex and gender—indeed, any words relating to sex and gender—are virtually absent, even in long sections on response patterns and self-selection, context effects, question interpretation, proxy reports, social interaction variables, and interviewer effects, sites where theory and research suggest that gender matters. Age and race, though grossly underrepresented, are at least acknowledged.

Like experiments, survey research enjoys a reputation for methodological rigor, soundness, and objectivity—a reputation to which feminist scholars take strong exception. Criticisms of survey research by feminist scholars can be seen as variations on standard criticisms of survey research, and even experiments: sexist or androcentric questions, biased sampling and response/nonresponse patterns, lack of appreciation for contextual factors (including the gender of the surveyor and the surveyed) and for the specific context created by the questionnaires (ordering and wording of questions and response categories), and problems with statistical inference. Because of the prestige and power of surveys, erroneous and biased findings can be very damaging to women and other disadvantaged groups, as when surveys consistently underreport rape, domestic violence, and sexual harassment or misleadingly proclaim that the division of household labor or parenting responsibilities is at or near parity.

The use of preexisting standardized questionnaires or closed-ended, investigator-developed ("tailored") instruments characterizes much research on gender. In support of the use of standardized instruments, scholars cite the virtues of planning in advance how to collect the information they need, the efficiency, reliability, and power of a focused analysis, and the ability to converse across studies for theory building and recommendations for practice (Huberman & Miles, 1994). But these measures may, superficially at least, seem antithetical to an appreciation of the complex, multidetermined, subjective, value-based nature of research. In detailing the arguments against prior instrumentation, Huberman and Miles note that predesigned and structured instruments can "blind the researcher to the site" (p. 34). It is possible that the most important elements at work in the construct are not in the instruments. Moreover, structured instruments are context-stripped: They "lust for" universality, uniformity, and comparability. Men and women, like people of different social classes, ages, and ethnicity, inhabit different social worlds in which common language structures assume different meanings (J.A. Cook & Fonow, 1990). Research suggests that people of different race and ethnicity, gender, and age may interpret items differently. For example, in an important study by Hope Landrine and her colleagues (Landrine, Klonoff, & Brown-Collins, 1992), White and non-White women took the Bem Sex-Role Inventory (S.L. Bem, 1974) and then were interviewed about why they responded as they did. Overall quantitative scores on the gender-stereotypic items were similar, but the interviews revealed that the different groups of women understood and defined key attributes quite differently. Relatedly, the match between the wording of a question and how the terms are spontaneously used by respondents is emerging as a critical variable in survey development (Schwarz, Groves, & Schuman, 1998). Further, different groups of people have different response sets, tendencies to respond in a characteristic manner, for example, to select the middle of the response scale. Marin and Marin (1991) write about such response tendencies among Hispanics. Obviously, such biases are particularly troublesome if a specific group of respondents has such tendencies whereas others do not, and artifactual differences between groups masquerade as "real" differences (Tashakkori & Teddlie, 1998).

Psychologists who study gender have been transforming the way instruments are developed and used. For example, after the qualitative examination of texts to get at "bedrock beliefs" about emotion in U.S. society, S.A. Shields and Crowley (1996) used open- and closed-ended questionnaires with women and men as part of a multimethod approach to the study of emotion. In an effort to understand beliefs about emotions, they explored who is identified as "emotional" and beliefs about the source and consequences of "being emotional." They found that emotion terms are mediated by observer judgments of the appropriateness of the emotional response, and that the meaning of specific emotion terms shifts when applied to men or to women. The questionnaires revealed that people have very different expectations about emotion in women and men—that emotion is a highly gendered construct.

Both established and new questionnaires need to be tested with a variety of respondents to determine their meaningfulness and utility. One respected category of techniques involves pretesting questionnaires by asking respondents across a spectrum of sociodemographic categories to articulate their thoughts as they answer questions (concurrent think-aloud procedures) or to reconstruct how they arrived at an answer after they have completed the questionnaire (retrospective think-aloud procedures). Less elaborately, respondents may be asked to paraphrase questions. Expert informants from various respondent groups can also be productive in identifying differing interpretations and concerns (Schwarz et al., 1998).

Survey methodologists and questionnaire crafters increasingly recognize the importance of social and psychological variables, but gender clearly deserves more attention than it has thus far received. For example, there is rapidly increasing use of computer assistance in questionnaire data collection, with attendant human-machine interface issues (Schwarz et al., 1998), some of which may be gender-related. Surveys and tests are complex and compromised measurement tools, and issues relating to their development and use are vital ones for gender scholars.

INTERVIEW RESEARCH

Interview research holds a prominent place in the history of feminist inquiry. As a research format, interviewing responds to several criteria that lie at the heart of gender study, feminist approaches to research, and alternative social science in general. It is probably the best known among the qualitative forms of research, while at the same time is an often misunderstood and inadequately theorized method.

Interview research was used in the disciplines of anthropology and sociology for decades before it was "discovered" for exclusive use, and a method in its own right, by feminist psychology (Kvale, 1996). Its success and spreading popularity owes partially to the special fit of the method to concerns about the nature of data typically used in social science research ("the torment of averages"; Thorne, 1993), issues of representation ("who is speaking for whom"; Kidder & Fine, 1997; see also C.L. Larson, 1997), and larger criticisms surrounding the roles of researchers and researched, including hierarchical relationships and the ethics of collecting information disconnected from, or running contrary to, the concerns of those who provide the information. Finally, interview research shifts the traditional alliances between psychology and the natural sciences by focusing exclusively on knowledge generation through social interactions, putting a human relationship, in the form of a two-way dialogue, at center stage of the research process, replacing the traditional one-way observation or manipulation of subjects.

Put in the service of the study of women, interview research has accomplished the important task of "recovering" women's "voice" (Gilligan, 1982; see Tolman & Brown, this volume). Contrary to the dictum of detachment and objectivity characterizing inquiry in the natural sciences and much traditional psychological research, interview formats allow for participatory meanings to emerge within the frame of empathic listening that validates meanings and theories existing in the lived worlds of the participants. This principle of "giving voice" has been used to study experiences previously "unheard," such as women's constructions of pregnancy (Talbot, Bibace, Bokhour, & Bamberg, 1996) and battered women's rights (L. Gordon, 1993), as well as accounts of (other) underprivileged, understudied and, in research, previously unknown populations (Espin, 1996; Hurtado, 1995; Lykes, 1994).

The relative lack of structure of most research interviews has many ramifications, both enhancing and troubling to this method's potential in the field of social inquiry. The special sensitivity produced during a successful interview leads to unique kinds of knowledge reflecting the complexities of multiple meanings shaping the experiences of a population or a single individual (Kvale, 1996). At the same time, much of what the interview accomplishes lies in the hands of the researcher's interpersonal skill, ability to make decisions on the spot, and capacity for empathy, understanding, and willingness to face a multitude of ethical issues. This makes the researcher explicitly, rather than implicitly, a part of the research processes; the researcher/interviewer role gains in theoretical, methodological, and ethical importance. Interview research is essentially a reflexive undertaking, in which both researched and researcher engage in a relationship to negotiate their understandings of a given topic and to gain new insights during the process. Kvale comments on the potential therapeutic value of the interview to the research participant who may receive a unique opportunity to formulate her or his beliefs around a relevant topic. The awareness-raising potential of an interview has been also noted by Espin (1996), yet some authors caution against assuming that being listened to is necessarily a validating experience for the informant, claiming that such assumptions are possibly patronizing (Burman, 1997). A more elusive aspect of the interview process is the transformative power of interviews on the researcher, who is often forced to reformulate her or his own understanding of the topic as well as to critically reflect on the purposes the interview is supposed to serve (Fine, 1994).

Reinharz (1992) describes some common hazards of interview research such as dilemmas pertaining to studying participants with whose experience one does not want to identify (but see Reitz, 1999, on "bracketing" employed in a study of women batterers), the traps of establishing boundaries of care during the process of research whose primary goal is to be helpful, and the dangers of being "seduced" by the accounts of the most articulate (most educated?) interviewees' accounts. In research on sexuality, interviewers frequently report feeling mixtures of embarrassment, sexual excitement, and emotional concern for the interviewed linked to the high stakes involved for people discussing such topics as high-risk behaviors or sexualized violence (Giami, Olumucki, & De Poplavsky, 1997). Other costs of conducting interview research include sharing in the pain of those to whom one listens, which can make it impossible for interviews to be completed, compared across researchers and participants, or analyzed (Reinharz, 1992).

Recent research on sexuality and drug use, among other sensitive topics, has compared the kinds and quality of information gathered using various forms of research and revealed other potential problems with interview research. Despite the opportunities it affords to explore sensitive problems in depth and hear respondents' descriptions in their own terms, interview research consistently underreports illicit and socially undesirable behaviors and overreports normative and desirable behaviors relative to self-administered questionnaires (Bancroft, 1997; see Gutek & Done, this volume, for a discussion of this problem in the area of sexual harassment). Nonetheless, interviews are often the only way to collect information from people whose language skills, attention problems, or other characteristics preclude the use of the long and complex written instruments that characterize much survey research today.

Recently, the search for innovative research methods in the psychology of gender has brought attention to a related methodology of conducting research with focus groups, sometimes called the group interview. This method typically employs a semistructured interaction among 8 to 10 participants around a given topic, moderated by a single researcher. Quite extensively used in marketing research, focus group methodology has been traditionally used for purposes of survey development, manipulation checking, and program evaluation; recently, its benefits have been noticed by qualitative-oriented researchers, including scholars of gender (D.L. Morgan, 1997; S. Wilkinson, 1999).

Sue Wilkinson (1999) has identified focus group research as uniquely suited to feminist research goals, based on several criteria: making research settings more naturalistic, bringing social context explicitly into the frame of the research design, and employing participatory strategies in service of promoting community action. In contrast to one-on-one interview formats, focus group research further diminishes the distance between the voice of the researcher and those who are studied, in shifting the center of the meaning-making process from interactions taking place between the researcher and the participants to those among the participants themselves (S. Wilkinson, 1999). This strategy results in (1) more naturalistic modeling of real-life interactions among people of equal status and with equal stakes in the research, increasing the "ecological validity" of the study; (2) the ability to observe ways in which meanings emerge in a social context rather than merely receive self-reports of these processes; and (3) incorporating disagreements among the group members as a strategy of differentiating multiple and often contradictory meanings around a given topic.

Again, the role of the group moderator is highlighted as it can alternately suppress or open up meanings that emerge during the group interaction. As J.A. Glick (1999) states, a focus group is inherently "a dialogic mode of encounter where ideas are not only expressed but also defended in relation to other ideas" (p. 116). The contradictory nature of a successful group interview revolves around disagreements among participants that, if left unchecked, may ultimately break up the research process. Yet, when disagreement is tolerated as an explicit group norm, it can result in participants using their most powerful frameworks to do the convincing and, in the course of doing so, letting the larger frameworks for thinking to surface. An unsuccessful moderator, on the other hand, may demand group consensus, or let the conversation wander "out of focus."

Sampling issues assume great importance in focus group design, because the group dynamic will drive what is being said in the course of the research. J. Kitzinger (1994) suggests that group members should be familiar with each other rather than come together as complete strangers, because the commonalties of experience will foster an atmosphere of trust, leading to a more dynamic group interaction. When comparisons among the meanings acquired by different groups are the goal of the research, multiple focus groups may be conducted and analytically compared.

Focus group research can be a greatly efficient method of collecting qualitative data to researchers who are concerned with accurately capturing the experience of others in their own voices, as compared to often time-consuming interviewing or ethnographic methods. Conducting two focus group sessions has been suggested to generate as much data as 10 individual interviews (Fern, 1982), thus reducing the time and costs to researchers who are underfunded and occupied by multiple commitments, a profile that, for better or worse, fits many scholars in the psychology of gender.

Finally, focus group research generates both individual and group-level data that can importantly enrich possibilities of interpretation (S. Wilkinson, 1999). Seal, Bogart, and Ehrhardt (1998) compared individual interview format with focus group format in studying men's attitudes about intimate and sexual relationships. Their results indicate that a greater range of responses and deeper meanings emerged as a function of an individual interview format; however, group dynamic analyses provided additional insights into the construction of these meanings as a function of group interactions, including the uses of nonverbal action. Some controversies about the extent of disclosure in public (focus group) versus private (interview) settings have been addressed with a view to conflicting findings in focus group research with men or women (J. Kitzinger, 1994), importantly suggesting that the nature of the group dynamic possibly varies by gender and relational styles of the participants.

After noting the usefulness of collecting data using interview and focus group formats, a few words are in order about the accuracy of narrative accounts. A substantial discussion now exists on the topic of the uneasy relationship between what people say, report, or remember and what has actually happened in their lives (Neisser, 1994). Sometimes posed as a distinction between a "narrative truth" and a "historical truth," this problem applies equally to qualitative researchers collecting interview data and survey and questionnaire users who seek to represent psychological events on the basis of paper-and-pencil reports. People have convincing memories of things that did not happen (Loftus, 1993). In reported accounts, research participants will alternately emphasize self-agency and self-victimization and even contradict their own words within a single interview session, and their response formats are likely to follow culturally constructed implicit theories of self-narration (Neisser, 1994).

Postmodern approaches, emphasizing the socially constructed nature of the self (K.J. Gergen, 1985), accept discontinuities in narratives as reflections, rather than errors, of the fundamentally fragmentary, pluralistic nature of the self, and this attitude has been echoed by many feminist researchers, attempting to portray the pluralistic complexities of a gendered experience (Burman, 1997). But the awareness of differences in accounts over time, place, and research setting also translates into a need for more reflective examination of the research process and its role in the construction of particular personal accounts. Meanings assigned to the research setting, the race and ethnicity of the researchers vis-à-vis the participants (Reinharz, 1992), and the distance, closeness, and investment of those involved in research should be closely examined to illuminate the ways in which a research encounter produces one particular set of understandings while suppressing others.

Archival Research

The study of gender has profited from appropriating cross-disciplinary methods and frameworks, resulting in a creative mix of techniques to illuminate the nature of gender and gender as lived in a particular culture and society. Archival research is a term borrowed from history, with parallel terms depicting a set of techniques under titles of content analysis, media analysis, text analysis, and narrative studies, a traditional domain of literary and linguistic studies (Reinharz, 1992). In this section, we comment on the benefits of utilizing archival research in the study of gender, most frequently conducted in the form of examining written texts and documents of the public sphere such as magazine and newspaper articles, fiction and nonfiction books, including textbooks, manuals, research publications, clinical records, and legal documents.

Archival research is a method used to analyze factors on the level of social discourse, including cultural norms and representations that define sets of behaviors and characteristics of men and women and the relations between them. These definitions are found typically in the form of expert knowledge (academic texts and manuals), legal documents (court transcripts and documents such as marriage and divorce records), and popular knowledge (TV programs, magazines, newspapers, and fiction). Unlike individual-level sources of data, collected by means of questionnaires or interviews, examinations of public records reveal regulatory forces operating on the level of society in which men and women perform their daily roles as mothers, husbands, lovers, workers, activists, or welfare recipients, among others. The focus on the role of social history in the construction of gender and gender-infused roles and the influence of cultural expectations act to de-essentialize our understanding of gender as an immutable category while highlighting the changing nature and historical construction of particular gender identities.

Studies of archival records can expose both the ways gender norms are reproduced and disseminated among particular populations, and also the ways that particular aspects of women's experiences have been silenced or are missing from these accounts (Reinharz, 1992). Not only can archival data delineate the content of particular accounts of women's and men's experiences, they can also point to discrepancies in the rate at which these portrayals are produced. The focus on the cultural production of knowledge thus depicts the ways women and men are differentially constructed in the public realm, with their particular perspectives alternately validated or ignored.

Durham (1998), in her study of teen magazines, identified the pervasive sexual double standards accompanying adolescent socialization of girls and the conflicts embodied in depicting girls both as objects of desire and as virginal at the same time. Methodologically speaking, such accounts are uniquely useful in illuminating parallel sets of contradictions often found in data collected from individuals, notably through formats allowing for multiple meanings to co-emerge (e.g., interviews). Rather than assuming inconsistency or incoherence in participants' articulations of their lived experience, the location of ambivalent or contradictory messages about women's roles in society points to the social construction of gender as a source of complex subjectivities (see also Haug, 1992b, on the construction of women's responsibility).

Analytic techniques used in analyses of archival data employ an eclectic range of qualitative and quantitative techniques and often combine methodologies to display a variety of factors construing a particular understanding of gender. Computer software packages have been used to track counts of words used in a specific text (e.g., nudist), and percentages can be offered to illustrate the proliferation of certain discourses over others. Content coding can be pursued in a deductive manner starting from a set of research questions, identifying a suitable source of information, and creating coding variables that will provide answers to the questions (F. Lee & Peterson, 1997). Inductive strategies are also used, where data are first scrutinized and hypotheses later formulated to adequately portray the range of accounts the data provide in a grounded research manner (Glaser & Strauss, 1967; Strauss & Corbin, 1994).

Combinations of research strategies can be particularly helpful in analyzing gender experiences on multiple levels simultaneously, such as employing diary studies together with works about women published by ministers, educators, and other authors (Cott, 1977), or examining written records not created for purposes of the study in combination with in-depth interviews (Luker, 1984). In fact, some of the most impressive examples of archival research have offered both individual and public (archival-based) perspectives on a given subject, successfully linking individuals' subjective experiences with the larger social structures in which these experiences were produced, providing rich, multilevel understandings of particular gender issues. Theodore (1986), in her research on academic women fighting employment discrimination, combined the study of court records, government briefs, and newspaper accounts of protest actions with extensive interviewing and detailed biographies of the women, including accounts of their personal and professional relationships and changes in campus climate relative to the protest actions. Methodological approaches that combine personal and institutional accounts also reject the assumption that consumers, readers, and subjects of law receive societal messages in a uniform manner, by positing individual interpretations as active ingredients of the meaning construction process (Radway, 1984).

Issues of sampling are crucial to most forms of archival research. Importantly, data collected from books, legal transcripts, and TV programs are not produced for the purposes of the research, and so the decisions regarding the sample frame will define, to a large extent, the results obtained. Most often, theoretical guidelines are used to select the appropriate data sample from the range of existing possibilities. For example, a historical analysis will typically employ a random sampling technique to identify texts representing each period within a given time frame. In other cases, however, historical events may be used as markers of changing societal perceptions and consequent constructions of gender (S.A. Shields & Koster, 1989). The question of how many texts (legal records, transcripts) of TV programs constitute a representative sample that ensures generalizability of the findings may be guided by statistical considerations (J. Cohen, 1988; Rossi, Wright, & Anderson, 1983). Sampling occurs on many levels, ranging from words, phrases, and sentences to chapters, books, writers, and contexts in which the texts were produced (Babbie, 1992). Specific to the study of gender, authorship of records is often defined as data useful in examining the differential production of public records by men and women, and oversampling by gender may be desirable to achieve balanced samples. The multiple considerations regarding issues of sampling, coding, and frequently complex statistical or qualitative analyses of archival data are, in the best examples of this research method, given detailed treatments in the research reports including the provision of coding manuals on request to interested colleagues.

MIXED METHODS IN RESEARCH

For more than 20 years, writings on research methods in the social sciences have called for methodological pluralism: the use of mixed or multiple methods within a single program of research or even within a single study. We will use *mixed methods* as our preferred term to highlight the fact that we are discussing here the use of qualitative and quantitative methods in a single study or program of research, not two or more qualitative or quantitative. Whether the authors are grounded in a qualitative (interpretive/hermeneutic or critical) or quantitative (experimental/nonexperimental) framework, it is hard to argue against the notions that different kinds of research questions are best answered by different methods, that each method has particular if not unique strengths, and that multiple, varied views of a phenomenon yield a fuller, more complete picture. Nonetheless, the relationships between epistemology and methodology and between what are known as qualitative and quantitative methods have been problematized and problematic, at least in the social sciences, for decades, with different trajectories and outcomes in different disciplines.

Obviously, it is beyond the scope of this chapter to review the history of the qualitative/quantitative debates, and many excellent reviews exist elsewhere (T.D. Cook & Reichardt, 1979; Reichardt & Rallis, 1994a; Shadish, 1995). Basically, some scholars see a necessary and important link between philosophical orientations (also called paradigms or worldviews) about the nature of reality and our ability to know it and the role of values in inquiry on the one hand, and the kind of research that is done on the other (Guba & Lincoln, 1989, 1994). Others do not see quantitative and qualitative approaches as based in inherently different and irreconcilable worldviews but simply as different strategies at the disposal of any broadly educated, well-equipped researcher—as different tools in the toolbox (Reichardt & Rallis, 1994b; Sechrest & Sidani, 1995; Shadish, 1995). These "paradigm wars," as they have been called, are not over, and their long history suggests that we should not expect an easy and final resolution. But at the present time, there appears to be greater acceptance of the use of mixed or multiple methods in mainstream psychology across the qualitative/quantitative divide than at any time in its recent history (see Marecek, Fine, & Kidder, 1997, for a discussion of psychology's [qualitative] past). Not coincidentally, funding opportunities for projects using qualitative methods are growing (Tashakkori & Teddlie, 1998), and for mixed method projects in fields like education, health, and program evaluation, they are particularly strong (M. Crawford & Kimmel, 1999).

The use of multiple methods may represent a conviction that each method adds an indispensable and irreplaceable part of the picture, or that good research is inherently multidimensional, as all methods are flawed, but not in the same way. In using multiple methods, one may also be trying to make a methodological point about how to deal with evaluating and integrating different kinds of results in a given area. Alternatively, the use of multiple methods may represent a shrewd calculation about the fate or reception of one's research effort. In the latter instance, the decision to use multiple methods is a pragmatic one made to expand one's publication prospects, potential audience and influence, or even one's standing with a particular group. Until recently, such efforts were often perfunctory, as when, for example, researchers added some standardized questionnaires to a qualitative study to make it more appealing to a mainstream audience, or "added voice" via a few quotes to a quantitative study to make it appear broader, more sensitive, or current. Increasingly, however, scholars are thinking creatively about how better to combine different methodological approaches and, just as important, actually combining them in their work.

Feminist psychologists are at the vanguard of the movement to use mixed model designs—research designs that combine features of qualitative and quantitative perspectives. For them, the questions about the relationship between theory and method have not ceased—indeed, they interrogate these relationships more and more critically than most scholars in psychology. But feminist engagement in the use of multiple methods reflects multiple commitments and concerns, as Shulamit Reinharz (1992) writes: "Feminists choose multiple methods for technical reasons, similar to mainstream researchers, and for particular feminist concerns that reflect intellectual, emotional, and political commitments. Feminist descriptions of multimethod research express the commitment to thoroughness, the desire to be open-ended, and to take risks. . . . Sometimes multiple methods reflect the desire to be responsive to the people studied" (p. 197). For many feminists, passionate commitments to the researched and to the importance of the question or the seriousness of the problem argue against the application of any single, limited research tool. Others seek new ways to stretch the boundaries of the field by integrating past and present, individual and social processes or to achieve new heights of rigor and understanding. For them, the question has moved from *Does* one use multiple methods? to *How does* one use multiple methods?

For many methodologists, including feminist methodologists, mixing methods is not like choosing discrete items from a menu. It is an altogether richer and more radical procedure of integrating multiple perspectives—including conceptual underpinnings of the methods—at all stages of the research process, from question formulation and review of the literature to the relationship of the researcher to the researched to data collection and description of the results. Creswell (1995) writes of the advantages of a truly mixed model approach: "This approach adds complexity to a design and uses the advantages of both the qualitative and quantitative paradigms. Moreover, the overall design perhaps best mirrors the research process of working back and forth between inductive and deductive models of thinking in a research study" (p. 178).

Methods can be combined in a *within-methods triangulation* (within qualitative or quantitative approaches) or *across-methods triangulation* (involving both qualitative and quantitative approaches) (Jick, 1979; J.C. Greene, 1994). Tashakkori and Teddlie (1998) cite five purposes for multimethod research of which *triangulation,* or seeking convergence of results across methods, is only one. Others are *complementarity,* examining different, possibly overlapping aspects of a phenomenon; *initiation,* or deliberately setting out to discover paradoxes, contradictions, and fresh perspectives; *development,* or using the methods sequentially so that the results early on inform the use of later methods; and *expansion,* using methods to enhance the breadth and scope of a project.

It is a truism in methods writing in psychology that qualitative research—case studies, interviews, archival research—are good for hypothesis generation, with refinement and precision best accomplished via quantitative hypothesis-testing means. This certainly reflects a certain view of the relative worth of the two approaches and dictates one kind of sequence for combining qualitative and quantitative work: rich, messy qualitative work first, followed by more controlled, elegant quantitative work. Recent thinking is more creative and experimental about the sequencing and status of qualitative and quantitative methods, developing taxonomies that differentiate designs according to their order (qual/quant; quant/qual; parallel and simultaneous) and the dominance of one method over another (QUAL/quant; QUANT/qual; QUAL/QUANT; QUANT/QUAL) (Tashakkori & Teddlie, 1998).

As we noted, a truly mixed model approach does not operate merely at the level of research design: It is applied through the entire study or program. At the level of data analysis, for example, qualitative data may be "quantisized" via a simple frequency count of themes, responses, behaviors, or events, or more elaborately, by means of more complex ratings of the strength and intensity of these expressions or behaviors. Quantitative data may be "qualisized" by means of creating profiles of modal or average respondents or distinct types of respondents. In these cases, means, modes, or statistical clusters may be embodied. In another approach, groups divided into qualitatively different types can be compared quantitatively on a variety of dimensions, and groups that differ quantitatively on some dimension can be compared qualitatively on others.

Recent work by feminist scholars illustrates the innovative and effective use of multiple methods. Tolman and Szalacha (1999) set out explicitly to show "how feminist psychology can bridge qualitative and quantitative methods while keeping lived experience at the center of an inquiry" (p. 7). The goal of their study was to understand adolescent girls' experience of their sexual desire. The questions they posed were grounded in feminist theory and research and were asked in ways consistent with qualitative epistemology and methodology: Tolman conducted intensive, semistructured interviews with the adolescent girls.

To ensure both that her findings would have more generality than many studies of this type and that she would be able to perform conventional quantitative analyses on the data, Tolman (Tolman & Szalacha, 1999) chose a random sample of 30 girls and collected several narratives from each. When it came to analyzing the data, the authors were guided by preformed questions as well as by questions that emerged from the data themselves. Both qualitative and quantitative approaches to data analysis were used, depending on the question: For how girls described desire, the authors used two qualitative approaches, including *The Listening Guide* (L. Brown, Debold, Gilligan, & Tappan, 1991). To determine whether urban and suburban girls differed in their experience of their own desire, the qualitative data were reduced or quantisized to frequency counts of associations of desire with pleasure, pain, and mixed experiences. In the end, their analyses yield a far richer, more nuanced view of adolescent girls' sexual desire than a monomethod study is likely to have done, and can be appreciated by a wider variety of scholars. Their work shows that attention to the voices of girls is not incompatible with seeking random samples, and that the different questions that thoughtful scholars have about their data require varied, flexible, multilayered approaches.

Another example of a mixed model approach to gender research is provided by R. Campbell and Salem (1999), who used concept mapping, a method used in program evaluation and public health research, to examine community response to rape. Concept mapping is a single method that integrates qualitative and quantitative methods. As Campbell and Salem describe it, "In both research and applied applications of concept mapping, the underlying approach is the same: a group of people are identified to discuss and 'unpack' an issue or concept, moving toward a group understanding of that concept. The group discusses the steps that would be needed to implement a new program, or the domains that should be included in theory or measurement. The collective understanding is then represented in an actual picture or map" (p. 68). Using a national sample of randomly selected rape victim advocates, they identified 12 clusters of changes needed to improve community responses to rape. The authors discuss limitations of the method, including intriguing questions about reliability and validity when subjectivities are the focus of the research.

There are now thoughtful practical guides to the use of mixed methods, including a recent volume by Tashakkori and Teddlie (1998), to which we are indebted in this section. But key issues remain unresolved. Despite widespread enthusiasm for mixed methodology, it is inadequately theorized at the present time. The linkages among the various methods and among the findings they yield are underspecified, although some serious attempts have been made to begin this work (cf. Kidder & Fine, 1987). It is most securely grounded in a pragmatic orientation in which metaphysical concepts such as truth, reality, and cause are eschewed, and its freewheeling philosophy can be summed up in the supremely unguided call to "study what is of value to you, study it in the different ways that you deem appropriate, and use the results in ways that bring about positive consequences in your value system" (Tashakkori & Teddlie, 1998, p. 30).

Beyond this, some scholars, including those who share the call for some kind of synthesis, are critical of calls to paper over the differences between qualitative and quantitative approaches. As

Kidder and Fine (1987) write, "Instead of homogenizing research methods, we would like to see researchers become bicultural. Rather than 'closing down the conversation' about quantitative-qualitative differences, we want to sustain it" (pp. 57–58). Erica Burman (1997) similarly cautions against a "too-friendly or harmonious rendering of the qualitative-quantitative relation" (p. 795) and argues for a complex view of that relationship as competing as well as complementary. For example, she notes that qualitative research regularly presents alternative interpretations to quantitative research, as well as demonstrates that there are arenas that quantitative research does not know, cannot theorize, or fails to recognize. She warns against the potential encroachment of quantitative evaluative criteria on qualitative research, and the potential dilution of qualitative research's progressive, disruptive mission.

Notwithstanding these serious concerns and without minimizing the work that needs to be done, we believe that mixed model research is one hopeful response to Unger's (1998) aforementioned challenge to the field. A thoughtful blend of qualitative and quantitative methods, of working back and forth between inductive and deductive models, of attention to validity/trustworthiness, reflexivity, and voice, of valuing lived experience and hypothesis testing, may be how we can best deal with the subjective without losing the objective.

CONCLUSION: METHODOLOGICAL PLURALISM, AUDIENCE, AND RESEARCH DILEMMAS

In this chapter, we have argued that methodological pluralism is the strategy of choice in addressing the complexity of gender arrangements in our society, and that the dilemmas facing scholars of gender are manifestations of competing and multiple philosophies in today's social scholarship. The range of methods available to social scientists necessitates the making of choices throughout the research process, with a reflective awareness that methodological choices have important consequences for researchers and participants alike, as well as for advancing claims with direct effects on the status quo. In research on gender, these considerations translate into such riddling questions as, do we emphasize or hide gender differences, whose interpretation is most valid and why, and how do we retain a unified agency while celebrating a diversity of voices, or how do we critique social arrangements that at the same time support our professional practice?

Many of the conflicts and contradictions encountered in various disciplines in psychology, including the psychology of gender, are contradictions resulting from the reality of speaking to multiple audiences. Slife and Williams (1997) discussed the increasing disciplinary fragmentation in the field of psychology that threatens its scientific status and the set of assumptions on which this status rests, the deep conflicts about what is worth knowing, and the accompanying differences in scholarly, social, and political agendas among psychologists. At the same time, these debates have provided unique opportunities to initiate new dialogues across disciplinary boundaries (D. Fox & Prilleltensky, 1997).

Different readerships, like different disciplines, expect and respect different claims, warrants, and evidence (Booth et al., 1995). The kinds of claims and evidence that are highly persuasive to some groups of scholars are often meaningless to others. Psychotherapists, lawyers, and physicians frequently find laboratory experiments using college sophomores as respondents useless to them and their profession, regardless of the topic area of the studies, how well the studies are done, and what the investigators claim to have found. To quantitatively trained scientists, evaluative criteria in qualitative research remain unarticulated and elusive (Jaffe, Kling, Plant, Sloan, & Hyde, 1999). As a practical matter, the types of questions, warrants, and evidence presented define and limit one's audience. When scholars seek to expand their audience, they often have a tough job, especially when retaining the traditional assumptions, techniques, and linguistic conventions of their respective field. Many of the current debates in and around psychology—the qualitative/quantitative debates and the clash of postmodern and evolutionary perspectives in psychology, for example—often have involved people talking past each other.

Yet, more important, connections and common themes among voices arising from different subdisciplines serve to advance competing social values in a more balanced manner than would be possible in a unified and hegemonic, if less problematized, enterprise of social science. We need to treat complex questions through complex approaches, thereby promoting a new democracy of voices in the "moral maze of value implementation" (Kane, cited in D. Fox & Prilleltensky, 1997). The commonalties of today's feminist and other movements and practices in psychology have to be forged rather than assumed (Burman, 1998), with common goals (rather than common methods) defining the basis of scholarly and political identity. The opportunities to connect across disciplines, to disseminate innovative work, and even to create new audiences for one's work have never been richer, with new opportunities increasing rapidly on the Internet as well as in more traditional venues (see M.M. Gergen, Chrisler, & LoCicero, 1999, for a list of research, publishing, and teaching resources). As always, greater choices mean more challenges, responsibilities, and anxieties, but researchers in gender are no strangers to these; instead, they have welcomed such contradictions as opportunities to interrupt the fixed choices of traditional science and inequitable social practices (Fine et al., 2000). Offering a dialogue emphasizing shared commitments to the seriousness of social problems and the quality of scholarship, this chapter is written with the hope of stimulating new and innovative research possibilities.

CHAPTER 4

Women, Psychology, and Evolution

PATRICIA ADAIR GOWATY

If it is true that "Nothing at all in biology makes sense except in the light of evolution" as T. Dobzhansky (1937) said, the evolution of human psychology is the critical piece of the puzzle of what it means to be human. It may also be critical to all life on Earth. What are the evolutionary forces that shape human sexual behavior and fertility variation, runaway resource exploitation, within- and between-group conflict, rape, war, and genocide? The answers are important. The rub is that it is not always clear *how* we can study minds and behavior "in the light of evolution."

The contentious issues surrounding human psychology probably began before Darwin, but the biggest brouhahas have occurred in the past quarter century. All have been over how to study selection and its effects. In this paper, I attempt to describe what all the fuss is about. Some of it is silly; much of it seems politically motivated—part and parcel of the stuff to be studied; but some of it seems dangerous, too, and not just to the credibility of scientific disciplines. The aspects that interest me the most are about methods, the ways in which we know.

The devil is in the details. If mainstream psychology and evolutionary biology are ever to be reconciled, researchers from both traditions must thoroughly understand the limits of Darwinian analysis, that is, the details. This may seem like a lot to ask given that evolutionary biologists are contentious among ourselves. I hope that this paper will be a productive part of the effort to get on with understanding the details and answering the important and (answerable) questions.

The paper is in four sections. First is a brief description of the types of evolutionists who study mind and behavior. Second is a critique of some evolutionary psychology. Third, I discuss a real-time alternative hypothesis to axiomatic parental investment theory to explain some often observed, but far from universal, differences between the sexes. It is based on the idea that individuals shape and create the real-time "ecological-social" problems that others must solve to reproduce. It is an idea about real-time, ongoing selection pressures, and its predictions are testable. Last is an incomplete catalogue of questions about women's psychology that Darwinian perspectives might productively inform, with some suggestions of where to go from here.

SOCIOBIOLOGISTS, BEHAVIORAL ECOLOGISTS, AND EVOLUTIONARY PSYCHOLOGISTS

Darwin's most important ideas, evolution by natural (1859) and sexual selection (1871), and modifications of Darwinian basics (R.A. Fisher, 1930; W.D. Hamilton, 1964) organize the evolutionary study of human behavior. Behavioral ecologists, sociobiologists, and evolutionary psychologists use ideas and data in sometimes only slightly different ways, but, as it is turning out, the differences among their approaches are increasingly the source of serious contention.

Sociobiologists are evolutionary biologists who study behavior and its proximate and ultimate causation. Sociobiologists are often those who focus specifically on humans. Sociobiologists who study humans call themselves evolutionary anthropologists, human behavioral ecologists, and evolutionary psychologists. Some prefer the umbrella term "sociobiologist" (Hrdy et al., 1996). All share interest in how selection and other evolutionary forces (e.g., drift and population bottle-necks) shape(d) the behavior of humans. Behavioral ecologists and many evolutionary anthropologists ask how environmental variation affects behavior and its proximate causes through differential survival and reproduction of individuals (and sometimes groups), and how individuals shape the environmental problems that other individuals have to solve to survive and reproduce. They want to know about the generalities of causes and consequences of selective processes in real time.

Evolutionary psychologists ask how selection shaped psychology, that is, the thoughts and feelings that proximately mediate the expression of behavior. Their work almost always depends on assumptions about selective pressures in our distance past. Often, their studies depend on assumptions about the selective pressures experienced by our hunter-gatherer Pleistocene ancestors.

In the beginning, sociobiology suffered a variety of criticisms. Concerns over genetic determinism were an early response (Lewontin, Rose, & Kamin, 1984). Genetic determinism implies that there is a one-to-one correspondence between possession of a particular coding region of DNA and particular traits. It is seldom, possibly never, the case, however, that environmental variation does not modify, organize, and control gene expression. Thus, few evolutionary biologists are genetic determinists anymore (Gowaty, 1995; Maynard Smith, 1997).

Other critics held that sociobiologists were "pan-selectionists," with a just-so story for every trait (S.J. Gould & Lewontin, 1979). Some regard as dangerous the ease with which adaptive storytelling proceeds because the evil-minded could use some adaptive stories for their own ends (as, of course, could not-so-evil others). One hopes that this criticism is irrelevant to the mature *science* of sociobiology. If an adaptive story is a type of hypothesis, the adaptive stories of any interest at all must be those that are empirically vulnerable, sporting assumptions or predictions subject to rejection or evaluation of their probable truth by controlled observations or experiments. Otherwise, they really are just-so stories.

The great problem is that it is impossible to eliminate all alternative possible selection pressures that may or may not have favored traits that are fixed, invariable, and universal (more about why below). This was the point of the famous "Spandrels" paper (S.J. Gould & Lewontin, 1979). It is likely that adaptive explanations for *fixed* traits in flies or people are not empirically vulnerable in most strongly inferential senses. If this is so, adaptive explanations for fixed traits will remain just-so stories no matter how intuitively reasonable they seem.

Does this mean that there is nothing to the business of the study of natural selection? No. For as Reeve and Sherman (1993) pointed out, evaluation of adaptive significance is possible for real-time (P. Sherman & Reeve, 1997), modern populations. Thus, some of the just-so stories are hypotheses with predictions vulnerable to controlled observation and experiment. Empiricists interested in how selective forces work on real-time, modern populations use comparative biology, observational and experimental study of fitness variation in natural or laboratory populations, and mathematical models to study how natural and sexual selection currently work.

The main goal of evolutionary psychology is to explain psychological mechanisms as solutions to survival or reproductive problems in our evolutionary past. Behavioral ecologists are interested in explaining trait variation in terms of current variation in survival and reproductive success of individuals as a function of currently operating selection pressures. Most evolutionary biologists, and behavioral ecologists in particular, prefer to study selective processes within populations, because within-population studies provide controls against extraneous sources of variation that may or may not be relevant to one's questions.

The goal of behavioral ecology might be characterized as the study of selection pressures: What are they? How do they work? What traits result from this or that selective mechanism given other selective pressures and constraints on evolution? What selective pressures or combination of selective pressures cogently explain the success of a trait variant? In contrast, evolutionary psychologists hypothesize a universal human psychology made up of "domain-specific mental modules," each an evolved solution to a particular adaptive problem from our evolutionary past. Evolutionary psychologists then look for supporting evidence, but have declared examinations of current adaptive significance beside the point, because they assume humans no longer live in the environment of evolutionary adaptedness.

No area of sociobiology is more controversial—inside or outside of evolutionary biology—than evolutionary psychology.

CONTROVERSIES ABOUT EVOLUTIONARY PSYCHOLOGY

Evolutionary psychologists recently set their discipline apart from others who study evolutionary aspects of human behavior (C. Crawford, 1998; Daly & Wilson, 1999) and stimulated a vigorous response from evolutionary anthropologists (E.A. Smith, Mulder, & Hill, in press), who study humans from behavioral ecological perspectives. Smith et al. (in press) noted several problems in the evolutionary psychology approach to the study of human behavior. First, they said, evolutionary psychology avoids using formal models allowing analysis of the trade-offs in fitness when behavior is costly in terms of one selection pressure but beneficial in terms of another. A classic example is associated with bizarre and elaborate traits in one sex that increase the vulnerability of individuals to predators, but also increase their likelihood of mating. Such fitness trade-offs are common fare in modern evolutionary studies of nonhuman animals (Andersson, 1994), so it is reasonable that the highly variable behavior of human individuals should also be confronted with explanatory models of fitness trade-offs.

Second, E.A. Smith et al. (in press) criticize evolutionary psychologists for emphasis on "domain-specific cognitive algorithms." They say that the central problem with "Darwinian algorithms" or "mental modules" is "that behavior is unlikely to be a simple expression of evolved psychological mechanisms, but rather a complex outcome of *interaction* between such mechanisms and psychological, social, and cultural dynamics." I add that it is not yet at all clear that we know what "evolved psychological mechanisms" are or even theoretically what a partial, much less a complete, set might contain. Nor is it clear to the majority of practicing evolutionary biologists how we should go about finding out.

Third, E.A. Smith et al. (in press), like many others, criticized evolutionary psychology for reliance on notions of adaptive lag and adaptation to past environments. This is a criticism of the environment of evolutionary adaptedness (EEA). Reliance on the claim that one should explain psychological mechanisms as evolved solutions to adaptive problems in the remote past effectively hamstrings any investigation of how selection actually works, in the distant past or now. Reliance on *assumptions* about selection pressures that operated in past environments sets evolutionary psychology apart, not only from other disciplines interested in the evolution of human behavior, but from mainstream evolutionary biology as well. After all, we do not yet have a time machine; thus, most practicing evolutionary biologists infer evolutionary process from critical examination of patterns through comparative biology or examination of predictions in controlled experimental or observational settings of how Darwinian parameters play out in contemporary populations. Pronouncements of the selective pressures favoring a particular psychological trait in past environments are likely guesses, even when they are educated guesses. Such guesses make skeptical evolutionists uneasy, because they seem immune from strongly inferential tests.

Fourth, E.A. Smith et al. (in press) criticize evolutionary psychologists for avoiding any measures of fitness consequences. Whether studying flies, mallards, mice, or humans, behavioral ecologists and most other evolutionary biologists examine fitness causes and consequences in real time, something that gives the most reliable view of how past environments might have worked on trait evolution. The main assumption underlying these studies might be paraphrased as there's nothing so like the organisms and environments of selective importance as modern organisms and their environments. Behavioral ecologists and other evolutionary biologists find it difficult to understand why it would not also be potentially valuable to examine the real-time fitness correlates—causes and consequences—of human thought processes and feelings.

THE SEARCH FOR HUMAN UNIVERSALS

Perhaps because evolutionary psychologists have effectively eliminated current selective process from their field, they rely on identifying human universals as the footprints of past selection. This is a stringent criterion, one that would seem to be particularly difficult to meet for human psychological processes, and that the past century of research suggests is highly variable. I find it difficult to name thought processes or feelings that are expressed universally in response to a *particular* stimulus, though, of course, when one is frightened enough, one may respond with flight-fight responses not dissimilar to those of other mammals (Darwin, 1872). And it does seem likely that most of us are capable of feeling love, anger, and fear. Nevertheless, claims that jealousy, xenophobia, and male sexual coercion; male desire for multiple mates; fear of stepmothers, snakes, and spiders; lack of solicitude for stepchildren; and male rape fantasy are *universal* psychological adaptations fail on first observation to fit the criterion of species-specific universals. Jealousy, xenophobia, aggressive male sexuality; male desire for multiple mates; fear of stepmothers, snakes, and spiders; lack of solicitude for stepchildren; and male rape fantasy are undeniably part of the human repertoire. Each begs explanation from the sociobiological perspective; and I share with other sociobiologists and many other evolutionary biologists a commitment to understanding both the nasty and nice aspects of human behavior. I am willing to entertain the possibility that current expressions of our emotions have no adaptive value. Nevertheless, I am intrigued by the possibility that variation in their expression leads to adaptive success in real time for some. Appeals to universality, however, miss the greater point. Simple observations tell us that people vary in their tendencies to be aggressive, indifferent, and loving, for example, in the face of identical stimuli. The greater challenge for evolutionary biology is explaining he enormous variation in human thought processes and feelings. What are the selective pressures that favor *that?*

THE HYPOTHETICAL SELECTION PRESSURES

Another criticism of evolutionary psychology is that the assumed set of selection pressures acting on given traits may be incomplete. It is not yet certain that we have a perfect catalogue of the selective pressures that would have resulted in the dominant or most important mechanisms of human psychology. Nor is it clear that rules inferred from these ideas, such as parental investment theory, really do predict or explain what they claim, even for flies; thus, the basis of some of the inferences of evolutionary psychologists may be thin ice.

Typically, evolutionary psychologists use concepts in evolutionary reasoning to infer the universals of human psychology. They have been most interested in how processes of sexual selection act on the psychology of individuals (C. Crawford & Krebs, 1998). Sexual selection is an aspect of natural selection (Darwin, 1871) having to do specifically with relative reproduction among males and among females (Andersson, 1994). Darwin emphasized two mechanisms of relative reproduction among the sexes: female choice of mates and male-male competition. Darwin argued that these two selective pressures could easily account for the often bizarre and elaborate traits of males that are difficult to explain by natural selection.

Parental investment theory (Bateman, 1948; Trivers, 1972; G.C. Williams, 1966) explains why females choose and males compete for access to females. It says that women are universally choosy about with whom they copulate, because for women, as for other mammals, the costs of any single copulation are potentially very high. If they become pregnant, their minimal investment will be a usually lengthy gestation and a period of lactation. For humans, of course, beyond gestation and lactation is an extensive period of offspring dependence. For the vast majority of mammals, and in many human families, the costs of extended periods of offspring dependency are borne by females alone. The high cost of reproduction for females, including women, means that the fundamental limiting factor on reproduction for them is access to resources; so, if females compete, they compete over access to resources. The high cost of reproduction for females implies that any mistake a female makes in terms of mate choice is very costly. Access to females fundamentally limits male reproduction, so males compete with other males for reproductive monopolization of as many females as possible. From this, evolutionary psychologists have expected that women prefer above all others older, "high-resource-accruing males," and that men universally want multiple sexual partners, and that their degree of mate choice is affected only by their likely future investment in the offspring of a particular woman.

Among the questions one might ask is how, then, can evolutionary theory explain multiple mating by women, or women's attraction to men of social classes lower than their own? How does evolutionary psychology account for monogamous men, quite happy in their real or fantasy lives with only one woman?

Besides their obvious lack of universality, there are other problems with the application of these logical arguments to humans. How does evolutionary psychology square the predictable and inevitable genetic disadvantages of mating with older men (T.F. Hansen & Price, 1995) with women's supposedly universal desire for older, wealthier men? Or consider parental investment arguments, which have enormous intuitive appeal, so much that they are seldom actually confronted with data (Altmann, 1997; Snowdon, 1997).

Recently, my colleagues and I confronted the parental investment arguments with data from three species of fruit flies. We discovered discriminating males and ardent females in three species, *Drosophila pseudoobscura, D. melanogaster,* and *D. hydei* (Gowaty, Steinecher, & Anderson, 2000). Two of the three species we tested are "typical," meaning that they have the usual patterns of greater investment in offspring by females than males (*D. pseudoosbscura* and *D. melanogaster*). So, our a priori predictions were that we would find ardent females and discriminating males only in *D. hydei,* in which the relative investment in the offspring by parents is equal or very close to equal. We found for all three species that females are sometimes as ardent as males and males sometimes as discriminating as females. We therefore argue for a revised view of the relative sex-role variation in these fly species.

Of course, our results on flies might have nothing at all to do with human psychology. On the other hand, if one finds reason to doubt the differential mating enthusiasm of sexes of flies, one might wonder if the old principals hold for humans too. After all, the distribution of parental investment among typical humans is much closer to parity than in typical fly species, or so it would seem. If Darwin did not completely describe the set of selection pressures potentially favoring human psychology, the assumption that different modes of sexual selection are the most likely candidates acting on human sex-role psychology is likely to be incomplete at best, wrong at worst.

We are now asking what selective pressures favor female ardency and male discrimination in *Drosophila* and other nonhuman organisms. If the answer is offspring viability selection (Gowaty, 1996a, 1996b, 1997b; Gowaty & Hubbell, 2000), we may have identified another critical selection pressure. This one, unlike variation in parental investment, has equal force on the behavior of both sexes and theoretically results in flexibly expressed discrimination and ardency by both sexes.

Offspring viability selection is not the only overlooked selection pressure. Consider, for example, how long it took evolutionary biologists to confront one of the obvious problems of humans: In comparison to other primates and even in comparison to socially monogamous birds, humans are odd in that women compete over access to men. The usual explanation that female-female competition over males is a consequence of women's requirement for help from fathers is being challenged from several perspectives (Hawkes, O'Connell, & Blurton Jones, 1989, 1995, 1997; Hawkes, O'Connell, Blurton Jones, Alvarez, & Charnov, 1998, 1999). At the same time, another, alternative explanation has been identified. Men may broker women's access to economic and other resources as a way to manipulate and control women's reproductive decisions (Gowaty, 1996a, 1996b, 1997b; Gowaty, 2000). Male coercion or manipulation of female reproductive decisions is a realistic mechanism of reproductive competition by males. B. Smuts and Smuts (1993) argued that mechanisms males use to coerce females are ways males increase reproductive success relative to rival males. They showed how coercive sexuality by males was a mechanism in sexual selection. Likewise, female resistance mechanisms, and female resistance psychology, may also be mechanisms of reproductive competition—among females. If female mate choice is favored by offspring viability selection (Gowaty, 1997b), females who resist coercive sexuality or less violent manipulations of their reproductive decisions by others will have a fitness benefit in terms of the viability of their offspring (Gowaty, 1996a, 1996b; Gowaty & Buschhaus, 1998). This means that variation among women within populations in their abilities to resist coercion or milder manipulation of their reproductive decisions by men and others will result in differential offspring viability. In turn, this means that female resistance mechanisms arise via differential reproductive success among women; that is, resistance mechanisms are mechanisms in sexual selection too. The force of this selective pressure on women's psychology has never been investigated. If these models are right, selective pressures on women to resist coercive or milder manipulations of their reproductive decisions are important shapers of the psychology of women, just as they may be in ducks (Gowaty & Buschhaus, 1998).

The point here is that reliance on the list of selection pressures that Darwin recognized is probably inadequate for explaining the breadth of human psychology. The recently recognized list of selective mechanisms that fit under sexual selection—female-female competition (Hrdy, 1981), male coercion of female reproductive decisions, female resistance mechanisms, and offspring viability selection—have extended Darwinian process and should be incorporated into considerations of the Darwinian shapers of real-time human psychology.

THE METHODS AND SOME EXAMPLES

In their search for the universals of human psychology, evolutionary psychologists examine how the metaphors we use when thinking about a problem affect our ability to solve it (Barkow, Cosmides, & Tooby, 1992). They predict the results of our emotions, such as patterns of homicide and spousal or child abuse (Daly & Wilson, 1988, 1998a, 1998b). They use self-report surveys asking people how they feel and behave. They also make direct observations of behavior in experimental situations.

Daly and Wilson (1998a, 1998b) confronted predictions about universal male sexual jealousy and sexual proprietariness with data on murder rates in several U.S. and Canadian cities. Their results were impressive in that the sociobiological considerations successfully predicted more of the variation in spousal homicides than the models used by criminologists. Using Triversian parental investment theory, they predicted that men would be more likely than women to kill their partners out of sexual jealousy. They made a priori predictions about sociological and demographic patterns among victims and their murderers—in relation to recorded motives in police records. Daly and Wilson typically also examine and often eliminate some other common explanations for the patterns they report, making their studies particularly valuable. Although they claim they are looking at evolved responses, their results are consistent also with the idea that the patterns result from currently acting selective forces. The devilish detail here and elsewhere is how to sort out whether their results are about selection from ancient environments or selection acting in much more recent and current environments.

THE PSYCHOLOGY OF MATE CHOICE: IS WHAT WE *SAY* WE WANT WHAT REALLY TURNS US ON?

Among the most controversial work of evolutionary psychologists is that of David Buss (1989). Original critics noted incorrect use of essential evolutionary concepts and methods (Borgia, 1989); incorrect interpretation of crucial evolutionary ideas and subsequent inappropriate predictions and tests (Nur, 1989); flawed sampling (Borgia, 1989); and incorrect statistical analyses (Hartung, 1989). Their arguments in a nutshell were these: "Predictions for particular behavioral traits, such as mating preference, are often complex and depend on the particular pattern of social arrangements existing in a society. Buss's typological analysis does not allow for these exceptions within the framework of an evolutionary hypothesis" (Borgia, 1989, p. 16). Thus, Borgia argued that Buss's characterization of the evolutionary hypothesis is inaccurate, something also pointed out by another sociobiologist, Dickemann (1989). Nur, a behavioral ecologist and population biologist, pointed out the inappropriate use of a universal value for women's age of maximum reproductive value, which arises from the fact that reproductive value varies with the age structure of populations and therefore varies across cultures. Predictions based on reproductive value of men's preference for age of women therefore must vary too, unless the age structure of human populations throughout human history has been constant (something that is unlikely and difficult to test). Buss's failure to grasp this basic point of evolutionary theory reinforces Bixler's (1989) suspicion that some evolutionary psychologists have a haphazard understanding of evolutionary theory. Borgia, a behavioral ecologist and population biologist, also argued that the sample was flawed in not being random or representative of the diversity of human cultures. Eighty-two percent of the samples were from cultures that were influenced by European culture or were European (Borgia, 1989), so claims to universality were bogus. Hartung had two criticisms of Buss's statistics. The first was that the data were nonparametric, so that use of parametric t-tests was inappropriate. The second was that Buss did not correct his P values for performing multiple tests. Given that the tests were planned a priori, the second criticism might not be of much concern, though skeptical approaches to one's data argue for their use anyway. Concern for the first criticism is less easy to assuage. T-tests on nonparametric data are simply inappropriate. Therefore, Buss provided no reliable evaluation of the variation in answers within sex relative to variation between sexes, an evaluation that is essential to Buss's claim of evolved sex differences.

Nur's (1989) and Borgia's (1989) criticisms are considered fatal flaws that would usually irrevocably inhibit publication. Bixler's (1989) and Hartung's (1989) suggest fixable difficulties. However, any one of these four criticisms alone would have kept this paper from publication in mainstream evolution journals, such as *American Naturalist* and *Evolution*. The copublication of these criticisms along with the original article begs the question of why, a decade after their original publication, Buss's (1989) 37 cultures data are still a topic of discussion.

Other criticisms also exist. Recently, Buss (1995a) summarized his research on human mate attraction. He began his article this way: "What do men and women *want* in a mate? . . . Would a Gijarati of India *be attracted* to the same traits in a mate as a Zulu of South Africa or a college student in the midwestern United States?" (p. 238). To answer these questions, the author treated his summary descriptions of survey data as though what we say to each other in surveys directly reflects the ancient evolutionary causes of our mating behavior. He concluded that similarity across cultures is evidence for species-typical desires. He recapitulated his earlier conclusions despite the overwhelmingly critical response to open peer commentary of his original article.

The form of Buss's investigation is not unique. He began with a theory of what selection pressures on women and men might have been, noted (incorrectly for some) what the predictions were, and designed a study to examine them. If these selection pressures operated, the proximate psychological mediators should take this or that form, and should be different in men and in women. He assumed, in keeping with many investigators using survey instruments, that subjects gave honest answers, based on reasonable self-knowledge, and reflected the force of selection on mate preferences. He also assumed that mate choice processes are conscious. He assumed that the sexually selected forces that acted on mate choices by each of the sexes were those in Triversian parental investment theory. He did not consider the developments in sexual selection theory post-Trivers (1972). Therefore, the study did not examine multiple hypotheses predicting mate preference criteria, as noted in original commentaries, mostly by practicing evolutionary biologists (Borgia, 1989; Caporael, 1989; Dickemann, 1989; Essock, 1989; Gladue, 1989; Nur, 1989; R.W. Smuts, 1989). It lacked controls against the potential sexist mind-set of the investigator and his collaborators. He did not institute controls against the possibility of nonindependence of samples that may have arisen if participants previously were exposed to Western media values. The study also lacked controls against lying by survey participants.

There are several alternative hypotheses to explain Buss's results. One is that answers are confounded by universal exposure to Western media (Yu & Shepard, 1998), something noted in original commentaries (Borgia, 1989; Caporael, 1989; Dickemann, 1989; Essock, 1989; Gladue, 1989; Nur, 1989; R.W. Smuts, 1989). A second is that subjects lied about their preferences. A third is that responses may have been deceptive self-presentation (R.D. Alexander, 1987). A fourth is that what we say to each other, especially about our conscious desires for a mate, is display behavior (Gowaty, 1992, 2000). This explanation says that communication is not so much about information, but what signalers do to manipulate the behavior of the receivers of the signals (Krebs & Dawkins, 1984), and it is a potential explanation for much of human communication (Trivers, 1985, 1991, in press). In other words, our responses to surveys may be part of a "propaganda campaign" designed to manipulate the behavior of the opposite sex for our own advantage. Our verbal answers to questions about our mate preferences may be especially vulnerable to the operation of deceit and self-deception (H. Kaplan, 1987). Buss did not consider the possibility that responses to surveys, or even what we *believe* about the causes of our own behavior, may reflect conscious deception, unconscious deception, self-deception, or all three (Trivers, 1985). He did not consider that what we say may be the construction of real-time selection pressures on each other, the construction of ecological problems to be solved to survive and reproduce. The devilish detail of this reasonable, deeply sociobiological alternative (more on it below) escaped his attention.

WHERE ARE THE CONTROLS FOR SEXIST STEREOTYPES?

Any studies of evolutionarily fixed sex differences in psychology must control for sexist stereotypes. Across-culture similarity in answers may be evidence for the pervasiveness of Western media forces (Yu & Shepard, 1998). If a culture has been exposed to Western media, an important aspect of surveys should be a critical examination of the possibility that similarities in response are due to the spread of sexist stereotypes. Another possibility is that similarities may represent beliefs that facilitate the institutionalized subordination of women, beliefs that could have arisen independently in each culture. Sexist beliefs may facilitate the advantage of many men (and a few women) at the expense of most women and many men. Buss's (1989) 37 cultures data in fact show that women's responses were correlated with their economic autonomy, the main criticism of Eagly and Wood (1999), who argued that Buss's data are consistent with a social-structural account of sex differences in mate preferences.

Urges, conscious desires, and displays are elements of psychological process that evolutionary psychologists investigate. Understanding the "urge to mate" (a proximate cause of mating behavior that may or may not be conscious) is one important task of evolutionary psychology. Understanding natural selection of conscious knowledge of "desire" is another. The function of self-reports about "what we want in a mate" (another proximate mediator or cause of mating behavior) is yet another. Survey studies that take answers at face value confound these possibilities. I would have little trouble believing that these three aspects of proximate causation correlate in ways that facilitate reproductive success and survival. *How* they correlate is an unanswered—never asked—important empirical question. How each of these proximate causes affect reproductive success and survival (ultimate causation) also is unknown.

Reasonable alternatives to Buss's (1989) conclusions include that men are more likely than women to *say* they are willing to mate. An individual's willingness to respond in a given way may be a function of who asked the question and how it was asked. How the researchers controlled for interviewer bias and "self-reports as a display" may have been important to the outcomes. Another alternative is that women *say* they are less willing to mate because of expectations about their "purity." Men may *say* they are more willing to mate because of expectations about their manliness. Obviously, controls against institutionalized, culturally sanctioned values also should be a part of survey studies. Women, because of the propagandistic features of the virgin-whore stereotype (roughly correlating with long- and short-term mateships), and men, because of similar social pressure to conform to manly stereotypes, may be less willing to describe or forthrightly tell about their (consciously perceived) desires. Buss (1995a) wrote "For the most part we are completely unaware of *why* we find certain qualities attractive in a mate" (p. 241). In fact, we may be completely unaware of *what* we find attractive in a mate. It is possible that we have little conscious access to what the qualities are in a mate that turn us on. Has anyone examined the correlations between what people *say* they desire and what turns them on? How often have surveys of this type been validated?

Buss's (1989) discussion of sexual selection includes male-male behavioral competition and female choice of mates. For the most part, he leaves aside female-female competition (Hrdy, 1981). Dickemann (1979a, 1979b, 1981) exposed the significance of female-female competition for mates in economically stratified societies. Given that humans are not typical mammals, it would seem important to evaluate how variation in male parental investment correlates with variation in the strength of male choice. It also seems important to evaluate how women's preferences are constrained when their access to economic resources is biased by sexual stereotypes, double standards, and customs that limit women's opportunities in paid workforces (Gowaty, 2000). How women under ecological and social constraints acquire resources for reproduction (including but not limited to those controlled by men) is an important point. What do women under social or ecological constraint *say* they want? How do they speak about what they want? What do they tell other people? Buss was insensitive to such concerns, as sadly illustrated by the caption to his Figure 6 (1995a), containing a photograph of female sex workers in Bangkok dancing on a bar stage while being watched by Caucasian men. The legend says, "Prostitution . . . solves the short-term problems of *males* who can minimize the commitment of resources and quickly identify women who are sexually accessible" (p. 243; emphasis mine). This partial and sexist analysis leaves out the "challenges" to resource acquisition for women in societies where economic resources are controlled by men and brokered to women though men (including those societies where women still do not earn equal pay for equal work, such as our own). Thus, Buss's characterization of women's and men's "reproductive challenges" leaves out natural selection favoring male attempts to control and manipulate women's reproductive decisions. It leaves out as well the challenge of women's resistance to male control attempts. And it leaves out the basic drive of mammalian females to nutritionally support their pregnancies and later their dependent children (Hrdy, 1999).

Buss's (1995a) response variable, "physical beauty," also seems to ridicule the complexity of forces shaping human perceptions of beauty. Beauty in modern and traditional societies includes modifications of girls' and women's bodies in deleterious ways (e.g., foot-binding, female genital mutilation, breast lifts, breast reductions, and face lifts). How do these cues correlate with fertility, reproductive success, and survival?

Juniors at a large Southern university wonder about these things too. One asked, "Wouldn't men who base partner or mate selection on smarts, strength, and resourcefulness be favored over men who base mate choice on cues of youthfulness and purity?" And why is it, if women are the choosier sex, men seem to use a wider set of cues than women, who, according to Buss, choose mates for resources almost exclusively? In response to Buss's (1995a) claim that nowhere do people in any culture "perceive wrinkled skin . . . to be attractive" (p. 244), one undergraduate quipped, "What explains Ted's attraction to Jane, then?" I wondered, as well, how Buss might explain the attractiveness of foot-bound women whose calves had no, not just poor, muscle tone. Just how is it that the infection-prone urigenital tracts and the putrefying urethral and vaginal discharges created by sewn-together labia of infibulated women do not render them "unattractive," but rather as preferred marriage partners? An evolutionary theory worth the trouble will explain these variations in mate attractiveness too.

Does a woman who *says* she wants an older, wealthy man for a mate end up having more grandchildren than a woman who says she wants a kind lover (Gladue, 1989)? Does a man who says he wants a chaste wife end up with more grandchildren than a man who says he wants a smart, resourceful mate? Buss (1995a) says the "universal features" of these desires are evidence that they are evolved, species-typical patterns. He does not consider that these stereotypical and sexist views may be myths that serve in real time the reproductive success and survival of some at the expense of others (Gowaty, 2000). Buss's interpretation assumes that these self-reported desires were favored in the past.

ALTERNATIVES TO AXIOMATIC PARENTAL INVESTMENT THEORY

There is another evolutionary possibility, as well. Because reproduction is such an important component of fitness, many evolutionists suspect evolutionary theories accounting for facultative expression of behavioral alternatives to be a good bet. In long-lived individuals in a species like ours with interated bouts of reproduction, individuals able to adjust behavior depending on the environment in which they find themselves would have been favored over individuals that lacked the ability to adjust behavior. Given that the environment of selective importance to most mating behavior of humans includes the responses of other individuals, the likelihood that long-lived human individuals would experience more than one set of selective circumstances seems high. Thus, flexibly expressed behavioral alternatives in people rather than "species-typical, fixed desires" make quite a bit of evolutionary sense.

Men who say they prefer young, chaste women as wives may be attempting to manipulate unconsciously the reproductive decisions of women for their own benefit. If men say they prefer young, chaste women, women may conform to this male expectation in an attempt to be marriageable. This is an evolutionary hypothesis. Fitness benefits could accrue to men (1) through direct benefits of paternity certainty, (2) through kin selection if his male kin enjoy an increase in paternal certainty, or (3) through reciprocal altruism if fitness benefits accrue for other men. If women routinely remained chaste before marriage, all married men would have higher paternity certainty, but this might come at a cost to conforming women. If this theory has merit, men's claims that they want young, chaste women for marriage partners can be seen as attempted manipulation of women's reproductive decisions. It may not mean that what turns men on is chaste women. Women who are vulnerable to such manipulation may forgo matings with other partners, perhaps even with those that "turn them on" by whatever means (vibes, chemistry, whatever), to increase the probability of mating with a man who will provide them essential resources. But why should women mate with this idealized "man who wants a chaste wife" instead of with a man who turns them on? What's in this evolutionary scenario for women? Perhaps nothing, if men don't have something to provide of equal or greater selective value to women in exchange for guarantees of paternity, which suggests why women may say they want men with resources as mates. If all women depend on male-controlled resources, all women may benefit from trades of "cues of paternity certainty" for access to male-controlled resources. In such cases, we might expect all women to want to marry rich men and to perhaps surreptitiously seek matings with men who "turn them on." However, women with autonomous control of the resources they need should be less likely to trade cues of paternity certainty for resources in marriage. Such women will be more likely seek relationships with men who "turn them on."

Many nonhuman primate females are able to provide their children with food, sleeping sites, protection from predators, and information about their environments, and feed themselves. Why is it that human females seem to be the only primate females unable to provide for their children without help? Or can they? Even in soft modern societies there is underlying variation in women's access to and control of resources necessary for reproduction (e.g., variation in metabolic rate, ability to store calories, etc.). Based on this evolutionary hypothesis, there should be within-sex variation in survey answers depending on how much autonomous control of economic resources and reproductive decisions women have. The results of Eagly and Wood (1999) are consistent with this evolutionary idea as well as with the social-constructionist idea that motivated their study.

Another alternative idea, the women's autonomy hypothesis (Gowaty & Hubbell, 2000) says that when women have autonomous control of resources, what they *say* they want in a mate will be different from what relatively less autonomous women say. When women have little autonomous control of reproductive decisions, they will *say* they want rich men for husbands and lovers. When women have less autonomous control of resources, women also will attempt to manipulate men's willingness to provide resources to them via "propaganda," that is, through what they *say* they want in a mate. Remember, what one *says* one wants in a mate may not be what "turns one on."

This theory predicts that variation in what men say they want in a mate will be a function of their own likelihood of mating and the degree of women's autonomy. If women lack economic and decision-making autonomy, as is often the case in economically stratified societies with institutionalized monogamy, men's mating prospects may be tied to their economic prospects. If so, what men say they want in a mate may vary as a function of their marriageability. Men with enough resources to marry are likely to say they want a young, chaste wife, because many men who marry will benefit from paternity certainty and thus have a stake in its manipulation. Among men too poor to marry, there will be more variation in what they *say* they want, because such men are not so readily guaranteed a mating advantage from "attractiveness propaganda."

In contrast to the predictions of parental investment theory, the predictions of this evolutionary hypothesis are based on within-gender variation in the answers, and not on the differences between the sexes. Variation in women's sociosexual environment is fundamental to this idea, and, as women's environments change, so will the predicted responses of individual women and individual men. This again demonstrates that evolutionary hypotheses can accommodate predictions about flexible, facultatively expressed behavior. This theory also can account for "odd" standards for women's beauty, such as those associated with bound feet.

SOCIOBIOLOGY'S SUCCESSES IN THE STUDY OF BEHAVIOR

Sarah Hrdy's (1974, 1976, 1977, 1979, 1981, 1997, 1999; Hrdy et al., 1996) original contributions spanning 25 years have helped create feminist consciousness within evolutionary biology as no other evolutionist before or since. Her pioneering efforts, along with those of J. Altmann, L. Fedigan, J. Alexander, and other feminist primatologists to "raise Darwinian consciousness," transformed evolutionary study of primatology (Haraway, 1989). Their scholarship paved the way for the many other evolutionary biologists of feminist consciousness (Gowaty, 1997a) also currently working in anthropology and behavioral ecology of nonhumans.

Of the many topics investigated by modern evolutionists, some resonate strongly with my own feminist consciousness. Two of these are sex ratio theory, explaining differential favoritism for daughters over sons, and hypotheses about adaptive female sexuality. These are of particular importance to discussions about genetic determinism, because each provides evidence against genetic determinism, while simultaneously demonstrating the utility of "natural selection thinking" (Charnov, 1982). This is because each of these evolutionary ideas posit flexible behavioral repertoires serving survival and reproduction of the individuals expressing them.

SEX ALLOCATIONS

Sex ratio theory was outlined by R.A. Fisher (1930). He realized that the reproductive value to the parents of daughters and of sons in out-bred, diploid (in which daughters and sons receive chromosomes from both parents) populations was necessarily equal, because the average reproductive success of males must equal the average reproductive success of females. Another way to say this is that because we each have a mother and a father, the value to a parent of a son or a daughter is the same. Fisher's logic explains why, in most sexual organisms, the sex ratio will be 1:1. Selection will act to equalize the costs of sons relative to daughters because the average reproductive value to the parents of a daughter or a son is the same. In the past 30 years, observation of sex ratios deviating from parity piled up, many of them in human populations. Each observed deviation in nonhuman animals has been explained by a failure of Fisher's assumptions, so that in each case of skewed sex ratios, either the cost or the benefit of sons or daughters differed from the other. Each exception has proved the rule; thus, some call sex ratio theory "evolutionary biology's crown jewel." Each has increased evolutionary biologists' confidence in Fisher's original insight. Charnov's (1982) classic review and development of the explanatory mathematics is the best extant discussion of the power of natural selection to explain flexibly expressed, adaptive patterns of parental sex allocation, that is, gender-balanced egalitarianism or gender-biased "favoritism and meanness" to their children.

Trivers and Williard (1973) realized that the reproductive value of sons and of daughters was not always the same. They explicitly considered the likelihood of flexibly produced adaptive sex ratios by mothers in polygynous societies in which many males fail to mate at all, while other males monopolize access to many females and most females mate and reproduce. (Polygynous populations are technically defined by evolutionary biologists as those in which the variance in mating success of males is greater than the variance in mating success of females.) Their simple but powerful insight was that if a mother's health or well-being (her "condition") had a predictable effect on the health, viability, and competitive abilities of her children, she should produce daughters rather than sons if her own condition was poor. This prediction followed directly from the technical definition of polygynous societies. Trivers and Williard argued that mothers would vary the sex ratio of their progeny as a function of their own health. According to basic sexual selection theory (Andersson, 1994; Darwin, 1871), in polygynous societies, the reproductive value of a healthy competitive son will be far greater than a less competitive son. In contrast, reproductive payoffs to parents of their daughters, whether the daughters are in good or poor health, will vary much less than for sons in good or poor health. This is for the simple reason that the limiting factors for female reproduction constrain the range of female success to smaller values than the factors limiting male reproduction. Thus, Trivers and Williard predicted that in polygynous societies, mothers in relatively good condition would produce son-biased sex ratios (they assumed that mother's condition was passed on to her children), and mothers in poorer condition daughter-biased sex ratios. This idea has been astonishingly successful in explaining sex ratio variation in nonhuman animals (Gowaty 1997c; Komdeur et al., 1997).

A variant of the maternal condition hypothesis explains the most dramatic variations in parental favoritism toward one sex of offspring over the other in humans. In extremely socially and economically stratified societies (often called "patriarchal"), prejudice against daughters is severe in the upper classes. Evidence of severe prejudice includes extreme values of offspring and adult sex ratios. These are noted by the United Nations (UN 1994) as missing girls and women. They are attributed to daughter-biased patterns of infanticide, childhood neglect, and abuse. Mildred Dickemann's (1979a, 1979b, 1981) important papers building on the Fisherian extensions of Trivers and Williard (1973) discussed why. In highly economically stratified societies, in which resources are controlled by men, women marry up social classes. To do so, they provide husbands and husbands' families with evidence of paternity certainty (e.g., purdah, infibulation, clitorectomies, modesty, chastity). In the highest social classes, there are few, sometimes no opportunities for daughters to marry. Thus, for parents, the reproductive value of their daughters is low relative to the reproductive value of sons. Low reproductive value of daughters leads to parental favoritism toward sons and parental meanness toward daughters, including daughter-biased sex selection, differential abortion, daughter infanticide, neglect, less education, and poorer health care. Hrdy (1999) offers a recent sensitive and insightful review of data in human populations consistent with this logic. In the lowest social classes, if mating is contingent on access to resources, sons are less likely to reproduce than daughters, so parental behavior favors daughters (son infanticide is known to occur, but much less frequently than daughter infanticide).

Lee Cronk's (1993, 1999) studies of the Mukogodo are particularly compelling in regard to these ideas about parental favoritism, because he worked with a group of people down, rather than up, the social ladder. The Mukogodo are Kenyan goat herders who are poorer neighbors of cattle-herding Masai. Mukogodo sons are less likely to marry than Mukogodo daughters, who marry up local socioeconomic ladders into Masai households. Mukogodo parents are more solicitous of their daughters than of their sons; they attend to their illnesses more carefully, for example, taking them to health clinics when they are sick more rapidly than they do their sons. Daughter favoritism is consistent with the greater expected reproductive payoff Mukogodo parents have of their daughters compared to their sons.

Fisherian sex allocation logic explains patterns of parental favoritism and meanness to daughters versus sons in eastern bluebirds, *Sialia sialis* (Gowaty & Droge, 1991). In this songbird species, fathers feed their daughters more than they feed their sons, but mothers feed sons and daughters equally. From a male nestling bluebird's point of view, fathers play favorites when they give their sisters more. These patterns are not explained by parental sex-role variation, and they occur despite the facts that sons and daughters are the same size and exhibit no differences in metabolic rates. But sons do remain near their natal territories when they grow up, whereas daughters disperse from their natal sites before breeding. This means that sons may continue to interact with their parents throughout life and may compete with both their parents over food, nesting sites, and roosting sites, but only with their fathers for mates. Thus, daughters are less costly to parents than sons, and, consistent with their lower cost to parents, daughters typically outnumber sons. Unlike mammals, it is mother birds that contribute the sex-determining chromosome, so mother bluebirds bias the sex ratio of their children in favor of the sex least costly to both parents. Consistent with sex allocation theory, though, fathers adjust the relative cost to themselves of their sons and daughters by feeding their daughters more often.

Similar attention to variation in parental favoritism or meanness to daughters versus sons within modern populations and in other nonhuman populations (Gowaty & Plissner, 2000) would be of interest. Other subtle patterns of gender-biased prejudice probably also occur in traditional and modern societies. How do these vary with perceived and actual reproductive value to parents of sons and daughters? How do these Darwinian parameters vary with expression of thoughts, feelings, and perceptions of parental favoritism and meanness—by parents and by children?

ADAPTIVE FEMALE SEXUALITY

In the late 1980s and early 1990s, Robin Baker and Mark Bellis (1988, 1989a, 1989b, 1993a, 1993b, 1995) moved the study of human sexuality forward by examining some of the most intimate of human behavior from a Darwinian perspective. Among the difficult topics they examined was the adaptive significance of masturbation in men and women. Their studies engendered controversy mostly over what they had to say about sperm competition in humans (R.R. Baker & Bellis, 1989a). What caught my attention was their hypothesis that masturbation in women was adaptive as a means of sometimes increasing and often decreasing the likelihood of fertilization. From their studies of sperm uptake during copulation as a function of the timing of the woman's orgasm, they reasoned that the cervix moved during orgasm. If a woman's orgasm was a minute before or within 20 minutes after her partner ejaculated, significantly more sperm were "sucked up" out of the cul-de-sac of the vagina, which received the ejaculate, and into the upper reproductive tract of the woman. They reasoned that a strong, uptake orgasm increased the likelihood of fertilization and subsequent pregnancy. Later, Desmond Morris provided filmed evidence that during orgasm of some women, anyway, the cervix moves. The neck of the cervix dips forward into the cul-de-sac gaping open at climax.

R.R. Baker and Bellis's speculations about female sexuality did not end with the *potential* adaptive significance of orgasm during copulation, but extended in an even more interesting way to "cryptic orgasms." They hypothesized that a potential mechanism of adaptive contraception arises from "intercopulatory orgasms," attained when women masturbate, perhaps while alone, between copulations. If the cervix also moves during intercopulatory orgasm (a supposition supported by the technicalities of Morris's film), the dipping down of the cervix into the cul-de-sac of the vagina could pick up cellular debris and vaginal secretions. These, then, may form a block to the movement of ejaculate into the woman's upper reproductive tract, unless during copulation the woman also experiences an uptake orgasm. Numerous predictions from this logic remain untested and offer fertile ground for interactions among reproductive physiologists, psychologists, psychiatrists, and evolutionary biologists.

Baker and Bellis's ideas lead to some further interesting speculations about the interactions of thoughts and feelings with the likelihood of fertilization: Do vaginal secretions associated with intercopulatory masturbation and orgasm vary as a function of women's conscious or unconscious preferences for her usual partner(s), and how? How might emotions associated with variation in preference affect vaginal secretions, the behavior of the cervix, and other aspects of physiology of the vaginal bowl? How do vaginal secretions kill or reduce the ability of sperm to get to upper reaches of women's reproductive tracts? Do some secretions work better as blocks to sperm movement than others? Do some vaginal secretions facilitate sperm movement? Does their secretion vary with the conscious thoughts and feelings or unconscious feelings of women?

These speculations are compelling from my feminist and scientific perspectives for a number of reasons. They are about active female sexuality. Predictions from the hypothesis are novel. The hypothesis provides for the first time a credible explanation of adaptive significance for the clitoris. R.R. Baker and Bellis's hypothesis raises the possibility, that, even though one does not have to have an orgasm to get pregnant, in noncontracepting populations one may have to have an orgasm ("cryptic") *not* to get pregnant. Whether this is true or not is an empirical question. Some of the predictions of the hypothesis are directly testable. Whether observations match prediction or not, new insights into women's sexuality will flow from the attempts to test their ideas. The implications of the Baker and Bellis hypothesis are enormously important. If they are right, "customs" such as clitorectomy and infibulation would take on new meanings beyond current understanding (Hosken, 1993) of their effects on the psychology, sexuality, and reproductive outcomes of the girls and women who suffer them. At the very least, these original ideas underscore our remaining ignorance of behavior, physiology, and morphology of human sexuality and reproduction.

WHERE DO WE GO FROM HERE?

Bringing traditional psychology and behavioral ecology closer together seems not so difficult when one is interested in the *current* fitness dynamics of trait variants. Evaluating long-term effects of psychological variants on survival and reproductive success need not cover the entire life of subjects, as it often does in studies of *Drosophila*. Productive, prospective studies that directly measure fitness variation among individuals with different trait variants in some cases could easily be accomplished in two to five years, just as they are in many epidemiological studies. It appears that the time may be right for collaboration between social-constructionist psychologists and behavioral ecologists.

CHAPTER 5

Gender Similarities and Differences as Feminist Contradictions

MEREDITH M. KIMBALL

Differences are inequality's post hoc excuse . . . its outcome presented as its origin . . . Inequality comes first; differences come after . . . A discourse of gender difference serves as ideology to neutralize, rationalize, and cover disparities of power, even as it appears to criticize them. Difference is the velvet glove on the iron fist of domination. This is as true when differences are affirmed as when they are denied . . .

(MacKinnon, 1987, p. 8)

When women want to escape from exploitation, they do not merely destroy a few "prejudices," they disrupt the entire order of dominant values, economic, social, moral, and sexual. They call into question all existing theory, all thought, all language, inasmuch as these are monopolized by men and men alone. They challenge *the very foundation of our social and cultural order*, whose organization has been prescribed by the patriarchal system.

(Irigaray, 1978/1985, p. 165)

Gender similarities and differences have been a matter of intense feminist debate for at least the past 200 years. They have also been the main focus of empirical investigations of gender within psychology. Between 1974 and 1995, over 26,000 studies of sex or gender comparisons were published, including more than 2,000 publications per year during the mid-1990s (Favreau, 1997; Worell, 1996). For both empirical and epistemological reasons, this chapter will not be a review of the psychological research on gender similarities and differences. Empirically, there are simply too many findings in too many areas to synthesize usefully. Epistemologically, I wish to move beyond the yes/no polarized debate within psychologies and feminisms that I am convinced will never be resolved. More important, attempts to argue one side or the other of this debate in its most essentialized construction are not useful for the creation of either feminist knowledge or political strategies. In a criticism of my earlier work on gender differences and similarities (Kimball, 1995), Eva Magnusson (1998) suggested: "We may do better by looking critically at the cultural obsession with differences vs. similarities . . ." I want to take up this suggestion and examine more closely why we continue to ask the question: Are women and men more similar or different? And why we continue to search for dichotomous answers to this question.

My main point for this chapter is that there are always similarities and differences in any comparison. This applies to gender as well as other social categories of dominance such as race, age, sexual orientation, class, abilities, and so on. It also applies at all levels of analysis including one individual at different points in time, any two (or more) individuals or groups, any situation or context at different points in time, and any two (or more) social contexts or institutions. The contradictions of simultaneously existing similarities and differences are always present. These contradictions have three important implications: (1) All similarities and differences, including those focused on gender, are constructed. (2) All constructions of similarities and differences are partial. Because they are partial, all constructions have both strengths and limitations. (3) One way to begin to challenge dichotomous thinking in which differences are constructed as hierarchies is to fully acknowledge both the strengths and limitations of one's own and others' partial constructions.

I begin this chapter with a brief historical overview of the presence and importance of gender similarities and differences in the history of feminisms. The continuing importance of both constructions in modern empirical, theoretical, and political feminisms is strengthened by a knowledge of their importance throughout the past. Neither similarities nor differences can be taken as a marker of historical progress. Next I turn to an analysis of the modern debate within feminist psychology over the question: Should feminists study gender (or sex) differences? Here I look at the yes/no structure of this debate and at the three epistemological contributions that have emerged: (1) statistical critiques of research on gender similarities and differences; (2) the focus away from definitions of gender based on individual characteristics; and (3) the focus on differences among women. In the final section, I examine some of the ways differences are constructed as hierarchies and suggest two ways in which this process might be resisted: (1) constructing dichotomies as necessary contradictions and (2) creating reflexivity thorough an examination of the strengths and limitations of all constructions. These points are illustrated through an examination of the debate over gender similarities and differences in relationship violence.

HISTORICAL OVERVIEW

The idea that women are different from men, more maternal, more nurturant, and less aggressive is very old. The use of this difference to argue for feminist goals such as access to education and against misogynist views of women is at least 600 years old (Pizan, 1405/1982). The idea that women are in most or all important ways similar to men and that gender differences are social and subject to change is more recent, dating back to the European enlightenment of the eighteenth century. However, for individual feminists and feminist organizations, these two ideas have often coexisted.

An excellent illustration of this coexistence is in Mary Wollstonecraft's *A Vindication of the Rights of Woman* (1792/1988). She argued for women's rights on the basis of both sexual equality and sexual difference. As human beings, women and men shared in basic human rights and duties, in particular the right and duty to develop virtue through the exercise of reason. Virtue required education in reason that ought to be equally available to both women and men. As many feminists before and after her argued, women should be given the same education as men of their social class and this experiment would prove whether women were equal or inferior to men in reason and virtue. She firmly believed that the results of this experiment would prove women equal to men, but even if she was wrong and the results showed women to be inferior, it would be in the quantity not the quality of virtue that had one essential and eternal standard. Although virtue was the same trait in both sexes, women and men were to use virtue to fulfill different duties: "Women, I allow, may have different duties to fulfill; but they are *human* duties, and the principles that should regulate the discharge of them, I sturdily maintain, must be the same" (p. 51). She argued that women ought to be trained for useful professions, so they could support themselves in the case they chose to remain single or became widowed. However, most women would choose to marry and raise children, jobs that would benefit greatly from training in reason and the practice of virtue.

Although the assumptions of different gender roles were predominant throughout Mary Wollstonecraft's work (1792/1988), in two places she made arguments crucial to the construction of gender similarities. In one she gave voice to an earnest wish "to see the distinction of sex confounded in society, unless where love animates the behaviour" (p. 57), and in the other, she dropped a hint that she planned to pursue later that women "ought to have representatives, instead of being arbitrarily governed without having any direct share allowed them in the deliberations of government" (p. 147). Both of these radical ideas she compromised and softened by assuming that she risked exciting laughter in the reader. Wollstonecraft was working in the increasingly conservative environment of British politics that sought distance from the French Revolution. In France where it was easier to be radical, several women active in the Revolution publicly demanded equal political rights for women, although without success (Offen, 1996).

Epistemologies of gender differences and similarities informed feminist politics during the "first wave" of feminist politics in the nineteenth and early twentieth centuries. Although in some organizations and for some individuals either gender similarities or differences predominated in feminist theories and political strategies, often both similarities and differences were advocated at different times or in different contexts. In Europe, maternal feminisms based on gender differences were most common, although equal rights arguments based on gender similarities were also present. Most important feminists of the time did not see maternalism as an antithesis to equal rights, but rather as an ethical basis through which to claim rights and change both public and private gendered relations. Although not always strongly in support of women's equal participation in the public economic and political spheres, maternal feminisms advanced some of the most radical critiques of the family advocating aid to unmarried mothers and their children, divorce reform, birth control, abortion, paternal responsibilities, and even lesbian rights. Furthermore, through the development of the concept of spiritual motherhood, women who chose not to marry or to have children also found a place within maternal feminisms. Maternal feminist political action both opened up and constricted opportunities for women. As motherhood became more of a public concern, some professions opened up for women. At the same time, these professions soon became ghettoized, devalued, and underpaid compared to male professions involving similar education and training. Feminists used maternal arguments to fight for a state that embodied maternal values and included real women as active participants. Male politicians used the same arguments to reinforce traditional roles and limit women to the home (A.T. Allen, 1991; Kimball, 1995; Koven & Michel, 1993; Yeo, 1997).

In North America, the suffrage movements of the nineteenth and early twentieth centuries also used both gender similarities and differences in forming rhetoric and policies. Suffrage organizations were more likely to focus on universal political responsibilities, visions of women as competent intelligent pioneers in new fields, and the importance of education and economic independence as prerequisites for political equality. In contrast, reform and temperance organizations focused more on women's differences from men, on consolidating women's power within traditional roles, and on particularistic social changes such as prohibition and other reforms that could be accomplished through suffrage. Although there were differences in focus, organization, and popular appeal, both suffrage and temperance organizations were crucial in the fight for women's suffrage, both supported suffrage, and there was overlap in both the membership and leadership of these organizations (E.C. DuBois, 1998; Giele, 1995).

Most of these feminist organizations, both maternal and equal rights, were predominately middle class and white in composition and focus. Many African American women in the United States supported suffrage and other feminist causes, and some were members of white organizations. However, as racism intensified in the mid- to late nineteenth century, most were active in African American women's organizations, including temperance organizations. In contrast to the gender division within the white political debate over suffrage, both male and female leaders in African American communities supported woman's suffrage (Giele, 1995; Terborg-Penn, 1998).

As middle-class feminists gained access to higher education in the late nineteenth century, they used arguments about gender similarities and differences to consolidate their own and other women's places in the professions. Early feminists within academic psychology took a strong gender similarities position in response to the many attempts couched in scientific jargon to use gender difference to define women's inferiority. Leta Stetter Hollingworth and others critiqued what passed for a science of sex differences, and were particularly concerned to disprove the hypothesis of greater male variability. Sharing with their male colleagues a faith in the progressive nature of positivist science, they argued that methodological reforms would ensure good and accurate science as well as gender similarities in all intellectual skills needed for academic achievement and professional success (Kimball, 1995; S.A. Shields, 1975a, 1982).

In contrast to these early academic psychologists, the women who first entered psychoanalysis accepted gender differences, especially women's greater nurturance. When Karen Horney took issue with Freudian theories of femininity, she accepted the existence of difference, even gender differences that originated in the biology of instincts. What she challenged was Freud's evaluation of masculinity as primary and femininity as a derivative version of masculinity. She argued for a primary femininity that was equal to although different from primary masculinity in the development of gender. Difference was accepted, variously explained, but not contested by early women analysts. Indeed assumptions about women's greater nurturance probably facilitated their participation in the profession, in particular the accumulation of power and influence as training analysts (Chodorow, 1986, 1989; Kimball, 1995).

This brief historical overview makes clear the persistence of constructions of both gender similarities and differences in feminist thinking over the past several centuries. This persistence is illustrative of the partial nature of attempts to construct and use gender similarities and differences. Both exist, both have meaning for feminists, and both are useful for feminist political actions. Neither constructions of similarities nor of differences have emerged as formulations that make the other unnecessary. At the same time, the debate among feminists over the study and use of gender similarities and differences has also not been resolved. As pointed out in the next section, the debate in its most dichotomous form has continued to the present among feminist psychologists. And it will continue as long as what is a necessary contradiction is viewed as a hierarchical dichotomy requiring a choice of one option over the other.

FEMINIST APPROACHES TO THE STUDY OF GENDER SIMILARITIES AND DIFFERENCES

Should feminist psychologists study gender (or sex) differences? This question has generated a great deal of debate among feminist psychologists. With few exceptions, this debate has been dichotomized into yes or no answers. The phrasing of the question is notable, it is never constructed in terms of studying gender similarities or studying both similarities and differences. It is gender difference that is contested and this is not surprising because it is gender difference that has been used in support of the status quo and to devalue women in political patriarchies. In answering this question, many different arguments have been proposed, and there are overlaps between the two positions in beliefs in the importance of socialization and the acknowledgment of biology. However, two factors differentiate the yes and no positions.

The first is that those who answer the question yes see science as a powerful tool in promoting feminist changes and believe that better research will give better answers. In contrast, those who answer the question no tend to view science as unable to reveal either truths or facts. Rather science is seen as a social institution that reflects the values of dominant society and therefore makes suspect the examination of gender differences (C. Kitzinger, 1994b). The second is that the yes and no sides are correlated with different definitions of gender. The yes side unquestioningly defines gender as individual gender (S. Harding, 1986) in which one is examining similarities and differences in traits and abilities that are constructed as residing within the individual. On the no side, views about gender are not so consistent, however, one dominant theme is a rejection of individual gender. Gender is redefined as residing not in the individual, but in social interactions, discourses, institutional structures, and relations of power.

I first review arguments on both sides of this debate. I then look at three contributions to feminist scholarship that have come from this debate. Ultimately I argue that yes and no are the wrong answers. And if dichotomous yes and no answers are rejected in favor of more contextually specific constructions, then the question itself becomes only one of many possible questions, each with its advantages and disadvantages.

Among the answers of yes, perhaps the strongest is that of Diane Halpern (1994) who argues that the only way to dispel stereotypes is through the scientific study of differences and that without such studies stereotypes and the status quo would rule the day. Furthermore, without gender differences, there is no justification for psychology of women courses. Both Alice Eagly (1987, 1994, 1995) and Janet Hyde (1994a, 1994b) agree that there are problems with studies of gender similarities and differences. Some of these problems include the biases against nonsignificant findings, failures to replicate findings of gender difference, failures to report effect sizes, interpretations of findings in ways that harm females, and assumptions of biological differences in the absence of biological data (Hyde, 1994b). Thus, not all studies of gender differences generated by scientific study are valid or useful. Science can be done well or poorly and it is the job of feminist scientists to do the best possible science. Alice Eagly summarizes this position well: "Although appropriate to sow uneasiness about science through emphasizing its social construction, science remains a rule-bound set of social activities that provides a powerful tool for examining relations between variables and for testing theories about these relations" (1994, p. 517). It is only through good scientific study of gender similarities and differences that we will be able to accurately judge what are the true gender similarities and differences, and to know the contexts that lead to larger, smaller, or no differences. Furthermore, Olga Favreau (1997) argues that detecting differences is useful in cases where differences require remediation, a process that can lead to elimination of inequalities.

There is more diversity among the no answers. One common theme is that it is wrong and politically dangerous to attribute gender differences to individuals as if gender is a series of traits, beliefs, and abilities that are internal, independent of context, and permanent. In epistemological terms, this is an argument against essentialist constructions of gender. Many feminist psychologists, among them Janis Bohan (1993), Stephanie Riger (1992), and Rhoda Unger (1998), argue for a definition of gender that arises out of interpersonal interactions. Thus people do gender, they do not have gender. Another approach to deconstructing gender as belonging to the individual is that of Rachel Hare-Mustin and Jeanne Marecek (Hare-Mustin & Marecek, 1994; Marecek, 1995a). They broaden definitions of gender to include cultural constructions of gender through discourses, institutions, and symbols. All of these arguments link gender to power relations in society. Of particular concern is the reinforcement of the status quo through the study of gender differences and similarities. This argument is made most strongly by Arnold Kahn and Janice Yoder (1989) in terms of the dangers of focusing on individual gender differences: ". . . a psychology of women that assumes that women and men are naturally different . . . or that differences are caused by factors internal to individuals . . . is necessarily supportive of the status quo, and hence, antithetical to a women's movement" (p. 428). Michelle Fine and Susan Gordon (1991) argue that the study of gender difference not only supports a gender hierarchy, but also legitimates heterosexuality through an unspoken presumption of complementarity. Others also point out that a focus on gender similarities can also result in inequalities, such as ignoring the needs of pregnant women or when overall similarities mask an important interaction of gender with other variables (Hare-Mustin & Marecek, 1994; Riger, 1992; Unger, 1998). Throughout these arguments is a pervasive belief that it is impossible to know the truth about gender similarities and differences. Because all similarities and differences are context dependent, we can construct a whole range of similarities and differences. Rhoda Unger (1979b, 1998, p. 125) offers the metaphor of a rainbow to show how comparisons change with context. If we compare two colors close in the spectrum, such as red and magenta, they seem quite different. But if we compare them within the full rainbow, they appear very similar.

Wendy Hollway (1994) presents a differently constructed no answer to the question of studying gender differences. Instead of moving away from the focus on individual gender, she chooses to go beyond the study of sex differences to study differences and similarities between and among women and men. Basically her argument is to take the singular focus off differences between women and men, and look at many differences and similarities all of which share the underlying psychodynamic mechanisms of splitting and identification. By broadening the possible comparisons, differences between genders become less important. Rhoda Unger (1992) makes a similar point when she argues that exploring more differences will result in less importance being attached to any one difference.

Because such different assumptions underlie the yes and no answers to the question: Should we study gender differences? Neither answer can be singularly right or wrong. Rather both have their advantages and disadvantages for feminist scholars. Thus, I turn next to the examination of three contributions to feminist scholarship that have come from this debate. Each of these contributions has strengths and limitations that I examine as I discuss each of them.

INCREASED STATISTICAL SOPHISTICATION IN THE QUANTITATIVE MEASUREMENT OF
SIMILARITIES AND DIFFERENCES

The commitment to constructing a better science of gender similarities and differences by feminist psychologists who believe in the importance of empirical findings has led to two important contributions to the study of quantitative gender similarities and differences. The first of these is effect size. Effect size is an important tool for the study of the existence or extent of a difference. It is a particularly important corrective to the problem that statistical significance is dependent on sample size. As the sample size increases, the size of the gender difference necessary to reach significance decreases. Thus, minuscule gender differences will be statistically significant if the sample size is large enough, and conversely, fairly large differences will fail to reach significance if the sample size is small. As a numerical description of the extent of a quantitative difference, effect size is most useful. Furthermore, it is possible through a meta-analysis to combine effect sizes from different studies and compute an average effect size that can be tested to see if it is significantly different from zero. If an average effect size is not different from zero, Janet Hyde (1994a) argues that one can take the "revolutionary step of *accepting* the null hypothesis" (p. 454). For example, the average gender difference in mathematics performance across many different studies employing representative samples is not significantly different from zero, a finding she describes as "a real feminist transformation" (p. 455).

Statistically, it is possible also to determine if all the effect sizes in a meta-analysis are homogeneous, that is if they are similar to one another in size, or if they are heterogeneous, in which case several groups of effect sizes are found that are reliably different from each other. As far as I am aware, every meta-analysis of gender similarities and differences has found heterogeneity of effect sizes. Explaining heterogeneity requires attention to context (i.e., what is different about one group of studies that found no differences and another that found substantial differences?). Context in meta-analysis can and does include factors like class and race (Hyde, 1994a; Hyde, Fennema, & Lamon, 1990) as well as differences among empirical methods used. In either case, attention to context and theory building is an important part of meta-analytic studies (Eagly, 1994). Advocates of effect size argue that they are more objective summaries of a group of studies than narrative reviews (Eagly, 1987) and that they provide a powerful tool to influence the media and counter assertions of inferior female performance (Hyde, 1994a).

Advocates of meta-analytic techniques have focused on strengths rather than limitations of this method. In keeping with my thesis that an exploration of both is important for understanding the partial nature of all knowledge, I explore a few of them here. One obvious limitation is that only quantitative studies can be included. There is no way to take account of qualitative studies within a meta-analysis, although they could help inform the theory used to explain heterogeneity of effect sizes. In a complementary fashion, quantitative studies may be most useful to determine the extent or existence of a difference and qualitative ones to describe the nature of a difference (Ussher, 1999). Furthermore, anyone undertaking a meta-analysis is limited to the operationalizations, samples, and experimental contexts used by other researchers. Thus if all the samples are white, and if the studies are laboratory experiments, race and the effects of real life contexts cannot be included in the analysis.

Because meta-analysis depends on fairly sophisticated statistical techniques, it is difficult to translate into language that can easily be used in a public debate, or understood by feminist scholars who are unfamiliar with the statistical jargon. Teaching about effect size to undergraduate psychology majors who have a background in statistics is not easy. To explain in terms readily accessible to the media would seem a difficult task. I agree with Janet Hyde (1994a) that potentially effect size is a powerful tool to counter media assertions of female inferiority. What I question is how effective it actually has been in doing so. I know of no study of media representations that attempts to validate this assertion. In contrast, there is evidence (Eccles & Jacobs, 1986) that media presentations of gender differences and female inferiority do influence the attitudes of parents concerning their children's mathematics performance.

Although meta-analyses may guard against some biases that could occur in a narrative review such as the overestimation or underestimation of an effect because of reliance on statistical significance, the interpretation of effect sizes is not at all straightforward. There are rough rules describing small, medium, and large effect sizes, with the assumption that large differences are more important. However, sometimes small differences can have important practical or theoretical consequences, and in turn some large differences may be trivial. Turning first to the issue of small differences, gender differences in risk taking in potentially dangerous activities such as driving or unprotected sex are very small in terms of absolute effect sizes. But when large numbers of people are involved, this can translate into a substantial gender difference in numbers of injuries and deaths (Byrnes, Miller, & Schafer, 1999). Small differences that aggregate over time may cumulatively attain considerable importance (Eagly, 1987). Deborah Prentice and Dale Miller (1992) have argued that very small differences can be important in demonstrating the strength of a social phenomenon through minimal manipulation. For example, ethnocentrism, or a bias in favor of one's own group and against a group of others, can be created in the laboratory by assigning people randomly to two different groups and telling them it was random. The effect size in such studies is very small, but that it exists at all in this highly contrived context, says something important about the power of ethnocentrism. Conversely, some large effect sizes are, or should be, minimally important in many contexts. Physical differences between females and males are often large, and in most contexts are irrelevant to the actual task at hand. However, because of the symbolic association of male characteristics such as height with power, these differences take on social and political importance. Because gender differences are mapped onto male-superior and female-inferior symbolic hierarchies, it becomes particularly difficult to find large gender differences that are irrelevant, although many feminists have argued that most of them should be in most contexts.

The second feminist contribution to the study of quantitative gender similarities and differences is an emphasis on distributions of scores for both genders. Olga Favreau (1997) has challenged the validity of examining mean differences to determine gender differences, whether significance testing or effect sizes are used. Both of these techniques depend on assumptions of a normal distribution of scores. This is an assumption that is met in less than 10% of the samples in one review of achievement studies (Micceri, 1989). The lack of normal distributions calls into question most tests of statistical significance and effect size. Practically, it also means that distributions are as important an aspect of describing gender similarities and differences as are means. If most men and women perform similarly on a task, but a few women have very high scores, this may result in a significant mean difference and a reasonable effect size, and yet the difference is not that most women perform better than most men on the task, but that most women and men perform similarly and a few women perform very well.

Although I am not optimistic that statistical improvements to the study of gender similarities and differences will create important feminist transformations in the larger society, I would argue that they are crucial feminist transformations within quantitative psychology and that we are far from implementing them. I would argue that every study of difference (whether a group difference such as gender or an experimental manipulation) should report effect sizes for all comparisons and should provide descriptions of the variability of scores for each group, preferably in the form of a frequency distribution. With this information it would be possible to form much more complex and contextually accurate descriptions of gender similarities and differences. And although I am not sure this alone is sufficient to make change in the larger society, I am sure it is necessary.

REMOVING GENDER FROM THE INDIVIDUAL

One of the major contributions to gender scholarship that has come from the work of those who answer the question should we study gender differences in the negative is shifting the focus from gender as an attribute of an individual to gender as an attribute of social and institutional contexts. Jeanne Marecek (1995a) identifies four possible constructions of gender that shift the focus away from internal individual differences to the interpersonal and institutional. First, one can define gender as personal and cultural accomplishments that are produced by social processes. Within this definition, sex difference research becomes one such cultural accomplishment. Second, one can look at gender as a system that organizes male-female relations in culturally specific ways. Third, gender can be thought of as performances through which individuals produce subjectivities. And fourth, gender can be understood as a marker of hierarchy, one of many that culturally define relations of power and subordination.

Rhoda Unger (1998) has also argued for shifting concepts of gender from individual sex differences that ignore institutional sexism and male authority, to interpersonal interactions that occur in social contexts. By changing the focus in this way, she proposes that useful comparisons shift from comparing individual women and men to comparing how people do gender in various contexts. For example, one might compare the same behaviors in the different social contexts of lab and field, public and private, groups of varying sex ratios, and what people say about themselves and what they say about others (p. 153).

A major focus in the move to shift away from individual gender has been the analysis of gender in terms of power. This argument is that gender differences can better be explained as power differences than as gender differences per se. Because in many situations men have more power and privilege than women, gender differences in behavior can be explained as differences between more and less powerful people, or between those who are dominant and those who are submissive. Nancy Henley (1977) pioneered this approach in her early work showing that gender differences in nonverbal behaviors such as touching and smiling could be attributed to power differences between women and men. Experimental work has also demonstrated importance of power over gender. For example, Sara Snodgrass (1985, 1992) demonstrated that when university students were assigned roles of boss and employee or teacher and learner in a laboratory setting, there were no gender differences in interpersonal sensitivity, but in each situation there were main effects for role showing that both men and women in a subordinate role demonstrated more interpersonal sensitivity than women and men in a dominant role. Her conclusions that subordination, not gender, explains interpersonal sensitivity is a powerful one. However, I would caution that reducing gender differences to power differences, may not be as simple in socially complex situations as in the lab. Certainly the dynamics of a male boss and female employee are not a simple reversal of the dynamics of a female boss and a male employee. Celia Kitzinger (Kitzinger et al., 1996) points out that although in most situations a researcher has more power than her or his participants, this can change in a situation of "studying up" where the research is focused on people who are socially more powerful than the researcher. A power analysis is crucial to understanding gender, however it is not a simple nor a one-way relationship, but rather an interaction between gender and power that plays out in complex and different ways in different situations.

The shift of focus from individual to social and institutional definitions of gender has been a crucial one for feminist psychologists to make in the process of understanding gender differences and similarities. However, the shift does not reduce the importance of analyzing gender differences and similarities, but rather moves the analysis to a different level. If gender is socially constructed through interpersonal and institutional contexts, then an analysis of gender differences within these contexts is crucial. Carol Cohn (1993) studied a group of defense intellectuals as a participant observer. She found that any concern that was marked as feminine, such as a concern with the human suffering involved in an exchange of nuclear weapons, could not be legitimately expressed by either men or women in this context.

One limitation of the move away from individual gender is the implication that either the individual or the social level is legitimate. By rejecting individual gender and choosing instead social and institutional definitions of gender, a dichotomy is set up in which only one level of gender is legitimate. I would argue that there are a number of levels to the construction of gender that are important. Certainly individual gender is not the only possible analysis nor a privileged level of analysis as much psychological scholarship would claim either explicitly or implicitly. But neither is the social. We would do better to entertain all possible constructions of gender, acknowledging advantages and disadvantages to each. Levels of gender are not mutually exclusive, rather they interact in many and complex ways. People bring symbolically gendered ideas with them into situations they encounter (Unger, 1998, p. 185). Gendered discourses define a range of possibilities that are variously used by different institutions. Individuals are not totally defined by institutional gender constraints, but are also not totally free of them. They are also constrained in different ways at different times, and resist these constraints in various ways.

Differences among Women

A major disadvantage of an emphasis on studying gender differences is that it essentializes women. That is, to generalize about how women are different from men, one must ignore differences among women. Furthermore because participants in psychology research are overwhelmingly white middle-class university students, these generalizations to "women" are particularly suspect (Bohan, 1993; Hare-Mustin & Marecek, 1994). Thus an important contribution of feminist researchers critical of gender differences research has been the search for differences among women, especially those related to differences of power such as race, ability, class, sexual orientation, age, and so on. In this work power differences among women become the epistemological starting point, and a knowledge of differences is constructed as a necessary part of understanding commonalties among women (Griscom, 1992). With this emphasis on differences among women has come a concern for the representation of the other, particularly where both the researcher and her participants are women. Recently, two special issues of *Feminism & Psychology* (Vol. 6, Nos. 1 & 2) were devoted to the issue of researchers' responsibilities to their participants, in particular ethical and political problems in dealing with issues of differences and similarities. With one exception, which involved the difference of HIV status between Adrian Coyle (1996) and his gay male participants, all of the articles focused on differences and similarities between women researchers and their participants.

There is a certain inconsistency in the rejection of research on gender differences as politically dangerous and the lauding of research on differences among women as politically liberating. Problems of essentialism are not absent in studies of differences among women. Indeed any comparison, particularly one across power dynamics, contains a necessary essentialism or generalization that masks some aspects of diversity. Thus comparisons of women across race may mask both differences across and similarities within class (P.T. Reid, 1993). This essentialism applies also to comparisons among situations, institutions, and discourses as well as comparisons among individuals or groups (J.R. Martin, 1994; Unger, 1998, pp. 151–154). Another risk in the focus on differences among women is that of focusing on smaller and smaller groups in order to minimize differences, risking an extreme identity politics of the individual, and undermining the possibility of broad based political solidarity in fighting specific oppressions.

In exploring this hierarchy that devalues gender difference research relative to research on differences among women, I propose three possible sources of this differential evaluation. First, for feminist researchers the chance to focus all one's energy on women is both validating and challenges main stream psychology's insistence that research on women alone is bad or biased (Fine & Gordon, 1991). Power dynamics also make studying only women a very different activity than studying only men that marked classical psychology. Second, it may be easier or more obvious to focus on context as the source of differences among women whereas gender differences are more likely to be reduced to essential biological or socialization causes, if not by the researcher, then by others who interpret the research. Gender is a more difficult difference because it appears so monolithic. When focusing on women, there are so many relevant differences that any single difference is less likely to be reduced to socialization, let alone biology. Cultural factors are more obviously front and center for both the researcher and the reader. Third, there may be some gain in avoiding gender comparisons, especially when they are painful for women, make one feel a victim or at a particular disadvantage. Pat Macpherson and Michelle Fine (1995) engaged in extensive conversations with a group of four adolescent women who were from various racial and class backgrounds. These young women consistently defined themselves as different from other girls who embodied the feminine and as similar to young men (i.e., one of the guys). Acknowledging gender differences seemed to shift their status down, even to bring on date rape, harassment, and subordination of one's needs to others, particularly men and children. "Doing [gender] difference means fixing hierarchies, becoming victim and losing power" (p. 195). Believing in their entitlement to equality and denying heterosexual danger, these young women felt alone and vulnerable when out of identity with young men. In contrast, they gained in power and status in constructing their differences from other girls, especially girls they judged as feminine.

I would argue that gender differences are neither more nor less important than differences among women and all differences are contextually specific partial constructions. Whether a comparison supports the status quo or is liberating is not inherent in the comparison, but in how it is constructed and interpreted. Just as there are many levels on which gender similarities and differences are mapped, so there are also many levels on which other power inequalities are mapped. Not only are there interactions among levels for any power dimension, but also among different dimensions of power within and across levels. There is much to be learned from the interaction of gender with other power dynamics. Even within the level of individual analysis these interactions have much to tell us. For example, in both mathematics achievement (Hyde et al., 1990) and in the endorsement of feminist beliefs (Henley, Meng, O'Brien, McCarthy, & Sockloskie, 1998) gender differences are larger for white samples than for minority samples. Gender as difference stands out more within the dominant culture because other differences seem irrelevant; within marginal cultures, gender as difference exists in a context of one or more other power differences.

DIFFERENCE AND HIERARCHY

Because there are always both similarities and differences—within one person over time, among individuals and groups, within one situation or context over time, and among situations, contexts, institutions, and discourses—I broaden my discussion to include an examination of constructions of similarities and differences on several different levels. I begin with an examination of the process of mapping difference onto hierarchy. Differences are not essentially hierarchical. However, there are powerful factors, both individual and social, that contribute to the mapping of difference onto hierarchy, creating from difference a social distinction based on power and status (Tajfel, 1984). After discussing what I see as some of these factors, I want to turn my attention to two suggestions as to how we as researchers might resist this process in our examination of similarities and differences. The first is constructing dichotomies as necessary contradictions rather than mutually exclusive alternatives. The second is increasing reflexivity through an examination of strengths and weaknesses of all partial constructions. I conclude with a detailed examination of gender similarities and differences in relationship violence to illustrate this reflexivity.

CONSTRUCTING DIFFERENCE AS HIERARCHY

In examining how difference becomes mapped onto hierarchy, I begin with the level of the individual and move from there to interpersonal processes. Finally I examine academic and political discourses. Wendy Hollway (1994) locates splitting as the psychodynamic process that produces and reproduces differences and identification as the process that produces and reproduces similarities. Splitting is a process whereby the good is retained for the self and the bad is projected onto the other, mapping hierarchy onto difference. As Deborah Marks (1996) says: " 'Other' is always a construction, that relies on the fears and fantasies we have about ourselves as much as the fears and fantasies we have about 'Others' " (p. 72). This splitting comes through interpersonal contexts as differing perceptions of the self and others. The fundamental attribution error arises because people have more information about their own than about others' behaviors. Thus one's own behavior is explained more by context and others' behavior more by traits. People also tend to see themselves as exceptions to any kind of group categorization (Unger, 1998, pp. 159–161). Members of minority groups claim that while others in their group are discriminated against, they are not (Clayton & Crosby, 1992). Often women victims of violence prefer to blame themselves than to categorize themselves as victims (S. Lamb, 1996, pp. 22–55). Suzanne Kessler (1998, pp. 100–104) found that university students asked to imagine they had been born with large clitorises or small penises were very likely to reject surgical reconstruction of their genitals as an option, or to have it delayed until they were adults and could decide for themselves. However, these same students, when asked what they would do if they had a child with different genitals, made more traditional choices, opting for surgery during infancy. Thus, they rejected choices for themselves that they endorsed for their sons and daughters. For themselves preserving sexual pleasure took precedence, for their children fitting in with their peers took precedence.

Another cognitive process that contributes to making hierarchies of differences is zero sum thinking. If dichotomies are constructed as mutually exclusive alternatives, then if one wins the other loses. If the victim is more to blame, then the perpetrator is proportionately less to blame in this kind of thinking (S. Lamb, 1996, pp. 91–96). Rhonda Reitz (1999) has demonstrated how zero sum construction of dichotomies in the discourses of violent men contributes to continued violence. These men construed many encounters as zero sum games in which one person would be good, big, and winner; the other bad, small, and loser. They engaged in violence to regain control of the big, good, and winning side battering their partner into positions of bad, little, and loser. However, the violence was unsuccessful in securing the winning position and therefore had to be repeated in an attempt to win in this very serious and ultimately unwinnable zero sum game.

Academic and political discourses are structured around creating hierarchy out of difference. The main way this is done is by claiming the strengths of one's own constructions and criticizing the weaknesses of others' constructions. This maximization of splitting and minimization of identification, in intellectual terms, sets up a zero sum contest among various positions, the more one is right or useful, the more the other is wrong or dangerous. Taking a different position is constructed as opposition.

In academic discourses, differences are constructed as hierarchies in the process of speaking for the other and in the process of speaking to each other. Psychology has long maintained that the researcher can claim to speak for the other with objectivity and distance, that is through splitting (Coyle, 1996). Furthermore, this process of distancing oneself from one's participants and claiming objective knowledge about them is alive and well, in spite of feminist methodological and epistemological critiques. This is perhaps most clearly constructed in methodology texts. Rebecca Campbell and Pamela Schram (1995) surveyed psychology and general science textbooks and found that except for the use of gender neutral language, the vast majority of the texts reinscribed the hierarchy between the researcher and participant and the superiority of scientific, quantitative, "objective" knowledge. Their results agree well with Michelle Fine and Susan Gordon's statement: "When feminism and psychology mate, our evidence has found that feminism seems to bear only recessive genes" (1991, p. 20). This persistent reinscription of researcher/participant hierarchy, makes understandable some feminists' claim that the very act of speaking for another is an act of colonization (S. Wilkinson, 1996b). However, this only reverses the hierarchy found in academic psychology.

Taking a critical view of the power dynamics between researcher and participant without rejecting the possibility of speaking for the other with respect, feminist psychologists have raised important issues. One such issue is what to do when you as the researcher do not agree with or actively dislike your participants (K. Davis & Gremmen, 1998; F.K. Grossman, Kruger, & Moore, 1999; C. Kitzinger & Wilkinson, 1997). Another is how shared similarities with one's participants can block one from understanding important differences (Hurd & McIntyre, 1996; Oguntokun, 1998). Some feminist researchers have even engaged in the process of negotiation with participants about how the results are constructed (S.J. Jones, 1997). However, speaking about or across difference remains in feminist scholarship a difficult process to negotiate and subject to various hierarchies. M. Brinton Lykes (1989) describes how her best attempts to write a consent form that empowered her participants served instead to reinscribe her power as a researcher and to undermine the trust she had previously established with the Guatemalan women whose life stories she recorded. Manjit Bola describes how her research on white women's experiences of pregnancy led either to her being labeled as a coconut—brown on the outside but white identified or to validation for turning the tables and investigating whites the way women of color have so often been investigated (C. Kitzinger et al., 1996, p. 219).

Academic hierarchies are also created in the ways we speak to each other in academic exchanges. Academic reputation has often been built on claiming all that is good for one's theory or methodology, and disproving or attempting to disprove alternative constructions. For feminists it is difficult to move beyond this, and academic exchanges, both in person and in writing, are far too often one-sided in pointing out only the inaccuracies or limitations of others' constructions that are responded to in kind (e.g., Bola et al., 1998; R. Edwards, 1998).

Political discourses also abound in hierarchies, many constructed in the same way as in academic discourses. One position or strategy is advocated and all others attacked or questioned as dangerous. Amanda Kottler (1996) describes how a discourse of similarities was the mainstay of anti-apartheid politics at the University of Cape Town, until Harriet Ngubane, a Zulu woman, joined the faculty and began to speak of cultural difference and pride. Because among the white, politically active faculty racial similarities was the main discourse used to fight apartheid, discourses of racial differences were seen a dangerous and wrong, a hierarchy that silenced differences. Diane Richardson (1996a) finds critiques of radical feminisms so one sided in their dismissal, that she both cannot recognize her own and other radical feminists' discourses, and fears that radical feminism is being set up in these arguments to carry all the failures of feminism. Marion Martin and Beth Humphries (1996) make the important point that institutional hierarchies can impose hierarchies on individuals who are attempting to work together across difference.

Deconstructing Difference as Hierarchy

Dichotomies as Necessary Contradictions

Hierarchies are created when dichotomies are treated as zero sum constructions—the more one side of the dichotomy is right or useful, the more the other is wrong, dangerous, or problematic. In order to reduce hierarchy, it is important to resist zero sum thinking. Instead both sides of a dichotomy can be constructed as necessary, if sometimes contradictory, aspects of reality. Indeed if reality embodies contradictions then our epistemologies should reflect these contradictions (Unger, 1998, p. 183). The dualisms of western psychology such as the personal and the social, the individual and society, nature and nurture are often constructed as mutually exclusive choices, as are methodological dualisms such as positivism and social constructionism or empiricism and theory. Only when one choice excludes the possibility of the other are the two poles of a dichotomy incommensurate. If instead all choices are partial and contextually specific with advantages and disadvantages, then exclusive choice is neither necessary, nor desirable. Rhoda Unger (1998, pp. 185–186) proposes the metaphor of optical illusions as a way of embracing paradox and contradiction. In the same way that the study of optical illusions leads to an understanding of how multiple perceptual realities are created, approaching dichotomies as necessary contradictions rather than hierarchies can promote an understanding of how multiple social realities are created. In much the same vein, I (Kimball, 1995) have argued that the metaphor of double visions, illustrated by a reversing figure-ground illusion, is a useful way to construct gender similarities and differences as multiple social realities rather than mutually exclusive choices.

When we try to convince others that we are right and they are wrong, they are naturally defensive of their position. Janet Hyde's (1998, p. 362) assumption that data, or the "real responses of real women" should lead to the modification of feminist theories creates a hierarchy in which data dominate theory. In response, Nancy Henley and William McCarthy (1998) make the important point that theoretical distinctions may be useful, even if these distinctions are not reflected in the responses of a particular sample of participants in an empirical study.

As will be obvious by now, I am arguing that an attempt to construct gender similarities and differences as a hierarchical dichotomy forcing a choice between one or the other is not very useful for knowledge construction nor for feminist politics. What may be less obvious and is critical for feminists is the dichotomy of gender itself with female and male, feminine and masculine poles in which the male and masculine have more power, and are more valued than female and feminine. Although many have argued that masculine and feminine need not be mutually exclusive choices, not many have questioned male and female as a natural dichotomy, even feminists who would argue for deconstructing the power associated with being male. Suzanne Kessler (1998) makes a powerful critique of gender as a natural dichotomy. Intersexed infants are born with ambiguous genitals, often very small penises or very large clitorises, making their assignment as male or female unclear. The medical profession responds to this natural variability by imposing a strictly dichotomous gender assignment followed as necessary by surgery, hormone treatment, and assurance to the parents that the child "really" is male or female based on the medical assignment. Many intersexed adults object to the treatments they received as infants—treatments that often both failed to create realistic-looking genitalia and severely compromised genital sexual pleasures. Some transgendered or transsexual adults choose to surgically alter their bodies to live as the "opposite" sex. However, some refuse surgery and choose to live as a male with female genitals or vice versa. Other dress and act in ways that cross or blur gender boundaries. The experiences of people who cross or blur gender boundaries challenge the naturalness of dichotomous gender. This is an important challenge because without dichotomous gender, the gender hierarchy is destabilized.

Embedded in all dichotomies are complex realities. "Dualism reduces complexity, but does not explain it" (Unger, 1998, p. 82). I would add that not only does the dualism not explain complexity, but also that one side of a conceptual dualism is particularly inadequate as an explanation of complexity. Embracing both sides of necessary contradictions means living with partial constructions. If we can acknowledge both advantages and disadvantages of all partial constructions, both those of ourselves and those of others, then we will make a contribution to the deconstruction of difference as hierarchy.

Reflexivity through Strengths and Limitations

Consistent with an emphasis on the study of differences among women, reflexivity is recognizing and analyzing the difference one's own differences make (S.J. Jones, 1997; Reay, 1996). Mary Crawford and Ellen Kimmel (1999b) define both a personal reflexivity that is how our identities and our work influence each other and a functional reflexivity that involves a sociological perspective of our academic discipline and how dominant paradigms and powerful institutions support each other. I argue for one very specific operationalization of reflexivity that incorporates aspects of the above definitions. As scholars and political activists, we should examine the strengths and limitations, advantages and disadvantages, powers and dangers of our own and others' partial constructions about similarities and differences. This is not an argument for relativism, although it is an argument against a positivist vision of a single truth about any particular aspect of reality. All that we are capable of as humans is partial constructions of reality. We cannot grasp the whole all at once, nor can we devise perfect strategies for change. Random factors and oppositional forces will partly determine the success of political strategies.

Although the following is a very select sample, I offer here several illustrations of this kind of reflexivity in action and in the following section I apply it in some detail to an analysis of gender similarities and differences in relationship violence. Celia Kitzinger and Deborah Powell (1995) provide an excellent example of an analysis of advantages and disadvantages of different constructions of the same data. They asked university students to respond to a projective cue about infidelity in a heterosexual relationship. There were many differences in the males' and females' responses. In interpreting these data, the authors provided both an essentialist reading that focused on these differences as reflections of sex differences in motives, needs, and beliefs; and a social constructionist reading that focused on the participants' use of various gendered social narratives and discourses about heterosexuality. Not only do both interpretations fit the data, both have advantages and disadvantages that the authors are careful to point out. Furthermore such a rich interpretation of the data helps to link it to other important information. For example, in the male participants' projective stories, violence was much more frequent no matter who the victim was. That is, they were more likely than the female participants to respond to both male and female infidelity with violent stories. When this finding is put together with the information that 28% of female but only 3% of male homicide victims are killed by a partner (Reitz, 1999), the combination informs both an essentialist and a social constructionist interpretation. It points to behavioral sex differences that are important consequences of the existence of socially constructed discourses. Clearly, no one would argue that telling violent stories leads directly to male violence in any particular individual. Most, hopefully all, of the young men who told these stories will not go on to murder a partner and the young women will not be murdered. However, whether one interprets these stories as reflecting individual gender differences in motives and beliefs or as reflecting culturally constructed discourses that the participants draw on in forming stories, there are important links to violent behavior. Unfortunately, we can predict that some of these young men do or will abuse their female partners and some of these young women will be victims of abuse.

Kathy Davis and Ine Gremmen (1998) give a nuanced analysis of the problems of wanting as feminist researchers to make heroines of their participants and having to cope with either disappointment or active dislike instead. They analyze various ways of resolving this dilemma that will both allow the differences they experience and also acknowledge on some level the similarity their own and their participants' constructions. They recognize in their desire for perfect informants their own desire to be perfect researchers. And the impossibility of either requires that they pursue both similarities and differences between themselves and their participants. Hannah Frith (1998) provides a discourse analysis that looks at specific aspects of group talk through which participants do similarities and differences. In this way, she and her participants are neither similar nor different but both at various times and about a variety of issues.

To engage in reflexivity about partial constructions of similarities and differences, interactions with people across differences are important. Liberation struggles require that we can identify across boundaries of difference (Chrisler, 1996b; Livia, 1996) and this identification is facilitated by relationships of friendship and trust as a context for dialogue (D. Bell, 1996), and through working relationships that incorporate differences (F.K. Grossman et al., 1999; Lykes, 1989; A.J. Stewart & Zucker, 1999).

Gender Similarities and Differences in Relationship Violence

As an illustration of reflexivity in the study of gender similarities and differences, I look at the debate over gender and violence in intimate relationships. On the one hand, feminists have emphasized abusive heterosexual relationships, the vast majority of which involve a male perpetrator and a female victim. Using information from hospitals, police records, shelters for battered women, and crime surveys, a picture of large gender differences has emerged (R.P. Dobash, Dobash, Wilson, & Daly, 1992; Kurz, 1993). On the other hand, family violence researchers using large random national surveys of violent behavior have constructed a picture of gender similarities (Straus, 1993). Largely this debate has been constructed as a mutually exclusive set of options, with one construction embodying the truth and the other a dangerous fiction. For example, in *Current Controversies in Domestic Violence* (Gelles & Loseke, 1993), the chapters reviewing each of these constructions are titled: "Physical assaults by husbands: A major social problem" (Kurz, 1993) and "Physical assaults by wives: A major social problem" (Straus, 1993). One feminist author has concluded that "the basic assumptions of the family violence and feminist approaches to domestic violence are irreconcilable" (Kurz, p. 98). Much of this literature is structured so that the reader must take sides, make a choice. The literature is replete with the strengths of one's own point of view and criticisms of alternative constructions. The goal of the rhetoric on both sides of the debate is to turn the reader into a believer in the exclusive truth of the author's point of view.

Is there an alternative? I firmly believe there is and that it is important for feminists to exit this debate and take a very different approach. My goal is to "usefully complicate" (Landsman, 1998, p. 94) the debate around gender differences in relationship violence. To show how this might be done, I turn to the work of Michael Johnson (1995) who argues that the family violence and feminist literatures are using constructions that capture two different and non-overlapping phenomena. Feminists have focused on a pattern he labels "patriarchal terrorism." Patriarchal terrorism involves one partner, almost always the male, seeking to control his partner and to display his control. The violence almost always escalates, the violence is frequent with incidents occurring on average once a week or more often, injury is frequent and severe, most of the violence is initiated by the male, and very few women fight back. In contrast in "common couple violence" partners are expressing momentary frustrations or angers that arise out of particular circumstances, but do not seek the absolute control over another that is involved in patriarchal terrorism. Common couple violence is reported by a similar proportion of both men and women in heterosexual relationships who both initiate and reciprocate acts of violent behavior, involves fewer incidents (average of one every two months), and does not show evidence of escalating over time. With the important exception of assaults resulting in physical injury, which is higher for male acts of violence (Straus, 1993), gender similarities predominate in studies of common couple violence.

To make sense of these two very different pictures, Michael Johnson (1995) examined the sampling techniques and methodologies that produce these two very different constructions. Studies of patriarchal terrorism have usually focused on statistics and stories gathered in the settings where the most extreme forms of partner abuse are seen, in shelters for battered women, in hospital emergency rooms, in divorce court proceedings, and in surveys of criminal behavior. Clearly these clinical samples are very selective and cannot be thought of as representative. What is less clear is how the national random surveys of violent behavior also are not representative. The crucial information here is that no random sample survey ever includes everyone who is originally identified for inclusion, and that those who do not participate are not necessarily representative of those who do. Indeed, the National Family Violence Survey response rates are as low as 60% if one excludes not only those who were eligible and refused to participate, but also an estimate of those who would have been eligible but who either refused to answer the screening questions or were never located after multiple calls (pp. 290–291). Thus there are enough nonresponses to cover the highest estimates of women who are battered and the men who engage in patriarchal terrorism against them. And it is reasonable to assume that men engaged in patriarchal terrorism and women who are victimized by this terrorism, will refuse to participate in surveys, even phone surveys, about family violence.

Is patriarchal terrorism a qualitatively different phenomenon from common couple violence, or is it an extreme point on a violence continuum? The difference can be usefully constructed as both a quantitative one and a qualitative one (Dutton, 1999). Both constructions are partial, and together they form a more complete picture. Using Olga Favreau's (1997) warning that it is always important to examine the distributions of scores, I hypothesize that patriarchal terrorism and common couple violence studies are sampling two different parts of the distribution. If one samples only situations in which there are no or relatively few acts of violence directed toward a partner (common couple violence), then the male and female distributions would overlap almost completely and the average amount of violence would be very similar. If instead situations are sampled where there are many acts of violence (patriarchal terrorism), one would find many more men than women. In statistical terms, the male distribution of violent acts is skewed toward the high end of the distribution. Linguistically it is accurate to say more men than women engage in patriarchal terrorism, but inaccurate to say men are more aggressive than women because for the vast majority of women and men the distributions of violent behaviors are very similar.

Qualitatively, I see two very different motivations. In patriarchal terrorism, the motivation is control or domination of the partner, it is purposive, and most important it is insatiable. Since another person cannot be totally dominated, the need will never go away, and will very likely escalate into more and more extreme forms as the possibility of control continually eludes one. Qualitative studies of both victims and perpetrators of patriarchal violence point to the motivation of control. Paige Smith, Jason Smith, and Jo Anne Earp (1999) developed their WEB (Women's Experience of Violence) Scale to reflect women's experiences of violence. This scale has 10 items that show how women victims of violence do feel highly controlled by their partners' violence (e.g., "I feel like he keeps me a prisoner," "I feel owned and controlled by him," and "I feel like I am programmed to react a certain way with him"). Rhonda Reitz's (1999) study of batterers' experiences of violence also point to the need to control the victim through violence as a never ending attempt to feel good, big, and a winner that is constructed as coming only from a position of absolute dominance.

In common couple violence, the motivation is more likely frustration and anger over a particular conflict that does not arise from a need to control the partner's behavior, and is more likely to be satisfied in the fight or violent behavior. Although the violence may very likely be repeated, especially if reinforced, it is much less likely to escalate into more serious violence. There are probably individuals, mostly men, who do begin with common couple violence and move onto patriarchal terrorism, but the majority of people who do engage in common couple violence never do.

Is the distinction between common couple violence and patriarchal terrorism unique to heterosexual couples or to couple violence? My guess is that it is not and here I examine what little is known about violence in gay and lesbian couples, and briefly consider child abuse. Although it is very difficult to determine rates of violence, it is clearly present in both gay and lesbian relationships. Most of the work of gay and lesbian violence has focused on what I am calling patriarchal terrorism—situations of serious abuse of high frequency that escalate over time, often result in injury, arise out of a motivation to control the partner, and are experienced by the victim as terrorism (B. Hart, 1986; Island & Letellier, 1991; Renzetti, 1992). An interesting question is whether patriarchal terrorism is a useful rhetoric, especially in lesbian relationships. It is useful in describing heterosexual abuse partly because it clearly identifies the common abuser as male (M.P. Johnson, 1995). I chose to use it with reference to lesbian relationships because it captures the ideas of dominance and control that are based on the legitimization and power of male authority, even when it is borrowed by a woman. There is only beginning to be work that examines common couple violence in gay and lesbian relationships. There are, however, community surveys that indicate levels of physical aggression in gay and lesbian relationships similar to those found in community samples of heterosexuals (Bartholomew, Landolt, & Oram, 1999; Lie, Schilit, Bush, Montague, & Reyes, 1991).

Much more work has been done examining child abuse, but little that examines the distinction that I am making between a motivation to control as completely as possible another person, in this case a child, and the use of violence occasionally and as a result of particular circumstances out of anger or frustration. One piece of evidence supports the idea that there may be two nonoverlapping phenomena in terms of the physical abuse of children. It is well known in the clinical literature that stepparents are much more likely to abuse their children than are parents. However, in the large scale random family violence surveys, this difference does not hold up and equal rates of violence against children are reported by parents and stepparents (R.P. Dobash et al., 1992). Although this finding has been used to argue against the validity of the Conflict Tactics Scale (CTS) which also does not yield gender differences, it is also possible that, as with gender, two different forms of violence and two different populations are being examined. Stepparents may direct more patriarchal terrorism against their children, but not more common couple forms of violence.

Because this discussion is meant to be illustrative of reflexivity and not a literature review, and because most of the debate has focused on physical violence, I have not considered other forms of violence including psychological, emotional, material, or sexual. These differing definitions of violence may also result in different constructions of gender similarities and differences. But in each case I would look for differences between what I am calling patriarchal terrorism and common couple violence. For example, emotional or verbal abuse can be used to hurt in a fight or disagreement, or it can be a systematic tool of control through humiliation and threat. Researchers in both heterosexual and lesbian violence are careful to point out that abuse and battering can occur in the absence of physical violence if the level of threat and intimidation through other means is high enough to control and terrorize the partner (B. Hart, 1986; M.P. Johnson, 1995).

Why consider both patriarchal terrorism and common couple violence as valid constructions of gender similarities and differences? As feminists, the existence of patriarchal terrorism must engage our energy and our activism. But is common couple violence only a patriarchal tactic to divert our attention? How can the information that women too are violent be useful to feminists? In keeping with my main point, I argue that both the constructions that I am calling patriarchal terrorism and common couple violence are partial visions, neither captures more truth than the other, but rather different subsets of truth. Both constructions have strengths and weaknesses and as feminists and/or family violence researchers, we need to be more aware of the problems with our own constructions and the strengths of the constructions with which we do not agree. To make my point, I am going to specifically examine what I see as both strengths and limitations of both patriarchal terrorism and common couple violence from my feminist perspective.

Turning first to patriarchal terrorism: The strengths, as I see them, are that it names the perpetrator as male, it emphasizes gender differences in serious violence, it calls attention to forms of violence that are highly destructive, both physically and psychologically in many women's lives, and it supports the need for social resources for victims of violence. The limitations or weaknesses of patriarchal terrorism are that it misses the violence that many women and men experience as both initiators and receivers. By insisting that the gender differences in patriarchal terrorism are representative of gender differences more generally, there is the risk that women's aggression will not be treated as legitimate and even pathologized. Women who murder their partners receive much longer sentences (15 to 20 years) than men who murder their partners (2 to 6 years) (J.W. White & Kowalski, 1994). Finally, patriarchal terrorism can be used as an excuse for women's violence, or a reason not to study or report it. Thus, one feminist researcher is careful to point out that men who beat their wives are also more likely to also abuse their children (Kurz, 1993, p. 92). However, without also including how the experiences of violence relate to women's abuse of children (Straus, 1983, pp. 229–230), the reader is left to wonder what is being hidden and may tend to doubt not only this reported fact, but also the author's argument more generally.

Common couple violence also has both strengths and weaknesses. Among the strengths are its usefulness in showing the widespread degree of violence in society, and that it acknowledges women's power. Women are not only victims, marriages are not only institutions of domination although both of these statements are partially accurate. But only partially. Women are also actors, even violent actors, often for some of the same reasons men are. In some contexts, women do stick up for themselves; they are neither controlled nor terrorized by the men in their lives. The limitations of focusing on common couple violence are that this can and has been misused to construct concepts like the "battered husband syndrome," and women's violence has been used to explain or even excuse male violence. One family violence researcher specifically argued that women's violence is important because it increases the probability of wife beating through the husband's retaliation and escalation (Straus, 1993, pp. 78–79). In addition to being incorrect, this argument contributes to blaming women for their own victimization. In this form, an emphasis on the gender similarities in violent behavior can and has used as an excuse for male violence. It also can and has been used to undermine resources for the protection and support of battered women.

Given that both constructions have strengths and weaknesses, what do we gain by considering both as potentially useful, if partial, constructions of feminist knowledge? I argue that we gain a more accurate vision of the complexity of gender similarities and differences. From this can come more powerful theories and better intervention strategies. On a practical level, it is important to know that patriarchal terrorism usually escalates over time. This is critical in helping victims understand why they need to leave relationships. However, common couple violence does not usually escalate, and this too is useful knowledge for couples who want to work to eliminate violence from their relationship. On a theoretical level, resisting the choice between patriarchal terrorism and common couple constructions of relationship violence helps to undermine the dualism of perpetrator/victim as a zero sum choice. When our culture creates discourses of innocent victims and monster perpetrators, an idealistic hierarchical dichotomy is created. When these idealizations break down, for example if a woman victim is shown to be in any way to blame or responsible for her victimization, then in a zero sum formulation, the perpetrator is less to blame or less responsible. The hierarchy can even reverse and be reconstructed as a guilty victim and helpless perpetrator (S. Lamb, 1996, pp. 88–127). A woman's aggression or any other behavior does not and should not undermine in any way the seriousness of her own victimization (S. Lamb, 1996; J.W. White & Kowalski, 1994). A nonhierarchical construction of perpetrator/victim responsibility leads Sharon Lamb to assert: "I hold victims responsible and blame perpetrators for their acts" (p. 185).

CONCLUSIONS

There will always be similarities and differences. And each construction of a comparison as a similarity or a difference will always be partial. I agree with Wendy Hollway (1994) we should study differences and similarities between and among women and men. I would extend her analysis and argue that these similarities and differences exist on many levels—individual, interpersonal, institutional, discursive, and symbolic. And at each of these levels gender and other differences interact with power such that the male and the masculine are associated with more power, authority, and influence than the female and the feminine. Just to make things even more complex, similarities and differences interact across as well as within levels of analysis.

The strength of this construction is the focus on complexity. Not only does this in my view make it potentially more accurate vision of reality, it also means that there are many different ways to make important contributions in terms of both action and knowledge. Through such an interactive view it is possible to see how important knowledge and social change can emerge at any point of the dynamic whole (Unger, 1998, p. 87). We do not have to be perfect researchers, nor search for the perfect study or political strategy. We can begin where there is meaning for us, proceed by examining the strengths and limitations of where we begin and compare our work with that of others in non hierarchical ways.

The limitation of this construction is in some ways also its complexity. It is one thing to say that dichotomies should be constructed as necessary contradictions rather than hierarchical dualisms. It is quite another thing to create this kind of thinking. Zero sum thinking is both common and difficult to change. Thus, people blame perpetrators less when they assume the victim had any responsibility or when they endorse victim blaming stereotypes (Hillier, 1995; S. Lamb & Keon, 1995). It is difficult to recognize white middle-class women as both powerless and privileged.

Furthermore, complexity is difficult to communicate. Just as I doubt that effect sizes and meta-analytic techniques will have a great deal of influence on the media and popular culture because of the difficulty of communicating the ideas, so I also doubt that deconstructing hierarchies and advocating partial constructions will have much effect on the popular culture. The media typically portray extreme positions. I became aware of this recently when I was giving a paper about recovered memories of childhood abuse in which I reject both extremes in the current debate (Kimball, 1999). The people promoting the talk contacted the local CBC radio station and the producer of one of the shows was very interested in doing an interview. However, when he and I began talking, it was clear very soon that he was back-peddling as fast as possible on any commitment to interview me. He kept saying "There isn't any hook" by which I took him to mean he wanted a more polarized position that would create a "hook."

Another limitation of what I advocate is the risk of relativism. Although I do not construct the examination of partial visions for their strengths and weaknesses as condoning relativism, I fear that it is all too easy to read it as such. If all partial visions have strengths and weaknesses, then what is there to choose between? Relativism is more easily avoided if one vision is held to be true or at least better than others for specific reasons. Sometimes we need to challenge others' taken-for-granted experiences (C. Kitzinger & Wilkinson, 1997). There is no easy negotiation of the issue of relativism once one gives up the positivist belief in one true reflection of reality that can be known if we follow the rules. But that does not mean giving up this belief relegates us to extreme relativism. The act of examining both strengths and limitations can help make clear what are better or more useful visions *in a particular context*. What becomes impossible is a better or more useful vision *for all contexts*.

The most important gain from acknowledging multiple partial constructions of gender differences and similarities is that feminist research will become less defensive and ultimately more powerful. Feminist research often is marginalized; it is a fight just to be heard. In the academic world as well as the media, extreme views often get more air time than complex and partial visions. However, that is not a reason to defend our own visions against all alternative constructions. We seek to change not only knowledge about women, but also how that knowledge is constructed. One aspect of that construction that should be changed is the dichotomization of knowledge as true or false. Critical as feminist knowledge construction has been of dichotomization and hierarchy, we have perpetuated just such constructions when we define positivist and social constructionist epistemologies, or person-centered and power-centered explanations of behavior as mutually exclusive. By emphasizing partiality of all that we and others do, we just might make a difference not only in the knowledge that is generated, but also in the process by which knowledge is constructed.

CHAPTER 6

Framing Gendered Identities

KAY DEAUX and ABIGAIL J. STEWART

I guess my feminism and my race are the same thing to me. They're tied in to one another, and I don't feel an alliance or allegiance with upper-class white women. I don't. I can listen to them and on some level as a human being I can feel great compassion and friendships; but they have to move from their territory to mine, because I know their world. They don't know mine.

—Sandra Cisneros (p. 461 in S. Cahill, Ed.,
Writing Women's Lives. New York,
Harper Perennial, 1994)

I got really sick of my mom asking me about guys, so I finally told her, "Mom, I'm a lesbian," or I think I said, "I'm queer," and she said, "Don't ever use that word." . . . It was horrible. The first thing she said was, "So you'll never be attorney general."

—Amy Goldberg (p. 182 in M. Miedzian and
A. Malinovich, *Generations: A century of women speak
about their lives*. Atlantic Monthly Press, New York, 1997)

My mother was a housewife and really loved taking care of the children. She made a very big business out of making three meals and cleaning. She had no other life. My mother was very bright. She loved books, but she was afraid to leave the confines of her kitchen. Women didn't work. My aunt, my mother's sister, went to law school and graduated and passed the bar. She never practiced.

—Sharon Goldberg (p. 75 in *Generations*)

I met my real mother one time, when I was seventeen, but I never kept in touch with her. She was the direct opposite of the mother that raised me. The mother that raised me was a very Godly woman, soft spoken, clean, just a very nice woman; and my own mother smoked and drank.

—Abigail Midgley (p. 19 in *Generations*)

Alas! Sometimes it feels sad to be a woman! Men seem to have so much more choice as to what they are intended for. Still, I suppose our position improves with the years, and I must be thankful not to have lived in Homeric Greece instead of 20th century England.

—Vera Brittain (March 4, 1913 diary;
Brittain,1982, pp. 30–31)

We would like to thank Yael Bat-Chava, Nida Bikmen, Bill Cross, Michelle Fine, Judy Schor, Rhoda Unger, David Winter, and Alyssa Zucker for their helpful comments on drafts of this chapter.

From the thousands of statements that women have made describing what it means to be a woman, we offer just a few. With these examples, we try to illustrate the range in which identity is framed—gendered, but also intertwined with race, class, sexual orientation, occupation, and history, among other possibilities. It is this richness and complexity that makes the topic of identity so fascinating and so challenging.

Have social scientists met the challenge? Can the work on identity that has been done over the past several decades take into account the lived experience of women such as those quoted above? We begin this chapter with a brief, admittedly selective, and inevitably incomplete survey of traditional research on gender identity, work that typically assumes a single identity acquired early. This work is extensive. Nonetheless, we find significant gaps and limitations and, in some cases, an inability of the theoretical models to encompass the multiple kinds of gendered experiences reflected in the quotations above. Moving from a critique of this work, we consider three issues that we believe are essential to a full understanding of what we conceptualize as gendered identities: historical and cultural context, intersectionality, and negotiation. Exploring these three areas and suggesting implications for future work, we hope to arrive at a position more able to encompass and illuminate the words of the women quoted previously.

DEFINING GENDER IDENTITY

Traditional definitions of gender identity refer to a generally early awareness of oneself as male or female. Thus Spence (1985), relying on earlier discussions by John Money and Anke Ehrhardt, defined gender identity as "a fundamental, existential sense of one's maleness or femaleness, an acceptance of one's gender on a psychological level that, with rare exceptions, parallels and complements awareness and acceptance of one's biological sex" (pp. 79–80). Similarly, Ruble and Martin (1998) pointed to the anatomic basis of gender identity, but observed that it also includes "the presentation of the self as a male or female sexual being" (p. 950).

What is notable in these and similar conceptions is how early and how inevitably gender identity is thought to emerge. The majority of investigators seem to agree that somewhere between the age of 24 and 36 months, most children have a sense of their gender identity (see Powlishta, Sen, Serbin, Poulin-Dubois, & Eichstedt, this volume). At the same time, considerable research has been devoted to those children whose course is outside of these established parameters. Perhaps the best-known of these investigations is the work of Money and Ehrhardt (1972), who assessed the developmental course of "atypical" children who are born with what are considered to be ambiguous genitalia. In this kind of work, investigators assume that there is a normal and standard definition of gender that most children will incorporate, one based in large part on an assumed link between the biological and the psychological.

Such an assumption of biological determinism may not be warranted, however. S.J. Kessler (1998), for example, documented how arbitrary and socially constructed gender assignment can be, beginning with the designation of sex immediately after birth. Imperato-McGinley and her colleagues studied individuals whose ambiguous genitals at birth resulted in medical and parental labeling of them as girls, but who experienced significant masculinization at puberty (Imperato-McGinley & Peterson, 1976; Imperato-McGinley, Peterson, Gautier, & Sturla, 1979; R.E. Peterson, Imperato-McGinley, Gautier, & Sturla, 1977; R.T. Rubin, Reinish, & Haskett, 1981). Called *guevedoce* (penis at 12) in the Dominican Republic, these individuals at least sometimes appear to shift gender relatively easily (for another view, see Zucker, this volume). These shifts in gender identity raise questions about the fixedness of early gender identification.

Although the biological basis of gender identity is often a starting point, most treatments of gender identity broaden the net to include a variety of other attributes and behaviors. Ruble and Martin (1998), in their extensive analysis of gender development that builds on the earlier work of Huston (1983), considered the manifestation of gender identity in a variety of content areas, including activities and interests, personal and social attributes, social relationships, verbal and nonverbal communication styles, and gender-related values. Although Ruble and Martin make a good case for the relevance of these varied domains, their review of the literature shows that investigators have for the most part concentrated on biological and trait domains, with little attention given so far to establishing the influence on gender identity of social relationships, physical appearance, styles, or symbols.

This expansion of gender identity, from a simple biological identification to a more varied set of social experiences and expectations, can unquestionably enrich the concept. It also forces us to address the question of how similar or varied individuals' experiences of gender are. In other words, we must ask whether all or most children engage in similar activities and learn similar associations to gender, perhaps as a result of prescribed norms and social representations of gender, or whether the variation in personal experience means that gender identity is defined differently by different people.

Traditional models of socialization typically balance some predictability of developmental course with a recognition of varied experience. Kohlberg (1966), for example, acknowledged that environmental variables may have consequences for children's sex-role attitudes and that age and intellectual and social maturity can shape cognitive beliefs about gender. At the same time, however, he emphasized "a constant, or categorical, gender identity" (p. 164) that is developed cognitively in a child's early years. Early applications of social learning theory to issues of gender identity put more emphasis on variability, not only among children but within the range of gender-linked behaviors that a single person might display (Mischel, 1966). Through observation, it was argued, children learn a variety of behaviors associated with both women and men. Reinforcement contingencies, however, are presumed to shape the display of behaviors, resulting in children's greater likelihood of acting in ways that are consistent with societal norms for their gender. Mischel's account stressed that gender-linked behaviors will not necessarily correlate highly among each other, because of the different reinforcement contingencies that children may experience. He gave less attention, however, to possible variation in the parental or societal norms that might influence variations among children, and to the possibilities of changes later in life.

In a more nuanced analysis of gender identity, Spence (1985) considered both how individual variations in masculinity and femininity evolve, as well as how gender identity itself becomes in some sense functionally autonomous. For Spence, the early role of gender identity in shaping attribute development and behavioral choice decreases over time. Rather, she suggested, "people strive to keep their sense of masculinity or femininity intact, using those gender-appropriate behaviors and characteristics they happen to possess to confirm their gender identity" (p. 84). In other words, gender identity is preserved, but it is a reflection of experience rather than a determinant.

These accounts in themselves do not speak to the issue of consistency across individuals as well as across time. Chodorow (1978) took on this issue, with a creative solution to the question of how gender roles get reproduced across history. She began with the premise that infants encounter gender extremely early in the person of their caretaker (as she encounters gender in them). If the caretaker is always a woman, then some children (girls) identify with her, whereas others (boys) press for differentiation. (As the opening quotation of Abigail Midgley illustrates, the definition of mother itself needs to be unpacked.) Although some have argued that it is problematic to assume that one and only one dimension of infants and mothers defines identification, the theory does offer an explanation of how a range of differences among boys and among girls might be subordinated to a powerful (because it is formed early) gender identity.

In her more recent theorizing, Chodorow (1999) considers a broader range of experiences. She indicates that from the time children are spoken to, read to, or put in front of the television set, a spectrum of stories contributes to their fantasies about gender. Investigations of life histories, biography, autobiography, and fiction also make clear how culturally available images, narratives, and gender scripts shape individuals' self-understandings and self-stories, and how great are the historical and cultural variations in gendered meanings. At the same time, Chodorow points out that "each person brings masculinity and femininity to life and develops a gender identity imbued with emotion and fantasy, including personal animation not just of difference itself but of differences in value and power" (p. 103).

Greater complexity is also evident in Bussey and Bandura's (1999) recent development of social cognitive theory as applied to gender development and differentiation. As in earlier versions of social learning theory, gender development is believed to derive from three major sources of influence: modeling, enactive experience, and direct teaching. More attention is given, however, to the influence of social structure beyond the immediate family, including the gendered practices of occupational systems. Further, by emphasizing self-efficacy, Bussey and Bandura incorporate possibilities for individual choice and change and extend the potential range of the theory to the full life course.

These more recent discussions of gender identity by Chodorow (1999) and Bussey and Bandura (1999), though representing quite different theoretical perspectives, nonetheless both offer an antidote to some of the more simplistic assumptions of earlier models. Our objections to the traditional models are threefold. These models have, for the most part, put forward a conception of gender identity that (1) assumes a strictly linear development leading to a stable outcome, (2) defines what is psychological too narrowly, and (3) posits a monolithic gender identity as opposed to multiple gendered identities. We comment briefly on each of these issues.

LINEAR DEVELOPMENT WITH STABLE OUTCOMES

Many models make gender identity appear to have a linear, predictable developmental course. From an early awareness of biological sex, the child goes on to acquire a set of other associations with gender, based on psychological readiness and cognitive abilities. The underlying developmental assumptions are based in part on a parallel with biological development. Thus, children move from childhood to puberty, at which time the sexual potential of gender becomes much more salient. At the same time, educational systems set up a series of age-graded gender expectations that further contribute to a consistent developmental sequence. Because of these consistent potentials and pressures, it is perhaps not unreasonable to assume that outcomes of the developmental course are predictable. However, experiences of gender can be much more varied and random than these developmental models suggest, as the opening quotations suggest. Depending on the particular context in which gender-related attributes are modeled or learned, the resultant gender identity can vary appreciably. For example, McGann (1995, 1999) argues that "tomboys," who deviate from one developmental trajectory of gender identity, are not a homogeneous group. It includes some women whose interests and identities are gender-normative by adolescence, and others who are "career tomboys" for life. In both groups, some women eventually identify as heterosexuals, whereas others are lesbians. This variability in the course of gender identity and its different linkage with sexual identities is not easy to account for with traditional theories.

The end point of developmental processes can also be questioned. In many discussions of the development of gender identity, investigators appear to assume a point at which one's sense of gender identity is fully acquired. But can such stability be assumed? In the dramatic cases of individuals who, as adults, shift their gender from male to female or vice versa, the answer is clearly no. Jazz musician Billy Tipton was raised female, but lived as a man from age 19 onward; despite most of a lifetime of "passing" from one gender to another, he left clear documentation of "the transformation of Billy from *she* to *he*" to be discovered at his death (Middlebrook, 1998). The economic historian Donald McCloskey (1999) pursued a sex change at age 53, after more than 30 years of heterosexual marriage, as did the writer James (now Jan) Morris (1974) a few decades earlier. Less dramatic life histories suggest a negative answer as well. For many, gender identity is a state in continual negotiation. Although "the fundamental, existential sense of one's own maleness or femaleness" (Spence, 1985, pp. 79–80) may continue relatively unquestioned, those attributes and behaviors associated with gender identity may shift noticeably across time and situation. Further, we argue that one's gender identity is a negotiated process, to be conceptualized as an active verb rather than a static noun (West & Zimmerman, 1987). One can think of the outcome of the socialization process as one that provides a repertoire of possible behaviors and attributes. The enactment of gender will necessarily draw on this repertoire, but it is a question of agency and selection among elements rather than the inevitable expression of an acquired gender identity that is considered here. Transsexual McCloskey (1999) suggested precisely that, in her or his experience, gender was performative and selective: "She has made herself a woman. But everyone does that. She has made herself a man, too, learning to suppress her femininity, becoming an athlete and lover and tough-guy debater. A male version and a female version are available for everyone, one's own sister or brother, mother or father" (p. 178). It is noteworthy how central, even if selected, gender was to McCloskey. She or he did not imagine a more random assortment of idiosyncratic characteristics—but two alternate persons, one male and one female, but both "the same." Transgender performer and activist Kate Bornstein advises, in contrast, "I'm neither a man nor a woman" (Bornstein, 1998, p. 169).

DEFINING THE LIMITS OF THE PSYCHOLOGICAL: IN THE HEAD OR IN THE WORLD?

In suggesting that gender changes across time and situation, we speak as well to the issue of psychological narrowness. Gender identity is, in our view, an inescapably social process, in which other people, changing situations, and social norms play a major role. Thus, gender first emerges not in a vacuum, determined only by internal psychological potentials, but in a rich cultural and historical context. From the perspective of symbolic interaction, gender identity, like other aspects of self, is created in the context of social interaction. Although these interactions may have idiosyncratic elements, they are also heavily shaped by the social representations of gender that exist in the society. Thus, as Duveen (in press) has argued, a child's gender identity emerges from the set of cultural beliefs about gender attributes and roles, and these cultural understandings become the basis of individual beliefs about self: "Before they are capable of independent activity in the field of gender (or any other social field), children are the objects of the representations of others. A child is always a construction before it is a reality, but a construction of others, and through this construction its parents and others extend to it a social identity, they locate it in a social space" (p. 4).

Further, we recognize that gender identities develop in *particular* historical and cultural contexts. As a result, the features most likely to define gender identity at one point in time may be quite different at another time and place. An understanding of these processes is possible only if we consider identity in context.

GENDER IDENTITY AS MONOLITHIC

As we have noted, conceptions of gender identity are often multidimensional, in that they recognize a range of attributes and behaviors that contribute to the global concept. Ruble and Martin (1998), as an example, use a framework first developed by Huston (1983) to delineate six separate aspects or dimensions of gender identity. Although such multidimensionality is undoubtedly appropriate in characterizing something as complex as gender identity, it does not address a problem that for us is more central. Specifically, we believe that we need to consider gender identity not as a single, monolithic concept, but rather as a set of intersecting, overlapping *gendered identities.*

Many of the more sociologically based models of identity adopt some principle of multiplicity, suggesting that people readily define themselves in terms of a number of different identities (see Hogg, Terry, & White, 1995; Stryker & Statham, 1985; Thoits & Virshup, 1997). Yet, simply to assume multiplicity does not really deal with the complexities of gender. Many other identities, such as occupation and sexual orientation, are heavily gendered in their definitions. Consider mother and father, for example, or nurse and pipe fitter. Gender is inherent in these identities, at the same time that they contain elements not necessarily associated with gender. Stryker (1986), in trying to deal with this question in his model of identity theory, suggested that gender, perhaps like ethnicity and age, should be considered a "master status." As such, the meanings associated with gender suffuse other roles that one might hold, such as being a spouse or having an occupation, and the performance of these more subsidiary roles is consistent with the master gender status. Skevington and Baker (1989) also spoke to the issue of multiplicity from the perspective of social identity theory, suggesting that the general concept of womanhood comprises several distinct social identities, such as mother and worker.

An alternative approach is to define the issue in terms of the intersections between gender and other identities, such as race and ethnicity. From this perspective, gender has no necessary priority but can be considered only in conjunction with other key elements of self. This concept of intersectionality not only looks to the interface between two often separated identities, but it also considers the emergent properties that such intersections can produce.

Our view of gender identity, as it has developed in the literature and as we see its limitations, led us to identify three key themes that characterize the framing of gender and should be reflected in future research: (1) the cultural and historical context of gender, (2) issues of multiplicity and intersection, and (3) the negotiation of and changes in gender identity.

THE HISTORICAL AND CULTURAL CONTEXTS OF GENDER

If the identities of individuals are created in social interaction, then the particularities of the social interactions involving and surrounding them, and their coherence in cultural patterns, will surely matter. This general point has been made by Cherry (1995). In focusing on some of the classic studies in social psychology, Cherry showed how a gendered reading, one that considered the particulars of who was interacting with whom for what purpose, can reveal new meanings and question old and accepted interpretations of the selected phenomena. Consider the often-cited study of the Westgate housing project by Festinger, Schacter, and Back (1950), which investigated social interaction in an apartment complex built for male veterans who were going to the university under the G.I. bill. Although the findings of this study are typically cited to show the significance of proximity as a generalizable principle of interaction (with an emphasis on the veterans themselves), Cherry's reanalysis shows that the shape of these interactions can be explained almost entirely by the characteristics of the wives. Whether women worked outside the complex or had children was functionally and critically important to the overall communication and interaction patterns, particularly as the women shared child-raising responsibilities.

The influences of context on gender development, and in turn identity, have been demonstrated in research that explores the microprocesses of gender socialization. In a classic study, J. Rubin, Provenzano, and Luria (1974) observed that parents described their newborn sons and daughters differently within 24 hours after childbirth. For example, they described their daughters as softer and more delicate than their sons, and their sons as better coordinated and hardier (despite the fact that male newborns have been found in some studies to be more irritable and in any case are more physically vulnerable than females). More recently, K.A. Martin (1998) used ethnographic observations to detail the many preschool teachers' interventions that shaped "appropriate" gender behavior in the children in their care, such as asking the already quieter girls to be quiet or to speak more softly or "nicely" three times more often than they did boys. Similarly, Thorne (1993) identified not only the actions of teachers, but also those of other children, in "policing" gender-normative behavior in older children. She argued that the "separate cultures" of boys' and girls' play reported by some developmental researchers (see, e.g., Maccoby, 1998) may exist because boys and girls who try to engage in cross-gender play are teased (e.g., called "sissies" and "tomboys"), excluded (e.g., girls often won't allow a boy to jump rope with them; boys often won't allow a girl to play baseball with them), and more gently pressured or encouraged into conformity with those separate cultures. The findings from these studies both shock us in their starkness and document things we know to be true—because the behaviors involved flow so directly from widely shared gender norms in our culture.

At the same time, we know that gender norms, like other norms, are not universally shared across cultures, stable over time, nor equally shared by subgroups within cultures (see, e.g., Lamphere, Ragone, & Zavella, 1997; Lancaster & di Leonardo, 1997). For example, though women are often viewed as more "religious" or "spiritual" than men in industrialized Western cultures, and men as more ambitious (see, e.g., ratings of Italian and English men and women in Eagly & Kite, 1987), Ortner (1996) describes the Nepalese Sherpa view that men are more spiritual and women more "material." Similarly, though men are viewed as tougher and more courageous than women in the United States, Schoenberger (1989) reports the South Korean explanation that island pearl divers are all women because men lack the necessary toughness to handle this dangerous job. Similarly, despite our cultural view of women as self-sacrificing, protective nurturers, Scheper-Hughes (1997) has described mothers' choices to allow some infants to die under conditions of drought, poverty, and hunger in a Brazilian village.

If particular identities are fashioned within particular contexts, it is important to bring those contexts into our study of identity. Erik Erikson is one theorist who attempted to do this. In offering the concept of cultural "identity" as critical to understanding personality, he noted that "the study of identity [is] as strategic in our time as the study of sexuality was in Freud's time" (Erikson, 1950/1963, p. 282). In making this assertion, Erikson observed that Freud's conception of the "ego" was somewhat different: "To him the ego stood like a cautious and sometimes shrewd patrician, not only between the anarchy of primeval instincts and the fury of the archaic conscience, but also between the pressure of upper-class convention and the anarchy of mob spirit. The bearer of such an identity could turn with dignified horror from mass developments which threatened to throw doubt upon the self-determination of the ego. Thus, preoccupied with symptoms which characterized the ego's defenses, psychoanalysis had, at first, little to say about the way the ego's synthesis grows—or fails to grow—out of the soil of social organization" (pp. 281–282). In contrast, Erikson grounded the problem of identity formation in that very soil. In his earliest work (Erikson, 1950/1963), he compared the nature of the task of identity formations in different national cultures at the same time (America, Germany, and Russia); later he focused on the particularities of history as well as culture in his psychobiographical studies of Luther (Erikson, 1958) and Gandhi (Erikson, 1969). Eventually, he formulated a method for scholars systematically to recognize their own historical and cultural embeddedness while studying the historical and cultural identities of their subjects (Erikson, 1975).

Within the field of personality, investigators have more often operated from the Freudian sensibility—that personality processes are universal—than from Erikson's. However, some investigations have examined the cultural and historical particularities that shaped identities, frequently making use of systematic case studies. As an example of this strategy, Stewart and her colleagues (Franz, 1995; B.E. Peterson & Stewart,1990; A.J. Stewart, Franz, & Layton,1988) used personal documents (diaries and autobiographies) produced over 40 years by Vera Brittain—an influential English feminist, pacifist journalist, and novelist—to show that Brittain's expression of identity themes was tied to personal and social events (e.g., the course of World War I, including the deaths of her brother and fiancé). Similarly, Espin, Stewart, and Gomez (1990) used the letters written by a dislocated Central American girl to her teacher to document identity creation in the context of exile.

Narrative methods have been used more widely to situate identity processes historically and socially. Mkhonza (1995), for example, showed how domestic workers in Swaziland fashion social identities in the context of a forced labor system: "Fear was pervasive in most of the interactions and encounters with the employers. There was fear of expulsion and also fear arising from ignorance of the other, especially in first encounters. The psychosocial maintenance of power of the whites in colonial Swaziland relied on creating fear of the whites. . . . Social identity was created in fearful situations" (pp. 181–182). Nagata (1999) used interview data to demonstrate how Japanese American women's identity formation was affected by their age at the time of their internment during World War II. She notes that although one purpose of the campus was to "speed up assimilation," in fact, "The placement of young Nisei in the all-Japanese environment of camp may actually have provided a context for shaping a Japanese identity more strongly than before the war" (p. 80).

A.J. Stewart and Healy (1989) offered a general model of linkage between personality development and social events that pointed to the central role of identity formation. Specifically, they argued that for some cohorts in particular cultures, the convergence of individual development and significant social changes results in a strong "generational identity" (examples would include those affected by World War I in England and by the Great Depression in the United States). A.J. Stewart and Healy (1986) used this theory to contrast the course of Vera Brittain's feminist and pacifist identities. They showed that her feminist consciousness formed early (in the context of her own distaste for the "unfairness" of her patriarchal family of origin, given theoretical force by the writings and teaching of early suffragists). Although particular issues changed somewhat over the course of her long life, her basic approach to "the woman question" and her identity as a feminist remained the same from adolescence onward. In contrast, Brittain began World War I as a patriotic supporter of the war but formed a powerful aversion to war as a result of her personal losses and her experiences as a nurse caring for both English and German troops. Over the interwar period, this aversion was gradually shaped into a formal ideology of pacifism, resulting in her adoption of the "peace pledge," her midlife "testament" against war, and her opposition to World War II. Though both political identities had strong roots in late adolescence (as Erikson would argue they should), one persisted nearly unchanged throughout her life, whereas the other took radically different shape in midlife.

A.J. Stewart (1994b) compared the different ways that three college-educated women who came of age in the 1960s formed their (feminist) identities in the context of the women's movement. For one woman, the first elements of the "second wave" of the women's movement (the publication of Betty Friedan's *The Feminine Mystique* in 1963) confirmed an intuitive understanding of the bankruptcy of "traditional" gender roles. For a second, the women's movement offered new ideas and new opportunities in early adulthood. For a third, the movement was initially of no interest, but she returned to it in her late 30s through a feminist theory study group and found a tremendous resource for interpreting and understanding her education and her young adulthood, as well as for launching a second career and marriage. For each of these women, a "feminist identity" was central, but identity formation was a late-adolescent process of confirmation of intuition in one case, of new ideological commitment in another, and of midlife rethinking in the third (see Cole, Zucker, & Duncan, this volume). For other women who came of age before the feminist movement, like the mother that Sharon Goldberg describes in her opening quotation, a feminist identity may never have emerged or, perhaps, as in the case of her aunt, may have developed less fully.

None of these studies assumes any simple deterministic role for the social context. Individual identities in any period and social situation are enormously diverse, and individuals fashion identities in reaction to, opposition to, and appreciation of dominant and local pressures. What these studies do, however, is articulate and examine the particular ways in which the context—forced labor, exile, war, women's suffrage, and women's liberation movements—provided specific pressures and opportunities for self-definition and self-construction. Although these studies sometimes focus on broad or common elements of identities (such as traits, ideological commitments, vocational self-definitions), they demonstrate how idiosyncratically these elements cohere within a single person, as well as how much they vary in stability over the life course (see, e.g., A.J. Stewart & Healy, 1986).

Recently, quantitative evidence from large samples has also pointed to the importance of historical time periods in the formation of personality traits that are often important elements of identity. Twenge (1997b) conducted a meta-analysis of over 100 psychological studies employing one of two widely used measures of personality attributes often associated with gender identity, the Bem Sex Roles Inventory (BSRI) and the Personal Attributes Questionnaire (PAQ), between the years 1973 and 1994. She showed that during that time, the magnitude of the differences between men's and women's scores significantly decreased, and that women's scores on the scales assessing so-called masculine or agentic personality characteristics dramatically increased. Men's scores on those characteristics also increased significantly, but less dramatically. Importantly, neither men's nor women's scores changed on what are termed the feminine traits of expressivity and communion.

Twenge (1997b) identified a number of cultural changes that might account for these results, mostly changes associated with the impact of the women's movement in American culture. These changes include increases in the rate of mothers working; increases in girls' aspirations for traditionally male careers; and increases in women's participation in activities such as sports that require assertion and instrumentality and that had previously excluded girls and women. Importantly, this work demonstrates that although most of the researchers who study these phenomena have not been interested in examining the social or historical context, they have generated data that, when combined and analyzed across time, convincingly demonstrates its impact.

Twenge has performed similar analyses on attitudes toward women over a 25-year period (1997a) and on other personality traits (1998) over a much longer period. All of these studies point to the impact of social and historical changes even in standardized measures that have been used unchanged over time. Research employing more open-ended material, in which the exact nature of the phenomenon can be examined more thoroughly, would surely reveal more, as work by Landrine, Klonoff, and Brown-Collins (1992) suggests. In a study of White women and women of color in the same historical moment, they offered research participants alternative meanings for the kinds of terms assessed in gender-stereotyped trait measures like the BSRI and the PAQ. They showed that despite similarities in self-attributions of these traits by White women and women of color, large differences were apparent in the intended "meanings" or interpretations of the traits in the two groups. For example, the preferred definition of "passive" by White women was "laidback/easygoing"; for women of color, in contrast, "passive" meant "not saying what I really think." This study is a powerful demonstration of how cultural and subcultural contexts matter, even when it may appear that they don't.

MULTIPLICITY AND INTERSECTIONS

We assume, as do many others, that self-conceptions include social identities (identities that are attached to social groups and statuses) and other personal characteristics (such as traits and core values). Because most people are attached to several groups and statuses and have an assortment of personality characteristics (which may be differentially associated with different social identities; see A. Reid & Deaux, 1996), the concept of identity is characterized by great complexity and diversity.

Many scholars have developed theories that emphasize the diversity of identity by focusing on the multiplicity of identity, on variation in the contents of identity, and/or on variations in the relative salience of particular identities in particular situations. Most theories that emerge from a sociological or social psychological framework stress some form of multiplicity. Social identity theory, for example, assumes that different identities emerge from different intergroup comparison contexts (see Skevington & Baker, 1989). More specific in dealing with multiplicity is Stryker's (1980; Stryker & Statham, 1985), identity theory in which a hierarchy of identities is proposed. From a more methodological perspective, S. Rosenberg and Gara (1985) show how identity structures can be described based on the overlapping use of defining traits. In each of these approaches, multiplicity is assumed, but (with the exception of the Rosenberg and Gara approach) the relationship between various identities is not of particular concern.

In contrast, a persistent theme in the personality literature (particularly among researchers drawing on Erikson's theoretical approach) is the notion that this complexity is organized and structured into a whole that is coherent and relatively stable. Thus Marcia (1966, 1994) and his colleagues have derived indicators of an individual's overall "identity status" by combining assessments across different domains (e.g., vocational, ideological, interpersonal). Similarly, Grotevant (1992) has argued that assigned components of identity (based on ascribed characteristics, such as race and gender) may have broad ramifications for identities that are chosen (such as vocation). Thus, the emphasis here, unlike in the sociological models, is on the internal structure and organization of identity components.

Although these two perspectives approach the question of identity differently, both run some risk of failing fully to appreciate the complexity that identity entails. Too much stress on the internal coherence of identity may ignore points of conflict and disjunction among identity components. From the other side, treating each social identity as a distinctive unit ignores the points of overlap and integration that may exist. (Consider Sandra Cisneros's statement at the beginning of the chapter that her feminism and her race are the same thing to her, and that distinctions based on social class are part of that identity as well.)

Many studies, perhaps the majority, examine a particular identity (e.g., race, gender, feminism) without considering the impact of other identities in shaping that definition. For example, studies of racial identity often include both men and women but do not examine gender identity; similarly, studies of gender identity often include people of different ethnic backgrounds but do not examine the possibility that ethnic background is an important context shaping gender identity. On a few occasions, however, researchers have considered relatively simple combinations of identities. For example, some scholars proposed that since both African American and female are subordinate identities, being an African American female results in "double jeopardy" (see discussion in L.A. Patterson, Cameron, & Lalonde, 1996).

One theoretical development that may offer some direction to our thinking in this area is the notion of "intersectionality." Most often identified with critical legal theorists concerned with both race and gender, intersectionality refers to the unique consequences of holding two (or more) social statuses (see Crenshaw, 1995; Crenshaw, Gotanda, Peller, & Thomas, 1995). Thus, people hold both a gender status and a racial-ethnic status at the same time, and experience in the particular race-inflected gender statuses is qualitatively different. The experience of "being a woman" is different for a Black woman and a White woman, because womanhood is defined and socially constructed differently for the two groups. Moreover, the individual woman can never separate her experience into some that are due to her race versus others due to her gender: She is always and everywhere both raced and gendered, and her experience cannot be wholly attributed to only one of these characteristics (see Essed, 1990, for many examples of this dilemma). The parallel reasoning also holds: Black men and Black women experience their race differently. Frankenberg (1993) shows that White women are often unable to articulate the implications of their race, but she draws on a variety of theorists to suggest that, nevertheless, their Whiteness "matters" (see especially P. McIntosh, 1998; Roediger, 1991, 1994). Hurtado and Stewart (1997) suggest that those accorded privilege by virtue of their social status are often unaware of their privileges, and propose that self-reports may be of less value in documenting the meaning of Whiteness than, for example, reports by subordinates, ethnographic observation, or even experimental behavior (see also Fine, Stewart, & Zucker, in press).

According to reasoning about intersectionality, even though we may think of gender identity as a characteristic of all persons, that identity may be crucially different as it intersects with some other identities (not only race). For example, the identity "parent" is generally assumed in our culture to be gendered: We imagine that motherhood and fatherhood are crucially different. Other identities (e.g., gardener) are much less gendered in our minds; however, those identities may, for a given individual, be deeply tied to her or his own gender identity.

The notion of intersectionality can produce a sense of the dizzying proliferation of potential intersecting social statuses: If "parent" is gendered, is it also "raced" and "classed"? Clearly it is in the public imagination; we have only to think of "welfare mothers" to conjure up a stereotype that includes gender, race, and class in a single image. What about sexual orientation? The current public debate about gay adoption suggests that sexual orientation, gender, and parent status produce qualitatively distinct images of gay and straight mothers and fathers. (And for Amy Goldberg's mother, as she describes her at the beginning of the chapter, sexual orientation has occupational implications as well.)

Yet, it must be said that not all identities seem generally or frequently to intersect in critical ways. For example, "parent" and "musician" or "parent" and "midwesterner" appear to be less critically intersecting than do some of the previous examples. Moreover, some identities may intersect crucially in some situations but not others. For example, many women assistant professors feel that their gender is very relevant when they are not "heard" in department meetings, but they may feel their gender is irrelevant when they are working on a journal article or talking with a student about a particular complex idea. Culturally, then, some social identities are deeply and pervasively gendered (or raced or classed), whereas others may not be. (And, of course, personal history may override cultural patterns for any given individual.)

Considerable research has formally or implicitly used the notion of intersectionality to examine the particular combination of race/ethnicity and gender. Gay and Tate (1998) used national survey data collected in 1984 and 1996 to examine how race and gender identities combined for Black women. They found that race and gender identities mutually reinforced one another and interacted in predicting attitudes toward certain public events and figures. Specifically, the combination of strong race and strong gender identity predicted more negative feelings about the Million Man March, Clarence Thomas, and O.J. Simpson. Using parallel measures of the stages of racial and gender identity development in both Black and White women, E.E. Parks, Carter, and Gushue (1996) found that Black women's developmental stages in the two domains were correlated, whereas they were unrelated to each other among White women.

In a qualitative study, Waters (1996) found that gender shaped the form and content of ethnic identity in Caribbean American teenagers: "Although there was no overall difference in the numbers of boys and girls in the choice of identity adopted, there were significant differences in the meanings they attached to being American. The two main differences were that girls were under greater restrictions and control from parents than boys and that racism appeared to have a different impact on boys than on girls. Boys discussed being black American in terms of racial solidarity in the face of societal exclusion and disapproval. Girls also faced exclusion based on race, but they discussed being American in terms of the freedom they desired from strict parental control" (p. 75).

In a study using an experience-sampling method of data collection, Aries and colleagues (1998) examined race and gender awareness and the importance of race and gender identity among White and non-White students in a predominantly White college setting. Although they found important (and different) effects for race and gender, they also found that among students for whom race or gender was particularly important, their awareness of that identity was more variable across situations, rather than (as one might expect from discussions of centrality) less. Further, when women—but not men—were aware of one aspect of social identity, they were less aware of the other. This study showed, then, that race and gender identity were in dynamic relationship to each other over time and across situations, and in different ways for women and men.

An intersectional approach has also been used to examine some other identities. Kurien (1999), for example, considered the interplay between religious and political identities for women and men of Hindu Indian background who immigrated to the United States. Her work showed how gender and ethnicity are interwoven in the process of immigration and relocation. In their study of the Metropolitan Community Church of New York, Rodriguez and Ouellette (2000) considered the intersections of four social identities: gay, male, Latino, and practicing Christian. For the men in their sample, these identities are integrated, even though many outsiders might assume that discord and conflict would be inevitable. M.F. Rogers and Lott (1997) showed that "Log Cabin Republicans"—gay members of the Republican Party—are overwhelmingly White, male and middle or upper class. They argued that this group's political views derive more from their holding of dominant (race, gender, and class) than of subordinate (sexual orientation) social statuses. They identified the particular "standpoint" or "intersection" of this group as one of being "virtual insiders." Marginalized by virtue of their sexual orientation, these men are privileged in many other ways; their political ideologies and commitments flow from their particular set of intersecting social identities. The intersection of vocational identity (lawyer) and class identity for working-class students in an elite academic institution was the focus of work by Granfield (1996). He showed that many students shifted from a posture of pride in their own background to a strategy of upward mobility and "passing" as middle class. These students carried with them a sense of "faking it" and concealment, and as a result were ambivalent about their new identities (Goffman, 1963; see also Steinitz & Solomon, 1986; J. Ryan & Sackrey, 1984).

The multiplicity of identities—their variety, shifting salience or importance, intersection, and mutual influence—is increasingly recognized in particular studies, especially of individuals occupying a subordinate social status. There is a need both for empirical research that is more consistently attentive to multiplicity and for theories that articulate the importance or irrelevance of the different kinds of multiplicity in different identity or social contexts.

IDENTITY NEGOTIATION AND CHANGE

The third key element in our analysis of gender identity is a recognition of the dynamics of its construction, which points to the possibilities for change. Rather than verifying static structural entities, research suggests to us that gender identities are negotiated and developed over time (see Deaux & Ethier, 1998). In the words of West and Zimmerman (1987), we *do* gender, and it is in the doing of gender that identities are shaped and altered.

The dynamics of gender can be considered in terms of one of two time frames. First, we are interested in those long-term, developmental processes through which an identity is developed and altered. Here the time frame is extended, considering months, years, or decades. For example, Josselson (1996) studied women's identities from the college years until middle age; A.J. Stewart and Healy (1986) explored Vera Brittain's feminist and pacifist identities over six decades. At the same time, it is important to study the more immediate process of identity presentation, wherein the framing of gender occurs, in part, "online," responsive to the pressures of the immediate situation (Deaux & Major, 1987). In this second approach, the time frame is very narrow, better characterized as a single snapshot in comparison to the extended photo album that long-term changes might be thought to represent. Both perspectives are important, we believe, to fully understand the dynamics of gender.

LONG-TERM IDENTITY DEVELOPMENT AND CHANGE

Developmental analyses of identity frequently offer stage models to describe a sequence of identity representations. Within the literature of Black identity, for example, Cross (1991, 1995) proposes five stages of nigrescence: preencounter, encounter, immersion-emersion, internalization, and internalization-commitment. Through this sequence, the meaning associated with being Black alters and the agenda for behavior changes as well. Phinney (1989) proposed a general three-stage model of ethnic identity consisting of the unexamined ethnic identity, identity search, and achieved ethnic identity. Using some of this work as a reference point, Downing and Roush (1985) developed a sequential model of feminist identity; Henderson-King and Stewart (1999) used it to assess the impact of women's studies courses on feminist identity development. Cass (1979) and S. Meyer and Schwitzer (1999) have developed parallel measures of homosexual and minority sexual orientation identity formation.

Although these models differ in both the focal identity and the particulars of various stages, each model assumes that identity changes over time in predictable ways. In line with our concerns in the previous section, however, most of these models place their emphasis on a single identity category and give little attention to the influence that other identity categories might have on the sequence and the particulars of change. Recently, Cross and Fhagen-Smith (in press) have repositioned their Black identity model within a life span perspective to account for identity variability, linear and nonlinear trends, and single focus as well as multiplicity patterns, as found in the contemporary Black identity literature. This reconfiguration suggests a shared concern for some of the issues we raise and points to directions for more complex conceptualizations.

Other analyses of long-term identity change have been less tied to a theoretical sequence of stages, focusing instead on the kinds of cognitive, emotional, and behavioral changes that accompany a particular developmental change. Many candidates present themselves as possibilities for this kind of analysis, but we limit our discussion to two: the acquisition of an identity as a mother, and the negotiations involved for immigrants to a new country.

Motherhood is a wonderful and complex example of identity change, particularly when we focus on women who are becoming mothers for the first time (Ethier, 1995; Ruble, Fleming, Hackel, & Stangor, 1988; J. Smith, 1991, 1999). During the period of pregnancy and postpartum, many women create an entirely new identity for themselves. This identity has biological aspects, it clearly draws from the social representations of motherhood that exist in the society, and it is shaped by the personal beliefs of the woman herself and the interactions that she has with family and friends (as the comments of Midgley at the beginning of the chapter about her two very different mothers would suggest).

Ethier (1995) tracked the development of the mother identity over the course of women's pregnancy, completing her study two months after the birth of the child. During this period, she was interested not only in how the identity of mother was constructed and elaborated, but also in the ways in which women's other identities shifted in importance or prominence in their overall identity structure. Not surprisingly, the importance of an identity as a mother and the richness of meaning associated with that identity increased over time. At the same time, however, some other identities were receding, such that women named significantly fewer identities after the birth of their child than they had six months prior to birth. Further, while the attributes associated with motherhood became increasingly more positive, the evaluation of other identities, such as spouse or occupation, became more negative and, in the case of work, less important. In brief, the identity of mother became very central for these women, engulfing the field of their identity definition.

As these data suggest, relationships with others change as the identity of mother gains prominence. In J. Smith's (1999) interviews with three women going through the transition to motherhood, an emergent theme is the relationship of self to other. Reflecting the dynamic interdependence that George Herbert Mead and others have assumed, these women comment on the ways their relationships with others are changing. Not only do they perceive that they are being treated differently by others, but they are also re-viewing their positions vis-à-vis other people in their lives.

Immigration offers a second domain for analysis of identity negotiation and change. Here, as suggested above, we can see a complex interplay of gender and ethnicity, as the cultural affordances can differ sharply for women and men. Kurien's (1999) analysis of Hindu Indian immigrants in the United States points to important differences in patterns of immigration, with men often coming initially as single students and women most often coming as the new wives of husbands who have returned to India to find a bride. Some women may come on their own as students, but these women do not become part of the organizations that represent Indians in

America and that foster a particular image of the group (a representation that is typically quite conservative and traditional).

Other studies of immigrants also point to significant gendered effects (Pessar, 1999). From the initial decision to immigrate to the satisfaction with the new country, men and women frequently show different attitudes and patterns of behavior. The decision to immigrate, once assumed to be the product of a collective household decision, is often contested. More markedly, members of a family do not necessarily come at the same time, a sequencing that can influence later gender roles (Pessar, 1999). Differential availability and variety of employment opportunities in the new country (a situation shaped by class as well as second-language facility) also impacts the ways in which gender identity is defined, as do the differing social networks that women and men create (see also Jamal, Lin, & Stewart, 1999). Further, the experiences in the new country cause shifts in meaning of both gender and ethnic identity, as research by Diaz, Martin, and Deaux (1999) suggests.

SHORT-TERM PRESENTATION OF IDENTITY

Over the short term, varying from one setting to another, people often show shifts in identity as well. These shifts do not, in most cases, represent any dramatic change in the overall pattern or structure of identity as a person conceptualizes herself or himself. Rather, they represent reactions to situations, wherein one aspect of one's identity may be more prominent, more important, or more relevant at one time than at another. Such fluctuation in identity does not necessarily indicate instability or fickleness on the part of the person. Instead, these variations can be seen as the often subtle exercise of agency and responsiveness to situations in which we find ourselves (see LaFrance, this volume).

As Deaux and Major (1987) proposed, gender enactment (and hence the conceptualization of "sex differences") is a process in which goals of the person, the forces of the environment, and a variety of modifying conditions can shape the interactions that occur. Though not threatening the assumption that there are internalized beliefs about one's gender, the model does assume that the potential repertoire of gender-related beliefs and behaviors is extensive and that one can draw differentially from that repertoire, depending on a variety of fluctuating factors.

Something as simple as the number of like people in one's environment can affect gender identity—not only the salience that gender has, but the beliefs that women have about gender and sex differences as well (Ely, 1995; Izraeli, 1983). Comparing women in law firms that were male-dominated with women in firms that were more successfully sex-integrated, Ely found that women in the former were more apt to generate traditional gender stereotypes (e.g., women are more sensitive, men are more analytical and self-confident) and to see sharper distinctions between the characteristics of women and of men. Ely also reported that women in sex-integrated firms "experienced less ambivalence about their gender identity, self-consciously enacting both masculine and feminine roles as they saw fit" (p. 625).

The enactment of one versus another aspect of one's identity can be shown in even more momentary and not necessarily conscious ways, as recent work on the phenomenon of stereotype threat has shown (Shih, Pittinsky, & Ambady, 1999). Asian American women who were influenced to think about either their identity as an Asian or their identity as a woman showed different levels of performance on a mathematics test, performing better when Asian identity was salient and worse when their identity as a woman was salient. Results such as these indeed show us how dynamic and subtle the process of gender presentation can be.

Clearly, the processes involved in long-term change are different from those at work in the short-term presentations just described. Yet both, we would argue, need to be considered when we think about framing gender identity. Judging from the research documenting them, we gain in understanding when we consider historical contexts as well as situational demands, look at internal values and external influences, and combine qualitative narratives with quantitative indices.

FRAMING THE STUDY OF GENDERED IDENTITIES

The past study of gender identity and the future study of gendered identities are inevitably shaped and influenced by larger trends and forces in academic scholarship, including interdisciplinary feminist scholarship (see Morawski, 1994; D. Stanton & Stewart, 1995). Much of the past research was conducted in the spirit of an empiricist, or at least a feminist empiricist, paradigm that has been critiqued from postmodern, poststructuralist perspectives as naturalizing and essentializing phenomena that are arbitrary, socially constructed, and changing (see Hare-Mustin & Marecek, 1988; Marecek, 1995b). In our view, by framing gender identity within history and culture, emphasizing multiplicity and intersectionality, and considering the negotiated process of identity change, the empirical study of gendered identities can gain from that critique and move forward to new levels of understanding.

In presenting our case for the analysis of gendered identities, we have focused primarily on women. This choice in part reflects the state of the literature, in which studies of male identities have been less frequent than studies of female identity. We firmly believe, however, that the issues and assumptions we make here apply equally well to variations in male identity. Further, as the writings on transgender illustrate so well, the analysis of gendered identities can not impose artificial boundaries between male and female.

Our discussion has emphasized the patterns and negotiations of identity among adults. This emphasis is in contrast to traditional models that tend to focus on the development of gender identity in childhood. In those discussions, major attention is most often directed to *when* gender identity develops, often leading to the assumptions of stability and inflexibility that we have critiqued. By looking at the dynamics and negotiations of adult identity, we read a different story and raise quite different questions for research. At the same time, we believe that this new story gives us tools we can use to return to the study of childhood development with a new set of questions about identity processes.

Listening to the words of the women whose statements began this chapter also gives us direction for future research. First, these varied statements illustrate well the multiplicity that characterizes gender identity. In speaking of intersections of gender and race, in referring to the influences of historical time and place, in describing how sexual orientation, occupation, and parental roles can be part of self-definition, these women challenge us to develop models complex enough to encompass their experience.

Their words also remind us that the exploration of gendered identities demands multiple methodologies. Quantitative work that can provide a set of clear reference points across time and place must be combined with the richness of the individual narrative to fully understand how gendered identities develop and are negotiated.

None of these recommendations for research suggests the task is easy. It is a tall order for us to figure out how exactly to study gendered identities framed this way, but we believe it's an order we must try to fill.

PART II

DEVELOPMENTAL ISSUES

CHAPTER 7

Biological Influences on Psychosexual Differentiation

KENNETH J. ZUCKER

OVERVIEW AND TERMINOLOGY

This chapter considers the role of biological influences on selected aspects of psychosexual differentiation in humans. As a point of departure, it is useful to provide a brief description of several terms that will be used throughout. These are (1) sex, (2) gender, (3) gender identity, (4) gender role (masculinity-femininity), (5) sexual orientation, and (6) sexual identity.

SEX

The term *sex* refers to attributes that, collectively and usually harmoniously, characterize biological maleness and femaleness. In humans, the most well-known attributes that constitute biological sex include the sex-determining genes, the sex chromosomes, the H-Y antigen, the gonads, sex hormones, the internal reproductive structures, and the external genitalia (Migeon & Wisniewski, 1998; Money & Ehrhardt, 1972). Over the past couple of decades, there has, of course, also been great interest in the possibility that the human brain has certain sex-dimorphic neuroanatomic structures that, perhaps, emerge during the process of prenatal physical sex differentiation.

It should be recognized that knowledge about biological sex has been a gradual, cumulative process. From historical studies, it is clear that knowledge about biological sex has included many false and flawed notions (Laqueur, 1992). In modern times, the common "person on the street" likely can identify the sex chromosomes as constituting an important component of biological sex; yet, it should be remembered that it was only in the 1950s that reliable techniques were developed to karyotype the sex chromosomes (K.L. Moore & Barr, 1955).

In the 1990s, there have been substantial developments in understanding aspects of biological sex that had been speculated about for several decades. For example, although it had long been surmised that the presence of the Y chromosome was necessary for the gonads to differentiate along male lines (i.e., testicular differentiation), it was only in 1990 that the testis-determining factor (TDF) was identified (Vilain & McCabe, 1998). As described by Haqq and Donahoe (1998), the TDF is located on the short arm of the Y chromosome, with subsequent identification of SRY (the sex-determining gene region of the Y chromosome) (Donahoe & Schnitzer, 1996). In addition, Mullerian inhibiting substance is another protein involved in the temporal sequence of events that leads to male sex differentiation, as it results in the regression of the Mullerian duct, the anlagen of the uterus, fallopian tubes, and the upper vagina.

GENDER

Gender is a term that is often used to refer to psychological or behavioral characteristics associated with males and females (Ruble & Martin, 1998). From a historical perspective, it is of interest to note that gender as a technical term is much younger than the technical term sex. Indeed, as late as the mid-1950s, the term gender was not even part of the professional literature that purported to study psychological similarities and differences between males and females. In fact, the first term introduced to the literature was that of *gender role* (not gender), which Money (1955) defined as "all those things that a person says or does to disclose himself or herself as having the status of boy or man, girl or woman, respectively. It includes, but is not restricted to, sexuality in the sense of eroticism" (p. 254).

Over the past four-plus decades, three major developments have occurred with regard to the usage of the terms sex and gender. First, as some scholars have noted, there has been a tendency, at least in some quarters, to conflate the use of the two terms, so that it is not always clear if one is referring to biological or psychological characteristics that distinguish males from females (Gentile, 1993). As noted by Unger and Crawford (1993), a good example of this is the title of a scholarly journal, *Sex Roles,* which began publishing in 1975. Because this journal typically publishes articles pertaining to psychological and behavioral characteristics associated with males and females, it might be more aptly titled *Gender Roles.*

Second, scholars have argued that the use of the terms sex and gender are related to assumptions about causality, in that the former is used to refer exclusively to biological processes and the latter is used to refer exclusively to psychological or sociological processes (for critiques of this division, see Maccoby, 1988; Money, 1985; Unger, 1979b; for a recent exchange on this point, see Deaux, 1993; Gentile, 1993; Unger & Crawford, 1993). As a result, some researchers who study humans employ such terms as *sex-typical, sex-dimorphic,* and *sex-typed* to characterize sex differences in behavior, because terms of this kind are descriptively more neutral with regard to putative etiology.

The third development, as noted by K.J. Zucker and Bradley (1995), is that Money's original use of the term gender role has been decomposed into three conceptually distinct component parts that are identified by the terms gender identity, gender role, and sexual orientation, which are defined next.

Gender Identity

Gender identity was introduced into the professional lexicon by Hooker and Stoller almost simultaneously in the early 1960s (see Money, 1985). For example, Stoller (1964) used the slightly different term *core gender identity* to describe a young child's developing "fundamental sense of belonging to one sex" (p. 453). This term was later adopted by cognitive-developmental psychologists, such as Kohlberg (1966), who defined gender identity in relation to the child's ability to accurately discriminate males from females and then to identify his or her own gender status correctly—a task considered by some to be the first "stage" in "gender constancy" development, whose end state is the knowledge of gender invariance (Eaton & Von Bargen, 1981; Kohlberg, 1966).

Gender Role

The term *gender role* has been used extensively by developmental psychologists to refer to behaviors, attitudes, and personality traits that a society, in a given culture and historical period, designates as masculine or feminine, that is, more "appropriate" to or typical of the male or female social role (Ruble & Martin, 1998). It should be recalled, however, that defining gender roles in this way assumes that they are completely arbitrary and social in origin, a view not universally shared by researchers in the field. In any case, from a descriptive point of view, the measurement of gender role behavior in young children includes several easily observable phenomena, including affiliative preference for same-sex versus opposite-sex peers, fantasy roles, toy interests, dress-up play, and interest in rough-and-tumble play. In older children, gender role has also been measured using personality attributes with stereotypic masculine or feminine connotations (Absi-Semaan, Crombie, & Freeman, 1993).

Sexual Orientation

The term *sexual orientation* is defined by a person's relative responsiveness to sexual stimuli. The most salient dimension of sexual orientation is probably the sex of the person to whom one is attracted sexually. This stimulus class is obviously how one defines a person's sexual orientation as heterosexual, bisexual, or homosexual. In contemporary sexological research, sexual orientation is often assessed by psychophysiological techniques, such as penile plethysmography and vaginal photoplethysmography (R.C. Rosen & Beck, 1988), although structured interview assessments have become increasingly common, particularly when respondents do not have a compelling reason to conceal their sexual orientation.

SEXUAL IDENTITY

It is important to uncouple the construct of sexual orientation from the construct of *sexual identity*. A person may, for example, be predominantly aroused by homosexual stimuli, yet not regard himself or herself as "a homosexual," for whatever reason. Sociologists, particularly those of the "social scripting" and "social constructionist" schools, have articulated this notion most forcefully, arguing that the incorporation of sexual orientation into one's sense of identity is a relatively recent phenomenon, culturally variable, and the result of a complex interplay of sociohistorical events (Gagnon, 1990; Weeks, 1991). Anthropologists, such as Herdt (1981), who have described ritualized, age-structured homosexual behavior in non-Western cultures, note that such behavior is not at all tied to a homosexual sexual identity, but rather is a rite of passage to mature, adult heterosexuality.

In contemporary Western culture, there are many individuals who are primarily or exclusively sexually responsive to same-sex persons, yet do not adopt a homosexual or "gay" identity (see, e.g., Ross, 1983). Moreover, there are also individuals who engage in extensive homosexual behavior, yet are not predominantly aroused by homosexual stimuli or consider themselves to "be" homosexual, such as among male adolescents who have sex with men for money. Thus, one must pay attention to the empirical evidence regarding disjunctions between sexual orientation and sexual identity (for a detailed analysis, see Laumann, Gagnon, Michael, & Michaels, 1994, Ch. 8). From a biological perspective, one might make the case that the relevant parameter of interest is sexual orientation, not sexual identity.

CONCEPTUAL MODELS

Psychosexual differentiation is an umbrella term that encompasses the constructs of gender identity, gender role, sexual orientation, and sexual identity and for which one seeks to understand the underlying mechanisms.

Only the most naïve reader will be unaware that debates regarding the determinants of psychosexual differentiation have long yielded polarized positions: nature versus nurture, congenital versus acquired, essentialism versus social constructionism, and so on. The main effect position, to use the language of factorial design, can be illustrated with two quotations from scholars in the field. Thorne (1993), for example, writes:

> While many still see gender as the expression of natural differences, the women's movement of the 1970s and 1980s launched a powerful alternative perspective: notions of femininity and masculinity, the gender divisions one sees on school playgrounds . . . the idea of gender itself—*all* are social constructions. . . . Parents dress infant girls in pink and boys in blue, give them gender-differentiated names and toys, and expect them to act differently. . . . peer groups . . . also perpetuate gender-typed play and interaction. In short, if boys and girls are different, they are not born, but *made* that way. (p. 2; italics in original)

In stark contrast to this view, theorists with a biological bent also emphasize single-factor influences. For example, Swaab, Gooren, and Hofman (1992) asserted that gender identity is very difficult to change, "probably because . . . [it is] fixed in the brain" (p. 52).

Other scholars have argued forcefully that this kind of polarization is a false dichotomy and should be abandoned, and that an interactionist or transactional perspective is both conceptually more complex and more in line with the extant data. In practice, however, adoption of the interactionist perspective remains a challenge and many scholars continue to succumb to the lure of either biological or psychological/sociological reductionism.

From the animal literature, recent data sets point quite strongly to the need to consider both biological and environmental processes to understand the degree to which there is plasticity and malleability in psychosexual differentiation. Three examples will suffice. First, Juraska (1998) has shown that the average number of neurons in the corpus callosum of rats shows a significant sex difference. However, this typical sex difference is exquisitely sensitive to, and modified by, the rearing environment. Second, Breedlove (1997) showed that copulatory experience in rats altered neural morphology, suggesting the possibility that differences in sexual behavior cause, rather than are caused by, differences in brain structure. Last, K. Wallen (1996) has recently summarized ways in which the social environment either attenuates or exacerbates typical sex differences in behavior among nonhuman primates, thus providing illustrations of how "nature needs nurture."

Thus, although this chapter reviews lines of evidence that suggest some ways in which biological factors influence psychosexual differentiation, it is important to understand that such factors should best be viewed as predisposing influences, rather than as fixed effects.

EMPIRICAL STUDIES

In this section, I review selected examples from the empirical literature that have examined the role of biological factors with regard to gender identity, gender role, and sexual orientation.

In the general population of males and females, these behavioral components show, on average, very strong sex differences: Most males have a male gender identity and most females have a female gender identity; most males have a masculine gender-role behavioral pattern and most females have a feminine gender-role pattern (e.g., in children with regard to sex-typed toy preferences); and most males are erotically attracted to females and most females are erotically attracted to males.

Although no one has attempted to systematically study these behavioral differences by meta-analysis and the effect size metric (J. Cohen, 1988), I have little doubt that the effects would be quite large. Indeed, I would wager that the effect sizes would be considerably larger than any other behavioral variable for which the sexes have been compared to date in meta-analytic investigations. Thus, there is a great deal of room to study the source of these differences, which can include biological mechanisms. Of course, it should also be recognized that there are important within-sex variations on these parameters. For example, heterosexual and homosexual men and heterosexual and homosexual women differ substantially in their recalled patterns of childhood sex-typed behavior, as reviewed in a meta-analytic study by J.M. Bailey and Zucker (1995). Thus, such within-sex variation can also be studied with regard to biological (and other) processes.

Gender Identity and Gender Role: Lessons from Intersexuality

Over the past half-century, there has been a great deal of interest in physical intersex conditions (hermaphroditism) from a behavioral and psychological point of view, particularly with regard to what it can teach us about normative or typical psychosexual development and differentiation. In this respect, research on hermaphroditism is a prototype example of the interface between the study of normal and abnormal development (cf. Cicchetti, 1993).

A common aspect of several physical intersex conditions involves the differentiation of ambiguous external genitalia. When this occurs, there is often uncertainty whether the neonate's *sex assignment* should be that of a male or a female and the *gender assignment* that of a boy or a girl.

Sex and gender assignment at birth are believed to be the first of a cascade of events that fall under the rubric of gender socialization (Ruble & Martin, 1998). But because the rearing of an infant as a boy or a girl is usually perfectly confounded with biological sex, researchers have long made the point that it is actually difficult to disentangle the relative contribution of biological and psychosocial influences. For some researchers, it was this methodological and interpretive dilemma that led to the study of children with physical intersex conditions in the hope of providing at least a partial resolution to this problem. In this regard, two aspects of psychosexual differentiation—gender identity and gender role—are of particular relevance.

First Steps: The Work of Money and Colleagues

Beginning in the 1950s, Money and colleagues began to report data on the psychosexual development of children born with physical intersex conditions and much of this work focused on gender identity differentiation. Money, Hampson, and Hampson (1957) noted that because hermaphrodites are "neither exclusively male or female, [they] are likely to grow up with contradictions existing between the sex of assignment and rearing, on the one hand, and various physical sexual variables, singly or in combination, on the other" (p. 333). Thus, Money et al. asked "whether the gender [identity] that a hermaphrodite establishes during the course of growing up is concordant with the sex of assignment and rearing, or whether it is predominantly concordant with one or another of the . . . physical sexual variables" (p. 333).

In a study of 105 hermaphrodites, Money et al. (1957) found that only 5 of 105 patients had a "gender role and orientation [that] was ambiguous and deviant from the sex of assignment and rearing" (p. 333). Thus, Money et al. concluded that "the sex of assignment and rearing is consistently and conspicuously a more reliable prognosticator of a hermaphrodite's gender role and orientation than is the chromosomal sex, the gonadal sex, the hormonal sex, the accessory internal reproductive morphology, or the ambiguous morphology of the external genitalia" (p. 333). Thus, in this early work, gender identity differentiation was deemed largely a function of psychosocial, not biological, influences.

Money et al.'s (1957) conclusion about the apparent malleability and plasticity in gender identity differentiation had one important caveat, namely, the advisability of an early decision about sex assignment. They recommended that when there was uncertainty about the appropriate sex of assignment, the final decision about it should certainly be made no later than 18 to 24 months, and argued that "uncompromising adherence to the decision is desirable" (p. 334). Otherwise, it was claimed that the child would be vulnerable to "psychologic nonhealthiness" (p. 334), which presumably was related to a more conflicted or ambiguous gender identity, which Stoller (1964) later referred to as a "hermaphroditic" gender identity.

In part, Money et al.'s (1957) recommendation of an early sex assignment was based on the observation that among intersexed children who experienced a sex reassignment after the neonatal period, 11 of 14 children adjusted to the change without complications if the reassignment occurred prior to 27 months, in contrast to only 1 of 4 children who adjusted to the change without complications if it occurred after 27 months (Fisher's exact test, $p = .0379$, one-tailed, my analysis).

Money et al. (1957) interpreted this age effect as evidence for a process akin to the phenomenon of imprinting, or a critical period, that had been described by ethologists with regard to other behavioral characteristics, such as attachment formation (Bowlby, 1969).

Since the 1950s, the critical period construct has been subject to a great deal of general empirical scrutiny, and the concept of a "sensitive" or an "optimal" period was introduced to expand the window of time in which certain environmental experiences might exert their greatest impact but without implicating the irreversibility that was believed to occur in the case of critical periods (M.H. Bornstein, 1989). Thus, the idea that there is a sensitive period for gender identity formation suggests that there be a window of time in which gender identity differentiation can more readily move in one direction or another but that afterwards, this becomes more difficult.

Appraisal of the Gender Identity Formation Data

To what extent have the original Money et al. (1957) data been substantiated by subsequent research on gender identity formation in children with physical intersex conditions? To answer this question, one can take advantage of the increased precision in identifying physical intersex conditions on a syndrome-by-syndrome basis. Moreover, one can consider the nature of the syndromes themselves and which aspects of physical sex differentiation are affected in each.

As noted by K.J. Zucker (1999), it is with regard to those physical intersex conditions in which there might be some uncertainty at birth regarding sex assignment that the relative importance of socialization versus biological influences can best be evaluated. In genetic females, the syndrome of congenital adrenal hyperplasia (CAH) is most relevant; in genetic males, the relevant syndromes include steroid 5α-reductase 2 deficiency (5-ARD), partial androgen insensitivity syndrome (pAIS), micropenis, penile agenesis, and cloacal exstrophy. Regarding gender identity differentiation, these syndromes share two characteristic features: (1) There is usually some uncertainty regarding sex assignment at birth, in part because the configuration of the external genitalia is severely affected and, as a result, there may be some uncertainty regarding the "optimal" gender in which the child should be reared; (2) either the prenatal hormonal milieu or the configuration of the external genitalia (and sometimes both) can be atypical in relation to the gender in which the child is reared. Here, data on psychosexual differentiation in one of these syndromes—CAH—are reviewed, in part because this syndrome has been studied with the greatest degree of methodological rigor (for the remaining syndromes, see K.J. Zucker, 1999).

Congenital Adrenal Hyperplasia in Genetic Females

In genetic females with CAH, the overproduction of androgenic steroids during fetal development, which has been documented from amniotic fluid assays in at-risk pregnancies (Forest, 1985), causes genital masculinization ranging from mild clitoral enlargement to complete fusion of the labioscrotal folds with a phallic urethra (New, Ghizzoni, & Speiser, 1996). It is this aspect of the syndrome that, at times, creates uncertainty with regard to sex assignment at birth. When the condition is properly diagnosed, several medical interventions typically ensue, including surgical "feminization" of the enlarged clitoris (Donahoe & Schnitzer, 1996) and cortisol-replacement therapy to control or eliminate postnatal virilization (New & Josso, 1988). Under these conditions, a female sex assignment is made and the infant is, invariably, raised as a girl. For further details on the syndrome itself, including recent understanding of its molecular genetic basis, see Pang (1997).

Gender Identity Differentiation. What do we know about the gender identity development of girls with CAH raised under these conditions? Ehrhardt, Epstein, and Money (1968) compared 15 girls with CAH and 15 control girls with regard to a variety of sex-dimorphic behaviors (M age = 10.5 years; range = 5–16 years). Based on interview data regarding gender identity, 7 (46.6%) of the CAH girls were classified as "content or prefers to be a girl," 5 (33.3%) were classified as "ambivalent," and 3 (20%) were judged to desire "expressly to be a boy." The corresponding percentages for the controls were 93.3, 0, and 6.7, respectively. Thus, there was some evidence that girls with CAH were less content with their gender identity than were the controls; however, Ehrhardt et al. remarked that only one of the CAH girls appeared to be severely gender-dysphoric and had markedly impaired general psychosocial functioning. In a similar study, Ehrhardt and Baker (1974) asked their youngsters whether it was better to be a girl or a boy. Of 17 girls with CAH (age range = 4.3–19.9 years), 6 (35%) indicated that they were undecided or thought that they might have chosen to be a boy if such a choice had been possible. In contrast, only 1 (9%) of 11 sisters gave a similar response. Ehrhardt and Baker noted, however, that "none of the [CAH] girls had a conflict with her female gender identity or was unhappy about being a girl" (p. 43).

Two more recent studies have also evaluated the gender identity of girls with CAH. Slijper, Drop, Molenaar, and de Muinck Keizer-Schrama (1998; Slijper, personal communication, April 18, 1999) assessed 18 girls with CAH (M age = 13.5 years; range = 2–27 years). Of these, 10 were assigned to the female sex at birth, but 8 others were initially assigned to the male sex (and subsequently reassigned to the female sex no later than age 6 months). Of the 18 girls, 2 (11.1%) were judged to meet the *DSM-IV* criteria for Gender Identity Disorder (American Psychiatric Association, 1994). The remaining 16 girls were deemed reasonably content with their female gender identity.

Berenbaum and Bailey (1998) studied 31 girls with CAH, an ad-recruited group of 7 "tomboys" without known somatic intersexuality, and 22 unaffected sisters of both CAH girls and boys and of the tomboys (M age = 10.9 years). A nine-item interview schedule assessed what was termed "continuous gender identity." On this measure, there was little evidence that the girls with CAH were uncomfortable being female. Item analysis indicated that the girls with CAH were more similar to the sister-control group but different from that of the tomboys. For the continuous measure, the girls with CAH had a mean score in between that of the other two groups. Berenbaum and Bailey concluded that their data confirmed earlier reports that girls with CAH "have female-typical gender identity."

Adult follow-up of women with CAH provides a more definitive picture with regard to gender identity differentiation. Over the years, there have been several follow-up reports pertaining to the gender identity development of women with CAH; in addition, inferences about gender identity development in adulthood can be gleaned from reports in which there is cursory mention of gender identity (typically, in the context of medical or surgical aspects of CAH).

In one study, K.J. Zucker et al. (1996) assessed the gender identity of 31 women with CAH (M age = 24.4 years) and 15 sister/female cousin controls (M age = 25.6 years). Gender identity was assessed via a semistructured interview and by a Gender Dysphoria/Identification self-report questionnaire.

At the time of assessment, all of the probands were living, in the broadest sense, as women; that is, they were known to others as females and were registered as such on legal or other official documents. For the interview ratings of current and lifetime gender dysphoria, the proband-control comparisons were not significant. On the self-report questionnaire, the two groups did not differ on the factor labeled Gender Dysphoria.

Although these data did not provide any clear evidence for gender dysphoria or discontent among the CAH probands, it should be noted that there were 10 additional potential probands who refused to participate in the study and 13 others could not be traced. Among the latter, two siblings were both raised as boys from infancy by parental decision. By virtue of an independent clinical referral, one of the refusers (age 19 years) had been previously assessed by me (in another hospital setting) because of extreme gender dysphoria. This proband was diagnosed with Trans-sexualism (with a homosexual sexual orientation) using the criteria in the *DSM-III-R* (American Psychiatric Association, 1987). Thus, of the 53 potential probands (excluding one who had died in infancy), 3 (5.7%) were currently living as men (for a review of "gender change" cases among women with CAH, see Meyer-Bahlburg et al., 1996).

This percentage was compared to one prevalence estimate of female-to-male transsexualism in genetic females, 1 in 30,400 (0.0000329%) (A. Bakker, van Kesteren, Gooren, & Bezemer, 1993). Using this baseline prevalence value, the odds ratio was 1823.70:1 that a genetic female with CAH in our sample was living, as an adult, in the male social role compared to genetic females in the general population living in the male social role (if we exclude the two CAH patients reared as boys from infancy, the odds ratio was 607.9:1).

Our group data appear to be comparable with other reports on the gender identity status of adult females with CAH. All of these studies indicate (or imply) that the vast majority differentiated a female gender identity (for references, see K.J. Zucker, 1999). One early study of women with CAH is of particular interest. Ehrhardt, Evers, and Money (1968) studied 23 CAH women (M age = 33 years) who were "late-treated"; that is, they did not receive early corticosteroid replacement therapy and thus had lived for many years with the "stigma of heavy virilization, sometimes uncorrected genital morphology and lack of feminine secondary sexual development" (p. 117). The mean age of treatment with cortisone was 26 years (range = 8–47 years). Although Ehrhardt et al. did not directly assess the gender identity of these patients, all were living as women and none were judged to be severely gender dysphoric.

In some cohorts of patients, a percentage of genetic females with CAH were assigned to the male sex at birth (invariably due to the extreme masculinization of the external genitalia) and subsequently raised as boys without apparent complications. For example, in one large cohort, Mulaikal, Migeon, and Rock (1987) reported that 9 (5.6%) of 158 genetic females with CAH were assigned to the male sex and reared as boys (for other references, see K.J. Zucker, 1999). The fact of genetic females with CAH reared as boys is interesting in its own right because it tells us that a male gender identity can differentiate in a person who, for example, has female sex chromosomes and internal reproductive structures. It is likely that the masculinization of the external genitalia, which go "uncorrected," work in concert with masculine gender socialization. Moreover, socialization as boys may well augment the putative prenatal androgenization of the central nervous system that predisposes such youngsters to behavioral masculinity.

Summary. The data on gender identity differentiation among genetic females with CAH generally support the Money et al. (1957) argument that gender identity differentiates primarily in accordance with gender of rearing. Nonetheless, there appears to be variability in the extent to which females with CAH are satisfied or content with their gender identity, and such variability appears to be greater than what is observed among control females.

Gender Role Differentiation. In contrast to gender identity differentiation, gender role differentiation among girls with CAH appears to be more masculinized, that is, shifted in the direction of behavior patterns more typical of boys than of girls.

Initial studies, which relied on interviews of both the proband and her mother, indicated that girls with CAH were more masculine and/or less feminine than control girls in several common behavioral domains, such as peer preference, toy preference, and roles in fantasy play (Ehrhardt & Baker, 1974; Ehrhardt, Epstein, et al., 1968).

Although these studies were subject to some legitimate methodological criticisms, such as the reliance on interview measures and rater's knowledge of the subject's status (proband vs. control) (for review, see Berenbaum, 1990), subsequent studies of genetic females with CAH, which have evaluated children, adolescents, and adults, have obtained similar findings using additional measurement approaches, including observation of overt behavior and the use of psychometrically sound questionnaires (Berenbaum, 1999; Berenbaum & Hines, 1992; Berenbaum & Resnick, 1997; Berenbaum & Snyder, 1995; Dittmann, 1992; Dittmann, Kappes, Kappes, Borger, Meyer-Bahlburg, et al., 1990; Dittmann, Kappes, Kappes, Borger, Stegner, et al., 1990b; Helleday, Edman, Ritzen, & Siwers, 1993; Hines & Kaufman, 1994; Leveroni & Berenbaum, 1998; Meyer-Bahlburg et al., 1999; K.J. Zucker et al., 1996).

Berenbaum and Hines (1992), for example, assessed the sex-typed play behavior of CAH girls and compared them with unaffected sisters or first cousins (some were relatives of CAH boys, who were also studied) in a free-play situation. The children were given the opportunity to play with stereotypical masculine, feminine, or neutral toys. Figure 7.1 shows that the CAH girls were more likely to play with the masculine toys and less likely to play with the feminine toys than were the controls; however, the two groups did not differ in their play with neutral toys. Compared to control boys, the CAH girls played about as much with the masculine toys and somewhat more with the feminine toys.

Berenbaum and Hines's (1992) data are remarkably similar to that obtained by K.J. Zucker et al. (1996), who found that women with CAH were significantly more likely than their unaffected sisters/cousins to recall masculine childhood gender role interests by questionnaire (see Table 7.1).

On the whole, the gender role data on CAH might be interpreted as consistent with data on lower animals in which experimental manipulation of the prenatal hormonal milieu alters the patterning of sex-dimorphic behavior (Dixson, 1998; K. Wallen, 1996). This interpretation has not, however, been universally accepted. Critics have appealed to alternative explanations of the CAH data, such as parental response to the ambiguous genitalia (which are sometimes not corrected until toddlerhood or later), expectancy effects for a child of ambiguous sex, and medication side effects (e.g., Bleier, 1984, pp. 97–101; Fausto-Sterling, 1985, pp. 133–138; S.J. Kessler, 1990; Quadagno, Briscoe, & Quadagno, 1977; L. Rogers & Walsh, 1982; Unger & Crawford, 1992, pp. 211–214).

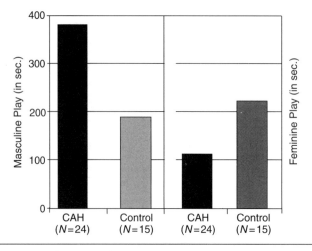

Figure 7.1 Time spent in play with sex-typed toys by girls with congenital adrenal hyperplasia (CAH) and control girls during 10 minutes of play (play with neutral toys not shown). From "Early Androgens Are Related to Childhood Sex-Typed Toy Preferences" by S.A. Berenbaum and M. Hines, 1992, *Psychological Science, 3,* p. 205. Copyright 1992 by the American Psychological Society. Adapted by permission.

Table 7.1
Mean Factor Scores on the Recalled Childhood Gender Identity Scale

Groups	Factor 1 M	SD	p	Factor 2 M	SD	p	N
CAH	2.54	.62	.060	2.94	.74	.009	31
Controls	2.25	.49		2.43	.47		15
CAH–SW	2.69	.55	.053	3.12	.55	.006	19
CAH–SV	2.29	.67		2.64	.92		12

Note. CAH = congenital adrenal hyperplasia; SW = salt-water; SV = simple virilizer. Factor 1 contains 10 items that index the subject's "felt sense" of childhood masculinity-femininity; Factor 2 contains 5 items pertaining to childhood gender-role preferences. For both factors, response scale ranged from 1 to 5. A higher score indicates more sex-atypical behavior.
Source: Data from Zucker et al., 1996.

Regarding genital effects, however, Berenbaum and Hines (1992) found no relation between measures of physical masculinization (e.g., clitoral length) and degree of behavioral masculinity. This finding is consistent with an important experimental study of female rhesus macaques (*Macaca mulatta*) by Goy, Bercovitch, and McBrair (1988). Goy et al. were able to induce behavioral masculinization in the absence of genital hermaphroditism by varying the timing of exogenous injections of testosterone propionate during pregnancy. From an interpretive point of view, this methodology is of interest because it rules out the possibility that the masculinized behavior is, in part, a function of how the social group reacts to the anomalous genitalia of the female offspring.

As partly depicted in Figure 7.2, early-exposed females, who were genitally virilized, showed increased rates of maternal- and peer mounting (male-typical behaviors) and lowered rates of grooming of their own mothers (a female-typical behavior) compared to normal females, but did not differ from normal females in their rates of rough play. In contrast, late-exposed females, who were not genitally virilized, showed increased rates of rough play and peer mounting, but did not differ from normal females in their rates of maternal mounting. The mothers of the early-exposed females were more likely to inspect their genitalia than were the mothers of normal females, but the mothers of the late-exposed females were not.

Although the genital effects hypothesis has not received any empirical verification, it should be recognized that important individual differences in the psychosexual differentiation of CAH

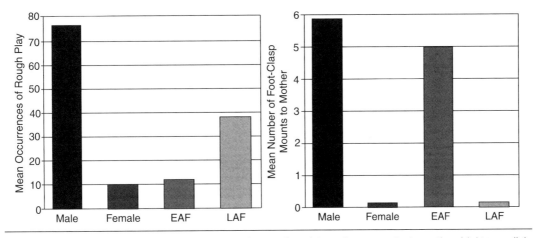

Figure 7.2 Mean occurrences of rough play (left panel) and foot-clasp mounts to mother (right panel) in normal male, normal female, early-androgenized female (EAF), and late-androgenized female (LAF) rhesus macaques. From "Behavioral Masculinization Is Independent of Genital Masculinization in Prenatally Androgenized Female Rhesus Macaques" by R.W. Goy et al., 1988, *Hormones and Behavior, 22,* pp. 559, 565. Copyright 1988 by Academic Press. Adapted by permission.

females have not, as of yet, been fully accounted for. Apart from "error variance," how might individual differences be explained? One possibility is that variation in exposure to prenatal androgens is associated with degree of atypical psychosexual sequelae.

Support for this hypothesis is hinted at in data on psychosexual behavioral differences between CAH females with the simple virilizing (SV) and salt-wasting (SW) forms of the disorder. In many individuals with CAH, there is also a deficiency in aldosterone, which causes low serum sodium levels, high serum potassium levels, and vascular collapse—the so-called salt-wasting crises in severe cases (New et al., 1996). Among patients with the 21-OH deficiency form of the disorder, it has been traditional practice to classify them as either SV or SW. From a psychosexual perspective, the SW-SV distinction is potentially important because there is some evidence that the SW group is, on average, more severely physically masculinized genitally (Prader stages) at birth (Qazi & Thompson, 1972; Verkauf & Jones, 1970), and data from Pang et al. (1985) suggest that prenatal androgen levels are particularly high in CAH probands with SW.

Available data suggest that CAH females with the SW form of the disorder are more masculinized behaviorally than those with the SV form (Dittmann, Kappes, Kappes, Borger, Meyer-Bahlburg, et al., 1990; Meyer-Bahlburg et al., 1999; Slijper, 1984; K.J. Zucker et al., 1996; see also Table 7.1), suggesting a prenatal androgen effect.

But even within the more affected SW subgroup, there are individual differences. Another possibility, then, is that social effects intensify or attenuate the presumed biological predisposition toward a male-typical bias in behavior. Unfortunately, little empirical work has assessed social influences directly. Thus, it is important to design future studies that focus more directly on social variables to test for variations that augment or reduce the likely biologic predisposition toward culturally defined masculinity in CAH girls and women.

Summary.   The data on gender role differentiation among genetic females with CAH suggest that the excessive prenatal exposure to androgens plays a role in the pattern of masculinization that has been observed across a variety of behavioral domains. The behavioral systems that appear affected include nurturance ("maternalism"), affiliation (nonsexual peer relations), aggression, and activity level, all of which show normative sex differences and which, at least in lower animals, have been shown to be affected by experimental manipulations in exposure to prenatal sex hormones, including androgens.

In humans, then, it may be the case that the behavioral components subsumed under the term gender role are influenced more strongly by prenatal sex hormones than is gender identity. In lower animals, it has not been possible to study the construct of gender identity, because its subjective, phenomenological nature defies direct inquiry. Indeed, gender identity may well be an aspect of psychosexual differentiation that is uniquely human, in contrast to the parallels that can be studied in both humans and lower animals with regard to elements of gender role differentiation.[1]

---

[1] As noted earlier, there are other physical intersex conditions in which the relative importance of socialization versus biological influences on gender identity and gender role differentiation can also be appraised. Unfortunately, for some of these syndromes, the study of psychosexual differentiation has not been assessed with the same rigor as it has for CAH (for review, see K.J. Zucker, 1999). From a psychosexual perspective, perhaps the best-studied intersex condition affecting genetic males is that of 5-ARD. For this syndrome, there is much more variability in gender identity differentiation, including well-documented instances of patient-initiated gender change from female to male (e.g., Imperato-McGinley, Peterson, Gautier, & Sturla, 1979; J.D. Wilson, 1999). Among 5-ARD patients with an apparent female gender identity, it appears that their gender role behavior is, on average, masculinized, consistent with a prenatal androgen effect.

Regarding the cases in which there is a patient-initiated change in gender, its interpretation depends on the answer to one key question: What is the evidence that the patient had been consistently, or reasonably consistently, raised as a girl? If there is clear evidence for "unambiguous" gender rearing, then the change might best be interpreted in favor of a biological influence overriding the rearing environment. On the other hand, if the gender rearing was ambiguous or ambivalent, then the interpretation of the change is more complex. As I have argued elsewhere (K.J. Zucker, 1999), the literature is deeply divided on the answer.

There is also a small case report literature on biologically normal males who have suffered a traumatic loss of the penis during infancy (e.g., due to a circumcision mishap). The most well-known case was first reported by Money and Ehrhardt (1972; see also Money, 1975) and later by Diamond (1982), Diamond and Sigmundson

Does sexual orientation have a biological basis? Many scholars have argued that this question is poorly formulated, because all behavior presumably has some kind of biological substrate (Schoenfeld, 1991). Thus, a reformulated question might be: What are the biological substrates that are involved in the differentiation of sexual orientation?

As noted by Gladue (1997), in the 1990s, there was an unparalleled increase in research on the possible biological substrates of sexual orientation. New research has explored a variety of domains relevant to a psychobiological understanding of sexual orientation, including molecular genetics, behavior genetics, prenatal sex hormones, neuroanatomy, neuropsychology, dermatoglyphics, and family demographics (for a review of some of this research, see K.J. Zucker & Bradley, 1995, Ch. 6).

Despite this new wave of psychobiological empirical inquiry, considerable caution is required in appraising the literature. For example, the three studies that reported postmortem neuroanatomical differences between heterosexual and homosexual men remain unreplicated (L.S. Allen & Gorski, 1992; LeVay, 1991; Swaab & Hofman, 1990). A molecular genetic study of homosexual men (Hamer, Hu, Magnuson, Hu, & Pattatucci, 1993), although replicated by the same team (Hu et al., 1995), was not replicated by an independent team (G. Rice, Anderson, Risch, & Ebers, 1999), and, in another study, the underlying assumption regarding X-linkage (i.e., maternal transmission) has been questioned (J.M. Bailey et al., 1999). Although studies comparing monozygotic and dizygotic twins have yielded differential concordance rates consistent with a genetic influence (J.M. Bailey & Pillard, 1991; J.M. Bailey, Pillard, Neale, & Agyei, 1993), the magnitude of the effect likely has been overestimated, in part due to methodological problems regarding subject ascertainment (J.M. Bailey, Dunne, & Martin, 2000). And even where the empirical database appears more solid, the underlying mechanisms remain poorly understood. Despite these caveats, a variety of new research studies hint at the importance of biological processes in sexual orientation differentiation. Some of this work is summarized next.

The Prenatal Sex Hormone Hypothesis

As a point of departure, let us consider the status of perhaps the most prominent and enduring biological model of sexual orientation development, namely, the influence of prenatal sex hormones (L. Ellis & Ames, 1987; Meyer-Bahlburg, 1984). The prenatal hormonal theory of sexual orientation differentiation in humans was stimulated by a large body of experimental research on lower animals, which had demonstrated rather conclusively the effects of prenatal or perinatal sex hormones on subsequent sexual "partner preference" (Adkins-Regan, 1988; J. Bakker & Slob, 1997; Dixson, 1998).

From this line of research, one hypothesis has been that the degree of prenatal androgenization accounts for normative heterosexuality (Collaer & Hines, 1995; Meyer-Bahlburg, 1984). Males, who are exposed to high levels of prenatal androgens, are predisposed to be attracted sexually to females, whereas females, who are exposed to much lower levels of prenatal androgens, are predisposed to be attracted sexually to males. By this account, men with a homosexual sexual orientation should be prenatally "demasculinized," whereas females with a homosexual sexual orientation should be prenatally "masculinized."

(1997b), and Colapinto (2000). This patient lost his penis at 7 months, was gender-reassigned at around 17 months, and received a gonadectomy at 22 months. Money reported apparent success in raising the patient as a girl, but long-term follow-up indicated that the patient eventually rejected the reassignment and began to live in the male social role during midadolescence. Thus, the "experiment of nurture" was viewed as an abject failure, and the "naturists" declared victory. Another case of a patient with ablatio penis was reported by Bradley, Oliver, Chernick, and Zucker (1998). In this case, penile loss occurred at 2 months, and the gender reassignment (and gonadectomy) occurred at 7 months. A follow-up at the age of 26 years indicated that a female gender identity had differentiated, serving as a striking contrast to the first case. In both cases, however, there was clear evidence of "girlhood" tomboyism, which would be consistent with a prenatal androgen influence. It is, of course, not clear which case would be representative of the typical outcome of such cases and, on this point, the literature is quite patchy, as minimal follow-up data are available on other known cases of ablatio penis. For additional analyses of these two cases, see Meyer-Bahlburg (1999) and K.J. Zucker (1999).

But many scholars have pointed out that the strong version of this hypothesis has limited empirical support. For example, there is very little evidence to support a relation between systemic (peripheral) sex hormone levels and sexual orientation in adulthood (Meyer-Bahlburg, 1977, 1979, 1984), although the relation between circulating sex hormones and prenatal hormone patterns is far from clear.

The study of sexual orientation in people with physical intersex conditions has, however, lent some support to the prenatal hormone hypothesis. For example, in women with CAH, there is some evidence for higher rates of a homosexual or bisexual sexual orientation, in either behavior or fantasy (Dittmann, Kappes, & Kappes, 1992; Money, Schwartz, & Lewis, 1984; K.J. Zucker et al., 1996). But the strong version of the hypothesis does not receive unequivocal support because the majority of women with CAH appear to have a heterosexual sexual orientation.

More important, the point has been made that most homosexual adults show no evidence of gross somatic intersexuality (e.g., as judged by ambiguously differentiated external genitalia), which might be linked to a sex-atypical prenatal sex hormone milieu (Byne & Parsons, 1993; Gooren, Fliers, & Courtney, 1990). Thus, the prenatal hormonal hypothesis required modification, such that it was posited that there might be subtle variations in prenatal hormone exposure that affect sexual orientation differentiation but not genital differentiation (Meyer-Bahlburg, 1984)—what some authors have dubbed "central nervous [system] hermaphroditism" (Dörner, 1976). As noted earlier, the experimental study by Goy et al. (1988) suggests that such a behavioral-genital dissociation is possible in nonhuman primates, but its applicability to human sex-dimorphic behavioral differentiation remains to be demonstrated.

Given the equivocal status of the strong version of the prenatal hormone hypothesis, what lines of evidence currently exist that suggest that prenatal biological factors might be operative in sexual orientation differentiation, including a role for prenatal sex hormones?

Dermatoglyphy.   One line of research has utilized a methodology familiar to that of physical anthropologists, namely, the study of fingerprint patterns (dermatoglyphy). J.A. Hall and Kimura (1994) noted that dermal ridges are formed by the 16th week of fetal life. It is known that the total ridge count on the fingertips is partly genetic, but can also be affected by prenatal environmental variables, such as alcohol ingestion and maternal stress (Ahuja & Plato, 1990; Newell-Morris, Fahrenbruch, & Sackett, 1989), and some data on nonhuman primates suggest an influence of variations in the prenatal hormonal milieu on dermatoglyphic patterns (Jamison, Jamison, & Meier, 1994).

Kimura and Carson (1993) reported that men have a higher ridge count than women and that there is also a sex difference in dermatoglyphic asymmetry: Women are more likely than men to have more ridges on the left hand than on the right hand. J.A. Hall and Kimura (1994) subsequently studied ridge patterns in 182 heterosexual men and 66 homosexual men. The two groups did not differ in total ridge count, but the percentage who showed a leftward asymmetry (i.e., more ridges on the left hand than on the right hand) was significantly greater in homosexual men than in heterosexual men (30.3% vs. 14.2%).

Three studies have attempted to replicate the findings by J.A. Hall and Kimura. L.S. Hall (1998, in press) measured total ridge count and directional asymmetry in monozygotic male and female twins either concordant or discordant for homosexuality. In the concordant pairs, the two dermatoglyphic measures were quite similar, which is consistent with an expected genetic influence. In the discordant pairs, however, there were differences on the two measures. In the discordant male twins, the homosexual twins showed more leftward asymmetry than the heterosexual twins (i.e., in the female-typical direction), but not on total ridge count. In the discordant female twins, the homosexual twins had a lower total ridge count than the heterosexual twins, but did not differ in directional asymmetry.

Green and Young (2000) studied the same variables in male-to-female and female-to-male transsexuals and male and female controls. In both the patient group and the controls, males had a higher total ridge count than females. Male-to-female transsexuals with a homosexual sexual orientation showed more leftward asymmetry than the male controls, but this difference was detected only with a more extreme definition of asymmetry than was used by J.A. Hall and Kimura (1994). There were no differences between the female-to-male transsexuals and the female controls. In another study of male-to-female and female-to-male transsexuals, Slabbekoorn, van Goozen, Sanders,

Gooren, and Cohen-Kettenis (2000) did not find evidence for greater directional asymmetry, using the original definition of J.A. Hall and Kimura.

Taken together, then, there are three studies of biological males that have found a relation between directional asymmetry in fingerprint patterns and sexual orientation. The findings for biological females appear weaker. Although it is imperative that there be additional replication studies, these findings are suggestive that some aspect of the prenatal environment accounts for the relation between fingerprint patterns and subsequent sexual orientation in males, including variations in prenatal hormonal exposure during the second trimester.

Finger-length ratios are also sex-dimorphic, more so on the right hand than on the left hand. In females, the index finger (2D, second digit) is, on average, almost the same length as the fourth digit (4D) whereas in males 2D is, on average, shorter than 4D, a sex difference that has been attributed to differential exposure to prenatal androgens (Manning, Scott, Wilson, & Lewis-Jones, 1998). T.J. Williams et al. (2000) found that women with a homosexual sexual orientation had a smaller (i.e., more male-typical) 2D:4D ratio than women with a heterosexual sexual orientation. No difference in the 2D:4D ratio was found between men with a homosexual vs. a heterosexual sexual orientation. In another study, however, S.J. Robinson and Manning (in press) found that men with a homosexual sexual orientation had a smaller 2D:4D ratio than men with a heterosexual sexual orientation, that is, the homosexual men had an "exaggerated" male-typical pattern in finger length ratio. This finding led S.J. Robinson and Manning to speculate that men with a homosexual sexual orientation are exposed prenatally to an excess of fetal androgens, not a deficiency, as postulated by the classical prenatal hormone theory of psychosexual differentiation (Dörner, 1976; Meyer-Bahlburg, 1984). Because the study of finger length ratios in relation to sexual orientation is so new, additional studies will be needed to establish the repeatability of these initial findings.

Otoacoustic Emissions.   Otoacoustic emissions (OAE) are weak sounds produced by elements of the inner ear. There are several types of OAE, including click-evoked otoacoustic emissions (CEOAE), which are echolike waveforms emitted in response to a brief transient sound, and spontaneous otoacoustic emissions (SOAE), which are tonal or narrow-band sounds that are continuously emitted by an ear in the absence of eliciting acoustic stimulation. Both CEOAE and SOAE show a sex difference: Beginning in infancy, CEOAE are stronger and SOAE are more numerous in females than in males (for review, see McFadden, 1998).

McFadden (1993) argued that the sex difference in OAE might, in part, be related to prenatal exposure to androgens, as females with a male cotwin had about half the average number of SOAE as females with a female cotwin or female nontwins. Thus, it was surmised that prenatal exposure to androgens (through diffusion from the male cotwin) had a masculinizing effect on the auditory system of the females.

In a subsequent study, McFadden and Pasanen (1998) found that CEOAE of homosexual and bisexual females were intermediate to that of heterosexual females and heterosexual males, but no difference was found between homosexual and heterosexual males. Similar findings were reported for SOAE (McFadden & Pasanen, 1999). It was concluded that this within-sex sexual orientation difference among females might be related to variations in prenatal exposure to androgens. No support, however, was found for such an effect among males.

Handedness.   About 90% of the general population favors the right hand in the execution of unimanual tasks. Handedness appears quite early in development; for example, Hepper, Shahidullah, and White (1991) found, using ultrasound, that 92% of fetuses who sucked their thumbs tended to choose the right thumb. There is, however, a small sex difference in handedness patterns: Males are somewhat more likely than females to be left-handed (Calnan & Richardson, 1976; Perelle & Ehrman, 1994). Handedness preference is influenced by both genetic and nongenetic factors, including indices of prenatal developmental instability (Thornhill & Moller, 1997), and some authors have speculated that the sex difference might be accounted for, in part, by differences in exposure to prenatal androgens (Geschwind & Galaburda, 1985).

Lalumière, Blanchard, and Zucker (2000) conducted a meta-analysis of 20 studies (20 contrasts for men; 9 contrasts for women) that compared the rates of non-right-handedness in heterosexual (14,808 men; 1,615 women) and homosexual (6,182 men; 805 women) adults. Homosexual adults had a 39% greater odds of being non-right-handed than heterosexual adults, and the average odds ratio for sexual orientation was stronger for females (1.91) than for males (1.34).

What are the candidate explanations that might account for these data? For males, Lalumière et al. (2000) noted that the results were inconsistent with the prenatal androgen hypothesis, as one would predict that homosexual men should be *less* likely to be left-handed (i.e., shifted in the direction of heterosexual females). For females, however, the data were consistent with the androgen hypothesis (i.e., shifted in the direction of heterosexual males).

An alternative explanation for the data borrows from the research literature on developmental instability, which can be caused by a variety of environmental factors, including pathogens, pollutants, and stress during pregnancy. Left-handedness has been associated with a number of indicators of reduced Darwinian fitness, including a smaller number of offspring, higher number of spontaneous abortions, lower birthweight, and several neurodevelopmental disorders. Thus, the higher rate of left-handedness in homosexual adults may be accounted for by factors that divert the development of erotic preferences away from the species-typical pattern of attraction toward opposite-sex adults, which may be related to more general factors that are associated with developmental instability. If this line of reasoning is correct, then one would predict that homosexual adults would be more likely to show, apart from atypical handedness patterns, other signs of developmental instability. As of yet, however, no systematic comparative study has evaluated such signs in homosexual and heterosexual adults.

Birth Order.   Birth order refers to a proband's position in the sibline. One method for quantifying birth order is Slater's (1958) index, in which the number of older siblings is divided by the number of older siblings and younger siblings, yielding a metric ranging from 0 (first born) to 1 (last born). This index cannot be calculated for only children (for additional methods of analysis, see Blanchard, 1997; M.B. Jones & Blanchard, 1998).

A number of recent studies, including reanalysis of old data sets, has consistently shown that birth order is associated with sexual orientation in males (with samples totaling 7,000+ subjects), but not females. On average, homosexual men have a greater number of older brothers than do heterosexual men. They do not, however, have a greater number of older sisters, once their number of older brothers has been taken into account. Because the probability that a man will be homosexual increases only in proportion to his number of older brothers, this phenomenon has been termed the *fraternal* birth order effect (for review, see Blanchard, 1997; Blanchard, Zucker, Siegelman, Dickey, & Klassen, 1998; L. Ellis & Blanchard, in press; D.W. Purcell, Blanchard, & Zucker, 2000).

Several biological explanations for the birth order effect have been proposed, including the role of genetic mutations, prenatal sex hormones, and immunologic effects. Only the last hypothesis will be discussed here. Because of the finding that older sisters have no influence on the sexual orientation of later-born males, Blanchard and Bogaert (1996) conjectured that male homosexuality may result from a maternal immune reaction, which is provoked only by male fetuses and which becomes stronger after each pregnancy with a male fetus (see also Blanchard & Klassen, 1997). This hypothesis is based, in part, on the argument that a woman's immune system would appear to be the biological system most capable of "remembering" the number of male (but not female) fetuses that she had previously carried and of progressively altering its response to the next fetus according to the current tally of preceding males.

Because steroid hormones are not ordinarily antigenic, Blanchard and Bogaert (1996) suggested that the relevant fetal antigen might be one of the male-specific, Y-linked, minor histocompatibility antigens, often referred to collectively as H-Y antigen. H-Y antigen almost certainly has some role in the sexual differentiation of vertebrates because it is usually present in the heterogametic and absent in the homogametic sex—in mammals, present in males and absent in females.

It should be noted that the maternal immune hypothesis does not predict a later birth order for homosexual females, because female fetuses do not produce H-Y antigen and they would not be targets of H-Y antibodies. Hence, the finding of no birth order effect in females is important for the maternal immune hypothesis of male homosexuality.

Although there is some evidence that maternal antibodies to H-Y affect sexual behavior in mice (Singh & Verma, 1987), the maternal immune hypothesis lacks a well-known human model; however, there is some evidence that male and female fetuses may have different effects on the outcomes of subsequent pregnancies that are sex-dimorphic (e.g., in birthweight). Nonetheless, a direct test of the maternal immune hypothesis has yet to be devised and evaluated.

SUMMARY

In summary, a variety of recent empirical studies suggest that specific biological factors may play a role in sexual orientation differentiation. It is hard to imagine that compelling psychosocial explanations could account for some of the sexual orientation effects described above, such as variations in OAE and handedness (for a review of psychosocial accounts of the birth order effect, see Blanchard, 1997). It is important, however, to keep in mind that some of these findings have been observed only in females and not males, and vice versa. Thus, there may be distinct psychobiological pathways in the differentiation of sexual orientation by sex. Moreover, the data also suggest that there are a multitude of biological pathways involved in sexual orientation differentiation. Last, these factors account for only a small portion of the variance. Apart from error variance, this can be interpreted as consistent with a multifactorial model of sexual orientation differentiation, which includes not only diverse biological pathways, but psychosocial pathways as well (see, e.g., D.J. Bem, 1996; Peplau, Spalding, Conley, & Veniegas, 1999). Thus, it is in the more precise identification of the transactional nature of psychobiological and psychosocial influences that future empirical inquiry must continue to invest its efforts.

CHAPTER 8

From Infancy through Middle Childhood: The Role of Cognitive and Social Factors in Becoming Gendered

KIMBERLY K. POWLISHTA, MAYA G. SEN, LISA A. SERBIN,
DIANE POULIN-DUBOIS, and JULIE A. EICHSTEDT

The process of becoming gendered begins virtually at birth. When confronted with the vast amount of information available in a complex world, adults and children alike tend to sort it into clusters to reduce information load and facilitate further processing. They do this by selectively attending to certain features in the environment, forming categories and making generalizations about objects and people. Such generalizations help us to organize and simplify, to make predictions, and to resolve ambiguities (Allport, 1954; Powlishta, Serbin, Doyle, & White, 1994; Quinn & Eimas, 1996; Serbin, Powlishta, & Gulko, 1993; S.E. Taylor, Fiske, Etcoff, & Ruderman, 1978; Tversky, 1977). When the resulting categories involve types of people, generalizations may take the form of social stereotypes. As children realize they belong to one of the social categories, they may come to value that category and the characteristics they associate with it. This emotional reaction sets social categories apart from nonsocial categories (e.g., furniture, animals, vehicles).

One of the first social categories children notice is sex. This dimension is relatively simple, consisting of only two distinct groups. In addition, whether a person is male or female is both perceptually salient and emphasized by society. It is not surprising, then, that children pay a great deal of attention to gender and rapidly acquire knowledge of the stereotypes associated with gender (C.L. Martin & Halverson, 1981; Serbin et al., 1993).

In addition to learning about gender categories and stereotypes, children also develop gender-typed preferences and behaviors from an early age. Sex-related differences are apparent in children's choice of toys, activities, and occupations, as well as in their personality traits and social behaviors (Ruble & Martin, 1998).

Cognitively oriented theories of gender-role development propose that such behaviors and preferences follow directly from the tendency to categorize on the basis of gender and to form gender stereotypes. That is, because of a desire to behave in a gender-consistent manner, children come to prefer people, activities, and objects associated with their own sex (Kohlberg, 1966; C.L. Martin & Halverson, 1981; Powlishta, 1995b). Social learning theory, on the other hand, places more emphasis on the impact of the social environment on gender-role development. Exposure to gender-typed models and reinforcement contingencies encourages children to behave in a gender-typed manner (Mischel, 1966).

The current chapter begins with a description of the development of gender-related cognitions. That is, we examine what children know about gender categories and stereotypes at various ages from infancy through middle childhood. Next, sex-related differences in children's toy, activity, and occupational interests and in their personality traits and social behaviors are described. Evidence linking these sex-related differences to cognitive and social-environmental factors is presented to test the assumptions underlying cognitive and social learning theories of gender-role development. Finally, ways in which cognitive and social variables may work together to create a gendered child are proposed.

CHILDREN'S KNOWLEDGE OF AND BELIEFS ABOUT GENDER

INFANTS AND TODDLERS

Even in infancy, children react differently to males and females. For example, male strangers tend to inspire more anxiety than do female strangers (e.g., Greenberg, Hillman, & Grice, 1973). Infants may even begin to form rudimentary gender categories by the middle of the first year. At this age, infants will lose interest in a particular face or voice when it is presented repeatedly; interest is renewed on presentation of a new face or voice only when the sex of the target has changed (Fagan & Shepherd, 1981; Fagan & Singer, 1979; P.A. Katz, 1996; Leinbach & Fagot, 1993; C. Miller, 1983). That is, even dissimilar faces or voices are treated as "the same" when they represent two males or two females, but are treated differently when they represent a male and a female. Apparently, infants rely primarily on relatively superficial perceptual cues (e.g., hair length, clothing style, or vocal pitch) to make these discriminations (Leinbach & Fagot, 1993; C. Miller, 1983). They also can match the gender of a face and voice by 6 months of age with dynamic displays (Walker-Andrews, Bahrick, Raglioni, & Diaz, 1991), and by 9 months with still displays (Poulin-Dubois, Serbin, Kenyon, & Derbyshire, 1994), reflecting the creation of intermodal gender categories.

These simple categories may enable infants to begin associating other attributes with gender. For example, when presented with male or female faces paired with objects, 10-month-olds show increased attention to new face-object pairs only when a face of one sex is paired with an object previously associated with the other sex. These findings suggest that infants can detect correlations between gender and other attributes, in a sense forming primitive stereotypes (G.D. Levy & Haaf, 1994).

Such knowledge of gender categories and stereotypes increases in the second year. By 18 months, girls are able to match gender labels (lady, man) with appropriate faces (Poulin-Dubois, Serbin, & Derbyshire, 1998). Similarly, by examining the sequence in which children touched various dolls, Johnston, Madole, Bittinger, and Smith (2000) demonstrated a sharp increase in children's tendency to categorize male and female dolls according to gender between 18 and 22 months.

Eighteen-month-olds also show some awareness that toys are associated with gender categories. Specifically, Serbin, Poulin-Dubois, Colburne, Sen, and Eichstedt (in press) found that girls looked more at a face (boy's face vs. girl's face) that "matched" the gender stereotyping of a previously presented toy (masculine or feminine) than at a face that did not match the toy. Similarly, when presented with toys from two categories (masculine- or feminine- and nongender-typed), 20- to 28-month-old boys and girls tend to touch in sequence toys stereotypically associated with their own sex more than would be expected by chance (G.D. Levy, 1999). In addition to this beginning awareness of toy stereotypes, 18-month-olds also have begun to form masculine metaphorical gender associations, linking fir trees, bears, and the color blue with males (Eichstedt, Serbin, Poulin-Dubois, & Sen, 2000).

By 24 months of age, toddlers have been shown to look more at a surprising, stereotype-inconsistent photograph (a man feeding a baby, ironing, or putting on makeup) than they do at a stereotype-consistent photograph (Poulin-Dubois, Serbin, Eichstedt, & Sen, 2000), reflecting some awareness of the typical activities of men and women. Such awareness is also demonstrated when young children are asked to imitate masculine and feminine activities. They tend to select a "sex-appropriate" doll when imitating a gender-stereotyped action (e.g., shaving the face, putting on lipstick). Such gender-matched imitation occurs by 24 months for girls; boys show evidence of this behavior by 31 months of age, at least for masculine activities (Poulin-Dubois et al., 2000). Similarly, Sen and Bauer (2000) found that 2-year-old boys were better able to imitate five-step sequences portraying masculine events than those portraying feminine events.

Results from these studies indicate that toddlers have fairly well-developed gender categories. Furthermore, they have begun to understand gender labels and have acquired at least implicit knowledge of the gender stereotyping of many common activities, metaphors, and toys.

THE PRESCHOOL YEARS

As children move into the preschool years, this knowledge about gender becomes more explicit, more verbal, and more extensive. For example, they are able to sort photographs on the basis of gender as early as 2 (P.A. Katz, 1996; Sen & Bauer, 2000) to 3 years of age (S.K. Thompson, 1975; Weinraub et al., 1984; M. Yee & Brown, 1994). Three-year-olds also attend to gender over other dimensions (e.g., activity, body stance, facial expression) when asked to choose a second picture that matches a target (Serbin & Sprafkin, 1986). Many children begin to use gender labels appropriately during the third year (P.A. Katz, 1996; Leinbach & Fagot, 1986; G.D. Levy, 1999; Sen & Bauer, 2000) so that, by the time they are 3, most children can use gender labels for themselves and others accurately (Leinbach & Fagot, 1986; Sen & Bauer, 2000; S.K. Thompson, 1975; Weinraub et al., 1984).

Preschoolers also have extensive knowledge about the characteristics associated with these gender categories, knowledge that they appear to acquire with great ease. For example, Gelman, Collman, and Maccoby (1986) taught 4-year-olds new sex-linked properties. The children were able to use gender labels to infer that newly encountered male and female targets would also possess these properties. Similarly, Bauer and Coyne (1997) assigned a different, traditionally gender-neutral preference to a boy and a girl figure. They then asked 3½-year-olds about the preference of a gender-ambiguous target identified with either the label "boy" or "girl" or with a masculine or feminine proper name. Children made stereotypical inferences (i.e., that the male target would prefer an object similar to the original boy and that the female target would prefer an object similar to the original girl) for the labeled targets ("boy" and "girl") as well as for targets with a proper name typical of the child's own sex.

Not only do preschoolers readily learn new gender-based associations in the laboratory, but they also know a great deal about real-world gender stereotypes. When asked whether certain objects, activities, or occupations are associated with males or females, their gender stereotype knowledge exceeds chance levels by 2 to 2½ years of age, with such knowledge increasing rapidly throughout the preschool years (Blaske, 1984; Edelbrock & Sugawara, 1978; Helwig, 1998; Kuhn, Nash, & Brucken, 1978; Ruble & Martin, 1998; S.K. Thompson, 1975; Vener & Snyder, 1966; Weinraub et al., 1984). Preschoolers also are quite knowledgeable about the gender typing of toys and clothing (P.A. Katz, 1996; C.L. Martin & Little, 1990; Ruble & Martin, 1998). Gender stereotypes include metaphorical associations (e.g., bears are for boys; butterflies are for girls) at this age as well (Leinbach, Hort, & Fagot, 1997).

Given that personality traits are more abstract than activities and objects (Livesley & Bromley, 1973), it is not surprising that knowledge of the gender stereotyping of traits is much more limited in the preschool years. Often, children of this age simply will assign positive traits to their own sex and negative traits to the other (Albert & Porter, 1983; Kuhn et al., 1978). However, some studies have found at least minimal awareness of some trait stereotypes in children as young as 2½ years of age (Albert & Porter, 1983; Cowan & Hoffman, 1986; Etaugh & Riley, 1979; Reis & Wright, 1982). Three-year-olds respond in a stereotypic manner when asked to attribute traits such as strong/weak, mad/scared, quiet/loud, and soft/hard to animals and infants labeled as male or female (Cowan & Hoffman, 1986; Haugh, Hoffman, & Cowan, 1980). In the preschool years, children show most awareness of trait stereotypes that portray males as high in power and that have negative connotations; females are more likely to be assigned traits conveying fear and helplessness, as well as those with more positive connotations (Ruble & Martin, 1998).

Even preschoolers can use their knowledge of stereotypes to make inferences about gender-unspecified people, at least when those people are described as having characteristics typical of the child's own sex. For example, when told about a person who likes a particular stereotyped toy, 4- to 6-year-olds predicted that the person would like other toys from the same gender category (C.L. Martin, Wood, & Little, 1990). Similarly, when told about a person with a stereotyped personality trait or occupation, 4½-year-olds predicted that the target would wear clothing consistent with that stereotype (e.g., a two-piece bathing suit vs. swim trunks; Bauer, Liebl, & Stennes, 1998).

Thus, by the time they are 5 years old, children have acquired expertise in the use of gender labels and are quite knowledgeable about the toys, clothes, objects, activities, roles, occupations, and metaphors stereotypically linked with gender. They also have some, albeit limited, awareness of the gender stereotyping of personality traits. Finally, they can use their knowledge of gender and gender stereotypes to make inferences about the characteristics of unfamiliar people.

THE ELEMENTARY SCHOOL YEARS

Gender remains an important social category throughout the elementary school years. For example, children rate two people as more similar to each other (Powlishta, 1994) or another person as more similar to themselves (M.B. Brewer, Ho, Lee, & Miller, 1987; Powlishta, 1995b) when the two are of the same sex. They also encode the gender connotations of words in memory, showing an increase in recall when the words to be remembered have shifted from one gender category (masculine or feminine) to the other (Kail & Levine, 1976).

Knowledge of activity and occupation stereotypes reaches ceiling on many measures during early childhood (Serbin et al., 1993; Signorella, 1987). However, some studies have found continued increases in such knowledge throughout the elementary school years (D.B. Carter & Patterson, 1982; Nadleman, 1974; Ruble & Martin, 1998; Trautner, Helbing, Sahm, & Lohaus, 1989; Vener & Snyder, 1966).

Increasing knowledge is even more apparent in the trait domain. Using measures in which children attribute a variety of personality traits to males or females, researchers have demonstrated substantial increases in stereotype knowledge between the ages of 5 and 11 in a variety of countries, with 11-year-olds performing similarly to adults (Beere, 1990a; Best, 1982; Best et al., 1977; Serbin et al., 1993; J.E. Williams, Bennett, & Best, 1975).

Despite this extensive knowledge, the tendency seen with preschoolers to assign positive traits to one's own sex and negative traits to the other persists in middle childhood. For example, boys and girls may agree that certain positive traits are masculine (e.g., strong) or feminine (e.g., gentle), but disagree on the degree of gender typing, with boys viewing the masculine traits as more masculine than do girls, and girls viewing the feminine traits as more feminine than do boys. Similarly, boys see negative, traditionally masculine traits (e.g., messy) and girls see negative, traditionally feminine traits (e.g., cries a lot) as less gender-typed than do children of the other sex (Powlishta, 1995a).

As was seen with preschoolers, stereotype knowledge also affects the inferences older children make about other people. Eight- to 10-year-olds predict that unfamiliar boys and girls (e.g., those portrayed in brief videotaped segments) will possess traditional gender-typed traits (e.g. daring and messy for boys; gentle and cries a lot for girls; Powlishta, 1995b). Several studies have asked children ranging in age (collectively) from 3 to 15 years and college students to predict the competencies, behaviors, toy preferences, personality traits, physical characteristics, roles, and occupations of a target child portrayed in either a stereotypical or counterstereotypical fashion. In all cases, participants used gender stereotypes to guide their predictions, making masculine predictions for boy targets and feminine predictions for girl targets, particularly in early childhood (Berndt & Heller, 1986; Biernat, 1991a; Cann & Palmer, 1986; C.L. Martin, 1989).

Even when the sex of the target is unspecified, older children can use their knowledge of gender stereotypes to make predictions. For example, C.L. Martin et al. (1990) told 6- to 10-year-olds about a target with a masculine or feminine characteristic in one of four domains (appearance, personality, occupation, or toy preferences). Children predicted that the target would possess other gender-typed characteristics as well, whether those characteristics were from the same or different domains. The degree of this stereotyping increased with age.

Furthermore, children are better able to remember information that is consistent with their stereotypes and, in fact, will even distort information to be stereotype-consistent (e.g., remembering a girl seen sawing wood as a boy; C.L. Martin & Halverson, 1983b; relabeling a male nurse as a doctor; Cordua, McGraw, & Drabman, 1979). This preferential memory for stereotype-consistent information becomes stronger with increasing age (Stangor & Ruble, 1987).

In middle childhood, even though knowledge of gender stereotypes increases, the use of such stereotypes sometimes becomes more flexible, at least when additional information is available. For example, in the previously described studies, older children's predictions were influenced not only by the target's specified gender, but increasingly by individuating information such as the current behavior (Berndt & Heller, 1986), the known toy preferences and labels ("tomboy," "sissy"; C.L. Martin, 1989), or the personality traits, physical characteristics, roles/behaviors, and occupational aspirations (Biernat, 1991a) attributed to the target. That is, older children recognize that a person with one masculine characteristic is likely to have other masculine characteristics, even if that person is a girl. Similarly, a boy with one feminine characteristic is predicted to have other feminine characteristics as well.

More direct measures of stereotype flexibility also show that gender stereotypes become less rigid with age. That is, by the end of the elementary school years, children are more willing to acknowledge that both males and females can participate in various stereotyped activities and occupations (D.B. Carter & Patterson, 1982; Emmerich & Shepard, 1982; Garrett, Ein, & Tremaine, 1977; P.A. Katz & Ksansnak, 1994; O'Keefe & Hyde, 1983; Serbin et al., 1993; W.O. Shepard & Hess, 1975; Signorella & Liben, 1984; Trautner et al., 1989) and can possess similar personality traits (Serbin et al., 1993; Trautner et al., 1989; Urberg, 1982). Girls are more likely than boys to show this increased flexibility, however (Serbin et al., 1993). Increasing flexibility does not mean that the tendency to categorize on the basis of gender disappears with age. However, as we get older, we become more willing to attend to other characteristics, particularly individuating characteristics (Powlishta, 1994; Serbin & Sprafkin, 1986).

Thus, in the elementary school years, children's knowledge of the gender stereotyping of activities and traits reaches ceiling. They are able to use this knowledge to make increasingly complex inferences about other people. At the same time, their use of these stereotypes becomes somewhat more flexible by middle childhood. That is, they begin to realize that not all members of a given sex are alike and that there is considerable overlap in the characteristics of males and females. As a result, they are increasingly likely to take individuating information into account when making inferences.

Developments in the Meaning of Gender

Not only does knowledge about gender and gender stereotypes become more explicit, extensive, and flexible, but children's very understanding of the meaning of gender, the origins of gender-typed characteristics, and the consequences of gender-norm violations also undergoes considerable change during the years from preschool to middle childhood. For example, children move from being able to identify the sex of self and others, to realizing that one's sex remains stable over time, to understanding, finally, that gender is a fixed attribute, unalterable by changes in activity or appearance (Slaby & Frey, 1975). Some researchers have argued that a complete grasp of this "gender constancy" is not attained until 6 or 7 years of age (e.g., Emmerich, Goldman, Kirsh, & Sharabany, 1977). However, procedures that discourage "pretend responding" (C.L. Martin & Halverson, 1983a), that ask children questions about familiar people (A. Miller, 1984), and that ask questions about pictures of undressed real boys and girls rather than the typical simple drawings (S.L. Bem, 1989) have revealed what appears to be gender constancy in children as young as 3 or 4 years of age (see Ruble & Martin, 1998, for a complete review).

Young children also believe that people possess gender-stereotyped properties automatically, simply from being male or female. That is, they emphasize nature over nurture in the origins of gender roles. Specifically, when told about a target child raised solely with individuals of the other sex, 4- to 8-year-olds thought that the target would nevertheless possess traditionally sex-appropriate characteristics. Nine- and 10-year-olds, in contrast, recognized the role of factors such as the social environment in shaping the stereotyped properties of boys and girls (M. Taylor, 1996).

As children become older, they also begin to distinguish between social conventions, which are potentially flexible, and universal social regulations that do not allow exceptions, placing gender roles in the former category (D.B. Carter & Patterson, 1982; Damon, 1977; Serbin et al., 1993). For example, Damon described the reactions of children when questioned about a boy ("George") who wanted to play with dolls. Preschoolers believed that George could do whatever he wanted to do, particularly if it was consistent with the child's own desires. In early childhood, they believed it was absolutely wrong for George to play with a doll. But by middle childhood, they made a distinction between moral rules that must be obeyed, and gender roles, which were viewed as customary and even desirable, but not absolutely binding. For example, a 9-year-old described George's doll playing in this way: "It's not really doing anything bad. . . . Because, like, if he was breaking a window, and he kept on doing that, they could punish him, because you're not supposed to break windows. But if you want to, you can play with dolls, but people really don't like you if you play with dolls" (quoted in Damon, 1977, p. 262).

G.D. Levy, Taylor, and Gelman (1995) provide further evidence that, although older children believe that gender roles *can* be violated, they don't necessarily approve of such violations. Males engaging in feminine behavior were evaluated particularly negatively by 8-year-olds, although these negative responses were not as extreme as they were for moral transgressions.

GROUP AND INDIVIDUAL DIFFERENCES IN THE DEVELOPMENT OF GENDER-RELATED COGNITIONS

The developmental patterns described thus far apply to virtually all children. That is, by middle childhood, nearly everyone has acquired extensive knowledge about gender and the attributes linked, either actually or stereotypically, with gender. However, the rate of such knowledge acquisition varies somewhat depending on the sex of the child and the nature of the knowledge assessed. For example, children show accelerated learning of stereotypes that portray their own sex favorably (i.e., positive own-sex traits and negative other-sex traits; Albert & Porter, 1983; Serbin et al., 1993).

Furthermore, children tend to acquire more in-depth knowledge for own-sex gender-typed information at an earlier age than they do for other-sex information (C.L. Martin, 1993). For instance, as described previously, toddlers show greater-than-chance sequential touching of same-sex gender-typed toys, but not of other-sex toys. This pattern suggests a greater awareness of own-sex than other-sex toy categories (G.D. Levy, 1999). Children also show greater exploration of and better memory for the name, function, and use of novel objects when those objects are introduced as being for their own sex than when the same objects are introduced as being for the other sex (Bradbard & Endsley, 1983; Bradbard, Martin, Endsley, & Halverson, 1986).

Moreover, children use own-sex stereotypes to make inferences about people before they use other-sex stereotypes (Bauer & Coyne, 1997; Bauer et al., 1998; C.L. Martin et al., 1990). For example, when told about a target whose sex is identified only by a proper name, children assumed that the target would have gender-consistent interests, but only when the target's name identified him or her as being of the child's own sex (Bauer & Coyne, 1997). Similarly, when told about a sex-unspecified child who possessed a particular masculine or feminine characteristic, 6-year-olds predicted that child would possess other stereotype-consistent characteristics as well, but only when given own-sex cues (i.e., when a boy is told about a target with a masculine characteristic or a girl is told about a target with a feminine characteristic). In contrast, 8- to 10-year-olds made stereotypic predictions when given either same-sex or other-sex cues (C.L. Martin et al., 1990).

Finally, children have better knowledge and recall of "scripts," that is, temporally ordered sequences of events, for own-sex activities than for other-sex activities (e.g., mowing the lawn vs. doing laundry; Boston & Levy, 1991; G.D. Levy & Boston, 1994). Similarly, 2-year-old boys show better imitation of own-sex than of other-sex sequences (Bauer, 1993; Sen & Bauer, 2000).

In addition to such sex-related differences, there also are *individual* differences in the extent to which children focus on gender in categorizing their social world and the extent to which they believe in the stereotypes associated with these gender categories (D.B. Carter & Levy, 1988; G.D. Levy, 1994; G.D. Levy & Carter, 1989; Powlishta, 1994; 1995b; Serbin et al., 1993). For example, S.L. Bem (1981) proposed that, because of exposure to different social environments, some individuals should be more highly gender-schematic than others. That is, gender roles should be particularly salient for such individuals, who are more likely than other people to organize or process social information along the gender-role dimension. Indeed, research evidence has revealed individual differences in gender schematicity as early as the preschool years, differences that are linked to other aspects of gender-role development (D.B. Carter & Levy, 1988). However, despite these individual differences, all children eventually acquire the ability to categorize on the basis of gender, as well as extensive knowledge of gender stereotypes (Serbin et al., 1993).

SEX-RELATED DIFFERENCES IN PREFERENCES AND BEHAVIORS

As noted above, from a very early age, children come to view males and females as very different from each other. They rely on gender when making similarity ratings and predictions. They believe that males and females possess different personality traits and interests. Although these beliefs become more flexible with age, even adults believe in the validity of many gender stereotypes (see Kite, this volume). To what extent are there actual differences in the preferences and behaviors of boys and girls?

When examining sex-related differences in behaviors and preferences, it is important to keep in mind that most studies focus on whether there are statistically significant mean differences between males and females. But even when such mean differences exist, they often are quite small, with a striking degree of overlap between the sexes on most characteristics. As Maccoby (1998) points out, there are a few behaviors that are highly differentiated by sex (playmate preferences, rough-and-tumble play, direct aggression, and the themes enacted in pretend play and storytelling). However, when significant sex-related differences are found on most other characteristics, they reflect highly overlapping distributions. In other words, there are extensive individual differences within each sex in the extent to which children display various preferences, interests, aspirations, traits, skills, and interpersonal styles.

TOYS, ACTIVITIES, AND OCCUPATIONS

Sex-differentiated toy preferences emerge early in life. For example, using a visual preference measure, Serbin et al. (in press) found that boys preferred trucks over dolls, with girls showing the reverse pattern, at 18 but not 12 months of age. Roopnarine (1986) found that even among 10-month-olds, girls played with dolls more than did boys in a free-play laboratory setting. Similarly, stereotypical preferences for dolls, tools, and trucks were seen for some children by 14 to 20 months during free-play periods in a day care center (M. O'Brien & Huston, 1985). By the age of 2 years, children quite commonly show gender-typed toy preferences for a variety of toys (Ruble & Martin, 1998).

Such toy preferences continue to be seen throughout the preschool and elementary school years, whether children are simply observed at play or are given forced-choice laboratory tasks (Blakemore, LaRue, & Olejnik, 1979; Bussey & Bandura, 1992; D.B. Carter & Levy, 1988; Connor & Serbin, 1977; Fagot, 1974; Fein, Johnson, Kosson, Stork, & Wasserman, 1975; P.A. Katz, 1996; D.G. Perry, White, & Perry, 1984; Serbin & Sprafkin, 1982). In one recent study, Etaugh and Liss (1992) had kindergarten through eighth-grade students complete questionnaires before and after Christmas and found that children generally wanted, asked for, received, and most liked gender-typical toys.

Stereotypical toy preferences are particularly strong for boys (D.B. Carter & Levy, 1988; Etaugh & Liss, 1992; Fagot, Leinbach, & Hagan, 1986; Lobel & Menashri, 1993; Sen & Bauer, 2000; also see Maccoby, 1998) and may appear at an earlier age in boys as well (M. O'Brien & Huston, 1985; Sen & Bauer, 2000). It should be kept in mind, however, that children (especially girls) are not simply interested in gender-typed toys; they show as much or more interest in gender-neutral toys (Downs, 1983).

In addition to differential toy interests, boys and girls also prefer different sorts of activities. For example, when asked to rank-order the desirability of several stereotypical behaviors depicted in drawings (e.g., sawing, playing baseball, feeding a baby, cooking), both preschoolers and older children show traditionally gender-typed preferences (Edelbrock & Sugawara, 1978; Serbin et al., 1993). In preschool classrooms, girls prefer activities in which an adult is present and providing structure, whereas boys prefer adult-absent, peer-oriented situations (Carpenter, Huston, & Holt, 1986; Carpenter & Huston-Stein, 1980; Powlishta, Serbin, & Moller, 1993). Girls spend more time in arts and crafts areas, whereas boys are more often found in block areas (Pellegrini & Perlmutter, 1989).

Sex-related differences in activities continue in middle childhood. For example, in a study in which elementary school–age children were asked to list the play activities they engage in with their friends, boys preferred ball sports, cars, and war games, whereas girls preferred outdoor games, dolls, and playing house (Etaugh & Liss, 1992). Ruble and Martin (1998) summarized other common patterns at this age: Compared to girls, boys prefer watching cartoons and adventure programs on television, spend more time in outdoor chores and leisure activities, engage more in sports, and are involved in activities that are less structured. In contrast, girls spend more time in indoor household tasks and chores and are involved in more shopping and socializing. As with toy interests, however, there are also striking similarities in boys' and girls' use of time (Timmer, Eccles, & O'Brien, 1985).

By the age of 4 or 5, children have highly sex-typed occupational aspirations as well, preferences that are firmly established in early childhood (Etaugh & Liss, 1992; Helwig, 1998; Papalia & Tennent, 1975; Sellers, Satcher, & Comas, 1999). Despite the fact that more occupations are now considered appropriate for both males and females, stereotypical aspirations have not disappeared in recent years. Girls have increased the number of different occupations to which they aspire, however, surpassing boys in this respect, at least by middle childhood (Helwig, 1998).

As with toy choices, boys frequently report activity and occupation preferences that are more traditionally gender-typed than do girls (Etaugh & Liss, 1992; Helwig, 1998; P.A. Katz & Walsh, 1991; Ruble & Martin, 1998; Serbin et al., 1993), a difference that often increases with age (DeLucia, 1963; Nadleman, 1974). This pattern occurs because interest in "sex-appropriate" activities and occupations sometimes increases for boys and/or decreases for girls during the elementary school years (Brinn, Kraemer, Warm, & Paludi, 1984; Etaugh & Liss, 1992; Helwig, 1998; P.A. Katz & Boswell, 1986; P.A. Katz & Walsh, 1991). However, even girls typically continue to prefer traditionally feminine over masculine activities and occupations in these studies (Helwig, 1998; Serbin et al., 1993). As Ruble and Martin summarized, "When preferences become less rigidly gender-typed during the middle grades, it is usually for girls only" (p. 954).

PERSONALITY TRAITS AND SOCIAL BEHAVIORS

In addition to differences in toy, activity, and occupation preferences, there are also sex-related differences in the personality traits and social behaviors that boys and girls endorse and/or possess. The latter differences typically are not as extensive or pronounced as the former, however (Huston, 1985). Preschoolers tend to describe themselves using traits that are socially desirable, regardless of the gender connotations of those traits (Cowan & Hoffman, 1986). This tendency is found, to a certain extent, among older children as well (Inoff, Halverson, & Pizzigati, 1983). Sex-related differences are apparent by middle childhood, however, at least on measures that include largely positive traits. That is, boys endorse more traditionally masculine or instrumental traits than do girls, and girls endorse more traditionally feminine or expressive traits than do boys (Biernat, 1991b; Boldizar, 1991; Ruble & Martin, 1998). Many traits are endorsed by children of both sexes, however (Boldizar, 1991).

Do boys and girls actually possess different personality traits and social behaviors that are consistent with their stereotypes and self-descriptions? Ruble and Martin (1998) recently summarized the empirical evidence on this issue. On average, boys are more aggressive, assertive, and active, better at physical activities, and have higher self-esteem than girls. Girls tend to be more socially oriented and sensitive than boys; for example, they are more accurate at decoding emotions and show more facial expressiveness. However, there is little evidence to support stereotypical expectations for other trait domains, such as prosocial behavior, moral reasoning, passivity, or dependence.

Sex-related differences in social behaviors are somewhat more apparent when we look at the characteristics of boys' and girls' *groups*. As early as 2½ years of age, children begin to prefer same-sex playmates. This phenomenon, known as gender segregation, increases in intensity throughout the elementary school years. By middle childhood, both boys and girls spend the vast majority of their social time being near and interacting with others of their own sex (see Maccoby, 1998, for a recent review).

Maccoby (1998) has argued that distinctive cultures emerge in these gender-segregated playgroups. Boys' groups tend to be larger than girls' groups. Their play is rougher, with more physical aggression. Themes in their pretend play often involve taking on the role of a heroic character and carrying out "dangerous" fantasy actions. The boys are much more concerned with issues of competition, dominance, and the maintenance of status. When talking with each other, boys frequently use direct imperatives and prohibitions, often rejecting suggestions made by other boys. There is more bragging, threatening, ignoring, demanding, daring, "dirty" talk, and conflict in boys' than in girls' groups. Boys tend to choose friends who share interests in similar activities; playing and discussing sports are common. Their friendships tend to be less intimate than are those of girls. Boys are more rejecting of the other sex and of things associated with the other sex. Finally, their groups are more separated from the world of adults.

In contrast, girls' groups are smaller, often involving pairs and trios. They engage in more cooperation and turn-taking than do boys' groups. Their pretend play often involves reciprocal interactions, such as enacting family roles. Themes of glamour and romance also are common. Girls' speech to each other is more cooperative than is boys', often building on something another person has said. When conflict occurs among girls, they are more likely to engage in "relational aggression" or social alienation (e.g., saying "I won't be your friend" or spreading negative gossip). They are also more likely to use conflict-mitigating strategies. Their friendships are more likely than boys' to be focused on shared personal characteristics. They frequently disclose secrets and confess weaknesses and fears to each other. Getting together to shop or merely for the sake of getting together is common. Finally, girls are less rejecting of the other sex and things associated with the other sex than are boys, and they spend more time interacting with adults (Maccoby, 1998).

Although children spend a great deal of time in these gender-segregated groups, interactions with the other sex are not uncommon. Using the distinctive interaction styles developed in same-sex groupings, boys are frequently able to dominate cross-sex encounters (Charlesworth & LaFreniere, 1983; LaFreniere & Charlesworth, 1987; Powlishta & Maccoby, 1990).

Maccoby (1998) contends that these distinctive cultures emerge as a result of gender-segregated play, but suggests that preexisting play style differences also may be one of the reasons why such segregation arises in the first place. For example, Serbin, Moller, Gulko, Powlishta, and Colburne (1994) observed 2½-year-olds during free-play periods at nursery school, noting each child's play partners. They asked teachers to rate the play styles of each child as well. Pairs of children identified as "best friends" had quite similar styles of play, regardless of whether they were of the same or opposite sex. Among children who were not yet showing gender segregation, no sex-related differences in play style were apparent. However, among the segregating children, girls showed a higher level of the "social sensitivity" play style than did boys. One possible interpretation for these findings is that children seek out peers with play styles that are similar to their own. As these styles become gender-typed, play partners are increasingly likely to be of the same sex.

However, play style compatibility cannot fully explain why children prefer same-sex peers. Children often react more positively to someone of their own sex even when they have had little or no exposure to that person's play style. For example, when provided with a verbal description, photograph, or brief videotape of people they have never met, children show same-sex preferences. Relative to individuals of the other sex, they predict they will like same-sex people more and they select them as preferred playmates (C.L. Martin, 1989; Serbin & Sprafkin, 1986). Children also show preferences for same-sex adults (Serbin & Sprafkin, 1986), for whom play styles have less relevance. Own-sex favoritism extends beyond a willingness to play with same-sex versus other-sex peers. Children's general attitudes toward individual or generic males and females reveal preferences for their own sex (Powlishta, 1994, 1995b; M. Yee & Brown, 1994). In general, children's perceptions of males and females are distorted such that their own sex is viewed more favorably than the other sex. Positive traits are rated as more masculine/less feminine by boys than by girls; negative traits are rated in the opposite manner (Powlishta, 1995a). That is, children do not simply like what they see in members of their own sex; they see what they like.

LINKS BETWEEN KNOWLEDGE ABOUT GENDER AND GENDER-TYPED PREFERENCES AND BEHAVIORS

Several theories of gender-role development propose that knowledge about gender concepts and the stereotypes associated with gender play an important part in children's acquisition of gender-typed preferences and behaviors (see Ruble & Martin, 1998; Serbin et al., 1993). For example, according to Kohlberg's (1966) cognitive-developmental theory, children use gender to categorize the self, other people, and aspects of the nonsocial world (e.g., activities, occupations, toys, clothing, traits). By observing males and females, they note correlations between gender and other characteristics, forming rigid stereotypes. To maintain cognitive consistency, children are motivated to behave in accordance with these stereotypes once they are able to identify their own sex consistently. As a result, same-sex imitation and behavioral enactment of stereotypic knowledge occur.

Similarly, according to an intergroup approach to gender-role development (Powlishta, 1995b), once children have categorized self and others into male and female groups, certain cognitive processes are set in motion, processes that can be seen even in experimentally created groups. Namely, people favor members of their own groups, they exaggerate differences between groups and similarities within each group, and they see other groups as more homogeneous than their own. A tendency to exaggerate differences between and similarities within the sexes would make children prone to create and believe in gender stereotypes. A tendency to favor one's own sex would lead them to value same-sex people as well as the traits and roles associated stereotypically with their own sex, thus providing the motivation for behaving in a stereotype-consistent manner.

Finally, according to gender schema theory (C.L. Martin & Halverson, 1981), children are thought to create naïve theories (gender schemas) concerning the characteristics of males and females. These schemas influence the ways children attend to, interpret, remember, and predict gender-relevant information, and help children to choose behaviors that are considered appropriate for their own sex (i.e., those that are schema-consistent).

All of these theories suggest that there should be clear links between gender-related cognitions and preferences or behaviors. That is, children's ability to categorize and/or label self and others on the basis of gender, their knowledge and acceptance of gender stereotypes, and the way they process gender-related information should all be related to the sorts of activities, roles, objects, and people they prefer, the traits they endorse, and the behaviors they enact.

The Impact of Gender Labels and Categories

Numerous studies have found evidence for such links (see Ruble & Martin, 1998). For example, some studies have found a relation between the ability to use gender labels appropriately and preferences for gender-typed toys, gender-segregated play, or aggressive behaviors among preschoolers (Fagot, 1985b; Fagot & Leinbach, 1989; Fagot et al., 1986; C.L. Martin & Little, 1990; M. O'Brien & Huston, 1985). Children who can verbally identify their own sex also have been shown to have more stereotypical toy preferences than those who cannot do so (Weinraub et al., 1984). Similarly, children who select a same-sex over an other-sex target as being most like themselves show stronger preferences for gender-typed toys and same-sex playmates (C.L. Martin & Little, 1990).

Furthermore, young children often display more interest in novel toys and objects when they are labeled as appropriate for their own sex (Cobb, Stevens-Long, & Goldstein, 1982; C.L. Martin, Eisenbud, & Rose, 1995; S.K. Thompson, 1975). Similarly, older children have been shown to perform better at tasks labeled sex-appropriate than those labeled sex-inappropriate (D.R. Davies, 1986; Montemayor, 1974). Such effects are found even in adults. For example, in a recent study, male college students did better on a mathematics achievement test than did females when told that the test had previously shown gender differences favoring men. There was no sex-related difference in the performance of the same men and women, however, when they believed the test was merely comparing Canadian and American students (M. Walsh, Hickey, & Duffy, 1999).

The Impact of Stereotype Knowledge and Flexibility

Links between stereotype knowledge and gender-typed preferences are sometimes found as well. For example, for both preschool-age boys (Edelbrock & Sugawara, 1978) and elementary school students (Serbin et al., 1993), greater knowledge of activity and occupation stereotypes predicts more traditional preferences in one or both of these domains. In addition, Serbin et al. found that children who were more knowledgeable about personality trait stereotypes had a greater preference for same-sex playmates relative to their peers.

Stereotype flexibility (i.e., acknowledging that both males and females can possess similar traits or engage in similar activities or occupations) has an even more consistent relation to behaviors and preferences than does stereotype knowledge for older children. Specifically, those with more flexible norms are less likely to have stereotypic activity and occupation (Serbin et al., 1993), toy (Lobel & Menashri, 1993), and peer (Kovaks, Parker, & Hoffman, 1996; Serbin et al., 1993) preferences.

THE IMPACT OF INFORMATION PROCESSING

Some studies also have found connections between information processing variables and gender-typed preferences. For example, preschoolers who have a strong gender schema (indicated by slower reaction times when asked to choose between two masculine or two feminine toys) are more highly gender-typed in their toy preferences relative to other children (D.B. Carter & Levy, 1988). Similarly, 2-year-olds who show better memory for same-sex than for other-sex events (as indicated by their ability to imitate those events) are more likely than their peers to choose an unattractive same-sex toy over an attractive other-sex toy (Sen & Bauer, 2000). Among older children, girls with gender-stereotyped activity preferences are more likely than other girls to pay attention to the gender connotations of words during a memory task (Kail & Levine, 1976). Similarly, children who have highly gender-typed activity preferences show poorer memory for role-irrelevant information than do less gender-typed children (List, Collins, & Westby, 1983).

WHEN COGNITIVE VARIABLES FAIL

Despite this positive evidence, links between gender-related cognitions and gender-typed preferences and behaviors are weak or absent in many other studies. For example, not all research has demonstrated a connection between gender-labeling ability and same-sex peer preferences (Serbin et al., 1994), toy preferences (Fagot et al., 1986), or activity preferences (Hort, Leinbach, & Fagot, 1991). Similarly, children do not always show better performance on or more interest in activities labeled sex-appropriate (Herzog, Enright, Luria, & Rubin, 1982). Furthermore, although there are exceptions, children's attainment of gender constancy generally fails to predict their behaviors (see Ruble & Martin, 1998).

Many studies of preschoolers find no connection between stereotype knowledge and gender-typed preferences (D.B. Carter & Levy, 1988; Hort et al., 1991; Weinraub et al., 1984). In fact, stereotypical toy preferences often are found before children appear to have knowledge of the corresponding stereotypes (Blakemore et al., 1979; D.G. Perry et al., 1984). Furthermore, P.A. Katz and Walsh (1991) failed to find a link between the flexibility of children's gender stereotypes and their willingness to perform behaviors traditionally associated with the other sex.

Preferential memory for stereotype-consistent over-inconsistent information is largely unrelated to a child's gender-typed activity preferences (C.L. Martin & Halverson, 1983a). Similarly, the tendency to make stereotypical inferences about others is unrelated to self-endorsement of gender-typed personality traits (Lobel, Bempechat, Gewirtz, Shoken-Topaz, & Bashe, 1993). Whether children are selecting toys (Johnston, 2000), providing reactions to stereotypic versus counterstereotypic toy play (Bussey & Bandura, 1992), or attributing personality traits (Cowan & Hoffman, 1986), they tend to be more gender-typed when making judgments of other people than of themselves. Adults, too, show more gender stereotyping in their trait ratings of other people than they show in their self-perceptions (B.P. Allen, 1995; C.L. Martin, 1987; Spence, Helmreich, & Stapp, 1975).

There are a number of reasons why gender-typed behaviors and preferences may not always be related to cognitions in accordance with theoretical predictions. First, it is important to keep in mind that gender is not a unitary construct (Spence & Hall, 1996). Relations are not always strong even within the preference (e.g., Biernat, 1991b; Downs & Langlois, 1988; P.A. Katz & Boswell, 1986) or cognitive (Hort et al., 1991) domains. Given the multidimensional nature of gender-role development, it is not surprising that a lack of coherence sometimes is found.

Second, a number of researchers have argued that traditional measures may underestimate very young children's knowledge about gender because of an overreliance on verbal techniques (G.D. Levy, 1999; Poulin-Dubois et al., 1994, 1998, 2000; Serbin et al., in press). Such knowledge cannot be expected to predict preferences and behaviors if it is inadequately assessed. Consequently, techniques that depend less on verbal abilities are being used more frequently in studies with very young children.

Third, it is important to use appropriate measures of gender-related cognitions in older children as well. By middle to late childhood, nearly everyone has expert levels of stereotype knowledge. Given the resulting lack of variability, it is not surprising that stereotype knowledge often fails to predict behaviors and preferences. C.L. Martin (1993) has suggested that we focus not on stereotype knowledge per se, but on how that knowledge is used. Specifically, the salience of stereotype knowledge for a given child, the sorts of stereotypical inferences the child makes, and the value the child attaches to gender stereotypes (e.g., are stereotypic violations considered acceptable?) may do a better job of predicting behaviors and preferences than traditional knowledge measures.

Finally, few if any researchers would argue that gender-role development results solely from cognitive factors. Instead, children's behaviors and preferences are likely to be multiply determined. There are certain to be biological underpinnings for some aspects of sex-differentiated behavior (see Zucker, this volume). Furthermore, as described below, a child's social environment also has a substantial impact on his or her acquisition of gender-typed preferences and behaviors.

LINKS BETWEEN SOCIAL ENVIRONMENTAL FACTORS AND GENDER-TYPED BEHAVIORS AND PREFERENCES

According to social learning theory (Mischel, 1966), the social environment to which a child is exposed has a direct impact on gender-role development. This view holds that children acquire gender-typed behaviors gradually, through observing such behaviors in others. They preferentially attend to and imitate same-sex or gender-appropriate models and are reinforced for stereotype-consistent behaviors and punished for inconsistent behaviors, either directly or vicariously. Children may use gender labels, knowledge of stereotypes, and other cognitive information to generalize from past experience and to infer probable response consequences (Bandura, 1977; Mischel, 1979). However, environmental factors play a more central role. That is, variations in the general environment in which a child is raised and the specific learning experiences the child has encountered should predict variations in gender-role development.

GENERAL ENVIRONMENTAL CORRELATES

Numerous studies have demonstrated links between gender-role development and broad aspects of children's social environments. For example, socioeconomic status is inversely related to the traditionality of children's gender-related attitudes and behaviors (Lackey, 1989; Nadelman, 1974).

There also are ethnic differences in gender typing. For example, African American children are more likely than European American children to have friends of the other sex (Kovacs et al., 1996). Similarly, among White children in a recent study, girls stood closer and showed more attraction to a baby than did boys; this traditional sex-related difference was not found among African American children (P.T. Reid & Trotter, 1993), with both boys and girls displaying as much interest in the baby as did White girls. P.T. Reid and Trotter suggest that the more egalitarian gender roles and greater maternal workforce participation in African American families relative to White families may account for these results.

Finally, cross-cultural variations are often found in children's gender-typed behaviors. For example, Safir (1986) reviewed studies examining sex-related differences in intellectual functioning in the United States and Israel. She found that differences favoring boys are larger and appear at an earlier age in Israel than in the United States, perhaps due to a patriarchal Jewish tradition and a greater parental valuing of education for boys than for girls. In contrast to the United States, where males show an advantage on some mathematical and spatial tasks and females show an advantage on some verbal tasks (see Ruble & Martin, 1998), males tend to outperform females even on verbal tasks in Israel. Furthermore, within Israel, sex differences are less pronounced among children raised in a more egalitarian kibbutz environment than among those raised in the city.

Thus, consistent with the predictions of social learning theory, general environmental variations are associated with variations in children's gender-typed behaviors and preferences. Is there evidence that children are acquiring these roles through the specific mechanisms proposed by social learning theory, namely, modeling and reinforcement?

EXPOSURE TO GENDER-TYPED MODELS

Children certainly do encounter models of gender-typed behavior in their natural environment. Despite changes in gender roles in recent years, men and women continue to divide household and child care tasks along traditional gender lines. Fathers are more likely to be involved in activities such as yard work, emptying the garbage, playing catch with the children, and putting toys together; mothers are more likely to be involved in activities such as cooking, doing the laundry, taking children on errands, and caring for infants (Serbin et al., 1993). Furthermore, fathers are employed outside the home more hours per week than are mothers (Wille, 1995).

Schools also provide children with models of sex-differentiated behavior. For example, women are more likely to be teachers, especially for early grades, whereas men hold a disproportionate number of administrative positions (Ruble & Martin, 1998).

Children frequently see models of gender stereotyping on television as well, particularly in children's programs (see Ruble & Martin, 1998). Gender stereotypes are modeled not only on the programs themselves, but also on television commercials (Furnham & Mak, 1999; Kaufman, 1999). In a review of studies from 11 different countries, Furnham and Mak found evidence for "the universality of sex-role stereotyping in television commercials" (p. 413). For example, men are more likely than women to be the central authority figures, to function as interviewers or professionals, to be portrayed as engaged in outdoor or leisure activities, to be middle-aged, and to be on commercials selling automobile or sports products. Women are more likely to be the users of the products, to fill dependent roles, to be portrayed in the home, to be young, and to be on commercials selling home and body products.

Traditional gender roles also are frequently portrayed in video games. In a recent survey (Dietz, 1998), over 40% of games with characters contained no females. When they appeared, females were frequently portrayed as victims. Only 15% portrayed women in hero or action roles, and even then, they were typically dressed in stereotypical colors or clothing. In nearly 30% of the video games, women were portrayed as sex objects; many other women were portrayed in villain, spectator, or supportive roles. In general, games contained a high level of aggression, with more than 20% including violence directed specifically at women.

Gender roles also are modeled in children's literature (P. Purcell & Stewart, 1990; Turner-Bowker, 1996). For example, males are more often depicted in titles and pictures than are females, and they are described as more potent, active, and masculine (Turner-Bowker, 1996). P. Purcell and Stewart note that gender stereotyping in children's readers was not as pronounced in 1989 as it had been in 1972, however.

THE IMPACT OF MODEL EXPOSURE

Does exposure to such stereotypical models influence children's behaviors and preferences? A number of studies have found correlations between various specific aspects of children's home environment and their gender roles (see Ruble & Martin, 1998, for a more complete review). For example, the availability of parental models is related to children's gender-role development. Boys from father-absent homes often display less traditional gender roles than do boys from father-present homes (Brenes, Eisenberg, & Helmstadter, 1985; Drake & McDougall, 1977), perhaps because they lack consistent exposure to male models. Similarly, children from single-parent homes are more likely to have at least one cross-sex friend than are children from two-parent families; this pattern is particularly true for African American boys (Kovacs et al., 1996).

The attitudes and personality characteristics of parents often are related to their children's attitudes, preferences, and behaviors as well. Preschoolers whose fathers endorse a relatively high number of feminine personality traits are less gender-typed in their toy preferences relative to their peers (Weinraub et al., 1984). Similarly, children are more likely to describe toys and occupations as appropriate for only one sex when their parents have traditional gender-typed personality traits (Repetti, 1984). Children from "nonconventional" families (i.e., those rejecting traditionally normative domestic arrangements and family practices) have more flexible attitudes about gender roles than do children from "conventional" families (Weisner, Garnier, & Loucky, 1994). Girls show more interest in and nurturance toward babies than do boys especially when their parents have traditional gender-stereotyped attitudes (Blakemore, 1998). Furthermore, girls from traditional families show a decline in math and science performance in early adolescence, whereas girls from families with egalitarian marital roles do not show this decline (Updegraff, McHale, & Crouter, 1996).

Maternal behaviors also are linked to their children's gender-role development. Children whose mothers work outside the home tend to be less gender-typed in their preferences and behaviors (Blaske, 1984; S.M. Miller, 1975) and to have more flexible attitudes about gender roles (G.D. Levy, 1989; Marantz & Mansfield, 1977; Signorella, Bigler, & Liben, 1993). Whether the mother is employed outside the home sometimes is unrelated to the child's gender-role development, however (Serbin et al., 1993). Instead, the nature of the mother's occupation may be more important. For example, higher-status maternal occupations predict greater flexibility in children's gender-role attitudes (Serbin et al., 1993). Furthermore, girls with mothers who have traditionally female careers are more likely than other girls to have stereotypic occupational aspirations (Marantz & Mansfield, 1977). Finally, mothers who engage in more traditionally male household and child care responsibilities have children who are less traditional in their own occupational aspirations and peer preferences (Serbin et al., 1993).

Variations in school environment also have been linked to children's gender-related preferences and behaviors, although fewer studies have investigated this issue. For example, children's preference for same-sex playmates is greater in a "traditional" preschool than in an "open" preschool with a curriculum and structure designed to minimize gender typing (Bianchi & Bakeman, 1978). Similarly, Koblinsky and Sugawara (1984) found that children's preferences for gender-typed activities over a six-month period decreased with exposure to a nonsexist curriculum but increased in a control condition. These effects were particularly strong for children with male teachers. Furthermore, children with same-sex teachers showed a greater increase in stereotypic preferences than did children with other-sex teachers, regardless of curriculum.

Children's gender-related behaviors and preferences are related to media exposure as well. A recent meta-analysis revealed that children who watch TV less frequently, who prefer educational over entertainment TV, and who have greater knowledge of nontraditional TV programs have more flexible attitudes about gender roles (Signorella et al., 1993). Similarly, children who like and/or see themselves as similar to other-sex characters in television shows, movies, and books show activity and occupational preferences that are less gender-typed than their peers (P.A. Katz & Boswell, 1986; P.A. Katz & Ksansnak, 1994). In a naturally occurring experiment, children in a Canadian town showed a dramatic increase in traditional gender-role attitudes in the two years after television first became available (Kimball, 1986). In another study, children's play with stereotypic toys increased following exposure to a gender-stereotyped book (Ashton, 1983).

The links between children's gender-typed behaviors or preferences and variations in their home life, school environment, and media exposure suggest that modeling plays an important part in gender-role development. There is also more direct evidence that children can acquire gender-typed behaviors by imitating models. However, they do not blindly imitate same-sex others. Instead, they imitate behaviors that they have reason to believe are sex-appropriate. For example, when children see several same-sex models behaving in a way that is distinctive from the behavior of other-sex models, they are more likely to imitate the same-sex models (Bussey & Perry, 1982; D.G. Perry & Bussey, 1979). Furthermore, children are more likely to imitate an individual model of their own sex if that model has behaved consistently with other same-sex models in the past (D.G. Perry & Bussey, 1979).

DIRECT ENCOURAGEMENT OF GENDER-TYPED BEHAVIOR

In addition to learning gender roles by modeling and imitation, social learning theory posits that children also are encouraged directly by adults and peers to behave stereotypically. Are boys and girls in fact treated differently, and in particular, do children receive direct pressure to behave in a gender-consistent way? In a recent meta-analysis of parents' socialization practices, Lytton and Romney (1991) reported striking similarities in the ways boys and girls are treated by parents. However, parents, especially fathers, did encourage gender-typed activities in their children. For example, adults provide gender-typed toys, even for toddlers (N. Eisenberg, Wolchik, Hernandez, & Pasternack, 1985; M. O'Brien & Huston, 1985). This pattern does not occur simply because children ask for such toys. When examining the toys children requested and received for Christmas, Etaugh and Liss (1992) found that they were less likely to receive requested gender-atypical toys.

As well as providing a gender-typed environment, parents also behave in ways that should encourage stereotypic behaviors. Roopnarine (1986) found that parents were more likely to pay attention to the block play (a stereotypically male activity) of their sons than of their daughters. Fagot and Hagan (1991) found that, relative to girls, 18-month-old boys received more positive responses from parents when engaged in male-typical toy play or when they were being negative, and fewer positive responses when engaged in female-typical toy play (fathers only) or when they attempted to communicate.

Such parental attitudes seem to influence children's behavior. For example, parents who report more traditional gender-role socialization practices (P.A. Katz & Boswell, 1986) or whose children perceive them as encouraging and modeling gender-typed behaviors (P.A. Katz & Boswell, 1986; P.A. Katz & Ksansnak, 1994) have children who are less flexible in their own gender-typed attitudes and preferences. Similarly, in a study by Raag and Rackliff (1998), preschool-age boys frequently reported that their fathers would think it was "bad" to play with cross-gender-typed toys. Boys' actual toy choices were the most stereotyped if they believed their fathers would react in this way. Fisher-Thompson and Burke (1998) found that, when experimenters discouraged activities stereotypically associated with the other sex, children were less likely to engage in such activities. Verbal encouragement of cross-sex activities, however, failed to influence children's behavior in this study. Other studies have demonstrated that children can be encouraged by adults to engage in cross-sex behaviors under some circumstances. For example, when children observed a peer model engaging in a gender-atypical behavior and receiving positive reinforcement, they were more likely to imitate that behavior than children who observed the model in the absence of such reinforcement (P.A. Katz & Walsh, 1991).

When it comes to socializing gender-typed personality traits, parents seem to treat boys and girls much more similarly than they do when socializing gender-typed activities (Lytton & Romney, 1991). However, Ruble and Martin (1998) suggest that "it may be premature to conclude that the only way parents treat boys and girls differently is by encouraging gender-typed activities" (p. 975). They argue that differential socialization practices are subtle, complex, and context-dependent, but that there are differences in the way parents use language, discuss emotions, and convey skill and ability expectations with sons compared to daughters.

Children also receive gender-typed socialization pressure from teachers and peers (see Ruble & Martin, 1998). For example, Fagot (1977) found that girls received more criticism from teachers than did boys when engaged in masculine behavior (playing in the sandbox). Boys received more criticism than girls from teachers and peers when playing dress-up, and more criticism from peers when playing with dolls (both feminine behaviors).

Children are responsive to such contingencies provided by peers and teachers. They are less likely to play with gender-atypical toys in the presence of an other-sex peer (Serbin, Connor, Burchardt, & Citron, 1979). Watching a model receive peer reinforcement for engaging in a gender-atypical behavior increases the likelihood that children will imitate that behavior, especially in the early elementary school years (P.A. Katz & Walsh, 1991). Similarly, rates of gender segregation decline substantially when teachers give positive attention any time they see a boy and girl playing together (Serbin, Tonick, & Sternglanz, 1977). Finally, when children anticipate that their best friend would react positively to gender-atypical behavior (P.A. Katz & Boswell, 1986), when they describe their best friend as having nonstereotypic preferences (P.A. Katz & Ksansnak, 1994), or when they identify with other-sex teachers (P.A. Katz & Ksansnak, 1994), they report less gender-typed preferences themselves.

Thus, social environmental factors encountered in one's general society, or in more specific home, school, or play settings, have a clear impact on gender-role development. These factors include exposure to and imitation of gender-typed models, as well as direct encouragement of stereotypic behaviors and preferences. Boys, in particular, receive pressure to behave in a gender-consistent manner (Fagot, 1977; P.J. Turner & Gervai, 1995). It should be kept in mind, however, that boys and girls are treated much more similarly than differently. Furthermore, not all studies find the expected links between socialization factors and gender-typed preferences and behaviors (Ruble & Martin, 1998). That is, gender-role development does not appear to occur solely because of the differential socialization of boys and girls.

THE JOINT INFLUENCE OF COGNITIVE AND SOCIAL FACTORS ON GENDER-ROLE DEVELOPMENT

The findings reported above provide evidence consistent with both cognitive and social learning accounts of gender-role development. These accounts are not mutually exclusive. Children's gender-typed behaviors and preferences may be influenced by their gender-related knowledge, attitudes, and information processing, as well as by the social environments and behavioral contingencies to which they are exposed. Indeed, numerous studies have demonstrated the additive influences of cognitive and social factors. For example, Serbin et al. (1993) found that children's gender-typed preferences for child activities, adult occupations, and same-sex peers were predicted both by social variables (the mother's participation in traditionally male household and child care activities) and by cognitive variables (knowledge and flexibility of activity and occupation stereotypes).

In addition to such additive effects, cognitive and social factors may work together to influence gender-role development in several more complex ways. First, the gender-related cognitions of socialization agents may impact the way they treat their children, which, in turn, may have an effect on children's gender-typed behaviors and preferences. For example, in a classic study, J. Condry and Condry (1976) showed adults a videotape of an infant responding in an ambiguous emotional fashion. Half of the subjects were told that the infant was a boy and half were told it was a girl. The same emotional reaction was labeled as anger when displayed by a "boy" and fear when displayed by a "girl." Parents also seem to perceive their own infants in gender-stereotypical ways. Newborn daughters are rated as finer-featured, less strong, more delicate, and more feminine than are newborn sons (Karraker, Vogel, & Lake, 1995). If adults believe that boys and girls are different, they might be expected to treat them differently as well. Indeed, S.M. Condry, Condry, and Pogatshnik (1983) found that females responded more quickly to a crying infant (actually a tape recording) that had been labeled a girl than to one that had been labeled a boy. Similarly, when interacting with an infant dressed in gender-neutral clothing, people encourage activity, provide more physical stimulation, and offer traditionally masculine toys when they believe the baby is a boy, but they vocalize more, display more nurturance, and offer traditionally feminine toys when they think it is a girl (Stern & Karraker, 1989). Such differential treatment may lead ultimately to sex-related differences in the characteristics of children.

Cognitive and social factors may work together in a second complex way as well. Children's gender-related cognitions may impact the way they interpret and respond to socialization variables, which, in turn, may have an effect on their preferences and behaviors. A study by D.G. Perry and Bussey (1979), described earlier, illustrates this point. When children watched same-sex and other-sex models make choices, they did not simply imitate the same-sex model. Instead, they did so only when that model had displayed gender-consistent choices in the past. That is, children cognitively processed the social information and imitated what they considered to be gender-appropriate behavior.

Third, socialization variables may have a direct influence on children's gender-related cognitions, which, in turn, may affect their behaviors and preferences. For example, in a longitudinal study, Fagot and Leinbach (1989) found that parents of 18-month-olds who gave more positive and negative responses to gender-typed toy play than did other parents were more likely to have children who could use gender labels accurately by 27 months of age. At 27 months, children who could use gender labels showed a greater preference for gender-typed toy play than did other children, even though behavioral differences in their parents were no longer apparent. Other studies have shown that children's preferences and behaviors are regulated not only by actual rewards and punishments, but also by the anticipation of such reactions from parents and peers

(P.A. Katz & Boswell, 1986; P.A. Katz & Ksansnak, 1994; Raag & Rackliff, 1998). Presumably, this anticipation is the result, at least in part, of past socialization experiences. Once again, then, cognitive factors are mediating the relation between socialization processes and children's gender-role development.

A fourth way in which social and cognitive factors may act together to influence gender-typed behaviors and preferences is through gender salience. Deaux and Major (1987) point out that some events (e.g., watching the Miss America Pageant) encourage us to think in gender-based terms, whereas other events (e.g., watching a news report of a hijacking) are less likely to do so. Similarly, some social environments may increase the salience of gender for children, thus causing them to pay more attention to the sex of others and to the stereotypic implications of their actions. We should see greater sex-related differences in children's attitudes, preferences, and behaviors in such gender-salient contexts. In fact, there is a great deal of evidence that children's gender-typed behaviors and preferences are context-dependent. For example, sex-related differences in behavior are most apparent when children are seen in same-sex groups rather than individually (Maccoby, 1998). Blakemore et al. (1979) found that 3-year-old girls showed gender-typed toy preferences only if they were first asked to identify the toys as boys' or girls'. In another study, boys showed the most stereotyped toy play when the toys had been labeled explicitly as being "for boys" or "for girls" (Raag & Rackliff, 1998). Playing in group settings, answering questions about stereotypes, and being exposed to gender labels are all likely to highlight the salience of gender. Similarly, when teachers make use of explicit boys' and girls' groups in the classroom, thereby increasing gender salience, children's gender stereotyping of occupations increases (Bigler, 1995). However, focusing children's attention on characteristics that boys and girls share seems to make gender less salient. For example, when children participate in groups that cross-cut gender (e.g., "blue" vs. "red" groups, each composed half of boys and half of girls), their tendency to favor their own sex (by predicting that same-sex classmates will outperform other-sex classmates on a task) disappears (Deschamps & Doise, 1978).

In conclusion, it is clear that children treat gender as an important social category from a very early age. They readily learn stereotypes associated with being male and female, and they use these stereotypes to guide their preferences, behaviors, and expectations of others. The social environment also influences gender-role development, both directly and indirectly, through its impact on children's beliefs about gender. However, it is important to keep in mind that children (especially girls) become somewhat more flexible in their gender-related beliefs, attitudes, and behaviors as they reach middle childhood. Furthermore, there are vast individual differences in the traits, skills, preferences, and behaviors of both boys and girls. Finally, the extent to which children think and behave in gender-typed ways varies greatly depending on the context.

CHAPTER 9

Adolescent Girls' Voices: Resonating Resistance in Body and Soul

DEBORAH L. TOLMAN and LYN MIKEL BROWN

> By voice I mean voice . . . to have a voice is to be human. To have something to say is to be a person. But speaking depends on listening and being heard; it is an intensely relational act.
>
> —Carol Gilligan (p. xvi, *In a Different Voice*, 1993)

One of the traditional characterizations of adolescence is that it is a time of intense interest in problems of social justice and also of rebellion against unfair and uncaring authorities. It offers a dress rehearsal of sorts for adulthood, with more and less wiggle room for experiments and errors, depending on teenagers' social circumstances. Because at this time in life new cognitive competencies emerge (Kagan, 1971), adolescents are likely to be acutely aware that they are multiply situated in the world and find themselves struggling with the many voices vying for their allegiance. As the ability to think abstractly and complexly develops, adolescents become able to "do the analysis." That is, they come to understand the existence of institutions and ideologies and how they create, maintain, and undermine systems of social injustice in both the public sphere and in their own lives, relationships, and bodies. Indeed, they are apt to struggle openly with their relationships to and interactions with the many overlapping borders they confront, whether they be the borders marking kinship, community, economic, or political spheres (Muñoz, 1997).

Listening to and conveying adolescent voices is a particular challenge, even as it offers particular opportunities. Adolescents are more likely to offer their social critique and commentary about how things go. As when women began to listen to women speaking about the realities of their experiences and heard very different stories than those that were told about them, listening to the voices of adolescents has greatly increased our understanding of how their experiences differ from the theories and cultural constructions of them, which have created a partial body of knowledge of the processes of adolescence. In this chapter, we report the "subjugated knowledge" (Bartky, 1990) or "situated knowledge" (Haraway, 1988) that researchers who have listened to adolescent girls' voices have heard, particularly when they have listened from a feminist standpoint perspective (Hartsock, 1983; Reinharz, 1992).

Listening to the voices of adolescents has been a subterfuge, underground, even marginalized activity within psychology, even more so than listening to the voices of women (Fine & Gordon, 1989). We have chosen in this paper to focus primarily on adolescent girls. Even though it is only as recently as the mid-1990s that articles in which girls' or even women's voices have appeared in the

---

The authors wish to thank Renée Spencer and Kate Collins for their help in preparing this chapter.

major journals even of feminist psychology, most voice-based research has been on girls. Whether because feminist psychologists have elicited their social critique more often or because it is more acceptable for girls to speak their thoughts and feelings or because girls experience or are more likely to name a relational crisis at this developmental juncture, we argue that listening to adolescent girls, White and of color, economically privileged and marginalized, offers particular insight into the contested borders between their experiences and conventional constructions of reality (L.M. Brown & Gilligan, 1992; Fine, 1990, 1991; Gilligan, 1990; J.M. Taylor, Gilligan, & Sullivan, 1995; Way, 1998).

We have also chosen to focus on the theme of resistance, because listening to voices is a pathway to psychological knowledge and because adolescent voices convey varied forms of resistance. Gilligan, Rogers, and Tolman (1991) observed that, in listening to girls, "The word resistance takes on new resonances, picking up the notion of healthy resistance, the capacity of the psyche to resist disease processes, and also the concept of political resistance, the willingness to act on one's own knowledge when such action creates trouble" (p. 2). The shift in methodology, from asking girls to choose from a set of preordained answers for questions that were not necessarily their own, to inviting them to speak about their experiences in their own voices, is significant. As M. Crawford and Maracek (1989) observed, "A method is a theory" (p. 159). What researchers have learned when acknowledging that research is a relational practice differs from, informs, and challenges other efforts to document or make sense of adolescent development. In this chapter, we do not compare voice-based research to, or disparage, other forms of inquiry into adolescence. Rather, we endeavor to tell a series of complex, contextualized stories that have emerged from this approach.

In listening to the voices of adolescents, researchers have heard adolescent girls' psychological and material resistance to their own thoughts, feelings, needs, and desires. Such resistance can be understood as a hallmark both of internalization and psychological response to White, middle-class cultural constructions of womanhood that demand a sacrifice or silencing of the self. Some adolescent girls, when asked to speak about what their lives are like and choose to speak about what they see and know and feel, what is important to them, express resistance to being suppressed and oppressed by social systems that do not and were never meant to support them. We anchor this chapter in the theme of resistance to highlight how listening to adolescent voices showcases the political nature of psychological research (Fine & Gordon, 1989).

Listening to female adolescent voices has challenged and changed not only how we understand female development but also has contributed to a redefinition of the central processes that define adolescent development and experience. Carol Gilligan (1993) observed in the preface to the new edition of *In a Different Voice* that "The different voice . . . is a relational voice: a voice that insists on staying in connection and most centrally staying in connection with women, so that psychological separations which have long been justified in the name of autonomy, selfhood, and freedom no longer appear as the sine qua non of human development but as a human problem" (p. xiii). Thus, listening to how adolescent girls articulate their struggle to maintain relationships in the face of social pressures to disconnect from self and from relationships, that is, how girls, on the cusp of adolescence, resist social constructions of reality that contradict their own experience and their struggle "to know what they know," tells us much about adolescent psychology.

In this chapter, we focus on two topics: how listening to adolescent voices provides a way of knowing about adolescents' lived experiences in the areas of (1) psychosocial development and (2) embodiment. Both of these topics underscore how girls resist pressures that are meant to keep them in line, socialize them to become "civilized" according to the status quo, muffle the voices of some, lead some to dissociate from their own voices and thus their knowledge and also their own bodies, and cause others to struggle with oppressive institutions, as well as with barriers to authenticity in their relationships, and within themselves.

VOICING DEVELOPMENT, DEVELOPING VOICES

> . . . this is how you smile to someone you don't like too much; this is how you smile to someone you don't like at all; this is how you smile to someone you like completely.
>
> —Jamaica Kincaid (p. 4, "Girl," 1985)

Carol Gilligan (1982) began her now-classic book *In a Different Voice* with a story of discovery and a central assumption: that the way people talk about their lives is of significance, that the language they use and the connections they make reveal the world that they see and in which they act. Though Gilligan traced the contrapuntal themes of justice and care across the life span, her preoccupation, here and elsewhere, is the juncture of childhood and adolescence, the developmental shift into convention or "civilization." In her book, she illustrates the power of convention to override or voice over not only girls' and women's voices, but also boys' and men's. Fundamentally, Gilligan suggests, development is a value judgment. Whose voice is heard and understood, taken seriously, and promoted has everything to do with power relations and one's social location within the dominant society. In the service of "civilization," some voices are legitimized while others are muted or rendered incoherent and thus deficient.

Articulating girls' and women's struggle to be heard and understood, under the weight of historical conceptions of adolescent development as a move toward separation and individuation, provided an opening for a critical analysis. Gilligan's (1982) analysis conveyed two invaluable lessons. First, to appreciate girls' voices, one must understand how they are positioned both developmentally and culturally. Second, if a girl's struggles to convey her knowledge point to her social location, a single girl's experiences cannot be the norm for all girls. That it has taken so long for psychologists to appreciate gender diversity between and within groups of girls is important to note. That many White feminist psychologists, urged on by the healthy and constructive critique of feminist theorists of color, are now doing so is crucial to psychological research on adolescent girls' voices and our understanding of human development. In discussing her belief that her White students can and need to read the work of Black women writers, bell hooks emphasizes the importance of contextualizing the interpreter, noting that "we should all be capable of learning about an ethnic/racial group . . . even if no person from that group is present. . . . However, I do recognize that as a black woman . . . I might have insights and interpretations that would be quite different from those of white male readers. . . . I would, however, consider my insights equally valuable" (hooks, 1989, p. 47).

For a variety of reasons, however, ranging from funding options to publishing pressures to a lack of critical consciousness, the developmental literature on adolescence had taken White middle class experience as the norm. Adolescents of color have been included in traditional psychological studies, but too often the result has been overgeneralization or symbolic annihilation (Dines, 1995), "a tendency to ignore certain groups in cultural representations and discourse or only to represent them in ways congruent with our socially rooted conceptions of them" (Ohye & Daniel, 1999, p. 116). And yet, as Signithia Fordham (1993) claims, "in a socially, culturally, and racially stratified society like the United States, culturally specific routes to [adulthood] are inevitable" (p. 8). If we don't make our understanding of this diversity clear and specific, she argues, we are, by default, referring to the White middle class as the norm. Acknowledging gender diversity allows us to racially mark the structures of feeling and parameters of experience available to adolescent girls and also the way skin privilege influences White girls' emerging identities and social constructions of reality. It enables women to appreciate the seduction of idealized middle-class femininity and its complicated relationship to the reproduction of White male power. It opens all of us, White and of color, to the indeterminacy of language and meaning in ways that immeasurably enrich our understanding of human development. It invites and compels us to resist the temptation to "voice over" the diverse experiences of girls (and everyone else) in the service of a consensus on what constitutes a "normal" developmental trajectory. It enables us to hear different girls narrating varying forms of resistance, which take on distinctive resonances depending on the circumstances of a girl's life.

With these reflections on how developmental psychology has in fact been voiced in mind, we turn to a nuanced description of girls' developing voices at adolescence. Our goal is to present neither a chorus of voices nor a cacophony, but to reveal the orchestration of voices spoken by adolescent girls from a range of experiences, contexts, and social locations and also to reveal the way voice-based research allows for the emergence of new understandings of adolescent development.

Discovering the Underground of Adolescent Girls' Lives

Listening to 100 educationally privileged girls over the course of five years, most of whom were White and middle class, L.M. Brown and Gilligan (1992) described a relational crisis at early adolescence. Defining crisis in the Eriksonian sense to mean a moment of both opportunity and danger, they heard girls at the edge of adolescence struggling with a problem of exclusion: whether to stay with their own experiences, thoughts, and feelings, which would bring them into conflict with White, middle-class cultural expectations of girls and ideals of femininity, or align with such ideals and risk their capacity to stay in touch with what they knew to be true from their observations and experience. Girls who in childhood were lively and outspoken, comfortable taking up space in the world, and quick to speak their thoughts and feelings directly began at early adolescence to voice their confusion and uncertainty about social reality and their place in a male-defined culture. They expressed their frustration with pressures to adopt an image of the " 'perfect girl'—a white, middle-class image put forth by parents and teachers and taken in through books and magazines and television—the perfect girl who has no bad thoughts or feelings, the kind of girl everyone wants to be with, who is worthy of praise and attention by adults, love and inclusion by peers" (p. 59). Girls described her as the girl who is always "nice and kind," never rude, mean, or bossy. Along with the image, Brown and Gilligan claimed, comes a kind of voice training by adults: Perfect girls, "nice girls" are always calm, controlled, and quiet, they are never noisy, they don't "cause a ruckus," they do not cause trouble (p. 61).

Knowing and feeling the pressure of this image—what L.M. Brown and Gilligan (1992) called "the tyranny of nice and kind" (p. 53)—the girls became adept at reading other people and social cues for approval and disapproval, and they modulated their voices accordingly. They began to cover over their feelings and thoughts to stay in relationships with others; that is, they took themselves out of genuine relationships for the sake of idealized, all-loving relationships they associated with "nice" girls. At early adolescence, girls narrated their fight to remain connected to themselves and eventually their increased disconnection or dissociation from their thoughts and feelings for the sake of such idealized relationships. They began to talk about knowing when they were being themselves and when they were pretending, performing, or impersonating the right kind of girl to maintain relationships or to approximate what others desired and wanted. For example, talking about a time when "a whole group of friends [were] mad at one of my really good friends," 11-year-old Jessie narrated such a struggle. If she chose to stay out of the disagreement, Jessie risked dissociating from herself and her feelings. She said, "I usually just stay away and I know how I act when that happens, I can tell. . . . I am not really me. I can tell when it's not really [me]." On the other hand, if she stayed with herself and her feelings and got involved in public confrontation, she risked that "they won't want me in the club." "You sort of get afraid to say it," she added, "because a lot of times they get really mad and it really terrifies you" (pp. 59–60).

At early adolescence, then, the girls in this study spoke of themselves, their thoughts and feelings, as "endangered" or "jeopardized" in their relationships; they began to narrate their disconnection from their thoughts and feelings and to name their anger, fear, and sadness in the face of pressure to accommodate to White middle-class ideals of femininity. They did not want, they said, to "disrupt" others. In situations of unequal power such as the classroom, they were often cautious, as some girls said, "discrete." In addition, at this time the phrase "I don't know" entered the interviews more frequently, signifying girls' confusion about what to believe and what to know and also their resistance to being known by others, including the interviewer.

Depending in part on their social location within the dominant culture and within the context of their privileged private school, the girls in this study negotiated different pathways through adolescence. While many of the girls took their strong opinions underground, protecting themselves by living a kind of double existence, others struggled so deeply with their desire to attain feminine ideals of perfection that they began to lose touch with their experiential reality and to show signs of psychological trouble. Still others boldly resisted the voice-over of the dominant culture, refusing to change their voices or narrow their feelings to fit such ideals. "The tendency for a healthy resistance to turn political and for a political resistance to turn into a psychological resistance [or dissociation] becomes central to our understanding of the difficulties and psychological suffering that many of these privileged girls experienced" (p. 16).

The "political resisters" were likely to be girls of color and White working-class girls, those who lived on the margins of their private girls' school and "who were so clearly at odds with the dominant models of female beauty and perfection as to reveal the cultural hand behind the standards" (p. 226). Listening to the voices of these girls in particular revealed that the patterns of loss and struggle the majority of girls in this study experienced had a great deal to do with their social location as White middle- and upper-middle-class females.

Although early adolescence may, indeed, be a watershed moment in girls' development (Block, 1990; L.M. Brown & Gilligan, 1992; Gilligan, Brown, & Rogers, 1990; L. Harris, Blum, & Resnick, 1991; Orenstein, 1994), the particular struggles around voice and the experience of relational crisis or impasse, as Brown and Gilligan described it, may be a primarily White middle-class girls' experience. Prohibitions against girls' and women's expression of strong feelings, particularly anger, in White middle-class culture play a large role in the psychological and political struggles with voice that these girls experience (Bernardez, 1991; L.M. Brown, 1998; L.M. Brown & Gilligan, 1992). There is a growing body of evidence to suggest, for example, that girls who uncritically adopt conventional images and understandings of White femininity—often but not exclusively White middle-class girls—are at particular risk for eating disorders (Steiner-Adair, 1986, 1991), depression (Schonert-Reichl, 1994; Tolman & Porche, 2000), and diminished sexual agency (Tolman, 1999b).

Such vulnerabilities may be difficult to detect through voice research, however, because the notions of conventional or idealized femininity that elite girls have internalized by definition prohibit voicing anger and open critique and endorse a kind of polite compliance (A. Rogers, Brown, & Tappan, 1993). Additional supporting evidence comes from more traditional avenues. For example, a survey of 36,284 predominantly White adolescents from Minnesota, half of whom were female, painted "a troubling portrait of quiet disturbance" in White girls (L. Harris, Blum, & Resnick, 1991, p. 119). The authors note that whereas there was a tendency for White boys to act out when they were under stress or in pain or angry, the adolescent girls in their survey tended to turn inward. White girls in particular appeared to act out their distress in self-directed, quietly disturbed ways. As a consequence, their cries for help may have been overlooked, harder to hear, and easier to ignore.

LISTENING TO GIRLS OF COLOR: CONTESTATIONS AND CRITIQUES

The research conducted to date suggests that voice is expressed and relational crises are experienced and negotiated differently for African American, Latina, and poor or working-class White girls. Whereas White middle-class girls may come up against the framework of the dominant culture for the first time in early adolescence, voice-based research with girls of color and White working-class girls indicates that they are likely to have named and struggled with this framework in more or less conscious ways since they were young children (L.M. Brown, 1998; H.J. Kim, 1991; Muñoz, 1995; B. Smith, 1991; Ward, 1990, 1996, 2000). Thus, listening to the voices of these girls, not only is the limited generalizability of earlier findings underscored, but we hear yet another set of stories of childhood and adolescence, stories in which experiential and discursive frameworks are grounded in an array of cultural constructions of femininity, and so developmental boundaries and pathways take on different contours.

For example, in a study of 26 culturally diverse, economically disadvantaged, "at-risk" adolescent girls who were followed over the course of three years in an urban public school system (J.M. Taylor et al., 1995), a group of researchers explored how culture and class differentially affect girls' development and future prospects, revealing tensions between what girls want and cultural norms and expectations, as well as tensions between personal goals and economic realities. The girls in this study tended to be outspoken and to resist sexist and racial stereotypes. Yet from eighth to tenth grade, they became more vulnerable to betrayal and loss and more likely to silence or judge themselves, "to experience their voice as 'my big mouth'" (p. 196) that got them into trouble. Their propensity for social critique and for speaking "painful or difficult truths" (p. 193) did not seem to put them at risk psychologically as compared to the White middle-class girls, yet they too struggled with "frequent losses or betrayals in relationships" and, over time, became "disconnected on some important levels from their own feelings and desires and from relationships with others" (p. 196). Such struggles were nuanced by race and class, however. There were similarities among the girls in this study, but cultural conventions of femininity seemed to restrict Portuguese and Latina girls from voicing opinions that were in conflict with the values and beliefs of their families and cultures in particular, rather than the dominant culture in general.

For instance, these girls refrained from speaking openly about sexuality. The poor working-class White girls and Black girls "tend[ed] to maintain their ability to express disagreement or anger, and many demonstrate[d] a willingness to speak about sexuality" (p. 40). In particular, the Black girls spoke of their mothers offering alternative constructions of femininity, including expressing oneself and looking after one's own interests in gender relations, which often brought them into conflict with institutional pressures to comply with middle-class standards of femininity, generating difficulties in school.

Gender, race, and class arrangements differentially affect adolescent girls' struggles to be taken seriously and to experience themselves as powerful and effective subjects. Though not a developmental study, lengthy conversations with four outspoken young feminists—two African American girls from poor and working-class families, and two elite girls, one White and one Asian—with two White middle-class women provide insights into these girls' different "cultures of womanhood." While the elite young women " positioned themselves in an ongoing, critical, hierarchical struggle with men," the African American young women constructed womanhood "horizontally—still in struggles situated with or near African-American men." Theirs was a "far less dichotomized and oppositional" construction and "far richer in a sense of connection to community" (Fine & Macpherson, 1992, p. 181).

Such different cultures deeply affected these girls' understandings of self in relationship and "body-in-relation" (p. 192). The close community ties and "deeply textured and relational lives" of the African American girls influenced their self-constructions and bodily boundaries in ways that contested an obsession with individualism and distinctions between public and private, hallmarks of White middle-class culture. The elite girls, in turn, experienced themselves as individuals separate from their communities and "deployed a language of bodily integrity" and "patrolled borders" (p. 192). Thus, the two groups of girls "parted sharply in terms of how they hibernated in privacy and how they revealed themselves through public talk" (p. 192). While the African American girls spoke their realities and brought their social critique into the public realm, the elite girls "absorbed, carried, and embodied their 'private troubles,' revealing that the 'costs of privilege' were in the internalizing, personalizing, and depoliticizing of gender dilemmas" (p. 193).

Niobe Way (1996; see also Way, 1998) further complicates and deepens our appreciation of the ways adolescent girls perceive, experience, and negotiate their realities. In a three-year longitudinal study of 12 urban, poor and working-class, ethnically and racially diverse adolescent girls, Way found that the girls she listened to were not silent, did not go underground or align with feminine ideals, but tended to speak their minds and express their opinions, dared to disagree, and spoke the truth in relationships with each other and with adults, although not necessarily with boys. These girls saw open conflict and honesty not only as an ideal but as necessary for their survival; they saw such expression as a sign of the life of relationships and depth of connection.

And yet, speaking out, Way emphasized, did not mean these girls had higher self-esteem or that they effectively or collectively resisted oppressive conditions or circumstances. Videotaping a group of poor and working-class White girls over the course of a year, L.M. Brown (1996, 1998) also heard girls' outspokenness and outward anger and the ways they used toughness as a form of defense against feelings of vulnerability, insecurity, and failure. Attempting to outline a clearer picture of these rural girls as "resisters" and to explore how social class and culture affected their resistance strategies, Brown documented how these girls challenged the unmarked and thus seemingly natural order of White middle-class ideals of femininity through their explicit talk of sexuality and desire, their stories of danger, daring, and invulnerability, and their propensity to fight both physically and verbally to protect themselves and those they love. Their videotaped identity shifts from tough girls to icons of idealized femininity, depending on the audience and the questions asked, revealed the performative nature of conventional femininity; their capacity to play with different identities underscored the instability of feminine ideals and, over time, the increasingly weakened power of such ideals to regulate and contain them.

Pastor, McCormick, and Fine (1996) found as well that the urban middle-school girls of color to whom they listened were assertive and outspoken and had developed a critical consciousness that allowed them "to know that much is wrong with the world and that they cannot hide or 'go underground' within white-dominated class-based institutions," because they know that "these institutions are often not designed to protect them or promote their interests" (p. 16). And yet, although they were "unstoppable in their desires to preserve and develop their personal integrity," these girls "do not seek each other out for collective action, which might address the inequities of which they are so critically conscious" (p. 16). Not only are there "few experiences in their lives to prepare them to work collectively," the authors explain, but they had perhaps adopted "traditional notions of feminine behavior which did not include collective action" (p. 16).

As conducted by all of these researchers, voice-based research reveals the complicated and often contradictory relationships between mind and body, language and experience, social and relational context and perceived reality. While research on White women and girls has tended to address issues of voice and silence, Signithia Fordham (1993) underscores in her analysis of the particular struggles of high- and low-achieving Black girls the historical and cultural contexts of the Black community. She described how the girls in her study "improvise" or "ad hoc" their lives in order to construct and express identities that do not violate their sense of self but fit within their group. Fordham unpacks and moves beyond dominant cultural (i.e., White) understandings of girls' use of voice and silence to develop new discursive forms. Although the high-achieving African American adolescent girls she listened to became voiceless or silent in school, for example, they did so as a form of resistance or defiance; their silences did not signal a loss of voice but a struggle with the tension between the burden of acting White and identification with their Black community. On the other hand, the low achievers, "those loud Black girls," were defined by their striking visibility and presence in school and the ways they creatively improvised to refuse to conform to standards of good behavior without actually entering the realm of bad behavior.

Janie Ward, too, creates a developmental framework derived from African American culture and experience (T. Robinson & Ward, 1991; Ward, 1990, 1996, 2000). In her interviews with 60 African American adolescents and their families in four locations across the United States, she further complicates our understanding of silence. Silence can signify a struggle with voice and self-confidence, but it can also signify defiance and resistance. Ward identified the reasons why African American girls do not experience the drop in self-esteem more evident among White girls at adolescence: Their closeness to their families as well as loyalty and identification with Black culture help to create an oppositional gaze (Fordham, 1988; Ogbu, 1989b). That is, identification with and support from the Black community in opposition to White culture enables girls to resist internalization of racism and to repudiate negative images. Black parents have high expectations of their adolescent daughters and emphasize their inner strength and perseverance; they support the dual roles of mother and wife and value Black women's voice and strength and their capacity to renegotiate those roles in a racist culture. Ward's terms—her choice of the phrase "resistance for liberation" as an alternate to L.M. Brown and Gilligan's "political resistance," and "resistance for survival" instead of "psychological resistance"—resonate more deeply with the African American community and its particular history of struggle.

Voice-based research with Latina adolescents further deepens our appreciation of cultural differences and serves again both to question the narrow construction of adolescence as conventionally defined and to introduce new language and imagery particular to the lives of Latina youth. Muñoz (1995, 1997) combines Erikson's understanding of wholeness or a sense of inner identity and his notion of meaningful work with a pedagogy at "las fronteras" (Anzaldúa, 1987) to articulate a model of identity developed through engagement with community. By invoking both Gloria Anzaldúa and Toni Morrison (1992a), Muñoz (1995) explicitly struggles to "redefine language by reconstructing metaphors, images, stereotypes, and romantic ideals" (p. 68). She focuses on the difficulty of translation and "the multiplicity of voice" (p. 6) as it relates to ethnic identity, as a "twin skin to linguistic identity" (Anzaldúa, 1987, p. 59).

Muñoz finds Anzaldúa's metaphor of the Chicana psyche as a frontera—"a bordertown, the edge and intersection where two cultures interact and where both are constantly being negotiated" (Anzaldúa, 1987, p. 56)—especially useful for conceptualizing the psychological development of Latina youth, who are bicultural and often bilingual. Listening to 56 Puerto Rican youths, half of whom were female, she described the complicated ways in which gender crosses borders of culture, class, and skin color to create different psychological and social patterns for girls. Listening to the voices of some of the poor girls in her study, she hears the particular contours of their struggle to integrate traditional feminine ideals with choosing work, with "being a mujer—being feminine, caring, attentive to others, never saying no," with "what they dream of doing as human beings" (Muñoz, 1995, p. 156).

Jill Taylor (1996) listened to this struggle as it played out between 12 Latina and Portuguese adolescent girls and their mothers in a three-year longitudinal study (see also J.M. Taylor, Gilligan, & Sullivan, 1995). She heard these girls struggle with the same kind of "fronteras," trying to be part of school culture even as it conflicted with their culture at home. In particular, she described the tension the girls felt between developing their own voices and the increasing tendency for them to accommodate to their cultures' expectations of femininity—that is, to be "dependent, obedient, responsible, and submissive, particularly to one's elders" (p. 123)—over the three years of the study. Taylor points out how the girls' attempts to accommodate and resist reflect their mothers' own struggles to raise daughters within two cultures.

INSIGHTS INTO SCHOOL: ADOLESCENT GIRLS SPEAKING TRUTH TO POWER

Listening to a diversity of girls' voices opens us to a deep appreciation of the complicated intersections of personal, familial, cultural, and material experiences and the ways these interwoven realities impact adolescent girls' subjectivities. Development occurs within and against and in spite of social and cultural contexts. Because most adolescents spend the majority of their time in school and because most voice-based research is conducted in school settings, we would be remiss if we did not mention the powerful role schooling has in the development of adolescent girls' voices.

There is ample evidence, from both traditional and voice-based research, to suggest that schools impact girls' sense of themselves and their perceived realities in negative ways (American Association of University Women [AAUW], 1990; L.M. Brown, 1998; Fine, 1991; Fine & Gordon, 1989; Fordham, 1988, 1993; Orenstein, 1994; Sadker, 1994; Way, 1998). It is perhaps not surprising, therefore, that much of voice-based research conveys adolescents girls' private and public struggles with and social critique of school practices and policies. Girls struggle with and against sexist, classist, racist, and homophobic messages often unwittingly inculcated in schools and, as we have seen, do so in ways informed by their social and material locations.

Schools primarily operate at the level of right and wrong and from a place of presumed neutrality, and knowledge in schools is constructed as linear. Because what is in fact a middle-class construction of reality is often viewed as objective truth, there is little room for contradiction and for the complexity of most girls' lives (Fine, 1991, 1992b). Indeed, schools can seem particularly out of step with the lives of urban girls of color because, as Michelle Fine (1991) observes, schools ignore many such girls' capacity to view the world from both inside and outside the margins. It is for this reason that often it is the most politically astute, most clear and full-voiced girls who drop out of public high schools in the service of their psychological survival (Fine, 1991). For example, low-income African American girls might put aside their own education or aspirations to support their brothers, understanding them to be "wrapped too tight" (p. 23) in a system that constantly works against them (Fine & Zane, 1989). The radical public-private split schools endorse further disconnects girls of color and White working-class girls from school by making their relational knowledge and their community values and ideals irrelevant. This split contributes as well to White middle-class girls' struggle for voice and agency by dismissing or pushing their relational strengths underground. If, as Gilligan (1993) has recently explained, "voice is a powerful psychological instrument and channel, connecting inner and outer worlds," and is "mediated through language and culture, diversity and plurality" (p. xvi), then most girls engage in a daily public struggle in school over the interpretation of reality and the contours of legitimate knowledge (L.M. Brown, 1998; Luttrell, 1993). This is an important point, because it prevents oversimplification or even idealization of girls of color or White working-class girls when we speak of their assertiveness, relational strengths, and capacities for voice, and from an underappreciation of the impact of oppressive policies and practices.

Because most schools operate from a White, male, heterosexist, and middle-class standpoint, adolescent girls struggle with pressures to fit in: to gender-pass as male, to face the "burden of acting White" (Fordham, 1993), to perform and negotiate compulsory heterosexuality (Rich, 1983) and to ventriloquate White middle-class femininity (L.M. Brown, 1998). White working-class girls and girls of color have described their awareness that their constructions of femininity are inherently disruptive in most schools and that their connections to their communities are dismissed as a knowledge base in school. Lesbian and bisexual girls have spoken about how their relational realities are constructed as perverted and dangerous (Friend, 1993; S. Thompson, 1995; Tolman, 1994a). The ways schools respond to and define "loud" girls and "quiet" girls, "good" girls and "bad" girls, "nice" girls and "mean" girls, "smart" girls and "stupid" girls cover over the multiply situated realities of girls' lives and ignore how girls resist, "passionate about and relishing their capacities to move between the nexus of power and powerlessness" (Fine & Macpherson, 1992, p. 178).

(MISS)EDUCATION OF ADOLESCENT GIRLS' BODIES

... this is how to behave in the presence of men who don't know you very well, and this way they won't recognize immediately the slut I have warned you against becoming.

—Jamaica Kincaid (p. 5, "Girl," 1985)

In the previous section, we concentrated on how girls internalize, experience, resist, negotiate, and perform femininity, as it is defined by dominant patriarchal norms and institutions, and the ways that girls have articulated psychological fallout and psychological resilience in the face of pressure to dissociate from their thoughts and feelings and to keep their authentic selves out of relationships. The dominant White middle-class cultural construction of femininity is not meant to regulate only girls' self-conceptions and relationships but also their embodiment. We turn now to what we have learned from girls through voice-based research that has focused on their experiences of their bodies and their sexuality to hear how girls in different social locations have capitulated, negotiated, and resisted institutionalized pressure to lose a fundamental connection with themselves, that is, not to "know" their bodies.

As an interruption in the recent flurry of concern about girls negative body image, Deborah Tolman and Elizabeth Debold (1993) noted a conflict between these two words that are often breathed so easily together: "Living in a body means feeling hunger and desire (for food, for sex), satiation and frustration, pleasure and pain. And what then is an image? An image is created when someone is looking. . . . An image is flat, has no feelings, is silent. An image can have no appetite, no hunger, no desire, and no power of its own. An image creates a 'no-body body'" (p. 301). An interview with an eleventh-grade, economically privileged White girl illustrates how girls' relationship with their bodies is not only shaped by a male gaze (both actual and internalized), but also is profoundly moderated by school context: "It would be a lot different if there were [boys at the school] because with the boys, we would—we wouldn't be ourselves at all, we wouldn't come to school without looking as good as we can" (Tolman & Debold, 1993, p. 305). Narratives told in interviews with girls in two previously described school-based studies, one in a primarily White private girls' school (Brown & Gilligan, 1992) and one in a racially and ethnically diverse public school (J.M. Taylor, Gilligan, & Sullivan, 1995), revealed a conflict between their embodied desires for food and for sex and the pressure they feel consciously, or have simply internalized as "normal," to monitor, curtail, and control their bodies, to dissociate from their own feelings, to be in compliance with appropriate femininity (Tolman & Debold, 1993).

The primary "curriculum of the body" (Lesko, 1988) for girls is not learning about menstruation or the mechanics of reproduction in school; the most pervasive and equally invisible curriculum is what feminist philosopher Sandra Bartky (1990) calls "the disciplinary project of femininity . . . [that] woman lives her body as seen by another, by an anonymous patriarchal Other" (p. 72). As Simone de Beauvoir observed, when the adolescent girl's body becomes a woman's body, she "becomes an object and she sees herself as object. . . . instead of coinciding exactly with herself, she now begins to exist outside" (1961, p. 316, cited in Bartky, 1990, p. 38). When asked, girls give voice to the often painful process of "the conventional story of female becoming" (L.M. Brown, 1991, p. 72). This bodily process of socialization, interwoven with specific plots and themes embedded in structural differences of race, ethnicity, class, sexual orientation, and ableness, occurs within and through what Adrienne Rich called "the institution of compulsory heterosexuality" (1983, p. 177). Through socialization, compulsory heterosexuality systematically and thus seamlessly constructs "normal" female sexuality as passive and organized around meeting male needs, yielding "feminine" women and "masculine" men, as well as silence about and denigration of female embodied experiences (Tiefer, 1995).

In asking girls to speak about their experiences with their bodies and sexuality, researchers have heard how some girls can and do resist this "(miss)education." Such resistance is consistently anchored in a girl's having access to critiques of this dominant cultural construction of female bodies and sexualities, that is, to an alternative "curriculum," such as feminism or Black and poor women's understanding that giving up the expectation of one's own desire and pleasure in exchange for male protection is not held out for them. However, when researchers have listened, they have heard diverse girls give voice to how well some have learned, and how many others struggle with, the meanings available to girls for understanding their own bodily experiences (G. Rubin, 1984).

CURRICULA OF EMBODIED FEMININITY: LESSONS LEARNED AND RESISTED

In our own projects of listening to girls' narratives, we have observed that it is at adolescence that intensified socialization into femininity (Galambos, Almeida, & Petersen, 1990; P.A. Katz & Ksansnak, 1994) and the specific plot of the larger "cultural story" ordering "normal" female adolescent sexuality gain importance in the education of girls' bodies (cf. L.M. Brown, 1998; Tolman, 1999a). In particular, we have noted the ways in which cultural stories of femininity and female sexuality differ depending on girls' social location, as well as how the master narrative positions and constructs diverse girls in relation to White girls, and vice versa. For instance, Tolman (1996) identified "the myth of the Urban Girl" by tracing how this "embodiment of (teenage) sexuality" reproduces a historical association of Black women (as well as other women of color) with sexuality and White women with asexual virtue (p. 256); that is, how the "goodness" of White women rests on the constructed "immorality" of Black women (Caraway, 1991). It is through and against these intersecting cultural stories that girls constitute themselves and speak, and through which researchers interested in what girls have to say about their experiences and relationships with their bodies have, with varying levels of awareness, listened.

There are two notable and intertwining characteristics of how adolescent girls come to know—and not to know (in the sense of learning to see rather than feel)—their bodies. This process occurs simultaneously with girls' physical development, and it is embedded in the daily life of school, as early as the elementary years. Barrie Thorne (1993) noticed the contradiction between how elementary schools are depicted as "sanitized and idealized images of innocence and safety" and the reality of "the physicality and sexuality of childhood" that pervades schools, if the observer is willing to see (p. 136); Valerie Walkerdine (1990) offers a similar analysis of elementary schools in the United Kingdom. In Thorne's observations of one Midwestern and one Californian elementary school (both approximately 75% White, with the remaining students Latina or Chicano, African American, Asian American, and Native American), she described how threats of kissing were evident among children of all ages, though they had a more explicitly sexual valence for the older ones. Thorne noted that by fifth and sixth grade, "the rituals of 'goin' with' become a central activity" (p. 151). Although most of these relationships were played out through notes, phone conversations, and being together at group activities, and were short-lived, discussion by peers of those participating in these relationships and supposition about the possible sexual quality of their interactions was a prevailing theme on the playground. Thorne noted in particular younger adolescent girls' efforts to comply with idealized and sexualized norms of femininity, "learning the skills" of teen culture, including the use of cosmetics, new modes of dress, and "heterosexualized ways of moving and holding one's body" (p. 158), that is, turning themselves into sexual objects.

In an ethnographic study of peer culture in a Midwestern middle school, Donna Eder and her colleagues (Eder, Evans, & Parker, 1995) found heterosexuality to be the fundamental organizing principle. Her analysis illustrated how school is a major site for gender socialization and how in middle school, when children cross into adolescence, sexuality is a key component of this socialization, which brings the script of heterosexuality to life in the lives and bodies of girls as well as, and importantly, in relation to boys. She observed boys perceiving girls as sexual objects for conquest and competing with other boys to garner sexual achievements. Girls became more concerned about their appearance at this age and more vulnerable to embracing their status as desirable sexual objects. She documented how the girls were judged by their sexual attractiveness. This constant judgment by boys contributes to the invisible curriculum of school for girls; learning the fine line that creates hierarchies in the paradigm of heterosexuality, having a "great body" so as to be attractive, but not drawing too much attention to one's sexuality by one's appearance or by initiating sexual actions, which renders girls "whores," "bitches," and "sluts" (p. 130; see also Larkin & Populeailk, 1994). Such commentary and assessment intensified as the adolescents moved from seventh to eighth grade and more boyfriends were lost to other girls. The control of girls' sexuality through such labeling was observed by Eder to be done by boys and especially by girls in school. As the girls became more aware of the denigration of active female sexuality, this labeling served as a strategy to enable girls to avoid associating with girls who could be considered promiscuous and thus keep themselves uncontaminated and safe from the negative consequences of being thrust into this denigrated category. In the hallways and cafeteria, Eder observed how girls and boys learned that active sexuality was "normal" for boys and "abnormal" for girls. At the same time, girls did not want to appear prudish or sexually innocent, but as sophisticated and knowledgable, dovetailing with their developing adolescent identities.

Girls must go through a physiological process of developing a woman's body, which ushers in their objectification. Karin Martin (1996) conducted a qualitative study of the experience of puberty with 55 working-class and middle-class boys and girls age 14 to 19. She found girls to be ambivalent and anxious about their developing bodies, and that girls had little subjective (i.e., experiential) knowledge of or even interest in their bodies, except for "their work on appearance—jewelry, hair, make-up, clothes . . . as one girl said, 'my hair is my accomplishment'" (p. 21). Having so little subjective knowledge and also often distorted information about menstruation, gender relations, and sex, going through puberty was rarely a positive experience for girls; it was "associated with sexuality, and sexuality and the female sexual body became associated with dirtiness, shame, taboo, danger, and objectification. As girls internalized these meanings, they began to feel bad about their new bodies and themselves" (p. 27). A working-class 18-year-old gave voice to the aura of danger that lurks around menarche: "A lot of girls that I hung around with thought as soon as you got your period at any moment you could spontaneously be pregnant" (p. 28). The denigration of female bodies infused menarche with negative meanings. Martin reported that girls were confused, ashamed, or "disgust[ed]." She noted, "The girls whom I interviewed gave only negative descriptions of their menstruating bodies. Their bodies made them feel 'yuck,' or 'sick,' or as if they had 'shit [their] pants'" (p. 30).

K. Martin (1996) notes that only late developers and girls who were pursuing femininity most intensely looked positively on breast development and menarche, as one working-class 18-year-old remembered: "I just wanted it so bad, just to feel older" (p. 33). Among the very few girls whose responses to Martin suggested resistance to these negative constructions of their bodies is one middle-class girl, whom Martin described as "particularly articulate" and "with more feminist sensibilities than most of the teenage girls" (p. 21). This adolescent talked about her impression that girls do not know their sexual bodies, and she herself resisted such ignorance by cultivating "subjective knowledge": "One thing I thought was really nice about using tampons is it in a way forces you to get to know your body. You kind of have to know what you're doing, and I think it does make you a little more comfortable with your body to be able to put a tampon in and out because . . . I think a pad is like, it's still outside your body, and you're still like not really dealing" (p. 21).

A simple lesson proffered is that becoming feminine demands a negation of a girl's embodiment. Elizabeth Debold (1991) has observed that "the ideals that [girls] take in and hold in their minds—ideals reflecting the construct of femininity—split their feelings for hunger, passion and play from their knowing" (p. 177). Lily, a 17-year-old Latina interviewed by Tolman in a study of girls' sexual desire (see below), illustrated how she had internalized the dictum to split herself (her mind) from herself (her body) in enacting femininity (Debold, Tolman, & Brown, 1996). When asked what makes her feel sexy, she talked about how her boyfriend evaluates her appearance every morning: "'When he says that I look sexy, that's one of my sexy days.' . . . she knows herself in the realm of 'sexy' as the object of male desire" (p. 109). Even after persistently asking Lily how she herself felt, she continued to explain what her boyfriend thought. Lily did not know her own sexiness as her feeling, only as his observations. Debold, Tolman, and Brown noted that "at this point, the incorporation of the Other's view of herself is so thorough that Lily herself acts as the thief. Listening to her, we hear a cultural discourse uncritically emerging from and creating her with the full force of its authority" (p. 109).

Girls from various social locations can and have described a common societal ideal of femininity that prescribes a specific construction of a desirable woman's body to which they do—or know they are supposed to—subscribe; reminiscent of a Barbie doll, this ideal woman is perfectly beautiful in conventional ways, that is, blonde, blue-eyed, large-breasted, tall, and thin. In concert with this narrowly conceived notion of beauty goes a set of personal qualities; this girl is "beautiful" not only in her appearance but also in her comportment, being always sweet, popular, and smart (but not too smart). But depending on race, ethnicity, class, sexual identity, and ableness, girls stand in different relationships to this ideal, and they name, appropriate, and resist it in very different ways. That is, girls may perform femininity, mouthing the accepted line for particular audiences, or they may openly resist individually or collectively, either aggressively and defiantly or by developing an oppositional stance to such ideals. Drawing from a survey, focus groups, and interviews with White and Black adolescent girls, Sheila Parker and her colleagues (1995) explored the impact of social location on girls' appropriation of such dominant ideals of femininity. They discovered that, whereas White girls were obsessed with being perfect and with narrow beauty ideals and were engaged in competitive behavior around such ideals, the Black girls they studied were clear about the distinction between such White ideals and Black ideals of beauty. When asked about their ideals, Black girls were apt to list personality traits rather than physical attributes, that is, to de-emphasize external beauty as a prerequisite for popularity (see also Tolman & Porche, 2000). An alternative curriculum of the body enabled these Black girls to resist White, middle-class cultural pressure.

In narratives that 32 14- to 18-year-old privileged White girls told in relation to questions about cultural values and images of women, Catherine Steiner-Adair (1986, 1990) noticed two patterns in girls' descriptions of how women are "supposed" to be and look: "Wise Women" were aware of societal values demanding thinness, among other qualities, and rejected and challenged such demands; "Super Women" produced an idealized image that included "remaking the body to fit a rigid beauty ideal . . . a tall, thin body" (p. 171). She found also that Super Women girls were more likely to have negative body images and to engage in disordered eating. Steiner-Adair offered the notion of the "body politic" as a way of understanding disordered eating to be a dangerous form of resistance to the relational and bodily demands of femininity, whereby girls utilize their bodies as a voiceless, resistant "voice." She suggested that girls who are not conscious or fully aware of, or not able to articulate their resistance are literally dying to be heard. J.M. Taylor et al. (1995) also heard some Portuguese and Latina girls using control of their bodies as a form of psychological resistance to being sexualized and objectified. Carla, a 16-year-old Latina, talked about her looks as being a problem for her: "I don't like, sometimes I feel like, I feel clumsy about myself sometimes . . . I think I'm fat. I feel like I'm overweight" (p. 103–104). Being overweight may be a resistant strategy against having to make decisions about sexual activity in a White middle-class cultural context where being desirable is equated with being thin—a strategy, however, that leaves her with negative feelings about herself.

In contrast, Niva Piran (2001) described a successful participatory action research project at a coed residential dancing school in Canada. Girls met with her in age-specific focus groups organized to create a space for them to evaluate their experiences with their bodies in school and to plan how to take action on their own behalf. In these groups, girls age 10 to 18 talked about their feelings and concerns about their bodies, and together developed a critical understanding of how these negative feelings were being "produced," as well as made action plans at the interpersonal and institutional levels to resist and reverse this unhealthy process. She described how one group of 13-year-olds started speaking about their discomfort with their bodies, especially with having their periods, a recent development for the first speaker: "I resent having to tell resident staff why I need to go to the pharmacy when I get my period. I feel that this is a private thing." Mary: "One time last year I was asked to prove that I had my period so I could go out. When I came to the staff room, there were three staff there; I felt that my body was public." Cindy: "Aaron told me that all the boys' washrooms have condoms, but we don't have Tampax machines in our washrooms. How come?" The group seemed struck by this comparison. Elizabeth: "I don't think that they respect the bodies of girls as much as boys. We should go together to the staff and demand that they install Tampax machines in all washrooms." Piran notes that this program of political resistance was carried through successfully. She is critical of unsuccessful didactic eating disorder prevention programs (Piran, 1995, 1997, 2001), in which adults do not listen to what girls have to say about their bodily experiences and what they need for healthy development. In this program, girls together developed a critical perspective on how they were individually feeling that their bodies were being mistreated by bringing this knowledge into relationship and resonance with other girls going through the same kinds of things. With support from adults, they were able to resist objectifying their bodies and denying their embodiment by making changes that resulted in diminished eating disorders in their schools.

CURRICULA OF DISEMBODIED SEXUALITY: LESSONS LEARNED AND RESISTED

The twinned lure of romance and threat of a bad reputation dominate the stories that many adolescent girls tell about their experiences with sexuality. They do not speak spontaneously about their experiences with their sexual feelings or their experiences with particular sexual behaviors. Reflecting the legitimated ways in which girls can approach relationships that involve sexual feelings or attraction, romance is the dominant discourse of how younger girls speak about their relationships. Linda Christian-Smith (1990) identified in an analysis of romance novels—which are the mainstay of many adolescent girls' reading diet—what she called the "code of romance": that romance is "a transforming experience giving meaning to heroines' lives and endowing heroines with prestige and is about the dominance of men and the subordination of women" (p. 17). Often, when girls have been asked to talk about their experiences with sexuality and relationships, they narrate their enactments of this code.

In interviews with 400 girls from racially, ethnically, socioeconomically diverse backgrounds and sexual identities (S. Thompson, 1990, 1992, 1995; Sharon Thompson observed that White, working-class heterosexual girls organize their relationships and their lives around what she calls "the quest romance." Among the heterosexual girls whom she interviewed, she heard "the same old story" of sexual progress and male pressure, of these girls trying to hold onto what they had to trade—their virginity—for a man who would ultimately marry and protect them and provide the life for which they hoped (Thompson, 1990, 1992). She observed that in this "bargain," girls may gamble for commitment in having sex with the hopes that they are found "worthy," enacting the construction of their bodies as sexual objects for the approval and enjoyment of boys who are romanticized rather than desired. Their expectations were not associated with sexual pleasure but with winning the lottery for a committed relationship. This same pattern was less audible in the narratives told to her by lesbian girls, perhaps because they must develop relationships in spite of and in opposition to this heterosexual script. Thompson noted that it was extremely rare for a teenage girl to tell a story about wanting to go further sexually than her partner, and nonexistent for White working-class girls.

K. Martin (1996) found that the girls in her study were "immersed in romantic culture" (p. 61). She theorizes that "many girls, especially working-class girls, find ideal love to be the only route (although often an alienated one) to attaining agency and sexual subjectivity, and it has a particularly strong force in girls' heterosexual relationships at this age" (p. 63). Girls told stories of ideal love in which the boy was the hero, stories stuffed with exquisite (or excruciating) detail, stories that Martin describes as "polished," as if they had been told and retold. For instance, one girl describes what she herself called a "fairy tale sort of story": "He's in the Marine Corps. . . . He's wonderful. . . . He's very secretive about his feelings. I've just started tapping into them myself. He'll do anything to help anyone out. . . . We communicate really good. He can mumble on about something for five minutes and someone else would be truly lost but I know exactly what he's talking about" (p. 63).

This association between conventional femininity and idealized romance that K. Martin found among older adolescent women has been identified and explored among younger girls as well. Tolman (1999b) conducted a study of early adolescent sexual health in which 148 White and Latina poor, working-class, and middle-class girls were surveyed about their sexual experiences and perspectives, and how conventional their beliefs about femininity were. She found a positive relationship between girls' conventional femininity ideology and the conventionality of their beliefs about romance. In interviews with 46 of these girls, some articulated their resistance to complying with conventions that render them passive or position them as potential victims of male sexuality. For example, one 13-year-old Latina described her resistance to being objectified and mistreated: "You need to worry what your breast size are. How your butt is formed. . . . First it's like the way you act around them [boys], then it's your body, and THEN comes like what's inside. . . . I don't like that. . . . I was straight up with my boyfriend. . . . I was like, 'If you think you're gonna be going on like from me to another girl and then another girl and stuff, you must be buggin', cause it ain't gonna be like that with me'" (p. 136).

In their middle school ethnography, Eder and her colleagues (1995) found that the young adolescent girls simultaneously performed, aspired to, and mocked very stereotypical gendered behavior by engaging in alternative behaviors; one girl explained to another: "You're not supposed to go (voice in a high lilt) 'Oh Jimmy'; you're supposed to go (with a blatantly sexual emphasis) 'Oh Jimmy,' after which she leaned back, clapped her hands, and laughed giddily" (p. 140). Eder et al. observed that the working-class girls in their study were willing to mock crying or whining or being sexually aggressive in their public peer interactions, though their teasing was dominated more by romantic than sexual themes. The authors noted the contradiction between working-class girls being more willing to talk about sexual themes in middle school and the increasingly traditional quality of their experiences as they moved into and through adolescence. They concluded that "mocking romantic messages alone is not enough to alter current patterns of gender domination. It is essential that girls also challenge social messages about female sexuality and even more essential that boys also begin to modify their sexual attitudes" (p. 146).

However, the constant fear of getting a bad reputation colors, contours, and constrains girls' experimentation with romantic relationships, as well as with their appearance and their friendships. In spending a year with eighth-graders at two California public schools, one primarily White and middle class, and one primarily African American and Latina, and working class. Peggy Orenstein (1994) listened to girls narrate, unaware, the hidden curriculum of their bodies. Among the White and Latina girls, she observed how the interlocking and contradictory constructions of girls' bodies as sexual objects for the use of male needs and the controlling punishment of a bad reputation meted out to girls who did not stay within these boundaries impaired girls' developing sense of self. Both Orenstein and Eder et al. (1995) illustrated how the school day is imbued with these concerns for girls, and how girls are aware of and can speak about how little control they have over what is said about them and then is taken to be "reality."

Orenstein (1994) related "a typical story" from the White school, about Evie, who was in love with a boy in sixth and seventh grades. When he asked her to have sex with him, she said no, and he ignored her for the next 12 months. When she managed to get his attention again at the end of sixth grade, she said yes, not wanting to be rejected again. Orenstein explained that "in truth, Evie didn't exactly say 'yes' . . . when he asked her over the phone if she would 'have sex' with him she was silent, and both of them interpreted her silence as consent" (p. 54). As the time neared, she began to fear that she would become a "slut" if she did have sex:

> I had thought girls like that were bad and terrible and they didn't give it a second thought . . . I think you're more pulled into it. It's not like you just decide to have sex; it's like you don't have a choice. You're so emotionally torn, you just say, "Do it, get it over with, nothing will happen." But socially, mentally, physically, something does happen. You change. Even your hairstyle changes. That girl [who in sixth grade would have sex with her boyfriend, and then he would drop her, who ended up in "a special school for troublemakers"] she'd had her hair back and pinned up and a happy face. Then suddenly it was down and across her face, over her eye. She started dressing in tight clothes, a tank top pulled down so it's low in front and high in back—one of those cropped tops. She'd lay on the grass on her belly and put her chin on her hand so the guys could see her breasts. It was dramatic: her whole opinion of herself changed and everyone else's opinion of her changed, too. . . . *Her* life changed, but the guy, he's still in school. He's popular. It didn't damage his image, just hers. . . . In my dreams, that's what happens to me. (p. 54)

After she decided not to have sex, the expected rejection occurred: "Even though I didn't actually do it, I feel like a total slut inside. I feel like a slut for considering it. It damaged my personality and my opinion of myself" (p. 54). Orenstein observed that "at thirteen, just as she is awakening to her own sexuality, she has learned she must suppress it immediately; she has learned, in fact, to convert it into feelings of disgust, and to make girls who express sexuality into untouchable 'sluts'" (pp. 54–55).

Comparing the girls at the two schools, Orenstein noted that while the White girls were worried about ruining their reputations yet sought to "lose themselves in love" anyway, academic-minded girls of color "view relationships with apprehension" (p. 238), the fear of losing their dreams of success outweighing their concern with their reputations. Other girls were aware of and internalized their parents' fear and anxiety in response to their maturing bodies. Marta, a Latina girl at the second school, was "reduced" to her sexuality by her parents, "using safety as their justification" (p. 203). Marta observed that her brothers were taught to have a "right to self determination," while she learned that for her, entering womanhood was "circumscribed by peril and repression" (p. 203). Marta said that she did not want to be a "little saint . . . I want to be how I am. I don't know how I am but that's what I want to be" (p. 204). Crying, she explained that "my dad used to be so different . . . he used to hardly even pay attention to me. Now he thinks I'll get pregnant, so he's after me all the time to stay away from boys . . . you're going to be a *puta*" (p. 204). Orenstein noted that the only kind of sexual encounter Marta could imagine is rape.

In studies with older adolescents, poor girls and girls of color do voice a fear of getting a reputation (i.e., Tolman, 1994a, 1994b, 1996), as sexual experiences become a more pervasive aspect of the majority of adolescents' lives. Girls from diverse cultural backgrounds, and their parents, voice concerns about preserving girls' reputations. In a focus group study of racially/culturally diverse (Black, Latina, Portuguese, Vietnamese, Haitian, White) male and female adolescents' and their parents' views of adolescent sexuality, Ward and J.M. Taylor (1992) found that the only theme to arise in every group they conducted was "the double standard," and the resulting problem of girls having to worry about getting a bad reputation. Potential consequences ranged from being thought of as "damaged goods" and thus less likely to be able to form relationships with peers, boys and girls, to bringing dishonor to the family and/or the community.

In her study of older adolescent girls in the UK, Sue Lees (1993) found that the most common response of girls to the constant onslaught of sexual insults and negative labels was to deny being a "slag," or in U.S. terms, a "slut." She observed not only what these girls said but also how they did not challenge the double standard that anchors the concept that girls can be categorized as bad girls or "whores." Some girls tried to ignore such comments or boys altogether, choosing to just accept such behavior and try not to take it seriously; others tried to call boys names in retaliation (a difficult task because there is no negative construction of boys' promiscuity). Such attempts put girls at risk for being labeled sluts just for asserting their thoughts and feelings. Some girls in Lees's study were becoming aware of the sexist nature of sexual labeling and of the implied double standard and were beginning to question its legitimacy in privileging boys and disenfranchising them. J. Holland, Ramazanoglu, and Thomson (1996) observed how young women became aware of the double standard and then were able to describe how fear of getting a sexual reputation produces conformity with "normative" female sexuality: "With girls you're brought up to be ladylike, because if you start being rampant you're called a slag or a slut or whatever, but with boys they can get away with anything, like they won't get called no major names, they just get called Casanova and things like that, but that's not really going to hurt them, like if a girl gets called a slag" (p. 242).

In such studies, girls rarely spoke of having resisted or even of feeling able to resist humiliating and often destructive sexual labeling. Girls can be labeled "whores" based solely on what someone considered an "overly sexual" appearance (Eder et al., 1995, p. 129). Eder et al. observed how difficult it was for girls to challenge sexual insults, but noted two instances where one sixth-grade girl was able to resist negative sexual labelling. Andrea, a large and strong girl who possessed particularly well-honed verbal skills, humor, and intelligence, was collecting money for a candy sale, when a former boyfriend called her a prostitute for collecting money. She responded by saying she "wasn't that low and wasn't that cheap." When he replied, "I don't owe you anything. You enjoyed it, didn't you?" and gave her a nickel, she retorted, "Well, I'm not that cheap." She also told her friends a story about "how a guy down the street from her . . . called her a bitch.

She had responded by punching him in the stomach and said he claimed he threw up on the way home because she had punched him so hard" (p. 135). Whether they capitulate to or resist the cultural story that gives sexuality to boys and romance and relationships to girls (Tolman, 1996), when they speak about their experience, the reality of sexual objectification is a "contrapuntal theme" (Gilligan, 1982) that weaves through how girls describe the course they steer through the rough seas of compulsory heterosexuality.

In the recently published report, *Voices of a Generation: Teenage Girls on Sex, School, and Self* (Haag, 1999) sponsored by the American Association of University Women (AAUW), girls illustrated how intertwined with their experiences of schooling such concerns about and experiences with a "bad" reputation were, and how these concerns contour the constant barrage of sexual harassment that they report having to deal with in school. Diverse girls participated in more than 150 summits and small group discussions, and then answered a series of six open-ended survey questions about how to improve education for girls. Based on analysis of 730 questionnaires, the report documents how "a numbing litany of incidents in which peers, primarily boys, call girls 'bitches,' 'sluts' and 'whores' and boys make crude requests for sex" is entrenched in girls' experience of school. They are "'policed'" in two divergent directions: boys push for sex and then punish both girls who comply and girls who resist. Girls made a "plea for schools to improve relations between the sexes" (p. 25).

Consistent with reports by Nan Stein (1999; N. Stein, Marshall, & Tropp, 1993), who listened to girls voice their educational experiences, the girls in this AAUW report said that they are aware of and desperate to dismantle what has been called a "culture of sexual harassment" in school (V.E. Lee, Croninger, Linn, & Chen, 1996). Such harassment is grounded in girls' vulnerability to bad reputations, and then having their sexual objectification narrated and operationalized in school hallways (Larkin, 1994; N. Stein, 1991, 1999; N. Stein et al., 1993). Sexual harassment produces not only a psychologically and even physically unsafe learning environment, but also can initiate and contribute to a girl's diminished sense of self (see Gutek & Done, this volume). As one girl noted in this AAUW report, "Someone said that I was a slut. You always try to pretend that what people say about you doesn't affect you, but it does. You slowly start to believe what's being said about you" (Haag, 1999, p. 23). Girls report consistently that sexual harassment in schools is everywhere. N. Stein and her colleagues (1993) conducted a survey of sexual harassment in schools through *Seventeen* magazine. Open-ended questions followed survey items to invite girls to describe their experiences; this survey elicited responses from over 4,000 girls, age 9 to 19. These young women, from diverse backgrounds and across the nation, described not only being harassed but the lack of response from teachers and administrators, even when they decided to speak up. But girls also reported that they were not simply passive recipients of unwanted and untoward behavior by boys and did in fact react to sexual harassment in ways that were designed to make it stop. However, they reported that their individual efforts were fruitless in the wake of adults' failure to do anything about observed harassment or complaints by girls. A White 14-year-old wrote: "I was in class and the teacher was looking right at me when this guy grabbed my butt. The teacher saw it happen. I slapped the boy and told him not to do that. My teacher didn't say anything and looked away and went on with the lesson like nothing out of the ordinary had happened . . . most of all, I felt really bad about myself because it made me feel slutty and cheap. It made me feel mad, too, because we shouldn't have to put up with that stuff, but no one will do anything to stop it. . . . it happens so much it almost seems normal" (Stein, 1995, p. 146). A Mexican American 12-year-old illustrated the oppressive and punitive quality of some sexual harassment that occurs in classrooms and hallways: "In my case there were two or three boys touching me, and trust me, they were big boys. And I'd tell them to stop but they wouldn't! This went on for about six months until finally I was in (one) of my classes in the back of the room minding my own business when all of them came back and backed me into a corner and started touching me all over. So I went running out of the room and the teacher yelled at me and I had to stay in my seat for the rest of class" (N. Stein et al., 1993, p. 10a).

Some girls have been able to resist such harassment effectively when the adults in their lives believed them and demanded that the problem be ameliorated. In some cases, adults have utilized the legal system on behalf of girls (as well as gay boys) to force schools to acknowledge and not tolerate sexual harassment through the threat of liability (N. Stein, 1999). Listening to girls voice their experiences and perspectives on such sexual harassment forces us to acknowledge that it exists, and to hear what the experience of harassment is like for them. It also illuminates how authorities' lack of response legitimates such harassment, which girls (and boys) observe, thereby failing to challenge or offer alternatives to the curriculum of girls' bodies organized by compulsory heterosexuality (see also Larkin, 1994).

Framed by compulsory heterosexuality, sexual harassers often use homosexual labeling as a form of denigration, as well as to target adolescents (male and female) who are thought to be gay or lesbian for harassment (Boxer, Cook, & Herdt, 1999; Eder et al., 1995; Friend, 1993). In an analysis of gay and lesbian adolescents' narratives about their experiences in school, Richard Friend relayed the experience of Gail, a lesbian "survivor," who ultimately graduated from high school in an environment that "attempted to silence [her] voice" (p. 210): "I'm 17 and a senior in high school. I'm not 'out' to everyone at school, but I am to most of my friends and my folks. My parents and friends have been terrific. A lot of my friends' reaction was 'oh, that figures.' I'm not out at school because it is potentially dangerous. Dangerous because I might get beat up, it would make life tough for my friends and because it would make it difficult to make new friends" (p. 200).

The voice of this lesbian "survivor" underscores the irony that adolescent girls' sexuality has actually been the target of much study, but defined almost exclusively in terms of heterosexual intercourse (S. Thompson, 1990; Tolman, 1994a). Lurking in this body of research is the implied perspective that girls' expression of their sexual feelings is not normative and that it is possible and necessary to separate the chaff of "bad girls" from the wheat of "good girls" to identify and characterize girls who have sex. Underpinning these studies is a romanticized and disembodied view of female adolescent sexuality. This view of adolescent girls is in fact the linchpin in how society organizes and regulates adolescent sexuality: Because boys are considered to have uncontrollable sexual urges, girls who want romance but not sexual experiences are necessary to keep adolescent sexuality under control (Fine, 1988; Tolman, 1994a, 1999a; Tolman & Higgins, 1996). Although much research has documented the timing and quantity of diverse girls' sexual behavior in relation to sexual intercourse, these questions and also these methods do not yield information about girls' experience of sexuality. This "partial" knowledge of female adolescent sexuality is not only the outcome of a methodological limitation, but also stems from inquiry that does not challenge conceptions of gender and the shaping role of the institution of heterosexuality in adolescent sexuality.[1]

In contrast, researchers who have thought or even wanted to ask girls about their experiences with their own sexuality and to listen to what they have to say are working within a feminist analysis of the education of girls' bodies. These researchers are committed to adolescent girls' right to and need for sexual subjectivity. Their perspective has generated questions and research contexts that have enabled girls to speak about an "unspeakable" part of their lives (Tolman, 1994b). For instance, when Sharon Thompson (1990, 1992, 1995) asked heterosexual girls to tell their stories about their experience of first (hetero)sexual intercourse, she found that this experience (which one girl described as "putting a big thing in a little hole") was rarely pleasurable (Thompson, 1990). Only a quarter of the heterosexual girls with whom she spoke talked about it in terms of pleasure: having expected and having had pleasure. These girls, whom she called

---

[1] For instance, the absence of resistant voices to conventional constructions of heterosexual relationships and sexuality in Martin's (1996) study is striking and stands in contrast to other feminist standpoint studies in which strains of girls' resistance were audible. We suggest that this study highlights and reflects the crucial importance of the questions that we ask girls and also boys to create "safe spaces" for them to voice what may be dangerous and counterhegemonic aspects of their experience. Martin's questions ("How did you/would you decide to have sex the first time? What happened? What do you think it will be like?"; p. 140) stayed squarely within the framework of institutionalized heterosexuality. As Tolman (1994a) has noted, it would be literally crazy for girls to volunteer information about their sexual desire or sexual pleasure without some assurance of safety; perhaps it is in part because Martin did not ask girls direct questions about sexual feelings that she heard consistently conventional stories of compliance with compulsory heterosexuality, especially among the middle-class girls in her sample. The onus is on researchers to invite and make it possible for adolescent girls to "say what they know" or to consider aspects of their sexuality and their bodies that they have come to understand as bad, taboo, or not normal—that is, to let girls know that we will hear and respect their resistance.

"pleasure narrators," had primarily White, middle-class, feminist mothers who talked to them in positive terms about female sexuality, enabling in their daughters a sense of entitlement to pleasure and desire and anchoring a resistance to the conventional terms of female sexuality that position them as passive and pleasing to male partners. In a later analysis of over 400 interviews with young women from across the United States who represent diverse racial, ethnic, and class backgrounds, and sexual orientations, Thompson (1995) found that adolescent girls narrated their romantic lives differently. These groups included "victims of love," girls who became teen mothers, "hell year" narrators, lesbian narrators, and girls who actively sought out adult lovers as a route to sexual experience. Each of these "genres" of storytelling involved girls speaking in distinct ways about how they related to their bodies and to others in their lives, and how they negotiated and experienced their sexuality. Two additional genres, popular narrators and successful girls, were grounded in girls' explicit and conscious orientation toward and understanding of their position in their educational worlds. For instance, Thompson noted how popular girls, who were exclusively middle class and White, "play[ed] the field," most often in the context of school and school events. They held relative power in relationships with boys in which they invested or actually felt very little; as one girl said, "I could just find another guy" (p. 62). Though they said they were having fun, Thompson noted that "they rarely described having it" (p. 75). These narrators tended to keep intimacy and sexual experience to a minimum. One girl who became involved with a college student outside of her school context broke up with him when he began initiating sexual intimacy. She described herself as having "the ability to 'build a wall' . . . I can put stops to feelings. . . . I consider it kind of a power that I have. . . . It does to a point where I feel that I'm in danger of being hurt. Or invaded. I can, I can make a wall. I can, I can stop it" (p. 64). Narrating her dissociation from her body and from her emotions, she sustained her status as a popular and desirable girl by refusing to risk the vulnerability that emotional and embodied feelings would bring, toppling the pedestal that a popular girl wants to and indeed must occupy.

Another question in Martin's study (see above) was whether there are gender differences in adolescents' experiences of sexual intercourse, agency, and sexual subjectivity, in part to answer the question of whether girls feel differently about their sexuality than boys do (K. Martin, 1996). Martin argues that "sexual subjectivity is a necessary component of agency and thus of self esteem. That is, one's sexuality affects her or his ability to act in the world, and to feel like she or he can 'will things and make them happen'" (p. 10). She found consistent compliance with traditional gender roles and norms of compulsory heterosexuality for both genders and both middle- and working-class groups. Martin argued for the importance of placing girls' voices in relation to what boys say. Boys reported that they were not supposed to reveal feelings of connection with girlfriends; as Scott, a working-class 18-year-old, explains, "I don't ever talk to my guy friends about my girlfriends except . . . well you never admit that you like her, never. You just say that she was a pain in the neck" (p. 71). In contrast, these girls framed their experiences in terms of romance and love, and working-class girls were even more oriented toward developing agency and sexual subjectivity through the route of ideal love. Their stories reflected romance and "magnified moments" (Hochschild, 1994, cited in K. Martin, 1996) rather than passion.

In high schools, adolescent sexuality is a palpable and often disquieting element of the school day (Tolman, 1994a), and the education of girls' bodies—both intended in classrooms and implicit in hallways—turns more explicitly toward sexuality. Sandra Kessler and her colleagues (1985) observed, "The gender regime of a high school is not an expression of sexual biology so much as a social means of dealing with it. . . . The result is a dialectic of biosocial development" (cited in Thorne, 1993, p. 138). In her now-classic article, "Sexuality, Schooling and Adolescent Females: The Missing Discourse of Desire," Michelle Fine (1988) offered an analysis of the debates over and content of sex education in public high schools, which occurs within and bolsters the gender-specific discipline of and against the body that Sandra Bartky (1990) has discussed. Fine found that girls encounter sex education organized by three discourses of adolescent sexuality: sexuality as violence, sexuality as victimization of girls, and sexuality as individual morality that demands that girls alone be responsible for maintaining premarital sexual abstinence. A fourth discourse, a discourse of desire—which Fine found essentially absent from socially condoned educational curricula—occasionally appeared as "an interruption of the ongoing conversation" (p. 36). Although rarely heard from authorities, Fine found that the low-income Latina and African American young women in her ethnography tried to introduce a discourse of female desire into their classes, which were organized around "superficial notions of male heterosexuality" (p. 36). These attempts were inevitably snuffed out by adults, conveying their own and society's ambivalence and anxiety about female adolescent sexuality. For example, Opal, a young Black woman, responded to her teacher's solicitation of topics for sex education by asking "What's an orgasm?" When the other students' laughter died down, the teacher offered a contradictory and confusing answer, in which not people but organs appear: "Sexual response, sensation all over the body. What's analogous to the male penis on the female?" A boy answered: "Clitoris." The teacher, who seemed to be trying to encourage the young women to become familiar with their own bodies, suggested that they "go home and look in the mirror . . . [because] it's yours." When the teacher then inquired why it is important for a girl to know "what your body looks like," Opal's response that "you should like your body" was immediately covered over by a warning that girls need to be able to recognize "problems like vaginal warts" (pp. 37–38).

Fine (1988) argued that in silencing a discourse of desire and positioning young women only as potential victims of male heterosexuality, "public schooling may actually disable young women in their negotiations as sexual subjects. Trained through and into positions of passivity and victimization, young women are currently educated away from positions of sexual self-interest" (p. 33). She outlines a genuine discourse of desire as an invitation for adolescents "to explore what feels good and bad, desirable and undesirable, grounded in experiences, needs, and limits. Such a discourse would release females from a position of receptivity, enable an analysis of the dialectics of victimization and pleasure, and would pose female adolescents as subjects of sexuality, initiators as well as negotiators" (p. 33).

Tolman's research has attended to the particulars of girls' discourse of desire, and several other studies also shed light on girls' desire in the United States (cf. Bartle, 1998; Boxer et al., 1999; Haag, 1999; Orenstein, 1994). She has focused her inquiry on whether and how girls can articulate their experiences of sexual desire and the place of their bodies in these experiences. In an in-depth qualitative study of 30 girls who were juniors in either an urban or a suburban public school, or participants in a gay and lesbian youth group, she asked explicit questions about their sexual feelings, inviting descriptions and narratives about sexual desire. These girls said that no adult had ever talked to them before about sexual desire and pleasure "like this"; more than half said they had never talked with anyone (Tolman, 1994a).

Although all but three of the girls reported that their own desire was part of their experience of their sexuality, speaking in an "erotic voice," a dilemma emerged in how these girls described their own desire and how they felt about and responded to these feelings: How is it possible for a girl to know about and respond to her own sexual feelings and still think of herself, and have others think of her, as a good, normal, and appropriate girl (Tolman, 1994a, 1994b, 1996)? Framed in these terms, this dilemma of desire is securely located in compulsory heterosexuality, straining and undermining girls' relationships with themselves and their own bodies, with boyfriends or girlfriends, with peers, family, and community—although these girls, with some notable exceptions, understood this "problem" as simply the way things are. As one girl in the AAUW report complained: "I wish that every girl who enjoys her sexuality was not considered slutty, and dirty. I wish that all the girls could walk around all schools with all the pride as guys have" (Haag, 1999, p. 27). The narratives told by girls in Tolman's study describe individual solutions to what is in fact a social problem, such as trying to hide their desire by drinking to be able to "blame it on the alcohol," or having "my mind tell my body no" and "not dancing reggae" to avoid getting aroused. Some girls managed to construct their desire within the cultural stories of male and female sexuality (Tolman, 1996), such as by feigning resistance to a boy's advances to cover her own desire with his.

Differences between the experiences of urban and suburban girls were audible. When the urban girls described how they responded to their own desire, themes of self-control, caution, and conflict were most evident; these girls made and fronted explicit connections between their own desire and danger. In contrast, the suburban girls spoke frequently about sexual curiosity, which competed and contrasted with their anxiety about controlling themselves when they felt desire. These girls rarely spoke of their desire in terms of material or social danger; they voiced an internal conflict between what they were feeling in their bodies and their internalized conception of passive female sexuality and appropriate female sexual behavior (Tolman, 1994b).

Some girls solved this dilemma with "silent bodies"; that is, they said that they did not experience sexual desire or feelings. Girls' dissociation from their bodily feelings leaves them vulnerable not only psychologically, but also in the eyes of the law (Tolman & Higgins, 1996). Jenny, one of the three girls in the study who reported not feeling desire, offered a description of her first time having sexual intercourse, about which she was confused. In telling her story, she said first, "I just, I sort of let it happen to me and never really like said no, I don't want to do this. I mean, I said no, but I never, I mean I never stopped him . . . I mean, he wasn't, he's not the type of person who would like rape me or whatever" (p. 213). Because Jenny did not have her own desire to inform her sexual experience, it was hard for her to know whether or not she was raped. Such confusion, which is a direct result of an absence of desire, diminishes young women's chances of making a legally defensible claim of rape. In contrast, very few girls in the study described their critique of and resistance to the double standard. Paulina, a recent immigrant from Eastern Europe, voiced a sense of entitlement to her sexual desire which served her well in her ability to make active sexual decisions, to have pleasurable and desired sexual experiences, and to know when she was being violated: "And he just like kept touching me, and I was just like, just get off me. He goes, you know that you want to, and I said no I don't. Get off me, I hate you" (p. 220).

In response to this dilemma of desire, most of these girls struggled either to stay in connection with their bodies or to disconnect from their bodies, with little awareness of institutionalized and, in most cases, internalized constructions of femininity, passive female sexuality, and "appropriate" gender relations. Ellen, an African American 17-year-old, understood her own desire as dangerous because it could threaten her educational aspirations. Ellen said she felt desire rarely; when she did so, it caused her distress. In describing an experience when a boy she liked kissed her, she said "I didn't want it to happen . . . kissing or whatever, my feelings, cause, you know . . . I'm afraid that, you know, liking the person so much, or maybe something will happen . . . that I might act upon it" (Tolman, 1996, p. 262). Ellen's fear about her sexuality is similar to that recounted by some of the girls of color in other studies who were trying to achieve academically (cf. Orenstein, 1994). Poor girls and girls of color often feel pressure to choose between their education and their sexuality, whereas White middle-class girls do not experience their sexuality as such a threat because safety nets, such as access to and information about contraception, are readily available to them (Tolman, 1996).

Lesbian sexuality is not without its dangers for adolescent girls. Melissa, one of three lesbian and bisexual girls in the study, was 16 years old and out at school and to her family. Yet she was very aware of how her sexual feelings made her vulnerable to harm, in particular other girls' anger or physical violence, because her desire violated the norms of compulsory heterosexuality. She managed these well-grounded fears by attempting to restrain her desire: "Whenever I start, I feel like I can't help looking at someone for more than a few seconds, and I keep, and I feel like I have to make myself not, stare at them or something" (Tolman, 1994a, p. 336). The constraints within which Melissa explored her desire affected her friendships with other girls and her attempts to make sense of her relationship with a new girlfriend. Through the course of her interview, by talking about sexual desire explicitly, Melissa began to untangle the different kinds of desires she felt and did not feel in this relationship. In another interview-based study of 202 (55 female) culturally diverse 14- to 21-year-olds participating in a gay and lesbian youth group, Boxer et al. (1999) found that, compared to the majority of the males, coming out was not a positive experience for more than half of the females. All of the girls reported that there was someone from whom they had to hide their sexual identity. They reported that teachers were not perceived as a source of support or protection.

When talking about their own experiences with sexuality, it is not surprising that some girls described experiences of sexual violence and/or abuse; in Tolman's study (Tolman, 1994a, 1994b; Tolman & Szalacha, 1999), a third of the girls did so (see also Tolman, 2000). In her study of young women living in poverty, Lisa Dodson (1998) heard African Americans and Latinas describe early sexualization and prevalent sexual abuse. These young women reported that sexual abuse made girls especially vulnerable to the persistent predatory male behavior that was part of the landscape of their lives, calling them "craving girls" (p. 62). One report on teen mothers conveyed how girls (in diaries and letters that were written as part of prevention programs) described persistent sexual abuse, such as "Still today I have problems with this terrible thing which has happened to me. . . . I was abused when I was five and believe me I'm seventeen years old today and I still carry the memory, hurt, and guilt with me" (Musick, 1993, p. 76).

A quantitative analysis of girls' desire narratives in Tolman's study revealed an interaction between girls' social location (urban or suburban) and reports of sexual violation or abuse in predicting how they experienced their own sexual desire (predominantly pleasurable, predominantly vulnerable, or neither); based on this analysis, the authors conducted another voice-based analysis of these girls' desire narratives (Tolman & Szalacha, 1999). They found a pocket of resilience among some of the urban girls who had reported sexual violence or abuse. Resonating with suburban girls who had not had such experiences, some of these girls described explicitly their conscious resistance to having "silent bodies." For instance, Barbara, a White 16-year-old, described her fight for sexual subjectivity in the wake of having been molested for years as a young girl: "I wanted to be able to feel pleasure . . . cause in the back of my mind, I knew that I couldn't just go on being this way, cause if I got married, I was never going to enjoy it. And I wanted to be able to enjoy it. And so I worked upon it myself a lot" (p. 32).

Researchers outside of the United States have also documented the complexity and frequent dangers associated with girls' active sexuality and desire. Janet Holland and her colleagues in the Women, Risk and AIDS Project (WRAP) collected accounts about heterosexual relationships from 150 young British women, age 16 to 21, from diverse cultural and class backgrounds. They documented girls' strategies for negotiating safer sex and obstacles to girls making safer choices (J. Holland, Ramazanoglu, Scott, Sharpe, & Thomson, 1991, 1992a, 1992b; J. Holland, Ramazanoglu, Scott, & Thomson, 1990; J. Holland, Ramazanoglu, Sharpe, & Thomson, 1992, 1994; J. Holland et al., 1996). They report "overwhelming documentation" of inequalities of power in sexual relationships and sexual experiences that are organized around boys' needs, desires, and interests in conjunction with an absence of a positive conception of female sexuality. Like U.S. girls, these young women virtually never mentioned their own bodily feelings.

J. Holland and her colleagues (1994) specifically identified "femininity" as "an unsafe sexual strategy" (p. 23). In these narratives, they heard girls describe the double bind of needing to take initiative in sexual situations to protect themselves (asking a young man to use a condom), which requires that they admit that they are being actively sexual, while wanting to maintain a sense of themselves as feminine, which requires sexual passivity and (at least the appearance of) sexual inexperience. In listening to this diverse group of heterosexual young women, they noted that girls' sexual subjectivity is contextualized by a spectrum of male coercion, ranging from verbal sexual persuasion ("It wasn't sort of physical, I mean, but in a way it was sort of like mental"; J. Holland et al., 1992a, p. 655), to verbal sexual pressure ("He was . . . older, he was very very persuasive and very pushy, and I was so frightened of him at the time that you don't want to say no"; p. 656), to physical sexual pressure, primarily intimidation ("He told me, 'whatever I do, don't say no, just say yes' and . . . 'you have to say yes, you have to listen to me.' . . . I was scared. . . . But every time I pushed him, he pulled my hair"; pp. 657–658) or the use or threat of force, in which young women described abusive relationships and being raped.

The WRAP collaborative concluded that young women may be "very active in resisting men's power, but their resistance may not necessarily be effective" (J. Holland, Ramazanoglu, & Scott, 1990, p. 354). They contend that, to diminish their risk, young women need to be empowered to construct a positive conception of female sexuality, both intellectually and in their practices. They observed young women's reports of the constant threat of male violence as a key deterrent to such empowerment and that "the effectiveness of health education for women will depend on the effectiveness of education for men" (p. 354).

VOICE PRAXIS: HOME PLACES AND SOME REFLECTIONS ON RESEARCH

Before we offer some final reflections, we want to remind the reader of the limited scope of this review of adolescent voices. Voice-based research is, we are excited to report, a growing approach to research on/of/into adolescence. A recent and crucial development is researchers who are turning and tuning their ears to boys' experiences of development, in the context of constructions of masculinity, which also pose dilemmas and constrain the humanity of young men of diverse backgrounds (i.e., H. Pinderhughes, 1997; Pollack, 1998; Way, 1998; Weis, 1993). Voice-based research has produced a deeper and more nuanced understanding of both female and male adolescents' experiences, including, for example, friendship (i.e., Way, 1998; Way & Pahl, 1999), schooling and dropping out (Fine, 1991; Fordham, 1996; Stevenson & Ellsworth, 1993), and cultural identity development (i.e., Jones, 2001; McGann, 1999; Nagata, 1999; H. Pinderhughes, 1997; Romero, 1999; Xiong & Tatum, 1999).

In conclusion, we note that listening to adolescent girls' voices has enabled a nuanced understanding of how conceptions, internalization, and enactments of conventional femininity leave out or even push out girls' experiences and their bodies as a source of knowledge. This body of research provides evidence of how some young women are undermined and compromised when their own realities are shoved under the carpet of femininity, as well as how others resist these particularly diminishing aspects of growing up female. In conclusion, we discuss possible ways of strengthening and "joining" these pockets of resistance (Gilligan, 1991) suggested by this research.

A thread that weaves through this chapter is the context of schooling, in which adolescent girls' voices develop, are nurtured, and are suppressed. In particular, possibilities for resisting the "(miss)education" of girls' bodies punctuate this scholarship. Sharon Thompson (1990) has argued for "erotic education" (p. 357). The obligation to educate young women about their entitlement to pleasure in the context of the reality of danger is a logical conclusion of listening to young women speak about their sexuality (Fine, 1988; Thomson & J. Holland, 1994; Tolman, 1994a, 1994b). As a 14-year-old in the AAUW report astutely remarks, schools should "educate everyone that there are other ways of showing affection besides sex" (Haag, 1999, p. 26). Many of girls' descriptions and recommendations in this most recent AAUW report seek adult recognition that girls are sexual subjects and that an array of social, cultural, and media pressures complicate the seemingly straightforward act of "just saying no."

Throughout this chapter, instances of girls' resistance have most often been individual and oriented toward survival in nature, as if they are throwing water on small bush fires while the flames of the forest fire continue to rage around them. Yet girls' and women's groups can offer "insular home places," both in schools and in communities, that can engage young women (separately, as well as with young men) (cf. Pastor et al., 1996). The key feature of such efforts is the desire to listen to young women and to encourage them to listen to one another, in and through the real barriers and difficulties that may separate them or have positioned them at odds with one another. This body of research indicates the importance of encouraging and supporting girls in the collective work of "resistance for liberation" and creating ways to see the shortcomings of the individual strategy of "resistance for survival" (T. Robinson & Ward, 1991).

In particular, these scholars illustrate how even one woman can make a difference in the lives of young women by listening to them and "backing them up." Niva Piran's (2001) participatory action project created spaces where girls could tell and share with each other the truth of their experiences with their bodies and the institutionalized harm they realized was part of their school. With Piran's commitment to help them, they were able to make changes in their school that supported their health and that reflected their perspectives. In L.M. Brown's (1998) research, one teacher brought girls together to give voice and also credibility to their understanding and experience of working-class constructs of femininity, which were so often at odds with the school's expectations of them. S. Thompson (1990) identified her small group of "pleasure narrators" of first intercourse as young women whose mothers had told them about female sexual pleasure, recalibrating their expectations for desire, enjoyment, and entitlement to an embodied active sexuality. In Tolman's research, simply giving voice to an aspect of girls' experience that is not supposed to exist or have legitimacy created an opportunity for young women to consider, construct, and name their embodiment—or to question its absence (cf. Tolman, 1994b, 1996, 2000). Catherine Steiner-Adair's (1990, 1991) research and practice paves the way for how feminist therapists, whose very task is to listen, can notice girls speaking with and through their bodies about parts of their lives that otherwise may not seem possible to voice. There is currently a cottage industry of popular books that collect and distribute girls' voices to convey the various meanings of female adolescence; though some of these anthologies work within and reify stereotypic portrayals of growing up female (Shandler, 1999), other volumes are anchored in resistance to such constructs (Carlip, 1995), and incite and invite girls' resistance, by interrupting silences, interweaving girls' real questions and observations with much-needed— and usually much-withheld—information (Drill, McDonald, & Odes, 1999).

If we believe that girls' resistance and social critique are responses to the intensification of cultural expectations and social regulation of them at adolescence, then voice-based research provides us a way to appreciate the impact of these expectations and how they do—and do not—become part of girls' identities and the meanings they make of their experiences. Simply asking or inviting girls to speak about their experiences is necessary but not sufficient. The work of researchers who have listened to adolescent girls resonating resistance marks the importance of asking questions that interrupt the seamless sense of reality associated with powerful conventions of femininity and romance, as well as the struggle to hear girls' voices through, in spite of, and because of one's own experiences of giving in, giving up, refusing, and resisting.

CHAPTER 10

Current Perspectives on Women's Adult Roles: Work, Family, and Life

LUCIA ALBINO GILBERT and JILL RADER

Gender theories and processes provide a critical framework for considerations of occupational work and family life. Participation in a culture also includes participation in the stories or discourses of that culture. Patriarchal power rests on the social meanings given to biological sex differences and to their reproduction as societal discourses. These power relations take many forms, from the sexual division of labor, to the structure of work, to the social organization of procreation, to internalized norms of femininity and masculinity. Thus, central to visions of women's adult roles are discourses about what it means to be a woman or a man—what is thinkable, what is possible, and what is doable. Such discourses are culturally specific and vary across cultures and time periods.

This chapter illuminates how the active processes of reproducing gender through societal discourses and structures influence normative developmental processes and participation in adult roles. We are in agreement with Unger (1998) that there cannot be any real progress in research and policy if "resisting gender" is the modus operandi. We first provide a bit of recent history and then present contemporary theories of gender. We then use these theories and perspectives to frame the realities and issues for women's contemporary adult roles. We include in this discussion current facts on adult women and employed women in the United States. These facts and figures describe the broader social context of women's adult roles today. We next discuss, in some detail, paradigms used to study women's work and family roles. Finally, we draw some overall conclusions. It is important to note that much of the research detailed in the chapter is grounded in the assumptions of a predominantly Western European, White, middle-class culture.

Our focus is largely on the combining of life roles both by individuals and by partners. Because of space limitations, we say relatively little about important distinctions associated with race, class, and sexual orientation. Although considerations of gender often go across race and class lines, the organizational and social views of women and men, and the constraints and opportunities they envision, vary by race, class, and sexual orientation. Also, our conclusions are largely based on studies that did not necessarily include diverse populations or compare individuals by ethnicity, race, sexual orientation, or socioeconomic class when they were included in a study.

A BRIEF HISTORICAL PERSPECTIVE

Notions of the working woman are hardly new. Women have always worked, most often in low-paying jobs, moving in and out of the workplace and rearing children. These concepts of working women do not necessarily challenge traditional assumptions about a woman's place. In contrast, notions of women seeking equal pay and equal opportunity do challenge traditional assumptions—and these are concepts only recently embraced in the United States.

EMERGENCE OF THE DUAL-CAREER FAMILY

The term "dual-career family," first used in 1969 by researchers working in England, described what was considered to be an unusual and "revolutionary" type of dual-wage heterosexual family emerging as the result of complex social changes (Rapoport & Rapoport, 1969). Revolutionary from their perspective was the dual-career families' apparent inconsistency with respect to traditional notions of gender. In these families, the woman and man both pursued lifelong careers, relatively uninterrupted, and also established and developed a family life that often included children. Contrary to tradition, women in these families viewed their employment as salient to their self-concept and life goals and pursued occupational work regardless of their family situations. Male partners, in turn, appeared less defined by the traditional "good provider role" long associated with male privilege and power.

The acknowledgment of the dual-career family form rocked the foundation of traditional marriage, which tethered a woman's destiny to her fertility. Social changes had brought about an evolution in what was considered "normal" for adult women. Women's normative adult roles were broadened to include preparing for both family and occupational roles. Much less focus, however, was given to the impact of such changes on men's socialization and their preparation for family and occupational roles (L.A. Gilbert, 1985).

Researchers working in the United States during this time also recognized early on the restructuring of gender roles that was occurring and the profound implications of this transformation for individuals, family life, and the workplace. Jessie Bernard (1975) wrote of the momentous changes impacting the roles of wife and mother, and of the new societal forms that would be necessary for women to plan their lives with wider latitude. Rosabeth Moss Kanter's (1977b) groundbreaking report, *Work and Family in the United States: A Critical Review and Agenda for Research and Policy,* spoke of the many forces focusing attention on the dynamic intersections of work and family systems in contemporary American society. She provided clear evidence that work and family are interconnected—socially, economically, and psychologically—thus foreshadowing the next two decades of research. Moreover, she argued that occupational and family roles are more accurately depicted as converging and mutually enhancing, rather than as separate and in opposition. We will see that these opposing depictions of work and family—oppositional and competitive versus converging and mutually enhancing—form a significant theme in the years of research to come. Bernard and Kanter focused more on what was needed to accommodate the role changes for women than on what was needed to accommodate role changes for men (e.g., flextime and organizational change and job redesign), as both recognized the resistance to these changes within the conventional institutions of marriage and occupational work (e.g., Bernard, 1981). Here, too, their focus and concerns anticipated themes of the subsequent two decades of research.

CONTEMPORARY DUAL-WAGE FAMILIES

The notion of the dual-*career* family marked a significant shift in views of women's roles in England and the United States because it recognized women as engaging in influential occupational positions or *careers* that had historically been open only to men. The term career generally refers to those positions requiring special education and training and undertaken or engaged in as a lifework. Also significant is that the dual-career family form assumed that women who prepared themselves for careers did not necessarily leave their careers for marriage and children. Because the dual-career family form signaled profound social change, a good deal of research in the 1970s and 1980s studied the women and men in these families, a population that is quite educated, well-off economically, and, in the United States, predominately White.

As women in the 1980s and 1990s became increasingly recognized as economic providers for their families and as desiring equitable employment, studies of dual-career families broadened to studies of dual-wage or dual-earner families, and thus to more diverse populations. This shift in focus reflected both the broader range and variation in women's continuous employment—from jobs to careers—and a blurring of the distinction between jobs and careers. Historically, in comparison to careers, jobs involved less commitment to the work involved, required less training, paid less, and were more likely to lack clear developmental stages and accumulation of experience.

Today, jobs and careers are not necessarily differentiated by demands, commitments, and responsibilities. Moreover, how a person views her or his involvement in a career or job may or may not reflect that person's self-concept and life goals. Finally, compared to 1970, across various ethnic groups in the United States, women and men today marry later, are more likely to divorce, have fewer children, and change jobs associated with their occupational work more often (Sandfort & Hill, 1996; Steil, 1997). All these factors inform contemporary perspectives on women's adult roles.

GENDER AS A FRAMEWORK FOR WOMEN'S ADULT ROLES

> Our wont is to put up with things, with the notion that men behave in one manner, and women in another. You might say it is a little side show we put on for ourselves, a way of squinting at human behavior, a form of complicity. Only think of how we go around grinning and winking and nodding resignedly or shrugging with frank wonderment! Oh well, we say with a knowing lilt in our voice, that's a man for you. Or that's just the way women are. (C. Shields, 1994, p. 121)

C. Shields's (1994) observation in *The Stone Diaries* illustrates the formidable pressure we feel to conform to gender roles that seem polarized, arbitrary, and contrived. This conformity to gender roles is normative in our culture and is a largely unconscious process for men and women. Gender theories and perspectives provide a critical framework with which to examine and understand such experiences.

Traditional views of women and men have emphasized differences historically attributed to biological sex. Stereotypical beliefs about women's biology, for example, are believed to be at the root of discriminatory employment practices and the homogenization of women's abilities and roles (Albee & Perry, 1998; Ely, 1995; Gutek, 1986; Heilman, 1995; Hesson-McInnis & Fitzgerald, 1997; C. Sherif, 1979; Valian, 1998). However, women and men are not born with their respective genders. Rather, they learn how to become women and men via complex social processes that vary across cultures, within cultures (e.g., ethnicity and class) and across historical periods. Contemporary gender theories emphasize the cultural assumptions about the sexes and how they are reproduced in a society, rather than the physiological differences between men and women. Broadening explanatory models to incorporate gender perspectives enables researchers to identify and study contextual variables that shape women's and men's experiences. In addition, these broader perspectives help to counter conventional norms and practices, practices that attribute women's and men's challenges and successes at work or in their families to inherent sex differences (L.A. Gilbert & Scher, 1999; C. Shields, 1994).

In this section, we use the many "faces of gender" described by L.A. Gilbert (1994) and L.A. Gilbert and Scher (1999) to investigate gender processes that are particularly salient in the workplace and in the family. These "faces" include gender as difference, gender as structure, and gender as discourse and interactive process. Such conceptualizations illuminate how gender processes impact all levels of women's experiences.

GENDER OPERATING AS DIFFERENCE

In Myra Ferree's (1990) decade review of feminism and family research, she noted the importance of moving our thinking about gender away from gender differences, functionalist gender roles, and separate spheres for women and men. Historically, views about the nature of women and men have emerged from an opposite-sex model (Deaux & LaFrance, 1999; C. Sherif, 1979). Differences between men and women have been exaggerated, and they have been assumed to have few common attributes and abilities. Beliefs in such differences remain persistent even in the face of empirical evidence that challenges such beliefs. For example, findings from meta-analyses present females and males as having largely overlapping traits and abilities (Hyde, 1994a). Such research employs contemporary notions of gender to challenge the assumption that men and women are inherently different, an assumption underlying, for example, participation in family nurturing roles.

Gender operating as difference is ever present in our society and culture. A number of recent studies use the concept of family discourse to investigate the systematic structuring of social relations surrounding family responsibilities and the practices of women and men in dual-earner families (cf. L. Thompson & Walker, 1995). These studies are particularly useful in elucidating how partners recreate day-by-day dominant societal discourses about women's and men's different worlds. Cases in point are studies of discourse analysis by Blain (1994), L. Thompson (1991), and others that identified themes characteristic of spouses' talk in the area of family work. Consistent with the notion of gender operating as difference, themes that emerged to explain one's own behavior and the behavior of one's spouse typically relied on supposedly essential characteristics on which women and men differ and ignored the sociopolitical context of women's and men's lives.

Societal discourses perpetuate inequities between women and men at work and at home. The explanatory theme "individual choice," for example, assumes that all tasks are chosen freely by partners, an explanation that ignores the context of household and parenting tasks and the larger social context of power relations in marriage. The theme "differential abilities," also used by partners to explain who does what in a marriage, presents women as good at caretaking and men as more competent in pursuits outside the home. This explanation ignores the fact that the abilities of women and men are more similar than they are different. Finally, the theme "women naturally nurture" to explain how family tasks are divided reflects the view that it is necessary for mothers, but not fathers, to bond to their children to ensure a "secure attachment." This theme ignores the fact that research on bonding was inspired by the popular belief that women are inherently suited for motherhood; it is hence situated in ideology rather than scientific research (Eyer, 1992). Moreover, there is no evidence that men are not suited for infant and child care (Silverstein, 1996).

Gender as difference shows its "face" in the workplace in a variety of forms. Wage inequality, unfair hiring and promotion decisions, and differential expectations regarding child care responsibilities (e.g., who takes family leave or uses flextime) are just a few examples. According to 1998 data released by the U.S. Department of Labor, women's median weekly earnings are 76% of men's (U.S. Bureau of Labor Statistics, 1999), up from 59% in 1975 and 64% in 1983. Women working full time earn a median weekly salary of $456, compared to men's $598 (U.S. Bureau of Labor Statistics, 1999). Wage inequities by sex are maintained across different ethnic groups, as well, with women of color receiving the least compensation (see Figure 10.1).

Differences between male and female earning power are also maintained across educational levels. For example, male high school graduates earn more than women with associate's degrees, and men with associate's degrees out-earn women with bachelor's degrees (U.S. Bureau of Labor Statistics, 1999). Table 10.1 presents annual income differences by education level, according to 1994 data.

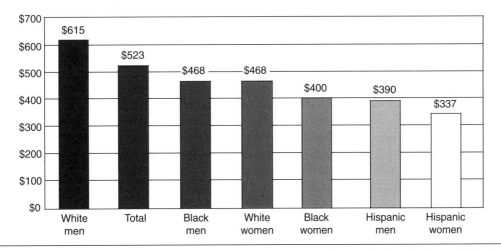

Figure 10.1 Median Usual Weekly Earnings of Full-Time Wage and Salary Workers by Sex and Ethnicity, 1998. *Source:* U.S. Department of Labor, 1999.

Table 10.1
Median Annual Income by Educational Attainment and Sex,
Year-Round, Full-Time Workers, 1994

Level of Education	Women	Men
9th to 12th grade (no diploma)	$15,133	$22,048
High school graduate	$20,373	$28,037
Some college (no degree)	$23,514	$32,279
Associate's degree	$25,940	$35,794
Bachelor's degree or more	$35,378	$49,228

Source: U.S. Department of Commerce, Bureau of the Census, 1994. *Income, Poverty, and Valuation of Noncash Benefits.*

Although men have more earning power across ethnic groups and educational levels, it is important to acknowledge that a sizable proportion of women today earn more than their spouse (Winkler, 1998). In fact, by 1993, more than 25% of wives earned hourly wages that were higher than those of their husband, and 20% of wives reported greater annual earnings than their husband (Winkler, 1998). It is estimated that women in dual-earner families contribute 40% of the family income. Furthermore, studies of wives' income and marital quality indicate that increases in wives' income do not significantly affect either spouses' perceptions of marital discord (e.g., S.J. Rogers, 1999).

Besides impacting salary decisions, notions of gender as difference influence how employers evaluate and promote female employees. In particular, sex stereotypes emphasizing differences between men and women play an important role in job performance ratings (Heilman, 1995). For example, empirical research suggests that men are evaluated more favorably than women on work performance ratings (A.H. Eagly, Makhijani, & Klonsky, 1992; Martell, 1991). Gender-based evaluations and perceptions have also been linked to glass-ceiling effects in corporate America (Frankforter, 1996).

In summary, gendered beliefs and discourses that women and men are inherently different have resulted in a multitude of workplace inequities. Studies indicate that one's internalized beliefs about gender roles are an important "hidden factor" explaining why employers promote women less than men, evaluate them less favorably on their work performance, and pay them lower salaries. At home, societal discourses perpetuate a sexual division of labor such that women are expected to assume a caretaking role and men are expected to focus their energies outside the family environment.

Gender Operating as a Structural and Organizing Factor

Carolyn Sherif (1982) argued that gender extends beyond the individual level to the social structure and operating "rules" of organizations. This assertion has been validated by investigations of formal and informal policies and laws and by current quantitative and qualitative research examining women's work experiences (J. Rosenberg, Perlstadt, & Phillips, 1993; R. Wright, 1996; Zuckerman, Cole, & Bruer, 1991).

A brief perusal of legislation over the past century illustrates the power associated with gender as an organizational force. Women were not granted the right to vote in the United States until 1920. Prior to the passage of the Pregnancy Discrimination Act in 1978, it was within an employer's right to fire women once they became pregnant. Other crucial U.S. legislation affecting adult women's roles was Title VII, which prohibited discrimination on the basis of sex, race, color, religion, or national origin with respect to compensation, terms, conditions, and privileges of employment, and which generally covered employers of 15 or more employees. The Family and Medical Leave Act (FMLA) was finally signed into law in 1993, after considerable resistance and debate about what this would mean to the traditional family and to corporate profit (Crampton & Mishra, 1995). The FMLA requires companies with 50 or more employees to allow up to 12 weeks of unpaid leave so that workers can care for newborn children or seriously ill family members. About 5% of all U.S. employers are covered by the law, and together they employ about 40% of all American workers.

Gender as structure is also apparent in the extent to which women are represented in certain occupations and among managerial levels. Many women and men still pursue careers that reflect traditional gender roles, and women as a sizable group continue to be employed in a far narrower range of occupations than men (Beck, 1998; J.W. Scott, 1982; Spain, 1988; U.S. Bureau of Labor Statistics, 1997). A large proportion of women are employed in female-dominated professions. Occupations most likely to be dominated by women include dental hygiene, nursing, secretarial work, prekindergarten and kindergarten teaching, and child care (U.S. Bureau of Labor Statistics, 1997). In 1995, for example, 93% of registered nurses and 84% of elementary school teachers were women, compared with 3 out of 10 computer system analysts and scientists, and fewer than 1 out of 10 engineers (Wooten, 1997).

In 1985, almost half of all working women were employed in female-dominated professions, according to the U.S. Department of Labor's Bureau of Labor Statistics (1997). By 1995, however, the proportion of women in female-dominated professions had dropped to 38%, indicating the movement of women into other fields. At the top business schools in the United States, women MBA students on average constitute 30% of the total. Women's share of employment in executive, administrative, and managerial positions increased more than 80% between 1975 and 1995, with women accounting for 40% to 60% of employees in most managerial fields. The most pronounced differences in occupational employment by sex are in precision production, craft, and repair occupations; in 1995 only 1% of auto mechanics and 1% of carpenters were women (U.S. Bureau of Labor Statistics, 1997). Thus, although occupational differences between women and men continue to decline, substantial differences still remain.

Some researchers theorize that the disproportionate representation of women in certain occupations may reflect the "masculine" nature of those fields. For example, R. Wright (1996) has explored how the "male culture" of the computing industry has created sex segregation within that field and discouraged women from continuing, or even pursuing, careers in technology. Wright also reports that the number of female computer workers, as well as women earning a bachelor's degree in computer science, has declined since the mid-1980s. Similar career disillusionment is evident among women MBAs and provides further support for the presence of gender as structure. Schneer and Reitman (1994) conducted a longitudinal study comparing male and female MBAs and found that although differences in women's and men's income and job satisfaction were negligible during the early phases of their respective careers, significant differences emerged by midcareer, with women earning less and reporting less satisfaction.

In addition, power and leadership positions in business organizations and academic institutions are still largely held by men (Rix, 1987; Valian, 1998). Sex segregation within organizations is particularly noticeable in male-dominated fields such as the natural sciences, computer technology, high finance, and law (Freeman, 1990; Wright, 1996; J. Rosenberg, Perlstadt, & Phillips, 1993; Zuckerman et al., 1991). A case in point is Fortune 500 companies. In 1996, only 10% of the 13,000 corporate officers at the Fortune 500 companies were women, up from 8.7% in 1994. Moreover, only 2% of the top wage earners in Fortune 500 companies were women, up from 1.2% in 1994. In addition, occupations dominated by women offer significantly lower starting wages in comparison to predominantly male professions (K.C. Duncan & Prus, 1992), and women in predominantly male occupations report being paid less than their male counterparts (Frieze, Olson, & Good, 1990).

Gender as structure also reveals itself in the rules and procedures that organizations implement to address the needs of its female and male employees. For example, a business's stance on sexual harassment affects how seriously the problem will be viewed by its employees. More specifically, organizations relying on more proactive approaches to combat the problem are more successful in reducing incidences of sexual harassment than those relying on more informal, "pass the word on" methods (Gruber, 1998). In summary, gender as structure poses challenges for adult women in such areas as vocational choice, advancement within organizations, and organizational policies (e.g., sanctions against sexual harassment, family leave).

Gender as structure also has a great deal to do with family policies provided by employers. Although the situation is improving somewhat, the United States does not provide the extensive day care that exists in other industrialized nations (Kamerman, 1991). Parents often create ways to combine work and family by using workplace family polices such as flextime, negotiating more flexible work schedules during preschool years, or working less-demanding jobs. Flexible work schedules are the most prevalent among work policies, with many companies offering flextime, part-time work (not always with benefits), and, to a lesser extent, job sharing, telecommuting, and a compressed work week. Other programs provided by employers include on- or near-site child care facilities, paternity leave, sick leave for dependent care, and flexible spending accounts.

Even when organizations respond to the needs of women and families, these responses can perpetuate cycles of inequity. For example, there is some evidence that work-family benefits are more geared toward women than men and that more women than men use existing work-family options (Pleck, 1996). In an illustrative study of 550 men from Wisconsin interviewed four months after becoming fathers, 78% responded that men should have a right to parental leave, 60% believed that the leave should be paid, and 51% believed that men should have the option of working part-time during the first month of the child's life (Hyde, Essex, & Horton, 1993). However, despite this fact, relatively few men use the benefits, although the numbers are increasing (Pleck, 1996). Most men use sick leave, vacation days, or other discretionary leave as a means to justify their absence, as opposed to formalized parental leave (Pleck, 1993). Factors that affect men's use of parental leave are the societal view that men should provide for families (Hyde et al., 1993) and employers' attitudes toward men who take leave (Pleck, 1988). Many men are implicitly and explicitly discouraged from taking leave, a practice that can greatly affect their willingness to utilize their rightful benefits.

As long as men continue to earn significantly more than women, it will make greater economic sense to families for the female partner to take leave, reduce her hours, or move to part-time work to ease the family situation. We thus perpetuate a situation in which women bring in the second income and do most of the caretaking and men progress in careers and control most of the power over social policy and legislation. Women's commitment to and rewards from occupational work would be limited and, in turn, so would be their leverage to challenge the gender structure of the workplace (Okin, 1989). Thus, rather than transcending traditional notions of gender and how they construct participation in family and career, we would be perpetuating them in slightly modified forms. A related concern is that we may be moving from husbands making decisions about wives' daily labor to employers and policymakers making decisions about women's and men's daily labor (C.A. Brown, 1987). That is, although individual families benefit when both spouses are actively involved in occupational work and family life, the structure of occupations and other societal institutions may work against these kinds of involvements.

GENDER OPERATING AS DISCOURSES AND INTERPERSONAL PROCESSES

Gender is also an interactive process that occurs in interpersonal, institutional, and societal contexts (Marecek, 1995a). As recent theorists have explained, gender does not reside within individuals; individuals construct or "do gender" within a social and cultural context (Bohan, 1993; L.A. Gilbert, 1994; West & Zimmerman, 1987).

Women and men are encouraged to act in ways deemed appropriate for their sex (B.M. Davis & Gilbert, 1989; Deaux, 1985; Ely, 1995; C. Sherif, 1982; Unger, 1990). Gender-related expectations, discourses, and interactions influence women and men from birth and play an important role in the development of their self-concept, behavioral repertoires, vocational choices, and possible selves. For example, gender processes affect girls' participation in math, science, engineering, and sports (AAUW, 1991; Eccles, Jacobs, & Harold, 1990; Valian, 1998).

Gender as an interactive process makes the workplace a very different place for women and men. For example, gendered beliefs about male entitlement and female sexuality contribute to working climates that condone sexual harassment (Fitzgerald, Drasgow, Hulin, & Gelfand, 1997; L.A. Gilbert, 1993; Gruber, 1998; Hesson-McInnis & Fitzgerald, 1997). Sexual harassment is a pervasive problem. In one investigation of 4,385 female government employees, more than 40% reported being sexually harassed within the prior two years (Hesson-McInnis & Fitzgerald, 1997).

Women working in male-dominated organizations or trades are most likely to experience sexual harassment (Gruber, 1998; Mansfield, Koch, Henderson, & Vicary, 1991). Research examining the psychological and professional impacts of sexual harassment is still in the early stages. One investigation that polled women in both private-sector and university jobs demonstrated that even low levels of sexual harassment have a significant negative impact on their psychological and occupational functioning, ranging from reduced job satisfaction to feelings of anxiety and depression (Fitzgerald et al., 1997; K.T. Schneider, Swan, & Fitzgerald, 1997).

Gender as interpersonal process is also apparent in how women conduct themselves at work. Working women report feeling pressured to conform to gender stereotypes to be successful in their careers, and that the use of these "gender management strategies" comes at a personal cost to them (Cassell & Walsh, 1997). Furthermore, both White women and women of color feel that they receive differential treatment at work in comparison to men (Weber & Higginbotham, 1997), and women as a whole report experiencing more discrimination on the job than do men (B.A. Browne, 1997). For instance, a qualitative study of women attorneys indicated that the small inequities of daily working life were a significant source of stress for 71% of respondents (Haslett & Lipman, 1997).

Virginia Woolf offered keen insights into how gender reproduces interactions between women and men. Women were described by Woolf as "providing men with looking glasses that possessed the magic and delicious power of reflecting the figure of man at twice its natural size" (1929/1957, p. 35). That is, women learn to interact with men in ways that preserve the societal view that men are stronger and more capable than women and that women play a crucial role in empowering men. Examples of such gender-producing interpersonal processes come from the current dual-earner literature on perceptions of fairness and equity in marriage.

Male partners may feel entitled to do less at home than their spouse, and many women may agree with that premise. This seemingly paradoxical finding likely reflects women's and men's different sense of personal entitlement about what they should put into and what they should obtain from marriage (Greenstein, 1996; Major, 1993). L. Thompson (1991) described how couples create within the family what she calls "a private culture," in which men get more credit than women for family provision through wage work, and women get less credit than men for family work. She found that this interactive process worked to undermine women's sense of entitlement for assistance with family responsibilities. Moreover, partners' expectancies can distort perceptions of attributions for entitlements, competencies, and interests (Blain, 1994; Sanchez & Kane, 1996; L. Thompson & Walker, 1989). Women, for example, may compare themselves with other women, rather than with their husbands, when making decisions about fairness. These many studies illuminate how personal entitlement not only is situated in societal norms about gender and the rights and roles of women and men, but also is played out and recreated in the day-to-day behaviors of spouses. Thus, employed women may do more of the child care and household chores than their male partner, and see this as fair because they view men's occupational success as being more important than women's (Steil, 1997).

To conclude, gender as an interactive process leads women and men to behave according to their proscribed roles, and this stereotypical behavior has deleterious effects on how women view and experience their work environments as well as their opportunities for advancement. Similar processes occur in family and marital contexts.

APPROACHES TO RESEARCH ON WOMEN'S ADULT ROLES

We are just beginning to know what we need to know. We are still handicapped by inadequate conceptualizations, models, paradigms, research techniques for finding the right questions to ask and ways to answer them. But we are learning. (Bernard, 1975, p. 1)

Since 1969, women's work/family role experiences have received a great deal of attention by researchers in a number of disciplines, most notably psychology, sociology, and organizational behavior. A particularly rich body of feminist research on housework and family work comes from the field of family studies within sociology (e.g., Sanchez, 1994; Sanchez & Kane, 1996; L. Thompson & Walker, 1995).

From a gender perspective, research on work and family roles can be viewed as falling into three somewhat distinct phases or paradigms: an early phase that we call women's role expansion, a later but continuing phase that we call multiple competing roles, and an emerging gender-informed phase that we call work-family convergence.

WOMEN'S ROLE EXPANSION

The 10-year period between 1975 and 1984 witnessed a dramatic increase in the labor force participation of women. The participation of women with children under age 18 increased from 47.3% in 1975 to 62.1% in 1985. For women with children under 6, participation rates increased from 38.8% in 1975 to 53.5% in 1985. Table 10.2 summarizes women's increasing participation in the labor force over the past three decades.

Because women's movement into the workforce was viewed as women's "expanding" their traditional role, questions were raised about the possible harm to women, and to their children and spouse, if they persisted in occupational work. Questions centered around how women could "do it all" and still minimize potential harm to their traditional responsibilities of caring for husbands and children. This phase assumed an essentialist model in which women were naturally suited to family work and were stretching themselves into male domains. Single-parent families were approached from a similar perspective.[1]

Implicit in the women's role expansion paradigm was that women's roles were changing but men's were not, and so women were expected to make any necessary accommodations. Close watch was kept on how women dealt with the stress of their "expanded role," how their children fared, and how happy their husbands were. Researchers, for example, looked for harm to children and compared children reared in traditional and dual-wage homes; however, results from the many studies conducted showed preschool-age children to be at no added risk if they received alternative child or day care instead of parental care for some portion of the day (Scarr & Eisenberg, 1993). It is important to note the implicit racism in such research. For example, by contrast, poor women—particularly poor women of color—have historically been expected to combine their work and child-rearing roles without considering the potential harm to their children.

MULTIPLE, COMPETING ROLES

The second phase, best characterized as gender-comparative, viewed women as engaging in "multiple roles." The proportion of women in the workforce had continued to increase (see Table 10.2). A woman's decision to pursue occupational work was viewed as "her right" as well as "her choice." Employed women in heterosexual families began to push for changes within the home and family, which in turn caused assumptions to change about how to arrange occupational work and family life. The earlier model of women's role expansion shifted to the more modern model of partner-sharing. This approach to work/family research, which is still quite prevalent today, poses such questions as: How much are men doing in the home compared to women? Do women and men cope in different ways? Are there gender differences in marital, occupational, or parenting satisfaction?

Within the multiple, competing roles perspective, women's decisions to pursue occupational work, although viewed as normative, are also viewed as causing conflict or requiring sacrifice. This almost exclusive focus on intraindividual conflict persists despite evidence first presented by Kanter (1977b) and later by Barnett and others, that many workers do not experience work-family conflicts and many report benefits of simultaneously meeting these various responsibilities (R.C. Barnett, 1998; R.C. Barnett & Rivers, 1996).

Many of these studies implicitly use a "gender as difference" atheoretical framework, although some do consider possible differences in the context of structural variables such as workplace

---

[1] The number of single mothers has remained constant at 9.8 million since 1995, but the number of single fathers has grown by 25% from 1.7 million to 2.1 million. Thus, men now constitute one-sixth of the nation's 11.9 million single parents (Work/Life Today, 1999).

Table 10.2
Population, Labor Force, and Labor Force Participation Rates of Women Age 16 Years
and Older by Age of Own Children, Selected Years, 1975–1996

Presence and Age of Own Children and Labor Force Status	1975	1980	1985	1990	1995	1996
Total women:						
Population	79,453	87,939	93,455	98,152	103,128	104,058
Labor force	36,496	44,934	50,891	56,138	60,538	61,229
Labor force participation rate	45.9	51.1	54.5	57.2	58.7	58.8
With children under 18:						
Population	30,597	31,456	32,295	33,262	35,413	35,194
Labor force	14,467	17,790	20,041	22,196	24,695	24,720
Labor force participation rate	47.3	56.6	62.1	66.7	69.7	70.2
With children 6–17:						
Population	16,182	17,489	16,929	17,123	18,721	18,679
Labor force	8,875	11,252	11,826	12,799	14,300	14,427
Labor force participation rate	54.8	64.3	69.9	74.7	76.4	77.2
With children under 6:						
Population	14,415	13,966	15,366	16,139	16,692	16,515
Labor force	5,592	6,538	8,215	9,397	10,395	10,293
Labor force participation rate	38.8	46.8	53.5	58.2	62.3	62.3

(Numbers in thousands)

Source: U.S. Department of Labor (1997, September). *Monthly Labor Review.*

policies and child care availability and quality. However, studies tend to focus on women and women's changing roles more than on men's, often with the assumption that women are more vulnerable and at risk psychologically and that work/family issues are women's issues (R.C. Barnett, 1998; Silverstein & Phares, 1996).

Another prevalent theme is the view that work and family are in competition, and that families need to accommodate to workplace structures and demands (R.C. Barnett, 1998; Pleck, 1996). A case in point is a discourse analysis of postgraduate women talking about family and career (Athanasiadou, 1997). A major conclusion of the study is that women construct an ideology of "personal choice" that reproduces gender. An illustration from the study is a woman who said, "I do not think that marriage limits women more than men. I want to have a family . . . if my marriage influences my career I will accept that because I want to have a family" (p. 325). Thus, a woman's wish to sacrifice a career for a family is represented as her own decision, a decision unrelated to the sociocultural context of women's lives and husbands' breadwinning role. Such research, of course, is based on the assumptions that all families are heterosexual and/or that all marriages result in children.

Gender-comparative research has provided, and continues to provide, valuable insights into the day-to-day life of working partners. As a body of literature, these studies have beautifully documented changes in women's and men's work and family behaviors and attitudes over the past two to three decades. They have also provided the data needed to challenge persistent societal myths about women's nature, women's place, and "working women." A main limitation of this phase and paradigm is using the behavior of individual women and men as the main focus of inquiry. We know that most employed individuals function in social systems including families, friends, schools, and community, and that these influences have an interactive mutuality, with conditions at work influencing social systems, and social systems influencing the structure of work. In addition, there is the danger of nonconsciously using gender comparisons derived from a primarily essentialist perspective that locates the cause for observed differences within the psychological makeup of women and men.

Work-Family Role Convergence

Employment is now widely recognized as an appropriate, normative, healthy, and intrinsically rewarding aspect of women's and men's adult lives. Similarly, connections with family—feeling loved and loving and providing interpersonal care and nurturance within families—are also widely recognized as appropriate, normative, healthy, and intrinsically rewarding aspects of women's and men's adult lives. Indeed, fewer than 3% of American families today fall into the category of breadwinner father and stay-at-home mother. For married women with children under 6 years old, 63.1% are in the labor force, and for married women with children under 18, approximately 71% are employed (U.S. Bureau of Labor Statistics, 1997). Among dual-earner families and across various ethnic groups, both spouses are employed full-time in three-fourths of the families (National Report on Work & Family, 1998). Dual-earner couples made up 60% of all marriages in 1996 and 45% of the labor force. Thus, almost half of the workforce is married to an employed spouse. Single-parent families add an additional 12 million people to the workforce who engage in work-family roles. Research suggests that marriage and work are good for us, and that we benefit from combining them in our lives. For example, it is well documented that marriage benefits men's health and well-being, and that the health benefits of traditional marriage are greater for husbands than for wives (Bernard, 1981; Steil, 1997). In addition, employed women report better physical and psychological health than women who are not employed (R.C. Barnett & Rivers, 1996). Though they have busy lives and often may feel stressed, as a group, they are in very good health overall.

The majority of spouses surveyed by Catalyst, a nonprofit group working to advance women in business, classified their career and family of equal importance and wanted to balance work and family (National Report on Work & Family, 1996). Many women who work outside the home enjoy their employment and (at least in theory) have access to a greater range of fields and positions than in earlier times. Women receive college degrees in roughly equal numbers to men and are more likely to complete high school. Approximately 40% of doctoral degrees were awarded to women in 1987. Women with higher education use that education; there is almost no difference between women and men in the numbers who are employed (Beck, 1998). In addition, research to date indicates a positive association between employers' offering flexible policies and parental leave and what is financially good for a company. A recent survey of 1,000 employers, for example, concluded that companies believe family-friendly policies can save money. Johnson & Johnson was cited as saving $4 in increased productivity for every $1 spent on its Life-Works program, a package that helps employees plan for parental leave and find child care (Beck, 1998). Flextime has been shown to decrease employee absenteeism, tardiness, and turnover in several studies (J.L. Glass & Estes, 1997). Flexible workdays have proven both profitable and essential to retain valuable employees (Bailyn, 1993).

This emerging paradigm of work-family role convergence explicitly recognizes that loving and working are human needs and endeavors, and that loving and working are compatible within the family and within the workplace. The supposed contrast between family and occupational roles has been overdrawn and exaggerated, not unlike the supposed contrast between women and men as opposite sexes. The "highly charged affective relations found in the family are also present in the occupational world and influence what goes on there, from job selection to job performance" (Aldous, 1969, p. 707). Interestingly, as R.C. Barnett (1998) noted, there has always been an assumed complementarity between men's enactment of their family and of their work roles. But when women assumed occupancy of roles in both domains, social scientists assumed doing so triggered conflict and incompatibility.

The results from many studies support the concept of role balance or what R.C. Barnett (1998) describes as "a model of human nature that restores the notion of 'one self,' a self that manages simultaneously to meet different needs that are sometimes in conflict, but often in concert" (p. 147). Kanter (1977b), it will be recalled, persuasively argued some time ago that the processes of working and loving are compatible. Many studies since the mid-1970s provide strong evidence that this is indeed the case (e.g., R.C. Barnett & Rivers, 1996; L.A. Gilbert, 1987; J.A. Levine & Pittinsky, 1997). Recent data on the division of family labor in dual-earner families indicate that the inevitability of a "second shift" for wives is overstated and that although some husbands do far less than their fair share, others are in a more equitable arrangement (R.C. Barnett & Rivers, 1996; Crouter & Manke, 1997; Pleck, 1996). Overall, men's participation in family work has continued to increase from 1970 to the present, more so in the area of parenting than in the area of household work (Pleck, 1996). At the same time, there is a good deal of variation among dual-earner families and how they manage work and family roles (L.A. Gilbert, 1993). On average, men in dual-earner families do 34% of the housework and larger percentages of the parenting, with a sizable number close to 50–50 in both areas (cf. Crouter & Manke, 1997; L.A. Gilbert, 1993; Milkie & Peltol, 1999).

Research exemplifying the work-family role convergence paradigm would place at the center of inquiry the assumption that work and family roles are compatible and that role strain occurs only when a person's total system of roles is overdemanding (S.R. Marks & MacDermid, 1996). Indeed, evaluating work/life initiatives using the concept of balance is at the heart of a large two-year initiative of national work/life projects sponsored by large companies such as Prudential, Motorola, Squibb, and Bristol-Meyers (Work/Life Today, 1999). From this perspective, structural variables like the kind of child care provided, definitions of optimal care, and the impact of employers' policies on family life and spouse well-being are conceptualized as central to an integrated self. Variables to consider in investigating the work-family role convergence paradigm include the following:

- Dominant discourses that prevail in the culture (e.g., the "women need men" and "women empower others but not themselves" discourses).
- Views of women and men as opposite and possessing nonoverlapping attributes and abilities (e.g., women as natural nurturers and men as breadwinners).
- Structure of work (e.g., are work hours flexible, are there health care benefits, and if so, are partners covered?).
- Employer's views (e.g., the kinds of family policy provided, general attitudes about employees who involve themselves in family life).
- Child care availability and quality.
- Support systems (family, friends, colleagues, place of worship, community).
- Racial and ethnic views/discrimination in social and employment systems.
- Economic and educational resources.

The integrated self is one that is situated in a community of roles organized in some unique way by the individual, rather than a self torn asunder by roles assigned in some hierarchical fashion by society (R.C. Barnett, 1998).

WHAT IS MISSING FROM OUR ANALYSIS

Our analysis, to a large extent, reflects what is missing from the literature we considered: perspectives of race, class, and sexual orientation. We briefly consider issues in each area to illustrate topics needing more considered attention.

RACE

Work and family roles converge in many of the same ways for African American and White women and men but with two important distinctions. First, African American women traditionally have had a high labor force participation rate, with both African American women and men holding the cultural expectation that African American women will be employed regardless of their marital status (Staples & Johnson, 1993; Vaz, 1995). In addition, African American women are less likely to marry. In 1990, 96.1% of White women had been married at some time by the age of 54, compared to 91.9% of Black women (Steil, 1997).

Important in understanding the context of African American women's employment are the limitations historically placed on Black men's employment opportunities and status. Societal views of male privilege, economic success, and power long associated with the White male have not extended to the Black male (A.G. Hunter & Davis, 1992). Second, the pervasiveness of racism may also intensify the effects of sexism for African American women (B. Greene, 1994). In her essay "Sexism: An American Disease in Blackface," Audre Lorde (1984a) asked, "If this society ascribes roles to Black men which they are not allowed to fulfill, is it Black women who must bend and alter our lives to compensate, or is it society that needs changing? And why should Black men accept these roles as correct ones, or anything other than a narcotic promise encouraging accep-tance of other facts of their own oppression?" (p. 62). According to Steil (1997), the limited data available suggest that Black women benefit less from marriage than any other group. Clearly, there is much to be studied and understood here.

CLASS

Women have worked outside the home since the Industrial Revolution; however, it was not until the mid-1970s and the return of upper- and middle-class women to the workforce that maternal employment surfaced as a major issue for research and policy (Ferree, 1990). Because much of the research literature addresses dual-career families, lower-income employed women have been overlooked as a separate group. The relatively few studies available indicate that working-class women are committed to their jobs and that their families are similar to other dual-earner families in men's participation in family roles (e.g., Dancer & Gilbert, 1993; Stegelin & Frankel, 1993; Thorne & Gilbert, 1998). Common stressors of lower-income working-class employed women with children relate to a lack of resources: money, time, and adequate child care. Some women, or their partners, are employed in shift work that places additional strains on families while sometimes easing child care. For families of lower-income employed mothers, unemploy-ment can be a stressor.

Low-income women with children have become the focus of recent national debates on welfare (Seccombe, James, & Walters, 1998). Congressional proposals and policies to reform the welfare system have sought to develop strategies for getting welfare mothers into the workplace. Fueling the impetus is the belief, contradicted by social science research, that reforming the welfare sys-tem will reduce other social problems, such as drug use, poverty, and illiteracy.

This debate has imbedded within it many biases related to class. For example, a key issue for working middle-class women in the 1980s and, to some extent, today is child care. Middle-class women are subtly pressured to return to their traditional family roles to save the family and to save society from such ills as violence and drug use. In contrast, welfare mothers are character-ized as using children as an excuse not to be self-sufficient. In both cases, gender is the primary lens used to focus blame on women, although this lens is used quite differently in each case to fit what best serves the rhetoric of conventional roles and the status quo.

A second and related issue centers around women and the notion of self-sufficiency. Few would question the importance of assisting poor single mothers to achieve greater self-sufficiency. How one does so for women in this vulnerable position, however, is complicated and involves a number of factors that mediate the effect of the assistance on later self-sufficiency (Sandford & Hill, 1996) and on the women's emotional involvement with their children (Reay, 1998). Such factors include child support, educational opportunities, and job training. Forcing individuals with young children into minimum-wage jobs that provide little opportunity for increased pay, social support, or self-esteem is clearly not the answer.

SEXUAL ORIENTATION

Work and family roles converge in many of the same ways for same-sex as for heterosexual cou-ples. The statistics for lesbian and gay dual-career couples are not readily available, although cur-rent statistics likely include women and men whose partners are of the same sex. Unlike a person's race or sex, an individual's sexual orientation cannot be determined on the basis of phys-ical cues. The pervading heterosexual bias (Morin, 1977) that is a part of our socialization usually leads to assumptions that everyone is heterosexual unless there is clear evidence to the contrary. Because our society discriminates heavily against those who are not heterosexual, lesbians often collude with this heterosexual bias to avoid the consequences of being identified as "deviant." In one study of working lesbians in committed relationships, 65% of the sample indicated that they had not disclosed their lesbianism to their employers, and 37% indicated that no one in their work environment knew they were lesbian (Eldridge & Gilbert, 1990). A significant proportion of these women had children.

The integrating and sharing of occupational and family roles, which is "emerging" for women and men in heterosexual dual-career relations, is normative among lesbian women. Lesbians grow up knowing that they will provide for themselves. Thus, the fact that women are earning higher median salaries and have better career opportunities improves the economic situation for women in lesbian families. Improved work-family benefits could also be somewhat helpful to lesbian families. Lesbian couples, however, may be reluctant to use policies that would require disclosing their lifestyle to employers. They also face the additional problem of not receiving medical benefits for partners and nonbiological children. Therefore, the extent to which partners can risk using work-family policies will largely determine how much such benefits can facilitate converging roles and role balance for single and partnered lesbian women.

CONCLUDING REMARKS

What is new and radical, and what emerges from our chapter on current perspectives, is the convergence of work and family norms for women and men. This situation presents a dramatically different view of normative development and how society should prepare women and men for their adult roles in the 21st century.

Male-female relationships have changed irreversibly in the past 30 years. Women have increased access to education, good job opportunities, laws to protect them from discriminatory practices, and a status and meaning separate from their affiliations with men. Marriage is more optional for women of "independent means." Marriage is also fairer when women have other options and can leave a situation that is stifling and disrespectful. Although household work and parenting remain unevenly divided in many marriages, the distribution of income and participation in family roles is more equitable than ever before in our history. Moreover, involvement in work and family roles confers improved health, well-being, and personal happiness on women, in addition to enhanced economic independence.

A number of studies report evidence that equity has an effect on marital satisfaction and marital stability, and not vice versa. For example, in Ray's (1990) sample of dual-career couples, greater marital satisfaction was related to greater equality and reciprocity in relationships. Couples experiencing greater marital satisfaction were apt to both give and take support, to be involved in each other's careers, to have equal commitment to the relationship, and to practice equal decision making. Spouses holding nontraditional sex-role attitudes and husbands approving of their wife's career were both related to higher marital satisfaction. Nicola and Hawkes (1986) reported support for the theory that partners in dual-career couples who share equally in the rights and duties of marriage will be bound closer together, and thus more committed, than partners in less egalitarian marriages. Sharing was found to contribute to self-reported marital satisfaction and commitment. Dancer and Gilbert (1993) reported that spouses in dual-earner families with comparable perceptions of fairness reported higher marital satisfaction. Finally, Milkie and Peltol (1999) were surprised to find that employed women and men reported similar levels of success and kinds of work-family trade-offs.

Thus, there is good reason to be optimistic, although the situation is clearly not improved for all women and overall improvement is still needed for women as a group. The absence of racial and ethnic diversity in studies investigating family roles and careers, in particular, is a serious limitation of current research. Nonetheless, we see gender perspectives as crucial to continuing the momentum that has been achieved. Gender processes thread interconnections among the individual, family, workplace, and societal variables examined by researchers and these gendered variables need to be recognized and acknowledged as such. Moreover, the unit of analysis in most studies is the individual, even though we know that most workers function in social systems that include families, friends, schools, and community. These influences have an interactive mutuality, with conditions at work influencing social systems, and social systems influencing the structure of work. Clearly, an understanding of gender theories and processes must guide these efforts. A gender theorist's work is never done.

CHAPTER 11

Motherhood and Mothering

ANNE WOOLLETT and HARRIETTE MARSHALL

In this chapter we bring together two disparate psychological approaches to motherhood. The first examines motherhood as a defining aspect of women's adult female identity, and the second examines mothering and the role mothers play in ensuring that children become well adjusted and competent members of society. These two aspects of motherhood—women's identities as mothers and their practices and impact on their children—draw on somewhat different research and theorising. Although both draw on psychodynamic accounts, motherhood and women's identities as mothers are frequently positioned within family theories and feminist ideas of women's development and subjectivities, with women's practice as mothers positioned within developmental psychology in terms of their influence on children and their development, rather than objects of study in their own right (Burman, 1994; Woollett & Phoenix, 1996). In this chapter, we examine a variety of psychological approaches, including attachment, ecological and systems theory, developmental psychology, feminist and critical psychology, and some ideas from the social sciences more broadly to examine the multifaceted and sometimes contradictory nature of ideas and findings about motherhood and mothering.

We start by considering some ideas and expectations about motherhood that are used to define mothering as "good/bad" and to present motherhood as providing "ultimate fulfillment" for all women. We draw on research about women who do not become mothers as well as those who do, and the ways in which childless women (i.e., women who reject as well as those who fail to achieve motherhood) serve to challenge expectations about motherhood as "normal" and "natural" for all women.

Women become mothers and bring up children in a wide range of contexts or settings. Some of these are designated as "good" and "appropriate" and others as "bad" and "inappropriate," based on factors such as women's age, their sexuality and able-bodiedness, whether they are single or partnered, their "race" and ethnicity, social class/economic position, and employment status. We argue that in concentrating on mother-child dyads, developmental psychology has failed to address the wider social, economic, and cultural context of mothering, including women's relations with other children, fathers, and relations outside their families.

Whereas for most women becoming a mother involves conception, pregnancy, and childbirth, stepparenting, adoption, and reproductive technologies also enable women to be/become mothers. We examine some tensions around models of pregnancy and childbirth as physical and biological events, requiring medical monitoring and management, and those that consider their social and psychological significance for women, partners, and others.

Psychological approaches to mothering are concerned largely with the identification of characteristics considered to facilitate and encourage the development of those aspects of children's competence of current interest, and that are the basis of dominant notions of "good" mothering. Psychological approaches are examined critically, with reference to research about mothering in a diversity of settings (including single-parent, Black, and ethnic minority families) and children's agency (as older and younger children, as "only" children and children with siblings) to question universal notions of mothering. We also consider some of the ways women resist these dominant notions of motherhood and negotiate ways of mothering appropriate to their social and cultural settings.

IDEAS AND EXPECTATIONS ABOUT MOTHERHOOD AND MOTHERING

In most societies, women are expected to become mothers and motherhood is construed as "normal" and "natural." Because motherhood is expected and taken for granted, it is often only when women do not become mothers (Morell, 1994) or when they experience fertility problems (Woollett, 1991) that they have to explain or account for themselves. As K. Gerson (1985), Currie (1988), and Woollett (1996b) argue, the taken-for-granted nature of motherhood also means that women's choices and decisions are not so much about whether or not to become mothers, but about when or in what situations to become mothers and how many children to have.

Ideas and expectations about mothering derive from a variety of psychological theories and research, including developmental psychology, psychodynamic theories, and attachment theories, as discussed by Birns and Hay (1988), Woodward (1997), and R. Parker (1995). A major concern for psychology is to identify how mothers ensure the development, competence, and adjustment of children: Maternal practice currently considered as optimal includes listening to children, being warm and responsive, but also setting high standards and monitoring children's activities (Wearing, 1984; Woollett, 1999; Woollett & Phoenix, 1991, 1996, 1997). These optimal practices, drawn from ideas about what is "good" for children, are then used to define "good" mothering, an ideal toward which all mothers are expected to strive and which all women are expected to find satisfying and rewarding (S. Brown, Lumley, Small, & Astbury, 1994; Elvin-Nowak, 1999).

These ideas about motherhood and mothering provide the context in which mothers—and others—make sense of what it means to be a mother and evaluate their mothering. Mothering is presented as "essential," that is, as applicable to all women regardless of the settings in which they become mothers and bring up children (Coll, Surrey, & Weingarten, 1998; Glenn, Chang, & Forcey, 1994; Sparks, 1996). Ideas about mothering are discussed in psychology largely as "facts," suggesting that there is a consensus about what constitutes "good" mothering (Nicolson, 1998; Phoenix & Woollett, 1991; Woollett & Phoenix, 1996, 1997). Equating "good" mothering with what is "normal" and "natural" suggests that women share these ideas and find it easy and satisfying to be "good" mothers. Although women do share many of these ideas, they also resist and challenge ideas and expectations about motherhood in the light of their situations and experiences (Sparks, 1996; Wearing, 1984; Wetherell, 1995; Woodward, 1997).

MOTHERHOOD AS ESSENTIAL, EXPECTED, AND COMPULSORY

Motherhood is presented as essential, normal, and natural for *all* women: Whatever else they do with their lives, women are expected to become mothers. However, not all women become mothers, either through choice (Morell, 1994), because of the circumstances of their lives, or because they are not able to have children (Currie, 1988; Sandelowski, 1993; Woollett, 1991). The situations in which women become mothers vary considerably. Many women become mothers by conceiving within heterosexual sexual relations and giving birth to their "own" children. However, some become mothers only after treatment for infertility, or through IVF and surrogacy; their numbers are small, but increasing in the Western world (S. Franklin, 1997; Stanworth, 1987). Women also become mothers through adoption, including the adoption of children from other countries (Brodzinsky & Schechter, 1990; B. Smith, Surrey, & Watkins, 1998). Women become mothers in a variety of relationships, as single women, in first and subsequent marriages/relationships, and in heterosexual and lesbian relationships (Benkov, 1998; Golombok, Murray, Brinsden, & Abdalla, 1999). As relations break down and new ones are established at an increasing rate, more women are becoming stepmothers, caring for the children of their partners as full-time residential stepmothers, as part-time nonresidential stepmothers, or by combining stepmothering with mothering their "own" children (Arendell, 1986; Baylies, 1996; Das Gupta, 1995). Some routes to motherhood, such as surrogacy, donor insemination for lesbian women, and adoption of children from abroad, are controversial and raise moral and practical questions for women and the wider society about what it means to be a mother, the morality and acceptability of some routes to motherhood, and who is considered "fit" to be a mother (Baylies, 1996; Rowland, 1987; Stanworth, 1990).

In their accounts, women often draw on the "essential" quality of motherhood to argue that motherhood is inevitable or a natural progression in a relationship (Oakley, 1979; Wearing, 1984; Weaver & Ussher, 1997; Woollett, Dosanjh-Matwala, & Hadlow, 1991). Although there is no evidence that the mothering of women who become mothers through IVF or adoption differs from that of other mothers, they are often keen to present themselves as "real" and "normal" mothers (Golombok et al., 1999; B. Smith et al., 1998). However, women's accounts also point to tensions between the essential nature of motherhood and women's other goals and activities: Though women often want to have children and become mothers, they also want to continue to have identities and lives outside motherhood. A common theme in accounts is the difficulty women experience in combining mothering with their other roles and activities (Elvin-Nowak, 1999; K. Gerson, 1985; Glenn, 1994; R. Parker, 1995).

MOTHERHOOD AS A/THE KEY ASPECT OF WOMEN'S ADULT IDENTITIES

Motherhood is often considered to be *the* key aspect of women's adult identities; other identities are added to motherhood but are not expected to replace it as women's central identity. Motherhood is considered a crucial component of the life course and as making "real" women of mothers (M-J. Gerson, Berman, & Morris, 1991; Nicolson, 1998; Rich, 1977; Russo, 1979). It is also constructed as a major source of well-being, emotional satisfaction, and fulfillment (Marshall, 1991; R. Parker, 1995). Comparisons of motherhood with fatherhood indicate the gendered nature of parenthood. Although motherhood and fatherhood are both sources of intense emotional satisfaction, fatherhood is more "optional" than motherhood, and men are expected to consider fatherhood as only one aspect of their adult male identities (M-J. Gerson, 1986; L.A. Gilbert, 1994; R.W. Larson, Richards, & Perry-Jenkins, 1994; L. Thompson & Walker, 1989; Woollett & Nicolson, 1998).

One consequence of the argument that motherhood is central to women's adult identities is that it may be difficult for women to acknowledge the constraints of motherhood. These constraints are acknowledged in women's accounts of their reproductive decision making, for example, about delaying pregnancy to enable them to "live and do things before you have children" or for work and career reasons (Currie, 1988; K. Gerson, 1985; Oakley, 1979; Woollett, 1991; Woollett & Nicolson, 1998). However, once they are mothers, women seem to find it more difficult to acknowledge ambivalent feelings without threatening their identities as "good" mothers (Nicolson, 1998; R. Parker, 1995; Weaver & Ussher, 1997). Nicolson links this to the ways psychology explains negative and ambivalent feelings in individualized terms, as women being "depressed" or failing to adjust, rather than, for example, as an understandable response to feeling isolated or being overworked. One way women deal with these tensions is with statements such as "I wouldn't be without her, but . . . ," acknowledging both their affection and enjoyment of their children as well as negative feelings.

NOT BECOMING A MOTHER: CHILDLESSNESS AND INFERTILITY

Ideas about motherhood impact *all* women, those with children and those without. The emphasis on motherhood as normal and natural means that women who are childless are considered "abnormal" and "unnatural" and their voices are often silenced (Ireland, 1993; Morell, 1994; Sandelowski, 1993; Woollett, 1991). Research with nonmothers examines the ways in which, because motherhood is taken for granted, childless women are defined as "other," in terms of the absence of children or their "deviation" from "normal" pattern, as Carolyn Morell (1994) argues: "Compensatory discourses make motherhood the natural condition for women by describing the activities and attachments of non-mothers as compensations for the original deficiency, *no child.* Every aspect of a childless woman's life may be interpreted through the lens of this deficiency. . . . *Whatever* a childless woman *does have* or *does* may be viewed as mere compensation for the missing real experience of motherhood" (p. 89). The taken-for-granted quality of motherhood is bolstered, Morell argues, by minimizing the value of women's other achievements or designating these as "mere compensation for the missing real experience of motherhood."

Women are childless or nonmothers for a variety of reasons. Some women are childless by choice (voluntary childlessness), whereas others are childless because of fertility problems (infertility/involuntary childlessness) (Ireland, 1993). For some women, being childless is a permanent condition. Women's feelings about being infertile or their reproductive refusal vary from woman to woman and over time (Morell, 2000; K. Gerson, 1985). For other women, including those who become mothers only after a delay and/or as the result of infertility treatment, childlessness is a temporary state and identity, and for some impinges on their experiences of motherhood (S. Franklin, 1977; Sandelowski, 1993; Stanworth, 1990).

Childless women are an anomaly, demonstrating that motherhood is not compulsory and women are not necessarily locked into biological reproduction (Glenn, 1994; Morell, 2000). However, rather than incorporating their experiences into theorizing about motherhood and challenging notions of the universal and obligatory character of motherhood, nonmothers and their experiences are marginalized by rendering them "deficient" and as lacking emotional fulfillment. This is reinforced by research that concentrates on the problems and not on the well-being of childless women (Morell, 2000; A.L. Stanton & Dunkel-Schetter, 1991; Stanworth, 1987). Similarly, approaches to women whose children have grown up and have left home—the so-called empty nest syndrome—imply a loss or void once women's primary functions as mother have passed (Arber & Ginn, 1991). In concentrating on deficit and what is missing from the lives of childless women, women's other activities, relationships, and identities (those of mothers as well as nonmothers) are dismissed as "mere compensation" for the absence of children rather than as having meaning and value in themselves.

Responses to childless women, and the ways women make sense of their nonmotherhood, are related to the reason for their childlessness. In their commitment to becoming mothers, women who want but can't have children (or have them only after a delay/treatment for infertility) share ideas about the value of motherhood. Urlich and Weatherall (2000) discuss how infertile women sometimes resist being identified in terms of the failure of their own (or a partner's) reproductive system (Stanworth, 1987; Woollett, 1996a). In contrast, women who are childless by choice are often considered to be rejecting motherhood and challenging ideas about the value of motherhood, although their ideas and choices are complex and fluid (Heaton, Jacobson, & Holland, 1999; Morell, 2000; Wager, 2000). Whereas infertile women are frequently considered "desperate" or objects of pity, women who are childless by choice are more likely to be criticized as selfish and unnatural (K. Gerson, 1985; Ireland, 1993; Stanworth, 1987). In spite of their differences, women who are childless all face the challenge of retaining a positive sense of themselves and experiencing their lives as worthwhile and fulfilled in the face of negative presentations of nonmothers (Ireland, 1993; Woollett, 1991).

WOMEN'S ACCOUNTS OF MOTHERHOOD

Ideas about motherhood and mothering provide a framework within which women make sense of mothering and their practices as mothers. Women's accounts suggest that they share many of the dominant ideas and expectations but are also aware of tensions and contradictions (Birns & Hay, 1988; Bjornberg, 1992; S. Brown, Small, & Lumley, 1997; Croghan, 1991; Everingham, 1994; Coll et al., 1998; K. Gerson, 1985; Glenn, 1994; Nicolson, 1998; Phoenix, 1991b; Reay, 1995; Wearing, 1984; Woodward, 1997). Motherhood and the production of children who are competent, well-adjusted, and effective citizens are publicly valued and give women a sense of being effective, powerful, and in control. Women consider motherhood a source of satisfaction, enjoyment, and pleasure, but they also experience it as costly in terms of time and energy and because they are expected to subordinate their needs and identities to those of their children (Oberman & Josselson, 1996). As S. Brown et al. (1994), Wearing (1984), and Woodward (1997) discuss, being "good" mothers gives women a sense of satisfaction, but they also often complain that committing themselves wholeheartedly to mothering constrains their individual development and achievement and limits other activities and relationships.

Psychological accounts tend to be written in terms of "the mother," on the assumption that the singular term can stand for and represent all mothers. However, women's accounts suggest powerfully that their experiences are moderated by the circumstances of their lives, the settings in which they mother, and their social relations. These settings include the age at which women become mothers (Furstenberg, Brooks-Gunn, & Morgan, 1987; Phoenix, 1991a, 1991b), their relationships and support for mothering (Silva, 1996; Silverstein and Phares, 1996), how many children they have (Munn, 1991), their health and able-bodiedness (Thomas, 1997), and their other roles, including employment (Birns & Hay, 1988; Brannen & Moss, 1991; L.A. Gilbert, 1994; Glenn et al., 1994). We consider here mothers' ideas and identities in some of these settings, the issues they raise for theorizing motherhood and mothering, and the ways they disrupt notions of the essential and normative nature of motherhood.

Although psychology acknowledges the diversity of motherhood and mothering, some settings are theorized as "good" and more appropriate than others. Psychological research and public debates about mothers who are single (Silva, 1996), homeless (Koch, Lewis, & Quinones, 1998), disabled (Thomas, 1997), lesbian (Benkov, 1998; C.A. Parks, 1998), were abused and taken into care as children (Croghan & Miell, 1998), or young (Flanagan, 1998; Phoenix, 1991a, 1991b) are conducted largely in terms of "bad" mothering and mothering in "unsuitable" settings. Women make sense of their "problem" mothering in ways that recognize how they are considered by others, but also by resisting and challenging ideas about the inadequacy of their mothering.

AGE AND MOTHERHOOD

Most women become mothers in their twenties and thirties, with relatively few "young" mothers. Figures for the 1980s and 1990s show variations among countries: Fewer than 2% of mothers are under 20 in Singapore and Japan, 8% in UK, between 13% and 16% in Argentina, Barbados, and the Czech Republic, rising to about 25% in the United States (Baylies, 1996; Brooks-Gunn & Chase Lansdale, 1995). Young mothers, especially those under the age of 16 years, are considered problematic because motherhood disrupts their education and training. As Brooks-Gunn and Chase Lansdale indicate, considerable concern is expressed about the effectiveness of young mothers and whether, as youngsters themselves, they can set aside their own needs to attend to those of their children. The assumption that women's youth is a problem is questioned by researchers such as Phoenix (1991a, 1991b), Furstenberg et al. (1987), and Flanagan (1998), who argue that the major problems young mothers face tend to be not so much to do with their youth as with a lack of money and support.

The number of older mothers has increased slightly, as women delay having children but also because new techniques of reproductive medicine allow older women to become pregnant (Berryman, 1991; Berryman, Thorpe, & Windridge, 1995; Kuchner & Porcino, 1988). Interest in "older" mothers focuses on their fitness, compared with younger women, to cope with the demands of pregnancy and mothering (in contrast to fathering, which age is rarely considered to compromise). Berryman et al. (1995) argue that any lack of fitness is more than compensated for by the greater financial security and strong commitment to motherhood of older mothers.

SINGLE MOTHERS AND MOTHERS WITH PARTNERS

Within developmental psychology, as in the wider community, stable heterosexual relations are considered the most appropriate setting for motherhood. Male partners are construed as necessary or important for a variety of reasons (L. Thompson & Walker, 1989). Drawing on gendered division of family roles and men's greater economic power, it is argued that fathers provide economically for children and hence enable mothers to devote themselves to the care of children and development of close attachments with them (Burman, 1994; R. Parker, 1995; Schnitzer, 1998). The absence of fathers is also considered problematic because of assumptions about their value as male role models for children (especially for boys) (Burman, 1994; Weintraub & Grisglas, 1995; D. White & Woollett, 1992). The extent to which fathers do provide support for women to develop close relations with children varies considerably. In settings such as lesbian relationships (Benkov, 1998; Tasker & Golombok, 1997) and in many extended and single-parent families, mothers are supported by other family members who are involved with the children (Aquilino, 1996; M. Cochran, Larner, Riley, Gunnarsson, & Henderson, 1990). For most children, therefore, fathers are only one of a range of male role models.

Reflecting public concern, there is considerable research and theorizing about single mothers. The proportion of single mothers has increased in most countries, although their numbers vary from country to country: In the mid-1980s, there were fewer single mothers in Japan (4%) than in France (10%), the former USSR (20%) and the United States (42%) (Baylies, 1996; Weintraub & Grisglas, 1995). There are also considerable variations among social and ethnic communities. In the United States, for example, there are more Black (56%) than Hispanic (29%) or White single mothers (19%) (Schnitzer, 1998; R.J. Taylor, Jackson, & Chatters, 1997). It is also important to remember that single mothers are not a unitary category (Silva, 1996). Some mothers are single because they were not in stable heterosexual relationship when they became mothers, whereas others were in relationships when their children were born but have become single mothers since (Aquilino, 1996; Weintraub & Grisglas, 1995). Many women are single mothers only for a short time because they move into new relationships, providing stepparents/fathers for their children. In these new relationships, women often act as stepmothers to their partner's children (Burghes, 1996). The term "single" relates to the type or structure of the nuclear family, but its usage is often extended, on the basis of little empirical support, to family processes and the mothering of single mothers. In many cases, single mothers and their children have the support and involvement of others, such as the members of their own family (and sometimes the family of an ex-partner), and resist assumptions that the absence of a father necessarily impacts negatively on the quality of their parenting and on their relations with their children. As they point out, even when fathers are resident, they are not necessarily highly involved in parenting, and fathers who do not live with their children may continue to be supportive and maintain relations with them (Arendell, 1986; Burghes, 1996; M. Cochran et al., 1990). More important than whether fathers are present or absent are the quality and the nature of children's relations with family members (Wetherell, 1995).

Even though some psychologists question simplistic associations between family type and the quality of parenting, single mothering continues to be considered problematic (Wetherell, 1995; Woodward, 1997). Research with families headed by mothers concentrates on "problems"—"bad" mothering and poor outcomes of children in single-parent families—and "good" mothering is researched largely in families with two heterosexual parents. As D. White and Woollett (1992) argue, this means that we have little information about mothering that is good or normal in single-parent families and or about problematic mothering in two-parent families, and hence little on which to make considered judgments about the quality of single mothering (Burman, 1994; Sparks, 1996; F. Walsh, 1993).

Burman (1994), Phoenix (1996), and Woollett and Phoenix (1996, 1997) are also critical of research on single mothers for the ways in which the "causes" of any problems are theorized. The circumstances in which single mothers bring up children often differ from those of partnered mothers: Single mothers are more likely to be poor and to live in poor quality housing in inner-city neighborhoods and their children are less likely than those of partnered children to attend successful schools. As Burghes (1996) and Sparks (1996) discuss, these circumstances combine to make it difficult for single mothers to engage in "good" mothering (Coll et al., 1996; Sidel, 1996). These differing circumstances are more likely than whether women are partnered or not to be the "cause" of any problems women have in mothering or in how children turn out (Weintraub & Grisglas, 1995). The accounts of single mothers portray vividly the tensions women experience as they try to balance being supportive and responsive to children with earning a living, "being there" for children and "having a life," and engaging in activities for themselves. Single mothers often challenge assumptions about the inadequacy of their mothering, in common with other women mothering in settings considered problematic. Phoenix indicates how the circumstances of the lives of single mothers often increase their competence, resourcefulness, and organization as mothers. Indeed, T. Gordon (1994) argues that for some single mothers, the lack of a partner enables them to give their children extra interest and attention, and hence to compensate children for any disadvantages of living in a single-parent household.

EMBODIMENT AND MOTHERHOOD

So far, we have emphasized the psychological and social meanings of motherhood. Becoming a mother is also a physical process and a biological event as women conceive, carry through a pregnancy, and give birth. These physical and biological processes are important in themselves but also because of the ways they are understood by women, their families, the wider society, and those who manage women's pregnancies and childbirth.

PREGNANCY AND CHILDBIRTH

Motherhood is usually the result of the birth of a child who is a couple's biological child, although adoption, stepparenting, and recent developments in reproductive technologies mean that the links among sexual intercourse, a couple's desire for a baby, and their genetic input may be separated (S. Franklin, 1997). Because of concerns about the lack of biological links between parents and adopted children (B. Smith et al., 1998) or children conceived as a result of reproductive technologies (S. Franklin, 1997; B. Smith et al., 1998; Stanworth, 1987), these routes are generally accepted only as a last resort, when a woman cannot otherwise become a mother. Feminist analyses of reproductive technologies often argue that they are exploitive because they increase medical control of women's reproduction, but also because the high costs of the technologies mean they are a solution only for a small proportion of women (S. Franklin, 1997; Stanworth, 1987; Urlich & Weatherall, 2000).

Pregnancy involves bodily and physical changes: Women put on weight and change their shape, they often experience physical symptoms such as sickness and nausea, and they have problems with mobility (Niven, 1992; Oakley, 1979; Woollett & Marshall, 1997). The impact of these physical changes and their meanings for women vary considerably, reflecting contradictory ideas about pregnancy and childbirth and their management. So, for example, employment during pregnancy is sometimes considered a matter of individual choice, related to the health of women, but also in economic terms, such as whether a family can forgo a women's financial contribution (Romito, 1997).

Feminists such as Davis-Floyd (1994), Rothman (1989), and Ussher (1989) call attention to tensions in Western societies between models of pregnancy and childbirth that emphasize their biological nature and the need for medical supervision and care, and models that emphasize their psychological significance for women, their identities and relations with others. Nicolson (1998) and Woollett and Marshall (1997) examine the ways in which women's accounts draw on both models. Women often draw on medical notions of "risk" and "safety" to argue that they want to make use of the technologies for monitoring pregnancy and childbirth. But they also want to be involved in decisions and to experience their pregnancies and childbirth as "natural" and emotionally fulfilling (E. Martin, 1989).

POSTNATAL DEPRESSION

Nicolson (1998) examines links between the embodied nature of motherhood and ideas about depression in the postnatal period (see also S. Brown et al., 1994; Woollett & Nicolson, 1998). Biological/medical approaches explain women's feelings postnatally in terms of physiological and hormonal events. These explanations are often considered beneficial for women because, by arguing that women's negative feelings are beyond their control, women cannot be blamed for their feelings (Mauthner, 1998; Nicolson, 1998; R. Parker, 1995; Weaver & Ussher, 1997). But biological/medical explanations can also mean that women's feelings are not taken seriously but are dismissed as "only their hormones" or as "something that will pass." Feminist explanations, in contrast, emphasize links between women's feelings and their life and identities, arguing that depression is often associated with tiredness and the changes motherhood brings to women's lives and relationships (S.E. Lewis & Nicolson, 1998; Nicolson, 1998). Postnatal depression alerts women and those around them to negative as well as positive feelings about and experiences of motherhood.

There has been less interest in women's physical recovery after childbirth and the impact of physical problems for women and their practice of mothering (Woollett & Nicolson, 1998). Feminist researchers point to the impact of tiredness and lack of sleep on women's health and well-being, making it difficult for women to engage in "good" (i.e., sensitive and child-centered) mothering and to maintain a sense of themselves as "good" and effective mothers (Nicolson, 1998; Popay, 1992).

MOTHERING AND MOTHER-CHILD RELATIONS

A major goal of developmental psychology has been to identify key aspects of maternal practice and how these influence children's competence and development. The main focus of developmental psychology is children; there is less interest in mothers, their experiences and feelings (their subjectivities), or personal, social, or economic factors that enable women to be more or less sensitive and child-centered (Woollett & Phoenix, 1991). A variety of aspects of mothering have been identified as influencing children's development and linked to children's cognitive, social, or emotional development.

The aspects of mothering that research explores varies according to the theoretical position of the psychologists involved. In general, mainstream developmental psychology accounts argue that "good" mothering—that is, mothering associated with children's competence, adjustment, and development—is responsive and child-centered (Burman, 1994; Woollett & Phoenix, 1991). Woollett and Phoenix (1996) indicate the variety of ways in which mothers are considered to demonstrate their child-centeredness, depending on the setting (e.g., whether they are observed in home or lab setting) and the age of the children. Most accounts of mothers' child-centeredness include being available, giving children time and attention, listening to them, and responding appropriately (Burman, 1994). But as Ribbens (1994) argues, "good" mothering also involves being directive, socializing and guiding children, and monitoring and controlling their activities to ensure they behave well, perform effectively, and fit in to society. As Walkerdine and Lucey (1989) indicate, mothers are expected to maintain control through discussion with children rather than a direct show of power (Dunn, 1993). Finally, as Wearing (1984) discusses, "good" mothering also requires that mothers express their feelings (especially their warmth and affection toward children) but also remain calm and patient, maintaining control over their emotions, and putting their needs aside to meet those of their child (Das Gupta, 1995).

Psychodynamic and attachment theory approaches emphasize the warmth and love mothers provide and their attachment to their children (Burman, 1994; R. Parker, 1995). Mothers are construed as "naturally" committed to their children, as taking pleasure in caring for them and establishing close relations that are characterized by sensitivity and mutuality, with mothers' "needs" reflecting those of their children (Birns & Hay, 1988; Oberman & Josselson, 1996; Woollett & Phoenix, 1991). Mothers' accounts suggest that they do often experience pleasure in caring for children and enjoy the companionship, shared activities, and close relations with them (S. Brown et al., 1997; S.E. Lewis & Nicolson, 1998; Wearing, 1984). There is, however, considerable variability in women's feelings, with some enjoying the practice of mothering more than others. Das Gupta (1995) examines the ways women's feelings vary from day to day and in terms of how busy they are and whether there are other people to help and support them (Everingham, 1994). Mothers also report ambivalent and negative feelings such as anger, guilt, and depression (Elvin-Nowak, 1999; Hock, Schirtzinger, & Lutz, 1992; Nicolson, 1998; Oberman & Josselson, 1996; R. Parker, 1995). These feelings and their expression, however, are often either ignored in mainstream discussions of "normal" mother-child relations or are explained in terms of individual pathology (Burman, 1994; Ong, 1985; F. Walsh, 1993; Woollett & Phoenix, 1996).

Women are expected to bring a strong educational or pedagogical component to mothering (Woollett & Phoenix, 1996). Within this framework, "good" mothers are those who encourage children's cognitive development and understanding of their worlds (showing interest in what children are doing, talking to them, modeling cause and effect) and who also make demands for children's competence. As Walkerdine and Lucey (1989) argue, mothers are exhorted to turn every activity into an opportunity for facilitating children's competence and educational achievement (Woollett & Phoenix, 1996). Mothering with a strong educational or pedagogical component is considered particularly effective when accompanied by warmth, firm control, and close monitoring of children (mothering sometimes labelled "authoritative") (Burman, 1994; Ribbens, 1994). Mothers, therefore, are expected to maintain a balance between being firm (making demands, setting clear limits) but not *too* firm (expressing warmth, giving children autonomy and space) (Brannen, Dodd, Oakley, & Storey, 1994; S. Brown et al., 1997; Everingham, 1994).

Within developmental psychology, the social/emotional aspects of mothering are often separated from cognitive/educational aspects, although, as Dunn (1993) and Tizard and Hughes

(1984) argue, they are closely linked. So, for example, secure attachment is often associated with children's later cognitive achievement, and children learn through their social relations about perspective taking and moral development (Burman, 1994).

Psychology operates within wider social and cultural contexts, and these inform psychological ideas about and approaches to mothering (Ingleby, 1986). The questions asked by psychologists about mothering and children are those considered important in the Western world, especially in the U.S. context. A major interest, therefore, is how mothers encourage children's individuality, independence, and assertiveness (Greenfield & Cocking, 1994; Ogbu, 1981). The findings of psychological research are often presented as objective facts and as legitimate sources of knowledge about mothering and children (in contrast, for example, to the subjective and "biased" information mothers provide) (Burman, 1994; Woollett & Phoenix, 1996, 1997). Accounts and theories based on these findings are presumed to be universally applicable, regardless of the diversity of settings in which women bring up children and their ideas about and values for children (Greenfield & Cocking, 1994; P.H. Collins, 1989, 1994; Woollett & Phoenix, 1996; Wyche & Crosby, 1996).

DIVERSITY AND DIFFERENCE

Psychology is interested in diversity as well as general patterns of mothering. Commonly explored are individual differences among mothers, such as their psychological state (especially whether they are depressed) and their personalities, and their implications for the sensitivity, child-centeredness, warmth, and demandingness of their mothering (Belsky, Robins, & Gamble, 1984; C. Lee, 1997; R. Parker, 1995). Another source of diversity relates to women's ideas and expectations of mothering, as explored by Wearing (1984) and Everingham (1994), and the settings in which they practice their mothering. Diversity in terms of women's age and whether mothers are single or partnered has been discussed earlier (Phoenix, 1991a, 1991b; Silva, 1996). Other sources of diversity examined include women's sexuality (C.J. Patterson, 1995), social class (Tizard & Hughes, 1984; Walkerdine & Lucey, 1989), "race" and ethnicity (P.H. Collins, 1989, 1994; Phoenix, 1997; Sparks, 1996), and their links with the physical, social, and financial circumstances in which they bring up their children (Das Gupta, 1995; Wearing, 1984). A number of studies examine how living in poverty or in poor housing can make it difficult for women to be responsive and child-centered and to encourage children to be autonomous (G.J. Duncan, Brooks-Gunn, & Klebanov, 1994; Huston, McLoyd, & Coll, 1994; Koch et al., 1998; Newson & Newson, 1968, 1976; Woollett & Phoenix, 1996).

Underlying interest in differences among mothers are often assumptions about some mothers being "better" or "worse" than others. This happens especially because research on difference is characterized in terms of a "normalized absence/pathologised presence" couplet (Phoenix, 1997). Phoenix argues that research on "normal" mothering is examined largely in White, middle-class, two-parent families and that the mothering of "other" mothers is largely absent from this research (normalized absence). Other mothers (such as mothers in Black, ethnic minority, and working-class families; young and single mothers; disabled and lesbian mothers) are the focus of research predominantly when problems and pathology are explored (pathological presence), lending support to notions that the mothering of Black women and working-class women is necessarily problematic. As Burman (1994) argues, although psychology has not created these negative views of "other" mothers, the ways it constructs and draws on notions of developmental "norms" and "good" mothering provide support for them (Walkderdine & Lucey, 1989; Woollett & Phoenix, 1996, 1997).

This concentration on the problematic nature of the mothering of single mothers and Black, ethnic minority, and working-class women is challenged by research that moves beyond notions of universal competencies and "good" mothering to examine how mothers encourage competencies relevant to the cultural context and ecological niches in which they and their children live (Glenn et al., 1994; P.H. Collins, 1994; J.K. Rice, 1994; Sparks, 1996). Research such as that discussed by P.H. Collins (1989) and Ogbu (1981) suggests, for example, that the skills and competencies important for success among White, middle-class U.S. children are not necessarily those that equip other children to do well and to do well in other settings, such as tough inner-city areas, or in other cultures (G.J. Duncan et al., 1994; Coll et al., 1996; Woollett, 1999). Lamborn, Dornbusch, and Steinberg (1996) suggest that the academic achievement of children in Black and ethnic minority families in the U.S. is linked to their mother's firm control and close monitoring, rather than to the sensitive and child-centered mothering associated with the competence of children in well-resourced families. This is also the case for Asian children who outperform White children in the U.S. educational system (Lamborn et al., 1996; C.A. Mason, Cauce, Gonzales, & Hiraga, 1996; Woollett, 1999).

CHILDREN: AGE, CHARACTERISTICS, AND AGENCY

There is tension in accounts of developmental psychology between approaches that consider mothers as the main influence on children's lives and development and those such as J.R. Harris's (1995), which argue that children actively engage with their social environments and are not merely passive consumers of "influence." Accounts sometimes fail to consider the ways children bring their biological and genetic characteristics to interactions and relations with others and how mothers respond to children in terms of their age, gender, temperament, and physical characteristics such as able-bodiedness, height, skin color, and appearance.

Because of the emphasis on the influence of mothering in developmental psychology, children's agency and their impact on mothering has been explored less extensively. Also because most research is conducted with young children, the impact of children's age is not often considered. Mothers of 7-year-olds (Newson & Newson, 1976) and adolescents (Allatt, 1996; Brannen et al., 1994) continue to be responsible for their children, but the nature of their mothering and their relations with the children change. These changes reflect notions prevalent in Western culture about the relative competence of older and younger children and the value of autonomy (Goodnow, 1988). Mothers encourage older children to take care of themselves, to manage their time, and to become independent. These children are often expected and encouraged to make a contribution to household tasks and finances (Goodnow, 1988). As Brannen et al. report, older children use their skills to discuss their ideas and expectations and to negotiate with mothers about family rules, such as what time they get home at night and keeping mothers informed of their whereabouts (Allatt, 1996; M. Moore, Sixsmith, & Knowles, 1996).

Mothers' ideas about children (their independence, contribution to the household) and mothering (negotiation of family rules and how to ensure children's compliance) are related to children's characteristics, such as their gender. Mothers generally allow boys greater independence than girls, but expect girls to contribute more to household tasks (Brannen et al., 1994; Everingham, 1994; Goodnow, 1988; Newson & Newson, 1976; Rowland & Thomas, 1996). There is also some evidence that mothering is related to the number of children in a family. Fertility rates have decreased worldwide and especially in Western Europe: Most women have fewer children than was the case in the past (Bjornberg, 1992), although they still expect to have more than one child, and "only" children are often considered problematic (e.g., Woollett et al., 1991). Even though there is more than one child in most families and research that suggests that the presence of second and subsequent children impacts on relations between mothers and firstborn children, psychological ideas about mothering are based largely on research with mother-child dyads (Dunn, 1993; Munn, 1991; R.B. Stewart, 1990). When there are two or more children, mothers are less responsive and child-centered and, as Munn reports, are concerned with managing relations between children, trying to ensure that each child gets a turn and get along together, in line with notions of "happy families" (Newson & Newson, 1968, 1976).

Examination of mother-child relations argues that "influence" is two-way: Children are not merely influenced by mothers but have agency and in their turn influence mothers and how they are mothered. Mothering is not static but undergoes change as mothers and children negotiate and renegotiate rules and relationships over time and as family circumstances change (Das Gupta, 1995; Woollett, 1999).

MOTHERING IN WIDER SOCIAL SETTINGS

Ideas about motherhood and mothering are related to more general cultural ideas and expectations about women and their relations with their wider social networks. In their home, women combine mothering and their relations with children with household tasks, relations with fathers and other family members, and sometimes in paid employment in the home (Silverstein & Phares, 1996; Tizard & Hughes, 1984; D. White & Woollett, 1992; Woollett & Phoenix, 1996). Mothering is also combined with women's engagement in settings beyond the home and family, especially employment outside the home, and relations with schools and the local neighborhood (M. Cochran et al., 1990; Das Gupta, 1995; L. Thompson & Walker, 1989; Tizard, 1991).

Positioning mothering in these wider settings involves greater recognition of aspects of mothering not often explored in psychological research (such as feeding children, keeping them warm and well-clothed, and ensuring they get to school on time) as well as household tasks such as shopping, washing clothes, and cleaning. Mothers often report tensions between being "good" mothers who are child-centered and engage with children, and getting on with their "work" (Brannen et al., 1994; Newson & Newson, 1968, 1976; Oakley, 1979; Wearing, 1984). As Oakley argues, mothering, like housework, is invisible but also relentless and never completed. Women report that they feel their mothering is noticed only when it is not done or is badly done, when children behave badly or do not have clean clothes. Wetherell (1995) contrasts women's family tasks with those of men: The family tasks in which men typically engage have a clear end to them and are noticed and appreciated by children.

MOTHERHOOD AND WOMEN'S RELATIONS WITH FATHERS

Developmental psychology tends to consider mothering in isolation from women's other relations. This means recognition of the value and influence of mothering but less consideration of women's other relationships and social networks in which motherhood is positioned, and how these impact on women's practices and experiences as mothers (Glenn, 1994; L. Thompson & Walker, 1989; Woollett & Phoenix, 1996).

At the same time, however, there is considerable interest in fathers and their contribution, often expressed in terms of the "problems" for mothers and children when fathers are absent. The contribution of fathers is often defined largely in terms of their financial provision, drawing on traditionally gendered models of families in which fathers are breadwinners and mothers are caretakers (Burman, 1994; Silva, 1996; L. Thompson & Walker, 1989). Increasingly, however, men's identities and subjectivities as fathers and men's relations with children are considered important in their own right, and are used to argue for "family-friendly" employment policies and for support of children's relations with fathers after divorce (Silverstein & Phares, 1996; Wetherell, 1995; D. White & Woollett, 1992). In many respects, fathering and mothering are construed in similar ways, for example, sharing the values of being responsive, child-centered and listening, and "being there" for children. However, it is often the differences that are emphasized, with these differences used to argue that fathers make a distinctive contribution to children's—especially boys'—life and development (Burman, 1994; Silverstein & Phares, 1996; Wetherell, 1995). One reason why families without fathers are considered to be problems is that boys are considered to lack male role models. However, the absence of fathers can mean that mothers are more sensitive and child-centered because they do not have to balance mothering with relations with male partners (D. White & Woollett, 1992).

The birth of children is an important event for parents and is often discussed in terms of "creating a family." But babies bring changes to mother-father relations and the distribution of household tasks. Women and men are often committed to sharing family roles and household tasks before they have children. However, once they become parents, roles usually become more gendered, with women taking major responsibility for household tasks as well as mothering (Backett, 1987; Croghan, 1991; Oakley, 1979; L. Thompson & Walker, 1989). As Croghan (1991) and Wearing (1984) discuss, women often explain these changes in terms of rational decision making, arguing that because men earn more, it "makes sense" for women to take responsibility for child care and household tasks and for men to continue to be employed. Nicolson (1998) discusses how this gendered division of tasks is sometimes also explained in terms of "instincts" and women's "natural" ability for housework and child care. In spite of these "commonsense" arguments, women often express dissatisfaction with traditionally gendered family roles and the mismatch between their own (and often partner's) expectations and commitment to equality and the reality of parenting (Backett, 1987; Croghan, 1991; Ruble et al., 1988). Women sometimes explain these mismatches in terms of individual differences among fathers, for example, as fathers being committed to child care but failing to wake up when the baby cries at night, as being less competent than mothers, or in terms of pressures at work that make their involvement difficult (Backett, 1987; Croghan, 1991; Croghan & Miell, 1992; Woollett & Parr, 1997).

Women's experiences of child care differ from that of fathers: Men usually have more choice about which child care tasks they engage in and can opt in and out of parenting tasks more readily than mothers. Another factor related to women's dissatisfaction is whether they consider that fathers understand and empathize with their feelings as mothers (Hackel & Ruble, 1992; Ruble et al., 1988; Wilkie, Ferree, and Ratcliff, 1998). It has been suggested that women with a more traditional approach to mothering and fathering may experience less dissatisfaction with their life as a mother of young children than is the case for women with a stronger commitment to equality and shared roles (Wetherell, 1995).

MOTHERHOOD AND EMPLOYMENT

One major aspect of the wider social context in which motherhood and mothering are positioned is employment. In Western societies, motherhood often brings changes to women's employment status, with women sometimes ceasing to be economically active, at least while their children are young. Traditionally, attachment theory has considered employment as antipathetic to notions of "good" mothering because it detracts from women's commitment to motherhood and their ability to be ever-present and child-centered (Tizard, 1991). However, women who give up employment outside the home when they become mothers often miss the status, social contacts, and economic independence associated with employment (S. Brown et al., 1994; K. Gerson, 1985; L. Thompson & Walker, 1989).

Many women combine motherhood with employment and return to paid employment even when their children are young (K. Gerson, 1985; Glenn et al., 1994; H. Graham, 1993; S. Lewis, 1991; Ozer, 1995; Wearing, 1984). The meanings for women of being an employed mother vary considerably. Some women identify as career women and employ other women/mothers to provide child care so they can continue with their full-time employment. Other mothers work for financial reasons, including single mothers who are increasingly encouraged to seek employment rather than live on welfare (Coll et al., 1998; Silva, 1996). Because they usually continue to be responsible for child care, mothers tend to take part-time employment that can be scheduled around school hours. Subsequently, their jobs are more likely to be unskilled, insecure, and badly paid compared with men's jobs and the jobs they had before they became mothers (H. Graham, 1993).

Women's feelings about combining employment and motherhood are complex. Motherhood is expected to remain central to women's identities, and so women are not expected to take their employment too seriously. This is reflected in women's accounts of fitting work around child care, in contrast to men, who are more likely to talk about fitting children around work (Brannen et al., 1994; Wearing, 1984). But employment outside the home is often associated with women's well-being and feelings of self-worth; it provides them with some financial independence and economic power in their families, and, as Ozer (1995) suggests, this may be the case especially when men's employment is uncertain (S. Lewis, 1991; Wearing, 1984).

When women are employed they make greater demands for involvement from fathers in child care and household tasks, although even mothers in full-time employment outside the home continue to take greater responsibility for child care and household tasks than do fathers (H. Graham, 1993; Wetherell, 1995). The impact of employment, therefore, is often to increase women's workload both within the home and because of the work involved in making arrangements for child care (H. Graham, 1993; S. Lewis, 1991). Child care arrangements often include elements of reciprocity, which further increase the workload of employed mothers as they take their turn in looking after children and taking children to and from school and after school activities.

MOTHERHOOD AND WOMEN'S OTHER RELATIONSHIPS

The centrality of motherhood in women's life and identity (those with as well as those without children) means that women's other relationships and friendships and the support they receive from other family members, friends, and neighbors tend not to be valued and explored in psychological research. Those studies that do examine women's relationships suggest that they often provide women with support and opportunities to talk about their experiences, discuss ways to negotiate child care and relations within families, and challenge ideas about motherhood (Brannen & Moss, 1991; H. Graham, 1993; Newson & Newson, 1976). Women with good support networks report more positive feelings about motherhood and are less likely to experience isolation and depression (S.E. Lewis & Nicolson, 1998; Nicolson, 1998; Phoenix, Woollett, & Lloyd, 1991).

BRINGING TOGETHER IDEAS ABOUT MOTHERHOOD AND MOTHERING

We have considered a number of approaches to motherhood and mothering, some of the issues they raise, and tensions and contradictions among the different approaches. One tension is the construction of motherhood as compulsory for women in the "right" circumstances (e.g., old enough, in a stable heterosexual relationship) so that if they do not become mothers, women are denied an adult female identity and their relationships are marginalized. At the same time, the mothering of many women and women in the "wrong" circumstances (e.g., single, Black, young, working-class, and in lesbian relationships) is rendered pathological, indicating how motherhood is compulsory but only for women in particular settings and relationships.

Constructions of motherhood and mothering as natural and as an ultimate fulfillment emphasize the close links between *woman* and *mother*. Motherhood is expected to be central to a woman's identity, and women who do not become mothers are considered not only as rejecting motherhood but as putting their identity as a woman at risk. In contrast to constructions of the "natural" quality of motherhood, motherhood is often demonstrated to be costly for women, requiring them to subordinate their own needs and identity to those of their children. The presentation of motherhood as natural serves to neutralize the physical and emotional work of mothering and renders women's ambivalence "unnatural" or pathological. This makes it difficult for women to talk about ambivalence and negative feelings and increases their guilt at their failure to live up to notions of "good/normal" mothering.

Psychology identifies key aspects of mothering in terms of what is considered to support and enhance children's competence and development. These are set up as "good" mothering and as goals to which all women should aspire. Dichotomies are set up between "good" and "bad" mothers (between those who are and are not sensitive, selfless, stimulating). The lack of consideration of mothers and their perspective in psychological accounts means that the personal, psychological, and social costs of mothering tend to be underestimated and underexplored. In contrast to the usual psychological approach to diversity, framed in terms of difference, problems or deviance, we have drawn on considerations of diversity within a framework of "normal" mothering.

We have suggested that although women share many of the culturally dominant ideas about motherhood and mothering, they also resist and challenge those ideas. We have pointed to some of those challenges and drawn on them to identify some limitations of psychological theorizing. In this way, we have attempted to theorize "good" mothering to include mothering in the diversity of settings in which women become mothers and bring up children.

CHAPTER 12

Older Adult Women: Issues, Resources, and Challenges

SILVIA SARA CANETTO

Aging can be thought of as the great equalizer because it happens to everyone, women and men, rich and poor, lesbian and heterosexual. In reality, differences between women and men are exaggerated, not diminished, by aging. For example, although all older people experience a decline in physical health, women and men differ in the health problems they experience and the resources they can count on to deal with these problems. In this chapter, I review common issues and experiences of women in late adulthood, and discuss the implication of these experiences for their well-being.

The boundaries of late adulthood are somewhat arbitrary, depending on life expectancy (i.e., how long one expects to live) and cultural beliefs (i.e., how cultures define old age). In the United States, late adulthood is typically defined as the time of life beyond age 60. In the United States, this stage of life can stretch for several decades. Life expectancy at birth is 79 years for women, and about seven years less for men. Women who survive to age 65 can expect to live beyond age 80 (Gatz, Harris, & Turk-Charles, 1995). Even in the United States, nonetheless, there are important variations in life expectancy and mortality related to ethnicity. The life expectancy of ethnic minority women is on the average five years less than that of women of European American descent. Older women of African American descent have the highest mortality rates, and women of Asian and Pacific Islander descent have the lowest mortality rates of all ethnic groups. Native American women experience slightly higher mortality than European American women between the ages of 55 and 64, but have lower mortality rates thereafter (Torrez, 1997).

Internationally, women outlive men by five to nine years in most industrialized nations, although the gap is usually smaller in developing countries (Kristof, 1996). In some countries, such as Nepal and Bangladesh, women's lives are shorter than men's (Kalache, 1998). In other countries, the gender gap in longevity is much wider in the United States. In Russia, for example, the life expectancy at birth was 70 years for women and 57 years for men in 1996. Countries that are geographically close but culturally different can present very different life expectancy patterns. For example, in 1996 in Haiti, women's life expectancy at birth was 51 years, and men's was 47 years. During the same year in Cuba, the life expectancy was 80 years for women, and 75 years for men (Kristof, 1996).

In most industrialized countries, late adulthood not only encompasses many years of life, but also a significant variety of experiences. In these countries, the kind of psychological, interpersonal, economic, and health issues faced by women in their sixties and early seventies are often different from the issues they experience in their late seventies and beyond. Thus, whenever possible, the experiences of the so-called young-old (women aged 60 to 75, approximately) will be addressed separately from those of the so-called old-old (women aged 75 to 85, approximately), and those of the oldest-old (women in their late eighties and beyond). An age-based analysis of older women's issues is not always feasible or useful for a number of reasons. First, available research has not consistently examined different age-groups of older adults separately.

Second, many issues can not be easily assigned to a specific late-adulthood age period. Third, there is inter-individual variability in the timing of many experiences, due to factors such as nationality, ethnicity, social class, health, and cohort status.

In this chapter, I rely on research and theories produced in English-speaking and/or industrialized countries. Thus, the picture of aging discussed in this chapter reflects primarily the experiences and values dominant in these countries. Women living in very different national and cultural settings than those covered in this chapter may experience very different patterns and issues of aging.

While this chapter focuses on women's unique experiences, as compared to men, a caveat is in order. Differences between older women and men co-exist with a large variability among women and men even within specific historical and national boundaries. This within-group variability is associated with a variety of factors, including social class, sexual orientation, and ethnicity. For example, within current cohorts of older women in the United States, there are important differences in health, income, and life expectancy, depending on ethnicity. This within-group variability is an important theme in this chapter.

ISSUES, RESOURCES, AND CHALLENGES FOR OLDER ADULT WOMEN

This section examines common issues, unique resources, as well as unique vulnerabilities for women in late adulthood. Issues related to cultural meanings of aging for women are addressed first. The life situations (e.g., living arrangements), transitions (e.g., widowhood), and health status typical of older women are described next. Finally, end-of-life issues are discussed.

MEANINGS OF AGING

Like gender, age functions as a system of social classification. It determines a person's location on the social map in terms of power, status, and access to resources (M. Crawford & Unger, 2000). Like gender, it also is associated with stereotypes.

What are the prevalent stereotypes of women and aging in the United States? First, women are perceived as reaching old age earlier than men (Drevenstedt, 1976; Seccombe & Ishii-Kuntz, 1991). In one study, for example, women were viewed as old when they were between the ages of 55 and 59, while men were considered old several years later, between the ages of 60 and 64 years (Seccombe & Ishii-Kuntz, 1991). In addition, older women tend to be evaluated more negatively than older men in terms of physical appearance (F.M. Deutsch, Zalenski, & Clark, 1986; M.B. Harris, 1994; Kite, Deaux, & Miele, 1991). More women than men are expected to, and do use age concealment devices, such as hair coloring (M.B. Harris, 1994).

Older women are also viewed as less competent, intelligent, wise (Canetto, Kaminski, & Felicio, 1995; Kite, Deaux, & Miele, 1991), and less independent (Canetto et al., 1995; O'Connell & Rotter, 1979) than older men. Some of these views may be grounded in the harsh reality of women and aging. For example, older women, due to their longevity, are more likely than older men to develop syndromes (such as dementia), which involve dependence and cognitive decline. Older women are also more likely to live alone and to be poor than older men, a consequence of which is that their needs and vulnerabilities become visible. Conversely, older men's dependence and cognitive problems may be less obvious because older men can often count on the assistance of their younger wives or paid help. The perception of older women as less intelligent and wise than older men, however, suggests the persistence of the sexist stereotypes documented for young adult women (Deaux & Kite, 1993).

At the same time, older women are perceived more positively than older men with regard to nurturance, warmth, and sensitivity (Canetto et al., 1995; Kite et al., 1991; O'Connell & Rotter, 1979). These perceptions are consistent with images of older women as grandmotherly (M.B. Brewer, Dull, & Lui, 1981; Facio, 1996; Hummert, 1990; Kite et al., 1991; Schmidt & Boland, 1986). The "nice grandmother" stereotype may enhance older women's likability, but may also lead to an expectation of care-giving, and possible disapproval of older women who do not fit the "fuzzy" grandmother type. The view of older women as nurturant may be uniquely problematic for those women who, having been socialized for self-sacrifice, have already spent their adult years caring for others. This view may interfere with the development of a healthy sense of entitlement and investment in the self-care activities, which, as we will see later, are crucial to physical and mental well-being.

In sum, older women face a more hostile cultural climate than older men. Images of older women are more limiting, if not always more negative, than older men's. Older women are perceived as nice, but unattractive and dull.

RETIREMENT

Retirement, defined as separation from paid employment, is traditionally conceptualized as a life transition involving changes in social status, power, income, activities, interpersonal interactions, and family roles (Abeles et al., 1997). This conceptualization is, however, a poor fit for women's experiences, because it is based on a male model (Calasanti, 1996). Until relatively recently, few women were employed in the kind of industries that offer retirement benefits. Of those women who did, few had accumulated the years of continuous employment to qualify for retirement benefits. Furthermore, women's typical jobs (i.e., sales, service, teaching, nursing, librarian, and clerical positions), and their status within those jobs, involve subordinate roles. Thus, retirement for women is less likely to lead to an important loss in status and power. In addition, women's retirement is more likely than men's retirement to be precipitated by external events (such as a spouse's retirement or a family illness) than by work-related events (Turk-Charles, Rose, & Gatz, 1996). Furthermore, for women, especially working class women, retirement from paid employment does not bring about the same freedom from labor that it does for men (especially upper to middle class men) (Calasanti, 1993, 1996).

Definitions of retirement as separation from paid employment are particularly inapplicable to the experience of homemakers whose labor has always been unpaid. A homemaker's labor may involve contributions to a family business, household work, and/or family care-giving. Independent of employment and marital status, most women are involved in unpaid family care-giving throughout their lifetime, and they rarely experience the clear end of labor activities that is basic to the concept of retirement.

The fact that women's experiences of retirement have been examined through a male model may account in part for the mixed findings on women's satisfaction with retirement. In general, retirement appears to be more difficult for women than for men (Hatch, 1987, 1992). Different factors have been associated with women's dissatisfaction with retirement in different studies. Women tend to retire earlier and to have lower incomes at retirement than men (Carp, 1997b). In some studies, but not in others, younger age, low income, and poor health at retirement were predictors of dissatisfaction for women. It is important to remember, however, that the majority of women (like the majority of men) look forward to, and are pleased with, retired life (Calasanti, 1996).

Women whose primary productive activities involved raising their children may experience some of the psychological dynamics traditionally associated with retirement when the children permanently leave home. Evidence suggests that the "empty nest" transition may be particularly stressful for women whose self-definition and self-worth depended on being a parent (Grambs, 1989). For example, one study found that children moving out of the home was more difficult for women who were born in the 1920s and 1930s, and who reached adulthood at a time when motherhood was viewed as a woman's exclusive vocation, than for women who were born between 1900 and 1910, and who were encouraged to join the workforce during World War II (Adelmann, Antonucci, Crohan, & Coleman, 1989). Typically, however, the "emptying of the nest" is associated with increased well-being and happiness in women (Grambs, 1989).

Some full-time homemakers may experience retirement vicariously through their husbands' retirement. For these women, retirement means adjusting to family and financial changes associated with their husband' retirement (Carp, 1997b).

A minority of women (8%) remain in the paid labor force after age 65. Divorced or single women are more likely to be employed after age 65 than married women. These women typically work part-time and in low-paying occupations, where more than half the workers are women (R.M. Rubin, 1997).

In sum, women are less likely than men to experience the labor and income patterns which allow them to identify themselves, or to be viewed as retired (Calasanti, 1993, 1996). Independent of employment and family situation, most women are involved in unpaid care-giving throughout their lifetime. As such, they rarely experience the clear-cut end of labor that is intrinsic to the traditional concept of retirement. These factors may account for the variable findings on women's satisfaction at retirement.

FINANCIAL RESOURCES

Poverty is a serious concern for older women. Surveys show that about two-thirds of poor older adults in the United States are women (Turk-Charles et al., 1996). A majority of these poor women are ethnic minorities (Gatz et al., 1995; Turk-Charles et al., 1996). In 1992, the median income for older women was $8,189, in contrast to $14,748 for older men. Older married women are better off than single women (R.M. Rubin, 1997). Older women living alone have five times the rate of poverty of men in the same situation (Gatz et al., 1995). Over 60% of African American women living alone are below the poverty line, as compared to 25% of European American women in the same situation (Hess, 1990). According to Hess, official statistics underestimate poverty among older women because many poor older women live with an adult child or become homeless.

International studies indicate that older women's poverty is a worldwide problem. According to data from the International Council on Social Welfare (Sadik, 1997), many older women are unable to meet their minimal needs for nutrition and shelter. Everywhere in the world "poverty has a female face" (p. 6).

Poverty in late adulthood usually reflects the accumulation of disadvantages through life (Gatz et al., 1995; Hess, 1990; Turk-Charles et al., 1996). For older women in the United States, these disadvantages include less education, low pay while employed, limited opportunities for retirement and health care benefits, family responsibilities which interfere with continuous employment, and nonpayment for household and family care-giving work. According to data from the International Council on Social Welfare (Sadik, 1997), women's poverty around the world is due to gender discrimination in education, employment, and access to economic resources (such as credit, land ownership, and inheritance property), as well as women's under-representation in political decision making.

Family illnesses place further strain on older women's financial resources. For example, older women tend to take care of their ill older husbands, a task that can deplete the family savings. When their husbands die, women's pensions often do not include survivor's benefits. The social security widows receive based on their own employment record is often much less than the one they received when their husbands were alive (Turk-Charles et al., 1996). Other strains on women's financial resources are women's own health problems (Chrisler, 2000). Women suffer from more chronic health problems and disabilities than men. Because women live longer and are less likely to have health insurance coverage, they are more likely to exhaust their financial resources on health-related expenses (Hess, 1990).

Financial problems are typically more serious for persons in advanced stages of adulthood. The income of all household units over age 85 is less than half of what it is for persons in the 65 to 69 age group (Schaie & Willis, 1996). The personal income of oldest-old women is two-thirds of that of men. This is "because men have income from more sources and higher amounts from those sources" (Bould & Longino, 1997, p. 215).

In conclusion, financial problems are a major concern for women in late adulthood. These problems are particularly serious for ethnic minority women, and worsen with advancing age. Women's poverty in late adulthood reflects the accumulation of disadvantages through life. These advantages include their low levels of education, family that interfere with continuous employment, low pay while employed, limited retirement and health care benefits, high rates of widowhood and living alone, poor health and longer lives in poor health, and a disproportionate contribution to unpaid care-giving.

FAMILY, FRIENDS, AND LIVING ARRANGEMENTS

In part because of differences in longevity, and in part because women tend to marry older men, women are far more likely to be widowed than men (United Nations, 1995). For women, widowhood starts earlier and lasts longer than for men (Barer, 1994). The average length of widowhood for women is 15 years (Carstensen & Pasupathi, 1993).

Moreover, when older women are widowed, they are less likely to remarry than older men in the same situation (Hess, 1990). In the United States, only about a quarter of women age 75 and older are married, as compared with 70% of men (Turk-Charles et al., 1996). Nearly all of women over 85 are widowed, while about half of men of the same age are not (Bould & Longino, 1997). The same situation is found in many other countries. For example, in Italy, only 15% of women over age 80 are married, in contrast to 61% of men over 80 (ISTAT, 1997).

In some countries, special limitations are applied to widows, but not to widowers. For example, in India, upper caste widows are not allowed to work and must live in their deceased husband's residence under restriction of diet, dress, and demeanor (United Nations, 1995). In parts of Papua New Guinea, older widows were ritually killed by their kin because they were considered a burden on their children. Widowers, however, were not treated as a burden, and were not ritually killed (Canetto & Lester, 1998).

The combination of women's longevity, with their high widowhood and low remarriage rates accounts in part for women's high rates of living alone. In Western countries, older women are more likely to live alone than older men (Hess, 1990; Ory & Warner, 1990; Turk-Charles et al., 1996; D.A. Wolf, 1995). For example, in the late 1980s in the United States, there were 6.5 million women among those age 65 and older living alone, in comparison with fewer than 2 million men in the same situation (Hess, 1990). This is a growing phenomenon. Living alone is increasingly common among women, including women age 75 and older (Carp, 1997a).

While living alone typically starts with widowhood or divorce, in many cases it becomes a choice (Carp, 1997b). A preference for living alone has been documented even in communities where women are assumed to prefer family living arrangements. For example, many of the older Chicanas interviewed by Facio (1996) reported choosing to live alone. They reported enjoying the independence brought by widowhood and sought ways to reduce involvement in family care-giving.

Another common arrangement for older women is to live with relatives and others. In the United States, about 20% of older women live with relatives or others, more than twice the rate of older men (R.M. Rubin, 1997).

What is the impact of widowhood on women's health? In some respects, women cope well with the transition to widowhood better than men. Although they report high levels of bereavement-related distress, they experience fewer physical and mental health problems than widowers. For example, widows are less likely to suffer from cardiovascular morbidity and mortality than widowers (L.F. Berkman et al., 1993). Widows are also less likely to suffer from depression than widowers (Siegel & Kuykendall, 1990; Umbertson, Wortman, & Kessler, 1992). When they do, it is often because of financial problems (Umbertson et al., 1992). Widows, unlike widowers, have low rates of alcohol abuse (Abeles et al., 1997) and low rates of suicide (Bock & Webber, 1972; Li, 1995; MacMahon & Pugh, 1965). The mortality risk for widows is lower than for widowers (C. Lee, 1998).

One reason older women adjust better to widowhood than men may be that marriage is more important for men's well-being and health than for women's (Joung et al., 1997; D.B. Preston. 1995). Men benefit more from, and report greater satisfaction with, marriage than women (Schone & Weinick, 1998). They also tend to be less close than women to their children and grandchildren. In contrast, older women have a greater number of friends, and feel closer to their friends than older men (Turk-Charles et al., 1996). Close friends are particularly important for older lesbians (A.H. Grossman, D'Augelli, & Hershberger, 2000). It is important to remember, however, that for women, having many close relationships may create more demands than support, because women are expected to give rather than to receive in relationships (D.B. Preston, 1995; J. Smith & Baltes, 1998).

Another reason that women cope relatively well with the loss of a spouse may be that widowhood is more normative and occurs at a younger age among women than among men. Women expect to spend part of the life as widows. They have more time to adjust to widowhood and to develop other relationships (Barer, 1994).

Finally, widows may be better prepared than widowers to live as single persons because of their practice running a household. Also, for widows, to assume responsibilities for tasks previously performed by their husbands, such as managing financial assets, may be psychologically rewarding because those are socially valued tasks. Conversely, widowers' self-image may be diminished by having to perform tasks, such as household cleaning or food preparation, which they may consider feminine and degrading (Blieszner, 1993).

While widows seem to do better emotionally and socially than widowers, they do significantly worse financially. Widows have the lowest income of all demographic groups. Widows are four times more likely to live in poverty after retirement than married women (R.M. Rubin, 1997). Financial problems are the main reason for the physical and mental health problems of widows (Joung et al., 1997; Umbertson, Wortman, & Kessler, 1992).

As noted earlier, a common consequence of widowhood for older women is to live alone. Older women living alone put high proportions of their small incomes into housing, which leaves little money for other budgetary categories. Older women living alone are overrepresented in housing with the most structural deficiencies and the poorest maintenance (Carp, 1997a).

Living alone also increases the risk for institutionalization, especially after an illness or disability create a need for assistance in daily activities. As their disabilities increase, older women living alone tend to change their living arrangements in order to have access to more help. For example, more women with self-care disabilities live with children and relatives than women with mobility limitations. Disabilities are also the primary reason that women enter a nursing home (Bould & Longino, 1997).

More women than men are permanent residents of nursing homes and other kinds of extended care facilities (Schaie & Willis, 1996). Three out of four nursing home residents are women (Turk-Charles et al., 1996). Among persons 85 and over, one in four women lives in a nursing home, in contrast to one in seven men (American Association of Homes for the Aging, 1991). Good nursing homes are expensive. Older women often can not afford quality nursing home care.

It is important to remember that some of the problems associated with widowhood are not the result of being single. Older women who never married are better off financially than previously married older women (widows, separated, or divorced women). Ever-single persons are also more likely than previously married persons to share a home with at least one other person, a pattern that reduces the need for residential care. Furthermore, when compared with the formerly married, ever-single older women report the best health and the fewest disabilities, conditions which otherwise are the major reason for admission to long-term facilities. When they develop disabilities, however, ever-single older women are at higher risk for institutionalization than previously married older women with the same condition. The greater financial and lesser familial resources of the ever-single older women influence the kind of care they use. For example, ever-single women are more likely than previously married women to rely on hired help (Newtson & Keith, 1997).

One limitation of the data on ever-single women is that they lump together women who are single for very different reasons, ranging from sexual orientation to religious vows. Older lesbians, for example, may be better equipped for the challenges of late adulthood as a result of practice in the negotiation of marginalization and resisting negative stereotypes (Sharp, 1997). Granted these limitations, the data on ever-single women make it clear that "being without a man" is not what puts widows at risk for negative outcomes later in life. Rather, many of the difficulties that widows face are the result of gender inequities that especially exploit married women (Carstensen & Pasupathi, 1993).

To summarize, older women are far more likely than men to be widowed than older men. Most widows remain single and live alone. Older women do not appear to suffer severe health, emotional or social problems as a result of widowhood. Nonetheless, they suffer economically. Widows have the lowest income of all demographic groups. Financial problems are the main reason for the physical and mental health problems of widows. Widows are also at increased risk of moving to extended care facilities when disabled. The economic problems associated with widowhood for women are not the result of being single. Ever-single older women are better off financially than previously-married older women. A limitation of the research on older women and relationships is that it has focused on heterosexual married and widowed women. The inclusion of a more diverse sample of women and relationships will help clarify whether the widowhood effects reported above are related specifically to the institution of marriage and heterosexual issues and dynamics, to general issues associated with the loss of an intimate partner, or to societal sexism. Many questions about the relationships of older lesbians remain to be investigated.

Older women are typically involved in a variety of care-giving activities. Like younger women, they provide more care and more kinds of care than men, independent of participation in the paid labor force (A.J. Walker, 1992). Older women may be involved, either sequentially or simultaneously, in the care of their husbands; significant others and friends; parents; other relatives; children; and grandchildren. A recent national survey of about 1,500 English-speaking family care-givers with telephones revealed that 73% were women, and that the older women were caring for the most disabled persons (National Alliance for Caregiving/AARP, 1997). Women also provide the majority of assistance with nonmedical care for terminally ill persons (Emanuel et al., 1999).

For some women, care-giving continues without interruption for several decades into late adulthood. While the amount of physical care-giving may decline after a certain age, the emotional care-giving may not. For example, in a study, old-old women reported providing more emotional care than old-old men (J. Smith & Baltes, 1998).

There are probably a number of reasons why women do most of the care-giving. These include attachment to care recipients, economic necessity, and socialized obligation (A.J. Walker, 1992). Care-giving can be rewarding and contribute to a person's sense of connection and purpose (Biegel & Schulz, 1999). It may also be frustrating and alienating. Regardless of the reasons and of the quality of the relationship with the care-recipient, the long-term care-giving typical of women involves costs (R. Schulz, O'Brien, Bookwala, & Fleissner, 1995). It interferes with activities related to economic independence, personal development, and self-care (A.J. Walker, 1992). Consequently, it can take a toll on the caregiver's physical and mental health. It also impinges on women's already limited financial resources, leading to economic strain. Thus, it is not surprising that women experience the more stress and mental health problems from care-giving than men (Neal, Ingersoll-Dayton, & Starrels, 1997; J.L. Yee & Schulz, 2000).

Women, like men, need more care as they get older. Care-receiving is related to disability and increases with age. Related to demographic reasons, most people in need of care assistance are women (Dwyer & Coward, 1992). In many ways, older women are disadvantaged with regard to care-receiving, relative to older men. For example, married women with disabilities are far less likely to receive care from their spouses than the other way around. In 1988, only 18% of women with disabilities were cared for by their spouses, in contrast to 55% of men with disabilities (Hess, 1990). Having a spouse results in reduced nursing home stay for men but not for women (V. Freedman, 1993). At the same time, women do not appear disadvantaged in terms of care received from other informal sources. Women experience shorter nursing home stays than men if they have an adult child (V. Freedman, 1993). In one study, community-dwelling women and men ages 75 to 84 were equally as likely to receive help from family and friends—although men were more likely to receive help from formal sources (Chipperfield, 1994). However, when they are terminally ill and dying, women, even when they are married, receive less assistance from family members, and they must rely on paid help to a greater extent than men (Emanuel et al., 1999).

In sum, older women provide more care and a greater variety of care than older men, and for reasons which may include attachment, socialized obligation, and economic necessity. Regardless of the reason, care-giving impinges on women's already limited resources, leading to emotional, physical, and economic strain. Social contact and self-care may be reduced, due to task overload. Care-receiving increases with age. In general, older women are less likely to receive care from their spouses than older men but they often get help from other informal sources, including children and friends. However, when women are terminally ill and dying, they are less likely than men to receive care from family members and friends and tend to rely on paid assistance. A limitation of the research on care-giving and care-receiving is the invisibility of the experience of older lesbians. Of significance in the lives of older lesbians are a variety of relationships, including partnerships, families of choice, and families of origin. The ways older lesbians deal with these relationships in terms of care-giving and care-receiving remains a neglected topic.

PHYSICAL HEALTH

A paradox characterizes women's health in late adulthood. Women have higher rates of physical illnesses and disabilities, but live longer than men (Gatz et al., 1995; Ory & Warner, 1990; J. Smith & Baltes, 1998; Turk-Charles et al., 1996). Because of their longevity, women tend to experience a long period of morbidity, together with frailty, incapacity, and dependence (J. Smith & Baltes, 1998).

Socioeconomic status has an important effect on health. Older women and men of lower socioeconomic status are more likely to experience health problems than those who are socioeconomically advantaged (Adler & Coriell, 1997; Gatz et al., 1995). Women's poor health, relative to men, may be a consequence of their lower socioeconomic resources. Ethnic minority women generally report worse health than European American women. For example, African American women have poorer self-rated health and higher specific mortality rates than European American women. Women of Hispanic heritage report poorer self-rated health and higher disability rates, but have similar mortality rates as European American women (Torrez, 1997). The role of sexual orientation on health is unclear. One self-report study of older lesbians found them to enjoy excellent health (Deevey, 1990).

Older women are more likely than older men to suffer from nonfatal but debilitating conditions, such as arthritis (D.E. Smith, 1990; Verbrugge, 1990). While co-morbidity is an issue for all older adults, it is particularly common among older women (Guralnik, LaCroix, Everett, & Kovar, 1989). Functional health problems are also more common in older women than in older men (Gatz et al., 1995), especially lower-body disabilities (R.J. Johnson & Wolinsky, 1994). Functional health problems lead to reduced mobility and risk for accidental injury, such as falls (S.J. O'Brien & Vertinsky, 1991).

Old-old women are particularly vulnerable to chronic conditions that interfere with their motivation to ambulate. According to a review by S.J. O'Brien and Vertinsky (1991), spinal degeneration and deformity, colitis, migraine headaches, bladder infections, varicose veins, and bunions are two to three times more prevalent in women over 75 than in men the same age. The same is true of conditions associated with stress such as stomach ulcers.

The gender gap in health increases at advanced stages of adulthood. Women who survive beyond the age of 85 suffer from more diseases and disabilities than men the same age. They are also less independent than similarly aged men. Many more women are alive at 95 but they do worse than men the same age in terms of physical health. It has been speculated that men who survive beyond their eighties represent an unusually vigorous group, and that this vigor gives them a health and survival advantage. For example, although women make up 80% of 100-year-olds, they represent only 60% of 105 year-olds. In a similar fashion, after age 75, African Americans are less likely to die than European Americans (Perl, 1995).

Older women do not seem to differ from older men with regard to self-rated health. Older adults, independent of sex, report more health problems than younger adults but are more optimistic about their health than might be expected based on physicians' health assessments (Gatz et al., 1995). Self-rated health, however, is a better predictor of mortality in men than in women of comparable ages. The relationship between self-rated health and mortality varies in different national settings (Jylhä, Guralnik, Ferrucci, Jokela, & Heikkinen, 1998).

Women report more medical visits than older men, but the care they receive is often of worse quality than that of men (Council on Ethical and Judicial Affairs, American Medical Association, 1991). Older women and older men with the same medical conditions receive different care, although this difference has no basis in research. Compared to men, women are over-prescribed tranquilizers and hypnotic drugs, and are underserved for cardiac catheterization, bypass surgery, renal dialysis, and renal transplant (Gatz et al., 1995). Women report higher use of legal prescription and nonprescription drugs than men (Verbrugge, 1990).

Older women have lower rates of hospitalization than older men. However, they remain longer in acute-care beds and are more likely to be transferred to long-term care facilities for their recovery (E. Segal, 1996). When discharged, older women are less likely than older men to have a spouse at home to take care of them. When older women get home care, it is from a female relative, usually a daughter (Turk-Charles et al., 1996).

In the United States, older women and men differ with regard to the kind of illnesses they experience, but die of the same diseases. The leading causes of death for women and men in the United States (and other industrialized countries) are heart disease, cancer, and stroke (Gatz et al., 1995). Women, however, live for a shorter time with life-threatening conditions, such as heart disease and cancer. There are, also, important differences in leading causes of mortality across ethnic groups. For example, diabetes is the fourth leading cause of death among African American, Native American and Hispanic-descent women, but only the seventh leading cause among European American women (Torrez, 1997). Suicide is among the ten leading causes of death for Native American or Alaskan Native and Asian or Pacific Islander women, but not for European American women, African American women, or women of Hispanic descent (Field & Cassell, 1997).

In sum, older women live longer than older men but in poorer health. They tend to experience a greater prevalence of nonfatal disabling conditions, especially those that interfere with mobility. Older women receive worse medical care than older men. They are less likely to receive costly medical procedures, but are over-prescribed psychotropic medication. Finally, while women and men die of the same diseases, women live less long with life-threatening conditions such as heart disease and cancer. Why women suffer from more nonfatal conditions is not clear. One factor may be their greater longevity. Behavioral factors may also play a role. Women exercise less than men in every age groups (C. Lee, 1998), a behavior that is probably related to socialization factors as well as limited resources. It has been estimated that regular exercise could halve age-related decline in physical functioning in older women (S.J. O'Brien & Vertinsky, 1991).

MENTAL HEALTH

Given that poverty and poor health are common among older women, it is perhaps not surprising that older women report less subjective well-being, more feelings of unhappiness and more frequent negative emotions than same-age men (J. Smith & Baltes, 1998). Older women are over-represented among the users of tranquilizers and sleeping pills. For example in Canada, 23% of women over age 65 use sleeping pills, as compared with 18% of same-age men, and 7% of women under 55 (S.J. O'Brien & Vertinsky, 1991).

At the same time, mental health disorders that plague women in early adulthood, such as eating disorders, disappear in late adulthood. Other mental syndromes, such as depressive and anxiety disorders, show similar rates for women and men in later life. In fact, the prevalence of depressive disorders is lower among persons age 65 and older than among those younger than age 65 (Gatz et al., 1995; George, 1990; R. Wolfe, Morrow, & Fredrickson, 1996).

There are more women than men among those suffering from dementia, the most common disorder leading to cognitive impairment among older adults. A reason may be women's longevity, since the diagnosis of dementia dramatically increases with age (Gatz et al., 1995). Women also live longer with cognitive impairment disorders (Turk-Charles et al., 1996). The large number of women with dementia has important consequences for the lives of women because dementia is a major factor in institutionalization. More women than men are permanent residents of nursing homes and other kinds of extended care facilities (Schaie & Willis, 1996). Among the consequences of institutionalization is the loss of the will to live, manifested as indirect suicidal behavior, such as refusing food or medication (Osgood & Eisenhandler, 1995).

It is possible that the low rates of diagnosed non-organic psychopathology observed in older adults represent an underestimate, due to diagnostic criteria and methods developed on the basis of observations of young samples (Gallagher-Thompson et al., 2000). Since older adults tend to express their distress through physical rather than psychological symptoms (Abeles et al., 1997; Gallo, Anthony, & Muthén, 1994), depression may be under-diagnosed in all older adults. Gatz and colleagues, however, warn that "while it is important not to minimize genuine distress, it is also important to be careful not to argue that rates of depression should be higher in older women. . . . due to the stress in their lives" (1995, p. 509). Many factors beside stress contribute to rates of mental disorders.

One mental health domain in which older women differ greatly from older men is suicide. Older women have very low rates of suicide, as compared to older men (Canetto, 1992). Men age 65 and older take their own lives six times the rate of women in the same age group. Among persons age 85 and older, the ratio of male to female suicide is even greater. For example, in 1990, the female to male suicide ratio for those ages 85 and older was 1:12 (Osgood & Malkin, 1997). Suicide is particularly high among older men of European American descent. It is important to note that the national data on older women and suicide hide important variations by ethnicity. For example, rates of suicide for Chinese American women rise after age 45 and reach a peak among the oldest-old. Also, after age 75, Japanese American women have rates of suicide that are higher than those of European American women (D. Yee, 1997). At the same time, African American women's suicide rates are lowest, relative to those of African American men and European American women (Ralston, 1997).

It is unclear what are the mechanisms responsible for women's low rates of non-organic mental disorders and suicidal behavior in late adulthood, as compared to young adulthood, and for the variations in suicide risk across ethnicity. Theories of geriatric psychopathology have tended to focus on older European American men, and to ignore questions of gender and ethnicity. Unfortunately, without the benefit of information on women across ethnicity and on ethnic minority men, it is impossible to make sense of older European American men's vulnerability to suicide. Also, mental health issues relevant to both women and men that would most readily emerge through the study of women and ethnic minorities are overlooked (Canetto, 1995). Another limitation of the research on psychopathology among older adults is its lack of attention to questions of sexual orientation.

Older adult suicide (in European American males) is often conceptualized as a response to the "losses of aging" (e.g., reduced financial resources, widowhood, living alone, and poor health), and the depression triggered by these losses. Older women, however, especially ethnic minority older women, are more likely to experience the losses that presumably lead older European American men to suicide (Canetto, 1992, 1995). Furthermore, rates of depression do not vary by sex among older adults, so it is not obvious why so many more men than women kill themselves.

A gender analysis sheds some light on older European American male suicide. Studies of predominantly European American respondents show that killing oneself is considered masculine and more permissible for men than women. Suicide by men is viewed as less wrong, less foolish, and stronger than suicide by women. Older European American men's suicides are narrated as acts of independence and courage in the face of adversity (Canetto, 1997).

Attention to cultural meanings of gender and suicide helps to make sense of important variations in suicide mortality across different-ethnicity women, specifically, the low rates for African American women, and the high rates among Chinese American and Japanese American women. Asian American women are not worse off than African-American women in terms of the stresses of aging (such as poverty, widowhood, or poor health); nor are African American women advantaged over European American women. Rather, Chinese American older women come from a tradition where suicide is a female behavior. In China, suicide is more common among women than men, especially in rural areas (Canetto & Lester, 1995).

Attention to gender scripts of suicidal behavior in different cultures also illuminates the relationships between gender, ethnicity, and suicide method. Older women and men tend to use the suicide method that is acceptable for them as women and men in their community. Among successive cohorts of Chinese and Japanese American older women, traditional suicide methods such as hanging are being replaced by firearms (J.L. McIntosh & Santos, 1986). Firearms is now the suicide method chosen by most older adults, accounting for about one-third of women's, and three-fourth of men's, suicides in the United States (M.S. Kaplan, Adamek, Geling, & Calderon, 1997).

In conclusion, the data on gender, culture, and mental health among older adults point to the inadequacy of a simple stress model of psychopathology. Older women, especially ethnic minority women, experience more adverse life conditions than older men. Older women report less well-being, but do not exhibit more psychopathology than older men. Perhaps the adversities women face tax their health and reduce their quality of life, but also foster psychological growth and resilience. Perhaps women's care-giving relationships provide a deterrent against killing oneself because of the feeling of being needed and a concern that others may be upset by one's suicide (Canetto, 1992). The variations in women's rates of suicide across cultures where women have similarly low social status point to the role of cultural scripts in gender and coping in suicide. People appear to resort to suicide when such an act is permissible and even expected under certain circumstances for persons like oneself in one's community—independent of social status, privilege, and objective quality of life. The cross-cultural data suggest that it is the association of suicide with masculinity that protects most U.S. older women from suicide. Once that association is reversed, as appears to be the case in Chinese communities, women are counted among the suicidal.

LONGEVITY

Life expectancy has increased enormously in the past century in the United States. In 1900, the average longevity was 47 years; by 1996, it had increased to 76 years, a gain of 29 years in less than a century (Pamuk, Makuc, Heck, Reuben, & Lochner, 1998). The gender gap in longevity has also increased. In 1900, women could expect to live only two to three years longer than men in most of North America and Western Europe (Kristof, 1996).

Currently, women live longer than men across a variety of national and ethnic groups. At the same time, the age at which women die, and the gender gap in longevity, vary according to nationality, ethnicity, and social class. Internationally, women's life expectancy is shorter where their status is very low, and their access to basic resources, such as food or health care, is systematically and drastically reduced. In these countries, women may eat less food and lower quality food, suffer from complications of frequent childbearing and sexually transmitted diseases (because they can not demand abstinence or condom use), and/or experience "infections and hemorrhages following genital mutilation, neglect of symptoms of illness until severe, and restricted access to modern health care" (Lorber, 1997b, p. 14).

In the United States, there are three older women for every two older men. Among those 85 and older, women outnumber men five to two (Gatz et al., 1995). Although there are important ethnic differences in longevity, women consistently outlive men across ethnic groups. For example, an African American woman can expect to live 74 years, as compared to 80 years for a European American woman, and 65 years for an African American man (Field & Cassell, 1997). Finally, the higher one goes in socioeconomic status, the lower the risk of mortality for both women and men (Adler & Coriell, 1997).

In sum, women live longer than men. Given women's high rates of morbidity and co-morbidity, a longer life does not necessarily mean a better life. It is not clear what accounts for the divergent gender trends on morbidity and mortality.

MEANINGS OF LONGEVITY

The world of the old-old is a world of women. Old-old women are the age elite. In the words of Bould and Longino, they are the survivors from the struggles of life, "the true pioneers of the aging society" (1997, p. 211). In the United States, survivors are usually admired. Yet, "to survive into advanced old age . . . is seldom considered heroic for women" note Bould and Longino. Old-old women are more likely to be "pitied . . . for having outlived their friends and family" and for being sick rather than to be "celebrated as victors" (p. 211). Their added years have been called a "bitter fruit," and perceived like a curse rather than blessing (S.J. O'Brien & Vertinsky, 1991, p. 347).

In fact, old-old women have not even been studied very much. Researchers have seemed more interested in older men who die than in older women who survive. "Both the Baltimore and the Framingham study initially examined men exclusively," observe Bould and Longino (1997, p. 210).

Some scholars have gone beyond treating longevity as uninteresting or personally burdensome. They have argued that longevity is a social burden. They contend that publicly financed resources such as health care should be rationed on the basis of old age and other criteria (Brody, 1992; Callahan, 1995). Their idea is that lifesaving resources should not be invested in persons who have reached a certain age, and fulfilled on the whole their life goals and obligations, thus completing their biographical narrative. It is argued that letting older persons die may be sad, but should be tolerable.

Since there are more women than men among the old-old, discussions about rationing resources based on age are essentially discussions about rationing resources for older women. In practice, age-based measures treat life beyond male life expectancy as expendable and excessive.

Because women have more years to live as old-old, in poorer health, and with fewer private resources than men, age-based rationing proposals disproportionately harm women (Jecker, 1991).

The inclusion of so called biographical considerations in resource-rationing proposals is also uniquely problematic for women (Canetto & Hollenshead, 1999). Given the perception that reproductive and care-giving work are women's life vocation (Gergen, 1990b), women's lives may be perceived as complete and even meaningless as soon as women can no longer function as caregivers. Sick older women who need (rather than provide) care-giving may be particularly vulnerable to seeing themselves, and to be viewed by others as burdensome. Several of the women whose death was hastened by Dr. Kevorkian fit this biographical profile. For example, an 82-year-old widow requested and was assisted in suicide on the grounds that she was old. She suffered from various age-related disabilities, but was healthy for her age. Before her death, she said she believed in assisted suicide on demand for anyone older than 80 (Canetto & Hollenshead, 1999).

In sum, women's longevity is not socially valued. Those who view longevity as a social burden have proposed that some resources be rationed on the basis of age. Age-based rationing policies, while not directed explicitly and exclusively at women, are uniquely harmful to women because women live longer and depend more on publicly financed programs than men.

LIFE-EXTENDING AND DEATH HASTENING DECISIONS

The experience of dying has changed in the past century in the United States (Field & Cassell, 1997). Death in hospitals has replaced death at home, and the dying process tends to more extended than it used to be, partly because medical interventions can control many immediate causes of death. Questions about life-extending interventions have thus become central issues for older and dying persons, their families, and clinicians. It has been argued that most deaths in the United States result from medical decisions about withdrawal or withholding of some death-delaying technology (Webb, 1997).

Very little is known on how decisions about life-extending care are made, and even less on how being an older woman affects these decisions. What we do know is that the seriously ill person is not usually the sole or even the primary decision maker about care at the end of life. A likely reason is that as many as half of those judged terminally ill do not meet the most minimal criteria for competence to make decisions (Mishara, 1999). Physicians typically make these decisions, with some degree of consultation with family members (Mishara, 1999). Furthermore, we know that family and professional surrogates do poorly when asked to predict a person's life-sustaining preferences (Fagerlin, Ditto, Danks, Houts, & Smucker, in press). In addition, individual preferences for life-sustaining medical treatments are only moderately stable within the short-term (up to a six-month interval), and even less stable over longer periods of time. Healthy individuals appear unable to predict their own preferences under states of impaired health (L.K. Lockhart, Ditto, Danks, Coppola, & Smucker, in press). In fact, people change their minds about these preferences without being aware of having done so (Gready et al., in press). Substantial fluctuations in the will to live have been documented even in terminally ill persons in palliative care (Cochinov, Tataryn, Clinch, & Dudgeon, 1999). Among the factors that appear to play a role in the refusal of life-saving treatments are depression and family support (Mishara, 1999). Concerns about costs influence the preferences of patients and family members about life-extending measures (Covinsky et al., 1996). One public opinion poll found that the most frequently expressed fear about death is the fear of being a burden to one's family (Foreman, 1996). Socioeconomic factors play a role in hospital decisions to withdraw life-sustaining interventions. Higher income persons are more likely to have a private attending physician, which is related to the maintenance of life-sustaining care (Mishara, 1999).

While studies have not examined whether being a woman makes a difference in life-extending decisions, we know that at the time these decisions are usually made, older women have significantly fewer personal, social, and economic resources than older men (Gatz et al., 1995; Hess, 1990). For example, they are more likely than men to live alone or in an institution, to be poor, and to rely on publicly funded health insurance. They receive less quality and less appropriate medical care than men. In addition, women have a lower sense of entitlement than men. Finally, they are exposed to cultural models that glorify self-sacrifice in women (Canetto & Hollenshead, 1999). As a result, older and seriously ill women may be particularly prone to seeing themselves, and/or to be seen by others as undeserving of life-extending care. However, one study of judicial reasoning about termination of treatment for incompetent persons found the opposite. In the absence of written directives, the courts were less likely to infer a preference to terminate life supports for women than for men (Miles & August, 1990). Women's past behaviors suggesting a preference for termination of life-supports tended to be discounted as immature and irrational. In this case, life-extending measures were maintained for women more than for men because women's judgment and agency were viewed as questionable.

While we do not know much about women and life-support decisions, there is some information on women and death-hastening decisions such as assisted suicide and euthanasia. In hastened death situations, life is terminated prematurely by days, months, or years. Assisted suicide involves providing information or access to a lethal method that the person may use to kill herself, while euthanasia involves implementing the lethal method (e.g., giving the lethal injection). In the United States, assisted suicide has recently become legal in Oregon for persons who are terminally ill and do not suffer from a mental disorder that impairs judgment. Assisted suicide was also practiced in Michigan by Dr. Jack Kevorkian between 1990 and 1998. In the Netherlands, assisted suicide and voluntary euthanasia for persons with unbearable suffering have been permissible for two decades (Canetto & Hollenshead, 1999). Voluntary euthanasia was legal for less than a year in the Northern Territory of Australia (Kissane, Street, & Nitschke, 1998).

Various surveys have established that women (like poor, less-educated, older, ethnic minorities, and religious persons) express less interest in, and less support of assisted suicide and euthanasia than men. These survey data have been interpreted as indicating that women, like other disadvantaged groups, may be more concerned about being pressured to die than about being forced to live (Canetto & Hollenshead, 1999). When we move from possibility to practice, however, women are as numerous as, or more numerous than men among the hastened death cases. Nearly all cases of assisted suicide or euthanasia for which information about ethnicity was available have involved White women. Women represent half of the assisted suicide cases in Oregon and the Northern Territory of Australia, and 70% of the Michigan Kevorkian cases. In the Netherlands, they constitute about one-third of assisted suicides but more than half of the voluntary euthanasia cases, a far more common death in that country. Finally, they represent half (in the Netherlands and Australia) to two-thirds (in the United States) of nonvoluntary or involuntary euthanasia cases (performed by clinicians and/or family members) (Canetto & Hollenshead, 2000). In the United States, dependence (i.e., incapacity, loss of autonomy, loss of control of bodily functions) and altruistic concerns (i.e., concerns about being a burden) appear to influence decisions for assisted suicide (Canetto & Hollenshead, 1999; A.E. Chin, Hedberg, Higginson, & Fleming, 1999; Sullivan, Hedberg, & Fleming, 2000). For women in the United States, these concerns may be particularly powerful given their limited resources. It is not clear why women of color have been nearly absent in the recorded cases of assisted suicide and euthanasia.

Nearly all cases of hastened death publicized in the media in the United States have also involved women (Canetto & Hollenshead, 1999). In the late 1970s, Jean Humphry's assisted suicide was documented in the book *"Jean's Way: A Love Story,"* written by her husband Derek Humphry and his second wife Ann Wickett, cofounders of The Hemlock Society. Ann eventually killed herself after being diagnosed with cancer. The famous case of the early 1980s was Elizabeth Bouvia, a woman with quadriplegia and advanced cerebral palsy who attempted to legally compel a hospital to help her die of starvation. Ten years ago, the case at the center of the professional debate on hastened death was Debbie. She died of involuntary euthanasia at the hands of a medical resident who reported the act in an anonymous article published in the *Journal of the American Medical Association*. Then came Dr. Kevorkian's string of female assisted-suicide cases. It took two years before a male died of suicide with Dr. Kevorkian's assistance. In the meantime, a New England physician published an article in *The New England Journal of Medicine* about assisting in the suicide of his patient Diane. Some years later, he wrote about assisting Jane. Louise's assisted suicide was the cover story in a 1993 issue of *The New York Times*. Her story was meant to illustrate the approach to assisted suicide taken by Compassion in Dying, an advocacy organization. In the same year, the president of a regional chapter of The Hemlock Society, dedicated his book, *The Struggle for Death with Dignity,* to seven women (Karen Anne Quinlan, Nancy Cruzan, Patti Rosier, Diane Trumbull, Janet

Adkins, Sherri Miller, Marjorie Wantz), whom he viewed as key cases in promoting the cause of hastened death (Cox, 1993). In Canada, a prominent case was that of Sue Rodriguez, a woman with amyotrophic lateral sclerosis who unsuccessfully attempted to change the Criminal Code concerning assisted suicide, and eventually killed herself with the help of a physician. The first person reported to have legally died of assisted suicide in Oregon was also a woman. She was presented by Compassion in Dying as a model of how well the Oregon system works (Hendin, Foley, & White, 1998). The use of female cases to promote assisted suicide and euthanasia may hold for the Netherlands as well. A well-known Dutch practitioner of hastened death was quoted as saying: "Have you noticed . . . that all of the cases that have broken new ground in Dutch law have been women?" (Hendin, 1994, p. 136).

In sum, life-extending and death-hastening policies and practices have particular relevance for women. Because of their high morbidity and scarce resources, older and seriously ill women in the United States may be uniquely vulnerable to viewing themselves, and to being viewed by others, as better off dead. The right to die may become a duty to die for women. It will be important for future research to account for the discrepancy between women's attitudes about, and mortality from assisted suicide and euthanasia. It will also be helpful to understand why hastened death has not, so far, been a mode of death chosen by women of colors. The question of women's high rates of hastened death, relative to their endorsement of its practice, acquires particular poignancy in the context of this country's managed care medicine, where a shortened end-of-life represents a cost-saving measure. The idea of tempting medical providers to persuade terminally ill persons to minimize costs by hastened death is no fantasy. For example, an economist proposed that financial incentives be offered for choosing physician-hastened death over life-extending interventions. He dedicated the article in which he made this proposal (titled "Dying for Money: Overcoming Moral Hazard in Terminal Illnesses Through Compensated Physician-Assisted Death") to his mother, whose death he wished had been hastened (Fung, 1993).

SUMMARY AND IMPLICATIONS

Women enjoy some unique advantages during late adulthood. For example, they live longer than men and seem to suffer from fewer emotional problems than younger women. Following widowhood, they are less likely than men in the same situation to experience severe physical or emotional problems. They have a greater number of close relationships, and feel closer to friends and family than older men. In contrast to older men, they do not exhibit high rates of mortality from suicide.

Older women, however, face serious challenges. They are expected to, and in fact perform a disproportionate amount of care-giving, but are less likely to be cared by their spouse even when they are married. They suffer from more ill health and disabilities than older men, but have fewer resources to deal with their health problems. Due to high rates of widowhood, older women tend to live alone, which increases costs as well as risks for institutionalization. More women than men are permanent residents of extended care facilities. Older women's health, economic, and social difficulties increase with advancing age. They are more likely to be pitied than celebrated for their longevity. Given their difficult lives and the cultural tradition of women's self-sacrifice, older women may particularly likely to view themselves, and/or be treated by others, as a burden. When they are terminally ill, they receive less help from family members and friends and are more likely to have to pay for assistance.

A person's situation at late adulthood reflects the accumulation of a lifetime of experiences and opportunities. The cohorts of women who reached older adulthood through the past century all experienced, in their lifetime, blatant, institutionalized gender discrimination in intellectual and physical education, professional training, employment, pay, access to resources and leisure, and political representation.

As a result, these women entered late adulthood with vastly different educational, economic, social, family, health, and psychological resources than men. They often thought and behaved differently than men as young adults. Many of the problems (e.g., poverty) these women experienced as older adults were clearly related to generational disadvantage. Considering the massive structural inequalities they experienced, they coped remarkably well with the challenges of late adulthood.

Women who are older adults in the third millennium include the largest number ever of well-educated women. They include the first cohort of women able to plan childbearing through effective contraception and legal abortion. Women who are older adults in the third millennium include the first generation of women to have access to parental leave from their employers. They contain the first substantial group of employed women who enjoy good pensions and benefits. They encompass the first sizable group of women with access to physical education, and a history of regular physical exercise. It will be interesting to see how the resources, health, behavior, and self-image of women in late adulthood change as gender customs, gender values, and forms of gender discrimination change.

As noted by Hendricks, the "circumstances of older women do not come about by chance; they are socially constructed and reflect social priorities" (1995, p. 57). This does not necessarily mean that there is a deliberate intention to harm older women. Older women's main problem may be one of invisibility. Their economic and social contributions are often overlooked. Their needs tend to be viewed as personal or family issues requiring private solutions. An improvement in older women's lives will only come about when older women's issues are treated as public issues with public solutions. Such improvement will require that public policies and planning affecting older adults (concerning matters such as retirement, health care, care-giving for dependents, housing) recognize women's unique life trajectories, and explicitly address their experiences and needs.

PART III

SOCIAL ROLES AND SOCIAL SYSTEMS

CHAPTER 13

The Psychology of Men and Masculinity: Research Status and Future Directions

GLENN E. GOOD and NANCY B. SHERROD

If your interests reside with the psychology of women and gender, you may wonder why this chapter on the psychology of men and masculinity is included in this volume. Indeed, hasn't the study of psychology historically been primarily the study of men anyway? Some readers might view this chapter with skepticism, as a token acknowledgment of the existence of the other sex. However, women's lives and the psychology of women and gender are intimately intertwined with societal notions of men and masculinity. We feel that women's lives and the psychology of women will be greatly enhanced through greater scientific examination of societal conceptions of men and masculinity and their implications for the lives of women and men. For example, if rape, sexual harassment, and domestic violence are dramatic examples of patriarchal oppression of women, people might seek to ameliorate these traumatic problems by developing more effective prevention and treatment programs for women. However, we believe that women's lives are more likely to be enhanced by also improving our understanding and interventions with the *men* who are perpetrating the oppressive acts, and with societal notions that support the problems. The importance of the psychology of men and masculinity to women and their lives is reflected in a story about responses to rape. Specifically, when a curfew for women was suggested to fight a growing number of rapes in Israel, Prime Minister Golda Meir suggested that the curfew instead be for men who were committing the rapes. After you read this chapter, we hope that you will agree, and will join us in seeking to advance research and practice in the psychology of men and masculinity.

Until the publication of Pleck's *The Myth of Masculinity* in 1981, social scientists had scarcely examined masculine gender roles. In the subsequent two decades, the psychology of gender has enjoyed great professional and public appeal. As in the popular media, researchers and theorists in the psychology of gender have increasingly sought to clarify the cultural and social pressures experienced by *both* women and men. This new arena of masculine gender-role research in psychology is seriously considering how men are socialized as men—what and how males learn ideologies of masculinity (e.g., G.R. Brooks & Good, in press; Good, Wallace, & Borst, 1994; Levant & Pollack, 1995). In 1997, the Society for the Psychological Study of Men and Masculinity (SPSMM; Division 51 of the American Psychological Association) was established "to advance knowledge in the psychology of men through research, education, training, public policy and improved clinical practice" (Division 51, 1998, p. 2; see also G.R. Brooks & Levant, 1999). This growing body of research has begun the process of informing our understanding of both women's and men's experiences.

In this chapter, we provide a broad view of many of the most salient issues in the current study of men and masculinity. We begin with a discussion of the terminology used to describe men and masculinity, prominent theories in the area, and measurement issues. Next, we discuss adverse and desirable aspects of masculinity. In this discussion, we include the relation of masculinity to such issues as violence, homonegativity, and family. We also include a brief section on developmental issues. We conclude with a discussion on the broad implications that the study of men and masculinity has for men, women, and society as a whole.

KEY TERMS

On the surface, defining concepts related to men and masculinity may appear simple. But amid the growing research on men and masculinity, significant definitional and conceptual ambiguity exists. Numerous authors have attempted to clarify the terminology and concepts related to men and masculinity (e.g., APA, 1994; Deaux, 1984, 1993; Gentile, 1993; Good & Mintz, 1993; Mintz & O'Neil, 1990; Pleck, Sonenstein & Ku, 1993b; Unger & Crawford, 1993). These authors point to the critical need to distinguish biologically determined sex-based characteristics (maleness) from societally/psychologically based conceptions of masculinity. For instance, having male genitalia is a biologically determined male characteristic, whereas being achievement-oriented is one socially and psychologically constructed view of how men should be. This area of societally/psychologically based conceptions of masculinity has been referred to by a variety of terms, including masculine gender roles, attitudes toward the male role, conceptions of masculinity, and masculinity ideologies. To avoid definitional ambiguity, the term "masculinity ideologies" is used throughout this review. Masculinity ideologies refer to sets of culturally defined standards of masculinity to which men are expected to adhere (Pleck, 1995). This plural term is desirable because it reflects the notion that there are multiple standards of masculinity, various groups have different dimensions that are salient in their conception of masculinity (Brod, 1987). It should be noted that there are significant variations in the extent to which North American men endorse a single standard regarding masculinity ideology. (In other words, and not surprisingly, there are within-group differences.) For example, current observations and research indicate that there are differing conceptions of masculinity among various ethnic/racial groups (Levant, Majors, & Kelley, 1998), religious groups (Brod, 1987), age cohorts (Cournoyer & Mahalik, 1995), affectional/sexual preference groups (J. Harrison, 1995), and geographical regions (Good et al., 1995).

Another common area discussed in masculinity research is that of masculine role conflict and stress. This refers to the degree of conflict and stress associated with men's efforts to meet the standards associated with masculinity ideologies. This concept has been called "sex role strain" (Pleck, 1981), "gender role conflict" (O'Neil, 1981), and "masculine gender role stress" (Eisler & Skidmore, 1987) by various researchers. Masculine role conflict and stress refers to such problems as restriction of emotional expression, need for success, and restriction of male friendships.

THEORIES AND MODELS OF MASCULINITY

Before we can examine the ways in which conceptions of masculinity are related to men's and women's lives, it is critical to review the many ways in which the concept of masculinity has been operationalized. A variety of theories have sought to explain "why men are the way they are." Some authors speculate a genetic or psychoevolutionary basis for male behavior (e.g., Archer, 1996; Buss, 1995b). However, this chapter examines masculinity as a primarily socially constructed phenomenon (e.g., Eagly & Wood, 1999). This view posits that most boys (and subsequently men) learn to adopt and adhere to culturally defined standards for masculine behavior (e.g., Bergman, 1995; M.S. Kimmel & Messner, 1992; O'Neil, 1981; Pleck, 1995). These cultural messages are learned through such routine developmental traumatic experiences as injuring oneself, experiencing pain, crying, and then receiving punitive responses to such tears. For example, when young boys are told "Big boys don't cry," they are being instructed explicitly that crying is an unacceptable avenue of expression for them. This message is typically accompanied by the message "Only girls cry." Hence, an implicit message that underlies the explicit one suggests that there are clearly demarcated realms of gender-related behavior differentiating boys/men from girls/women. If crying (and feeling pain) is feminine and not masculine, crying becomes a sign of weakness and vulnerability associated with femininity. Conversely, repressing emotions becomes a sign of strength and invulnerability associated with masculinity. Therefore, to be viewed as masculine, boys typically learn to repress emotions that might be associated with vulnerability. Boys are often called various derogatory names referring to girls (or gay men) if they express any sign of vulnerability and, hence, fail to meet cultural standards of masculinity. This process of being shamed, ridiculed, and physically assaulted is highly aversive, one that most boys learn to avoid at all costs. Further, some boys subsequently reinforce these beliefs and behaviors with their peers through the process of identification with their aggressors (J. Miller, 1998). Hence, the process of indoctrination into masculine ways continues intrapersonally and interpersonally, without conscious examination of its harmful effects.

Although theories and models of masculinity ideologies have progressed, the most complete descriptions remain the "blueprint for manhood" (Brannon, 1976) and "the masculine mystique" model (O'Neil, 1981), which are based on research conducted primarily with dominant, White, Western European participants in the United States. According to these models, men are typically socialized toward characteristics that can be broadly categorized as independence and achievement (instrumentality, personal agency), restriction and suppression of emotions (rationality), and avoidance of characteristics associated with femininity and homosexuality (interpersonal dominance). Also mentioned in several models are the notions that men are socialized toward physical aggressiveness, toughness, and status seeking (Brannon, 1976; E.H. Thompson & Pleck, 1986).

In addition to writings and research seeking to describe masculine socialization, a related area of research has examined masculine role conflict and stress. As mentioned earlier, these are stresses many men experience in attempting to meet or resist societal and internalized demands to live up to the cultural standards for masculinity. For example, restricting expression of emotions appears to contribute to greater psychological distress and fear of intimacy (Good et al., 1995). Issues associated with efforts to empirically assess masculinity ideologies, masculine role conflicts, and their correlates are reviewed next.

MEASUREMENT OF MASCULINITY-RELATED CONSTRUCTS

Central to an understanding of the current status of research on masculinity ideologies are issues related to the measurement of the constructs. Although a significant amount of research purports to examine aspects of masculinity, the vast majority of earlier studies employed instruments of limited utility to the investigation of masculinity. For example, the two most widely used "gender role" instruments were the Bem Sex Role Inventory (BSRI; S.L. Bem, 1974) and the 24-item version of the Personal Attributes Questionnaire (PAQ; Spence & Helmreich, 1978). Although there has been significant controversy about the relative merits of these two scales (e.g., Spence, 1991), it is now clear that *neither* measures masculinity ideologies (i.e., the extent to which individuals endorse numerous aspects of socialized masculine gender roles). Despite their differences, both the BSRI and the PAQ appear to tap the degree to which individuals (males or females) report *instrumental* ("masculinity") and *expressive* ("femininity") traits of a gender-related and socially desirable nature as being descriptive of their personalities (Spence, 1984, 1991; Spence, Losoff, & Robbins, 1991). Hence, the PAQ and BSRI "masculinity" scales should be viewed as assessing whether individuals report possessing a single personality trait that is socially desirable for males in this culture (namely, instrumentality or personal goal-directedness; Good, Wallace, & Borst, 1994). In our society, masculinity is far more complex; multiple dimensions are necessary to describe a single conception of masculinity ideology (Fischer, Tokar, Good, & Snell, 1998; E.H. Thompson & Pleck, 1995).

Instruments designed to assess more specifically masculinity-related constructs do exist, however. Broadly speaking, two approaches to assessing masculinity are currently in favor (E.H. Thompson & Pleck, 1995). One approach assesses dimensions of masculinity ideologies primarily derived from Brannon's (1976) "blueprint for manhood" (e.g., Brannon & Juni, 1984; Fischer et al., 1998; E.H. Thompson & Pleck, 1986) and typically includes dimensions such as status, toughness, and antifemininity. E.H. Thompson and Pleck (1995) examined 17 peer-reviewed scales developed since 1977 that were either attitude measures that tap ideologies about men and masculinities, or inventories for other masculinity-related constructs that reveal how males might experience their gender. They concluded that masculinity ideology appears to be distinct from and to have different correlates from gender-role orientation, gender relations in general, and gender ideologies about women. They suggested that scales seeking to assess masculinity ideology should (1) avoid using gender-comparative items, (2) separate the concepts of gender-based personality orientation and masculinity ideology, and (3) employ broader definitions of masculinity.

The second approach attempts to assess the degree of masculine role stresses and conflicts associated with endorsement of traditional conceptions of masculine gender roles (Eisler & Skidmore, 1987; O'Neil, Helms, Gable, David, & Wrightsman, 1986). Specifically, the Masculine Gender Role Stress scale (MGRS; Eisler & Skidmore, 1987) is posited to assess five dimensions of masculinity-related stress, and the Gender Role Conflict Scale (GRCS; O'Neil et al., 1986) assesses four dimensions of conflict with male gender roles. These two scales tap stress and/or conflict associated with culturally defined masculinity, such as restricted emotions, need for success, and restricted male friendships. Additionally, the GRCS has been subjected to numerous studies of its psychometric properties, with findings strongly supporting the scale's factor structure (e.g., Good et al., 1995; Moradi, Tokar, Schaub, Jome, & Serna, 2000). Not surprising, research using indicators of masculinity-related stress/conflict typically identifies larger relations with men's psychosocial and biomedical concerns than does research using indicators of masculinity ideologies (e.g., Eisler, 1995; Good et al., 1995; Good, Robertson, Fitzgerald, Stevens, & Bartels, 1996; O'Neil, Good, & Holmes, 1995).

J.C. Wade's (1998) theory of "reference group identity" attempted to account for both conformity to and variability in standards of masculinity for individual men. This theory suggests that men's gender-role self-concepts (attributes, attitudes, and behaviors) are related to their level of ego identity development (Erikson, 1968) and linked to their specific reference group (M. Sherif, 1962). In other words, this scale is designed to assess the extent to which a male's gender-role self-concept is dependent on a specific male reference group. The research utility of this new model is yet to be established. In the future, it would also appear desirable to assess the degree of *salience* various aspects of masculinity ideology have for respondents (e.g., "How important is it to you that you are perceived as successful and powerful?").

ADVERSE AND DESIRABLE IMPLICATIONS OF SOCIALLY CONSTRUCTED ASPECTS OF MASCULINITY

A growing body of research documents both the positive and detrimental implications of traditional conceptions of masculinity. The negative consequences will be examined in greater detail subsequently; a number of positive features associated with traditional conceptions of masculinity warrant acknowledgment first. Specifically, men holding more traditional conceptions of masculinity may have strengths in such areas as problem solving, logical thinking, risk taking, anger expression, and assertive behavior that may be especially beneficial in times of crisis (Levant, 1995). Examples of how these positive aspects of more traditional masculinity ideologies may manifest include the ability to remain calm and problem-focused in times of crisis (mental "compartmentalizing") and subsuming personal needs to the greater duty of protecting and providing for one's family or country (personal sacrifice). In contemporary times, the perceived lack of need for these qualities associated with traditional conceptions of masculinity is causing distress for some men (e.g., Faludi, 1999).

In relationships, clearly defined gender roles can provide expedient guides for division of household responsibilities and allocation of tasks. We note, however, that all too often these responsibilities and tasks have not been divided equitably along gender lines. Qualities embodied by more traditional masculinity ideologies can be simultaneously beneficial and injurious. This "double-edged sword" (noting both the pros and cons associated with some aspects of traditional masculine gender roles) is one of the reasons that men and women struggle in our society about what roles and behaviors are acceptable and appropriate for men. Although this chapter primarily focuses on research investigating the ways in which masculinity ideologies and masculine role conflicts are deleterious for men and others in their lives, it is important to acknowledge that both men and women receive some benefits from aspects of "traditional" masculinity-related behaviors.

Deleterious aspects of "traditional" masculinity ideologies are examined next. Men acknowledging greater masculinity-related conflict associated with traditional masculinity ideologies have been found to be more psychologically distressed (e.g., Good et al., 1995), to have more difficulty with interpersonal intimacy (e.g., Fischer & Good, 1997), to have greater biomedical concerns (e.g., Watkins, Eisler, Carpenter, Schechtman, & Fischer, 1991), and to hold more negative attitudes toward their use of mental health services (Blazina & Watkins, 1996; Good, Dell, & Mintz, 1989). We examine the implications of masculinity messages associated with the strong and silent ideal (restricted experience and expression of emotions), toughness and violence, self-sufficiency, being a stud, avoiding "sissy stuff," and seeking power and success.

STRONG, SILENT TYPES

As mentioned earlier, being viewed as unemotional is central to the "strong, silent type" aspect of most masculine ideologies (e.g., Brannon, 1976; Eisler, 1995; Fischer et al., 1998; O'Neil et al., 1995). Conforming to this standard may help boys and men avoid some of the immediate consequences of failing to live up to masculine role expectations. However, the longer-term adverse consequences for individuals of having an emotionally restrictive style are becoming increasingly apparent. Levant (1992) initiated the theoretical discussion of the problem of alexithymia (meaning literally "without words for emotions") as a potential result of masculine socialization. In the empirical literature, restricted emotionality has been found to be associated with men's greater levels of alexithymia (Fischer & Good, 1997; D.S. Shepard, 1994), increased paranoia and psychoticism (Good et al., 1996), fear of intimacy (Fischer & Good, 1997; Good et al., 1995), higher levels of depression (Good & Mintz, 1990; Good et al., 1996), greater hostile-submissive personality styles (Mahalik, 2000), and higher levels of anxiety, anger, and personality styles similar to substance abusers (Blazina & Watkins, 1996). Of note, men who perceived their relations with their fathers as having been more secure and positive reported less emotional restriction and inexpressiveness in their own lives (Fischer & Good, 1998).

Efforts to provide an alternative "ideal" to which boys and men may strive have included the notion of "emotional competence" that emphasizes that courage and strength are required "to feel, experience, and communicate the full range of human emotions" (Good, 1998, p. 1). Indeed, it appears that the way men are being portrayed in the popular media may be evolving. For example, in contrast to TV shows of past decades (e.g., *Dragnet*'s Sgt. Joe Friday's "Just the facts, Ma'am"), male characters in the leading situation comedies of the 1998–1999 season were found to disclose about themselves on a relatively frequent per episode basis (M.J. Porter, Good, & Dillon, 1999). However, the extent to which society appears ready to accept and value the expression of the full range of emotions by men is still uncertain.

TOUGHNESS AND VIOLENCE

One of the common prescriptions of masculinity ideologies is that men should be tough and "give 'em hell" (Brannon, 1976). This stance of toughness and aggression can lead to violence. As mentioned previously, when boys learn to be tough, they all too frequently do so by suppressing all emotions potentially associated with vulnerability. These messages and the coping styles subsequently associated with them "have dysfunctional health consequences for many men and for those with whom they come into contact" (Eisler, 1995, p. 208). For example, unable to openly express honest emotions of sadness and grief, men might turn to alternative (and less healthy) coping mechanisms, such as substance abuse. Indeed, men are three times more likely than women to die from alcohol-related ailments (Doyle, 1996), with 39% of males having some level of psychological dependency on alcohol in their lifetime (Lemle & Mishkind, 1989). Overall, men are three times more likely than women to die of suicide (U.S. Bureau of the Census, 1997). Specific age groups of men are at particularly heightened risk; men age 15 to 19 have four times the suicide risk, and men age 20 to 24 have six times the suicide risk compared to women in the same age groups (National Center for Health Statistics, 1991). Efforts that assist men in developing truly healthy conceptions of masculinity are needed. These revisions of masculinity recognize that stoicism does not produce emotional strength. Indeed, rather than producing strong men, stoicism produces brittle men (Fischer & Good, 1997).

Other related cultural messages about masculinity include prescriptions that men must be aggressive, fearless, and invulnerable. As with repression of emotions, aggressiveness and attempts to be fearless can contribute to health problems and premature death. Often, the extent to which a man is considered masculine is defined by his willingness to engage in extreme behaviors attesting to his supposed indestructibility. For example, men may be valued for their ability to consume large amounts of alcohol. Likewise, the faster the car, motorcycle, or boat or the higher the ski jump, the more masculine the man. In this vein, men are far more likely than women to take risks while driving motor vehicles. The main cause of early death in males under the age of 35 is accidents, with about half of these due to motor vehicle injuries (U.S. Bureau of the Census, 1997). Indeed, men are involved in fatal crashes three times more often than women (Li, 1998).

As a group, men do not make adequate use of preventative health care measures. Many deaths of men due to accident and disease are considered premature because they are often preventable (Courtenay, 1998). Men are far less likely than women to seek health care during illness or following injury (Courtenay, 1998). Similarly, men are far more likely than women to eschew health maintenance and prevention activities, such as gaining health information (Weiss & Larson, 1990), using sunscreen to prevent skin cancer (B.A. Banks, Silverman, Schwartz, & Tunnessen, 1992), and scheduling cancer screening exams (R.C. Katz, Meyers, & Walls, 1995). For example, only 20% of men have been checked for testicular cancer, whereas 46% of women have been tested for breast cancer (Men's Health, 1998). The U.S. National Institutes of Health and the National Cancer Institute reported that men contracted 12 of 14 types of cancer at a higher rate than women; breast and pancreatic cancers were the only types contracted at a higher rate by women. Preventative exams for women such as mammograms, pap smears, and breast self-exams have helped to curb death rates from breast and uterine cancer. Testicular and prostate cancer are corresponding male cancers that can be successfully treated after early detection. Although testicular cancer is the most common type found in young men, few men are taught to perform a testicular self-examination. Efforts are needed to help men approach their real physical vulnerabilities, as opposed to encouraging repression and disregard of actual physical vulnerabilities (e.g., use of sunscreen, seat belts, and helmets).

Despite statistics to the contrary, most American men appear to believe in their own invulnerability to injury and illness (Courtenay, 1998; H. Goldberg, 1977; J. Harrison, 1978). Hence, it is not surprising that, despite dying on an average of seven years younger than women, male patients ask their physicians fewer questions than do female patients. Beliefs about men's ruggedness are often replicated in the health care community; physicians spend less time with male patients than with female patients (U.S. Bureau of the Census, 1997) and make less effort to warn male patients about health risks (J.A. Foote, Harris, & Gilles, 1996). Such behavior may reinforce the myth of male invulnerability. In reality, because male patients account for only 40% of physicians' office visits, men's higher rates of illness, injury, and death suggest that physicians need to modify their services to attract and serve male patients better. In addition to making their services more "male-friendly," physicians should consider intentionally spending more time with their male patients.

Evidence suggests that men's discomfort with their emotions is associated with their reluctance to use health care services (Komiya, Good, & Sherrod, 2000). Seeking help may imply dependence, vulnerability, or even submission to someone with more knowledge (such as a physician). If men succumb to illness, they may be threatened by feelings of helplessness and loss of power—feelings that directly contradict societal pressures demanding their independence and invulnerability (Cowling & Campbell, 1986; Pollack, 1995; Sutkin & Good, 1987). Hence, men may perceive submitting to (health-sustaining) annual prostate exams or performing testicular self-exams as unnecessary, humiliating, and "unmanly" activities.

Statistics about men's health problems and practices suggest that adhering to the belief that men should be "tough" has many detrimental consequences for men. Being tough, fearless, and aggressive and restricting emotions may be considered ways men harm themselves. Such behaviors may also lead to detrimental consequences for others, particularly in the area of violence. Men, women, and children all suffer from the effects of male-perpetrated violence in American society. Men disproportionately perpetrate most forms of violence. Statistics suggest that men commit 95% of all reported violent crimes in the United States (Sourcebook of Criminal Justice Statistics, 1994).

Male violence against women has received particular attention in recent years. Researchers estimate that 21% to 34% of American women will be slapped, kicked, beaten, choked, or attacked with a weapon by their intimate partners (L.A. Goodman, Koss, Fitzgerald, Russo, & Keita, 1993). In 1997, husbands or partners killed 29% of female murder victims (FBI Uniform Crime Reports, 1997). The National Crime Victim Center (1992) reported that at least 12.1 million American women had been victims of forcible rape at some point in their life. Over half (61%) of these assaults involved victims who were less than 17 years old, with 29% being raped before the age of 11. Since the age of 14, approximately one in four college women have been the victim of either rape or attempted rape (Koss et al., 1987). Research shows that boys, as well as girls, are sexually abused at alarming rates (Lisak & Luster, 1994). Dating violence also appears common, with estimates ranging from 22% to 67% of couples experiencing some form of violence (Straus & Gelles, 1988).

Following the brutal murders at Columbine High School in April 1999, many Americans searched for a way to explain how such violence could happen. Americans looked to the availability of guns, the popularity of violence in the media, and parental uninvolvement to explain the Columbine and other high school killings. However, it is noteworthy that all the perpetrators of these crimes were boys. Statistics suggest that boys account for 94% of all juvenile killers (Courtenay, 1999). Boys are also more frequently the victims of juvenile crime, with 85% of all murder victims age 5 to 24 being male (Department of Health and Human Services, 1996). About 1 in 10 male high school and college students carry a gun (Centers for Disease Control, 1997). Although guns are a problem in our culture, "we take it for granted that boys, not girls, use guns" (Courtenay, 1999, p. 141). Boys' violence is an underexamined trend that continues in adulthood, with 89% of murders committed by those 18 and over being perpetrated by males (FBI Uniform Crime Reports, 1997).

As with juvenile murders, both violence that receives media attention (e.g., hate crimes) and less publicized crimes are most often perpetrated by males. Male violence against other males is by far the most common type of violent crime in the United States (FBI Uniform Crime Reports, 1997). In 1997, 77% of all murder victims were male, with 88% of male murder victims being killed by male assailants (FBI Uniform Crime Reports, 1997). Criminals may see perpetration of violence as a way of affirming or defending their sense of masculinity. For example, one of the convicted murderers in the June 1998 racially motivated assault on an African American man in Jasper, Texas, reportedly compared killing his first "nigger" to losing his virginity (National Public Radio, 1998). Another example is Majors and Billson's (1992) "cool pose" concept, in which inner-city men kill one another if they perceive that they are being "dissed" (disrespected).

Theorists and researchers have looked to masculine gender-role socialization and masculinity ideologies to explain why men disproportionately perpetrate most forms of violence. Early on, boys and men may learn that violence is a way to cope with their own problems and with problems in interpersonal relationships. Teaching boys to be "men" may involve a certain amount of physical violence (e.g., hitting followed by the statement, "This is for your own good, boy") in addition to emotional violence (e.g., name calling). Some boys are encouraged to learn to fight to "build character" and keep from being bullied (Levant & Pollack, 1995). It may be considered acceptable for men to fight with other men to cope with their feelings of frustration, helplessness, or inadequacy. Violence and aggression may be ways that boys and men try to compensate for the discomfort of feeling vulnerable and ashamed (Bergman, 1995). Instead of dealing with their emotions, men may externalize their distress by "taking it out on others."

Violence may be a way that some men try to convince others of their invulnerability. Perpetrating violence may also give them a sense of power over others when they are feeling powerless. One example of male externalization of distress into violence could be "gay bashing." Some men may feel threatened by others' homosexuality because they feel it violates male role norms or because they do not wish to deal with their own sexual feelings. Therefore, they may externalize this confusion into violence against those who make them uncomfortable (but the discomfort comes from within them, not from the outside).

Many forms of violence against men are condoned and encouraged in American culture. For example, in some primarily male groups (e.g., the military, college fraternities), a certain amount of violent peer hazing is considered an acceptable way of initiating men into an exclusive masculine "club." Popular sports such as boxing and wrestling in which men purposefully injure one another may also be considered forms of socially condoned male violence against males. Coaches' support of violence may lead to an admiration of violence (Pollack, 1995). Boys and men may learn that violence is, at least to some extent, a socially acceptable way to express themselves. Some boys and men may not learn to separate aggression and violence that occurs within the context of a sporting event with aggression and violence against others outside of the sports arena.

SELF-SUFFICIENCY

Recent advances in self psychology theories have promoted the notion that young boys typically experience "forced disidentification" from their mothers too early in their development (Bergman, 1995; Pollack, 1995, in press). From this perspective, these traumatic experiences subsequently produce men who are "defensively self-sufficient" (Pollack, 1995, 1998). As a result, men might be expected to be particularly uncomfortable with "attaching" to others or with "needing" assistance from others, including their partners or health care professionals, or with dependency associated with serious injuries or illnesses. Defensive self-sufficiency may be associated with the observation that many men are uncomfortable with being nurturing either to others or to themselves (Good, 1998). All too often men associate nurturing with women and femininity; as noted earlier, empathy and nurturance in men are often punished by their peers and by society. Indeed, nurturance involves gentleness and interdependence—a mutuality that involves the risk of being connected with, and potentially hurt by, another person. Obviously, risking being emotionally hurt runs counter to the defensive self-sufficiency men learn to feel most comfortable with.

Problems associated with young boys' development may be prevented by several different methods. Most obviously, boys could be allowed to disidentify from their mothers at their own pace. Additionally, providing opportunities for boys to develop their nurturing skills could help them learn how to connect with, nurture, and care for others. For example, having boys help care for toddlers at preschools may develop their nurturing skills. While learning to care for others better, these boys could also learn the value of interpersonal connection and self-care. In other words, men who are more nurturing to others might better recognize (i.e., be attuned to, rather than attempting to suppress) their own biomedical needs (e.g., for adequate rest) and psychosocial health needs (e.g., meaningful social support). Third, encouraging fathers to be more actively involved in raising their children would help improve men's connection with the members of their families. "Involved fathers" have been found to have better psychological health and to have more psychologically healthy offspring than have less involved fathers (Fischer & Good, 1998; Good, 1998; Pleck, 1987; Silverstein, 1996; Silverstein & Auerbach, 1999).

BEING A STUD

Sexuality is a normal component of human development. However, a variety of societal messages and traumatic experiences can deflect young men's sexual development onto problematic trajectories. As mentioned previously, boys often learn to suppress the extent to which they allow themselves to care for and connect with others. Hence, when sexuality enters their lives, it is often of an unconnected and nonrelational nature (Good & Sherrod, 1997; Levant, 1997). Nonrelational sex is a tendency to experience sex primarily as lust without any requirements for relational intimacy or emotional attachment. Although for some men engaging in nonrelational sex is a useful stage of exploration during their life journey, for others it becomes a problematic, self-perpetuating stage from which they have difficulty progressing (e.g., G.R. Brooks, 1995; Good & Sherrod, 1997).

According to many masculinity ideologies, nonrelational sex is valued and, in the context of a committed relationship, sex is devalued. Targets of sexual desire are often objectified and at times are not even people in one's life (e.g., women's bodies or parts of women in pornographic books or videos). These targets of desire are pursued in an agentic fashion to meet one's needs, which, in addition to the release of sexual tension, include needs for nurturance and affirmation of one's adequacy as a man (Levant, 1997). Nonrelational sex is encouraged by the media (in rock and rap songs, MTV, TV, movies, and magazines) and reinforced in most men's peer groups. Nonrelational sex has many variations and can exist to various degrees. It includes not just men's behavior, but also men's attitudes and the consequences for men and women, which occur within the context of gender socialization and patriarchy (see concept of "rape domain"; M. Stevens, 1985). Similarly, nonrelational sexual behavior can be viewed as occurring along a continuum. One pole of this continuum is reflected by consensual casual sex with a likewise nonrelational sex–oriented partner, the middle by casual sex with an intimate sexual relations–oriented partner, and the other pole is forced (Good & Sherrod, 1997).

G.R. Brooks (1995, 1997) hypothesizes that many men have the "centerfold syndrome," whereby they are "programmed" to relate to women in terms of voyeurism, objectification, masculinity validation, and trophyism. Voyeurism refers to the idea that men are socialized to focus on looking at women and women's bodies. Voyeurism can include use of pornography, which has become a major entertainment and moneymaking industry in the United States (Gaylor, 1985). Under the male gaze, women are often experienced as objects of lust. Thus, men's behavior and attitudes toward women can reflect a view of women as objects to satisfy their sexual needs rather than as humans. In addition, women's bodies may be used to validate men's sense of masculinity. Part of being a man means feeling "virile," and he may need power over a woman's body to feel that way. Finally, women as objects may be viewed as something to be collected. A successful conquest may be equivalent to a boost in self-esteem. Therefore, men may assume that numerous sexual partners will lead to an increase in self-esteem. This phenomenon is referred to as trophyism, whereby men attempt to collect "trophies" in the form of sexual conquests. A related idea is that of the "trophy wife"; the man who has the most beautiful woman by his side is thought to have the biggest trophy. However, because living women trophies age and may lose some of their beauty, a man may feel the need to discard his old trophy in favor of a newer one to reaffirm his sense of masculinity. This concept of trophyism is also prevalent in gay culture (Gonzales & Meyers, 1993; Hatala & Prehodka, 1996; Siever, 1994).

Men's fears of vulnerability and shame lead to a fear of intimacy in sexual relations (G.R. Brooks, 1995). Thus, men "learn that the safest form of sex is the 'slam-bam-thank-you-ma'am' variety" (p. 35). In other words, the safest expression of sexuality for many men may be nonrelational. Having multiple sexual partners with whom little communication occurs and little caring is shared increases the risk of exposure to a variety of sexually transmitted diseases. For example, HIV was the leading cause of death for men age 25 to 44 in 1995 (National Center for Health Statistics, 1998).

No Sissy Stuff

For the majority of people who have a dualistic way of viewing the world (W.G. Perry, 1970), the corollary of being traditionally masculine is to *not* display any features associated with femininity or homosexuality. In this vein, characteristics that are potentially associated with femininity (such as emotional sensitivity) and homosexuality (which involves connection with other men) must be avoided. This concept has been referred to as "no sissy stuff" by Brannon (1976) and "fear of femininity" by O'Neil (1981). Men's fear of homosexuality is sometimes called "homophobia," and is perhaps more accurately termed "homonegativity" (Mayfield, 1999). Research has supported the importance of these concepts. For example, men scoring higher on the GRCS's Restrictive Affectionate Behavior among Men scale have been found to employ more immature psychological defenses, such as projection and turning against the object (Mahalik, Cournoyer, DeFranc, Cherry, & Napolitano, 1988), and to acknowledge more symptoms of paranoia, psychoticism, and personal inadequacy (Good et al., 1996). These notions of paranoia and turning against the (threatening) object appear to be exemplified by the murderers of Matthew Shepard (an unimposing gay man in Wyoming). Indeed, men with an insecure sense of their masculinity may be highly prone to a variety of hypermasculine assertions of their heterosexuality.

Be Powerful and Successful

An additional message endorsed by American culture is the idea that men should be competitive and successful (Brannon, 1976; O'Neil, 1981). Though competition may be a fun and important aspect of sports activities, competition in the workplace is theorized to be a significant source of stress, contributing to elevated blood pressure and other cardiovascular health problems (Good, Sherrod, & Dillon, 2000). Men have twice the age-adjusted death rate from heart disease as women (National Center for Health Statistics, 1992), with 48% of men who die suddenly of coronary heart disease having had no previous symptoms (American Heart Association, 1998). The influence of masculine roles on cardiovascular problems first drew the interest of researchers in the 1950s and 1960s, when successful, hard-working, middle-class men displayed coronary heart disease at alarming rates (Darbyshire, 1987). These men had achieved the American dream, but they also appeared to be dying from the effort. Conventional wisdom at the time identified excess stress and the "Type A" personality as the culprits (Rosenman et al., 1975). Type A behavior includes characteristics such as impatience, high drive for achievement, hostility, high need for control, competitiveness, and inability or unwillingness to express oneself. Many of these qualities are valued as ideals of American masculinity (Cowling & Campbell, 1986; O'Neil et al., 1995).

More recently, Type A behavior has been associated directly with masculine gender role stress in working adults (Watkins et al., 1991). Health professionals increasingly believe that factors related to masculine gender roles account for increased rates of several serious health problems in men. One of the most serious discrepancies between men's and women's health is that of death rates. Men have higher death rates than do women across various age groups. Higher rates of disease also contribute to earlier deaths for men. For instance, men die from coronary heart disease at twice the rate of women (Eisler, 1995). There is further evidence suggesting that conceptions of masculinity effect multiple areas of men's health. For example, the MGRS has been used to assess the relations between masculinity-related stressors and health problems in men (Eisler & Skidmore, 1987). Eisler and his colleagues found that men having higher levels of masculine stress were more prone to anger, high blood pressure, and high-risk health behaviors. Hence, the research to date suggests that masculine role stresses are important contributors to the development of cardiovascular disease, a leading cause of premature death in males (Eisler, 1995).

In terms of psychosocial implications, men with higher scores on the Success, Power, and Competition subscale of the GRCS have been found to display more controlling and rigid interpersonal behavior (Mahalik, 2000), more immature psychological defenses (Mahalik et al., 1988), and more paranoia (Good et al., 1996). Clearly, more research is needed to clarify the correlates and consequences of masculine role conflict and stress.

DEVELOPMENTAL PERSPECTIVES

The nature and salience of conceptions of masculinity may evolve over a man's life span. Concerns about masculinity begin in childhood, when boys are instructed according to a particular masculinity ideology. As a result, Pollack (1998) proposes that "boys today are in serious trouble" (p. 7). Boys are increasingly having academic difficulties, with higher rates of learning disorders and Attention-Deficit Disorder (ADD). Boys also appear to be confused about gender roles and what is expected of them as a male in American society. Often, boys feel pressure to project an air of self-confidence that does not reflect their true inner feelings of insecurity and sadness. Many boys report feelings of loneliness and alienation (Pollack, 1998). As boys grow up, their feelings of uncertainty and confusion may transform into a reluctance to become men (Pollack, 1998). During adolescence and young adulthood, young men's subscription to traditional values of masculinity may increase. At this time, young men are more likely to engage in high-risk behaviors ranging from casual sex to violence.

It is thought that later, toward midlife, some men may come to see increased value in stereotypical "feminine" qualities of nurturance and interdependency (Levinson, 1978). Research suggests that middle-aged men feel less gender-role conflict in the areas of success, work, power, and competition than do college-age men. Middle-aged men demonstrated more gender-role conflict in the areas of work and family responsibility than college men did. The two age groups did not differ in their amount of conflict over restrictive emotionality and restrictive affectionate behavior between men (Cournoyer & Mahalik, 1995). In contrast, another study found no differences in the aforementioned areas for three age groups (Stillson, O'Neil, & Owen, 1991).

There are also indications that men tend to respond to divorce differently from women. Specifically, men seem to have more psychological problems and commit suicide more often than women following divorce. However, men are also likely to remarry more quickly than women (Price & McKenry, 1988).

During midlife, many men begin to realize that they are never going to achieve "alpha male" status (i.e., they will never become "top dog" or "king of the hill"). This self-realization might occur when they become aware that they have risen about as far as they are going to in their occupation, that they have passed the zenith of their physical strength, or when a physical illness or injury jars them into the realization of their mortality. For some men, this can be shocking, producing the famed "midlife crisis." Some men will seek to vanquish the specter of midlife by redoubled efforts to restore their lost sense of personal power. Such misguided efforts are illustrated when men suddenly "run off" with much younger women in an attempt to restore their sense of potency (Good & Sherrod, 1997). Such men may also attempt to bolster their self-image through the purchase of ego props, such as expensive sports cars, speedboats, and motorcycles. Rarely in our society do men receive messages encouraging self-nurturance through healthy diets, contact with supportive friends, cardiovascular exercise, and sufficient sleep as a means for coping with the challenges of midlife.

When men advance beyond 45 years of age, health concerns often become more salient. This is typically a time when goals and progress in the areas of work, relationships, and the self are evaluated. Men may be left feeling empty and bored, even when they have reached their career goals (Collison, 1987). They may also face the important tasks of redefining relationships (such as when adult children move out of the house or when a partner dies). Distinct physical losses that severely detract from previous capabilities may underscore the fact of aging. Negative societal attitudes about aging are reflected in such statements as being beaten in an athletic event by an "old man," and "humorous" yet morbid parties typically given when people turn 40 or 50 years old (Collison, 1987). As men grow older, the meanings associated with physical prowess and sex become important considerations in healthy adjustment. If men's self-worth has been based on the importance of physical and sexual performance, these may indeed become the "declining years." Conversely, men may learn to appreciate the possibilities of their present life situations in new and different ways. For example, this may become a time when increased focus on a healthy lifestyle, including better nutrition, exercise, interpersonal connection, and relaxation, improve the quality of men's lives (Good, Sherrod, & Dillon, 2000).

MULTICULTURAL PERSPECTIVES

Masculinity ideologies have been presented as culturally prescribed norms and expectations imposed on men. Because masculinity ideologies are culturally defined and enforced, it stands to reason that masculinity ideologies will vary depending on the culture in which they have been supported. There is some research to support variations in cultural beliefs within the United States. Men living in the southern region of the country have been found to endorse more traditional conceptions of masculinity, including acceptance of violence (e.g., D. Cohen, 1996; D. Cohen, Vandello, Puente, & Rantilla, 1999; Levant, Majors, & Kelley, 1998; Nisbett, 1993). African American men have been found to hold more traditional conceptions of masculinity in general (Levant & Majors, 1997), but are more likely to feel that it is appropriate for mothers with school-age children to work (Lyson, 1986).

According to D.B. Lee and Saul (1987), Asian men may relate differently to other men and women than do European American men. Specifically, Asian men may be more comfortable in male-male relationships than in male-female relationships. In Asian cultures, men appear to be able to relate to one another more comfortably without fear of being labeled "gay." Asian men may be discouraged from relating to women in an emotional way, because they are expected to avoid disclosing emotions or signs of "weakness." The type of masculinity ideology adopted by Asian men in American society may depend on the man's degree of acculturation (D.W. Sue, in press).

Acculturation is also an important factor for Hispanic and Latino men (Valdes, Baron, & Ponce, 1987). Acculturation refers to the extent to which individuals incorporate aspects of the predominant culture. A concept highly associated with Latino men is that of machismo. Valdes et al. point out that in English, this term has become associated negatively with the ideas of chauvinism and sexism. In Spanish, however, the term is more closely associated with the concept of chivalry and connotes physical strength, attractiveness, and virtue. Masculinity in Hispanic culture emphasizes dignity, respect, and family; however, Hispanic men are often stereotyped as aggressive, promiscuous, and dominant. Masculinity ideologies are thought to be problematic in Hispanic culture, just as they are in the predominant culture, but not more so, as the stereotypes may suggest.

Caldwell and White (in press) and Washington (1987) note that dominant culture stereotypes about African American men affect the way they think about their masculinity. For example, whereas European American men may be thought of as powerful, moneymakers, self-determined, and privileged, African American men may be thought of as angry, lazy, unmotivated, unemployed, and subservient. Because this description goes against what is put forth as desirable by the dominant culture's conception of masculinity ideology, African American men may deal with increased gender-role conflict and strain. Further, African American men may deal with increased amounts of stress due to the disproportionate amount of murders, imprisonment, unemployment, suicide, drug abuse, and lowered access to education in their community. In a comparison of European American and African American men, African American men were found to have slightly more traditional views in the areas of fear and hatred of homosexuals, self-reliance, achievement status, and restrictive emotionality (Levant, Majors, & Kelley, 1998). However, masculinity in the African American community may be expressed in unique ways, such as adopting a "cool pose," exhibiting streetwise behavior, and "rapping" (Washington, 1987).

IMPLICATIONS

In this chapter, we have noted that issues relating to the psychology of women and the psychology of men and masculinity are intimately connected. Further, we note that masculinity is not unidimensional; rather, conceptions of masculinity are complex and have differential relations to aspects of men's roles and behaviors. Several implications arise from this review. The information has implications for advancing research and theory in the psychology of men and masculinity. Efforts are needed to expand what is currently understood and empirically supported about the nature of masculinity and its impact on men, women, and families. The information in this chapter also has implications for creating changes on the individual, relationship, and societal levels.

Although progress has been made in understanding the psychology of men and masculinity, there is a dearth of research in the area. Research is needed to improve ways of measuring masculinity and the effect of masculine role conflict on psychological well-being, and to expand our understanding of the interaction between cultural factors and masculinity ideologies (Good, Wallace, & Borst, 1994). Recent studies suggest that masculinity ideologies are multidimensional, rather than unidimensional, constructs. Fischer and Good (1997) found that masculinity ideology can be divided into five patterns. Future research could examine if certain patterns of masculinity ideology are related to certain behaviors. For example, patterns of masculinity ideology in which violent toughness is endorsed likely lead to a greater risk of physical violence, sexual assault, and gay bashing (Fischer & Good, 1997). Specific patterns of masculinity ideologies may predict other problems such as domestic violence, sexual harassment, psychological distress, and substance abuse. Some research suggests a relation between gender-role conflict and psychological distress; however, more research is needed to understand these dynamics (Good, Wallace, & Borst, 1994).

Research could also further elucidate developmental issues for men throughout the life span. Such investigations may involve longitudinal designs. Research is needed to support/disprove current theory about masculinity, improve measurement of masculinity-related constructs, and establish causation. Investigations into men's development may also shed light on the development and evolution of masculinity ideologies.

Because so little is known about the effects of nonrelational sex, a broad, exploratory approach may be most useful to further understanding of this phenomenon and its effect on others. For example, more research could be done on the effects of objectification of women on men's relationships and mental health. More interventions could be investigated that aim to teach men the value of intimacy and emotional expression in sexual relationships.

Although some research supports the connection between masculine gender roles and men's health, more specific investigations could investigate which aspects of masculinity are most directly associated with which specific biomedical and psychosocial health concerns. A greater emphasis on empirically based, scientifically rigorous outcome studies of education efforts could identify effective interventions worthy of broader implementation. More broadly, to conduct important research in this area, financial support from governmental and/or private funding sources would be needed. However, financial support is unlikely to be provided until the severe problems associated with men's health receive greater public attention. It is our hope that improving men's health will soon be a top priority for medicine, the social sciences, business, and the public.

The advancement of research and theory in the area of men and masculinity will likely contribute to more practical improvements for men, women, and society as a whole. For example, a recent study found that male advanced doctoral students were unable to differentiate college men who were at a particularly high risk for perpetrating sexual assault from those who were at a particularly low risk for perpetrating sexual assault (Sherrod & Good, 1999). The implications of this are notable, especially for survivors of sexual assault. Self-blame is common following a rape or sexual assault (Resick, 1993). Survivors and their friends or family may believe that they should have been able to detect violent tendencies in their attacker. However, evidence from this research suggests survivors are not alone in their inability to detect a potential rapist. Education about this finding could provide emotional relief and facilitation of recovery to survivors who take responsibility for their own assault. This finding also suggests that our current understanding of the causes of sexual assault is lacking. Understanding the connection between masculinity ideologies and violence could be essential in developing ways to prevent sexual assault, domestic violence, and child abuse.

Little research examines the interaction between culture and masculinity ideologies. More research is needed to understand the unique cultural aspects of different masculinity ideologies. Research suggests that culturally relevant interventions are more effective with specific cultural groups than are culturally neutral interventions (Heppner et al., 1999). Research is needed to understand more about the effects of culturally relevant interventions on changing conceptions of masculinity to improve men's psychological well-being. Additionally, research in the area of masculinity could further understanding of hate crimes. Such crimes are not only most often perpetrated by men, but are also more specifically perpetrated by *White* men. Perhaps this reflects a feeling that White male power and privilege are diminishing in light of recent gains made by women and ethnic minorities in American culture (see Branscombe, Ellemers, Spears, & Doosje, 1999).

A better understanding of men and masculinity could provide information useful for improving relationships between men and women as well as family relationships. Future investigations may go beyond the popular "Venus" and "Mars" conceptions of male-female interactions and discover ways that both men and women can work to improve relationships. Interventions designed to improve men's health and fathering will likely improve conditions for many families.

Meaningful efforts to improve current masculinity ideologies will likely involve changing society's view of masculinity. Remedial and preventative efforts must occur within a cultural context—most often, the same environment containing the typical and pervasive messages endorsing the misguided features of traditional conceptions of masculinity (G.R. Brooks & Good, in press). Crucial as it may be, changing the dominant paradigm of masculinity will be a major undertaking. Calls for this type of change are not new (e.g., H. Goldberg, 1977; J. Harrison, 1978); however, these voices have been overshadowed by pervasive messages supporting the traditional conceptions of masculinity that are associated with poorer health, violence, and other problems. Changing masculinity involves challenging widely accepted myths dictating how men, and women, should think, behave, and be. Meaningful change will likely involve countering advertisers' masculinity-related messages and their pitch to the subsequent insecurities they have fostered in potential consumers. Such a change also requires countering peer-group pressures associated with adolescence that support conformity to these messages. It would mean

Table 13.1
Resources

Society for the Psychological Study of Men and Masculinity (SPSMM)
Division 51 Membership Services, American Psychological Association
750 First Street, NE
Washington, DC 20002-4242
(202) 336-6013
http://web.indstate.edu/edu/spsmm/home.html

American Men's Studies Association (AMSA)
Membership Office
329 Afton Avenue
Youngstown, OH 44512-2311
(216) 782-2736

breaking the cycle by which older generations transmit traditional masculine beliefs to younger generations, who subsequently pass them on. Messages must come from many community sources or risk being lost in the continual waves of contradictory messages essential to marketing need-based products. Schools, religious institutions, health care providers, and community public service announcements could all promote change via appeals designed for the male population. Although individual efforts to find solutions to the problems associated with masculinity are vital, collective efforts are also needed to create broader social change associated with these important issues (see Table 13.1).

CHAPTER 14

Changing Times, Changing Gender Roles: Who Do We Want Women and Men to Be?

MARY E. KITE

The first women's rights convention in the United States took place in July 1848. In the more than 150 years since that event, women's opportunities have changed on many fronts. Women can now vote, own land, and file for divorce. They can also hold doctoral degrees, compete in sports, and succeed at all levels in the workplace. The ground has shifted, and along with it our ideas about what women and men can and should do have radically changed. With these changes, however, has come uncertainty and mixed messages about appropriate gender roles. Some glass ceilings have been shattered, but others remain. Men are encouraged to take greater interest in the father role, but are discouraged from taking this role too seriously. Once, women and men "knew their place." Now that place has expanded, and we struggle with the ambiguities that these changes have brought. How do we feel about changing gender roles and those who occupy these new positions? This chapter addresses our attitudes and beliefs about women and men and discusses how these perceptions vary across roles and settings.

GENDER BELIEF SYSTEMS

The gender belief system model (Deaux & Kite, 1987; Kite & Whitley, 1996) proposes that our perceptions about men and women are influenced by societal expectations. These expectations are reflected in "a set of beliefs and opinions about males and females and about the purported qualities of masculinity and femininity. This belief system includes, but is not limited to, gender stereotypes, attitudes toward appropriate roles for the sexes, and perceptions of those who violate the modal pattern" (Deaux & Kite, 1987, p. 97). According to this model, people's expectations reflect the belief that gender-associated attributes are bipolar: What is masculine is not feminine, and vice versa. That is, people expect someone who is described by stereotypically masculine traits to also possess stereotypically masculine physical characteristics and to adopt stereotypically masculine roles. Similarly, the knowledge that a person is stereotypically feminine on one dimension leads to the inference that the person is stereotypically feminine on other dimensions (Berndt & Heller, 1986; Deaux & Lewis, 1984). Apparently, people expect gender-related attributes, such as roles, traits, and physical appearance, to form a coherent package. Thus, when judging others, people believe that knowledge about one gender-associated component informs about the other components. At the individual level, people differ widely in the extent to which they endorse these beliefs, but most of us can readily identify the general societal expectations Americans hold for the sexes. Moreover, people automatically utilize gender stereotypes, even if they do not explicitly endorse them (Banaji & Hardin, 1996; Greenwald & Banaji, 1995) and even though they can later override the influence of this automaticity (I.V. Blair & Banaji, 1996).

This chapter examines how the gender belief system influences our perceptions of and reactions to women and men in nontraditional roles. The work described in this chapter is based largely on the beliefs of heterosexual, White, middle-class college students. Although these beliefs have been shown to generalize across a variety of cultures and settings (e.g., Williams & Best, 1990a), the perspectives of ethnic minorities, gay men and lesbians, and members of other social classes are not well-represented in this work. Similarly, this chapter describes research that, implicitly or explicitly, represents evaluations and perceptions of White women and men. The picture is likely more complicated when targets are described by both ethnicity and sex. When ethnicity of the stimulus person is taken into account, for example, free-response assessments of these more specific targets are quite distinct; White women and men are not described in the same way as Black or Asian women and men (e.g., Niemann, Jennings, Rozelle, Baxter, & Sullivan, 1994). I acknowledge the limitations of the current tendency to rely on White, middle-class targets and respondents and, whenever possible, discuss the available research that examines gender-role beliefs from a broader perspective (see Howard & Hollander, 1997, for a discussion of how race and social class issues cross-cut gender issues). An exception to this narrow perspective is the number of studies demonstrating that beliefs about gay men and lesbians are strongly linked to the gender belief system; this research is described in the section on gender-role nonconformity.

STEREOTYPIC CHARACTERISTICS OF WOMEN AND MEN

The early studies of Paul Rosenkrantz and Inge Broverman (Broverman et al., 1972; Rosenkrantz et al., 1968) charted the traits typically associated with women and men. These authors identified a competence cluster, typically associated with men, that includes characteristics such as confident, independent, and controlling (labeled agentic or instrumental), and a warmth-expressiveness cluster, typically associated with women, that includes characteristics such as warm, kind, and concerned for others' welfare (labeled communal or expressive). These associations have been replicated many times and across many cultures (e.g., Spence & Helmreich 1978; Williams & Best, 1990a). Extending this work, Deaux and Lewis (1984) document that the sexes are stereotypically differentiated on other dimensions as well (see also Cejka & Eagly, 1999). Men's physical characteristics are believed to include strong, rugged, and broad-shouldered, whereas women's physical characteristics are believed to included dainty, pretty, and graceful. Similarly, people believe women's gender roles include caring for children and taking care of household tasks and men's gender roles include being head of the household and handling financial matters. As discussed above, these components of the gender belief system are interrelated, in that information about one dimension influences inferences about other dimensions (Deaux & Lewis, 1984; L.A. Jackson & Cash, 1985).

Young children do not utilize gender-associated information as readily as adults do, but rather, are more likely to base judgments strictly on biological sex. Boys described as having feminine interests, for example, are still thought to prefer boy's activities (C.L. Martin, 1989). By around age 9, children begin to associate gender-related information, rather than merely biological sex, with activities and interests. Yet even young children are well aware of gender-associated expectations and make judgments based on those assumptions. Young children can readily identify which toys are appropriate for their sex (Blakemore, LaRue, & Olejnik, 1979) and they know which activities are stereotypically associated with women and men (G.D. Levy & Fivush, 1993). Children assume that if they like a gender-neutral toy, other members of their sex will also like it and children of the other sex will not. Moreover, they will like even very attractive toys less if they learn they are designed for the other sex and assume their peers will feel the same (C.L. Martin et al., 1995).

Once stereotypic beliefs are developed, they have remarkable staying power; studies in a variety of settings and cultures show that men are believed to be higher in agency than women, whereas women are believed to be higher in communion than men (Eagly, 1987; Williams & Best, 1990b). These beliefs are also fairly stable across time (Lueptow, Garovich, & Lueptow, 1995), although there is some evidence that the male gender role is being viewed less positively than in the past (Werner & LaRussa, 1985), a point that I return to later. Yet, as mentioned earlier, these ratings most strongly reflect beliefs about middle-class Whites. Landrine (1985) found that Black women and lower-class women were seen as feminine, but less so than White women and middle-class women. Similarly, Deaux and Kite (1985) found that gender-associated beliefs about Black and White men are similar, but that Black women are seen as more similar to Black men than to White women on male-associated traits.

ASSESSING THE GENDER BELIEF SYSTEM

A number of influential instruments have been developed to assess components of the gender belief system (see Beere, 1990a, 1990b; Frieze & McHugh, 1997). I describe next measures of overt and subtle sexism toward women, ambivalent sexism measures, and measures assessing a belief in a masculine ideology. I discuss briefly the overlap between these measures and, finally, contrast them with agency and communion measures. Attitudes toward women and men as individuals are described in a later section.

ATTITUDES TOWARD WOMEN'S RIGHTS AND RESPONSIBILITIES

One aspect of the gender belief system that has received a great deal of attention is attitudes toward women's rights and responsibilities. For nearly three decades, measures such as the Attitudes toward Women Scale (AWS; Spence & Helmreich, 1972a) have been used to document people's beliefs about the appropriate place for women in society. Women more readily endorse egalitarian attitudes than do men, and Southerners' attitudes toward women's roles are more conservative than are the attitudes of those from other regions of the United States (Twenge, 1997a). Accompanying the marked changes in women's roles since the AWS and similar measures were developed, attitudes of both men and women have shifted toward considerably greater acceptance of women's rights (Spence & Hahn, 1997; Twenge 1997a). Recent studies find a significant number of respondents, particularly women, are scoring at the extremely positive end of the AWS (Spence & Hahn, 1997). The progress demonstrated by these studies is indeed heartening; overtly sexist attitudes are declining. Unfortunately, claims of universal acceptance for women in nontraditional roles are premature. The subtle sexism measures, described next, indicate that the obstacles women face can be a moving target.

MEASURES OF SUBTLE SEXISM

Measures such as the Modern Sexism scale (MS; Swim et al., 1995), the Ambivalent Sexism Inventory (ASI; P. Glick & Fiske, 1996), and the Neosexism Scale (NS; Tougas, Brown, Beaton, & Joly, 1995) reflect the complexities of our current beliefs about women's roles. Swim's work documents how sexist beliefs can go unnoticed, disappearing into the fabric of cultural and societal norms. Even those who consider themselves supporters of women's rights can exhibit these subtly sexist behaviors. Swim et al. hypothesized and found that modern sexists overestimated the percentage of women in traditional male professions (e.g., engineers, architects). These modern sexists also believed that gender-based job segregation is rooted in biological differences between the sexes rather than socialization or discrimination, and they preferred a male candidate for public office. Traditional gender-role attitudes, as measured by Swim et al.'s Old-Fashioned Sexism scale, did not predict voting preferences or attributions about the causes of job segregation.

Tougas et al. (1995) define neosexism as "a manifestation of a conflict between egalitarian values and residual negative feelings toward women" (p. 843). Neosexists believe it is important to maintain the current balance between women's and men's roles and believe that, if this balance shifts, their group stands to lose more than it gains. For neosexist men, affirmative action for women represents such a shift and, as predicted by the neosexism model, these men were less accepting of affirmative action (Tougas et al., 1995). Similarly, neosexist women and men are generally unsupportive of the women's movement and hold more negative attitudes toward gay men and lesbians than do nonsexist respondents (B. Campbell, Schellenberg, & Senn, 1997). Also central to the theory is the notion that men's belief in their collective interest contributes to sexist attitudes; men who strongly identify with their collective interest are more likely to be sexist and to oppose affirmative action (Tougas et al., 1995).

Ambivalent sexism theory (P. Glick & Fiske, 1996, 1997, 1999a; Goodwin & Fiske, this volume) posits that people's feelings about the other sex are fundamentally ambiguous and can be both subjectively benevolent and hostile. This ambiguity comes from the fact that women and men differ in terms of status and power but at the same time are intimately linked in social and/or romantic relationships. Hence, women and men view each other in both positive and negative terms. Benevolent male sexists feel protective toward women, believing them weaker and necessarily dependent on men. As with the modern sexist, the benevolent male sexist does not recognize the ways those beliefs patronize and limit women. The hostile male sexist, in contrast, holds derogatory beliefs about women that serve as justification for the sexual exploitation of women. These beliefs are measured by the ASI (P. Glick & Fiske, 1996). Women's attitudes toward men, assessed by the newly developed Ambivalence toward Men Inventory (AMI; P. Glick & Fiske, 1999a), also reflect both hostility and benevolence. Women's hostile sexism reflects a resentment of men's higher status and power. Women's benevolent sexism stems from their emotional and economic dependence on men, leading to materialism, or the belief that women must protect and nurture men. Both hostile and benevolent sexism are rooted in traditional gender-role beliefs and both serve to justify and maintain traditional patriarchal social structures.

The psychometric properties of the subtle sexism instruments have been well-established and all have excellent reliability and validity. Comparisons of the subtle sexism toward women measures are available (see B. Campbell et al., 1997; P. Glick & Fiske, 1996, 1999a; Masser & Abrams, 1999; Swim & Cohen, 1997), and there is no strong evidence that one scale is superior to the others. These measures all correlate with traditional measures of women's rights, but account for unique variance above and beyond those traditional measures (P. Glick & Fiske, 1996, Swim & Cohen, 1997; Tougas et al., 1995). Because the AMI is new, work comparing this instrument to other subtle sexism measures is limited. P. Glick and Fiske (1999a) report that the AMI correlates with the ASI and measure of attitudes toward men, but that only the AMI successfully distinguishes between subjectively positive and subjectively negative beliefs about men. Similarly, only the Benevolent Sexism scale of the ASI assesses the subjectively positive side of sexism toward women (Masser & Abrams, 1999). Because the theoretical bases for these measures differ in important ways, authors should examine their research question carefully and rely on theoretical justifications for selecting a relevant measure. Future research will likely further clarify the differences and similarities among these instruments.

ATTITUDES TOWARD MEN'S GENDER ROLES

Parallel to measures of attitudes toward women's rights, measures of masculine ideology assess the belief that men should conform to culturally defined standards for male behavior (E.H. Thompson, Pleck, & Ferrara, 1992). Measures designed to assess this construct include the Brannon Masculinity Scale (BMS; Brannon & Juni, 1984) and the Male Role Norm Scale (MRNS: E.H. Thompson & Pleck, 1986). The MRNS does correlate with the AWS, but the measure also assesses constructs that are distinct from those gender-associated beliefs.

The theoretical basis for measures such as the MRNS and the BMS is the proposition that a masculine ideology exists that limits men, just as the traditional feminine gender role limits women. Conceptually, a masculine ideology stems from the cultural constraints of the traditional male role. These constraints, in turn, produce gender-role strain that is harmful to men (Pleck, Sonenstein, & Ku, 1993a). Failure to fulfill masculine role expectations, for example, can lead to low self-esteem, whereas fulfilling these role expectations may be rooted in an unhealthy socialization process that, in the long run, has negative consequences for men. Supporting this perspective, adolescents who endorse a masculine ideology are more likely to report problematic behavior such as drug use and suspension from school (Pleck et al., 1993a), reduced likelihood of condom use and lessened concern about the sexual partner's perspective (Pleck et al., 1993b), and more negative attitudes toward gay people (Pleck, Sonenstein, & Ku, 1994). These results are similar for Whites, Blacks, and Hispanics (Pleck et al., 1993b, 1994). This research documents that both men and women are constrained by societal expectations and that the process, although related to the same cultural scripts, is manifested differently for women and men. I will return to this point when I discuss the consequences of gender-role violation.

MEASURES OF AGENCY AND COMMUNION

A common misconception is that measures such as the Personal Attributes Questionnaire (PAQ; Spence & Helmreich, 1978) and the short form of the Bem Sex Role Inventory (BSRI; S.L. Bem, 1979) assess attitudes toward women and men, masculinity/femininity, or gender-role orientation. In fact, these instruments measure agency (self-assertiveness) and communion (interpersonal orientation). Spence (1993) and others (Deaux, 1985; Deaux & Lewis, 1984) have convincingly argued, with considerable empirical support, that constructs such as gender role and masculinity/femininity are more complex than those concepts measured by the BSRI and the PAQ. (The longer form of the BSRI [S.L. Bem, 1974] contains items such as "masculine" and "feminine" that are not components of agency and communion. See Spence, 1993, for a discussion of the psychometric consequences of this.) This is not to suggest that agency and communion scores are similar for women and men. Research in a variety of settings and cultures has consistently shown that men self-report greater agency and women self-report greater communion than their other-sex counterparts (see Eagly, 1987; Spence, 1993; Williams & Best, 1990b). The PAQ and the BSRI are also successfully used to assess the gender-stereotypic beliefs that men are agentic and women are communal, discussed above. Measures of agency and communion have a well-established place in the gender-role literature and, when used appropriately, are excellent choices for examining those gender-associated constructs.

A complete discussion of the measurement of gender-related constructs is beyond the scope of this chapter. The point here is that evaluating people's views about women and men is complex, and different measures represent distinct aspects of the gender belief system. Researchers should take care that the instruments they have chosen represent the constructs they intend. Excellent overviews of available measures can be found in Beere (1990a, 1990b), Frieze and McHugh (1997), and E.H. Thompson et al. (1992).

EVALUATIONS OF WOMEN AND MEN

The measures discussed thus far examine gender stereotypes and attitudes toward women's and men's gender roles. As Eagly and her colleagues have noted (Eagly, Mladinic, & Otto, 1991), reviewers of this research have traditionally concluded that men are viewed as superior to women. In light of this common assumption, Eagly and Mladinic's (1989) finding that women are evaluated more positively than men was unexpected. Yet, subsequent studies have replicated this result (Eagly et al., 1991; Haddock & Zanna, 1994), with effect sizes for this sex comparison ranging from .38 to .54 (see Eagly & Mladinic, 1994). Moreover, Eagly and Mladinic's (1994) review of this literature points to earlier documentation of this result (e.g., Werner & LaRussa, 1985). Although early research showed that men were evaluated more favorably than women (Sherriffs & McKee, 1957), it appears that changing social roles have erased any tendency to evaluate the general category "woman" negatively.

Despite its replicability, the suggestion that women are viewed more favorably than men is clearly inconsistent with the discrimination women face in many aspects of their lives. In many settings, and particularly in high-achievement settings, women are less valued than men (e.g., Fouad et al., in press; E.D. Kahn & Robbins, 1985; Sandler & Hall, 1986). One plausible hypothesis is that negative attitudes toward women emerge at the subtype level, rather than toward the general social category "woman" (see Eagly et al., 1991). This issue is explored next.

SUBTYPES OF WOMEN AND MEN

People possess a variety of identifiable gender subtypes that differ in significant ways from the more general categories "woman" and "man." Although the identified categories vary somewhat, subtypes of women as housewives, sexy women, and nontraditional women consistently emerge (e.g., Clifton, McGrath, & Wick, 1976; Deaux, Winton, Crowley, & Lewis,1985; Six & Eckes, 1991). The subtypes of men are somewhat less clear-cut, but the cluster of male subtypes typically includes "macho man," "businessman," "blue-collar worker," and "family man" (e.g., Deaux et al., 1985; G.H. Edwards, 1992; Six & Eckes, 1991).

Evidence further suggests that attitudes toward these subtypes vary. The family man is viewed as more likable than are athletes, businessmen, or blue-collar workers; ratings of these latter categories are similar and neutral (G.H. Edwards, 1992). Macho men are viewed more negatively than any other subtypes (J. Carter, Lane, & Kite, 1991). Feminists are viewed less positively than are housewives (Haddock & Zanna, 1994), and feminists and sexy women also fare less well than mothers or businesswomen (J. Carter et al., 1991). Our evaluation of both women and men, then, differs depending on the roles the individuals occupy. Yet, whether the roles are traditional or nontraditional does not completely explain these varied reactions. Men with primarily masculine characteristics, for example, fare less well than any other subtypes of women or men (J. Carter et al., 1991). Housewives and mothers are preferred to feminists, but the traditional sexy woman is also viewed relatively negatively. People do seem to prefer subtypes associated with communal characteristics (e.g., housewives and family men). This is consistent with Eagly and Mladinic's (1994) suggestion that women are preferred over men because women are associated with warmth and kindness. Yet, the benefit may not extend to lower-class women or to Black women; these women are generally described in less positive terms than middle-class or White women (Landrine, 1985).

Recent work suggests that these evaluations also depend on the gender-role attitudes of the respondents. Those scoring high on the MS, for example, exhibit a bias in favor of men and against women (Swim & Cohen, 1997). Glick and his colleagues (P. Glick, Diebold, Bailey-Werner, & Zhu, 1997) argue that sexist men divide women into polarized subtypes, representing "good" and "bad" women. In support of this proposition, they showed that, overall, sexist and nonsexist men evaluated subtypes of women similarly. Ambivalent sexist men, however, were polarized in their evaluations of subtypes of women. Hostile sexist men were particularly derogatory toward the subtypes they spontaneously generated; in contrast, benevolent sexist men were particularly complimentary toward the subtypes they generated. Regardless of their score on the ASI, women did not display these polarized attitudes. In a second study (P. Glick et al., 1997), these authors demonstrated that men's hostile sexism scores predicted less favorable attitudes toward career women, whereas men's benevolent sexism scores predicted more favorable attitudes toward homemakers.

There is no easy answer to the question of which sex is held in higher esteem. At the global category level, people show a preference for women over men. Yet, at the subtype level, beliefs are considerably more complicated. Evaluations of the sexes depend both on who you ask—traditional or nontraditional women and men—and whom you ask about. As I'll describe next, our beliefs about the sexes also depend on whether people's gender-associated characteristics are consistent with society's expectations for their sex.

GENDER-ROLE VIOLATORS

The importance of gender-role conformity is learned early, both from parents and peers. A meta-analysis found that parents treated boys and girls differently only in regard to gender-role socialization; parents, especially fathers, encouraged gender-typed activities in their children (Lytton & Romney, 1991). On the 18 other behaviors these authors reviewed, parents were found to treat boys and girls similarly. By about age 3, sex segregation in playgroups becomes the norm, and evidence shows that these sex-segregated playgroups have markedly different concerns. In boys' playgroups, the focus is dominance and constriction of interaction, whereas in girls' playgroups, the focus is cooperation and facilitation (see C.L. Martin, 1999, for a review).

The pressure to stay within gender-appropriate boundaries is strong: Children as young as 3 punish their peers for gender-role nonconformity (M.E. Lamb, Easterbrooks, & Holden, 1980; M.E. Lamb & Roopnarine, 1979). Preschool children, especially preschool boys, are less likely to play with cross-sex toys in the presence of an other-sex peer (Serbin et al., 1979). From an early age, then, we come to expect girls to be girls and boys to be boys: Girls should play with dolls and be passive; boys should play with trucks and be active. Adult men should be strong and independent, and head the household, whereas adult women should be warm and small-framed and take care of children (e.g., Cejka & Eagly, 1999; Deaux & Lewis, 1984). The reality, of course, is that many women head households and many men are warm. To what extent do we accept these variations? One answer to this question comes from research examining perceptions of gender-role violators—those individuals who take on stereotypic roles and characteristics of the other sex.

At first glance, it appears that gender-role violators are disliked. Three independent studies by Costrich and her colleagues (Costrich, Feinstein, Kidder, Marecek & Pascale, 1975), for example, revealed that passive, dependent men and aggressive, assertive women were rated as less likable and in greater need of therapy than their non-role-violating counterparts. Moreover, role violators described mainly by characteristics of the other sex are viewed less favorably than gender-role-congruent individuals (Costrich et al., 1975; Rajecki, De Graaf-Kaser, & Rasmussen, 1992). When individuals with a mixed gender role are examined, however, the outcome is less clear-cut. L.A. Jackson and Cash (1985) found that individuals who endorsed either strictly incongruent or strictly congruent gender-role behaviors were evaluated unfavorably, but individuals who exhibited both male and female role behaviors were rated as most likable and well-adjusted. Similarly, Laner and Laner (1979) compared the likability of hypothetical heterosexual and homosexual men; in a separate, similar study, they compared the likability of hypothetical heterosexual and homosexual women (Laner & Laner, 1980). Heterosexual men and women with mixed gender-role descriptions were most liked. In contrast, in both studies and regardless of described gender role, homosexual targets were either moderately or greatly disliked. Overall, these studies suggest there is greater likability for heterosexuals, but not for gay people, who have combined masculine and feminine characteristics. Apparently, there can be penalties for role transgressions, but some violations are considered more acceptable than others.

An important point is that evaluations may change depending on whether the role violation is represented by traits or other dimensions. Many studies in this area manipulate only the congruency of gender-associated traits. This is unfortunate because trait information itself conveys likability (S.E. Lee & Kite, 1998). Specifically, these results are difficult to interpret because it cannot be discerned whether the raters based their evaluations on the traits presented, which themselves indicate likability, or on whether those traits violated gender roles. It does appear that, regardless of the stimulus person's sex, heterosexuals described by communal traits (e.g., kind, warm) are generally liked better than heterosexuals described by agentic traits (e.g., independent, self-confident). Heterosexuals described as primarily agentic are not liked as much as heterosexuals described as primarily communal (S.E. Lee & Kite, 1998; McCreary, 1994). Similarly, grade school children prefer peers who have communal rather than agentic traits, although this preference is stronger for girl respondents than for boy respondents (Hibbard & Buhrmester, 1998). Such results are consistent with the above suggestion that subtypes associated with communal characteristics are preferred to subtypes associated with agentic characteristics. Simply put, gender-role violation may be acceptable when the individual exhibits communal characteristics. Yet, a seemingly small change in how targets are described produces a different result. Men described as "feminine" and women described as "masculine" were the least preferred hypothetical characters, compared to those described by more specific communal and instrumental traits (Leaper, 1995). Studies that remove the confounding between the likability and the gender-role congruency of the dimensions will provide a clearer picture of how gender-role violators are perceived.

Perceptions of role violators may also depend on whether the described person deviates from the norm on many or just a few gender roles. O'Leary and Donoghue (1978) found single role violations were not seen as problematic. A man choosing the traditional male job of successful businessman was not preferred over the male choosing the traditional female job of elementary school teacher. Similarly, a man recommending a dispute be resolved by talking was not rated less favorably than the man who recommended fighting as a resolution. Cano and Kite (1998) manipulated whether a target's traits, physical characteristics, or role behaviors were gender-role-congruent. Liking did not depend on which gender-associated component was varied. However, targets who were gender-role-congruent on all categories were liked most, followed by those congruent on two categories; those who were incongruent on all categories were liked least. It may be that a single role violation is not viewed as particularly serious, but that, at some point, people cross the line and take on too many other-sex characteristics to be acceptable.

As with the literature on evaluations of gender subtypes, no one explanation accounts for all the results of studies on gender-role violators. Whether people are penalized for role violation appears to depend on which characteristics are deviant and their number. People may also be more bothered by children's gender-role violations than by adults' similar violations, perhaps because of a concern that gender-role violation in children indicates homosexual tendencies (e.g., C.L. Martin, 1990). When participants learn the adult role violator is heterosexual, they are less concerned about gender-related characteristics (e.g., Laner & Laner, 1979, 1980). The association between gender-role nonconformity and sexual orientation is discussed in more detail below. Another possibility is that richer, more complex stimuli engage research participants and thus produce more accurate results. Studies using broader descriptions (e.g., include role information) or photographs of the gender-role violator find stronger evidence that the nonconformist is disliked (Costrich et al., 1975; L.A. Jackson & Cash, 1985). A meta-analytic review of this literature would clarify when and why gender-role deviants are rejected. Experimental studies do suggest that when role violators are devalued, males are particularly susceptible to negative evaluations. Data supporting this claim are described next.

THE COSTS OF MEN'S GENDER-ROLE VIOLATIONS

Although both women's and men's behavior is governed by roles and scripts (S.L. Bem, 1993), gender-role deviance appears to present special problems for men and boys (Fagot, 1977, 1985a; Feinman, 1981, 1984; McCreary, 1994). Gender-associated traits and gender-associated physical appearance both are more rigidly defined for males than for females (e.g., Hort, Fagot, & Leinbach, 1990), and men themselves report more congruence in their gender roles than do women (Twenge, 1999). Moreover, people react more negatively to men who possess female-associated characteristics than to women who possess male-associated characteristics (Feinman, 1984; McCreary, 1994). Role-deviant men, for example, are viewed as poorly adjusted in their careers, their relationships, and their sexuality. They are also thought to have emotional difficulty and to be in need of psychiatric help. Role-deviant women, however, are generally seen as well-adjusted (Tilby & Kalin, 1980).

A similar pattern emerges in studies of children's gender-role nonconformity. Girls who display masculine behavior, such as playing with trucks or playing sports, are not seen as a cause for alarm, but boys who display feminine behavior, such as playing with dolls, are not viewed complacently. Boys as young as toddlers send negative feedback to other boys exhibiting feminine behavior, but they usually ignore girls exhibiting masculine behavior (Fagot, 1985a). Teachers similarly criticize cross-sex behavior in boys but accept cross-sex behavior in girls (Fagot, 1977). Students of all ages, but particularly older students, believe that feminine boys are likely unpopular, whereas girls' perceived popularity is unaffected by their gender-associated characteristics (Berndt & Heller, 1986). College students report that they would feel worse if their son were a sissy than if their daughter were a tomboy (C.L. Martin, 1990). Boys' preference for a potential boy friend becomes increasingly negative with each feminine behavior he exhibits, and exclusively masculine boys are seen as happier than exclusively feminine boys (K.J. Zucker, Wilson-Smith, Kurita, & Stern, 1995). Girls' preferences for boy friends are less pronounced, but they do prefer feminine boys to masculine boys. K.J. Zucker et al. also demonstrated that girls prefer feminine girls and boys prefer masculine girls but, again, these preferences were less pronounced than were preferences about boy playmates. These authors interpret these results as further evidence that cross-sex behavior is less acceptable for boys than for girls.

Two explanations have been proposed to account for the contrasting evaluations given to the cross-gender behavior of males and females. One explanation is based on the hypothesis that gender-role violators, particularly male gender-role violators, are perceived to be gay (e.g., C.L. Martin, 1990; McCreary, 1994). A second explanation derives from the hypothesis that male gender roles are higher status than female gender roles (e.g., Feinman, 1984; Unger, 1976).

PERCEIVED SEXUAL ORIENTATION

According to the perceived sexual orientation explanation, negative attitudes toward gender-role violators stem from the inference that these individuals are likely to be gay or lesbian (e.g., Deaux & Lewis, 1984; McCreary, 1994). According to this perspective, it is not necessarily the gender-role violation that is problematic, but rather the association of this role violation with homosexuality.

The association between homosexuality and gender-role nonconformity has been well-established. Heterosexuals believe that gay men have the gender-associated characteristics of heterosexual women and that lesbians have the gender-associated characteristics of heterosexual men (e.g., Kite & Deaux, 1987). Bisexuals also are thought to have characteristics of the other sex, but not to the same extent as gay people (Weakland & Kite, 1999). These results emerge both when people freely list the attributes they associate with a group and when they report on standard measures of gender-associated characteristics such as the PAQ or the Deaux and Lewis (1984) component measure. Similarly, people are likely to conclude that men with female-associated characteristics are gay and, to a lesser extent, that women with male-associated characteristics are lesbian (Deaux & Lewis, 1984; Helgeson, 1994b). Also supporting this viewpoint is that traditional gender-role attitudes are associated with antigay attitudes (Kerns & Fine, 1994). People also make assumptions about sexual orientation based on physical appearance: Men with feminine, rather than masculine, facial features are thought more likely to be gay; similarly, women with masculine, rather than feminine, facial features are more likely presumed lesbian (Dunkel & Francis, 1990). Both women and men see unattractive women as more likely than attractive women to be lesbian (Dew, 1985; Unger, Hilderbrand, & Madar, 1982), but only women rate unattractive men as more likely to be gay than attractive men (Unger et al., 1982).

McCreary (1994) has proposed that males acting in feminine ways are more likely to be perceived as gay than females acting in masculine ways. This possibility, labeled the sexual orientation hypothesis, has received a great deal of empirical support. First, the association between men's femininity and gay male sexuality is stronger than the association between women's masculinity and lesbianism (Deaux & Lewis, 1984; Kite & Deaux, 1987; Weakland & Kite, 1999). McCreary, for example, found that men described by female-associated characteristics were more strongly perceived as being or becoming gay than men with traditional gender-role characteristics. Judgments of women's likelihood of being or becoming lesbian did not depend on their gender-associated characteristics. Similarly, men who use women's language are seen as likely to be gay, but estimates of women's lesbianism are not affected by their language use (Rasmussen & Moely, 1986). C.L. Martin (1990) found that people believe tomboys will outgrow some of their cross-sex behavior, but that sissies will not; she also showed that people believe sissy boys are more likely than tomboy girls to be maladjusted and gay. Finally, the label "homosexual" was listed as the worst insult that can be hurled at a man, but this did not hold for insults about women (K. Preston & Stanley, 1987). These findings all lend support to the sexual orientation hypothesis.

Males' discouragement of cross-sex behavior begins as young as preschool. Lamb and his colleagues (M.E. Lamb et al., 1980; M.E. Lamb & Roopnarine, 1979) found that boys were much more likely than girls to negatively reinforce other children's gender-role deviance. Boys are also more effective in changing their peers' gender-associated behavior than are girls or teachers (Fagot, 1985a). This rejection of feminine men unfortunately does not end when men reach adulthood (Herek, 1986; Herek & Glunt, 1993).

Men's and boys' intolerance for gender-role deviance may well account for why heterosexual men hold more negative attitudes toward homosexuality than do heterosexual women (e.g., Kite & Whitley, 1996, 1998; LaMar & Kite, 1998; Pleck et al., 1994). If the male gender role is indeed more rigid than the female gender role, tolerance for those who are perceived as violating those roles (e.g., gay men) would be especially discouraged (Herek, 1986; Herek & Glunt, 1993). Teaching males to eschew all things feminine undoubtedly leads to a rejection of feminine men, and gay men are so perceived. Because women, in contrast, may have more gender-role latitude, lesbianism is seen as relatively more acceptable (see S.L. Bem, 1993). Supporting this proposition, people, but especially men, hold more negative attitudes toward gay men than toward lesbians (Kite & Whitley, 1996). A similar pattern is found for ratings of bisexuals. Both women and men are accepting of bisexual women, but heterosexual men's view of bisexual men is as negative as their view of gay men (Nollen

& Whitley, 1998). The exception to this pattern emerges on measures of attitudes toward contact with gay men and lesbians. On these measures, women are more negative toward lesbians than are men (LaMar & Kite, 1998).

ROLE STATUS

The advantages of the male gender role in American society have long been noted. Men earn higher salaries and often command more respect than women do (see Betz, 1993, for a review). One reason traditionally male occupations are attractive to women, for example, is that they are more positively valued than women's occupations. Closely related to the perceived higher status of the male role (Conway, Pizzamiglio, & Mount, 1996; Henley, 1977; Unger, 1976) is the power that accompanies this more valued position. Because Goodwin and Fiske (this volume) provide an excellent summary of the importance of power in gender-associated interactions and perceptions, this issue is not discussed in this chapter.

The higher status of the male gender role has been offered as a reason why women's gender-role violation is viewed more positively than men's similar violations (Feinman, 1981, 1984). That is, women's cross-gender-role behavior can be seen as an attempt to gain social standing, whereas men's cross-gender-role behavior can be seen as giving up their higher social status (Tilby & Kalin, 1980). Indeed, Tilby and Kalin have proposed that women who strive to gain acceptance in a man's world are met with positive reinforcement and societal rewards. In contrast, men lose social acceptance and prestige by joining in traditional female-associated activities. Supporting this, Spence and Helmreich (1972b) found that a woman who described herself as competent in a variety of traditional male roles was preferred over a woman who described herself as competent in traditional female roles or as incompetent in either male or female roles. More recently, Cejka and Eagly (1999) showed that people believe occupations with higher prestige require skills associated with a masculine personality or cognitive ability and that jobs requiring these characteristics should pay more than jobs requiring feminine characteristics. These findings suggest that women who pursue a traditionally male occupation are moving up the status hierarchy. Interestingly, once traditionally male occupations gain significant numbers of women, the status of that occupation declines (Reskin & Roos, 1990). Cejka and Eagly argue that the association between gender-linked characteristics and occupational prestige is used to justify the sex-based division of labor. If so, one might predict that having significant numbers of women enter traditionally male occupations would result in the perception that the skills required for those jobs are now feminine.

Unfortunately, research directly testing the social status explanation for rejection of gender-role violators has produced mixed results. Feinman's (1984) work supports this viewpoint. He found that people who displayed high-status behavior gained in approval, but those who displayed low-status behavior lost in approval. McCreary (1994) measured status by both approval of the behavior and estimates of the number of friends the target likely had, but his results showed no support for the status hypothesis. S.E. Lee and Kite (1998) measured social status by characteristics such as "holds a position of authority" and "is a leader." They, too, failed to find support for the status hypothesis. Yet, these failures to support the status hypothesis stemmed from studies in which gender-role deviance was manipulated by traits, which has the limitations previously noted. Findings in the leadership arena, which show women are penalized more than men for gender-incongruent behavior, also call the status hypothesis into question. Eagly et al. (1992) found that women leaders were especially devalued when their leadership style was autocratic (e.g., traditionally male) compared to when it was democratic (e.g., traditionally female) or was not gender-stereotypic. Men and women who used a democratic leadership style were evaluated similarly. Because the status of the male and the female gender roles is markedly different (e.g., Conway et al., 1996), it is important that research continue to examine the effects of this status difference on our evaluations of the sexes.

WOMEN IN NONTRADITIONAL ROLES

One criticism that can be levied at the research described thus far is that, by and large, results are based on impoverished stimuli. That is, participants read or hear information about women and men whom they have never met and with whom they do not interact. Although such research can offer important insights into the theoretical underpinnings of our beliefs about and attitudes toward the sexes, it is fair to question whether these results completely describe the experiences of women and men who actually occupy nontraditional gender roles.

Jan Yoder (1985) poignantly described her experiences in such a role; she served for a time as one of the first two civilian female faculty members appointed at West Point. Her first-person account details the loneliness and isolation she experienced and how quickly her self-esteem declined during her time there. She was pigeonholed as either a wife (and thus expected to bring food to events when her male colleagues were not) or as a feminist/libber (who, after objecting to sexist actions, came to be unwelcome and ignored). She describes her double bind this way: "Because I was different, I could not be a good team member; but, not being part of the team helped make me different and increased my isolation" (p. 64). Caplan (1993) has likened these experiences to "lifting a ton of feathers," noting that each individual action or event can be waved away as minor or inconsequential. The cumulative impact for those whose daily work lives involve such interactions, however, is demoralizing and often devastating.

The double bind that women in nontraditional roles can experience is illustrated by what happens in the college classrooms. Women faculty report they are not taken seriously and that students make hostile and rude remarks, going so far as to question their credentials. Men faculty may also experience these behaviors, but this rarely occurs to the same degree it does for women faculty. V.R. Brooks (1982) found that male students interrupted both male and female professors more often than female students did, but that male students were particularly likely to interrupt when the professor was a woman.

Such events likely stem from the conflict between expectations about the faculty role and women's roles in the United States. Faculty members are expected to be directive, assertive, and knowledgeable; women are expected to be warm, nurturant, and supportive. Women who fit the traditional female gender role fare better in students' eyes than women who do not (Bennett, 1982), but even those women walk a fine line: If they are too nurturant, they are not behaving as a professor should; if they are not nurturant enough, they are not behaving as a woman should (see Sandler, 1991). In contrast, the male role and the professor role are not incongruent; because of this, men professors do not face this role conflict. Resolving this double bind is complicated because women professors are sometimes held to different standards than male professors. When professors choose a less-structured classroom style, women professors report more negative student reactions than do men professors (Statham, Richardson, & Cook, 1991). Similarly, women professors who are described as socializing out of class receive higher ratings than women not so described, but perceptions of male professors are unaffected by out-of-class socializing (Kierstead, D'Agostino, & Dill, 1988). There is no easy solution to this double bind. As Statham et al. (1991, p. 6) put it, "Whether she resolves the conflict along gender-stereotypic or gender-innovative lines, such resolution might create secondary problems. For example, if she adopts a male-typed teaching style, she might be resented; if she adopts a female-typed teaching style, she might be judged incompetent." Consider the work showing that expectations differ by student gender. Winocur, Schoen, and Sirowatka (1989) found that women who used an affiliative lecture style were devalued by male students. In contrast, women who used an instrumental lecture style were devalued by female students. These differences did not emerge for men lecturers. These data suggest that women in the college classroom truly are damned if they do and damned if they don't.

Negative classroom experiences are unpleasant in their own right, but they can also affect women's pocketbook and livelihood. Salary, promotion, and tenure in the academy, for example, often depend on one's classroom performance—usually assessed by student ratings. Yet, such ratings are potentially biased and at best provide only one perspective on how well faculty teach (McKeachie, 1997). Relative to the issues discussed here, a number of gender-associated biases have been identified as potential problems, including the gender-typed characteristics of the instructor, the gender-typing of the discipline, teacher rank, and the types of questions asked (see Basow, 1998, for a review). Discrimination is also more likely for individuals who teach in disciplines that are nontraditional for their gender. Evaluations of women chemistry instructors, for example, are more likely to be gender-biased than are evaluations of women English instructors (Basow, 1995; Basow & Silberg, 1987). Women professors experience similar forms of subtle discrimination in their research and service activities (Benokraitis, 1998). Moreover, the impact of even a small gender-based bias can be dramatic. Results of a computer simulation showed that when a mere 1% of the variance in performance ratings was due to gender, only 35% of top-level positions were filled by women. This occurred even when equal numbers of women and men joined the organization at entry level (Martell, Lane, & Emrich, 1996).

The experiences of women professors illustrate the process by which subtle and overt discrimination can limit advancement, but such experiences are in no way limited to women or the academy. The career success of ethnic minorities in the academy is similarly hindered by subtle biases (Brinson & Kottler, 1993), and women and ethnic minorities in other occupations report parallel experiences that limit their advancement and effectiveness (Benokraitis & Feagin, 1995; Fiske, Bersoff, Borgida, Deaux, & Heilman, 1991; Kanter, 1977a). Yoder and Aniakudo (1997), for example, recount the experiences of Black women firefighters, pointing to the exclusion, coworker hostility, and lack of support they experienced in this traditionally male profession. The settings may change, but the process is strikingly similar. These experiences are most vivid when members of a lower-status group enter a profession dominated by a higher-status group. That is, just being a numerical minority does not alone lead to subtle or overt job discrimination: Men entering traditionally female occupations are rarely disadvantaged by, and often benefit from, their minority status (see Yoder, 1991, for a review). It is lower role status, combined with being a "solo" in a dominant work group, that leads to discriminatory behavior.

This general process is illustrated by the experiences of women in leadership positions. A recent meta-analysis comparing the effectiveness of women and men in managerial and leadership roles showed no sex differences in leadership effectiveness overall (Eagly, Karau, & Makhijani, 1995). Yet, both sexes were more successful when their leadership style minimized the gender-role violation: Men were more effective when the leadership task called for traditionally masculine role behaviors and women were more effective when the leadership task called for traditionally feminine role behaviors. Supporting Yoder's (1985) experiences at West Point, for example, men were rated as more effective leaders, compared to women, in the traditionally male military setting. Consistent with the work on minority status, described above, men were also more effective when their work group had a high percentage of men. Gender-role incongruency hinders a leader's effectiveness, as does being female in a predominately male work group. These results are similar to those of Eagly et al.'s (1992) meta-analysis of the experimental literature on leadership effectiveness, described above. Both meta-analyses support the proposition that women, and sometimes men, fare better in our esteem when they occupy gender-congruent roles.

Women and ethnic minorities are well aware of these stereotypic expectations and may internalize them. Unfortunately, doing so may hinder their academic performance. According to Steele (1997), stereotypes become threatening "when one is in a situation or doing something for which a negative stereotype about one's group applies" (p. 614). Because negative stereotypes about women's mathematical abilities exist, for example, when women face math-achievement-oriented situations, such as test taking, they are confronted with the possibility of confirming the group's negative stereotype. This extra burden may impede their performance in certain situations. Supporting this, Spencer, Quinn, and Steele (cited in Steele, 1997) found that women who believed the achievement test they were completing generally showed sex differences (with men outperforming women) did worse than when they believed the test did not produce sex differences. These women were as capable as the men, but the threat that a negative stereotype might be applicable in their situation harmed performance. Similar results have been shown when Blacks believed a test usually showed inferior performance for their group (Steele & Aronson, 1995) or when low-socioeconomic-status (SES) participants believed their group scored worse on a test than high-SES participants (Croizet & Clair, 1998).

SUMMARY

Without question, the gender belief system guides our perceptions of and interactions with women and men. These expectations about what women and men *should be* guide and shape how women and men actually are. This process begins in infancy and continues throughout our lives. Although these beliefs are informative, providing a road map for our interactions with others, they are also limiting. Research on subtle sexism demonstrates the ways in which even well-intended gender-stereotypic beliefs limit women (e.g., P. Glick & Fiske, 1996; Swim et al., 1995; Tougas et al., 1995). Studies of gender nonconformity, as well as work on masculine ideology (e.g., Pleck et al., 1993b, 1994), highlight how boxing men into gender roles can have negative consequences. Research on women in nontraditional roles highlights the challenges women face when breaking new ground.

This chapter has outlined how both women and men are compromised when we evaluate others' potential based on gender-role expectations. As I have discussed, sometimes men benefit more than women do when these expectations are violated, and sometimes the reverse is true. The conflicting patterns of results reflect the complexities of our gender belief system. They also likely reflect our uncertainties about changing gender roles. Although the outcomes of our prejudgment are not always parallel, neither sex benefits when gender roles are rigidly defined. Gender roles are changing, and over time, our gender-associated beliefs have become less traditional (Spence & Hahn, 1997). People expect that gender roles will continue to change, predicting that differences between the sexes will decrease over time (Diekman & Eagly, 1999). Accepting these changes can only broaden opportunities for both men and women.

CHAPTER 15

Gender and Language

MARY CRAWFORD

For as long as feminism has been a social movement, language has been a battleground. With the emergence of second-wave feminism in the late 1960s, feminist scholars and activists alike drew attention to how language shapes social reality and how it can be an agent of change. Language and naming are sources of power (M. Crawford & Unger, 2000).

Aspects of reality that are named become "real" and can be talked about and thought about more easily. Names allow people to share experiences and teach others to name their own experiences in the same way. Moreover, when certain aspects of reality are granted names, unnamed aspects get overshadowed and thus become more difficult to think about and articulate. Unnamed experiences are less visible and, therefore, in a sense, less real to the social world (P.L. Berger & Luckmann, 1966). The idea that language shapes and constrains thought (sometimes called the Whorfian hypothesis) was proposed over 50 years ago by Benjamin Whorf and Edward Sapir. In its strong form (sometimes called *linguistic determinism*), the Whorfian hypothesis posits that a speaker's native language determines his or her perception of reality. In a weaker form (sometimes called *linguistic relativity*), it posits that the native language has a strong influence on one's perception of reality. The Whorfian hypothesis still provides many unanswered and interesting questions for psychology (Henley, 1989).

The study of gender and language has always been an interdisciplinary field, with theory and research coming from communication, linguistics, anthropology, sociolinguistics, history, literary studies, and philosophy as well as psychology. By the mid-1970s, the already large research literature had been catalogued in a hundred-page bibliography by Nancy Henley and Barrie Thorne (1975), and new books and articles began to appear at a rapidly increasing rate (Lakoff, 1975; Spender, 1980; Stannard, 1977; Thorne, Kramarae, & Henley, 1983).

Research on gender, language, and communication was framed initially in terms of three questions that guided the field (Thorne et al., 1983):

- Do women and men use language differently?
- How does language reflect and help perpetuate gender inequality?
- How can sexist language be changed?

In this chapter, I focus mainly on research from 1990 onward, because there are excellent summaries, reviews, and evaluations of earlier work available and because research has taken important new directions in the past decade. I discuss how the three questions posed by Thorne, Kramarae, and Henley have been answered, challenged, and reframed. Their first question, about gender differences, has come to be seen as less interesting and important over time; I discuss the

---

Portions of this chapter were adapted from M. Crawford (1995) and M. Crawford and Unger (2000).

reasons for that change. Their second question, on language and inequality, has been and remains an important topic of research. I discuss research on how masculinity and femininity are expressed linguistically and how names and word usage can perpetuate or redress inequality. Their third question, on language change, has been answered affirmatively through feminist language reform: coinage of new words, reclaiming old words, and the movement toward nonsexist language. Together, these areas of gender and language research provide a dynamic picture of the power of language in social interaction.

THE QUESTION OF GENDER DIFFERENCES

Of the three questions that have guided research on gender and language, the first—Do women and men use language differently?—would seem to be the simplest and the easiest to answer. Researchers could simply compare men's and women's talk to find out how they differ (and how they are similar) (Canary & Dindia, 1998). People certainly *believe* that women and men talk (and think) differently; consider the immense popularity of advice books that tell women how to interpret the talk and behavior of men (e.g., *Why Can't Men Open Up*, Naifeh & Smith, 1984), how to improve their own ways of talking (*The New Assertive Woman*, V. Bloom, Coburn, & Perlman, 1975), and how to communicate across the "gender gap" (*You Just Don't Understand*, Tannen, 1990; *Men Are from Mars, Women Are from Venus*, Gray, 1992). However, despite a very large number of studies on gender differences in speech style, there have been few definitive answers (Thorne et al., 1983).

Many influential feminist scholars have suggested that this area of research should not be given priority (cf. Thorne & Henley, 1975; Thorne et al., 1983; Torres, 1992). Their doubts are related to the broader question of whether social scientists should study gender-related differences at all (C. Kitzinger, 1994b). Some researchers maintain that scientific data on gender-related differences and similarities can dispel myths and stereotypes about women (Canary & Dindia, 1998; Hyde, 1994b). Others maintain that focusing on differences is a mistake (M. Crawford & Marecek, 1989b; Hare-Mustin & Marecek, 1994; Unger, 1979a, 1989a, 1992).

In the case of gender and language research, there are some negative consequences of a focus on difference: It encourages us to think of women and men as opposites, when there is much more gender similarity than difference; it distracts attention from issues of power and dominance in language; it impedes understanding of the diversity of women; and it treats gender as a fixed, static attribute of individuals (M. Crawford, 1995). I discuss each of these consequences briefly before describing some new directions in gender and language research.

WHAT IS SO OPPOSITE ABOUT THE "OPPOSITE SEX"?

In every area of language use where women and men have been compared, the similarities are more apparent than the differences. When researchers choose to focus on the differences, they are making a value judgment about what is important.

For example, suppose a study demonstrates that women use more adverbs than men. How large does that difference have to be before we are justified in labeling men and women more different than similar? Should its importance be judged in terms of a hypothetical average woman/man, in terms of the extremes of difference, or in terms of overlap? And what does that tell us about "human nature"? The answers to these questions involve value judgments about the meaning of difference (see Kimball, this volume).

Even when a reliable difference is found, we know little about its causes because it is difficult to separate gender from all the other factors it is related to in our society. Because gender is linked to many differences in background and status, researchers can rarely know whether their female and male samples are really comparable. When the effects of two or more variables are mixed in a research study, it becomes impossible to decide which variable is causing a particular result to occur (Jacklin, 1981). Despite the most careful matching of samples, women and men who are in "identical" situations may be functioning in different social worlds *because of others' social reactions to them as women or men* (M. Crawford & Unger, 2000; see LaFrance, this volume). Moreover, others react not only to a person's gender as a cue for how to behave toward them, but to race, (dis)ability, attractiveness, age, and other important social markers.

GENDER AND POWER: ERASURES

Power has been a very difficult concept to theorize for psychologists. Although power is a word we all use in everyday meanings, it is often left undefined and implicit in psychological research (C. Kitzinger, 1991). The difference approach has been criticized for not paying enough attention to power relations. What appears to be a "sex difference" may actually reflect linkages among gender, status, and power. For example, a hesitant, weak speech style originally called "women's language" (Lakoff, 1975) was later shown to be used by both males and females when they are lower in power or status than their conversational partners (O'Barr & Atkins, 1980).

According to critics of the difference approach, naming and studying dominance in communication are very important. To understand power and dominance in language and naming, researchers should focus less on static gender differences in speech patterns and more on the functions of language in discourse (C. Kitzinger, 1991). Much research is now based on this more dynamic view (West, Lazar, & Kramarae, 1997).

GENERIC WOMAN

The difference approach treats women as a unitary category. But women (and men) are located along other socially salient dimensions, too, such as race, (dis)ability, sexuality, class, and age. Foregrounding gender as the only or most important difference moves these other dimensions to the background. Researchers on differences often did not consider the diversity of women as they chose samples for study or offered interpretations of their findings. For example, the landmark book by linguist Robin Lakoff, *Language and Woman's Place* (1975), which claimed that there is a distinctive woman's style that is hesitant, weak, and deferential, influenced research for at least the next two decades as researchers tried to validate her claims (M. Crawford, 1995). However, Lakoff's book was based entirely on her observations of educated, White, middle-class speakers, not a more representative or diverse group of women (Henley, 1995). When a research study concludes that women are different from men, it is important to ask, "Which women do we mean?" (Bohan, 1993).

Incorporating the diversity of women into research is a complex process (P. McIntosh, 1983; Spelman, 1988). Using more diverse samples in gender and language research is not very enlightening if the study is asking the same old questions about differences between women and men. Instead, researchers must work to understand how people use language within their speech communities (Coates & Cameron, 1988; P.C. Nichols, 1980, 1983). Because speech communities are local cultural constructions, factors such as race/ethnicity, social class, and gender affect communication differently in each.

ESSENTIAL WOMAN

The difference approach is an *essentialist* approach. That is, it views gender as a fundamental, essential part of the individual. Essentialism conceptualizes gender as a set of properties residing in one's personality, self-concept, or traits. Gender is something women and men *have* or *are;* it is a noun (Bohan, 1993). Some examples of essentialist claims are the beliefs that women as a group lack the skills to speak assertively and that women universally value cooperative, intimacy-enhancing speech styles. These essentialist views portray women's speech as relatively uniform across situations. They imply that women speak in particular ways *because they are women.* The supposedly fundamental attributes of women and men (which define femininity and masculinity) are believed to determine gendered roles and actions. But research on social interaction shows that gender is continually negotiated and reenacted in discourse.

THE TURN TO DISCOURSE: FROM SEX AS A VARIABLE TO MEANING IN CONTEXT

Because of problems in resolving the matter of gender differences in language and speech style, the field has largely moved on from merely trying to catalogue differences and has turned to research methods that allow different, more profound questions to be asked. These current methods are based on a social constructionist view. In contrast to an essentialist stance, the social constructionist views gender as a social construct—a system of meaning that organizes interactions and governs access to power and resources. From this view, gender is not an attribute of individuals but a way of making sense of transactions. Gender is conceptualized as a verb, not a noun. The term "doing gender" (West & Zimmerman, 1987) reflects the social constructionist view that gender is a salient social and cognitive category through which information is filtered, selectively processed, and differentially acted on to produce self-fulfilling prophecies about women and men.

How does this approach apply to language? From a social constructionist perspective, language is viewed as a set of strategies for negotiating the social landscape, an action-oriented medium in its own right (Potter & Wetherell, 1987). Because social constructionists conceptualize language as dynamic and fluctuating in response to speakers' goals and intentions in particular social circumstances and speech communities, they endorse the use of interpretive research strategies such as ethnomethodology (Garfinkel, 1967), speech act analysis (Gervasio, 1987; Gervasio & Crawford, 1989), and discourse analysis (M. Crawford, 1995; Potter & Wetherell, 1987; S. Wilkinson & Kitzinger, 1995).

From a social constructionist perspective, talk is a powerful resource that is used in influencing other people, enlisting their help, offering them companionship, protecting ourselves from their demands, saving face, justifying our behavior, establishing important relationships, and presenting ourselves as worthwhile, admirable people. Whether we are talking informally among friends or engaged in more formal or task-oriented interaction, such as a job interview, we use the same system of conversational interaction which we adapt for each situation (Nofsinger, 1991). The reality constructed through language forms the basis of social organization (M. Crawford, 1995; Heritage, 1984; Potter & Wetherell, 1987).

As gender and language have been placed in a social constructionist framework, new research questions have emerged. Texts—written language and transcriptions of spoken language—are now analyzed for how they support or challenge constructions of gender. Discursive research, rather than focusing on differences per se, addresses the second question that has guided the field: How is inequality created and maintained in interaction? Proceeding from a discursive framework, we can ask interesting questions about how masculinity and femininity are constructed—and resisted— through talk.

LOVE YOUR MARTIAN FOREVER: MEDIATED DISCOURSES

"As many feminist researchers have shown, that which we think of as 'womanly' or 'manly' behavior is not dictated by biology, but rather is socially constructed. And a fundamental domain in which gender is constructed is language use. . . . Language does not merely reflect a preexisting sexist world; instead, it actively constructs gender asymmetries within specific sociohistorical contexts" (West et al., 1997, pp. 119–120). This assertion by Candace West and her colleagues reflects the view that to understand how gender relations are maintained, we need to look at social processes. As Simone de Beauvoir famously said, "One is not born, but rather *becomes* a woman." In Western societies, beliefs about gender are mediated by public discourses. I briefly analyze two genres that present discourses of idealized femininity and masculinity— romance novels and relationship advice books—before turning to the construction of masculinity and femininity in conversation.

In virtually every supermarket and shopping mall bookstore in the United States, romance novels are prominently displayed. Their covers feature women (usually young, always beautiful) gazing rapturously up into the eyes of tall, strong, handsome men. Their titles and their plots tell women that "love is everything."

Romance novels are read by more than 50 million American women, constitute 46% of U.S. mass-market paperback sales, and create a $1 billion industry each year (Associated Press, 1996). Over 120 new titles are published every month, aimed at women of all ages and diverse ethnic and cultural backgrounds. Romance novels aimed specifically at adolescents have been sold through public school book clubs since about 1980, gaining in popularity every year (Christian-Smith,

1993). Although most romance novels are published in the United States, England, and Canada, their readership is global (Puri, 1997).

Romance novels follow a predictable script: "Woman meets (perfect) stranger, thinks he's a rogue but wants him anyway, runs into conflicts that keep them apart, and ends up happily in his arms forever" (E.A. Brown, 1989, p. 13). The woman attracts her man without planning or plotting. In fact, she often fights her attraction, although her knees go weak, her head spins, her heart pounds, and her pulse quickens. The hero is usually portrayed as cold, insensitive, and rejecting, but by the end of the novel the reader learns that his coldness has been merely a pretense. Swept away by love, the independent, rebellious heroine finally gives in to the power of desire (M. Crawford & Unger, 2000).

What is the discourse of femininity and love in romance novels? A close analysis of a sample of 34 teen romances showed that they portrayed girls' sexuality as dangerous until it is channeled into heterosexual pairing. Girls' bodies are positioned as the site of a struggle for control among boyfriends, themselves, and their parents. Girls respond to boys' cues, but never take the lead themselves (Christian-Smith, 1993). In these novels, the lives of the heroines are made meaningful only by their heterosexual relationships.

Why do so many women enjoy these fantasies? For adolescent girls, they provide a discourse for interpreting their own emerging sexuality (Christian-Smith, 1993). For older women, they provide a reassuring fable of women transforming men. Although the hero is cold, scornful, sometimes even brutal, he actually loves the heroine, and it is the power of her love that transforms him into a sensitive, passionate, and caring lover. In reading the romance, women may learn to interpret the insensitivity of their own boyfriend or lover as evidence that underneath the gruff exterior is a manly heart of gold, and thus to tolerate unsatisfying heterosexual relationships without complaint (Radway, 1984).

However, reading romance novels is not only a form of re-creating cultural scripts of femininity. It can also be a form of resistance. India, where most marriages are arranged and romantic love has little or nothing to do with choosing a life partner, may be the world's largest sales outlet for romance novels. A study of young, single, middle-class Indian women explored reading romance novels as a form of cultural resistance. These women used the novels as examples of alternative, more "liberated" kinds of relationships with men. They admired the rebellious, feminine-but-strong heroines. And they used the novels as a source of information about sexuality. As one woman said, she had learned about the biology of sex at school, but from the romance novels she learned that there is nothing wrong with sex—indeed, that it is pleasurable. For better and for worse, romance novels are part of the globalization of Western culture (Puri, 1997).

It is not just novels that tell women what an ideal heterosexual relationship is like. In the United States and other Western countries, there is a plethora of self-help books aimed at women that promise to help them communicate better and therefore have more fulfilling relationships with their partner. Unfortunately, they almost always rely on a discursive representation of gender as essential difference, a position that was discussed earlier in this chapter and found inadequate. *Men Are from Mars, Women Are from Venus* (Gray, 1992), one of the most spectacularly successful relationship advice books in recent years, will serve as an example of their discourse of masculinity/femininity.

John Gray's book *Men Are from Mars, Women Are from Venus,* first published in 1992, had sold 6 million copies by 1997. Sequels—*Mars and Venus in the Bedroom, Mars and Venus in Love, Mars and Venus on a Date, Mars and Venus Together Forever*—have sold another 4 million. The book, available in virtually every bookstore in the United States, has been published in 38 languages. In addition to the books, there are Mars/Venus audiotapes and videotapes, greeting cards, calendars, a CD-ROM, an infomercial, package holidays, a CD of Mars/Venus pop songs, a syndicated "Dear Abby"–type advice column, and a one-man Broadway show. Gray has also trained a large number of "facilitators" who run his weekend couples' workshops, and expanded this profitable venture by devising the first fast-food-style franchise for the professional market. For a price, psychologists can buy the right to call their therapy practice a "Mars/Venus Counselling Center." Although Gray has a mail-order Ph.D. and is not licensed to practice psychology, his Mars/Venus franchise has been advertised in the *Monitor,* an official publication of the American Psychological Association (Bruning, 1998; Gleick, 1997; Marano, 1997).

Gray's perspective on heterosexual marriage is loosely based on a theory of gender and communication previously popularized by Deborah Tannen's best-seller *You Just Don't Understand* (1990). This model (Maltz & Borker, 1982) claims that male-female conversations are fraught with difficulty because women and men have different (opposing) conversational goals. Gray carries the model to its logical conclusion: Women and men are fundamentally and properly different; these differences are inherent, inevitable, and healthy. As their titles proclaim, his books dichotomize and stereotype women and men to extremes:

> Centuries before the Martians and Venusians got together they had been quite happy living in their separate worlds. Then one day everything changed. The Martians and Venusians on their respective planets suddenly became depressed. . . . When the Martians became depressed, everyone on the planet left the cities and went to their caves for a long time. They were stuck and couldn't come out, until one day when a Martian happened to glimpse the beautiful Venusians through his telescope. . . . The sight of these beautiful beings inspired the Martians. . . . *Suddenly they felt needed.* They came out of their caves and began building a fleet of spaceships to fly to Venus.
>
> When the Venusians became depressed, to feel better they formed circles and began talking with one another about their problems. But this didn't seem to relieve the depression. They stayed depressed for a long time until through their intuition they experienced a vision. Strong and wondrous beings (the Martians) would be coming across the universe to love, serve, and support them. *Suddenly they felt cherished* . . . they happily began preparing for the arrival of the Martians. . . .
>
> Men are motivated and empowered *when they feel needed* . . . women are motivated and empowered *when they feel cherished.* (Gray, 1992, pp. 42–43; emphases in original)

Every aspect of personality, motivation, and language is polarized. Women's speech is indirect, men's is direct. Women respond to stress by becoming overwhelmed and emotionally involved, men by becoming focused and withdrawn. Women and men even lunch in restaurants for different reasons: For men, it is an efficient way to approach the task of eating; for women, it is an opportunity to build a relationship.

Women and men are so irredeemably and fundamentally different that they need translators to help them communicate (a Martian/Venusian phrase dictionary is provided). They also need rules and routines to bridge the gender gap. The book is full of lists: 23 things not to say, 101 ways to score relationship points with a woman (e.g., offer to carry the groceries), 5 points to include in love letters, 5 tips for motivating a man, 15 things to do when your man won't talk to you (e.g., go shopping, take a bubble bath), the 6 primary love needs of women and the 6 (different) primary love needs of men.

In this book, middle-class heterosexual families follow all the scripts. Martians come home after a long day at the office to waiting Venusians. Martians are obsessed with paid work and money, Venusians with home and feelings. Venusians seem to do almost all the domestic work, from taking children to the dentist to cooking, cleaning, and calling elderly relatives. Martians may be asked to help, but only if Venusians are very careful about how they ask and if they recognize that Martians have every right to refuse. Helpful tips are provided for "Programming a Man to Say Yes" and "The Art of Empowering a Man." If all else fails, one can read the section on "How to Give Up Trying to Change a Man."

Self-help books that tell women how to pacify their husbands and accept inequality in domestic arrangements fit a conservative agenda that glosses over the social structures that sustain inequality, and distract attention from the need for collective action on behalf of gender equality. As Deborah Cameron (1996) puts it, "Saving a woman's marriage is a far cry from producing a critique of marriage itself" (p. 35).

Relationship advice books also contrast with other advice books for women. Throughout the 1970s and 1980s, there was a publishing and therapeutic fad on assertive speech, which produced a very large number of books, training courses, videos, and other media aimed at helping people become more assertive. Although there was never any solid research evidence that women are less assertive than men, many of these books were aimed specifically at women (M. Crawford, 1995). In them, women are instructed to speak clearly, forcefully, and directly, with the promise that they will then achieve respect and status. The examples of speech in assertiveness training books are often quite artificial and seem based on stereotypical masculine speech. And when women use these artificial speech styles, they are often seen as less warm and likable (M. Crawford, 1988).

The self-help genre, then, has prescribed different—and strikingly contradictory—strategies for women to use at home and at work (Cameron, 1995). Career advice tells women that, to get ahead, they must learn to talk more like men. For example, the February 1999 issue of *New Woman* magazine advises women to "bridge the language gap" by "talking his way." According to *New Woman*, talking like a man means using numbers, direct commands, and "I" statements. In contrast, relationship advice tells women that they should learn to accept that men and women are just different, and work hard to understand their man's meanings.

Together, self-help books and romance novels, along with other cultural vehicles such as television and advertising, create a complex discourse of femininity/masculinity that might be summarized as follows:

- Women and men are fundamentally and naturally different.
- To lead fulfilling lives, women need men.
- To get and keep the approval of men, women must emulate them at work and defer to them at home.

Ordinary social talk takes place within this larger discourse and is permeated by it. Linguist Deborah Cameron (1996) summarizes the outcome: "If I talk like a woman this is not just the inevitable outcome of the fact that I am a woman; it is one way I have of becoming a woman, producing myself *as* one. There is no such thing as 'being a woman' outside the various practices that define womanhood for my culture—practices ranging from the sort of work I do to my sexual preferences to the clothes I wear to the way I use language" (p. 46).

GIRL TALK: THE SOCIAL CONSTRUCTION OF FEMININITY

Exactly how is gender reproduced in the ways we use language? For a clear-cut case, let us consider a site where women's language is overtly "bought, sold, and custom-tailored" for customer satisfaction: the 900-number fantasy lines (K. Hall, 1995). These services allow telephone callers (usually male) to engage in a verbal sexual encounter with a woman who is paid to do so. The women who are employed on the fantasy lines work from their homes and may choose to accept or reject the fantasy requests of particular callers. The worker never meets her male client, and they know nothing about each other.

Because the telephone as a medium does not allow for visual stimulation, the fantasy must be created in words alone. To create the illusion of intimacy, the women draw on the discourse of male pornography. Their training manuals for the job tell them to create different (stereotypical) characters, such as the ideal woman, bimbo, nymphomaniac, mistress, slave, lesbian, and virgin. They are also instructed to be "bubbly, sexy, interesting, and interested" (K. Hall, 1995, pp. 190–91).

In interviews with a small but diverse group of phone sex workers, Kira Hall (1995) found that they were very aware of what kind of women's language is marketable. They consciously created "sexy talk" by using "feminine" or "flowery" words, inviting and supportive comments, and a dynamic intonation pattern (breathy, excited, varied in pitch, "lilting"). These are features often characterized as "women's language," submissive and powerless (Lakoff, 1975). However, the women on the fantasy lines did not feel powerless; they generally felt quite superior to their male callers, whom they characterized as unintelligent and socially inept. (When a caller insisted on a domination scenario in which the woman was allowed to respond only briefly and meekly, one woman said she used the call to get a lot of dishes done on the job.)

This study illustrates the social constructionist position that meaning depends on context. Within the context of the fantasy lines, women manipulate "women's language" in a way that brings them some power; they can use their creativity to generate characters and scripts, they can earn a great deal of money, and they can play at sex anonymously with no fear of violence or social sanction. To the male callers, the fantasy woman constructed entirely through language was presumably satisfying.

The construction of the feminine woman on the fantasy lines is an unusual case because it is overt, a form of game playing. Usually, femininity is constructed outside of conscious awareness, as a "natural" part of social interaction.

Consider the talk of adolescent girls. Girls do many different things in talk. One of their most important accomplishments is to create and sustain friendships by sharing experiences and feelings in supportive ways. Another discursive accomplishment is "doing femininity"; that is, they enact and perform what it is to be a real girl in their particular community and culture. For example, Jennifer Coates (1996) recorded a conversation among four 16-year-old British girls who were talking about one of their group as she tried on another girl's makeup. In complimenting her ("Doesn't she look really nice?" "She *does* look nice." "You should wear make-up more often."), they are being supportive friends. At the same time, however, they are co-constructing a social reality where looking good is very important and working on one's appearance is expected.

Discursive research on gender and language also looks for sources of resistance. In one study of Latina girls in a residential therapeutic institution, interaction in group therapy sessions was analyzed (Houghton, 1995). Much of the talk in these sessions is about female identity, relationships, contraception, and sexuality. Clients do most of the talking, but the therapist actively controls the talk. Therapists might interrupt clients and challenge their way of speaking, but clients cannot do the same. In one instance, a client said during a discussion of teen pregnancy, "You know how it is when you just want to have a baby, just something that is yours and belongs to you." The therapist interrupted and directed her to use "I" instead of "you." From the therapist's perspective, this would encourage the client to "own" the views she expressed. However, the client's use of "you" expressed a commonality of experience with the other girls in the group, a kind of sisterhood of shared meanings. The therapist's act of controlling language by prescribing the "correct" way to talk about feelings allowed her, as a member of a more powerful social group, to privilege one (culturally legitimated) system of meanings and social reality over another; the girl's meaning is positioned as less valid. The structures of dominance involve not only the power to put girls in institutions "for their own good," but to control the form, content, and meaning of their talk.

Nevertheless, the girls in this study were resistant to control. A common form of linguistic resistance was to mimic the therapist's professional language in ways that could not easily be challenged. For example, after one girl told a tearful story in group therapy, another might say, "How does that make you feel?" In this case, the therapist cannot easily challenge the questioner because he or she cannot tell whether the girl is really concerned or is just reminding the other girls of the therapist's insincere and formulaic questions.

Other research on the talk of young women shows discursive practices that construct femininity in unexpected ways. A study of the conversation of several overlapping groups of Australian university students, some heterosexual and some lesbian, showed that their talk was often subversive (Coates & Jordan, 1997). These women thought of themselves as feminists and antipatriarchal women, and their friendships crossed gay/straight boundaries. Their conversation showed that their social construction of themselves as feminists subverted the larger societal discourse about gender and sexuality. For example, here are a few of the comments made by a group of three friends when they hear that the mother of a friend of theirs is planning to marry a man she has been having an affair with for only a month:

Oh my god what?

Oh my god that is sick.

That is awful.

That is terrible.

That is horrible.

That is foul.

That is really foul.

I just thought "oh god how shit."

It's awful horrible horrible.

Oh yuk that's gross.

They go on to talk about marriage in negative terms ("the M-word") and question why any woman in her right mind would do such a thing:

> I thought at least she could have come to her senses after a few weeks.

> Fling, affair, relationship, these things I can deal with, marriage I can't.

Their talk is more than just a comment on one particular situation; what it accomplishes is "an overturning of the hegemonic discourse that represents marriage as the be-all-and-end-all of women's lives" (Coates & Jordan, 1997, p. 217–218).

Women's informal use of humor in conversation is often a site of resistance (M. Crawford, 1995). Humor is an exceptionally flexible conversational strategy. With it, people can introduce taboo topics, silence others, create group solidarity, express hostility, educate, save face, ingratiate, and express caring for others. The power and flexibility of conversational humor is related to its indirectness (Mulkay, 1988). It allows the unspeakable to enter the discourse.

Mercilee Jenkins (1985) studied women's humor through participant observation. In Jenkins's study of a group of mothers of young children who met weekly at a neighborhood church, she found examples of humor that gently mocked unrealistic expectations of mothers (One mother to another: "I don't know about you, but my children are perfect."). She also noted a collaborative storytelling style. Instead of a single speaker holding the floor and leading up to the climax or punch line of a story in linear fashion, speakers told stories of their own experiences by first presenting the main point and then recounting the tale with the encouragement and participation of the other group members. Susan Kalcik (1975) observed a similar dynamic in women's rap groups, in which the "kernel" of a story would be told first so that hearers could participate in the telling, knowing the direction and point of the story all along in collaboration with the teller. Although the collaborative style of storytelling is not unique to women, it may serve their interests better than more individualistic styles when they are in all-women groups.

Sexuality is a favorite source of humor in situations where direct talk about it is not socially acceptable (M. Crawford, 1995, 2000a). Folklorist Rayna Green (1977) has described the sexual humor of U.S. Southern women based on her own (White, lower-middle-class) social network. Most of the humor she describes occurred at family gatherings at which men congregate outdoors while women and children are in the kitchen. Many of the most outspoken of the bawdy humorists were old women. Like many traditional cultures, the U.S. South allows increasing license to old women, and Green notes that the women she observed took full advantage in presenting themselves as wicked: "Once, when my grandmother stepped out of the bathtub, and my sister commented that the hair on her 'privates' was getting rather sparse, Granny retorted that 'grass don't grow on a racetrack'" (p. 31).

Among these women, frequent sources of humor were men's boasts, failures, or sexual inadequacies. Also, preachers were the butt of many jokes, in reaction to the power of evangelical Christian traditions. However, there was a marked absence of racism and hostility in humor about sexuality. Instead, these women engaged in creative wordplay, inventing comic names for genitals that mocked the euphemisms expected of them. Thus, children were told, "Wash up as far as possible, down as far as possible, and then wash possible." Women's pubic areas were affectionately called "Chore Girl" (after a bristly scrubbing pad) or "wooly booger"; male genitals were "tallywhackers."

The women's humor had several functions. First, the storyteller gained respect and admiration as an inventive and entertaining user of language. Second, it was educational. Green (1977) suggests that the sexual information children gleaned from stories of lustful young married couples, cynical prostitutes, rowdy preachers, impotent drunks, and wicked old ladies was at least as accurate as a parental "sex ed" lecture, and much more fun. Finally, women's bawdy humor was subversive of the cultural rules controlling women's sexuality: "The very telling defies the rules. . . . Women are not supposed to know or repeat such stuff. But they do and when they do, they speak ill of all that is sacred—men, the church, marriage, home, family, parents" (p. 33).

Green (1977) speculates that in their humor, the women vent their anger at men, offer alternative modes of understanding to their female hearers, and, by including the ever-present children in the circle of listeners, perform "tiny act(s) of revenge" on the men who have power over their lives.

As women began to question received wisdom about gender roles and relations in the consciousness-raising groups and political organizations of the 1970s, they evolved a distinctive humor that is expressed in public and private settings and is a powerful tool of political activism (M. Crawford, 1995). Much of this humor subverts the premise that women are less competent than men and cannot wield power. A feminist aphorism on T-shirts and lapel buttons in the 1970s stated, "To be seen as equal, a woman has to be twice as good as a man. Fortunately, that isn't difficult." It also mocks the idea that women need men to fulfill their sexual and emotional needs and cannot survive without them. Another 1970s feminist aphorism is " A woman without a man is like a fish without a bicycle." A more recent example of feminist humor that pokes fun at women's presumed obsession with men is Nicole Hollander's 2-panel cartoon seen on T-shirts and calendars. The first panel, titled "What men hope women are saying when they go to the washroom together," depicts two women bragging about the skill of their lovers. The second, "What they're really saying," shows the women's actual conversation: "Do you think cake is better than sex?" "What kind of cake?" (Hollander, 1994).

In an interview, Hollander noted, "Men are frightened by women's humor because they think that when women are alone they're making fun of men. This is perfectly true, but they think we're making fun of their equipment when in fact there are so many more interesting things to make fun of—such as their value systems" (quoted in Barreca, 1991, p. 198).

A great deal of feminist humor can be thought of as the humor of a culturally subordinated group in that it acknowledges men's ability to define reality in ways that meet their needs. Yet, in making that acknowledgment public, it subverts men's reality by exposing its social construction. As Florynce Kennedy said, "If men could get pregnant, abortion would be a sacrament." Gloria Steinem's essay "If Men Could Menstruate" (1978) describes how "menstruation would become an enviable, boast-worthy, masculine event" and "sanitary supplies would be federally funded and free." Women would, of course, suffer from acute cases of "menses envy" (p. 110).

How do feminists differentiate themselves as feminists in and through their humor? Cindy White (1988) asked self-identified feminists to keep diaries of feminist humor in mundane settings over an eight-week period. From an analysis of three diaries, White concluded that the values expressed were generalized positive evaluation of women, celebration of women's experiences, affirmation of women's strengths and capabilities, and autonomy and self-definition for women. The rarity of antimale humor suggested to White that these diary writers also valued men and that they made a distinction between men as individuals and patriarchal culture.

The value of autonomy and self-definition for feminists is suggested by the following diary entry, quoting a woman who presented a paper on lesbian sexuality at a conference: "Politically correct sex lasts at least three hours, since everyone knows we're process-oriented and not goal-oriented. If we do have orgasms, those orgasms must be simultaneous. And we must lie side by side. Now I know that some people think that orgasms are patriarchal. But I've given up many things for feminism, and this isn't going to be one of them" (p. 83). Just as feminist humor subverts the inflexible gender roles of the dominant culture, it mocks inflexibility in feminism (C. White, 1988). In the orgasm example, a feminist jokes about how the notion of political correctness can be coercive for women, and asserts her own autonomy, placing limits on the influence she will allow to feminist doctrine in her own life.

The most important role for humor in the creation of a feminist culture may be the articulation of common meanings (C. White, 1988). By creating and affirming their own meanings, feminists create a sense of community. When common meanings express ingroup/outgroup relationships, they help set the boundaries for feminist culture. These factors allow women to self-identify as feminists and re-create (enact) their feminism in everyday interaction.

GUY TALK: DISCOURSES OF MASCULINITY

Feminist researchers have tended to pay more attention to women's talk than to men's for several reasons. It is easier for female researchers to get access to the talk of all-female groups and impossible for them to participate in and observe all-male groups. Moreover, feminist research on men may be criticized as treating men as (still) more important than women (Cameron, 1998).

Nevertheless, research on men's talk is increasing, based on the understanding that masculinity does not exist in isolation from femininity. Rather, their meanings depend on each other. Men's behavior is just as "gendered" as women's.

In one recent study using interview data from a diverse sample of British men, Margaret Wetherell and Nigel Edley (1999) investigated how men create and take on the social identity of "being a man" in their talk. Using critical discourse analysis, the researchers identified three patterns that men used to describe their masculinity and position themselves socially as men. In the first pattern, dubbed "heroic positions," men aligned themselves with standard masculine ideals: being in charge at work or in competitive athletics, outdoing other men, and being courageous, physically tough, and able to stay "cool." In the second pattern, "ordinary positions," men described themselves as just normal, average guys, not macho men. In the third pattern, "rebellious positions," they described themselves as flouting social expectations of masculinity. These "gender rebels" reported that they could and did cry, cook, knit, wear jewelry and bright colors, and so on.

Constructing masculinity as ordinariness or rebellion may be forms of resistance against the heroic ideal. However, Wetherell and Edley (1999) argue, these constructions may still function to reproduce male power. Even when the men saw themselves as ordinary or rebellious, they explained and justified their difference from other men in terms of their personal strength, independence, and autonomy—all aspects of heroic masculinity.

Because masculinity is so largely defined as having power, many studies of men's talk have focused on how men position themselves with respect to less powerful groups. Michael Mulkay (1988) examined how women are represented in men's sexual humor, based on comic routines in British pub acts. Mulkay found that the themes of this humor objectified women, emphasized their sexual availability (all women always want sex even if they deny it), and silenced women's voices.

In a study of male U.S. college students' conversation while watching a basketball game on television, Deborah Cameron (1997) noted that in addition to sports talk, the young men talked about daily events—their classes, doing the food shopping—and their sexual exploits with women. (The male student who collected the data summarized their talk as "wine, women, and sports.") However, another important topic was gossip about other (despised) men, whom they called "gay." Rather than accurately reflecting sexual orientation, their characterizations of other men as "gay" seemed to be a way of displaying their own heterosexual masculinity. Like the men in Mulkay's (1988) study, who distinguished themselves from mere women by objectifying and sexualizing them, these men distinguished themselves from "unmasculine" men by denigrating them as "artsy fartsy fags" and "homos." Cameron notes that this kind of discursive strategy "is not only *about* masculinity, it is a sustained performance *of* masculinity" (p. 590).

FEMINISM AND LANGUAGE CHANGE

While some researchers have focused on conversation and discourse, others have focused on characteristics of language itself: the lexicon, grammatical structures, word usage, and so on. The term *linguistic sexism* refers to inequitable treatment of gender issues that is built into the language. When people choose a particular way of speaking, they are making choices that are not only practical but political. Feminists have worked to change sexist language on the grounds that through our choice of words, each of us either accepts and thereby helps perpetuate the status quo, or rejects linguistic sexism and helps to change it (West et al., 1997).

In the 1970s, a great deal of research analyzed sexism in language. Patterns of everyday language sometimes *omitted* women, for example, through the use of *he, his,* and *man* to refer to people in general. They sometimes *trivialized* women, for example, with the use of gender-marked terms such as "poetess." Some language *denigrated* women: There were far more negative sexual terms for women than for men, and words referring to women tended to acquire negative meanings over time (M. Schulz, 1975). For example, "master" connotes expert status for a male, but the corresponding female noun, "mistress," has acquired less positive, more sexual meanings. Males were taken as the norm, with terms such as "working woman" and "woman doctor" marking the exceptions to the rule. And women were often described primarily in terms of their relationships to men (Stannard, 1977). Even ordinary courtesy titles advertised women's marital status (Miss or Mrs. were the only alternatives), whereas men, married or single, were simply "Mr." It seemed that everywhere one looked, the English language encoded androcentrism and sexism in its structure, content, and usage: It portrayed women as different, less important, and unequal to men (Pauwels, 1998; Spender, 1980; West et al., 1997).

Feminists from many cultures and societies began to take action to change linguistic sexism through *feminist language reform* (Pauwels, 1998). They began to reshape language by critically analyzing the linguistic representation of women and men and by proposing specific changes. Here, we look at some "success stories": language reforms that were initiated and widely adopted through feminists' efforts. We also look at some examples of attempted language reform that were less successful, and consider what factors influence the success or failure of language reforms.

Feminist language reform consists of eliminating the gender bias found in the structure, content, and usage of language and providing linguistic alternatives such as novel expressions, phrases, grammatical forms, and word coinage. It can also involve reclaiming formerly negative words about women. Therefore, it involves both modifying old language and creating new language. We will look at examples of both kinds of changes.

Linguistic sexism has been documented in a great variety of texts, including educational and reference materials (children's readers, textbooks, dictionaries), the mass media, and the discourses of law, medicine, and religion (F.W. Frank, 1989; Pauwels, 1998). In the 1970s and early 1980s, most of the research was on the English language, and very little attention was paid to linking race or ethnicity with linguistic bias (Henley, 1995). Since then, there have been studies of many other European languages as well as Japanese, Chinese, Thai, and some African languages (Pauwels, 1998). Attempts to reduce or eliminate linguistic sexism have been correspondingly broad; a thorough review is beyond the scope of this chapter. Here, I focus on English and on two areas of general interest: the critique of allegedly generic masculine language and the creation of guidelines for nonsexist language use. I then turn to feminists' attempts to create new language to encode feminist meanings and values.

HE/MAN LANGUAGE: DOES "MAN" INCLUDE WOMEN?

In many languages, the word for man is used to refer to humans in general: in Italian, *uomo*; in French, *homme*; in Spanish, *hombre* (Pauwels, 1998). In English, too, traditional usage reflected this "generic" use of man, in such phrases as "the rights of man" and such book titles as *The History of Man*. Moreover, English lacks a gender-neutral singular pronoun, so that speakers must always choose "he" or "she." In practice, forms of *he* were used to refer to both females and males, as in the sentence "Each student must bring his notes to class."

A great deal of research has shown that these "generic" masculine terms are not really generic at all (Henley, 1989). When people read "man" in educational materials such as textbooks (e.g., a chapter titled "Industrial Man"; J. Schneider & Hacker, 1973) or job advertisements (e.g., "repairman"), they think not of people in general but of men. And this perception affects their behavior. Sex bias in job advertisements affected both women's and men's willingness to apply for gender-incongruent jobs (S.L. Bem & Bem, 1973). And when college students read an essay titled "The Psychologist and His Work," which referred to the psychologist throughout as "he," the women students remembered the facts in the essay less well than when they read the same essay in a gender-inclusive ("he or she") version (M. Crawford & English, 1984). The results of these and many other studies show that the "generic" masculine does not function generically (Henley, 1989).

Feminists used the evidence from studies like these to argue for language reform. They advocated replacing *man* and words that included it as part of a compound (policeman, chairman) with gender-inclusive alternatives (humans, people, police officer, chairperson, chair). This suggestion provoked a great deal of ridicule, with terms like "huperson" (for human) and "personhole cover" being a favorite source of humor. Feminists also suggested alternatives to the pseudo-generic *he* and *his*, including using "they" and "their" (Each student should bring their notes), "he or she" (Each student should bring his or her notes), alternating "he" and "she," or using the generic "she." Some even suggested adopting an entirely new pronoun, such as "tey." Although these suggestions were often resisted, even ridiculed, they drew attention to issues of language reform. Moreover, articulating how the grammar and usage of English excluded women led the way to important efforts to make changes in public discourse, in the form of guidelines for nonsexist language.

NONSEXIST LANGUAGE GUIDELINES

Women's groups within professional organizations, various feminist collectives, and task force groups in the early 1970s began to influence their organizations to eliminate gender-biased language from professional and educational materials—indeed, from all kinds of written materials in the public arena. Bolstered by research showing that the use of "generic" masculine language actually encoded masculinist bias, these groups of women succeeded in implementing guidelines to nonsexist language use. By the mid-1970s, major educational publishers (McGraw-Hill, Scott, Foresman and Company, Macmillan, and Random House) and professional organizations (American Psychological Association, National Council of Teachers of English, International Association of Business Communication) had all adopted guidelines for nonsexist language in their publications (Pauwels, 1998). The Modern Language Association, which is one of the largest and most influential professional organizations of scholars and teachers of language and literature, took much longer; its "Guidelines for Nonsexist Usage" did not appear until 1989 (F.W. Frank & Treichler, 1989).

Another impetus for language change came from government agencies that moved to eliminate gender bias in occupational titles to comply with antidiscrimination laws. For example, the U.S. Department of Labor did so in 1975. Similar changes were made in Germany (1986), Italy (1986), France (1984–1986), French-speaking Canada (1979), and Spain (1988) by governmental commissions or agencies (Pauwels, 1998).

Typically, guidelines for nonsexist language aim to sensitize their users to the issue of sexism in language and to offer alternatives to sexist usage. Anne Pauwels (1998) analyzed the contents of published guidelines in English, German, French, Italian, Dutch, and Spanish. She found a great deal of similarity in the areas of language they covered, the examples of sexist language they used, and the alternative forms they suggested. They typically discussed the pseudo-generic *man*, for example, and suggested similar alternatives to it. They also suggested changes in occupational titles and pseudo-generic pronouns, and they showed how to avoid linguistic asymmetry, where women are referred to in nonparallel or derivative ways (salesman and salesgirl, men and ladies, man and wife, the inhabitants and their women).

Mainly, these guidelines dealt with changing individual words or isolated forms of grammar. They did not address more subtle aspects of linguistic sexism, such as the use of passive voice to hide male agency (The woman was raped), or more blatant ones such as sexualized and negative terms for women. In line with their goal of changing public practice, they presented their proposed changes as more sensible, clear, and accurate usages. And they were careful not to accuse anyone of deliberate sexism. Rather, "the use of sexist language is usually portrayed as the result of lack of awareness or knowledge or subconscious habit rather than as a deliberate language practice. Changes are seldom presented in a compulsory manner: usually a range of alternatives to a sexist expression are listed and the selection of the preferred alternative is left to the reader" (Pauwels, 1998, p. 167).

Have nonsexist language guidelines succeeded in changing public discourse? In some cases, change is very evident. Occupational titles, used in job descriptions and employment notices, have become virtually gender-neutral, with terms such as "barman," "handyman," "cleaning lady," "stewardess," and "waitress" replaced by ones that do not mark sex. In other cases, guidelines appear to have destabilized traditional usage and led to more variability in the language used to talk about women and men. Many of the "ridiculous" suggestions of feminists have now become part of everyday usage. Today, "letter carrier" has replaced "mailman," "flight attendant" has superseded "steward/stewardess," "chairpersons" is more common than "chairmen," and politicians, educators, and other public speakers routinely use "he or she." Studies of he/man usage show a dramatic drop in the use of pseudo-generic masculine terms over time in American newspapers and magazines (R. Cooper, 1984), New Zealand news publications (Meyerhoff, 1984, cited in Pauwels, 1998), and university documents in the United States (Markowitz, 1984), and Canada (Ehrlich & King, 1992). Although no single alternative form predominates, various alternatives to sexist language do seem to be spreading (Pauwels, 1998).

NEW TERMS FOR NEW TIMES: FEMINIST ADDITIONS TO THE LEXICON

Feminists brought many new terms to the language: "sexism," "male chauvinism," "date rape," and "herstory" are just a few examples. Some coinages, such as herstory, were aimed at raising awareness of hidden sexism. Others were acts of naming the unspeakable—acts that were powerful political statements. The writer Gloria Steinem (1983) perhaps best expressed the importance of the power of naming and the influence of feminist activism on language change: "We have terms like 'sexual harassment' and 'battered women.' A few years ago, they were just called 'life'" (p. 149).

Language change as a result of feminist activism is evident in many domains. One example is the widespread use of "Ms." as a parallel title to "Mr." When Ms. was first proposed, it was considered dangerously radical, and it quickly became a target of ridicule and outrage. The feminists who proposed it thought of the idea as eminently sensible: There should be a term of address for women that paralleled Mr., one that did not mark marital status. However, they were accused of being "women's lib redhots" who were bent on "warping" and "mutilating" the English language with "ugly neologisms" (M. Crawford et al., 1998).

Given the controversy over Ms., researchers became interested in how the term itself and women who used it were perceived. Their studies showed that women who chose to use Ms. were seen as more assertive, competent, and dynamic, but less warm and likable, than those who chose the more traditional titles (K.L. Dion, 1987). The title Ms. evoked connotations of masculinity; women who used it were seen as much more like men than like other women. Today, however, the use of Ms. has become the norm. The stereotype connected to it has changed, too; its association with a masculine stereotype has decreased, and Ms. now evokes the same connotations as the other women's titles, probably because it is no longer seen as a radical feminist choice (M. Crawford et al., 1998).

A once radical concept has become common usage; a new gender-related word has become part of the language. The practical implications of this change are clear: Women can now choose whether or not to reveal their marital status with a term of address, an option that did not exist two decades ago and that came about through feminist language activism.

Lesbian, gay, bisexual, and transgender activists have also added many new terms to the language. "Gay" and "straight," as alternatives to the psychiatric-label connotations of "homosexual" and "heterosexual," emerged earliest. "Coming out" (originally, "coming out of the closet," meaning to acknowledge one's lesbian or gay sexuality) and "outing" (announcing in public that someone else is gay) were named. Most recently, the neologisms LGB and LGBT are increasingly used in spoken and written language as inclusive terms for nonstraight sexual orientations. And the growing visibility of bisexual people has led to the use of the shortened "bi." Like the coinage of the word sexism a generation earlier, social activism led to the coinage of "heterosexism," "homophobia," and "biphobia." Another interesting new word is "gaydar" (from the words gay and radar, referring to an individual's ability to recognize another person as LGBT in social interaction) (M.L. Murphy, 1997; Zwicky, 1997). Of course, all language change grounded in social movements has political significance. For example, the term "sexual orientation" has replaced "sexual preference," which was objectionable to many LGBT activists because it implied that one could freely choose to be gay or straight, a view that coincided with the religious right's position.

In addition to coining new words and phrases, gay activists, feminists, and people of color have demanded the right to rename themselves and their experiences. For all these groups, renaming and reclaiming words has been a vehicle for empowerment (Van Den Bergh, 1987). Just as African Americans rejected the words "colored people" and "Negroes" and reclaimed "Black" as a symbol of identity in the Black Pride Movement, women rejected the use of "girl" to describe an adult woman. And feminists reclaimed many words that had been used to denigrate women. A crone, according to Mary Daly (1978), is a wise and independent old woman; witches, hags, and spinsters are women to be admired. Daly's efforts at linguistic creativity (always with a purpose of exposing patriarchal thought and naming radical feminist alternatives) are collected in her *Wickedary,* a feminist dictionary (1987). Cheris Kramarae and Paula Treichler (1985) collected entries from a large and diverse group of women to compile another interesting feminist dictionary.

Examples of reclaiming that originated in lesbian activism include taking up epithets such as "queer" and "butch" and using them positively. "Dyke," formerly an insulting term for lesbian, has been adopted with pride by many women and is the title of a popular comic strip by Alison Bechtel, *Dykes to Watch Out For.*

CONTESTED MEANINGS: THE STRUGGLE FOR CONTROL

How influential are feminist-inspired changes in language? Many of the more successful attempts to change language were at the level of words and phrases: changing "housewife" to "homemaker," "girls" to "women," "Miss" to "Ms.," and "he" to "he or she." However, even these small changes were not always as successful as they seemed. For example, the much resisted move to replace the word "chairman" with the gender-neutral "chairperson" seems to have resulted in a new gender-specific usage. Some recent studies of written documents (reviewed in Pauwels, 1998) show that men are more often referred to as chairs or chairmen, and women more often as chairpersons. Of course, change is an ongoing process, and perhaps the usage of chair and chairperson will continue to evolve.

As discursive and social constructionist approaches to gender and language became more prominent, changes in word usage, even when they succeeded, began to seem less important because this kind of change was based on the assumption that meaning and usage are normally fixed and static. From a social constructionist perspective, however, they are continually re-created in interaction. Therefore, ongoing resistance to feminist attempts to control meaning can be expected. And attempts to eliminate sexist language will have limited effects as long as the society remains sexist (Cameron, 1998).

According to a social constructionist perspective, making meaning in discourse is more complex than just choosing nonsexist words. A person who wants to express sexist meanings can easily do it in nonsexist language. Imagine an attorney who, cross-examining a female witness, repeatedly and somewhat sarcastically refers to her as *Ms.* Smith. The attorney may succeed in damaging her credibility by connecting her with a negative stereotype of women who use Ms. If the stereotype changes—if Ms. no longer connotes an aggressive, masculinized woman—the attorney's strategy would not be effective. (As discussed earlier, the Ms. stereotype does seem to have changed in recent years.) But as long as sexism is embedded in societal structures (e.g., stereotyping in the mass media) and individual cognitive schemas (e.g., individual attitudes and beliefs about sex differences), the attorney easily could find other linguistic ways to denigrate a female witness. From a social constructionist perspective, it is unsurprising that not all feminist attempts to change language have worked and that there has been a backlash of new antifeminist and sexist usage. Consider, for example, the terms "feminazi" and "politically correct."

Although people may use Ms., he or she, and chairperson, some of the most fundamental concepts of feminism have been eroded in the struggle to control meaning. Two examples are the meaning and use of the words "feminist" and "feminism," and the naming of violence against girls and women.

At each historical period when women actively pursue equality, feminists and feminism are represented negatively in public discourse. First-wave feminists were caricatured as ugly, angry man-tamers who wanted nothing to do with natural womanly functions such as mothering (M. Crawford & Unger, 2000). Second-wave feminists, too, were portrayed in the 1970s as "shrill, overly aggressive, man-hating, ball-busting, selfish, hairy, extremist, deliberately unattractive women with absolutely no sense of humor" (S.J. Douglas, 1994, p. 7). As second-wave feminism made gains for women, the media immediately declared that it was dead (Faludi, 1991).

As a result of this antifeminist public discourse, being labeled feminist is a form of stigma. In a recent study, women made less positive statements about the "feminist" movement than about the "women's" movement, demonstrating that simply using the "f-word" (feminist) induces more negative thinking about a group (Buschman & Lenart, 1996). Although the majority of U.S.

women endorse the goals of the women's movement, they are reluctant to identify themselves as feminists. In one recent study, 63% of women supported feminist goals but did not label themselves feminists (R. Williams & Wittig, 1997).

As discussed earlier, one of the most important contributions of feminist language reform has been to spotlight abuses of girls and women through naming. Such terms as "male chauvinism," "sexism," "battered woman," "sexual harassment," and "date rape" entered the language because of feminist activism and research. However, precisely because these terms draw attention to abuses of power, and thereby threaten those with more social influence, they have been subject to discursive regulation—thus, they have changed in meaning, becoming less threatening and more vague.

Masculinity is highly agentic: Traits stereotypically linked to men and masculinity include aggressive, independent, dominant, active, and athletic. However, there is one place where language functions to hide male agency: when the topic is violence against girls and women. When feminists first drew attention to physical, sexual, and emotional abuse of women by their partners, they used the direct, confrontive terms "wife beating," "woman battering," and "marital rape." Over time, professional journal articles and the popular press alike switched to "gender-neutral" terms such as "domestic violence" and "spouse abuse." However, in this case, the gender-neutral term is not accurate and not an improvement. It works to obscure the fact that the great majority of abuse in intimate relationships is perpetrated by men against women (J.W. White, Bondurant, & Donat, 2000). Before feminist activism focused on violence against women, male agency was hidden simply by not naming these crimes; now it is hidden by the linguistic device of presenting them as gender-neutral crimes.

Discursive research can be very useful in uncovering the processes by which male agency, and the harm done by violence against women, are continually rendered invisible. For example, consider the terms "date rape" and "acquaintance rape," coined by feminists to draw attention to evidence that most sexual assaults are not committed by the prototypical strange-man-jumping-out-of-the-bushes-at-night, but by acquaintances and dating partners. Psychological research on trauma indicates that acquaintance rape has even more serious psychological consequences than stranger rape, because it involves not only physical violation but a violation of trust (J.W. White et al., 2000). In a discourse analysis of a radio talk show in which experts discussed the causes of rape on college campuses, speakers did use the feminist term "date rape." However, they subtly made distinctions between date rape and "real rape," contrasting the two and discursively rendering date rape less serious than stranger rape (M. Crawford, 1995). Thus, a term coined to draw attention to intimate violence and its consequences was actively corrupted and trivialized.

The term "sexual harassment" has also been corrupted and trivialized. Originated by feminists to describe an experience of male violence common to most women and to facilitate taking action against it, the term is an excellent example of "women's renaming of the world" (C. Kitzinger & Thomas, 1995). In one sense, this act of naming is a feminist success story. Behavior that went unnoticed or uncriticized because it had no name has now been described, classified, pronounced illegal, widely surveyed for prevalence, and regulated by codes of practice and grievance procedures. A form of violence named by feminists has been officially recognized and prohibited.

However, official codes do not capture how sexual harassment is understood and socially constructed in everyday interaction. Celia Kitzinger and Allison Thomas (1995), in a discursive study, interviewed women and men about their understanding of the term, asking for examples from their own experience and whether their understanding of specific incidents had changed over time. They found that people used several discursive strategies to erase and obscure sexual harassment, with somewhat different strategies being preferred by women and men. Women were more likely to deny having been harassed because they refused to think of themselves as victims. Men were more likely to maintain that (1) it's not harassment because it's a normal part of male-female interaction, (2) it's not harassment if it's not motivated by a desire to have sex, and (3) it's not harassment because it's really about asserting status and power. C. Kitzinger and Thomas state, "These strategies together work a form of magic—and with the sleight of hand of a vaudeville conjurer, sexual harassment simply disappears by definitional fiat" (p. 46).

CONCLUSIONS

Feminist research on gender and language has developed and changed since its resurgence in the early 1970s. There is less emphasis on cataloguing differences in the speech of women and men and more interest in analyzing what people accomplish with talk. As a result of this shift in emphasis, more diverse groups of speakers are being studied and more is understood about how people create and maintain social realities through "doing gender" in everyday talk.

Moreover, feminists have coined new words and adopted new usages of old words to express women's perspectives and create a more gender-balanced language. They have worked for changes in language guidelines among publishers and professional associations, so that nonsexist language is now a hallmark of good professional writing. These changes have taken place in a context of ongoing resistance to women's controlling language. Despite resistance, feminist efforts to change language have gone forward in the realization that language is more than just talk. In using language, we create our social reality. By changing language, we can contribute to changing that reality.

CHAPTER 16

Gender and Social Interaction

MARIANNE LaFRANCE

For anyone who has ears to hear and eyes to see, it seems patently obvious that women and men have different social interactional styles. We are told that men and women in conversation "just don't understand" each other (Tannen, 1990). We hear that women and men come from different planets (Gray, 1992), that they inhabit different cultures (Maltz & Borker, 1982). According to numerous popular books, the sexes are "worlds apart"; they encounter "barriers" when they attempt to communicate; their talk is marked by a "communications gap"; there is an acute need for "healing dialogues." That the sexes have different styles of interacting has seemed so incontrovertible that it has appeared that the only thing to be established was *why* and not *whether.*

The present chapter challenges the core notion that there are basic and stable sex differences in social interaction. To be sure, there are some gender-related aspects of social interaction. The goal here is to expand the questions that need to be asked about the relationship between gender and social interaction. Instead of probing the various ways that women and men differ in how they interact, we will look more closely into context: who else is present; what social identities they have; in what settings such interactions are taking place; and especially what functions the interaction is serving. In short, I view gender as a highly contextualized and multifunctional set of phenomena and processes. Social interaction is not only a context for understanding gender but is itself always embedded in particular social contexts in which gender may or may not be particularly salient (Deaux & Major, 1987).

Of late, there has been considerable debate about the best way to approach the study of gender and social interaction. For much of the 20th century, three perspectives have held sway: the *deficit model,* the *cultural difference model,* and the *dominance model.* The predominant view early on, and still strong in some quarters, is a deficit view that holds that the communication style of one sex, typically women, is problematic. Jesperson (1922) was one of the first linguists to single out the language of women as a special case. He argued that women are quicker to learn, hear, and answer than men—on the face of it, positive qualities. However, Jesperson attributed men's slower time in answering to their greater desire to be accurate and clear. He also believed that women were more indirect and linguistically conservative than men, again qualities that suffered by comparison to men's purported greater effectiveness and inventiveness with language. A half century later, Lakoff (1975) noted that it was women who showed greater hesitancy and indecision, such as ending sentences with a rising pitch and adding questions after statements. Lakoff argued that such features convey uncertainty, although she placed the locus for these linguistic deficiencies on social forces designed to keep women in a separate and unequal place.

In response to the idea that women's interaction styles were deficient in one way or another, others countered that women's interactional styles were not deficient relative to men's, they were merely different. They acknowledged that sex-related differences existed but noted that one sex's interactional mode was not inherently better than the other's. In several books, Tannen (1990, 1993, 1994) went to considerable lengths to argue that differences in male/female conversational style are the result of men and women being socialized into different cultures. For example, Tannen posed that women are more concerned with the "rapport" aspects of social engagement, whereas men are more concerned with the "report" aspects, leading each sex to use different styles. Thus, women use more conversational strategies aimed at eliciting disclosure and reducing conflict and enhancing solidarity. Men, on the other hand, are ostensibly more concerned with clarity, comprehensibility, and economy.

According to Tannen (1990), these different strategies stem from the fact that men inhabit a hierarchical social order in which conversation serves as a negotiating device for preserving independence and avoiding failure. Women, Tannen argues, communicate for the central purpose of building connections through which they acquire and pass along confirmation and support. Although there may be hierarchies in women's communities, for Tannen, these collectives are designed preeminently to sustain intimacy and ward off social isolation (pp. 24–25). These gender distinctions thus involve deep "meaning-of-life" issues about personal goals and moral principles as well as beliefs about the appropriateness of various interactional processes.

Tannen (1990) has hesitated to draw conclusions about the origins of such gender distinctions. She suggests environmental origins but does not argue for them in any detail, noting only that differences in conversational styles are observed in very young children. Persons familiar with evolutionary accounts of human behavior (Buss, 1995b) will no doubt find it hard to resist a partial explication of Tannen's data in neo-Darwinian terms. For instance, competition among males to establish hierarchical position is common in other species and has seemingly been part of the human experience from its beginnings (J.Q. Wilson, 1993). But it is obvious to those familiar with the nature/nurture debate that neither side alone can make sense of complicated human interactional behavior.

This difference framework, whether there from the beginning (essentialist) or acquired through socialization (cultural), has been found wanting by those who argue that it fails to recognize gender inequalities at the societal level (Henley & Kramarae, 1991). The difference perspective assumes that men and women are oriented toward different aspects of human relationships. Hence, differences in how they communicate arise from women and men adopting different agendas and/or having learned different ways of interacting. But once discrepancies in the power men and women hold in society is acknowledged, as it is by those who argue for a dominance model, then what appear to be sex differences in interactional style are really differences in dominance. According to a dominance model, people who show more concern with the rapport aspects of interaction do so because they have less power. Conversely, those who are focused on control and things being settled are likely to have more power.

The deficit, the difference, and the dominance models are now being challenged by those who view gender in performance terms. From a performance perspective, gender is a dynamic acting-out or ongoing construction of perceivable behaviors, with self and others as the audience. Such performances are not set early (as a difference perspective would argue) or in response to established structural arrangements (as a dominance perspective would argue). Rather, people "do gender" in social relationships rather than having a gender or occupying static roles (West & Zimmerman, 1987).

The performative perspective partly arose due to the rich set of tools that have been developed for analyzing the dynamics of ongoing social interaction. Also, a new domain has opened up that is ripe for study: the relationship of sexuality to social interaction and language use. Recent edited collections such as *Language and Masculinity* (S. Johnson & Meinhof, 1997), *Language and Desire* (Harvey & Shalom, 1997), *Queerly Phrased* (Livia & Hall, 1996), *Language and Gender* (Coates, 1998), *Rethinking Language* (Bergvall, Bing, & Freed, 1996), and *Gender Articulated* (K. Hall & Bucholtz, 1995) suggest a research field that is just beginning to be explored.

A core assumption of this chapter is that to understand gender and social interaction requires understanding how face-to-face communication reflects, creates, and sustains gender divisions in society and how gender performances affect face-to-face interactions. In what follows, I describe how two communicational elements, *tag questions* and *directives*, can be understood from different perspectives. More specifically, my aim is to show the advantages of viewing these and other interactional behaviors from a functional or performative perspective. A functional perspective considers how the behavior is used to accomplish some interactional goal or end. A performative perspective focuses on the communicator and inquires as to what interactional arrangement is being enacted.

FUNCTIONS OF INTERACTIONAL STYLE:
TAG QUESTIONS AND DIRECTIVES

Consider how one might understand the gendered nature of tag questions. Tag questions are characterized by attaching a query to a declaration, such as, "It's a nice day, isn't it?" In her ground-breaking book, *Language and Women's Place,* Robin Lakoff (1975) proposed that tag questions were one of several speech modes used more frequently by women than by men. Other speech modes seemingly distinctive to women were *rising intonation* where one might expect to find a falling intonation, *empty adjectives,* and *speaking in italics.* In what looks like a deficit and/or difference approach, Lakoff claimed that tag questions had the effect of making women sound more hesitant and unsure than men. There is indeed support for the idea that some linguistic forms result from being unsure. V.L. Smith and Clark (1993) found that when people did not know the answer to a question, often they answered with rising intonation, used hedges such as "I guess," and added "uh" or "um," self-talk, and other face-saving comments.

Following Lakoff's (1975) assertion, a score of researchers began to look more closely at whether women use more tag questions and other signs of communicational hesitancy. Like the pattern found elsewhere, initial findings of broad sex differences were succeeded by awareness that tag questions, like other features of social interaction, were neither monolithic nor singularly indicative of hesitancy.

So, instead of tag questions representing a single category, several subtypes emerged. Moreover, when all the subtypes were considered, it became clear that different forms of tag questions served different interactional purposes. For example, women were found to use tag questions to facilitate interaction, whereas men tended to use forms aimed at seeking verification (Cameron, McAlinden, & O'Leary, 1988). More generally, it became apparent that both men and women used tag questions more when they were called on to facilitate interaction (Hochschild, 1983). In contrast, people in competitive or achievement situations are more likely to place greater emphasis on directness, thus eschewing tag questions (S.M. Clancy & Dollinger, 1993).

Cameron and her colleagues (1988) also examined tag questions in a large corpus of conversations of White, middle-class, southern London speakers, called the Survey of English Usage project. They found that women and men in "powerful" roles use tag questions to generate talk from other participants. However, in "powerless" roles, both sexes use them to seek reassurance for their opinions. In sum, tag questions are used not exclusively by women, nor do they always express uncertainty. Rather, they serve a variety of functions depending on who is speaking, whether the format is a discussion, negotiation, or argument, and who has the power (Holmes, 1990).

Consider another linguistic style previously linked with gender, namely, the tendency to tell people what to do. M.H. Goodwin (1990) observed African American boys and girls at play and noted that boys made greater use of directives, that is "utterances designed to get someone else to do something" (p. 65). Girls, on the other hand, were found to use directives much less. Instead of saying "Gimme some," as boys were found to do, girls were more likely to say "Let's ask."

At first glance, these stylistic differences within the context of play seem understandable from a difference perspective: Boys are assertive; girls are accommodating. But M.H. Goodwin (1990) recorded not just which sex used directives but also where the directives occurred and what social functions they served. Adopting this approach showed that girls, too, use directives, but they were more inclined than boys to use directives in the context of infractions or arguments. They also use them more with boys than with other girls. Had she focused only on all-girl play, M.H. Goodwin might have concluded that girls show greater politeness because they used fewer directives. However, in looking at social context, it was possible to see that directives *function* to create a particular type of interaction. In other words, recognition that a particular feature changes depending on who else is present necessarily requires one to reconsider simple deficit or difference models.

GENDER AND MANAGING CONVERSATIONS

Everyday conversation provides a rich domain in which to examine whether, how, and when gender-related behavior shows itself. We start by acknowledging pervasive stereotypes about which sex talks and which listens; about which sex interrupts and which provides encouragement to continue; and about whose interactions are task-oriented and whose are socioemotional in character. This section reviews research exploring how gender impacts several of these aspects of conversation, specifically talk-time, task and socioemotional, interrupting, and listening contributions. Like the work described earlier, the initial search for basic sex differences in these modalities has been superseded by a more complex understanding of the multidimensional nature of each of these interactional processes.

GENDER AND TALK-TIME

Despite the stereotype that women talk more than men, evidence indicates the contrary to be true (Mulac, 1989). For example, males are more likely than females to speak up in classrooms and boardrooms (LaFrance, 1991). But this greater talk by males relative to females is moderated by dominance or status indicators. When explicit cues as to power are unavailable, men out-talk women in mixed-sex groups, but talk-times are equivalent in same-sex groups. When women become the majority in mixed-sex groups or when women are the experts in mixed-sex pairs, they talk more than their male partners (Bilous & Krauss, 1988; Leet-Pellegrini, 1980; Yamada, Tjosvold, & Draguns, 1983).

There is also research demonstrating that men use talk somewhat differently from women when they are primarily in the position of listening to someone else's talk (Fishman, 1983; Zimmerman & West, 1975). For example, in a study of conversations among New Zealanders, supportive questions and comments were used by both females and males as they listened to someone telling a story. However, one particular kind of "listening behavior" was shown more by men, namely, making distracting, challenging, undermining comments and asking disruptive questions (Holmes & Stubbe, 1997). J. Pilkington (1992) noted that men regarded such challenging insertions as normal, friendly behavior, in contrast to women, who tended to regard them as more intrusive.

GENDER AND CONTRIBUTING TO THE TASK OR THE SOCIOEMOTIONAL ASPECTS OF SOCIAL INTERACTION

Is there reason to believe that women and men contribute different things to conversation? A good deal of research has been aimed at exploring whether women are more oriented toward the socioemotional dimension of interaction and men are more focused on the task. For men, participation is thought to take the form of proffering ideas, challenging others' ideas, and directing the course of the conversation. Women's participation is thought to be of a different sort, namely, characterized by a greater receptivity to ideas, showing more concern, and stressing interpersonal relations.

Empirical validation came first from Strodtbeck and Mann (1956). They reported that women made fewer task contributions in mixed-sex jury groups. Those findings have been followed by others attesting to the idea that in mixed-sex groups, men make more task contributions and offer more task-related suggestions (Aries, 1976; Borgatta & Stimson 1963; J.A. Kelley, Wildman, & Urey, 1982; Lockheed & Hall, 1976; Mabry, 1985; Piliavin & Martin, 1978; W. Wood & Karten, 1986).

Why would this be the case? Status characteristics theory argues that sex operates as a "diffuse status characteristic" (J. Berger, Ridgeway, Rosenholtz, & Webster, 1986). When no identifying information is provided about a person's competence or ability, people tend to rely on external status as a clue to competence. A person's sex is an important status cue; specifically, the status assumption is that men and women are differentially valued. Observations of adult conversations show that men's verbal contributions get more attention (Ridgeway, 1981).

Thus, in a society where men have greater status, there will be higher expectations for men's competence and ability. If a task is not specifically gender-typed as being one that women are particularly good at, then the default performance expectations will be higher for men than for women. Groups give more floor time to people they believe to have more ability; the result is that men talk more, in general, and in particular make more task contributions than women. As the result of others holding lower expectations for females, women will engage in more supportive and reactive behaviors. Furthermore, if the task is additionally gender-typed as masculine, the differences in task behavior between men and women will be increased even more than for a "neutral" task. Only when a task is defined as women's turf would we expect higher task contributions by women in mixed-sex interactions.

The picture in same-sex groups is much less clear. Some studies (Lockheed & Hall, 1976; Yamada et al., 1983) report that men and women initiate equal amounts of task behavior in same-sex groups. Other studies (Carli, 1989; Mabry, 1985; Piliavin & Martin, 1978) report that even in all-female groups, women make fewer task contributions than do men in single-sex contexts.

These conflicting results in same-sex groups are puzzling. Status characteristics theory accounts well for why women in mixed-sex groups may make fewer task contributions: Men are implicitly ascribed more status and believed to be more competent; the effect is that men take up the mantle of leader. But why would women appear to make fewer task contributions in all-female groups? One explanation focuses on the scoring method used to determine levels of task contributions. Studies typically report the proportion of an individual's overall behavior that falls into a given interactional category. Consequently, the rate of any category of behavior reported for an individual is dependent on the behavior that person exhibits in other categories. So, if women engage in more socioemotional behavior than men, they would, by definition, exhibit lower rates of task behavior: Increases in socioemotional behavior would necessarily subtract from task-related behavior. Indeed, there is solid evidence to support the idea that women are more likely to engage in behaviors coded as socioemotional; namely, they smile and laugh in interaction more than men (LaFrance & Hecht, 1999). In sum, given the way data are typically aggregated in these studies, differences in socioemotional behaviors would produce gender differences in relative rates of task behaviors, with the result that women would *appear* to be making fewer task contributions.

This explanation has been advocated by a number of researchers (Carli, 1989; Shelly & Munore, 1999). The latter study put it to the test and found that in same-sex groups, women do not engage in less task behavior than men when socioemotional behavior is measured independently of task behavior. Thus, the more appropriate comparison involves looking at rates of socioemotional behavior for women and men separately from rates of task behavior for women and men. By looking at it this way, Aries (1996) concluded that polarized descriptions of women and men fall by the wayside, because "women, like men, direct the majority of their interaction to task behavior" (p. 38).

GENDER AND CONVERSATIONAL INTERRUPTIONS

In conversation, there are several ways to make suggestions: One can listen while another is talking; one can wait until the speaker has come to a full stop, then take one's own verbal turn; or one can begin by talking over someone else who has yet to finish. Verbal insertions of the last kind are generally considered interruptions. Although an interruption can be said to occur when the talk of one person overlaps the talk of another person, not all overlapping speech constitutes an interruption. For example, listeners sometimes overlap with a primary speaker's talk when they are merely indicating active attention and involvement. Such verbal contributions by listeners are sometimes called back-channel responses (S. Duncan & Fiske, 1977).

Interruptions are clearly overlapping speech of another kind, namely, that which occurs when one person's talk is cut short by another person's verbal insertion. Gender aspects of interruptions came to the research forefront when investigators became interested in whether differential rates of conversational infractions, such as interruptions, might correspond to the differential status and power possessed by men and women. If men have more power, then they take advantage of their position by interrupting women more than they themselves are interrupted. According to one formulation, an interruption is "a device for exercising power and control in conversation" because it involves "violation(s) of speakers' turns at talk" (West & Zimmerman, 1983, p. 103).

Early findings seemed to indicate strong support for just such a prediction. In several studies, West and Zimmerman observed that interruptions occurred more in mixed-sex encounters than in same-sex encounters, and, in the former, it is men who initiate more of the interruptions (West, 1979, 1982, 1984; West & Zimmerman, 1983; Zimmerman & West, 1975). Nonetheless, not every study has found men interrupting women more than the reverse (Dindia, 1987; Kennedy & Camden, 1983; Smith-Lovin & Brody, 1989). Indeed, a narrative review of the interruption literature concluded that there was little evidence for the premise that men interrupt more than women either in same-sex or opposite-sex encounters (D. James & Clark, 1993).

Is this hodge-podge made sensible by including factors that have helped to make sense of other interactional phenomena such as tag questions and directives? That is, would distinguishing among types of interruptions, attending to different functions of interruptions, and taking other aspects of the interactional context into account bring order to the mixed findings linking gender to interruptions? The short answer is yes.

In a recent meta-analysis of this literature, K.J. Anderson and Leaper (1998) reported that several factors significantly moderated the finding that women are more likely to be interrupted by men than the reverse. In terms of subtypes of interruptions, K.J. Anderson and Leaper found that gender differences in interruptions are larger when "intrusive interruptions" are specifically coded. Intrusive interruptions differ from other types of speech overlap by virtue of the fact that they describe active attempts by the previous listener to usurp the primary speaker's conversational turn. They are further distinguished from such types of speech overlap as back-channel responses, which are vocalizations by listeners designed to encourage the speaker to continue or to convey signs of continuing attention.

K.J. Anderson and Leaper (1998) did not find that sex composition moderated the size of the sex-related difference. In other words, across the sample of studies, men were no more likely to interrupt women than they were to interrupt men. However, they found that the environmental setting and activity structure of the interaction did affect the size of the sex difference. Specifically, they found that sex differences in intrusive interruptions were greater in naturalistic settings than in laboratory or office settings, and greater when the participants were observed in unstructured activities than in structured ones. Thus, it appears that men are more likely to interrupt women outside the bounds of research studies and outside the bounds of structured activities—a finding that suggests that when men and women are otherwise unconstrained by task demands, men interrupt women more than the reverse.

There is also indication that the situation of women interrupting men is met with considerably more disapproval than in other sex combinations. In one experimental study, male and female judges rated target individuals they heard via audio recordings. Results showed that particular gender combinations affected ratings of interrupters. Specifically, when a woman interrupted a man, the ratings on disrespect and assertiveness were significantly higher than in the other sex pairs (LaFrance, 1992). In other words, it appears that conversational infractions are gendered in the sense that infractions in some sex pairings are perceived to be more serious than in others. Perhaps women are considered more polite than men and hence are more harshly judged when they interrupt men. Or perhaps, because sex is a diffuse status characteristic, interruptions of a higher-status person (male) by a lower-status person (female) are considered more grave conversational infractions.

GENDER AND BEING A RESPONSIVE LISTENER

Listening is as essential to conversation as is talk. Listeners contribute to conversation in various ways, including uttering well-timed vocal behaviors such as "mm-hmm," as well as brief requests for clarification or completing a speaker's thought. Termed back-channel responses, these behaviors appear to be more the province of women than men (Bilous & Krauss, 1988; Carli, 1990). Moreover, as in other interactional behaviors, women and men tend to use back-channel responses differently. Fishman (1983), for example, concluded that women use back channels to encourage their male partners to elaborate on what they are saying. In contrast, males appeared to insert back-channel responses more in response to the requirement to express some token sign of attention or interest; they do this by inserting back channels only after fairly long remarks by women and after some pause. The effect of delayed back channeling is to discourage partners from continuing. And, similar to other conversational devices such as tag questions, back-channel responses are used to facilitate interaction. For example, back-channel responses are more likely to occur in cooperative than in competitive exchanges (Trimboli & Walker, 1984).

Listening responses can also be nonverbal, such as head nods and smiles. In the realm of smiling, research consistently shows that women smile more than men (LaFrance & Hecht, 1999). This appears partly due to norms that call for women to be more interactionally expressive than men.

We tested this idea in a recent study in which participants responded to another person's "good news" with or without a smile. Specifically, male and female research participants were presented with a vignette where they were asked to imagine interacting with someone who described to them a recent success he or she had had. After being asked to imagine that they either did or did not smile in response to this person's declared good news, participants indicated on several scales how they felt about their behavior and how they thought the other would react to it (LaFrance, 1998). Results strongly supported the idea that women feel more obligation to respond positively than do men. Specifically, nonsmiling females felt significantly less comfortable and less appropriate than nonsmiling men. Women also reported that the other would regard them as significantly less friendly, less genuine, less caring, and less polite than men who do not smile, as well as more cold and more rude. Finally, females also believed that the other's impression of them would change more if they did not smile than if they did, whereas men reported that whether they smile or not does not affect the other's impression of them.

Stoppard and Gunn Gruchy (1993) also found that women anticipate greater costs and fewer rewards when they fail to express positive emotion in response to someone else's success. Even in competitive contexts, women are expected to be cheerful (J. Graham, Gentry, & Green, 1981). Adolescent girls are taught to look happy even when they are uncomfortable or disappointed (Eder & Parker, 1987), and researchers at the National Institute for Healthcare Research found women are more apt than men to say "Thank you" (C.R. Snyder & McCullough, 2000). Once again, the data show that men's relative reluctance to thank other people is particularly true of men's interactions with other men. Whereas women often express appreciation to their male and female friends, men frequently express appreciation only to their female friends.

Gender-based demands for greater positivity by women are, in fact, part of a general demand that women be more nonverbally expressive than men. Such expressivity demands, also called display rules, are the prescriptive parts of gender stereotypes. Such prescriptive expectations shape nonverbal gender differences through self-socialization and through conformity to others' real or imagined expectations (J.A. Hall & Briton, 1993).

Moreover, these social consequences are applied relatively early in life. For example, Block (1984) investigated parents' views on appropriate emotional expressivity for their daughters and sons. The parents in these studies had children who ranged in age between 3 and 20 years and who came from a variety of ethnic and socioeconomic backgrounds. Across all samples, mothers and fathers tended to encourage their sons to control emotional expressions, but they encouraged their daughters to be expressive.

Finally, many observed gender differences in expressivity in social contexts may be based more on the roles women and men occupy than on their sex per se. For example, occupants of jobs that require interpersonal responsiveness, such as flight attendants, personal assistants, and day care workers (more often occupations of women than of men), evidence greater expressivity than do those in jobs that are less interpersonally oriented (Hochschild, 1983).

GENDER AND MANAGING INTERPERSONAL ENGAGEMENT

GENDER AND MANAGING CONFLICT

A concern of those who study interaction of intimate heterosexual couples is that it is often marked by a particular kind of tension. Specifically, research has focused on a problematic interchange described as the demand/withdraw pattern. This particular kind of interaction has been characterized as one of the most central, most intractable, and most destructive patterns of marital interaction (Christensen, 1988). In the demand/withdraw situation, one partner attempts to engage the other in a problem-solving discussion to which the other partner responds with avoidance. The "demander" suggests and complains; the "withdrawer" becomes silent and withdrawn. The pattern takes hold when the withdrawal and the demand behaviors become both stimulus and response: Withdrawal leads to more demand, which in turn causes more withdrawal, which elicits more demand, and so on. Moreover, there appears to be a gender pattern, with women tending to be demanders and men tending to be withdrawers (Christensen & Heavey, 1990). This gender-related behavior, like many others, should be seen as relative rather than absolute: Wives tend to demand and husbands tend to withdraw in about 60% of heterosexual couples; the reverse characterizes 30% of couples, and in about 10% of cases, wives and husbands demand and withdraw equally (Klinetob & Smith, 1996).

There have been two kinds of explanations for the gender link to this particular interactional process. One approach has been to focus on individual differences, that is, differences in how women and men approach social interaction. Another approach has been to eschew individual differences and to look instead at social structural factors such as power inequities. The sex difference orientation is seen in Gottman and Levenson's (1988) proposal that men are more physiologically reactive than women. As a result, they apparently withdraw more from conflict than do women in an attempt to reduce discomfort. Another sex difference perspective draws more heavily from the view that women and men are socialized into having different social agendas. In this view, women's acquired orientation toward interpersonal relationships is in forming and maintaining them; in contrast, men develop a self that is organized around being separate from others (Sagrestano, Heavey, & Christensen, 1993).

Social structural explanations for the gender link to the demand/withdraw pattern draw instead on the differential power possessed by men and women. Thus, men's greater social power affords them the right to pay less attention to women's entreaties as well as the right to be less adept at interpreting a whole range of communicational cues (Noller, 1993). According to Noller, men's interaction practices subscribe to the following guidelines: Do not acknowledge another person's contribution; act as though the normal rules of conversation do not apply to oneself; adopt the stance of expert. According to Christensen and Heavey (1990), such behaviors result in topics initiated by women being ignored by men, especially those that are emotionally charged. As Peplau and Gordon (1985) put it, "If men have greater power in a relationship, they have nothing to gain by discussing problems with their partner and may benefit from avoidance. If women have lesser power, they may see confrontation as the only way to protect or to enhance their own positions" (p. 256).

It is worth reiterating that such interactional behaviors are not "built into" being male or being female. Rather, they are the result of social structural arrangements. Men and women are assigned respectively to roles with greater and lesser status. These roles are what provide the engine of sex-differentiated behavior. In other words, distribution into different roles triggers different social and psychological processes by which men and women seek different outcomes in accord with what has been socially established (Eagly & Wood, 1999). Women's affiliation with domestic and child-rearing roles, along with female-dominated occupations, favors a pattern of socioemotional behaviors. Men's affiliation with the breadwinner role along with their own male-dominated occupations favor a pattern of task-oriented and independent behaviors. In sum, gender roles derive from the different work expected from each sex, which itself is dictated by a hierarchical social structure.

Empirical Examination of the Gender Link to Demand/Withdrawal

A number of investigators have focused on disentangling a sex difference from a social structural explanation for why women are more often found "demanding" and men "withdrawing." First, Christensen and Heavey (1990) found that both husbands and wives are more demanding when it comes to their own issues and more withdrawing on partner issues, suggesting a position rather than a person explanation. They also found, as predicted, that on wives' issues, wife demand/husband withdraw predominated; however, there were no differences on the demand/withdraw role on the husbands' issues; that is, men and women were not as likely to withdraw in that case. The combined results appear to suggest both the existence of sex-related differences and the influence of the structures in which marriage exists.

A later study expanded the range of topics to be discussed by husbands and wives (Klinetob & Smith, 1996). In keeping with a social structural explanation, they found greater husband demand/wife withdraw during discussion of his issue and greater wife demand/husband withdraw during discussion of her issue. In other words, one's interactional stance (i.e., demand or withdraw) corresponds to which partner wants change and which does not. The spouse supporting the status quo is more likely to withdraw as the spouse seeking change makes his or her demands.

GENDER AND INTERACTION IN GROUPS

GENDER AND LEADERSHIP STYLE

In explicit leadership roles, women tend to be viewed less positively than men (Eagly et al., 1992) and this differential evaluation can be seen in subtle interactional behaviors directed at male versus female leaders. An experimental study found, for example, that group members direct more negative nonverbal behaviors toward female leaders than male leaders even when they offer the same suggestions and arguments (D. Butler & Geis, 1990).

The less than positive view of women as leaders likely stems from the fact that the communication behaviors associated with women look to be incompatible with the communicational behaviors associated with leadership. The latter tend to be associated more in people's minds with the communicational strategies adopted by men. In fact, people who show more masculine-typed behaviors are more likely to be perceived as leaders (Kent & Moss, 1994).

Males are more likely to become leaders in initially leaderless groups in short-term situations and when the task does not require complex social interaction. As we noted earlier in our discussion of task contribution, sex is a diffuse status characteristic that is used to infer competence (Carli, 1991). However, when the implicit association of males with status and competence is overridden by making the group task explicitly neutral, then men and women are equally likely to emerge as leaders (Goktepe & Schneier, 1988).

In sum, the data indicate that men are more likely to emerge as leaders because they interact in a manner that more closely fits the stereotypic view of what leaders do or what they are expected to do. What has not been addressed, however, is whether female and male leaders actually adopt different communication styles when they are in leadership positions. Mirroring the results described earlier for conversational inputs, differences have also been noted for leadership contexts: Women are more interpersonally oriented and men are more task-oriented (Forsyth, Schlenker, Leary & McCown, 1985).

And, like the results described previously, these gender-based stylistic differences are moderated by a number of contextual factors. A meta-analysis found that women are more interpersonally oriented than men (although no less task-oriented) specifically in two kinds of settings: laboratory studies and self-assessment studies (Eagly & Johnson, 1990). There were no stylistic differences between women and men leaders in real organizational settings. Presumably, in more complex organizational settings, existing structures and established roles are more critical in affecting leadership style. The roles and structures thus have a compelling influence on what interactional behaviors are shown.

Most groups require effectiveness in both task and socioemotional domains. The association between these domains and gender may also make it more likely that women are maneuvered into a more socioemotional managerial style and men coaxed into a more task-oriented style in mixed-sex groups. As support for this, Eagly and Karau (1991) found a strong tendency for men to emerge as task leaders and general leaders and a weaker tendency for women to emerge as social leaders, in part because men and women step into the roles that others nudge them toward.

Women also tend to adopt a more democratic leadership style and men tend to adopt a more autocratic one (Eagly & Johnson, 1990). The question is far from settled as to why this might be the case. Women may prefer a more democratic style of leadership. Indeed, members of all-female groups are more likely than all-male groups to participate equally (W. Wood, 1987). Alternatively, the choice of a democratic over an autocratic style by women may be a combination of gender-based expectations and context. This may work in the following way. Particular types of women and men are recruited into leadership roles because of presumed sex differences in management style (Eagly & Johnson, 1990): When an organization needs a leader who is particularly assertive and authoritative, the search might be restricted to male candidates; when the situation calls for a more democratic manager, expectations might then induce a search for a woman to fill the role.

Also, women might lead in a more democratic style as a way of dealing with subordinates' reservations about women leaders. We know, for example, that subordinates are more satisfied with leaders who behave in gender-stereotypic ways (Petty & Miles, 1976). We also know that agentic female job applicants are viewed as less socially skilled than agentic males and that this perception results in hiring discrimination for the "feminine" job (Rudman, 1999). Consequently, women may have a better chance of succeeding if they manage using an expected socioemotional manner.

It is likely that female leaders encounter contradictory expectations. As women, they are expected to be more socioemotional; as leaders, they are expected to be task-focused. They can do both by adopting a nonhierarchical style that adapts to rather than dominates subordinates (Leary, 1989). In fact, women leaders are evaluated more positively than men leaders when they demonstrate a leadership style based on consideration of members (Bartol & Butterfield, 1976).

Finally, having less power may have something to do with why women adopt a more democratic leadership style. Specifically, those in lower-level positions have been found to adopt a more democratic style when assigned to a leadership position (Chusmir & Mills, 1989).

INTERPERSONAL INFLUENCE

Gender has repeatedly been implicated in the processes by which people attempt to bring others around to their way of thinking. The gender aspects of interpersonal influence, however, are not reducible to assertions that men are more persuasive than women or that women are more easily persuaded than men. For example, being masculine was a better predictor than being male of who is more convincing in a dyadic situation (Sayers, Baucom, & Tierney, 1993).

Power also affects influence attempts. In one study, participants were given scenarios describing a situation in which a man or a woman was trying to influence a person of the other sex. Some scenarios provided information regarding the sex of the actors, and other scenarios provided status information as well (e.g., bank vice president vs. bank teller). When status cues were provided, participants believed that men and women of equal status had equal influence. When information about a person's sex was the only information, participants inferred that the man held higher status and would be more successful in his influence attempts (Eagly & Wood, 1982).

Another study also showed how gender operates as a diffuse status characteristic in influence situations. Both men and women used more direct influence strategies when they had high power than when they had low expert power or when no information about their expertise was provided (Driskell, Olmstead, & Salas, 1993). But it is not always the case that directness works for women, at least with males. Carli (1990) studied the effect of tentativenss in speech as conveyed by tag questions, hedges, and disclaimers. For a male audience, tentative women were more influential and were perceived as more trustworthy than confident women. For a female audience, confident speakers were more influential than tentative speakers, regardless of their sex.

Sex operating as a diffuse status characteristic is also evident in attempts to exert influence in intimate relationships (Sagrestano, 1992). The observed variability in influence strategies used by men and women heterosexual American couples is due at least in part to the higher status and assumed greater expertise of men relative to women.

When power differences are explicitly measured in intimate couples, power better predicts choice of influence strategy than does sex. Among heterosexual, lesbian, and gay couples, individuals who perceived themselves as having less power than their partner report using more indirect and unilateral influence tactics to get their way (Falbo & Peplau, 1980). Similarly, individuals who have less control over resources than their partner in intimate same-sex and mixed-sex couples (e.g., less income, more dependent on the relationship) are more likely to use indirect strategies such as manipulation and supplication than those who have more resources (Howard, Blumstein, & Schwartz, 1986). Although this latter study reported no main effect for sex in terms of who makes an influence attempt, a main effect for target sex was observed. Specifically, both men and women used indirect influence strategies when the target was a man than a woman.

The fact that both men and women adopt more indirect strategies with a male partner shows how important sex composition is to a full understanding of the influence of gender on interaction processes. When both men and women become more indirect in persuading a man, it is likely because people have different expectations of male than female targets. Such expectations may then become self-fulfilling; that is, men will prove harder to influence than women.

Besides using different verbal strategies, males and females attempting to influence also adopt different nonverbal styles. Women tend to display more submissive nonverbal behaviors in such a position (Ridgeway, 1987). As we saw in our discussion of women's tendency to adopt more democratic styles of leadership, a more dominant attempt at influence by a nonleader woman might be perceived as a violation of both gender and status expectations. Research shows that both male and female speakers are perceived to be more likable and more influential when they adopt a competent as opposed to a dominant nonverbal style. Nonetheless, male raters tended to find women who exhibited a competent style to be less likable, more threatening, and less influential than men exhibiting the same style (Carli, LaFleur, & Loeber, 1995).

CONCLUSIONS

Gender clearly makes a difference in interaction, but it takes layers of context and construction to direct the route that it takes. When investigators first turned their attention to how women and men communicate and act in the company of others, they often found differences and just as often made invidious comparisons. It was not merely that the sexes showed different interactional behaviors, but the behaviors women showed were less competent and more unproductive than those of men.

There was some dispute about the precise cause of these differences; some argued for distinct evolutionary-based mechanisms, others posited different socialization histories, and still others suggested the constraints imposed by gender roles and unequal status. Those who adhered to a dominance perspective found the difference perspective flawed in ignoring real and pervasive differences in the social status ascribed to women and men. One's sex affects expectations about one's underlying attributes and likely worth, and it's natural to assume that assumed worth affects the way one interacts. Others found dominance explanations wanting, arguing instead that sex differences in interactional behavior could not be adequately accounted for by status alone. When sex is salient, women and men are expected to show different levels of competence (J. Berger et al., 1986). But they are also expected to show different personalities, abilities, and preferences (Eagly, 1987). In short, a person's sex is neither a simple nor a transparent stimulus. Rather, it is a repository of possibilities.

More recently, the deficient, difference, and dominance perspectives are giving way to the view that social interactions are dynamic and affected by multiple purposes and pressures. Social encounters take place in different settings with different combinations of males and females, and they are enacted by individuals with varying status and skills, agendas and attitudes. Women and men enter social situations knowing something about appropriate gender behavior. But even as they enter social interactions, the interactions themselves are being defined and redefined by the people who populate them. Gender is an important cause and outcome of these definitions. Social interaction is one venue where these processes can be observed.

CHAPTER 17

Gender and Relationships

KAREN K. DION and KENNETH L. DION

The Internet is revolutionizing the domain of relationships, much as it is changing many other aspects of contemporary life. Although exact figures are unavailable to document the extent of the phenomenon, unquestionably many women and men in countries around the world are developing relationships with one other "electronically" in the computer medium, including very intimate relationships and sometimes sexual ones. Some Internet relationships remain exclusively electronic; others proceed to actual meetings "offline."

An important feature of these Internet relationships is that, in the absence of physical contact, first impressions develop without the usual cues revealed in face-to-face interactions, such as gender, facial and physical attractiveness, age, weight, socioeconomic status, and so on. In particular, individuals can and do misrepresent aspects of themselves, including their gender, and experiment with alter egos. Two such cases were reported by Lea and Spears (1995). One is a case of a "double bluff," in which a woman presented herself as a man and developed an electronic relationship with a man who, in turn, was misrepresenting himself as a woman (Reid, 1994, as cited in Lea & Spears, 1995). Their relationship was threatened by the mutual deception but survived the point when they revealed their actual genders to one another. They eventually married after subsequently beginning their acquaintance again using the telephone as well as the computer and, hopefully, greater honesty.

A more disturbing case of misrepresented gender on the Internet involved a middle-aged, male psychiatrist from New York City who wanted to experience life as a woman and the intimacy of women's friendships and embarked on a grandly deceptive and ethically questionable "experiment" (Van Gelder, 1985, as cited in Lea & Spears, 1995). He misrepresented himself on the Internet as a neuropsychologist named Joan, who had allegedly been disabled and disfigured in a terrible car accident in which her boyfriend had been killed. Allegedly, after recovering from a long depression, "Joan" became a considerable presence in chat groups on the Internet, championing the cause of disabled women and developing deep friendships, including intense online romances, with dozens of women. These duped women were understandably shocked and disillusioned when they later learned that "Joan" was neither disabled nor even a woman after all. "Joan's" story is obviously a cautionary tale advising women (and men) to take care in developing Internet relationships and not blithely to assume that everything is as it seems or claimed with those with whom they develop online relationships.

These apocryphal stories of Internet relationships provide a way to introduce our chapter on gender and relationships. That women and men can convincingly play the role of someone from the other sex suggests that societal gender roles are well-known to members of both sexes and crucial in defining expectations for how women and men are supposed to act with one another in

---

Both authors contributed equally to writing this chapter. Correspondence concerning this chapter can be addressed to Karen K. Dion, Division of Life Sciences, University of Toronto, Scarborough, Ontario, Canada, M1C 1A4 (Email address: dionkk@psych.utoronto.ca) or Kenneth L. Dion, Dept. of Psychology, University of Toronto, Toronto, Ontario, Canada, M5S 3G3 (Email address: dionkl@psych.utoronto.ca).

developing and maintaining a close relationship. Some popular books and advocates of the "different cultures" perspective both suggest that because they are literally from different worlds, women and men in heterosexual relationships do not and perhaps cannot understand one another. However, if that were true, the deceptions in the aforementioned Internet relationships could never have occurred.

Social science researchers interested in gender and/or relationships are conducting research that helps us to understand how, why, and in what ways women and men in relationships are similar as well as different from one another. This goal is of relatively recent vintage. When we reviewed what was known about the relation of gender and heterosexual, romantic love in the mid-1980s (see K.K. Dion & Dion, 1985), the literature was very limited, consisting of perhaps only a half-dozen studies, several of which were our own investigations. That situation has changed considerably, with a fast-growing literature, burgeoning research, and a growing cadre of researchers from several disciplines and countries around the world, working on the common project of understanding gender and relationships.

Space limitations preclude exhaustively reviewing all of the research on gender and relationships that currently exists as of this writing. Indeed, the literature has grown so quickly and haphazardly that it cannot be easily or coherently organized within a single chapter. Rather, our approach is to focus on central themes emerging from the social science literature, especially the psychological one, at the intersection of gender and relationships. We have organized the chapter into three general sections. The first presents theoretical perspectives and models in the relationships literature that either incorporate gender as a central aspect or are nevertheless clearly relevant for understanding the role of gender in relationships. The second section presents a selective sampler of research topics concerning relationships in which gender is clearly implicated as a relevant factor. Last, but perhaps most important, the third section considers gender and culture together as interrelated processes for better understanding relationships across countries and cultures as well as within ethnocultural groups in a specific country, such as the United States or Canada.

GENDER AND RELATIONSHIP THEORIES

EVOLUTIONARY PSYCHOLOGY VERSUS SOCIAL STRUCTURAL EXPLANATIONS

The song "Summertime" from George Gershwin's opera *Porgy and Bess* aptly sums up each sex's allegedly principal attributes as a parent in the line: "Your daddy's rich and your mommy's good-looking." With such assets, the song implied, a child need not worry and could well sleep comfortably. The line epitomizes a widely held belief that given a choice of a mate's qualities, a man will select as attractive a woman as possible, and a woman will choose that partner from among her suitors with the greatest wealth and resources. Although few would be shocked or surprised by such gender differences in heterosexual mate preferences, *why* they occur is more controversial.

From theorizing in evolutionary psychology, Buss (1989) predicted and also found from a large cross-cultural study of 37 samples in 33 countries comprising more than 10,000 respondents that men valued youth and physical attractiveness in a potential mate more than women, whereas women emphasized more than men qualities such as "good financial prospects" and "ambition and industriousness." Men's preferences were predicted on the premise that youth and physical attractiveness signal a woman's reproductive capacity; and women's preferences, a potential partner's resources for parental investment in offspring. By these diverging choices in mate preferences, each sex presumably furthers its reproductive success.

This evolutionary psychology account for gender differences in mate preferences is, however, weakened in several regards. First, cultural differences are far more pronounced than gender differences in Buss's (1989) own data, respectively accounting for 13.45% versus 2.4%, on average across traits, of the variance (Buss et al., 1990). Second, Kalick, Zebrowitz, Langlois, and Johnson (1998) showed with a longitudinal sample that physical attractiveness is unrelated to actual physical health across the life cycle (thus not serving as a marker for a woman's health) and, in fact, masks the relationship between perceived and actual health.

Gender differences in mate preferences can also be accounted for by social structural explanations as well as a sociobiological one. Indeed, the magnitude of the gender differences in mate preferences observed by Buss correlated negatively with indicators of economic development (see Glenn's comment in Buss, 1989) as well as gender empowerment and gender-related development (Eagly & Wood, 1999), such that they are less apparent in modern, industrialized societies where women's rights are recognized and their opportunities encouraged. Eagly and Wood proposed social role theory, which emphasizes differential distributions of women and men in social and societal roles, as an alternative metatheory for explaining gender differences in mate preferences that is as compelling as evolutionary psychology. The aforementioned gender differences in mate preference that implicitly assume women are the homemakers and men the breadwinners are more muted in societies where women are empowered and participate more equitably in the workforce.

Although evolutionary psychology and social structural theory explanations for gender differences in mate preferences are equally viable, the passage of time may allow us to differentiate between them. If social structural theory is correct, gender differences in mate preference should slowly abate and perhaps eventually disappear in several decades in places, such as the United States, Western Europe, and Canada, where women's and men's participation in the workforce and managerial ranks is increasingly equal. By contrast, according to the evolutionary psychology account, such changes in the social structure should not matter insofar as they do not directly affect one's reproductive success, so gender differences in mate preferences should be evident for many eons hence.

ATTACHMENT THEORY

Many relationship researchers today believe that attachment and love are not the same for everyone (e.g., see K.K. Dion & Dion, 1985, 1993; K.L. Dion & Dion, 1988). People differ in the ways they form attachments to others and love them and in their characteristic attachment styles and love styles. These styles are relatively stable, enduring individual differences that help us to understand and predict many different aspects of individuals' orientations to close relationships and their relationship experiences.

An infant's bond with its principal caretaker(s), especially the mother, lays the basis for its *attachment style*—a characteristic way of relating to parents and intimate others—that endures from infancy to adolescence and throughout adulthood. Pioneering attachment theorist and researcher Mary Ainsworth (1982) was among the first to propose that the infant's temperament, together with the caregiver's consistency of responding to it, yield (at least) three different attachment styles: (1) *secure* (a consistently responsive caretaker and a confident, easily soothed infant); (2) *anxious-ambivalent* (a fussy, temperamental, difficult-to-soothe child whose caretaker is inconsistently responsive); and (3) *avoidant* (a mutually unresponsive mother and child). Developmental psychologists following the same children from infancy to early adolescence in longitudinal studies have found some evidence of continuity and stability in attachment styles initially identified in infants around their first year from observations of mother-child interactions (e.g., Weinfeld, Sroufe, Egeland, & Carlson, 1999).

Proposing that these same attachment styles also apply to adults, Hazan and Shaver (1987) developed a simple one-item measure with statements describing each style (without the label provided) with which individuals classified themselves. In relation to self-reports of their romantic relationships, the principal features for the secure attachment style are trust, friendship, and positive emotions; for the anxious-ambivalent style, they are obsession, anxiety, and turbulent emotions; and for the avoidant style, fear of closeness and lack of trust are prototypical.

Using this and related attachment style measures, relationship researchers have since found that they relate to many aspects of adults' romantic and sexual relationships. For example, L.A. Kirkpatrick and Davis (1994) explored relationship stability over three years in heterosexual couples who began dating seriously in university. Some pairings of attachment styles, such as pairs of avoidant or anxious-ambivalent persons, never occurred. Moreover, relationships of avoidant men and of anxious-ambivalent women were surprisingly stable and enduring, despite negative ratings of the relationships by themselves and their partners.

The paradoxical stability of relationships for these "insecure" attachment styles was interpreted as reflecting their respective congruency with masculine and feminine gender roles. The avoidant style, characterized by a fear of closeness and emotional distance from one's partner, is congruent with the male gender role and typifies the stance of some men in close relationships. By contrast, the anxious-ambivalent style, with its obsessive fear of losing one's partner that motivates attentiveness to the relationship, is more compatible with the female gender role and women's role as "relationship specialists" who do most of the work in maintaining relationships. Thus, gender role interacts with attachment style in accounting for relationship stability. Even those with "insecure" attachment styles may have long-lasting, if not entirely satisfying, relationships with their romantic partners.

An infant's interactions with its caretakers also lead to cognitive representations or "mental models" of self and others that are positive or negative, providing the basis for a recent fourfold classification of adult attachment style (Bartholomew & Horowitz, 1991). Positive models of self and others define the "secure" style, and negative models of both identify a "fearful" style. The "dismissing" style consists of a positive self-model and a negative model of others. Finally, the "preoccupied" style comprises a negative self-model and a positive model of others and is also equivalent to the anxious-ambivalent style in the original three-category classification by Hazan and Shaver (1987). Basically, the original "avoidant" style from the three-category system is differentiated into separate "fearful" and "dismissing" categories in the fourfold scheme.

Researchers using the fourfold classification find consistent gender differences in two of these styles, with men scoring higher than women on the "dismissing" style (one of the two avoidant styles), and women scoring higher than men on the "preoccupation" or anxious-ambivalent style, whether the attachment style classifications are based on self-reports or ratings by interviewer or one's partner (Bartholomew & Horowitz, 1991; Scharfe & Bartholomew, 1994). As noted above, these respective styles are congruent with masculine and feminine gender roles.

LOVE STYLES THEORY

Canadian sociologist John Lee has identified six different styles of love from interviewing people in love (for a recent description of this theory, see Lee, 1998). *Storge* is a companionate type of love, where love develops from a deeply caring friendship with one's partner. *Ludus* is a playful, noncommital style of love, in which the relationship is viewed as a "game" each partner tries to win. *Mania* is an obsessive love style characterized by strong emotions, such as jealousy, anxiety, and depression, and is similar to the anxious-ambivalent or "preoccupied" attachment style. *Agape* is a selfless love style characterized by altruism and sacrifice for one's partner, without expectation of reciprocity. *Pragma* is a logically oriented, "shopping list" love style in which one's choice of partner is carefully planned according to a checklist of desired qualities or traits. Finally, *eros* is a love style characterized by a strong, but unobsessive, physical and sexual attraction to a partner.

Gender differences have been found for most of these love styles except eros. Psychological studies in Canada (K.L. Dion & Dion, 1993) and the United States (S.S. Hendrick & Hendrick, 1995) have shown that on questionnaire measures of love styles, men reject the ludic style less vigorously than women, and women endorse the storgic and pragma love styles more strongly than men. Further, combining several of their studies that were conducted in the United States, the Hendricks have also reported that women scored higher on the manic love style than men, and men outscored women in attitudes toward "sexual permissiveness" (i.e., a positive orientation to casual, noncommital sex).

S.S. Hendrick and Hendrick (1995) have interpreted these gender differences as explainable by both evolutionary psychology and social learning perspectives. For example, the game playing, sexually permissive approach favored by men more than women is consistent with a male reproductive strategy in which a man tries to maximize his reproductive success by impregnating as many female partners as possible. Similarly, the pragmatic and friendship-oriented love styles favored by women more than men are congruent with a reproductive strategy in which male partners are carefully selected for their potential investment in the relationship and their suitability as potential parents in an exclusive, long-lasting relationship.

By contrast, the social learning perspective views these gender differences in love styles as reflecting traditional gender roles, in which men are encouraged to be sexually exploratory as part of the traditional male role, whereas the female gender role focuses women toward restraining male sexuality and orients them to take a practical and sensible approach to love. The social learning explanation gains credence from the fact that gender-role orientation correlates with reported love styles. For example, respondents with a feminine gender-role orientation have been found to be less likely to endorse the ludic love style than those whose gender orientations were classified as masculine, androgynous, or undifferentiated (W.C. Bailey, Hendrick, & Hendrick, 1987).

The role of social learning in influencing love styles is also suggested by ethnocultural differences in love styles independently found in large multicultural cities in the United States and Canada. C. Hendrick and Hendrick (1986) classified University of Miami students in Florida into one of five categories: Black, White non-Hispanic, White Hispanic, Oriental, or an "other" category. Compared to their White non-Hispanic counterparts, Oriental students endorsed more companionate and more pragmatic but less erotic love styles.

In Toronto, Canada, K.L. Dion and Dion (1993) explored gender and ethnocultural comparisons in love styles by classifying University of Toronto students into four categories: Anglo-Celtic, European, Chinese, and "other Asian" (i.e., Japanese, Vietnamese, East Indian, and Pakistani). Chinese and "other Asian" respondents scored higher on storge than those from either Anglo-Celtic or European backgrounds. Gender also interacted with ethnocultural background in relating to love styles. "Other Asian" women were less ludic than their male counterparts or women from other ethnocultural backgrounds, which was interpreted as reflecting greater gender-role differentiation for those from Asian communities. "Other Asian" women were also more agapic than Anglo-Celtic women, perhaps reflecting the interdependent or "relational" self typical of collectivistic, Asian cultural traditions.

The Investment Model: Satisfaction, Commitment, and Relation Stability/Longevity

Caryl Rusbult (1980, 1983) has proposed an investment model to predict satisfaction with and commitment to relationships, whether romantic (including other-sex and same-sex) or nonromantic (e.g., friendships, business relationships, job-related feelings and behaviors). Rusbult's investment model is based on the theory of interdependence (H.H. Kelley & Thibaut, 1978; Thibaut & Kelley, 1959)—a general psychological theory of social behavior—which assumes that individuals are primarily motivated to maximize rewards and minimize costs. To that end, individuals presumably sustain interpersonal relationships that are rewarding and terminate those that are costly. Like the theory of interdependence, the investment model assumes that relationship satisfaction (SAT) is a function of outcomes (O) (i.e., rewards minus costs) that exceed one's comparison level (CL), defined as a personal standard for evaluating the attractiveness of a relationship based on one's previous relationship experiences. Thus, the equation $SAT = O - CL$ reflects the investment model's prediction that satisfaction will be greater to the extent that net relationship outcomes increase and these outcomes increasingly exceed one's expectations for a relationship. Satisfaction determines one's attraction to, or the extent of positive feeling for, a given relationship.

Commitment (COM) is defined in the investment model as the intent to continue a relationship and a feeling of attachment to it. Commitment is assumed by the model to depend on satisfaction as well as two other factors that define one's dependency on the relationship: alternatives (ALT) and investment size (INV). Thus, the investment model equation $COM = SAT - ALT + INV$ signifies that commitment to a relationship is theoretically expected to increase directly with both satisfaction and investments but to decrease with better alternatives to one's present relationship.

"Alternatives" include dating several other people simultaneously, dating someone else exclusively, or preferring to be alone and uninvolved in a relationship. "Investment size" refers to how much an individual has invested in a relationship and includes direct, "intrinsic" investments in the relationship, such as time, money, and expended effort, as well as "extrinsic" investments that were originally extraneous to the relationship but that have become entwined in it and might be wholly or partly forgone were the relationship to dissolve (e.g., a home, children, mutual friends). The greater one's investments in a relationship and the less acceptable the alternatives, the more dependent one is on a given relationship.

An important implication of interdependence theory and the investment model is the notion that one may be "entrapped" and continue in an unsatisfying relationship because of inadequate or worse alternatives and/or because one has invested too much in the relationship to quit it. This situation of *nonvoluntary dependence* characterizes some women who stay in abusive relationships and those in otherwise unhappy and unsatisfying relationships who feel compelled or constrained to stay in them because the alternatives are even less palatable.

Substantial evidence supports the validity of the investment model for understanding satisfaction and commitment in relationships. For example, longitudinal studies in the 1980s and 1990s that have followed college student relationships over several months (Rusbult, Martz, & Agnew, 1998), over 17 months (Rusbult, 1983), and even over 15 years (Bui, Peplau, & Hill, 1993) strongly support investment model predictions regarding the determinants of commitment and the temporal stability of both women's and men's relationships. These studies also suggest that, as assumed by the investment model, commitment is *the* dimension that mediates the effects of rewards, costs, alternatives, and investments on the stability of relationships and one's decision to continue or leave a relationship.

Although gender differences are not invariably found in investment model research, they do arise. When they do, it is typically women who show greater commitment, higher satisfaction, and greater dependency (i.e., worse alternatives, larger investments)—in short, greater overall investment in the relationship—than men (Rusbult et al., 1998). Showing the applicability of the investment model for understanding abusive relationships, Rusbult and Martz (1995) had access to intake interviews of women who had left an abusive relationship and sought refuge in a shelter, along with telephone follow-ups of their subsequent behavior. As predicted by the model, abused women's commitment, if not entrapment, in the abusive relationship was greater if they had poorer alternatives (e.g., low education, low income, no alternative means of financial support) and had made greater investments in the relationship (e.g., were married, had children, had a long-standing relationship). Abused women highly committed to their relationship were also more likely to return to it in the year subsequent to their shelter visit and to do so sooner than those less committed to them.

Having discussed a number of relationship perspectives relating to gender, let us turn now to consider selected research issues at the intersection of gender and relationships research.

SELECTED RESEARCH ISSUES ON GENDER AND RELATIONSHIPS

LONG-DISTANCE RELATIONSHIPS

Long-distance relationships (hereafter, LDRs), especially among college students, are interesting to relationship researchers for several reasons. For one, such relationships are fairly common, with prevalence estimates suggesting they account for between 25% and 33% of all college student relationships, with sometimes higher percentages (e.g., Dellman-Jenkins, Bernard-Paolucci, & Rushing, 1994). LDRs also allow investigators to explore the effects of being separated from one's relationship partner and of being exposed to a chronic relationship stressor (viz., separation). In fact, though, evidence suggests LDRs do *not* differ from geographically close relationships (hereafter, GCRs) in breakup rate (Van Horn et al., 1997), nor do they differ on most relationship quality indices, such as satisfaction, most types of intimacy, intimacy of self-disclosure, and affection for one's partner (Guldner & Swensen, 1995; Van Horn et al., 1997). However, those in LDRs have been found to be more likely to report depression and anxiety symptoms (Guldner, 1996) and to believe that the relationship will not endure (Helgeson, 1994a), a relationship belief that is itself a stressor.

Gender also plays a role in LDRs. Helgeson (1995) found gender differences in adjusting to the stress of an LDR and also in response to breakups of these relationships, in a longitudinal study where participants' stress level and adjustment were assessed at two times in a sample of college students: at the beginning of the academic year and three months later. Approximately a third of the LDRs broke up over this period. Helgeson (1994a) explored whether gender differences in marital relationships, whose beneficial effects are usually less evident for women's well-being than for men's but whose dissolution is typically more deleterious to men than to women, would also be evident in LDRs. These expected gender differences were premised on the notion that among heterosexuals, men depend more on a relationship with an other-sex partner than do women for emotional intimacy and social support, whereas women can draw on a wider social network, including family and same-sex friends, to satisfy such needs. Consistent with this view, among those whose LDRs remained intact, women scored higher than men on "global distress," a measure including anxiety, depression, and hostility scales. By contrast, men whose LDRs had broken up were more distressed than men in intact ones.

Helgeson (1994a) also observed interesting, though complex, gender differences in response to the LDR's breakup and which partner had initiated its breakup. Men whose partners had initiated the breakup were the most distressed, perhaps because they had not anticipated it. Men adjusted better to the breakup if they initiated it themselves. By contrast, in LDRs whose breakup had been initiated by the man, women were better adjusted and had more positive emotion than men, perhaps in part because they had given greater consideration to the possibility of a breakup than their male counterparts. However, other studies yield divergent findings in this regard. Although they did not take the breakup's initiator into account, Wilmot, Carbaugh, and Baxter (1985) found no gender differences in regrets or emotional reactions in LDRs that terminated within 15 months but observed that women used direct verbal strategies more than men to terminate them.

Finally, Dellman-Jenkins et al. (1994) have found several suggestive gender differences between women and men in LDRs. Women reportedly daydreamed more than men in LDRs and also wrote more to their partners than women in GCRs. Men in LDRs were less satisfied than their female counterparts because they felt their partners were not supportive of their pursuing higher education. Regardless of whether they were in an LDR or a GCR, women outscored men on several kinds of intimacy (social, sexual, intellectual, and recreational).

WHICH GENDER HAS THE GREATER ROMANTICISM?

"Romanticism" is a set of interrelated beliefs that idealizes the romantic love experience, seeing it as unique and special ("one true love"), as lasting forever, as occurring at "first sight," and overcoming any and all obstacles. Because romanticism relates to other important relationship attitudes and behaviors, including marital satisfaction, the relation of gender to romanticism, if any, is relevant for those interested in gender and/or relationship processes.

If asked which gender is the most romantic, most people would perhaps confidently wager that women exceed men in romanticism, reflecting a traditional and long-standing stereotype in the United States and Canada. If so, they would lose the bet, at least as regards college students. From the 1950s to the late 1980s, most studies examining gender differences in romanticism among U.S. and Canadian college students have consistently shown that men outscore women on questionnaire measures of romanticism, including the specific beliefs noted above (see reviews by K.K. Dion & Dion, 1985, pp. 224–227; Sprecher & Metts, 1989). Although it does not qualify this gender difference, feminine gender-role orientation is also associated with greater romanticism (Sprecher & Metts, 1989).

Interpretations most often given for the gender difference in romanticism—a functionalistic perspective (K.K. Dion & Dion, 1985) and social role theory (Sprecher & Metts, 1989)—stress the respective economic roles and positions of women and men in the United States and Canada. Historically and even today, women in the United States, Canada, and elsewhere typically contribute less to the family's economic subsistence than do men. Women, especially those following a traditional gender-role pattern of primarily being a homemaker, typically determine their standard of living when choosing a husband. Accordingly, women may view romantic love more pragmatically as a basis for marriage rather than in more purely idealistic terms. By contrast, being socialized to become economically self-sufficient, men can afford to be less pragmatic and more idealistic in their view of romantic and marital relationships and their choice of romantic and marital partners. These interpretations further suggest that gender differences in romanticism would decline, if not disappear, in those societies where and when women gain genuine economic equality with men.

There are already some welcome signs of change in this regard. Kephart (1967) surveyed a large sample of college students in the Philadelphia area and asked: "If a boy (girl) had all the other qualities you desired, would you marry this person if you were not in love with him (or her)?" Whereas a solid majority of men (65%) said no, only 24% of the women did so. This same question, with minor changes in wording ("man/woman" instead of "boy/girl"), was repeated in later surveys in 1976 and 1984 by other researchers (see Simpson, Campbell, & Berscheid, 1986). In these studies, the gender difference in reported willingness to marry without love had virtually disappeared, with more than 80% of both women and men answering the question negatively. Thus, recent evidence suggests that women are as unlikely as men to countenance the possibility of entering a loveless marriage.

CROSS-SEX FRIENDSHIPS

Heterosexual men may be the more romantic gender, but they are also more prone to see sexual interest in an other-sex partner or friend where there may, in fact, be none. In the movie *When Harry Met Sally*, Harry suggested somewhat outrageously, though perhaps honestly, to Sally that a man could not be interested in friendship with a woman without the prospect of a sexual relationship developing from it. As he bluntly put it: "No man can be friends with a woman . . . [because] . . . he always wants to have sex with her." Can a woman and a man never be "just friends," at least as far as the man is concerned? Do men see sexual interest when and where a woman is only being friendly?

A survey of 138 college students by Monsour, Harris, Kurzweil, and Beard (1994) found that only 6% of males and 8% of females indicated sexual overtones were problematic when asked an open-ended question about "challenges" in a cross-sex relationship. A more recent study of 200 college students by D.L. Kaplan and Keys (1997) using more direct questions about sexual aspects of cross-sex friendships reported much higher percentages, with proportionally more men than women (57% vs. 32%) indicating moderate or higher levels of sexual attraction toward their closest, other-sex, "platonic" friend. However, for both sexes, feelings of love were more strongly related to sexual attraction toward the cross-sex friend than was the participant's sex. So, although Harry's extreme claim is not sustained by existing research, his contention has more than a kernel of truth.

GENDER DIFFERENCES IN PERCEIVING FRIENDLINESS VERSUS SEXUAL INTEREST

In the United States (and probably elsewhere), men are clearly more prone than women to feel sexual undertones in cross-sex friendships; in some cases, men may enter into such a relationship in the hope of its later becoming sexual. Considerable evidence suggests that in interactions between strangers, men are more likely than women to misperceive friendliness on the part of the woman as sexual interest toward them. Abbey (1982) had a male-female pair engage in a five-minute discussion about university life (the actors) while another male-female pair observed their interaction (the observers). On postinteraction ratings, male actors and observers judged the female actor as having been more "sexual" (i.e., promiscuous, flirtatious, and seductive) than did women considering the male actor; the men were also more sexually attracted to the female actor than women were with regard to their other-sex actor counterparts.

Shotland and Craig (1988) had participants judge male-female interactions where the male and female actors deliberately acted either friendly or sexually interested, and they confirmed and extended Abbey's (1982) previous findings. Both sexes were indeed capable of differentiating between friendly and sexually interested behavior between a woman and a man, but men had a demonstrably lower threshold for perceiving a woman's friendly behavior as sexually interested than did women in viewing a man's friendly behavior in this way. Men also misclassify "tie signs"—nonverbal cues signifying a relationship such as hug or a pat—as reflecting physical or sexual attraction, whereas women are more apt to see them as expressions of intimacy (Afifi & Johnson, 1999).

These gender differences—men perceiving sexual interest from an other-sex partner more readily than women—even emerge when judging static photographs of couples, regardless of whether or not nonverbal cues suggest a close relationship exists between the woman and the man (Abbey & Melby, 1986). The causes of these gender differences remain unclear, though differential socialization of the genders, greater readiness toward sexual arousal in men, and high testosterone levels in young adult men have all been proposed as possible explanations. Regardless of cause(s), though, these gender differences undoubtedly play a role in explaining relationship miscommunications between the genders and in understanding and perhaps developing strategies for avoiding date rape by having members of each sex communicate clearly as well as perceive one another's intentions accurately.

GENDER AND RELATIONSHIP VALUES: IDEALS AND REALITIES

Do women and men value the same qualities in personal relationships? Much of the research addressing this topic has focused on heterosexual relationships among single young adults (typically, university student samples) and/or heterosexual couples. Some studies also have examined relationship values among same-sex couples. Although there appears to be considerable similarity in relationship values, gender may be differentially related to the realization of these ideals. The remainder of this section discusses research findings pertaining to this issue.

For example, S.D. Cochran and Peplau (1985) identified two components of values in heterosexual relationships among single, White male and female university students, which they labeled *dyadic attachment* and *egalitarian autonomy.* The authors noted that similar components had also been identified in research on relationship values among same-sex couples (Peplau & Cochran, 1981; Peplau, Cochran, Rook, & Padesky, 1978), suggesting that these two components were important across different types of relationships. Dyadic attachment reflected valuing intimacy, sexual exclusivity, and commitment to one's partner. There were no gender differences on dyadic attachment. The second factor, egalitarian autonomy, did reveal a gender difference, with women endorsing this relationship value more than men. The items in this factor concerned the importance of independent careers for both partners, equal power in the relationship, and the importance of friendships and other interests outside the relationship.

Forming and maintaining close relationships in adulthood is related to the physical and psychological well-being of women and men (Worell, 1993a). As illustrated by S.D. Cochran and Peplau's (1985) research, members of both sexes report valuing dyadic closeness. However, women and men have been found to differ in their reported satisfaction with different types of adult relationships. For example, various studies have found greater dissatisfaction with some aspects of the marital relationship for wives compared to husbands. Some of this dissatisfaction suggested a discrepancy between women's desired and perceived intimacy with their spouse. Moreover, women's greater reported marital dissatisfaction during certain phases of family development might also reflect pressures associated with primary responsibilities for parenting (K.K. Dion, 1985). Research on other types of personal relationships (e.g., friendships) similarly suggests that although intimacy is important for men's and women's well-being, women contribute more to perceived intimacy (Steil, 1997).

Why this gender difference occurs is a matter of debate. Cancian (1987) argued that the conceptualization of love in the United States and in the social science literature has been feminized, defining love mainly in terms of expressing feelings and self-disclosure. She suggested that men were more likely to express love by instrumental actions such as offering help, sex, spending time with their partner, and shared interests and activities. In essence, she hypothesized gender differences in preferred modes of expressing love for one's partner. From this perspective, gender differences in marital satisfaction might be attributable to these hypothesized feminine and masculine styles of love.

A similar type of conceptual framework is reflected in the "two cultures" controversy, which has captured both scholarly (e.g., J.T. Wood, 1997) and popular attention. As discussed by Wood, this account suggests that in a given society, there are various "speech communities," with gender being one type of differentiation. Within a given group, there are different styles and goals of interpersonal communication, leading to the potential for misunderstanding and miscommunication between members from different groups. Metts (1997) commented that if there are "different social and relational cultures," then the development and maintenance of personal relationships between women and men becomes an "intercultural enterprise," with each side learning the rules of each other's behavior.

Vangelisti and Daly (1997) examined whether men and women differ in the importance they assign to different relationship qualities, contending that from a "different cultures" perspective, gender differences would be expected. The participants were adults whose average age was in the mid-30s. They evaluated how important each of 30 qualities was for the success of a long-term romantic relationship and indicated the degree to which their current relationship fulfilled each of these qualities. On average, respondents had been involved in their current relationship for nearly 12 years. Their reported discrepancy between valuing and achieving various relational standards was negatively related to relationship satisfaction, as assessed by a measure of marital quality.

Both on a composite measure and on most subscales, there were no gender differences on the perceived importance of various relationship qualities. However, there were gender differences in the extent to which men and women believed that these standards were met in their current relationship. Compared to men, women were less likely to report that their expectations about standards for a successful relationship were fulfilled. Vangelisti and Daly (1997) suggested that the pattern of findings supported a "different experiences" rather than a "different cultures" interpretation about the relation between gender and relational standards. In other words, women and men seemed to share the same worldview as applied to relationship values, but they differed in the reported likelihood of realizing these goals/ideals. Additional discussion/debate of these findings and related issues can be found in J.T. Wood's (1997) and Burleson's (1997) commentaries.

One important factor that may contribute to the realization of relationship standards and ideals is relationship equality. In S.D. Cochran and Peplau's (1985) research, egalitarian autonomy was one of the two factors identified, and young women endorsed this value more strongly than their male counterparts. Rosenbluth, Steil, and Whitcomb (cited in Steil, 1997) asked White, dual-career, married couples (on average, in their early 30s) about the characteristics defining equality and inequality in others' marriages, and also how they would personally define equality in a marital relationship. When considering others' marriages, division of responsibility for tasks, especially domestic tasks, was frequently used as a criterion for judging the degree of perceived equality. However, the more general question as to what defines marital equality elicited responses related to relationship qualities such as respecting and supporting one another.

Although both women and men endorsed the importance of equality in their marriage, an egalitarian marriage—defined as equal sharing of domestic tasks and equal valuing of both partners' careers—was reported by only a minority of the sample. Steil (1997, p. 70) suggested that the respondents' emphasis on relationship qualities rather than division of labor to define equality might represent one way of "coping with inequality when equality is the stated ideal." By contrast, in their discussion of lesbian and gay families, Demo and Allen (1996) stated that one consistent finding has been that compared to heterosexual couples, same-sex couples tend to be more egalitarian.

What is the relation between gender roles and equality in marital relationships? Scholars writing from both microsocial (psychology) and macrosocial (sociology) perspectives have suggested that traditional gender roles are dysfunctional for optimal heterosexual relationships. Ickes (1993) contended that women and men who endorse traditional gender-role orientations have less optimal relationships compared to androgynous women and men. Based on research from the United States and other societies, Steil (1997) has similarly argued that separate gender roles contribute to inequality in the relationship between marital partners. In the context of separate gender roles, women traditionally have been regarded and have functioned as primary nurturers in relationships.

In his cross-cultural analysis of 90 nonindustrialized societies, Coltrane (1988) hypothesized and found that men's involvement in active nurturing behavior—specifically, the care of young children—was related to a more egalitarian view of gender. In societies with high father involvement in parenting, women had positions of greater public authority. This finding occurred across societies that differed on a number of other structural dimensions. As Coltrane (1996) noted, men's involvement in a nurturant family role has implications for gender equality. Whether paternal nurturance results in or reflects the presence of gender equality remains to be determined; it is likely that the relation is bidirectional.

Paternal nurturance in the form of active involvement in the care of young children may also contribute to greater marital intimacy because of the impact of parenting itself on adult development. For example, Coltrane (1996) commented on the implications of his previous research in which couples identified as "shared parenting" families were interviewed. Both spouses were employed at least half-time, and the couple had two or more school-age children. The interviews suggested a positive "spillover" effect between men's learning to be a sensitive parent and improvement in the couple's marital relationship. These couples also reported spending much of their time together discussing parenting, which, as Coltrane noted, also enhanced their sense of commitment to each other. (See also F.M. Deutsch, 1999, for further discussion of issues pertaining to shared parenting.)

GENDER, CULTURE, AND RELATIONSHIPS

Social psychological theory and research on relationships typically has not explicitly considered the role of cultural processes. However, for over a decade, we have contended that cultural perspectives should be an integral part of the psychology of personal relationships (K.K. Dion & Dion, 1993, 1996; K.L. Dion & Dion, 1988). As discussed previously, Buss and his colleagues (1990) found that culture accounted for more variance than gender in their cross-cultural study of mate preferences. Sprecher and her colleagues (1994) found culture-related differences on most of variables included in their cross-cultural study of love relationships. Cultural factors also contribute to gender differences in relationship processes. For example, Ting-Toomey (1991) found gender differences in reported expressions of intimacy in Japan and the United States, but not in France. These studies reflect a growing interest in cultural comparisons in the field of psychology. Recognition of the importance of cultural factors has the potential to encourage dialogue among scholars from different fields in the social and behavioral sciences and those from different cultural traditions (K.K. Dion & Dion, 1996).

CROSS-CULTURAL PERSPECTIVES: INDIVIDUALISM AND COLLECTIVISM

This point is well-illustrated by considering the impact of Hofstede's (1984) seminal cross-cultural study of values, which has played a significant role in stimulating research interest in individualism and collectivism (see U. Kim, Triandis, Kagitcibasi, Choi, & Yoon, 1994). Commenting on the impact of his book on cross-cultural psychology, Hofstede (1994, p. ix) noted that "surprisingly, *Culture's Consequences* is not really a psychological treatise at all. It does not belong to any single social science discipline." In the initial study, conducted in the late 1960s and early 1970s, survey data were collected from respondents in 40 countries who were all employees in the same multinational corporation. Individuals' survey responses within each society were averaged, and the resultant country-level scores were factor analyzed. Four societal dimensions were identified based on these analyses: power distance, uncertainty avoidance, individualism, and masculinity. Each society in the sample was characterized in terms of the score received on each of these four dimensions. This approach provided a conceptual framework that integrated previously disparate findings of bicultural contrasts (Bond, 1994).

Individualism and collectivism are heuristic, culture-related dimensions for understanding relationship processes and outcomes for women and men. At core, these constructs address the relation between the individual and society, and their respective defining characteristics concern the relative importance assigned to the needs/priorities of the individual versus the group. As discussed by Hofstede (1984), in societies characterized as individualistic (e.g., the United States, Canada, and Australia), there is an emphasis on individual rights (rather than duties), self-realization, personal autonomy, and individual initiative. By contrast, in collectivistic societies (e.g., Taiwan, Singapore, Hong Kong), loyalty to the in-group is valued, which in turn protects and looks after the needs of its individual members. Other important features of collectivism include emotional dependency on groups and organizations and personal identity based on one's place in the group.

It is important to distinguish conceptually between societal and personal levels of individualism and collectivism (U. Kim et al., 1994). Members of a given society are likely to differ in the extent to which they endorse cultural values. For example, in a society characterized as individualistic, it cannot be assumed that all its members personally endorse this value orientation. The terms *societal* and *psychological* individualism and collectivism help to distinguish among different levels of analysis for these constructs (K.K. Dion & K.L. Dion, 1993). Hui and Triandis (1986) suggested that individualism at the personal level is reflected in showing less concern for others' needs and highly valuing one's independence, whereas the interdependence underlying collectivism is manifested in concern about bonds with others and responsiveness to their needs. We suggested that there are culture-related differences in self-construal and that these differences are related to the experience of love and intimacy in heterosexual relationships (K.L. Dion & Dion, 1988).

Subsequently, we presented a more fully elaborated conceptual framework on the relation between individualism/collectivism and relationships (K.K. Dion & Dion, 1993). We suggested that at the societal level, individualism is associated with valuing love as a basis for marriage and personal fulfillment through emotional intimacy in marriage. However, some aspects of individualism at the psychological level—notably, valuing personal autonomy and self-reliance—make it more difficult to experience these desired outcomes. For example, we have found that psychological individualism, particularly "self-contained individualism," in which personal autonomy is highly valued, was negatively related to affective involvement with one's romantic partner. This finding occurred after controlling for age and sex as well as psychological collectivism (K.K. Dion & Dion, 1991). It is possible that there are other forms of psychological individualism that facilitate forming and maintaining relationships, and this possibility represents one direction for future research.

Societal collectivism fosters valuing interdependence; however, at the personal level, psychological intimacy less likely to be centered in the relationship with one's spouse but rather is apt to be diffused in a broader set of family relationships (K.K. Dion & Dion, 1993). Iwao (1993) contrasted women's and men's expectations about marriage in Japan and the United States. In contrast to the high expectations for personal fulfillment in marriage among U.S. women and men, among Japanese men and women, many of these needs were fulfilled in other relationships (other family members, friends, coworkers). As discussed by Iwao, the findings from a large sample survey in 1990 comparing U.S. and Japanese women and men documented differences in expectations about marriage. Japanese women rated financial security and having children as more important compared to U.S. women. U.S. women and men viewed romantic love and a good sexual relationship in marriage as more important compared to Japanese women and men. Younger Japanese women attributed greater importance to factors such as "keeping romance alive" in marriage compared to Japanese older women, but the perceived importance of these factors was still less compared to the U.S. sample.

Other researchers have similarly found that U.S. university students endorsed romantic beliefs more strongly than Japanese students (Sprecher et al., 1994). When university students from three countries (France, Japan, and the United States) were asked about the intimacy of a current relationship with an other-sex close friend, Ting-Toomey (1991) found that U.S. and French respondents reported greater "love commitment" (e.g., feelings of attachment) and "disclosure maintenance" (e.g., level of personal disclosure in the relationship) compared to Japanese respondents. U.S. respondents also reported more "relational ambivalence" (e.g., uncertainty about continuing the relationship, feeling pressured or trapped) than Japanese respondents, which may well reflect concerns about maintaining personal freedom and is one aspect of psychological individualism described earlier in this section.

Kamo (1993) found a positive relation between the husband's income and both spouses' reported satisfaction with their marital relationship in a sample of Japanese couples. This relation was absent among U.S. couples, consistent with a more instrumental view of marriage among the Japanese couples. However, a more pragmatic view of marriage does not necessarily imply a lack of caring in the marital relationship. Although U.S. couples reported greater levels of companionship than Japanese couples, companionship was positively related to marital satisfaction for both Japanese and U.S. wives and husbands (Kamo, 1993). Similarly, Iwao (1993, p. 77) noted that given the formality expected in nonfamily social relationships in Japan, the relationship between spouses was unique because both parties could "effortlessly depend on each other."

A qualitative study of a small sample of older U.S. and Japanese couples identified several themes (Ingersoll-Dayton, Campbell, Kurokawa, & Saito, 1996). On average, both groups had been married over four decades. The interview data revealed that both groups reported intimacy with their spouse, but the development of intimacy and the role relationship between spouses showed culture-related differences. U.S. couples characterized their marriage as a partnership from the earliest stages, often referring to themselves as a team. In older adult-hood, an issue for the U.S. women and men interviewed, especially the retired women, was to "negotiate a separate identity and space in which to develop autonomously" (p. 394). The themes identified in this sample of older U.S. couples reflected valuing a high level of psycho-logical intimacy throughout marriage, combined with concerns about maintaining or develop-ing personal autonomy.

By contrast, the Japanese couples in Ingersoll-Dayton et al.'s (1996) study characterized the early phases of their marriage (which, for most of them, had been "arranged") as reflecting "sep-arate spheres of influence." The husband's responsibilities were to his extended family and his work, and the wife's obligations centered around her husband's family. However, Japanese cou-ples reported the development of greater intimacy with their spouse later in their marriage. This change was attributed to various factors, including the husband's greater willingness and ability to express affection; change of the wife's health, requiring more assistance from the husband; and the loss of other close family ties in which a high level of psychological intimacy was previously invested. Themes emerging from the interviews with the Japanese couples suggested that mar-riage was embedded in a larger context of family relationships. Changes in reported intimacy re-flected, in part, changes in the family system.

Cross-cultural analyses of gender and relationships must consider the contribution of societal change and related cohort differences. The participants in the research conducted by Ingersoll-Dayton and her colleagues (1996) were from an earlier cohort of U.S. and Japanese couples. One trend identified in surveys conducted in several Asian societies over the past two decades has been an increase in individualistic value orientations among recent cohorts, especially among university student samples (Cha, 1994; Yang, 1996). This trend can coexist with endorsement of some traditional collectivistic values. It is, therefore, important to examine the structure of con-structs such as psychological individualism and collectivism within different societies when as-sessing their contribution to personal relationships (K.K. Dion & Dion, 1996).

Cross-Cultural Perspectives: Other Cultural Values

Constructs such as individualism and collectivism offer one framework for examining culture and relationships by comparing and contrasting relationship processes in different societies. An-other approach to studying the cultural context of relationships is to examine culturally specific concepts and their implications beyond the society in which they originated. There are many such concepts pertaining to relationships that merit attention in the study of gender and relationships. One illustrative example is the Chinese concept of *yuan,* which at core refers to a type of "rela-tional fatalism" (R. Goodwin & Findlay, 1997). The development of a relationship is believed to be affected by contextual factors beyond the control of the individual; hence, its success or failure is less attributable to individual qualities (R. Goodwin & Tang, 1996).

R. Goodwin and Findlay (1997) compared beliefs in yuan and correlates of these beliefs in Hong Kong Chinese university students and British students. Cultural differences were found, with Chi-nese students endorsing this concept more strongly. However, British students, too, showed some endorsement of beliefs concerning "fated" aspects of relationships. There were no gender differ-ences nor interaction between gender and culture on the overall scale. Beliefs in yuan were posi-tively related to pragmatic and altruistic attitudes toward love but negatively related to erotic beliefs about love, using a standard "love styles" measure.

A content analysis of Chinese (mainland China and Hong Kong) and U.S. popular love songs from the late 1980s and early 1990s revealed no differences for themes of "intense desire," but the Chinese songs were more likely to express negative outcomes and suffering associated with love (Rothbaum & Tsang, 1998). Rothbaum and Tsang suggested that this greater expectation of suf-fering was consistent with yuan. If the romantic partners did not have this predestined affinity, the relationship would falter regardless of personal effort. Although the concept of yuan reflects distinct religious and philosophical traditions, as R. Goodwin and Findlay (1997) noted, this con-cept has parallels with Western views of romantic love as a mysterious force, with lovers predes-tined to be together. This point illustrates that indigenous cultural concepts, such as yuan, can be relevant for understanding relationship processes beyond a specific society.

GENDER AND ETHNOCULTURAL DIVERSITY IN PERSONAL RELATIONSHIPS:
INTRACULTURAL PERSPECTIVES

Cultural perspectives on personal relationships focus attention not only on comparisons across different societies but also on ethnocultural diversity within societies (see Gaines, 1997; McAdoo, 1999; Mindel, Habenstein, & Wright, 1988a). Within a specific society, the relation of gender to different domains of adulthood may differ depending on cultural values. For example, many issues identified as important for understanding the psychology of women have been mostly based on research with White, middle-class women (K.K. Dion, 1985; Peplau, Veniegas, Taylor, & DeBro, 1999). There are signs, however, of greater convergence between the study of gender and of ethnocultural factors (Veniegas, Taylor, & Peplau, 1999).

Ethnic groups have been defined as those that "share a unique social and cultural heritage that is passed on from generation to generation" (Mindel, Habenstein, & Wright, 1988b, p. 5). In the United States, scholarly discussions of ethnicity have increasingly moved away from the metaphor of the melting pot to other images (Mindel et al., 1988b). Canada, with its policy of multiculturalism, officially recognizes diversity; salient themes in research conducted by psychologists and other social scientists in Canada have included topics such as ethnic identity, intergroup processes, and the social psychology of language (K.L. Dion, 2000). The remainder of this section examines research illustrating the contribution of ethnocultural values when studying gender and relationships. The examples cited are from the United States, but the importance of considering culture-related values can be applied to other ethnically diverse societies.

A number of scholars have suggested that among Black Americans, an African American worldview is reflected in collectivistic values such as interdependence, mutual support, and cooperation (e.g., Asante, 1980; Gaines, 1997; Nobles, 1978). Y.R. Bell, Bouie, and Baldwin (1990) found that African self-consciousness (Baldwin & Bell, 1985) was positively related to Afrocentric values in the context of heterosexual relationships. The relationship attributes surveyed included qualities preferred in an ideal mate, heterosexual attitudes, and responses to a hypothetical scenario about a relationship crisis/hardship. A distinctive feature of this research was the inclusion of four different groups of Black respondents: university students, unskilled workers, professionals, and older adults drawn from Black churches. Compared to their younger and more educated counterparts, older and less educated adults were more likely to endorse unconditional support (i.e., the more communal alternative) when asked how they would respond to the hypothetical crisis (dealing with unemployment or illness of one's partner that resulted in one's bearing most of the responsibility for the family).

In a nationally representative survey of Black men and women in the United States, high levels of family solidarity were reported by over 90% of the sample (Hatchett & Jackson, 1999). There were, however, several sociodemographic variables related to interaction with and aid from kin. In other words, Hatchett and Jackson's and Y.R. Bell et al.'s (1990) research illustrates the need to examine the structural and individual variables that contribute to personal relationships within an ethnocultural community.

Another example of an important culture-related value is familialism/familism, which, along with other values such as "simpatia" (valuing interpersonal harmony), contributes to understanding personal relationships among Hispanic Americans (Chahin, Villarruel, & Viramontez, 1999). Familialism refers to valuing strong identification with the family unit and solidarity among family members (Chahin et al., 1999). For example, comparing Anglo-American and Mexican American young adults (mostly university students), Freeberg and Stein (1996) examined the relation between "felt obligation" to one's parents and several cultural values. Of interest here, Mexican American men and women endorsed collectivism and familism on separate measures more strongly than did their Anglo-American peers. Felt obligation was defined in terms of respondents' expectations as to how they should behave with family members in areas such as participation in family rituals, avoiding conflict, giving help. Among the Mexican American but not the Anglo-American respondents, cultural values (especially collectivism and familism) predicted the extent of felt obligation to family, specifically one's parents (scores averaged across expectations for behavior toward each parent).

Women's role in maintaining family bonds and values is evident across diverse ethnocultural communities. For example, Mexican American and Anglo-American respondents reported a greater sense of felt obligation to their mothers compared to their fathers (Freeberg & Stein, 1996). Consistent with other research, Hatchett and Jackson (1999) found that Black women reported more frequent interaction with kin than did Black men. The importance of American Indian women for preserving and transmitting cultural values has likewise been repeatedly documented (Kawamoto & Cheshire, 1999; LaFromboise, Heyle, & Ozer, 1999).

Cultural values are also important for understanding both other-sex and same-sex personal relationships between individuals from different ethnic or racial groups. These individuals often must contend with not only their own development as a couple but also the reactions of family members and others within and outside their respective communities (see Blea, 1992; K.L. Dion & Dion, 1996; Morales, 1990). The prevalence of interethnic and interracial marriage has increased, with the frequency and type of intermarriage in the United States varying for different groups (see D. Wilkinson, 1999). A sensitive discussion of some of the issues that can arise is presented in Rosenblatt, Karis, and Powell's (1995) qualitative study, conducted with a small group of interracial heterosexual couples in which one partner was Black and the other White. The interviews not only suggested areas for future study but also challenged views of these relationships. When asked about their relationship, most couples emphasized "feeling ordinary." Rosenblatt and his colleagues suggested that this view of their relationship might serve to challenge others' reactions (e.g., family opposition, stares from strangers). However, the researchers also noted that one cost of this stance might be a tendency for couples to deny or minimize differences in culture-related values. If so, relationship-related stresses might be attributed to the partner's personality, rather than acknowledging and working out ways of resolving differences in values (Rosenblatt et al., 1995).

Explicitly examining cultural values offers several insights about the contribution of gender to personal relationships within ethnically heterogeneous societies. As various scholars have noted (e.g., Gaines, 1997; Le Espiritu, 1997), it is important to challenge stereotypic assumptions about relationships and interpersonal behavior attributed to women and men from various ethnocultural groups. Research that addresses culture-related issues is one way of contributing to this process. Illustrating this point, since the mid-1970s, the social science literature on ethnicity and family relationships has increasingly documented the strength and cohesion of families from diverse groups rather than focusing only on problems in family functioning (D. Wilkinson, 1999). Finally, it is also important to study the factors that contribute to individual differences within ethnocultural communities in endorsing specific values, such as familism, collectivism, and individualism, and the implications of these differences for personal relationships.

CONCLUDING REMARKS

Our goal in writing this chapter has been to provide a framework that not only discusses current theory and research but also suggests promising directions for future research. In current theories of relationships, for the most part, it has been those theories rooted in biosocial and evolutionary assumptions that have explicitly focused on gender. In other major theories, such as attachment theory and investment theory, gender per se has not been a central focus. The guiding assumption in this latter group of theories is that once basic relationship processes are identified, gender similarities and differences in the outcomes of these processes can be studied, along with their applicability to gender-related issues (e.g., applying the investment model to understand the behavior of women in abusive relationships). This approach is a valuable one, and we have reviewed some of this research in this chapter.

However, as some other research in this chapter illustrates, gender can also be the starting point for interesting hypotheses about relationship processes. For example, research such as Coltrane's (1996) suggests the importance of the social construction of gender for understanding relationship processes. Hopefully, researchers interested in the study of gender and relationships will consider this type of approach when formulating theories of relationships.

Another promising direction for future research is the explicit consideration of cultural context when studying gender and relationships. We have devoted a major section of this chapter to examining culture-related factors, specifically, the role of cultural values. This perspective is relevant at several levels. Theories of personal relationships themselves emerge from particular cultural contexts and may or may not be applicable across different societies. One attempt to address this issue in cross-cultural psychology has been the search for culturally universal or etic dimensions to permit comparison. Some of these dimensions have been heuristic when applied to the study of women's and men's personal relationships. However, it is also the case that more culture-specific (emic) constructs can offer insights. Moreover, given the ethnic heterogeneity of many societies and related trends such as immigration and geographic mobility within societies, ethnocultural perspectives will be increasingly important in the 21st century. Ultimately, the inclusion of cultural factors in theory and research will contribute to a more comprehensive understanding of gender and personal relationships.

CHAPTER 18

Sexualities

CELIA KITZINGER

It has become a truism of contemporary feminist scholarship that sexuality and gender are intimately interrelated. What exactly this means, and what its implications might be for developing theory, research, and practice is rather less clear. Over most of the course of their long histories, research on sexuality and on gender have remained largely distinctive fields of inquiry. In sexuality research, gender has generally been treated as no more than a variable to be factored in (along with class, race/ethnicity, age, etc.) as a pre-defined property of research participants and correlated with different sexual experiences (e.g. Kinsey, Pomeroy, & Martin, 1948; Kinsey, Pomeroy, Martin, & Gebhard, 1953; Masters & Johnson, 1966). The role of gender in the construction of sexual behaviors and identities was barely considered, such that "maleness and masculinity provide the normative base line for understanding all human sexuality" (B.E. Schneider & Gould, 1987, p. 131). With the development of lesbian and gay psychology in the mid-1970s, gender achieved a much higher profile although rarely from a specifically feminist perspective. It remains true that most research on sexuality is not informed by feminist concerns and that, through the assumptions built into its design, it actively precludes an understanding of the co-construction of genders and sexualities.

Not surprisingly, then, sexuality research—including the relatively new field of lesbian and gay (and, subsequently, bisexual and transgender) psychology—has not been very attractive to feminist psychologists, and (with some important exceptions, e.g. Tiefer, 1978), few feminist psychologists have ventured into this field until recently. Most feminist psychology continues to assume a generic heterosexual woman: by and large it ignores or glosses over sexual diversity and demonstrates a wilful ignorance of lesbian, gay, bisexual, and transgender (henceforth LGBT) issues (see C. Kitzinger, 1996). The observation (frequently made in psychology of women) that oppressions are "interconnected" or "braided" often functions as a throw-away remark—an attempt to "acknowledge diversity"—rather than as a move toward theorising just *how* they are interrelated, and the implications of that. As someone who works both in psychology of women and in LGBT psychology, I am struck by the gulf between them: each proceeds without much awareness of advances in the other, and there is an extraordinary lack of cross-referencing. An important aim of this chapter is to bridge the gulf by demonstrating the importance, for those concerned with women and gender, of taking sexuality research seriously.

Psychology of women/gender has a lot to gain from a more sustained and committed engagement with LGBT psychology (as, of course, does LGBT psychology from feminism, C. Kitzinger, 1987). This chapter is organized around three such benefits. First, LGBT psychology has evolved its own theories of oppression and analyses of resistance which, although often developed apparently in complete independence of the theories developed by feminists, nonetheless show some important parallels. We can develop a more sophisticated feminist understanding of oppression and resistance if we consider how such issues are theorized in other arenas, and the political costs and benefits associated with those theories. Second, as feminists have noted, women have traditionally been defined in purely sexual terms—by which is meant *hetero*sexual terms. However, with a few notable exceptions—some of them explicitly written as responses to *lesbian* theorizing of heterosexuality (e.g. Hollway, 1993; L. Segal, 1994; see also Tolman & Brown, this volume)—psychology of women/gender has "naturalized" rather than interrogated heterosexuality and has occluded the experiences both of women and of men who do not engage in heterosexual sex. Taking lesbian and gay psychology seriously means more than simply "adding in" lesbians (and gay men) to heterosexual feminist psychology. It means re-thinking established feminist theories, reworking feminist models of development, and creating a renewed psychology of women. Third, although some early feminist psychology addressed the interrelationship of genders and sexualities as social constructions (e.g., S.J. Kessler & McKenna, 1978), this has never been a central area of psychology of women, and is relatively rare in contemporary (especially empirical) work (see C. Kitzinger, 1994b). By contrast, the notion that lesbian and gay identities are constructed has been one thread of lesbian and gay social science at least since the late 1960s (e.g., M. McIntosh, 1968, see also Weeks, 1998), and this is particularly the case since the emergence of social constructionist, postmodern, and Queer theory, which has challenged not just lesbian, gay, and heterosexual as essentialist categories, but also male and female. LGBT psychology's greater involvement with social constructionist and postmodern theorizing poses important challenges for the psychology of women/gender.

The organization of this chapter is as follows. The development of LGBT psychology is first outlined as a field, and discussed in terms of the contribution it can make to psychology of women/gender in relation to the three themes just outlined: theories of oppression, heterosexist assumptions in psychology of women, and the development of social constructionist approaches to genders/sexualities. All three themes point in different ways to the importance of the complex interrelationship between genders and sexualities, and their implications are highlighted in the concluding section.

In charting the development of LGBT psychology and in outlining these three themes, this chapter draws on research using a range of different (and sometimes incompatible) methodologies, theories, and epistemologies. Although both psychology of women/gender and LGBT psychology share mainstream psychology's preoccupation with quantification, positivist-empiricism and essentialism, both also embrace some social constructionist and postmodern work. Elsewhere I have argued for the political value of *both* essentialism/positivism and social constructionism/postmodernism in charting and resisting oppression (C. Kitzinger, 1995a) and my aim in this chapter is to speak to adherents of both positions, rather than to engage in a lengthy defense of one or attack of the other. Here, then, I work with both approaches—each on its own terms (for discussion of the contradictions between different approaches see Wilkinson, this volume). My primary aim is to illustrate that, irrespective of one's broader theoretical/epistemological allegiance, researchers working in the field of psychology of women/gender need more comprehensively to draw on, and to integrate into their own work, research and theory derived from LGBT psychology.

LGBT PSYCHOLOGY: THE DEVELOPMENT OF THE FIELD

Just as the contemporary field of psychology of women developed in response to the male power and female oppression, so the contemporary field of LGBT psychology developed in response to social and political discrimination against anyone who is not (or who is assumed not to be) heterosexual. This oppression is far-reaching and deep-seated across a range of cultures and societies, including those in which feminist psychologists are developing their own theories—theories which, overwhelmingly, do *not* recognize or address the pervasive effects of compulsory heterosexuality (as much on the psychology of heterosexuals as on lesbians and gay men).

Lesbians, gay men, and other nonheterosexuals are discriminated against and oppressed to varying degrees in laws and social policies across the world. Until the early 1990s, nearly one half of the states in the United States outlawed private consenting homosexual acts, and their right to do so had been upheld by the U.S. Supreme Court in 1986 (Herek, 1998). Same-sex sexual acts are still illegal in more than seventy countries and are punishable with prison sentences (e.g., Bermuda, Nigeria, Trinidad, Romania); beatings (e.g., India, Pakistan); and execution (e.g., Iran, Kuwait, Saudi Arabia) (Amnesty International, 1997). In the United States, where, according to one recent survey, 54% of the population believe homosexuality to be a "sin" (Peyser, 1998), crimes of violence and harassment against lesbians and gay men are endemic. A comprehensive overview of antigay violence and victimization found that up to 92% of lesbians and gay men report having been the targets of anti-gay verbal abuse or threats, 24% report physical attack, and 75% expected to be the targets of future harassment because of their sexual identity: attacks are often not reported for fear of secondary victimization by the police or the courts (Herek & Berrill, 1992). In most countries, lesbians and gay men also face widespread discrimination in education, in the workplace, and in healthcare (Bradford & Ryan, 1988; D. Epstein & Johnson, 1998; D. Herman & Stychin, 1995; Saphira & Glover, 1999; see also Chrisler, this volume). Heterosexual privilege is manifested in the U.S. Congress Defense of Marriage Act, explicitly restricting the institution of marriage to opposite-sex partners—a restriction which, to date, applies across the world—and in widespread legislation that gives these married opposite-sex partners rights which are denied to same sex couples. Lesbians and gay men are denied the rights extended to heterosexuals in relation to the custody, adoption, and fostering of children; access to fertility services; domestic partner benefits; including insurance, health and pension schemes; tax and inheritance rights for couples; housing; and immigration rights (S.J. Ellis, 1999). Florida and New Hampshire, for example, have enacted legislation that prohibits gays and lesbians from qualifying as foster or adoptive parents (McLeod & Crawford, 1998). These forms of discrimination are increasingly recognized as human rights violations.

Historically, psychology collaborated in the oppression of lesbians and gay men. Heterosexist legislation and social discrimination was justified and excused with reference to psychological research demonstrating homosexual pathology. With the emergence of the new science of psychology at the turn of the last century, the Judeo-Christian legacy of homosexuality as sin was translated into homosexuality as sickness (e.g., Bloch, 1909; Forel, 1908; Krafft-Ebing, 1882). From then until the mid-1970s, the vast bulk of this research supported the view that lesbians and gay men were sick in one way or another—the products of disturbed upbringings, or the perverted results of genetic mishaps (see Rosario, 1997 for a review of this literature). In the same way as feminist activists challenged androcentric research, so lesbian and gay liberation activists challenged these heterosexist views. In 1973, activists caused major disruption at the meetings of the American Psychiatric Association, which subsequently conceded that homosexuality, in and of itself, was not an illness, and removed it as such from its *Diagnostic and Statistical Manual*. It took a further twenty years before (in 1993) homosexuality was removed from the World Health Organization's International Classification of Diseases, the diagnostic handbook generally used outside North America. The American Psychological Association adopted, in 1975, the official policy that homosexuality per se does not imply any kind of mental health impairment, and urged mental health professionals "to take the lead in removing the stigma of mental illness that has long been associated with homosexual orientation" (see Rothblum & Bond, 1996, p. x). However, no such statement has ever been made by other national psychological organizations. The British Psychological Society, for example, has so far remained conspicuously silent during various political debates in which other professional groups challenged heterosexist legislation (e.g., Section 28 of the Local Government Act that prevents the "promotion" of homosexuality as a "pretended family relationship"; and the discriminatory Age of Consent legislation of eighteen for a man with a male partner, compared with sixteen for a man with a female partner).

The field of "lesbian and gay psychology" was given institutional recognition with the formation, in 1984 of a formal Division (Division 44) within the American Psychological Association, devoted to the psychological study of lesbian and gay issues, and since the mid-1980s, lesbian and gay psychology has established itself within North American psychology. In 1995, a Special Interest Group in Lesbian and Psychology was established within the Australian Psychological Society, and in 1998, after a nine-year campaign, and three rejected proposals (in part a consequence of the refusal of the BPS Psychology of Women Section to support the proposal, see C. Kitzinger, 1996), a parallel grouping for lesbian and gay psychologists was finally established within the British Psychological Society (Comely, Kitzinger, Perkins, & Wilkinson, 1993; C. Kitzinger, 1999b; C. Kitzinger, Coyle, Wilkinson, & Milton, 1998). Although informal groupings of lesbian and gay psychologists exist in other countries, no other national psychological societies have established parallel subsystems: in New Zealand, for example, the first lesbian and gay psychologists' caucus meeting was held at the 1978 national psychology society meeting at Massey university (Lapsley & Ritchie, 1997, p. 28) and a lesbian psychologists' group existed for a while, but without any official affiliation to the New Zealand Psychological Society—although there has been some informal discussion of this as a possibility (Lapsley & Paulin, 1994, p. 25; Lapsley & Ritchie, 1997, p. 28).

Although anti-gay prejudice and discrimination is still apparent within some psychological theory and practice (see Annesley & Coyle, 1995; Chernin, Holden, & Chandler, 1997; C. Kitzinger, 1990a, 1996; Milton & Coyle, 1998; Simoni, 1996), it does not now receive explicit support from psychological bodies, or from expert researchers, and it is rare to find overt reference, within Anglo-American psychological writing, to homosexuality *per se* as pathology (Morin & Rothblum, 1991). There are exceptions: individual psychologists sometimes display absurdly anachronistic heterosexist prejudices (e.g., M. Davis, 1995; V. Hamilton, 1995) and there are a few mavericks whose more sustained anti-lesbian and anti-gay arguments make them much courted by the media (see Herek, 1998). However, in general, feminist psychologists are doing nothing to distinguish themselves from the mainstream of psychology when they proclaim lesbian mental health or "normality." As Squire (1989, pp. 39–40) pointed out some time ago—and it is still more the case today—"as conventional psychological studies of lesbians become more tolerant, and egalitarian-feminist psychological studies of these subjects become more psychological, it is increasingly difficult to distinguish between the two."

There is, however, a backlog of nearly a century of psychological research that assumes homosexual pathology and near-universal "natural" heterosexuality, and contemporary psychology (both mainstream and feminist) continues to base its theories and practices on a taken-for-granted but never explicitly articulated substrate of heterosexuality. The classic models of lifespan development, interpersonal attraction, relationship formation and dissolution, parenting, personality, stress and coping, and so on are based on an unacknowledged assumption of heterosexuality just as surely as they are based on sexist assumptions of masculinity and femininity. When psychology (including psychology of women) incorporates into its theory and practice an unstated assumption that virtually everyone is unproblematically heterosexual (with nonheterosexuals assigned tokenistic mentions under the heading of "diversity" or "difference" it perpetuates an "unexamined heterocentricity" (Rich, 1989), and this is still the case for much psychology of women today (see C. Kitzinger, 1996). Simply challenging the "sexism" of traditional psychology is not enough. The psychology of women/gender needs to engage with lesbian/gay psychology to understand and to challenge the heterocentricity built into theories of women/gender, without which oppression of women cannot be properly understood.

THEORIZING OPPRESSION

The earliest formulation of oppression, within lesbian and gay psychology, as within psychology of women, was as a personality or attitude problem. Paralleling the early focus of research within psychology of women on attitudes toward women, some of the earliest research by lesbian and gay psychologists was directed to exploring the causes and correlates of anti-lesbian and anti-gay attitudes and behaviors, and this has remained an important area of the field.

The term *homophobia* first began to appear in psychology in the late 1960s and early 1970s and was defined as "an irrational persistent fear or dread of homosexual" (A.P. MacDonald, 1976) or "an irrational fear or intolerance of homosexuality" (Lehne, 1976). Subsequently, homophobia scales were developed (e.g., G.L. Hansen, 1982; Herek, 1988; Larsen, Reed, & Hoffman, 1980) and these are still widely used in studies which correlate individual levels of antilesbian and antigay prejudice with various personality traits, or which carry out laboratory experiments on people with differing levels of "homophobia." High levels of homophobia are purportedly associated with being more authoritarian, less well-educated, more religious, more politically conservative and endorsing traditional sex roles (e.g., Haddock, Zanna, & Esses, 1993), and many studies report that people are significantly more likely to be homophobic if they have a religious affiliation (e.g., C.S. Berkman & Zinberg, 1997) and if they are male (e.g., Donnelly et al., 1997; Schellenberg, Hirt, & Sears, 1999). Many LGBT psychologists pre-empted the arguments of queer theorists in other disciplines (who draw from psychoanalysis rather than from psychometric scaling, e.g., Sedgwick, 1990) in claiming that fear and anxiety about homosexuality stems "from personal insecurities about personal adequacy in meeting gender-role demands" (Herek, 1986, p. 566). It is, however, almost always men's homophobia (hatred of gay *men*) which is discussed as a way of displaying masculinity, and which is described as being "inherent in the cultural construction of heterosexual male role and identity" (Harry, 1992; Herek, 1986, p. 566; see also Herek, 1990) and there is virtually no discussion of *women's* prejudices, or of antilesbianism under the "gender panic" rubric.

While neatly reversing the diagnostic label, such that it is now "homophobes" rather than homosexuals who are "sick," this work has been criticized for its narrowly individualistic focus (e.g., C. Kitzinger & Perkins, 1993) that ignores the oppression of lesbians and gay men as a *social* phenomenon, incorporated into the fabric of society, rather than caused by the actions of a few "sick" individuals suffering from a diagnosable phobia. Antilesbian and antigay expression is in fact *normal* in a heterosexist society: for example, a U.S. national survey of males aged 15 to 19 found that few (12%) felt they could have a gay friend and that most (89%) considered sex between males to be "disgusting" (Marsiglio, 1993). Even right-wing researchers are willing to accept a construction of "homophobia" as pathological, and use this definition to exempt their own antilesbian and antigay arguments—as illustrated by this extract from a publication produced by Focus on the Family:

> Genuine homophobia requires professional help. To be genuinely homophobic, a person must manifest an *irrational* fear or hatred of homosexuals. [. . .] What isn't homophobic is a reasoned, principled, even compassionate denial of the moral normalcy of homosexual acts. Nor is it homophobic to oppose social policies and legislation which grant protected status to those who engage in homosexual acts. (Burtoft, 1994, p. 80)

Moreover, the concept of homophobia, initially developed to pathologize *heterosexuals,* was very quickly applied to lesbians and gay men, who were supposed to suffer from internalized homophobia ("the oppressor within," Margolies, Becker, & Jackson-Brewer, 1987, p. 229). Work on internalized homophobia has been described as "a central organizing concept for a gay and lesbian affirmative psychology" (Shidlo, 1994, p. 176), and work in this area parallels early (and continuing) work in psychology of women on women's alleged low self-esteem, fear of success, loss of voice, false consciousness, and internalization of patriarchal discourses (see Wilkinson, 1999 for an overview). The idea that lesbians and gay men are psychologically damaged by heterosexism (just as women are psychologically damaged by sexism) runs throughout lesbian and gay psychology and has been used to explain the many ways in which lesbians and gay men allegedly oppress themselves. According to some of this literature, we are unable to accept our own homosexuality, riddled with guilt and self-hatred, and hence deliberately seek out situations in which we can experience pain and failure. Lesbians and gay men may "maintain a victim attitude" (B. Decker, 1983, p. 40), and "develop a need for self-punishment" which becomes "a self-fulfilling prophecy" (Groves, 1985, p. 20), when they "set themselves up for rejection with poorly planned and impulsive disclosure in an environment that is likely to produce a harsh response" (Gonsiorek, 1995, p. 34). Lesbian, gay, and bisexual people are now supposed to suffer from "minority stress" which is associated with adverse mental health consequences (I.H. Meyer, 1995).

Worrying political implications attach themselves to the concept of homophobia, including, for example, court cases in which the murderers of gay men have pleaded provocation (i.e., in the form of sexual advances from their victims), and contended that they are suffering from homophobia, using this alleged mental health problem as a reason for a reduction in their sentence (Forde, 1999). By contrast, other research locates the problem of antilesbian and antigay attitudes and behaviors not in individual psychologies but in social, political, and institutional organization, for example, research on institutional "climate" for lesbians and gay men (e.g., Eliason, 1996; Malaney, Williams, & Geller, 1997) work taking an explicitly human rights perspective (e.g., S.J. Ellis, 1999), and research on hate crimes. The latter, in particular, has been successful as a sociopolitical intervention in lobbying for the inclusion of "sexual orientation" in the (North American) Hate Crimes Statistics Act, which required the Department of Justice to collect and publish annual statistics on crimes that manifest prejudice based on race, religion, and ethnic origin: this was achieved in 1990, so enabling documentation of the problem of antilesbian and antigay violence (Herek & Berrill, 1992).

The psychology of women/gender embodies (sometimes implicit) theories of oppression which in many ways parallel those of lesbian and gay psychology (e.g., sexism as individual psychological pathology, as a "chilly climate" problem, as a human rights violation). Yet despite acknowledgment of the intersections between gender and sexuality, there has been little attempt seriously to address the relationship between these theories of gender oppression and sexuality oppression, or to explore the implications of these parallel approaches. On the contrary, it has sometimes been the case—both within and beyond psychology—that attempts have been made to advance women's liberation *at the expense of* lesbians (and, equally, to advance gay liberation *at the expense of* women) (C. Kitzinger, 1996).

Psychology of women/gender can gain in theoretical sophistication and explanatory power by routinely addressing heterosexism, whatever the research topic. Generally invoked only when LGBT-identified individuals are included in the research sample, the concept of compulsory heterosexuality and the insights of LGBT research are relevant even in research in which there are (as far as is known) no LGBT participants. For example, LGBT research on the experiences of young people with same-sex sexual experience graphically illustrates the power of compulsory heterosexuality in shaping people's lives. Up to half of lesbian and gay male adults report having experienced some form of victimization in school (Berrill, 1990) or at home (J. Hunter, 1990), and one study found that more than a third reported having been verbally abused, and 10% physically assaulted by a family member because of their sexual orientation (N.W. Pilkington & D'Augelli, 1995). There is also an increased rate of suicide attempts and suicides among lesbian, gay, and bisexual youth (Remafedi, Farrow, & Deisher, 1991). Young people with same-sex experiences (irrespective of the sexual identities they later adopt) experience near universal conflicts about same-sex sexuality: "because a primary developmental task of adolescence is the consolidation of personal identity, the growing awareness of homo-erotic desires during this time, along with the knowledge that these feelings are condemned by others, may lead to considerable intrapsychic conflict and anxiety" (Savin-Williams, 1994, p. 174). Fear of being (or being seen as) lesbian or gay is one reason for unwanted heterosexual activity in adolescence (for both girls and boys) and this may be particularly the case for young people who fail to conform to cultural ideals of sex-appropriate masculine or feminine behavior, and who (whether or not they have same-sex sexual interests) are often subjected to heterosexist bullying at school (Savin-Williams, 1994). It is increasingly recognized that it is in part the threat to *gender* posed by lesbians, bisexuals, and gay men that underlies heterosexism. Through heterosexism "any male who refuses to accept the dominant culture's assignment of appropriate masculine behavior is labelled early on as a 'sissy' or 'fag' and then subjected to bullying" (K. Franklin, 1998, p. 7) and "any woman who opposes male dominance and control can be labelled a lesbian and attacked" (K. Franklin, 1998, p. 8; see also A. Hunter, 1993). Recent feminist psychological work has begun seriously to address the intersection of gender and sexuality oppression includes studies of the ways in which the institutional power of compulsory heterosexuality shapes *heterosexual* people's experience, for example, how it circumscribes the same-sex friendships of both heterosexual females (Griffin, 2000) and heterosexual males (Wetherell & Edley, 1999).

Heterosexism, then, is one of the ways in which strict adherence to gender role stereotypes is enforced, and gender oppression maintained. Theories of gender oppression and sexuality oppression have a lot to learn from each other, and there is value for feminists in understanding the practical contingencies and the successes and failures of the various approaches taken within LGBT research, and relate them to their own.

MORE THAN "INCLUSION": MOVING HETEROSEXUALITY OUT OF THE SHADOWS

There has been, for some time, a move to "include" lesbian and bisexual women in research purporting to address "women's" experience, and this is, of course, an important development. Just as traditional psychology apparently did not notice its assumption of "male as norm" and its exclusion of women, so psychology of women often has not noticed its own assumption of "heterosexual" as norm, and its exclusion of alternatives. Although most feminist psychology textbooks do now index a few pages on lesbians, we are still excluded from—or given merely token acknowledgment in—many psychology of women books. For example, lesbians are not mentioned at all in Carol Tavris' (1992) (otherwise excellent) *The Mismeasure of Women*—although lesbians have undeniably borne the brunt of a great deal of psychological mismeasurement; there are only two passing references to lesbians (a sentence each) in Ussher and Nicolson's (1992) *Gender Issues in*

Clinical Psychology, and Choi and Nicolson's (1994) volume on *Female Sexuality* deals with lesbian-ism in a chapter called "Sexual Orientation in Women," and lesbians are ignored elsewhere in the book including, for example, in chapters on postnatal sexuality and sexuality and the menopause, both of which use the terms *sex* and *intercourse* interchangeably. Nonheterosexual women are often "included" only as items in a list of "inessential" (Spelman, 1988) identities, flagged under headings such as "diversity" or "difference," and sometimes (in textbooks) boxed off from the main text. This serves only to illustrate the persistent assumption of heterosexuality from which we differ:

> One group of women have taken their own situation to be that of "women in general," and now, in order not to have an account of "the condition of women" that is as exclusionary as masculinist accounts of "the situation of man," differences among women must be discussed. (Spelman, 1988, p. 182)

Lesbian and gay psychologists have pointed out "the fallacy of assuming that everyone is het-erosexual, or that all important research questions shall be defined from the point of view of heterosexuals" (Garnets & Kimmel, 1993, p. 600).

Leaving lesbians and bisexuals out of the research group referred to simply as "women" (and leaving gays and bisexuals out of the research group referred to simply as "men") obviously has the effect of rendering lesbians, bisexuals, and gay men invisible. But more than this, it also makes *heterosexuality* invisible—just as maleness/masculinity was rendered invisible in tradi-tional research with exclusively male participants, whose maleness was never interrogated, and who were treated as representing not men, but humanity (see Tavris, 1992). One benefit of includ-ing lesbians in research on women is that it makes *heterosexuality* visible. There is of course a great deal of psychological research on and about heterosexual people, but most treats its (assumed) heterosexual participants as generic persons and rarely interrogates the specific implications of their heterosexuality.

For example, most psychological research of heterosexuals *as heterosexuals* still exists largely as an offshoot of research on other sexualities for which heterosexuals are constituted as a control group. This comparative research is usually aimed at demonstrating that lesbians (or whoever) are "just as" something (just as mentally healthy, just as feminine, just as good mothers, etc.) as heterosexual women. We can, however, inspect comparative research of this type, and the LGBT literature more generally, for what it reveals about *heterosexuality*. In some of the earliest lesbian and gay psychological research, standard psychological tests administered to both heterosexual women and lesbians revealed that heterosexual women score *higher* on neuroticism (Siegelman, 1972; M. Wilson & Green, 1971), tension (Hopkins, 1969), anxiety (Ohlson & Wilson, 1974) and de-pression (Siegelman, 1972) which might have led us to ask what it is about heterosexuality that makes women neurotic, tense, anxious, and depressed. Instead, of course, lesbian and gay re-searchers simply treated heterosexual women as the control group and used their findings to demonstrate that lesbians are at least as mentally healthy as heterosexual women; and (heterosex-ual) feminist psychologists followed their lead in reporting the results in this way, without ever apparently wondering what this meant about *heterosexuality* for women. Although the classic study by Gove (1972) revealed that marriage is good for men's psychological health and bad for women's, this has been used to argue for more egalitarian marriages, rather than to interrogate heterosexuality per se.

Similarly, research on lesbian and gay parenting has been overwhelming designed as respon-sive to the general assumption that, compared with heterosexual parents, gay and lesbian parents have adverse effects on the psychological and social development of their children (C.J. Patterson, 1992). Some of this research literature offers evidence of possible *benefits* of lesbian/gay parent-ing, including greater interpersonal intimacy between parents and children (Bigner & Bozett, 1990), and the development of greater empathy for others and tolerance for alternative viewpoints in the children of lesbians and gays (C.J. Patterson, 1992): Again, this might lead us to ask what it is about heterosexual parenting that might inhibit these desirable characteristics. Most of it, though, simply demonstrates that lesbians and gay men can create couple relationships as stable as those of heterosexuals, have parenting skills as effective as do heterosexuals, and that the chil-dren of lesbian and gay parents do not differ from the children of heterosexual parents in overall social or psychological adjustment, nor are they any more likely than heterosexuals' children to be lesbian or gay themselves (Flaks, Ficher, Masterpasqua, & Joseph, 1995; Golombok & Tasker, 1996; C.J. Patterson, 1994). It is repeatedly found that "gay parents and their children do not differ significantly from the norm" (McLeod & Crawford, 1998, p. 211). If this is the case, then, as Tasker and Golombok (1997) point out, it necessitates a fundamental reworking of the way we conceive of child development within psychology, in that parental influence (particularly in the development of gender and sexuality) is far less significant than previously thought. Just as adding women in to traditional psychology necessitated some fundamental rethinking of established theories, so too adding LGBT people in to feminist (and mainstream) psychology cannot be adequately achieved without reworking existing models.

Lifespan developmental research in LGBT psychology (see D'Augelli & Patterson, 1995 for an overview) has likewise posed challenges to heterosexual psychology in this area. Research on midlife lesbians is a case in point. By midlife, many lesbians have spent their years learning to define themselves independently of other people's reactions. By contrast, as D.C. Kimmel and Sang, 1995 point out, for many traditional heterosexual women midlife is a time when women whose lives have been oriented around care taking, finally begin to search for their own identity, separate from children and husbands. Compared with lesbians, midlife heterosexual women are less likely to have had a continuous work history prior to midlife, and are half as likely to be living alone (17% vs. 27%) (Bradford & Ryan, 1991). And whereas menopausal lesbians, overwhelmingly (75%) report that their sex lives are as good or better than ever, menopausal heterosexual women express a great deal of concern about their changing sexuality (E.R. Cole & Rothblum, 1991).

In writing these paragraphs, I have had systematically to reverse the claims I am reporting: in each case, the original took heterosexual women, not lesbians, as the point of comparison (i.e., I have rewritten sentences which read "compared with heterosexuals, lesbians as twice as likely. . . ." as "compared with lesbians, heterosexuals are half as likely . . ."). Just as much sex differences research takes male-as-norm (C. Kitzinger, 1994a), so LGBT and feminist research has too often taken heterosexual-as-norm. This unaccustomed reversal, dislocating maleness and heterosexuality from their taken-for-granted position at the center of the conceptual universe, typically causes incomprehension, discomfort, or anger in those who are used to their own experience taking center-stage (see, for example, many of the responses to the *Heterosexuality* Special Issue of *Feminism & Psychology*, reprinted in S. Wilkinson & Kitzinger, 1993a). As it happens, my own social constructionist perspective means that I am not particularly convinced by the results of the psychometric and comparative research cited above (irrespective of whether or not they represent lesbians in a "good" light). My aim is not to claim that heterosexual women are psychologically less healthy than lesbians, but simply to point out that there is already in existence a literature which *could* (but has not) been interpreted in this way, and to draw attention to the assumptions that underlie it. While lesbians and gay men (at least within psychology) have rarely protested about being assessed in relation to heterosexual control groups, many heterosexual feminists are apparently outraged about being judged in relation to lesbians.

The *exclusion* of LGBT people and perspectives is only one problem: the other is the (increasingly common) *inclusion* of LGBT issues as if they were simply lifestyle choices toward which (heterosexual) psychologists should extend a liberal inclusive welcome. For example, until recently, virtually all psychological research on adult love relationships has focused on heterosexual dating and marriage, and lesbian and gay relationships are still omitted from the interpersonal attraction section of most standard undergraduate psychology textbooks. Much of the existing research on lesbian and gay male couples is framed within a heterosexual context, and informed by a liberal humanistic framework that emphasizes the similarities between homosexuals and heterosexuals. Features of lesbian and gay partnerships are often measured using scales originally formulated for use with and/or developed exclusively on heterosexual samples—and these are reported unproblematically and without comment within the psychology of women/gender literatures (see C. Kitzinger & Coyle, 1995).

Similarly, lesbian and gay levels and patterns of sexual activity appear to diverge markedly from heterosexual norms with gay men having "too much" sex—often outside their established couple relationships (P.M. Davies, Hickson, Weatherburn, & Hunt, 1993)—and lesbians (particularly those in long-term couple relationships) having "too little" and pathologized as suffering from "erotophobia" or "inhibited sexual desire" (M. Nichols, 1987). The heterosexual norm of what constitutes "sex" is part of what is at issue here. Challenging the claim of lower levels of sexual activity among lesbian couples, Marilyn Frye (1990) suggested that this finding is an artefactual consequence of measuring lesbian sexual activity in terms of a metric derived from heterosexual intercourse, and some feminist psychologists are now explicitly challenging the discourses which regulate the frequency of sexual interaction in heterosexual couples, and the "coital imperative" that defines "real" sex in terms of penile-vaginal penetration (Gavey, 1993; Gavey, McPhillips, & Braun, 1999).

The emphasis in psychological research on the personal and interpersonal characteristics of lesbian and gay relationships risks ignoring their social context. Lesbian and gay couples are struggling to build and to maintain relationships in the context of a society that often denies their existence, condemns their sexuality, penalizes their partnership, and derides their love for each other. Even among those sufficiently open about their homosexuality to risk taking part as subjects in research, it is consistently found that about three-quarters engage in various forms of subterfuge—including careful conformity with gender-role stereotypes, introducing partners as "friends," avoiding conversations about personal matters, inviting a gay person of the opposite sex to meet parents and colleagues, changing pronouns, and inventing (or even acquiring) a fiancé(e) or spouse (M.P. Levine & Leonard, 1984; Schneider, 1984). When families are told of a lesbian or gay relationship, they often refuse to accept it (Kurdeck & Schmitt, 1987) and key aspects of the couple's joint life (anniversaries, the birth or adoption of children, house purchases, job changes, retirement) go unacknowledged. Serious illnesses and injuries can be doubly traumatic given the heterosexism of the health care system (Bradford, Ryan, & Rothblum, 1994; S. Butler & Rosenblum, 1993; Fish & Wilkinson, 2000), and if a couple separate, or a partner dies, denial of the nature and/or significance of the relationship that has been lost may exacerbate the distress experienced. In the workplace, it is usual for heterosexuality to be everywhere flaunted—engagement and wedding rings, photographs of spouses on the desk, casual conversations about weekend activities, and flirtation between colleagues, all of which confirm its normative status and the "deviance" of the lesbian or gay worker. In addition to the psychological and interpersonal costs this imposes, there are also material costs. A study of "the wage effects of sexual orientation discrimination" (Badgett, 1995) found both gay and bisexual male and female workers earn less than their same-sex counterparts, and lesbians and gay men are also disadvantaged by anti-gay clauses in contracts of conditions of service, such as pension schemes or relocation allowances that exclude a same-sex partner; denial of child-care, sports, or canteen facilities to a same-sex partner; definitions of paternity leave which exclude lesbian co-mothers; and compassionate leave limited to the spouse and blood relatives of the employee. Emphasis on questions of similarity and difference within and between homosexual and heterosexual relationship has diverted attention away from broader political concerns about the social context within which these relationships are located.

DOING SEXUALITIES, DOING GENDERS

Until a decade or so ago, lesbian and gay psychology was, almost without exception, rooted in essentialist theories. That is, sexual orientation was assumed to be an inner state or essence which the individual represses or discovers, denies, or acknowledges. The vast bulk of LGBT psychology still relies upon notions of an underlying fundamental and relatively stable essential sexuality (either innate or acquired early in life) which determines a person's sexual response. Research within an essentialist framework may measure homosexual and heterosexual characteristics or responses and report similarities and differences, and/or may aim to "recover the authentic voice of queer experience" (Norton, 1997, p. 11). The small amount of social constructionist work that has emerged within lesbian and gay psychology (e.g., Bohan, 1997; C. Kitzinger, 1987; Tiefer, 1987) challenges this view and draws its intellectual inheritance from landmark papers in sociology such as those by M. McIntosh (1968), Gagnon and Simon (1973), and (later) Foucault (1978). This work shifts the research focus from the characteristics and life experiences of homosexual people, to an examination of the ways in which societies construct "the homosexual" and to the meanings and definitions attached to that concept. Subsequent interdisciplinary research has focused on the history of the development of "homosexuality" (Weeks, 1977, 1981); the social uses to which it is put in different cultures (Plummer, 1981, 1992) and the ways in which individuals construct lesbian and gay identities in specific social contexts (J. Hart & Richardson, 1981; C. Kitzinger, 1987; E. Stein, 1992). Whereas ways of "doing" and "experiencing" sexuality had previously consolidated the gay or lesbian person into a type of being with a sexual orientation, now the person, far from expressing an "essential self" through sexuality, is conceptualized as an actor whose identity is a performance, complying with or transgressing (socially constructed) scripts (J. Butler, 1989, 1993; Sedgwick, 1990, 1994). Instead of searching for truths about homosexuals and lesbians, much contemporary social science research asks about the discursive practices, the narrative forms, the social and political contexts by which, and within which, homosexuals and lesbians are produced and reproduced (e.g., C. Kitzinger & Wilkinson, 1995; Plummer, 1992).

The debate between essentialists and social constructionists (and, later, postmodernists) formed a central motif of LGBT research in the late 1980s and early 1990s (see C. Kitzinger, 1995a for an overview). Neither side has convinced the other, and research now proceeds within both traditions without much reference to the other. On the one hand there is continuing essentialist research that focuses on biological determinant or concomitants of homosexuality (e.g., Hamer et al., 1993; LeVay, 1993; Rahman, 1999) or which continues to posit the existence of homosexual and heterosexual persons whose mental health, social adjustment, and personal habits can then be compared across a range of dimension (see *Journal of Homosexuality* for a wide selection of work of this nature). This research parallels psychology of women/gender research that focuses on the biological differences between the sexes, or that continues the long tradition of sex differences research: in both LGBT and psychology of women/gender research of this type, heterosexuals and homosexuals, men and women exist as pre-given categories. On the other hand, there is research with labels such as social constructionist, postmodern, or queer that aims radically to deconstruct these very categories, and in so doing parallel feminist work deconstructing gender categories (e.g., Dreger, 1998; Fausto-Sterling, 2000; S.J. Kessler, 1998; van den Wijngaard, 1997). (Note that while the distinction between these two traditions is fairly straightforward—one takes for granted the sexuality/gender categories which the other deconstructs—the labels assigned to them are not. In particular, virtually nobody accepts the label "essentialist" for themselves—although this is the dominant position in both psychology of women/gender and in lesbian and gay psychology; my use of this term is not intended as an insult, but simply to demarcate work which accepts male and female, heterosexual and lesbian as reasonable working categories in studies which, for example, compare suicide risks, assess mental health, or compare coming out experiences. The vast majority of the research cited so far in this chapter is of this type.)

A number of concerns have been expressed about social constructionist/postmodern perspectives in LGBT research. First, much of it has focused on the analysis of lesbians or gay men as socially constructed categories without explicit and analogous consideration of the socially constructed nature of heterosexuality. Although social constructionists have said that "the awareness of a dispersal of homosexualities must also mean the awareness of a dispersal of heterosexualities" (Plummer, 1992, p. 14), there has been very little within psychology on the construction of heterosexuality. (Though, see J.N. Katz, 1995 for a historical perspective and Richardson, 1996b for a sociological perspective.) Instead, in typical victimology mode, it is virtually always homosexuality rather than heterosexuality that constitutes the analytic focus. It is homosexuals, not heterosexuals, whose lifestyles are questioned, whose problems are analyzed, and whose very existence is rendered problematic by social scientists.

Second, some activists have argued that the "love that dare not speak its name" is silenced today not only by overt discrimination and oppression, but also by scholarly assertions that its name is historically and socially constructed, unstable, fragmented, diverse, even—in Judith Butler's words (1991, p. 13)—a "phantasm." Agonizing over signifiers and signification, the postmodern postlesbian abandons essentialist slogans like "glad to be gay" or "every woman can be a lesbian" in favor of radical doubt and uncertainty about "being" anything at all. Judith Butler, for example, writes of her anxiety at "appear[ing] at political occasions under the sign of lesbian [. . .] I would like to have it permanently unclear what precisely that sign signifies" (J. Butler, 1991,

p. 14). Opponents of postmodernism and queer theory point to the political necessity for lesbian and gay self-naming (Jeffreys, 1994), announcing that "we'll deconstruct when they deconstruct" (J. MacDonald, 1990, p. 89).

Essentialist—especially *biological*—arguments are often favored by those who want to promote lesbian and gay rights because they are seen as enabling a shared identity around which to organize effectively. It is, moreover, an identity, which many people experience as authentically "real": according to Rictor Norton (1997) "social constructionism violates commonsense" (p. 27) because "if anything suggests that experiential reality exists outside of discourse, it is the feeling of thousands of homosexuals of a desire *for which they have no name*" (p. 25, italics in original). Essentialist arguments are often also described as offering a kind of moral neutrality: "it seems pointless to judge the outcome of a biological process in moral terms. It would be equally absurd to disapprove of the fact that tadpoles turn into frogs" (Moir & Jessel, 1989, p. 112). This approach has a distinguished pedigree—it goes right back to the early campaigners for sex reform like Havelock Ellis and Radcliffe Hall who used essentialist arguments that depicted homosexuality as innate and based their pleas for tolerance on that basis. Instead of sinners or criminals, we are "congenital inverts" or "the third sex"—people with an inherent orientation who ought not to be blamed for a condition over which we have no control. These same arguments are sometimes resurrected in political debate—as in the British Age of Consent debate in 1999 when members of parliament (resolutely ignoring the last thirty years of constructionist research) spoke in favor of equality for gay men on the grounds that "people do not choose their sexual nature." Critiquing social constructionist perspectives, S. Epstein (1992, p. 261) complains that from these academic theories "a folk constructionism comes to be disseminated: the view that sexual identities are wilful self-creations"—an argument that has rarely, if ever, been useful in the struggle for LGBT liberation. On the other hand, we might equally note that when the British media reported LeVay's (1993) "gay hypothalamus" and Hamer et al.'s (1993) gay gene theory as "proving" a biological basis for homosexuality, this did not herald a new tolerance for lesbians and gay men. Instead, there was a flurry of newspaper headlines advocating a prenatal "search and destroy" mission: former Chief Rabbi Lord Jacobovitz called for Jews to undergo voluntary genetic engineering to eradicate homosexual tendencies, and a triumphant headline in a national newspaper proclaimed, "Abortion hope after 'gay gene' findings" (see discussion in C. Kitzinger, 1995a). The problem with biological theories of homosexuality is that they assume the "naturalness" of *heterosexuality* (the biologically determined orientation for 96 to 98% of all women according to LeVay, 1993, p. 108), which runs directly counter to theories of heterosexuality as a compulsory institution. Feminists have spent more than a century challenging concepts of the natural that relegate women to the kitchen and the bedroom and that justify and condone male subjectation of women, and these very theories arise again in LeVay's ruthlessly reductionist account that extrapolates wildly from rats to human beings, and ignores sociopolitical context. Why, for example, are women more involved in childcare than men?

> The short answer is: hormones [. . .] the levels of androgens usually present in male fetuses, while certainly not preventing the organization of circuits for maternal behavior, in some way restrict the range of circumstances in which such behavior is exhibited. (LeVay, 1993, pp. 64, 69)

Arguing about the proper definition of nature only evades and obscures the political context defining the terms of the debate.

Reviewing biological research on homosexuality, one commentator has suggested that "if one's sexual orientation is caused by having a certain gene, then social constructionism is wrong" (E. Stein, 1992, p. 352). Conversely, reviewers of research on women whose sexual identities shift from heterosexual to lesbian in midlife (C. Kitzinger & Wilkinson, 1995), have suggested that this should be treated as evidence of that essentialist and biological explanations are wrong (and have even chastised, as insufficiently committed to the scientific enterprise, those who refuse to interpret it this way (see Baumrind, 1995). In fact, genetic findings do not act as counterevidence for social constructionism, and findings of sexual change and fluidity do not act as counter-evidence for biological theories because biology and social constructionism are not, in fact, competing explanations for the same phenomena. Rather social constructionists view biology itself as discursively constructed, and science as the grand narrative or rhetoric through which such constructions are warranted. Social constructionists treat biological and other scientific arguments not as factual claims to be assessed against the evidence, but as rhetorical claims to be inspected for their ideological and political assumptions. As Fausto-Sterling (2000, p. 5) puts it: "truths about human sexuality created by scholars in general and by biologists in particular are one component of political, social, and moral struggles about our cultures and economies." This line of research has been particularly fruitful in exploring the intersections of genders and sexualities in relation to transgender issues.

With some notable exceptions (e.g., S.J. Kessler, 1990, 1998; S.J. Kessler & McKenna, 1978; see M. Crawford, 2000b), transgender issues—which are, technically, as the term suggests, gender rather than sexuality issues (although, of course, they are both) have been raised *not* by people working in psychology of women/gender, but by lesbian and gay researchers, as witnessed by the new addition of T to LGB. The birth of intersex infants (born either/or or neither/both—*hermaphrodites* in an older terminology) is relatively common (in the order of 1.7% of all live births, Fausto-Sterling, 2000, p. 53, Table 3.2): they are surgically constructed as either female or (less often) male to uphold our cultural belief that there are two and only two sexes. It has been estimated that about five intersexed children have their genitals cut into in U.S. hospitals every day, a procedure performed by accredited surgeons and covered by all major insurance plans (Fausto-Sterling, 2000, p. 226). Sex assignation is made primarily on the basis of the appearance of the genitals and their presumed future suitability for heterosexual intercourse. Babies with small or non-existent penises (even XY babies, as in the infamous John/Joan case, Colapinto, 2000), are assigned female, and vaginoplasty (creation of a neo-vagina) performed. A "successful" vagina is defined as one which, in adulthood, will hold a "normal-size" penis (S.J. Kessler, 1998, p. 58). These genital surgeries are "closely related to ideas regarding the functioning of the penis or vagina in heterosexual intercourse" (van den Wijngaard, 1997, p. 89) and "make little allowance for the possibility of 'normal' lesbianism or homosexuality" (van den Wijngaarad, 1997, p. 95). One team of clinicians argues that the most serious mistake in gender assignment is to create "an individual unable to engage in genital [heterosexual] sex" (S.J. Kessler, 1998, p. 26), and the (heterosexual) marriage of intersex persons is taken as proof of surgical success. On the grounds that "you can make a hole but you can't build a pole" about 90% of anatomically ambiguous infants are assigned as female and their genital tissue excised (Chase, 1998). Intersex adults upon whom this kind of surgery was performed have spoken out about the loss of sensation, painful genital scarring, infection, orgasmic incapacity, and emotional trauma caused by early genital surgeries performed without their informed consent, and the Intersex Society of North America (ISNA) is campaigning against all forms of cosmetic genital surgery on infants, and is supported by leading intersex researchers (M.A. Diamond & Sigmundson, 1997a).

Until very recently, however, the vast bulk of psychology of women/gender has accepted as given, the "natural, biological" separation of human beings into two (and only two) sexes, with heterosexuality as normative. This is particularly clear from psychology of women/gender textbook descriptions of John Money's work on sex reassignment, both with intersex infants and with John/Joan. Textbook authors adopt without question the language Money used to describe genital surgery as "corrective" (Frieze, Parsons, Johnson, Ruble, & Zellman, 1978, p. 89), "reconstructive" (Renzetti & Curran, 1995, p. 29; Williams, 1987, p. 117) or "feminizing" (Lips, 1997, p. 145), nor is there any challenge to Money's assumption of the over-riding need for people to be equipped with genitals capable of performing heterosexual intercourse. Psychology of women/gender textbook reports of the decision to raise, as a girl, a boy whose penis was severely damaged, are notable for the *absence of explanation* offered to justify this decision (e.g., "the doctors recommended that the boy be given an artificial vagina, which was the simpler operation, and be raised as a girl," Basow, 1992, p. 28).

Conventionally, transsexuals have also often been used to prop up a two-gender system: they are women in men's bodies (or vice verse), leaving the binary classification intact. Queer theorists explode this traditional version and instead embrace transsexuality as occupying a position outside the binary oppositions of gendered discourse. Queers born with penises may keep them, but *also* have breast implants; queers born with vaginas and clitorises may leave them intact but have mastectomies and use hormones to deepen their voice and grow facial hair (K. Bornstein, 1994). According to Prosser (1998, p. 174), "The need, even the desire, to head toward recognizably sexed homes (male *or* female, man *or* woman) can no longer be assumed." These products of "transsexualism interruptus" avoid genital surgery as interfering with sexual pleasure; some identity themselves as women with penises or men with vaginas, some as neither male nor female, just "queer." And they may have sexual relationships with men and with women and with each other, transgressing and subverting both the binary gender system and the very concepts of heterosexuality and homosexuality.

Gender and sexuality are inextricably linked. Historically, people who do same sex sexual activities were seen as "the third sex," "psychic hermaphrodites," or "the intermediate sex" (H. Ellis, 1934). Being a "proper" women has been taken to mean heterosexuality—even if, for XY people assigned as female (e.g., John/Joan, transsexuals, and women with AIS, see C. Kitzinger, 2000b), this means sex with another XY person. Not being heterosexual has been taken to signal lack of proper female characteristics, hence the long search for "mannish" characteristics of lesbians: early sexology claimed to find long clitorises, narrow hips, small breasts, and deep voices in lesbians; both early and later sexology debated whether or not we had masculine personality characteristics such as independence, assertiveness, and an interest in the sciences. Explicit links were made between lesbianism and first wave feminists' rejection of stereotypical feminine behavior (see Jeffreys, 1985 for an overview). Similarly, for men—a "real" man is taken to be heterosexual, such that gay men are allegedly more less masculine than heterosexual men: Eysenck and Wilson (1979, p. 39) claim that "homosexual males tend to have feminine-type pelvises" and LeVay (1993) finds gay male brains to be more like women's than heterosexual men's.

In deconstructing scientific (medical and biological) arguments, rather than engaging with them—endorsing some and attempting to refute others—social constructionist (postmodern/queer) perspectives have enabled a radical interrogation of the relationship between sexualities and genders.

IMPLICATIONS FOR PSYCHOLOGY OF WOMEN/GENDER

Psychology of women/gender embraces a wide variety of different theoretical and methodological perspectives, but LGBT research has a place (in one way or another) within *all* of them (see Braun, 2000). At the very least, there needs to be a greater awareness of the findings of research on LGBT issues such that (heterosexual) feminists no longer invoke what I have referred to elsewhere (C. Kitzinger, 1996) as "the privilege of ignorance." Within LGBT psychology, there is now a wealth of research on topics varying from the challenges of LGBT adolescence, midlife, and old age; parenting issues, anti-LGBT discrimination, cultural/racial/ethnic diversity, therapy, workplace issues, and more (see B. Greene & Croom, 2000 for a recent overview). Feminist psychologists repeatedly assert that they are ignorant of this work: see for example the edited collection of essays on *Motherhood* which as only one indexed reference to lesbians which reads (implausibly enough!) "there has been little research on lesbian mothers" (Phoenix et al., 1991). Even prior to 1990 when the book presumably went to press, this simply isn't true (e.g., Falk, 1989; Gibbs, 1988; Rohrbaugh, 1988), and with the enormous growth of LGBT psychology over the last decade, every feminist psychologist, whatever her area of expertise, should assume that there is LGBT psychology relevant to her work.

Moreover, when LGBT experience *is* explicitly discussed in psychology of women/gender, this often seems to prompt writers to a defensive rationalization of *heterosexuality* as an equally legitimate lifestyle choice for women, creating a false parallelism that overlooks the role of compulsory heterosexuality in constructing lesbianism and heterosexuality as very different "lifestyles." For example, across a range of recent psychology of women textbooks, it is common to find "violence against women" described as perpetrated by men (e.g., rape, sexual harassment, domestic violence) whereas "violence against lesbians" is routinely described as perpetrated by other lesbians (i.e., lesbian battering). I do not want to deny the existence or seriousness of lesbian battering, but I do want to draw attention to the way in which these presentations overlook and thereby obscure male harassment of and violence against lesbians: In many psychology of women/gender textbooks there are no references at all to either the "homophobia" or "hate crimes" research, and the concept is likewise absent from much feminist theorizing.

As should be clear from the preceding discussion, my argument is not simply that it is morally right or politically correct for feminists to support LGBT visibility (although I think there are both moral and political reasons why they should do so); rather I am suggesting that an analysis of heterosexual domination and the challenges posed by LGBT existence can enrich (heterosexual) feminist theory and practice. This means incorporating a consideration of heterosexism into *all* feminist research—studies that analyze the experiences only of heterosexuals, as well as those that include LGBT participants. Heterosexual women—as much as lesbians—are strongly influenced by the interrelationship between sexuality and gender, and for many heterosexual women who experience their gender authenticity as somehow in question (e.g., women with polycystic ovarian syndrome, Wilmott, 2000; women with androgen insensitivity syndrome, C. Kitzinger, 2000b), doing heterosexuality (dating, intercourse, marriage) may serve the symbolic function of asserting and affirming their femaleness in the face of apparently disconfirming evidence (such as lack of menstruation/fertility, facial hair, or XY chromosomes). Heterosexuality, like heterosexism, is a way of dealing with a threatened gender identity: heterosexuality is a way of doing gender. When psychology of women deals with heterosexism only in relation to lesbians under the heading of "difference" or "diversity," it obscures some potentially important questions about *heterosexual* women's development and experience, qua heterosexuals.

In sum, the development of strong feminist psychologies and politics will depend upon further interrogating and integrating the study of sexualities and genders across the full range of our research and practice.

PART IV

GENDER AND PHYSICAL AND MENTAL HEALTH

CHAPTER 19

Gendered Bodies and Physical Health

JOAN C. CHRISLER

Why include a chapter on physical health in a handbook on the psychology of women? Health and illness are biopsychosocial phenomena. Biological sex differences affect both morbidity (i.e., the number of cases of particular diseases) and mortality (i.e., the number of deaths due to particular diseases or causes). Psychological and social factors lead to gendered behaviors and situations that influence health and illness. For example, women's greater concern about physical appearance and body weight has led girls and women to start (and continue) to smoke cigarettes because of the appetite-suppressant effect of nicotine. Smoking behavior, in turn, affects women's lung cancer and coronary heart disease morbidity rates.

The women's health movement in the 1960s grew out of the women's liberation movement, which taught us that sexism affects all aspects of women's lives, and the consumer movement, which taught us that people should educate themselves rather than depend solely on experts and that we should demand the products and services we want. The early focus of the women's health movement was on reproductive health. Women gathered in small groups to learn about their bodies (e.g., by learning to do cervical exams and menstrual extractions) and to share what they had learned with others. The latter goal later led to the founding of several important organizations that are still active today: the Boston Women's Health Book Collective (publishers of *Our Bodies, Ourselves*), the Washington, D.C.–based National Women's Health Network, and the Atlanta-based National Black Women's Health Project. These groups have performed important educational and political work over the years, including lobbying for abortion rights and uniform labeling of tampon absorbency and demanding a choice of birthing alternatives.

Scholars inspired by the women's health movement have documented ways that sexism, racism, classism, ageism, and homophobia have affected women's health care. Physicians, the majority of whom were men, paid greater attention to diseases that affected themselves and people they knew, were ignorant about the lives and problems of people who were different from themselves, preferred working with people who could pay for their services (jokes were often made about doctors who specialized in "diseases of the rich"), and held attitudes and beliefs about women that were influenced more heavily by stereotypes than by reality. These problems began to change in the 1970s, after affirmative action programs opened medical school admissions to a more diverse set of students.

Medical researchers and the funding agencies that support their work have also been heavily criticized by feminist scholars. Women were rarely included as participants in medical research projects, and, when they were included, gender comparative statistics were rarely computed, the samples of women were more often homogeneous than diverse, life span development was not often taken into account, and researchers tended to focus on diseases that are more common in men than in women (Rodin & Ickovics, 1990). These omissions only began to be taken seriously in the 1990s, after a group of congresswomen forced the issues during a debate on federal funding of the National Institutes of Health. We have a long way to go yet to fill in the gaps in our knowledge of women's health and illness.

A focus on women's health will help us to better understand and treat diseases of women (e.g., ovarian cancer), diseases that occur disproportionately in women (e.g., breast cancer, rheumatoid arthritis, systemic lupus erythematosus), and diseases that manifest themselves differently in women than in men (e.g., AIDS, coronary heart disease). A focus on women's health will help us to provide more sensitive (e.g., culturally appropriate) care and more accurate treatment (e.g., drug doses designed for and tested in women's bodies). A focus on gendered aspects of health and illness will also benefit men's health. For example, if we shift the focus from why men die younger to why women live longer, we may learn lessons about benefits such as social support that men could utilize (Crose, 1997). Furthermore, gender roles affect men's morbidity and mortality, too. For example, the greater tendency of boys and men to take physical risks (e.g., accept dares, ignore seat belt warnings) has led to their higher rates of death and disability from accidents.

It is impossible to cover all the interesting gendered aspects of health in the space allotted, but I have tried to give an overview of some important areas. To learn more about the gender psychology of health, see Dan (1994), Gallant, Keita, and Royak-Schaler (1997), Kato and Mann (1996), Lorber (1997a), K.J. Peterson (1996), Sabo and Gordon (1995), and A.L. Stanton and Gallant (1995).

WOMEN'S EXPERIENCES IN THE HEALTH CARE SYSTEM

UTILIZATION OF SERVICES

There are well-documented gender differences in the utilization of health care services. The results of most studies (e.g., Cleary, Mechanic, & Greenley, 1982; Dennerstein, 1995; Verbrugge, 1979, 1980) indicate that women use health services more often than men do. Because women of childbearing age make the most visits to physicians and clinics (Dennerstein, 1995), we can assume that many of these visits are for pre- and postnatal care. However, when pregnancy and birth-related visits are factored out, women are still more likely than men to utilize health care services (S.E. Taylor, 1995).

A number of factors probably combine to predict women's greater utilization of services. First, women may be more "in tune" with their bodies than men are, and thus more likely to notice the emergence of signs or symptoms that may indicate a need for medical attention. The emphasis in Western societies on menstrual cycle–related changes encourages women to attend to their bodies and to make attributions about the causes of bodily experiences (Chrisler, 1996a). It has also been suggested (Leventhal, Nerenz, & Strauss, 1982) that women have better homeostatic mechanisms than men do because of their greater olfactory acuity, pain sensitivity, and accuracy in detecting body temperature changes.

Second, the way medical services for women are organized often means more visits for basic preventive care. Whereas men may visit an internist or general practitioner for an annual checkup, women may have to visit an internist, a gynecologist, and a mammography center for their basic checkup (S.E. Taylor, 1995). In recent years, medical professionals (e.g., M. Harrison, 1992; K. Johnson, 1992; Wallis, 1992) have been debating the pros and cons of establishing a specialty in women's health care. An important point in favor of such a specialty is a decrease in the fragmentation of health services for women, which would result in fewer office visits. An argument against it is the concern that if there were a specialty in women's health, it would "absolve" other specialists of the obligation to learn about and address women's health and illnesses.

Third, aspects of gender-role socialization encourage women to be more concerned about health and to seek medical attention when they need it. Women's role as nurturer includes caring for ill family members and encouraging healthy practices (e.g., good nutrition), as television commercials about "Dr. Mom" regularly remind us. Women's magazines publish many more articles about health than men's magazines do; thus, women tend to know more about health and illness. Because of their greater knowledge, women may be more likely than men to recognize when symptoms need medical attention. Furthermore, women may believe that they need to remain healthy themselves in order to take good care of those who depend on them, and they may be more familiar with and comfortable than men in medical settings, as they more often accompany their dependents (e.g., children, pets, aging parents) to medical appointments. Finally, gender-role socialization discourages men from admitting their weaknesses and seeking help when they need it and encourages them to appear strong and carry on despite pain, fatigue, and other symptoms. It is acceptable for women to ask for help and to depend on experts for advice and support; thus, we should not be surprised that women are more likely than men to use medical (and psychotherapy) services.

ATTITUDES AND BELIEFS OF HEALTH CARE PRACTITIONERS

Physicians' attitudes toward women patients directly affect the quality of care women receive as well as women's ability to make informed decisions about their health. For example, there is evidence that physicians do not take women's complaints as seriously as men's (Corea, 1977; J. Wallen, Waitzkin, & Stoekle, 1979; Weisman & Teitelbaum, 1985). Many physicians believe that women are prone to minor ailments; that women patients are likely to be neurotic, difficult, overly emotional, or depressed; and that women tend not to understand medical explanations because they "feel" rather than "think" (Chrisler & Hemstreet, 1995; Fidell, 1980; S. Fisher & Groce, 1985; Marris, 1996). These biased assumptions hinder accurate diagnosis of women's illnesses (V.N. Anderson & Walsh, 1998; Chrisler & Hemstreet, 1995; Grace, 1995a), lead to the overprescription of psychotropic medications to women (Cooperstock, 1971; Corea, 1977; Lack, 1982; Ogur, 1986; J. Wallen et al., 1979), and contribute to the lesser likelihood that women will be referred to specialists for neuropsychological testing, cardiovascular interventions, and other services (M.E. Banks, Ackerman, & Corbett, 1995; Hsia, 1993; Travis, Gressley, & Phillippi, 1993; Weinstein & Reeves, 1995).

Heterosexist assumptions and homophobia occur often in medical settings and have raised concerns about how they affect lesbians' willingness to seek care and the quality of care they receive. Surveys (C.E. Randall, 1989; P.E. Stevens, 1992; Trippet & Bain, 1992; E.W. Young, 1988) of lesbians have revealed that disclosure of sexual orientation to health care providers has resulted in reactions of shock, pity, fear, repulsion, embarrassment, and overt hostility. Researchers (C.J. Douglas, Kalman, & Kalman, 1985; Eliason & Randall, 1991; C.E. Randall, 1989; E.W. Young, 1988) have found that many physicians and nurses are not only uncomfortable providing care for lesbian patients but also believe that lesbians are immoral, criminal, or mentally ill. Lesbian patients who are honest with their physicians run the risk of being inappropriately pathologized and finding that their sexual orientation rather than their presenting complaint has become the focus of treatment (Reagan, 1981; P.E. Stevens, 1992).

Attitudes toward and stereotypes about ethnic minority and elderly women also affect their health care. Medical school faculty reinforce the idea that minority women are immature, irresponsible, and unlikely to return for follow-up care (M. Harrison, 1982). Such attitudes no doubt contribute to the reasons why African American (Lillie-Blanton, Bowie, & Ro, 1996) and Latina (Ramirez, 1996) women have been found to be less satisfied than European American women with their health care providers. Furthermore, if providers believe that ethnic minority women are irresponsible about making and keeping appointments, they may be less likely to refer them for specialized preventive services. Both African Americans and Latinas are less likely than European American women to have had mammograms (Lillie-Blanton et al., 1996; Ramirez, 1996), and Latinas are significantly less likely than other women to have regular pelvic and clinical breast exams (Ramirez, 1996). Beliefs about the behavior and abilities of groups of women may interfere with practitioners' ability to respond to the needs of individual patients. Perhaps because physicians do not expect their Latina patients to smoke, drink alcohol, or use street drugs, those who do are less likely than other women to have been counseled by their doctors about their habits (Ramirez, 1996). Similarly, if physicians believe that depression and cognitive impairment are endemic to aging, they may not refer elderly women for psychiatric or neurological evaluations (Gatz et al., 1995).

DOCTOR-PATIENT COMMUNICATION

Impatience and a need to reassert control often lead physicians to cut off responses to their questions before the patients have adequately conveyed their concerns, which can lead to the loss of information that is important for diagnosis (Waitzkin & Waterman, 1974; A.L. Wright & Morgan, 1990). Women, particularly those who are not well educated or not fluent in English, are most likely to be interrupted by their physicians. Despite their tendency to underestimate women's ability to understand medical information, physicians often use highly technical language when talking to their patients (S.E. Taylor, 1995). This compounds the problems of immigrant women, who must try to communicate during medical crises with physicians who not only do not understand their language and are impatient with their hesitant English, but who come from a different economic class and cultural background and know little about the cultural assumptions of immigrant groups (Chrisler & Hemstreet, 1995). Latinas are particularly likely to report that it is difficult to talk to their doctors (Ramirez, 1996). When women patients encounter men physicians who interrupt them and intimidate them, they may retreat into more traditional feminine behavior; that is, they may become passive and submissive, and thus less likely to ask for and get the attention and information they need.

One of the biggest complaints that both men and women have about their health care is that their doctors do not spend enough time talking to them and answering their questions (S.E. Taylor, 1995). Managed care and other financial pressures have forced physicians to see more patients per day, which means less time to spend with each one, and, until recently, medical students did not receive training in communication skills. Furthermore, there is evidence that doctor-patient communication is even poorer when doctors encounter patients they would prefer not to treat; researchers have found that physicians of both sexes prefer male patients and those who are healthier, acutely rather than chronically ill, better educated, and of similar socioeconomic and ethnic backgrounds (S.E. Taylor, 1995).

Women patients have told researchers that their doctors did not listen to them or show concern about their problems; did not explain the diagnosis adequately; and treated them dismissively by making them feel they had wasted the doctor's time, by not taking their pain seriously, or by telling them that they had caused their own problems (V.N. Anderson & Walsh, 1998; Grace, 1995b; Marris, 1996; Savidge, Slade, Stewart, & Li, 1998). When symptoms are vague and illnesses are difficult to diagnose, physicians may take out on their patients their frustration at not finding the cause by suggesting that there is really nothing wrong with the patients or that their problems are psychological rather than physical. Women of lower socioeconomic status are probably more likely to experience this type of blame from their physicians (Grace, 1995b).

Poor communication is a major cause of patient dissatisfaction, which can have direct effects on women's health. Dissatisfaction often keeps patients from returning for follow-up visits (S.E. Taylor, 1995) that may be necessary for proper diagnosis or treatment. Remember that ethnic minority women have been found to be less satisfied than European American women with their health care. If they do not return because they found their doctors to be insensitive, insulting, or incomprehensible, they may inadvertently reinforce their physicians' stereotypes about them. Poor communication may also affect patients' ability to adhere to the treatment recommendations their physicians have given them (S.E. Taylor, 1995). This happens when patients do not understand the recommendations; when physicians do not check to see whether the patients have understood; when physicians ignore, are unaware of, or do not listen when a patient mentions cultural, economic, or other constraints that may interfere with their ability to adhere to the treatment; or when the physicians' intimidating behavior makes patients anxious or angry, which interferes with their ability to remember the instructions they have been given.

A number of researchers (S. Fisher & Groce, 1985; Malheux, Pineault, Lambert, Beland, & Berthiaume, 1989; van den Brink-Muinen, Bensing, & Kerssens, 1998; Waller, 1998) have found that women physicians spend more time with their patients and are more likely than men to emphasize, listen, teach, practice preventive medicine, and involve their patients in decision making. At least in the short run, women patients may be more satisfied with their health care if they can see women physicians from a similar ethnic background. However, this is often not possible, especially in geographic areas where there are few physicians from which to choose or in medical specialties dominated by European American men.

ACCESS TO HEALTH CARE SERVICES

Many women work in low-paying jobs that do not provide medical benefits or that require large deductibles and cost shares and often specifically exclude payments for prenatal care and birthing, which makes the insurance less expensive for employers and nearly worthless for employees (Perales & Young, 1988). Insurance policies often prohibit payment for treatment of preexisting conditions (including pregnancy), which discriminates against people with chronic illnesses and may make it impossible for them to change jobs. HMOs vary considerably in what they consider to be essential health care needs. Some will pay for treatment of erectile dysfunction and male infertility but not for female infertility or contraceptives. Several states have recently had to enact laws to require HMOs and insurance plans to cover the costs of mammography. Furthermore, many employers restrict insurance benefits to their employees' "legal" dependents. This means that lesbian, gay, and cohabiting but unmarried heterosexual employees may find that their families cannot share their health insurance coverage.

Women of color are overrepresented in occupations that pay low wages and carry high risk of occupational injuries that result from secondary exposure to chemicals (e.g., laundry workers, hairdressers) or from repetitive movements (e.g., factory workers, word processors). Such injuries develop over time, and so do not have the exact "date of injury" that is typical of men's industrial accidents. The date of injury is often among the criteria required for coverage by worker compensation policies (Stellman, 1988). Thus, they may be ineligible for proper medical treatment or disability leaves.

Although Medicaid is a federal welfare program designed to provide medical care for the poor and near poor, eligibility is determined by formulas that vary from state to state. The result of this complex web of qualifications is that many of the nation's poor do not qualify, people who move from one state to another may lose their medical coverage, and therefore as many as half of the people Medicaid was designed to help receive fragmented, episodic care or none at all (Perales & Young, 1988). Several states have attempted to pass laws to exclude undocumented immigrants from Medicaid coverage, which could have a devastating effect on immigrant women. Elderly women, who often suffer from multiple chronic illnesses that require medications and monitoring by physicians, frequently fall into the poor or near poor category. Even economically advantaged women may find themselves with low financial means as they grow older due to divorce, lack of pensions for homemakers, or a history of low-paying jobs that results in minimal social security payments. Medicare, like many private insurance carriers, provides better coverage for conditions that primarily affect men, and it does not cover expenses for hearing aids, dentures, custodial home care, or preventive examinations (C.M. Clancy & Massion, 1992; Perales & Young, 1988; Sofaer & Abel, 1990; Woolhandler & Himmelstein, 1988).

Clinics, physicians' offices, and other health care services are often scarce in inner cities and rural communities, where physicians (and psychotherapists) are less likely to want to live and work. For example, 84% of U.S. counties had no abortion services in 1992 (Henshaw, 1998), and that number has probably increased since then as clinic personnel have been harassed and intimidated out of business. Access to health care may require a car or money for transportation and child care, as well as time to travel, that many low-income women do not have. Thus, women of color, the elderly, the working poor, welfare recipients, lesbians, and women with physical or psychiatric disabilities often have difficulty obtaining adequate medical care as well as significant problems in being treated with respect by health care practitioners (Christmas, 1983).

WOMEN AND CHRONIC ILLNESS

It has been estimated that at least 50% of Americans have some chronic illness that needs medical management (S.E. Taylor, 1995), and the likelihood of developing a chronic illness increases with age. Because women live longer than men, they are at greater risk of developing at least one chronic illness. The (U.S.) National Center for Health Statistics (cited in Ferrini & Ferrini, 1989) reported that 45% of women and 35% of men age 60 to 65 and 70% of women and 53% of men age 80 and over have at least one chronic illness. In a recent study (Ormel et al., 1998) of more than 5,000 people (age 57 and over) in the Netherlands, 30.8% had no chronic illnesses, 31.7% had one diagnosis, 19.3% had two, and 18.3% had three or more chronic illnesses. It would not, therefore, be very unusual to meet an older woman with diabetes, arthritis, heart disease, and hypertension—four chronic illnesses that each require medical and behavioral management.

Chronic illnesses are defined (Lubkin, 1995) as irreversible, accumulative, or latent diseases or impairments that require a high degree of medical and self-care to prevent further disability.

Patients who have been diagnosed with a chronic illness must face the fact that they may never be well again. Learning to live with a chronic illness means adjusting to what G. Gordon (1966) termed "the impaired role," in which one maintains normal behavior and responsibilities within the limits of the health condition. Rather than being motivated to "recover," the patients' challenge is to figure out what they can and cannot accomplish under which conditions. In addition to coping with physical symptoms, newly diagnosed patients must cope with changes in roles, self-concept, and body image. Adjustment to life with a chronic illness can be difficult, and it should not be surprising that many patients also struggle with depression.

Adjustment is made more difficult when symptoms or illness management routines interfere with multiple roles or with particularly valued roles. Women report considerable distress when their symptoms interfere with parenting (Lanza & Revenson, 1993; Reisine, Goodenow, & Grady, 1987), and they worry that displacing household duties onto family and friends will strain their relationships (Chrisler & Parrett, 1995; Mauriello & Chrisler, 1999). Caring for a disabled wife is a role reversal for a man who entered marriage thinking that she would be taking care of his needs (Chrisler & Parrett, 1995), and people often assume that women with disabilities are "burdens" and that any man associated with them is either a "saint" or a "loser" (Asch & Fine, 1988). Such expectations and assumptions may contribute to the fact that women with multiple sclerosis (Gulick, 1994) and cancer (Stahly, 1992) are more likely than men with the same diagnoses to be abandoned by their partners. Increasing disability may eventually result in the loss of valued roles, but well-meaning relatives, friends, and health care practitioners may urge women to give up employment or other social roles too soon (Karasz, Bochnak, & Ouellette, 1993). Gender-role stereotypes are particularly likely to affect medical advice on work and disability (S. Russell, 1989), as both physicians and patients may be influenced by the belief that employment is more important for the self-esteem of men than of women (Chrisler & O'Hea, 2000).

Living with chronic illness can be stressful, and this is especially likely to be the case with diseases such as multiple sclerosis, lupus, AIDS, and cancer that alternately flare up and go into remission. Coping with illness is also more stressful when patients cannot afford the medication, surgery, or routine health care they need, when patients live alone and/or lack a social support system, and when the quality of their doctor-patient relationships are poor. When their illnesses are difficult to diagnose or their primary symptoms are invisible (e.g., pain, fatigue, weakness), coping is likely to be complicated by the beliefs and attitudes of other people. Physicians are not the only ones who believe that women exaggerate their symptoms, complain of minor ailments, and mistake psychological problems for physical disorders. Many women (Marris, 1996) complain that formerly supportive friends, relatives, and coworkers lose patience with them and begin to withdraw help and sympathy when their chronic symptoms persist.

Stress also exacerbates the symptoms of many chronic illnesses, and it has been known to induce symptom flare-ups. Poverty is connected to many conditions that have been repeatedly found by behavioral scientists to cause stress, including unemployment, uncontrollable events, crowding, role overload, chronic strain, daily hassles, unsanitary conditions, urban violence, and noise (Chrisler & O'Hea, 2000). This is important because poverty and factors associated with it have been found to predict worse outcomes in many chronic diseases. Continual struggles to survive despite poverty, racism, and sexism mean that many women of color in the United States live in a state of continual psychological stress (A.Y. Davis, 1990). Recently, researchers have devised ways to measure how sexism (Klonoff & Landrine, 1995; Landrine, Klonoff, Gibbs, Manning, & Lund, 1995) and racism (R. Clark, Anderson, Clark, & Williams, 1999; Landrine & Klonoff, 1996) increase stress and to demonstrate that they have a direct impact on health status.

In the rest of this section, I highlight several types of chronic illness and discuss ways that sex and gender affect women's morbidity, mortality, and experiences of living with coronary heart disease, autoimmune disorders, and breast cancer.

CORONARY HEART DISEASE

Coronary heart disease (CHD) is the leading cause of death for both women and men in the United States (Sharpe, Clark, & Janz, 1991), although many women do not seem to realize this. In a telephone survey of over 1,000 American women, Legato, Padus, and Slaughter (1997) found that

58% of their participants thought that they were more likely to die of breast cancer than heart disease, 44% considered themselves to be somewhat or very unlikely ever to have a heart attack, and only 50% reported that their doctors had ever talked to them about CHD or suggested a cholesterol screening.

Over the past 35 years, mortality from CHD has substantially decreased for men at the same time that it has increased for women (Dittrich et al., 1988; Liao, Cooper, Ghali, & Szocka, 1992; Tobin et al., 1987), and mortality rates for Black women and Latinas are even higher than for White women (Liao et al., 1992). Erroneous beliefs (e.g., CHD is more severe in men; women's chest pains are due to anxiety; estrogens protect women from CHD; women's smaller blood vessels make coronary artery surgery more dangerous for them) have interfered with physicians' ability to diagnose and properly treat CHD in their women patients (Steingart et al., 1991; Tobin et al., 1987). Because most research on CHD was conducted with male participants, knowledge about ways women's disease profiles may differ from men's was scarce. However, new information is coming to light that should improve women's diagnosis and treatment. We now know, for example, that women are more likely than men to seek medical advice for reasons other than an initial heart attack (Shumaker et al., 1997), that congestive heart failure is much more common in women than in men (Samuel, Hausdorff, & Wei, 1999), and that treadmill tests and nuclear imaging are less predictive of CHD for women than for men (Hsia, 1993).

Researchers have only recently begun to examine gender and ethnic differences in risk factors for CHD, but some interesting information is beginning to emerge. In a recent study of over 5,000 women (Winkleby, Kraemer, Ahn, & Varady, 1998), African American and Mexican American women were found to be higher than European American women on most risk factors, and low-SES women in all three groups were at greater risk than those who had higher income. In a study of a small group of African American and European American women (Eck, Logan, Klesges, & Slawson, 1997), European Americans were more likely to report that they smoked for weight control or to increase their energy levels; African American women were more likely to report that they smoked because others in their families were smokers and to take more inhalations per cigarette. Finally, Type A behavior is more likely to predict eating disorders than heart disease in women (Watkins, Cartiglia, & Champion, 1998).

The belief that CHD is more common or more severe in men has resulted in 10 times as many men as women undergoing such cardiac exams as radioactive heart scan, exercise/stress tests, and angiography (Ayanian & Epstein, 1991; Hsia, 1993; Tobin et al., 1987) and significantly fewer women than men undergoing such cardiac procedures as catheterization, angioplasty, and bypass surgery (Travis et al., 1993). Some researchers (Fiebach, Viscoli, & Horwitz, 1990; Steingart et al., 1991) have concluded that women's higher mortality rate during and after coronary bypass surgery is primarily due to the fact that women are on average seven years older than men at the time of the surgery and have more advanced CHD largely because their initial complaints were not taken as seriously as men's, and so they were "watched" for a longer period of time before surgery was scheduled. Men generally undergo cardiac surgery on an elective basis, but it is more often performed on an emergency basis for women, which further contributes to their higher mortality rate (Tobin et al., 1987).

Women are also less likely than men to be referred to a cardiac rehabilitation program despite similar medical profiles and functional capacities (Ades, Waldmann, Polk, & Coflesky, 1992; R.F. Young & Kahana, 1993). After cardiac surgery, men typically return to the workforce, secure in the knowledge that their wives will support them by taking charge of household maintenance and preparing meals in accordance with their dietary regulations. Women are considered less likely to need rehabilitation because they are older on average than men after heart attack or surgery, because physicians believe that it is less necessary psychologically for women to return to work, and because the description "return to the workforce" is inapplicable to many women who have been full-time homemakers. However, whether or not women work for pay, they are usually engaged in various types of work (e.g., cooking, cleaning, and running their households) that can affect levels of fatigue, pain, and stress. Researchers have recently documented high levels of post–heart attack fatigue in women (Varvaro, Sereika, Zullo, & Robertson, 1996) and postsurgical depression in low-income women (Ai, Saunders, Peterson, Dunkle, & Bolling, 1997). Furthermore, complete remission of symptoms after surgery is less common in women than in men; women generally continue to report angina, shortness of breath, and other problems (Sharpe et al., 1991; Vroman, 1983). Thus, women would be likely to benefit from rehabilitation programs and should be given the option to try them.

AUTOIMMUNE DISORDERS

Autoimmune disorders result when the immune system fails to discriminate between self and non-self, and thus produces autoantibodies that attack the body's own cells. Autoantibodies may be specific to particular organs of the body, or they may be nonspecific, systemic antibodies. Autoantibodies may either destroy the target tissue or achieve their effects by deranging the function of an organ or system. Many inflammatory, degenerative, and atrophic disorders are now attributed to probable or possible autoimmune reactions. Among the more common of these disorders are multiple sclerosis (MS), rheumatoid arthritis (RA), Graves' disease, Hashimoto's thyroiditis, pernicious anemia, Type 1 diabetes mellitus, chronic active hepatitis, systemic lupus erythematosus (SLE), Sjogren's syndrome, glomerulonephritis, scleroderma, and myasthenia gravis. Chronic fatigue syndrome, irritable bowel syndrome, vasculitis, and other chronic disorders of unknown etiology are currently under investigation for evidence of autoimmunity (Chrisler & O'Hea, 2000). Together, these disorders represent a significant proportion of the total incidence of chronic illness; approximately 1 in 20 Americans has some form of autoimmune disease (Faustman, 1997).

Women are diagnosed with autoimmune disorders more often than men, and in the case of some disorders, the sex difference in prevalence is substantial. The female-to-male ratio of patients with SLE, Sjogren's syndrome, and Hashimoto's thyroiditis is 9:1. The ratio is 6:1 for Grave's disease, and 3:1 for RA, chronic active hepatitis, scleroderma, and myasthenia gravis (Ollier & Symmons, 1992). The peak age of onset of autoimmune disorders tends to be in midlife, which violates our cultural expectations that chronic illnesses primarily affect the elderly. The reasons why individuals develop autoimmune disorders are not yet clear, but the following mechanisms have been postulated: (1) the body's own antigens have been altered by some substance (e.g., drug, virus, environmental toxin) that causes them to become antigenic and provoke autoimmune reactions; (2) cross-reacting antibodies against foreign substances are formed that then attack the body's own tissues; or (3) the body's regulator T-lymphocytes are defective and misregulate the immune system's responses (Crowley, 1997).

The greater frequency of autoimmune disorders in women and age distributions that show increased incidence coinciding with periods of marked alterations in endocrine functioning (e.g., greater reproductive activity, perimenopause) have led researchers to suggest that gonadal hormones may contribute to their etiology (Kiecolt-Glaser & Glaser, 1988). Evidence for the involvement of estrogenic hormones has been noted in women with SLE and RA. Oral contraceptives can exacerbate the symptoms of SLE, flare-ups are common during pregnancy and postpartum, and both women and men with disorders that involve excessive estrogen exposure are at increased risk of developing SLE (Achterberg-Lewis, 1988; Kiecolt-Glaser & Glaser, 1988). RA is rare before puberty, and its incidence is much greater in women than in men during the reproductive years than it is after menopause (Ollier & Symmons, 1992). Furthermore, RA often goes into remission during pregnancy and flares up postpartum; its symptoms may be ameliorated and its progression slowed by the use of oral contraceptives (L.L. Alexander & LaRosa, 1994; Kiecolt-Glaser & Glaser, 1988). Several animal studies have provided support for the role of gonadal hormones in autoimmunity (Ollier & Symmons, 1992), and researchers are currently examining the efficacy of exogenous hormones in the treatment of various autoimmune disorders (Van Vollenhoven & McGuire, 1994).

Genetic and environmental factors are implicated in autoimmune disorders. Relatives of patients with autoimmune disorders tend to show a higher than expected incidence of the same autoimmune disorders, and the prevalence of autoimmune disorders is high in people with Klinefelter's syndrome and higher in monozygotic than in dyzogotic twins (Merck Research Laboratories, 1992; Ollier & Symmons, 1992). The genetic contribution may be one of predisposition or susceptibility to damage by environmental agents (e.g., viral infection in the case of MS, or tissue damage from ultraviolet light in the case of SLE). SLE is more common in women of African and Chinese descent (Ollier & Symmons, 1992), and it occurs three times more often in African American than in European American women (Carr, 1986). RA is more common among some Native Americans, such as the Chippewa and Yakima (H. Weiner, 1991), than among other population groups. MS is five times more common in temperate than in tropical climates (Merck Research Laboratories, 1992), and Graves' disease is more common in developed countries (Ollier & Symmons, 1992). Scleroderma has been found in clusters around airports, which has led researchers to suggest that exposure to airplane fuel may be a risk factor (Ollier & Symmons, 1992). Among the other suspected toxins that have been investigated as triggers of autoimmunity are hair dyes (Liang et al., 1991), breast implants (Coleman et al., 1994), silicon, and vinyl chloride (Ollier & Symmons, 1992).

Autoimmune disorders present unique coping challenges because periods of active disease, which may last for weeks, months, or years, alternate with spontaneous improvement or even remission of symptoms. Flare-ups may be relatively mild or quite severe, and it is difficult to plan one's activities around them. Furthermore, the onset of autoimmune disorders is usually insidious, and the symptoms are vague and transient, which makes them difficult to diagnose. The symptoms of SLE resemble those of more than 20 other diseases; the first signs of MS often appear months or even years before it can be definitively diagnosed; and even RA, whose symptoms are clearly characteristic of the disorder, may take some time to diagnose because a number of other diseases (e.g., SLE, Lyme disease, Sjorgen's syndrome, gout) have symptoms that overlap with it (Chrisler & Parrett, 1995).

Patients with autoimmune disorders must cope not only with their symptoms, but with an uncertain future, with stigma, and with other people's ignorance. Although the autoimmune disorders as a group occur frequently, individual disorders are less common, and patients' friends and relatives may not know anything about them. The disorders are usually diagnosed at a time of life when people are expected to be busy and active, and healthy people may assume that people with autoimmune disorders are fine when they are not because they look normal. People with autoimmune disorders fit neither the sick role nor the healthy role much of the time (Thornton & Lea, 1992), and others may not know what to think of them. Fatigue, pain, and weakness are common to many of the autoimmune disorders, and these symptoms can be difficult to describe to others. We all get tired; in fact, many women are tired much of the time due to their many roles (Marris, 1996). Thus, these symptoms may be categorized by healthy people as illegitimate (Thornton & Lea, 1992). Perhaps because they are labeled as women's diseases, autoimmune disorders have not received the attention they deserve from biomedical or psychosocial researchers. We need to learn much more about them in order to develop adequate treatments and prevention strategies.

BREAST CANCER

The American Cancer Society has estimated that one in nine women in the United States will be diagnosed with breast cancer at some time in her life. More than 185,000 women were diagnosed with breast cancer in 1994, and 46,000 died of it (Kasper, 1995). These statistics, plus Americans' cultural obsession with breasts (Latteier, 1998) as objects of beauty and sexual signals, no doubt account for women's fear of breast cancer. Women with breast cancer have often been described in the medical, psychoanalytic, and psychological literature as hysterical, frustrated, depressed, masochistic, unable to express anger, sexually inhibited, or suffering from maternal or gender-role conflicts (Hiller, 1989). Despite the lack of empirical evidence to support any of these claims, they have been used by health care professionals, as well as laypeople, to suggest that women are to blame for their cancer (Hiller, 1989).

Although a genetic marker for breast cancer has been found (Travis, 1988), it is not present in every case, which is one reason why medical researchers believe that breast cancer is not one but several diseases. The cause of any individual woman's breast cancer is rarely known, but large epidemiological studies have identified a number of risk factors. These include increasing age, family history of breast or ovarian cancer, early menarche, late menopause, nulliparity or late (after age 35) birth of first child, high-fat diet, obesity, smoking, alcohol consumption, dense breast issue, and extended use of exogenous hormones (L.J. Lewis, Ritenbaugh, & Aickin, 1995). The connection of breast cancer to reproductive history has been known since the early 1700s, when a higher than average incidence was noticed in nuns (Hiller, 1989). More recently, women professors were discovered to have a higher than expected breast cancer rate (L.J. Lewis et al., 1995), and lesbians (Lauver et al., 1999; Rankow, 1995) are also believed to be at higher than average risk, although it has been difficult to gather the data necessary to verify this. Low birthrate may be the factor that links these groups. Ethnic differences in breast cancer experience have also been found. White women have higher morbidity rates, but Black women have higher mortality rates, probably due to later diagnosis and worse medical care. In one study of Black and White women in Maryland (Chaulk, Kazandjian, & Pipesh, 1995), Black women were not only more likely to die of breast cancer, but were significantly younger at diagnosis, more likely to have other chronic illnesses, and more likely to be poor or near poor (i.e., on Medicaid).

Advances in cancer treatment have greatly increased the survival rate of women with breast cancer, especially when the cancer is detected early. This means that women should be encouraged to utilize screening procedures: clinical breast examinations, breast self-examinations (BSE), and mammography. Although most American women are aware of these screening procedures, they do not regularly engage in them for a variety of reasons (e.g., cost, availability, uncertainty about how to perform BSE, fear of pain or radiation from mammography, or fear of the discovery of cancer) (Lauver et al., 1999; S.E. Taylor, 1995). Even in well-educated groups such as university faculty, only about half regularly practice BSE, although almost all are familiar with the procedure (L.J. Lewis et al., 1995). Cultural variables (e.g., modesty) also affect women's willingness to undergo breast cancer screening. Latinas and Asian American women are most likely to report that it is embarrassing to receive a clinical breast exam from a male physician and that they are not comfortable examining their own breasts (Dibble, Vanoni, & Miaskowski, 1997; Mo, 1992; J.A. Stein, Fox, & Murata, 1991).

Grady (1988) reported that confidence in one's ability to perform BSE properly is the best predictor of regular BSE practice, and Trotta (1980) found that although pamphlets and physicians' verbal descriptions were the most common sources of BSE information, those women who were taught by direct, person-to-person, hands-on instruction practiced BSE most frequently. Person-to-person instruction, although time-consuming, may be the best way both to teach the technique and to increase women's confidence in their abilities. Regular reminders from health care professionals are also helpful in increasing the practice of BSE, perhaps especially among low-income (Russ & Winett, 1996) and older women (Grady, 1988).

The best predictor of ever having had a mammogram is physician recommendation (J.D. Johnson & Meischke, 1994), and older women are especially likely to say they would have one if a doctor told them to do it (Rimer & King, 1992). Women with a family history of breast cancer are more likely to have had mammograms, as are women who worry about breast cancer, who believe they are vulnerable to breast cancer, who have a personal history of breast abnormalities, or know someone who's had breast cancer (J.D. Johnson & Meischke, 1994; McCaul, Branstetter, Schroeder, & Glasgow, 1996). In one study (Lauver et al., 1999), lesbians who had never had a mammogram gave as their reasons that they thought mammograms were unnecessary, that they distrusted the medical community's advice, or that they had encountered instances of homophobia or racism in health care practitioners. In a study of why older women don't get mammograms (Rimer & King, 1992), 94% of the participants said that they did not realize that the risk of breast cancer increases with age.

The most common cancer sites in women are the breasts, lungs, and colorectal system. Although the incidence of breast cancer is more than twice that of lung cancer, lung cancer kills significantly more women each year than breast cancer does. In their review of the psychosocial literature on women and cancer, Meyerowitz and Hart (1995) found that gender-role stereotypes have apparently affected researchers' decisions about which cancers to study and which psychological concerns to emphasize. They found that a substantial majority of articles in the medical and psychological databases concerned women's breast and reproductive cancers, whereas fewer than 15% of medical and fewer than 5% of psychological articles concerned men's reproductive cancers. This focus is inconsistent with cancer mortality rates in both sexes; more research is needed on reproductive cancers in men, and more research is needed on other cancer sites in women. Women were less likely than men to be included in studies of cancers to which both sexes are subject. Furthermore, psychosocial studies of women with cancer tended to examine body image, emotional reactions, and family roles. Studies of men with cancer tended to examine work roles, fertility, and insurance coverage. Obviously, both women and men have concerns in each of these areas, yet only gendered information is available to clinical practitioners who are trying to support their patients.

Much of the psychosocial literature on breast cancer is informed by the assumption that mastectomy is psychologically devastating to women, much more so than any other type of amputation would be. This reflects the cultural obsession with women's breasts and the belief that breasts are central to womanhood (Latteier, 1998). Thus, clinicians and American Cancer Society volunteers focus their efforts on body image issues, encourage women to apply makeup and appear "feminine" immediately after surgery, and urge them to have breast reconstruction for mental health reasons (Kasper, 1995; S. Wilkinson & Kitzinger, 1993b). However, in their review of the literature, Meyerowitz and Hart (1995) found that women with breast cancer do not report more distress than women with other types of cancer or than men with cancer. Women's main concerns are more likely to be survival, obtaining the best medical advice they can, worries about cancer recurrence, and questions about strength and physical activity after cancer treatment. For a personal account that illustrates how sexism, racism, heterosexism, and gender stereotypes affect treatment of and advice to breast cancer patients, see Audre Lorde's (1980, 1990) writings about her experiences.

PHYSICAL HEALTH CONSEQUENCES OF GENDERED BEHAVIORS

Aspects of gendered behavior can have direct effects on women's physical health status. In this section, I briefly discuss possible health effects of interpersonal power inequalities and the pursuit of beauty and unrealistically low body weight.

INTERPERSONAL POWER INEQUITIES

Earlier in this chapter, I discussed ways that institutional power inequalites (e.g., medical practice, insurance, scientific research, funding agencies) affect women's health and health care services. Power imbalances between individuals can also have health effects. In this section, I focus on power inequalities between couples, particularly, but not necessarily, heterosexual couples. Gender-role socialization can lead to aggression and domineering behavior in men that erupts into violence, and it can lead to passivity and subservience in women, especially where sex and romance are concerned.

The most frequent cause of injuries to women is battering, usually perpetrated by intimate partners. It accounts for as many as one in five of women's visits to hospital emergency rooms (Stark & Flitcraft, 1988). An estimated 25% of pregnant women are victims of domestic violence (Stark & Flitcraft, 1988); in one study of 358 low-income women (O'Campo, Gielen, Faden, & Kass, 1994), 65% reported having experienced verbal or physical abuse by their male partners or a family member during their pregnancies. Homicide is the 11th leading cause of death in the United States, and nearly 30% of women victims were killed by their intimate partners (Horton, 1992). Perhaps these numbers would be lower if states that require physicians to report suspected cases of abuse of children and the elderly also required them to report suspected cases of battering of women (Horton, 1992).

As many as one in five women have been raped (Koss, 1993), and about 25% of rape victims are physically injured seriously enough during the incident to require medical attention (Horton, 1992). Marchbanks, Lui, and Mercy (1990) examined the medical records of rape victims and reported that 82% had black eyes and swelling; 25% had bites, burns or scaldings, and injuries from physical restraints or bindings; 19% had internal injuries and experienced unconsciousness; 8% had broken bones or teeth; and 2% had knife or gunshot wounds. Rape victims also frequently experience vaginal injuries and bruises or other external trauma, usually on the mouth, throat, breasts, and thighs (M.E. Banks et al., 1995).

Violence against women has long-term as well as immediate health consequences. Researchers (e.g., Koss, 1994) typically find that victims of violence increase their frequency of health care utilization; the more severe the violence, the more physician visits women make. Koss (1994) found that rape victims, for example, increased their physician visits by 56%, from an average of 4.1 visits the year before the rape to an average of 7.3 visits the year after. Letourneau, Holmes, and Chasedunn-Roark (1999) found that women who had ever been victims of physical or sexual abuse were more likely than those who had not to report severe dysmenorrhea, pain during sexual intercourse, and one or more STDs. Victims of violence also commonly reported experiencing migraines, infections, gastrointestinal disorders, hypertension, and musculoskeletal problems. Eby, Campbell, Sullivan, and Davidson (1995) found high rates of somatic complaints in their study of women who had experienced physical or sexual abuse within the previous six months. More than 50% of their 110 participants reported experiencing the following symptoms, which they believed were related to the abuse: low energy, sleep problems, headaches, muscle tension/soreness, constant fatigue, weight change, back pain, nightmares, dizziness, poor appetite, acid stomach or indigestion, weakness, stomach pain, pounding or racing heart, trembling limbs, severe aches and pains. Health problems of the type these researchers have found could be the result of residual effects of injuries sustained during the violent incident, stress-induced changes in immune functioning, posttraumatic stress disorder, or an intensified focus on physical sensations as a result of postviolence concerns about bodily integrity (Koss, 1994).

STDs and unintended pregnancies can have serious consequences for women's health. In addition to their immediate symptoms, certain STDs can lead to urinary tract infections, pelvic inflammatory disease, cervical cancer, infertility, and even death. The inability to plan and space pregnancies negatively impacts women's physical and mental health. Feminine gender-role socialization that encourages deferential and submissive behavior, putting others' needs and desires ahead of one's own, and going to any lengths to maintain an intimate relationship can put women at risk for STDs and unintended pregnancies. Fear of violence and inability to resist emotionally coercive pronatal pressures also put women at risk.

Standard public health messages about how to avoid contracting an STD urge people to discuss medical and sexual histories with their partners and to use condoms. The advice assumes sexual equality in intimate relationships, which is often not the case. If a woman begins to ask a man about his sexual history, it may appear that she is trying to question his authority or fidelity. It takes considerable self-esteem and courage for women to assert themselves in an intimate relationship, and some women will not want to run the risk of being rejected by their partners for asking questions (S.D. Cochran & Mays, 1989; Leonardo & Chrisler, 1992). In their study of 146 women college students, Sheahan and her colleagues (Sheahan, Coons, Seabolt, Churchill, & Dale, 1994) found that only 31% had ever discussed with their partners their own or their partners' sexual histories. Yet, 38% of the women had had between one and four episodes of STDs, and only 12% regularly utilized condoms.

Winter (1988) found that having a positive self-concept is positively correlated with contraception use; that is, women who admit to being sexually active and perceive themselves as at risk for STDs or pregnancy are most likely to decide to use contraception. This may seem like an obvious point, but, in a society that has traditionally divided good women and sexual women into different groups, many women are ashamed of their sexual needs and thus may deny them (Leonardo & Chrisler, 1992). Acquiring contraceptives means that one is planning to have sex, and women who view sex as an event that happens to them, as when they are romantically "swept away," rather than as an event they can control are not likely to use contraceptives (Leonardo & Chrisler, 1992). Furthermore, traditional gender roles require women to follow the lead of their partners in romantic and sexual situations. To ask a man to use a condom violates these expectations. Because condom use has to be renegotiated with each sexual encounter, the issue of control is brought up repeatedly, and each time women are vulnerable to vicissitudes of their current relationships (Worth, 1989).

It is interesting that, in addition to affordability, availability, sexual self-concept, and partner cooperation, variables that have been found to predict regular contraception use include health orientation, achievement orientation, educational goals (Costa, Jessor, Foretenberry, & Donovan, 1996), communication skills (Burger & Inderbitzen, 1985), self-esteem, self-efficacy, and nontraditional gender-role ideology (Sable & Libbus, 1998).

THE PURSUIT OF BEAUTY

Individuals' concerns about what others think of them can lead them to engage in behaviors that affect their health status (Leary, Tchividjian, & Kraxberger, 1994). For example, to fit in with a group they'd like to impress, people may take up smoking or drug use, drink alcohol to excess, exercise obsessively or not at all, or stay out in the sun too long, which can increase their risk of skin cancer (Leary et al, 1994). Gendered concerns are also relevant to impression management. For example, men may use steroids to build up their muscles or engage in risky behaviors (e.g., drag racing) to appear strong and brave. In this section, I highlight ways that women's pursuit of beauty can expose them to health risks.

There is considerable evidence that women's physical attractiveness is judged more harshly than men's (Saltzberg & Chrisler, 1995), and this is particulary true as people age. Women are acutely aware of this double standard. At all ages, women are more concerned than men about body weight and physical appearance and have lower appearance self-esteem; those women who define themselves as feminine are the most concerned about their appearance and have the lowest self-esteem (Pliner, Chaiken, & Flett, 1990). Beauty is an elusive commodity, which varies across cultures and changes with time (Fallon, 1990). The value of beauty depends in part on the high costs of achieving it; the costs involved may be physical, temporal, economic, or psychological (Saltzberg & Chrisler, 1995).

Physical costs include health risks. Perhaps the most obvious of these are the health effects that can result from weight loss strategies. Women have died from unsafe products such as rainbow pills and liquid protein, and they have become malnourished from very-low-calorie diets or diets that require them to cut out whole food groups. Very lean bodies can result in delayed menarche or prolonged amenorrhea, both of which are associated with factors that compromise bone density (Graber, Brooks-Gunn, & Warren, 1999) and thus put girls and women at risk for bone fractures, osteoporosis, and scoliosis.

Much has been written about the mental health effects of eating disorders, which also have serious physical consequences that can be fatal. As many as 5% to 10% of anorexics die from either starvation or suicide; the severe malnutrition can result in bone marrow failure and cardiac decompensation, arrhythmia, or failure (de Zwaan & Mitchell, 1993). Liver dysfunction and acute pancreatitis can result from refeeding (i.e., the ingestion of large amounts of carbohydrates that is necessary to reverse anorexia nervosa) (M.J. Turner & Shapiro, 1992). Many bulimics experience dehydration and electrolyte imbalances due to their purging behaviors, and erosion of the surface of the teeth is common in those who vomit frequently (Robb & Smith, 1996). Potassium depletion often causes heart arrhythmia and affects muscular transmission in general; therefore, bulimics often experience fatigue and muscle weakness (Hofland & Dardis, 1992). Kidney and endocrine abnormalities, brittle hair and nails, and edema are common to both anorexics and bulimics (M.J. Turner & Shapiro, 1992).

Cosmetic surgery has become so accepted and so common that, although it's quite expensive, surgeons advertise their services on television. These ads often mention the mental health "benefits" of enhancing appearance, but it is important to remember that there are potentially serious side effects to any surgery, especially if general anesthesia is necessary. Hemorrhages, scars, nerve damage, and occasional deaths do result. Surgery is currently performed to reduce the size of lips, ear lobes, nose, buttocks, thighs, abdomen, and breasts; rebuild the face; remove wrinkles; and add "padding" to almost any body part. Most cosmetic surgery patients are women (Hamburger, 1988), and many affluent women have had multiple procedures. Increasing numbers of Asian, Jewish, and African American girls and women have had facial surgery (Faludi, 1991) in order to come closer to a beauty standard that idealizes features most common in northern Europeans.

It is not surprising that a large percentage of cosmetic surgeries are for the augmentation or reduction of the breasts. The cultural obsession with breasts had led many physically normal women to be self-conscious about the size and shape of their breasts (R.J. Freedman, 1984), even to the point of valuing form over function (Latteier, 1998). The FDA has estimated that about 2 million American women have undergone breast augmentation surgeries; 80% of the procedures were for purely cosmetic reasons (Latteier, 1998). As early as 1950, physicians invented the term "micromastia" to describe small breasts, and thus they defined a disorder that needed correction and added a "health" concern to already existing appearance concerns (Latteier, 1998). Ruptures in silicone breast implants have been linked to autoimmune disorders; although it is difficult to "prove" a connection to the extent required to win lawsuits, the FDA has banned the further use of silicone, and surgeons are now using saline implants. Among the health consequenceses that can result from breast implants are the formation of scar tissue that can harden, interference with clear reading of mammographic images, and possible inability to breastfeed (Latteier, 1998).

Makeup use causes an allergic reaction known as acne cosmetica in about one-third of girls and women (R.J. Freedman, 1984). This can result in a vicious cycle, as the appearance of the acne leads to the use of more makeup to cover it, which then leads to more acne (R.J. Freedman, 1984). Other fashion-related health problems include allergies from scented products; podiatric problems due to pointy-toed, high-heeled shoes; lower back pain from the use of high heels and heavy shoulder bags; infections from tatooing and body piercing with unsanitary instruments; scalp burns from hair-straightening techniques; injuries from long hair and dangling earrings that get caught in machinery; and increased vulnerability to assaults when clothing such as high heels and tight skirts make it difficult to run from danger (Saltzberg & Chrisler, 1995).

CONCLUSION

Medicine has had a peculiar and ambivalent interest in women's health throughout its history. On the one hand, physicians have increased the number of office visits for health care services that women must make by redefining normal experiences (e.g., the menstrual cycle, pregnancy, birth, and menopause) as medical emergencies that must be managed (Chrisler, 1996a; Gannon, 1998; Wertz, 1983). On the other hand, physicians complain that women seek care unnecessarily for minor ailments or problems for which they would receive more appropriate care from a psychotherapist (Corea, 1977; Fidell, 1980). While they have been busy inventing disorders such as micromastia and premenstrual syndrome and discovering cures for natural developmental phenomena such as menopause, they have neglected to study the causes and natural histories of chronic illnesses such as SLE that disproportionately affect women and have not done the research necessary to be certain that pharmacologic cures and treatments for common diseases will work as well in women as in men.

Health psychologists have also neglected the study of behavioral interventions for disorders more common in women, and the research they have done, for example, on coping with cancer diagnosis and treatment, has often contained sexist assumptions and hypotheses influenced by gender stereotypes. Thus, although we've come far in our knowledge of women's health and illnesses since the rise of the women's health movement in the 1960s, we still have far to go to reach parity in our medical and psychosocial understanding of women's needs.

An understanding of women's physical health and health care needs is as important to the study of the psychology of women as an understanding of women's mental health. In fact, the two can rarely be clearly divided from one another, as psychological variables affect physical health and vice versa. Gendered knowledge affects both physical and mental health. Gender influences not only what we do but how we feel, not only how we are perceived but how we are diagnosed and treated. Gendered behavioral prescriptions and limitations can literally mean life or death for both women and men.

CHAPTER 20

Disorderly Constructs: Feminist Frameworks for Clinical Psychology

JEANNE MARECEK

L ike other progressive movements of the sixties, the Women's Liberation Movement took a dim view of the mental health professions. Feminists protested the power of the mental health professions to enforce the status quo by labeling nonconformity and dissent as mental illness. Psychoanalytic theory, then the reigning paradigm in the mental health field, made a particularly obvious and easy target (Buhle, 1998). Penis envy, women's "inner space," marriage and motherhood as criteria of female maturity, women's alleged capacity for double orgasm, and the disparagement of clitoral sexuality—all these psychoanalytic notions came under fire and did not survive the attack.

The first critiques of the mental health professions were leveled by feminists on the outside but feminists in the mental health professions quickly joined in. The Association for Women in Psychology was launched in 1969, followed by the Division of the Psychology of Women in 1973. Three influential works set the tenor of early feminist research and activism in clinical psychology. One was Naomi Weisstein's *Psychology Constructs the Female* (first published in 1968b), subsequently reprinted 30 times under various titles. Weisstein's well-honed ire was directed toward clinical and personality psychology. Her critique was two-pronged: (1) What is advanced as scientific dogma about women often merely recycles cultural stereotypes; and (2) psychology's claims about women's nature grossly under rate the influence of social context. Phyllis Chesler's *Women and Madness* (1972) charged the therapy professions with placing women in a double bind: behaviors that were aspects of normative femininity (such as emotional expressiveness and dependence) were also symptom criteria for mental disorders such as hysteria and dependent personality disorder. Chesler also criticized psychotherapy, charging that male therapist/female patient dyads (then the most common configuration) replicated the cultural norm of male dominance and female subordination and thus were damaging to women clients. Broverman and her colleagues (1970) provided empirical evidence to support claims of therapists' biases. Using adjective checklists, they showed that therapists' views of the ideal man resembled a mentally healthy person, while their views of the ideal woman resembled a typical mental patient. All these issues—that cultural biases permeate scientific constructs; that psychologists too readily ignore or underplay the social context; that sexist and other biases are sedimented in concepts of disorder; and that the power difference in therapy relationships can work against clients' interest—still thread through the tapestry of feminist clinical psychology today.

At the beginning, feminist work in clinical psychology was largely reactive, seeking to correct outmoded and pejorative ideas and to produce empirical warrants for challenges to sexist theories and therapy practices. However, feminists soon moved from a solely reactive stance to producing new knowledge and treatment approaches as well. Soon feminists were asking their own questions about the experiences of women and girls, the role that gender and other markers of social status play in psychological disorder, and the best concepts and methods of therapy and research. Today, three journals, *Women and Therapy,* the *Journal of Feminist Family Therapy,* and *Affilia* are devoted to feminist clinical practice. In addition, *Feminism & Psychology* and *Psychology of Women Quarterly* frequently include research on clinical disorders and therapy.

In this chapter, I describe five frameworks of feminist knowledge in clinical psychology. These are not successive stages of development; workers are currently active in all five. My goal is not to catalogue all the work that has been accomplished by feminist scholars and practitioners thus far, a task that verges on the impossible. Instead, I seek to look at the work from new vantage points, to focus on forests rather than trees, in hopes of stimulating further insights and questions.

FRAMEWORK 1: ASSESSING CLINICAL BIAS

The work of Broverman and her colleagues suggested that therapists' values and beliefs about women inflected their clinical judgments. Following their study, scores of studies addressing therapists' judgments were carried out. Most rely on analogue methods. Typically, therapists receive information (for example, case descriptions, clinical assessment scores, or video- or audiotapes) about a hypothetical client described as either a man or a woman. They then make clinical assessments such as ratings of the severity of the patient's problem, a diagnosis, suitability for treatment, or likelihood of treatment success. These early studies yielded a mixed bag of results (reviewed by C.V. Abramowitz & Dokecki, 1977; J.A. Sherman, 1980), in part because analogue methods tend to be fraught with methodological and interpretive problems. When questionnaires are distributed to large samples of therapists, low response rates and self-selection often cloud the interpretation of the results. Often the intent of the study is transparent, leading therapists to modify their judgments in accord with the perceived demands of the situation. Moreover, the value of an analogue study depends on its external validity: Does the contrived situation mimic real-life clinical practice? In most cases, the information given about the hypothetical client is scant, in part so that it can plausibly describe both a man and a woman. In an actual clinical situation, a therapist would be likely to suspend judgment until sufficient information was available. Moreover, some analogue studies have required therapists to make judgments that are not usually part of a clinical assessment.

We can ask whether a difference in therapists' perceptions of men and women should be considered bias. Should an action or presenting complaint hold a single meaning and have the same diagnostic significance regardless of the social location of the actor? Gender is a central feature of social life and personal identity; men and women typically experience different strains, have different resources, and operate under different constraints. For each gender, there are normative ways of expressing distress and seeking relief. A therapist who is aware of the gender norms that govern social life and the gendered social hierarchy may well interpret the same behavior differently depending on the gender of the individual. Taken in context, the "same" behavior is not the same (Hare-Mustin & Marecek, 1990a). Thus, researchers have broadened the scope of inquiry from individual judgments to questions about assessment instruments and diagnostic categories (Worell & Remer, 1992).

Overdiagnosing, Underdiagnosing, and Misdiagnosing

Initial concerns about gender bias centered on the possible overdiagnosis of women because feminists saw that diagnoses can serve as regulatory devices that pathologize women who violate the norm. However, underdiagnosis, that is, overlooking psychological problems, also occurs. Until recently, for instance, alcohol abuse among women (at least middle-class women) often went unrecognized. Even when it was recognized, shame and embarrassment often kept women out of treatment (Sandmaier, 1980). Although alcohol abuse among women is no longer an unspeakable matter, underdiagnosis and lack of access to treatment for other problems persists among women from disadvantaged groups and from cultural subgroups in which therapy is not acceptable (Raja, 1998).

Psychiatric diagnosis can also be used to protect the interests of dominant groups. Leslie Camhi's (1993) fascinating study of the emergence of kleptomania in the nineteenth century traces it to the invention of department stores, which displayed goods within consumers' reach. The diagnosis kleptomania turned shoplifting from a crime into an illness. The diagnosis was used selectively to shield upper-class women from prosecution and to distinguish their actions from the common thievery of ordinary women. Diagnosing a woman with kleptomania thus preserved not only her personal reputation and dignity but also the moral superiority of the upper classes. In this instance, diagnostic bias served to protect a certain class of women as well as to preserve the class hierarchy.

DANGEROUS DIAGNOSES

Viewed from a feminist perspective, the constitution of certain diagnostic categories reveals a troubled—and troubling—relationship to women. In the past, diagnoses such as nymphomania, hysteria, neurasthenia, erotomania, kleptomania, and masochism have enforced women's conformity to norms of domesticity, subordination, and subservience to men's sexual needs; at times diagnoses enforce class distinctions as well (cf., Camhi, 1993; Groneman, 1994; King, 1990; Showalter, 1985).

Concern about diagnostic categories is not confined to the past. Consider the recent addition of premenstrual dysphoric disorder to the *Diagnostic and Statistical Manual of Mental Disorders* (*DSM*, American Psychiatric Association, 1994), an addition seems to echo Hippocrates' idea that the female psyche is governed by the reproductive tract (Vieth, 1965). Moreover, if women's anger, depression, and discontent are mistakenly interpreted as byproducts of unruly reproductive physiology, women will be deterred from making changes in difficult and unjust life circumstances. In the view of feminist social scientists, the scientific evidence did not warrant labeling premenstrual difficulties as a psychiatric (as opposed to medical) disorder, nor their inclusion in the *DSM* (Parlee, 1989). As Mary Parlee (1993) has documented, premenstrual dysphoric disorder was positioned at the intersection of the economic interests of pharmaceutical companies, gender politics, and rivalries between medical specialties. Scientific considerations could hardly carry the day in the debates over its inclusion in the *DSM*.

Borderline personality disorder (BPD) is another diagnostic category of special concern to feminists (Becker, 1997). At least three times as many women as men receive diagnoses of BPD. Individuals with BPD are notorious as unsavory therapy clients—difficult to work with, troublesome, and unlikely to make progress. Yet the symptom criteria for BPD are vague and over-inclusive, overlapping with those of other personality disorders. The criteria lack specificity, leaving it to a therapist to decide whether a client's behavior reaches the threshold of pathology required for a diagnosis. Examples include "inappropriate" intense anger, "marked" reactivity of mood, and "markedly" unstable self-image. Therapists who specialize in working with women who have been victims of intimate violence have pointed out that a diagnosis of BPD is often mistakenly given to such women. They should be diagnosed with posttraumatic stress disorder (J. Herman, 1992). This diagnostic error prevents women from receiving appropriate therapy. Moreover, therapy clients diagnosed with BPD carry the onus of the therapist's negative expectations and this may well impede the therapy.

Sexuality and sexual expression have far-reaching implications for women's lives. Feminists have struggled against moral, legal, religious, and medical strictures that have regulated women's sexuality and limited their self-determination, pleasure, and safety. Diagnostic categories for sexual problems, which have proliferated in recent editions of the *DSM*, are based on the model of human sexuality developed by Masters and Johnson in the 1960s. As Leonore Tiefer (1992, 1995) has argued, the model reflects a view of sexuality that is centered in male and heterosexual experience. Moreover, the model reduces sex to a set of physiological responses focused on genital sensation and orgasm. As Tiefer notes, this focus excludes many sensual, sexual, and pleasurable experiences that women say they value and enjoy. Moreover, it fails to acknowledge that sexual difficulties are often embedded in personal or relationship problems. Tiefer (2000) has described the emerging category of female sexual dysfunction, which its proponents say affects up to 80% of women. Female sexual dysfunction is closely tied to the interests of pharmaceutical companies seeking to market Viagra-like remedies for women. Not surprisingly, the diagnostic criteria emphasize physiological indices of sexual arousal. The category of female sexual dysfunction may further divorce sex from its psychological and relational context.

The diagnoses given to women are not the sole concern that feminists have about clinical bias. For instance, feminists have objected to the pattern of blaming mothers for the difficulties and disorders of their offspring, a tradition of long standing in the mental health professions. A review of the clinical literature showed that a broad array of behavioral problems (ranging from arson to xenophobia) in children and adults has been attributed to faulty mothering practices (Caplan & Hall-McCorquodale, 1985). Such mother blaming is not grounded in scientific evidence, but instead echoes mother blaming in the culture (Caplan, 1989). As Nancy Chodorow (1978) has pointed out, in contemporary post-industrial societies, the burden of responsibility placed on mothers has enlarged from meeting children's physical needs to nurturing their psychological development as well. Mothers are held responsible for the lifelong cognitive, emotional, and moral status of their offspring, a standard that is diffuse, open-ended, and ultimately impossible.

The clinical literature on sexual abuse and violence in intimate life reflects yet another gender-linked bias—a tendency to exonerate men from responsibility for acts of violence. The use of the passive voice (e.g., "Patient was hit in the face by a fist.") and other linguistic practices in articles in professional writing serve to obscure male agency and responsibility for battering (S. Lamb, 1991). These patterns of linguistic avoidance persist to this day, even after nearly a decade of criticism and high attention to the problem of intimate violence (D. Phillips & Henderson, 1999). A review of the family therapy literature showed ways in which blame for incest is sometimes shifted away from men. When incest is conceptualized as a problem in the family system, fathers are largely absolved of responsibility for their actions (K. James & MacKinnon, 1990). Women may be blamed for being sexually unavailable to their husbands or for failing to detect or deter their husbands' incestuous behavior. Thus, we see a complementary pattern in which women are held to an extreme standard of responsibility for the welfare of their families and responsibility is shifted off men (see Fine & Carney, this volume).

THE *DSM* IN CRITICAL PERSPECTIVE

Some feminists have moved beyond a critique of specific diagnoses to challenge the epistemological and ontological assumptions of the *DSM*. The *DSM* embodies a disease model, construing psychological problems in medicalized terms. In the disease model, disorders are considered real entities that, as R.J. Kessler (1990) puts it, "have an existence independent of the patient" (p. 141). The disease model ignores everyday identities and social categories—such as gender, race/ethnicity, and social class—that shape experience and life chances. Instead, it defines disorders in terms of discrete symptoms devoid of personal meanings. The disease model is inconsistent with the feminist emphasis on the social context, especially the power relationships within that context. Moreover, it is inconsistent with feminists' commitment to exploring women's lives in the terms dictated by women themselves, a strategy that has uncovered important new knowledge (A.J. Stewart, 1994a).

The *DSM* imposes sharp boundaries around each disorder, implying that there is a clear distinction between normal and abnormal, as well as between disorders. But its category system does not carve nature at its joints. For example, the boundary that separates a clinical eating disorder from the eating practices of many women is an artificial one. In reality, eating problems fall along a continuum. Moreover, in real life, distinctions between categories of disorder are blurred and textbook cases are seldom seen (Nurcombe & Gallagher, 1986).

The number of categories in the *DSM* has inflated with each successive edition, beginning with 198 in 1952 and rising to 340 in 1994 (Hare-Mustin & Marecek, 1997). From the perspective of a feminist critical psychologist, this means that more and more areas of life are brought under the scrutiny of mental health authorities and subjected to judgments of normality and abnormality. The *DSM* thus operates as a regulatory device, enforcing conformity in the name of "good health." Ironically, in spite of the proliferation of diagnostic categories in successive editions, the *DSM* does not map the universe of problems for which individuals seek psychological help. According to one estimate, 60% of individuals who seek the help of a mental health professional present with a problem that does not fit in any *DSM* category (Wylie, 1995).

FRAMEWORK II: HIGH-PREVALENCE DISORDERS

High-prevalence disorders are disorders with an "association with the female gender, either in terms of the large number of women affected or because of their specific relationship to women's role issues" (Brodsky & Hare-Mustin, 1980, p. 391). This term was introduced at a 1979 conference on women and psychotherapy sponsored by the American Psychological Association and the National Institute of Mental Health, which was convened to set priorities for research on women. The high-prevalence disorders identified by conference participants were depression, agoraphobia, hysteria, anorexia, obesity, and marital and family conflict.

In the twenty years since the conference, the specific disorders that appear to be of high prevalence among women have shifted dramatically. At this writing, posttraumatic stress disorder and other consequences of gender-linked violence loom large as women's problems. Hysteria is seldom diagnosed or discussed in the literature; indeed, it is not included in the *DSM.* Agoraphobia seems to occur only infrequently. Bulimia has emerged as a pattern of disturbed eating at least five times more common than anorexia. In short, prevalence rates seem quite unstable, whether because the true prevalence of the disorder changes, the number of people who seek treatment shifts, or therapists alter their diagnosing practices. Whatever the cause of the variability in prevalence rates, it seems unwise to set a research agenda on the basis of them.

The high-prevalence disorders identified by the APA-NIMH conference participants were more prevalent among women than men at the time. However, in terms of absolute numbers, not all of them affected large numbers of women. Disorders that have high base rates among women, regardless of their gender distribution, deserve attention too. Moreover, we cannot assume that gender is irrelevant because a disorder is diagnosed with equal frequency among men and women. Sheer prevalence rates reveal very little. Looking beyond them, we often find that features such as risk factors or trigger events, the onset and course of a disorder, and treatment response differ for men and women. Clinical depression provides a good example. Marriage offers men some protection from depression, but it raises women's risk for depression. Unhappy marriage constitutes a serious risk of depression for women; one study showed that 50% of women in unhappy marriages were clinically depressed. However, even in supposedly happy marriages, almost five times as many women as men experienced depression (McGrath, Keita, Strickland, & Russo, 1990). There are further differences among women depending on class, ethnic background, generation, and culture.

Even when prevalence rates of a disorder appear equal for men and women, gender remains an important consideration. Medical and societal responses to clinical conditions depend on the gendered meanings attached to them. For example, Holstein (1987) studied discharge hearings for patients hospitalized for schizophrenia. Judgments about readiness for discharge differed sharply for men and women. For men, key factors were their propensity to violence and the need to protect others from them; for women, the key concerns were to guard them against sexual involvement and to insure the safety of their living arrangements. Although schizophrenia appears to occur equally often in men and women, African Americans—particularly men—are disproportionately diagnosed with schizophrenia. Clinicians attribute different symptoms to African Americans than to Whites; moreover, they base diagnoses of schizophrenia on different configurations of symptoms depending on an individual's race (Treirweiler et al., 2000).

Even when mental health problems occur more frequently among men than women, important questions about the treatment of women remain. Substance abuse provides a provocative example. The experiences of women with substance abuse problems have been shaped by shifting ideas about women, as well as class and racial biases. Indeed, many of the chemical addictions of women over the past century are directly attributable to medical practices. Physicians and other practitioners indiscriminately provided women with opium-based patent medicines in the 1800s, amphetamine-based diet pills in the 1960s, and tranquilizers such as Librium and Valium in the 1970s (Kandall, 1999). In summary, gender is a primary category of social identity. Actions and emotions—including those constituting psychological disorder—carry gender-linked meanings. Thus, all diagnostic categories merit attention, not merely those that are (perhaps only temporarily) of high prevalence among women.

FRAMEWORK III: WOMEN'S DIFFERENCE

Since the earliest days of psychology over a century ago, psychologists have made claims about women's nature and male-female difference. Classical personality theories—especially psychoanalytic theories—laid out different developmental trajectories for men and women, normative personality traits, capacities, and interests for each, and different criteria for maturity and mental health. For decades, these personality theories formed the bases for psychotherapy practice, as well as for criteria of mental health and illness. Sharp disagreements about women's nature pepper the history of psychoanalytic personality theory. Indeed, the debates on what was sometimes known as the "woman question" constitute some of its most contentious chapters (Buhle, 1998).

Two lines of work on women follow the personological framework of earlier psychodynamic theorists. One is "women's voice" theory, which centers on the work of Carol Gilligan and her students (Gilligan, 1980). The other is self-in-relation theory (recently renamed the relational/cultural model) of the Stone Center. The Stone Center writings directly concern mental health and psychotherapy, so I will concentrate on them here. The Stone Center enjoys a large following among feminist-identified therapists and women therapists and counselors who specialize in work with women. Indeed, self-in-relation theory, along with women's voice theory, tends to dominate the spoken discourse and training workshops for feminist-identified practitioners (Chodorow, 1999).

The work of the Stone Center, a group of therapists led by Jean Baker Miller, adopts the personological framework of earlier psychodynamic theories, albeit from a woman-centered perspective. In an early and well-received book, *Toward a New Psychology of Women* (1976), Miller examined women's experiences of subordination in the intimate setting of marriage and family life. In her view, women experience a distinct and often hidden emotional life; moreover, their experiences give rise to a special set of feminine qualities, including intuition, capacities for empathy and relatedness, and a propensity for nurturing and caring for others. Although these characteristics can lead to psychological problems, Miller nonetheless applauded them. In her words, feminine characteristics are "closer to psychological essentials and are, therefore, the bases of a more advanced form of living" (1976, p. 27).

The subsequent work of the Stone Center was cast within a narrower frame than *Toward a New Psychology of Women*. The model they developed, called the self-in-relation model, shifted away from Miller's attention to cultural norms and societal practices and substituted a focus on individual development (Jordan et al., 1991). In the self-in-relation model, the childhood experiences of girls (particularly mother-daughter interactions) give rise to a self-structure that is uniquely female. This self-structure seeks connection to others and requires such connections to flourish. This developmental trajectory is the source of women's unique relational capacities and needs. A context of empathic relationships is a necessity for women's psychological growth and well being; absent this context, psychological difficulties (such as work inhibitions, depression, anger, impaired relationships) result. As one might expect, the self-in-relation model of therapy centers on the quality of the therapist-client relationship (J.B. Miller & Stiver, 1997). Healing takes place through mutuality, empathic understanding, and the attunement of the therapist and the client to each other's emotional needs. Women therapists, because their own relational capacities for empathy and connection match those of their clients, are specially suited for work with women.

Stone Center workers have targeted their work to therapists and other human service workers, such as nurses, counselors, and social workers. They have elected to disseminate their ideas largely through training institutes and workshops for practitioners and through in-house working papers. Stone Center workers rarely, if ever, write for refereed journals or edited volumes other than in-house ones. As a result, as Nancy Chodorow (1999) has noted, the writings of the Stone Center are seldom read or cited by either psychodynamic thinkers or feminist scholars or researchers.

By positioning itself at some distance from the scholarly world, the Stone Center has denied itself opportunities for engagement with feminist scholars. Such engagement could serve to clarify elements of the model. For example, some psychodynamic theorists have pondered how the self-in-relation model of development overlaps with Kohutian self-psychology, as well as with some of Winnicott's ideas about the mother-child relationship. For others, the model of therapy seems hard to distinguish from Rogerian client-centered therapy and other humanist approaches. For scholars seeking a more precise understanding of the self-in-relation model, it would be helpful to know what its developers see as the similarities and differences between their model and related bodies of theory.

Another set of questions concerns the connections between self-in-relation theory and similar bodies of feminist theory. Some readers have simply merged Chodorow's (1978) theory of gender development, women's voice theory, and self-in-relation theory. Yet, Chodorow (1999) has taken pains to dispute this reading of her work (and indeed a careful reading of her work reveals striking differences). What consistencies and divergences do the Stone Center theorists themselves see? Many scholars also wish for more precise and concrete definitions of key concepts of the model. These include relationality, connectedness, self-structure, empowerment, growth, and healing in therapy.

A third set of questions concerns what self-in-relation therapy shares with feminist therapies. It is not clear whether the Stone Center workers consider self-in-relation therapy to be a type of feminist therapy, although many of its adherents do. Is the silence regarding the vast literature on feminist therapy to be read as a sign of agreement or a tacit rejection? Are the principles of feminist therapy (discussed next) germane to self-in-relation therapy? Can the self-in-relation model offer guidance to therapists hoping to translate feminist principles into concrete practices? Stone Center workers have been developing their model of women's psychology and women's psychotherapy for over twenty years. Yet almost no empirical research has been undertaken to verify its claims of women's difference or the elements of the developmental model. Moreover, with more and more practitioners receiving training and certification in the Stone Center's model of therapy, it seems important to evaluate its effectiveness and efficacy.

Like other feminist difference theories, the self-in-relation model poses an alternate universalism to traditional personological theories of gender difference, one that celebrates the redemptive possibilities of women's ways of being. It makes claims about how women are and, by implication, how they should be. This universalism raises a variety of questions. First, which women are included in the theory? Until recently, the Stone Center seemed to focus primarily on the experiences of women who were white, middle-class, heterosexual, educated, and in therapy. How must the model change when women from different backgrounds are included? For instance, can we speak about "the" mother-child relationship, as if mothering practices remained the same in spite of varying cultural values, economic resources, and historical changes? (Indeed, in the past 25 years, the changes associated with feminism altered mothering practices among white middle-class women considerably.) Moreover, the focus on the qualities that are presumed to distinguish women from men tends to mask the differences among women. As Spelman (1988) has written, "The claim of commonality can be very arrogant indeed" (p. 139). Instead of establishing a general model and then adding on the exceptions, it is better to begin with the heterogeneity of women's experiences. Mapping this diversity of experiences and interests of women then becomes the project.

Theories of women's difference tend to overgeneralization. They push aside evidence of similarity or overlap between men and women. Furthermore, because the differences are tied to early childhood experience, the theories pay little attention to the fluctuating significance of gender in different social circumstances. Moreover, the self-in-relation model seems to assume that socialization is unidirectional, flowing from mothers to children and from early experiences to later life. This overlooks the extent to which children regulate their own behavior and the behavior of their peers. Moreover, it may underestimate children's capacities for resisting or rebelling against their socialization.

FRAMEWORK IV: DISORDERS IN SOCIAL CONTEXT

Psychological health and disorder is tied to the social context of women's lives, particularly to conditions that maintain women in subordinate relations. This is the premise that distinguishes feminist therapy from conventional approaches, which typically focus on individuals in isolation. The question for feminist researchers has been to make the link between risk for disorder and particular features of the lives of particular groups of women. Researchers have studied the micropolitics of gender in intimate relationships and families; stressful events such as reproductive crises, marital and relationship problems, childbirth and mothering; gender-linked violence and abuse; patterns of economic disadvantage; social dislocation, such as homelessness and immigration; and the absence of social support networks. Some have looked at conditions such as state-sponsored torture and terrorism, social upheaval related to war and natural catastrophes.

Feminist work on eating disorders provides an excellent example of the power of this framework. Eating problems—anorexia, bulimia, and binge eating—are culture-bound syndromes. They are highly specific to our time and place, suggesting that they must be understood within the social and cultural context of contemporary North American society. More than 90% of those who suffer from clinical eating disorders are women, strongly implicating contemporary practices of femininity in the culture. Moreover, the eating problems of those who receive *DSM* diagnoses represent only the tip of the iceberg of eating problems that women and girls face.

Much work traces eating practices to a prevailing "culture of thinness," pointing to the glamorization of ultra-thin female bodies in the mass media, cultural equations of thinness with heterosexual attractiveness, and the proliferation of diets and diet foods. The "culture of thinness" model suggests that girls and women internalize "messages" about the desirability of thin bodies, leading to intense preoccupation with their body shape and size, a distorted body image, and rigorous dieting to achieve a thin body. Although there is ample evidence for a "culture of thinness," a mono-causal model that explains eating problems solely on the basis of cultural "messages" about thinness is too simplistic. It does not explain why some women develop clinical eating disorders, but most do not. Moreover, if the culture of thinness were solely responsible for eating problems, we might expect that some groups of women and girls—such as those with high academic or professional aspirations, lesbians, and feminists—who are less concerned with attractiveness to men would be less prone to develop eating problems. There is little evidence that this is true; indeed, high-achieving college students may be at greater risk than other women.

Three lines of feminist work on eating problems go beyond the notion of a thin ideal to interrogate the many additional culture-specific meanings of gender that bear on women's body size, eating practice, and identities. Psychodynamic and postmodern feminist theorists have examined the gender-laden motifs and themes invoked by body size and fat, and by dieting, self-nurturance, and food itself. They have also focused on the strong positive value placed on self-control, virtuous self-restraint, and, for women, self-abnegation (C. Bloom, Gitter, Gutwill, Kogel, & Zaphiropoulos, 1994; Bordo, 1993). The controlled body signifies the mind's control over the body and thus confers a sense of power. Food is figured as temptation and thus, indulging in eating can seem like moral corruption. Malson (1998) traces the ways that these discourses thread through the talk of women diagnosed with anorexia, constructing both their identities as women and their relations to their bodies.

A second line of work, called objectification theory, ties women's eating problems to social processes that lead to objectification (Fredricksen & Roberts, 1997). Contemporary Western culture is saturated with sexualized evaluations of women. The (hetero)sexualized gaze—that is, the visual inspection of women's bodies—often is an objectifying one. It separates a woman's body parts or sexuality from her personhood and represents her solely in terms of the former. Sexualized gazing and the sexual objectification of women are constantly present in women's mundane lives, both in actual interpersonal encounters and in visual media. Women and girls internalize this evaluative gaze and come to adopt an attitude of self-scrutiny and evaluation. This self-conscious body monitoring can lead to shame, anxiety, and depression, as well as vigorous efforts to meet cultural ideals.

A third line of work, carried out by Becky Thompson (1995), challenges the idea that eating problems among women are always tied to the desire to meet cultural ideals of (hetero)sexual attractiveness and beauty. Thompson conducted life history interviews to learn about the ways in which women themselves understood and explained their eating problems. She chose to study women who are not ordinarily thought of as being at risk for eating problems and who thus constitute an understudied population: women of color, lesbian women, and women from impoverished backgrounds. The women she recruited described themselves as recovering from eating problems; none had had formal treatment. All reported that their eating problems had persisted over long periods of time.

In the interviews, the women related the beginning of their eating practices to a time of severe emotional strain. Examples included adolescent struggles over coming out as a lesbian; childhood experiences of repeated incest; facing intense parental demands to lose weight; and serious financial crises. Binge-eating and dieting served as a means of managing emotional distress. Women could comfort themselves, distract themselves, or temporarily "numb out." Even among women who linked their eating problems to a wish to be thin, this wish was not necessarily tied to a desire to be attractive to men. One woman, for example, recounted that she was pressured to lose weight by her father as his social status rose. In her father's eyes, having a slender wife and slender daughters would confirm his upward mobility. Thompson's work challenges the stereotype that eating disorders are limited to White and middle-class adolescents. It also suggests that we might consider a range of possible pathways by which eating disorders come about, rather than rely on just one causal explanation. Moreover, for Thompson, the reliance on the "culture of thinness" as the sole explanation for eating problems is not only inaccurate, but also demeaning to women. It represents women as victims of the culture, unable to resist or rebel against its dictates. Thompson's work suggests that taking women's own accounts of their disturbed eating seriously can enlarge this picture. In her participants' own eyes, they did not simply fall victim to eating problems; instead their eating practices were active means of coping in situations when no other means are available.

FRAMEWORK V: FEMINIST THERAPY

The rise of feminist forms of psychotherapy is a hallmark of second-wave feminism. The concept of feminist therapy was first introduced in the early 1970s. Centers for feminist therapy and counseling soon appeared in major U.S. cities, spurred by the activist spirit of the movement, as well as its commitment to female solidarity and working outside the system (M. Elias, 1975). Therapists in these centers espoused many principles that remain part of feminist therapy today: a respect for women's competence, dignity, and worth; therapy goals of empowerment and self-determination; a desire to establish egalitarian relationships with clients; and a commitment to activism and social change.

The initial descriptions of feminist therapy emphasized consciousness-raising (CR), a technique borrowed from the small-group practice of the Women's Liberation Movement (Brodsky, 1973; Kirsh, 1974). In its original form, CR was a tool for women to comprehend the sociopolitical structures of gender by analyzing their personal experiences. It was also intended to inspire solidarity among women and incite them to collective action for societal change. When CR moved into therapy, however, its focus shifted to personal change and self-knowledge; goals of political mobilization and societal transformation were often put aside. Some feminists who were not therapists deplored this appropriation of CR, viewing it as co-optation (for example, Hanisch, 1971). The project of forging a connection between psychotherapy, a technology of individual change, and feminist goals of societal transformation continues to the present. Indeed, in 1998 *Women and Therapy* devoted an entire issue to the question of therapy as a political act (Hill, 1998).

Feminist ideas, critiques, and values have been interpellated into many systems of therapy (Enns, 1997b). Feminists have devised therapeutic interventions for disorders such as eating problems (C. Bloom et al., 1994), sexual difficulties (Barbach, 1975; M. Hall, 1998), depression (Jack, 1999), childhood sexual abuse (Courtois, 1996; J. Herman, 1992), and relationship violence (Goldner, 1999). Moreover, concepts and practices of feminism have been extended to work with couples and families (McGoldrick, Anderson, & Walsh, 1989), as well as men and boys. Deborah Luepnitz (1988), for example, describes feminist-informed family therapy with a young African American man from the inner city and his family. McLean, Carey, and White (1996) present accounts of innovative feminist interventions directed toward issues such as bullying by boys, intimate violence by men, and relationship problems in gay couples.

The voluminous literature produced by and for feminist practitioners boils over with rich ideas, strong convictions, and practical wisdom. This literature moves in many different directions at once. This is hardly surprising, as its authors represent a multiplicity of therapeutic orientations and a diverse array of feminisms. The practice knowledge of feminist therapists has far outstripped the pace of research. Again, this is not surprising; for the most part, feminist therapy has been developed by practitioners operating outside of research settings. Their focus has been pragmatic and close to their clinical experience; empirical verification has not been the priority. An important question for the field is how to bring the rich vein of nuanced thinking, practice knowledge, and clinical evidence into fruitful relation with feminist research without sacrificing its richness and depth.

Feminist therapy is a philosophy of therapy, not a set of specific techniques, nor a theoretical orientation. As such, it is a broad umbrella under which a wide variety of practitioners and practices can flourish. Nonetheless, a consensus has emerged concerning the basic principles of feminist therapy. These are honoring the client's own perspective on her life; placing the person and her problems in a social context; attending to the power relationship in therapy; scrutinizing a client's situation for multiple sources of oppression in addition to gender; and fostering social change (Hill & Ballou, 1998). Marcia Hill and Mary Ballou (1998) asked whether there are also consistencies in the ways that feminist therapists do therapy. They surveyed 35 members of the Feminist Therapy Institute, all active therapists. Their goal was to examine how expert feminist therapists, regardless of their theoretical orientation, translated feminist principles into actual practice. Their work revealed a number of ways in which therapists self-consciously enacted the principles of feminist therapy in the ongoing dialogue of therapy, as well as in the application of specific techniques. Lynne Parker (1998) conducted a qualitative study with a small group of expert feminist family therapists. For these therapists, challenging unequal distributions of power between partners was key to their way of working with couples in therapy. Based on a review of the literature, Damon Robinson and Judith Worell (1991) have developed a 52-item checklist of behaviors and beliefs of self-identified feminist therapists (the *Therapy With Women Scale*). This work offers a promising start on the task of identifying procedural consistencies of feminist therapy.

Diane Kravetz and I gathered a large sample of therapists and counselors who identified themselves as feminists. Using open-ended interviews, we asked these therapists to describe how their feminism entered their practice of therapy (Marecek & Kravetz, 1998a). Not surprisingly, more diversity emerged in this sample than in the groups of experts discussed above. The therapists articulated a wide range of feminisms, from mainstream liberal views to ecofeminism and neopaganism. More importantly, the use of open-ended questions and discourse analytic techniques enabled us to explore uncertainties and contradictory ideas that many of our participants voiced. For example, nearly all struggled with a variety of dilemmas engendered by the backlash against feminism and its effects on their work (Marecek, 1999b). Moreover, the translation of abstract principles—such as sharing power with clients—was far from straightforward. Sometimes therapists faced situations in which two feminist principles were in conflict. One example is respecting a client's right to self-determination even if she chooses a self-defeating or potentially dangerous course of action versus protecting her welfare. Using a discourse analytic technique, we explored the ways in which three feminist therapists talked about feminism, women's empowerment, and power relations in their therapy (Marecek & Kravetz, 1998b). For all three, power relations were a key consideration in their therapy. But beyond that, there was little that their approaches shared.

An important part of documenting the process of feminist therapy is examining the experiences of clients in feminist therapy. For example, feminist writers have argued that therapists' self-disclosures (when used judiciously and to meet the client's needs) serve to put the relationship between therapist and client on a more equal footing and to dispel any tendencies to idealize the therapist (L. Brown, 1994). An empirical study of clients' reactions could verify that therapists' self-disclosures are indeed received positively. Also, some feminists have advocated the use of written contracts between client and therapist as a means of putting the relationship on an equal footing and clarifying the responsibilities of therapist and client. Some therapists have reported, however, that their clients were suspicious of contracts and reluctant to "sign anything." Many feminist therapists avoid using formal diagnostic labels, because they feel that those labels demean and stigmatize clients. Yet, some women in therapy have reported that receiving a diagnosis sparked relief and hope (Griffin, personal communication, 1999). A diagnosis signified that others shared their problem and that treatments for it were available. Last, clients from different backgrounds may respond differently to aspects of feminist process. Sheila Raja (1998) has noted that clients from certain cultural backgrounds may have learned to respect authority; such clients may be dismayed when a therapist repeatedly shifts the power onto the client (Raja, 1998). Documenting the variety of responses and reactions that clients have to feminists' intervention will produce a body of knowledge that can refine the use of these interventions. Feminist principles are grounded in a philosophical stance and cannot be proven or disproved. However, we can evaluate what are the best ways to put those principles into practice.

Understanding what goes on in feminist therapy and what various practices contribute to clients' experiences of therapy is important, but key questions still remain: What is the outcome of feminist therapy? Does feminist therapy benefit clients more than conventional therapy? For which clients, for what kinds of problems, and under which circumstances is it beneficial? Two early studies

(M. Johnson, 1978; Marecek, Kravetz, & Finn, 1979) offered preliminary empirical assessments of the outcomes of feminist therapy. Marilyn Johnson compared a small sample of clients at the Feminist Therapy Collective in Philadelphia with clients in the Penn Psychotherapy Study. The two groups had similar backgrounds, as well as similar problems and levels of severity; their satisfaction with therapy and the degree of change they experienced were also similar. The similarity in outcome is striking because the Collective clients were in short-term group psychotherapy (the only modality offered there at the time), while the Penn clients were in long-term psychoanalytically-oriented psychotherapy. Diane Kravetz, Steven Finn, and I drew on the database of a large national study of consciousness-raising groups. We compared women who reported that they were in therapy with a feminist therapist with those who reported being in therapy but not with a feminist therapist. We too found little difference in demographic backgrounds and pretherapy complaints between women in feminist therapy and women in conventional therapy. However, women who identified themselves as feminists were more likely to enter therapy with a feminist. Moreover, feminist-identified women were more satisfied with therapy when their therapist was a feminist. These studies stand as preliminary efforts. They assessed feminist therapy at its beginnings. Even though there are still few formal training programs in feminist therapy, feminist therapists now have a far greater knowledge base and more training resources available to them. Thus, feminist therapy today is likely to be more powerful and more effective. Feminist therapy aims to produce changes in women's lives beyond the narrow goal of symptom reduction. Outcome studies documenting the difference that feminist therapy makes are long overdue.

IN CONCLUSION: LOOKING BACKWARD AND FORWARD

Feminist clinical psychology has an extensive record of accomplishments. Feminists have achieved concrete changes in the relation of the mental health professions to women. For example, feminist activists in psychology succeeded in putting in place a requirement that training programs for clinical psychologists include coverage of gender and cultural diversity. They also put in place an ethical principle that prohibited psychologists from having sexual relations with therapy clients. Moreover, some of the ideas of early feminist therapists that were once regarded as iconoclastic (such as declaring autonomy a therapy goal for women; encouraging women to seek employment outside the home; and promoting gender equality in marriage) have now become unexceptional in therapy and in the culture at large. Today, the number of therapists who are women has increased dramatically; it is no longer considered unusual or risky for a woman to choose a woman as her therapist, as it was when feminist therapy first came into being (Phillipson, 1993).

Feminists in the mental health professions have successfully called attention to the prevalence of gender-linked violence and the devastating effects it can have on victims. Moreover, they have contributed important and widely used models of therapy for people whose intimate lives involve physical violence, as well as for women who have experienced sexual abuse or assault. Feminist clinical psychologists have helped to design treatment protocols for use by emergency room personnel, shelter workers, hotline counselors, and police rape squads. Moreover, many feminist psychologists have provided expert testimony in cases of gender-linked violence. Others have been engaged in policy formation in the American Psychological Association and in local and national government. All in all, feminist work on gender-linked violence has wrought sweeping changes.

Although the *DSM* is far from a feminist treatise, feminists have had some influence on its recent revisions. The diagnosis of posttraumatic stress disorder is included in the *DSM* and applied widely in cases of sexual assault, rape, and battering. Feminists also mobilized to exclude certain proposed diagnoses. For example, they supplied evidence to refute the claim of a post-abortion trauma syndrome, showing that although some women may find the decision to have an abortion difficult, most women experience relief. Feminists delayed or averted the inclusion of the categories of self-defeating personality disorder and paraphilic rapism in the *DSM*. Although feminist activism to prevent inclusion of premenstrual dysphoric disorder was not successful, it nonetheless served to let the authors of the *DSM* know that categories and constructs inimical to the interests of women and other minority groups will be challenged. The protests of feminists and other activists also made it clear that the *DSM* is not a pristine scientific document, but a provisional product of many interests, including economic and political ones.

Feminist clinical psychologists have produced a vast library of work on clinical disorder, therapy approaches, and contextual forces that influence women's well being and distress. This work has become increasingly more attentive to the experiences of women in different social locations, leading to a body of knowledge that is more specific and nuanced, as well as more comprehensive. Feminist psychologists from diverse ethnic backgrounds, cultures, and sexualities now play a crucial role in the process of remaking and enlarging our knowledge about women. Moreover, feminist clinical psychology has come to encompass an increasingly diverse set of methods for producing knowledge.

What directions should we pursue in the future? How can we continue to develop a body of knowledge and practice that challenges received wisdom, that is grounded in feminist ideals of social justice, and that acknowledges the diversity of women's lives? What intellectual practices and social relations would further the development of feminist clinical psychology? I close with some personal answers to these questions.

1. *We need to devote attention to neglected populations of women.* The lives and treatment experiences of women with schizophrenia and other chronic mental illnesses have rarely been examined from a feminist perspective. Yet, the prevalence of schizophrenia among women compares with that of anorexia. We also do not know enough about women from working class and poor backgrounds and their experiences of psychological disorder. Moreover, feminist psychologists have made important strides toward addressing the gap in knowledge about women of color, but there is far more to learn about ethnic and cultural differences in risk, resilience, coping, and social supports. Another important question to explore is how discriminatory practices may raise the risk of psychological disorders.

2. *Researchers and clinicians need to write with and for each other.* Collaboration between clinicians and researchers is rare. Many feminist psychologists study clinical problems, but therapists do not find their work accessible or useful. This lack of accessibility is part of a pattern in clinical psychology in general that has been decried for decades, but not remedied. At the same time, many researchers are uninformed about the works that compose the knowledge base of feminist practitioners. (The writings of the Stone Center are a case in point.) Although clinicians are upbraided as anti-intellectual and even unethical for ignoring the research literature, researchers are not chastised for ignoring clinical writings. This implicit hierarchy of worth leads me to my next wish.

3. *We need to bring writings grounded in clinical, theoretical, political, and ethical frameworks into conversation with research reports.* Psychologists in the United States are heirs to a century-long tradition that disparages theory in favor of empirical data. *Psychology of Women Quarterly* has reinscribed this tradition; its editorial policy describes the journal as the "scientific voice" of feminist psychology and commits it to preserving an "empirical, scientific tradition" (Russo, 1995a). This publication policy places research at a far remove from practice knowledge, theory, ethical, and political considerations. Bringing the ideas generated within these diverse frameworks into juxtaposition would serve to enrich feminist knowledge.

4. *We must generalize with more caution and precision.* Can the behavior of college students participating in half-hour study as a course requirement tell us about clinical depression in women? What can convenience samples of White, middle-class women tell us about the lives of women who are neither White nor middle class? How much do studies of eminent feminist therapists reveal about what ordinary practitioners do? False generalizations abound in psychological research, yet we often sweep the doubts they raise under the rug.

   The common practice of denying the historicity of psychological knowledge is another form of overgeneralization. We need to stop generalizing from studies that are decades old to the present. Social and cultural contexts change. For example, the struggles of girls over eating and body image problems today are not the same as those of girls thirty years ago. The present generation of girls have mothers who themselves were subjected to cultural pressures for thinness from their childhood. Moreover, girls today are subject to widespread acceptance of cosmetic surgery and liposuction, even for teenagers. They may well have even more acute concerns about weight and body image than girls of previous generations.

Overgeneralization is often coded into the language of research reports. Discussion sections of research reports often shift the style of language from the particular to the general and from the simple past to the ongoing present. These shifts represent a linguistic universalism that falsely implies that the findings of a single, particular study can be recast as general laws of human behavior.

5. *We must use the medical model with care.* The medical metaphor implies that disorders are akin to physical diseases, that is, fixed entities residing inside the person, characterized by objectively defined symptoms, and unaffected by the social context. The skyrocketing rates of conditions such as eating disorders, multiple personality, and attention deficit disorder should lead us to reject that conception. Instead of seeing psychological disorders as fixed entities, we can construe them as idioms of distress that depend on cultural dictates and on the social roles available to the sufferer. In such a conception, for example, dissociation, multiple personality disorder, and possession states might be seen as idioms of displaced agency. Social anthropologists and cultural studies scholars have elaborated this more fluid conception of psychological symptoms (cf. Haaken, 1998). It does not deny the reality of the suffering of the individual, but it does not turn that suffering into a reified entity. A similar idea is advanced by Ian Hacking (1998), who uses the term *niche disorders* for disorders that emerge and disappear as idioms of distress shift.

6. *We need to make more room for innovative methods.* These methods include field-based, interpretive, discursive methods, and phenomenological methods. I do not advocate that we abandon conventional methods of research but rather that we enlarge the scope of the field enough to incorporate additional methods. Journal editors need to adjust page limits and style requirements to accommodate reports of qualitative work.

Meaning-centered and interpretive methods can provide knowledge about women's experiences as women themselves perceive it. Virginia Goldner (1999) tells of one woman who refused a referral to a support group for battered women, because she adamantly rejected the label *battered* woman, even though she and her partner had entered treatment for violent couples. As a result of listening to the women, Goldner's research group stopped using the terms violent man and battered woman. In Goldner's (1999) words,

> Such an act of naming consigns the person to a stigmatized social identity . . . , reducing a complex individual to this singular, shameful aspect. Instead of essentializing violent behavior by making it an attribute of the perpetrator or the victim, we talk about violence as an action and victimization as its effect. (p. 331)

More generally, interpretive approaches can highlight the range of experiences women have. Such approaches provide a counterpoint to conventional psychological research methods, which seek modal tendencies. Moreover, when researchers listen to participants speaking in their own voices, they hear uncertainty, contradiction, and multiplicity; this provides a counterpoint to the unified self and singular point of view that conventional research seeks. A recent series of qualitative studies of women and depression, edited by Janet Stoppard and Linda McMullen (1999), illustrates the value of these approaches.

7. *Feminist clinical psychologists can look to other disciplines for inspiration and innovative ideas.* Questions about women and the mental health professions and mental health have been fruitfully investigated by feminist scholars in fields such as critical science studies, social history, anthropology, sociology, and sexuality studies (e.g., queer theory and gay, lesbian, bisexual, and transgender studies). This work offers a variety of different perspectives that can enrich and "thicken" the results of conventional psychological approaches. Often it also provides alternative conceptual frameworks and different theoretical and epistemological commitments. For example, Leonore Tiefer (1995) has noted that the efforts of scientific sexology researchers are being overshadowed by the work on sex emerging from disciplines such as cultural studies, queer theory, and feminist theory.

8. *We should consider clinical disorders as cultural products that tell us about the sex/gender system.* Historians, sociologists of science, philosophers, and literary critics have examined women's disorders and diagnoses and their medical management as a means to understand how gender is constructed and regulated. Clinical psychologists are in an excellent position to contribute to this effort, because they combine familiarity with theory, first-hand knowledge of the inner life of women in treatment, and training in interpretive skills. Janice Haaken (1998), for example, has examined the intricacies of women's experience of sexual abuse, female agency, narratives of the self, and the complex cultural landscape in which the current controversies over truth and memory emerged.

9. *We must maintain the feminist tradition of skeptical vigilance.* For over thirty years, feminists in psychology have monitored clinical psychology for biased, inadequate, and discriminatory conceptions and treatment practices. There is no reason to relax our vigilance at this point. Indeed, the pressures of managed care organizations and pharmaceutical companies work to promote treatments that focus on the individual. The promotion of biologically based treatments threatens to marginalize considerations of the social and political context, indeed, even of the psychological context (Marecek & Hare-Mustin, 1991). Laura Brown, a prominent feminist practitioner and theorist, says that she must "voice her doubts to those she teaches, trains, and writes for" and remind her audiences of "the fact that the first feminist responses to psychotherapy were to identify its destructive and controlling influences on women" (1992, p. 240). I concur with Brown that feminist clinical psychology must retain its skeptical sensibility, along with its willingness to challenge established ways of doing things and accepted categories of meaning.

CHAPTER 21

Therapy with Women: Feminist Frameworks

JUDITH WORELL and DAWN JOHNSON

Concerns for women's health and well-being have been addressed only recently in the psychological literature. Prior to 1970, few books or articles included issues of women's physical or mental health. Across the following decade, even major handbooks of psychotherapy practice and research (e.g., Bergin & Garfield, 1971; Garfield & Bergin, 1978; Meltzoff & Kornreich, 1970) included no chapters related to psychotherapy with women, diagnosis and treatment of high-incidence disorders for girls and women, or the issues that might motivate women to seek community or psychological help.

With the advent of renewed activism in the women's movement and changing roles for women and men, a surge of interest arose that targeted the historical neglect of women's psychological well-being. The reawakening of attention to women's issues stimulated both academic and clinical groups in psychology to examine the stereotyping and gender bias that appeared to pervade the fields of mental health practice and research. At the same time, new models of intervention for women's concerns emerged in the literature, calling for a revision of traditional approaches to women and to their focal issues. New approaches to intervention and psychotherapy for women were being crafted that brought women's lives into focus in ways never before articulated.

In this chapter, we review some of the factors that marked the early beginnings of feminist interventions for women, the major streams of theory and practices that have characterized their development, applications to selected populations, research evidence in support of these practices, and some of the limitations of current theory and practice. We conclude with a call for further research to explore the effectiveness of feminist interventions for diverse populations across a range of the issues that motivate women to seek services.

EARLY BEGINNINGS

Three primary factors stimulated the movement toward the development of new approaches to mental health services for women: mounting dissatisfaction with the current traditional models of women's mental health, the new psychology of women and gender that provided an alternative set of lenses through which to view the lives of girls and women, and grassroots feminist movements. The introduction of "nonsexist" therapy was one early response to the call for change.

Dissatisfactions with Traditional Treatment

Traditional models of therapy have been described as those "that put an emphasis on therapist objectivity, analytical thinking, therapist expertness and control of procedures, emotional distance from clients, and intrapsychic dynamics" (Worell & Remer, 1992, p. 84). What were the major sources of dissatisfaction with traditional approaches to mental health treatment for women? At the base of these concerns were theories and practices that assumed that the lives and experiences of men, of the dominant male culture (Rawlings & Carter, 1977), and of middle-class heterosexual White women (B.A. Greene, 1986; Sang, 1977) provided the standards for "normal" and desirable human behavior. Among the more serious of these practices were those that:

1. Stereotyped "healthy" women as relatively passive, dependent, overemotional, suggestive, and irrational (Broverman et al., 1970; Fabrikant, 1974).
2. Evaluated personality traits traditionally attributed to women as less healthy and desirable than those attributed to men (Broverman et al., 1970), or evaluated minority women's behavior as less healthy than that of White women (B.A. Greene, 1986).
3. Judged social roles traditionally assigned to men as more important and valuable than those traditionally reserved for women, thereby excluding women from positions of power, leadership, and social influence (Kirsh, 1974).
4. Reflected evidence of gender, racial, and sexuality bias and stereotyping in diagnosis and psychotherapy with women, translating normative behaviors as illness and some role-resistant behaviors as pathology (American Psychological Association, 1975; Chesler, 1972; M. Kaplan, 1983; Sang, 1977; J.A. Sherman, 1980).
5. Attributed women's malaise and distress to intrapsychic causes rather than to inequities in the sociocultural environment (G.W. Brown & Harris, 1978; Greenspan, 1983; Rawlings & Carter, 1977).
6. Employed therapeutic approaches that disadvantaged women by actively or passively supporting asymmetrical gender and power arrangements that maintained the interpersonal and societal status quo (J.D. Rice & Rice, 1973).
7. Assumed the existence of the generic woman, taking the experiences of White middle-class women as reflective of all women and ignoring the diversity among them (B.A. Greene, 1986).

These sources of dissatisfaction with traditional practices in mental health services for women provided some of the impetus to create alternative opportunities for progress and change. The growing tide of reaction to these social conditions was mirrored in new advances in the psychology of women and gender.

THE NEW PSYCHOLOGY OF WOMEN AND GENDER

The second major factor that provided an impetus to alternative models of intervention for women was the developing corpus of research and knowledge about the lives of girls and women. Major outcomes of innovative research on women and gender included new information about women's lives in contemporary society; revised views of gender, sex, gender roles, and gender-related behavior; the rise of feminist theory, which guided subsequent research and practice; and applications of these innovations to professional practice (Worell & Remer, 1992). The more recent contributions of theory and research about the lives of diverse groups of women have broadened and enriched the field, leading to the development of a more inclusive feminist psychology (B.A. Greene & Sanchez-Hucles, 1997).

GRASSROOTS MOVEMENTS

The early consciousness-raising (C-R) groups enabled women to examine and challenge gender roles, social norms, and social institutions (Kravetz, Marecek, & Finn, 1983). Through C-R, feminists determined that violence against women was widespread and underreported (K. Kahn, 1995). Not only did the C-R movement give women a forum through which to understand and speak about violence against women, it also led to feminist organizing for social change (Schechter, 1982). Examples of other feminist grassroots movements born in the early 1970s include rape crisis centers and battered woman shelters.

Consciousness-Raising Groups

In C-R, small groups of women gathered informally to explore their lives and to identify their commonalities through an analysis of women's oppression and their subservient place in society (Kravetz, 1978). C-R groups veered from the traditional structure and goals of psychotherapy. Whereas traditional psychotherapy focuses on the individual's maladaptive attitudes, behaviors, and emotional states that require change, C-R groups viewed institutional structures and social norms as legitimate frames of analysis.

The early C-R groups were typically egalitarian and leaderless; thus, they avoided reproducing the hierarchical nature of the traditional therapist-client relationship. The sharing of personal experiences in the context of social and political awareness enabled group members to become aware of "the connections between that unique experience and the external reality of a patriarchal sociopolitical context" (L.S.Brown, 1994, p. 50). What may have appeared to each participant as her personal flaws and failures could thus be reconstructed and reframed as a reflection of the dominant power structures of society.

Discussions in C-R groups led to the theme "the personal is political." This theme implies that "women's personal conflicts and distress are embedded in inequalities in the political, economic, legal, and social structures of society that disempower and disadvantage women" (Worell, 2000). Through such C-R groups, the growing awareness of asymmetrical gender-role socialization and institutionalized sexism led many of these groups to adopt an activist agenda that demanded social change (Kirsh, 1974; Kravetz, 1980). Thus, to alleviate women's personal distress, changes must be made in the sexist and oppressive social structures that characterized a patriarchal society.

The empowering and beneficial aspects of these groups provided a useful model for both personal and social change (Brodsky, 1973, 1977; Kirsh, 1974). In addition to forming the foundation of modern feminist theorizing, C-R groups also resulted in positive outcomes for women. Women in C-R groups have been found to develop an increased autonomy, self-respect, self-confidence, and feminist identity and worldview (e.g., Kravetz, Marecek, & Finn, 1983). Subsequently, many of the core beliefs of the C-R groups have been incorporated into contemporary models of feminist therapy.

Rape Crisis Centers and Battered Women's Shelters

Because early feminist analysis tended to focus on the sexual exploitation of women, one of the earlier movements to grow out of women's raised consciousness was the antirape movement (Heise, 1996). Aside from its benefits to women in crisis, the antirape movement contributed to feminist theory and therapy by translating rape as an act of aggression, rather than simply a sexual act (A.W. Burgess & Holstrom, 1979). The antirape movement preceded and served as a model for the battered women's movement. The battered women's movement emerged after rape crisis lines became overwhelmed with calls from women seeking escape from abusive partners (Heise, 1996). Awareness and concern for the pervasive violence that dominated the lives of many women promoted the establishment of community-based spouse abuse shelters, providing these women and their children with a refuge from abusive and battering relationships (Schechter, 1982; Wharton, 1987).

Feminist analyses of violence against women characterized both these movements. Feminists "contend that male violence against women has been condoned throughout history" (Murray, 1988, p. 76). Therefore, violence against women is a problem that affects all women. Many feminist theorists conceptualize violence against women as a purposeful act intended to keep women submissive; men are seen as using violence to control women and keep them from obtaining power (K. Kahn, 1995). Such theorizing served as the basis for modern trauma therapies that adopt a feminist perspective (cf. L.E. Walker, 1994).

GENDER-NEUTRAL AND NONSEXIST THERAPIES

The growing awareness in professional psychology of gender stereotyping in treatment for women stimulated discussions of gender-neutral or nonsexist therapy (cf. Brickman, 1984; Foxley, 1979; Rawlings & Carter, 1977). A nonsexist approach allows clients to determine their own destiny without prescribing socially constructed gender-role stereotypes. Although the terms feminist, gender-neutral, and nonsexist therapy have sometimes been applied interchangeably, Rawlings and Carter (1977) distinguished some of the differences between the models. Specifically, they suggested that feminist therapies incorporate feminist political values and philosophies (i.e., equality between women and men in personal, institutional, and economic power, and egalitarian interpersonal relationships). Therefore, all feminist therapies are potentially nonsexist, but nonsexist therapies are not necessarily feminist. Indeed, most nonsexist therapists do not label their therapy feminist.

Although contemporary feminist therapists adopt the assumptions consistent with nonsexist therapy, their conceptualization, approach to therapy, and expected outcomes have evolved from the more radical feminist theorizing of earlier C-R groups. Newer models of feminist therapy have emerged that render the discussion of nonsexist therapy relatively obsolete. In its place are alternative models of feminist therapy that introduce multiple perspectives and new controversies. From an examination of the current range of feminist perspectives in psychotherapy, it becomes clear that feminist therapies represent much more than "just good therapy."

THEORETICAL VARIATIONS OF FEMINIST THERAPY

There is no unified definition of feminist therapy; many variations of feminist theory and therapy have been proposed. Feminist therapy is typically considered an approach to therapy rather than a system of therapy in itself (Betz & Fitzgerald, 1993; Wyche & Rice, 1997). However, Wyche and Rice (1997) identified three themes that have recurred in the feminist therapy literature: (1) conceptualizing gender as a salient variable in therapy process, evaluation, and outcome; (2) emphasizing a sociocultural understanding of a woman's life in addition to an intrapsychic perspective; and (3) personal empowerment as a goal of therapy.

In defining feminist therapy, Carolyn Zerbe Enns (1997a) identified basic principles that all feminist therapists tend to share. According to Enns, the specific theoretical framework that the therapist employs will determine how these principles are interpreted and applied in practice. These principles help distinguish feminist therapies from traditional and nonsexist approaches to therapy.

1. Feminist therapies adopt perspectives born from the C-R era (i.e., the personal is political). Thus, the political and social contexts in which a woman lives influence her personal problems.
2. Clients are coping with stressors to the best of their ability; therefore, "symptoms" are viewed as adaptive coping skills.
3. Clients are seen as competent and therefore the best expert on their own experiences.
4. Feminist therapists acknowledge issues of power imbalance and emphasize the need to strive for egalitarian relationships both inside and outside of the therapy relationship.
5. It is impossible to practice value-free psychotherapy.
6. Feminists pay special attention to clients' rights as consumers; they share their relevant feminist values with clients.

These principles in turn reflect recurrent themes in the feminist theories that form the foundations of feminist approaches to therapy. The major feminist theories have been identified in the literature as liberal, radical, Marxist, socialist, cultural, and women of color or multicultural (Donovan, 1985; Jagger & Rothenberg, 1993). We have condensed these positions according to their primary themes as applied in therapy. Although differences among feminist therapies exist in theory, there is no empirical evidence documenting how therapists who subscribe to different feminist therapies apply feminist principles differentially in practice. Furthermore, there is no empirical evidence that feminist therapists consistently adhere in practice to one specific theory.

LIBERAL/REFORM FEMINISMS

Liberal or reform feminisms are based on the principles of egalitarianism and rationality (i.e., all people are rational beings who deserve to be treated equally; Whalen, 1996; Whelehan, 1995).

Within this perspective, women are rational beings and therefore deserve to be treated equally to men. Sexism and oppression are caused by irrational prejudice and sex-role socialization. Therefore, the focus typically has been on issues such as individual freedom, autonomy, self-fulfillment, dignity, and equality. Liberal/reform feminists have traditionally attempted to work within existing systems when promoting reform and have not challenged the basic assumptions of major institutions. Given the emphasis on equality of opportunity, liberal/reform feminists have advocated for a wide variety of nontraditional behaviors for both women and men. The extensive literature on the personal advantages of androgyny (e.g., E.P. Cook, 1985; Whitley, 1984; Worell, 1978) attests to the broad appeal of the liberal/reform perspective in mental health.

Feminist therapies that reflect a liberal/reform perspective "facilitate women's awareness of how social conditioning influences their lives, and assist women in making choices based on their personal strengths and interests" (Enns, 1992, p. 456). Gender-role flexibility is seen as a strength, but must be freely chosen. A gender-role analysis enables the woman to explore for herself the risks and advantages of expanded gender roles, enabling her to reduce self-blame for her current choices and to consider alternative possibilities (L.S. Brown, 1986). Assertiveness training may be used in helping clients to overcome their reluctance to ask for equity in interpersonal or work-related settings (Jakubowski, 1977).

In the spirit of helping women achieve equity, liberal/reform therapists have been in the forefront of attention to women's career development (e.g., Betz & Fitzgerald, 1987). In particular, women's nontraditional career choices and home-career conflicts are explored. Feminist career counseling assists women in examining their internalized messages about responsibility to self and others, and their career-related self-efficacy expectations and aspirations. Of particular concern to feminist career counseling are the structural barriers to women's career advancement, such as sexual harassment, occupational segregation, inequitable salaries, and devaluation of women's competency.

RADICAL/SOCIALIST FEMINISMS

In contrast to liberal/reform feminisms, radical/socialist feminisms label oppression as the root of women's problems. Patriarchy, male domination, and men's control over women's bodies are responsible for women's oppression and sexism (Enns, 1997a; Henley et al., 1998; Whalen, 1996; Whelehan, 1995). Borrowing from the socialist tradition, women are seen as equally oppressed by gender, race, nationality, and class. Therefore, the radical/social feminist typically recognizes multiple forms of oppression. A broad goal for radical/socialist feminisms is to transform gender relationships and eliminate patriarchy and all patriarchal forms of oppression.

The politics of asymmetrical gender relations become apparent in the process and content of therapy. The feminist goal of empowerment replaces the traditional goal of "adjustment." Although gender-role analysis remains a basic approach in therapy, power analysis and the exploration of interpersonal power relationships become paramount. Therapists engage in multiple strategies toward encouraging client empowerment, including an egalitarian stance, judicious self-disclosure, demystification of the therapy process, validation of client perceptions and experience, and support of both personal and social change (Worell & Remer, 1992). Because of their commitment to social change, radical/socialist feminist therapists are frequently involved in social action and women's advocacy. They view social advocacy as a desired outcome of therapy and encourage redirection of anger toward social change (Enns, 1992).

CULTURAL/INTERPERSONAL FEMINISMS

Cultural feminisms (sometimes referred to as gender or interpersonal feminisms) embrace the idea that a woman's experience is distinctly different from that of a man's experience (Enns, 1992, 1997a; Tong, 1998; Whalen, 1996). Drawing on the work of Nancy Chodorow (1978), Carol Gilligan (1982), and others, women are viewed as more relational than men (e.g., ethic of care vs. ethic of justice). Sexism and oppression are seen as caused by devaluation of feminine values and overvaluation of masculine and patriarchical values (Donovan, 1985; Tong, 1998; Whalen, 1996). Cultural feminists advocate for the revaluing of characteristics considered traditionally feminine and the redefinition of these traits as strengths. There is a celebration of women's traditional values of caring, cooperation, peace, gentleness, and emotionality, in contrast to the "masculine" values of aggressiveness and emotional avoidance (Donovan, 1985). Therefore, they are less likely to advocate for the reconstruction of gender roles. Instead, cultural feminists anticipate that greater flexibility for both women and men will occur through the feminization of culture (Enns, 1992).

Cultural feminist therapists stress the importance of self-knowledge and women's relationships and emphasize empathy as a therapeutic intervention (Jordan, Surry, & Kaplan, 1991). Therefore, many cultural feminists adopt an interpersonal or psychodynamic perspective to therapy. One of the more popular models, self-in-relation therapy, has been proposed by feminists at the Stone Center at Wellesley College (e.g., Jordan, Kaplan, et al., 1991; Jordan & Surrey, 1986; J.B. Miller, 1976). The self-in-relation model of psychotherapy adopts a developmental perspective and emphasizes the mother-daughter relationship in the woman's development, leading to a capacity for empathy, nurturance, and caring (Jordan, 1991; Surrey, 1991). Relationship-differentiation is viewed as central to a woman's identity development rather than the traditional assumption of individuation and separation (Surrey, 1991). As the outcome of self-in-relations therapy, Judith Jordan (1991) concluded that "feeling connected and in contact with another . . . allows us our most profound sense of personal meaning and reality; at its best, therapy works toward developing and honoring this relational process" (p. 289).

Women of Color Feminisms

Criticism of the White, middle-class feminism of the early 1960s and 1970s centered on its neglect of the needs and experiences of women of color. In assuming the ethic of universal sisterhood, early feminists failed to acknowledge the differing life experiences of women from diverse ethnic, racial, national, and multicultural backgrounds (Comas-Diaz & Greene, 1994; P.T. Reid & Kelly, 1994). Unlike women from the dominant White community, women of color are faced with several unique circumstances. In North American society, people of color are generally seen as "the other," whereby difference is defined as deficiency. In addition, women of color are faced with conflicting loyalties, in which solidarity with their racial or ethnic group often takes priority over gender. Being asked to view men as the source of women's oppression denies their sense of group bonding both with the boys and men that they love and with other men in their community and support networks. On the other hand, "women of color are not only exposed to oppression within the dominant group, but also experience sexism and oppression within their own ethnic and racial communities as well" (Comas-Diaz & Greene, 1994, p. 5). Thus, issues of equity and power imbalance do not disappear.

As a consequence of considerations such as these, women of color have developed a rich literature that considers the multiple pluralisms that characterize their communities (Comas-Diaz, 1999; Landrine, 1995, 1999; Raja, 1998). Therapeutic models and strategies that target specific groups of ethnic women have evolved into a "multicultural feminism" that addresses the complex issues of multiple social locations and how they impact the situated lives of women of color. With a multicultural feminist therapist, women of color can explore their experiences of racism, sexism within and from outside their communities, their personal and cultural identities, internalization of their negative experiences with the dominant culture, and their need to distance or remain interconnected with their ethnoracial group (Comas-Diaz & Greene, 1994). As a therapeutic goal, social activism is also important for women of color "as a means of coping and transforming their realities, potentially enabling them to achieve more control over their lives" (Comas-Diaz, 1991, p. 601).

Across such pluralism of cultures, gender roles may be more rigid or more flexible for women with differing group identities (T.L. Robinson & Howard-Hamilton, 2000; C. Wade & Tavris, 1999). Thus, gender roles may be relatively structured and prescribed within some cultural groups, whereas other cultures may allow more space for individual choice. For example, issues of power, status, and empowerment may assume very different contextual frames for members of individualistic cultures as compared to those from more collective or interconnected cultures (Vandello & Cohen, 1999). The interdependency of personal and social identities may also differ within and across ethnic and racial groups (Gutierrez & Nagata, 1996). And, for many women of color, issues of bicultural and immigrant identity as well as multicultural loyalties may be of continuing concern.

The tasks of the multicultural feminist therapist thus require mature cultural sensitivity and multiple competencies. In support of incorporating pluralism and diversity into feminist practice, Lillian Comas-Diaz (1991) concluded that women of color "are collaborating with their feminist sisters and brothers in the transformation of an integrative feminist psychology that will be relevant to all women" (p. 607).

Toward an Integrative Model of Feminist Practice

In supplement to the four models outlined above, there are a number of feminist approaches to practice with women that emphasize particular populations or specific concerns. Examples of these include lesbian feminism (e.g., L.S. Brown, 1989), ecofeminism (e.g., Sturgeon, 1997), and Marxist feminism (e.g., Whelehan, 1995), each of which might reflect differing worldviews and stimulate a variation in procedures with clients. Further exploration of these variations is worthwhile but is beyond the scope of this chapter.

Each of the feminist theories and its associated practices may stand alone or may be integrated within more comprehensive approaches. Recognizing that each approach has merit, Worell and Remer (1992, 2000) proposed an empowerment model of feminist therapy that incorporates some elements of theory and associated practices from each of the four major models above. This integrative model contains four principles, with strategies and goals that are consistent with each principle.

Principle 1, *The Personal Is Political,* reflects mainstream feminist thought and is the overarching principle that provides a broad umbrella for feminist intervention. This principle emphasizes the importance of locating the client's "pathology" in a social and political context; clients are helped to separate the internal from the external sources of their problems. Under this principle, therapists address issues of gender-role socialization, institutionalized sexism, and oppression from many sources. Examples of therapy goals consistent with this principle include awareness of how gender-role socialization has impacted her life; developing more flexible behaviors that are not dictated by gender or cultural-role stereotypes; reframing pathology as "best-attempt" coping strategies; and social activism at either micro (proximal and personal) or macro (distal and structural) levels.

Principle 2, *Personal and Social Identities Are Interdependent,* incorporates aspects of the women of color and multicultural feminist perspectives, as well as the plurality of women's identities. It addresses the importance of exploring a woman's personal identity in the context of the larger culture and the groups with which the woman identifies and is socially identified. Examples of therapy goals associated with this principle include becoming aware of one's social location with respect to gender, ethnicity, social class, sexual orientation, physical characteristics, or ablism; identifying internal from external representations of these locations; mediating conflicting loyalties; and functioning comfortably within this interdependence.

Principle 3, *Relationships Are Egalitarian,* reflects themes from both liberal and radical perspectives. It addresses women's lower power and status compared to men, power differentials among women, and the inequality of minority groups within the dominant culture. To address the unequal balance of power, therapists may use self-disclosure, collaborative goal setting, honoring clients' experience, and affirming client strengths. Examples of therapy goals consistent with this principle include developing egalitarian relationships both within and outside of therapy, assertiveness, and economic independence.

Principle 4, *Female Perspectives Are Valued,* finds its roots in cultural feminism. This principle concerns the importance of revaluing traditional female perspectives within the cultural contexts of clients' experience. Goals reflecting this principle include helping the client to identify her personal strengths, trusting her own experience, translating perceived weakness into strengths, and bonding with other women.

To extend the theory and practice of feminist practice to outcome assessment, the goals of personal and social empowerment for women were further articulated by Worell (1993b) in an empowerment model of women's mental health. The 10 broad outcomes of the model were intended to match the four integrative principles listed above. These outcomes advance the assessment of therapy outcomes beyond symptom reduction or returning the woman to her "premorbid" status.

Each of the 10 goals embodies a range of possible strategies for feminist intervention; the goals do not define the means by which they can be realized. Further, each hypothesized outcome can be reliably measured with standardized assessments currently available or in progress.

The 10 hypothesized outcomes are (1) positive self-evaluation; (2) a positive comfort-distress ratio; (3) gender- and culture-role awareness; (4) personal control and self-efficacy; (5) self-nurturance and self-care; (6) effective problem-solving skills; (7) competent use of assertiveness skills; (8) access to facilitative social, economic, and community resources; (9) gender and cultural flexibility; and (10) socially constructive activism. These broad outcomes are supported by the broad literature on women's health and well-being. The model offers a theoretical conceptualization that can guide therapy goals, choice of interventions, and evaluation of effective therapy outcomes.

One of the contributions of empowerment feminist therapy is its applicability to integration with several more structured theoretical approaches; for example, it has been integrated successfully in several cognitive-behavioral formats (Toner, Segal, Emmott, & Myran, 2000; Worell & Remer, 1999). The resulting product is a model that incorporates a set of empirically validated procedures with feminist strategies, taking advantage of the strengths of both approaches.

APPLICATIONS TO SPECIAL POPULATIONS

Feminist approaches to intervention with women have prompted applications to a wide range of populations and presenting issues. We list a sample of these applications here: feminist marital and family therapy (Skerrett, 1996; C.I. Wright & Fish, 1997), lesbian and bisexual issues in counseling (P. Ellis & Murphy, 1994; Garnets, Hancock, Cochran, Goodchilds, & Peplau, 1998; M. Nichols, 1994), feminist sex therapy (Tiefer, 1996), feminist approaches for women with disabilities (O. Prilleltensky, 1996), feminist ethics in therapy (Rave & Larson, 1995), feminist group therapy, and feminist therapy with men (the last two discussed further below). Feminist principles have also been incorporated into specific interventions, such as those designed for woman battering (McClosky & Fraser, 1997; Rinfret-Raynor & Cantin, 1997; L.E. Walker, 1994), incest and rape survivors (Koss et al., 1994a), eating disorders (Kearney-Cooke & Striegel-Moore, 1996; Rees, 1996), depression and anxiety (Fishel, 1995), and irritable bowel syndrome (Toner et al., 2000). In the sections below, we consider two widely used applications, feminist group therapies and feminist therapy with men.

FEMINIST GROUP THERAPIES

In contrast to most forms of individual therapy, group therapy minimizes the power differential between the therapist and clients (Burden & Gottlieb, 1987; Rawlings & Carter, 1977). Additionally, group is a valued and effective mode of therapy for many of today's women's concerns. For example, group therapy has been described as useful for addressing the concerns of battered women (e.g., Dutton, 1992; L.E. Walker, 1994), rape survivors (e.g., Resick & Schnicke, 1996), child sexual abuse survivors (e.g., Chard, Weaver, & Resick, 1997; Sprei, 1987), and women with eating disorders (e.g., Hotelling, 1987). Furthermore, group is typically the preferred modality for assertiveness training, a concern for many women (Jakubowski, 1977). Therefore, feminist therapists commonly utilize group therapy alone or in conjunction with individual therapy.

Some feminist groups apply C-R principles (e.g., countering gender-role socialization; Burden & Gottleib, 1987) in reaction to many of the sexist concerns inherent in more traditional group therapies (Lerman, 1987); other feminist and woman-centered groups emphasize the normalizing effect inherent in groups where women share similar experiences (e.g., Resick & Schnicke, 1996). From a feminist perspective, an advantage of group therapy lies in its ability to give women a voice in a society were women have been historically and consistently silenced.

Burden and Gottlieb (1987) describe many of the major components of feminist group-work. Specifically, they emphasize that feminist group therapy needs to counteract the deleterious effects of gender-based socialization and the need for therapists to attend to the ways in which women typically respond in group situations. They describe five characteristics of feminist group therapy: (1) countering gender-role socialization, (2) emphasizing support and decreasing women's isolation through normalizing their problems, (3) distinguishing between personal problems and those that are socially constructed, (4) emphasizing education and skill building, and (5) incorporating a problem-solving approach that empowers women. Some feminists suggest that feminist therapy is most effective in a group format because of its ability to dilute the power of the therapist and its ability to support and validate women (e.g., Rawlings & Carter, 1977). However, a group framework may not be sufficient for some women to address all their concerns (e.g., battered women; Dutton, 1992; L.E. Walker, 1994). Therefore, group therapy may prove more useful as an ancillary to individual therapy. Consequently, feminist therapists working with clients individually typically refer clients to psychoeducational, support, and/or skill training groups.

Feminist Therapy with Men

A common question related to feminist therapy is whether it can be effective only for women. As early as 1978, *Counseling Psychologist* devoted an entire issue to counseling men, with a number of articles that reflected feminist concerns. These included the impact of male socialization on men's ability to be flexible in their behavioral repertoires, especially with respect to expressions of tenderness and positive emotionality, and their socialized needs for power, control, and achievement. Subsequent work on male socialization extended these ideas, pointing out that it leads typically to homophobia, restricted emotionality, and excessive focus on competition and success. Mintz and O'Neill (1990) discuss how this pattern of "masculine gender-role conflict" may become an issue in psychotherapy with men. These authors see the pattern as normative in American society for men but also dysfunctional for them in many ways, both in their work and in their close interpersonal relationships.

The feminist position that traditional socialization is disabling for women can be applied to men as well. Given that men have generally been depicted as reluctant consumers of therapy, unwilling to share or relinquish power and suspicious of self-disclosure, particular strategies for therapy with men have been proposed (Bograd, 1990; Ganley, 1988; Good, Gilbert, & Scher, 1990). The range of strategies includes both process and content. The process variables involve the therapeutic relationship; for the female therapist with a male client, these might include uncovering beliefs about women, men's fear of vulnerability, and issues of power and control in session. The content variables cover topics that relate to traditional masculinity norms and the specific masculinity ideology endorsed by the male client (Pleck et al., 1993a). In particular, the focus might include the client's conceptions of achievement, intimacy in relationships, power and control, entitlement, and expressions of emotionality.

Although it is important that masculinity variables are explored within a sociocultural context, a recent measure of masculine ideology across three cultures suggested that there may be more commonalities than differences among men across diverse groups (Doss & Hopkins, 1998). In a study using the Multicultural Masculinity Ideology Scale, Brian Doss and Roy Hopkins found two components that were consistent across groups of White, Black, and native Chilean college males: hypermasculine posturing and achievement. Some culturally specific variables appeared as well, such as toughness, sensitivity, and sexual responsibility. However, across all three cultures, men were consistently different from women on this scale. These results highlight the importance of attending to both gender and culture in feminist therapy with men and couples.

EMPIRICAL VALIDATION OF FEMINIST THERAPY PROCESS AND OUTCOMES

As is true of most applied programs, the progress of feminist interventions at the scholarly and practice levels exceeds their empirical support. Specific programs designed to treat particular conditions (e.g., rape, bulimia; Chambless et al., 1998) have been at the forefront of insistence on validating their procedures with outcome research. The average feminist practitioner, however, probably has little control of who walks in the door, and typically treats a wide range of women's problems. There has been relatively little research providing empirical support for most of the theoretical positions discussed above. What is the evidence that any of these feminist approaches to therapy are as effective as more traditional and established interventions?

If the various forms of feminist therapy are to take their place among the major intervention approaches, it is critical to establish both their unique components as well as the outcome validity of these interventions (Worell, in press-a). In this section, we review several recent research studies that were designed to define the unique parameters of feminist therapy from the perspectives of both therapists and clients, and assess the effectiveness of feminist practice using short- and long-term outcome data.

ARE FEMINIST THERAPIES UNIQUE?

The first question addresses a commonly stated view that feminist therapy or counseling is no different from any other "good therapy." In response to this question, we review several studies that have developed instrumentation to compare the attitudes and behaviors of feminists with nonfeminists who practice counseling and psychotherapy.

Therapist Reports of Therapy Behaviors

One approach to answering the first question about feminist therapy behaviors is to elicit that information with a structured rating scale directly from practitioners. The Therapy with Women Scale (TWS; D. Robinson & Worell, 1991) was constructed following an intensive review of the principles, beliefs, and strategies reported in the feminist therapy literature. The scale contains 40 declarative statements, such as "I consider my clients' problems through a gender-role perspective." From the responses of a stratified, randomized sample of 266 female and male practitioners, two factors were extracted, which we named empowerment of the client and advocacy for women. Both factors of the scale discriminated significantly between those practitioners who identified as either feminist or woman-centered and those who identified otherwise (D. Robinson, 1994).

A recent survey using selected items of the TWS was conducted with 208 clinician psychologists equally divided as women-centered or not in their theory and practice. Six factors were extracted that characterized therapist behaviors; five of the six factors significantly differentiated the responses of the feminist from the nonfeminist practitioners. We named these feminist therapy factors affirming the client, gender-role perspective, woman-centered activism, therapist self-disclosure, and egalitarian stance. Similarly, feminist or woman-centered practitioners were more likely than others to endorse the following four goals for their clients: improved self-esteem and self-regard, improved well-being or quality of life, flexible use of gendered behaviors, and personal activism toward social change (Task Force on Outcomes in Feminist Therapy, 1999). These studies confirm prior research that feminist therapy differs in substantial ways from those intervention approaches that do not identify as feminist or woman-centered.

Consumer Reports of Therapist Behaviors

A second approach to validating feminist therapy behaviors is to assess the experiences of the clients who are consumers of that therapy. A mirror image scale of the TWS, the Client TWS (CTWS; Worell, Chandler, & Robinson, 1996) reflects the individual's report of whether her counselor or therapist demonstrated these behaviors with her. In a follow-up study using the TWS with therapists, almost all the responses on the CTWS of 45 clients in eight student counseling centers reflected those of their therapists on the TWS (Worell, Chandler, Robinson, & Cobulius, 1996). Thus, with this method of assessing feminist therapy behaviors, clients clearly experienced in sessions the behaviors their counselors indicated they used.

Another method of assessing client experience of therapy behaviors was developed by Niva Piran (1999) in a study with 112 therapy clients in Toronto. The Feminist Frame Scale asks 43 specific questions about the therapy experience in the form of "Did your therapist ask you about . . . ?" This scale revealed three major factors: respectful validation, empowerment, and unsilencing trauma. Comparing client reports on the Feminist Frame Scale from three sets of practitioner offices—feminist, client-centered, and traditional medically informed—Piran found that adherence to feminist principles was significantly higher by feminist therapists than by either the humanistic or traditional therapists. Once again, clients validated their therapists' feminist stance.

Finally, in a third study on feminist therapy by Anne Cummings (in press), novice counselors were instructed and coached on the use of four feminist strategies: empowering the client, decreasing power differentials, exploring gender-role conflict, and placing client concerns within a sociocultural context. At the end of training, counselor scores on the TWS and their written diaries following each session confirmed that they were using feminist strategies. Further, client responses on the CTWS further confirmed that clients experienced these strategies in their sessions. These three studies corroborate that feminist therapy principles can be reliably measured, can be taught to novice counselors, are experienced as feminist by clients, and are more likely to be implemented by feminist as compared to nonfeminist practitioners.

ARE FEMINIST THERAPIES EFFECTIVE?

The question of therapy outcome effectiveness must be considered in the context of the goals of the intervention. Many traditional therapies focus mainly on "symptom reduction," whereby the disorder or problem for which the client seeks relief is remediated or reduced in severity. Although feminist therapists also aim to reduce personal distress, they tend to focus on client strengths rather than deficits. Concomitantly, they regard symptoms as adaptive strategies in the context of an oppressive environment (Wyche & Rice, 1997). An overall goal for many feminist therapists and counselors is to affirm client empowerment. The experience of empowerment prepares individuals to confront and deal with both internal and external threats to their current and future well-being. Standard measures of therapy outcome that assess symptom reduction are therefore unsuitable for most feminist therapy goals.

To establish a reliable measure of feminist therapy outcomes, Worell and Chandler (1996) matched the goals of the empowerment model and the principles of empowerment feminist therapy described above as a composite map of women's optimal mental health and well-being. We envisioned the healthy woman in a healthy environment as self-aware and self-confident, assertive within her cultural constraints, and aware of the limitations imposed by unbalanced gender and intercultural relations. She has effective problem-solving and coping skills for dealing with internal and external barriers and stressors, is relatively free of dysfunctional patterns of thinking and behavior, and has effective access to the interpersonal and community resources that are important to her. In brief, she is confident, strong, connected to a supportive community, and resilient. From this model we generated a 35-item Personal Progress Scale (PPS) that assesses an individual's personal and social empowerment.

When included as one of several therapy outcome measures with diverse samples and mixed diagnoses, the PPS has demonstrated validity for both short- and long-term outcomes (Chandler, Worell, Johnson, Blount, & Lusk, 1999; Cummings, in press). Following either brief therapy (four sessions or fewer) or extended therapy (more than seven sessions), clients reported moderate to high scores on the PPS, suggesting that even brief intervention from a feminist perspective can impact a sense of personal empowerment. Further, in a long-term follow-up study of feminist therapy outcomes (Chandler et al., 1999), scores on the PPS correlated well with client self-ratings of improvement over time. The PPS scores also increased significantly more over time than scores on a standard measure of personal well-being. We interpret this finding as an indication of increased empowerment, or resilience, over time, as a function of earlier experiences with feminist-oriented interventions. In both studies, women's qualitative written reactions also reflected most components of the empowerment goals.

These preliminary studies on measuring process and outcomes in feminist therapy are suggestive and encouraging. They suggest that feminist therapy, when articulated in a structured and clearly defined model, is a unique and measurable form of intervention that provides positive outcomes for women in personal distress. The results also caution us to extend the findings to diverse populations and to those with more severe indices of distress and dysfunction. We look to future researchers to continue this work with carefully designed effectiveness studies that will enhance our understanding of both the process and the range of outcomes for feminist therapies. The challenge for all forms of feminist therapy is to validate their applied practices with research that establishes the effectiveness of their procedures for women's well-being.

CAUTIONS AND CONCLUSIONS

In this chapter, we have discussed feminist intervention from a variety of perspectives—its history and rationale, its major tenets, the forms of feminist theory that gave birth to feminist interventions, some examples of the range of feminist applications to therapy, and a brief introduction to recent research studies to validate its processes and outcomes. This review would be incomplete, however, without some commentary on cautions and critiques regarding the theories and practices of feminist therapies.

CAUTIONS AND CRITIQUES

There have been a number of criticisms in the literature of feminist approaches to therapy. We list some of these reservations to acknowledge the voices that have raised important issues. In doing so, we recognize that each concern is both complex and controversial and each deserves a separate forum for further discussion. Readers are invited to draw their own conclusions. We consider seven major critiques:

1. Psychotherapy is a form of professionalized compliance to an oppressive society. By helping women one by one to adjust to an unfair system, we are sustaining and supporting the status quo rather than resisting and restructuring it. In contrast, this point of view proposes that only organized social activism will effectively remediate women's inequality and subordination by dramatically changing the institutions that oppress them. By implying to women that psychotherapy can make them "feel better," feminists are undermining the goals of the feminist movement (Perkins, 1996).
2. From a contrary view, feminist therapy is better defined as politics, not therapy. Social activism is political and has no place in therapy. Therapists should not "impose" their political values on clients (Task Force on Outcomes in Feminist Therapy, 1999).
3. Feminist therapy is the invention of middle-class, heterosexual, White women and has little relevance for those who are less privileged. For example, in insisting on women's right to paid employment, they have ignored poor women's equal right not to work outside the home. From a multicultural perspective, gender is only one of the many oppressions that are central in women's lives. Oppression occurs across all women's social locations, including race, ethnicity, sexual orientation, class, ablism, appearance, and so on. Women from the intersections of any of these social locations with gender have been made relatively invisible (B.A. Greene & Sanchez-Hucles, 1997; P.T. Reid & Kelly, 1994).
4. Feminist therapies are vaguely defined and represent a philosophy or belief system about the importance of gender rather than an established, theory-driven set of procedures (Rampage, 1998).
5. Feminist theories that posit special qualities for women are essentially biased and sexist (M. Crawford, 1989). By suggesting that qualities such as nurturance, the ethic of caring, and relational connection are unique to women as compared to men, these feminist therapies "essentialize" women and denigrate men. The essential qualities of women are assumed to be inherent in women's nature rather than shaped and socialized by the dominant culture. This position relegates therapy to intrapsychic rather than external change.
6. Feminist therapy contains an inherent paradox between feminist principles of empowerment and the implicit power of the therapist. Therapists cannot relinquish power without sabotaging the process of therapy. Empowerment of clients is questionable when dealing with self-destructive or self-damaging behavior (Sesan & Katzman, 1998).
7. Finally, we have pointed out here that feminist therapies have been slow to establish empirical validity. Major proponents have failed to document the effectiveness of their interventions with outcome studies that demonstrate client or community change.

Progress in feminist therapy will be enhanced when satisfactory responses to these concerns have been addressed.

CONCLUSIONS

The science and practice of health care for women provide us with a rich arena for innovative feminist interventions. At the present time, the field of feminist therapy is multidimensional and unsystematic. There are many different approaches to intervention with women that emanate from divergent theories about women's unequal status within the social structure. However, aside from certain structured approaches, most feminist therapies adhere to a broad set of principles that may be relatively independent of specific procedures or specific goals. In the absence of detailed manuals, it would appear that there is little cohesiveness or validation of procedures across these interventions for women.

On the other hand, the possibility of research on the process and effectiveness of feminist practice should not be dismissed. For example, several research studies have found broad, identifiable strategies that are endorsed by most feminist practitioners. Among these are affirming and empowering the client, providing a gender-role perspective, exploring multicultural and gender-role conflicts, modeling social activism, self-disclosing relevant experiences, and promoting egalitarian relationships (Cummings, in press; D. Robinson, 1994; Task Force on Outcomes in Feminist Therapy, 1999). Further, many of these strategies have been operationalized and taught successfully to novice trainees (Cummings, in press; Worell, Stilwell, Robinson, & Oakley, 1999).

As we develop more standardized procedures and diverse measures of feminist principles, it may be feasible to validate our feminist strategies through closely controlled experimental procedures. From a feminist perspective, effectiveness studies provide us with unique opportunities for creative clinician-researcher collaboration. By bringing researchers and practitioners together in mutual efforts, our complementary areas of expertise can enrich our methods for exploring therapy effectiveness.

Finally, we need to move away from symptom-focused research toward more inclusive variables that will predict personal strength and empowerment, positive thriving, resilience in the face of stress, and maintenance of psychological well-being over time. Symptom-focused practice has been shown to result in immediate relief but high relapse rates. In contrast, we need to articulate useful and testable models of the healthy woman in a healthy environment and work toward achieving this goal. We presented one such model here that provides an example of partnership between practice and research that must remain active, vigorous, and creative.

CHAPTER 22

Sociocultural Issues in
Counseling for Women of Color

KAREN FRASER WYCHE

I think it is fair to assume that all mental health professionals hope to be effective helpers for their clients. They want the individuals, families, and groups who seek their services to feel understood and helped through the journey of problem solving and resolution. Naturally, some mental health professionals are more effective helping certain clients more than others. There are many reasons for this, but one reason that is often overlooked is the counselor's understanding of culture and level of skill in using cultural knowledge. That is, how competent are those in the mental health profession in helping women, men, families, and children who differ from themselves racially and ethnically? To understand this interactive process and to improve one's existing knowledge require ongoing learning. Such learning involves a sophisticated understanding of the multiple ways behavior is shaped by who we are and where we come from. This learning requires a recognition that social context and ecological factors are salient in understanding variations within environments. Unfortunately, the extent to which counselors actively improve their cultural knowledge in this process is often not the focus of either training or supervision. Of course, understanding culture does not mean knowing the particulars of every client's social environment: "Culture does not mean knowing everything about every culture. It is instead respect for difference, eagerness to learn, and a willingness to accept that there are many ways of viewing the world . . . a tolerance for cultural mysteries" (Lynch & Hanson, 1998, p. 493).

In addition to acquiring cultural understanding of clients, mental health professionals need self-awareness. They come to the profession with multiple cultural identities, situated in the context of self, family, group, and community. Their awareness of these levels of consciousness can vary from person to person and follow a developmental pattern that I hypothesize in the following order: a naïveté and lack of understanding; a beginning encounter with these issues; an evaluation of specific factors related to self; a reflection on self as a cultural being; and finally, a sophisticated multiperspective integration of cultural understanding. Although I have described this as a stage-like process, it should not be assumed that these stages are mutually exclusive. There is a cognitive process of reappraisal, reshaping, and new learning as one interacts with others who differ from oneself along various dimensions. This new learning can happen in several ways. It can relate to language: the relative nuances of meaning and interpretation given a conversation between a bilingual woman and a monolingual woman. It can relate to differences in understanding of religion and spirituality, age, sexual orientation, physical issues, socioeconomic status, immigration experiences, and/or ethnicity. Finally, it can relate to distinctions between the client's social environment and the mental health professional's perception of that environment. This challenge is ongoing, involving a refinement of one's perspectives and integration of new ways of learning.

The process I just described is the focus of this chapter. The goal of this chapter is to provide a framework that mental health professionals can use in assessing cultural factors that influence the treatment of ethnic minority women. These women are those whom Ogbu (1989a) describes as lacking power in the United States. They are African American, Afro-Caribbean, Latina American, Native American, and Asian American. These are the women the reader should keep in mind while reading this chapter. These women share different immigration histories and/or patterns of discrimination in the United States. They are influenced by different sociopolitical forces that impact their lives and shape their worldview (cf. D.W. Sue & Sue, 1999). They also show within-group differences that are very important to keep in mind when reading any chapter on culturally competent mental health treatment.

This chapter discusses the biases that characterize a lack of cultural and gender understanding in mental health assessment and treatment, and themes that are important for understanding the interactive aspects of gender, culture, and ethnicity. The chapter concludes with suggestions for cultural and gender-informed assessments, with examples of cognitive behavioral techniques that can be used in clinical assessment and treatment.

BIAS IN THE DELIVERY OF MENTAL HEALTH SERVICES TO MINORITY WOMEN

What is bias in the delivery of mental health services? It involves cultural or group bias that operates to stereotype and to define the culture of one group as superior and, in doing so, demeans another cultural group. On the individual level, personal bias influences the treatment decisions that affect the well-being of persons within a particular cultural group. On an institutional level, bias appears in formal or informal policies of private and governmental agencies (local, state, governmental) (Dana, 1998). Women are often the brunt of these policies, resulting in multiple oppressions from the theoretical paradigms that locate the origins of psychological problems within the woman while ignoring the sociopolitical context. Bias can also be related to theoretical orientation. Those counselors who use the medical model can be prone to bias in diagnosis because sociocultural factors are often excluded in diagnosis and treatment (Malgady & Rogler, 1987). Moreover, Western models of psychopathology are cognitively and biologically based (McLachlan, 1997) and can be simultaneously racist, sexist, heterosexist, and classist when used inappropriately (B. Greene, 1997, 1999).

Models used to train mental health professionals can include biased assumptions regarding normality and abnormality that go unquestioned (M.H. Glass & Beiber, 1997; D.W. Sue, 1998). Guidelines from a European American perspective do not fit some cultural groups. Psychiatric diagnostic formulations can have cultural explanations of illness that differ from White, middle-class norms. As Lum (1996) discusses, these can be expressions of stress discussed in culturally specific ways, such as "nerves," possessing spirits, somatic complaints, or misfortune; perceptions of severity of symptoms related to the cultural group norms of the reference group; local illness categories used to identify culture-bound syndromes; and explanatory notions of the symptoms.

Bias in Diagnostic Categories

Garb (1997) discusses how race, social class, and gender bias can occur when the mental health professional's accuracy of clinical judgments vary based on these attributes. He focuses on accuracy of judgments, not judgments used to make this distinction. He provides several examples: The diagnostic criteria for the diagnosis may be more valid for males than females; the self-report personality measures used to make a diagnosis may be more invalid for a particular population; or counselors may hold stereotyped views about race, social class, and gender that are used to confirm their hypothesis regarding clients. Diagnostic bias also relates to assessment bias. For example, test scores for one group can have very different meaning on a criterion for another group. Such forms of test bias in cross-cultural assessment occur in item construction, predictive validity, and criterion bias (Cuellar, 1998).

Diagnostic labeling also becomes influenced when cultural misunderstanding leads a counselor to infer that some clients' behaviors are maladaptive. J. Allen (1998) provides an example in his reviews of studies of depressive symptoms among American Indians and Alaska Natives. His findings suggest a potential for confusion between the Western psychiatric disorder of depression and indigenous forms of illness, raising serious questions about the universality of the construct of depression. Fleming's (1996) case study of a Salish American Indian woman provides another example. The woman's grief reaction to her grandmother's death included hearing her grandmother's voice in the months following death and experiencing dreams and hallucinations; these were not considered abnormal grief reactions by her tribal community. After the 12-month observance of grieving ended, a memorial dinner, the purpose of which was to bring a sense of peace, was held among family and friends. As Fleming discusses, if the grieving were to continue in intensity after this ceremony, there would be cause to consider unresolved grieving. This discussion of depression is a good example of the possibility that depression can be expressed in different ways in different cultures. Interestingly, some cultures, such as the Taluli of New Guinea and the Toraja of Indonesia, have no word for depression and apparently no occurrence of it (MacLachlan, 1977). Understanding this distinction can be difficult in Western cognitive and biologically based models of psychopathology.

The message seems clear: We need to understand the interaction of person variables across cultures to work multiculturally. Otherwise, therapist bias becomes related to values, assumptions, and beliefs about groups of people who are different from the dominant culture (Bermudez, 1997).

The diagnosis of schizophrenia is another category where cultural misunderstanding can occur. For example, research indicates that African American and Puerto Rican patients are more likely than Whites to be diagnosed as schizophrenic, even when measures of psychopathology do not indicate that a diagnosis of schizophrenia is justified (Able-Kim, 1996; Garb, 1997). Conversely, some believe that Asian Americans have lower incidences of mental health problems than do African Americans or Latino Americans because of low utilization rates by Asian Americans of mental health services. A more accurate appraisal is that Asian Americans' low utilization rates relate not to a lack of need, but rather to the failure of traditional mental health services to meet the needs of the Asian American community (J. Chin, De Lacancela, & Jenkins, 1993; Homma-True, Greene, Lopez, & Trimble, 1993).

RACE BIAS

Kutchins and Kirk (1997) report on race-based conclusions from studies of diagnosis using the *Diagnostic and Statistical Manual of Mental Disorders (DSM)*. There findings indicate that psychiatrists were more likely to diagnose African American women and men as having paranoid personality disorder compared to White women and men, although the presenting case material was similar.

Race bias has been well documented in the prescription of antipsychotic medications. African American patients are often prescribed more antipsychotic medications than other patients even when they are not more psychotic (D.R. Brown, 1990; Poussiant, 1990). Affective symptoms are often undertreated in patients who are African American or Latino compared to Whites (Garb, 1997). Brown suggests that lower rates of depression diagnosed in African Americans may be attributed to the European roots of American psychiatry, where depression was viewed as class-based, that is, associated with middle- and upper-class persons. Pouissant points out the stressful life circumstances of many African Americans (poverty, racism, unemployment, high-crime neighborhoods) and wonders if coping strategies of humor are misunderstood and therefore depression is not considered.

GENDER BIAS

Feminist therapists have written widely on the topic of gender bias, criticizing theoretical approaches that are used to exploit women by maintaining the status quo. This has been especially true of psychoanalytic approaches, and family psychology approaches that posit an assumption of power equity that does not exist in the typical male-dominated family (Nutt & Gottleib, 1993; Worell & Remer, 1992). Females are more likely than males to be diagnosed as having histrionic personality disorder (Garb, 1997). Women have higher rates of reported depressive disorders, schizophrenia, and somatization disorder (Russo, 1995b; Worell & Remer, 1992). Men have higher rates of alcohol and drug abuse and dependence and antisocial personality disorder (Russo, 1995b). Males are more likely to be diagnosed as having an antisocial personality disorder even when female and male clients do not differ in symptomology (Garb, 1997). Worell and

Remer (1992) provide a discussion of the most prevalent diagnostic disorders for females and males. They point out that therapist bias can occur when mental health professionals mislabel and misevaluate women's responses to their environment as pathological rather than as coping strategies for dealing with society's oppression.

However, there is also misdiagnosis based on the assumption that only certain groups of women are prone to the disorder. For example, eating disorders are viewed primarily as occurring in White, younger women, and not in African American, Latina, or Asian American women. Epidemiological studies on binge eating disorder have compared rates of binge eating among African American women and men and White women and men. Findings are that both groups of women and White men have comparable rates of binge eating, but African American men have the lowest rate (D. Smith, Marcus, Lewis, Fitzgibbon, & Schreimer, 1998). In a study of overweight, dieting women (African American, Asian American, and White), more purging was reported among African American women (LeGrange, Stone, & Brownell, 1998). These examples point to the need for mental health professionals to not assume eating disorders are problems only for White women. As Klonoff and Landrine (1995) discuss, health studies in the area of obesity and exercise are a literature about women with mostly White participants, and as a result fail to provide a comprehensive view of these health issues for all women.

Gender bias in counseling is exhibited in unexamined assumptions about women and men that guide treatment with clients; lack of separation between a client's concerns and the social context in which problems occur; focus on intrapsychiatric dynamics to work with clients' concerns; assessment of healthy behavior and psychological functioning based on gender-stereotypic behaviors (L.A. Gilbert & Scher, 1999); and higher rates of medication prescribed for females than males (Nutt & Gottleib, 1993). In the counseling process, a minority woman's way of coping can be misunderstood. For example, a spiritual woman can construct meaning for her life in a belief system that can be both behavioral (e.g., attending a religious service) and cognitive (e.g., prayer) (Wyche, 1998). A counselor who views a woman's spirituality as a passive rather than active way of coping fails to understand this as a form of spiritual expression drawn on for therapeutic change.

The sociopolitical status of minority women is not well understood by many therapists (Nahmias & Froehlich, 1993). An understanding of the issues involved would include an emphasis on the social inequality of women and its effects on power, social identity, and emotional processes. Poverty and violence continue to be two central components of the social context of women's health and need to be examined in relation to caretaking roles, psychological stress, and physical demands (Rieker & Jankowski, 1995). The practitioner who ignores life status variables that can predispose minority women to mental health problems has failed to understand the multiplicative nature of gender roles (mother, partner, worker, daughter, sister, etc.) that carry both cultural and societal expectations of role behavior (Wyche, 1995). For example, in some cultures, the involvement and importance of an extended kinship network serve a social support function as protective factors in times of crisis and stress. These networks are female-dominated and important across the life course. They are characterized by strong feelings of loyalty, reciprocity, and solidarity among members of the network (L.P. Anderson, 1991). Conversely, these social support networks can also be a source of stress as requests for reciprocity in relationships can become a burden (Wyche, 1998). The counselor who fails to assess this situation (i.e., the positive and negative effects of social support relationships) or who assumes that all social supports are positive for minority women will have difficulty being an effective helper. This lack of understanding becomes a treatment bias because of a failure to understand the distinct historical, economic, social, and psychological experiences tied to women's minority status.

Bias and Sexual Orientation

How sexual orientation, race, and gender interact with mental health issues receives little attention. B. Greene (1993, 1997) observes that lesbian and gay populations of color are ignored in the mental health literature. She states that therapists working with these populations need to be culturally competent in addition to having an understanding of the special needs of lesbian and gay clients. Homophobia or a belief system that values heterosexuality as superior to homosexuality will result in biased therapy. Therapists may also fail to understand the interactive factors that impinge on the lives of lesbians and gay clients of color. A focus on a single factor, as opposed to the multiple factors, of a person's life is not uncommon. That is, the therapist may minimize the significance of heterosexism's negative impact on a client's life, or focus on the client's sexual orientation as pathological and the source of problems, and in doing so ignore racial issues (B. Greene, 1997).

BIAS AND SOCIAL CLASS

The social class of clients also influences diagnosis. Clients with lower socioeconomic status are generally viewed as more seriously disturbed than those with higher socioeconomic status (Able-Kim, 1996). African Americans in lower social classes are more likely to be diagnosed as schizophrenic than those from middle to upper classes (D.R. Brown, 1990). Mental health professionals can misunderstand how social class influences a person's life. For instance, people's perception of their social class within their community is a more appropriate way to conceptualize class as a treatment variable than the traditional definitions of income and education (Wyche, 1996). Perhaps the most glaring point about social class issues in the United States health care system is the inequality of access to mental health care for all lower-income citizens.

WHY IS CULTURAL COMPETENCE IMPORTANT?

Mental health professionals can begin to address these various forms of bias by developing cultural competence. Such competence is a critical aspect of providing quality mental health care to ethnic minority populations. The cultural context of therapy becomes shaped by the ethnocultural factors of race, ethnicity, nativity, acculturation, religion, gender, age, class, sexual orientation, and other variables that interact to form the personal characteristics of those who come for help. Without this understanding of who gets sick, how they get sick, and how they are diagnosed and treated, the effectiveness of clinical interventions is limited (Able-Kim, 1996). Sometimes, these factors are completely ignored. I remember attending a grand round presentation at a child psychiatric hospital where a psychiatric fellow presented the case of an 11-year-old, White, blue-eyed girl who wanted to be called Pocahontas. There was no discussion of why the child chose the name of a Native American princess; the choice was meaningless to the presenter and was not factored into the treatment. The child's self-identity label was ignored and viewed as unimportant to assessment, diagnosis, and treatment.

Perhaps this understanding is less important for therapists who want to see people who are like them—often referred to as the YAVIS (young, attractive, verbal, intelligent, and successful) clients (Toupin, 1980). But for counselors who are interested in improving their skills in working with minority clients, acknowledging and becoming aware of their own culture is crucial to understanding the ethnic heritage and culture of their clients (Fuller, 1995), and a way to monitor their own bias.

Differences are always present in any helping relationship. These can be differences based on racial or ethnic group membership or the gender of client and counselor. Often, minority women clients see a White female counselor. In this situation, the counselor must assess her level of comfort with clients who may differ either by skin color, English fluency, English spoken with an accent, or all of the above. These recognizable client characteristics can constrain the helping relationship, resulting in inappropriate assumptions and unrealistic expectations (Proctor & Davis, 1994). Sometimes, differences are experienced by counselors as frightening or pitiful, or are altogether ignored.

There are many reasons minority women seek counseling. One reason is because of racism and/or experiences with discrimination. In this case, several important questions need to be addressed: Does the counselor understand the client's survival needs? Does the counselor have past experiences with discrimination? Does the counselor understand his or her privilege, and if so, what does that understanding entail? These are difficult questions to answer. At the university where I teach, there are some White, middle-class graduate students who experience, for the first time in their lives, the concept of difference. Many of their career objectives are to enter private practice. They are surprised when assigned a field placement where clients differ from them by race, ethnicity, and income. Sometimes, these students are in an agency where they are the numerical minority; when they enter the agency or walk from the bus or subway, their "minority" status is salient. Some of them request placements at another agency, stating that the current neighborhood is not safe, therefore they should not be placed there. These students fail to understand their own biases regarding racism and discrimination. They are at the stage of White privilege that is characterized by an absence of self as a racial person (R. Carter & Helms, 1991; Frankenberg, 1993). My response to them is Why did you choose a school in New York City? The privilege of class and race dominates their discourse. Not wanting to use subways or work in "bad" neighborhoods is more than fear; it is sometimes racism disguised as fear of difference. Many of these students do not want to confront the issues of race, class, and White privilege.

No relationship is value-free. Personal values can also influence helping relationships in several ways. Counselors transmit values directly or indirectly to prospective clients who come to them for help. Therefore, we can assume that by understanding one's own cultural self, we gain not only in sensitivity in becoming a more effective counselor, but also in our own value clarification (Okun, 1987). Personal values interact with beliefs about family, religion, work, race, authority, lifestyle, sexual orientation, money, and other variables by which individuals differ. Professions have codes of ethics that help guide in value clarification and emphasize dignity and respect for clients. We cannot assume that everyone shares the same worldview, and not all counselors will feel comfortable working with every client. Some counselors become judgmental when working with clients because of stark value differences between themselves and their clients. Several forms of personal bias can influence this process: ageism (Arean & Gallagher-Thompson, 1996), sexism, racism, homophobia, and ethnocentrism are just a few (B. Greene, 1993, 1999; Klonoff & Landrine, 1995; Landrine & Klonoff, 1996). Within the therapeutic dyad, a counselor's emotional reactions to a client—empathy, dislike, fear, sadness, and so on—will eventually become discernible and create an impasse in the therapeutic work (Perez-Foster, 1996). When a counselor is uncomfortable, the treatment process becomes influenced in subtle and not so subtle ways, with a treatment outcome that is always unfavorable for the client. When such a value discrepancy occurs between counselor and client, several options are available: Seek consultation; limit the relationship to discussion of achieved goals at the point of impasse; discuss these achieved goals with the client; or transfer the client to another counselor (Okun, 1987).

GENDER, ETHNICITY, AND CULTURAL UNDERSTANDING

Individuals construct their reality and worldview based on their multiple identities. Gender, culture, and ethnicity are major identities that remain with us over the life span. Lum (1996) makes a helpful distinction between culture and ethnicity: Culture is the ideas, customs, skills, and arts of a group of people that have been cultivated and passed on from generation to generation; ethnicity is a group's sense of identity that is based on loyalty to a distinctive cultural pattern that is expressed by common ancestry, nation, religion, language, historical continuity, and/or race. On the individual level, ethnicity gives a person a sense of belonging. Other important identities we incorporate into our view of self and that interact to make us unique relate to sexual orientation, religion, physical abilities, and social class. These identities shape who people are as we move from childhood through old age (see Deaux and Stewart, this volume). For minority women, the experience of racism and discrimination in the United States filters the salience of gender, culture, ethnicity, and race. I include race because, although it is a socially constructed category, it has sociopolitical and historical importance with the institutionalized racism imposed on African American, Asian American, Native American, and Latina American women. These multiple identities all become crucial determinants of our life experiences, roles, behaviors, opportunities, and orientation to the world around us. People construct their realities based on a self-identity that is gendered and situated within a cultural and ethnic framework. For mental health professionals to understand women, they must be able to develop an awareness and appreciation of how women identify themselves as gendered, ethnic, and cultural persons (Starrett, 1997).

How a minority woman self-identifies or labels herself may differ substantially from the label the counselor may use. For example, racial definitions can change from country to country. A Puerto Rican woman may self-identify as a White Puerto Rican woman, but her European American woman counselor may view her only as a Puerto Rican woman, or as a Latina (a less distinctive description). As Unger (1995) has argued, a person's skin color can evoke differing so-cial responses from others. In this example, the misunderstanding of the meaning of skin color can influence the quality of treatment, creating a void between the client's perspective and the counselor's awareness. Here, a counselor who views skin color as a proxy for race has not under-stood that skin color can have multiple meanings within an ethnic group. However, these nuances of meaning change when interacting with those who are not members of one's ethnic group. Eth-nic group bonding provokes a sense of "peoplehood," and within-group distinctions are not re-vealed to outsiders.

Starrett (1997) argues that to understand women's cultural identification we need to consider the ways women are affected by ongoing support of family. In addition to ethnic or racial forces that impinge on her life, her family's view of sexuality, how values are defined and exhibited, and how abilities and disabilities are handled are all important factors. Social class is not included in this conceptualization, but it is an important influence on self-identity and self-perception (Wyche, 1996). As N.L. Baker (1996) discusses, social class definitions and descriptions are part of American culture's covert discourse, carrying value-laden meanings. Counselors are in a privi-leged position vis-à-vis minority women clients, who often differ from them by social class job status (e.g., manual labor or low prestige) even when they are ethnically or racially similar. It would be a mistake, however, to assume that all minority women are poor (Wyche, 1996). Devel-oping an understanding of ethnic group patterns can help in understanding the culturally spe-cific ways feelings are expressed, stress is acted on, and mental health is viewed (Wyche, 1995). This is an argument against the notion of the homogeneity of minority women. African American women born in the United States cannot be assumed to be completely similar to Afro-Caribbean women, who have come from specific countries and who may experience acculturative stress. A Jamaican woman is not the same as a woman from Haiti or Trinidad (Brice-Baker, 1994). Similarly, as immigrant Latina lesbian women's narratives eloquently highlight, the issues of culture and sexuality are multiple identities in their definition as women (Espin, 1997).

DEVELOPING SELF-AWARENESS AND SELF-EVALUATION: THE MENTAL HEALTH PROFESSIONAL

In trying to understand oneself as a cultural being with values, biases, stereotypes, and unique communication patterns, a counselor can begin the process of self-examination. The personal goal is to become a culturally skilled counselor. In this process, one becomes aware of cultural assump-tions, biases, stereotypes, and the limitations of one's background (Fuller, 1995). Self-awareness be-comes a way to monitor these biases so as to not impose one's own values on clients either verbally or nonverbally. It is not necessary that everyone share the same worldview, but one certainly can learn to monitor biases. It is a process of discovering and understanding our ethnic and cultural identity and the ways in which gender shapes who we are. This exploration must incorporate an analysis of privilege and power in our interactions with others. This includes examining how dif-ferences are conceptualized, being aware of the influences of oppression on clients, and a willing-ness to work within culturally appropriate treatment frameworks that facilitate personal and social change (J. Chin et al., 1993). Survey data from White mental health practitioners (psychologists and social workers) employed in multiethnic urban institutional settings provide information about how these professionals define ethnically sensitive practice (Zayas, Torres, Malcolm, & DesRosiers, 1996). They reported that ethnically sensitive therapy comprises four elements: (1) being aware of the existence of differences between the client and oneself; (2) having knowledge of a client's cul-ture; (3) distinguishing between culture and pathology in assessment; and (4) understanding how culture influences the therapeutic process.

O.J. Williams (1992) describes the process by which practitioners struggle with questions of di-versity, self-awareness, and self-evaluation in working with ethnic minority populations. I have incorporated gender sensitivity as part of his model. Although Williams focuses on White practi-tioners in conceptualizing these stages, this model can be applied to any practitioner (regardless of ethnicity or gender) who views difference as deviance.

The first stage is called cultural resistance. In this stage, the counselor denies that minority clients should be viewed any differently from White clients. This is the homogeneity assump-tion, whereby a counselor adheres to standard treatment approaches for all clients. This type of counselor denies prejudice, views cultural and gender differences as part of the presenting problem, and evaluates treatment failure as the client's problem. Understandably, this type of counselor has a low comfort level with minority women clients.

The second stage is color blindness. In this stage, a counselor is more open to working with minority clients, but believes that all clients should be treated the same. This is really an argument against learning how culture and gender issues may influence presenting problems as well as treatment approaches. If any ethnic- and gender-sensitive material or treatment approaches have been learned, they are rigidly applied to all minority clients without assessing the extent to which such information fits a particular client. This type of counselor thinks that clients should be matched by gender and ethnicity. They have medium comfort levels, with little success in working with most minority clients.

O.J. Williams (1992) labels the last stage cultural sensitivity. In this stage, practitioners engage in self-examination and self-awareness of their attitudes and feelings regarding minority clients. Their cultural sensitivity is shown by the amount of attention given to understanding a client's worldview as it relates to the presenting problem. They attempt to build trust with clients by utilizing ethnic- and gender-sensitive approaches in evaluating the client's uniqueness. These practitioners are comfortable working with issues of difference between themselves and their clients. Although this model is not empirically tested, it provides an evaluative framework to assess counselors who are being trained in gender and cultural sensitivity.

ASSESSMENT AND TREATMENT ISSUES

The bias that occurs in diagnosis, assessment, and subsequent treatment fails to take into account the major cultural, class, age, gender, and sexual orientation differences between racial minorities and White women and men. As previously discussed, invalid conclusions regarding the type and degree of mental health problems are often the result. This situation becomes complicated further by the reality of the managed care environment that disadvantages racial minorities in a system that values low costs and rationed access to mental health services. Women and men minority group members can be blocked from gaining access to treatment because of the cultural limitations of the *DSM-IV*, language barriers, and the cultural expression of symptoms of mental illness (e.g., somatization of symptom expressions) (Able-Kim, 1996). These factors, together with services provided in public mental health outpatient units where many ethnic minority people enter the counseling world, often result in assignment to the more inexperienced clinicians or trainees.

Social class factors influence the referral patterns of clients, with middle-class persons more likely to be recommended for psychotherapy because of the assumption that they will be more successful in psychotherapy than lower-class individuals (Garb, 1997; McPhatter, 1991). Because African Americans, Latino Americans, Native Americans, and some Asian Americans (especially Southeast Asians) are disproportionately represented in the lower classes in the United States, they are more likely to get supportive counseling rather than insight-oriented psychotherapy (Garb, 1997). Supportive counseling relieves the counselor from helping to empower the client for change, and gives a subtle message to clients to accept their fate.

CULTURAL ASSESSMENT: ETHNIC GROUP PATTERNS

Counselors use various theories of practice to inform their clinical interventions. Adding the cultural component to these theories can be difficult for counselors who have not viewed their clinical work from a cultural lens. One way to sharpen the cultural lens is to become more aware of the cultural meanings of behaviors. Research on cultural themes of groups indicates dimensions that distinguish between broad patterns of behavior and norms of groups (Phinney & Rotheram, 1989). These cultural themes can be used for understanding the clinical assessment process (Rotheram-Borus & Wyche, 1994). These ethnic group patterns should be understood as interacting with a client's age, gender, social class, and acculturation level. Broad themes that distinguish ethnic groups are a view of the self as family- and group-oriented, and cooperative versus individualistic, assertive, and competitive; a passive or nondirective style of interaction and communication that involves nonverbal communication versus an open expression of feelings; relationships that can be authoritarian and hierarchial versus egalitarian; expressive versus restrained emotionality, a present versus future time orientation, and a view of mental illness that makes few distinctions between mind and body, or use of folk explanations versus a distinction between physical and mental well-being.

These dimensions become tools to guide the counselor in asking culturally important questions that will inform the assessment process and subsequent therapy. Because these are broad themes, it is important to contextualize this information to understand the uniqueness of each client. How does the discussion of symptoms differ for Hmong people versus Japanese? Each culture will have unique ways of talking about mental health problems. As Canada and Phacbtong (1992) point out, Southeast Asian clients who are Buddhist will have unique ways of handling psychological difficulties. Asian clients will often find somatic complaints that are culturally sanctioned ways of dealing with underlying psychological distress because of the stigma attached to mental illness and the feeling of shame for a client and family seeking treatment (Okazake, 1998; True, Greene, Lopez, & Trimble, 1993). Emotional problems and perspectives on mental illness can be viewed within a religious framework for Latinos, as the integration of mind and body for Native Americans, or as different forms of spirituality for African Americans. These various conceptualizations differ from the Western, White, middle-class cultural view that makes a distinction between physical and mental illness (MacLachlan, 1997).

Another difference is time orientation. African Americans, Asian Americans, Native Americans, and Latino Americans come later to therapy than White middle-class individuals (Rotheram-Borus & Wyche, 1994; D.W. Sue & Sue, 1999). Sometimes, the reason is shame, lack of understanding of the therapeutic process, lack of success in obtaining problem relief from other courses, or mistrust. But, whatever the reason, once help is sought, the expectation is that relief will come quickly. This poses a difficult problem for the counselor who does not understand these factors.

Gender and age factors also interact with cultural patterns of behavior. Knowing which cultural groups have patriarchal societies, privilege male authority, and make women's roles subservient or traditional will influence the assessment process. Though this may be more true of Asian American groups, in Latino groups the social class of the client may be a modifying influence (J. Chin et al., 1993; D.W. Sue & Sue, 1999). The point is that counselors should attempt to understand how this may influence what is normative or not within a cultural group. It is also important to understand that I mean normative within the ways cultural groups function in the United States and within the laws of this country. Sometimes, this distinction is misunderstood. For example, sexual harassment is not normative in this country, and there are laws in the workplace that govern this behavior. A man who engages in sexual harassment of his female coworkers should not be excused for this behavior on the grounds that in his former country this is permitted. Similarly, severe physical punishment of children is reportable to state child welfare agencies in the United States, but the same behavior might not be reported to governmental officials in a country where an abusing parent was born. In these examples, cultural differences are not excuses for inappropriate behavior.

Communication patterns also shape group patterns of behavior. African Americans are very verbal and communicate with expression of feelings, whereas Native American, Latino, and Asian American patterns of communication are more reserved, especially with persons of higher status (Rotheram-Borus & Wyche, 1994). However, this is not a blanket generalization, for within each group, age, social class, and acculturation factors influence these patterns. For clients who speak English as a second language, what is discussed in English may have a different emotional meaning and tone than if it was expressed in their first language (Perez-Foster, 1996). A simple question for counselors is Does the client understand what the counselor is saying? The behavioral manifestations may falsely lead the therapist to believe the client understands. One cannot have good therapy without comprehension, and for this reason, clinicians need to become attuned to the multiple ways language influences therapeutic outcomes.

Organizing these structural domains of behavior can be done through the use of culturagrams (Congress, 1994), eco-maps, or genograms (Hartman, 1978; McPhatter, 1991). The culturagram is described by Congress as a family-focused assessment tool for assessing cultural background, family values, immigration history, and acculturation. The eco-map draws from within and outside of the family to assess internal and external subsystems that are related to family functioning (e.g., individuals and institutions). A genogram can help in the process of developing self-awareness; drawing a genogram enables the counselor to understand the heritage, culture, and the idiosyncratic nature of the ways families express cultural norms and behaviors. All of these tools are powerful visual assessment instruments with which to understand the cultural meanings of behavior for the purposes of assessment and treatment.

Cognitive Behavioral Interventions as a Useful Tool for Cultural Interventions

As discussed earlier, African Americans, Asian Americans, Native Americans, and Latino Americans often come later for clinical help for a variety of reasons, and with an expectation that relief will come quickly. These factors, together with short-term treatment as the preferred modality of managed care companies, force counselors to develop effective clinical treatment tools. Cognitive Behavioral Therapy (CBT) approaches to treatment offer several solutions to this situation. The assumptions of this model is that cognitive activities affect behavior and can be monitored and altered, and that the desired behavior change can take place from that process (Dobson & Block, 1999; Ivey, 1987; S.Y. Lewis, 1994). The CBT paradigm focuses on the present to provide clients with the skills to confront their situation. This action can be helpful to minority clients who have tried other solutions before seeking help. Because quick relief is a desired goal, the counselor can discuss issues that provide cognitive clarity about the nature of the problems and potential solutions while giving reassurance and hope. This structured approach allows minority clients to respond to an active, empathetic response from counselors. Client and counselor work together to define the problem, outline solutions, and work toward alternatives. This solution-focused, joint collaboration has the goal of empowering clients toward change in their life and equalizing the power differential between client and counselor. This aspect is especially important for racial and ethnic minority people who have come from experiences of racism and discrimination and distrust clinicians of another race. Because clients are active in their treatment, they can take credit for successes via positive self-attributions, and reevaluate setbacks. For many clients, it is the first time they have some control over their lives (especially those in poverty and discriminatory situations) (S.Y. Lewis, 1994).

Feminist therapy (see Worell & Johnson, this volume) is one means with which to engage in cognitive behavioral techniques. The special focus is on helping women find unique meaning in life, examining cultural issues, using community resources, and sharing information. Feminist therapy is a therapeutic process centered in a dialogue about social and interpersonal justice. The personal validation of women as unique is valuable, and a focus on self-understanding and empowerment useful. The analysis of power in the realities of the woman's life builds on an active and participatory counseling style (Wyche & Rice, 1997). The focus on empowerment enables clients to gain or regain the ability to interact with the environment in ways that enhance their needs, gratification, well-being, and satisfaction. But, to gain a sense of power, essential resources must be available in the environment. For minority women, the multiple effects of racism, sexism, and poverty are salient. By using an empowerment approach to assessment (J. Lee, 1996), the counselor can begin to understand the role of oppression currently and in the past, and the experience of oppression. In this framework, minority women are encouraged to speak of these experiences (oppression, racism, and discrimination) to analyze powerlessness. That is, they can begin to understand how these situations influence their understanding of the situation and the subsequent behaviors.

There are many definitions of empowerment (E. Pinderhughes, 1983; B.L. Simon, 1990), but they share the focus on clients' change in perception of themselves as powerless, to being able to change that status, to actively working to gain skills to change their lives. Gutierrez (1990) has developed a process of empowering minority women that focuses on enhancing self-esteem, increasing self-efficacy, and developing group consciousness, with the goal of mobilizing resources (personal and institutional) toward developing a plan of action to solve the problem. Empowering women of color to enhance self-esteem would begin by valuing their definition of the problem, defining the helping relationship as one of collaboration, expressing a desire to understand, respect, and use culturally relevant solutions to the client's problem, and identifying and building on existing strengths of the woman. Often with women of low income, the counselor needs to be proactive in securing essential resources (e.g., housing, health care).

Techniques of cognitive restructuring are used to attack dysfunctional patterns and include cultural values and practices to facilitate personal empowerment. Forms of spirituality (prayer, meditation, visualization) so common for minority women are behaviors transferable to therapy using imagery techniques and positive self-statements (S.Y. Lewis, 1994). Spirituality issues raised by the client can help counselors design cognitive interventions such as visualization techniques (Neal-Barnett & Smith, 1997).

Other techniques that require active responses from clients are behavior logs. For example, if a woman presents with depression or anxiety, a behavioral log can be used to record where and when she feels depressed or anxious (Dobson & Block, 1999). These data are used by the woman and the counselor to develop cognitive strategies, such as restructuring her self-statements, to change behavior to gain mastery over their situation. Other client-centered techniques are art therapy, genogram, cultragram, eco-map, and bibliotherapy. Role playing can help develop skills to deal with stressful situations such as acculturative stress based on immigration history (M.H. Glass & Beiber, 1997) or school difficulties (Elligan, 1997). Because a cultural norm for minority clients is a present-time focus, these tools are viewed as valid and serve as a way to engage the client in painful memories or situations. Writing in a log, drawing family information, or reading enables clients to engage material that may be difficult to talk about because of family norms of silence, language difficulties, or lack of trust in the therapy process.

Cognitive behavioral techniques provide useful tools for engaging all clients—minority and nonminority. Therapeutic change is continually monitored by client and counselor; contracting for therapeutic goals is made specific rather than vague. It is my hope that counselors from various theoretical orientations will be able to incorporate CBT techniques within a cultural assessment framework. We all want good therapeutic outcomes for our clients. This is one tool to help us provide culturally appropriate and sensitive mental health practice.

PART V

INSTITUTIONS, GENDER, AND POWER

CHAPTER 23

A Developmental Examination of Violence against Girls and Women

JACQUELYN W. WHITE, PATRICIA L.N. DONAT, and BARRIE BONDURANT

In spite of images of loving, supportive families and caring, protective lovers, intimate relationships may be plagued by alarming levels of aggression and violence. Although men are usually the victims of nonintimate crimes, girls and women are much more likely than men to be the victims of violence in intimate relationships. Physical violence against women takes many forms, including childhood sexual abuse, dating violence, acquaintance rape, battering and wife abuse; nonphysical forms of violence include sexual harassment, stalking, and pornography. All these forms of violence share in common the fact that they frequently are committed by men known to the girls and women. Unlike other crimes, they are crimes in which others, as well as the victim herself, tend to blame the victim for what happened. By blaming the individual victims, attention and responsibility are shifted away from the perpetrators and from the social context that contributes to violence against women (R. Elias, 1986). The present chapter suggests that the roots of violence against women can be found in the childhood experiences of girls and boys, and that the messages learned in and the consequences of these early experiences are repeated and reinforced in adolescence and young adulthood. In this chapter, we discuss these experiences from a developmental perspective and conclude with a model for examining the commonalities among the various forms of violence against women.

A developmental perspective is important for three reasons. First, violence toward women occurs across the life cycle. Second, childhood victimization increases the risk of further victimization during adolescence, and adolescent victimization increases the risk of revictimization during adulthood. Third, there are serious and long-term psychological and physical consequences of victimization at all ages.

GENDERED VIOLENCE IN CHILDHOOD

The gendered nature of violence is evident early in childhood and establishes a framework for patterns of interactions between adult women and men. Children are at great risk for victimization because of their small physical stature and dependency on adults; they have little choice over whom they live with and few opportunities to leave an abusive home. From the beginning, they learn the major lesson of patriarchy: The more powerful control the less powerful. Furthermore, children learn that power is gendered and associate men and masculinity with power and dominance. Victimization is also gendered. During childhood, boys experience more physical aggression and girls experience more sexual aggression. Among adolescents, girls are at a greater risk than boys for both physical and sexual victimization (Finkelhor & Dziuba-Leatherman, 1994).

GENDER DIFFERENCES IN SUBJECTIVE MEANING OF AGGRESSION

There is a rich developmental literature that shows gender-related patterns in the understanding and use of various types of aggressive behavior (Archer & Parker, 1994; Crick, Bigbee, & Howes, 1996; Crick, Casas, & Ku, 1999). Women and men have different understandings of anger and aggression (Archer & Haigh, 1999). Girls are taught to be less direct in expressing aggression (Bjorkqvist, Lagerspetz, & Kaukiainen, 1992; Lagerspetz et al., 1988) and regard relational aggression more positively than boys, who judge physical aggression more positively (Crick & Werner, 1998). For adults, men see anger expression as a means of reasserting control over a situation, whereas women see anger expression as a loss of control (A. Campbell, Muncer, Guy, & Banim, 1996). Men perceive women's aggression as expressive, and women judge men's aggression to be instrumental (A. Campbell et al., 1996). Apparently, women and men share the belief that *his* aggression is a means of control and *hers* is a signal of loss of control. Thus, women come to experience aggressive behavior as a loss of emotional control, whereas men find aggression rewarding and an effective way to control others (A. Campbell, 1993).

CHILDREN'S PLAY EXPERIENCES AND AGGRESSION

Play is the "work" of children and the context within which they learn gender-role expectations (Crawford & Unger, 2000). Girls and boys learn very early that boys are supposed to be stronger than girls and that girls should follow boys. In particular, children receive very specific messages about aggression. Given that children often play in same-sex groups, it is not surprising that the forms of aggression expressed in these groups differ. For example, girls are more likely to use verbal persuasion, whereas boys are more likely to establish dominance physically, for instance, by shouldering (Charlesworth & Dzur, 1987). This leads boys to be the targets of physical aggression in play situations more often than girls.

School-age girls and boys show definite preferences for gender-segregated play. The pressure for children to differentiate themselves from other-sex playmates is strong at this age. Although both boys and girls run from, chase, and tease each other, key differences in the play styles of girls and boys exist. Boys establish their identity as male by defining girls as different and inferior, scorn girl-type activities, and exclude girls from their play. In fact, boys' rougher play may be one reason for same-sex segregated play groups (Maccoby, 1998). Jean Baker Miller (1986) has suggested that girls learn to protect themselves from boys' displays of dominance by avoiding them. Girls develop a wariness of boys that they carry into adolescence. These patterns explain why girls and women may develop greater anxiety and feelings of guilt regarding aggressive behavior.

GENDER AND PARENTAL PUNISHMENT

In both normal and abusive homes, children receive gendered messages about aggression and violence. Children, especially those from abusive homes, have many opportunities to learn that the more powerful person in a relationship can use aggression to successfully control the less powerful person. The majority of parents in American homes use verbal and physical aggression as disciplinary tactics. Murray Straus and Richard Gelles (1990) report that over 90% of children are spanked sometime in their youth, with many parents (62%) reporting physical aggression against their children; this aggression includes pushing, shoving, and slapping. Fewer parents (11%) report using severe aggression, including hitting, kicking, beating, threatening, and using weapons against their children.

Punishment does not appear to be uniform, however; the sex of the child and the parent affect the pattern and outcome (Strassberg, Dodge, Pettit, & Bates, 1994). During early childhood, boys are at greater risk than girls for severe abusive punishment, whereas during preadolescence and adolescence, girls' risk increases (Straus, Gelles, & Steinmetz, 1980). This is presumably because of boys' increased ability to inflict harm on others as they physically mature. Although parents do not differ in the frequency with which they spank girls and boys (Lytton & Romney, 1991), the effects of the spanking are different. Paternal spanking leads to reactive (angry) aggression in both girls and boys, but only boys show unprovoked bullying aggression against others when spanked by their fathers. Strassberg and his colleagues (1994) conclude that fathers' spanking of boys communicates a "gender-based approach to interpersonal disagreements, that of physical dominance, . . . explicitly transmitting gender-stereotypic notions" (p. 457). Moreover, parents' reactions to their children's aggressive behavior differs. Although parents generally see aggression as an undesirable attribute for children, they view it as a tolerated *masculine* behavior (Eron, 1992). Thus, boys expect less parental disapproval than girls for aggression directed toward peers (Huesmann, Eron, Lefkowitz, & Walder, 1984), although they are punished more harshly for aggression than are girls (D.G. Perry, Perry, & Weiss, 1989).

CHILDHOOD SEXUAL ABUSE

The message that the more powerful can control the less powerful is also learned in a sexual context for a minority of girls and boys. The best information to date comes from three published national probability samples. In a telephone survey of *children* between the ages of 10 and 16, researchers found that 15% of girls and 6% of boys reported being sexually victimized (Boney-McCoy & Finkelhor, 1995). In a telephone survey of *adults*, 27% of women and 16% of men recalled childhood sexual abuse experiences (Finkelhor, Hotaling, Lewis, & Smith, 1990), whereas in face-to-face interviews, only 17% of women and 12% of men reported experiencing childhood sexual abuse (Laumann et al., 1994).

The sexual victimization of children is an abuse of interpersonal power and a violation of trust. What makes the statistics even more tragic is the fact that most children are victimized by people they know and trust to protect them. Almost 90% of children who are raped are victimized by someone known to them (Greenfeld, 1997). Boys are more likely to be sexually abused by someone outside the family, whereas girls are more likely to be sexually abused by a family member or a quasi–family member (e.g., mother's boyfriend). Betrayal of the trust vested in those who have power is central to understanding childhood sexual abuse, its consequences, and the systems that sustain it (Freyd, 1997).

David Finkelhor (1984) proposed a model that describes the preconditions for abuse. For abuse to occur, the abuser must possess a motivation to offend and an ability to overcome internal barriers, external barriers, and the resistance of the child. There may be a cyclical pattern in perpetrator-victim incestuous relationships (Simon-Roper, 1996; S. Wolf, 1985). Prior to an abusive incident, perpetrators may engage in nurturant, "grooming" behaviors (i.e., buying the child toys, tucking him or her into bed at night, asking the child to spend time with them). Following the abusive incident, perpetrators may experience transitory guilt and promise themselves and the child that they will not victimize him or her again. This pattern of violation mixed with contrite, loving behavior perpetuates the cycle of abuse.

Although specific intrapersonal characteristics of the perpetrator have been identified by researchers, the risk factors for who will be victimized are situational ones, outside the child's control, rather than victim characteristics. Any child may be victimized by an adult family member, but specific family variables are associated with childhood sexual abuse (Carson, Gertz, Donaldson, & Wonderlich, 1990; J.J. Edwards & Alexander, 1992; J.L. Jackson, Calhoun, Amick, Maddever, & Habif, 1990; Yama, Tovey, & Fogas, 1993).

Characteristics of Abusive Families

In a recent review of the literature, Draucker (1996) identified three key factors present in sexually abusive families: (1) Families members are emotionally distant and open displays of affection often are absent; (2) families have a rigid, traditional family structure, in which fathers are the head of the household and women are viewed as subordinate to their husbands, children subordinate to their parents, and obedience and control permeate all aspects of the parent-child relationship; and (3) families have numerous conflictual relationships among family members, particularly between parents.

The family system in which parent-child incest typically occurs is headed by a father who is authoritarian, punitive, and threatening (Storer, 1992). Children who are victimized often feel powerless to stop the abuse and feel they have nowhere to turn for help, comfort, and support. The child's ability to confront and refuse sexual contact is overwhelmed by the feelings of loyalty and trust that the child may have developed for the perpetrator. The adult is in a position of authority (and often one of trust as well) and communicates to the child that the behavior is part of an exclusive, secretive, and special relationship. The perpetrator may even come to believe and attempt to convince the child that the relationship is a mutually loving and caring one (Gilgun, 1995). For children who may otherwise be neglected and emotionally isolated, the special attention and inappropriate sexual contact with the adult may be confusing and may complicate the coping process.

Ethnicity and Childhood Sexual Abuse

The relationship between racial ethnicity and victimization is currently being studied. No statistical differences between the percentages of Black (57%) and White (67%) women reporting childhood sexual victimization have been reported (Wyatt, 1985). Similarly, 49% of the women in a Southwestern American Indian tribal community reported childhood sexual victimization (Robin, Chester, Rasmussen, Jaranson, & Goldman, 1997). Using a more restrictive definition of sexual abuse, Arroyo, Simpson, and Aragon (1997) also found no significant differences in the prevalence of childhood sexual abuse among Hispanic and non-Hispanic women, with 27.1% of Hispanic women and 33.1% of non-Hispanic White women reporting victimization as children. Thus, girls from several ethnic groups appear to be at risk for becoming a victim of sexual abuse.

SUMMARY

As studies of play patterns in girls and boys, parental punishment, and childhood sexual abuse suggest, boys receive numerous messages that distance them from girls and tolerate their using aggression to express interpersonal power and control. Girls, on the other hand, receive messages that encourage submission and discourage them from defending themselves physically against aggression. Additionally, some girls and boys learn that their bodies are not their own, and that caretakers may use them sexually. These experiences set the stage for patterns of behavior that emerge during adolescence when intimate, heterosexual interactions develop. Boys and girls learn, through observations in the home, peer interactions, and media depictions of male-female interactions, that boys are dominant and girls are submissive, that boys are agentic and girls are passive.

GENDERED VIOLENCE IN ADOLESCENCE

During adolescence, young men and women experience extreme pressure to conform to traditional gender roles. Unfortunately, part of establishing a masculine identity for young men often involves distancing oneself socially and psychologically from anything feminine (A. Kahn, 1984). "Thus, to turn away and distance oneself from a woman is what a man does because he is a man, and what boys do in relation to girls because they are boys. Such behavior is expected, is tacitly approved, often goes unnoticed, and contributes to the implicit definition or understanding of manliness in a sexist society" (Lott, 1995a, p. 20). Young men seek out companionship from other men and distance themselves from women except in social contexts involving "power-enhancing" or sexual opportunities (Lott, 1995a).

IMAGES OF THE OTHER SEX AND ATTRACTIVENESS

Sexualized images of women's bodies are prevalent not only in sexually explicit materials, but in general media images (e.g., advertising). Women become the objects of men's gaze and evaluation. Women learn that their bodies are evaluated by others. Objectification theory states that a cultural context such as this socializes girls to view themselves as objects for evaluation and approval by others (Fredrickson & Roberts, 1997). Moreover, the girls themselves come to internalize an observer's perspective on self and may come to evaluate their self-worth based on the responses and evaluations of others.

One in-depth study of college women's peer cultures discovered that young women believed that being good-looking, attracting men, and having dates and boyfriends were very important (D.C. Holland & Eisenhart, 1990). The young women believed they would be judged more favorably if they had a relationship with an attractive man. Furthermore, college women seem to believe that when the woman is more attractive than the man, he must treat her especially well as a means of equalizing power in the relationship, but if the woman is less attractive than the man, he can treat her poorly to compensate for her unattractiveness. The woman, if less attractive than the man, reduces her expectation for good treatment. Women also come to use a man's treatment as an index of her relative attractiveness. When mistreated, they blame themselves rather than the man for their victimization (D.C. Holland & Eisenhart, 1990).

THE IMPACT OF PORNOGRAPHY ON YOUNG MEN AND WOMEN

In the extreme, the sexual objectification of women as depicted in pornography may have an impact on both adolescent women and men. Pornographic images include "verbal or pictorial explicit representations of sexual behavior that . . . have as a distinguishing characteristic the degrading and demeaning portrayal of the role and status of the human female as a mere sexual object to be exploited and manipulated sexually" (Longino, 1994, p. 154).

Although women rate pornography negatively (Seen & Radtke, 1990) and experience increased negative affect during the viewing of degrading, sexually explicit images (Krafka, 1985), repeated exposure to these images results in desensitization to the disturbing images presented. Moreover, it appears that women may be more likely to fail to reject certain myths about rape following exposure to R-rated films that portray coercive sex (B.A. Scott, 2000). Women were more likely to endorse statements describing rape as a sexual act and male sexuality as uncontrollable.

The evidence of an impact of repeated exposure to pornography on young men is well documented. Exposure to pornography increases men's sexual callousness toward women, desensitizes men to violence against women, and increases men's acceptance of rape myths and willingness to engage in aggressive behavior toward women in the laboratory (B.A. Scott, 2000). In a recent study conducted by Malamuth (1998), pornography consumption was identified as an important risk factor in sexual aggression. Malamuth examined differences in pornography consumption for men who were high in hostile masculinity and promiscuity. Seventy-two percent of men who also were high in pornography consumption reported engaging in sexually aggressive behavior, and 44% of the men who were low in pornography consumption reported sexually aggressive behavior. Although correlational in design, such results suggest that pornography, at the very least, contributes to the social context in which men and women learn about gendered relationships.

DATING VIOLENCE

The gender-related patterns learned in childhood are played out in adolescent dating and committed relationships. Young people usually begin dating in high school, although children as young as kindergartners talk about having boyfriends and girlfriends. The idea of being paired with a member of the other sex is pervasive in our society. Traditionally, it has been assumed that children's "playing house" and, later, dating provide a context for socialization into later roles, including husband, wife, lover, and confidante (F.P. Rice, 1984). Dating also offers opportunities for companionship, status, sexual experimentation, and conflict resolution. However, courtship has different meanings for young women and men (Lloyd, 1991). Whereas for men, courtship involves themes of "staying in control," for women, themes involve "dependence on the relationship." Violence is one of the tactics used to gain control in a relationship.

Dating and Sexual Scripts

It appears that dating violence and sexual assault among adolescents and college students is so prevalent, in part, because of the overall structure and meaning of dating in our culture, which give men greater power. Adolescent dating patterns follow a fairly well-defined script that has not changed much over several decades. A dating script is a set of rules to be followed by girls and boys that affords men greater power relative to women because they are expected to initiate and pay for dates, and because relationships generally are perceived as more important to women than to men (Breines & Gordon, 1983). Women are assumed to be responsible for "how far things go," and if things "get out of hand," it is their fault.

Relationship Traps for Women

Romantic relationships may become "destructive traps" for women when they feel they must put maintenance of the relationship above their own self-interests (Carey & Mongeau, 1996). Violence is more likely to occur in serious than in casual relationships (Pedersen & Thomas, 1992). Women who experience ongoing victimization often report more commitment to and love for their partner; they are less likely to end the relationship because of abuse and they allow their partner to control them. These women also report more traditional attitudes toward women's roles, justify their abuse, and tend to romanticize relationships and love (Follingstad, Rutledge, McNeill-Hawkins, & Polek, 1992). Many students believe dating violence is more acceptable in serious relationships (Bethke & DeJoy, 1993) and is not sufficient grounds for ending the relationship (Bethke & DeJoy, 1993; O'Keeffe, Brockopp, & Chew, 1986). Violence also is more likely in relationships plagued by problems, which include jealousy, fighting, interference from friends, lack of time together, breakdown of the relationship, and problems outside the relationship (Riggs, 1993), as well as disagreements about drinking and sexual denial (Roscoe & Kelsey, 1986). These conflicts lead to feelings of confusion and anger, and result in violence (Sugarman & Hotaling, 1989).

Incidence and Prevalence of Dating Violence

Studies indicate that dating violence during the teen years is pervasive, with as many as 35% of female and male students surveyed reporting at least one episode (O'Keeffe et al., 1986), with fewer experiencing recurring violence (Burcky, Reuterman, & Kopsky, 1988). A national survey of approximately 2,600 college women and 2,100 college men revealed that within the year prior to the survey, 81% of the men and 88% of the women had engaged in some form of verbal aggression, either as perpetrator or victim (J.W. White & Koss, 1991). Approximately 37% of the men and 35% of the women inflicted some form of physical aggression, and about 39% of the men and 32% of the women sustained some physical aggression. In this survey, all types of heterosexual relationships were included, from the most casual to the most serious, thus providing a comprehensive estimate of the scope of courtship violence. The measures of verbal aggression included arguing heatedly, yelling, sulking, and stomping. Physical aggression included throwing something at someone, pushing, grabbing, shoving, and hitting. The ubiquity of courtship violence among college students is apparent in that comparable rates of violence have been observed across gender, ethnic group, and type of institution of higher learning, such as private or public, religious or secular (M.L. Clark, Beckett, Wells, & Dungee-Anderson, 1994; J.W. White & Koss, 1991). All the evidence to date suggests that it would be unusual to find a high school or college student who had not been involved in some form of verbal aggression and a substantial number who have not been involved in physical aggression. Also, it appears that the same people who report inflicting some form of violence are the ones who report experiencing violence.

Motives for Dating Violence

Some studies suggest that women and men do not appear to differ in the frequency with which they report engaging in aggressive acts (Bookwala, Frieze, Smith, & Ryan, 1992; J.W. White & Koss, 1991; see J.W. White, Smith, Koss, & Figueredo, 2000, for a critique of studies examining sex differences in intimate partner aggression). However, this cannot be taken to mean there are no gender-related differences in aggression. On the contrary, studies have shown that the motives and consequences for such behavior are different for women and men (J.W. White, Koss, & Kissling, 1991). Most data suggest that women are more likely to engage in aggression for self-defense, whereas men report that they aggress to instill fear and to intimidate.

Predictors of Dating Violence

The underlying processes involved in courtship violence for women and for men appear different. The results of studies are quite consistent. Although the best predictor of being aggressive is having an aggressive partner (Bookwala et al., 1992; J.W. White, Merrill, & Koss, 1999), other predictors are different for women and men. Men who are quick to react to anger, believe that violence will aid in winning an argument, and have successfully used violence in other situations are likely to do so again (Riggs & Caufield, 1997; White et al., 1991). Similarities between men who engage in courtship violence and wife batterers have been found (K.M. Ryan, 1995). Drug use, divorced parents, stressful life events, beliefs that violence between intimates is justifiable, and less traditional sex-role attitudes also have been identified as predictors (Bookwala et al., 1992; A. Mason & Blankenship, 1987; Tontodonato & Crew, 1992).

For women, on the other hand, a history of parent-child abuse (Tontodonato & Crew, 1992; Sappington, Pharr, Tunstall, & Rickert, 1997), as well as anxiety, depression (J.W. White et al., 1991), and drug use (Tontodonato & Crew, 1992), have been related to courtship violence. It is likely that these latter factors are reactions to childhood experiences with violence, rendering women more vulnerable to being the target of a violent partner, which in turn increases the likelihood of being violent. Learning about violence in the home and associating with peers who endorse the use of violence may provide a backdrop of social norms that legitimate violence. Violence is learned as a tactic of dealing with interpersonal conflict (Reuterman & Burcky, 1989; Worth, Matthews, & Coleman, 1990).

However, women may be the initiator of aggression in dating relationships (DeMaris, 1992). White and colleagues have shown that prior experience with sexual victimization (Humphrey & White, 1991) as well as physical victimization in a dating context (P.H. Smith, White, & Humphrey, 1999) during adolescence predicts being physically aggressive in dating situations during the first year of college. Prior experience with violence may disinhibit aggression, thus enabling women to overcome gender-related constraints on aggressive expression (J.W. White et al., 1991). A recently developed theory (Hammock & Richardson, 1997) proposes that threat and perceptions of threat underlie relational violence. Past victimization experiences, including witnessing and experiencing parental aggression, may increase women's expectations of harm from male partners. Thus, offensive aggression may actually be preemptive aggression. Feelings of isolation resulting from prior victimization (reflected in passivity) may contribute to a greater awareness of threat associated with the intimidating behaviors of their male partners, resulting in the perceived need not only for self-defensive efforts, but for offensive (or initiating acts) as well (White & Humphrey, 1999).

SEXUAL VIOLENCE

As men and women establish intimate relationships, dominance and violence also surface in the form of sexual aggression. Although the legal definition of rape appears straightforward, both the social meaning of the term rape and the circumstances surrounding an act of forced sexual intercourse make some reluctant to use the label. The term rape has been shown to have different meanings for women and men. College students in general, and sexually aggressive men in particular, believe that sexual precedence (i.e., a past history of sexual intercourse) reduces the legitimacy of sexual refusal (Shotland & Goodstein, 1992). Moreover, some people are hesitant to label forced sex as rape if consent was not explicitly verbalized, even if threats, intimidation, or incapacitation are present (Sawyer, Pinciaro, & Jessell, 1998). Although a woman may not realize that forced sexual intercourse by an acquaintance during a date is rape, this does not change the legal definition of the act as rape, nor does it reduce the culpability of the perpetrator (Koss, 1996). Furthermore, whether a sexual assault is labeled rape does not alter the consequences for the victim.

Frequency of Sexual Victimization

A comprehensive survey asked over 3,000 college women from 32 institutions of higher education across the United States about sexual experiences since the age of 14 (Koss et al., 1987). Of those surveyed, over half of the women (53.7%) had experienced some form of sexual victimization; 15.4% had experienced acts by a man that met the legal definition of rape (though only 27% labeled the experience rape), and 12.1% had experienced attempted rape. An additional 11.9% had been verbally pressured into sexual intercourse, and the remaining 14.4% had experienced some other form of unwanted sexual contact, such as forced kissing or fondling with no attempted penetration. More recent studies confirm these high numbers among college students in the United States (Humphrey & White, in press) and among Canadians (DeKeseredy, 1997), as well as among a probability sample of 8,000 women in the United States (Tjaden & Thoennes, 1998).

High school women also appear to be at greater risk for rape than previously thought. A recent survey of 834 entering college students found that 13% reported being raped between the ages of 14 and 18, and an additional 16% reported being victims of an attempted rape (Humphrey & White, in press). Most victims knew the perpetrator, and the assaults frequently occurred in a dating context. Similar rates of reported sexual assault have been found among adolescents, indicating that sexual assault is not just a problem for college campuses. It is a frequent experience during the high school years as well.

The Koss survey (Koss et al., 1987) described earlier also examined the sexual experiences of over 2,900 college men. Of this group, 4.4% admitted to behaviors meeting the legal definition of rape, 3.3% admitted to attempted rape, 7.2% to sexual coercion, and 10.2% to forced or coerced sexual contact; thus, 25.1% of the college men admitted to some form of sexual aggression. Similar rates have been reported in college samples (Calhoun, Bernat, Clum, & Frame, 1997; White & Humphrey, 1993) and in a community college sample (J.W. White, Holland, Mazurek, & Lyndon, 1998).

Risk Factors for Sexual Victimization

Numerous studies have been conducted to identify risk factors for sexual victimization, most with little success. Simply being female is the greatest risk factor for sexual victimization. Men are less likely, although not invulnerable, to sexual victimization. Age is also a risk factor, with adolescence being the period of greatest vulnerability; during adolescence, the risk of first being victimized increases steadily from age 14 to 18 and declines thereafter (Humphrey & White, in press). Being a college student is another risk factor; sexual victimization rates are about three times higher among college students than in the general population (Aizenman & Kelley, 1988; Koss et al., 1987, but not Zweig, Barbee, & Eccles, 1997). Other risk factors have been difficult to determine. Several researchers have confirmed that the best predictor of victimization is past victimization. Childhood victimization typically increases the risk of adolescent victimization, which in turn increases the risk of victimization as a young adult (M.E. Collins, 1998; Gidycz, Coble, Latham, & Layman, 1993; Humphrey & White, in press; Mills & Granoff, 1992; Wyatt, Guthrie, & Notgrass, 1992). Additionally, childhood victimization has been related to earlier age of menarche and sexual activity that may increase the perpetrator's attraction to the victim (Vicary, Klingman, & Harkness, 1995).

Alcohol is implicated in sexual assault in several ways. Women with a history of victimization may turn to alcohol as a means of coping. Unfortunately, alcohol use also may make it more difficult for women to read the danger cues present in an impending assault; more important, her alcohol use may suggest, erroneously, to the perpetrator that she is sexually available and/or that she will be less able to resist an assault (Hammock & Richardson, 1997).

Risk Factors for Perpetration

The typical acquaintance rapist appears to be a "normal" guy. He is not a crazed psychopath, although he may display psychopathy-related traits (Kosson, Kelly, & White, 1997). Among college students, alcohol use (Koss & Gaines, 1993; J.W. White & Humphrey, 1994), athletic affiliation (Frintner & Rubinson, 1993; T.L. Jackson, 1991; Koss & Gaines, 1993), and fraternity membership (Frintner & Rubinson, 1993, but not Koss & Gaines, 1993) have been associated with sexual aggression toward women. Other significant correlates of sexual assault include a history of family violence; an early and varied sexual history, including many sexual partners; a history of delinquency; acceptance of rape myths; an impulsive personality; hedonistic and dominance motives for sex; lower than average sense of self-worth; and lower religiosity; as well as peers who condone and encourage sexual conquests (J.W. White & Koss, 1993). Finally, sexually aggressive men are more likely to perceive a wider range of behaviors as indicative of sexual interest than do nonsexually aggressive men (Bondurant & Donat, 1999) and are attracted to sexual aggression (Calhoun et al., 1997).

It appears that sexual promiscuity and hostile attitudes combine to characterize sexually aggressive men (Malamuth, Sockloskie, Koss, & Tanaka, 1991), particularly in men who tend to be self-centered and have little regard for others (i.e., low in empathy) (Dean & Malamuth, 1997). Sexually aggressive men tend to be more domineering with women, using "one-up" messages aimed at "gaining control of the exchange" (e.g., bragging about oneself and criticizing the other person) (Malamuth & Thornhill, 1994). Domineeringness in conversation may be a test sexually aggressive men use to identify vulnerable targets. A woman who resists the domination may be seen as unavailable, but a subordinate response from a woman may indicate that she is a potential target. Furthermore, it is likely that a woman experiencing the helplessness and powerlessness associated with a previous victimization will be less likely to resist the man's domineering behavior than women without a victimization history. This may help us understand why and how perpetrators target vulnerable women.

Ethnicity and Sexual Assault

Dating violence and sexual assault pose additional problems among adolescents who are not White, middle class, and heterosexual. Although it is difficult for any young person to admit being victimized by a dating partner, it is especially so for ethnic minorities. The legacy of slavery and distrust of White authority figures have made it difficult for African American teens to report abusive dating relationships (E.C. White, 1991). Asian/Pacific women, too, are reluctant to disclose abuse because of cultural traditions of male dominance and reticence to discuss private relationships in public (Yoshihamana, Parekh, & Boxingston, 1991). For lesbian teens, the problem is complicated by the fact that, in reporting abuse, they may have to reveal their sexual orientation, something they may not be psychologically ready to do (B. Levy & Lobel,1991).

SUMMARY

The various themes of "boy versus girl" that were learned in childhood are reinforced and played out with serious consequences for numerous young women and men during adolescence. Experiences with verbal, physical, and sexual aggression and violence are all too common. Young men continue to believe it is acceptable to dominate young women in ways that are not only harmful to their partner, but that increase the risk of continuing these patterns of behaviors in young adulthood. Young women who are victimized during childhood and adolescence are at great risk for further victimization in young adulthood (Humphrey & White, in press). Furthermore, young men who were victimized as children and were perpetrators of sexual and physical aggression during adolescence are at increased risk for further perpetration during early adulthood (Humphrey & White, 1992; Humphrey, White, & Smith, 1999).

VIOLENCE IN MARRIAGE AND OTHER COMMITTED RELATIONSHIPS

The patterns established during adolescence may continue in adulthood. The greatest threat of violence to adult women is from their intimate partners; for men, the greatest threat is from other men (A. Browne, 1993). Women are more likely to be physically or sexually assaulted by an intimate partner than by a stranger. It is estimated that 2 to 3 million women are assaulted by male partners in the United States each year and that at least half of these women are severely assaulted (i.e., punched, kicked, choked, beaten, threatened with a knife or gun, or had a knife or gun used on them) (Straus & Gelles, 1990). As many as 21% to 34% of women will be assaulted by an intimate partner during adulthood (A. Browne, 1993; Straus & Gelles, 1990). Further, it is estimated that 33% to 50% of all battered wives are also the victim of partner rape (Peacock, 1998; T. Randall, 1990). Studies have shown that 22% to 40% of the women who seek health care at clinics or emergency rooms are victims of battering (Stark & Flitcraft, 1996).

Intimate violence may escalate, resulting in homicide. Approximately 66% of family violence deaths are women killed by their male partners; over 50% of all murders of women are committed by current or former partners (A. Browne & Williams, 1989). In contrast, only 6% of male murder victims are killed by wives or girlfriends (Uniform Crime Report, 1985). Murder-suicides are almost always cases where the man kills his partner or estranged partner and then kills himself (Stuart & Campbell, 1989). He also may kill his children or other family members before he kills himself. Although there are instances where a woman murders a partner who has been abusing her, this happens less frequently than men killing partners they have abused chronically (A. Browne, 1993).

When women kill their partners, they are often reacting to abuse rather than initiating it. A study of women who killed partners found several common factors (A. Browne, 1987). The women were in abusive relationships and the abuse was increasing in frequency and severity. The increased violence was associated with a rise in the number and seriousness of the women's injuries. It was common for these men to have raped their spouses, forced them into other sexual acts, and made threats against their lives. The men typically used excessive alcohol daily and used recreational drugs. The effects of this intense and repeated abuse has prompted attorneys to use "the battered-woman syndrome" in court cases to describe the psychological state of battered women who kill (A. Browne, 1987).

RISK FACTORS FOR PERPETRATION

Social acceptance of wife beating has been common in the United States until recent years (Goldstein, 1983; Straus, Kantor, & Moore, 1997). People with more traditional attitudes toward male and female roles tend to blame the victim more and the perpetrator less for wife assault (Hillier & Foddy, 1993). Moreover, clergy who counsel women often hold traditional attitudes that blame women for their abuse (A.D. Wood & McHugh, 1994).

Frustration, stress, and a lack of coping skills may explain why some men are violent toward their partners (Howell & Pugliesi, 1988). Abusive men are more likely to have a history of alcohol abuse, to have more life stress, and to lack coping skills (O.W. Barnett & Fagan, 1993; Hale, Duckworth, Zimostrad, & Nicholas, 1988). Other characteristics include low self-esteem, a need to dominate, depression, dependency on others to meet emotional needs, and hostility toward women (Dewhurst, Moore, & Alfano, 1992; Hale et al., 1988). Age, ethnicity, education, and income have been associated with domestic violence (Sorenson, Upchurch, & Shen, 1996). Factors such as being under age 30, being an urban dweller, being Black, having less than a high school education, and earning less than $40,000 a year are associated with wife violence. Wife abuse occurs, however, in all social classes (Gelles & Straus, 1988).

Aldarondo and Kantor (1997) found that persistent perpetrators of violence were older, had been in their current relationship longer, had considerably more financial resources, and had experimented more with "hard-core" illicit drugs than men who ceased their abusive behavior. Aldarondo and Sugarman (1996) also found that marital conflict, socioeconomic status (SES), and witnessing violence in the family of origin were strong predictors of continuing marital violence. They also found that high levels of marital conflict and low SES were associated with the continuity of wife abuse over time.

RISK FACTORS FOR VICTIMIZATION

Studies of abusive couples have found little evidence that battered women have certain personalities that put them at risk (M. Russell, Lipov, Phillips, & White, 1989). Asking women why they stay in abusive relationships rather than asking men why they abuse assumes that women are weak, unable to protect themselves, and responsible for the abuse (M.D. Schwartz, 1989). Because research typically focuses on women who are married or in relationships with abusers, women who *do* leave abusive relationships often are not studied. A follow-up study of 51 battered women found that after 2.5 years, only 25% of the previously battered women were still in a violent relationship (M.D. Schwartz, 1989).

ETHNICITY AND INTIMATE PARTNER VIOLENCE

Community-based surveys have found that 25% of African American women (Wyatt, 1991) and 8% of Hispanic women (Sorenson & Siegel, 1992) reported at least one physical sexual assault experience in their lifetime. However, when norms regarding violence approval, age, and economic stressors are held constant, Kantor, Jasinski, and Aldarondo (1994) did not find differences between Hispanic Americans and Americans in their odds of wife abuse. However, they did find that being born in the United States increases the risk of wife assaults by Mexican and Puerto Rican American husbands. Importantly, they found that in any group, regardless of SES, the presence of norms sanctioning wife assaults is a risk factor for wife abuse.

However, even when rates of domestic violence do not vary, the predictors and consequences of men's and women's violence may be different. For example, Laura Vogel (1999) found that for African American and Mexican American women, but not European American women, the fear of injury or death by one's partner was found to mediate the relationship between violence and posttraumatic stress disorder (PTSD; nightmare, flashbacks, difficulty concentrating, difficulty sleeping, and anxiety). Furthermore, for African American women, PTSD as a result of violence was affected by past partner violence as well as childhood violence and sexual assault. On the other hand, for European American women, current environmental stressors, such as lack of safety and frequency of crime in the neighborhood, moderated the impact of violence on PTSD. Finally, no variables moderating the effects of violence on PTSD were found for Mexican American women.

For men and women in Israel, the West Bank, and the Gaza Strip, acceptance of patriarchal values is associated with acceptance of wife beating. Despite growth in educational and career opportunities for women in Arab countries, religious and family values condone wife abuse and provide women few avenues for escape (Haj-Yahia, 1996, 1998). Women in many countries such as Bangladesh and India also suffer from wife abuse (Fernandez, 1997; Schuler, Hashemi, Riley, & Akhter, 1996).

VIOLENCE IN LESBIAN RELATIONSHIPS

Relationship abuse is not limited to heterosexual relationships. Although there have been no prevalence studies, research with convenience samples indicates that partner abuse is a significant problem for lesbian women and gay men (Island & Letellier, 1991; L.L. Lockhart, White, Causby, & Isaac, 1994; Renzetti, 1992). Gay male couples report slightly less sexual abuse than lesbian couples, but more severe physical violence (Waterman, Dawson, & Bologna, 1989). Apparently, violence in committed relationships is not simply a gender issue. Issues of power and control arise in all relationships, and provide the basis for abuse. Partner abuse has been associated with issues of power and dependency in both lesbian (Hart, 1986; Renzetti, 1992) and heterosexual couples (Finkelhor, 1984). For lesbians and gay men, the internalization of societal homophobic attitudes may, in part, lead to aggression against partners and reduce reporting due to threats that they may be "outed" by their partner (Renzetti, 1997). For gay men, the fear of AIDS or the stress of having AIDS or caring for a partner with AIDS may be associated with abuse (Letellier, 1996). Fortunately, shelters and organizations are slowly beginning to assimilate information on the issue (Suh, 1990). For gay men, there are still few resources (Letellier, 1996).

ELDER ABUSE: VIOLENCE TOWARD ELDERLY WOMEN

Power inequalities between women and men continue into the later years and result in the continued victimization of older women by men (Crichton, Bond, Harvey, & Ristock, 1999; Whittaker, 1997). Pillemer and Finkelhor (1988) suggest that elder abuse is often spouse abuse that has continued for years. Although most data on elder abuse do not look specifically at spouse abuse or sexual assault, some patterns do emerge from the available data. In one of the only random-sample-based surveys examining elder abuse, Finkelhor and Pillemer found that in the over-65 population of Boston, 2% were the victims of physical abuse, with 58% of those being abused by a spouse and 24% by an adult child. Victimization by adult children reflects the change in relationship dynamics as parents age. Adult children gain power and the aging lose power in a social context that values youth and devalues maturity. Although half the victims were men, women were much more severely injured than men. Aronson, Thornewell, and Williams (1995) concluded that submissiveness, self-blame, self-doubt, and lack of social support mediate the effects of older woman abuse.

Even less in known about the sexual abuse of older women. This remains a taboo topic (Glendenning, 1997), although there is growing recognition that the problem needs attention (Ker, 1996). Clinical evidence suggests that older women may be raped in their homes as well as in institutions (such as residential treatment facilities and nursing homes). A. Burgess (1998) and Aitken and Griffin (1996) have described examples of the sexual abuse of women in nursing homes and the difficulties with verification because of dementia and other memory-related problems among this group. Holt (1993), in a study of elder sexual abuse in Great Britain, reported a ratio of 6:1 female:male victims; they found that the perpetrators were more likely to be sons than husbands. Muram, Miller, and Cutler (1992) compared the rape experiences of a group of older women (age 55 to 87) with those of a younger group and found evidence of greater injury. Additionally, one study suggests that men who sexually assault older women may suffer from more severe psychopathological processes and that their assaults are more brutal and motivated by anger and a need for power (Pollock, 1988).

Another area of research has begun to examine gender-related patterns of death in cases of assisted suicide and euthanasia. In two studies, Silvia Canetto (Canetto & Hollenshead, 1999; 2000) has documented a consistent pattern of women being more likely to be the target and men to be the agent of death. Although there are as yet no data, she speculated that gender-related attitudes toward suffering, being a burden on others, and caregiving, coupled with sexist attitudes toward older women, contribute to this pattern (also see Canetto, this volume, discussion of end-of-life decisions). Finally, research has documented the continued long-term effects of childhood sexual abuse (Allers, Benjack, & Allers, 1992) and domestic violence (Wolkenstein & Sterman, 1998) in the later years. Symptoms may include depression and revictimization. Diagnosis of symptoms related to prior abuse in the elderly is complicated by age and may result in misdiagnosis as dementia or mental illness (Allers et al., 1992).

The American Association of Retired Persons (1992) produced a report identifying similarities between elder abuse and other forms of violence against women. The report identified power imbalances, secrecy and isolation, personal harm to victims, social expectations and sex roles, inadequate resources to protect victims, and the control perpetrators have over their actions. The report further suggested that life span factors pose unique problems for elder abuse.

SUMMARY

In many ways, it appears that violence in marriage and other committed relationships in adulthood is a continuation of patterns of aggression and violence that emerge during adolescence. Although it has been documented that violence and aggression decline with age, negative consequences of earlier patterns of interpersonal violence persist. Aldarondo (1996) found that over half of the men who had been violent in the year prior to his survey had ceased or interrupted their violence and showed significant reduction in their psychological aggression during the course of the study. However, Aldarondo (1992) also found that even among men who cease to batter, negative relationship outcomes persist. Similarly, Malamuth, Linz, Heavey, & Barnes and his colleagues (1995) found that men who were sexually aggressive in college continued to have conflictual relationships with their intimate partners 10 years later.

CONSEQUENCES OF VIOLENCE AGAINST GIRLS AND WOMEN

The developmental pattern of continuing gendered violence is mirrored in an escalation of the consequences for victims. Beginning in childhood, victimization experiences influence subsequent psychological, social, and emotional development. For example, sexually victimized girls suffer from several problems including traumagenic sexualization (Finkelhor & Browne, 1996), that is, age-inappropriate sexualization that leads to many difficulties. These include impaired self-esteem, feelings of betrayal, and lack of trust. It is highly likely that these factors contribute to an increased risk of revictimization during adolescence. Young women who experience physical or sexual violence during adolescence are more likely to be injured and to feel surprised, scared, angry, and hurt by a partner's aggression than are men (Makepeace, 1986). Although men are 2 to 4 times more likely to use severe forms of violence, women are 3 to 4 times more likely to report injuries (Makepeace, 1986; Sugarman & Hotaling, 1989). An additional serious consequence of courtship violence is a possible increased risk of marital violence, either with the same or a different partner. For example, it is not known what percentage of women who were victimized during courtship are victimized in marriage, but for women who are victimized in marriage, there is evidence that some were victimized during courtship. In 25% of violent marriages, the violence began before marriage (Gayford, 1975). For battered women, the key factor linking marital battering with earlier courtship violence was the woman's acceptance of traditional gender roles as a result of being raised in a patriarchal home (Avni, 1991).

There are many consequences of assault beyond immediate physical trauma necessitating medical care. Abused women are at higher risk for a range of health problems that are not a direct consequence of physical blows to the body. These include clinical depression, sexually transmitted infection, gastrointestional disorders, PTSD, frequent urinary tract and vaginal infections, and decreased perceived health status (Gleason, 1993; Plictha, 1996; McCauley, Kern, Kolodner, Dill, & Schroeder, 1997; P.H. Smith, Edwards, & DeVellis, 1998). They also show a range of adverse behavioral outcomes such as suicide and substance use. There also are social and economic consequences. The abused woman's partner may limit access to household resources and control decision making, the quality of life for children in the home, and the woman's employment patterns (J.C. Campbell & Lewandowski, 1996; Plitcha, 1996; Tjaden & Thoennes, 1998). Domestic violence influences a woman's earnings and ability to remain in a job (A. Browne, Salomon, & Bassuk, 1999), reduces her educational attainment and income (Hyman, 1993), and reduces her participation in public life, lessening her contribution to social and economic development (Carillo, 1992). Violent partners also may prevent women from seeking immediate care even when it is needed. This is especially true among rural women, where one of the common forms of domestic violence is denial of access to means of transportation and communication (D. Coker, 1999).

Children witnessing abuse have many of the same problems as their abused mothers, including more emotional and behavioral problems and more physical health complaints. Children are abused in 30% to 60% of the families where husbands abuse their wives (Appel & Holden, 1998; Edleson, 1999). Jejeebhoy (1998) found that, in Nicaragua, women who were beaten were significantly more likely than nonabused women to have an infant death or pregnancy loss from abortion, miscarriage, or stillbirth. Furthermore, the children of these women were more likely to be malnourished and six times more likely than other children to die before age 5. Rao (1998) found that, in India, children of mothers who were beaten received less food than other children.

COMMONALITIES AMONG ALL FORMS OF VIOLENCE AGAINST WOMEN

Jacquelyn White and Robin Kowalski (1998) proposed a model that examines individual behavior in context. The model integrates a wide range of factors across various forms of violence against women at five levels: sociocultural (including historical and cultural values), interpersonal (i.e., social networks and groups), dyadic, situational, and intrapersonal. The model assumes that patriarchy operating at the historical/sociocultural level affects power dynamics in all relationships. Historical and sociocultural factors create an environment in which the growing child learns rules and expectations, first in the family network and later in peer relationships. Early experiences define the context for later experiences (Huesmann & Eron, 1992; Olweus, 1993; J.W. White & Bondurant, 1996). Power dynamics become enacted at the interpersonal level and result in the internalization of gendered values, expectations, and behaviors.

The sociocultural level encompasses sexual inequalities, gender-role prescriptions, and cultural myths about women, men, children, family, sex, and violence, as well as scripts for enacting relationships. Cultural norms governing aggression as a tool of the powerful to subdue the weak interact with gender inequalities to create a context conducive to violence against women (see Neft & Levine, 1997, for a chronicle of violence against women internationally). Whether discussing childhood sexual abuse, courtship violence, sexual assault, or wife abuse, a common underlying theme is societal endorsement of male dominance. The fear of violence imbued in women serves to disempower them (Rozee, 1993, 1996).

The social network level of analysis reveals how gendered norms and expectations are transmitted through the various social networks of which we are a part, including the family, peer groups, school, church, and work groups. Witnessing or experiencing family violence as a child is related to various forms of violence against women (Ewing, 1993; Hotaling & Sugarman, 1986). Many households in which violence occurs are characterized by patriarchal family structures where traditional gender roles are encouraged.

The dyadic level of analysis addresses the power and status differences between perpetrator and victim. Because of historical and sociocultural traditions, women and children are perceived as weaker and more passive than men and are supposed to be dependent on men. Such culturally prescribed dependence affects communication patterns (Lakoff, 1990) and other relationship dynamics to increase women's vulnerability to abuse.

However, for male violence against women to occur, the situation must be conducive to the violence. A number of situational variables influence the likelihood of violence. For example, situations that reduce open dialogue between women and men and that establish distant and hostile, yet sexually charged interactions may contribute to assault (Boswell & Spade, 1996). The situation affects the opportunity for violent acts (i.e., times when privacy is available and detection minimal). Alcohol and drug use also increases the risk of violence (J.W. White & Humphrey, 1994).

Finally, similar intrapersonal variables appear to underlie various forms of male violence toward women. These attitudinal, motivational, and personality characteristics include endorsement of traditional gender-role stereotypes, acceptance of cultural myths about violence, and a need for power, dominance, and control over women and children. Other characteristics include antisocial tendencies and nonconformity, as well as impulsivity, irresponsibility, hypermasculinity, affective dysregulation, and self-centeredness coupled with insensitivity to others. The extent to which these specific intrapersonal variables influence the incidence of violence against women depends on the degree to which cultural norms and the influence of social groups affect individual mental representations of situations and relationships with girls and women.

UNDERSTANDING VIOLENCE AGAINST GIRLS AND WOMEN

The pattern of intimate violence, where women are the victims and men are the perpetrators, is not due to biological destiny. Women are not born victims and men are not biologically predetermined to be aggressors. Rather, stereotypes of how women and men are supposed to behave, experiences that reinforce stereotypical behaviors, and a social structure that supports power inequities between women and men all contribute to violence against women.

To understand violence against girls and women we must first recognize that culturally based socialization practices encourage men to be aggressors and women to be victims. In societies where there is no formal hierarchy that privileges one group over another and in which women and men exercise relatively equal power, general levels of aggression and male violence against women are low (Lepowsky, 1994). As this chapter has described, gendered violence is learned early in life and continues in our different relationships as we age. Statistics allow us to examine larger social influences and overall patterns found in society. They reveal that women are the victims of intimate violence more often than men at every stage of development, with the exception of early childhood physical abuse.

Although women also may be the perpetrators of aggression, this does not destroy the argument that intimate violence is related to gender and social roles. The reason is that patriarchy as a social system carries with it the message that the more powerful are entitled to dominate the less powerful. Aggression and violence are inherently gendered; even when girls and women act aggressively, they are responding to and enacting male models of behavior and control, models our culture has endorsed. Because men more often hold higher-status positions than women, it follows that men will abuse more than women; because adults are more powerful than children, children will be victimized more than adults; and because the young are more powerful than the elderly, the aged are more at risk.

Inequality in relationships, coupled with cultural values that embrace domination of the weaker by the stronger, creates the potential for violence. The more powerful partner can control money, resources, activities, and decisions. Partner abuse has been associated with issues of power and dependency in both lesbians (Renzetti, 1992) and heterosexual couples (Finkelhor, 1984). Both men and women learn that violence is a method people use to get their way. When individuals use violence and get their way, they are reinforced and thus more likely to use aggression in the future; however, men have historically received greater rewards for aggression and violence than have women. Women are as likely as men to aggress in situations that are congruent with their gender identities and where they hold relatively more power (Towson & Zanna, 1982).

Traditionally, secrecy and myths regarding male-female relationships trivialized and/or justified male violence against women. The women's movement has done much to bring to public awareness the extent of the harm done to women by men and has prompted redefinitions that acknowledge the violence. Thus, for example, no longer is rape defined as a sexual act, sexual harassment as standard working conditions, and wife abuse as a legitimate way to "show the little woman who is boss"; rather, each are seen as acts by men intended to dominate and control women.

Violence against women, in its various forms, is now recognized as a public health and social problem. Hence, research has moved from focusing on individual psychopathology to identifying the sociocultural factors that contribute to such violence. Also, communities, institutions, and organizations are combating violence against women by developing interventions that not only help individuals but also promote change in values and attitudes at the societal level.

CHAPTER 24

Power and Gender: The Double-Edged Sword of Ambivalence

STEPHANIE A. GOODWIN and SUSAN T. FISKE

A truth about structural power: Men have more than women. Power differences persist despite the narrowing of gender gaps and changes in attitudes that have characterized the past century (for reviews, see Secord, 1983; United Nations Development Programme, 1998; U.S. Department of Labor, 1999). With regard to economic power, men control more resources of value than do women, and, not surprisingly, they benefit more from having such control. In the United States, for example, women occupy almost half of midlevel management positions but receive 28% to 30% less pay than their male counterparts (U.S. Department of Labor, 1999). Moreover, women rarely proceed to the highest echelons of organizational power (Eagly, 1999; A. Sinclair, 1995); only one of the world's 500 largest corporations—Hewlett-Packard—currently is headed by a female executive officer. At the other extreme of economic disparity, women are more likely than men to live below the poverty level in almost all societies (United Nations Development Programme, 1998). Power differences are not limited to economic domains; women generally fare worse with regard to legal and political power as well (United Nations Development Programme, 1998).

The present chapter does not address *whether* men have a relative power advantage, but rather *why*. It is perplexing that gender-based power differences are so resilient in modern societies. Given the nature of intimate contact between the sexes, egalitarian norms, and technologies that diminish the necessity of gender-role differentiation along traditional divisions of labor, one might predict the eradication of gender inequality. Gender inequality is admittedly a complex problem, influenced by both macrolevel social and microlevel individual factors (Ferree, Lorber, & Hess, 1999). The present analysis adopts a social psychological perspective, addressing how both the person and the situation contribute to the current status of gendered power inequalities. Social psychology provides a unique intersection among the social, situational, interpersonal, and intraindividual explanations of gender and power.

Social psychologists have explored numerous phenomena that contribute to gender inequities (for a recent review, see Deaux & LaFrance, 1998), which form this chapter's sections: *Sexism, gender stereotypes,* and *situational power* all facilitate gendered power differences. Ambivalent beliefs about women (P. Glick & Fiske, 1996) result from gendered power relations. On the positive side, women are universally pictured as mothers and housewives—supportive, and warm. On the negative side, women are also characterized as sirens and shrews—manipulative, deceitful, and cold. This ambivalence, coupled with the ideologies that underlie it, justifies and maintains status quo power differentials between the sexes (P. Glick & Fiske, in press).

SEXISM

"Such duty as the subject owes the prince, even such a woman oweth to her husband." (Shakespeare, *The Taming of the Shrew*, Act V, Scene 2)

Sexism may be generally defined as "attitudes, beliefs, or behaviors that support the unequal status of women and men" (Swim & Campbell, 2000). Sexism is therefore of central relevance to any discussion of gender and power. Both the conceptualization and measurement of sexism have evolved significantly since the Attitudes toward Women Scale (AWS; Spence & Helmreich, 1972a) first asked "Who likes competent women?" (for recent comprehensive historical reviews, see Deaux, 1999; Swim & Campbell, 2000). Whereas initial research focused heavily on understanding explicit endorsement of traditional gender roles and stereotypes, recent theorists have addressed subtle and complex forms of gender bias (P. Glick & Fiske, 1996; Swim et al., 1995; Tougas et al., 1995).

OLD-FASHIONED VERSUS MODERN SEXISM

Perhaps the most influential measure of sexism to date, the AWS (Spence & Helmreich, 1972b) measures what now is considered "old-fashioned" sexism, that is, support for traditional gender roles (i.e., men as providers, women as homemakers) accompanied by negative attitudes and stereotypic beliefs about women's competence. Patterns in Americans' sexist attitudes trace back over several decades, owing to the AWS's widespread adoption within the field and careful collection of longitudinal data. As one would expect, responses to the AWS have changed markedly over time; although women's scores continue to be more egalitarian than men's, scores for both men and women have moved toward decreased sexism in recent decades (Spence & Hahn, 1997). These changes occur in related measures as well (Eagly & Karau, 1991; Twenge, 1997), leading some to conclude that sexism is history, that any residual gender inequality will soon fade.

Contemporary theorists have argued, however, that changes in attitudes toward women reflect a shift toward more modern forms of sexism, as opposed to a genuine decline in the prevalence of sexism (Swim et al., 1995; Tougas et al., 1995). Drawing from the literature on modern and aversive racism (e.g., Dovidio & Gaertner, 1986; McConahay, 1983, 1986), these theorists argue that modern sexists are torn by positive beliefs in egalitarianism that conflict with simultaneously held negative beliefs about women. Similar to modern racists, the modern sexist resolves this value conflict by opposing social policy changes that would benefit women. That is, rather than directly acknowledging sexism, modern sexists seek to maintain status quo gender inequalities. Measures of this more subtle form of bias—the Modern Sexism Scale (Swim et al., 1995) and the Neosexism Scale (Tougas et al., 1995)—assess beliefs about current levels of gender discrimination and potential remedial efforts. These measures significantly correlate with the AWS (Spence & Buckner, 2000; Swim et al., 1995; Tougas et al., 1995). Hence, the modern measures overlap with the old-fashioned negative attitudes about women. Most old-fashioned sexists are also modern sexists, but not vice versa; all show antipathy toward women.

AMBIVALENT SEXISM

In contrast to sexism as pure antipathy, P. Glick and Fiske (1996, 1999b) argue that sexism arises from ambivalent attitudes toward women, based on relationships between men and women. The Ambivalent Sexism Inventory (ASI; P. Glick & Fiske, 1996) captures two opposing evaluative ideologies: *hostile sexism* and *benevolent sexism*. Hostile sexism embodies the traditional antipathy associated with dominative and competitive prejudice toward women (e.g., "Most women fail to appreciate fully all that men do for them"; "Once a woman gets a man to commit to her, she usually tries to put him on a tight leash"). Benevolent sexism comprises attitudes that are likewise stereotypic but are distinct in their subjectively positive (to the bearer) feeling tone (P. Glick & Fiske, 1996). Unlike hostile sexism, which stresses domination, competition, and sexual hostility, benevolent sexism embraces protective paternalism (e.g., "Women should be cherished and protected by men"), complementary roles, and intimacy-seeking behaviors (e.g., "Every man ought to have a woman whom he adores"). These two forms of sexism, though positively correlated, represent divergent ideologies about women that both justify and perpetuate male dominance (P. Glick & Fiske, in press). Both scales correlate cross-nationally with gender inequality, across countries that are, by U.N. indices, relatively traditional (Chile, Korea) and relatively progressive (the Netherlands, Australia) (P. Glick et al., 2000).

Whence do these ideologies arise? P. Glick and Fiske (in press) argue that interdependencies inherent to gender relations give rise to both hostile and benevolent forms of sexism. More specifically, although men have greater structural power related to economics and politics, women have greater dyadic power, related to relationships and reproduction (Secord, 1983). At a minimum, heterosexual men need women for childbearing. At a higher level, men often rely on women (e.g., mothers and wives) for interpersonal intimacy (Berscheid, Snyder, & Omoto, 1989). The ASI captures three important components of men's dyadic dependence on women: *gender-role differentiation*, *heterosexuality*, and *power dynamics*. Each of these dimensions is characterized by ambivalence and beliefs that sustain male dominance.

Gender-Role Differentiation

"The moment that I step outside, so many reasons for me to run and hide. I can't do the little things I hold so dear 'cause it's those little things that I fear. 'Cause I'm just a girl" (Stefani & Dumont, 1995).

Traditional gender-role differentiation involves male laborers and female homemakers (Eagly, 1987). Although many women now work outside the home, role differentiation is evident in both men's and women's career and educational outcomes (United Nations Development Programme, 1998; U.S. Department of Labor, 1999). For example, American women continue to dominate professions such as teaching and social work, and men dominate positions in engineering and computer technologies (U.S. Department of Labor, 1999). In addition, women continue to maintain high levels of gender-based responsibilities within the home (e.g., child rearing, domestic tasks) despite higher participation in the labor market (S.L. Blair & Lichter, 1991; F.M. Deutsch, 1999).

Eagly's social role theory (1987; Eagly & Steffen, 1984) argues that existing gender-role differences result from self-perpetuating social arrangements. Traditional roles create descriptive expectations for what men and women are like, as well as prescriptions for what they *ought* to be like. Hence, existing gender roles shape what men and women believe about their own skills, and whether certain skills can or should be developed (Hoffman & Hurst, 1990).

Regardless of origin, gender-role differentiation justifies status differences via social ideologies. Stereotypes also explain existing gender roles: Women are disproportionately homemakers because they are believed to be communal, and men are disproportionately breadwinners because they are believed to be agentic. *Competitive* gender differentiation justifies male structural power via women's perceived incompetence. Because women are perceived as physically and mentally inferior to men, men are seen as better suited for positions of greater status and structural power. In contrast, *complementary* gender differentiation develops from men's dependence on women (and vice versa) and accompanying positive views of women as mothers, wives, and lovers. Women's roles in the home complement men's roles outside the home. In this sense, women stereotypically complete what is missing in men (e.g., social warmth and nurturance), and vice versa (e.g., strength and intelligence).

Heterosexuality

"We can force our husbands to negotiate peace, ladies, by exercising steadfast self-control—by total abstinence . . . from sex!" (Aristophanes, *Lysistrata*)

Unlike other social groups (e.g., based on ethnicity), men and women often engage in intimate contact (Fiske & Stevens, 1993). Heterosexual contact with women can be both positive and negative for men, contributing to their ambivalence toward women. On the one hand, heterosexual men seek sexual intimacy with women to achieve closeness and happiness (Berscheid et al., 1989). On the other hand, being dependent on subordinate women for such happiness creates an atypical situation for the typically dominant male. Long before psychologists came around to an empirical test (Zillmann & Weaver, 1989), the Greek comedian Aristophanes identified one of men's greatest fears: Women act as gatekeepers to sex and therefore can gain power to control men. Such beliefs foster hostility toward women and possibly motives to dominate them (P. Glick & Fiske, in press; Lorber, 1999).

Power Dynamics

Little evidence suggests that matriarchies have ever existed. To the contrary, most cultures are biased toward patriarchy, with men controlling economic, legal, and political structures (M. Harris,

1991). Paternalism, a primary characteristic of power dynamics between the sexes, can be differentiated into *dominative* and *protective* forms. Dominative paternalism endorses a male-over-female hierarchy. As with gender-role differentiation, dominative paternalism is justified by women's alleged inferior capacities; like children, women are perceived as less capable of leading organizations, ruling countries, and making complex judgments. Women therefore should submit to men's superior capacities and authority in all domains. In contrast, protective paternalism obligates men to protect women because of their alleged weaknesses. Advocates of this more seemingly benevolent position argue that men are obligated to be providers as well as champions. In combination, these two forms of paternalism reflect the ambivalence inherent in attitudes toward women. Both justify male dominance.

AMBIVALENT SEXISM MAINTAINS POWER INEQUITIES

Ambivalent sexism maintains power differentials in at least three ways. First, men may adopt benevolent ideologies to justify their own power. To the extent that men believe in stereotypes of women as physically and mentally inferior, men's own dominance is justified at both the dyadic and societal levels (cf. Jost & Banaji, 1994). In this sense, benevolent ideologies serve as "hierarchy-legitimizing myths" that justify the existing social structure (Pratto, Stallworth, Sidanius, & Siers, 1997).

Second, women may likewise adopt benevolent ideologies and self-stereotype the in-group as a means of maintaining positive interactions with men. In a society where women rely on men for economic, political, and interpersonal outcomes, it is to women's advantage to have smooth relationships with men. Moreover, at the individual interpersonal level, women frequently depend on men for intimacy; such needs further motivate adopting benevolent ideologies that do not challenge male dominance. Gender differences in hostile versus benevolent sexism support this possibility. Although women score significantly lower overall on the ASI, gender differences in benevolent sexism are significantly smaller than differences in hostile sexism, suggesting that women are less reluctant to reject benevolent ideologies (P. Glick & Fiske, 1996; P. Glick et al., in press; Masser & Abrams, 1999).

Finally, hostile sexists punish women who challenge traditional gender roles. Hostile sexism correlates with negative evaluations of career women and feminists (P. Glick & Fiske, 1996). One need not look far for additional evidence that nontraditional women are perceived negatively on interpersonal dimensions. The terms "feminist" and "career woman" have become synonymous with derogatory stereotypes of women who are not nice and not feminine enough (Fiske, Xu, & Cuddy, 1999). Ann Hopkins's experience at Price Waterhouse illustrates the consequences for women who fail to toe the gender line: Despite unquestionably strong job skills, she was denied partnership and referred to charm school (Fiske et al., 1991).

In addition to anecdotal evidence, meta-analyses of leadership studies further reveal patterns of dominative punishment toward nontraditional women (Eagly et al., 1992, 1995). Female leaders, for example, are disliked in comparison to their male counterparts, especially when these women adopt stereotypically masculine (i.e., autocratic) leadership styles (Eagly et al., 1992). Consistent with these data, female leaders' effectiveness suffers in nontraditional occupations; women are least effective in stereotypically masculine leadership roles, most effective in stereotypically feminine leadership roles (Eagly et al., 1995). Similar patterns do not appear with regard to male leaders in masculine versus feminine roles. The perceived legitimacy of the leader's role is related to these phenomena. Women leaders who are legitimated by authorities tend to fare better than those who are not (Yoder, Schleicher, & McDonald, 1998). Finally, experimental investigations of gender and self-promotion suggest women are penalized for standing up for their own abilities. Rudman (1998) asked participants to evaluate the competency, attractiveness, and hireability of a male or female job applicant who behaved in either a self-promoting (i.e., masculine) or self-effacing (i.e., feminine) manner. Self-promotion increased competency ratings regardless of target gender. Nevertheless, the self-promoting female was rated as less attractive and less hireable (see also Rudman & Glick, 1999).

Unfortunately, negative reactions to nontraditional women are more the rule than the exception; reports of sexual harassment and sex discrimination continue to increase in the United

States, despite laws and norms that challenge such behaviors (Hulin, Fitzgerald, & Drasgow, 1996; E. Frank, Brogan, & Schiffman, 1998; Rospenda, Richman, & Nawyn, 1998). Gender and sexual harassment are explicit forms of male dominance. Surveys of American high school students indicate that sexual harassment as a form of male dominance emerges well before adulthood (AAUW, 1993; Fineran & Bennett, 1999; N. Stein, 1981). In a survey of 1,600 randomly sampled students, 87% of the girls reported peer sexual harassment in school. Fineran and Bennett surveyed 212 high school girls regarding the specific forms of harassment they encountered; 43% reported they had been called sexually offensive names, 57% reported being touched or cornered in a sexual way, and 24% reported being pressured to do something sexual against their will. These alarming statistics reaffirm that male domination begins long before women enter the workforce.

GENDER STEREOTYPES

"I'm a bitch. I'm a lover. I'm a child. I'm a mother. I'm a sinner. I'm a saint . . . you wouldn't want me any other way." (M. Brooks and S. Peiken, 1997)

Gender stereotypes—beliefs about how men and women do and ought to behave—run the gamut from physical characteristics to emotional dispositions (Deaux & Kite, 1993), yet several consistencies emerge across cultures (J.E. Williams & Best, 1990a). Men are stereotyped as being more agentic, independent, aggressive, and physically strong, but not as nice as women. Women are stereotyped as more communal, caring, emotionally expressive, and responsive to others, but also passive, submissive, and weak. These ambivalent expectations about agency and communion map onto traditional gender roles (Eagly & Steffen, 1984).

Fiske, Xu, et al. (1999) have recently proposed that two underlying dimensions reflect sociability and competence in stereotypes of out-groups. According to this analysis, some traditionally oppressed groups are perceived as *not warm* but *competent*. Stereotypes of Jews, for example, which include traits such as *educated, wealthy,* and *sly,* fit this category. In contrast, other groups are perceived as *warm* but *incompetent;* stereotypes about the elderly fit this classification. Importantly, gender subtypes (e.g., housewife vs. career woman) map onto stereotypes of traditional versus nontraditional stereotypes of women, which in turn fit nicely into the Fiske, Xu, et al. framework. Cluster analyses of the stereotype content for these gender subtypes support the underlying stereotype dimensions. *Career women* and *feminists* are stereotyped as not nice but competent; perceptions of these subtypes cluster with stereotypes of other groups that include Asians, Jews, rich people, and Black professionals. In contrast, housewives are stereotyped as nice but incompetent; perceptions of this subtype cluster with stereotypes of groups that include elderly, mentally retarded, blind, and physically handicapped individuals.

HOUSEWIVES VERSUS FEMINISTS

Beliefs about traditional versus nontraditional women maintain power differentials between the sexes in a variety of ways (P. Glick & Fiske, in press). First, traditional women invite paternalistic praise (P. Glick & Fiske, 1996). For men, benevolent sexism corresponds with more favorable evaluations of housewives (P. Glick & Fiske, 1996). Society rewards women who fulfill their roles as housewives and mothers, often with tangible benefits. For example, women who bear the first child of the new year or who bear an unusually high number of children at once can expect no less than a lead story in the local news, and in some cases, food, clothing, or other financial rewards. Interviews with parents about their roles both in and out of the home indicate differential patterns of praise and criticism for men and women (F.M. Deutsch & Saxon, 1998). Women are praised by others for successfully fulfilling their family roles, and criticized when they do not. Men, in contrast, are criticized for too little involvement in work or too much involvement at home. These data allude to the socialization processes that encourage women to adopt traditional caregiving roles.

On the flip side, nontraditional women invite dominative punishment. Lesbians, for example, challenge heterosexual male dominance. Women who choose same-sex intimate partners thwart the status quo in gender relationships, implicitly denying any need to rely on men for intimacy, financial support, or even, more than briefly, for reproduction. Several naïve explanations for lesbianism (e.g., lesbians are women who have not yet found the right man or who have been sexually abused) support theories of male dominance and superiority. Thus, feminists—women who seek gender equality—are frequently stereotyped as lesbians and derogated for being too masculine. Although feminists are perceived as competent, they threaten the status quo male dominance and are therefore not likable (Fiske, Xu, et al., 1999b).

In occupational settings, women who pursue nontraditional careers that require intellectual or physical strength (e.g., math or welding) face economic and interpersonal discrimination as well as sexual harassment. Sexual harassment is frequent in occupational settings where women occupy solo or near solo status (Fitzgerald, Drasgow, et al., 1997). Rape or threat of rape may similarly be seen as an extreme form of dominative punishment wherein men assert physical power as a means of restoring their own control over women (Sanday, 1981). Interviews with convicted rapists support this argument. In contrast to other felons, men convicted of rape are distinguished by hostility toward women and beliefs that men should be tough and fearless (Scully, 1990). Although none of the rapists interviewed for this research completed the ASI, one could speculate that these men would score high in hostile sexism.

Finally, as Eagly's (1984) social role theory argues, gender roles and stereotypes maintain male dominance by shaping identity development and later life choices. Gender-typed career choices likely stem from a combination of factors including gender-identity development, attitudes toward stereotypically gender-congruent careers, normative pressure, and the adoption of benevolent sexist ideologies, each of which is influenced by gender roles and stereotypes. With regard to gender-identity development, children begin to categorize themselves and others along gender lines as early as 26 months of age (for reviews of the developmental issues, see Ruble & Goodnow, 1998; Zemore, Fiske, & Kim, 2000; Powlishta et al., this volume). Gender-typed play and gender identification follow soon after, with little girls fantasizing about motherhood and teaching while little boys imagine lives as doctors and firemen. As gender identities become increasingly salient during adolescence, a corresponding decline occurs in girls' performance in traditionally male academic domains. In elementary school, girls and boys perform comparably in math and science, yet by adolescence, girls begin to perform significantly worse than boys in these domains (Eccles, 1994).

Gender differences in implicit and explicit attitudes toward traditionally male domains (e.g., math and science) versus traditionally female domains (e.g., the arts and humanities) may lie at the heart of later-life choices. Men and women differ in their explicit liking for math versus art. A web-based measure of implicit attitudes tests the hypothesis that men and women differ in their implicit (i.e., automatic) liking for math versus art (Nosek & Banaji, 2000). Sampling over 10,000 participants, researchers found a large, reliable gender difference in the predicted direction. Men implicitly preferred math relative to art, whereas women exhibited the reverse attitudinal pattern.

Research investigating stereotype threat (Steele & Aronson, 1995) and self-objectification theory (Fredrickson & Roberts, 1997) further suggests that gender stereotypes shape life choices and outcomes. For example, women who are primed to think about gender prior to taking difficult math tests are more likely to suffer performance deficits as compared to men (Shih et al., 1999; Spencer, Steele, & Quinn, 1999; Steele & Aronson, 1995). These responses hold even for women who pursue careers in math and science and who therefore presumably like these topics. Making women especially aware of their physical attributes by manipulating their clothing during a test has similar effects on cognitive performance. Women who completed a math test while wearing a swimsuit performed significantly worse than a comparable group of women who completed the same test while wearing a bulky sweater (Fredrickson, Roberts, Noll, Quinn, & Twenge, 1997). For men, comparable clothing and thinking about gender does not have the same effect on cognitive performance. These findings suggest that stereotypes operate not only at explicit, conscious levels but also at automatic, nonconscious levels, constraining women's life choices in more insidious ways.

SITUATIONAL POWER: SEXISM AND STEREOTYPES IN SOCIAL CONTEXT

Situations that involve power relations further escalate the effects of sexism and gender stereotypes in maintaining status quo power differences between the sexes. Situational power—having asymmetric control over others' outcomes—aggravates stereotype use (Fiske, 1993; S.A. Goodwin, Gubin, Fiske, & Yzerbyt, 2000; S.A. Goodwin, Operario, & Fiske, 1998). When perceivers have situational power, they attend more to information about their subordinates that fits stereotypes and are more likely to integrate this stereotypic information into their impressions of subordinates, as compared to perceivers who do not have power. In contrast, powerless perceivers attend to information that challenges stereotypes when evaluating those on whom they depend. These data correspond with evidence regarding the accuracy of intergroup perceptions. On average, members of groups with less status and power in society (e.g., women and ethnic minorities in the United States) have more accurate knowledge about the traits and characteristics of groups with greater status and power (e.g., men and Whites in the United States) than vice versa (Fiske & Taylor, 1991).

Situational power additionally aggravates behavioral confirmation processes during social interaction (Copeland, 1992). Adapting the classic behavioral confirmation paradigm (M. Snyder, Tanke, & Berscheid, 1977), Copeland manipulated men's power over women in a telephone interview. Expectations about female applicants were manipulated prior to the interview. Female applicants were most likely to engage in behaviors that confirmed male interviewers' expectations when interviewers were alleged to have power, as compared to no power.

One could speculate that stereotype threat (as described earlier, Steele & Aronson, 1995) would further add to these effects; if women become aware of gender stereotypes during interviews, cognitive deficits may result, interfering with performance and further confirming stereotypes. Situations that involve between-sex power are especially problematic because the cognitive activation of stereotype beliefs may not only lead power holders to behave in ways that elicit confirmation biases but may also lead subordinates to experience stereotype threat, creating a cycle of self-fulfilling prophecies. Evidence regarding nonverbal power displays supports this possibility. Women are more likely to display low-power behaviors (e.g., increased smiling, greater visual displays of submission) when discussing masculine tasks in mixed-sex dyads (Dovidio, Brown, Heltman, & Ellyson, 1988). Training in the tasks, however, eliminates sex differences in visual displays of dominance (C.E. Brown, Dovidio, & Ellyson, 1990). These data suggest that women adopt nonverbal behaviors that confirm gender stereotypes and roles in situations where they lack information. Mixed-sex power relations apparently activate gender stereotypes, possibly increasing stereotype threat. Because men are statistically more likely to occupy powerful roles in society, these biases are likely to further maintain gender inequities.

Similarly, one might argue that sexism, stereotypes, and situational power could interact to magnify confirmation biases. For example, powerful men who are higher in hostile sexism might have especially negative interactions with subordinate women, in turn increasing behavioral confirmation biases. Such processes might contribute to the glass ceilings that prevent women from ascending to higher levels of power. These important empirical questions remain untested.

CONCLUSION: ESCAPING THE DOUBLE-EDGED SWORD OF AMBIVALENCE

"I have a brain and a uterus, and I use both." (U.S. Representative Patricia Schroeder)

The ambivalence that underlies sexism and gender stereotypes may be especially difficult to overcome, owing to both cognitive and motivational factors. On the cognitive front, attacking gender stereotypes and attitudes may be difficult because these types of bias may occur automatically, outside of conscious awareness (Bargh, 1997; Greenwald & Banaji, 1995). I.V. Blair and Banaji (1996), for example, have demonstrated the speed with which gender stereotypes become cognitively available. In their priming research, participants were faster at identifying male versus female names when the names were preceded by gender-congruent prime words (e.g., "aggressive," "nurturing"). These data suggest that gender stereotypes may be activated automatically, outside of perceiver awareness. Nevertheless, motivation to change biased behavior is contingent on awareness of one's biases (Devine & Monteith, 1993). People who aspire to nonbiased behaviors try harder to avoid biases when they become aware of behaviors that are inconsistent with their egalitarian views (Devine & Monteith, 1993; Monteith, Zuwerink, & Devine, 1994).

Even if one is motivated to challenge benevolent or hostile ideologies, the subtle ways in which these influence social life may be difficult to recognize and therefore difficult to attack. Because these ideologies are so integral to the social fabric across cultures (P. Glick et al., 1999), their normative nature may mask their presence and influence for the average person. Challenging the "unseen" proves problematic.

With regard to motivation, women may be both motivated to adopt benevolent ideologies and to deny the relevance of discrimination in their personal lives. Some of the benefits of benevolent sexism may be enticing to women (Kiliansky & Rudman, 1998). For example, beliefs that women are less physically strong or more emotionally sensitive allow women to decline distasteful activities ranging from taking out the garbage to fighting in wars. The failure of the Equal Rights Amendment in the United States in the 1970s suggests that, at least for some women, being on a pedestal is not so bad. Moreover, the personal-group discrimination discrepancy suggests that women deny the impact of gender bias on their own outcomes (D.M. Taylor, Ruggiero, & Louis, 1996). Although women perceive aggregate-level discrimination against women, they do not report personal experiences of discrimination (Crosby, 1984; Major, 1989). In experimental manipulations of gender discrimination, women are extremely reticent to acknowledge discrimination as a factor in their negative outcomes (Ruggiero & Major, 1998). Only when the probability for gender discrimination was 100% were women participants willing to accept this as an explanation for negative evaluations. Women may be motivated to deny gender discrimination as a means of maintaining a sense of personal control over future outcomes (Ruggiero & Taylor, 1995). If so, one would predict a sense of false consciousness and lack of incentive to seek changes in the current economic and political system.

A final hurdle on the road to gender equality lies in overcoming the effects of situational power on stereotype use in impression formation. A large body of evidence indicates that accuracy motives are central for reducing biases during impression formation (for reviews, see Fiske, 1998; Fiske, Lin, & Neuberg, 1999). When people are directly instructed to be more accurate, they can and do form less stereotypic impressions (Fiske & Neuberg, 1990). Direct instruction to avoid bias may not be especially practical across all situations. Fortunately, several factors promote accuracy motives and hence less stereotyping: the internalization of egalitarian values, interdependence, and accountability to third parties (Fiske, 1998). With regard to egalitarian values, one might argue that many people already share egalitarian beliefs, at least in many Western societies. Indeed, as noted, ambivalent sexism is lower in those countries where women have better economic and social outcomes (P. Glick et al., in press). The causal relationship between these factors is unclear, but suggests avenues for empirical investigation.

Interdependence decreases stereotyping because people want to have more accurate impressions of those on whom they depend (Fiske & Neuberg, 1990). People have more potential control over their own outcomes when they form accurate impressions of people with whom they share outcomes. Empirically, people who are mutually outcome-dependent attend less to stereotype-confirming information and form less stereotypic impressions, as compared to people who are not outcome-dependent (for a review, see Fiske, Lin, et al., 1999). Thus, teamwork with peers undercuts bias. In spite of men's relative power advantage, powerful men may still have outcomes that depend on women's task performance. For example, in occupational settings, where men are more likely to control women's outcomes than vice versa, male managers may nevertheless have outcomes (e.g., pay raises, promotions, bonuses) that are contingent on the productivity of their female subordinates. In these cases, one would predict less gender bias (Fiske, 1993). This would, however, depend on men's awareness of their outcome dependence on women. Reminding powerful men of the ways in which their outcomes depend on subordinate women may prove a simple means of reducing bias in power situations. Hostile sexists, however, may be threatened by such reminders and respond more negatively to their subordinates.

Accountability to third parties (Tetlock, 1999) also reduces individual and institutional biases in power situations (Fiske, 1993, 1998). Within hierarchies, higher-level authorities set the tone for whether or not bias or harassment will be tolerated or even endorsed (I. Decker & Barling, 1998; Fitzgerald, Drasgow, et al., 1997; Glomb, Munson, Hulin, Bergman, & Drasgow, 1999). In experimental settings, people who are held accountable for their impressions of others are less likely to rely on stereotypes (Tetlock, Skitka, & Boettger, 1989). Simply anticipating that one must justify one's decisions is enough to reduce the impact of stereotyping (Tetlock, Skitka, & Boettger, 1989). Of course, accountability will reduce gender bias only if third parties believe and behave in accordance with gender-egalitarian values.

In conclusion, although women continue to have less power, all hope for equality is not lost. Ambivalent gender attitudes may indeed be resilient, but they arise from the fundamental interdependencies between men and women. It is these interdependencies that provide potential for change. As our scientific understanding of these complex phenomena continues to unfold, we can anticipate dulling the sword of ambivalence.

CHAPTER 25

Sexual Harassment

BARBARA A. GUTEK and ROBERT S. DONE

Sexual harassment is a topic that is more complex than it might have appeared 20 years ago. It is illegal—or at least some of it is. Sexual harassment continues to be prevalent and somewhat confusing to people, even as the term has become a household word. It does not appear to be easily controlled. Furthermore, the topic is inherently multidisciplinary. Sexual harassment is a psychological issue, to be sure, but it is also a legal issue, a management issue, a sociological phenomenon (see Welsh, 1999), and cutting across these disciplines, it is a feminist issue. Legal scholars have written extensively, often from a feminist perspective, about sexual harassment (e.g., Abrams, 1989, 1998; A. Bernstein, 1997; Bratton, 1980; K.R. Browne, 1997; Burns, 1994; Estrich, 1991; Franke, 1997; MacKinnon, 1979; Schultz, 1998). Their careful thinking about the topic could be helpful to researchers as a source of ideas (see M.S. Stockdale, Visio, & Batra, 1999, for an example). Scholars in history, anthropology, literature, and the classics have also addressed the topic of sexual harassment (see, for example, Brant & Too, 1994; Morrison, 1992b). Just within psychology, there are multiple perspectives from which to study sexual harassment: social psychological, clinical, forensic, psycholegal, industrial, and organizational. Sexual harassment has been the focus of at least five issues of psychology journals (*Basic and Applied Social Psychology*, 1995; *Journal of Social Issues*, 1982, 1995; *Journal of Vocational Behavior*, 1993; *Psychology, Public Policy and Law*, 1999), and several recently edited books (see O'Donohue, 1997; M.S. Stockdale, 1996).

In this chapter, we will consider some of what we now know about sexual harassment, based on theory, research, and practice. We review the following topics: a short history of sexual harassment, definitions and measurement, prevalence, theories, and models of sexual harassment, characteristics of initiators and recipients, consequences of harassment, and research on perceptions and judgments about harassment. Advice to targets of harassment (e.g., VanHyning, 1993) or to companies (e.g., Tamminen, 1994) will not be reviewed here.

A SHORT HISTORY OF SEXUAL HARASSMENT

It is no doubt safe to assume that the behavior we now call sexual harassment has been around for a long time, but it has been labeled, studied, and legislated for only about 20 years. Benson and Thomson (1982) cite a 1976 study by *Redbook* magazine (Safran, 1976) as the first attempt to study sexual harassment. In 1978, journalist, Lin Farley wrote *Sexual Shakedown* to bring attention to the phenomenon. In 1979, legal scholar, Catharine MacKinnon wrote an influential book that would provide a legal framework for dealing with sexual harassment. MacKinnon argued that sexual harassment was a form of sex discrimination and therefore Title VII of the 1964 Civil Rights Act, which forbade discrimination on the basis of sex (among other social categories), should apply. (For reviews, see Burns, 1995; Conte, 1997.) A year after her book was published, the Equal Employment

We wish to thank Maureen O'Connor, Peggy Stockdale, and Rhoda Unger for their very helpful comments on an earlier draft of this chapter.

Opportunity Commission (1980) established influential guidelines on sexual harassment as behavior that was prohibited by Title VII. Early empirical studies of sexual harassment in the workplace (Gutek, Nakamura, Gahart, Handschumacher, & Russell, 1980) and academia (Benson & Thomson, 1982) started appearing in print about the same time.

The combination of studies and reports documenting the prevalence of sexual harassment, MacKinnon's (1979) book, and the recognition of discrimination claims in the EEOC Guidelines eventually resulted in litigation charging sexual harassment as a form of sex discrimination made illegal under Title VII of the 1964 Civil Rights Act. Since then a number of highly publicized events—Professor Frances Conway's resignation from Stanford Medical School in response to continuing sexual harassment, the confrontation between Anita Hill and Clarence Thomas during his Senate confirmation hearing, Paula Jones' sexual harassment charge against then-Governor Bill Clinton to name a few—have made sexual harassment a household word. Despite the fact that some of these events do not fit a legal definition of sexual harassment, they have helped make it a widely discussed and debated phenomenon.

Since the EEOC issued its guidelines in 1980, the U.S. Supreme Court has weighed in with a number of key rulings that have given shape to sexual harassment law. In 1986, the Court held that sexual harassment, including hostile work environment sexual harassment, was a form of sex discrimination covered by Title VII (*Meritor Savings Bank v. Vinson*, 1986). In 1993, the Court decided that plaintiffs were not required to show harm to their psychological well-being in order to establish a claim of hostile work environment harassment (*Harris v. Forklift Systems*, 1993). In 1998, the Court clarified confusion over same-sex sexual harassment by stating that Title VII's language, that it covered discrimination "because of . . . sex," did not preclude actionable sexual harassment when the harasser and the target were of the same sex (*Oncale v. Sundowner Offshore Services, Inc.,* 1998). In its most recent decisions dealing with workplace harassment, the Court has begun to delineate the scope of employer liability for the harassing behavior of its employees (*Burlington Industries, Inc. v. Ellerth,* 1998; *Faragher v. City of Boca Raton,* 1998).

RESEARCH ON SEXUAL HARASSMENT

While the legal rulings have answered some key questions about sexual harassment, other questions remain. Social scientists have been exploring some of them from a psychological perspective for over two decades. In many respects, the research on sexual harassment has proceeded in a manner similar to many other phenomena of interest to social scientists. Researchers have grappled with defining the phenomenon, trying to measure it, and providing information on its prevalence. While still struggling with these issues, other researchers focused on both antecedents and consequences or outcomes of sexual harassment; others examined specific contexts like coal mines (Yount, 1991) or restaurants (Giuffre & Williams, 1994). A number of scholars have attempted to provide a descriptive model of sexual harassment, including antecedents, consequences, and mediating and moderating processes (e.g., Bowes-Sperry & Tata, 1999; Fitzgerald, Drasgow, et al., 1997). Others have provided theoretical perspectives on why it exists (Gutek, 1985; Gutek & Morasch, 1982; Studd & Gattiker, 1991; Tangri, Burt, & Johnson, 1982) or discussed the connections between sexual harassment and consensual sexual activities and workplace romances (Pierce & Aguinis, 1997; C.L. Williams, Giuffre, & Dellinger, 1999).

Although there are many similarities between the development of research on sexual harassment and other areas of interest to psychologists, in other respects, the research on sexual harassment is different because sexual harassment is illegal. Relative to the development of research on other concepts (say, self-esteem or job satisfaction), an inordinate amount of research on sexual harassment has focused on perceptions or judgments about sexual harassment, and the factors that affect these judgments. The sexual politics of sexual harassment—he said, she said—have focused interest on the examination of gender differences. Finally, the fact that sexual harassment is illegal has also spawned a growing number of studies that address specific legal issues. Some researchers have empirically examined legal innovations (for example, the utility of using a reasonable woman standard to replace the traditional reasonable person standard [Gutek et al., 1999]). Legal developments have also strongly affected the development of policies and procedures of employing organizations. Thus, some scholars have focused on employers' legal responsibilities, including the effectiveness of sexual harassment policies, procedures and training (e.g., Done, 2000; Gutek, 1997; Rowe, 1996).

DEFINITIONS OF SEXUAL HARASSMENT

Fitzgerald, Swan, and Magley (1997) contend that it is important to separate sexual harassment as defined by the law from a psychological definition of sexual harassment. Their psychological definition: sexual harassment is "unwanted sex-related behavior at work that is appraised by the recipient as offensive, exceeding her resources, or threatening her well-being" (p. 15). While their definition bears some resemblance to the definition of sexual harassment provided by the Equal Employment Opportunity Commission (EEOC) when it first issued its guidelines on sexual harassment in 1980, it is notable for its emphasis on the perspective of the target of the unwelcome sex-related behavior.

The EEOC guidelines (1980) define sexual harassment as "unwelcome sexual advances, requests for sexual favors, and other verbal or physical conduct of a sexual nature" that are either a condition of employment (quid pro quo harassment) or create an intimidating or hostile work environment. In the first case, getting or keeping a job or other conditions of employment are contingent on granting sexual favors or other sexual activity. In the case of a hostile work environment, these unwelcome behaviors must be severe and/or pervasive enough to meet a reasonable person's and the complainant's standard of a hostile work environment.

While psychologists have explored sexual harassment from the standpoint of its impact on the recipient, the courts have focused on the recipient's view, but in combination with the view of an objectively, reasonable person in the same or similar circumstances. In other words, sexual harassment must meet a "subjective" criterion (i.e., the recipient must find it to be severe or pervasive), and an "objective" criterion (i.e., a reasonable person would find the behavior sufficiently severe or pervasive to meet a legal definition). This latter requirement is necessary, according to the law, to prevent frivolous lawsuits by hypersensitive plaintiffs who see sexual harassment in otherwise innocent or harmless behavior.

MEASUREMENT OF SEXUAL HARASSMENT

In the early 1980s, researchers frequently used the term "social-sexual behaviors" to distinguish a set of behaviors that might be considered sexual harassment in that they were not work-related and they invoked a potentially inappropriate infusion of sex, sex-roles, gender, or sexuality into the workplace (see, for example, Gutek, 1985; Gutek et al., 1980). Such a set of behaviors typically included behaviors that would be unlikely to satisfy the legal requirements for sexual harassment. By including a broad range of behaviors, researchers could learn whether people's views of specific behaviors differed over time (or across samples). It also allowed researchers to see whether different categories of social-sexual behaviors have common antecedents and consequences. That is, do sexual harassment stories that end up in litigation look similar to each other, but different than the types of harassing experiences that are tolerated, or that do not produce legal action?

More typically, however, researchers claim to be measuring sexual harassment, with no clear distinction between behaviors that are annoying or unwanted and behaviors that would clearly meet the definition of unlawful sexual harassment. This has caused confusion because data gathered in this way tends to suggest that the percent of the workforce that would have experienced any of a broad range of social-sexual behaviors at work is the same as those who have a strong legal claim of sexual harassment. In fact, we know of no research that has attempted to make such an assessment. (Indeed, if one could accurately determine with a questionnaire when illegal sexual harassment had occurred, it would relieve the court of a great deal of work!) Because some confusion exists in this area, some scholars now make explicit the point that a lay definition of sexual harassment does not necessarily imply that a law has been broken (e.g., Bowes-Sperry & Tata, 1999).

Researchers may not have attempted to capture or distinguish the legal definition of sexual harassment from the broader category of behaviors for a number of reasons. For one, psychologists are not necessarily trained to think about the setting in which their work might be applicable, or the implications of what they are doing for that setting, in this case the law. Also, the legal defini- tion changes as the law develops, so the legal definition is a moving target. More importantly, the negative consequences of sexual harassment from a psychological standpoint are not limited to situations in which the harassment rises to meet a legal definition. Furthermore, from a psycho- logical standpoint, we can learn a great deal about workplace relationships, gender issues, power, sex-roles, psychological trauma, and many other topics without focusing on whether particular behavior would rise to the level of actionable conduct in a court of law.

MEASURING SEXUAL HARASSMENT WITH GLOBAL ITEMS

One approach to measuring sexual harassment is to simply ask, "Have you ever been sexually ha- rassed?" This global item approach is rarely used with a few exceptions. The Navy Equal Oppor- tunity/Sexual Harassment survey (NEOSH), "one of the most widely distributed surveys that has not been modified with each administration" (Culbertson & Rodgers, 1997, p. 1958) that was first administered in 1989 (Rosenfeld, Culbertson, Booth-Kewley, & Magnusson, 1992), measures sex- ual harassment with these two items: During the past year, have you ever been sexually harassed while on duty? and During the past year, have you ever been sexually harassed on base or ship while off duty?

Global items are used infrequently because some researchers contend that these measures would result in an under-reporting of the phenomenon (see Cortina, Swan, Fitzgerald, & Waldo, 1998; Fitzgerald, Swan, et al., 1997), as workers seem reluctant to acknowledge that they have been sexually harassed (Barak, Fisher, & Houston, 1992; Chan, Tang, & Chan, 1999; Jaschik & Fretz, 1992; B.E. Schneider, 1982; M.S. Stockdale & Vaux, 1993; M.S. Stockdale, Vaux, & Cashin, 1995). In addition, asking respondents if they have been sexually harassed places a great cognitive load on them, as they would have to determine first what constitutes sexual harassment and then determine if they had experienced any behavior that met those criteria.

In many studies, a single question asking the respondent if he or she has been sexually ha- rassed is used as an indicator of acknowledging or labeling sexual harassment (e.g., Adams-Roy & Barling, 1998; Cortina et al., 1998; Magley, Hulin, Fitzgerald, & DeNardo, 1999; M.S. Stockdale et al., 1995), rather than an indicator of sexual harassment, per se.

MEASURING SEXUAL HARASSMENT WITH A LIST OF BEHAVIORS

Studies that do not use one or more global items tend to ask respondents if they have experienced a list of behaviors that might be considered sexual harassment (e.g., J.W. Adams, Kottke, & Pad- gett, 1983; Chan et al., 1999; Grauerholz, 1989; Gutek, 1985; Gutek et al., 1980; USMSPB, 1981, 1988, 1995). These measures are generally (but not always) designed to be suitable for both sexes.

In some cases (e.g., Gutek, 1985), respondents are asked both whether they have experienced a list of behaviors that might be considered sexual harassment, and later in the survey which of those behaviors they consider sexual harassment. This procedure allows the researcher to deter- mine which of a broad range of behaviors the respondents have experienced and to determine which of those behaviors they consider sexual harassment (although they might not consider their own experience to be sexual harassment).

Using a list of behaviors also allows the researcher to determine the frequency of specific be- haviors and their particular antecedents and consequences (Grauerholz, 1989). This was an espe- cially important issue when sexual harassment was first being studied. What actually happened to people who were sexually harassed was not known. Learning that a sample had a mean score of 1.32 on a 3-point scale was less useful than knowing what percentage of women (or women and men) experienced each kind of potentially sexually harassing behavior. We believe this approach still has merit. It also allows readers to determine for themselves whether they think the respon- dents have been sexually harassed according to their own or a legal definition.

Every multi-item measure of sexual harassment we could find is based on a list of behaviors that people may have experienced. Although there are other measures (e.g., Gruber's [1992] Inventory of Sexual Harassment [ISH]), the best known is the Sexual Experiences Questionnaire (SEQ), a multi- item measure developed by Louise Fitzgerald and her colleagues (Fitzgerald et al., 1988; Fitzgerald,

Gelfand, & Dragow, 1995), and used extensively by their very productive research group at the University of Illinois (but also by other researchers, e.g., Barak et al., 1992; L. Brooks & Perot, 1991; Houston & Hwang, 1996; O'Hare & O'Donohue, 1998). Based on a typology developed by Till (1980), the SEQ has experienced many changes and its refinement is ongoing (Fitzgerald, personal communication, November, 1999). The SEQ has been modified in the number of questions, in the wording of questions, and in the way the responses are scored (sum vs. mean vs. number of non-zero responses of the whole scale vs. subscales). The number of subscales that emerge from it has also changed over time so it is important to keep in mind that all the studies using the SEQ are not necessarily using the same set of questions, scored the same way.

Unlike many of the other measures used that are designed for both sexes, the SEQ is designed for women only (but a male version has recently been designed [see Waldo, Berdahl, & Fitzgerald,1998]) and measures the extent to which women have experienced each of a number of harassing behaviors within the past year (see Barak, Pitterman, & Yitzhaki, 1995) or, in most cases, the past two years. There are two versions, the SEQ-E designed for students and the SEQ-W, designed for workers. More recently, another form of the SEQ, the SEQ-DoD has been developed for use in the U.S. Armed Forces (Fitzgerald, Magley, Dragow, & Waldo, 1999). In a 1995 report of the status of the SEQ (Fitzgerald, Gelfand, et al., 1995), it consisted of 19 items. In a 1999 article, the SEQ contained 18 items (Glomb et al., 1999). Some recent studies have used a short form (SEQ-s) containing eight items (Cortina et al., 1998). And the armed forces version (SEQ-DoD) contains 24 items (Fitzgerald et al., 1999).

The SEQ generally yields three components of sexual harassment: sexual coercion, unwanted sexual attention, and gender harassment (although early versions yielded five factors and they are sometimes still used in some analyses [e.g., Barak et al., 1995]). (An attempt to obtain these three factors from the list of behaviors used in the U.S. Merit Systems Protection Board studies [M.S. Stockdale & Hope, 1997] has been moderately successful.) In addition, the SEQ-DoD contains four components (Fitzgerald et al., 1999). The 1995 version of the SEQ (Fitzgerald, Gelfand, et al., 1995) contained 5 items measuring gender harassment, 7 items measuring unwanted sexual attention, and 5 items measuring sexual coercion. The sexual coercion alpha is low (alpha = 0.42) because the behaviors it assesses are not common. It sometimes has a mean of 1.01 and standard deviation of 0.01 (Fitzgerald, Drasgow, et al., 1997; see also Barak et al., 1995). Nevertheless, it is worth noting that the three components are not equally robust. Fitzgerald and her colleagues view sexual coercion as quid pro quo harassment while unwanted sexual attention and gender harassment are hostile work environment harassment, although they readily acknowledge that the items in the SEQ may not reflect current legal interpretations of sexual harassment. Furthermore, the intercorrelations among the three components are very high. Their average: $r = 0.74$ (Fitzgerald, Gelfand, et al., 1995).

In some publications, the SEQ score is the sum of the items (Glomb et al., 1999) and in other publications, the scores are dichotomized: those reporting none of the behaviors are compared with those respondents who have experienced one or more of the behaviors one or more times (e.g., Cortina et al., 1998). In at least one study, the answers to the individual items were dichotomized and then summed across items for each of the three components (O'Hare & O'Donohue, 1998). Thus, it would be difficult to use the SEQ to compare the incidence of sexual harassment across time, detect variations across samples, or compare the incidence in academia to various workplaces, occupations, and industries because the SEQ itself has undergone continuing development, there are multiple forms containing different numbers of factors, and it is scored in multiple ways.

Although there has been a lot of research attention given to measuring sexual harassment, more effort is indicated. Fitzgerald and her colleagues are still working on the SEQ. In addition, it might be useful to try to develop a multi-item global measure of sexual harassment. A number of scholars (e.g., Gutek & Koss, 1993; Pryor & Whalen, 1997) have noted that sexual harassment usually consists of a pattern of behavior over a period of time, suggesting the advisability of developing a measure that captures the whole episode.

One other area deserves attention. Only a small subset of the behaviors currently studied is likely to survive as a credible claim of unlawful behavior. Perhaps by trying to capture the EEOC's definition of sexual harassment researchers could assess some aspect of unlawful behavior (e.g., behavior that is likely to result in a judgment favorable to the plaintiff, or behavior that would sur-vive a motion to dismiss the case).[1] For example, a few flirtatious comments would not be a credi-ble complaint but a continuing barrage of obscene comments might.

In any measurement effort, it is important to separate legal behaviors from illegal behaviors, if for no other reason than to retain credibility and avoid confusion among the public or legal deci-sion makers. If in the mind of the public the term "sexual harassment" implies behavior that would be illegal in a court of law, then perhaps we should not claim to be measuring "sexual ha-rassment" when we are not limiting our focus to behaviors that could form the basis of a success-ful sexual harassment claim.

DEVELOPMENT OF OTHER MEASURES TO STUDY SEXUAL HARASSMENT

Rather than restricting their list of social sexual behaviors to those experienced by the respondents, some researchers have asked, for example, if respondents have had any experience with teachers telling sexist jokes (see Mazer & Percival, 1989). Both men and women who have had such an expe-rience are then considered to have been sexually harassed, thus inflating the percentage of those people the researchers consider to have been sexually harassed. Neither a man hearing a sexist joke about women nor a woman hearing someone put down men is likely to feel sexually harassed in the same way as the woman who is the target of the sexist joke or the man who is being put down.

We do not consider measures that focus on individual or organizational tolerance for social-sexual behavior to be sexual harassment per se. Such measures that describe the work environment were not available when the first author began studying sexual harassment in 1978, but a number of scales are now available. For example, Lott, Reilly, and Howard (1982; Reilly, Lott, & Gallogly, 1986) developed a 10-item measure, the Tolerance for Sexual Harassment Inventory (TSHI), yielding three factors, labeled "flirtations are natural," "provocative behavior," and "feminist beliefs." The TSHI measures the respondent's beliefs about men and women (e.g., "An attractive woman has to expect sexual advances and should learn how to handle them."), not organizational norms. Hulin et al. (1996) describe the development of their measure, the Organizational Tolerance for Sexual Ha-rassment Inventory (OTSHI), using a sample of employees at a regulated utility company. This 18-item measure which focuses on the respondent's view of the organization's tolerance for harassment, contains three subscales: risk of reporting, likelihood of being taken seriously, and probability of sanctions. This measure has subsequently been used in a structural equation model involving employees at the same company (Fitzgerald, Drasgow, et al., 1997). Developed as part of the navy's study (NEOSH), Culbertson and Rodgers' (1997) article includes nine items measuring sexual harassment climate perceptions. Their scale measures the extent to which sexual harassment occurs, if it is a problem, if anything is being done to stop it, and if respondents know what actions and words are considered sexual harassment. Finally, Gutek, Cohen, and Konrad (1990) used eight items to measure the extent to which the work environment is sexualized.

THE PREVALENCE OF SEXUAL HARASSMENT

We know of no research that has attempted to determine the prevalence of illegal sexual harass-ment. This makes a certain amount of sense because the legal definition is still in the process of evolving. On the other hand, the reported figures are sometimes interpreted either as all refer-ring to behavior that could form the basis of a successful sexual harassment claim and/or criti-cized for overstating the problem (i.e., including behavior that is not illegal or that is trivial) (e.g., Arvey & Cavanaugh, 1995; Lengnick-Hall, 1995).

What are the strengths of the research on the prevalence of sexual harassment? A number of studies have relied on random sample surveys including studies of the federal workforce (USMSPB,

---

[1] We were unable to find any examples of measures of sexual harassment that focus on the legal require-ments. However, there are studies of perceptions of sexual harassment that either ask if the behavior in ques-tion constitutes quid pro quo harassment or hostile work environment harassment (Gutek et al., 1999) or is severe, unwelcome, or pervasive criteria established by the legal system for illegal sexual harassment (see Wiener, Hurt, Russell, Mannen, & Gasper, 1997).

1981, 1988, 1995), the military (Culbertson, Rosenfeld, Booth-Kewley, & Magnusson, 1992; Martindale, 1991), specific geographical areas (Gutek, 1985), and specific work organizations (Fitzgerald, Drasgow, et al., 1997). Some of these (e.g., Gutek, 1985; USMSPB, 1981) have obtained quite high response rates. Another strength of the sexual harassment literature is that some studies have been conducted in Spanish as well as in English (Gutek, 1985; Magley et al., 1999). A few longitudinal analyses have also been conducted (e.g., Glomb et al., 1999; Murrell, Olson, & Frieze, 1995).

In determining the prevalence of sexual harassment, it is important to take into account the time frame being considered. Are respondents being asked to determine if they have been sexually harassed in the past year, the past 24 months, on their current job, or at any time during which they have been employed? If the goal of the research is to examine the effects of workplace factors on sexual harassment, then using the current job is an appropriate frame of reference. If a goal is to determine the percentage of women who have had the experience, then lifetime employment is an appropriate reference. Using total employment as a reference point means that respondents are not all considering the same number of years in their assessments of their experiences. Limiting questions about sexual harassment to the past year or two years may be an outcome of researchers' concerns that respondents will not remember sexual harassment that happened many years ago. Although Arvey and Cavanaugh (1995) are critical of studies that ask respondents to engage in retrospective self-reporting because of the possibility of inaccuracy and/or bias, it might be just as difficult to determine if one is currently being subjected to unwelcome social-sexual behavior (as they suggest researchers might do) than it is to determine if one has been subject to unwelcome social-sexual behavior in the past. In fact, Kidder, Lafleur, and Wells (1995) provide convincing examples in which events initially not labeled sexual harassment came to be so labeled at a later date. In addition, it seems probable that when people are recalling events from years ago, they are more likely to forget trivial incidents and are relatively more likely to remember serious incidents. It is clear that the percentage of men and women who experience different kinds of social-sexual behavior does not increase all that much when they are asked to consider any job they have ever held versus only their current job (see Gutek, 1985, p. 46). Presumably, when one considers events of years or decades ago, only the most significant will be remembered.

Another factor to take into account is the measure used to assess sexual harassment. Results obtained with the SEQ have been used to show that the prevalence rate is quite different if it is measured with a single global item or with the SEQ. More specifically, when a single item is used, the amount of sexual harassment seems to be under reported. What under reporting usually means in this context is that the respondents who check at least one item on the SEQ respond in the negative when they are asked if they were sexually harassed. For example, Barak et al. (1992) found that 57.8% of their respondents (female students at a university) scored above zero on a version of the SEQ but only 4.3% answered in the affirmative when they were asked if they were sexually harassed. In their sample of working women in urban Israel and in Israeli Kibbutzim, Barak et al. (1995) found that 91.7% of urban women and 95% of women in Kibbutzim said that they had "never been sexually harassed in the workplace" (p. 508). While these results strongly suggest under reporting, it is worth reiterating that these results do not mean that either 57.8% or 4.3% of women students experienced illegal sexual harassment (as it is defined in Israel or the United States). It does strongly suggest that people who experience behaviors that are often considered sexual harassment do not necessarily label their own experience as such. Thus, as noted above, the single global item is often used as an indicator of acknowledging sexual harassment rather than as a measure of experiencing sexual harassment.

In the following sections, we consider some of what we know about the prevalence of sexual harassment. Studies have been done in education (including students, faculty, and staff at high schools, and faculty and undergraduate and graduate students at colleges and universities), the military, industry, and the government.

SEXUAL HARASSMENT OF WOMEN

The random-sample studies together suggest that from about 35% to 50% of women have been sexually harassed at some point in their working lives, where sexual harassment refers to behavior that most people consider sexual harassment (Gutek, 1985), but estimates are higher among certain groups such as women who work in male-dominated occupations (LaFontaine & Tredeau, 1986). In a review of 18 studies, Gruber (1990) computed the median percentage of women who have ever experienced sexual harassment at work as 44%. In some of these studies, the researchers concluded that anyone who had experienced one of the behaviors included in their list of sexually harassing behavior had been sexually harassed. In other cases, the figures are based on judgments of the respondents (i.e., behavior they experienced and also met their own definition of sexual harassment [Gutek, 1985]). A relatively high percent reporting some form of sexual harassment has also been found in samples of undergraduate and graduate students (see Cammaert, 1985; Ivy & Hamlet, 1996; Richman, Flaherty, & Rospenda, 1996).

The most commonly reported social-sexual behaviors are the less severe ones, involving sexist or sexual comments, undue attention or body language (see Fitzgerald, Drasgow, et al., 1997; Grauerholz, 1989; Gutek, 1985; Piotrkowski, 1998; USMSPB, 1981, 1988, 1995). Sexual coercion is, fortunately, much rarer, involving 1% to 3% of many samples of women (Barak et al., 1995; Chan et al., 1999; Fitzgerald, Drasgow, et al., 1997; Gutek, 1985). In contrast, a study of allegations in cases tried in court showed a much higher incidence of severe behaviors (Paetzold & O'Leary-Kelly, 1996); for example, 22% included physical assault, 58% involved nonviolent physical contact, and 18% involved violent physical contact.

The incidence of sexual harassment of women appears to be rather stable. The U.S. Merit Systems Protection Board studies allow us to track changes over time because they have used the same method to assess sexual harassment in multiple surveys of the same population and they report prevalence rates. The three studies spanning 14 years show that 42% to 44% of women in the federal workforce have experienced at least one episode of sexual harassment over the previous 24 months, where sexual harassment refers to having experienced one or more of a list of potentially sexually harassing behaviors. In addition, the number of charges filed with the EEOC leveled off in the range of 15,000 to 16,000 per year for the period 1995 through 1998. This is in contrast to a change from 10,532 in 1992 to 15,549 in 1995 (EEOC, 1999). (Approximately 80% of complaints made to the EEOC from 1995 to 1998 are either administrative closures or closed for "no reasonable cause.")

SEXUAL HARASSMENT OF MEN

Men have been included in studies of sexual harassment from the very beginning. Many early studies (e.g., Gutek, 1985; Gutek et al., 1980) surveyed both men and women. In her study of a random sample of working men and women in Los Angeles County, Gutek (1985) found that some time during their working lives, from 9% to 35% of men (depending on definition of harassment), had experienced some behavior initiated by one or more women that they considered sexual harassment. The U.S. Merit Systems Protection Board studies (1981, 1988, 1995) found that from 14% to 19% of men in the federal workforce experienced at least one episode of a sexually harassing experience (initiated by either men or women) within the previous two years. As in the case of women, the most frequently reported harassment consisted of less severe behaviors. And as in the case of women, the figures for students are roughly similar to workers (Ivy & Hamlet, 1996; Richman et al., 1996).

The 1981 and 1995 USMSPB surveys revealed that about one-fifth of the harassed men were harassed by another man. Using data from the 1988 Department of Defense Survey of Sex Roles in the Active Duty Military, C.L. DuBois, Knapp, Faley, and Kustis (1998) found that about one-third of the men (but about 1% of the women) experiencing at least one of nine types of uninvited, unwanted sexual attention during the previous 12 months, reported that the initiator was the same sex. Using a male version of the SEQ that has recently been designed, Waldo et al. (1998) reported that more men reported being harassed by men than by women. The harassment of men by other men tended to be of two types: lewd comments that were considered offensive and attempts to enforce male gender role behaviors (see also Franke, 1997). Harassment by women was somewhat different, consisting of negative remarks and/or unwanted sexual attention.

The available research on sexual harassment of men, admittedly much less than the research on women, suggests that many of the behaviors women might find offensive are not considered offensive to men when the initiators are women (Gutek, 1985) and/or they report few negative consequences (C.L. DuBois et al., 1998; Gutek, 1985). In addition, a disproportionate percentage of men's most distressing experiences of sexual harassment come from other men (see C.L. DuBois et al., 1998). M.S. Stockdale et al. (1999), analyzing the Department of Defense's (J.E. Edwards, Elig, Edwards, & Riemer, 1997) nationally representative survey of military personnel which used a 25-item version of the SEQ, found that 37% of men in the sample were sexually harassed (measured by scoring greater than zero on the SEQ total scale score), but over half of those responding to a question about "the most distressing experience" reported that the offender was a man. Presumably these are especially distressing because the recipient's masculinity, manhood, and/or sexual orientation are being called into question.

The U.S. Supreme Court's decision in *Oncale v. Sundowner Offshore Services, Inc.* (1998) has opened the door for more same sex claims of sexual harassment. Indeed, the percentage of sexual harassment complaints filed with the EEOC by men has been increasing in recent years and as of 1998 represents 12.9% of all cases, up from 9.9% in 1994 and 1995 (EEOC, 1999).

OTHER CHARACTERISTICS OF TARGETS OF SEXUAL HARASSMENT

Relatively few studies have either focused on or found consistent differences in the experience of sexual harassment beyond the consistent differences reported by women versus men. It may be the case that younger and unmarried women are somewhat more likely targets of sexual harassment than older and married women (see Benson & Thomson, 1982; Gutek, 1985; LaFontaine & Tredeau, 1986). It may also be the case that lesbian women are more likely to be sexually harassed than heterosexual women, but more likely they are simply to label their experiences sexual harassment (see B.E. Schneider, 1982). Although several authors have suggested that in the United States, women of color (Asian, African American, Hispanic, and American Indian) are more likely to be targets of sexual harassment than Caucasian women (see Defour, 1990; Karsten, 1994; MacKinnon, 1979), the evidence is far from clear. Several random sample surveys found no clear link between ethnicity and the experience of sexual harassment (Gutek, 1985; USMSPB, 1981). Essed (1992) found frequent references by black women to sexual harassment by white men, but no comparative data were presented. Similarly, Segura (1992), studying Chicanas in white-collar jobs, Chan et al. (1999) studying secretaries and students in Hong Kong, and Mecca and Rubin (1999) studying African American students in the United States, found relatively many reporting behaviors often considered sexual harassment.

Murrell (1996), reviewing this literature, noted that two kinds of arguments have been advanced for reasons why minority women might experience relatively more sexual harassment. A direct argument relies on stereotyping of minorities. Although the stereotypes of African American women differ from stereotypes of Chicanas or Asian American women, in each case the stereotype might place these women at greater risk. An indirect argument relies on concepts of power and marginality. As women of color are less powerful and more marginal by virtue of their ethnicity than are White women, they may be more prone to sexual harassment (see also J.H. Adams, 1997). As Murrell (1996) noted, in order to understand the sexual harassment experiences of minority women, it is also necessary to understand if there are differences in the way each ethnic group defines sexual harassment relative to the Caucasian population. In addition, there may be differences in willingness to acknowledge social-sexual behaviors.

We were unable to find much research on other characteristics of men that affect their likelihood of being sexually harassed. Gutek (1985) found that single men were more likely to report social-sexual overtures from women than married male workers. She did not find any differences by ethnicity, but the number of men of the different minority categories were not large, despite the fact that the sample of men was relatively large ($N = 405$).

THEORIES OF SEXUAL HARASSMENT

Why sexual harassment exists has been of interest to psychologists since the phenomenon acquired a label (Tangri et al., 1982). A review of this literature (Tangri & Hayes, 1997) provides an excellent overview of the explanations for sexual harassment. In the space allotted, we cannot do justice to Tangri and Hayes' review, so the interested reviewer should read their work. Tangri and

Hayes subsume the various explanations into four categories: natural/biological perspectives, organizational perspectives, sociocultural explanations, and individual differences perspectives. There are two natural/biological perspectives: a hormonal model and an adaptive/evolutionary explanation. Likewise, there are two organizational perspectives: sex-role spillover and organizational power. All of these explanations tend to be broad in scope, not easily testable in a laboratory. Of them, the sex-role spillover perspective has probably been studied most widely. In this section, we review these four categories of theories plus some legal theories that can be examined empirically.

NATURAL/BIOLOGICAL PERSPECTIVES

The first of these, a hormonal explanation in which sexual harassment is a normal expression of men's stronger sex drive, does not, according to Tangri and Hayes (1997), fit the data on sexual harassment. A more elaborate argument is an evolutionary adaptation model (see K.R. Browne, 1997; Studd & Gattiker, 1991). The argument presented by Studd and Gattiker, while intriguing, lacks internal logic and is not falsifiable, as the authors themselves note that the existing research supports two aspects of the theory that predict opposite behavior. They argue that one strategy used by men to ensure reproduction, the "pursuit of short-term, low-cost, and low-commitment sexual liaisons," might produce sexual harassment (p. 253). They also argue that women, who have a higher reproductive investment (of time, energy, and risk), are more cautious in forming liaisons and "have evolved a generally negative emotional response to unsolicited sexual attention from men" (p. 256). Tangri and Hayes rightfully point out that if women have evolved a negative emotional response to unsolicited attention from men, then usual mating behavior would be initiated by women (since women, but presumably not men, respond negatively to unsolicited sexual attention). In addition, if sexual harassment is a reproductive strategy used by some men, it is an unusually inept strategy. Sexual harassment rarely results in sexual intercourse (Gutek, 1985; USMSPB, 1981, 1995).

Although probably not a successful short-term strategy for ensuring reproduction, some forms of what is considered sexual harassment might have roots in evolved behavior. For example, K.R. Browne (1997, p. 72) offers this food for thought: "Because of the importance of status and dominance in male hierarchies, men are very attentive to signs of weakness in others and correspondingly reluctant to reveal weakness and vulnerability in themselves. Where they see weakness, they may attack. People sensitive to sexually oriented attacks—women and particularly sensitive men—are likely to be attacked in this way." His analysis is consistent with some descriptions of hostile work environments reported by both women and men (M.S. Stockdale et al., 1999; Waldo et al., 1998; Yount, 1991).

ORGANIZATIONAL PERSPECTIVES: SEX-ROLE SPILLOVER

A number of organizational practices and conditions make it relatively easier for one employee to sexually harass another, but most do not explain why some workers take advantage of these conditions and others do not. "One theory that does provide an explanation for why workers sexually harass other workers is the sex-role spillover theory . . ." (Tangri & Hayes, 1997, p. 116). Sex-role spillover, defined as the carryover into the workplace of gender-based expectations that are irrelevant or inappropriate to work, occurs because gender role is more salient than work role and because under many circumstances, men and women fall back on sex-role stereotypes to define how to behave and how to treat those of the other sex (Gutek, 1985; Gutek & Morasch, 1982). Sex-role spillover tends to occur most often when the gender ratio is heavily skewed in either direction, that is, when the job is held predominantly either by men or by women. In the first situation (predominantly male), nontraditionally employed women are treated differently than their more numerous male coworkers, are aware of that different treatment, report relatively frequent social-sexual behavior at work, and tend to see sexual harassment as a problem. In the second situation (predominantly female), female workers hold jobs that take on aspects of the female sex-role and where one of those aspects is sex object (e.g., cocktail waitress, some receptionists), women are likely to be targets of unwanted sexual attention, but may attribute the way they are treated to their job, not their gender. Gutek and Morasch argued that there should be less sexual harassment in gender-integrated jobs where job is not sex-typed and gender is less salient (neither sex stands out as unusual in the setting).

Some research supports various aspects of sex-role spillover as it applies to women (D. Burgess & Borgida, 1997a, 1997b; Gutek & Morasch, 1982; Sheffey & Tindale, 1992). Gutek and Morasch found that nontraditionally employed women and traditionally employed women who worked predominantly with men (e.g., female secretary in male engineering group) reported relatively more sexual harassment than women in sex-integrated jobs.

While sex-role spillover was developed to take account of the experiences of workers, several researchers have attempted to apply it to the way outsiders evaluate the experiences of working women. Sheffey and Tindale (1992), in an experiment examining the way in which skewed occupational sex ratios influence perceptions of sexual harassment, found that when women were employed in traditionally female jobs, research participants rated sexually ambiguous behavior (e.g., "Why don't we go where we can speak more privately?") to be relatively more appropriate and less harassing. They interpreted these findings as supportive of sex-role spillover: because the traditional female's gender role overlapped her work role, ambiguous sexual advances toward her were perceived as appropriate to the workplace. D. Burgess and Borgida (1997b) followed this with an experiment in which they examined the way the occupation of the female target affects the way in which different types of sexual harassment are perceived. They used more severe sexual behaviors of three types: unwanted sexual attention, gender harassment, and sexual coercion (taken from Fitzgerald & Hesson-McInnis, 1989). They used scenarios in which the work environment was predominantly male, the harassment was relatively severe (e.g., "walked by and put an obscene centerfold on her desk. Mike has done this before"), and perpetrators were coworkers rather than supervisors. They found that sexual coercion, the type of sexual harassment most clearly labeled as harassment by both sexes, was least likely to be labeled sexual harassment when a woman was in a nontraditional job. Under those circumstances, research participants were also least likely to endorse corrective action.

D. Burgess and Borgida (1997a) followed this study with another set of analyses showing that scenarios about traditionally and nontraditionally employed female targets elicited different gender subtypes and different attributions of harasser motives, depending on the type of sexual harassment experienced. Sexual coercion provides a case in point: A woman in a nontraditional job was less likely to be perceived as sexually coerced because she did not fit into the traditional female subtype of needing protection. In contrast, women in traditionally employed jobs who experienced sexual coercion were most likely to be viewed "in terms of the traditional female subtype: weak and vulnerable" (p. 305). Burgess and Borgida suggest that feelings of vulnerability and femininity may be essential to the perception of sexual coercion and gender harassment. A women in a nontraditional job may be perceived as an "iron lady" (Kanter, 1977a), not needing protection or support and able to take sexual jokes and comments without being offended. If she views the behavior as sexual harassment, others may be surprised. Surely she knew what the environment was like and chose to work there anyway, presumably because she is tough and not easily offended. D. Burgess and Borgida (1997a) further note that "on the surface . . . unwanted sexual attention may bear the closest resemblance to 'normal' courtship behavior" (p. 306). Their results suggest that for unwanted sexual attention, employees in traditionally female occupations may be perceived to be more sexual than women in nontraditional jobs, and harassment may more likely be attributed to benign heterosexual motives (i.e., sexual interest).

Interestingly, in an early article, M.B. Brewer (1982) suggested a rather similar integration. She suggested, for example, that the natural/biological model might best explain sexual harassment that is more like courting behavior (unwanted sexual attention) and might occur more often in gender-integrated jobs, relative to other kinds of sexual harassment.

Sex-role spillover theory is not symmetrical, that is, it does not make completely parallel arguments for men and women for two reasons: male and female sex roles are different, and an accumulating body of evidence suggested that Kanter's (1977a) theory of gender ratios did not apply equally to men and women. Furthermore, there is less research on sex-role spillover as it affects male employees. One reason is that there are relatively few men in nontraditional jobs or sex-integrated jobs (Gutek, 1985, chap. 8). Nevertheless, some predictions have been made. Compared to men who work with few women, men who work with many women are more likely to receive sexual comments and looks meant to be complimentary from women and are more likely to be sexually touched by women. But, consistent with sex-role expectations, Gutek (1985) argued that work environments where men predominate would to be more sexualized (i.e., more sexual jokes, comments, posters, etc.) than predominantly female work environments. Thus, because men are in these environments more than women, men should tell more sexual jokes and the like, women should more often be the targets of such comments, and women should experience more sexual harassment than men. But men who are offended by a sexualized work environment, should also report more sexual harassment when they work predominantly with men than with women.

In their analysis of men in the military, M.S. Stockdale et al. (1999) found some support for sex-role spillover. They found that the most same-sex sexual harassment among men in the military happened to men who worked in groups that were almost all male, were currently serving on board a ship, and had a male supervisor. Conversely, opposite-sex sexual harassment for men in the military was more likely when they had a female supervisor and worked in less male-dominated work environments.

Overall, the research on sex-role spillover has produced some supportive results. These results suggest that type of sexual harassment and perhaps motive for sexual harassment need to be considered in the theory. A more thorough analysis of the differences expected, based on both the perspective of the actor and the observer, also needs to be done. In short, there is room for more research as well as room for a restatement and refinement of the theory in light of new empirical findings.

ORGANIZATIONAL PERSPECTIVES: POWER

As Tangri and Hayes (1997) note, the earliest writings on sexual harassment were about men abusing the power that comes from their positions in organizations to coerce or intimidate subordinate women (e.g., Backhouse & Cohen, 1981; Bularzik, 1978; Farley, 1978). Some subsequent statements on the power perspective are gender neutral, suggesting that although men tend to harass women, in principle if women occupied more positions of power, they might harass men in equal measure. The culprit, then is power, formal organizational power, which will inevitably be abused. As Tangri and Hayes note, the interpretation of sexual harassment as an abuse of organizational power is contraindicated by research showing that about half or more of harassment comes from peers (Gutek, 1985; USMSPB, 1995). In addition, both customers (see Hughes & Tadic, 1998) and subordinates (see McKinney, 1992) are also sources of harassment. Sexual harassment by subordinates has been documented primarily in academic settings where, for example, one study found nearly half of female faculty surveyed at a university had experienced one or more sexually harassing behaviors by male students (Grauerholz, 1989).

Nevertheless, while power cannot explain all sexual harassment, it remains a powerful explanation for at least some sexual harassment. Cleveland and Kerst (1993) draw on a large body of organizational research to explain how various kinds of power—formal organizational power and informal power stemming from ability to influence—are used, are often linked to gender, and help explain sexual harassment. For example, the fact that sexual harassment by customers is fairly common can be explained, at least in part, by the emphasis employers place on customer satisfaction and the notion that the "customer is always right" (Hughes & Tadic, 1998).

SOCIOCULTURAL PERSPECTIVES

Tangri and Hayes (1997) note that there are at least two ways of thinking of the broader sociocultural context. One is that behavior at work is merely an extension of male dominance that thrives in the larger society. Variations on this sociocultural explanation have been proposed by MacKinnon (1979), Pryor (1987), J.E. Stockdale (1991), and Vaux (1993). Summarizing some of the common themes in these perspectives, Tangri and Hayes note: "There is general agreement in the literature about the characteristics of the sex stratification system and the socialization patterns that maintain it. Men are expected to exercise, and are socialized for, dominance, leadership, sexual initiative and persistence, and self-interest. Women are expected to exercise, and are socialized for, submissiveness, nurturing, sexual gatekeeping, and self-abnegation" (pp. 120–121). Men can sexually harass women when they are overly exuberant in pursuing sexual self-interest at work, or they feel entitled to treat women as sex objects, or when they feel superior to women and express their superiority by berating and belittling the female sex.

The second way of thinking of the broader sociocultural context, according to Tangri and Hayes (1997), is to examine the sociocultural system itself and how and why status is assigned. According to this view, sexual harassment is an organizing principle of our system of heterosexuality, rather than the consequence of systematic deviance. If it is the case that sexual harassment at work is an extension of male behavior outside the workplace, then we might expect that societies in which men do not dominate would produce less sexual harassment. We found few studies that speak to this issue. Barak et al. (1995) attempted to examine the effect of power differentials in sexual harassment by comparing people who live in an Israeli kibbutz (relatively egalitarian) versus employed urban Israeli women (relatively less egalitarian). Using a Hebrew version of the SEQ (in this case, a 34-item instrument based on Fitzgerald et al., 1988), they found no differences between of the women living in the kibbutz and those living in urban areas in "overall sexual harassment, specific types of sexual harassment, and any specific sexual harassment behavior" (p. 510). Kauppinen-Toropainen and Gruber (1993) found greater differences when they compared the experiences of women in Scandinavian countries with the experiences of women in the United States and a sample of engineering technicians from the former Soviet Union. The fact that Scandinavian women reported fewer "unfriendly" experiences relative to the other two samples was attributed to general social and economic policies that have attempted to eradicate gender inequality, providing some support for the view that the sociocultural system is important.

LEGAL THEORIES WITH BEHAVIORAL COMPONENTS

Legal scholars are concerned with the issue: Why is sexual harassment illegal? MacKinnon (1979) argued, at bottom, that sexual harassment was illegal because it disadvantages women in the workplace and therefore discriminates against them. But as the law has progressed, a number of other theories have emerged, some of which have interesting behavioral implications.

Franke (1997), for example, argues that most forms of sexual harassment are forms of sexism. For her, the issue is not that sexual harassment is sexual, but that it enforces strict gender norms. Women are sexually harassed in two ways: either because they do not conform to gender norms (and are punished for it, often by having their heterosexuality questioned) or by being expected to be a sex object (one aspect of female gender norms). Sexual harassment by men against other men, according to Franke (1997), typically occurs when men do not meet other men's standards of masculinity. Franke's view is consistent with sex-role spillover; either the target is expected to serve as a sex object or is punished for not meeting sex-role expectations. Several researchers (D. Burgess & Borgida, 1999; M.S. Stockdale et al., 1999) have attempted to examine empirically some of Franke's predictions.

Another perspective is taken by Schultz (1998) who believes the courts have put too much emphasis on sex and not enough on work. In short, she argues that sexual harassment has little to do with sexual or social relations between the sexes but has everything to do with undermining women in the workplace. Sexual harassment is a form of sex discrimination because it disadvantages women relative to men. It is a barrier to equal opportunity. This perspective is important because discrimination by disparaging women, their accomplishments, and their ability or treating them in a demeaning manner, all of which constitutes gender harassment, is typically much more common than sexual coercion or unwanted sexual attention (Barak et al., 1995; Fitzgerald et al., 1988; Gutek, 1985; see Gruber, 1997).

INDIVIDUAL DIFFERENCE EXPLANATIONS

Although the data suggest that most sexual harassers are men, most men (and women) are not sexual harassers. This makes the study of personality characteristics particularly relevant. Thus, another kind of explanation views sexual harassment as an outcome of individual differences. As Tangri and Hayes (1997) and Pryor and Whalen (1997) note, the search for individual-level characteristics of perpetrators does not negate any of the other explanations, but helps to determine, for example, which men in a male-dominated society or which men in powerful positions in organizations harass women when most men do not.

Encouraged by the willingness of college men to admit to a propensity to rape, Pryor (1987) developed a measure of the Likelihood to Sexually Harass (LSH) in men. The Likelihood to Sexually Harass scale consists of 10 vignettes that place the respondent in a position to grant someone a job benefit in exchange for sexual favors and is currently the most widely known individual difference measure used in the study of sexual harassment. Although the words, sexual harassment, do not appear, the scenarios "essentially represent the likelihood of [the respondent] performing acts of quid pro quo sexual harassment" (Pryor & Whalen, 1997, p. 131). Thus, the measure does not assess the likelihood of engaging in hostile work environment harassment. The LSH is designed to be filled out by men.

The LSH has been validated in a number of studies. Pryor (1987) found that undergraduate men who scored relatively high on the LSH demonstrated more sexual behavior in a lab experiment than did those who reported a lower likelihood to sexually harass. Rudman and Borgida (1995) found that in a sample of undergraduate men, those who reported a higher likelihood to sexually harass also demonstrated more sexualized behavior in a lab experiment than men who reported a lower likelihood to sexually harass. And in a sample of men, Driscoll, Kelly, and Henderson (1998) found that those who scored higher on the LSH also gave lower performance ratings to a female subordinate in a lab experiment than men who reported a lower likelihood to sexually harass.

Pryor (1987) found that undergraduate men who scored higher on the LSH also held negative attitudes toward women. Pryor and Stoller (1994) found that in a sample of undergraduate men, those who reported that they were likely to sexually harass were also more confident of their memory of sexuality and dominance word pairs than control word pairs in a lexical recall experiment. Bargh, Raymond, Pryor, and Strack (1995) found that in a sample of undergraduate men, those who reported that they were likely to sexually harass also demonstrated an automatic link between power and sex. Consistent with other research on the gender distribution of sexual harassment, E.L. Perry, Schmidtke, and Kulik (1998) found that in a sample of undergraduate students who completed a cross-sex version of the Likelihood to Sexually Harass scale, men reported significantly higher average scores than women.

The LSH is not the only individual difference factor that has been studied. Drawing on the fields of sociology and criminology, Done (2000) studied the relationship between self-control and sexually harassing behavior. Gottfredson and Hirschi (1990) suggest that those who commit crime do so because they lack the self-control to overcome the impulse to immediately gratify desire. Whether or not a specific incident of sexual harassment is in violation of a law, sexual harassment may be an attempt to immediately gratify the desire for discrimination, intimidation, or sexual pleasure. This interpretation suggests that those with low self-control are also more likely to sexually harass. Done found preliminary support for this theory, as both men and women with lower self-control were also significantly more likely to report a higher likelihood of engaging in sexually harassing behavior (measured by scores on the LSH scale) than those with higher self-control. The self-control perspective contributes to our understanding of sexual harassment, which has been built, in large part on gender-specific differences.

Yet another approach to individual differences was taken by Fiske and Glick (1995; P. Glick & Fiske, 1996) with the development of their Ambivalent Sexism Inventory, which consists of two components: hostile sexism and benevolent sexism. Hostile sexism refers to a generalized hostility toward women and benevolent sexism refers to a set of beliefs focusing on women's differences from men. More specifically, benevolent sexism measures a subjectively positive, yet sexist, attitude toward women, including a protective paternalistic power, an obligatory heterosexual intimacy, and complementary gender identification. In comparison, hostile sexism measures a more obviously negative attitude toward women and includes dominating power relations, heterosexual hostility, and competitive gender identity. Fiske and Glick suggest that hostile sexism might be especially predictive of hostile work environment sexual harassment.

The results on the relationship between the measures of hostile and benevolent sexism and sexual harassment have, so far, been mixed (see Gutek et al., 1999; Wiener et al., 1997).

EMPIRICAL STUDIES OF ANTECEDENTS OF SEXUAL HARASSMENT

Some researchers focus less on broad theoretical perspectives and more on the types of variables that need to be included in models of sexual harassment (e.g., Fain & Anderton, 1987; Fitzgerald, Swan, et al., 1997; Pryor, LaVite, & Stoller, 1993; Terpstra & Baker, 1986). Thus far, the following organizational factors have been identified as correlates of sexual harassment: contact with the other sex, unprofessional and/or sexualized work environment.

CONTACT AND SEX RATIOS

Contact with the other sex is a prerequisite for heterosexual sexual harassment and contact itself is associated with both harassing and nonharassing social-sexual behavior (Gutek et al., 1990). Solo status, being the only woman in a workgroup, such that all contact within the workgroup is with the other sex, can make a worker especially vulnerable. Contact in combination with organizational position is also important. For example, women who have male supervisors are more likely to report being recipients of social-sexual behavior than women with female supervisors (Gutek, 1985).

Finally, sex ratios are important. Three sex ratios, sex ratio of the occupation, the job in the particular organization, and the work group or department, may all affect one's chances of being sexually harassed at work (Gutek & Morasch, 1982). The sex ratio of the workgroup may reflect both opportunity for contact and gender roles. Fitzgerald, Drasgow, et al. (1997) use the term "job-gender context" to refer both to the group sex ratio and the traditional or nontraditional nature of job duties and tasks. They see both as denoting the gendered nature of the workgroup. Gutek and colleagues consider both in their theory of sex-role spillover, discussed earlier (see Gutek, 1985; Gutek & Dunwoody, 1987, pp. 259–265).

UNPROFESSIONAL OR SEXUALIZED WORK ENVIRONMENT

Another set of factors that are antecedents of sexual harassment refer to aspects of the organization's culture: whether it is characterized by an unprofessional ambience (e.g., workers are asked to do tasks unrelated to work, workers are treated disrespectfully) and/or a sexualized environment (e.g., being attractive is important, sexual jokes are common, workplace norm supports women and men flirting with each other on the job). Gutek (1985) found that both were related to social-sexual behavior that might be considered sexual harassment. Subsequent research using a variety of different measures (e.g., Culbertson & Rodgers, 1997; Decker & Barling, 1998; Fitzgerald, Drasgow, et al., 1997; O'Hare & O'Donohue, 1998) provides additional support for the notion that an unprofessional and sexualized work environment is related to the prevalence of sexual harassment. Using their Organizational Tolerance for Sexual Harassment Inventory (OTSHI), Fitzgerald, Drasgow, et al. (1997) found through structural equation modeling that such a tolerance is associated with higher scores on the SEQ.

Experimental studies also offer support for the view that an unprofessional or sexualized work environment makes it easier for sexual harassment to occur. More specifically, either priming men with sexually explicit material (McKenzie-Mohr & Zanna, 1990) or providing a harassing role model (Pryor et al., 1993) increases the likelihood of sexually harassing behavior.

RESPONSES TO SEXUAL HARASSMENT

In the past decade, a number of researchers have proposed typologies or categories of responses to sexual harassment (Fitzgerald, Swan, & Fischer, 1995; Gutek & Koss, 1993; Knapp, Faley, Ekeberg, & DuBois, 1997). A major finding is that most targets of sexual harassment do not file a formal complaint (L. Brooks & Perot, 1991; C.L. DuBois et al., 1998; Gutek, 1985; USMSPB, 1981,

1995). A minority tend to blame themselves (Jensen & Gutek, 1982) and many do not tell anyone about their experiences. Fitzgerald, Swan, et al. (1995) provide a review and discussion of the reasons why most are not more public about their experiences. These reasons include fear or retaliation, concern about being labeled a troublemaker, and believing that "nothing will be done" (Gutek, 1985; see also Rudman, Borgida, & Robertson, 1995). Adams-Roy and Barling (1998) found that filing a complaint was associated with a lower score on perceived fairness and justice of their organization's procedures.

A recent U.S. Supreme Court decision may make it more difficult for victims of harassment who do not file a formal complaint (*Burlington Industries, Inc. v. Ellerth,* 1998). If an organization has implemented a sexual harassment policy and complaint procedures, failure to take advantage of those remedies may constrain a claimant's legal options. Thus, we need to better understand the reasons why workers do or do not report sexual harassment and the consequences of both doing so and not doing so.

CONSEQUENCES OF SEXUAL HARASSMENT

Available research suggests that targets of sexual harassment may experience a variety of negative outcomes. Many of the outcomes reported here are found even when the social-sexual behaviors are relatively mild (see Fitzgerald, Drasgow, et al., 1997; Gutek, 1985). The research in this area does not rely on a legal definition of sexual harassment.

Research on the consequences of sexual harassment was reviewed by Gutek and Koss (1993); they and others (e.g., Terpstra, 1996) note that more needs to be done. Because this research focuses almost exclusively on women targets (except for research done in the military; see C.L. DuBois et al., 1998; M.S. Stockdale et al., 1999), several scholars have suggested more work be done on male victims (see W.E. Foote & Goodman-Delahunty, 1999; Waldo et al., 1998). Almost all the research on this topic consists of cross-sectional data using samples of workers or students. Gutek and Koss note that the emotional and physical damage ostensibly due to sexual harassment could be attributable instead to a pre-existing condition or affect. In addition, causal direction is unclear; having psychological or physiological problems may increase the likelihood of being a target of sexual harassment. Fortunately, there are now some laboratory studies and some longitudinal studies, but more are needed (see Glomb et al., 1999; Satterfield & Muehlenhard, 1997).

Based on the research available, we focus on four types of outcomes: self-esteem and self-confidence, emotional and psychological well-being, mental health consequences (i.e., posttraumatic stress disorder and depression), and job satisfaction and commitment.

SELF-ESTEEM AND SELF-CONFIDENCE

Results of early research on the effects of sexual harassment on self-esteem and self-confidence (e.g., Gruber & Bjorn, 1982), reviewed by Gutek and Koss (1993), has been underscored by more recent qualitative and quantitative studies of students and employee (Luft & Cairns, 1999; Vukovich, 1996). In their review of the effects of sexual harassment on women, Gutek and Koss report that a decrease in self-esteem and perceived competence may result when rewards may have been based not on ability but on sexual attraction. Satterfield and Muehlenhard (1997) found this to be the case in two experiments and extended this work to men. In the first experiment, a male confederate posing as an advertising executive asked the sample of undergraduate women to draw a design for a perfume advertisement. The confederate praised the work of the subjects in both the experimental and control groups, but engaged in flirtatious behavior with the experimental group and did not flirt with the control group. Post-experiment self-creativity ratings improved for the subjects in the control group but decreased for the subjects in the experimental group.

The second experiment replicated the first experiment except that a female confederate posed as the advertising executive for the male subjects. As in the first experiment, the post-experiment scores of the female subjects in the experimental group decreased significantly while the scores of the control group did not significantly change, but no such effect was found for men.

Satterfield and Muehlenhard (1997) suggest that the explanation for these findings is related to the attributions of the subjects. They suggest that because women are more likely than men to have been praised in the past based on their looks rather than their performance, they are more likely than men to attribute praise to nonperformance criteria in the context of flirtatious behavior. Conversely, men (whose performance is more often evaluated on its own merits) are more likely to discount flirtatious behavior in their attribution of praise. These findings suggest women's self-perceptions suffer when praise for performance is commingled with praise for looks (see also Heilman, 1994).

EMOTIONAL AND PHYSIOLOGICAL CONSEQUENCES

Other negative outcomes can occur. Jayaratne, Vinokur-Kaplan, Nagda, and Chess (1996) found that social workers who reported experiencing sexual harassment also reported significantly more depression and irritability than those who had not been sexually harassed. In an analysis of the USMSPB sexual harassment survey data, Thacker and Gohmann (1996) found that those who reported experiencing sexual harassment also reported a worse emotional condition. Fitzgerald, Drasgow, et al. (1997) found that women employed at a utility company who endorsed at least one item on the SEQ also reported significantly higher levels of psychological distress (see also Glomb et al., 1997). In a sample of U.S. Army soldiers, L.N. Rosen and Martin (1998) found that men's and women's reports of deliberate, repeated unwelcome sexual advances, requests for sexual favors, and other verbal or physical conduct of a sexual nature within the preceding year was associated with reduced psychological well-being. Similarly, the endorsement of at least one item on each of the gender harassment, unwanted sexual attention, and sexual coercion scales of the SEQ was significantly associated with reduced psychological well-being for both men and women. The National Women's Study of 3,006 adult women found that having experienced sexual harassment was positively associated with the experience of major depressive episodes (as measured by *DSM-III-R* criteria) (Dansky & Kilpatrick, 1997).

Beyond emotional harm, sexual harassment can affect one's physical condition. In their analysis of the USMSPB sexual harassment survey data, Thacker and Gohmann (1996) found that those who reported experiencing sexual harassment also reported a significantly worse physical condition. Experiencing sexual harassment and discrimination was associated with reporting headaches and nausea among a sample of female construction workers (Goldenhar, Swanson, Hurrell, Jr., Ruder, & Deddens, 1998). Failure to label or recognize sexual harassment does not appear to attenuate these effects, as Magley et al. (1999) found. Whether or not the women labeled their experience as sexual harassment, those women who were targets of sexual behavior in the workplace were more likely to report negative outcomes (e.g., severe headaches, shortness of breath, and exhaustion).

MENTAL HEALTH CONSEQUENCES (POSTTRAUMATIC STRESS DISORDER AND DEPRESSION)

Gutek and Koss (1993) note that similarities have been observed between the symptoms following sexual harassment and the symptoms of posttraumatic stress disorder (PTSD). Although empirical evidence was limited at the time of that review, Dansky and Kilpatrick (1997) provided additional information from their national survey of women conducted by the research team at the Crime Victims Research and Treatment Center at the Medical University of South Carolina. They found a positive association between sexual harassment and the experience of PTSD. "The prevalence of lifetime PTSD differed among four sexual harassment groups in that it was lowest among respondents who reported that they have never experienced any potentially harassing behavior (9.0%) . . . and highest among women in the Sexual Harassment Victim group (29.7%)" (p. 166). (The Victim group consisted of women who approximately met the EEOC criteria for sexual harassment: experienced potentially sexually harassing behavior, perceived the behavior as sexual harassment, and it had an impact on the job.)

Additional support for the relationship between sexual harassment and PTSD was presented by J. Wolfe et al. (1998) for both the severity and frequency of sexual harassment. These authors surveyed U.S. Army women (enlisted soldiers, noncommissioned officers, and commissioned officers) about sexual harassment and PTSD symptoms. Women who were sexually assaulted reported significantly higher levels of PTSD than women who were not sexually harassed or than women who experienced only physical (e.g., unwanted sexual touching) or verbal (e.g., pressure for sexual favors) sexual harassment. PTSD symptoms were significantly predicted by the overall frequency of sexual harassment. These findings support not just the suggested relationship between sexual harassment and PTSD, but also the intuitive notion that more severe and more frequent sexual harassment is more likely to be associated with PTSD symptoms.

JOB SATISFACTION AND ORGANIZATIONAL COMMITMENT

Finally, sexual harassment can impact job attitudes. Gutek and Koss (1993) observe that sexual harassment can decrease job satisfaction and organizational commitment. In fact, even mild social-sexual behavior (like sexual comments meant to be complimentary) may be associated with lower job satisfaction of women (Gutek, 1985, chap. 7). Recent studies, using both civilian and military samples, report similar findings. In a sample of women office workers, Piotrkowski (1998) found that gender harassment was associated with reduced job satisfaction. Rosenfeld, Newell, and Le (1998) found that among female U.S. Navy officers and enlisted men and women, those who reported experiencing gender discrimination relative to those who reported not experiencing gender discrimination, also reported plans to leave the navy, general dissatisfaction with the navy, and the intention to not stay in the navy for 20 years.

Research by Louise Fitzgerald and her colleagues has also contributed to our understanding of the effect of sexual harassment on job satisfaction and organizational commitment. In a sample of employed women, K.T. Schneider et al. (1997) found that the best predictors of those who endorsed at least one item on the SEQ were dissatisfaction with coworkers, dissatisfaction with supervisors, and work withdrawal. Women employed at a utility company who reported being sexually harassed by endorsing at least one item on the SEQ also reported significantly lower levels of job satisfaction as evidenced by more absenteeism and intentions to leave (Fitzgerald, Drasgow, et al., 1997). Ambient sexual harassment (a sexualized work environment) was associated with reduced job satisfaction as well (Glomb et al., 1997). Finally, Glomb et al. (1999) successfully replicated the model suggest by Fitzgerald, Drasgow, et al. (1997) and found that sexual harassment was negatively related to job satisfaction in a longitudinal study of university women.

Thus, a number of studies have reported a variety of negative outcomes associated with women's (and to a less extent, men's) reports of social-sexual behaviors that might be considered sexual harassment. R.I. Simon (1996) suggests that those who have been sexually harassed may initially experience self-doubt and confusion. Uncertainty may lead to feelings of guilt when the targets of harassment wonder if they somehow encouraged or invited the harassment. These feelings give way to anxiety over employment status and the possibility of sexual assault. The downward spiral accelerates as anxiety leads to depression and diminished self-confidence. Finally, helplessness sets in and job performance is devalued (see also Dansky & Kilpatrick, 1997; Salisbury, Ginorio, Remick, & Stringer, 1986).

FACTORS AFFECTING JUDGMENTS OF SEXUAL HARASSMENT

The most widely published area of research on sexual harassment measures people's perceptions about sexual harassment. We could not find any study that asked respondents how they define sexual harassment. Instead, this set of studies falls into two categories. One set attempts to understand which specific behaviors (e.g., repeated requests for a date; sexual touching, stares, or glances; a sexually oriented joke) respondents consider to be sexual harassment. Respondents read a series of behaviors and are asked whether each behavior is sexual harassment. The other set of studies attempts to understand factors that affect the way respondents evaluate vignettes in which various factors are manipulated. The factors that are manipulated include characteristics of the behavior (e.g., touching versus comments), characteristics of the situation (e.g., the relationship between the initiator and recipient), and characteristics of the initiator and recipient (e.g., sex, age, attractiveness, occupation). In addition, characteristics of the rater (e.g., sex, age) may be measured. The choice of manipulated and measured variables seems generally to be based on curiosity or common sense. For example, one study (Hendrix, Rueb, & Steel, 1998) examined

(1) work status (student vs. employee), (2) gender of the initiator, (3) gender of the respondent to the survey, (4) age of the initiator, (5) position power of the initiator (supervisor or peer), (6) success status of the initiator, and (7) attractiveness of the initiator. The dependent variables in these studies are a series of judgments about the events in the scenario. A judgment of sexual harassment may be, but is not always, included. In very few studies are respondents asked to render a judgment about the legality of the events (but see Gutek et al., 1999) or evaluate the events in terms of legal criteria such as severity or pervasiveness (but see Wiener et al., 1997).

In general, the factors studied in the research on perceptions of harassment are not influenced either by theory or findings from legal proceedings (but see M. O'Connor, Stockdale, Gutek, Melançon, & Geer, 2000). Nor are there many attempts to compare the relative influence of rater characteristics (e.g., sex, age) with, for example, situational factors (e.g., status of initiator vis-à-vis target).

SEX DIFFERENCES IN PERCEPTIONS

Sex of the rater is the most frequently studied feature in studies about perceptions of sexual harassment. A recent compilation of the literature (1996–1999) by the second author yielded 103 articles on sexual harassment, of which 30 dealt with sex differences in perceptions about sexual harassment. Hundreds of studies have been done, although few have attempted to explain why sex differences might exist (but see Konrad & Gutek, 1986; Wiener et al., 1997). This body of research has been reviewed using traditional methods (Frazier, Cochran, & Olson, 1995; Gutek, 1995) and meta-analyses (Blumenthal, 1998; M. O'Connor, 1998).

Blumenthal (1998) reviewed more than 100 effect sizes from 111 articles and unpublished theses from 1982 through 1996 that met these criteria: (1) the study measured respondent's sex and/or status of initiator and at least one potential moderator of that effect, and (2) enough information was available to measure effect size. His analysis yielded a sex effect size r of 0.171, and "can be characterized as slightly larger than a 'small' effect" (p. 43). Whereas Blumenthal included studies that addressed sexual harassment or a related topic, such as appropriateness, M. O'Connor (1998) restricted her analysis to studies in which respondents were asked to make a judgment about sexual harassment specifically. Her analysis of 79 studies yielded an unweighted mean effect size (Meta r) of 0.16. M. O'Connor (1998) also examined differences between men and women on individual stimulus items for those studies in which respondents evaluated more than one scenario or kind of behavior (e.g., Terpstra & Baker, 1986) and found that 44% showed a significant sex difference. The bottom line: Women are slightly more likely than men to define a situation as sexually harassing or to perceive situations as slightly more harassing.

What do these results mean? Blumenthal (1998), M. O'Connor (1998), and Gutek (1995) all agree that these results challenge claims of a "wide divergence" between men and women's perceptions. O'Connor pointed out that sex differences were not consistently found, and Blumenthal noted that sex effects tend to be smaller when legal scenarios were used. These results are particularly important because it would appear that these studies have had an indirect influence on the Ninth Circuit's decision in *Ellison v. Brady* (1991) (Gutek & O'Connor, 1995). In that case, the court adopted a new legal standard in hostile environment cases of sexual harassment, the reasonable woman standard, which replaces the traditional reasonable person standard in that Circuit. Juries are asked to evaluate the events from the perspective of a reasonable woman: taking into account all the facts, would a reasonable woman consider the plaintiff to be sexually harassed? As Gutek and O'Connor (p. 152) explained, the predominant claim of the new standard is that it would force judges and juries to look at the case from the perspective of the complainant, who is typically a woman. This would presumably make it less difficult for a plaintiff to make a convincing claim of hostile work environment harassment.

The adoption of a new legal standard in some (but not all) jurisdictions leads to the obvious question of whether it results in different judgments by decision makers. The legal standard may exhibit a main effect (under the reasonable woman standard, evaluators give more pro-plaintiff judgments) or it may interact with gender (the modest sex difference in perceptions may disappear as men take into account the perspective of the complainant). Gutek et al. (1999) conducted analyses of seven different samples (students, managers, and jury pool members) using a variety of stimulus materials (short scenario, long scenario, video trial, pictures plus long scenario, multimedia presentation). They found that the reasonable woman standard has modest, if any, effects on the judgments studied including judgments about legality and monetary damages. Furthermore, they found relatively few significant gender effects, which generally were not reduced by the use of a reasonable woman standard. Gutek discusses the reasons why a reasonable woman standard as currently implemented may not result in different judgments than the traditional reasonable person standard. In any event, the magnitude of the gender gap in perceptions about sexual harassment may not justify a change in standards, regardless of the effect of standard itself. Wiener et al. (1997) note that the existence of a reasonable woman standard may have effects beyond the courtroom. It might, for example, influence corporate policies and training on sexual harassment.

OTHER FACTORS AFFECTING PERCEPTIONS

Although gender is far and away the most widely studied factor in the study of sexual harassment perceptions, other factors, as noted above, have been studied. Blumenthal (1998) included one other variable in his meta-analysis: the status of the initiator relative to the recipient. Although there were many fewer studies examining the effect of status of the initiator vis-à-vis the recipient, Blumenthal found a larger effect for status than for sex of respondent. In general, when the initiator is higher status than the recipient, judges respond more positively toward the recipient, more negatively toward the initiator, and perceive more harassment than when the initiator is not a supervisor.

Other rater characteristics that may have an effect on perceptions of sexual harassment are age and sexist attitudes. Several studies comparing students with workers find that students in Hong Kong as well as in the United States have a broader, more lenient view of social-sexual behavior relative to samples of workers who are presumably somewhat older (see D.D. Baker, Terpstra, & Cutler, 1990; Chan et al., 1999; Frazier et al., 1995; Gutek et al., 1999; Reilly et al., 1986). Blumenthal (1998) did not examine the direct effects of age in his meta-analysis; he did check to see if age moderated the relationship between sex and perceptions and found no effect.

CONTINUING AND EMERGING ISSUES

Much needs to be done before we have a full understanding of sexual harassment. Here we raise two methodological issues that surfaced in our review: the quality of sexual harassment research and the continued use of scenarios in sexual harassment research.

A number of papers have been written criticizing the research on sexual harassment (e.g., Arvey & Cavanaugh, 1995; Lengnick-Hall, 1995). Some criticisms seem to be politically motivated (e.g., McDonald & Lees-Haley, 1995). This is, after all, a controversial topic. Not all of the published research is exemplary. We have found published studies in which the independent variable was treated as the dependent variable in the analysis, several studies in which too little information was presented to follow the analyses reported, several studies in which scores on multi-item measures were not explained (e.g., whether the score is the mean or sum of the items or something else, number of items in the measure), and a study in which scales were reverse-coded without saying so in the article. Certainly there is some weak research that has been published and other studies that should have gone through one or two more revisions before publication. But overall the quality compares favorably to any other area of research. More funding for research on this topic would certainly help.

Perhaps because funding is scarce or because the research is simple to do, the use of scenarios or vignettes is prevalent (see Gutek, 1995, for a discussion). E.A. Cooper and Bosco (1999) found that about 15% of the research studies on gender and work in mainstream journals (including *Psychology Women Quarterly* and *Journal of Applied Psychology*) use scenarios or vignettes for stimulus materials. Needless to say, scenario studies are common in many other fields of psychology as well. So it was surprising to us to find virtually no guidance on how to construct a good scenario. For example, should they be short, reporting on only those variables that are being manipulated or should they try to capture all the important elements and richness of real situations? Research methods books do not deal with this issue. We suggest that in the case of sexual harassment, scenarios will be more applicable to real-world situations (litigation, employers' investigations) if the facts in these scenarios are contested. Rarely in real life are all the facts agreed upon and the only decision to be made is whether or not sexual harassment has occurred. More typically, if one version of the facts is accepted, sexual harassment has occurred, but if another version of the facts is accepted, it has not. Rather than calling for a moratorium on scenario studies (which has been done but to no avail), why not address the twin issues of when scenarios are appropriate and what kind of scenarios are most valid under what circumstances?

CHAPTER 26

Women, Gender, and the Law: Toward a Feminist Rethinking of Responsibility

MICHELLE FINE and SARAH CARNEY

In this chapter, we articulate a feminist analysis of the social psychology of responsibility as it is reflected in the treatment of girls and women in courtrooms. In particular, we analyze the gendering, classing, and racializing of responsibility, and we document the extent to which teenage girls and women, particularly those who are poor and of color, carry social responsibilities for the culture and in the law.

TOWARD A WORKING DEFINITION OF RESPONSIBILITY

Political theorist Joan Tronto (1993), in her book *Moral Boundaries,* views responsibility as the "taking care of" (p. 3). Distinguishing responsibility from obligation, Tronto sees the former as "embedded in a set of implicit cultural practices, rather than . . . a set of rules or series of promises" (p. 132).

From within traditional social psychology, the notion of responsibility has been embedded in familiar concepts such as blame, diffusion of responsibility, attribution theory, self-blame, and illusion of control. Very important work has been done on men's and women's views and experiences of unjust social relations at work, at home, on the streets, or in the laboratory, typically without much analysis of gender, race, or class (see Mikula, Petri, & Tanzer, 1990). Equally important work informs us about the conditions under which justice is conceived, injustice is awakened, and perpetrator and victim are held accountable for the inequities (M. Deutsch, 1983). Shaver (1985) has studied the knotty relations of blame, responsibility, and cause, and B. Weiner (1995), 10 years later, defined responsibility as "a judgment made about a person . . . [what] he or she 'should' or 'ought to have' done" (p. 8), assuming that "judgments of responsibility presuppose human causality" (p. 11). This line of work most clearly demarcates responsibility as blame. Citing his own work along with Skitka and Tetlock (1992), B. Weiner explains that when the source of a person's need is viewed as internal and controllable, responsibility, disgust, and anger are heightened. In contrast, when the cause of need is viewed as either external or internal/uncontrollable, sympathy and pity prevail.

Blending the arguments of Tronto (1993) and B. Weiner (1995), we theorize at the feminist intersection of care and blame, offering a feminist spectrum of responsibility. We relocate *responsibility* within unequal raced, classed, and gendered power relations, thereby opening notions of responsibility well beyond individual responsibility to interrogate collective, structural responsibility for currently unjust social formations. It has long been recognized by the trenchant theoretical work of feminist scholars ranging from Baker Miller (1976) to Apfelbaum (1999) to Rollins (1985) to Unger (1998) that assumptions about responsibility sit in a well-tilled field of power relations. In 1979, Erica Apfelbaum, for instance, argued: "Power expresses itself in [a] dependency relation between two groups when one group appropriates the rights and privileges and sets the limits on these for the other group. . . . Neither power, nor either of the two groups, can exist independently, outside of the relationship binding them" (1999, p. 268).

We take up four tasks in this chapter. First, we trace the extent to which contemporary women across racial and ethnic groups are considered accountable to care for "public" and "private" life. We present evidence on how thoroughly girls and women are presumed responsible for self, for others, for kin, for community, and for controlling the behaviors of men. Second, we document the extent to which girls and women are blamed for the "troubles" of both "public" and "private" life. We try to understand why, when there is a "problem"—a child is abused at home, a woman is harassed at work, a mother remains with an abusive husband, a secretary receives inadequate pay for 20 years, a male professor is accused of sexual harassment, a football star is accused of date rape—girls/women are disproportionately held accountable. Why didn't she save the child? Report the harasser? Leave the husband? Complain about her pay? Transfer out of his class? Why did she go to his room? Third, we seek to understand the conditions under which girls and women resist and break the silence, embracing social movements to right social wrongs (see Matsuda, 1996; Payton, 1984). Fourth, as a concrete instance, we analyze how women who expressly transgress social expectations, that is, women accused of breaking the law for failing to protect their children from harm, are viewed in terms of their responsibilities to care, to keep silent, and to be blamed.

We provide substantial social science evidence that reinforces the point that women are viewed disproportionately as the cause, the problem, the provocateurs, and the whistle-blowers deserving of punishment for betraying the social conditions that depend on these very women's silence and complicity. With the wisdom of Crenshaw (1997), we launch this analysis through "intersectionality." Looking explicitly and concurrently through race, class, and gender, we offer interpretations that enrich, complicate, and sometimes contradict gender- or race-only explanations, "Because women of color experience racism in ways not always the same as those experienced by men of color and sexism in ways not always parallel to experiences of White women" (p. 360).

RESPONSIBILITY AS CARE: WOMEN'S WORK

Women—regardless of their race, ethnicity, class, or sexual orientation—are held responsible for the emotional work in asymmetric social relations at home, in communities, on the streets, and at work. In contexts of gendered domination (see Miller, 1976; Benjamin, 1988; P.H. Collins, 1990; Irigaray, 1990; L. Phillips, 2000), being female carries a particular burden/gift–responsibility/ obligation: to sustain and nurture the most intimate, "private" unit—the family. We do not dispute that some of these responsibilities are chosen, filled with pleasure, surprise, the delights of interdependence, fluidity, and reciprocity. Nevertheless, we recognize that these responsibilities fall primarily to women, whether elected or not, chosen or not, pleasurable or not, fluid and reciprocal or not (Ruddick, 1989).

With a pen toward social critique, Haug (1992a), a German Marxist feminist psychologist, deliberately provokes when she writes, "Female responsibility is a mistake, a social deprivation which points to a general disorder in society" (p. 81). Haug continues, "Individual responsibility always appears when general rules stop working . . . individual responsibility is unthinkable in the absence of other people's irresponsibility" (p. 81). Haug is perhaps at her most frightening, and telling, when she argues, "Women's acceptance of being torn apart by demands they cannot satisfy leads to a stance we may call masochistic. The attempt is then made to locate the source of this stance in women's inner being . . . instead of assigning the blame to specific social formations" (p. 86).

If this were simply an issue of a "diffusion of responsibility" or "belief in the just world," the distribution of responsibility and blame would be more random. It would not keep falling on women across racial/ethnic groups. How does this happen? An analysis of gender is crucial. How did women get to be so powerful and powerless at the same time?

Further, when caring for the family unit is refused, or when the shape of the family "deviates" from heterosexual marriage, as with lesbian women (Espin, 1996) and mothers without men (Polakow, 1993), or when inherent flaws of the family grow obvious, as in the case of women who leave violent or dissatisfying relations, women's obligation to care without deviation may get converted into an opportunity to blame. The price paid for the challenge by women can be enormous, ranging from shame, embarrassment, silence, and depression, to the loss of her children, violence, and death.[1] This dynamic is especially evident when the country is in trouble and we can't find/invent external enemies. It is then to girls and women, poor and of color, that the national finger of blame typically points. Note the welfare reform debates (see Belle, 1999; Boris, 1998; Kittay, 1998; Mink, 1998).

Whether we review feminist research on housework, child care, emotional work in the family or in the labor force, baby nurturance, elder care, community organizing, or the "second shift," women consistently carry the emotional and relational work at home, in the community, and in the workplace (see Fine & Asch, 1988, for an important exception; i.e., women with disabilities are assumed fundamentally incapable of assuming responsibilities for others or for themselves).

WOMEN DO THE WORK AT HOME: AN INEQUITABLE DISTRIBUTION

Almost 20 years ago, Hartmann (1981, reprinted in 1994) authored a theoretically rich and empirically fastidious essay on the family as a site of gendered labor. Hartmann documents how the family, organized through gendered inequities, operates as a unit designed to support capitalist economic relations. As such, she argues, the family must be conceptualized as a site of struggle rather than a site of consensus on the radically inequitable distribution of housework that men and women undertake:

> First the vast majority of time spent on housework is spent by the wife, about 70 percent on the average, with both the husband and the children providing about 15 percent on average. Second the wife is largely responsible for child care. The wife takes on the excess burden of housework in those families where there are very young or very many children; the husband's contribution to housework remains about the same whatever the family size or the age of the youngest child. It is the wife who, with respect to housework at least, does all of the adjusting to the family life cycle. (p. 184)

Rollins (1985) extends this argument, demonstrating how women of color who work as domestics for White women not only provide physical and emotional work, but also labor to comfort, contain, and sanitize domestic life while subordinating (at least in public) their own desires, yearnings, passions, and needs. They are paid to stabilize the White heterosexual family on the stressed backs of color. At the intersection of patriarchy, capitalism, and heterosexism, sexism operates always in relation to racism (P.H. Collins, 1990; Crenshaw, 1997; A. Davis, 1995; Hartmann, 1994; Rollins, 1985), often with White privileged women and working-class and/or women of color positioned and engaged in relations of opposition, not solidarity.

Fast forward to the 1990s, and philosopher Mann (1998) argues in "Toward a Post-patriarchal Society":

> It seemed obvious that insofar as women were leaving the home each morning alongside men to work and contribute to the economic maintenance of the family, when women and men returned home at night they should share the various familiar and household responsibilities equally, as well. . . . What did happen was that women worked all day in the public workforce and returned each night to what sociologist Arlie Hochschild labeled a "second shift" in the home. While divorces increased greatly during this period, the lives of single and married mothers had become structurally similar, in that both now tended to be employed in the public workforce, returning home to a second familial shift. (Cited in Haber & Halfon, 1998, p. 94)

Haug (1992a) would tell us that such maldistribution of the caring function onto women, scaffolded by race and class, and acceptance of that work by women, occur most obviously when both the economy and the state systematically retreat from care, refusing responsibility for the collective

---

[1] Indeed, part of the punishment of women is to deprive them of these "private" and intimate relationships. Black slave mothers in the past and women in prison today have been denied access to and relations with their kin. Further, part of the devaluation of women with disabilities is that they are often assumed incapable of providing such emotional work (Fine & Asch, 1988).

well-being of children, adults, and the elderly. Such a retreat, accelerated by the rise of the New Right and the victory of conservative Republicans in the 1990s, requires that someone pick up the work. And, disproportionately, that someone is often a woman (Blackman, 1996).

Empirical study after empirical study confirms that women perform more housework, more child care, and more elder care than men. Steil (1999), in her remarkably comprehensive book *Marital Equality*, documents how thoroughgoing the gendered inequities are inside heterosexual marriages: "Despite the growing public endorsement of equality, most marriages continue to be unequal . . . wives are still more likely to be unemployed, to work part time, to earn less and to be in lower status jobs than their husbands. Even among dual career couples in high status positions, the wife's career is still more likely to be considered secondary" (p. 4). Steil reviews the existent literature, enriched by her own work: "In three recent studies, the percentage of husbands in dual earner families who shared the work of the home equally ranged from a low of approximately 2% to a high of 20%. . . . Employed wives in the late 80's did 60% to 64% of the total housework, compared to the 67% to 70% of all household labor they did in the late 70's" (p. 5). Citing studies of housework, we learn from Huber and Spitze (1988) that full-time homemakers spend an average of 52 hours per week, employed wives 26 hours per week, and husbands 11 hours per week on housework. Hochschild's (1989) now well-known second shift is confirmed by the systematic documentation of such overproduction by working women, once they get home.

Turning from housework to child care, we find both women and men agree that women are more involved in the micropractices of child rearing (Steil, 1999). According to Destefano and Colasanto (1990), 89% of national survey respondents report that when a child is sick, the mother reorganizes her worklife to accommodate. In a study conducted by Staines and Pleck (1986), women report cutting back on family time (minimally) when they work full time, but still spend significantly more time with family than do male partners. Steil and Weltman (1991) found that women who earned one-third more than their husbands bore somewhat less responsibility for children than women who earned one-third less, but for women and men, domestic responsibilities were never equally shared. Walzer (1996), who writes on the responsibility for "thinking about baby" (p. 218), notes, "The tendency for women and men to become more differentiated from each other in work and family roles upon becoming parents has been documented in longitudinal studies of transitions into parenthood" (p. 219). Walzer confirms that this division of labor appears to be associated with new mothers' marital dissatisfaction and "violated expectations" of more shared parenting. She finds that on dimensions of worrying, processing information about parenting, and managing the division of labor, women do the lion(ess's) share of visible and invisible work. She argues that because mothering is viewed as "natural, universal and unchanging . . . There is a much greater threat to [new mothers'] social identities . . . than there is for fathers if, in any particular moment, they are not taking responsibility for their baby" (p. 230).

A number of studies shed light on those heterosexual couples who work to redistribute responsibility for domestic work or income. Biernat and Wortman (1991) report that in couples in which academic women earn more than their partners, these husbands engage in *less* child care than men in couples where men earn more. "High earning wives absolve their husbands from child care responsibilities in order to compensate for the negative feelings evoked by their higher salaries" (Steil, 1999, p. 34). Hochschild (1989), too, documents that heterosexual couples go out of their way to camouflage the earnings of a "high-earning" woman, especially if her male partner earns less. Philliber and Hiller (1983) explain that women in "non-traditional managerial and professional positions are more likely to become divorced, to leave the labor force or move to a lower status position than women in traditional jobs, and this pattern is more salient when the wife's position is similar in status to her husband's than when it is of lower status" (reviewed in Steil, 1999, pp. 34–35).

When women take on economic responsibility and surpass their partner's earnings, if that partner is male, they may risk far more than the loss of partner pride or child care. Gauthier and Bankston (1997) have studied spousal homicide rates as they correlate with women's economic well-being and find that, "although males account for about 85% of all murders and non-negligent manslaughters in the United States . . . there is one category of killing in which the sex ratio is more equitable: the killing of intimate partners in domestic relationships" (p. 577). Indeed, whereas 7% of male-initiated murders are "intimate," a full 44% of female-initiated murders are classified as such. However, more frightening and relevant to the present discussion, these authors find, "In cities where females are experiencing relatively high economic advantage compared to males, sex ratios of killing intimate partners tend to be biased in favor of males as killers" (p. 593). The conclusion is simple: "High levels of high economic well being may intensify male violence, including homicide, in attempts to control women as economic/status resources" (p. 593). Tangri and Jenkins (1997) concur when they find, "Strong commitment to one's career still produces more conflict, which must be tolerated in order to sustain the career. It may be that as couples mature, the wife's more advanced and increasingly demanding career . . . may become more difficult for the husband to support" (p. 744). There may be severe costs for reversing traditional distributions of emotional and financial responsibilities.

Almost all women, but women of color in particular, manage ever more exhausting lives of intimacy and caring (see Romero & Stewart, 1999b). Often alone. Usually with inadequate resources. And if they are poor or working class, they are undoubtedly nurturing many, amidst punishing public surveillance (see Fine & Weis, 1998; Mink, 1998). Women of color are responsible not only for the care of kin and home and for contributing economically to family well-being but also for sustaining culture and community alongside racial and ethnic oppression (Alicea, 1997; Benmayor, Juarbe, Alvarez, & Vazques, 1987; Espin, 1996; Gilkes, 1988; Hurtado, 1996). In her book *Women Crossing Boundaries*, Espin (1999) describes the joys and burdens of immigrant girls and women who carry the responsibilities of preserving culture, typically at the expense of their gendered and sexual agency:

> The self-appointed "guardians of morality and tradition" that are ever present among immigrant communities are deeply concerned with women's roles and sexual behavior (Yuval-Davis, 1997). These guardians include religious or community leaders, older women and men, and even younger people who feel a need to preserve old values at all costs. Since immigrant communities are often besieged with rejection, racism and scorn, those self-appointed guardians have always found fertile ground from which to control women's sexuality in the name of preserving tradition. (pp. 6–7)

Thus, for social arrangements to proceed *as they are,* for culture, home, and family to be sustained, girls and women must assume responsibility for sets of social relations disproportionately neglected by men, the state, the economy, and other members of the community and family. This is where Haug's (1992a) writings grow so profoundly important. Haug reminds us that when the state retreats from social responsibility, women move to the discursive and material foreground with the obligation to reproduce good citizens, often without resources or full citizenship opportunities themselves. Reminded of their "duties" routinely, women can be vilified when disasters befall their children, parents, kin, the women themselves, their men, and their communities. As the horrific assault on women of color becomes visible—during the "welfare reform" debates, for example (Mink, 1998)—poor women of color are assumed responsible for emotional relations and physical well-being within profoundly unjust social arrangements in which women are oppressed and for which women, especially women of color, are then held accountable. And few rise to their defense, as welfare activist Mink has written: "Given the degree of harm inflicted on poor single mothers by the new welfare law, why were there no candlelight vigils like there were against O.J. Simpson? Why were there no marches like there have been to defend *Roe v. Wade*? Why were there no boycotts waged like there were against the film *The People v. Larry Flynt?*" (p. 57).

RESPONSIBILITY AS BLAME: WHEN VIOLENCE HITS WOMEN

When we theorize about violence in communities, it is important to look at how understanding and experience are structured by the material conditions of poverty and systemic exclusion from power. Intervening or turning away are behaviors best understood in historical and cultural context. The circumstances of [Kitty] Genovese's murder that I originally understood in individual behavioral terms became, during the 1970's, an instance of the general failure to intervene in the prevention of violence towards women. . . . I think it is the task of social psychology to theorize a socio-politics of intervention starting with increased knowledge of the long and complex history of non-intervention in instances of violence against powerless groups—women, the aged, children, racial minorities and the poor. . . . (Cherry, 1995, p. 29)

We turn now to the second reading of "responsibility": responsibility as blame. For a thorough review of the violence against women literature, we refer you to the chapters in this handbook authored by White, Donat, and Bondurant; Kimball; Good and Sherrod; and Kitzinger. Our focus, however, concerns how girls and women view violence against their bodies, and how men and women attribute blame for violence against women (see Cherry, 1995, on how social psychology has constructed our discipline to erase historical and structural conditions of inequity in the search for individual blame).

We know from studies of youth and adults that Blacks, girls, women, and people in the working class and in poverty are more fearful of violent victimization than are Whites, boys/men, and the middle class/elites (see Fishkin, Rohrbach, & Johnson, 1997). Ferraro (1996) argues that women's overall heightened fears of victimization stem from a profound daily terror of sexual assault. The more that women constrain their behaviors in an effort to avoid sexual assault, the more they fear the possibility. Thus, the ongoing terrors of victimization, lodged in racial, class, and/or gendered assault, hover in the minds and souls of women across racial and ethnic groups.

The literature on personal experience with and witnessing of domestic violence suggests astonishingly high rates of both fear and actual cumulative violence for girls and women, with serious consequences (see A. Browne & Bassuk, 1997; Richie, 1996; for counterarguments, see Pearson, 1997).

Turning to domestic violence nationally, a full 60% of women killed in the United States have been killed by a husband or boyfriend; 25% of female psychiatric patients who attempt suicide are victims of domestic violence; 85% of women in substance abuse programs have experienced domestic violence; between 40% (Castelano, 1997) and 63% (A. Browne & Bassuk, 1997) of New York's homeless families are fleeing abuse at home; and over 70% of women entering the New York State prison system have had a history of physical and/or sexual abuse (New York State Department of Corrections [NYSDOC], 1997).

Given the depth of evidence of gendered victimization, it is remarkable that a plethora of social psychological studies points to the following consistent finding: When girls and women are violated by men (through sexual harassment, domestic violence, or rape), the attributional questions nevertheless hover around the woman. In a clever study of sexual harassment, Roberts (in Fine, Genovese, Ingersoll, Macpherson, & Roberts, 1996) provided female students with the following vignette of sexual harassment: A female student enters the office of a male faculty member in the evening to discuss a grade. The professor closes the door and tries to kiss her. Students who responded to the case study were primarily female and included White, African American, Latino, and "other" students. Instead of simple accountability measures, participants were asked to generate three questions for the hypothetical victim and three questions for the hypothetical accused. Across 29 subjects, 84 questions were asked of the woman/victim and 84 of the male/harasser. Roberts found that the focus of the questions for the woman/victim differed enormously from the focus of the questions subjects asked of the man/harasser.

Over 75% of the questions posed to the woman/victim focused on her *behavior:* What did you wear? Why did you visit his office? Have you filed a complaint before? Why didn't you push him away? In contrast, 47% focused on the man's behavior, and 28% targeted his *social status,* that is, the broader context of his life: Are you married? How long have you taught? Do you work well with students? Do you have children? In contrast, only 5% of the questions posed to the woman asked about her social status.

Roberts (in Fine et al., 1996) concluded that the women were searching for behavioral explanations for male violence in the woman. They fixed their gaze squarely on the woman and, in particular, on her behavior. The participants were much less interested in the man's motives and much more interested in gathering information about the social circumstances that might "explain away" his behavior. The eye of blame focused on the woman, with little attention to male accountability (see Fine et al., 1996, p. 140).

Scores of studies repeat these finding: Women who charge men with violence are more often than not held accountable for that same violence. The men are, with surprising frequency, not seen as accountable (for an important exception, see A.J. Stewart & Maddren, 1997). H.C. Sinclair and Bourne (1998) report, "The percentage of reported rapes that result in a conviction has been estimated to be as low as 2.5% . . . and as high as 19.85%. . . . Most authorities agree however that the conviction rate for forcible rape is well below that of other violent crimes" (p. 576). They continue, "Most rape cases are classified as 'unfounded' by police, and therefore dropped, e.g., 92% of all rapes reported in 1992. Once a rape case reaches the court, 'not guilty' is the most typical verdict reached. In 1992, more than 8% of rape reports made it to trial, but only 3.6% warranted a conviction" (p. 576). H.C. Sinclair and Bourne attribute the low conviction rates to the broad-based acceptance of rape "myths," citing a "comprehensive 10 year study of juries in Indianapolis by LaFree (1989) which found that preestablished beliefs in such myths correlated with a verdict more reliably than any objective evidence presented at trial" (p. 576).

Convinced that rape myths are likely to discredit women in rape trials, H.C. Sinclair and Bourne (1998) were concerned that not-guilty verdicts—the vast majority of rape case decisions—serve to reinforce three rape myths: that most rape accusations should not be believed, that most victims are not credible, and that most defendants are not guilty. These authors predicted that not-guilty verdicts would both reflect and create public opinion. Testing this hypothesis in a jury simulation study, they presented subjects with a case in which a defendant was found not guilty, guilty, or "no information about the verdict." Attitudes Toward Rape Myth scores rose significantly after a not-guilty verdict and dropped after a guilty verdict, but only for men. Deploying a just-world model, female subjects, regardless of verdict, sought to distance themselves from the victim. Thus, women, more than men, sought to distinguish themselves from the victim.

In contrast to the H.C. Sinclair and Bourne (1998) study, Dexter, Linz, Penrod, and Saunders (1997), in an ethically very troubling study of violent pornography and its effects on victim blame, found evidence for the defensive attribution effect. In this study, women attributed lower levels of responsibility to "similar" victims and higher levels to "dissimilar" victims. This finding suggests that the race and class of a victim may affect jurors' ratings such that poor and working-class women, as well as women of color, may be more likely to be blamed than White women if middle-class and White women are doing the rating.

Ullman (1997) conducted a study in which women reported on the social reactions to their experiences of sexual assault. Ullman found greater attribution of responsibility to rape victims by male observers for victims of date rape, victims who are sexually active, victims who are less respected, victims who were nonresisting, victims who consumed alcohol prior to the assault, and victims who engaged in nontraditional gendered behavior. In a path analysis, negative social reactions (e.g., self-reports of being treated differently, having someone else take control, distraction) were significantly related to increased incidence of psychological symptoms and lower rates of recovery in the women. Ullman writes, "Reactions of victim blame were related to poorer victim recovery . . . whereas those who reported being believed had better current self-rated recovery" (p. 520).

In addition to the literature on *gender* and *attribution*, there are a set of studies on *gender attitudes* and attributions of blame in situations of violence against women. The trends in this literature are reviewed by Caron and Carter (1997), who find that women are less accepting of rape than men; are more likely to see women as innocent when victimized; are more likely to view rape as an extension of masculinity; and are less tolerant of rapists. Beyond gender, however, and perhaps even more important, for both men and women attitudes of egalitarianism correlate with intolerance of rape. Of particular relevance to our earlier discussion of the unequal distribution of domestic responsibilities, Caron and Carter find that nonegalitarian attitudes about parenting roles predict attributions of blame toward female victims. The inequitable division of responsibility at home noted above may be related to the broad-based tendency to blame female victims.

In a related vein, a number of studies point to the same conclusions regarding the power of rape myths: A person's gender may not be a strong predictor of victim blame in rape studies, but rape myth acceptance is. Krahe (1988) states, "It is not male attitudes but stereotypic rape myths held across the genders that have to be changed in the social perception of victims of rape" (p. 57). Krahe finds that men and women who endorse stereotypic ideas about rape are more likely to blame women in hypothetical rape scenarios, and are particularly likely to blame the victim when she engages in "role-discrepant" behaviors. Shotland and Goodstein (1983) found a similar pattern in their study of rape attributions. Although these researchers report no sex-related differences, they too find that "attitudes toward women" are significant predictors of victim blame, and that in circumstances of low force and late onset of protest, women victims are viewed as more responsible for the assault than in circumstances of high force and early onset of protest.

Beyond gender and gender attitudes, there is a small literature on *cultural variation* of blame and responsibility. For instance, Heaven, Connors, and Pretorius (1998) found that the culture of the subjects is a stronger predictor of victim blame than victim characteristics. For example, White South Africans are significantly more likely to blame the victim than Australian respondents. White South Africans also scored higher on the Just World Scale. National histories of injustice and oppression may help to create a cultural view that disproportionately fixes responsibility onto (or off of) victims of social injustice.

Turning from *victim blame* to *self-blame,* we note Janoff-Bulman's pioneering work (1979), which distinguished characterological self-blame (with the most adverse long-term consequences) from behavioral self-blame (which may be a way for a woman to resume a sense of control over her life circumstances). Challenging the then widely held assumption that self-blame is maladaptive and predictive of poor psychological outcomes over time, Janoff-Bulman demonstrated that "the self-blame in which most rape victims engage may represent a control maintenance strategy, a functional response to a traumatic event" (p. 1807). Since that time, researchers have been trying to explain the persistent finding of self-blame by women and men who have endured social injustice, violence, and/or traumatic accidents. C. Davis, Lehman, Silver, Wortman, and Ellard (1996) documented a pervasive tendency for respondents (men and women with spinal cord injuries) to self-attribute personal blame. Respondents tend to view their blame in terms of "self-implicating perceptions of avoidability" (p. 564). Given that avoidability and ratings of blame were found to be highly correlated among these respondents, C. Davis et al. see avoidability as an important forward-looking motivation contributing to elevated ratings of self-blame.

Ironically orthogonal to the literature on self-blame, another finding has begun to emerge across studies: A substantial proportion of girls and women refuse to cast themselves as victims, even after they have been victimized. Following on the heels of Crosby et al.'s (Crosby, Pulfall, Snyder, O'Connell, & Walen, 1989) well-documented finding of the "denial of personal disadvantage," L. Phillips (2000), in a study of sexual violence against girls and women, reports that the young women in her sample who reported experiences that fit the legal definition of date rape overwhelmingly refused to classify these experiences as date rape. When asked how they would define it if this same experience happened to a friend, most of these women did then agree to classify the experience as a date rape. Phillips concludes that these women, largely White and middle class, actively exempt themselves from the category of victim. They reframe their personal experiences as explicitly not violent, not abusive, and not unjust. If a woman considers *their* relationship and, in particular, *his* pleasure, to be *her* responsibility, then she may go out of her way to avoid claims of discrimination, violence, or rape. She does this, Phillips suggests, not only because she blames herself and she seeks to control the future (although both of these motivations are certainly operating). In addition, however, she fights the category of victim because she feels broadly responsible for the well-being of her partner and their relationship. To grieve or complain would be to reveal *her own* failings.

Blackman (1989), in a study of domestic abuse among middle-class suburban residents, finds, like L. Phillips (2000), an eerie distancing in the narratives of women who have been victimized by intimate violence. Blackman theorizes women's refusal to see themselves as victims, their commitment to tell the story from "his" perspective, and, often, their denial of histories of violence to be evidence of abuse, not counterevidence. Psychological inconsistencies narrated by women surviving in unjust contexts may be seen as evidence of the psychological torture they have endured, rather than challenges to assertions of abuse (see Bertram, 1998).

And yet, though speaking out, refusing blame, and protesting are profoundly important, Pamela Reid (1993) has asked about poor women, "If a woman cries in the forest, and no one listens, does she make a sound?" This question takes us to women's third responsibility: After care and blame, there comes silence.

RESPONSIBILITY AS SILENCE: ON KEEPING SECRETS

Speaking secrets is never easy. In many cultures it is considered bad form because secrets stigmatize families and community, separate one from loved ones, and leave bad impressions. . . . I address the politics of comfort and the revelations of discomfort that permeate our Chicana feminist discussions. I am not entirely convinced that revealing secrets or describing them is a good strategy or even necessary, but I feel that if we are to change the institutions . . . in this society, spaces need to exist for new dialogues born in feminist praxis, women of color discussions. (Gonzalez, 1998, p. 46)

Inspired by Gonzalez (1998) and borrowing from Baker Miller (1976), we extend our analysis of responsibility to recognize that a substantial part of women's work is not only to know and oil the workings of unjust social arrangements, but to remain mute, seemingly complicit, in these arrangements.

At home, work, and on the streets, women's job is to soothe—at least publicly—the tattered edges of patriarchal, racialized, sexualized (Espin, 1996), and classed arrangements. We know from feminist investigations that women are nestled not only inside relationships but precisely inside the most contradictory moments of social arrangements. Indeed, it is often women's work to be stuffed inside such spots and to testify that no contradiction exists (D. Smith, 1987). Ironically, women are then often blamed or viewed as complicit, as facilitators of injustice, or "willing." Wives are not supposed to give away the secret of male dependence, although they have plenty of evidence; secretaries are not supposed to tell about male incompetence, affairs, or the incoherence they make presentable; lesbian mothers are not supposed to "flaunt" their sexualities, lest they risk losing their children (Nestle, 1983); mistresses are not supposed to tell about the contradictions inside heterosexuality, monogamy, and promises of marriage; women with disabilities are not supposed to expose social obsessions with attractiveness and illusions of life-long independence and health; prostitutes are not supposed to tell about the contradiction of intimacy and sexuality; daughters are not to speak of incest; and maids or domestics are not supposed to talk about the world of paid work and family life under advanced capitalism (Fine & Gordon, 1991).

Major and Forcey (1985) conducted a set of studies in which they and colleagues determined that women are likely to be silent—that is, neither notice nor grieve injustice in the form of gendered pay discrepancies—when they compare their outcomes to "similar others," that is, other underpaid women. In the "absence of social comparison standards, women paid themselves less than men for comparable or better work relative to men and said that less money was fair pay. Conversely, when paid a fixed amount of money and asked to do as much work as they thought was fair for the amount paid, women worked longer, did more work, and compared more correct work than men" (Major, cited in Steil, 1999, p. 38).

Crosby (1982) has collected data that confirm this pattern of seeming complacency, denial, and silence. Crosby finds that although wives bear disproportionate responsibility for childbearing and domestic labor, they speak little in the way of grievance. "Even though employed wives did twice as much work at home as their husbands they were no less satisfied" (Crosby, cited in Steil, 1999, p. 41). Biernat and Wortman (1991) also found that among financially successful women who had primary responsibility for children and housework, fewer than 25% indicated that their husband did too little. In her review, Steil (1999) suggests that women's "lack of grievance reflects women's limited sense of entitlement to compare their own outcomes to those of men" (p. 45). The labors of silence, however, come at a cost, as we see below with women who do not feel entitled to grieve even about domestic violence.

Fine and Weis (1998) conducted a large-scale oral history project with 156 poor and working-class White, African American, and Latino men and women living in urban poverty. They found important race and ethnic distinctions in how women respond to domestic violence, in particular, the extent to which they kept it a secret. Women across racial and ethnic groups, with terrifying consistency, described vivid, vicious stories of childhood and adult domestic abuse. However, though experiences of violence were common across ethnicities, their responses to the violence varied dramatically by race and ethnicity. White women had the lowest rates of having ever told anyone about the violence—even though their rates of experiencing domestic violence were as high as Latinas and higher than African Americans in this sample. In this study, White women had significantly fewer orders of protection, fewer times in which they had called the police, sought refuge in a battered women's shelter, threw the batterer out of their home, or alerted family or friends about the violence. Instead, they "coped." They put up with the violence because "I was ashamed," or "There's nothing I can do about it," or "That's what men do to their wives." These women did not necessarily blame themselves for the violence, but they felt it was their duty to assure peace in their homes and were ashamed when that peace was violated.[2] Latinas, also shamed, quietly exited their homes with children in hand, hoping to find safer spaces to raise their family. In sharp contrast to the White women and the Latinas, African American women in this sample, for the most part, did not feel responsible to represent their homes as safe or tranquil or to camouflage male violence. Deeply committed to finding safe spaces for their children, these women were nevertheless eager to speak aloud, quite publicly, about violence they had endured and their strategies for fighting back or leaving. The African American women in the sample reported securing many orders of protection, visits to shelters, throwing men out of the house, fighting back, and alerting brothers and fathers who would then exact revenge. All of these women expressed what Ruddick (1989) calls a "duty to protect," and therefore a "duty to resist": to find peace and not to remain silent in the face of male violence.

Because we know much about the press for silence, we also know the enormous price women can pay for speaking. In an oral history with Stella Seliok, a migrant woman from rural Papua New Guinea and Tabubil, Polier (1998) writes:

> A resolute *bikhet* (recalcitrant female) . . . , Stella refused marriage to the Golgobip man selected as a spouse and eventually fled the village. . . . the most difficult story for Stella to tell is that of her gang rape in girlhood. The narrative moments of this telling were marked by ellipses, denial and evident regret. Stella initially told the story of the patrol officer without recounting her rape. "It didn't happen," she told me once; "It happened," she said later, "and I could not stop it." The fuller story emerged over time, and despite Stella's disgust with kinsmen and a rational representation of herself as their victim, she was laden with guilt for the retributive violence of her rape. . . . She has simultaneously opposed and internalized secular and ecclesiastical representations of herself as a *rabis meri* (a corrupt, rubbish woman). . . . Stella's social silencing—her reputation and dismissal as a bikhet and a rabis meri by members of her ethnic group—is an act of violence to which she repeatedly submits and resists. (pp. 522–523)

Meredith Tax (1999) argues that feminism as a global social movement, in each of its local forms, has emerged as a voice, the critical voice for women, against patriarchal cultural structures. As such, it is a primary target for emergent cultural movements. She suggests that "nationalist, communalist, and religious fundamentalist social movements have surfaced all over the world, moving into the power vacuum created as local elites have been overwhelmed by the new global financial ruling class" (p. 24). Naming, for instance, the Taliban, the Serbian nationalist movement, Islamic fundamentals, the Israeli settler movement in the West Bank, and the militantly patriarchal Christian groups, including Operation Rescue, Tax takes the position that these movements have "in common a desire for racial, ethnic and religious homogeneity; an apocalyptic vision of purification through bloodshed, and a patriarchal view of women and families . . . [at root, such movements seek the] control of women" (p. 24). As a consequence, Tax continues and we agree, feminism must be silenced, with cultural movements targeting and censoring feminist intellectuals and organizers who "stir up the others" (p. 24).

With every story of repression, we also know, over time, that silences are—and must be—reversible, even if such organizing is risky. In a fascinating action research project designed to "break the silence" around domestic violence and educate a full community, Fawcett, Heise, Isita-Espejel, and Pick (1999), working in Iztacalco, a low-income community on the outskirts of Mexico City, engaged community women as change agents, working collectively through focus groups, individual interviews, and hypothetical cases of abused women. Fawcett et al. note that

---

[2] Note that "Shalom be it" or "peace in the home" is an argument given by orthodox rabbis to women who complain about violent or abusive husbands (Unger, 1999, personal communication).

women initially did not see "unequal power relations" as the root cause of domestic violence. Indeed, some girls and women indicated the opposite:

> Violence was an expected consequence of women not having complied with their (gender) roles, thus implying a sense of responsibility on their part. Male participants blamed men's violence on external factors. . . . Male denial of responsibility has been documented in research from other countries. . . . And it is closely related to the self-blame that many battered women suffer. Our fictitious character, Rosita, was therefore not only considered responsible for provoking violence but also for not setting limits, not being able to communicate with her partner and not being able to "make him behave." (p. 44)

Because these researchers unearthed a strong "prejudice about responsibility for violence against women" (p. 44) and a strong sense, from abused women, that violence was to be considered a "private matter" (p. 45), they designed an intervention based on peer outreach, small-scale media, popular theater, and other special events. With their community campaign, they trained a cadre of community women, especially mothers, to provide support. In addition, they generated posters, leaflets, buttons, "photo stories," and community events designed to:

> Shift the community perception of domestic violence from a private problem that should not be interfered with to a community problem that is the responsibility of all . . . to reduce victim blaming of women and encourage more useful support responses on the part of family and friends to women living in violent relationships, and . . . to help individual women move . . . to action by advertising the types of violence, the elements of the new domestic violence laws and where to go for help. (pp. 47–48)

Across the studies in discrimination and violence against women, there is an understated but consistent theme: Girls and women of color are more likely to speak out against and challenge social (domestic and/or workplace) injustice, to go public with their outrage. In contrast, White girls and women are more likely to remain silent, internalize blame (Poran, 1998), or, as Crosby (1982) has found in the workplace, to "deny personal disadvantage" (p. 79). If women learn about inequities case by case rather than in the aggregate, they are less likely to be outraged (Crosby, Pufall, Snyder, O'Connell, & Whalen, 1989; Major & Forcey, 1985). If women see their rejection as personal rather than as discrimination, they are less likely to complain (K.L. Dion, 1975). If women feel responsible for the well-being of the organization or family, they are less likely to protest publicly. Silence thus operates as a collective self-fulfilling prophecy. Silence keeps women from knowing other women's experiences with discrimination, violence, and harassment, constituting an aggregate experience. Silence buries a history of oppression and laminates the status quo.

FIGHTING BACK, BREAKING THE SILENCE, AND RESISTANCE: WOMEN'S NEWEST RESPONSIBILITY

There is a growing (wo)mandate that may be cast as the newest responsibility for women: to speak out against social injustice; to resist assault; to report instances of harassment; to flee abuse; to challenge when inequity prevails. Although we have much sympathy for this move (and at least Michelle is implicated in her writings for such resistance), we worry about foisting yet another responsibility, the responsibility for challenging social injustice, onto individual women.

FIGHTING BACK/RESISTING SEXUAL ASSAULT

A substantial literature now confirms that, in the face of sexual assault, active resistance is the most effective strategy for minimizing adverse effects (Murzynski & Degelman, 1996). This oft-repeated press for resistance deserves a cautious reconsideration. Ullman (1997) reviews this literature and provides just such reflection on this field. Ullman begins her analysis with the well-confirmed finding that "completed rape victims experience more psychological problems than attempted rape victims . . . and that completed rape victims whose assaults involved additional physical injury and weapons are significantly more likely to suffer from post traumatic stress disorder" (p. 178). She notes, however, that Fischhoff, Furby, and Morgan (1987) have found forceful resistance strategies to correlate with more physical injury. Ullman worries that "evidence concerning the effectiveness of resistance combined with societal expectations that women force-fully resist rape may continue to shift responsibility for rape prevention onto women and perpet-uate societal blame and victim self-blame for victims unable to resist attack" (p. 182).

White, Donat, and Bondurant (this volume) found that resistance strategies such as running away and screaming were used less often in acquaintance rapes than in stranger rapes. As L. Phillips (2000) has found, women are less able to classify an intimate/known experience as a date rape, much less resist such a rape, when the assailant is known than when he is a stranger. Thus, it is understandable that Finkelhor and Yllo (1982), in their investigation of marital rape, found that women tended not to resist; these women did not resist out of fear of further anger-ing their husbands, their desire not to terrify their children, and their hopes for getting through the violence as quickly as possible. Ullman (1997) concludes that forceful resistance may be the most effective rape avoidance strategy, but she also insists on a much more cautious, situation-specific understanding of the conditions surrounding any particular assault: the possibilities for any potential positive as well as negative consequences of forceful resistance.

BREAKING THE SILENCE ON WHITE MALE VIOLENCE

Fine et al. (1996) found that in a series of four sexual harassment/rape cases in which individual girls/women actively resisted and confronted elite White males as students, daughters, and strangers, these same women paid an incredible price. Powerful institutions within which the men worked or lived—including universities, schools, police forces, churches, and government bodies—defended the men and attacked the young women (see Lefkowitz, 1997). Fine et al. write:

> Across the scenes, about the time when the institutions began to protect the men, we heard a surpris-ing but consistent shift in the plots. In the beginning, across the scenes, a young, assaulted woman tells another woman—teacher, counselor, therapist, mother—about abuse at the hands of a respected, White elite boy/man. The woman who hears the story may decide to do nothing, to deny or bury the story, to protect the man. . . . She may decide to carry the story to a "legitimate" institutional audi-ence. The carrier expects a sympathetic hearing. She is shocked to find little sympathy and not much of a hearing. (p. 138)

In these four cases, very differently crafted, the young women were consistently recast as the violators of an otherwise peaceful community, whereas the young and older men were portrayed as victims of the young women making accusations. The authors continue:

> Soon thereafter the institution discovers a local storyteller who narrates a revised text. Enter the shift. The . . . shift in blame sounds like "He's not to blame—she is." . . . [In a more elite setting] the shift moves from blame to tragedy. A simple changing of the subject maneuvers the focus onto the man [and off the girl/woman]. Sad tragedy, but he needs his job. What about his reputation? What about his wife and children? What about his health? What about all the good he's done? The conse-quences to the girl/woman, with the accountability of the male, are gently escorted off-stage. (p. 138)

These girls and women resisted, and *they were cast as the violators of school/family/community peace.*

FLEEING THE ABUSE: RESISTANCE AND DOMESTIC ASSAULT

The pressure to resist can also be found in the battered women's literature; the social mandate is that battered women resist by fleeing or by getting the man arrested. With profound despair, we feel obliged to quote from the work of Castelano (1997): "In one study of spousal homicide, over one half of the male defendants were separated from their victims. . . . In another study in Philadelphia and Chicago . . . almost 25% of the women killed by male partners were separated and divorced from the men who killed them; another 29% were attempting to end the relationship when they were killed" (p. 11). In addition, a national comparison of the homicide rates between the years 1976–1979 and 1980–1984 indicate an increase in the killing of women partners after separation in 72% of the states (Jones, 1990, cited in Castelano, 1997). The evidence suggests that women may be more vulnerable to male violence if they leave than if they stay. L. Walker (1999) reminds us, "Many batterers continue to harass, stalk, and harm the woman long after she has left him, sometimes even resulting in someone's death. . . . in one U.S. study, 70% of the reported injuries from domestic violence occurred after the separation of the couple" (p. 24). L. Walker also speaks to the consequences of mandatory arrest policies: "Many working in the field believe that an arrest and incarceration for domestic violence is the most successful technique for getting violent men to stop their abuse. . . . Others have found that arrest can increase physical violence in some cases, particularly when the man does not have good community ties or a need for social conformity" (p. 25).

WOMEN WHO BREAK THE LAW: WHEN CARE, BLAME, SILENCE, AND RESISTANCE COLLIDE

In this section, we would like to make our discussion of women's responsibility—for care, for blame, for silence, and for resistance—more concrete. To do so, we enter, as Blackman (1994) invites us to, a room frequently overlooked by social scientists, feminist or otherwise; it is a courtroom, and the main characters in this setting are the child, his or her abandoning, neglectful, or otherwise irresponsible mother, and the prosecutor, defender, social worker, and judge. It is, as Blackman suggests, a room where the abandoned child is taken and the mother is either left alone or, alternatively, imprisoned. This location offers us a glimpse at the ways female responsibility is fixed and defined—the ways responsibility is rewarded and affirmed as well as the ways female behavior deemed irresponsible becomes punishable by law.

There exist social sites where the beliefs and myths of popular culture(s) and those of politics, history, and even social science meet, mix together, clash, become hybridized, and may even codify into something more solid than myth or belief—into law or policy. We look, then, to the courtroom as a place where cultural conceptions of responsibility are contested and defined and where violations of responsibility mandates are sanctioned and punished.

We look to the site of the courtroom and the event of the trial to help us clarify notions of women's responsibility and to provide examples of its power. We do so by examining cases where responsibility is specifically (and publicly) questioned and assigned: in cases where women/mothers fail to protect their children. Whether these women fail to protect their children from violence, from the effects of maternal drug addiction, or from neglect, it will become clear from these examples that in each case, regardless of the details, women, and mothers in particular, carry the burden of responsibility. When things go wrong, women, especially poor women and women of color, are to blame, and sometimes they are implicated in surprising ways. We have examined four such cases, briefly described here and considered more in depth throughout this section. These stories of failure to protect, we hope, will serve as concrete examples of what happens to women who violate social mandates for their behavior and cultural prescriptions for female responsibility.

CASES OF FAILURE TO PROTECT

The stories of failure to protect discussed here reflect a variety of types of events and situations. For instance, the first case is that of Vickie Gray and involves the abuse of her daughter at the hands of her second husband and her own eventual arrest and imprisonment for failing to protect her child from his violence (V. Kincaid, 1993; Runquist, 1992a, 1992b, 1992c, 1992d; S. Wade, 1993; "Mom Gets Jail in Abuse Case," 1993). A similar case is that of Sarah Snodie; it involves the murder of her son by her boyfriend and her eventual arrest for failure to protect, physical abuse, and neglect (D. Cole, 1997; Rutledge, 1997). A third example comes from the story of Myrtle Lacey, a crack addict, who was arrested and charged with manslaughter after her newborn son died of malnutrition (Bryan, 1992; B. Smith, 1992a, 1992b). Finally, a fourth case involves the story of Michiko Kamiyama, a single mother arrested and convicted of child abuse when she left her 8-year-old daughter home alone while she worked (Parsons, 1998; Pasco, 1998).

These cases come from a vast and still growing literature; failure-to-protect laws now encompass all sorts of events involving children left alone at home, children who are born under the influence of alcohol, children who suffer from heart disease due to obesity, and children murdered by an abusive parent. In our examination of this literature, we are reminded again of Blackman's

(1994) urging us to enter this room, to acknowledge and include the lives of these previously ignored women in our scholarship and to recognize the ways their up-to-now absence has distorted
"our vision of the landscape of problems that women face" (p. 150).

Cases of Failure to Protect and Themes of Responsibility

The cases of women who have been charged with crimes such as failure to protect make visible
the mandate on women to *care about* and *care for* the other people in their lives. The women across
all of these cases are punished, in essence, for not caring. In addition, however, they make clear
the paradoxical responsibility women have to resist violence in their own lives and homes and
their responsibility to maintain the myths and idealized images (i.e., keep the secrets) of the family. Finally, these stories underscore the ways in which women are held accountable for the violence directed at them as well as at their own children. Let us look, then, at several themes of
responsibility that emerge from our consideration of the literature thus far and cases of failure to
protect. What do these cases reveal about the responsibility of women?

Resources Count.   The first theme in the literature and across available case studies is that
those without resources are assigned more responsibility and more blame—and are scrutinized
more thoroughly—than those who have the means to buy privacy or even the ability to pay others
to be responsible (Blackman, 1990, 1994; Chamallas, 1992; Fine & Weis, forthcoming; Fraser, 1993;
Roberts, 1997). For instance, Fine and Weis suggest that the standards for "good mothering" occur
"in a particular context; a context of money, time and excess. In the absence of these conditions, it
is far too easy to 'discover' bad mothering" (p. 5). The state and the media do not scrutinize elite
or middle-class mothers or fathers, they suggest, but instead focus their attention squarely on
"the least equipped and least resourced women, holding them to standards of mothering that
most of us could not and do not achieve" (p. 5).

The assumption and the acceptance of White middle-class standards for mothering means that
much of the mothering that goes on in families in poor communities is labeled deficient, neglectful, deprived, or even abusive. Roberts (1997) states that poor women and women of color are "the
least likely to obtain adequate prenatal care, the most vulnerable to government monitoring, and
the least able to conform to the white middle-class standard of motherhood" (p. 127). Blackman
(1994) writes similarly: "Those without the resources to ensure that their rights are protected are
the most likely to be held individually responsible when they act . . . destructively or self-
destructively" (p. 148).

Poor women and women of color, furthermore, are the primary targets of governmental control
(Fine & Weis, 1998; Roberts, 1997). Wary of systemic intrusion and aware of potential punishment,
they may stay away from the very agencies that exist to provide them with much-needed assistance. Welfare agencies, health care clinics, drug treatment centers, and the like, while ostensibly
offering help to those in need also act as primary gateways to increased state surveillance and
even potential punishment. Roberts writes that poor women are afraid to obtain health care (prenatal or postnatal) because they are afraid of the scrutiny and surveillance that accompanies such
assistance. But shying away from these agencies brings with it a backlash: Women are then held
individually responsible when conditions of poverty, addiction, and lack of resources produce
tragedy. Similarly, though some programs do offer drug and alcohol treatment to expectant mothers, for every one woman who has been helped by such programs there exist multiple stories of
prosecution, babies taken away at birth, and jail for mothers who abuse drugs or alcohol during
pregnancy.

Myrtle Lacey is one such story. Twenty-seven years old, addicted to crack, and homeless, Myrtle
gave birth to her son, Damon, in conditions most would consider deprived (Bryan, 1992). When
Damon tested positive for traces of cocaine in his blood, Family Services was contacted. The agency
determined that the Lacey home (Myrtle's mother's house) was appropriately safe, and the social
worker who visited the home twice after his birth found no reason to suspect that Damon's health
was in jeopardy. In fact, she wrote in her report that the home was well cared for and that the family seemed genuinely concerned for the child's welfare (B. Smith, 1992b). At 8 weeks old, however,
Damon died of malnutrition; he was said to be emaciated and had lost one pound since arriving
home from the hospital (Bryan, 1992). Myrtle Lacey was charged with manslaughter, with her

addiction to cocaine and her uncertain living conditions cited as the reasons she had *allowed* her child to starve to death. That perhaps other institutions—or social conditions—were at least *as* responsible for the death of her child was a possibility that went unexplored and unquestioned.

When does the legal system relieve women of responsibility for failure-to-protect cases? Blackman (1990) suggests that the response of the criminal justice system to cases of maternal failure to protect is influenced by racist, classist, and sexist assumptions, with women, particularly poor women of color, being blamed and held responsible most often. She cites the case of Hedda Nussbaum as an example of race and class bias operating to protect a White middle-class professional woman from charges of child murder. Despite the fact that she had no health insurance, Nussbaum was sent via court order to a private inpatient psychiatric facility, and it was eventually determined that she lacked the capacity to protect her daughter from the abuse inflicted by her husband, Joel Steinberg. She was never indicted. Blackman states that the difference between the treatment Nussbaum received at the hands of the court and that received by poor women or women of color (such as Myrtle Lacey) is remarkable and worth underlining. Resources, then, whether in the form of financial assets or race/class privilege, appear again and again in both the literature and in actual case studies as affecting cultural/legal assignments of female (and very likely, male) responsibility and blame.

Be a Good Girl.   A second theme that appears in much of the literature we have reviewed and that emerges strikingly in the case studies selected is that women who do not conform to traditional gender-role expectations are deserving of punishment. The ideal woman in U.S. society today is constructed out of better/worse dichotomies; for instance, she is White, not of color; she is middle class, not poor; she is nurturing and mothering, not self-satisfying; she is passive, not aggressive; she is feminine, not masculine (Roberts, 1997). These oppositional dichotomies not only perpetuate the division between male-public and female-private, they set up and make possible the splits between ideal and nonideal, good and bad, deserving and nondeserving, exonerated and punished—and they translate into widely held cultural beliefs about responsibility and culpability that guide the legal system today. Woe to the woman who does not match the cultural standard for a "good" woman, for whether her failure is due to lack of resources, ethnicity/skin color, country of origin, mental/physical illness, or political choice, she will be considered suspect, and her actions, her behavior, and her intentions will be scrutinized even more carefully. The nonconforming woman is seen as disruptive; she upsets the social order and the community-at-large (Fernandes, 1997).

This theme of role conformity runs throughout the literature on women and responsibility. It is a common finding in the important research on victims of rape and the successful prosecution/conviction of male perpetrators of rape and physical abuse or battery (Caron & Carter, 1997). Krahe (1988), for instance, states that victims of crimes such as rape who engage in behaviors that do not conform to the traditional female role—he calls these "provocative" behaviors (hitchhiking, for example, or drinking)—are assigned more blame (and responsibility) than victims who are "nonprovocative" or who behave in a manner that is role-conforming. He concludes that attributions of blame or responsibility toward a victim of a crime are partly made based on the gender-role-conforming or -nonconforming characteristics of the victim.

Wesson (1992) suggests that actions such as hitchhiking, drinking, going to bars without male companionship, having sex outside of marriage, or even entering the car or house of the accused offender willingly make up a list of behaviors classified as "victim nonconformity," and these circumstances or contextual factors have a tremendous impact on the decisions made by the arresting officers, the judge, and the eventual jury. The ways women appear to be nonconforming to gender-role expectations, she argues, override in importance the medical evidence, the evidence that the rapist had a weapon, and even eyewitness testimony. She concludes: "For police, judges, and especially jurors, the behavior of the victim of an alleged sex crime, particularly the degree to which she succeeded or failed in conforming to gender expectations, was an important determinant of their judgment as to whether she had been the victim of a crime" (p. 17). As Polakow states (cited in Fine & Weis, 1998), the further women stray from the standards set by the patriarchal model, the more blamable, and therefore punishable, they become.

How do these notions of gender-role expectations and responsibility play out when we consider women defendants rather than victims? What happens when we take this theme with us into the room from which Blackman beckons? It appears that constructions of gender-appropriate behavior work in much the same way; if anything, role nonconformity plays an even more important part in the punishing of women who are considered criminal than in considering the blameworthiness of women who are the victims of crime. Female aggression, drug use, violence, neglect of mothering responsibilities—these are all qualities that differ even more dramatically from those characteristics of the ideal woman, and thus they become deviance of an even higher order. Wesson (1992) writes: "Violence . . . is perhaps even more incompatible with prevailing cultural images of femininity than nonconformity to conservative sexual behavior" (p. 21). According to Wesson, violent women are punished by jurors more severely than violent men. Their aggressive nature places them outside the standard of the ideal, reasonable woman; they become fringe characters, abhorrent and menacing.

We can see how a woman's failure to protect her child may become particularly punishable, especially when this failure to protect is framed as a woman's stepping outside gender expectations. The cultural ideal of the "good mother" is that the woman is always powerful, always present, and always nurturing (P. Davis, 1994). A good woman, furthermore, is also supposed to be a good mother (Walzer, 1996). A bad mother—*a bad woman*—is especially dangerous; she represents a direct threat to the social system and, as such, is condemned with particular vehemence.

Vickie Gray was subjected to this special form of severe censure when her behavior was seen as violating gender-role expectations about good women and good mothers. Unable to (or unwilling to) understand the effect of Vickie's suffering at the hands of her husband, and unable to grasp how much her terror and fear of her husband had kept her from acting quickly to prevent the abuse of her 2-year-old daughter, the judge at her sentencing stated that he could not understand how Vickie had ignored what he called "a mother's basic instinct" (S. Wade, 1993, p. 1–B) to help her child. A mother's instinct—a woman's instinct—for nurturing children is her responsibility above all else, despite the very real threat of further or accelerated violence. Vickie's responsibility becomes all the more clear when we recognize that her husband's fatherly instincts are never questioned or scrutinized. Although his actions were certainly believed to be punishable, he was not believed to have abdicated a unique responsibility by severely injuring his wife and stepdaughter. The obligation for nurturance and care was Vickie's alone.

Similarly, Michiko Kamiyama was punished with special severity when her life choices were seen as violating gender-role prescriptions for good mothers and good women. Making the decision, as many single mothers must everyday, to leave her 8-year-old daughter home alone for a few hours while she worked resulted in her arrest and conviction for child abuse (Pasco, 1998). During Michiko's sentencing hearing it was clear that, to most, her decision to leave 8-year-old Julie Ann alone when she was having a tantrum was perhaps a lapse in judgment but hardly a crime. However, it was her role-nonconforming job—she was a "bar singer"—that attracted the most attention (Parsons, 1998) and contributed to her eventual conviction and jail time. Let us underline this point: It was not her daughter's identification as a "latchkey child" that led to her conviction for abuse; indeed, the existence of children who stay home alone is now a common White, middle-class phenomenon. The real issue was Michiko's choice of job. Clearly operating within the case of Michiko Kamiyama as well as in the case of Vickie Gray is the notion that women who fail—by chance, by threat, or by circumstance—to conform to the idealized images of the good mother/good woman (whose privilege goes unquestioned) risk severe punishment in the event that things go wrong: when babysitters don't show up, when husbands threaten homicide.

Women Are Responsible for the "Staffing" and the "Policing" of the Household

Earlier in our discussion, we elaborated on women's special responsibility for care; women are believed to be primarily responsible for caring for and about their children, their aging relatives, their own husbands, and their homes. Walzer (1996) defines three categories of "invisible" mental labor. First, she suggests that women are the ones who worry about their children and other dependents. Worrying, she writes, is an expected part of being a good mother. Second, women are responsible for processing information; they are the ones to consult experts and obtain information when such knowledge is needed. Women are then responsible for conveying that information to the men in their lives. Walzer's third category of mental labor is most important for the third theme that emerges when we consider case studies of failure to protect. Women, she argues, are responsible for managing the household division of labor. They manage the babies and they manage the activities and behavior of the fathers. Women determine what jobs need to be done, and it is then their task to delegate effectively to get those jobs done. It is this third task of mental labor—management of the household-at-large—that is exposed when we pause to consider the cases of women who fail to protect their children. Women are assumed to be responsible for the household, for its maintenance and also for the tasks and behaviors of its inhabitants. When households erupt, it is the managers—women—who are then held accountable.

That women carry the task of household "management" is quite evident in the assumptions that underlie many cases of failure to protect. Indeed, when women fail to protect children from the abuse of husband or boyfriend, this duty to manage the private sphere of family and home—and by implication, to control the behavior of its occupants—becomes most visible.

When Sarah Snodie's son, Drake, was murdered by her boyfriend, Sarah herself was charged with four counts of child abuse. Donell McKennie, Sarah's boyfriend at the time, beat Sarah and then her son over a period of eight hours, during which time he shook the 17-month-old, hit him, threw him across the room, and poured chili powder into his mouth (D. Cole, 1997). Drake died of massive head trauma the next day. During her trial, Sarah reported that Donell had beaten her savagely as well. In addition, he had promised Sarah that he would kill Drake if the boy made noise while Donell took an afternoon nap. Fearing for her son's life as well as her own, Sarah struggled to keep her son from crying while Donell slept (Rutledge, 1997). At trial, the prosecutor claimed and the judge affirmed that Sarah was responsible for the death of her son. Her guilt, they reasoned, came from the fact that she had failed to notify the authorities or leave her home with her son. Sarah's fear had led her to neglect the needs of her baby. But Sarah was also charged because she had violated a basic (unspoken, perhaps, but powerful) female responsibility: that of controlling, of managing the behavior and the actions of other household members. She failed to effectively control the violence of her boyfriend; in our culture, the management of the household tasks, including the policing of violence, is a task consistently assigned to the women of the house.

Sarah, argued her lawyer, was 18 years old; she was frightened, she was isolated from family and friends, and she had been violently beaten. Though the court acknowledged these circumstances, at the same time, it reaffirmed her responsibility. Young, scared, and isolated, Sarah and women like her who fail to protect their children from violence are held accountable for the actions of husbands or boyfriends who are often much stronger and much more powerful than they. Their failure, then, is not *only* to protect their children. Rather, it is to effectively manage their homes and their coinhabitants. When the men in their lives become violent, the women who, either voluntarily or through force, renounce the cultural obligation to manage become punishable as well.

But failure-to-protect case studies expose more than a simple failure to manage. They make clear a hidden sociopolitical ideology. We have seen that, throughout the literature and implicated in the case studies of failure to protect, women carry much of the burden of managing the physical and psychological health of household members, whether they are children or other adults. Legal enactments of failure-to-protect charges, furthermore, seem to bear out Walzer's (1996) notions about the invisible work of household management. We are suggesting in addition, however, a third managing task: Women are required to become "police" and resist domestic violence and child abuse with force lest they be held accountable and responsible for the violence and abuse perpetrated by fathers or boyfriends. If men become violent (due, perhaps, to ineffective management), women bear the responsibility to resist that violence physically: to throw themselves between the abuser and the child at risk. The U.S. cultural imperative for motherhood to be linked with selflessness and self-sacrifice (P. Davis, 1994) means that women who fail to rescue or save their children from violence at the hands of other people are punishable by law.

That such an attempt at rescue, through physical force, would undoubtably fail matters not at all. It is the gesture—the overt semblance of protest—that counts. The absence of such a gesture is interpreted by the courts as indicating that the woman has not only failed as a household manager, she has failed as a household police officer as well. For instance, rather than seen as indicators of the severity of Donell's destructiveness, Sarah's efforts to keep her baby quiet while Donell slept were interpreted as collusion with, as acceptance of, his violence. Similarly, Vickie Gray's attempts to get her relatives to take her baby became interpreted by the courts as signs of abandonment and neglect rather than as a successful survival strategy. Male violence becomes invisible. These legal interpretations reveal cultural longings at the same time that they make visible social definitions of female responsibility. Under the law, women are required to protect as well as serve.

KEEPING SECRETS AND GUARDING FAMILIES

As U.S. society moves increasingly toward privatization, the ideal of the family is more and more vehemently idolized by the state (Fraser, 1993). A rhetoric of personal responsibility and individual accountability comes to dominate the social and political discourse. Fraser writes that under current conditions of Western capitalism, moral explanations (for poverty, for mental illness, for drug addiction, etc.) replace structural theories. We suggest that it is during these periods of conservatism that gatekeepers or guardians of cultural ideology—usually women—are particularly burdened and doubly threatened. Working under conditions of shifting resources and dwindling social services, women adhere even more strongly to the ethic of individualism and family lest they, their families, and communities be further penalized.

These cases of women who are accused of failing to protect their children reveal, then, this fourth theme of female responsibility: Women are responsible for maintaining socially and culturally held values and beliefs about the sanctity of the family, and they are responsible for keeping the injustices, ironies, and contradictions inherent in those beliefs secret. Social ideals related to families include the notion that families are loving, safe places, that families need and deserve privacy, and that families are entitled to be autonomous entities (Blackman, 1990). They include the belief that parents act in the best interests of and do not harm their children (McConnell, 1992). They reflect an assumption that husbands do not abuse wives and children do not abuse parents (Fine & Weis, 1998). They suggest a qualitative difference from the danger of the public sphere—"the street," for instance—and the sanctity and protection of the home (Fine & Weis, 1998; Pastor et al., 1996). They reaffirm the capitalist doctrine of the value of independence and the pathology of dependence (Blackman, 1990). These ideals, these myths of the family, are closely held and fiercely guarded. They are, furthermore, myths that are guarded by the state, which refuses to see the contradictions inherent in families, contradictions that would threaten to upend capitalist notions of responsibility for care and issues of privilege. They are protected, in addition, by the law, which acts to punish those whose lives perhaps call their assumptions into question. And they are guarded as well by the families themselves, particularly the women in them, who carry responsibility for managing and living within the incongruity of the "private" (understanding, as we do, the complicated nature of this term), hiding the secret that, in fact, families may be dangerous, violent, unhealthy places that stifle rather than enhance life.

That women bear the responsibility of keeping the "dirty laundry" of the family secret is especially obvious when we look at actual cases of women who have either failed or refused to do so. When women, by virtue of circumstance or desire, offer (or scream) alternative versions of the nature of the family—as violent, as incestuous, or as unsafe, for example—they have the potential to threaten the social order, shattering fragile yet closely held beliefs. These women either refuse to or cannot deny the incongruity of the law versus their experience. They expose cultural secrets and shame: Husbands are batterers, grandfathers are molesters, and family friends are potential kidnappers. The act of exposure marks "offending" women as threats, and, as with any threat to the social system, the state moves quickly through the law to punish the transgressor and reestablish the truth of social myths. Such punishment has the further effect of privatizing the family (Blackman, 1990), with the consequence being that women will most likely have to struggle even more mightily to keep the secrets that victimized them in the first place.

Certainly, the cases of Vickie Gray and Sarah Snodie partially demonstrate what happens to women who reveal the existence of terrorism in the home. Sadistic abuse, as implied by the story of Vickie Gray, can be a daily occurrence rather than an aberrant or bizarre event. Vickie could not keep the secret that many women live daily with violence, that abuse of horrific proportions can be a way of everyday life. And, once such a secret was exposed, the machinery of the state moved quickly to reestablish a social discourse of individual responsibility, swiftly sweeping away questions regarding the devastation of domestic violence and replacing them with legal definitions of maternal neglect and failure to protect. Among all of the other things for which Vickie was punished—for her failure to achieve a middle-class lifestyle, her deviance from traditional definitions of motherhood, and her inability to either effectively manage or physically resist her violent husband—Vickie is in addition punished for revealing a rupture, an incongruity that exists within the Western cultural ideal of the family as safe haven.

Similarly, the legal system rushed to label Michiko Kamiyama neglectful and abusive, focusing public attention and outrage on her individual lack of parenting skills (and inappropriate occupation) to cover the secret her case revealed: that cultural requirements for the preservation/protection of the family unit are almost inaccessible to poor, immigrant, single mothers who lack adequate resources for child care. Steering the eyes of the public away from the ways individualist, capitalist economies handicap poor families and focusing them squarely on questions of individual responsibility, the legal system effectively patched over larger social questions and made the inconsistency of cultural myths invisible—a secret once more.

As cultural presumptions about the entitlements and values of families continue to proliferate (and the social/structural resources/agencies for relief decline), women will be pushed more and more into guarding the secret of the paradox of the private realm. In a virtually uninterrupted circle, the increasing value of privacy will allow violent families to grow more violent (Blackman, 1990), while at the same time, the punishment of women who expose a violence they cannot manage essentially works to ensure the preservation of cultural secrets. Such punishment poses a challenge to the development of women's sense of critical consciousness and their potential to resist social institutions that oppress them.

CONCLUSIONS

At the intersection of race, class, and gender, we are called on to focus our gaze clearly on ways in which the apparatus of the state reinforces tidy notions of female responsibility. We have seen in the cases of Sarah Snodie, Vickie Gray, Myrtle Lacey, and Michiko Kamiyama that more than anything else, the explicitness and vividness of female responsibility belie the absence of accounts of male responsibility. Men are only rarely charged with failure to protect, failure to act, or failure to resist. Fathers are not often brought up on charges when their wives murder the children. The absence of such conceptions of male responsibility as well as the work of authors such as Blackman (1990) and Roberts (1997) on issues of responsibility, gender, race, and class underscore our first conclusion: that courts are racialized, classed, and gendered sites, and the decisions made within their parameters reflect race/class discrimination. The values and assumptions—indeed, the foundations—of the law comprise those of the dominant ruling class, and punishment, when meted out, falls most severely on those individuals who stand further and further outside the borders of White, middle-class patriarchy.

Our second conclusion is that women who are charged with breaches of responsibility—of, in this case, failure to protect—may "redeem" themselves, but to do so, they must, in essence, plug up the holes they revealed in the social order. They must return to the fold of "decent" civilization; they must reaffirm their femininity, deny the normalcy of violence and abuse, affirm their own individual responsibility, and promise never to reveal the conflicting nature of the family. Vickie Gray, for instance, speaks this language of reform and repentance. She says, "I'm going to make it up to her. I am going to finish my education so that I can get a good job and be able to care for my children and myself" (quoted in S. Wade, 1993). Michiko Kamiyama took classes in English and parenting so that she could better raise her child (Pasco, 1998). These "reformed" women learn the language of responsibility; they conform to White, middle-class expectations and they reaffirm cultural values. They re-present themselves, in a sense, as conforming, and thus nonthreatening, responsible women (Fernandes, 1997).

At the same time, however, we wish to recognize with hope that this return to the fold may not indicate complete acceptance of a racist, patriarchal social order. L. Gordon (1993) describes the ingenious ways women, faced with conservative, male, dominant political regimes, have of encoding family violence and affecting social change—methods that overturn laws indirectly and obliquely. Women, she writes, have had a long history of being able to rewrite oppression in ways that work toward its dismantling; as an example, she describes how women in the late 1800s redefined wife beating as an issue of chivalry and thus worked to delegitimize domestic abuse without directly attacking men, marriage, or patriarchy. L. Gordon reminds us that resistance, and the actions that become defined as resistant, are constructions after all. What looks like reproduction—such as Vickie Gray avowing an individualist, self-blaming perspective on the violence she experienced—may in fact be careful strategy or successful defiance.

Finally, we conclude that courts, as they exist now, more often than not reaffirm the dominant cultural ideology of individual and personal responsibility (Gurin, 1987). Dependence, seen as an indication of weakness, is devalued and independence is glorified and applauded. Conceptions of "the public" are used pejoratively to stigmatize the poor (Fraser, 1993). Charity becomes seen as psychically damaging to its recipients, who, the state reasons, would be better off earning their assistance, however menially. Individual merit rather than a sense of the "common good" is revered (Gurin, 1987). The ideal citizen is the wage earner and taxpayer, and services directed toward the poor, the part-time worker, and the domestic worker are limited in the name of their own "best interest" (Fraser, 1993; J. O'Connor, 1996). The effect of this disavowal of dependence and commitment toward independence is to support current capitalist withdrawal of public support, placing the burden of moral and physical responsibility back on the families themselves. As the state relinquishes its social responsibility toward a "politics of privatization" (Eisenstein, 1997, p. 142), moral questions and questions of responsibility for care, for secret keeping, and for resistance point more and more toward the family, and so to women in particular. Legally defined blame, then, when families erupt or children get hurt, falls squarely on the shoulders of the women who have been assigned the responsibility of maintaining the private sphere of the family.

Thus, when we consider cases of female responsibility, and specifically cases where women fail to protect their children, it is important to make clear how individualistic rhetoric hides and protects social structures that might bear some responsibility themselves. Roberts (1997) suggests that governments could choose to help women have healthy pregnancies rather than punish them for addiction or illness. Austin (1995) suggests that blame for social "problems" such as Black teenage pregnancy might be "shared by an educational system that fails to provide black youngsters with either the desire or the chance to attend college, a labor market that denies them employment that will supply the economic indicia of adulthood, and a health care system that does not deliver adequate birth control, abortion, or family services" (p. 431).

Myrtle Lacey, for instance, was found guilty of murdering her son, although it was clear that the social services agent who had examined the home found no reason to suspect that her son was dying of malnutrition (B. Smith, 1992a). That this agent or the agency itself might also have been charged with neglect was a question that went unexplored at the time. Also unquestioned, though perhaps justifiably implicated, is a health care system that denies access to adequate medical assistance to those who are uninsured, as well as a drug treatment system that is overcrowded and inaccessible. Similarly, though Michiko Kamiyama was legally declared responsible for causing her child "unjustifiable mental suffering" (Parsons, 1998), can we not also question the nonavailability of affordable child care as responsible? Individualistic explanations of personal responsibility for care hide the ways the state fails to support its citizens, particularly its poor and disenfranchised. Allowed to emerge unscathed (at least legally) within the rhetoric of personal responsibility are the capitalist labor market, the educational system, the health care/drug treatment system, child care services, social services for families, the welfare system, and the absence of services for women who live with violence and abuse, all of whom may rightly carry some responsibility for cases where mothers fail to protect their children.

Cases of failure to protect demonstrate clearly the thin line between intention and negligence, the thin line between responsibility as care and responsibility as blame. Our goal in this section of the chapter has been to demonstrate concretely how notions of women's responsibility become visible within the site of the courtroom, how issues of social negligence are overlooked, how women get punished when the state withdraws its assistance, and how individual blame becomes codified into law. Our goal has also been to stretch these personal notions of responsibility and to suggest the inclusion of the state and corporate worlds, so that the larger social context might be viewed as responsible for what has been heretofore considered private: the lives of women, families, and homes.

RESISTING RESPONSIBILITY/RESPONSIBLY RESISTING

Critical legal and race scholar Austin (1995) writes:

> I grew up thinking that "Sapphire" was merely a character on Amos 'n' Andy, a figment of a White man's racist, sexist comic imagination. Little did I suspect that Sapphire was a more generally employed appellation for the stereotypical Black Bitch—tough, domineering, emasculating, strident and shrill. Sapphire is the sort of person who we look at and wonder how she can possibly stand herself. All she does is complain. Why doesn't that woman shut up?
>
> Black bitch hunts are alive and well. . . . There are so many things to get riled about that keeping quiet is impossible. We really cannot function effectively without coming to terms with Sapphire. Should we renounce her, rehabilitate her or embrace her and proclaim her our own? (p. 426)

In her essay "Leaving the Confederate Closet," Strickland (1997) remembers:

> In spite of the best efforts of the church, I still found time to sin. I cheated on Bible drills, beat up my little brother and lusted in my heart after other girls. Although I had no experiences of the flesh, I surely wished for some. I searched the Scriptures for anything I could find on sin and sexuality, especially homosexuality. Much was made of "men shouldn't lie with men," but I thought this meant that guys weren't supposed to sleep in the same bed together. The Bible was a little weak on women, except that Ruth could forsake all others and live with Naomi. I did get the distinct impression that every kind of sexuality, whether of the spirit or of the flesh, was sinful, and I resigned myself to everlasting hell. This in spite of the fact that the whole of my rather limited sexual activities consisted of being fondled by a church deacon and the man who ran our neighborhood dry cleaners. (p. 41)

If girls or women mouth off, as Sapphire has done, or challenge, as Strickland did, they betray the hetero deal that requires women to endure and not speak the secrets of intragroup domination between men and women (see E.R. Cole & Stewart, 1996; Espin, 1996; Gilkes, 1988; Henderson-King & Stewart, 1997). To speak out, protest, and organize is yet another fundamental, wonderful, and vibrant piece of women's work.

Social psychologically, we come to the question What conditions are necessary for women to see social injustice, resist self-blame, and engage a broader politic for social responsibility? In response to this question, P.H. Collins (1990) invites us to consider the power of "righteous rage," when she writes: "Although political struggle requires good ideas, it also needs much more. Without some sense of where we're going and why we want to go there, and some 'righteous rage' to spur us on, we won't even know if we're headed in the right direction" (p. 7). In a similar spirit, critical legal theorist Matsuda (1995) implores theorists, researchers, activists, and politically engaged citizens to collectively recognize our moral responsibility to correct social injustice, to speak out as we witness, to organize. Toward this end, in psychology, there is a sparse but growing literature within social psychology about the political organizing by and for women in response to the maldistribution of emotional and social responsibilities.

Like critical race theorist Austin, psychologist Ward (1996) is intrigued by the question of how to raise political, race-conscious, and activist resisters. In her essay, Ward studies how, "in the safety of a home space of care, nurturance, refuge, and truth, black mothers have learned to skillfully weave lessons of critical consciousness into moments of intimacy between a parent and child to cultivate resistance against beliefs, attitudes and practices that can erode a black child's self-confidence and impair her positive identity development" (pp. 85–86). Ward documents the micropolitics of hair brushing, dinner talk, and sporting events, when African American mothers enable "healthy psychological resistance fostered through a liberating truth telling" (p. 97). Perhaps ironically, this is yet one more responsibility foisted on Black mothers: to build the next generation of critical, engaged, outraged, but not brutalized young women.

Finally, we have traced a set of intellectual and political biases that saturate social psychology, as they permeate the larger culture, about women's endless responsibilities to care and, in the likely event of failure, to be blamed for social inequities. We invite researchers and activists to recast our net so that responsibilities are distributed widely through history, culture, the state, men, community, and families, and resist the temptation to locate this kind of social work squarely and painfully on the already burdened backs of women, particularly poor and working-class women and women of color. We imagine research that interrogates the suspect areas of silence with respect to social responsibility—that is, why is the state so off the hook in the United States but not in Sweden? Under what conditions do women refuse responsibility, and with what consequences? Under what conditions do men, corporations, elites, or the community accept social responsibility, and how are these commitments sustained?

As feminist researchers, we may have the responsibility to document the existent, but also to challenge the foundations of prevailing "common sense" in the Gramscian (1971) sense of the term. That is, we must identify the larger social forces that loom safely in the shadows of social injustice, as the media, the law, communities, and sometimes men and other women blame individual women for social atrocities.

CHAPTER 27

Changing Society, Changing Women (and Men)

ELIZABETH R. COLE, ALYSSA N. ZUCKER, and LAUREN E. DUNCAN

Few would argue that the second-wave women's movement engendered profound changes in the American social fabric, regardless of one's opinion of these changes. Both through legislation and changing social expectations and mores, the movement led to broad-scale transformations of family life and enlarged women's opportunities to participate, and even become leaders, in spheres that had previously been closed to them, including work, higher education, and conventional party politics. These social and political changes are well documented (Klein, 1984).

Yet, if asked to describe the impact of the women's movement in their life, many women who came of age during the most active years of this movement emphasize a slightly different aspect of these changes: As they developed a new political consciousness of gender and power and saw its application all around them, this awareness led to profound *personal* transformations in their sense of self and in their personal relationships. The reflections below, written by women who came of age during the early years of the second wave of the women's movement, suggest that for some women, the linkages between personal and social change were both profound and enduring:

> The realization that women's position was structurally similar to that of racial minorities and the economically disadvantaged was a cataclysm in my life; I will never view life the same since that clarifying vision. And the ongoing and progressive empowerment of women by the women's movement has empowered me every year, every decade of my life since then.[1]
>
> It is hard to imagine what my life would have been like without the [women's] movement. It changed how I viewed myself and my "role" in life. It created opportunities for education and employment that were not realities when I graduated from high school in 1964. It also shaped my current husband's attitudes toward women and male responsibility to family and home. Without the movement, I do not think my current marriage and career would have been possible.

However, relatively little research has attempted to understand the impact of this movement on the experiences of individual women. This is surprising, given the importance to the movement of the insight that "the personal is political." Indeed, a central mechanism of the feminist movement has been the active struggle to transform society through personal change, realizing at the same time that social change may prompt individuals to change.

---

[1]Quotations of college alumnae here and throughout are drawn from the data of the Women's Life Paths Study, a longitudinal study of women graduates of the University of Michigan class of 1967 (see Tangri & Jenkins, 1986), and from two parallel follow-up studies, one of African American alumnae of the UM classes of 1967 to 1973 (see E.R. Cole & Stewart, 1996) and another of women student activists, also alumnae of the classes of 1967 to 1973 (see E.R. Cole, Zucker, & Ostrove, 1998). All quotations, unless otherwise noted, are based on questionnaire responses to the open-ended question "In what ways have you been affected by the women's movement?" asked in 1992, when the women were at midlife.

In this chapter, we document the dynamic interplay between social change and change in the lives of individuals and families. In doing so, we pay special attention to the ways that the experience of social change can be mediated by the different social locations women occupy. Although early feminist scholarship attempted to think about "women" as a minority group (e.g., Hacker, 1951), the feminist movement has not affected all women in the same ways. Indeed, an important obstacle faced by the feminist movement has been that differences among women have made it difficult to articulate a coherent feminist agenda that speaks to the needs of all women. Thus, to understand the impact of a broad social movement on individuals, it is crucial to recognize the diversity of individual women's lives. In this chapter, we attempt to do this by outlining the contours of these changes as experienced by women who vary by age, race/ethnicity, class, and family context.

COHORT EFFECTS: PLACING THE WOMEN'S MOVEMENT IN DEVELOPMENTAL CONTEXT

Social scientists have long pondered the link between social history and individual lives. Notably, sociologist Karl Mannheim (1972) argued that the coincidence of historical events with the life course of a particular birth cohort can create "political generations," consisting of people with shared experiences of the possibilities of their world that "thereby limit them to a specific range of potential experience, predisposing them for a certain characteristic mode of thought and experience, and a characteristic type of historically relevant action" (p. 106). Within such a generation, there may be a number of "generational units" formed around other types of group memberships (e.g., race, gender, political ideology). The young people who took part in the student movements of the 1960s, including feminism, have often been discussed in light of Mannheim's analysis. In psychology, Erik Erikson (1963) noted that the development of individuals was inextricably intertwined with their social context. For example, he viewed the youth of the 1960s as using activism to establish their new identities in the social world (1968). Thus, the collective developmental press of a generation may express itself in political movements and social transformation.

Building from the work of Mannheim, Erikson, and others, A.J. Stewart and Healy (1989) suggested that the sociohistorical environment has different effects on individuals as a function of their age or life stage. They posited that the social climate and historical events experienced in childhood and early adolescence affect people's fundamental values and expectations. In terms of the women's movement, anecdotal accounts show that women who were children during or after the movement tend to take for granted the opportunities achieved by the movement, seeing them as a natural part of the environment (Glickman, 1993; Heywood & Drake, 1997; Kamen, 1991).

During late adolescence and early adulthood, when individuals negotiate how they fit into the world, social and historical events tend to affect perceptions of work and family options and identity formation. For example, many young adults who came of age during the late 1960s still define themselves in terms of political protest, the Vietnam War, and the women's movement (Braungart & Braungart, 1990; E.R. Cole, Zucker, & Ostrove, 1998; A.J. Stewart & Gold-Steinberg, 1990). This is eloquently expressed by one alumna of the college class of 1967 in her response to the question "What effect did the student movements [of the late 1960s] have on your life?"

> [Student movements] were how I identified myself. As the depression era defined my parents, their values and attitudes, so did the protest movements define me. I took part in the first Vietnam teach-in, and that defined my attitudes toward the Vietnam war. I was part of the civil rights protest movement and that defined my racial attitudes, and helped define my response to the women's movement, and the way I raise my children and teach.

Events experienced in early middle adulthood, after work and family commitments have been made, should affect behavior, but not necessarily identity. Women who had begun their careers and families before the height of the women's movement were able to take advantage of liberalized divorce laws and affirmative action education and work programs; however, they probably did not change their fundamental identities formed before the movement (see A.J. Stewart & Healy, 1989, for a similar argument about women during the Second World War).

Finally, at midlife, when careers are well-established and day-to-day demands of child rearing have diminished, social events affect perceptions of new opportunities and choices, perhaps spurring identity revision for some. Thus, midlife women with grown children may have seen opportunities in the women's movement of the late 1960s and early 1970s to change their beliefs and identities; they may have started careers, gone back to school, or ended unsatisfactory marriages (L.E. Duncan & Agronick, 1995). Thus, the responses to feminism of women coming of age before, during, and after the women's movement can best be understood by considering for each cohort the developmental stage coinciding with the movement.

Most of the research on the effects of the women's movement on women's personalities, careers, and families has relied on samples of women who were young adults or in early middle adulthood when the women's movement was at its peak (women's movement and pre–women's movement cohorts). Most of the participants in these studies have been White and college-educated. However, the life outcomes of members of privileged samples are of particular interest, because they are more likely to reflect the effects of a movement first, as members of these populations are in a position to take advantage of new opportunities opened by a movement (A.J. Stewart & Healy, 1989). These studies found that the women's movement had a profound impact on these women's lives.

L.E. Duncan and Agronick (1995) found that 65% of women in the Mills College classes of 1958 and 1960 (pre–women's movement cohort) rated the women's movement as somewhat or very personally meaningful. These percentages are smaller than they are for women just a few years younger, who were young adults during the movement. For example, 90% of Radcliffe College class of 1964 alumnae rated the movement as somewhat or very personally meaningful. These cohort differences are consistent with those found recently by A.N. Zucker (1998) and support arguments about the centrality of the young adult life stage for identity-formative experiences (Delli Carpini, 1989; L.E. Duncan & Agronick, 1995; Erikson, 1963; Schuman & Scott, 1989; A.J. Stewart & Healy, 1989). However, although anecdotal accounts show that post–women's movement cohorts of women seem to take gains of the movement for granted, two recent studies have found that these women do not rate the movement as less personally meaningful than do women of the women's movement cohort (L.E. Duncan & Stewart, in press; A.N. Zucker, 1998). Although women raised after the women's movement may be unable to imagine a time when women were not considered equal to men, they do recognize the importance of the movement that gained these rights. Thus, the impact of social events occurring during *childhood* can be recognized at later life stages by those affected; individuals are not unaware of the forces that shape our fundamental values.

Research on cohorts of women who were in midlife or later adulthood at the time of the movement shows that although these women may not have been able to make real changes in their lives as a result of the movement, the vast majority of them view the movement in a positive light (R.L. Cohen & Alwin, 1993; Yohalem, 1993). Cohen and Alwin's comparison of the Bennington College class of 1939 with national samples of college-educated women show that this favorable view of the movement is evident among their less liberal age peers as well, though not to the same extent.

Perhaps more than any of the other social movements of the late 1960s and early 1970s, the women's movement envisioned transformations that spanned every aspect of people's lives: as individuals, as contributors to the public spheres of work and politics, and as members of families. The changes engendered by the movement were reflected in women's personalities, career opportunities, and family choices. We consider each of these domains next.

PERSONALITY

Finding the women's movement personally meaningful was associated with the development of assertive and independent personality characteristics by midlife for at least one pre–women's movement cohort of women: graduates of the Mills College classes of 1958 and 1960 (Agronick & Duncan, 1998; L.E. Duncan & Agronick, 1995). In contrast, for women just a few years younger than the Mills College graduates, society's broader acceptance of assertive and independent characteristics in women was reflected in the young adult personalities of women graduating in 1964 from Radcliffe College. The women in this cohort affected by the women's movement showed no greater evidence of personality change by midlife on these characteristics than their peers who were not affected (L.E. Duncan & Agronick, 1995). In fact, there was evidence of identity search and revision for the older women affected by the movement, but not for the younger women. These findings are consistent with A.J. Stewart and Healy's (1989) idea that the values of social movements coinciding with young adulthood are likely to be incorporated into identity, and it is only those social movements coinciding with later life stages that necessitate identity revision to accommodate value changes.

To date, there has been little research on the personality characteristics of women of the post–women's movement generation. However, although the definition of femininity has changed very little over time (including such characteristics as dependence, nurturance, and passivity), American society today is more accepting of women who display assertive and independent characteristics (O'Heron & Orlofsky, 1990). As many feminists have noted, women who take on valued masculine characteristics are more tolerated than men who take on feminine characteristics, perhaps in part because society is slow to embrace what has historically been devalued (Lobel, 1994; Unger & Crawford, 1996). Thus, it might be hypothesized that women of the youngest cohorts would continue to show the assertive and independent personality characteristics found in earlier generations of women who benefited from the movement; however, it could also be the case that the "backlash" against feminism (Faludi, 1991) has tempered these changes. This is clearly an area for further research.

CAREERS

One of the goals of the women's movement was to allow women access to male-dominated careers with their corresponding high salaries and prestige. However, there has been more progress in some fields than in others. For example, in 1994, women made up 36.5% of MBA recipients (up from 3.9% in 1971), 38% of medical degree recipients (up from 8% in 1970), and 43% of law degree recipients (up from 5.4% in 1970). On the other hand, high-paying skilled trades have been relatively unaffected by the entrance of women. For example, in 1996, women made up only 1.3% of carpenters, which was virtually unchanged since 1983 (U.S. Bureau of the Census, 1997). More than older cohorts, younger women have been able to take advantage of affirmative action programs, and changes in the acceptability of girls studying math and science have increased the number of women in these fields. For example, the percentage of students earning biological or life science bachelor's degrees has increased from 29% women in 1971 to 51% in 1994 (U.S. Bureau of the Census, 1997).

However, even older cohorts of women have been able to benefit from new educational and career opportunities, and this is especially true of women who have embraced the women's movement. For example, responsiveness to and participation in the women's movement is associated with higher educational attainment, entrance into formerly male-dominated careers (e.g., doctors, lawyers, academicians), higher career status, and higher income levels in both the pre–women's movement and women's movement cohorts (Agronick & Duncan, 1998; L.E. Duncan & Agronick, 1995; Klein, 1984). Yohalem's (1993) study of women graduating from Columbia University graduate school between 1945 and 1951 found that most strongly supported the women's movement, perhaps because of their exposure to sexism in the workplace. Thus, in terms of education and career attainment, the correlates of finding meaning in the movement do not seem to differ for the older and younger cohorts.

FAMILY LIFE

Since the social movements of the 1960s and 1970s, there has been a well-documented increase in the divorce rate, and average family size (consisting of parents and children) is down from 3.58 members in 1970 to 3.20 members in 1996 (U.S. Bureau of the Census, 1997). There seem to be few differences in divorce rates and family size between women who acknowledge the impact of the women's movement on their lives and those who do not, suggesting that broad, societal-level changes have influenced marriage and family size (Carroll, 1989).

Women in post–women's movement cohorts are starting their careers in their early 20s and getting married and having children later than women of earlier cohorts. Current research suggests that women coming of age during and after the women's movement are less likely than their predecessors to feel that they must choose between career and family (Giele, 1993). In fact, there has been an explosion of scholarly and popular literature discussing the balancing act modern women face when combining career and family (e.g., R.C. Barnett & Rivers, 1998; Chira, 1999; Kaltreider, 1997; McGinnis, 1997; Peters, 1998). Although combining career and family is difficult for most women, those who are able to make it work may enjoy mental and physical health benefits from this role combination (R.C. Barnett & Rivers, 1998; Baruch, Barnett, & Rivers, 1983; Crosby, 1991; M. Miller, Moen, & Dempster-McClain, 1991; A.J. Stewart & Vandewater, 1993; Vandewater, Ostrove, & Stewart, 1997).

However, it is also true that each individual woman (or family) has to reinvent the wheel in some sense, coming up with her own unique way to care for children and advance her career, because, in general, U.S. industries have not responded much to changes in women's lives. For example, although the Family and Medical Leave Act (1993) allows men to take time off from work to care for a new child, only a small percentage of men take advantage of this opportunity. Most men, however, say they would like to spend this time with their families, but corporate culture (unofficially) frowns on men who do so (Hyde et al., 1993; Silverstein, 1996). For working-class women, and many women of color and single mothers, such role combination is not a result of the women's movement, but rather a way of life that is due to racial and economic oppression. For women who work in low-paying, low-status jobs, evidence shows that role combination is much more stressful than for women with "careers," often because the money they earn just covers child care expenses and low-status work may not be intrinsically rewarding or meaningful (Baruch et al., 1983; Colen, 1986; Greenglass & Burke, 1988; Statham, Miller, & Mauksch, 1988).

LIMITATIONS OF THE RESEARCH TO DATE

Unfortunately, most of the research conducted on the effects of the women's movement has been limited to samples of college-educated White women. There are a number of reasons why this may be so: These women were most visibly at the front of the women's movement; such women are easily accessible to academic researchers; and, by virtue of their conspicuous entry into previously male-dominated careers, perhaps their lives seem to exemplify changes brought about by the movement. Alternatively, the effects of the women's movement on these women may be studied more because the movement has mainly worked to improve the lives of privileged women. The fact that we find that less-educated samples of women feel they have been less affected by the movement than better-educated samples supports the argument that the movement has been one organized by, and on behalf of, the relatively privileged, at least up to now (see, e.g., Hulbert & Schuster, 1993).

To summarize, as a direct result of the women's movement, White, educated women have been able to take on socially valued assertive and independent personality characteristics, attain higher levels of education and employment in more prestigious male-dominated fields, and create new ways to combine work and family. These changes are more true of younger cohorts of women than they are of older cohorts of women. Perhaps the best that can be said about the research reviewed here is that it gives us an idea of what gains a privileged group of women can make in the wake of a movement devoted to improving their lives.

EFFECTS OF DIVERSITY: RACE AND SOCIAL CLASS

The women's movement is a middle-class White concern. When people see me—they see color first, gender second. My first priority is to my race. If the racial barriers are lessened, then all my people are free. The issues of White women are very different than those of Black women.

The women's movement has put women of color into the spotlight and let them have voices that might not otherwise have been heard. New alliances have been formed, particularly among women of color. The literature available has grown. All of these things have helped me in my personal development. I'm more grounded. I have an added sense of perspective regarding my place in the world. It has also helped me to personally redefine my own boundaries, to explore more my own sexuality, to deal with my own sexual abuse, and to allow my daughter some of the freedoms that I've only dreamed of.

As these two quotations illustrate, the women's movement did not have the same effects on all women. Even within subgroups of women, like the two African Americans quoted here, individual women experienced the women's movement in profoundly different ways. What is important is that women's experience of the women's movement was filtered through the prism of their multiple identities—and this is particularly salient for ethnicity and social class.

Although some women became involved with social change through the women's movement, other women's first experiences working in broad-based social movements concerned politicized identities other than gender. For instance, many African American and some White women first became politically active in the civil rights movement; some of these women later became active in the women's movement (Evans, 1979; Giddings, 1984).[2] In another example, Kingsolver (1989) documented how women who became active in a coal mining strike that centered around social class issues became politicized as women. There are relatively few psychological studies that examine how social identities intersect with women's work for social change. Many of the arguments we review here are based on theory and critical analysis of historical events, or only a few cases rather than large, rich data sets. Furthermore, the majority of the studies based on particular identity categories focus only on members of the group that is targeted with oppression (e.g., people of color, working-class people); much less research has attempted to understand allies of these movements who belong to dominant groups, for instance, middle-class people's class-based activism or White women working to eliminate racism.

At least three caveats must precede this section. First, because this chapter is concerned with the effects of the women's movement and the gains made by other progressive movements of the 1960s, we discuss only left-wing activism here. Second, our goal is not to be comprehensive; in fact, each of these topics merits volumes of its own. Rather, we aim to review each area briefly and choose to highlight research that illustrates the way women's multiple identities shape their activism. A final, and related, caveat is that although we consider for simplicity's sake the separate effects of race and social class on women's participation in social change activism, we must remember that it is artificial to consider any of these identities in isolation. Many of the studies described in this section consider the role not only of race and gender, for example, but also of social class, which may be affected by still other identities, such as immigrant status. The interaction among these identities is important as well; for example, race and gender tend to interact with social class in particular ways, such that people of color and some White women have less access to direct class privileges (Hurtado, 1989).

RACE

There is a growing literature on the role that both African American and White women played in the civil rights and Black Power movements in the United States (B.M. Barnett, 1996; Blumberg, 1990; Evans, 1979; Giddings, 1984; Irons, 1998; McAdam, 1992; C. Payne, 1990). Although many accounts of civil rights activism have rendered women's roles "invisible," women, particularly African American women, did in fact contribute to all forms of participation and leadership (B.M. Barnett, 1996). In some areas, there was even an "overparticipation" of women relative to their demographics (C. Payne, 1990). Women participated in these struggles at great personal risk; they often were fired from employment and were in physical danger. Payne suggested that women's participation was related to deeply held religious beliefs and to friendship networks (see F.C. Harris, 1994, for a discussion of the role of religion in African American political activism generally). Although the form that both Black and White women's participation was allowed to take was clearly

---

[2] It should be noted that women of color, particularly African American women, have a long history of both obvious and subtle everyday resistance to racism, which predates the civil rights movement, and which has been described as a form of activism (P.H. Collins, 1991).

limited by sexist assumptions (E.R. Cole, 1994; Giddings, 1984; McAdam, 1992), they were nonetheless crucial to the movement.

Scholars have considered the intersection of race and gender in political domains other than the civil rights movement. E.R. Cole and Stewart (1996) compared educated Black and White women's general political participation at midlife. They found that Black women scored higher on measures of political consciousness and participation than their White peers. The path to adult political participation differed slightly for the two racial groups. Although social responsibility played an important role for both groups, student activism was important for Black women only, whereas a collectivist political identification (i.e., believing the political realm is personally meaningful and that collective actions are the best responses to social problems) was important for White women only. This suggests that Black and White women's historical and political contexts imbued their political activities with different meanings.

Gay and Tate (1998) examined the issue of the double bind for Black women—that is, the question of whether race and gender identification compete with each other in political attitudes and behavior. They found that Black women identified as strongly on the basis of gender as on race, but that race affected political attitudes and activism more strongly. The one exception was in the cases where race and gender interests were in direct conflict with each other. For example, those women who were strongly identified as both Black and female rated political issues in which both race and gender were central, such as the Million Man March, the Clarence Thomas Supreme Court nomination, and the O.J. Simpson murder trial, more negatively than those women who were not high on both dimensions.

Similar issues are relevant to the political participation of Asian women. A surge of Asian American political activism grew out of the Black Power and women's movements and the general ethos of student protest in the 1960s and 1970s (Chow, 1989; Omatsu, 1993; Shah, 1993) and continues on college campuses today (Gupta, 1998). Asian American women have formed many women's groups, both those for women from a single, shared ethnic background, and pan-Asian groups. Often, these groups began as support networks and then became politically active in a variety of domains that addressed the immediate needs of the community, such as immigration issues, domestic violence, and lesbian/gay issues (Shah, 1993). Some groups organized specific grassroots movements; for instance, the Asian Immigrant Women Advocates in the San Francisco area created the Garment Workers' Justice Campaign, which staged protests and raised consciousness about the mistreatment of immigrant Asian women in the U.S. fashion industry (Omatsu, 1993). One barrier to Asian American women's full participation in feminist movements has been the movement's traditional focus on White women and/or a limited view of "women of color" as consisting of Black women only (Chow, 1989; Shah, 1993). Furthermore, cultural prescriptions of gender-appropriate behavior and divisions within Asian cultures based on ethnicity, social class, and immigrant status made the relationship to feminism complex (Chow, 1989; Shah, 1993).

Research on political participation and involvement by Latinas has been relatively scarce (Hardy-Fanta, 1997). Nonetheless, several key interview and participant observation studies demonstrate that Latinas are involved in the political realm in a variety of ways. These range from informal organizing of immigrant domestic workers (Hondagneu-Sotelo, 1998), to grassroots community-based organizing (Abrahams, 1996; Pardo, 1997, 1998), to electoral politics (Hardy-Fanta, 1997). Pardo demonstrated that, despite conflicts between women with different social class and immigration statuses, a number of Mexican American women in East Los Angeles became politically mobilized for community issues in their neighborhoods, schools, and churches and were able to take on state political forces. Pardo argued that these women were able to transform their traditional networks and resources that were based on family and household responsibilities into a powerful grassroots political activism, and that such a transformation appeared to be a natural extension of their other responsibilities. In some ways, the basis for these Mexican American women's actions is similar to that of the mothers of the Plaza de Mayo in Argentina (Bouvard, 1994).

It is clear that the importance of women's participation in race-based struggles for equality has often been overlooked. However, both women of color and White women have participated in these movements (Evans, 1979; McAdam, 1992). This participation may take different forms than men's (Schlozman, Burns, & Verba, 1994) and is sometimes explicitly gendered. For instance, in Pardo's (1997, 1998) studies, Latinas became politicized through their roles as mothers on behalf of issues that affected the young people in their communities. Although it was unusual for these women to be politically active, the activism was in a "traditional" domain, and thus more easily accepted by others. Women of color in the United States are often in positions of "multiple jeopardy"; that is, they are targeted with a great deal of oppression based on gender, race, and social class. Although those experiences can lead to feelings of inefficacy, it nonetheless is evident that women can achieve activist status on any one or a combination of these issues. Such activism, which may start because of a particular social concern, may even result in a stronger political consciousness and in continued activism on a variety of causes (see, e.g., E.R. Cole & Stewart, 1996).

SOCIAL CLASS

Much of the research concerning the relation between social class and women's activism has centered on working-class struggles to organize, either to develop unions or to strike to achieve favorable contracts. Researchers have documented the experience of those subject to both gender- and class-based oppression by studying several different types of occupations: those dominated by women, such as waitressing (Cobble, 1990); those dominated by men, but in which women play a large role in strike support (Beckwith, 1998; Fonow, 1998; Kingsolver, 1989; Maggard, 1990), such as industrial work (mining, steel work, etc.); and those male-dominated fields in which women have made inroads due to federal desegregation orders, such as construction (S. Eisenberg, 1998).

In a historical study of women's involvement as waitresses in the Hotel Employees and Restaurant Employees International Union, Cobble (1990) documented the gendered nature of the profession and of women's activist strategies. She found that some of the most active women were single or divorced and thus slightly removed from direct patriarchal influences in their day-to-day home lives. The creation of single-sex union locals also assisted women in organizing on their own behalf, away from men. They organized around issues specific to being working *women* and fought for equal representation at national union events.

The research on women's involvement in mining strikes demonstrates the complexity of gender and class influences on activism. Both Kingsolver (1989) and Maggard (1990) have documented mining strikes in which women, who previously identified as only housewives or miners' wives, became extremely active in union and strike efforts. In both cases, this activity strengthened bonds among women, disrupted traditional gender dynamics, and led to women's ability to see themselves as political actors. Women from striking communities were profoundly changed by their activist experience, perhaps because "the initial decision to join the women's picket line was a political act that required a shift in gender consciousness for these women" (Maggard, 1990, p. 95). After the strike, some of these women went on to get more education, find employment outside the home, or continue union activism in other areas. In this way, becoming politically mobilized around a specific issue had a profound and lasting impact on their lives.

There is less research about middle- or upper-class women's participation in class-based social change (either on behalf of their own group or of others'). Some studies have documented a relationship between social class and activism, such that middle- and upper-class individuals tend to be more involved (e.g., J.C. Jenkins & Wallace, 1996), perhaps because of greater political efficacy associated with being raised middle-class in the current educational system (Paulsen, 1991). However, these middle-class people tend not to be involved in activism that is class-based or that acknowledges class privilege. In fact, some women's movement activists have been criticized for being "unconsciously middle class," in that the "woman" whose women's rights they are fighting for is middle-class, and her struggles do not apply equally to working-class and poor women, who are disproportionately women of color (e.g., Giddings, 1984; Shah, 1994).

It is misleading to examine women's political and social change roles without exploring the other social identities that influence them. We have demonstrated here that one important source for and domain of women's activism is their experiences defined by race/ethnicity and social class/immigration status, or some combination of these factors. One element that cuts across these different identities is the importance of single-sex organizing. Whether it is Mexican American mothers in a working-class neighborhood or waitresses in a union, the value of having space to organize as women, away from men, seems critical to at least the initial stages of women's feminist activism across the board.

Both types of identities that we have examined here tend to involve a community of similar others who live, work, and/or socialize in close proximity, and may create the basis for a collective, activist orientation on behalf of the larger group. Yet, much political learning takes place in a smaller, more intimate group: the family. We now turn from considering these broad social variables to more individual-level variables, examining how feminism may be transferred from individual parents to their daughters and sons.

INTERGENERATIONAL EFFECTS: THE FEMINIST LEGACY

Can social change, or the impact of participating in social change, have a "ripple effect" across generations? Many of the women who participated in our studies believe that the women's movement has changed the social world that their children will inherit as adults, and they described the ways they helped socialize their children to prepare for it. For some, this is the most salient long-term impact of the movement. For example, although these women were asked to assess the impact of the women's movement in their own lives, they answered in terms of what these changes will mean for their children:

> Although my work in the business world largely preceded the movement, I think the movement has affected my years at home somewhat. I talk to my boys about being able to do dishes, etc., because it is likely that they may have to share household jobs. Moreover now it's easier to encourage my daughter to aim for anything she wants to do.
>
> I especially feel it has helped my daughter in that she doesn't have to mold herself into a "gender correct" career. She is *very* aware of sexist teachers (physical education particularly) and won't get caught in that trap.
>
> Because of increased awareness I think my divorcing my ex-husband was easier for other people to understand. . . . I certainly talked to my daughter, and sons, more about these issues and was more aware of stereotypes in raising children.

For some women, the feminist transformation of consciousness engendered by the women's movement is so valuable that they purposefully attempt to pass it on to their children. Some have found this a difficult project. Although there is only limited research on the topic, anecdotal accounts suggest that some feminists who took part in the early days of the movement now lament that their daughters have not fully embraced feminist activism even as they benefit from activists' hard-won gains. Rose Glickman's (1993) description of women of her daughter's generation is both vivid and painful: "Some issues that seem to us absolutely central to feminism are at best uninteresting, at worst irrelevant to them. I still grind my teeth when I recall my daughter's adolescent dismissal of my hortatory lectures: 'lighten up Mama, lighten up'" (p. xii). In this section, we explore whether parents with feminist attitudes have been able to transmit corresponding attitudes to their children. First, we briefly review the literature in political science on the intergenerational transmission of political attitudes generally, then we look in more depth at two studies focusing on the daughters of feminists.

Taken as a whole, research suggests that the relationship between parents' and children's political attitudes is modest at best. In perhaps the best-known study in this area, Jennings and Niemi (1981) surveyed parents and their high-school-age children in 1965. They found that correlations between the attitudes of parents and of children were smaller than had previously been believed: Few correlations between the generations' attitudes were strong or even moderate. However, relations between parents' and offsprings' attitudes were stronger for attitudes that were concrete, salient, or frequently reinforced, and for those in which parents were in agreement with each other. Jennings and Niemi followed up these families in 1973, when many of the offspring had begun to accept the adult responsibilities of work and family. The data yielded even weaker relations between parents' and adult children's attitudes. What is more, factors such as similarity to parents in age and education, amount of contact, and geographical proximity were all unrelated to correlations between parents' and children's attitudes! Of course, Jennings and Niemi were studying a fairly unique cohort of young people, the products of the post–World War II baby boom, and one must be cautious when generalizing from their experiences.

Be that as it may, Jennings and Niemi (1981) did find that correlations between parents' and children's attitudes varied for different attitudinal domains; for example, the strongest relationship was found for political knowledge. In addition, more recent research on the personality characteristic of right-wing authoritarianism has shown remarkable intergenerational consistency (correlations ranging from .44 to .48 in recent research; Altemeyer, 1988, p. 85; B.E. Peterson & Duncan, 1999). If we ignore the opposing politics of authoritarianism and feminism, we might argue that feminism and authoritarianism are similar *types* of variables, ones that color our perceptions of most aspects of life (B.E. Peterson & Duncan, 1999), and which may be more likely to be transmitted across generations than simple attitudinal variables.

Thus, it is reasonable to look specifically at the rates of mothers' transmission to their children of attitudes related to feminism. Again, research in this area does not suggest that feminists are reproducing themselves through parenting. Acock and Bengtson (1978) found that mothers' attitudes were more predictive of youths' political attitudes than were fathers' attitudes, and this was true for both daughters and sons. However, this pattern did *not* hold for traditional sex norms. In this case, fathers' attitudes were more predictive of daughters' than were mothers'; curiously, fathers had no independent influence on sons' attitudes toward sex norms. In their study of three-generation families, J. Glass, Bengston, and Dunham (1986) found modest intergenerational transmission of political and gender-role ideology; but for gender attitudes, children's effects on their parents were stronger than parents' effects on their children! Similar findings were reported by Alwin, Cohen, and Newcomb (1991) in their longitudinal study of women who attended Bennington College in the 1930s and 1940s. Women whose children belonged to the birth cohorts who were college students during the period of student protest in the late 1960s had greater change in political attitudes than did other women in the sample.

Nevertheless, this literature does suggest that under certain circumstances, feminists have raised children who share their views. First, Bohannon and Blanton (1999) found that mothers' and daughters' attitudes toward childbearing, marriage, and career were not significantly different either in early adolescence or when the daughters were in their late 20s. Second, there is reason to believe that similarity between mothers and daughters may aid in the transmission of gender-role attitudes. M.D. Smith and Self (1980) found that women college students' sex-role attitudes were better predicted by their mother's attitudes than by demographic qualities of their mother (such as age, education, occupation, or marital status). More important, for both liberal and conservative mothers, mothers' and daughters' attitudes were more similar in families with college-educated mothers. The authors theorized that education enhances the effectiveness of transmission from mother to daughter. This may be because women students view their mother as more similar to themselves when they are also college-educated.

Third, we must be cautious in our generalization of these findings to the cohort whose parents took active part in the women's movement during the 1970s. Jennings and Niemi (1981) speculate that the rate of intergenerational transmission of political attitudes may vary in different historical periods. The youth in their sample, and in most of the studies reviewed here, correspond roughly to the cohort that would be expected to be most affected by the social movements of the late 1960s. Thus, these findings may or may not describe the relationship between the attitudes of individuals who were youths in 1965 and those of their own offspring, many of whom are currently young adults. Indeed, the single study to support the transmission of gender-role attitudes (Bohannon & Blanton, 1999) was based on the youngest cohort of offspring. However, because of the small size of their sample ($N = 40$), their results are not definitive. Clearly, this is a question that begs further research.

Finally, it may be especially difficult to transmit political attitudes from parents to children because these views are often communicated only indirectly; if children are to be influenced by their parents' views, they must first assess them accurately. Indeed, there is some evidence suggesting that children's perceptions of parents' attitudes are more predictive of the children's attitudes than are the parents' actual opinions (R.M. Lerner & Knapp, 1975). Thus, if parents are to influence their children's political views, they must effectively make their political views obvious to their children (Acock, 1984). This implies that intergenerational transmission might be most effective in families in which parents express their views explicitly and visibly model behavior associated with their political attitudes—in other words, families in which the parents are politically active. The literature in this area, although small, suggests that this is the case. For example, historical research suggests that some activists in the social movements of the 1960s were not rebelling against their parents, but actually viewed their own parents as role models for activism (Evans, 1979; J. Miller, 1987). More recently, L.E. Duncan and Stewart (1995) found that students who protested the Persian Gulf War in 1991 were influenced, in part, by their own parents' involvement in protest against the Vietnam War.

However, there is a paucity of research investigating whether daughters of feminists share their mothers' attitudes and proclivity to political participation. Those studies that do exist are qualitative in methodology, and thus their findings cannot be directly compared to the literature on intergenerational transmission of political attitudes. However, they do provide us a richer and more nuanced picture of the dynamics of the transmission of political attitudes and behavior from parents to children.

To date, two book-length projects (C.L. Baker & Kline, 1996; Glickman, 1993) have explored the relationship between feminists and their adult daughters. What is striking in both books, particularly in light of the survey data finding little convergence between the political attitudes of parents and of adult children, is the extent to which adult daughters embrace the ideals of feminism, even though their involvement in activism is less than their mothers'. It is certainly reasonable to argue that families in which daughters have rejected the values of their feminist mother would be less likely to take part in such interviews. However, it is also the case that having a feminist activist mother could be expected to render feminist issues concrete, salient, and frequently reinforced—just the qualities that lead to high concordance between parents' and children's views (Jennings & Niemi, 1981).

At least two other themes presented in these books are relevant to the question of intergenerational transmission of feminist attitudes and activist behavior. The first concerns the nature of individual mother-daughter relationships and its relation to the transmission of feminist activism. Both books at times depict these relationships as fraught with conflict. But the voices in these texts tell many other stories. Certainly, some daughters express a longing for their mothers, who were often away from home (although it must be noted that, without a control group, we can't know whether this is merely a cohort effect). However, perhaps an equal number argued that their mothers' political involvements communicated to them the myriad avenues of possibility in their own lives.

A second strong theme recurring throughout these daughters' narratives was the sense in childhood that they were different from other children at school and in their neighborhoods by virtue of their mothers' feminism: different because their mothers were publicly visible, marched in protests, did not wear makeup or feminine clothing, were not home baking cookies, or, for some, because their mother's work as activists necessitated a lower material standard of living for the family. One daughter recalled a classmate's taunt: "At least my Mom's not some kind of women's libber, and she can afford to buy me designer jeans" (C.L. Baker & Kline, 1996, p. 261). It was just this sense of difference that many of the same women later came to regard, and even cherish, as something special about themselves. For these women, their mothers' feminism blazed a trail for them not only in the tangible accomplishments of the movement, but as models who demonstrated how it was possible for women to lead lives outside the constraints of convention.

To be sure, these two studies only scratch the surface; the question of whether the generation that mobilized for the second wave of the feminist movement will successfully transmit that charge to their daughters (and sons) remains to be answered, not only empirically, but more important, politically. For now, these studies are particularly valuable in that they remind us that parents transmit political behavior and values at the same time that they socialize their children in many other ways. Even as we attempt to envision societal transformations, such change necessarily takes place against the backdrop of each generation's normative, predictable developmental challenges. At the same time that they both admire and resent their parents, emulate them and rebel against them, and attempt to fashion their own independent identities, children will absorb, critique, and transform these lessons, making a new feminism that is their own.

TOWARD A PSYCHOLOGY OF SOCIAL TRANSFORMATION

Thus far, we have attempted to document the changes in diverse women's lives that accompanied the women's movement. But what if we consider again our chapter's title, "Changing Society, Changing Women," this time thinking of "changing" as a verb? That is, how are women mobilized to change society in general, and on behalf of women in particular?

THINKING FEMINIST

From a social identity perspective, this involves developing a specific set of cognitions, values, evaluations, and emotions (Tajfel, 1982). Gurin and her colleagues (Gurin, 1985; Gurin & Markus, 1989; Gurin, Miller, & Gurin, 1980; Gurin & Townsend, 1986) have demonstrated that a combination of awareness about both an individual's relationship to others in her or his social group and the relation of that social group to other groups is crucial for political consciousness. An awareness of sexism does not seem to be sufficient without a greater collective consciousness (Sigel, 1996). Both Gurin and Sigel have decried the American emphasis on the individual as detracting from people's abilities to think about themselves as part of a collective—to notice that injustices may be enacted communally rather than individually, and to realize that collective, political solutions may be more powerful than individual striving.

For many young women, an important route to feminist consciousness is enrollment in women's studies courses (Bargad & Hyde, 1991; L.E. Duncan, 1999; Henderson-King & Stewart, 1999; Stake, Roades, Rose, & Ellis, 1994; Thomsen, Basu, & Reinitz, 1995). One of the most effective ways to break down the negative stereotypes of feminists often seen in the mass media (S.J. Douglas, 1994; Faludi, 1991) seems to be participation in college-level women's studies classes. Exposure to the history, core issues, and theories of feminism seems to empower women (and men) to identify as feminists, taking on all the baggage that goes with the label (L.E. Duncan, 1999; Henderson-King & Stewart, 1999; Kamen, 1991; A.N. Zucker, 1998). Moreover, although enrollment in women's studies courses is not associated with a history of feminist activism, after the course, women's studies students are more likely than others to engage in activism (Stake & Rose, 1994). Similarly, reading feminist texts, even in contexts other than women's studies classes, often has a profound consciousness-raising impact (e.g., Findlen, 1995). Many of the women in one study described the transformative effect that reading such classic books as *The Feminine Mystique* (Friedan, 1963) had on their lives, causing them to recognize and reevaluate the sexism in their middle-class but unhappy lives and heralding in a new feminist era (A.N. Zucker, 1998).

A second route toward feminism involves personal experiences women have that raise their consciousness. Personal experiences of sexism are often the transforming moments in which women suddenly realize that they live in a sexist society (see, e.g., Evans, 1979; Giddings, 1984; Ruddick & Daniels, 1977). One study found that salient negative experiences, such as sexual harassment and rape, were related to support for feminism (Buschman & Lenart, 1996). L.E. Duncan (1999) found that for both educated, White, midlife women and reproductive rights activists of all ages, identifying as lesbian or bisexual, experiencing sexual harassment, and surviving sexual violence were all associated with increased levels of feminist consciousness and women's rights activism.

A third route is cohort-specific experiences. For instance, taking part in one of the many explicit consciousness-raising groups in the late 1960s and 1970s was effective for many women (R. Morgan, 1970; Popkin, 1990). Women who came of age after the height of the second wave of the women's movement usually lacked the opportunity to participate in such groups; Kamen (1991) suggested that this is one reason Generation X young adults are resistant to feminism (however, see Rosenthal, 1984, for a reevaluation of the political efficacy of such groups). However, these young adults do have other cohort-specific experiences that may make them more likely to endorse feminism. For instance, many of them grew up with the expectations that even White, middle-class women should work outside the home, that household labor should not be exclusively gendered, and that girls can grow up to be doctors, presidents, and athletes (A.N. Zucker, 1998). Thus, the changes already made in terms of social roles and expectations may have a positive effect in promoting further change.

ACTING FEMINIST

Yet, attitudes alone are not enough to create feminist activists; there is certainly a well-developed literature in social psychology describing the discrepancies that often exist between attitudes and behaviors. In the area of feminist attitudes, Sigel (1996) revealed a disturbing paradox: American women in general show high levels of awareness of discrimination and express a great deal of anger about the discrimination they encounter; however, few of the women in her samples either advocated or took part in political action to redress these problems (see also Crosby et al., 1989). Indeed, Sigel found that women in focus groups could readily describe instances of gender discrimination that they or others had experienced, but very few were willing to advocate collective action to redress the problem, instead endorsing individual-level solutions.

Sigel (1996) theorized several possible explanations for most women's reluctance to become politically active. First, women's sex-role socialization traditionally has worked against their political participation. Second, women may generally feel powerless to make political change. Third, the American ethos of individualism does not support taking collective action on behalf of group interests. But for women who actively took part in the social movements of the 1960s, including the women's movement, E.R. Cole et al. (1998) found that all three of these barriers may be lessened: At midlife, women who had had the socializing experience of political participation as young adults also scored higher on political efficacy and collectivist orientation. Thus, the experience of activism itself can be an initiation into political participation with long-lasting effects (E.R. Cole & Stewart, 1996).

For some women, this socialization may take place in the family of origin. Scholars have noted that people from particular ethnic backgrounds with activist traditions (e.g., Jewish, African American) or those who were raised in a particular political culture (e.g., red diaper babies) are likely to have early and sustained activist commitments (S.I. Abramowitz & Abramowitz, 1971; Braungart & Braungart, 1990; V. Harding, 1991; M. Lerner & West, 1995; A.D. Morris, 1984). It seems that a shared element among these different backgrounds is a commitment to *community;* that is, a common element of political socialization for individuals from these groups includes an emphasis on the well-being of an entire group of people, rather than on individual success.

BARRIERS TO CHANGE

Unfortunately, there remain a number of barriers to developing a politicized gender consciousness and becoming an agent of feminist change. As noted earlier, stereotypes about feminism and feminists are rampant. Feminism is often perceived as constituting a threat to the hegemonic, heterosexual discourse by virtue of its association with lesbianism, assertiveness, and other behaviors that are the antithesis of traditional notions of femininity (M. Fox & Auerbach, 1983; Griffin, 1989; Kamen, 1991; A. Stein, 1997). Other barriers to raising consciousness and mobilizing feminist activism are embedded in our political and economic structure; from this perspective, change in individuals' attitudes and behaviors may be relatively easy to bring about. For example, research shows that men of younger cohorts have more feminist attitudes and are more accepting of feminists than older generations of men, and they also are more equitable in their sharing of household responsibilities (K.O. Mason & Lu, 1988; P. Schwartz, 1994).

However, corporate America is generally conservative, changing slowly and often only in response to legislation. Functionally, this may be the same as no change at all. For example, despite the opposition to the Family and Medical Leave Act of 1993, employees of large organizations are now eligible to take up to 12 weeks of unpaid leave to care for their family members under certain circumstances. Yet, because *paid* parental leave is still a rarity for most employees, particularly those in low-wage jobs, many families may not be able financially to avail themselves of such leave. This example and others like it suggest that dominant groups in our society may be willing to make some minor concessions to feminist demands, while simultaneously resisting changes that mean real sacrifice or real changes in the distribution of power (and wealth).

Because in some ways society has not really changed very much, some women have become antifeminist, lamenting that changes in expectations have made their lives worse than before the women's movement. These critics of feminism say that now women are expected to excel in the work world *and* at home, instead of just at home (Klatch, 1987). Yet, they place the blame for increasing the expectations of women on feminism, rather than on market forces requiring two earners for families to maintain a middle-class income, combined with a lack of real social change supporting families (e.g., child and elder care). Judging from the spate of recently published books (e.g. Crittenden, 1999; Roiphe, 1994; Shalit, 1999), this view seems to be gaining an increasing audience. This perhaps speaks to the frustration of women who are conscious of discrimination but have no skills for collective action or are disapproving of it. Although individual women may have reaped the benefits of the women's movement, conditions will not change permanently for women until society at large and individual men and women change—and this is perhaps most true for women who are not economically privileged. As we look toward the start of the next millennium, there is still much to do for those of us who call ourselves feminists.

References

Abbey, A. (1982). Sex differences in attributions for friendly behavior: Do males misperceive females' friendliness? *Journal of Personality and Social Psychology, 42,* 830–838.

Abbey, A., & Melby, C. (1986). The effects of nonverbal cues on gender differences in perceptions of sexual intent. *Sex Roles, 15,* 283–298.

Abeles, N., Cooley, S., Deitch, I.M., Harper, M.S., Hinrichsen, G., Lopez, M.A., & Molinari, V.A. (1997). *What practitioners should know about working with older adults.* Washington, DC: American Psychological Association.

Able-Kim, J.S. (1996). Cultural competence and quality of care: Issues for mental health service delivery in managed care. *Clinical Psychology, 3,* 273–295.

Abrahams, N. (1996). Negotiating power, identity, family and community: Women's community participation. *Gender and Society, 10*(6), 768–796.

Abramowitz, C.V., & Dokecki, P.R. (1977). The politics of clinical judgment: Early empirical returns. *Psychological Bulletin, 84,* 460–476.

Abramowitz, S.I., & Abramowitz, C.V. (1971). Parents' religious affiliation and family support for student activism. *Psychological Reports, 29,* 1078.

Abrams, K. (1989). Gender discrimination and the transformation of workplace norms. *Vanderbilt Law Review, 42,* 1183–1248.

Abrams, K. (1998). The new jurisprudence of sexual harassment. *Cornell Law Review, 83,* 1169–1230.

Absi-Semaan, N., Crombie, G., & Freeman, C. (1993). Masculinity and femininity in middle childhood: Developmental and factor analysis. *Sex Roles, 28,* 187–206.

Achterberg-Lewis, J. (1988). Musculoskeletal disorders. In E.A. Blechman & K. Brownell (Eds.), *Handbook of behavioral medicine for women* (pp. 222–235). New York: Pergamon Press.

Acock, A.C. (1984). Parents and their children: The study of intergenerational influence. *Sociology and Social Research, 69,* 151–171.

Acock, A.C., & Bengtson, V.L. (1978). On the relative influence of mothers and fathers: A covariance analysis of political and religious socialization. *Journal of Marriage and the Family, 40,* 519–531.

Adams, J.H. (1997). Sexual harassment and Black women: A historical perspective. In W. O'Donohue (Ed.), *Sexual harassment: Theory, research, and treatment* (pp. 213–224). Boston: Allyn & Bacon.

Adams, J.W., Kottke, J.L., & Padgett, J.S. (1983). Sexual harassment of college students. *Journal of College Student Personnel, 24,* 484–490.

Adams-Roy, J., & Barling, J. (1998). Predicting the decision to confront or report sexual harassment. *Journal of Organizational Behavior, 19,* 329–336.

Adelmann, P.K., Antonucci, T.C., Crohan, S.E., & Coleman, L.M. (1989). Empty nest, cohort, and employment in the well-being of midlife women. *Sex Roles, 20,* 173–189.

Ades, P.A., Waldmann, M.L., Polk, D.M., & Coflesky, J.T. (1992). Referral patterns and exercise response in the rehabilitation of female coronary patients aged 62 years or over. *American Journal of Cardiology, 69,* 1422–1425.

Adkins-Regan, E. (1988). Sex hormones and sexual orientation in animals. *Psychobiology, 16,* 335–347.

Adler, N.E., & Coriell, M. (1997). Socioeconomic status and women's health. In S.J. Gallant, G.P. Keita, & R. Royak-Schaler (Eds.), *Health care for women: Psychological, social, and behavioral influences.* Washington, DC: American Psychological Association.

Afifi, W.A., & Johnson, M.L. (1999). The use and interpretation of tie signs in a public setting: Relationship and sex differences. *Journal of Social and Personal Relationships, 16,* 9–38.

Agronick, G.S., & Duncan, L.E. (1998). Personality and social change: Individual differences, life path, and importance attributed to the women's movement. *Journal of Personality and Social Psychology, 74,* 1545–1555.

Ahuja, Y.R., & Plato, C.C. (1990). Effect of environmental pollutants on dermatoglyphic patterns. In N.M. Durham & C.C. Plato (Eds.), *Trends in dermatoglyphic patterns* (pp. 123–135). Boston: Kluwer Academic.

Ai, A.L., Saunders, D.G., Peterson, C., Dunkle, R.E., & Bolling, S.F. (1997). Gender differences in distress and depression following cardiac surgery. *Journal of Gender, Culture, and Health, 2,* 305–319.

Ainsworth, M.D. (1982). Attachment: Retrospect and prospect. In C.M. Parkes & J. Stevenson-Hinde (Eds.), *The place of attachment in human behavior* (pp. 3–30). New York: Basic Books.

Aitken, L., & Griffin, G. (1996). *Gender issues in elder abuse*. London: Sage.

Aizenman, M., & Kelley, G. (1988). The incidence of violence and acquaintance rape in dating relationships among college men and women. *Journal of College Student Development, 29*, 305–311.

Albee, G.W., & Perry, M. (1998). Economic and social causes of sexism and of the exploitation of women. *Journal of Community and Applied Social Psychology, 8*(2), 145–160.

Albert, A.A., & Porter, J.R. (1983). Age patterns in the development of children's gender-role stereotypes. *Sex Roles, 9*, 59–67.

Aldarondo, E. (1992, December). The cessation of marital violence.*Dissertation Abstracts International, 53*(6–B), 3147.

Aldarondo, E. (1996). Cessation and persistence of wife assault: A longitudinal analysis. *American Journal of Orthopsychiatry, 66*, 141–151.

Aldarondo, E., & Kantor, G. (1997). Social predictors of wife assault cessation. In *Out of darkness: Contemporary perspectives on family violence* (pp. 183–193). Thousand Oaks, CA: Sage.

Aldarondo, E., & Sugarman, D.B. (1996). Risk marker analysis of the cessation and persistence of wife assault. *Journal of Consulting and Clinical Psychology, 64*, 1010–1019.

Aldous, J. (1969). Occupational characteristics and males' role performance in the family. *Journal of Marriage and the Family, 31*, 707–712.

Alexander, L.L., & LaRosa, J.H. (1994). *New dimensions in women's health*. Boston: Bartlett & Jones.

Alexander, R.D. (1987). *The biology of moral systems*. New York: Aldine de Gruyter.

Alicea, M. (1997). A chambered nautilus: The contradictory nature of Puerto Rican women's role in the social construction of a transnational community. *Gender and Society, 11*, 597–626.

Allatt, P. (1996). Conceptualising parenting from the standpoint of children: Relationship and transition in the life course. In J. Brannen & M. O'Brien (Eds.), *Children in families: Research and policy* (pp. 130–144). London: Falmer Press.

Allen, A.T. (1991). *Feminism and motherhood in Germany, 1800–1914*. New Brunswick, NJ: Rutgers University Press.

Allen, B.P. (1995). Gender stereotypes are not accurate: A replications of Martin (1987) using diagnostic vs. self-report and behavioral criteria. *Sex Roles, 32*, 583–600.

Allen, J. (1998). Personality assessment with American Indians and Alaska Natives: Instrument considerations and service delivery style. *Journal of Personality Assessment, 70*, 17–42.

Allen, L.S., & Gorski, R.A. (1992). Sexual orientation and the size of the anterior commissure in the human brain. *Proceedings of the National Academy of Sciences, USA, 89*, 7199–7202.

Allen-Burge, R., Storandt, M., Kinscherf, D.A., & Rubin, E.H. (1994). Sex differences in the sensitivity of two self-report depression scales in older depressed inpatients. *Psychology and Aging, 9*, 443–445.

Allers, C.T., Benjack, K.J., & Allers, N.T. (1992). Unresolved childhood sexual abuse: Are older adults affected? *Journal of Counseling and Development, 71*, 14–17.

Allport, G. (1954). *The nature of prejudice*. Cambridge, MA: Addison-Wesley.

Altemeyer, B. (1988). *Enemies of freedom: Understanding right-wing authoritarianism*. San Francisco: Jossey-Bass.

Altheide, D.L., & Johnson, J.M. (1994). Criteria for assessing interpretive validity in qualitative research. In N.K. Denzin & Y.S. Lincoln (Eds.), *Handbook of qualitative research* (pp. 485–499). Thousand Oaks, CA: Sage.

Altmann, J. (1997). Mate choice and intrasexual reproductive competition: Contributions that go beyond acquiring more mates. In P.A. Gowaty (Ed.), *Feminism and evolutionary biology: Boundaries, intersections, and frontiers*. New York: Chapman & Hall.

Alwin, D.F., Cohen, R.L., & Newcomb, T.M. (1991). *Political attitudes over the life span: The Bennington women after fifty years*. Madison: University of Wisconsin Press.

American Association of Homes for the Aging. (1991). *Fact sheet: Nursing homes*. Washington, DC: Author.

American Association of Retired Persons. (1992). *Abused elders or older battered women?* Washington, DC: Author.

American Association of University Women. (1990). *Shortchanging girls, shortchanging America*. Washington, DC: Greenberg Lake, The Anaylsis Group & American Association of University Women.

American Association of University Women Education Foundation. (1991). *Short-changing girls, short-changing America*. (Available from AAUW, 1111 16th NW, Washington, DC 20036–4873)

American Association of University Women Education Foundation. (1993). *Hostile hallways: The AAUW survey on sexual harassment in America's schools* (No. 923012). Washington, DC: Harris/Scholastic Research.

American Heart Association. (1998). *Cardiovascular disease: 1998 heart and stroke statistical update*. Dallas, TX: Author.

American Psychiatric Association. (1987). *Diagnostic and statistical manual of mental disorders* (3rd ed., rev.). Washington, DC: Author.

American Psychiatric Association. (1994). *Diagnostic and statistical manual of mental disorders* (4th ed.). Washington, DC: Author.

American Psychological Association. (1975). Report of the task force on sex bias and sex-role stereotyping in psychotherapeutic practice. *American Psychologist, 30,* 1169–1175.

Amnesty International. (1997). *Breaking the silence: Human rights violations based on sexual orientation.* London: Author.

Anderson, K.J., & Leaper, C. (1998). Meta-analyses of gender effects on conversational interruption: Who, what, when, where, and how. *Sex Roles, 39,* 225–252.

Anderson, L.P. (1991). Acculturative stress: A theory of relevance to Black Americans. *Clinical Psychology Review, 11,* 685–702.

Anderson, V.N., & Walsh, J.E. (1998). Women with interstitial cystitis: Uncertainty and psychosocial adjustment. *Journal of Gender, Culture, and Health, 3,* 51–57.

Andersson, M. (1994). *Sexual selection.* Princeton, NJ: Princeton University Press.

Annesley, P., & Coyle, A. (1995). Clinical psychologists' attitudes to lesbians. *Journal of Community and Applied Psychology, 5,* 327–331.

Anzaldúa, G. (1987). *Borderlands/La Frontera.* San Francisco: Aunt Lute.

Apfelbaum, E. (1999). Relations of domination and movements for liberation: An analysis of power between groups. In W.G. Austin & S. Worchel (Eds.), *Social psychology of intergroup relations* (pp. 188–204). Belmont, MA: Brooks/Cole. (Original work published 1979)

Appel, A.E., & Holden, G.W. (1998). The co-occurrence of spouse and physical child abuse: A review and appraisal. *Journal of Family Psychology, 12,* 578–599.

Aquilino, W.S. (1996). The life course of children born to unmarried mothers: Childhood living arrangements and young adult outcomes. *Journal of Marriage and the Family, 58,* 293–310.

Arber, S., & Ginn, J. (1991). *Gender and later life: A sociological analysis of resources and constraints.* London: Sage.

Archer, J. (1996). Sex differences in social behavior: Are the social role and evolutionary explanations compatible? *American Psychologist, 51,* 909–917.

Archer, J., & Haigh, A. (1999). Sex differences in beliefs about aggression: Opponent's sex and the form of aggression. *British Journal of Social Psychology, 38,* 71–84.

Archer, J., & Parker, S. (1994). Social representations of aggression in children. *Aggressive Behavior, 20,* 101–114.

Arean, P.A., & Gallagher-Thompson, D. (1996). Issues and recommendations for the recruitment and retention of older ethnic minority adults into clinical research. *Journal of Counsulting and Clinical Psychology, 64,* 875–880.

Arendell, T. (1986). *Mothers and divorce: Legal, economic and social dilemmas.* Berkeley: University of California Press.

Aries, E.J. (1976). Interaction patterns and themes of male and female, and mixed sex groups. *Small Group Behavior, 7,* 7–18.

Aries, E.J. (1996). *Women and men in interaction: Reconsidering the differences.* New York: Oxford University Press.

Aries, E.J., Olver, R.R., Blount, K., Christaldi, K., Fredman, S., & Lee, T. (1998). Race and gender as components of the working self-concept. *Journal of Social Psychology, 138,* 277–290.

Aronson, J., Thornewell, C., & Williams, K. (1995). Wife assault in old age: Coming out of obscurity. *Canadian Journal on Aging, 14,* 72–88.

Arroyo, J.A., Simpson, T.L., & Aragon, A.S. (1997). Childhood sexual abuse among Hispanic and non Hispanic White college women. *Hispanic Journal of Behavioral Sciences, 19,* 57–68.

Arvey, R.A., & Cavanaugh, M.A. (1995). Using surveys to assess the prevalence of sexual harassment: Some methodological problems. *Journal of Social Issues, 51,* 39–52.

Asante, M. (1980). *Afrocentricity: A theory of social change.* Buffalo, NY: Amulefi.

Asch, A., & Fine, M. (1988). Introduction: Beyond pedestals. In M. Fine & A. Asch (Eds.), *Women with disabilities: Essays in psychology, culture, and politics* (pp. 1–37). Philadelphia: Temple University Press.

Ashton, E. (1983). Measures of play behavior: The influence of sex-role stereotyped children's books. *Sex Roles, 9,* 43–47.

Associated Press. (1996, October 27). *Some facts about the $1 billion romance fiction industry from Harlequin.*

Astin, H.S. (1969). *The woman doctorate in America.* New York: Russell Sage Foundation.

Athanasiadou, C. (1997). Postgraduate women talk about family and career: The discursive reproduction of gender difference. *Feminism and Psychology, 7,* 321–327.

Atkinson, J.M., & Heritage, J. (Eds.). (1984). *Structures of social action: Studies in conversation analysis.* Cambridge, England: Cambridge University Press.

Austin, R. (1995). Sapphire bound! In K. Crenshaw, N. Gotanda, D. Peller, & K. Thomas (Eds.), *Critical race theory: The key writings that formed the movement.* New York: New Press.

Avni, N. (1991). Battered wives: Characteristsics of their courtship days. *Journal of Interpersonal Violence, 6*(2), 232–239.

Ayanian, J.Z., & Epstein, A.M. (1991). Differences in the use of procedures between women and men hospitalized for coronary heart disease. *New England Journal of Medicine, 325,* 221–225.

Babbie, E. (1992). *The practice of social research.* Belmont, CA: Wadsworth.

Backett, K. (1987). The negotiation of fatherhood. In C. Lewis & M. O'Brien (Eds.), *Reassessing fatherhood: New observations on fathers and the modern family* (pp. 74–90). London: Sage.

Backhouse, C., & Cohen, L. (1981). *Sexual harassment on the job: How to avoid the working woman's nightmare.* Englewood Cliffs, NJ: Prentice-Hall.

Badgett, M.V.L. (1995). The wage effects of sexual orientation discrimination. *Industrial and Labor Relations Review, 48,* 726–739.

Bailey, J.M., Dunne, M.P., & Martin, N.G. (2000). Genetic and environmental influences on sexual orientation and its correlates in an Australian twin sample. *Journal of Personality and Social Psychology, 78,* 524–536.

Bailey, J.M., & Pillard, R.C. (1991). A genetic study of male sexual orientation. *Archives of General Psychiatry, 48,* 1089–1096.

Bailey, J.M., Pillard, R.C., Dawood, K., Miller, M.B., Farrer, L.A., Trivedi, S., & Murphy, R.L. (1999). A family history study of male sexual orientation using three independent samples. *Behavior Genetics, 29,* 79–86.

Bailey, J.M., Pillard, R.C., Neale, M.C., & Agyei, Y. (1993). Heritable factors influence sexual orientation in women. *Archives of General Psychiatry, 50,* 217–223.

Bailey, J.M., & Zucker, K.J. (1995). Childhood sex-typed behavior and sexual orientation: A conceptual analysis and quantitative review. *Developmental Psychology, 31,* 43–55.

Bailey, W.C., Hendrick, C., & Hendrick, S.S. (1987). Relation of sex and gender role to love, sexual attitudes, and self-esteem. *Sex Roles, 16,* 637–648.

Bailyn, L. (1993). *Breaking the mold: Women, men and time in the new corporate world.* New York: Free Press.

Baker, C.L., & Kline, C.B. (1996). *The conversation begins: Mothers and daughters talk about living feminism.* New York: Bantam Books.

Baker, D.D., Terpstra, D.E., & Cutler, B.D. (1990). Perceptions of sexual harassment: A re-examination of gender differences. *Journal of Psychology, 124,* 409–416.

Baker, N.L. (1996). Class as a construct in a "classless" society. In M. Hill & E.D. Rothblum (Eds.), *In classism and feminist therapy: Counting costs* (pp. 13–23). New York: Haworth Press.

Baker, R.R., & Bellis, M.A. (1988). "Kamikaze" sperm in mammals? *Animal Behaviour, 36,* 937–980.

Baker, R.R., & Bellis, M.A. (1989a). Elaboration of the kamikaze sperm hypothesis: A reply to Harcourt. *Animal Behaviour, 6,* 887–909.

Baker, R.R., & Bellis, M.A. (1989b). Number of sperm in human ejaculates varies in accordance with sperm competition theory. *Animal Behaviour, 37,* 867–869.

Baker, R.R., & Bellis, M.A. (1993a). Human sperm competition: Ejaculate adjustment by males and the function of masturbation. *Animal Behaviour, 46,* 861–865.

Baker, R.R., & Bellis, M.A. (1993b). Human sperm competition: Ejaculate manipulation by females and a function for the female orgasm. *Animal Behaviour, 6,* 887–909.

Baker, R.R., & Bellis, M.A. (1995). *Human sperm competition: Copulation, masturbation and infidelity.* London: Chapman & Hall.

Bakker, A., van Kesteren, P.J.M., Gooren, L.J.G., & Bezemer, P.D. (1993). The prevalence of transsexualism in the Netherlands. *Acta Psychiatrica Scandinavica, 87,* 237–238.

Bakker, J., & Slob, A.K. (1997). Sexual differentiation of the brain and partner preference in the male rat: Behavioral, neuroanatomical, and neuroimmunocytochemical studies. In L. Ellis & L. Ebertz (Eds.), *Sexual orientation: Toward biological understanding* (pp. 91–106). Westport, CT: Praeger.

Baldwin, J., & Bell, Y. (1985). The African Self-Consciousness Scale: An Africentric personality questionnaire. *Western Journal of Black Studies, 9*(2), 61–68.

Banaji, M.R., & Hardin, C.D. (1996). Automatic stereotyping. *Psychological Science, 7,* 136–141.

Bancroft, J. (1997). Introduction and overview. In J. Bancroft (Ed.), *Researching sexual behavior* (pp. ix–xvi) Bloomington: Indiana University Press.

Bandura, A. (1977). *Social learning theory.* Englewood Cliffs, NJ: Prentice-Hall.

Banks, A., & Gartrell, N.K. (1996). Lesbians in the medical setting. In R.P. Cabaj & T.S. Stein (Eds.), *Textbook of homosexuality and mental health* (pp. 659–671). Washington, DC: American Psychiatric Press.

Banks, B.A., Silverman, R.A., Schwartz, R.H., & Tunnessen, W.W. (1992). Attitudes of teenagers toward sun exposure and sunscreen use. *Pediatrics, 89,* 40–42.

Banks, M.E., Ackerman, R.J., & Corbett, C.A. (1995). Feminist neuropsychology: Issues for physically challenged women. In J.C. Chrisler & A.H. Hemstreet (Eds.), *Variations on a theme: Diversity and the psychology of women* (pp. 29–49). Albany: State University of New York Press.

Barak, A., Fisher, W.A., & Houston, S. (1992). Individual difference correlates of the experience of sexual harassment among female university students. *Journal of Applied Social Psychology, 22,* 17–37.

Barak, A., Pitterman, Y., & Yitzhaki, R. (1995). An empirical test of the role of power differential in originating sexual harassment. *Basic and Applied Social Psychology, 17*, 497–518.

Barbach, L. (1975). *For yourself*. New York: Anchor Books.

Bardwick, J.M. (1971). *Psychology of women: A study of bio-cultural conflicts*. New York: Harper & Row.

Barer, B.M. (1994). Men and women aging differently. *International Journal of Aging and Human Development, 38*, 29–40.

Bargad, A., & Hyde, J.S. (1991). Women's studies: A study of feminist identity development in women. *Psychology of Women Quarterly, 15*, 181–201.

Bargh, J.A. (1997). The automaticity of everyday life. In R.S. Wyer, Jr. (Ed.), *The automaticity of everyday life: Advances in social cognition* (Vol. 10, pp. 1–61). Mahwah, NJ: Erlbaum.

Bargh, J.A., Raymond, P., Pryor, J.B., & Strack, F. (1995). Attractiveness of the underling: An automatic power-sex association and its consequences for sexual harassment and aggression. *Journal of Personality and Social Psychology, 68*, 768–781.

Barkow, J.L., Cosmides, L., & Tooby, J. (1992). *The adapted mind: Evolutionary psychology and the generation of culture*. New York: Oxford University Press.

Barnett, B.M. (1996). Invisible southern Black women leaders in the civil rights movement: The triple constraints of gender, race, and class. In E.N. Chow, D. Wilkinson, & M.B. Zinn (Eds.), *Race, class and gender: Common bonds, different voices* (pp. 265–287). Thousand Oaks, CA: Sage.

Barnett, O.W., & Fagan, R.W. (1993). Alcohol use in male spouse abusers and their female partners. *Journal of Family Violence, 8*, 1–25.

Barnett, R.C. (1998). Toward a review and reconceptualization of the work/family literature. *Genetic, Social and General Psychology Monographs, 124*(2), 125–182.

Barnett, R.C., & Rivers, C. (1996). *She works/He works: How two-income families are happier, healthier, and better off*. New York: HarperCollins.

Barnett, R.C., & Rivers, C. (1998). *She works/he works: How two-income families are happy, healthy, and thriving*. Cambridge, MA: Harvard University Press.

Barreca, R. (1991). *They used to call me Snow White . . . But I drifted*. New York: Viking.

Bartholomew, K., & Horowitz, L.M. (1991). Attachment styles among young adults: A test of a four-category model. *Journal of Personality and Social Psychology, 61*, 226–244.

Bartholomew, K., Landolt, M., & Oram, D. (1999). *Report of the West End relationship project*. Unpublished manuscript, Simon Fraser University, Burnaby, Canada.

Bartky, S.L. (1990). *Femininity and domination: Studies in the phenomenology of oppression*. New York: Routledge.

Bartle, N. (1998). *Venus in blue jeans*. Boston: Houghton Mifflin.

Bartol, K.M., & Butterfield, D.A. (1976). Sex effects in evaluating leaders. *Journal of Applied Psychology, 61*, 446–454.

Bartol, K.M., & Martin, D.C. (1986). Women and men in task groups. In R. Ashmore & F. Del Boca (Eds.), *Social psychology of female-male relations* (pp. 259–310). New York: Academic Press.

Baruch, G.K., Barnett, R.C., & Rivers, C. (1983). *Lifeprints: New patterns of live and work for today's women*. New York: New American Library.

Basow, S.A. (1992). *Gender stereotypes and roles* (3rd ed.). Pacific Grove, CA: Brooks/Cole.

Basow, S.A. (1995). Student evaluations of college professors: When gender matters. *Journal of Educational Psychology, 87*, 656–665.

Basow, S.A. (1998). Student evaluations: The role of gender bias and teaching styles. In L.H. Collins, J.C. Chrisler, & K. Quina (Eds.), *Career strategies for women in academe: Arming Athena* (pp. 135–156). Thousand Oaks, CA: Sage.

Basow, S.A., & Silberg, N. (1987). Student evaluations of college professors: Are female and male professors rated differently? *Journal of Educational Psychology, 79*, 308–314.

Bateman, A.J. (1948). Intra-sexual selection in Drosophila. *Heredity, 2*, 349–368.

Bauer, P.J. (1993). Memory for gender-consistent and gender-inconsistent event sequences by twenty-five-month-old children. *Child Development, 64*, 285–297.

Bauer, P.J., & Coyne, M.J. (1997). When the name says it all: Preschoolers' recognition and use of the gendered nature of common proper names. *Social Development, 6*, 271–291.

Bauer, P.J., Liebl, M., & Stennes, L. (1998). Pretty is to dress as brave is to suitcoat: Gender-based property-to-property inferences by 4½-year-old children. *Merrill-Palmer Quarterly, 44*, 355–377.

Baumrind, D. (1995). Commentary on sexual orientation: Research and social policy issues. *Developmental Psychology, 31*(1), 130–136.

Baylies, C. (1996). Diversity in patterns of parenting and household formation. In E.B. Silva (Ed.), *Good enough mothering? Feminist perspectives on lone motherhood* (pp. 76–96). London: Routledge.

Beck, B. (1998, July 18). For better, for worse (A survey of women and work). *Economist, 348*, S3–S6.

Becker, D. (1997). *Through the looking glass: Women and borderline personality disorder*. Boulder, CO: Westview Press.

Beckwith, K. (1998). Collective identities of class and gender: Working-class women in the Pittston coal strike. *Political Psychology, 19,* 147–167.

Beere, C.A. (1990a). *Gender roles: A handbook of tests and measures.* Westport, CT: Greenwood Press.

Beere, C.A. (1990b). *Sex and gender issues: A handbook of tests and measures.* Westport, CT: Greenwood Press.

Belenky, M.F., Clinchy, B.M., Goldberger, N.R., & Tarule, J.M. (1986). *Women's ways of knowing: The development of self, voice and mind.* New York: Basic Books.

Bell, D. (1996). White women can't speak? *Feminism & Psychology, 6,* 197–203.

Bell, Y.R., Bouie, C.L., & Baldwin, J.A. (1990). Afrocentric cultural consciousness and African-American male-female relationships. *Journal of Black Studies, 21,* 162–189.

Belle, D. (1999). *The after-school lives of children: Alone and with others while parents work.* Mahwah, NJ: Erlbaum.

Belsky, J., Robins, E., & Gamble, W. (1984). The determinants of parental competence: Towards a contextual theory. In M. Lewis (Ed.), *Beyond the Dyad* (pp. 251–279). New York: Plenum Press.

Bem, D.J. (1996). Exotic becomes erotic: A developmental theory of sexual orientation. *Psychological Review, 103,* 320–335.

Bem, S.L. (1974). The measurement of psychological androgyny. *Journal of Consulting and Clinical Psychology, 42,* 155–162.

Bem, S.L. (1979). Theory and measurement of androgyny: A reply to Pedhazur-Tetenbaum and Locksley-Colten critiques. *Journal of Personality and Social Psychology, 37,* 1047–1054.

Bem, S.L. (1981). Gender schema theory: A cognitive account of sex typing. *Psychological Review, 88,* 354–364.

Bem, S.L. (1989). Genital knowledge and gender constancy in preschool children. *Child Development, 60,* 649–662.

Bem, S.L. (1993). *The lenses of gender: Transforming the debate on sexual inequality.* New Haven, CT: Yale University Press.

Bem, S.L., & Bem, D.J. (1970). Training the woman to know her place: The power of a nonconscious ideology. In D.J. Bem (Ed.), *Beliefs, attitudes, and human affairs.* Belmont, CA: Brooks/Cole.

Bem, S.L., & Bem, D.J. (1973). Does sex-biased job advertising "aid and abet" sex discrimination? *Journal of Applied Social Psychology, 3,* 6–18.

Benjamin, J. (1988). *The bonds of love.* New York: Pantheon Books.

Benkov, L. (1998). Yes, I am a swan: Reflections on families headed by lesbians and gay men. In C. Garcia Coll, J.L. Surrey, & K. Weingarten (Eds.), *Mothering against the odds: Diverse voices of contemporary mothers* (pp. 113–133). New York: Guilford Press.

Benmayor, R., Juarbe, A., Alvarez, C., & Vazques, B. (1987). *Stories to live by: Continuity and change in three generations of Puerto Rican women.* New York: Centro de Estudios Puertorriqueños.

Bennett, S.K. (1982). Student perceptions of and expectations for male and female instructors: Evidence in relation to the question of gender bias in teaching evaluation. *Journal of Educational Psychology, 74,* 170–179.

Benokraitis, N.V. (1998). Working in the ivory basement: Subtle sex discrimination in higher education. In L.H. Collins, J.C. Chrisler, & K. Quina (Eds.), *Career strategies for women in academe: Arming Athena* (pp. 3–43). Thousand Oaks, CA: Sage.

Benokraitis, N.V., & Feagin, J. (1995). *Modern sexism: Blatant, subtle, and covert discrimination* (2nd ed.). Englewood Cliffs, NJ: Prentice-Hall.

Benson, D.J., & Thomson, G.E. (1982). Sexual harassment on a university campus: The confluence of authority relations, sexual interest and gender stratification. *Social Problems, 29,* 236–251.

Berenbaum, S.A. (1990). Congenital adrenal hyperplasia: Intellectual and psychosexual functioning. In C.S. Holmes (Ed.), *Psychoneuroendocrinology: Brain, behavior, and hormonal interactions* (pp. 227–260). New York: Springer-Verlag.

Berenbaum, S.A. (1999). Effects of early androgens on sex-typed activities and interests in adolescents with congenital adrenal hyperplasia. *Hormones and Behavior, 35,* 102–110.

Berenbaum, S.A., & Bailey, J.M. (1998, May). *Variation in female gender identity: Evidence from girls with congenital adrenal hyperplasia, tomboys, and typical girls.* Paper presented at the meeting of the Midwestern Psychological Association, Chicago.

Berenbaum, S.A., & Hines, M. (1992). Early androgens are related to childhood sex-typed toy preferences. *Psychological Science, 3,* 203–206.

Berenbaum, S.A., & Resnick, S.M. (1997). Early androgen effects on aggression in children and adults with congenital adrenal hyperplasia. *Psychoneuroendocrinology, 22,* 505–515.

Berenbaum, S.A., & Snyder, E. (1995). Early hormonal influences on childhood sex-typed activity and playmate preferences: Implications for the development of sexual orientation. *Developmental Psychology, 31,* 31–42.

Berger, J., Ridgeway, C.L., Rosenholtz, S., & Webster, M.A. (1986). Status, cues, expectations, and behavior. In E.J. Lawler (Ed.), *Advances in group processes: Theory and research* (pp. 1–22). Greenwich, CT: JAI Press.

Berger, P.L., & Luckmann, T. (1966). *The social construction of reality.* Harmondsworth, England: Penguin.

Bergin, A.E., & Garfield, S.L. (1971). *Handbook of psychotherapy and behavior change: An empirical analysis*. New York: Wiley.

Bergman, S.J. (1995). Men's psychological development: A relational perspective. In R.F. Levant & W.S. Pollack (Eds.), *A new psychology of men* (pp. 68–90). New York: Basic Books.

Bergvall, V.L., Bing, J.M., & Freed, A.F. (1996). *Rethinking language and gender research: Theory and practice*. New York: Longman.

Berkman, C.S., & Zinberg, G. (1997). Homophobia and heterosexism in social workers. *Social Work, 42*(4), 319–332.

Berkman, L.F., Seeman, T.E., Albert, M., Blazer, D., Kahn, R., Mohs, R., Finch, C., Schneider, E., Cotman, C., & McClearn, G. (1993). High, unusual and impaired functioning in community-dwelling older men and women: Findings from the MacArthur Foundation Research Network on Successful Aging. *Journal of Clinical Epidemiology, 46*, 1129–1140.

Berman, D. (1997). At ease, men. *Canadian Business, 70*(11), 105–106.

Bermudez, J.M. (1997). Experimental tasks and therapist bias awareness. *Contemporary Family Therapy, 19*, 253–267.

Bernard, J. (1975). *Women, wives, and mothers*. Chicago: Aldine.

Bernard, J. (1981). The good provider role: Its rise and fall. *American Psychololologist, 36*, 1–12.

Bernardez, T. (1991). Adolescent resistance and the maladies of women: Notes from the underground. In C. Gilligan, A.G. Rogers, & D.L. Tolman (Eds.), *Women, girls and psychotherapy: Reframing resistance* (pp. 213–222). Binghamton, NY: Haworth Press.

Berndt, T.J., & Heller, K.A. (1986). Gender stereotypes and social inferences: A developmental study. *Journal of Personality and Social Psychology, 50*, 889–898.

Bernstein, A. (1997). Treating sexual harassment with respect. *Harvard Law Review, 111*, 445–527.

Bernstein, M.D., & Russo, N.F. (1974). The history of psychology revisited: Or up with our foremothers. *American Psychologist, 29*, 130–134.

Berrill, K.T. (1990). Anti-gay violence and victimization in the United States: An overview. *Journal of Interpersonal Violence, 5*, 274–294.

Berryman, J. (1991). Perspectives on later motherhood. In A. Phoenix, A. Woollett, & E. Lloyd (Eds.), *Motherhood: Meanings, practices and ideologies* (pp. 103–122). London: Sage.

Berryman, J., Thorpe, K., & Windridge, K. (1995). *Older mothers: Conception, pregnancy and birth after 35*. London: Pandora Press.

Berscheid, E. (1992). A glance back at a quarter century of social psychology. *Journal of Personality and Social Psychology, 63*, 525–533.

Berscheid, E., Snyder, M., & Omoto, A.M. (1989). The Relationship Closeness Inventory: Assessing the closeness of interpersonal relationships. *Journal of Personality and Social Psychology, 57*(5), 792–807.

Bertram, C. (1998). Fitful narratives. In J. Ayala, C. Bertram, S. Carney, C. Centrie, K. Cumiskey, M. Fine, K. Foster, A. Galletta, S. Lombardo, S. Massey, T. McFarlane, R. Morton, R. Roberts, K. Tocke, J. Valentin-Juarbe, L. Weis, & S. Weseen (Eds.), *Speedbumps: Reflections on the politics and methods of qualitative work* (pp. 61–65). Buffalo: State University of New York, Graduate School of Education.

Best, D.L. (1982). An overview of findings from children studies of sex-trait stereotypes in 23 countries. In R. Roth, H.S. Asthana, D. Sinha, & J.B.H. Sinha (Eds.), *Diversity and unity in cross-cultural psychology* (pp. 261–271). Amsterdam: Swets.

Best, D.L., Williams, J.E., Cloud, J.M., Davis, S.W., Roberston, L.S., Edwards, J.R., Giles, H., & Fowles, J. (1977). Development of sex-trait stereotypes among young children in the United States, England, and Ireland. *Child Development, 48*, 1375–1384.

Bethke, T.M., & DeJoy, D.M. (1993). An experimental study of factors influencing the acceptability of daing violence. *Journal of Interpersonal Violence, 8*(1), 36–51.

Betz, N.E. (1993). Women's career development. In F.L. Denmark & M.A. Paludi (Eds.), *Psychology of women: A handbook of issues and theories* (pp. 627–684). Westport, CT: Greenwood Press.

Betz, N.E., & Fitzgerald, L.F. (1987). *The career psychology of women*. New York: Academic Press.

Betz, N.E., & Fitzgerald, L.F. (1993). Individuality and diversity: Theory and research in counseling psychology. *Annual Review of Psychology, 44*, 343–381.

Bianchi, B.D., & Bakeman, R. (1978). Sex-typed affiliation preferences observed in preschoolers: Traditional and open school differences. *Child Development, 49*, 910–912.

Biddle, B.S. (1993). *Health status indicators for Washington area lesbians and bisexual women: A report on the lesbian health clinic's first year*. Washington, DC: Whitman-Walker Clinic.

Biegel, D.D., & Schulz, R. (1999). Caregiving and caregiver interventions in aging and mental illness. *Family Relations, 48*, 345–354.

Biernat, M. (1991a). Gender stereotypes and the relationship between masculinity and femininity: A developmental analysis. *Journal of Personality and Social Psychology, 61*, 351–365.

Biernat, M. (1991b). A multicomponent, developmental analysis of sex typing. *Sex Roles, 24,* 567–586.

Biernat, M., & Wortman, C. (1991). Sharing of home responsibilities between professional employed women and their husbands. *Journal of Personality and Social Psychology, 60,* 844–860.

Bigler, R.S. (1995). The role of classification skill in moderating environmental influences on children's gender stereotyping: A study of the functional use of gender in the classroom. *Child Development, 66,* 1072–1087.

Bigner, J.J., & Bozett, F.W. (1990). Parenting by gay fathers. In F.W. Bozett & M.B. Sussman (Eds.), *Homosexuality and family relations* (pp. 155–176). New York: Harrington Park Press.

Billig, M. (1999a). Conversation analysis and the claims of naivety. *Discourse and Society, 10*(4), 573–576.

Billig, M. (1999b). Whose terms? Whose ordinariness? Rhetoric and ideology in conversation analysis. *Discourse and Society, 10*(4), 543–558.

Bilous, F.R., & Krauss, R.M. (1988). Dominance and accommodation in the conversational behaviors of same- and mixed-gender dyads. *Language and Communication, 8,* 183–194.

Birns, B., & Hay, D.F. (Eds.). (1988). *The different faces of motherhood.* New York: Plenum Press.

Bixler (1989). Diversity: A historical/comparative perspective. *Behavioral and Brain Sciences, 12,* 15–16.

Bjorkqvist, K., Lagerspetz, K.M.J., & Kaukiainen, A. (1992). Do girls manipulate and boys fight? Developmental trends in regard to direct and indirect aggression. *Aggressive Behavior, 18,* 117–127.

Bjornberg, U. (Ed.). (1992).*European parents in the 1990s: Contradictions and comparisons.* New York: Transaction.

Blackman, J. (1989). *Intimate violence: A study of injustice.* New York: Columbia University Press.

Blackman, J. (1990). Emerging images of severely battered women and the criminal justice system. *Behavioral Sciences and the Law, 8,* 121–130.

Blackman, J. (1994). At the frontier: In pursuit of justice for women. In B. Sales & G. Vandenbos (Eds.), *Psychology in litigation and legislation: The master lecturer* (pp. 141–173). Washington, DC: American Psychological Association.

Blackman, J. (1996). Battered women: What does this phrase really mean? *Domestic Violence Report, 23,* 1–11.

Blain, J. (1994). Discourses of agency and domestic labor: Family discourse and gendered practice in dual-career families. *Journal of Family Issues, 15,* 515–549.

Blair, I.V., & Banaji, M.R. (1996). Automatic and controlled processes in stereotype priming. *Journal of Personality and Social Psychology, 70,* 1142–1163.

Blair, S.L., & Lichter, D.T. (1991). Measuring the division of household labor: Gender segregation of housework among American couples. *Journal of Family Issues, 12*(1), 91–113.

Blakemore, J.E. (1998). The influence of gender and parental attitudes on preschool children's interest in babies: Observations in natural settings. *Sex Roles, 38,* 73–94.

Blakemore, J.E., LaRue, A.A., & Olejnik, A.B. (1979). Sex-appropriate toy preference and the ability to conceptualize toys as sex-role related. *Developmental Psychology, 15,* 339–340.

Blanchard, R. (1997). Birth order and sibling sex ratio in homosexual versus heterosexual males and females. *Annual Review of Sex Research, 8,* 27–67.

Blanchard, R., & Bogaert, A.F. (1996). Homosexuality in men and number of older brothers. *American Journal of Psychiatry, 153,* 27–31.

Blanchard, R., & Klassen, P. (1997). H-Y antigen and homosexuality in men. *Journal of Theoretical Biology, 185,* 373–378.

Blanchard, R., Zucker, K.J., Siegelman, M., Dickey, R., & Klassen, P. (1998). The relation of birth order to sexual orientation in men and women. *Journal of Biosocial Science, 30,* 511–519.

Blaske, D.M. (1984). Occupational sex-typing by kindergarten and fourth-grade children. *Psychological Reports, 54,* 795–801.

Blaxter, M. (1983). The causes of disease: Women talking. *Social Science and Medicine, 17,* 59–69.

Blazina, C., & Watkins, C.E. (1996). Masculine gender role conflict: Effects on college men's psychological well-being, chemical substance usage, and attitudes toward help-seeking. *Journal of Counseling Psychology, 43,* 461–465.

Blea, I.I. (1992). *La Chicana and the intersection of race, class, and gender.* New York: Praeger.

Bleier, R. (1984). *Science and gender: A critique of biology and its theories of women.* New York: Pergamon Press.

Blieszner, R. (1993). A socialist-feminist perspective on widowhood. *Journal of Aging Studies, 7,* 171–182.

Bloch, I. (1909). *The sexual life of our time.* London: Heinemann.

Block, J. (1984). *Sex role identity and ego development.* San Francisco: Jossey-Bass.

Block, J. (1990). *Ego resilience through time: Antecedents and ramifications. Resilience and psychological health.* Paper presented at the Symposium of the Boston Psychoanalytic Society.

Bloom, C., Gitter, A., Gutwill, S., Kogel, L., & Zaphiropoulos, L. (1994). *Eating problems: A feminist psychoanalytic treatment model.* New York: Basic Books.

Bloom, V., Coburn, K., & Perlman, J. (1975). *The new assertive woman.* New York: Delacorte.

Blumberg, R.L. (1990). White mothers as civil rights activists: The interweave of family and movement roles. In G. West & R.L. Blumberg (Eds.), *Women and social protest* (pp. 166–179). New York: Oxford University Press.

Blumenthal, J.A. (1998). The reasonable woman standard: A meta-analytic review of gender differences in perceptions of sexual harassment. *Law and Human Behavior, 22,* 33–58.

Bock, E.W., & Webber, I.L. (1972). Social status and the relational system of elderly suicides: A reexamination of the Henry-Short thesis. *Life-Threatening Behavior, 2,* 145–159.

Bograd, M. (1990). *Feminist approaches for men in family therapy.* New York: Haworth Press.

Bohan, J.S. (1992a). *Re-placing women in psychology: Readings toward a more inclusive history.* Dubuque, IA: Kendall/Hunt.

Bohan, J.S. (1992b). *Seldom seen, rarely heard: Women's place in psychology.* Boulder, CO: Westview Press.

Bohan, J.S. (1993). Regarding gender: Essentialism, constructionism, and feminist psychology. *Psychology of Women Quarterly, 17,* 5–22.

Bohan, J.S. (1997). *The psychology of sexual orientation.* New York: Routledge.

Bohannon, J.R., & Blanton, P.W. (1999). Gender role attitudes of American mothers and daughters over time. *Journal of Social Psychology, 139,* 173–179.

Bola, M., Drew, C., Gill, R., Harding, S., King, E., & Seu, B. (1998). Representing ourselves and representing others: A response. *Feminism and Psychology, 8,* 105–110.

Boldizar, J.P. (1991). Assessing sex typing and androgyny in children: The children's sex role inventory. *Developmental Psychology, 27,* 505–515.

Bond, M.H. (1994). Into the heart of collectivism: A personal and scientific journey. In U. Kim, H.C. Triandis, C. Kagitçibasi, S-C. Choi, & G. Yoon (Eds.), *Individualism and collectivism: Theory, method, and applications* (pp. 66–76). Thousand Oaks, CA: Sage.

Bondurant, B., & Donat, P.L.N. (1999). Perceptions of women's sexual interest and acquaintance rape: The role of sexual overperception and affective attitudes. *Psychology of Women Quarterly, 23,* 691–706.

Boney-McCoy, S., & Finkelhor, D. (1995). Psychosocial sequelae of violent victimization in a national youth sample. *Journal of Consulting and Clinical Psychology, 63,* 726–736.

Bookwala, J., Frieze, I.H., Smith, C., & Ryan, K. (1992). Predictors of dating violence: A multivariate analysis. *Violence and Victims, 7,* 297–311.

Booth, W.C., Colomb, G.G., & Williams, J.M. (1995). *The craft of research.* Chicago: University of Chicago Press.

Bordo, S. (1993). *Unbearable weight: Feminism, Western culture, and the body.* Berkeley: University of California Press.

Borgatta, E.F., & Stimson, J. (1963). Sex differences in interaction characteristics. *Journal of Social Psychology, 60,* 89–100.

Borgia, G. (1989). Typology and human mating preferences. *Behavioral and Brain Sciences, 12,* 16–17.

Boring, E.G. (1951). The woman problem. *American Psychologist, 5,* 679–682.

Boring, E.G. (1961). *Psychologist at large.* New York: Basic Books.

Boris, E. (1998). Scholarship and activism: The case of welfare justice. *Feminist Studies, 24,* 27–31.

Bornstein, K. (1994). *Gender outlaw: On men, women, and the rest of us.* New York: Routledge.

Bornstein, K. (1998). *My gender workbook.* New York: Routledge.

Bornstein, M.H. (1989). Sensitive periods in development: Structural characteristics and causal interpretations. *Psychological Bulletin, 105,* 179–197.

Boston, M.B., & Levy, G.D. (1991). Changes and differences in preschoolers' understanding of gender scripts. *Cognitive Development, 6,* 412–417.

Boswell, A.A., & Spade, J.Z. (1996). Fraternities and collegiate rape culture: Why are some fraternities more dangerous places for women? *Gender and Society, 10,* 133–147.

Bould, S., & Longino, C.F. (1997). Women survivors: The oldest old. In J.M. Coyle (Eds.), *Handbook on women and aging* (pp. 210–222). Westport, CT: Greenwood Press.

Bouvard, M.G. (1994). *Revolutionizing motherhood: The mothers of the Plaza de Mayo.* Wilmington, DE: Scholarly Resources.

Bowes-Sperry, L., & Tata, J. (1999). A multiperspective framework of sexual harassment. In G. Powell (Ed.), *Handbook of gender and work* (pp. 263–280). Thousand Oaks, CA: Sage.

Bowlby, J. (1969). *Attachment and loss: Attachment* (Vol. 1). New York: Basic Books.

Boxer, A.M., Cook, J.A., & Herdt, G. (1999). Experiences of coming out among gay and lesbian youth: Adolescents alone. In *The adolescent alone: Decision making in health care in the United States* (pp. 121–138). Cambridge, England: Cambridge University Press.

Bradbard, M.R., & Endsley, R.C. (1983). The effects of sex-typed labeling on preschool children's information-seeking and retention. *Sex Roles, 9,* 247–260.

Bradbard, M.R., Martin, C.L., Endsley, R.C., & Halverson, C.F. (1986). Influence of sex stereotypes on children's exploration and memory: A competence versus performance distinction. *Developmental Psychology, 22,* 481–486.

Bradford, J., & Ryan, C. (1988). *The National Lesbian Health Care Survey.* Washington, DC: National Lesbian and Gay Health Foundation.

Bradford, J., & Ryan, C. (1991). Who we are: Health concerns of middle-aged lesbians. In B. Sang, J. Warshow, & A. Smith (Eds.), *Lesbians at midlife: The creative transition* (pp. 147–163). San Francisco: Spinsters.

Bradford, J., Ryan, C., & Rothblum, E. (1994). National lesbian health care survey: Implications for mental health care. *Journal of Consulting and Clinical Psychology, 62,* 228–242.

Bradley, S.J., Oliver, G.D., Chernick, A.B., & Zucker, K.J. (1998). Experiment of nurture: Ablation penis at 2 months, sex reassigment at 7 months and a psychosexual follow-up in young adulthood. *Pediatrics, 102,* E91–E95. Available: http://www.pediatrics.org/cgi/content/full/102/1/e9

Brannen, J., Dodd, K., Oakley, A., & Storey, P. (1994). *Young people, health and family life.* Buckingham, England: Open University Press.

Brannen, J., & Moss, P. (1991). *Managing mothers: Dual earner household after maternity leave.* London: Unwin.

Brannon, R. (1976). The male sex role: Our culture's blueprint for manhood, what it's done for us lately. In D. David & R. Brannon (Eds.), *The forty-nine percent majority: The male sex role* (pp. 1–49). Reading, MA: Addison-Wesley.

Brannon, R., & Juni, S. (1984). A scale for measuring attitudes about masculinity. *Psychological Documents, 14*(6), 2012, 2612.

Branscombe, N.R., Ellemers, N., Spears, R., & Doosje, B. (1999). The context and content of social identity threat. In N. Ellemers, R. Spears, & B. Doosje (Eds.), *Social identity: Context, commitment, content* (pp. 35–58). Oxford, England: Blackwell.

Brant, C., & Too, Y.L. (1994). *Rethinking sexual harassment.* London: Pluto Press.

Bratton, E.K. (1980). The eye of the beholder: An interdisciplinary examination of law and social research on sexual harassment. *New Mexico Law Review, 17,* 91–114.

Braun, V. (2000). Heterosexism in focus group research: Collusion and challenge. *Feminism and Psychology, 10*(1), 133–140.

Braun, V., & Gavey, N. (1999). "With the best of reasons": Cervical cancer prevention policy and the suppression of sexual risk factor information. *Social Science and Medicine, 48,* 1463–1474.

Braun, V., & Kitzinger, C. (2000). *Telling it straight: Dictionary definitions of women's genitals.* Manuscript in preparation.

Braungart, M.M., & Braungart, R.G. (1990). The life-course development of left- and right-wing youth activist leaders from the 1960s. *Political Psychology, 11,* 243–282.

Breedlove, S.M. (1997). Sex on the brain. *Nature, 389,* 801.

Breines, W., & Gordon, L. (1983). The new scholarship on family violence. *Signs, 8,* 490–531.

Brenes, M.E., Eisenberg, N., & Helmstadter, G.C. (1985). Sex role development of preschoolers from two-parent and one-parent families. *Merrill-Palmer Quarterly, 31,* 33–46.

Brewer, M.B. (1982). Further beyond nine to five: An integration and future directions. *Journal of Social Issues, 38,* 149–157.

Brewer, M.B., Dull, V., & Lui, L. (1981). Perceptions of the elderly: Stereotypes as prototypes. *Journal of Personality and Social Psychology, 41,* 656–670.

Brewer, M.B., Ho, H., Lee, J., & Miller, N. (1987). Social identity and social distance among Hong Kong school children. *Personality and Social Psychology Bulletin, 13,* 156–165.

Brewer, R.M. (1993). Theorizing race, class and gender: The new scholarship of Black feminist intellectuals and Black women's labor. In S.M. James & A.P.A. Busia (Eds.), *Theorizing Black feminisms* (pp. 13–30). London: Routledge.

Brice-Baker, J. (1994). West Indian women: The Jamaican woman. In L. Comas-Diaz & B. Greene (Eds.), *Women of color: Integrating ethnic and gender identities in psychotherapy* (pp. 139–160). New York: Guilford Press.

Brickman, J. (1984). Feminist, non-sexist, and traditional models of therapy: Implications for working with incest. *Women and Therapy, 3,* 49–67.

Brinn, J., Kraemer, K., Warm, J.S., & Paludi, M.A. (1984). Sex-role preferences in four age levels. *Sex Roles, 11,* 901–910.

Brinson, J., & Kottler, J. (1993). Cross-cultural mentoring in counselor education: A strategy for retaining minority faculty. *Counselor Education and Supervision, 32,* 241–253.

Brittain, V. (1982). *Chronicle of youth: The war diary: 1913–1917.* New York: Morrow.

Brod, H. (Ed.). (1987). *The making of masculinities: The new men's studies.* Winchester, MA: Allen & Unwin.

Brodsky, A.M. (1973). The consciousness-raising group as a model of therapy for women. *Psychotherapy: Theory, Research, and Practice, 10,* 24–29.

Brodsky, A.M. (1977). Therapeutic aspects of consciousness-raising groups. In E.I. Rawlings & D.K. Carter (Eds.), *Psychotherapy for women: Treatment toward equality* (pp. 300–309). Springfield, IL: Thomas.

Brodsky, A.M., & Hare-Mustin, R.T. (1980). *Women and psychotherapy.* New York: Guilford Press.

Brody, H. (1992). Assisted death: A compassionate response to a medical failure. *New England Journal of Medicine, 327,* 1384–1388.

Brodzinsky, D.M., & Schechter, M.D. (Eds.). (1990).*Psychology of adoption.* Oxford, England: Oxford University Press.

Bronfenbrenner, U. (1992). *The ecology of human development.* Cambridge, MA: Harvard University Press.

Brooks, G.R. (1995).*The centerfold syndrome: How men can overcome objectification and achieve intimacy with women.* San Francisco: Jossey-Bass.

Brooks, G.R. (1997). The Centerfold syndrome. In R. Levant & G. Brooks (Eds.), *Men and sex: New psychological perspectives* (pp. 28–57). New York: Wiley.

Brooks, G.R., & Good, G.E. (Eds.). (in press). *The new handbook of psychotherapy and counseling for men: A comprehensive guide to settings, problems, and treatment approaches.* San Francisco: Jossey-Bass.

Brooks, G.R., & Levant, R.F. (1999). A history of Division 51 (the Society for the Psychological Study of Men and Masculinity). In D. Dewsbury (Ed.), *Unification through division: Histories of the divisions of the American Psychological Association* (Vol. 3, pp. 197–222). Washington, DC: American Psychological Association.

Brooks, L., & Perot, A.R. (1991). Reporting sexual harassment: Exploring a predictive model. *Psychology of Women Quarterly, 15,* 31–47.

Brooks, M., & Peiken, S. (1997). Bitch [Recorded by M. Brooks]. On *Blurring the edges* [CD]. Capitol Records.

Brooks, V.R. (1982). Sex differences in student dominance behavior in female and male professors' classrooms. *Sex Roles, 8,* 683–690.

Brooks-Gunn, J., & Chase Lansdale, P.L. (1995). Adolescent parenthood. In M. Bornstein (Ed.), *Handbook of parenting: Status and social conditions of parenting* (Vol. 3, pp. 113–149)). Hillsdale, NJ: Erlbaum.

Broverman, I.K., Broverman, D.M., Clarkson, F.E., Rosenkrantz, P.S., & Vogel, S.R. (1970). Sex-role stereotypes and clinical judgments of mental health. *Journal of Consulting and Clinical Psychology, 34,* 1–7.

Broverman, I.K., Vogel, S.R., Broverman, D.M., Clarkson, F.E., & Rosenkrantz, P.S. (1972). Sex-role stereotypes: A current appraisal. *Journal of Social Issues, 28,* 59–78.

Brown, C.A. (1987). The new patriarchy. In C. Bose, R. Feldberg, & N. Sokoloff (Eds.), *Hidden aspects of women's work* (pp. 137–160). New York: Praeger.

Brown, C.E., Dovidio, J.F., & Ellyson, S.L. (1990). Reducing sex differences in visual displays of dominance: Knowledge is power. *Personality and Social Psychology Bulletin, 16*(2), 358–368.

Brown, D.R. (1990). Depression among Blacks: An epidemiological perspective. In D.S. Ruiz (Ed.), *Handbook of mental health and mental disorder among Black Americans* (pp. 245–258). New York: Greenwood Press.

Brown, E.A. (1989, June 9). Happily ever after. *Christian Science Monitor,* p. 13.

Brown, G.W., & Harris, T. (1978). *The social origins of depression: A study of psychiatric disorder in women.* London: Tavistock.

Brown, L. (1994). *Subversive dialogues: Theory in feminist therapy.* New York: Basic Books.

Brown, L. (1996). Educating the resistance: Encouraging girls' strong feelings and critical voices. *High School Journal, 79*(3), 221–230.

Brown, L., Debold, E., Gilligan, C., & Tappan, M. (1991). Reading narratives of conflict for self and moral voice: A relational method. In W. Kurtines & J. Gewirtz (Eds.), *Handbook of moral behavior and development: Theory, research, and applications* (pp. 43–62). Hillsdale, NJ: Erlbaum.

Brown, L.M. (1991). Telling a girl's life: Self-authorization as a form of resistance. In C. Gilligan, A.G. Rogers, & D.L. Tolman (Eds.), *Women, girls and psychotherapy: Reframing resistance* (pp. 71–86). Binghamton, NY: Haworth Press.

Brown, L.M. (1998). *Raising their voices: The politics of girls' anger.* Cambridge, MA: Harvard University Press.

Brown, L.M., & Gilligan, C. (1992). *Meeting at the crossroads: Women's psychology and girls' development.* Cambridge, MA: Harvard University Press.

Brown, L.M., & Gilligan, C. (1993). Meeting at the crossroads: Women's psychology and girls' development. *Feminism and Psychology, 3*(1), 11–35.

Brown, L.S. (1986). Gender-role analysis: A neglected component of psychological assessment. *Psychotherapy: Theory, Research, and Practice, 23,* 243–248.

Brown, L.S. (1989). New voices, new vision: Toward a lesbian/gay paradigm for psychology. *Psychology of Women Quarterly, 13,* 445–458.

Brown, L.S. (1992). While waiting for the revolution. *Feminism and Psychology, 2,* 237–253.

Brown, L.S. (1994). *Subversive dialogues: Theory in feminist therapy.* New York: Basic Books.

Brown, L.W. (1989). New voices, new visions: Toward a lesbian/gay paradigm for psychology. *Psychology of Women Quarterly, 13,* 445–458.

Brown, S., Lumley, J., Small, R., & Astbury, J. (1994). *Missing voices: The experience of motherhood.* Melbourne, Australia: Oxford University Press.

Brown, S., Small, R., & Lumley, J. (1997). Being a "good mother." *Journal of Reproductive and Infant Psychology, 15,* 185–200.

Browne, A. (1987). *When battered women kill.* New York: Macmillan.

Browne, A. (1993). Violence against women by male partners: Prevalence, outcomes, and policy implications. *American Psychologist, 48,* 1077–1087.

Browne, A., & Bassuk, S. (1997). Intimate violence in the lives of homeless and poor housed women: Prevalence and patterns in an ethnically diverse sample. *American Journal of Orthopsychiatry, 67,* 261–278.

Browne, A., Salomon, A., & Bassuk, S.S. (1999). The impact of recent partner violence on poor women's capacity to maintain work. *Violence against Women, 5,* 393–426.

Browne, A., & Williams, K.R. (1989). Exploring the effect of resource availability and the likelihood of female-perpetrated homicides. *Law and Society Review, 23,* 75–94.

Browne, B.A. (1997). Gender and beliefs about work force discrimination in the United States and Australia. *Journal of Social Psychology, 137*(1), 107–116.

Browne, K.R. (1997). An evolutionary perspective on sexual harassment: Seeking roots in biology rather than ideology. *Journal of Contemporary Legal Issues, 8,* 5–77.

Bruning, F. (1998, February 17). The man from Mars. *Newsday.*

Bryan, B. (1992, February 2). Addict charged in death, malnutrition blamed: Baby's mother is held. *St. Louis Post Dispatch.*

Buhle, M.J. (1998). *Feminism and its discontents.* Cambridge, MA: Harvard University Press.

Bui, K-V.T., Peplau, L.A., & Hill, C.T. (1993, August 22). *Testing the investment model of relationship commitment and stability in a 15-year study of heterosexual couples.* Paper presented at the annual convention of the American Psychological Association, Toronto, Canada.

Bularzik, M. (1978). Sexual harassment at the workplace: Historical notes. Reprinted in pamphlet from *Radical American.* Boston: New England Free Press.

Burcky, W., Reuterman, N., & Kopsky, S. (1988). Dating violence among high school students. *School Counselor, 35,* 353–358.

Burden, D.S., & Gottlieb, N. (1987). Women's socialization and feminist groups. In C.M. Brody (Ed.), *Women's therapy groups: Paradigms of feminist treatment* (pp. 24–39). New York: Haworth Press.

Burger, J., & Inderbitzen, H. (1985). Predicting contraceptive behavior among college students: The role of communication, knowledge, sexual activity, and self-esteem. *Archives of Sexual Behavior, 14,* 343–350.

Burgess, A. (1998, November). Keynote address at North Carolina Coalition against Sexual Assault, annual meeting, Asheville, NC.

Burgess, A.W., & Holmstrom, L.L. (1979). *Rape: Crisis and recovery.* Bowie, MD: Bardy.

Burgess, D., & Borgida, E. (1997a). Refining sex-role spillover theory: The role of gender subtypes and harasser attributions. *Social Cognition, 15,* 291–311.

Burgess, D., & Borgida, E. (1997b). Sexual harassment: An experimental test of sex-role spillover theory. *Personality and Social Psychology Bulletin, 23,* 63–75.

Burgess, D., & Borgida, E. (1999). Who women are, who women should be: Descriptive and prescriptive gender stereotyping in sex discrimination. *Psychology, Public Policy, and Law, 5,* 665–692.

Burghes, L. (1996). Debates on disruption: What happens to the children of lone parents. In E.B. Silva (Ed.), *Good enough mothering? Feminist perspectives on lone motherhood* (pp. 157–174). London: Routledge.

Burleson, B.R. (1997). Second response. A different voice on different cultures: Illusion and reality in the study of sex differences in personal relationships. *Personal Relationships, 4,* 229–241.

Burlington Industries, Inc. v. Ellerth, 118 S.Ct. 2257 (1998).

Burman, E. (1994). *Deconstructing developmental psychology.* London: Routledge.

Burman, E. (1997). Minding the gap: Positivism, psychology, and the politics of qualitative methods. *Journal of Social Issues, 53,* 785–802.

Burman, E. (1998). *Deconstructing feminist psychology.* Thousand Oaks, CA: Sage.

Burman, E., Aitken, G., Alldred, P., Allwood, R., Billington, T., Goldberg, B., Gordo-Lopez, A.J., Heenan, C., Marks, D., & Warner, S. (1996). *Psychology discourse practice: From regulation to resistance.* London: Taylor & Francis.

Burman, E., & Parker, I. (Eds.). (1993). *Discourse analytic research: Repertoires and readings of texts in action.* London: Routledge.

Burns, S.E. (1994). Evidence of a sexually hostile workplace: What is it and how should it be assessed after *Harris v. Forklift Systems, Inc.? Review of Law and Social Change, 21,* 357–431.

Burns, S.E. (1995). Issues in workplace, sexual harassment law, and related social science research. *Journal of Social Issues, 51,* 193–210.

Burtoft, L. (1994). *Setting the record straight: What research really says about the social consequences of homosexuality.* Focus on the Family.

Bury, M. (1982). Chronic illness as biographical disruption. *Sociology of Health and Illness, 4,* 167–182.

Buschman, J.K., & Lenart, S. (1996). "I am not a feminist, but . . .": College women, feminism, and negative experiences. *Political Psychology, 17,* 59–75.

Buss, D.M. (1989). Sex differences in human mate preferences: Evolutionary hypotheses tested in 37 cultures. *Behavioral and Brain Sciences, 12,* 1–49.

Buss, D.M. (1995a). Human mate selection. *American Scientist, 73,* 47–51.

Buss, D.M. (1995b). Psychological sex differences: Origins through sexual selection. *American Psychologist, 50,* 164–168.

Buss, D.M. (1996). The evolutionary psychology of human social strategies. In E.T. Higgins & A.W. Kruglanski (Eds.), *Social psychology: A handbook of basic principles* (pp. 3–38). New York: Guilford Press.

Buss, D.M., Abbott, M., Angleitner, A., Asherian, A., Biaggio, A., & et. al. (1990). International preferences in selecting mates: A study of 37 cultures. *Journal of Cross-Cultural Psychology, 21,* 5–47.

Bussey, K., & Bandura, A. (1992). Self-regulatory mechanisms governing gender development. *Child Development, 63,* 1236–1250.

Bussey, K., & Bandura, A. (1999). Social cognitive theory of gender development and differentiation. *Psychological Review, 106,* 676–713.

Bussey, K., & Perry, D.G. (1982). Same-sex imitation: The avoidance of cross-sex models or the acceptance of same-sex models? *Sex Roles, 8,* 773–785.

Butler, D., & Geis, F.L. (1990). Nonverbal affect responses to male and female leaders: Implications for leadership evaluations. *Journal of Personality and Social Psychology, 58,* 48–59.

Butler, J. (1989). *Gender trouble.* London: Routledge.

Butler, J. (1990). *Gender trouble: Feminism and the subversion of identity.* New York: Routledge.

Butler, J. (1991). Imitation and gender insubordination. In D. Fuss (Ed.), *Inside/out: Lesbian theories, gay theories.* London: Routledge.

Butler, S., & Rosenblum, B. (1993). *Cancer in two voices.* London: Women's Press.

Byne, W., & Parsons, B. (1993). Human sexual orientation: The biologic theories reappraised. *Archives of General Psychiatry, 50,* 228–239.

Byrnes, J.P., Miller, D.C., & Schafer, W.D. (1999). Gender differences in risk taking: A meta analysis. *Psychological Bulletin, 125,* 367–383.

Cahill, S. (1994). *Writing women's lives.* New York: Harper Perennial.

Calasanti, T.M. (1993). Bringing in diversity: Toward an inclusive theory of retirement. *Journal of Aging Studies, 7*(2), 133–150.

Calasanti, T.M. (1996). Gender and life satisfaction in retirement: An assessment of the male model. *The Gerontologist, 51B,* S18–S29.

Caldwell, L.D., & White, J.L. (in press). African-centered therapeutic and counseling interventions for African American males. In G. Brooks & G. Good (Eds.), *The new handbook of psychotherapy and counseling for men.* San Francisco: Jossey-Bass.

Calhoun, K.S., Bernat, J.A., Clum, G.A., & Frame, C.L. (1997). Sexual coercion and attraction to sexual aggression in a community sample of young men. *Journal of Interpersonal Violence, 12*(1), 392–406.

Callahan, D. (1995). *Setting limits: Medical goals in an aging society.* New York: Simon & Schuster.

Calnan, M., & Richardson, K. (1976). Developmental correlates of handedness in a national sample of 11-year-olds. *Annals of Human Biology, 3,* 329–342.

Cameron, D. (1995). *Verbal hygiene.* London: Routledge.

Cameron, D. (1996). The language-gender interface: Challenging co-optation. In V.L. Bergvall, J.M. Bing, & A.F. Freed (Eds.), *Rethinking language and gender research: Theory and practice* (pp. 31–53). New York: Addison-Wesley.

Cameron, D. (1997). Performing gender identity: Young men's talk and the construction of heterosexual masculinity. In S. Johnson & U.H. Meinhof (Eds.), *Language and masculinity* (pp. 47–64). Oxford, England: Blackwell.

Cameron, D. (1998). Gender, language, and discourse: A review essay. *Signs, 23,* 945–973.

Cameron, D., McAlinden, F., & O'Leary, K. (1988). Lakoff in context: The social and linguistic functions of tag questions. In J. Coates & D. Cameron (Eds.), *Women in their speech communities: New perspectives on language and sex* (pp. 74–93). London: Longman.

Camhi, L. (1993). Stealing femininity: Department store kleptomania as sexual disorder. *Differences, 5,* 26–50.

Cammaert, L.P. (1985). How widespread is sexual harassment on campus? *International Journal of Women's Studies, 8,* 388–397.

Campbell, A. (1993). *Men, women, and aggression.* New York: Basic Books.

Campbell, A., Muncer, S., Guy, A., & Banim, M. (1996). Social representations of aggression: Crossing the sex barrier. *European Journal of Social Psychology, 26,* 135–147.

Campbell, B., Schellenberg, E.G., & Senn, C.Y. (1997). Evaluating measures of contemporary sexism. *Psychology of Women Quarterly, 21,* 89–101.

Campbell, D.T. (1999a). Science policy from a naturalistic sociological epistemology. In D.T. Campbell & M.J. Russo (Eds.), *Social experimentation* (2nd ed., pp. 163–173). Thousand Oaks, CA: Sage.

438 REFERENCES

Campbell, D.T. (1999b). Sociology of scientific validity. In D.T. Campbell & M.J. Russo (Eds.), *Social experimentation* (2nd ed., pp. 179–202). Thousand Oaks, CA: Sage.

Campbell, D.T., & Stanley, J. (1966). *Experimental and quasi-experimental design for research.* Chicago: Rand-McNally.

Campbell, J.C., & Lewandowski, L.A. (1996). Mental and physical health effects of intimate partner violence on women and children. *Psychiatric Clinics of North America, 20,* 353–374.

Campbell, R., & Salem, D.A. (1999). Concept mapping as a feminist research method. *Psychology of Women Quarterly, 23,* 65–89.

Campbell, R., & Schram, P.J. (1995). Feminist research methods: A content analysis of psychology and social science textbooks. *Psychology of Women Quarterly, 19,* 85–106.

Canada, E., & Phacbtong, T. (1992). Buddhism as a support system for Southeast Asian refugees. *Social Work, 37,* 61–67.

Canary, D.J., & Dindia, K. (Eds.). (1998). *Sex differences and similarities in communication.* Mahwah, NJ: Erlbaum.

Cancian, F.M. (1987). *Love in America: Gender and self-development.* New York: Cambridge University Press.

Canetto, S.S. (1992). Gender and suicide in the elderly. *Suicide and Life-Threatening Behavior, 22,* 80–97.

Canetto, S.S. (1995). Elderly women and suicidal behavior. In S.S. Canetto & D. Lester (Eds.), *Women and suicidal behavior* (pp. 215–233). New York: Springer.

Canetto, S.S. (1997). Gender and suicidal behavior: Theories and evidence. In R.W. Maris, M.M. Silverman, & S.S. Canetto (Eds.), *Review of suicidology* (pp. 138–167). New York: Guilford Press.

Canetto, S.S., & Hollenshead, J. (1999). Gender and physician-assisted suicide: An analysis of the Kevorkian cases, 1990–1997. *Omega: Journal of Death and Dying, 40,* 165–208.

Canetto, S.S., & Hollenshead, J. (2000). Older women and mercy killing. *Omega: Journal of Death and Dying.*

Canetto, S.S., Kaminski, P.L., & Felicio, D.M. (1995). Typical and optimal aging in women and men: Is there a double standard? *International Journal of Aging and Human Development, 40,* 1–21.

Canetto, S.S., & Lester, D. (1995). Gender and the primary prevention of suicide mortality. *Suicide and Life-Threatening Behavior, 25,* 58–69.

Canetto, S.S., & Lester, D. (1998). Gender, culture and suicidal behavior. *Transcultural Psychiatry, 35,* 163–191.

Cann, A., & Palmer, S. (1986). Children's assumptions about the generalizability of sex-typed abilities. *Sex Roles, 15,* 551–558.

Cano, M.A., & Kite, M.E. (1998, August). *Gender role violations: Perceived homosexuality as a mediating variable.* Paper presented at the meeting of the American Psychological Association, San Francisco.

Caplan, P. (1993). *Lifting a ton of feathers: A woman's guide to surviving in the academic world.* Toronto, Canada: University of Toronto Press.

Caplan, P., & Hall-McCorquodale, I. (1985). Mother-blaming in major clinical journals. *American Journal of Orthopsychiatry, 55,* 345–353.

Caplan, P.J. (1989). *Don't blame mother.* New York: Harper & Row.

Caplan, P.J. (1991). Delusional Dominating Personality Disorder (DDPD). *Feminism and Psychology, 1(1),* 171–174.

Caplan, P.J., McCurdy-Myers, J., & Gans, M. (1992). Should "premenstrual syndrome" be called a psychiatric abnormality? *Feminism and Psychology, 2(1),* 27–44.

Caporael, L.R. (1989). Mechanisms matter: The difference between sociobiology and evolutionary psychology. *Behavioral and Brain Sciences, 12,* 17–18.

Capshew, J.H. (1986). Networks of leadership: A quantitative study of SPSSI presidents, 1936–1986. *Journal of Social Issues, 42,* 75–106.

Capshew, J.H., & Lazlo, A.C. (1986). "We would not take no for an answer": Women psychologists and gender politics during World War II. *Journal of Social Issues, 42,* 157–180.

Caraway, N. (1991). *Segregated sisterhood: Racism and the politics of American feminism.* Knoxville: University of Tennessee Press.

Carey, C.M., & Mongeau, P.A. (1996). Communication and violence in courtship relationships. In D.D. Cahn & S.A. Lloyd (Eds.), *Family violence from a communication perspective* (pp.127–150). Thousand Oaks, CA: Sage.

Carillo, R. (1992). *Shattered dreams: Violence against women as an obstacle to development.* New York: United Nations Development Fund for Women.

Carli, L. (1989). Gender differences in interaction style and influence. *Journal of Personality and Social Psychology, 56,* 565–576.

Carli, L. (1990). Gender, language and influence. *Journal of Personality and Social Psychology, 59,* 941–951.

Carli, L.L. (1991). Gender, status and influence. In E.J. Lawler, B. Markovsky, C. Ridgeway, & H.A. Walker (Eds.), *Advances in group processes* (Vol. 8, pp. 89–113). Greenwich, CT: JAI Press.

Carli, L.L., LaFleur, S.J., & Loeber, C.C. (1995). Nonverbal behavior, gender and influence. *Journal of Personality and Social Psychology, 68,* 1030–1041.

Carlip, H. (1995). *Girl power: Young women speak out.* New York: Warner Books.

Carlson, E.R., & Carlson, R. (1960). Male and female subjects in personality research. *Journal of Social and Abnormal Psychology, 61,* 482–483.

Carlson, E.R., & Carlson, R. (1961). Male and female subjects in personality research. *Journal of Abnormal and Social Psychology, 61,* 482–483.

Carlson, R. (1972). Understanding women: Implications for theory and research. *Journal of Social Issues, 28,* 17–32.

Caron, S., & Carter, D. (1997). The relationships among sex role orientation, egalitarianism, attitudes toward sexuality and attitudes toward violence against women. *Journal of Social Psychology, 137,* 568–587.

Carp, F.M. (1997a). Living arrangements for midlife and older women. In J.M. Coyle (Ed.), *Handbook on women and aging* (pp. 253–270). Westport, CT: Greenwood Press.

Carp, F.M. (1997b). Retirement and women. In J.M. Coyle (Ed.), *Handbook on women and aging* (pp. 112–128). Westport, CT: Greenwood Press.

Carpenter, C.J., Huston, A.C., & Holt, W. (1986). Modification of preschool sex-typed behaviors by participation in adult-structured activities. *Sex Roles, 14,* 603–615.

Carpenter, C.J., & Huston-Stein, A. (1980). Activity structure and sex-typed behavior in preschool children. *Child Development, 51,* 862–872.

Carr, R. (1986). *Lupus erythematosus: A handbook for physicians, patients, and their families.* Rockville, MD: Lupus Foundation of America.

Carroll, S.J. (1989). Gender politics and the socializing impact of the women's movement. In R.S. Sigel (Ed.), *Political learning in adulthood* (pp. 306–339). Chicago: University of Chicago Press.

Carson, D.K., Gertz, L.M., Donaldson, M.A., & Wonderlich, S.A. (1990). Family-of-origin characteristics and current family relationships of female adult incest victims. *Journal of Family Violence, 5,* 153–171.

Carstensen, L.L., & Pasupathi, M. (1993). Women of a certain age. In S. Matteo (Ed.), *American women in the nineties: Today's critical issues* (pp. 204–212).Boston: Northeastern University Press.

Carter, D.B., & Levy, G.D. (1988). Cognitive aspects of early sex-role development: The influence of gender schemas on preschoolers' memories and preferences for sex-typed toys and activities. *Child Development, 59,* 782–792.

Carter, D.B., & Patterson, C.J. (1982). Sex roles as social conventions: The development of children's conceptions of sex-role stereotypes. *Developmental Psychology, 18,* 812–824.

Carter, J., Lane, C., & Kite, M.E. (1991, June). *Which sex is more likable? It depends on the subtype.* Paper presented at the meeting of the American Psychological Society, Washington, DC.

Carter, R., & Helms, J. (1991). Relationships of White and Black racial identity, attitudes and demographic similarity to counselor preferences. *Journal of Counseling Psychology, 38,* 446–457.

Cass, V.C. (1979). Homosexuality identity formation: A theoretical model. *Journal of Homosexuality, 4,* 219–235.

Cassell, C., & Walsh, S. (1997). Organizational cultures, gender management strategies and women's experience of work. *Feminism and Psychology, 7*(2), 224–230.

Castelano, C. (1997). *Domestic violence and conceptions of home.* New York: City University of New York, Graduate Center, Environmental psychology dissertation proposal.

Cejka, M.A., & Eagly, A.H. (1999). Gender-stereotypic images of occupations correspond to the sex segregation of employment. *Personality and Social Psychology Bulletin, 25,* 413–423.

Cha, J-H. (1994). Aspects of individualism and collectivism in Korea. In U. Kim, H.C. Triandis, C. Kagitçibasi, S-C. Choi, & G. Yoon (Eds.), *Individualism and collectivism: Theory, method, and applications* (pp. 157–174). Thousand Oaks, CA: Sage.

Chahin, J., Villarruel, F.A., & Viramontez, R.A. (1999). *Dichos y refranes:* The transmission of cultural values and beliefs. In H.P. McAdoo (Ed.), *Family ethnicity: Strength in diversity* (2nd ed., pp. 153–167). Thousand Oaks, CA: Sage.

Chamallas, M. (1992). Feminist constructions of objectivity: Multiple perspectives in sexual and racial harassment litigation. *Texas Journal of Women and the Law, 1,* 95–142.

Chambless, D.L., Baker, M.J., Baucom, D.H., Beutler, L.E., Calhoun, K.S., & et al. (1998). Update on empirically validated therapies, II. *Clinical Psychologist, 51*(1), 3–16.

Chan, D. (1998). Functional relations among constructs in the same content domain at different levels of analysis: A typology of composition models. *Journal of Applied Psychology, 83,* 234–246.

Chan, D.K.S., Tang, C.S.K., & Chan, W. (1999). Sexual harassment: A preliminary analysis of its effects on Hong Kong Chinese women in the workplace and academia. *Psychology of Women Quarterly, 23,* 661–672.

Chandler, R., Worell, J., Johnson, D., Blount, A., & Lusk, M. (1999). *Measuring long-term outcomes of feminist counseling and psychotherapy.* Paper presented at the annual meeting of the American Psychological Association as part of a symposium titled: Measuring process and outcomes in short- and long-term feminist therapy, J. Worell (Chair), Boston.

Chard, K.M., Weaver, T.L., & Resick, P.A. (1997). Adapting cognitive processing therapy for child sexual abuse survivors. *Cognitive and Behavioral Practice, 4*, 31–52.

Charlesworth, W.R., & Dzur, C. (1987). Gender comparisons of preschoolers' behavior and resource utilization in group problem-solving. *Child Development, 58*, 191–200.

Charlesworth, W.R., & LaFreniere, P. (1983). Dominance, friendship, and resource utilization in preschool children's groups. *Ethology and Sociobiology, 4*, 603–615.

Charnov, R. (1982). *The theory of sex allocation*. Princeton, NJ: Princeton University Press.

Chase, C. (1998). Hermaphrodites with attitude: Mapping the emergence of intersex political activism. *GLQ, 4*, 189–211.

Chaulk, C.P., Kazandjian, V.A., & Pipesh, F. (1995). Racial differences in illness and mortality among Maryland women hospitalized with breast cancer under an all-payer hospital system. *Journal of Women's Health, 4*, 27–33.

Chernin, J., Holden, J.M., & Chandler, C. (1997). Bias in psychological assessment: Heterosexism. *Measurement and Evaluation in Counseling and Development, 30*, 68–76.

Cherry, F. (1995). *The "stubborn particulars" of social sychology: Essays on the research process*. London: Routledge.

Chesler, P. (1972). *Women and madness*. New York: Doubleday.

Chesler, P. (1995). A leader of women. In P. Chesler, E.D. Rothblum, & E. Cole (Eds.), *Feminist foremothers in women's studies, psychology, and mental health*. New York: Haworth Press.

Chetwynd, J., & Hartnett, O. (1978). *The sex role system: Psychological and sociological perspectives*. London: Routledge & Kegan Paul.

Chin, A.E., Hedberg, K., Higginson, G.K., & Fleming, D.W. (1999). Legalized physician-assisted suicide in Oregon: The first year's experience. *New England Journal of Medicine, 340*, 577–583.

Chin, J., De Lacancela, V., & Jenkins, Y. (1993). *Diversity in psychotherapy: The politics of race, ethnicity and gender*. Westport, CT: Prager.

Chipperfield, J.G. (1994). The support source mix: A comparison of elderly men and women from two decades. *Canadian Journal on Aging, 13*(4), 434–453.

Chira, S. (1999). *Mother's place: Choosing work and family without guilt or blame*. New York: HarperCollins.

Chodorow, N.J. (1978). *The reproduction of mothering: Psychoanalysis and the sociology of gender*. Berkeley: University of California Press.

Chodorow, N.J. (1986). Varieties of leadership among early women psychoanalysts. In L. Dickstein & C.C. Nadelson (Eds.), *Women physicians in leadership roles* (pp. 47–54). Washington, DC: American Psychiatric Press.

Chodorow, N.J. (1989). Seventies questions for thirties women: Gender and generation in a study of early women psychoanalysts. In *Feminism and psychoanalytic theory* (pp. 199–218). New Haven, CT: Yale University Press.

Chodorow, N.J. (1999). *The power of feelings*. New Haven, CT: Yale University Press.

Choi, P.Y.L., & Nicolson, P. (Eds.). (1994). *Female sexuality: Psychology, biology and social context*. London: Harvester Wheatsheaf.

Chow, E.N. (1989). The feminist movement: Where are all the Asian American women? In Asian Women United of California (Eds.), *Making waves: An anthology of writings by and about Asian American women* (pp. 362–377). Boston: Beacon Press.

Chrisler, J.C. (1996a). PMS as a culture-bound syndrome. In J.C. Chrisler, C. Golden, & P.D. Rozee (Eds.), *Lectures on the psychology of women* (pp. 106–121). New York: McGraw-Hill.

Chrisler, J.C. (1996b). Politics and women's weight. *Feminism and Psychology, 6*, 181–184.

Chrisler, J.C. (2000). Gendered bodies and physical health. In R.K. Unger (Ed.), *Handbook of the psychology of women and gender* (pp. 289–302). New York: Wiley.

Chrisler, J.C., & Hemstreet, A.H. (1995). The diversity of women's health needs. In J.C. Chrisler & A.H. Hemstreet (Eds.), *Variations on a theme: Diversity and the psychology of women* (pp. 1–28). Albany: State University of New York Press.

Chrisler, J.C., & O'Hea, E.L. (2000). Gender, culture, and autoimmune disorders. In R.M. Eisler & M. Hersen (Eds.), *Handbook of gender, culture, and health* (pp. 321–342). Mahwah, NJ: Erlbaum.

Chrisler, J.C., & Parrett, K.L. (1995). Women and autoimmune disorders. In A.L. Stanton & S.J. Gallant (Eds.), *Psychology of women's health: Progress and challenges in research and application* (pp. 171–195). Washington, DC: American Psychological Association.

Christensen, A. (1988). Dysfunctional interaction patterns in couples. In P. Noller & M.A. Fitzpatrick (Eds.), *Perspectives on marital interaction* (pp. 31–52). Philadelphia: Multilingual Matters.

Christensen, A., & Heavey, C.L. (1990). Gender and social structure in the demand/withdraw pattern of marital conflict. *Journal of Personality and Social Psychology, 59*, 73–81.

Christian, B. (1985). *Black feminist criticism: Perspectives on Black women writers*. New York: Pergamon Press.

Christian-Smith, L.K. (1990). *Becoming a woman through romance*. New York: Routledge.

Christian-Smith, L.K. (1993). Voices of resistance: Young women readers of romance fiction. In L. Weis & M. Fine (Eds.), *Beyond silenced voices: Class, race and gender in United States schools* (pp. 169–189). Albany: State University of New York Press.

Christmas, J.J. (1983). Sexism and racism in health policy. In M. Fooden, S. Gordon, & B. Highley (Eds.), *Genes and gender IV: The second X and women's health* (pp. 205–215). New York: Gordian Press.

Chusmir, L.H., & Mills, J. (1989). Gender differences in conflict resolution styles of managers: At work and at home. *Sex Roles, 20,* 149–163.

Cicchetti, D. (1993). Developmental psychopathology: Reactions, reflections, projections. *Developmental Review, 13,* 471–502.

Cisneros, S. (1994). Sandra Cisneros (1954–). In S. Cahill (Ed.), *Writing women's lives* (pp. 459–468). New York: Harper Perennial.

Clancy, C.M., & Massion, C.T. (1992). American women's health care: A patchwork with gaps. *Journal of the American Medical Association, 268,* 1918–1920.

Clancy, S.M., & Dollinger, S.J. (1993). Photographic depictions of the self: Gender and age differences in social connectedness. *Sex Roles, 29,* 477–495.

Clark, M.L., Beckett, J., Wells, M., & Dungee-Anderson, D. (1994). Courtship violence among African American college students. *Journal of Black Psychology, 20,* 3, 264–281.

Clark, R., Anderson, N.B., Clark, V.R., & Williams, D.R. (1999). Racism as a stressor for African Americans: A biopsychosocial model. *American Psychologist, 54,* 805–816.

Clayton, S.D., & Crosby, F.J. (1992). Justice, gender, and affirmative action. Ann Arbor: University of Michigan Press.

Cleary, P.D., Mechanic, D., & Greenley, J.R. (1982). Sex differences in medical care utililization: An empirical investigation. *Journal of Health and Social Behavior, 23,* 106–119.

Cleveland, J., & Kerst, M. (1993). Sexual harassment and perceptions of power: An under-articulated relationship. *Journal of Vocational Behavior, 42,* 49–67.

Clifton, A.K., McGrath, D., & Wick, B. (1976). Stereotypes of women: A single category? *Sex Roles, 2,* 135–148.

Clinchy, B., & Norem, J.K. (Eds.). (1998). *Gender and psychology reader.* New York: New York University Press.

Coates, J. (1996). *Women talk.* Oxford, England: Blackwell.

Coates, J. (Ed.). (1998). *Language and gender: A reader.* Oxford, England: Blackwell.

Coates, J., & Cameron, D. (Eds.). (1988). *Women in their speech communities: New perspectives on language and sex.* London: Longman.

Coates, J., & Jordan, M.E. (1997). Que(e)rying friendship: Discourses of resistance and the construction of gendered subjectivity. In A. Livia & K. Hall (Eds.), *Queerly phrased: Language, gender, and sexuality* (pp. 214–232). Oxford, England: Oxford University Press.

Cobb, N.J., Stevens-Long, J., & Goldstein, S. (1982). The influence of televised models on toy preference in children. *Sex Roles, 8,* 1075–1080.

Cobble, D.S. (1990). Rethinking troubled relations between women and unions: Craft unionism and female activism. *Feminist Studies, 16,* 519–548.

Cochinov, H.M., Tataryn, D., Clinch, J.J., & Dudgeon, D. (1999). Will to live in the terminally ill. *Lancet, 354,* 816–819.

Cochran, M., Larner, M., Riley, D., Gunnarsson, L., & Henderson, C.R. (Eds.). (1990). *Extending families: The social networks of parents and their children.* Cambridge, England: Cambridge University Press.

Cochran, S.D., & Mays, V.M. (1989). Women and AIDS-related concerns: Roles for psychologists in helping the worried well. *American Psychologist, 44,* 529–535.

Cochran, S.D., & Peplau, L.A. (1985). Value orientations in heterosexual relationships. *Psychology of Women Quarterly, 9,* 477–488.

Cohen, D. (1996). Law, social policy and violence: The impact of regional cultures. *Journal of Personality and Social Psychology, 70,* 961–978.

Cohen, D., Vandello, J., Puente, S., & Rantilla, A. (1999). "When you call me that, smile": How norms for politeness, interaction styles, and aggression work together in Southern culture. *Social Psychology Quarterly, 62,* 257–275.

Cohen, J. (1988). *Statistical power analysis for the social sciences* (2nd ed.). Hillsdale, NJ: Erlbaum.

Cohen, R.L., & Alwin, D.F. (1993). Bennington women of the 1930s: Political attitudes over the life course. In K.D. Hulbert & D.T. Schuster (Eds.), *Women's lives through time* (pp. 117–139). San Francisco: Jossey-Bass.

Cohn, C. (1993). Wars, wimps, and women: Talking gender and thinking war. In M. Cooke & A. Woollacott (Eds.), *Gendering war talk* (pp. 227–246). Princeton, NJ: Princeton University Press.

Coker, D. (1999). Enhancing autonomy for battered women: Lessons from Navajo peacemaking. *UCLA Law Review, 47,* 1–111.

Colapinto, J. (2000). *As nature made him: The boy who was raised as a girl.* New York: HarperCollins.

Cole, D. (1997, January 28). Defense lawyer wants gag order on abuse case: Woman, 18, is accused of failing to protect infant son from fatal beating. *Milwaukee Journal Sentinel.*

Cole, E.R. (1994). A struggle that continues: Black women, community and resistance. In C. Franz & A.J. Stewart (Eds.), *Women creating lives: Identities, resilience, and resistance* (pp. 309–324). Boulder, CO: West-view Press.

Cole, E.R., & Rothblum, E. (1991). Lesbian sex after menopause: As good or better than eer. In B. Sang, J. Warshow, & A. Smith (Eds.), *Lesbians at midlife: The creative transition* (pp. 184–193). San Francisco: Spinsters.

Cole, E.R., & Stewart, A.J. (1996). Meanings of political participation among Black and White women: Political identity and social responsibility. *Journal of Personality and Social Psychology, 71,* 130–140.

Cole, E.R., Zucker, A.N., & Ostrove, J.M. (1998). Political participation and feminist consciousness among women activists of the 1960s. *Political Psychology, 19,* 349–370.

Coleman, E.A., Lemon, S.J., Rudick, J., Depuy, R.S., Fuer, E.J., & Edwards, B.K. (1994). Rheumatic disease among 1167 women reporting local implant and systemic problems after breast implant surgery. *Journal of Women's Health, 3,* 165–177.

Colen, S. (1986). "With respect and feelings": Voices of West Indian child care and domestic workers in New York City. In J.B. Cole (Ed.), *All American women: Lines that divide, ties that bind* (pp. 46–70). New York: Macmillan.

Coll, C.G., Lambery, G., Jenkins, R., McAdoo, H.P., Crnic, K., Wasik, B.H., & Garcia, H.V. (1996). An integrative model for the study of developmental competencies in minority children. *Child Development, 76,* 1891–1914.

Coll, C.G., Surrey, J.L., & Weingarten, K. (Eds.). (1998). *Mothering against the odds: Diverse voices of contemporary mothers.* New York: Guilford Press.

Collaer, M.L., & Hines, M. (1995). Human behavioral sex difference: A role for gonadal hormones during early development? *Psychological Bulletin, 118,* 55–107.

Collins, M.E. (1998). Factors influencing sexual victimization and revictimization in a sample of adolescent mothers. *Journal of Interpersonal Violence, 13,* 3–24.

Collins, P.H. (1989). The meaning of motherhood in Black culture and Black mother/daughter relationships. In M.M. Gergen & S.N. Davis (Eds.), *Toward a new psychology of gender.* New York: Routledge.

Collins, P.H. (1990). *Black feminist thought: Knowledge, consciousness and the politics of empowerment.* Boston: Unwin Hyman.

Collins, P.H. (1991). *Black feminist thought.* New York: Routledge.

Collins, P.H. (1994). Shifting the center: Race, class, and feminist theorising about motherhood. In E.N. Glenn, G. Chang, & L.R. Forcey (Eds.), *Motherhood: Ideology, experience and agency.* New York: Routledge.

Collison, B.B. (1987). Counseling aging men. In M. Scher, M. Stevens, G. Good, & G. Eichenfield (Eds.), *Handbook of counseling and psychotherapy with men* (pp. 165–177). Newbury Park, CA: Sage.

Coltrane, S. (1988). Father-child relationships and the status of women: A cross-cultural study. *American Journal of Sociology, 93,* 1060–1095.

Coltrane, S. (1996). *Family man: Fatherhood, housework, and gender equity.* New York: Oxford University Press.

Comas-Diaz, L. (1991). Feminism and diversity in psychology: The case of women of color. *Psychology of Women Quarterly, 15,* 597–610.

Comas-Diaz, L. (1999). Feminist therapy with mainland Puerto Rican women. In L.A. Peplau, S.C. DeBro, R.C. Veniegas, & P.L. Taylor (Eds.), *Gender, culture, and ethnicity: Current research about women and men* (pp. 323–335). Mountain View, CA: Mayfield.

Comas-Diaz, L., & Greene, B. (1994). *Women of color: Integrating ethnic and gender identities in psychotherapy.* New York: Guilford Press.

Comely, L., Kitzinger, C., Perkins, R., & Wilkinson, S. (1993). Anti-lesbianism in the British Psychological Society. *Self & Society, 21*(1), 7–9.

Condry, J., & Condry, S. (1976). Sex differences: A study of the eye of the beholder. *Child Development, 47,* 812–819.

Condry, S.M., Condry, J., & Pogatshnik, L.W. (1983). Sex differences: A study of the ear of the beholder. *Sex Roles, 9,* 697–704.

Congress, E.P. (1994). The use of culturegrams to assess and empower culturally diverse families. *Families in Society, 75,* 531–540.

Connor, J.M., & Serbin, L.A. (1977). Behaviorally based masculine- and feminine-activity-preference scales for preschoolers: Correlates with other classroom behaviors and cognitive tests. *Child Development, 48,* 1411–1416.

Conte, A. (1997). Legal theories of sexual harassment. In W. O'Donohue (Ed.), *Sexual harassment: Theory, research, and treatment* (pp. 50–83). Boston: Allyn & Bacon.

Conway, M., Mount, L., & Pizzamiglio, M.T. (1996). Status, community, and agency: Implications for stereotypes of gender and other groups. *Journal of Personality and Social Psychology, 71,* 25–38.

Cook, E.P. (1985). *Psychological androgyny.* New York: Pergamon Press.

Cook, J.A., & Fonow, M.M. (1990). Knowledge and women's interests: Issues of epistemology and methodology in feminist sociological research. In J.M. Nielson (Ed.), *Feminist research methods: Exemplary readings in the social sciences* (pp. 69–93). Boulder, CO: Westview Press.

Cook, T.D., & Campbell, D.T. (1979). *Quasi-experimentation: Design and analysis issues for field settings*. Boston: Houghton Mifflin.

Cook, T.D., & Reichardt, C.S. (Eds.). (1979). *Qualitative and quantitative methods in evaluation research*. Newbury Park, CA: Sage.

Cooper, E.A., & Bosco, S.M. (1999). Methodological issues in conducting research on gender in organizations. In G. Powell (Ed.), *Handbook of gender and work* (pp. 477–493). Newbury Park, CA: Sage.

Cooper, R. (1984). The avoidance of androcentric generics. *International Journal of the Sociology of Language, 50,* 5–20.

Cooperstock, R.A. (1971). A review of women's psychotropic drug use. *Canadian Journal of Psychiatry, 24,* 29–34.

Copeland, J.T. (1992). Motivational implications of social power for behavioral confirmation. *Dissertation Abstracts International, 52*(8-B), 4518–4519.

Cordua, G.D., McGraw, K.O., & Drabman, R.S. (1979). Doctor or nurse: Children's perception of sex typed occupations. *Child Development, 50,* 590–593.

Corea, G. (1977). *The hidden malpractice: How American medicine treats women as patients and professionals*. New York: Morrow.

Cortina, L.M., Swan, S., Fitzgerald, L.F., & Waldo, C. (1998). Sexual harassment and assault: Chilling the climate for women in academia. *Psychology of Women Quarterly, 22,* 419–441.

Costa, F.M., Jessor, R., Fortenberry, J.D., & Donovan, J.E. (1996). Psychosocial conventionality, health orientation, and contraceptive use in adolescents. *Journal of Adolescent Health, 18,* 404–416.

Costrich, N., Feinstein, L., Kidder, L., Marecek, J., & Pascale, L. (1975). When stereotypes hurt: Three studies of penalties for sex-role reversals. *Journal of Experimental Social Psychology, 11,* 520–530.

Cott, N.F. (1977). *The bonds of womanhood: "Woman's sphere" in New England, 1780–1835*. New Haven, CT: Yale University Press.

Cournoyer, R.J., & Mahalik, J.R. (1995). Cross-sectional study of gender role conflict examining college-aged and middle-aged men. *Journal of Counseling Psychology, 42,* 11–19.

Courtenay, W.H. (1998). College men's health: An overview and call to action. *Journal of American College Health, 46,* 279–290.

Courtenay, W.H. (1999). "Youth" violence? Let's call it what it is. *Journal of American College Health 48*(3), 141–142.

Courtois, C.A. (1996). *Healing the incest wound: Adult survivors in therapy*. New York: Norton.

Covinsky, K.E., Landefeld, C.S., Teno, J., Connors, A.F., Jr., Dawson, N., Youngner, S., Desbiens, N., Lynn, J., Fulkerson, W., Reding, D., Oye, R., & Phillips, R.S. (1996). Is economic hardship on the families of the seriously ill associated with patient and surrogate care preferences? *Archives of Internal Medicine, 156,* 1737–1741.

Cowan, G., & Hoffman, C.D. (1986). Gender stereotyping in young children: Evidence to support a concept-learning approach. *Sex Roles, 14,* 211–224.

Cowling, W.R., & Campbell, V.G. (1986). Health concerns of aging men. *Nursing Clinics of North America, 21,* 75–83.

Cox, D.W. (1993). *Hemlock's cup: The struggle for death with dignity*. Buffalo, NY: Prometheus Books.

Coyle, A. (1996). Representing gay men with HIV/AIDS. *Feminism and Psychology, 6,* 79–85.

Craib, I. (1998). *Experiencing identity*. London: Sage.

Crampton, S.M., & Mishra, J.M. (1995). Family and medical leave legislation: Organizational policies and strategies. *Public Personal Management, 24*(3), 271–289.

Crawford, C. (1998). The theory of evolution in the study of human behavior: An introduction and overview. In C. Crawford & D.L. Krebs (Eds.), *Handbook of evolutionary psychology: Ideas, issues, and applications* (pp. 3–40). Mahwah, NJ: Erlbaum.

Crawford, C., & Krebs, D.L. (Eds.). (1998). *Handbook of evolutionary psychology: Ideas, issues, and applications*. Mahwah, NJ: Erlbaum.

Crawford, M. (1988). Gender, age, and the social evaluation of assertion. *Behavior Modification, 12,* 549–564.

Crawford, M. (1989). Agreeing to disagree: Feminist epistemologies and women's ways of knowing. In M. Crawford & M. Gentry (Eds.), *Gender and thought: Psychological perspectives* (pp. 128–145). New York: Springer-Verlag.

Crawford, M. (1995). *Talking difference: On gender and language*. London: Sage.

Crawford, M. (1997a). Agreeing to differ: Feminist epistemologies and women's ways of knowing. In M.M. Gergen & S.N. Davis (Eds.), *Toward a new psychology of gender* (pp. 267–284). New York: Routledge.

Crawford, M. (1997b). Claiming the right to know: A personal history. In M. Crawford & R.K. Unger (Eds.), *In our own words: Readings on the psychology of women and gender* (pp. 5–9). New York: McGraw-Hill.

Crawford, M. (2000a). Only joking: Humor and sexuality. In C.B. Travis & J.W. White (Eds.), *Sexuality, society and feminism* (pp. 213–236). Washington, DC: American Psychological Association.

Crawford, M. (Ed.). (2000b). A reappraisal. *Gender: An Ethnomethodological Approach, 10*(1), 7–72.

Crawford, M., & English, L. (1984). Generic versus specific inclusion of women in language: Effects on recall. *Journal of Psycholinguistic Research, 13,* 373–381.

Crawford, M., & Kimmel, E. (Eds.). (1999a). Innovative methods for feminist research [Special issue]. *Psychology of Women Quarterly, 23,* 1–2.

Crawford, M., & Kimmel, E. (1999b). Promoting methodological diversity in feminist research. *Psychology of Women Quarterly, 23,* 1–6.

Crawford, M., & Marecek, J. (1989a). Feminist theory, feminist psychology. *Psychology of Women Quarterly, 13,* 477–491.

Crawford, M., & Marecek, J. (1989b). Psychology reconstructs the female, 1968–1988. *Psychology of Women Quarterly, 13,* 147–166.

Crawford, M., Stark, A.C., & Renner, C.H. (1998). The meaning of Ms: Social assimilation of a gender concept. *Psychology of Women Quarterly, 22,* 197–208.

Crawford, M., & Unger, R.K. (2000). *Women and gender: A feminist psychology* (3rd ed.). New York: McGraw-Hill.

Crenshaw, K. (1989). *Demorginalizing the undersection of race and sex.* Chicago: University of Chicago League Forum.

Crenshaw, K. (1995). Mapping the margins: Intersectionality, identity politics, and violence against women of color. In K. Crenshaw, N. Gotanda, G. Peller, & K. Thomas (Eds.), *Critical race theory* (pp. 357–383). New York: Free Press.

Crenshaw, K., Gotanda, N., Peller, G., & Thomas, K. (Eds.). (1995). *Critical race theory.* New York: Free Press.

Creswell, J.W. (1995). *Research design: Qualitative and quantitative approaches.* Thousand Oaks, CA: Sage.

Crichton, S.J., Bond, J.B., Jr., Harvey, C.D.H., & Ristock, J. (1999). Elder abuse: Feminist and ageist perspectives. *Journal of Elder Abuse and Neglect, 10,* 115.

Crick, N.R. (1997). Engagement in gender normative versus nonnormative forms of aggression: Links to social-psychological adjustment. *Developmental Psychology, 33,* 610–617.

Crick, N.R., Bigbee, M.A., & Howes, C. (1996). Gender differences in children's normative beliefs aggression: How do I hurt thee? Let me count the ways. *Child Development, 67,* 1003–1014.

Crick, N.R., Casas, J.F., & Ku, H. (1999). Relational and physical forms of peer victimization in preschool. *Developmental Psychology, 35,* 376–385.

Crick, N.R., & Werner, N.E. (1998). Response decision processes in relational and overt aggression. *Child Development, 69,* 1630–1639.

Crittenden, D. (1999). *What our mothers didn't tell us: Why happiness eludes the modern woman.* New York: Simon & Schuster.

Croghan, R. (1991). First-time mothers' accounts of inequality in the division of labour. *Feminism and Psychology, 1,* 221–246.

Croghan, R., & Miell, D. (1992). Accounts of intimate support relationships in the early months of mothering. In J.H. Harvey, T.L. Orbuch, & A.L. Weber (Eds.), *Attributions, accounts and close relationships* (pp. 221–243). New York: Springer-Verlag.

Croghan, R., & Miell, D. (1998). Strategies of Resistance: "Bad" mothers dispute the evidence. *Feminism and Psychology, 8,* 445–466.

Croizet, J-C., & Clair, T. (1998). Extending the concept of stereotype threat to social class: The intellectual underperformance of students from low socioeconomic backgrounds. *Personality and Social Psychology Bulletin, 24,* 588–594.

Cronk, L. (1993). Parental favoritism toward daughters. *American Scientist, 81,* 272–279.

Cronk, L. (1999). *The complex whole: Culture and the evolution of human behavior.* Boulder, CO: Westview Press.

Crosby, F. (1982). *Relative deprivation and working women.* New York: Oxford University Press.

Crosby, F. (1984). The denial of personal discrimination. *American Behavioral Scientist, 27,* 371–386.

Crosby, F.J. (1991). *Juggling: The unexpected advantages of balancing career and home for women and their families.* New York: Free Press.

Crosby, F.J., Pufall, A., Snyder, R.C., O'Connell, M., & Whalen, P. (1989). The denial of personal disadvantage among you, me, and all the other ostriches. In M. Crawford & M. Gentry (Eds.), *Gender and thought* (pp. 79–99). New York: Springer-Verlag.

Crose, R. (1997). *Why women live longer than men . . . , and what men can learn from them.* San Francisco: Jossey-Bass.

Cross, W.E., Jr. (1991). *Shades of Black.* Philadelphia: Temple University Press.

Cross, W.E., Jr. (1995). The psychology of nigrescence: Revising the Cross model. In J.G. Ponterotto, J. Manuel Casas, L.A. Suzuki, & C.M. Alexander (Eds.), *Handbook of multicultural counseling* (pp. 93–122). Thousand Oaks, CA: Sage.

Cross, W.E., Jr., & Fhagen-Smith, P. (in press). Patterns of Black identity development: A life span perspective. In B. Jackson & C. Wijeyesinghe (Eds.), *The development of racial identity*. New York: New York University Press.

Crouter, A.C., & Manke, B. (1997). Development of a typology of dual-earner families: A window into the difference between and within families in relationships, roles and activities. *Journal of Family Psychology, 11*, 62–75.

Crowley, L.V. (1997). *Introduction to human disease* (4th ed.). Sudbury, MA: Jones & Bartlett.

Cuellar, I. (1998). Cross-cultural clinical psychological assessment of Hispanic Americans. *Journal of Personality Assessment, 70*, 71–86.

Culbertson, A.L., & Rodgers, W. (1997). Improving managerial effectiveness in the workplace: The case of sexual harassment of Navy women. *Journal of Applied Social Psychology, 27*, 1953–1971.

Culbertson, A.L., Rosenfeld, P., Booth-Kewley, S., & Magnusson, P.O. (1992). *Assessment of sexual harassment in the Navy: Results of the 1989 Navy-wide survey* (NPRDC TR-92-11). San Diego, CA: Navy Personnel Research and Development Center.

Cummings, A. (in press). Assessing the process and outcome of short-term feminist therapy. *Counselor Education and Supervision*.

Currie, D. (1988). Re-thinking what we do and how we do it: A study of reproductive decisions. *Canadian Revue of Sociology and Anthropology, 25*, 231–253.

Daiute, C., Jones, H., Rawlins, C., & Stern, R. (1999). *Narrating social conflict: Opportunities for boys' and girls' non-stereotypical development*. Unpublished manuscript.

Daly, M. (1978). *Gyn/Ecology: The metaethics of radical feminism*. Boston: Beacon Press.

Daly, M. (with Caputi, J.). (1987). *Webster's first new intergalactic wickedary of the English language*. Boston: Beacon Press.

Daly, M., & Wilson, M. (1988). *Homicide*. Hawthorne, NY: Aldine de Gruyter.

Daly, M., & Wilson, M. (1998a). The evolutionary social psychology of family violence. In C. Crawford & D.L. Krebs (Eds.), *Handbook of evolutionary psychology: Ideas, issues, and applications* (pp. 431–456). Mahwah, NJ: Erlbaum.

Daly, M., & Wilson, M. (1998b). *The truth about Cinderella: A Darwinian view of parental love*. London: Weidenfeld & Nicolson.

Daly, M., & Wilson, M. (1999). Human evolutionary psychology and animal behaviour. *Animal Behaviour, 57*, 509–519.

Damon, W. (1977). *The social world of the child*. San Francisco: Jossey-Bass.

Dan, A.J. (1994). *Reframing women's health: Multidisciplinary research and practice*. Thousand Oaks, CA: Sage.

Dana, R. (1998). *Understanding cultural identity in intervention and assessment*. Thousand Oaks, CA: Sage.

Dancer, L.S., & Gilbert, L.A. (1993). Spouses' family work participation and its relation to wives' occupational level. *Sex Roles, 28*, 127–145.

Dansky, B.S., & Kilpatrick, D.G. (1997). Effects of sexual harassment. In W. O'Donohue (Ed.), *Sexual harassment: Theory, research, and treatment* (pp. 152–174). Boston: Allyn & Bacon.

Darbyshire, P. (1987). Danger man. *Nursing Times, 83*(48), 30–32.

Darwin, C. (1859). *On the origin of the species by means of natural selection*. London: Murray.

Darwin, C. (1871). *The descent of man, and selection in relation to sex*. London: Murray.

Darwin, C. (1872). *The expression of emotions in man and the animals*. London: Murray.

Das Gupta, P. (1995). Growing up in families. In P. Barnes (Ed.), *Personal, social and emotional development in children* (pp. 83–129). Buckingham, England: Open University Press.

D'Augelli, A.R., & Patterson, C.J. (1995). *Lesbian, gay and bisexual identities over the lifespan*. New York: Oxford University Press.

Davies, D.R. (1986). Children's performance as a function of sex-typed labels. *British Journal of Social Psychology, 25*, 173–175.

Davies, P.M., Hickson, F.C.I., Weatherburn, P., & Hunt, A.J. (1993). *Sex, gay men and AIDS*. London: Falmer Press.

Davis, A. (1995). *Art and work: A social history of labor in the Canadian graphic arts industry in the 1940s*. Montreal, Canada: McGill–Queen's University Press.

Davis, A.Y. (1990). Sick and tired of being sick and tired: The politics of Black women's health. In E.C. White (Ed.), *The Black women's health book: Speaking for ourselves* (pp. 18–26). Seattle: Seal Press.

Davis, B.M., & Gilbert, L.A. (1989). Effect of dispositional and situational influences on women's dominance expression in mixed-sex dyads. *Journal of Personality and Social Psychology, 57*, 294–300.

Davis, C., Lehman, D., Silver, R., Wortman, C., & Ellard, J. (1996). Self blame following a traumatic event: The role of perceived avoidability. *Personality and Social Psychology Bulletin, 22*, 557–567.

Davis, K. (1994). What's in a voice? Methods and metaphors. *Feminism and Psychology, 4*(3), 353–361.

Davis, K., & Gremmen, I. (1998). In search of heroines: Some reflections on normativity in feminist research. *Feminism and Psychology, 8*, 133–153.

Davis, M. (1995). Letter. *Psychologist, 8*(4), 151–152.

Davis, P. (1994, April 12). *The good mother: A new look at psychological parent theory.* Paper presented at the conference Helping Families in Crisis: The Intersection of Law and Psychology, Rutgers School of Law–Newark, Rutgers School of Law-Camden, and Seton Hall School of Law.

Davis-Floyd, R.E. (1994). The technocratic body: American childbirth as cultural expression. *Social Science and Medicine, 38,* 1125–1140.

Dean, K.E., & Malamuth, N. (1997). Characteristics of men who aggress sexually and of men who imagine aggressing: Risk and moderating variables. *Journal of Personality and Social Psychology, 72,* 449–455.

Deaux, K. (1971). Honking at the intersection: A replication and extension. *Journal of Social Psychology, 84,* 159–160.

Deaux, K. (1984). From individual differences to social categories: Analysis of a decade's research on gender. *American Psychologist, 39,* 105–116.

Deaux, K. (1985). Sex and gender. In L. Porter & M. Rosenzeig (Eds.), *Annual review of psychology, 1985* (Vol. 36, pp. 49–81). Palo Alto, CA: Annual Reviews.

Deaux, K. (1993). Sorry, wrong number: A reply to Gentile's call. *Psychological Science, 4,* 125–126.

Deaux, K. (1999). An overview of research on gender: Four themes from 3 decades. In W.B. Swann, Jr., J.H. Langlois, & Gilbert, L.A. (Eds.), *Sexism and stereotypes in modern society: The gender science of Janet Taylor Spence* (pp. 11–33). Washington, DC: American Psychological Association.

Deaux, K., & Ethier, K.A. (1998). Negotiating social identity. In J.K. Swim & C. Stangor (Eds.), *Prejudice: The target's perspective* (pp. 301–323). San Diego, CA: Academic Press.

Deaux, K., & Kite, M.E. (1985). Gender stereotypes: Some thoughts on the cognitive organization of gender-related information. *Academic Psychology Bulletin, 7,* 123–144.

Deaux, K., & Kite, M.E. (1987). Thinking about gender. In B.B. Hess & M.M. Ferree (Eds.), *Analyzing gender: A handbook of social science research* (pp. 92–117). Beverly Hills, CA: Sage.

Deaux, K., & Kite, M. (1993). Gender stereotypes. In F.L. Denmark & M.A. Paludi (Eds.), *Psychology of women: A handbook of issues and theories* (pp. 107–139). Westport, CT: Greenwood Press.

Deaux, K., & LaFrance, M. (1998). Gender. In D.T. Gilbert, S.T. Fiske, & G. Lindzey (Eds.), *Handbook of social psychology* (4th ed., Vol. 2, pp. 788–827). Boston: McGraw-Hill.

Deaux, K., & Lewis, L.L. (1984). The structure of gender stereotypes: Interrelationships among components and gender label. *Journal of Personality and Social Psychology, 46,* 991–1004.

Deaux, K., & Major, B. (1987). Putting gender into context: An interactive model of gender-related behavior. *Psychological Review, 94,* 369–389.

Deaux, K., Winton, W., Crowley, M., & Lewis, L.L. (1985). Level of categorization and content of gender stereotypes. *Social Cognition, 3,* 145–167.

de Beauvoir, S. (1961). *The second sex.* New York: Bantam Books.

Debold, E. (1991). The body at play. In C. Gilligan, A.G. Rogers, & D.L. Tolman (Eds.), *Women, girls and psychotherapy: Reframing resistance* (pp. 169–184). Binghamton, NY: Haworth Press.

Debold, E., Tolman, D., & Brown, L.M. (1996). Embodying knowledge, knowing desire. In N.R. Goldberg, J.M. Tarule, B.M. Clinchy, & M.F. Belenky (Eds.), *Knowledge, difference, and power* (pp. 89–125). London: Basic Books.

Decker, B. (1983). Counseling gay and lesbian couples. *Journal of Social Work and Human Sexuality, 2,* 39–52.

Decker, I., & Barling, J. (1998). Personal and organizational predictors of workplace sexual harassment of women by men. *Journal of Organizational Health Psychology, 3,* 7–18.

Deevey, S. (1990). Older lesbian women: An invisible minority. *Journal of Gerontological Nursing, 16*(5), 35–39.

Defour, D.C. (1990). The interface of racism and sexism on college campuses. In M.A. Paludi (Ed.), *Ivory power: Sexual harassment on campus* (pp. 45–52). Albany: State University of New York Press.

DeKeseredy, W.S. (1997). Measuring sexual abuse in Canadian university/college dating relationships: The contribution of a national representative sample survey. In M.D. Schwartz (Ed.), *Researching sexual violence against women: Methodological and personal perspectives* (pp. 43–53). Thousand Oaks, CA: Sage.

Delli Carpini, M.X. (1989). Age and history: Generations and sociopolitical change. In R.S. Sigel (Ed.), *Political learning in adulthood.* Chicago: University of Chicago Press.

Dellman-Jenkins, M., Bernard-Paolucci, T.S., & Rushing, B. (1994). Does distance make the heart grow fonder? A comparison of college students in long-distance and geographically close dating relationships. *College Student Journal, 28,* 212–219.

DeLucia, L.A. (1963). The toy preference test: A measure of sex-role identification. *Child Development, 34,* 107–117.

DeMaris, A. (1992). Male versus female initiation of aggression: The case of courtship violence. In E.C. Viano (Ed.), *Intimate violence: Interdisciplinary perspectives* (pp. 111–120). Washington: Hemisphere.

Demo, D.H., & Allen, K.R. (1996). Diversity within lesbian and gay families: Challenges and implications for family theory and research. *Journal of Social and Personal Relationships, 13,* 415–434.

Denmark, F.L. (1980). Psyche: From rocking the cradle to rocking the boat. *American Psychologist, 35,* 1057–1065.

Denmark, F.L., Russo, N.F., Frieze, I.H., & Sechzer, J.A. (1988). Guidelines for avoiding sexism in psychological research: A report of the APA ad hoc committee on nonsexist research. *American Psychologist, 43,* 582–585.

Dennerstein, L. (1995). Gender, health, and ill health. *Women's Health Issues, 5,* 53–59.

Deschamps, J.C., & Doise, W. (1978). Crossed category memberships in intergroup relations. In H. Tajfel (Ed.), *Differentiation between social groups* (pp. 141–158). London: Academic Press.

Destefano, L., & Colasanto, D. (1990). The gender gap in America. *Gallup Poll News Service, 54,* 1–7.

Deutsch, F.M. (1999). *Having it all: How equally shared parenting works.* Cambridge, MA: Harvard University Press.

Deutsch, F.M., & Saxon, S.E. (1998). The double standard of praise and criticism for mothers and fathers. *Psychology of Women Quarterly, 22*(4), 665–683.

Deutsch, F.M., Zalenski, C.M., & Clark, M.E. (1986). Is there a double standard of aging? *Journal of Applied Social Psychology, 16,* 771–785.

Deutsch, H. (1944). *Psychology of women: A psychoanalytic interpretation.* New York: Grune & Stratton.

Deutsch, M. (1983). Current social psychological perspectives on injustice. *European Journal of Social Psychology, 13,* 305–319.

DeVault, M.L. (1990). Talking and listening from women's standpoint: Feminist strategies for interviewing and analysis. *Social Problems, 37*(1), 96–116.

Devine, P.G., & Monteith, M.J. (1993). The role of discrepancy-associated affect in prejudice reduction. In D.M. Mackie & D.L. Hamilton (Eds.), *Affect, cognition, and stereotyping: Interactive processes in group perception* (pp. 317–344). San Diego, CA: Academic Press.

Dew, M.A. (1985). The effect of attitudes on inferences of homosexuality and perceived physical attractiveness in women. *Sex Roles, 12,* 143–155.

Dewhurst, A.M., Moore, R.J., & Alfano, D.P. (1992). Aggression against women by men: Sexual and spousal assault. *Journal of Offender Rehabilitation, 18,* 39–47.

Dexter, H., Linz, D., Penrod, S., & Saunders, D. (1997). Attributing responsibility to female victims after exposure to sexually violent films. *Journal of Applied Social Psychology, 27,* 2149–2171.

de Zwaan, M., & Mitchell, J.E. (1993). Medical complications of anorexia nervosa and bulimia nervosa. In A.S. Kaplan & P.E. Garfinkel (Eds.), *Medical issues and the eating disorders* (pp. 60–100). New York: Brunner/ Mazel.

Diamond, M.A. (1982). Sexual identity, monozygotic twins reared in discordant sex roles and a BBC follow-up. *Archives of Sexual Behavior, 11,* 181–186.

Diamond, M.A., & Sigmundson, H.K. (1997a). Management of intersexuaity: Guidelines for dealing with persons with ambiguous genitals. *Archives of Adolescent and Pediatric Medicine, 151,* 1046–1054.

Diamond, M.A., & Sigmundson, H.K. (1997b). Sex reassignment at birth: Long-term review and clinical implications. *Archives of Pediatrics and Adolescent Medicine, 151,* 298–304.

Diaz, R., Martin, D., & Deaux, K. (1999). *How first-generation Latinas describe gender and ethnic identity.* Unpublished data, City University of New York Graduate Center.

Dibble, S.L., Vanoni, J.M., & Miaskowski, C. (1997). Women's attitudes toward breast cancer screening procedures: Differences by ethnicity. *Women's Health Issues, 7,* 47–54.

Dickemann, M. (1979a). The ecology of mating systems in hypergynous dowry societies. *Social Science Information, 18,* 163–195.

Dickemann, M. (1979b). Female infanticide, reproductive strategies, and social stratification: A preliminary model. In N. Chagnon & W. Irons (Eds.), *Evolutionary biology and human social behavior: An anthropological perspective* (pp. 321–367). North Scituate, MS: Duxbury Press.

Dickemann, M. (1981). Paternal confidence and dowry competition: A biocultural analysis of purdah. In R.D. Alexander & D.W. Tinkle (Eds.), *Natural selection and social behavior: Recent research and new theory* (pp. 417–438). New Yoirk: Chiron.

Dickemann, M. (1989). Aggregates, averages, and behavioral plasticity. *Behavioral and Brain Sciences, 12,* 18–19.

Diekman, A.B., & Eagly, A.H. (2000). Stereotypes as dynamic constructs: Women and men of the past, present, and future. *Personality and Social Psychology Bulletin, 26,* 1171–1188.

Dietz, T.L. (1998). An examination of violence and gender role portrayals in video games: Implications for gender socialization and aggressive behavior. *Sex Roles, 38,* 425–442.

Dindia, K. (1987). The effects of sex of subject and sex of partner on interruptions. *Human Communication Research, 13,* 345–371.

Dines, G.H., & Hume, J.M. (1995). *Gender, race, and class in media: A text-reader.* Thousand Oaks, CA: Sage.

Dion, K.K. (1985). Socialization in adulthood. In G. Lindzey & E. Aronson (Eds.), *Handbook of social psychology* (3rd ed., Vol. 2, pp. 123–148). New York: Random House.

Dion, K.K., & Dion, K.L. (1985). Personality, gender, and the phenomenology of romantic love. In P.R. Shaver (Ed.), *Self, situations, and behavior: Review of Personality and Social Psychology* (Vol. 6, pp. 209–239). Thousand Oaks, CA: Sage.

Dion, K.K., & Dion, K.L. (1991). Psychological individualism and romantic love. *Journal of Social Behavior and Personality, 6,* 17–33.

Dion, K.K., & Dion, K.L. (1993). Individualistic and collectivistic perspectives on gender and the cultural context of love and intimacy. *Journal of Social Issues, 49*(3), 53–69.

Dion, K.K., & Dion, K.L. (1996). Cultural perspectives on romantic love. *Personal Relationships, 3,* 5–17.

Dion, K.L. (1975). Women's reactions to discrimination from members of the same or opposite sex. *Journal of Research in Personality, 9,* 294–306.

Dion, K.L. (1987). What's in a title? The Ms stereotype and images of women's titles of address. *Psychology of Women Quarterly, 11,* 21–36.

Dion, K.L. (2000). Canada. In A.E. Kazdin (Chief Ed.), *Encyclopedia of psychology.* New York: Oxford University Press and the American Psychological Association.

Dion, K.L., & Dion, K.K. (1988). Romantic love: Individual and cultural perspectives. In R.J. Sternberg & M.L. Barnes (Eds.), *Psychology of love* (pp. 264–289). New Haven, CT: Yale University Press.

Dion, K.L., & Dion, K.K. (1993). Gender and ethnocultural comparisons in styles of love. *Psychology of Women Quarterly, 17,* 463–473.

Dion, K.L., & Dion, K.K. (1996). Chinese adaptation to foreign cultures. In M. Bond (Ed.), *Handbook of Chinese psychology* (pp. 457–478). Hong Kong: Oxford University Press.

Dittmann, R.W. (1992). Body positions and movement patterns in female patients with congenital adrenal hyperplasia. *Hormones and Behavior, 26,* 441–456.

Dittmann, R.W., Kappes, M.E., & Kappes, M.H. (1992). Sexual behavior in adolescent and adult females with congenital adrenal hyperplasia. *Psychoneuroendocrinology, 17,* 153–170.

Dittmann, R.W., Kappes, M.H., Kappes, M.E., Borger, D., Meyer-Bahlburg, H.F.L., Stegner, H., Willig, R.H., & Wallis, H. (1990). Congenital adrenal hyperplasia: II. Gender-related behavior and attitudes in female salt-wasting and simple-virilizing patients. *Psychoneuroendocrinology, 15,* 421–434.

Dittmann, R.W., Kappes, M.H., Kappes, M.E., Borger, D., Stegner, H., Willig, R.H., & Wallis, H. (1990). Congenital adrenal hyperplasia: I. Gender-related behavior and attitudes in female patients and sisters. *Psychoneuroendocrinology, 15,* 401–420.

Dittrich, H., Gilpin, E., Nicod, P., Cali, G., Henning, H., & Ross, J. (1988). Acute myocardial infarction in women: Influence of gender on mortality and prognostic variables. *American Journal of Cardiology, 62,* 1–7.

Division 51. (1998). *Membership brochure.* Washington, DC: American Psychological Association.

Dixson, A.F. (1998). *Primate sexuality: Comparative studies of the prosimians, monkeys, apes, and human beings.* Oxford, England: Oxford University Press.

Dobash, R.P., Dobash, R.E., Wilson, M., & Daly, M. (1992). The myth of sexual symmetry in marital violence. *Social Problems, 39,* 71–89.

Dobson, K.S., & Block, L. (1999). Historical and philosophical bases of the cognitive-behavioral therapies. In K.S. Dobson (Ed.), *Handbook of cognitive-behavioral therapies* (pp. 3–38). New York: Guilford Press.

Dobzhansky, T. (1937). Nothing in biology makes sense except in the light of evolution. *American Biology Teacher, 35,* 125–129.

Dodson, L. (1998). *Don't call us out of name: The untold lives of women and girls in poor America.* Boston: Beacon Press.

Doise, W. (1997). Organizing social-psychological explanations. In C. McGarty & S.A. Haslam (Eds.), *Message of social psychology* (pp. 63–76). Cambridge, MA: Blackwell.

Doise, W., Clemence, A., & Lorenzi-Cioldi, F. (1993). *The quantitative analysis of social representations.* New York: Harvester/Wheatsheaf.

Donahoe, P.K., & Schnitzer, J.J. (1996). Evaluation of the infant who has ambiguous genitalia, and principles of operative management. *Seminars in Pediatric Surgery, 5,* 30–40.

Done, R.S. (2000). *Self-control and deviant behavior in organizations: The case of sexually harassing behavior.* Unpublished doctoral dissertation, University of Arizona, Tucson.

Donnelly, J., Donnelly, M., Kittelson, M.J., Fogarty, K.J., Procaccino, A.T., & Duncan, D.F. (1997). An exploration of attitudes on sexuality at a northeastern urban university. *Psychological Reports, 81*(2), 677–678.

Donovan, J. (1985). *Feminist theory: The intellectual traditions of American feminism.* New York: Unger.

Dörner, G. (1976). *Hormones and brain differentiation.* Amsterdam: Elsevier.

Doss, B.D., & Hopkins, J.R. (1998). The multicultural masculinity ideology scale: Validation from three cultural perspectives. *Sex Roles, 38,* 719–741.

Douglas, C.J., Kalman, C.M., & Kalman, P.T. (1985). Homophobia among physicians and nurses: An empirical study. *Hospital and Community Psychiatry, 36,* 1309–1311.

Douglas, S.J. (1994). *Where the girls are: Growing up female with the mass media.* New York: Times Books.

Dovidio, J.F., Brown, C.E., Heltman, K., Ellyson, S.L., & Brown, C.E. (1988). Power displays between women and men in discussions of gender-linked tasks: A multichannel study. *Journal of Personality and Social Psychology, 55*(4), 580–587.

Dovidio, J.F., & Gaertner, S.L. (1986). Prejudice, discrimination, and racism: Historical trends and contemporary approaches. In J.F. Dovidio & S.L. Gaertner (Eds.), *Prejudice, discrimination, and racism* (pp. 1–34). Orlando, FL: Academic Press.

Downing, N.E., & Roush, K.L. (1985). From passive acceptance to active commitment: A model of feminist identity development for women. *Counseling Psychologist, 13*, 695–709.

Downs, A.C. (1983). Letters to Santa Claus: Elementary school-age children's sex-typed toy preferences in a natural setting. *Sex Roles, 9*, 159–163.

Downs, A.C., & Langlois, J.H. (1988). Sex typing: Construct and measurement issues. *Sex Roles, 18*, 87–100.

Doyle, R. (1996). Deaths caused by alcohol. *Scientific American, 275*, 30–31.

Drake, C.T., & McDougall, D. (1977). Effects of the absence of a father and other male models on the development of boys' sex roles. *Developmental Psychology, 13*, 537–538.

Draucker, C.B. (1996). Family-of-origin variables and adult female survivors of childhood sexual abuse: A review of the research. *Journal of Child Sexual Abuse, 5*, 35–63.

Dreger, A.D. (1998). *Hermaphrodites and the medical invention of sex.* Cambridge MA: Harvard University Press.

Drevenstedt, J. (1976). Perceptions of onsets of young adulthood, middle age, and old age. *Journal of Gerontology, 31*, 53–57.

Drill, E., McDonald, H., & Odes, R. (1999). *Deal with it.* New York: Pocket Books.

Driscoll, D.M., Kelly, J.R., & Henderson, W.L. (1998). Can perceivers identify likelihood to sexually harass? *Sex Roles, 38*, 557–588.

Driskell, J.E., Olmstead, B., & Salas, E. (1993). Task cues, dominance cues, and influence in task groups. *Journal of Applied Psychology, 78*, 51–60.

DuBois, C.L.Z., Knapp, D.E., Faley, R.H., & Kustis, G.A. (1998). An empirical examination of same- and other-gender sexual harassment in the workplace. *Sex Roles, 39*, 731–749.

DuBois, E.C. (1998). Woman suffrage and women's rights. New York: New York University Press.

Duncan, G.J., Brooks-Gunn, J., & Klebanov, P.K. (1994). Economic deprivation and early childhood development. *Child Development, 65*, 296–318.

Duncan, K.C., & Prus, M.J. (1992). Starting wages of women in female and male occupations: A test of the human capital explanation of occupational sex segregation. *Social Science Journal, 29*(4), 479–493.

Duncan, L.E. (1999). Motivation for collective action: Group consciousness as mediator of personality, life experiences, and women's rights activism. *Political Psychology, 20*, 611–635.

Duncan, L.E., & Agronick, G.S. (1995). The intersection of life stage and social events: Personality and life outcomes. *Journal of Personality and Social Psychology, 69*, 558–568.

Duncan, L.E., & Stewart, A.J. (1995). Still bringing the Vietnam war home: Sources of contemporary student activism. *Personality and Social Psychology Bulletin, 21*, 914–924.

Duncan, L.E., & Stewart, A.J. (in press). A generational analysis of women's rights activists. *Psychology of Women Quarterly.*

Duncan, S., Jr., & Fiske, D.W. (1977). *Face to face interaction: Research, methods, and theory.* Hillsdale, NJ: Erlbaum.

Dunkle, J.H., & Francis, P.L. (1990). The role of facial masculinity/femininity in the attribution of homosexuality. *Sex Roles, 25*, 157–167.

Dunn, J. (1993). *Young children's close relationships: Beyond attachment.* London: Sage.

Durham, M.C. (1998). Dilemmas of desire: Representations of adolescent sexuality in two teen magazines. *Youth and Society, 29*, 369–389.

Dutton, M.A. (1992). *Empowering and healing the battered woman: A model for assessment and intervention.* New York: Springer.

Dutton, M.A. (1999). Multidimensional assessment of woman battering: Commentary on Smith, Smith, and Earp. *Psychology of Women Quarterly, 23*, 195–198.

Duveen, G. (in press). Representations, identitites, resistance. In K. Deaux & G. Philogene (Eds.), *Representations of the social: Bridging theoretical traditions.* Oxford, England: Blackwell.

Dwyer, J.W., & Coward, R.T. (1992). Gender, family, and long-term care of the elderly. In J.W. Dwyer & R.T. Coward (Eds.), *Gender, families and elder care* (pp. 3–17). Newbury Park, CA: Sage.

Dziech, B.W., & Weiner, L. (1984). *The lecherous professor: Sexual harassment on campus.* Boston: Beacon Press.

Eagly, A.H. (1987). *Sex differences in social behavior: A social-role interpretation.* Hillsdale, NJ: Erlbaum.

Eagly, A.H. (1994). On comparing women and men. *Feminism and Psychology, 4*(4), 513–522.

Eagly, A.H. (1995). The science and politics of comparing women and men. *American Psychologist, 50*, 145–158.

Eagly, A.H. (1999, April). *The power elite: Why so few women?* Presidential address presented at the 71st annual meeting of the Midwest Psychological Association, Chicago.

Eagly, A.H., & Johnson, B.T. (1990). Gender and leadership style: A meta-analysis. *Psychological Bulletin, 108,* 233–256.

Eagly, A.H., & Karau, S.J. (1991). Gender and the emergence of leaders: A meta-analysis. *Journal of Personality and Social Psychology, 60,* 685–710.

Eagly, A.H., Karau, S.J., & Makhijani, M.G. (1995). Gender and the effectiveness of leaders: A meta-analysis. *Psychological Bulletin, 117*(1), 125–145.

Eagly, A.H., & Kite, M. (1987). Are stereotypes of nationalities applied to both men and women? *Journal of Personality and Social Psychology, 53,* 451–462.

Eagly, A.H., Makhijani, M.G., & Klonsky, B.G. (1992). Gender and the evaluation of leaders: A meta-analysis. *Psychological Bulletin, 111*(1), 3–22.

Eagly, A.H., & Mladinic, A. (1989). Gender stereotypes and attitudes toward women and men. *Personality and Social Psychology Bulletin, 15,* 543–558.

Eagly, A.H., & Mladinic, A. (1994). Are people prejudiced against women? Some answers from research on attitudes, gender stereotypes, and judgments of competence. In W. Stroebe & M. Hewston (Eds.), *European review of social psychology* (Vol. 5, pp. 1–35). New York: Wiley.

Eagly, A.H., Mladinic, A., & Otto, S. (1991). Are women evaluated more favorably than men? An analysis of attitudes, beliefs, and emotions. *Psychology of Women Quarterly, 15,* 203–216.

Eagly, A.H., & Steffen, V.J. (1984). Gender stereotypes stem from the distribution of women and men into social roles. *Journal of Personality and Social Psychology, 46*(4), 735–754.

Eagly, A.H., & Wood, W. (1982). Inferred sex differences in status as a determinant of gender stereotypes about social influence. *Journal of Personality and Social Psychology, 43,* 915–928.

Eagly, A.H., & Wood, W. (1999). The origins of sex differences in human behavior: Evolved dispositions versus social roles. *American Psychologist, 54*(6), 408–423.

Eaton, W.O., & Von Bargen, D. (1981). Asynchronous development of gender understanding in preschool children. *Child Development, 52,* 1020–1027.

Eby, K.K., Campbell, J.C., Sullivan, C.M., & Davidson, W.S. (1995). Health effects of experiences of sexual violence for women with abusive partners. *Health Care for Women International, 16,* 563–576.

Eccles, J.S. (1994). Understanding women's educational and occupational choices: Applying the Eccles et. al. model of achievement-related choices. *Psychology of Women Quarterly, 18*(4), 585–609.

Eccles, J.S., & Jacobs, J.E. (1986). Social forces shape math attitudes and performance. *Signs, 11,* 367–380.

Eccles, J.S., Jacobs, J.E., & Harold, R.D. (1990). Gender role stereotypes, expectancy effects, and parents' socialization of gender differences. *Journal of Social Issues, 46*(2), 183–201.

Eck, L.H., Logan, P.S., Klesges, R.C., & Slawson, D.L. (1997). Smoking patterns and topography in Euro-American and African-American women. *Journal of Gender, Culture, and Health, 2,* 263–269.

Edelbrock, C., & Sugawara, A.I. (1978). Acquisition of sex-typed preferences in preschool-aged children. *Developmental Psychology, 14,* 614–623.

Eder, D., Evans, C., & Parker, S. (1995). *School talk: Gender and adolescent culture.* New Brunswick, NJ: Rutgers University Press.

Eder, D., & Parker, S. (1987). The cultural production and reproduction of gender: The effect of extracurricular activities on peer group culture. *Sociology of Education, 60,* 200–213.

Edleson, J.L. (1999). The overlap between child maltreatment and woman battering. *Violence against Women, 5,* 134–154.

Edwards, D. (1997). *Discourse and cognition.* London: Sage.

Edwards, D., & Potter, J. (1992). *Discursive psychology.* London: Sage.

Edwards, G.H. (1992). The structure and content of the male gender role stereotype: An exploration of subtypes. *Sex Roles, 27,* 533–551.

Edwards, J.E., Elig, T.W., Edwards, D.L., & Riemer, R.A. (1997). *The 1995 armed forces sexual harassment survey: Administration, datasets, and codebook* (Rep. No. 95–015). (DTIC/NTIS No. AD A323–945). Arlington, VA: Defense Manpower Data center.

Edwards, J.J., & Alexander, P.C. (1992). The contribution of family background to the long-term adjustment of women sexually as children. *Journal of Interpersonal Violence, 7,* 306–320.

Edwards, R. (1998). A rejoinder. *Feminism and Psychology, 8,* 383–386.

Ehrhardt, A.A., & Baker, S.W. (1974). Fetal androgens, human central nervous system differentiation, and behavior sex differences. In R.C. Friedman, R.M. Richart, & R.L. Vande Wiele (Eds.), *Sex differences in behavior* (pp. 33–51). New York: Wiley.

Ehrhardt, A.A., Epstein, R., & Money, J. (1968). Fetal androgens and female gender identity in the early-treated adrenogenital syndrome. *Johns Hopkins Medical Journal, 122,* 160–167.

Ehrhardt, A.A., Evers, K., & Money, J. (1968). Influence of androgen and some aspects of sexually dimorphic behavior in women with the late-treated adrenogenital syndrome. *Johns Hopkins Medical Journal, 123,* 115–122.

Ehrlich, S., & King, R. (1992). Gender-based language reform and the social construction of meaning. *Discourse and Society, 3,* 151–166.

Eichstedt, J.A., Serbin, L.A., Poulin-Dubois, D., & Sen, M.G. (2000). *Of bears and men: Infants' knowledge of conventional and metaphorical gender stereotypes.* Manuscript submitted for publication.

Eisenberg, N., Wolchik, S.A., Hernandez, R., & Pasternak, J. (1985). Parental socialization of young children's play: A short-term longitudinal study. *Child Development, 56,* 1506–1513.

Eisenberg, S. (1998). *We'll call you if we need you: Experiences of women working construction.* Ithaca, NY: Cornell University Press.

Eisenstein, Z. (1997). Women's publics and the search for new democracies. *Feminist Review, 57,* 140–167.

Eisler, R.M. (1995). The relationship between masculine gender role stress and men's health risk: The validation of the construct. In R.F. Levant & W.S. Pollack (Eds.), *A new psychology of men* (pp. 207–225). New York: Basic Books.

Eisler, R.M., & Skidmore, J.R. (1987). Masculine gender role stress: Scale development and competent factors in the appraisal of stressful situations. *Behavior Modification, 11,* 123–136.

Eldridge, N.S., & Gilbert, L.A. (1990). Correlates of relationship satisfaction in lesbian couples. *Psychology of Women Quarterly, 14,* 43–62.

Elias, M. (1975, April). Sisterhood therapy. *Human Behavior,* 56–61.

Elias, R. (1986). *The politics of victimization: Victims, victimology, and human rights.* New York: Oxford University Press.

Eliason, M.J. (1996). A survey of the campus climate for lesbian, gay and bisexual university members. *Journal of Psychology and Human Sexuality, 8*(4), 39–58.

Eliason, M.J., & Randall, C.E. (1991). Lesbian phobia in nursing students. *Western Journal of Nursing Research, 13,* 363–374.

Elligan, D. (1997). Culturally sensitive integration of supportive and cognitive behavioral therapy in the treatment of a bicultural dysthymic patient. *Cultural Diversity and Mental Health, 3,* 207–213.

Ellis, H. (1934). *Psychology of sex.* London: Heinemann.

Ellis, L., & Ames, M.A. (1987). Neurohormonal functioning and sexual orientation: A theory of homosexuality-heterosexuality. *Psychological Bulletin, 101,* 233–258.

Ellis, L., & Blanchard, R. (in press). Birth order, sibling sex ratio, and maternal miscarriages in homosexual and heterosexual men and women. *Personality and individual differences.*

Ellis, P., & Murphy, B.C. (1994). The impact of misogyny and homophobia on therapy with women. In M.P. Mirkin (Ed.), *Women in context: Toward a feminist reconstruction of psychotherapy* (pp. 48–73). New York: Guilford Press.

Ellis, S.J. (1999). Lesbian and gay issues are human rights issues: The need for a human rights approach to lesbian and gay psychology. *BPS Lesbian and Gay Psychology Section Newsletter, 3,* 9–14.

Ellison v. Brady, 924 F.2d 872 (9th Cir. 1991).

Elvin-Nowak, Y. (1999). *Accompanied by guilt: Modern motherhood the Swedish way.* Stockholm: Stockholm University.

Ely, R.J. (1995). The power in demography: Women's social constructions of gender identity at work. *Academy of Management Journal, 38*(3), 589–634.

Emanuel, E.J., Fairclough, D.L., Slutsman, J., Alpert, H., Baldwin, D., & Emanuel, L.L. (1999). Assistance from family members, friends, paid care givers, and volunteers in the care of terminally ill patients. *New England Journal of Medicine, 341*(13), 956–963.

Emmerich, W., Goldman, K.S., Kirsh, B., & Sharabany, R. (1977). Evidence for a transitional phase in the development of gender constancy. *Child Development, 48,* 930–936.

Emmerich, W., & Shepard, K. (1982). Development of sex-differentiated preferences during late childhood and adolescence. *Developmental Psychology, 18,* 406–417.

Enns, C.Z. (1992). Toward integrating feminist psychotherapy and feminist philosophy. *Professional Psychology: Research and Practice, 23,* 453–466.

Enns, C.Z. (1997a). *Feminist theories and feminist psychotherapies: Origins, themes, and variations.* New York: Harrington Park Press.

Enns, C.Z. (1997b). *Feminist theories and feminist therapies.* New York: Haworth Press.

Epstein, D., & Johnson, R. (1998). *Schooling sexualities.* Buckingham, England: Open University Press.

Epstein, S. (1992). Gay politics, ethnic identity: The limits of social constructionism. In E. Stein (Ed.), *Forms of desire.* New York: Routledge.

Equal Employment Opportunity Commission. (1980). Guidelines on discrimination because of sex (Sect. 1604.11). *Federal Register, 45,* 74676–74677.

Equal Employment Opportunity Commission. (1999, January 14). Available: http://www.eeoc.gov/stats/harass.html

Erikson, E.H. (1958). *Young man Luther.* New York: Norton.

Erikson, E.H. (1963). *Childhood and society.* New York: Norton. (Original work published 1950)

Erikson, E.H. (1968). *Identify, youth and crisis.* New York: Norton.

Erikson, E.H. (1969). *Gandhi's truth.* New York: Norton.

Erikson, E.H. (1975). *Life history and the historical moment.* New York: Norton.

Eron, L.D. (1992). Gender differences in violence: Biology and/or socialization? In K. Bjorkqvist & P. Nieme-lae (Eds.), *Of mice and women: Aspects of female aggression* (pp. 89–97). New York: Academic Press.

Espin, O. (1996). Race, racism, and sexuality in the life narratives of immigrant women. In S. Wilkinson (Ed.), *Feminist social psychologies: International perspectives* (pp. 87–103). Buckingham, England: Open University Press.

Espin, O. (1997). Crossing borders and boundaries: The life narratives of immigrant lesbians. In B. Greene (Ed.), *Psychological perspectives on lesbian and gay issues: Ethnic and cultural diversity among lesbians and gay men* (Vol. 3, pp. 225–250). Thousand Oaks, CA: Sage.

Espin, O. (1999). *Women crossing boundaries: A psychology of immigration and transformations of sexuality.* New York: Routledge.

Espin, O.M. (1995). "Race," racism and sexuality in the life narratives of immigrant women. *Feminism and Psychology, 5*(2), 223–238.

Espin, O.M., Stewart, A.J., & Gomez, C. (1990). Letters from V: Adolescent personality development in sociohistorical context. *Journal of Personality, 58,* 347–364.

Essed, P. (1990). *Everyday racism.* Claremont, CA: Hunter House.

Essed, P. (1992). Alternative knowledge sources in explanations for racist events. In M.L. McLaughlin, M.L. Cody, & S.J. Read (Eds.), *Explaining one's self to others: Reason-giving in a social context* (pp. 199–224). Hillsdale, NJ: Erlbaum.

Essock, S.M. (1989). Spouse preference shifts with age. *Behavioral and Brain Sciences, 12,* 19–20.

Estrich, S. (1991). Sex at work. *Stanford Law Review, 43,* 613–861.

Etaugh, C., & Liss, M.B. (1992). Home, school, and playroom: Training grounds for adult gender roles. *Sex Roles, 26,* 129–147.

Etaugh, C., & Riley, S. (1979). Knowledge of sex stereotypes in preschool children. *Psychological Reports, 44,* 1279–1282.

Ethier, K.A. (1995). *Becoming a mother: Identity acquisition during the transition to parenthood.* Unpublished doctoral dissertation, City University of New York.

Evans, S. (1979). *Personal politics: The roots of women's liberation in the civil rights movement and the new left.* New York: Vintage Books.

Everingham, C. (1994). *Motherhood and modernity: An investigation into the rational dimension of mothering.* Buckingham, England: Open University Press.

Ewing, W. (1993). The civic advocacy of violence. In A. Minas (Ed.), *Gender basics: Feminist perspectives on women and men* (pp. 200–205). Belmont, CA: Wadsworth.

Eyer, D.E. (1992). *Mother-infant bonding: A scientific fiction.* New Haven, CT: Yale University Press.

Eysenck, H.J., & Wilson, G. (1979). *The psychology of sex.* London: J.M. Dent.

Fabrikant, B. (1974). The psychotherapist and the female patient. In F. Franks & V. Burtle (Eds.), *Women in therapy: New psychotherapies for a changing society* (pp. 83–110). New York: Brunner/Mazel.

Facio, E. (1996). *Understanding older Chicanas.* Thousand Oaks, CA: Sage.

Fagan, J.F., & Shepherd, P.A. (1981). Theoretical issues in the early development of visual perception. In M. Lewis & L. Taft (Eds.), *Developmental disabilities in preschool children* (pp. 9–34). New York: Spectrum.

Fagan, J.F., & Singer, L.T. (1979). The role of simple feature differences in infants' recognition of faces. *Infant Behavior and Development, 2,* 39–45.

Fagerlin, A., Ditto, P.H., Danks, J.H., Houts, R.M., & Smucker, W.D. (in press). Projection in surrogate decisions about life-sustaining medical treatments.

Fagot, B.I. (1974). Sex differences in toddlers' behavior and parental reaction. *Developmental Psychology, 10,* 554–558.

Fagot, B.I. (1977). Consequences of moderate cross-gender behavior in preschool children. *Child Development, 48,* 902–907.

Fagot, B.I. (1985a). Beyond the reinforcement principle: Another step toward understanding sex role development. *Developmental Psychology, 21,* 1097–1104.

Fagot, B.I. (1985b). Changes in thinking about early sex role development. *Developmental Review, 5,* 83–98.

Fagot, B.I., & Hagan, R. (1991). Observations of parent reactions to sex-stereotyped behaviors: Age and sex effects. *Child Development, 62,* 617–628.

Fagot, B.I., & Leinbach, M.D. (1989). The young child's gender schema: Environmental input, internal organization. *Child Development, 60,* 663–672.

Fagot, B.I., Leinbach, M.D., & Hagan, R. (1986). Gender labeling and the adoption of sex-typed behaviors. *Developmental Psychology, 22,* 440–443.

Fain, T.C., & Anderton, D.L. (1987). Sexual harassment: Organizational context and diffuse status. *Sex Roles, 17,* 291–311.

Fairclough, N. (1995). *Critical discourse analysis: Papers in the critical study of language.* New York: Longman.

Falbo, T., & Peplau, L.A. (1980). Power strategies in intimate relationships. *Journal of Personality and Social Psychology, 38,* 618–628.

Falk, P.J. (1989). Lesbian mothers. *American Psychologist, 44,* 491–497.

Fallon, A. (1990). Culture in the mirror: Sociocultural determinants of body image. In T. Cash & T. Pruzinsky (Eds.), *Body images: Development, deviance, and change* (pp. 80–109). New York: Guilford Press.

Faludi, S. (1991). *Backlash: The undeclared war against American women.* New York: Doubleday.

Faludi, S. (1999). *Stiffed: The betrayal of American men.* New York: Morrow.

Faragher v. City of Boca Raton, 118 S.Ct. 2275 (1998).

Farley, L. (1978). *Sexual shakedown: The sexual harassment of women on the job.* New York: McGraw-Hill.

Faustman, D.L. (1997). Gender is important: Lessons in autoimmunity. *Journal of Women's Health, 6,* 521–522.

Fausto-Sterling, A. (1985). *Myths of gender: Biological theories about women and men.* New York: Basic Books.

Fausto-Sterling, A. (2000). *Sexing the body: Gender politics and the construction of sexuality.* New York: Basic Books.

Favreau, O.E. (1997). Sex and gender comparisons: Does null hypothesis testing create a false dichotomy? *Feminism and Psychology, 7,* 63–81.

Fawcett, G., Heise, L., Isita-Espejel, L., & Pick, S. (1999). Changing community responses to wife abuse: A research and demonstration project in Iztacalo, Mexico. *American Psychologist, 54,* 41–49.

Fein, G., Johnson, D., Kosson, N., Stork, L., & Wasserman, L. (1975). Sex stereotypes and preferences in the toy choices of 20-month-old boys and girls. *Developmental Psychology, 11,* 527–528.

Feinberg, L. (1996). *Transgender warriors: Making history from Joan of Arc to Ru Paul.* Boston: Beacon Press.

Feinman, S. (1981). Why is cross-sex-role behavior more approved for girls than for boys? A status characteristics approach. *Sex Roles, 7,* 289–300.

Feinman, S. (1984). A status theory of the evaluation of sex-role and age-role behavior. *Sex Roles, 10,* 445–456.

Fern, E.F. (1982). The use of focus groups for idea generation: The effects of group size, acquaintanceship, and moderator on response quantity and quality. *Journal of Marketing Research, 19,* 1–13.

Fernandes, L. (1997). Beyond public spaces and private spheres: Gender, family, and working class politics in India. *Feminist Studies, 23,* 525–547.

Fernandez, M. (1997). Domestic violence by extended family members in India: Interplay of gender and generation. *Journal of Interpersonal Violence, 12,* 433–455.

Ferraro, K. (1996). Women's fear of victimization: Shadow of sexual assault? *Social Forces, 75,* 667–690.

Ferree, M.M. (1990). Beyond separate spheres: Feminism and family research. *Journal of Marriage and the Family, 52,* 866–884.

Ferree, M.M., Lorber, J., & Hess, B.B. (Eds.). (1999). *Revisioning gender.* Thousand Oaks, CA: Sage.

Ferrini, A.F., & Ferrini, R.L. (1989). *Health in the later years* (2nd ed.). Dubuque, IA: Brown & Benchmark.

Festinger, L., Schacter, S., & Back, K. (1950). *Social pressures in informal groups: A study of human factors in housing.* New York: Harper.

Fidell, L.S. (1970). Empirical verification of sex discrimination in hiring practices in psychology. *American Psychologist, 25,* 1094–1098.

Fidell, L.S. (1980). Sex role stereotypes and the American physician. *Psychology of Women Quarterly, 4,* 313–330.

Fiebach, N.H., Viscoli, C.M., & Horwitz, R.I. (1990). Differences between women and men in survival after myocardial infarction. *Journal of the American Medical Association, 263,* 1092–1096.

Field, M.J., & Cassell, C.K. (1997). *Approaching death: Improving care at the end of life.* Washington, DC: National Academy Press.

Findlen, B. (1995). *Listen up: Voices from the next feminist generation.* Seattle, WA: Seal Press.

Fine, M. (1988). Sexuality, schooling, and adolescent females: The missing discourse of desire. *Harvard Educational Review, 58*(1), 29–53.

Fine, M. (1989). Coping with rape: Critical perspectives on consciousness. In R.K. Unger (Ed.), *Representations: Social constructions of gender* (pp. 186–200). Amityville, NY: Baywood.

Fine, M. (1991). *Framing dropouts: Notes on the politics of an urban high school.* Albany: State University of New York Press.

Fine, M. (1994). Working the hyphens: Reinventing self and other in qualitative research. In N.K. Denzin & Y.S. Lincoln (Eds.), *Handbook of qualitative research* (pp. 70–82). Thousand Oaks, CA: Sage.

Fine, M., & Asch, A. (1988). *Women with disabilities: Essays in psychology, culture and politics.* Philadelphia: Temple University Press.

Fine, M., Genovese, T., Ingersoll, S., Macpherson, P., & Roberts, R. (1996). Insisting on innocence: Accounts of accountability by abusive men. In B. Lykes, A. Banuazizi, R. Liem, & M. Morris (Eds.), *Myths about the powerless* (pp. 128–158). Philadelphia: Temple University Press.

Fine, M., & Gordon, S.M. (1989). Feminist transformations of/despite psychology. In M. Crawford & M. Gentry (Eds.), *Gender and thought: Psychological perspectives* (pp. 146–174). New York: Springer-Verlag.

Fine, M., & Gordon, S.M. (1991). Effacing the center and the margins: Life at the intersection of psychology and feminism. *Feminism and Psychology, 1,* 19–27.

Fine, M., & Macpherson, P. (1992). Over dinner: Feminism and adolescent female bodies. In M. Fine (Ed.), *Disruptive voices.* Albany: State University of New York Press.

Fine, M., Stewart, A.J., & Zucker, A. (in press). White girls and women in the contemporary United States: Supporting or subverting race and gender domination? In C. Squire (Ed.), *Culture in psychology.* New York: Routledge.

Fine, M., & Weis, L. (1998). Crime stories: A critical look through race, ethnicity, and gender. *Qualitative Studies in Education, 11,* 435–459.

Fine, M., & Weis, L. (2000). Working without a net but with a spotlight: Mothering in poverty. In G. Noblit (Ed.), *Post-critical ethnography.* Cranhill, NJ: Hampton Press.

Fine, M., Weis, L., Powell, L.C., & Wong, L.M. (Eds.). (1997). *Off White: Readings on race, power, and society.* New York: Routledge.

Fine, M., Weis, L., Weseen, S., & Wong, L. (2000). For whom? Qualitative research, representations, and social responsibilities. In N.K. Denzin & Y.S. Lincoln (Eds.), *Handbook of qualitative research* (pp. 107–131). Thousand Oaks, CA: Sage.

Fine, M., & Zane, N. (1989). Bein' wrapped too tight: When low-income women drop out of high school. In L. Weis, E. Farrar, & H. Petrie (Eds.), *Dropouts from school: Issues, dilemmas, and solutions* (pp. 23–54). Albany: State University of New York Press.

Fineran, S., & Bennett, L. (1999). Gender and power issues of peer sexual harassment among teenagers. *Journal of Interpersonal Violence, 14*(6), 626–641.

Finkelhor, D. (1984). *Child sexual abuse: New theory and research.* New York: Free Press.

Finkelhor, D., & Browne, A. (1986). The traumatic impact of child sexual abuse: A conceptualization. *Annual Progress in Child Psychiatry & Child Development,* 632–648.

Finkelhor, D., & Dziuba-Leatherman, J. (1994). Victimization of children. *American Psychologist, 49,* 173–183.

Finkelhor, D., Hotaling, G.T., Lewis, I.A., & Smith, C. (1989). Sexual abuse and its relationship to later sexual satisfaction, marital status, religion, and attitudes. *Journal of Interpersonal Violence, 4,* 379–399.

Finkelhor, D., & Yllo, K. (1982). Forced sex in marriage: A preliminary research report. *Crime and Delinquency, 54,* 459–478.

Fischer, A.R., & Good, G.E. (1997). Masculine gender roles, recognition of emotions, and interpersonal intimacy. *Psychotherapy, 34,* 160–170.

Fischer, A.R., & Good, G.E. (1998). Perceptions of parent-child relationships and masculine role conflicts of college men. *Journal of Counseling Psychology, 45,* 346–352.

Fischer, A.R., Tokar, D.M., Good, G.E., & Snell, A.F. (1998). More on the structure of male role norms: Exploratory and multiple sample confirmatory analyses. *Psychology of Women Quarterly, 22,* 135–155.

Fischoff, B., Furby, L., & Morgan, M. (1987). Rape prevention: A typology of strategies. *Journal of Interpersonal Violence, 2,* 292–308.

Fish, J., & Wilkinson, S. (in press) Lesbians and cervical cancer. In J. Ussher (Ed.), *Women's health: An international reader.* Leicester, England: British Psychological Society.

Fishel, A.H. (1995). Mental health. In C.I. Fogal & N.F. Woods (Eds.), *Women's health-care: A comprehensive handbook* (pp. 323–362). Thousand Oaks, CA: Sage.

Fisher, R.A. (1930). *The genetical theory of natural selection.* New York: Dover.

Fisher, S., & Groce, S. (1985). Doctor-patient negotiation of cultural assumptions. *Sociology of Health and Illness, 7,* 342–374.

Fisher-Thompson, D., & Burke, T.A. (1998). Experimenter influences and children's cross-gender behavior. *Sex Roles, 39,* 669–684.

Fishkin, S., Rohrbach, L., & Johnson, C. (1997). Correlates of youths' fears of victimization. *Journal of Applied Social Psychology, 27,* 1601–1616.

Fishman, P. (1983). Interaction: The work women do. In B. Thorne, C. Kramarae, & N. Henley (Eds.), *Language, gender and society* (pp. 89–102). Rowley, MA: Newbury House.

Fiske, S.T. (1992). Thinking is for doing: Portraits of social cognition from daguerreotype to laserphoto. *Journal of Personality and Social Psychology, 63,* 877–889.

Fiske, S.T. (1993). Controlling other people: The impact of power on stereotyping. *American Psychologist, 48*(6), 621–628.

Fiske, S.T. (1998). Stereotyping, prejudice, and discrimination. In D.T. Gilbert, S.T. Fiske, & G. Lindzey (Eds.), *Handbook of social psychology* (4th ed., Vol. 2, pp. 357–411). Boston: McGraw-Hill.

Fiske, S.T., Bersoff, D.N., Borgida, E., Deaux, K., & Heilman, M.E. (1991). Social science research on trial: Use of sex stereotyping research. In *Price Waterhouse v. Hopkins. American Psychologist, 46*(10), 1049–1060.

Fiske, S.T., & Glick, P. (1995). Ambivalence and stereotypes cause sexual harassment: A theory with implications for organizational change. *Journal of Social Issues, 51*, 97–115.

Fiske, S.T., Lin, M., & Neuberg, S.L. (1999). The continuum model: Ten years later. In S. Chaiken & Y. Trope (Eds.), *Dual-process theories in social psychology* (pp. 231–254). New York: Guilford Press.

Fiske, S.T., & Neuberg, S.L. (1990). A continuum model of impression formation: From category-based to individuating processes as a function of information, motivation, and attention. In M.P. Zanna (Ed.), *Advances in experimental psychology* (Vol. 23, pp. 1–108). San Diego, CA: Academic Press.

Fiske, S.T., & Stevens, L.E. (1993). What's so special about sex? Gender stereotyping and discrimination. In S. Oskamp & M. Costanzo (Eds.), *Gender issues in contemporary society: Claremont Symposium on Applied Social Psychology* (Vol. 6, pp. 173–196). Newbury Park, CA: Sage.

Fiske, S.T., & Taylor, S.E. (1991). *Social cognition* (2nd ed.). New York: McGraw-Hill.

Fiske, S.T., Xu, J., & Cuddy, A.C. (1999). (Dis)respecting versus (dis)liking: Status and interdependence predict ambivalent stereotypes of competence and warmth. *Journal of Social Issues, 55*, 473–489.

Fitzgerald, L.F. (1996). Sexual harassment: The definition and measurement of a construct. In M.A. Paludi (Ed.), *Sexual harassment on college campuses: Abusing the ivory power* (pp. 25–47). New York: State University of New York Press.

Fitzgerald, L.F., Drasgow, F., Hulin, C.L., Gelfand, M.J., & Magley, V.J. (1997). Antecedents and consequences of sexual harassment in organizations: A test of an integrated model. *Journal of Applied Psychology, 82*(4), 578–589.

Fitzgerald, L.F., Gelfand, M.J., & Drasgow, F. (1995). Measuring sexual harassment: Theoretical and psychometric advances. *Basic and Applied Social Psychology, 17*, 425–445.

Fitzgerald, L.F., & Hesson-McInnis, M. (1989). The dimensions of sexual harassment: A structural analysis. *Journal of Vocational Behavior, 35*, 309–326.

Fitzgerald, L.F., Magley, V.J., Drasgow, F., & Waldo, C.R. (1999). Measuring sexual harassment in the military: The Sexual Experiences Questionnaire (SEQ–DoD). *Military Psychology, 11*, 243–264.

Fitzgerald, L.F., Shullman, S., Bailey, N., Richards, M., Swecker, J., Gold, Y., Ormerod, A.J., & Weitzman, L. (1988). The incidence and dimensions of sexual harassment in academia and the workplace. *Journal of Vocational Behavior, 32*, 152–175.

Fitzgerald, L.F., Swan, S., & Fischer, C. (1995). Why didn't she just report him? The psychological and legal implications of women's responses to sexual harassment. *Journal of Social Issues, 51*, 117–138.

Fitzgerald, L.F., Swan, S., & Magley, V.J. (1997). But was it really sexual harassment? Legal, behavioral, and psychological definitions of the workplace victimization of women. In W. O'Donohue (Ed.), *Sexual harassment: Theory, research, and treatment* (pp. 5–28). Boston: Allyn & Bacon.

Flaks, D.K., Ficher, I., Masterpasqua, F., & Joseph, G. (1995). Lesbians choosing motherhood: A comparative study of lesbian and heterosexual parents and their children. *Developmental Psychology, 31*, 105–114.

Flanagan, P. (1998). Teen mothers: Countering the myths of dysfunction and developmental disruption. In C. Garcia Coll, J.L. Surrey, & K. Weingarten (Eds.), *Mothering against the odds: Diverse voices of contemporary mothers* (pp. 238–254). New York: Guilford Press.

Flax, J. (1987). Postmodernism and gender relations in feminist theory. *Signs, 12*(4), 621–643.

Fleming, C. (1996). Cultural formulation of psychiatric diagnosis. Case No. 01: An American Indian woman suffering from depression, alcoholism, and childhood trauma. *Culture, Medicine and Psychiatry, 20*, 145–154.

Follingstad, D.R., Rutledge, L.L., McNeill-Hawkins, K., & Polek, D.S. (1992). Factors related to physical violence in dating relationships. In E.C. Viano (Ed.), *Intimate violence: Interdisciplinary perspectives* (pp. 121–135). New York: Hemisphere.

Fonow, M.M. (1998). Protest engendered: The participation of women steelworkers in the Wheeling-Pittsburgh steel strike of 1985. *Gender and Society, 12*(6), 710–728.

Fonow, M.M., & Cook, J.A. (1991). Back to the future: A look at the second wave of feminist epistemology and methodology. In M.M. Fonow & J.A. Cook (Eds.), *Beyond methodology: Feminist scholarship as lived research* (pp. 1–15). Bloomington: Indiana University Press.

Foote, J.A., Harris, R.B., & Gilles, M.E. (1996). Physician advice and tobacco use: A survey of 1st-year college students. *Journal of American College Health, 45*, 129–132.

Foote, W.E., & Goodman-Delahunty, J. (1999). Same-sex harassment: Implications of the Oncale decision for forensic evaluation of plaintiffs. *Behavioral Sciences and the Law, 17*, 123–139.

Forde, J. (1999, December). Homo-cide: Homophobia and the provocation defense in R.V. Campbell (Ed.), *Queer in New Zealand symposium*, 3–5. Massey University, New Zealand, School of Sociology and Women's Studies.

Fordham, S. (1988). Racelessness as a factor in Black students' school success: Pragmatic strategy or pyrrhic victory? *Harvard Educational Review, 58*(1), 54–84.

Fordham, S. (1993). "Those loud Black girls": (Black) women, silence, and gender "passing" in the academy. *Anthropology and Education Quarterly, 24*(1), 3–32.

Fordham, S. (1996). *Blacked out: Dilemmas of race, identity, and success at Capital High.* Chicago: University of Chicago Press.

Forel, A. (1908). *The sexual question: A scientific, psychological, hygienic and sociological study* (C.F. Marshall, Trans.). New York: Physicians and Surgeons Books.

Foreman, J. (1996, October 4). 70% would pick hospice, polls finds. *Boston Globe.* [On-line]

Forest, M.G. (1985). Pitfalls in prenatal diagnosis of 21-hydroxylase deficiency by amniotic fluid steroid analysis? A six-year experience in 102 pregnancies at risk. *Annals of the New York Academy of Sciences, 458,* 130–147.

Forsyth, D., Schlenker, B.R., Leary, M.R., & McCown, N.E. (1985). Self-presentational determinants of sex differences in leadership behavior. *Small Group Behavior, 16,* 197–210.

Fouad, N., Brehm, S., Hall, C.I., Keita, G.P., Kite, M.E., Hyde, J.S., & Russo, N.F. (2000). *Women in academe: Two steps forward, one step back. Report of the Task Force on Women in Academe.* Washington, DC: American Psychological Association.

Foucault, M. (1978). *The history of sexuality: Volume I.* London: Penguin.

Fox, D., & Prilleltensky, I. (Eds.). (1997). *Critical psychology: An Introduction.* London: Sage.

Fox, M., & Auerbach, D. (1983). Whatever it is, don't call me one: Women students' attitudes toward feminism. *International Journal of Women's Studies, 6,* 352–362.

Foxley, C.H. (1979). *Non-sexist counseling: Helping women and men redefine their roles.* Dubuque, IA: Kendall/Hunt.

Frank, E., Brogan, D.J., & Schiffman, M. (1998). Prevalence and correlates of sexual harassment among U.S. women physicians. *Archives of Internal Medicine, 158,* 352–358.

Frank, F.W. (1989). Language planning, language reform, and language change: A review of guidelines for nonsexist usage. In F.W. Frank & P.A. Treichler (Eds.), *Language, gender, and professional writing* (pp. 105–133). New York: Modern Language Association.

Frank, F.W., & Treichler, P.A. (Eds.). (1989). *Language, gender, and professional writing.* New York: Modern Language Association of America.

Franke, K. (1997). What's wrong with sexual harassment? *Stanford University Law Review, 49,* 691–772.

Frankenberg, R. (1993). *White women, race matters: The social construction of whiteness.* Minneapolis: University of Minnesota Press.

Frankforter, S.A. (1996). The progression of women beyond the glass ceiling. *Journal of Social Behavior and Personality, 11*(5), 121–132.

Franklin, K. (1998). Unassuming motivations: Contextualizing the narratives of antigay assailants. In G.M. Herek (Ed.), *Stigma and sexual orientation: Understanding prejudice against lesbians, gay men and bisexuals.* London: Sage.

Franklin, M. (1997). Making sense: Interviewing and the narrative representation of women artists' work. In M. Gergen & S.N. Davis (Eds.), *Toward a new psychology of gender* (pp. 99–116). New York: Routledge.

Franklin, S. (1997). *Embodied progress: A cultural account of assisted conception.* London: Routledge.

Franz, C.E. (1995). A quantitative study of longitudinal changes in identity, intimacy, and generativity. *Journal of Personality, 63,* 27–46.

Franz, C.E., & Stewart, A.J. (Eds.). (1994). *Women creating lives: Identities, resilience and resistance.* Boulder, CO: Westview Press.

Fraser, N. (1993). Clintonism, welfare, and the antisocial wage: The emergence of a neoliberal political imaginary. *Rethinking Marxism, 6,* 9–23.

Frazier, P.A., Cochran, C.C., & Olson, A.M. (1995). Social science research on lay definitions of sexual harassment. *Journal of Social Issues, 51,* 21–37.

Fredrickson, B.L., & Roberts, T.A. (1997). Objectification theory: Toward understanding women's lived experiences and mental health risks. *Psychology of Women Quarterly, 21,* 173–206.

Fredrickson, B.L., Roberts, T.A., Noll, S.M., Quinn, D.M., & Twenge, J.M. (1998). That swimsuit becomes you: Sex differences in self-objectification, restrained eating, and math performance. *Journal of Personality and Social Psychology, 75*(1), 269–284.

Freeberg, A.L., & Stein, C.H. (1996). Felt obligation towards parents in Mexican-American and Anglo-American young adults. *Journal of Social and Personal Relationships, 13,* 457–471.

Freedman, R.J. (1984). Reflections on beauty as it relates to health in adolescent females. *Women and Health, 9*(2/3), 29–45.

Freedman, V. (1993). Kin and nursing home lengths of stay: A backward recurrence time approach. *Journal of Health and Social Behavior, 34,* 138–152.

Freeman, S.J.M. (1990). *Managing lives: Corporate women and social change.* Amherst: University of Massachusetts Press.

Freyd, J. (1997). Violations of power, adaptive blindness and betrayal trauma theory. *Feminism and Psychology, 7,* 22–32.

Friedan, B. (1963). *The feminine mystique.* New York: Dell.

Friend, R.A. (1993). Choices, not closets: Heterosexism and homophobia in schools. In L. Weis & M. Fine (Eds.), *Beyond silenced voices: Class, race, and gender in United States schools* (pp. 209–235). New York: State University of New York Press.

Frieze, I.H., & McHugh, M.C. (Eds.). (1997). Measuring beliefs about appropriate roles for women and men [Special issue]. *Psychology of Women Quarterly, 21,* 1–170.

Frieze, I.H., Olson, J.E., & Good, D.C. (1990). Perceived and actual discrimination in the salaries of male and female managers. *Journal of Applied Social Psychology, 20*(1), 46–67.

Frieze, I.H., Parsons, J.E., Johnson, P.B., Ruble, D.N., & Zellman, G.L. (1978). *Women and sex roles: A social psychological perspective.* New York: Norton.

Frintner, M.P., & Rubinson, L. (1993). Acquaintance rape: The influence of alcohol, fraternity membership, and sports team membership. *Journal of Sex Education and Therapy, 19,* 272–284.

Frith, H. (1998). Constructing the "other" through talk. *Feminism and Psychology, 8,* 530–536.

Frith, H., & Kitzinger, C. (1998). "Emotion work" as a participant resource: A feminist analysis of young women's talk-in-interaction. *Sociology, 32*(2), 299–320.

Frye, M. (1990). Lesbian sex. In J. Allen (Ed.), *Lesbian philosophies and cultures* (pp. 197–214). Albany: State University of New York Press.

Fuller, J. (1995). Getting in touch with your heritage. In N. Vacc, S. DeVaney, & J. Wittmer (Eds.), *Experiencing and counseling multicultural and diverse populations* (pp. 10–26). Bristol, PA: Taylor & Francis.

Fung, K.K. (1993). Dying for money: Overcoming moral hazard in terminal illnesses through compensated physician-assisted death. *American Journal of Economics and Sociology, 52*(3), 275–288.

Furnham, A., & Mak, T. (1999). Sex-role stereotyping in television commercials: A review and comparison of fourteen studies done on five continents over 25 years. *Sex Roles, 41,* 413–437.

Furstenberg, F.F., Brooks-Gunn, J., & Morgan, S.P. (1987). *Adolescent mothers in later life.* Cambridge, England: Cambridge University Press.

Furumoto, L., & Scarborough, E. (1986). Placing women in the history of psychology: The first generation of American women psychologists. *American Psychologist, 41,* 35–42.

Gagnon, J.H. (1990). The explicit and implicit use of the scripting perspective in sex research. *Annual Review of Sex Research, 1,* 1–43.

Gagnon, J.H., & Simon, W. (1973). *Sexual conduct.* New York: Aldine.

Gaines, S.O., Jr. (1997). *Culture, ethnicity, and personal relationships.* New York: Routledge.

Galambos, N.L., Almeida, D.M., & Petersen, A.C. (1990). Masculinity, femininity, and sex role attitudes in early adolescence: Exploring gender intensification. *Child Development, 61,* 1905–1914.

Gallagher-Thompson, D., McKibbin, C., Koonce-Volwiler, D., Menendez, A., Stewart, D., & Thompson, L.W. (2000). *Psychotherapy with older adults.* In C.R. Snyder & R. Ingram (Eds.), *Handbook of psychological change: Psychotherapy processes and practices for the 21st century* (pp. 614–637). New York: Wiley.

Gallant, S.J., Keita, G.P., & Royak-Schaler, R. (1997). *Health care and women: Psychological, social, and behavioral influences.* Washington, DC: American Psychological Association.

Gallo, J.J., Anthony, J.C., & Muthén, B.G. (1994). Age differences in the symptoms of depression: A latent trait analysis. *Journal of Gerontology: Psychological Sciences, 49,* P251–P264.

Ganley, A.L. (1988). Feminist therapy with male clients. In M.A. Dutton & L.E.A. Walker (Eds.), *Feminist psychotherapies: Integration of therapeutic and feminist systems* (pp. 186–205). Norwood, NJ: Ablex.

Gannon, L. (1998). The impact of medical and sexual politics on women's health. *Feminism and Psychology, 8,* 285–302.

Garb, H.N. (1997). Race bias, social class bias, and gender bias in clinical judgment. *Clinical Psychology, 4,* 99–120.

Garfield, S.L., & Bergin, A.E. (1978). *Handbook of psychotherapy and behavior change: An empirical analysis* (2nd ed.). New York: Wiley.

Garfinkel, H. (1967). *Studies in ethnomethodology.* Englewood Cliffs, NJ: Prentice-Hall.

Garnets, L.D., Hancock, K.A., Cochran, S.D., Goodchilds, J., & Peplau, L.A. (1998). Issues in psychotherapy with lesbians and gay men: A survey of psychologists. In D.R. Atkinson & G. Hackett (Eds.), *Counseling diverse populations* (2nd ed., pp. 297–316). Boston: McGraw-Hill.

Garnets, L.D., & Kimmel, D.C. (Eds.). (1993). *Psychological perspectives on lesbian and gay experience.* New York: Columbia University Press.

Garrett, C.S., Ein, P.L., & Tremaine, L. (1977). The development of gender stereotyping of adult occupations in elementary school children. *Child Development, 48,* 507–512.

Gatz, M., Harris, J.R., & Turk-Charles, S. (1995). The meaning of health for older women. In A.L. Stanton & S.J. Gallant (Eds.), *Psychology of women's health: Progress and challenges in research and application* (pp. 491–529). Washington, DC: American Psychological Association.

Gauthier, D., & Bankston, W. (1997). Gender equality and the sex ratio of intimate killing. *Criminology, 35,* 577–595.

Gavey, N. (1989). Feminist poststructuralism and discourse analysis: Contributions to feminist psychology. *Psychology of Women Quarterly, 13,* 459–475.

Gavey, N. (1992). Technologies and effects of heterosexual coercion. *Feminism and Psychology, 2*(3), 325–351.

Gavey, N. (1993). Technologies and effects of heterosexual coercion. In S. Wilkinson & C. Kitzinger (Eds.), *Heterosexuality: A feminism and psychology reader.* London: Sage.

Gavey, N. (1996). Women's desire and sexual violence discourse. In S. Wilkinson (Ed.), *Feminist social psychologies: International perspectives* (pp. 51–65). Buckingham, England: Open University Press.

Gavey, N., McPhillips, K., & Braun, V. (1999). Interruptus coitus: Heterosexuals accounting for intercourse. *Sexualities, 2*(1), 35–68.

Gay, C., & Tate, K. (1998). Doubly bound: The impact of gender and race on the politics of Black women. *Political Psychology, 19,* 169–184.

Gayford, J.J. (1975). Wife-battering: A preliminary survey of 100 cases. *British Medical Journal, 1,* 194–197.

Gaylor, L. (1985, July/August). Pornography: A humanist issue. *The Humanist,* 34–40.

Gelles, R.J., & Loseke, D.L. (Eds.). (1993). *Current controversies in domestic violence.* Newbury Park, CA: Sage.

Gelles, R.J., & Straus, M.A. (1988). *Intimate violence: The definitive study of the causes and consequences of abuse in the American family.* New York: Simon & Schuster.

Gelman, S., Collman, P., & Maccoby, E. (1986). Inferring properties from categories versus inferring categories from properties: The case of gender. *Child Development, 57,* 396–404.

Gentile, D.A. (1993). Just what are sex and gender, anyway? A call for a new terminological standard. *Psychological Science, 4,* 120–122.

George, L.K. (1990). Gender, age and psychiatric disorders. *Generations, 14,* 22–27.

Gergen, K.J. (1985). The social constructionist movement in modern psychology. *American Psychologist, 40,* 266–275.

Gergen, M.M. (1990a). A feminist psychologist's postmod critique of postmodernism. *Humanistic Psychologist, 18,* 95–104.

Gergen, M.M. (1990b). Finished at 40: Women's development within the patriarchy. *Psychology of Women Quarterly, 14,* 471–493.

Gergen, M.M., Chrisler, J.C., & LoCicero, A. (1999). Innovative methods: Resources for research, publishing, and teaching. *Psychology of Women Quarterly, 23,* 431–456.

Gergen, M.M., & Davis, S.N. (Eds.). (1997). *Toward a new psychology of gender.* New York: Routledge.

Gerson, K. (1985). *Hard choices: How women decide about work, careers and motherhood.* Berkeley: University of California Press.

Gerson, M-J. (1986). The prospect of parenthood for women and men. *Psychology of Women Quarterly, 10,* 49–62.

Gerson, M-J., Berman, L.S., & Morris, A.M. (1991). The value of having children as an aspect of adult development. *Journal of Genetic Psychology, 152,* 327–339.

Gervasio, A.H. (1987). Assertiveness techniques as speech acts. *Clinical Psychology Review, 7,* 105–119.

Gervasio, A.H., & Crawford, M. (1989). Social evaluations of assertiveness: A critique and speech act reformulation. *Psychology of Women Quarterly, 13,* 1–25.

Geschwind, N., & Galaburda, A.M. (1985). Cerebral lateralization. Biological mechanisms, associations, and pathology: I. A hypothesis and a program for research. *Archives of Neurology, 42,* 428–459.

Getz, S. (1997). The development of feminist practice in Canadian psychology. *History and Philosophy of Psychology Bulletin, 9,* 21–29.

Giami, A., Olumucki, H., & De Poplavsky, J. (1997). Surveying sexuality and AIDS: Interviewer attitudes and representations. In J. Bancroft (Ed.), *Researching sexual behavior* (pp. 61–77). Bloomington: Indiana University Press.

Gibbs, E.D. (1988). Psychosocial development of children raised by lesbian mothers: A review of research. *Women and Therapy, 8,* 55–75.

Giddings, P. (1984). *When and where I enter: The impact of Black women on race and sex in America.* New York: Morrow.

Gidycz, C.A., Coble, C.N., Latham, L., & Layman, M.J. (1993). Sexual assault experience in adulthood and prior victimization experiences: A prospective analysis. *Psychology of Women Quarterly, 17,* 151–168.

Giele, J.Z. (1993). Women's role change and adaptation, 1920–1990. In K.D. Hulbert & D.T. Schuster (Eds.), *Women's lives through time* (pp. 32–60). San Francisco: Jossey-Bass.

Giele, J.Z. (1995). *Two paths to women's equality: Temperance, suffrage, and the origins of modern feminism.* New York: Twayne.

Gilbert, D.T., Fiske, S.T., & Lindzey, G. (Eds.). (1998). *Handbook of social psychology* (4th ed., Vol. 1). Boston: McGraw-Hill.

Gilbert, L.A. (1985). *Men in dual-career families: Current realities and future prospects.* Hillsdale, NJ: Erlbaum.

Gilbert, L.A. (Ed.). (1987). Dual-career families in perspective [Special issue]. *Counseling Psychologist, 15*(1).

Gilbert, L.A. (1993). *Two careers/One family: The promise of gender equality.* Beverly Hills, CA: Sage.

Gilbert, L.A. (1994). Reclaiming and returning gender to context: Examples from studies of heterosexual dual-career families. *Psychology of Women Quarterly, 18,* 539–558.

Gilbert, L.A., & Scher, M. (1999). *Gender and sex in counseling and psychotherapy.* Boston: Allyn & Bacon.

Gilgun, J.F. (1995). We shared something special: The moral discourse of incest perpetrators. *Journal of Marriage and the Family, 57,* 265–281.

Gilkes, C. (1988). Building in many places: Multiple commitments and ideologies in Black women's community work. In A. Bookman & S. Morgan (Eds.), *Women and the politics of empowerment* (pp. 53–76). Philadelphia: Temple University Press.

Gill, R. (1995). Relativism, reflexivity and politics: Interrogating discourse analysis from a feminist perspective. In S. Wilkinson & C. Kitzinger (Eds.), *Feminism and discourse: Psychological perspectives* (pp. 165–186). London: Sage.

Gilligan, C. (1980). *In a different voice.* Cambridge, MA: Harvard University Press.

Gilligan, C. (1982). *In a different voice: Psychological theory and women's development.* Cambridge, MA: Harvard University Press.

Gilligan, C. (1990). Teaching Shakespeare's sister. In C. Gilligan, N. Lyons, T. Hanmer (Eds.), *Making connections: The relational worlds of adolescent girls at Emma Willard School.* Cambridge, MA: Harvard University Press.

Gilligan, C. (1991). Joining the resistance: Psychology, politics, girls, and women. *Michigan Quarterly Review, 29,* 501–536.

Gilligan, C. (1993). Letter to readers, 1993. *In a different voice* (2nd ed.). Cambridge, MA: Harvard University Press.

Gilligan, C., Brown, L.M., & Rogers, A. (1990). Psyche embedded: A place for body, relationships, and culture in personality theory. In A.I. Rabin, R. Zucker, R. Emmons, & S. Frank (Eds.), *Studying persons and lives.* New York: Springer.

Gilligan, C., Rogers, A.G., & Tolman, D.L. (1991). Introduction. In C. Gilligan, A.G. Rogers, & D.L. Tolman (Eds.), *Women, girls and psychotherapy: Reframing resistance* (pp. 1–3). Binghamton, NY: Haworth Press

Giuffre, P.A., & Williams, C.L. (1994). Boundary lines: Labeling sexual harassment in restaurants. *Gender and Society, 8,* 378–401.

Gladue, B.A. (1989). Missing link in mate prefence studies: Reproduction. *Behavioral and Brain Sciences, 12,* 21.

Gladue, B.A. (1997). Foreword. In L. Ellis & L. Ebertz (Eds.), *Sexual orientation: Toward biological understanding* (pp. xiii–xviii). Westport, CT: Praeger.

Glaser, B.G., & Strauss, A.L. (1967). *The discovery of grounded theory: Strategies for qualitative research.* Chicago: Aldine.

Glass, J., Bengston, V.L., & Dunham, C.C. (1986). Attitude similarity in three-generation families: Socialization, status inheritance, or reciprocal influence? *American Sociological Review, 51,* 685–698.

Glass, J.L., & Estes, S.B. (1997). The family responsive workplace. *Annual Review of Sociology, 23,* 289–313.

Glass, M.H., & Beiber, S. (1997). The effects of acculturative stress on incarcerated Alaska Natives and non-native men. *Cultural Diversity and Mental Health, 3,* 175–191.

Gleason, W.J. (1993). Mental disorders in battered women: An empirical study. *Violence and Victims, 8,* 53–68.

Gleick, E. (1997, June 16). Tower of psychobabble: Self-help author John Gray's empire. *Time, 149*(24), 68–71.

Glendenning, F. (1997). The mistreatment and neglect of elderly people in residential centres: Research outcomes. In P. Decalmer & F. Glendenning (Eds.), *The mistreatment of elderly people* (2nd ed., pp. 151–162). London: Sage.

Glenn, E.N. (1994). Social constructions of mothering: A thematic overview. In E.N. Glenn, G. Chang, & L.R. Forcey (Eds.), *Motherhood: Ideology, experience and agency* (pp. 1–29). New York: Routledge.

Glenn, E.N., Chang, G., & Forcey, L.R. (Eds.). (1994). *Motherhood: Ideology, experience and agency.* New York: Routledge.

Glick, J.A. (1999). Focus groups in political campaigns. In D.D. Perlmutter (Ed.), *The manship school guide to political communication* (pp. 114–121). Baton Rouge: Louisiana State University Press.

Glick, P., Diebold, J., Bailey-Werner, B., & Zhu, L. (1997). The two faces of Adam: Ambivalent sexism and polarized attitudes toward women. *Personality and Social Psychology Bulletin, 23,* 1323–1334.

Glick, P., & Fiske, S.T. (1996). The Ambivalent Sexism Inventory: Differentiating hostile and benevolent sexism. *Journal of Personality and Social Psychology, 70*(3), 491–512.

Glick, P., & Fiske, S.T. (1997). Hostile and benevolent sexism: Measuring ambivalent sexist attitudes toward women. *Psychology of Women Quarterly, 21,* 119–135.

Glick, P., & Fiske, S.T. (1999a). The Ambivalence toward Men Inventory: Differentiating hostile and benevolent beliefs about men. *Psychology of Women Quarterly, 23,* 519–536.

Glick, P., & Fiske, S.T. (1999b). Gender, power dynamics, and social interaction. In M.M. Ferree, J. Lorber, & B.B. Hess (Eds.), *Revisioning gender: The gender lens* (Vol. 5, pp. 365–398). Thousand Oaks, CA: Sage.

Glick, P., & Fiske, S.T. (in press). Ambivalent stereotypes as legitimizing ideologies: Differentiating paternalistic and envious prejudice. In J.M. Jost (Ed.), *Psychology of legitimacy.*

Glick, P., Fiske, S.T., Mladnic, A., Saiz, J., Abrams, D., & et al. (2000). Beyond prejudice as simple antipathy: Hostile sexism across cultures. *Journal of Personality and Social Psychology, 79,* 763–775.

Glickman, R.L. (1993). *Daughters of feminists.* New York: St. Martin's Press.

Glomb, T.M., Munson, L.J., Hulin, C.L., Bergman, M.E., & Drasgow, F. (1999). Structural equation models of sexual harassment: Longitudinal explorations and cross-sectional generalizations. *Journal of Applied Psychology, 84,* 14–28.

Glomb, T.M., Richman, W.L., Hulin, C.L., Drasgow, F., Schneider, K.T., & Fitzgerald, L.F. (1997). Ambient sexual harassment: An integrated model of antecedents and consequences. *Organizational Behavior and Human Decision Processes, 71,* 309–328.

Gluck, S.B., & Patai, D. (Eds.). (1991). *Women's words: The feminist practice of oral history.* London: Routledge.

Goffman, E. (1963). *Stigma: Notes of the management of spoiled identity.* Englewood Cliffs, NJ: Prentice-Hall.

Goktepe, J.R., & Schneier, C.E. (1988). Sex and gender effects in evaluating emergent leaders in small groups. *Sex Roles, 19,* 29–36.

Goldberg, A. (1997). Dad, I'm a lesbian, you probably know. In M. Miedzian & A. Malinovich (Eds.), *Generations: A century of women speak about their lives* (pp. 178–183). New York: Atlantic Monthly Press.

Goldberg, H. (1977). *The hazards of being male.* New York: Nash.

Goldberg, P.A. (1968, April 28–30). Are women prejudiced against women? *Transaction.*

Goldberg, S. (1997). My mother was a housewife. In M. Miedzian & A. Malinovich (Eds.), *Generations: A century of women speak about their lives* (p. 75). New York: Atlantic Monthly Press.

Goldenhar, L.M., Swanson, N.G., Hurrell, J.J., Jr., Ruder, A., & Deddens, J. (1998). Stressors and adverse outcomes for female construction workers. *Journal of Occupational Health Psychology, 3,* 19–32.

Goldner, V. (1999). Morality and multiplicity: Perspectives on the treatment of violence in intimate life. *Journal of Marital and Family Therapy, 25,* 325–336.

Goldstein, D. (1983). Spouse abuse. In A. Goldstein (Ed.), *Prevention and control of aggression* (pp. 37–65). New York: Pergamon Press.

Golombok, S., Murray, C., Brinsden, P., & Abdalla, H. (1999). Social versus biological parenting: Family functioning and the socioemotional development of children conceived by egg or sperm donation. *Journal of Child Psychology and Psychiatry, 40,* 519–527.

Golombok, S., & Tasker, F. (1996). Do parents influence the sexual orientation of their children? Findings from a longitudinal study of lesbian families. *Developmental Psychology, 32,* 3–11.

Gonsiorek, J.C. (1995). Gay male identities: Concepts and issues. In A.R. D'Augelli & C. Patterson (Eds.), *Lesbian, gay and bisexual identities over the lifespan: Psychological perspectives.* New York: Oxford University Press.

Gonzales, M.H., & Meyers, S.A. (1993). "Your mother would like me": Self-presentation in the personal ads of heterosexual and homosexual men and women. *Personality and Social Psychology Bulletin, 19,* 131–142.

Gonzalez, D. (1998). Speaking secrets: Living Chicana theory. In C. Trujillo (Ed.), *Living Chicana theory* (pp. 46–77). Berkeley, CA: Third Woman Press.

Good, G., Gilbert, L.A., & Sher, M. (1990). Gender aware therapy: A synthesis of feminist therapy and knowledge about gender. *Journal of Counseling and Development, 68,* 376–380.

Good, G.E. (1998). Missing and underrepresented aspects of men's lives. *Society for the Psychological Study of Men and Masculinity Bulletin, 3*(2), 1–2.

Good, G.E., Dell, D.M., & Mintz, L.B. (1989). Male role and gender role conflict: Relations to help seeking in men. *Journal of Counseling Psychology, 36,* 295–300.

Good, G.E., & Mintz, L.B. (1990). Depression and the male gender role: Evidence for compounded risk. *Journal of Counseling and Development, 69,* 17–21.

Good, G.E., & Mintz, L.B. (1993). Towards healthy conceptions of masculinity: Clarifying the issues. *Journal of Mental Health Counseling, 15,* 403–413.

Good, G.E., Robertson, J.M., Fitzgerald, L.F., Stevens, M.A., & Bartels, K.M. (1996). The relation between masculine role conflict and psychological distress in male university counseling center clients. *Journal of Counseling and Development, 75,* 44–49.

Good, G.E., Robertson, J.M., O'Neil, J.M., Fitzgerald, L.F., Stevens, M., Debord, K.A., & Bartels, K.M. (1995). Male gender role conflict: Psychometric issues and relations to psychological distress. *Journal of Counseling Psychology, 42*, 3–10.

Good, G.E., & Sherrod, N. (1997). Men's resolution of non-relational sex across the lifespan. In R. Levant & G. Brooks (Eds.), *Men and sex: New psychological perspectives* (pp. 182–204). New York: Wiley.

Good, G.E., Sherrod, N., & Dillon, M. (2000). Masculine gender role stressors and men's health. In R. Eisler & M. Hersen (Eds.), *Handbook of gender, culture, and health* (pp. 63–81). Mahwah, NJ: Erlbaum.

Good, G.E., Wallace, D.L., & Borst, T.S. (1994). Masculinity research: A review and critique. *Applied and Preventive Psychology, 3*, 3–14.

Goodman, N. (1983). *Fact, fiction, and forecast* (4th ed.). Cambridge, MA: Harvard University Press.

Goodman, L.A., Koss, M.P., Fitzgerald, L.F., Russo, N.F., & Keita, G.P. (1993). Male violence against women: Current research and future directions. *American Psychologist, 48,*(10), 1054–1058.

Goodnow, J.J. (1988). Children's household work: Its nature and functions. *Psychological Bulletin, 103*, 5–26.

Goodwin, M.H. (1990). *He-Said-She-Said: Talk as social organization among Black children.* Bloomington: Indiana University Press.

Goodwin, R., & Findlay, C. (1997). "We were just fated together." Chinese love and the concept of yuan in England and Hong Kong. *Personal Relationships, 4*, 85–92.

Goodwin, R., & Tang, C.S.-k. (1996). Chinese personal relationships. In M.H. Bond (Ed.), *Handbook of Chinese psychology* (pp. 294–308). Hong Kong: Oxford University Press.

Goodwin, S.A., Gubin, A., Fiske, S.T., & Yzerbyt, V.Y. (2000). Power can bias impression formation: Stereotyping subordinates by default and by design. *Group Processes and Intergroup Relations, 3*, 227–256.

Goodwin, S.A., Operario, D., & Fiske, S.T. (1998). Situational power and interpersonal dominance facilitate bias and inequality. *Journal of Social Issues, 54*(4), 677–698.

Gooren, L., Fliers, E., & Courtney, K. (1990). Biological determinants of sexual orientation. *Annual Review of Sex Research, 1*, 175–196.

Gordon, G. (1966). *Role theory and illness: A sociological perspective.* New Haven, CT: College and University Press.

Gordon, L. (1993). Women's agency, social control, and the construction of "rights" by battered women. In S. Fisher & K. Davis (Eds.), *Negotiating on the margins: The gendered discourses of power and resistance* (pp. 122–144). New Brunswick, NJ: Rutgers University Press.

Gordon, T. (1994). Single women and familism: Challenge from the margins. *European Journal of Women's Studies, 1*, 165–182.

Gottfredson, M.R., & Hirschi, T. (1990). *A general theory of crime.* Stanford, CA: Stanford University Press.

Gottman, J.M., & Levenson, R.W. (1988). The social psychophysiology of marriage. In P. Noller & M.A. Fitzpatrick (Eds.), *Perspectives on marital interactcion* (pp. 182–200). Philadelphia: Multilingual Matters.

Gould, M. (1985). Innovative sources and uses of qualitative data. In M. Gould (Ed.), *Innovative sources and uses of qualitative data* [Special issue]. *Qualitative Sociology, 8*, 303–308.

Gould, S.J. (1981). *The mismeasure of man.* New York: Norton.

Gould, S.J., & Lewontin, R.C. (1979). The spandrels of San Marco and the Panglossian paradigm: A critique of the adaptionist program. *Proceedings of R. Soc. Lond. B 205*, 581–598.

Gove, W.R. (1972). The relationship between sex roles, marital status and mental illness. *Social Forces, 51*(1), 34–44.

Goves, P.A. (1985). Coming out: Issues for the therapist working with women in the process of identity formation. *Women and Therapy, 4*, 17–22.

Gowaty, P.A. (1992). Evolutionary, biology and feminism. *Human Nature, 3*(3), 217–249 .

Gowaty, P.A. (1995). False criticisms of sociobiology and behavioral ecology: Genetic determinism, untestability, and inappropriate comparisons. *Politics and the Life Sciences, 14*, 12–18.

Gowaty, P.A. (1996a). Battles of the sexes and origins of monogamy. In J.L. Black (Ed.), *Black partnerships in birds* (pp. 21–52). Oxford, England: Oxford University Press.

Gowaty, P.A. (1996b). Field studies of parental care in birds: New data focus questions on variation in females. In C.T. Snowdon & J.S. Rosenblatt (Eds.), *Advances in the study of behaviour* (pp. 476–531). New York: Academic Press.

Gowaty, P.A. (Ed.). (1997a). *Feminism and evolutionary biology: Boundaries, intersections, and frontiers.* New York: Chapman & Hall.

Gowaty, P.A. (1997b). News and views: Birds face sexual discrimination. *Nature, 385*, 486–487.

Gowaty, P.A. (1997c). Sexual dialectics, sexual selection, and variation in mating behavior. In P.A. Gowaty (Ed.), *Feminism and evolutionary biology: Boundaries, intersections, and frontiers* (pp. 351–384). New York: Chapman & Hall.

Gowaty, P.A. (2000). *Mate choice, components of fitness, politics, and institutionalized monogamous marriage: A Darwinist and feminist perspective.* Manuscript submitted for publication.

Gowaty, P.A., Anderson, W.W., & Steinechen, B. (2000). *Ardent females and discriminating males: Sex role variation in three species of Drosophila.* Manuscript submitted for publication.

Gowaty, P.A., & Buschhaus, N. (1998). Ultimate causation of aggressive and forced copulation in birds: Female resistance, the CODE hypothesis and social monogamy. *American Zoologist, 38,* 207–225.

Gowaty, P.A., & Droge, D.L. (1991). Sex ratio conflict and the evolution of sex-biased provisioning. *Acta XX Congressus Internationalis Ornithologici,* Volume II, 932–945.

Gowaty, P.A., & Hubbell, S.P. (2000). *Fertility variation, gender equity, and the Red Queen: The women's autonomy hypothesis.* Manuscript submitted for publication.

Gowaty, P.A., & Plissner, J.H. (2000). *Sexually-dimorphic, sex-biased parental favoritism and meaness in eastern bluebirds, Sialia sialis, and the parent-parent conflict over the sex ratio hypothesis.* Manuscript submitted for publication.

Goy, R.W., Bercovitch, F.B., & McBrair, M.C. (1988). Behavioral masculinization is independent of genital masculinization in prenatally androgenized female rhesus macaques. *Hormones and Behavior, 22,* 552–571.

Graber, J.A., Brooks-Gunn, J., & Warren, M.P. (1999). The vulnerable transition: Puberty and the development of eating pathology and negative mood. *Women's Health Issues, 9,* 107–114.

Grace, V.M. (1995a). Problems women patients experience in the medical encounter for chronic pelvic pain: A New Zealand study. *Health Care for Women International, 16,* 509–519.

Grace, V.M. (1995b). Problems of communication, diagnosis, and treatment experienced by women using the New Zealand health services for chronic pelvic pain: A quantitative analysis. *Health Care for Women International, 16,* 521–535.

Grady, K.E. (1981). Sex bias in research design. *Psychology of Women Quarterly, 5,* 628–636.

Grady, K.E. (1988). Older women and the practice of breast self-examination. *Psychology of Women Quarterly, 12,* 473–487.

Graham, H. (1993). *Health and hardship in women's lives.* London: Harvester/Wheatsheaf.

Graham, J., Gentry, K., & Green, J. (1981). The self-presentational nature of emotional expression: Some evidence. *Personality and Social Psychology Bulletin, 7,* 467–474.

Grambs, J.D. (1989). *Women over forty: Visions and realities.* New York: Springer.

Gramsci, A. (1971). *Selections from the prison notebooks of Antonio Gramsci* (Q. Hoare, Ed. and G. Smith, Trans.). New York: International Publishers.

Granfield, R. (1996). Making it by faking: Working-class students in an elite academic environment. In S.J. Ferguson (Ed.), *Mapping the social landscape* (pp. 120–133). Mountain View, CA: Mayfield.

Grauerholz, E. (1989). Sexual harassment of women professors by students: Exploring the dynamics of power, authority, and gender in a university setting. *Sex Roles, 21,* 789–802.

Gray, J. (1992). *Men are from Mars, women are from Venus.* New York: HarperCollins.

Gready, M., Ditto, P.H., Coppola, K.M., Lockhart, L.K., & Smucker, W.D. (in press). Perceived versus actual stability of life-sustaining preferences. *Journal of Clinical Ethics.*

Green, R. (1977). Magnolias grow in dirt: The bawdy lore of Southern women. *Southern Exposure, 4,* 29–33.

Green, R., & Young, R. (2000). Fingerprint asymmetry in male and female transsexuals. *Personality and Individual Differences, 29,* 933–942.

Greenberg, D.J., Hillman, D., & Grice, D. (1973). Infant and stranger variables related to stranger anxiety in the first year of life. *Developmental Psychology, 9,* 207–212.

Greene, B. (1993). Human diversity in clinical psychology: Lesbian and gay sexual orientation. *Clinical Psychologist, 46,* 74–82.

Greene, B. (1994). African-American women. In L. Comas-Diaz & B. Greene (Eds.), *Women of color: Integrating ethnic and gender identities in psychotherapy* (pp. 10–29). New York: Guilford Press.

Greene, B. (Ed.). (1997). *Psychological perspectives on lesbian and gay issues: Ethnic and cultural diversity among lesbian and gay men.* Thousand Oaks, CA: Sage.

Greene, B. (1999, January 28). *Multiple oppressions.* Paper presented at the National Multicultural conference and summit, Newport Beach, CA.

Greene, B., & Croom, G.L. (2000). *Education, research and practice in lesbian, gay, bisexual and transgendered psychology: A resource manual.* Thousand Oaks, CA: Sage.

Greene, B.A. (1986). When the therapist is White and the patient is Black: Considerations for psychotherapy in the feminist heterosexual and lesbian communities. In D. Howard (Ed.), *The dynamics of feminist therapy* (pp. 41–66). New York: Haworth Press.

Greene, B.A., & Sanchez-Hucles, J. (1997). Diversity: Advancing an inclusive feminist psychology. In J. Worell & N.G. Johnson (Eds.), *Shaping the future of feminist psychology: Education, research, and practice* (pp. 173–202). Washington, DC: American Psychological Association.

Greene, J.C. (1994). Qualitative program evaluation. In N.K. Denzin & Y.S. Lincoln (Eds.), *Handbook of qualitative research* (pp. 530–544). Thousand Oaks, CA: Sage.

Greenfeld, L.A. (1997, February). *Sex offenses and offenders: An analysis of data on rape and sexual assault* (NJC-163392). Washinton, DC: U.S. Department of Justice, Office of Justice Programs, Bureau of Justice Statistics.

Greenfield, P.M., & Cocking, R.R. (1994). *Cross-cultural roots of minority child development.* Hillsdale, NJ: LEA.

Greenglass, E.R. (1973). Women: A new psychological view. *Ontario Psychologist, 5,* 7–15.

Greenglass, E.R., & Burke, R.J. (1988). Work and family precursors of burnout in teachers: Sex differences. *Sex Roles, 18,* 215–229.

Greenspan, M. (1983). *A new approach to women and therapy.* New York: McGraw-Hill.

Greenstein, T.N. (1996). Husbands' participation in domestic labor: Interactive effects of wives' and husbands' gender ideologies. *Journal of Marriage and the Family, 58,* 585–595.

Greenwald, A.G., & Banaji, M.R. (1995). Implicit social cognition: Attitudes, self-esteem, and stereotypes. *Psychological Review, 102,* 4–27.

Griffin, C. (1989). I'm not a women's libber but . . . : Feminism, consciousness and identity. In S. Skevington & D. Baker (Eds.), *The social identity of women* (pp. 173–193). London: Sage.

Griffin, C. (2000). Absences that matter: Constructions of sexuality in studies of young women's friendships. *Feminism and Psychology, 20*(2), 227–245.

Griscom, J.L. (1992). Women and power: Definition, dualism, and difference. *Psychology of Women Quarterly, 16,* 389–414.

Groneman, C. (1994). Nymphomania: The historical construction of female sexuality. *Signs, 19,* 337–367.

Grossman, A.H., D'Augelli, A.R., & Hershberger, S.L. (2000). Social support networks of lesbian, gay, and bisexual adults 60 years of age and older. *Journal of Gerontology: Psychological Sciences, 55*(3), P171–179.

Grossman, F.K., Kruger, L., & Moore, R.P. (1999). Reflections on a feminist research project: Subjectivity and the wish for intimacy and equality. *Psychology of Woman Quarterly, 23,* 117–135.

Grotevant, H.D. (1992). Assigned and chosen identity components: A process perspective on their integration. In G.R. Adams, T.P. Gullotta, & R. Montemayor (Eds.), *Adolescent identity formation* (pp. 73–90). Newbury Park, CA: Sage.

Gruber, J.E. (1990). Methodological problems and policy implications in sexual harassment research. *Population Research Political Review, 9,* 235–254.

Gruber, J.E. (1992). A typology of personal and environmental sexual harassment: Research and policy implications from the 1990s. *Sex Roles, 22,* 447–464.

Gruber, J.E. (1997). An epidemiology of sexual harassment: Evidence from North America and Europe. In W. O'Donohue (Ed.), *Sexual harassment: Theory, research, and treatment* (pp. 84–98). Boston: Allyn & Bacon.

Gruber, J.E. (1998). The impact of male work environments and organizational policies on women's experiences of sexual harassment. *Gender and Society, 12*(3), 301–320.

Gruber, J.E., & Bjorn, L. (1982). Blue-collar blues. *Work and Occupations, 9,* 271–298.

Guba, E.G., & Lincoln, Y.S. (1989). *Fourth generation evaluation.* Newbury Park, CA: Sage.

Guba, E.G., & Lincoln, Y.S. (1994). Competing paradigms in qualitative research. In N.K. Denzin & Y.S. Lincoln (Eds.), *Handbook of qualitative research* (pp. 105–117). Thousand Oaks, CA: Sage.

Guldner, G.T. (1996). Long-distance relationships: Prevalence and separation-related symptoms in college students. *Journal of College Student Development, 37,* 289–295.

Guldner, G.T., & Swensen, C.H. (1995). Time spent together and relationship quality: Long-distance relationships as a test case. *Journal of Social and Personal Relationships, 12,* 313–320.

Gulick, E.E. (1994). Social support among persons with multiple sclerosis. *Research in Nursing and Health, 17,* 195–206.

Gupta, A. (1998). At the crossroads: College activism and its impact on Asian American identity formation. In L.D. Shankar & R. Srikanth (Eds.), *A part, yet apart: South Asians in Asian America* (pp. 127–145). Philadelphia: Temple University Press.

Guralnik, J.M., LaCroix, A.Z., Everett, M.S., & Kovar, M.G. (1989). *Aging in the eighties: The prevalence of comorbidity and its association with disability.* Advance data from vital and Health Statistics of the National Center for Health Statistics, No. 170 (DHHS Publication No. PHS 89–1250). Hyattsville, MD: National Center for Health Statistics.

Gurin, P. (1985). Women's gender consciousness. *Public Opinion Quarterly, 49*(2), 143–163.

Gurin, P. (1987). The political implications of women's statuses. In F. Crosby (Ed.), *Spouse, parent, worker: On gender and multiple roles* (pp. 167–198). New Haven, CT: Yale University Press.

Gurin, P., & Markus, H. (1989). Cognitive consequences of gender identity. In S. Skevington & D. Baker (Eds.), *The social identity of women* (pp. 152–172). London: Sage.

Gurin, P., Miller, A., & Gurin, G. (1980). Stratum identification and consciousness. *Social Psychology Quarterly, 43,* 30–47.

Gurin, P., & Townsend, A. (1986). Properties of gender identity and their implications for gender consciousness. *British Journal of Social Psychology, 25,* 139–148.

Gutek, B.A. (1985). *Sex and the workplace.* San Francisco: Jossey-Bass.

Gutek, B.A. (1995). How subjective is sexual harassment? An examination of rater effects. *Basic and Applied Social Psychology, 17,* 447–468.

Gutek, B.A. (1997). Sexual harassment policy initiatives. In W. O'Donohue (Ed.), *Sexual harassment: Theory, research, and treatment* (pp. 185–199). Boston: Allyn & Bacon.

Gutek, B.A., Cohen, A.G., & Konrad, A.M. (1990). Predicting social-sexual behavior at work: A contact hypothesis. *Academy of Management Journal, 33,* 560–577.

Gutek, B.A., & Dunwoody, V. (1987). Understanding sex in the workplace. In A.H. Stromberg, L. Larwood, & B.A. Gutek (Eds.), *Women and work: An annual review* (pp. 249–269). Newbury Park, CA: Sage.

Gutek, B.A., & Koss, M. (1993). Changed women and changed organizations: Consequences of and coping with sexual harassment. *Journal of Vocational Behavior, 42,* 28–48.

Gutek, B.A., & Morasch, B. (1982). Sex-ratios, sex-role spillover, and sexual harassment of women at work. *Journal of Social Issues, 38,* 55–74.

Gutek, B.A., Nakamura, C., Gahart, M., Handschumacher, I., & Russell, D. (1980). Sexuality in the workplace. *Basic and Applied Social Psychology, 1,* 255–265.

Gutek, B.A., & O'Connor, M.O. (1995). The empirical basis for the reasonable woman standard. *Journal of Social Issues, 51,* 151–166.

Gutek, B.A., O'Connor, M.O., Melançon, R., Stockdale, M.S., Geer, T., & Done, R.S. (1999). The utility of the reasonable woman legal standard in hostile environment sexual harassment cases: A multimethod, multistudy examination. *Psychology, Public Policy, and Law, 5,* 596–629.

Gutierrez, L.M. (1990). Working with women of color: An empowerment perspective. *Social Work, 35,* 149–153.

Guttentag, M., & Secord, P. (1983). *Too many women?* Beverly Hills, CA: Sage.

Guttierez, G., & Nagata, D.K. (1996). Intraethnic and interethnic diversity: Researching the Japanese American and Mexican American communities. In K.F. Wyche & F.J. Crosby (Eds.), *Women's ethnicities: Journeys through psychology* (pp. 167–182). Boulder, CO: Westview.

Guy-Sheftall, B. (Ed.). (1995). *Words of fire: An anthology of African-American feminist thought.* New York: New Press.

Haag, P. (1999). *Voices of a generation: Teenage girls on sex, school, and self.* Washington, DC: American Association of University Women Educational Foundation.

Haaken, J. (1998). *Pillar of salt.* New Brunswick, NJ: Rutgers University.

Haber, J., & Halfon, M. (1998). *Norms and values: Essays on the work of Virginia Held.* Lanham, MD: Rowman and Littlefield.

Hackel, L.S., & Ruble, D.N. (1992). Changes in the marital relationship after the first baby is born: Predicting the impact of expectancy disconfirmation. *Journal of Personality and Social Psychology, 62,* 944–957.

Hacker, H.M. (1951). Women as a minority group. *Social Forces, 30,* 60–69.

Hacking, I. (1998). *Mad travelers: Reflections on the reality of transient mental illness.* Charlottesville: University of Virginia Press.

Haddock, G., & Zanna, M.P. (1994). Preferring "housewives" to "feminists": Categorization and the favorability of attitudes toward women. *Psychology of Women Quarterly, 18,* 25–52.

Haddock, G., Zanna, M.P., & Esses, V.M. (1993). Assessing the structure of prejudical attitudes: The case of attitudes toward homosexual. *Journal of Personality and Social Psychology, 65,* 1105–1118.

Haj-Yahia, M.M. (1996). Wife abuse in the Arab society in Israel: Challenges for future changes. In J.L. Edleson & Z.C. Eisikovits (Eds.), *Future interventions with battered women and their families* (pp. 87–101). Thousand Oaks, CA: Sage.

Haj-Yahia, M.M. (1998). Beliefs about wife beating among Palestinian women: The influence of their patriarchal ideology. *Violence against Women, 4,* 533–558.

Hale, G., Duckworth, J., Zimostrad, S., & Nicholas, D. (1988). Abusive partners: MMPI profiles of male batterers. *Journal of Mental Health Counseling, 10,* 214–224.

Hall, J.A., & Briton, N.J. (1993). Gender, nonverbal behavior and expectations. In P. Blanck (Ed.), *Interpersonal expectations: Theory, research and applications* (pp. 276–295). New York: Cambridge University Press.

Hall, J.A., & Kimura, D. (1994). Dermatoglyphic asymmetry and sexual orientation in men. *Behavioral Neuroscience, 108,* 1203–1206.

Hall, K. (1995). Lip service on the fantasy lines. In K. Hall & M. Bucholtz (Eds.), *Gender articulated: Language and the socially constructed self* (pp. 183–216). New York: Routledge.

Hall, K., & Bucholtz, M. (Eds.). (1995). *Gender articulated: Language and the socially constructed self.* New York: Routledge.

Hall, L.S. (1998). *Dermatoglyphic analysis of monozygotic twins discordant for sexual orientation (homosexuality, prenatal environment, maternal stress).* Unpublished doctoral dissertation, Temple University, Philadelphia.

Hall, L.S. (in press). Dermatoglyphic analysis of total finger ridge count in female monozygotic twins discordant for sexual orientation. *Journal of Sex Research.*

Hall, M. (1998). *The lesbian love companion.* San Francisco: Harper.

Halpern, D.F. (1994). Stereotypes, science, censorship, and the study of sex differences. *Feminism and Psychology, 4,* 523–530.

Hamburger, A.C. (1988, May). Beauty quest. *Psychology Today,* pp. 28–32.

Hamer, D.H., Hu, S., Magnuson, V.L., Hu, N., & Pattatucci, A.M.L. (1993). A linkage between DNA markers on the X chromosome and male sexual orientation. *Science, 261,* 321–327.

Hamilton, V. (1995). Letter. *Psychologist, 8*(5), 151.

Hamilton, W.D. (1964). The genetical evolution of social behavior, I and II. *Journal of Theoretical Biology, 7,* 1–52.

Hammock, G.S., & Richardson, D.R. (1997). Perceptions of rape: The influecne of closeness of relationship, intoxication, and sex of participant. *Violence and Victims, 12*(3), 237–246.

Hanisch, C. (1971). The personal is political. In J. Agel (Ed.), *The radical therapist* (pp. 95–103). New York: Ballantine Books.

Hansen, G.L. (1982). Measuring prejudice against homosexuality (heterosexism) among college students: A new scale. *Journal of Social Psychology, 117,* 233–236.

Hansen, T.F., & Price, D.K. (1995). Good genes and old age: Do old mates provide superior genes? *Journal of Evolutionary Biology 8*(6), 759–778.

Haqq, C.M., & Donahoe, P.K. (1998). Regulation of sexual dimorphism in mammals. *Physiological Reviews, 78,* 1–33.

Haraway, D. (1988). Situated knowledges: The science question in feminism and the privilege of partial perspective. *Feminist Studies, 14*(3), 575–600.

Haraway, D. (1989). *Primate visions: Gender, race and nature in the world of modern science.* New York: Routledge.

Haraway, D.J. (1991). *Simians, cyborgs and women: The reinvention of nature.* London: Free Association Books.

Harding, S. (1986). *The science question in feminism.* Ithaca, NY: Cornell University Press.

Harding, S. (1991). *Whose science? Whose knowledge?* Ithaca, NY: Cornell University Press.

Harding, S. (1993). Rethinking standpoint epistemology: What is "strong objectivity?" In L. Alcoff & E. Potter (Eds.), *Feminist epistemologies* (pp. 49–82). London: Routledge.

Harding, V. (1991). Community as a liberating theme in civil rights history. In A.L. Robinson & P. Sullivan (Eds.), *New directions in civil rights studies* (pp. 17–29). Charlottesville: University Press of Virginia.

Hardy-Fanta, C. (1997). Latina women and politics in Boston: Somos la vida, la fuerza, la mujer [We are the life, the force, the woman]. In F.C. Garcia (Ed.), *Pursuing power: Latinos and the political system* (pp. 190–207). Notre Dame, IN: University of Notre Dame Press.

Hare-Mustin, R.T. (1983). An appraisal of the relationship between women and psychotherapy: 80 years after the case of Dora. *American Psychologist, 38,* 593–601.

Hare-Mustin, R.T., & Marecek, J. (1988). The meaning of difference: Gender theory, postmodernism, and psychology. *American Psychologist, 43,* 455–464.

Hare-Mustin, R.T., & Marecek, J. (1990a). *Making a difference: Psychology and the construction of gender.* New Haven, CT: Yale University Press.

Hare-Mustin, R.T., & Marecek, J. (1990b). The meaning of difference: Gender theory, postmodernism, and psychology. In B. McVicker Clinchy & J.K. Norem (Eds.), *The gender and psychology reader* (pp. 125–143). New York: New York University Press.

Hare-Mustin, R.T., & Marecek, J. (1994). Asking the right questions: Feminist psychology and sex differences. *Feminism and Psychology, 4*(4), 531–537.

Hare-Mustin, R.T., & Marecek, J. (1997). Abnormal and clinical psychology. In D. Fox & I. Prilleltensky (Eds.), *Critical psychology: An introduction* (pp. 105–120). London: Sage.

Harris v. Forklift Systems, 114 S.Ct. 367 (1993).

Harris, B., Unger, R.K., & Stagner, R. (1986). 50 years of psychology and social issues. *Journal of Social Issues, 42*(1).

Harris, F.C. (1994). Something within: Religion as a mobilizer of African-American political activism. *Journal of Politics, 56*(1), 42–68.

Harris, J.R. (1995). Where is the child's environment? A group socialization theory of development. *Psychological Review, 102,* 458–489.

Harris, L., Blum, R., & Resnick, M. (1991). Teen females in Minnesota: A portrait of quiet disturbance. *Women and Therapy, 11*(3/4), 119–135.

Harris, M. (1991). *Cultural anthropology* (3rd ed.). New York: HarperCollins.

Harris, M.B. (1994). Growing old gracefully: Age concealment and gender. *Journal of Gerontology: Psychological Sciences, 49,* P149–P158.

Harrison, J. (1978). Warning: The male role may be dangerous to your health. *Journal of Social Issues, 34*(1), 65–86.

Harrison, J. (1995). Roles, identities, and sexual orientation: Homosexuality, heterosexuality, and bisexuality. In R.F. Levant & W.S. Pollack (Eds.), *A new psychology of men* (pp. 359–382). New York: Basic Books.

Harrison, M. (1982). *A woman in residence.* New York: Random House.

Harrison, M. (1992). Women's health as a specialty: A deceptive solution. *Journal of Women's Health, 1,* 101–106.

Harry, J. (1983). Gay male and lesbian relationships. In E. Macklin & R. Rubin (Eds.), *Contemporary families and alternative lifestyles: Handbook on research and theory* (pp. 216–234). London: Sage.

Harry, J. (1992). Conceptualising anti-gay violence. In G. Herek & K. Berrill (Eds.), *Hate crimes.* Newbury Park, CA: Sage.

Hart, B. (1986). Lesbian battering: An examination. In K. Lobel (Ed.), *Naming the violence: Speaking out about lesbian battering* (pp. 173–189). Seattle, WA: Seal Press.

Hart, J., & Richardson, D. (Eds.). (1981). *The theory and practice of homosexuality.* London: Routledge & Kegan Paul.

Hartman, A. (1978). Diagrammatic assessment of family relationships. *Social Casework, 59,* 465–476.

Hartmann, H. (1994). The family as the locus of gender, class and political struggle: The example of house-work. In A. Herrmann & A. Stewart (Eds.), *Theorizing feminism: Parallel trends in the humanities and social sciences.* Boulder, CO: Westview Press.

Hartnett, O., Boden, G., & Fuller, M. (1979). *Sex-role stereotyping.* London: Tavistock.

Hartsock, N. (1983). The feminist standpoint: Developing the ground for a specifically feminist historical materialism. In S. Harding & M. Hintikka (Eds.), *Discovering reality: Feminist perspectives on epistemology, metaphysics, methodology and philosophy of science* (pp. 283–310). Dordrecht, The Netherlands: Reidel.

Harvey, K., & Shalom, C. (1997). *Language and desire: Encoding sex, romance and intimacy.* London: Routledge.

Haslett, B.B., & Lipman, S. (1997). Micro inequities: Up close and personal. In N.V. Benokraitis (Ed.), *Subtle sexism: Current practice and prospects for change* (pp. 34–53). Thousand Oaks, CA: Sage.

Haste, H. (1994). You've come a long way babe: A catalyst of feminist conflicts. *Feminism and Psychology, 4*(3), 399–403.

Hatala, M.N., & Prehodka, J. (1996). Content analysis of gay male and lesbian's personal advertisements. *Psychological Reports, 78,* 371–374.

Hatch, L.R. (1987). Research on men's and women's retirement attitudes: Implications for retirement policy. In E.F. Borgatta & R.J.V. Montgomery (Eds.), *Critical issues in aging policy: Linking research and values* (pp. 129–160). Newbury Park, CA: Sage.

Hatch, L.R. (1992). Gender differences in orientation toward retirement from paid labor. *Gender and Society, 6,* 66–85.

Hatchett, S.J., & Jackson, J.S. (1999). African American extended kin systems: An empirical assessment in the National Survey of Black Americans. In H.P. McAdoo (Ed.), *Family ethnicity: Strength in diversity* (2nd ed., pp. 171–190). Thousand Oaks, CA: Sage.

Haug, F. (1992a). *Beyond female masochism: Memory work and politics.* London: Verso.

Haug, F. (1992b). *Responsibility as masochism: Memory-work and politics.* London: Verso.

Haugh, S.S., Hoffman, C.D., & Cowan, G. (1980). The eye of the very young beholder: Sex typing of infants by young children. *Child Development, 51,* 598–600.

Hawkes, K., O'Connell, J.F., & Blurton Jones, N.G. (1989). Hardworking Hadza grandmothers. In V. Standen & R. Foley (Eds.), *Comparative socioecology of mammals and man* (pp. 341–366). London: Blackwell.

Hawkes, K., O'Connell, J.F., & Blurton Jones, N.G. (1995). Hadza children's foraging: Juvenile dependency, social arrangements and mobility among hunter-gatherers. *Current Anthropology, 36,* 688–700.

Hawkes, K., O'Connell, J.F., & Blurton Jones, N.G. (1997). Hadza women's time allocation, offspring production, and the evolution of long postmenopausal life spans. *Current Anthropology, 38,* 551–577.

Hawkes, K., O'Connell, J.F., Blurton Jones, N.G., Alvarez, H., & Charnov, E.L. (1998). Grandmothering, menopause, and the evolution of human life histories. *Proceedings of the National Academy of Sciences, USA, 95,* 1336–1339.

Hawkes, K., O'Connell, J.F., Blurton Jones, N.G., Alvarez, H., & Charnov, E.L. (1999). The grandmother hypothesis and human evolution. In L. Cronk, N. Chagnon, & W. Irons (Eds.), *Evolutionary anthropology and human social behavior: Twenty years later.* Hawthrone, NY: Aldine de Gruyter.

Hazan, C., & Shaver, P.R. (1987). Romantic love conceptualized as an attachment process. *Journal of Personality and Social Psychology, 52,* 511–524.

Heaton, T.B., Jacobson, C.K., & Holland, K. (1999). Persistence and change in decisions to remain childless. *Journal of Marriage and the Family, 61,* 531–539.

Heaven, P., Connors, J., & Pretorius, A. (1998). Victim characteristics and attribution of rape blame in Australia and South Africa. *Journal of Social Psychology, 138,* 131–133.

Heilman, M.E. (1994). Affirmative action: Some unintended consequences for working women. *Research in Organizational Behavior, 16,* 125–169.

Heilman, M.E. (1995). Sex stereotypes and their effects in the workplace: What we know and what we don't know. *Journal of Social Behavior and Personality, 10*(6), 3–26.

Heise, L.L. (1996). Violence against women: Global organizing for change. In J.L. Edleson & Z.C. Eisikovits (Eds.), *Future interventions with battered women and their families* (pp. 7–33). Thousand Oaks, CA: Sage.

Helgeson, V.S. (1994a). Long-distance romantic relationships: Sex differences in adjustment and breakup. *Personality and Social Psychology Bulletin, 20,* 254–265.

Helgeson, V.S. (1994b). Prototypes and dimensions of masculinity and femininity. *Sex Roles, 31,* 653–682.

Helgeson, V.S. (1995). The effects of self-beliefs and relationship beliefs on adjustment to a relationship stressor. *Personal Relationships, 1,* 241–258.

Helledey, J., Edman, G., Ritzen, E.M., & Siwers, B. (1993). Personality characteristics and platelet MAO activity in women with congenital adrenal hyperplasia (CAH). *Psychoneuroendocrinology, 18,* 343–354.

Helwig, A.A. (1998). Gender-role stereotyping: Testing theory with a longitudinal sample. *Sex Roles, 38,* 403–423.

Henderson-King, D., & Stewart, A. (1997). Feminist consciousness: Perspectives on women's experience. *Personality and Social Psychology Bulletin, 23,* 415–426.

Henderson-King, D.H., & Stewart, A.J. (1999). Educational experiences and shifts in group consciousness: Studying women. *Personality and Social Psychology Bulletin, 25,* 390–399.

Hendin, H. (1994). Seduced by death: Doctors, patients, and the Dutch cure. *Issues in Law and Medicine, 10*(2), 123–168.

Hendin, H., Foley, K., & White, M. (1998). Physician-assisted suicide: Reflections on Oregon's first case. *Issues in Law and Medicine, 14*(3), 243–270.

Hendrick, C., & Hendrick, S.S. (1986). A theory and method of love. *Journal of Personality and Social Psychology, 50,* 392–402.

Hendrick, S.S., & Hendrick, C. (1995). Gender differences and similarities in sex and love. *Personal Relationships, 2,* 55–65.

Hendricks, J. (1995, June). Older women in social and economic development. *Ageing International,* 55–58.

Hendrix, W.H., Rueb, J.D., & Steel, R.P. (1998). Sexual harassment and gender differences. *Journal of Social Behavior and Personality, 13,* 235–252.

Henle, M. (1983). Autobiography. In A.N. O'Connell & N.F. Russo (Eds.), *Models of achievement: Reflections of eminent women in psychology* (pp. 221–232). New York: Columbia University Press.

Henley, N.M. (1973). Status and sex: Some touching observations. *Bulletin of the Psychonomic Society, 3,* 91–93.

Henley, N.M. (1977). *Body politics: Power, sex, and nonverbal communication.* Englewood Cliffs, NJ: Prentice-Hall.

Henley, N.M. (1989). Molehill or mountain? What we do know and don't know about sex bias in language. In M. Crawford & M. Gentry (Eds.), *Gender and thought* (pp. 59–78). New York: Springer-Verlag.

Henley, N.M. (1995). Ethnicity and gender issues in language. In H. Landrine (Ed.), *Bringing cultural diversity to feminist psychology* (pp. 361–396). Washington, DC: American Psychiatric Association.

Henley, N.M., & Freeman, J. (1975). The sexual politics of interpersonal behavior. In J. Freeman (Ed.), *Women: A feminist perspective* (391–401). Palo Alto, CA: Mayfield.

Henley, N.M., & Kramarae, C. (1991). Gender, power, and miscommunication. In N. Coupland, H. Giles, & J.M. Wiemann (Eds.), *Miscommunication and problematic talk* (pp. 18–43). Newbury Park, CA: Sage.

Henley, N.M., & McCarthy, W.J. (1998). Measuring feminist attitudes: Problems and prospects. *Psychology of Women Quarterly, 22,* 363–369.

Henley, N.M., Meng, K., O'Brien, D., McCarthy, W.J., & Sockloskie, R.J. (1998). Developing a scale to measure the diversity of feminist attitudes. *Psychology of Women Quarterly, 22,* 317–348.

Henley, N.M., & Thorne, B. (1975). She said he said: An annotated bibliography of sex differences in language, speech and non-verbal communication. Pittsburgh, PA: KNOW.

Henshaw, S.K. (1998). Barriers to access to abortion services. In L.J. Beckman & S.M. Harvey (Eds.), *The new civil war: The psychology, culture, and politics of abortion* (pp. 61–80). Washington, DC: American Psychological Association.

Henwood, K., Griffin, C., & Phoenix, A. (Eds.). (1998). *Standpoints and differences: Essays in the practice of feminist psychology.* London: Sage.

Henwood, K., & Pigeon, N. (1995). Grounded theory and psychological research. *Psychologist, 8*(3), 115–118.

Hepper, P.G., Shahidullah, S., & White, R. (1991). Handedness in the human fetus. *Neuropsychologia, 29,* 1107–1111.

Heppner, M.J., Neville, H.A., Smith, K., Kivlighan, D.MK., Jr., & Gershuny, B.S. (1999). Examining immediate and long-term efficacy of rape prevention programming with racially diverse college men. *Journal of Counseling Psychology, 46,* 16–26.

Herdt, G. (Ed.). (1994). *Third sex, third gender: Beyond sexual dimorphism in culture and history.* New York: Zone.

Herdt, G.H. (1981). *Guardians of the flute: Idioms of masculinity.* New York: McGraw-Hill.

Herek, G. (1986). On heterosexual masculinity: Some psychical consequences of the social construction of gender and sexuality. *American Behavioral Scientist, 29*(5), 563–577.

Herek, G. (1988). Heterosexuals' attitudes toward lesbians and gay men. *Journal of Sex Research, 25*(4), 451–477.

Herek, G. (1990). The context of anti-gay violence. *Journal of Interpersonal Violence, 5*(3), 316–333.

Herek, G.M. (1991). Stigma, prejudice, and violence against lesbians and gay men. In J.C. Gonsiorek & J.D. Weinrich (Eds.), *Homosexuality: Research implications for public policy.* Newbury Park, CA: Sage.

Herek, G.M. (1998). Bad science in the service of stigma: A critique of the Cameron groups survey studies. In G.M. Herek (Ed.), *Stigma and sexual orientation: Understanding prejudice against lesbians, gay men, and bisexuals.* London: Sage.

Herek, G.M., & Berrill, K.T. (1992). *Hate crimes: Confronting violence against lesbians and gay men.* London: Sage.

Herek, G.M., & Glunt, E.K. (1993). Interpersonal contact and heterosexuals' attitudes toward gay men: Results from a national survey. *Journal of Sex Research, 32,* 95–105.

Heritage, J. (1984). *Garfinkel and ethnomethodology.* Cambridge, England: Polity.

Herman, D., & Stychin, C. (Eds.). (1995). *Legal inversions: Lesbians, gay men, and the politics of law.* Philadelphia: Temple University Press.

Herman, J. (1992). *Trauma and recovery.* Basic Books.

Herzog, W.W., Enright, M., Luria, Z., & Rubin, J.Z. (1982). Do gender labels yield sex differences in performance, or is label a fable? *Developmental Psychology, 18,* 424–430.

Hess, B.H. (1990). The demographic parameters of gender and aging. *Generations, 14,* 12–16.

Hesson-McInnis, M.S., & Fitzgerald, L.F. (1997). Sexual harassment: A preliminary test of an integrative model. *Journal of Applied Social Psychology, 27*(10), 877–901.

Heywood, L., & Drake, J. (1997). *Third wave agenda.* Minneapolis: University of Minnesota Press.

Hibbard, D.R., & Burhmester, D. (1998). The role of peers in the socialization of gender-related social interaction styles. *Sex Roles, 39,* 185–202.

Hill, M. (Ed.). (1998). Feminist therapy as a political act [Whole issue]. *Women and Therapy, 21*(2).

Hill, M., & Ballou, M. (1998). Making therapy feminist: A practice survey. *Women and Therapy, 21,* 1–16.

Hiller, J.E. (1989). Breast cancer: A psychogenic disease? *Women and Health, 15*(2), 5–18.

Hillier, L. (1995). How language betrays us: Explaining violence against women in the 1990s. *Feminism and Psychology, 5,* 118–125.

Hillier, L., & Foddy, M. (1993). The role of observer attitudes in judgements of blame in cases of wife assault. *Sex Roles, 29,* 629–644.

Hines, M., & Kaufman, F.R. (1994). Androgen and the development of human sex-typical behavior: Rough-and-tumble play and sex of preferred playmates in children with congenital adrenal hyperplasia (CAH). *Child Development, 65,* 1042–1053.

Hochschild, A. (1983). *The managed heart: Commercialization of human feeling.* Berkeley: University of California Press.

Hochschild, A. (1989). *The second shift: Working parents and the revolution at home.* New York: Viking Press.

Hock, E., Schirtzinger, M.B., & Lutz, W. (1992). Dimensions of family relationships associated with depressive symptomatology in mothers of young children. *Psychology of Women Quarterly, 16,* 229–241.

Hoffman, C., & Hurst, N. (1990). Gender stereotypes: Perception or rationalization? *Journal of Personality and Social Psychology, 58*(2), 197–208.

Hofland, S.L., & Dardis, P.O. (1992). Bulimia nervosa: Associated physical problems. *Journal of Psychosocial Nursing, 30,* 23–27.

Hofstede, G. (1984). *Culture's consequences: International differences in work-related values* [Abridged ed.]. Thousand Oaks, CA: Sage.

Hofstede, G. (1994). Foreword. In U. Kim, H.C. Triandis, C. Kagitçibasi, S-C. Choi, & G. Yoon (Eds.), *Individualism and collectivism: Theory, method, and applications* (pp. ix–xiii). Thousand Oaks, CA: Sage.

Hogg, M.A., Terry, D.J., & White, K.M. (1995). A tale of two theories: A critical comparison of identity theory with social identity theory. *Social Psychology Quarterly, 58,* 255–269.

Holland, D.C., & Eisenhart, M.A. (1990). *Educated in romance: Women, achievement, and college culture.* Chicago: University of Chicago.

Holland, J., Ramazanoglu, C., & Scott, S. (1990). *Sex, risk, danger: AIDS education policy and young women's sexuality.* London: The Tufnell Press.

Holland, J., Ramazanoglu, C., Scott, S., Sharpe, S., & Thomson, R. (1991). Between embarrassment and trust: Young women and the diversity of condom use. In P. Aggleton, G. Hart, & P. Davies (Eds.), *AIDS: Responses, interventions and care* (pp. 127–148). Bristol, PA: Falmer Press.

Holland, J., Ramazanoglu, C., Scott, S., Sharpe, S., & Thomson, R. (1992a). Pressure, resistance, empowerment: Young women and the negotiation of safer sex. In P. Aggleton, P. Davies, & G. Hart (Eds.), *AIDS: Rights, risk and reason* (pp. 142–162). Washington, DC: Falmer Press.

Holland, J., Ramazanoglu, C., Scott, S., Sharpe, S., & Thomson, R. (1992b). Risk, power and the possibility of pleasure: Young women and safer sex. *AIDS Care, 4*(3), 273–283.

Holland, J., Ramazanoglu, C., Scott, S., & Thomson, R. (1990). Sex, gender and power: Young women's sexuality in the shadow of AIDS. *Sociology of Health and Illness, 12*(3), 336–350.

Holland, J., Ramazanoglu, C., Sharpe, S., & Thomson, R. (1992). Pleasure, pressure and power: Some contradictions of gendered sexuality. *Sociological Review, 40*(4), 645–674.

Holland, J., Ramazanoglu, C., Sharpe, S., & Thomson, R. (1994). Power and desire: The embodiment of female sexuality. *Feminist Review, 46*, 21–38.

Holland, J., Ramazanoglu, S.S., & Thomson, R. (1996). Reputations:Journeying into gendered power relations. In J. Weeks & J. Holland (Eds.), *Sexual cultures: Communities, values, and intimacy* (pp. 239–260). New York: St. Martin's Press.

Hollander, N. (1994). T-shirt advertisement. *Funny Times, 9*, 22.

Hollway, W. (1989). *Subjectivity and method in psychology: Gender, meaning and science.* London: Sage.

Hollway, W. (1993). Theorising heterosexuality. *Feminism and Psychology, 3*, 412–417.

Hollway, W. (1994). Beyond sex differences: A project for feminist psychology. *Feminism and Psychology, 4*(4), 538–546.

Hollway, W. (1995). Feminist discourses and women's heterosexual desire. In S. Wilkinson & C. Kitzinger (Eds.), *Feminism and discourse: Psychological perspectives* (pp. 86–105). London: Sage.

Holmes, J. (1990). Hedges and booseter in women's and men's speech. *Language and Communication, 10*(3), 185–205.

Holmes, J. (1995). *Women, men and politeness.* London: Longman.

Holmes, J., & Stubbe, M. (1997). Good listeners: Gender differences in New Zealand conversation. *Women and Language, 20*(2), 7–20.

Holstein, J.A. (1987). Producing gender effects on involuntary mental hospitalization. *Social Problems, 34*, 141–155.

Holt, M. (1993). Elder sexual abuse in Britain. In C. McCreadie (Ed.), *Elder abuse: New findings and guidelines* (pp. 16–18). London: Age Concern Institute of Gerontology,

Homma-True, R., Greene, B., Lopez, S.R., & Trimble, J.E. (1993). Ethnocultural diversity in clinical psychology. *Clinical Psychologist, 46*, 50–63.

Hondagneu-Sotelo, P. (1998). Latina immigrant women and paid domestic work: Upgrading the occupation. In N.A. Naples (Ed.), *Community activism and feminist politics: Organizing across race, class, and gender* (pp. 199–211). New York: Routledge.

hooks, b. (1989). *Talking back: Thinking feminist, thinking Black.* Boston: South End Press.

hooks, b. (1990). *Yearning: Race, gender and cultural politics.* Boston: South End Press.

Hopkins, J. (1969). The lesbian personality. *British Journal of Psychiatry, 115*, 1433–1436.

Horner, M.S. (1972). Toward an understanding of achievement-related conflicts in women. *Journal of Social Issues, 28*, 157–176.

Hort, B.E., Fagot, B.I., & Leinbach, M.D. (1990). Are people's notions of maleness more stereotypically framed than their notions of femaleness? *Sex Roles, 23*, 197–212.

Hort, B.E., Leinbach, M.D., & Fagot, B.I. (1991). Is there coherence among components of gender acquisition? *Sex Roles, 24*, 195–208.

Horton, J.A. (1992). *The women's health data book: A profile of women's health in the United States.* New York: Elsevier.

Hosken, F.P. (1993). *The Hosken Report: Genital and sexual mutilation of females* (4th ed., rev.). Boston: Women's International Network News.

Hotaling, C.T., & Sugarman, D.B. (1986). An analysis of risk markers in husband and wife violence: The current state of knowledge. *Violence and Victims, 1*, 101–124.

Hotelling, K. (1987). Curative factors in groups for women with bulimia. In C.M. Brody (Ed.), *Women's therapy groups: Paradigms of feminist treatment* (pp. 241–251). New York: Springer.

Houghton, C. (1995). Managing the body of labor: The treatment of reproduction and sexuality in a therapeutic institution. In K. Hall & M. Bucholtz (Eds.), *Gender articulated: Language and the socially constructed self* (pp. 121–142). New York: Routledge.

Houston, S., & Hwang, N. (1996). Correlates of the objective and subjective experiences of sexual harassment in high school. *Sex Roles, 34*, 189–204.

Howard, J.A., Blumstein, P., & Schwartz, P. (1986). Sex, power, and influence tactics in intimate relationships. *Journal of Personality and Social Psychology, 51*, 102–109.

Howard, J.A., & Hollander, J. (1997). *Gendered situations, gendered selves.* Thousand Oaks, CA: Sage.

Howell, M., & Pugliesi, K. (1988). Husbands who harm: Predicting spousal violence by men. *Journal of Family Violence, 3*(1), 15–27.

Hrdy, S.B. (1974). Male-male competition and infanticide among the langurs (Presbytis entellus) of Abu, Rajasthan. *Folia Primatologica, 22*, 19–58.

Hrdy, S.B. (1976). The care and exploitation of nonhuman primate infants by conspecifics other than the mother. *Advances in the Study of Behavior, 6,* 101–158.

Hrdy, S.B. (1977). *The langurs of Abu: Female and male strategies of reproduction.* Cambridge, MA: Harvard University Press.

Hrdy, S.B. (1979). Infanticide among animals: A review, classification, and examiniation of the implications for the reproductive strategies of females. *Ethology and Sociobiology, 1,* 13–40.

Hrdy, S.B. (1981). *The woman that never evolved.* Cambridge, MA: Harvard University Press.

Hrdy, S.B. (1997). Raising Darwin's conciousness: Female sexuality and the prehomind origins of patriarchy. *Human Nature, 8,* 1–50.

Hrdy, S.B. (1999). *Mother nature: A history of mothers, infants, and natural selection.* New York: Pantheon Books.

Hrdy, S.B., Rodman, P., Charnov, E.L., Seger, J., Hawkes, K., Emlen, S., Foster, S.A., Gowaty, P.A., Haig, D., Hauser, M., & Jacobs, L.F. (1996). Sociobiology's successes. *Science, 274,* 162–163 .

Hsia, J. (1993). Gender differences in diagnosis and management of coronary disease. *Journal of Women's Health, 2,* 349–352.

Hu, S., Pattatucci, A.M.L., Patterson, C., Li, L., Fulker, D.W., Cherny, S.S., Kruglyak, L., & Hamer, D.H. (1995). Linkage between sexual orientation and chromosome Xq28 in males but not in females. *Nature Genetics, 11,* 248–256.

Hubbard, R. (1996). Gender and genitals: Constructions of sex and gender. *Social Text, 46/47,* 157–165.

Huber, J., & Spitze, G. (1988). Trends in family sociology. In N. Smelser (Ed.), *Handbook of sociology* (pp. 425–448). Newbury Park, CA: Sage.

Huberman, A.M., & Miles, M.B. (1994). Data management and analysis methods. In N.K. Denzin & Y.S. Lincoln (Eds.), *Handbook of qualitative research* (pp. 428–444). Thousand Oaks, CA: Sage.

Huesmann, L.R., & Eron, L.D. (1992). Childhood aggression and adult criminality. In J. McCord (Ed.), *Facts, frameworks, and forecasts* (pp. 137–156). New Brunswick, NJ: Transaction.

Huesmann, L.R., Eron, L.D., Lefkowitz, M.N., & Walder, L.O. (1984). The stability of aggression over time and generations. *Developmental Psychology, 20,* 1120–1134.

Hughes, K.D., & Tadic, V. (1998). Something to deal with: Customer sexual harassment and women's retail service work in Canada. *Gender, Work and Organization, 5,* 207–219.

Hui, C.H., & Triandis, H.C. (1986). Individualism-collectivism: A study of cross-cultural researchers. *Journal of Cross-Cultural Psychology, 17,* 225–248.

Hulbert, K.D., & Schuster, D.T. (Eds.). (1993). *Women's lives through time.* San Francisco: Jossey-Bass.

Hulin, C.L., Fitzgerald, L.F., & Drasgow, F. (1996). Organizational influences on sexual harassment. In M.S. Stockdale (Ed.), *Sexual harassment in the workplace* (pp. 127–150). Newbury Park, CA: Sage.

Hummert, M.L. (1990). Multiple stereotypes of elderly and young adults: A comparison of structure and evaluations. *Psychology and Aging, 5,* 182–193.

Humphrey, J.A., & White, J.W. (1992, November). *Perpetration of sexual assault: Social psychological predictors.* Paper presented at American Society of Criminology, New Orleans, LA.

Humphrey, J.A., & White, J.W. (in press). Women's vulnerability to sexual assault from adolescence to young adulthood. *Journal of Adolescent Health.*

Humphrey, J.A., White, J.W., & Smith, P.H. (1999, July). *The onset and persistence of sexual assalt: Consideratioan of the self-control and routine activities formulations.* Paper presented at symposium on Developmental Antecedents of Violence against Women: A longitudinal approach at the 6th International Family Violence Research conference, Durham, NH.

Hunter, A. (1993). Same door, different closet: A heterosexual sissy's coming out party. In S. Wilkinson & C. Kitzinger (Eds.), *Heterosexualty: A feminism and psychology reader* (pp. 150–168). London: Sage.

Hunter, A.G., & Davis, J.E. (1992). Constructing gender: An exploration of Afro-American men's conceptualization of manhood. *Gender and Society, 6,* 464–479.

Hunter, J. (1990). Violence against lesbian and gay male youths. *Journal of Interpersonal Violence, 5,* 295–300.

Hurd, T.L., & Brabeck, M.M. (1997). The presentation of women and Gilligan's ethic of care in college texts, 1970–1990: An examination of bias. *Teaching of Psychology, 24,* 159–167.

Hurd, T.L., & McIntyre, A. (1996). The seduction of sameness: Similarity and representing the other. *Feminism and Psychology, 6,* 86–91.

Hurtado, A. (1989). Relating to privilege: Seduction and rejection in the subordination of White women and women of color. *Signs, 14,* 833–855.

Hurtado, A. (1995). Relating to privilege: Seduction and rejection in the subordination of White women and women of color. In B.M. Clinchy & J.K. Norem (Eds.), *The gender and psychology reader* (pp. 698–716). New York: New York University Press.

Hurtado, A. (1996). *The color of privilege: Three blasphemies in race and feminism.* Ann Arbor: University of Michigan Press.

Hurtado, A. (1999). Underground feminisms: Inocencia's story. In M. Romero & A. Stewart (Eds.), *Outside the master narratives: Women's untold stories.* New York: Routledge.

Hurtado, A., & Stewart, A.J. (1997). Through the looking-glass: Implications of studying Whiteness for feminist methods. In M. Fine, L. Powell, L. Weis, & L.M. Wong (Eds.), *Off White: Readings on race, power and society* (pp. 297–311). New York: Routledge.

Huston, A.C. (1983). Sex-typing. In E.M. Hetherington (Ed.), *Handbook of child psychology: Socialization, personality, and social development* (Vol. 4, pp. 388–467). New York: Wiley.

Huston, A.C. (1985). The development of sex typing: Themes from recent research. *Developmental Review, 5,* 1–17.

Huston, A.C., McLoyd, V.C., & Garcia Coll, C. (1994). Children and poverty: Issues in contemporary research. *Child Development, 65,* 275–282.

Hyde, J.S. (1994a). Can meta-analysis make feminist transformations in psychology? *Psychology of Women Quarterly, 18,* 451–462.

Hyde, J.S. (1994b). Should psychologists study gender differences? Yes, with some guidelines. *Feminism and Psychology, 4*(4), 507–512.

Hyde, J.S. (1998). Measuring feminist attitudes: A possible rapprochement between feminist theory and empirical data? *Psychology of Women Quarterly, 22,* 361–362.

Hyde, J.S., Essex, M.J., & Horton, F. (1993). Fathers and parental leave: Attitudes and experiences. *Journal of Family Issues, 14,* 616–638.

Hyde, J.S., Fennema, E., & Lamon, S.J. (1990). Gender differences in mathematics performance: A meta-analysis. *Psychological Bulletin, 107,* 139–155.

Hyde, J.S., & Plant, E.A. (1995). Magnitude of psychological gender differences: Another side to the story. *American Psychologist, 50,* 159–161.

Hyde, J.S., & Rosenberg, B.G. (1974). *Half the human experience: The psychology of women.* Lexington, MA: Heath.

Hyman, B. (1993). *Economic consequences of child sexual abuse in women.* Unpublished doctoral dissertation, Brandeis University, Heller School of Public Policy, Waltham, MA.

Ibanez, T., & Iniguez, L. (Eds.). (1997). *Critical social psychology.* London: Sage.

Ickes, W. (1993). Traditional gender roles: Do they make, and then break, our relationships? *Journal of Social Issues, 49*(3), 71–85.

Imperato-McGinley, J., & Peterson, R.E. (1976). Male pseudohermaphrodism: The complexities of male phenotypic development. *American Journal of Medicine, 61,* 251–272.

Imperato-McGinley, J., Peterson, R.E., Gautier, T., & Sturla, E. (1979). Androgens and the evolution of male-gender identity among male pseudohermaphrotes with 5 alpha-reductase deficiency. *New England Journal of Medicine, 300,* 1233–1237.

Ingersoll-Dayton, B., Campbell, R., Kurokawa, Y., & Saito, M. (1996). Separateness and togetherness: Interdependence over the life course in Japanese and American marriages. *Journal of Social and Personal Relationships, 13,* 385–398.

Ingleby, D. (1986). Development in a social context. In M. Richards & P. Light (Eds.), *Children of social world: Development in social context* (pp. 297–327). Cambridge, England: Polity.

Inoff, G.E., Halverson, C.F., Jr., & Pizzigati, K.A.L. (1983). The influence of sex-role stereotypes on children's self- and peer-attributions. *Sex Roles, 9,* 1205–1222.

Ireland, M.S. (1993). *Reconceiving motherhood: Separating motherhood from female identity.* New York: Guilford Press.

Irigaray, L. (1980). When our lips speak together. *Signs, 6*(1), 69.

Irigaray, L. (1985). *This sex which is not one* (C. Porter, Trans.). Ithaca, NY: Cornell University Press. (Original work published 1978)

Irons, J. (1998). The shaping of activist recruitment and participation: A study of women in the Mississippi civil rights movement. *Gender and Society, 12,* 692–709.

Island, D., & Letellier, P. (1991). *Men who beat the men who love them: Battered gay men and domestic violence.* Binghamton, NY: Haworth Press.

ISTAT. (1997). *Anziani in Italia.* Bologna, Italy: Il Mulino.

Ivey, A.E. (1987). *Counseling and psychotherapy.* Englewood Cliffs, NJ: Prentice Hall.

Ivy, D.K., & Hamlet, S. (1996). College students and sexual dynamics: Two studies of peer sexual harassment. *Communication Education, 45,* 149–166.

Iwao, S. (1993). *The Japanese woman: Traditional image and changing reality.* New York: Free Press.

Izraeli, D.N. (1983). Sex effects or structural effects? An empirical test of Kanter's theory of proportions. *Social Forces, 62,* 153–165.

Jack, D.C. (1999). Ways of listening to depressed women in qualitative research: Interview techniques and analysis. *Canadian Psychology, 40*(2), 91–101.

Jacklin, C. (1981). Methodological issues in the study of sex-related differences. *Developmental Review, 1,* 266–273.

Jackson, J.L., Calhoun, K.S., Amick, A., Maddever, H.M., & Habif, M. (1990). Young adult women who report childhood intrafamilial sexual abuse: Subsequent adjustment. *Archives of Sexual Behavior, 19,* 211–221.

Jackson, L.A., & Cash, T.F. (1985). Components of gender stereotypes: Their implications for inferences on stereotypic and nonstereotypic dimensions. *Personality and Social Psychology Bulletin, 11,* 326–344.

Jackson, T.L. (1991). A university athletic department's rape and assault experiences. *Journal of College Student Development, 32,* 77–78.

Jaffe, S., Kling, K.C., Plant, E.A., Sloan, M., & Hyde, J.S. (1999). The view from down here: Feminist graduate students consider innovative methodologies. *Psychology of Women Quarterly, 23,* 423–430.

Jagger, A.M., & Rothenberg, P.S. (1993). *Feminist frameworks: Alternative theoretical accounts of the relations between women and men* (3rd ed.). New York: McGraw-Hill.

Jagose, A. (1996). *Queer theory.* Dunedin, New Zealand: University of Otago Press.

Jakubowski, P.A. (1977). Self-assertion training procedures for women. In E.I. Rawlings & D.K. Carter (Eds.), *Psychotherapy for women* (pp. 168–190). Springfield, IL: Thomas.

Jamal, A., Lin, A.C., & Stewart, A.J. (1999, August 13). *Gender consciousness among Arab immigrants to the United States.* Paper presented at conference on immigrants and immigration, sponsored by Society for the Psychological Study of Social Issues, Toronto, Canada.

James, D., & Clark, S. (1993). Women, men and interruptions: A critical review. In D. Tannen (Ed.), *Gender and conversational interaction* (pp. 281–312). New York: Oxford University Press.

James, K., & MacKinnon, L.K. (1990). The "incestuous family" revisited: A critical analysis of family therapy myths. *Journal of Marital and Family Therapy, 16,* 71–88.

Jamison, C.S., Jamison, P.L., & Meier, R.J. (1994). Effect of prenatal testosterone administration on palmar dermatoglyphic intercore ridge counts of rhesus monkeys (*Macaca mulatta*). *American Journal of Physical Anthropology, 94,* 409–419.

Janoff-Bulman, R. (1979). Characterological vs. behavioral self-blame: Inquiries into depression and rape. *Journal of Personality and Social Psychology, 37,* 1798–1809.

Jaschik, M., & Fretz, B. (1992). Women's perceptions and labeling of harassment. *Sex Roles, 27,* 19–23.

Jayaratne, S., Vinokur-Kaplan, D., Nagda, B.A., & Chess, W.A. (1996). A national study on violence and harassment of social workers by clients. *Journal of Applied Social Sciences, 20,* 1–14.

Jecker, N.S. (1991). Age-based rationing and women. *Journal of the American Medical Association, 266,* 3012–3015.

Jeffreys, S. (1985). *The spinster and her enemies: Feminism and sexuality 1880–1930.* London: Pandora Press.

Jeffreys, S. (1994). *The lesbian heretic.* London: Women's Press.

Jejeebhoy, S.J. (1998). Associations between wife-beating and fetal and infant death: Impressions from a survey in rural India. *Studies in Family Planning, 29,* 300–308.

Jenkins, J.C., & Wallace, M. (1996). The generalized action potential of protest movements: The new class, social trends, and political exclusion explanations. *Sociological Forum, 11*(2), 183–207.

Jenkins, M. (1985). What's so funny? Joking among women. In S. Bremner, N. Caskey, & B. Moonwomon (Eds.), *Proceedings of the First Berkeley Women and Language conference.* Berkeley, CA: Berkeley Women and Language Group.

Jennings, M.K., & Niemi, R.G. (1981). *Generations and politics.* Princeton, NJ: Princeton University Press.

Jensen, I.W., & Gutek, B.A. (1982). Attributions and assignment of responsibility in sexual harassment. *Journal of Social Issues, 38,* 121–136.

Jespersen, O. (1922). The woman. In *Language, its nature, development, and origin* (pp. 237–254). London: Allen & Unwin.

Jick, T.D. (1979). Mixing qualitative and quantitative methods: Triangulation in action. *Administrative Science Quarterly, 24,* 602–611.

Johnson, J.D., & Meischke, H. (1994). Factors associated with adoption of mammography screening: Results of a cross-sectional and longitudinal study. *Journal of Women's Health, 3,* 97–105.

Johnson, K. (1992). Women's health: Developing a new interdisciplinary specialty. *Journal of Women's Health, 1,* 95–99.

Johnson, M. (1978). An approach to feminist therapy. *Psychotherapy: Theory, Research, and Practice, 13,* 72–76.

Johnson, M.P. (1995). Patriarchal terrorism and common couple violence: Two forms of violence against women. *Journal of Marriage and the Family, 57,* 283–294.

Johnson, R.J., & Wolinsky, F.D. (1994). Gender, race and health: The structure of health status among older adults. *The Gerontologist, 34,* 24–35.

Johnson, S., & Meinhof, U.H. (1997). *Language and masculinity.* London: Blackwell.

Johnston, K.E. (2000). *Influences on preschoolers' toy choices for the self and others.* Manuscript in preparation, Pennsylvania State University, University Park.

Johnston, K.E., Madole, K.L., Bittinger, K., & Smith, A. (in press). Developmental changes in infants' and toddlers' attention to gender categories. *Merrill-Palmer Quarterly.*

Jones, M.B., & Blanchard, R. (1998). Birth order and male homosexuality: Extension of Slater's index. *Human Biology, 70,* 775–787.

Jones, S.J. (1997). Reflexivity and feminist practice: Ethical dilemmas in negotiating meaning. *Feminism and Psychology, 7,* 348–353.

Jones, S.J. (2000). Embodying working-class subjectivity and narrating self: "We were the hired help." In D.L. Tolman & M. Brydon-Miller (Eds.), *From subjects to subjectivities: A handbook of interpretive and partici- patory methods.* New York: New York University Press.

Jordan, J.V. (1991). Empathy and the mother-daughter relationship. In J.V. Jordan, A.G. Kaplan, J.B. Miller, I.P. Stiver, & J.L. Surrey (Eds.), *Women's growth in connection: Writings from the Stone Center* (pp. 28–34). New York: Guilford Press.

Jordan, J.V., Kaplan, A.G., Miller, J.B., Stiver, I.P., & Surrey, J.L. (Eds.). (1991). *Women's growth in connection: Writings from the Stone Center.* New York: Guilford Press.

Jordan, J.V., & Surrey, J.L. (1986). The self-in-relation: Empathy and the mother-daughter relationship. In T. Bernay & D.W. Cantor (Eds.), *Psychology of today's woman: New psychoanalytic visions* (pp. 81–104). Hillsdale, NJ: Erlbaum.

Jordan, J.V., Surrey, J.L., & Kaplan, A.G. (1991). Women and empathy: Implications for psychological devel- opment and psychotherapy. In J.V. Jordan, A.G. Kaplan, J.B. Miller, I.P. Stiver, & J.L. Surrey (Eds.), *Women's growth in connection: Writings from the Stone Center* (pp. 27–50). New York: Guilford Press.

Josselson, R. (1996). *Revising herself: The story of women's identity from college to midlife.* New York: Oxford Uni- versity Press.

Jost, J.T., & Banaji, M.R. (1994). The role of stereotyping in system-justification and the production of false consciousness. *British Journal of Social Psychology, 33*(1), 1–27.

Joung, I.M.A., van de Mheen, H., van Poppel, F.W.A., van der Meer, J.B.W., & Mackenbach, J.P. (1997). The contribution of intermediary factors to marital status differences in self-reported health. *Journal of Mar- riage and the Family, 59,* 476–490.

Juraska, J.M. (1998). Neural plasticity and the development of sex differences. *Annual Review of Sex Research, 9,* 20–38.

Jylhä, M., Guralnik, J.M., Ferrucci, L., Jokela, J., & Heikkinen, E. (1998). Is self-rated health comparable across cultures and genders? *Journal of Gerontology, 53B,* S144–S152.

Kagan, J. (1971). A conception of early adolescence. In J.C. Kagan (Ed.), *Twelve to sixteen: Early adolescence* (pp. 997–1012). New York: Norton.

Kahn, A. (1984). The power war: Male response to power loss under equality. *Psychology of Women Quarterly, 8,* 234–247.

Kahn, A.S., & Yoder, J.D. (1989). The psychology of women and conservatism: Rediscovering social change. *Psychology of Women Quarterly, 13,* 417–432.

Kahn, E.D., & Robbins, L. (Eds.). (1985). Sex discrimination in academe [Special issue]. *Journal of Social Issues, 41.*

Kahn, K. (Ed.). (1995). *Frontline feminism 1975–1995: Essays from Sojourner's first 20 years.* San Francisco: Aunt Lute.

Kail, R.V., Jr., & Levine, L.E. (1976). Encoding processes and sex-role preferences. *Journal of Experimental Child Psychology, 21,* 256–263.

Kalache, A. (1998, Spring). The World Health Organization perspective on gender, ageing, and health. *Ageing International,* 39–48.

Kalick, S. (1975). ". . . like Ann's gynecologist or the time I was almost raped": Personal narratives in women's rap groups. *Journal of American Folklore, 88,* 3–11.

Kalick, S.M., Zebrowitz, L.A., Langlois, J.H., & Johnson, R.M. (1998). Does human facial attractiveness hon- estly advertise health? Longitudinal data on an evolutionary question. *Psychological Science, 9,* 8–13.

Kaltreider, N.B. (1997). *Dilemmas of a double life: Women balancing careers and relationships.* Northvale, NJ: Aronson.

Kamen, P. (1991). *Feminist fatale: Voices from the "twenty-something" generation explore the future of the "women's movement."* New York: Donald I. Fine.

Kamerman, S.B. (1991). Child care policies and programs: An international overview. *Journal of Social Issues, 47*(2), 179–196.

Kamo, Y. (1993). Determinants of marital satisfaction: A comparison of the United States and Japan. *Journal of Social and Personal Relationships, 10,* 551–568.

Kandall, S.R. (1999). *Substance and shadow: Women and addiction in the United States.* Cambridge, MA: Harvard University Press.

Kanter, R.M. (1977a). *Men and women of the corporation.* New York: Basic Books.

Kanter, R.M. (1977b). *Work and family in the United States: A critical review and agenda for research and policy.* New York: Russell Sage Foundation.

Kantor, G., Jasinski, J.L., & Aldarondo, E. (1994). Sociocultural status and incidence of marital violence in Hispanic families. *Violence and Victims, 9,* 207–222.

Kaplan, D.L., & Keys, C.B. (1997). Sex and relationship variables as predictors of sexual attraction in cross-sex platonic friendships between young heterosexual adults. *Journal of Social and Personal Relationships, 14,* 191–206.

Kaplan, H. (1987). Human communication and contemporary evolutionary theory. In S.J. Sigman (Ed.), *Research on language and social interaction* (Vol. 20). Edmonton, Canada: Boreal Scholarly.

Kaplan, M. (1983). A woman's view of *DSM-III. American Psychologist, 38,* 786–792.

Kaplan, M.S., Adamek, M.E., Geling, O., & Calderon, A. (1997). Firearm suicide among older women in the U.S. *Social Science and Medicine, 9,* 1427–1430.

Karasz, A.K., Bochnak, E., & Ouellette, S.C. (1993, August). *Role strain and psychological well-being among lupus patients.* Paper presented at the meeting of the American Psychological Association, Toronto, Canada.

Karraker, K.H., Vogel, D.A., & Lake, M.A. (1995). Parents' gender-stereotyped perceptions of newborns: The eye of the beholder revisited. *Sex Roles, 33,* 687–701.

Karsten, M.F. (1994). *Management and gender: Issues and attitudes.* Westport, CT: Praeger.

Kasper, A.S. (1994). A feminist, qualitative methodology: A study of women with breast cancer. *Qualitative Sociology, 17*(3), 263–281.

Kasper, A.S. (1995). The social construction of breast loss and reconstruction. *Women's Health: Research on Gender, Behavior, and Policy, 1,* 197–219.

Kato, P.M., & Mann, T. (1996). *Handbook of diversity issues in health psychology.* New York: Plenum Press.

Katz, J.N. (1995). *The invention of heterosexuality.* New York: Dutton.

Katz, P.A. (1991). Women, psychology, and social issues research. *Psychology of Women Quarterly, 15,* 665–676.

Katz, P.A. (1996). Raising feminists. *Psychology of Women Quarterly, 20,* 323–340.

Katz, P.A., & Boswell, S.L. (1986). Flexibility and traditionality in children's gender roles. *Genetic, Social, and General Psychology Monographs, 112,* 105–147.

Katz, P.A., & Ksansnak, K. (1994). Developmental aspects of gender role flexibility and traditionality in middle childhood and adolescence. *Developmental Psychology, 30*(2), 272–282.

Katz, P.A., & Walsh, P.V. (1991). Modification of children's gender-stereotyped behavior. *Child Development, 62,* 338–351.

Katz, R.C., Meyers, K., & Walls, J. (1995). Cancer awareness and self-examination practices of young men and women. *Journal of Behavioral Medicine, 18,* 377–384.

Kaufert, P.A. (1998). Women, resistance and the breast cancer movement. In P.A. Kaufert (Ed.), *Pragmatic women and body politics* (pp. 287–309). Cambridge, England: Cambridge University Press.

Kaufman, G. (1999). The portrayal of men's family roles in television commercials. *Sex Roles, 41,* 439–458.

Kauppinen-Toropainen, K., & Gruber, J.E. (1993). Antecedents and outcomes of woman-unfriendly experiences: A study of Scandinavian, former Soviet, and American women. *Psychology of Women Quarterly, 17,* 431–456.

Kawamoto, W.T., & Cheshire, T.C. (1999). Contemporary issues in the urban American Indian family. In H.P. McAdoo (Ed.), *Family ethnicity: Strength in diversity* (2nd ed., pp. 94–104). Thousand Oaks, CA: Sage.

Kearney-Cooke, A., & Striegel-Moore, R.H. (1996). Treatment of childhood sexual abuse in anorexia nervosa and bulimia nervosa: A feminist psychodynamic approach. In M.F. Schwartz & L. Cohn (Eds.), *Sexual abuse and eating disorders* (pp. 155–175). New York: Brunner/Mazel.

Keller, E.F. (1982). Feminism and science. *Signs, 7,* 589–602.

Kelley, H.H., & Thibaut, J.W. (1978). *Interpersonal relations: A theory of interdependence.* New York: Wiley.

Kelley, J.A., Wildman, H.E., & Urey, J.R. (1982). Gender and sex role differences in group decision-making social interactions: A behavioral analysis. *Journal of Applied Social Psychology, 1,* 112–127.

Kennedy, C.W., & Camden, C. (1983). Interruptions and nonverbal gender differences. *Journal of Noverbal Behavior, 8,* 91–108.

Kent, R.L., & Moss, S.E. (1994). Effects of sex and gender role on leader emergence. *Academy of Management Journal, 37,* 1335–1346.

Kephart, W. (1967). Some correlates of romantic love. *Journal of Marriage and the Family, 29,* 470–479.

Ker, H.J. (1996). Training residential staff to be aware of sexual abuse in old age. In R. Clough (Ed.), *The abuse of care in residential institutions* (pp. 166–171). London: Whiting and Birch.

Kerns, J.G., & Fine, M.A. (1994). The relation between gender and negative attitudes toward gay men and lesbians: Do gender role attitudes mediate this relation? *Sex Roles, 31,* 297–306.

Kessler, R.J. (1990). Models of disease and the diagnosis of schizophrenia. *Psychiatry, 53,* 140–147.

Kessler, S.J. (1990). The medical construction of gender: Case management of intersexed infants. *Signs, 16*(1), 3–26.

Kessler, S.J. (1998). *Lessons from the intersexed.* New Brunswick, NJ: Rutgers University Press.

Kessler, S.J., & McKenna, W. (1978). *Gender: An ethnomethodological approach.* New York: Wiley.

Kidder, L.H., & Fine, M. (1987, Fall). Qualitative and quantitative methods: When stories converge. In M.M. Mark & R.L. Shotland (Eds.), *Multiple methods in program evaluation: New directions for program evaluation* (Vol. 35, pp. 57–75). San Francisco: Jossey-Bass.

Kidder, L.H., & Fine, M. (1997). Qualitative inquiry in psychology: A radical tradition. In D. Fox & I. Prilleltensky (Eds.), *Critical psychology: An Introduction* (pp. 34–50). London: Sage.

Kidder, L.H., Lafleur, R.A., & Wells, C.V. (1995). Recalling harassment, reconstructing experience. *Journal of Social Issues, 51,* 117–138.

Kiecolt-Glaser, J.K., & Glaser, R. (1988). Immunological competence. In E.A. Blechman & K. Bownell (Eds.), *Handbook of behavioral medicine for women* (pp. 195–205). New York: Pergamon Press.

Kierstead, D., D'Agostino, P., & Dill, H. (1988). Sex role stereotyping of college professors: Bias in students' ratings of instructors. *Journal of Educational Psychology, 80,* 342–344.

Kiliansky, S.E., & Rudman, L.A. (1998). Wanting it both ways: Do women approve of benevolent sexism? *Sex Roles, 39,* 333–352.

Kim, H.J. (1991). Do you have eyelashes? In C. Gilligan, A.G. Rogers, & D.L. Tolman (Eds.), *Women, girls and psychotherapy: Reframing resistance* (pp. 201–212). Binghamton, NY: Haworth Press.

Kim, U., Triandis, H.C., Kagitçibasi, C., Choi, S-C., & Yoon, G. (Eds.). (1994). *Individualism and collectivism: Theory, method, and applications.* Thousand Oaks, CA: Sage.

Kimball, M.M. (1986). Television and sex-role attitudes. In T.M. Williams (Ed.), *The impact of television: A natural experiment in three communities* (pp. 265–301). Orlando, FL: Academic Press.

Kimball, M.M. (1995). Feminist visions of gender similarities and differences. Binghamton, NY: Haworth Press.

Kimball, M.M. (1999). Acknowledging truth and fantasy: Freud and the recovered memory debate. In M. Rivera (Ed.), *Fragment by fragment: Feminist perspectives on memory and child sexual abuse* (pp. 51–72). Charlottetown, Prince Edward Island, Canada: Gynergy.

Kimmel, D.C., & Sang, B.E. (1995). Lesbians and gay men in midlife. In A.R. D'Augelli & C.J. Patterson (Eds.), *Lesbian, gay and bisexual identities over the lifespan.* Oxford, England: Oxford University Press.

Kimmel, M.S., & Messner, M.A. (1998). *Men's lives* (4th ed.). Boston: Allyn & Bacon.

Kimura, D., & Carson, M.W. (1993). Cognitive pattern and ridge asymmetry. *Society for Neuroscience Abstracts, 19,* 590.

Kincaid, J. (1985). Girl. In *At the bottom of the river.* New York: Vintage Books.

Kincaid, V. (1993, February 11). Clark County: Mother gets probation in abuse. *Courier Journal.*

King, C.A. (1990). Parallels between neurasthenia and premenstrual syndrome. *Women and Health, 15,* 1–23.

Kingsolver, B. (1989). *Holding the line: Women in the great Arizona mine strike of 1983.* Ithaca, NY: ILR Press.

Kinsey, A., Pomeroy, W.B., & Martin, C.E. (1948). *Sexual behavior in the human male.* Philadelphia: Saunders.

Kinsey, A., Pomeroy, W.B., Martin, C.E., & Gebhard, R.H. (1953). *Sexual behavior in the human female.* Philadelphia: Saunders.

Kirkpatrick, C. (1936). The construction of a belief pattern scale for measuring attitudes toward feminism. *Journal of Social Psychology, 7,* 421–437.

Kirkpatrick, L.A., & Davis, K.E. (1994). Attachment style, gender, and relationship stability: A longitudinal analysis. *Journal of Personality and Social Psychology, 66,* 502–512.

Kirsh, B. (1974). Consciousness-raising groups as therapy for women. In V. Franks & V. Burtle (Eds.), *Women in therapy: New psychotherapies for a changing society* (pp. 326–354). New York: Brunner/Mazel.

Kissane, D.W., Street, A., & Nitschke, P. (1998). Seven deaths in Darwin: Case studies under the Rights of the Terminally Ill Act, Northern Territory, Australia. *Lancet, 352,* 1097–1102.

Kite, M.E., & Deaux, K. (1987). Gender belief systems: Homosexuality and the implicit inversion theory. *Psychology of Women Quarterly, 11,* 83–96.

Kite, M.E., Deaux, K., & Miele, M. (1991). Stereotypes of young and old: Does age outweigh gender? *Psychology and Aging, 6,* 19–27.

Kite, M.E., & Whitley, B.E., Jr. (1996). Sex differences in attitudes toward homosexual persons, behaviors, and civil rights: A meta-analysis. *Personality and Social Psychology Bulletin, 22,* 336–353.

Kite, M.E., & Whitley, B.E., Jr. (1998). Do heterosexual women and men differ in their attitudes toward homosexuality? A conceptual and methodological analysis. In G.M. Herek (Ed.), *Psychological perspectives on lesbian and gay issues: Stigma and sexual orientation: Understanding prejudice against lesbians, gay men, and bisexuals* (Vol. 4, pp. 39–61). Thousand Oaks, CA: Sage.

Kittay, E. (1998). Dependency, equality and welfare. *Feminist Studies, 24,* 32–45.

Kitzinger, C. (1987). *The social construction of lesbianism*. London: Sage.

Kitzinger, C. (1990a). Heterosexism in psychology. *Psychologist, 4*(9), 391–392.

Kitzinger, C. (1990b). Resisting the discipline. In E. Burman (Ed.), *Feminists and psychological practice* (pp. 119–136). London: Sage.

Kitzinger, C. (1990c). The rhetoric of pseudoscience. In I. Parker & J. Shotter (Eds.), *Deconstructing social psychology* (pp. 61–75). London: Routledge.

Kitzinger, C. (1991). Feminism, psychology, and the paradox of power. *Feminism and Psychology, 1,* 111–129.

Kitzinger, C. (1994a). Anti-lesbian harassment. In Y.L. Too & C. Brant (Eds.), *Rethinking harassment* (pp. 125–147). Boulder CO: Westview Press.

Kitzinger, C. (Ed.). (1994b). Should psychologists study sex differences? Editor's introduction. *Feminism and Psychology, 4,* 501–546.

Kitzinger, C. (1995a). Over our dead bodies: The scientific construction of gay biology [Review]. *Theory and Psychology, 5*(2), 309–311.

Kitzinger, C. (1995b). Social constructionism: Implications for lesbian and gay psychology. In A. D'Augelli & C. Patterson (Eds.), *Lesbian, gay and bisexual identities over the lifespan: Psychological perspectives* (pp. 136–161). New York: Oxford University Press.

Kitzinger, C. (1996). The token lesbian chapter. In S. Wilkinson (Ed.), *Feminist social psychologies: International perspectives* (pp. 119–144). Buckingham, England: Open University Press.

Kitzinger, C. (1999a). Intersexuality: Deconstructing the sex/gender binary. *Feminism and Psychology, 9*(4), 493–498.

Kitzinger, C. (1999b). Lesbian and gay psychology: Is it critical? *Annual Review of Critical Psychology, 1,* 50–66.

Kitzinger, C. (2000a). Doing feminist conversation analysis. *Feminism and Psychology, 10*(2), 163–193.

Kitzinger, C. (2000b). Women with androgen insensitivity syndrome in J. Ussher (Ed.), *Women's health: An international reader*. Leicester, England: British Psychological Society.

Kitzinger, C., Bola, M., Campos, A.B., Carabine, J., Doherty, K., Frith, H., McNulty, A., Reilly, J., & Winn, J. (1996). Speaking of representing the other. *Feminism and Psychology, 6,* 217–235.

Kitzinger, C., & Coyle, A. (1995). Lesbian and gay couples: Speaking of difference. *Psychologist, 8*(2), 64–69.

Kitzinger, C., Coyle, A., Wilkinson, S., & Milton, M. (1998). Towards lesbian and gay psychology. *Psychologist, 11*(11), 529–533.

Kitzinger, C., & Frith, H. (1999). Just say no? The use of conversation analysis in developing a feminist perspective on sexual refusal. *Discourse and Society, 10*(3), 293–316.

Kitzinger, C., & Perkins, R. (1993). *Changing our minds: Lesbian femnism and psychology*. New York: New York University Press.

Kitzinger, C., & Powell, D. (1995). Engendering infidelity: Essentialist and social constructionist readings of a story completion task. *Feminism and Psychology, 5,* 345–372.

Kitzinger, C., & Thomas, A. (1995). Sexual harassment: A discursive approach. In S. Wilkinson & C. Kitzinger (Eds.), *Feminism and discourse: Psychological perspectives* (pp. 32–48). London: Sage.

Kitzinger, C., & Wilkinson, S. (1995). Transitions from heterosexuality to lesbianism: The discursive construction of lesbian identites. *Developmental Psychology, 31,* 95–104.

Kitzinger, C., & Wilkinson, S. (1997). Validating women's experience? Dilemmas in feminist research. *Feminism and Psychology, 7*(4), 566–574.

Kitzinger, J. (1994). Focus groups: Method or madness? In M. Boulton (Ed.), *Challenges and innovation: Methodological advances in social research on HIV/AIDS* (pp. 159–175). London: Taylor & Francis.

Klamen, D.L., Grossman, L.S., & Kopacz, D.R. (1999). Medical student homophobia. *Journal of Homosexuality, 37*(1), 53–63.

Klatch, R.E. (1987). *Women of the new right*. Philadelphia: Temple University Press.

Klein, E. (1984). *Gender politics*. Cambridge, MA: Harvard University Press.

Klinetob, N.A., & Smith, D.A. (1996). Demand-withdraw communication in marital interaction: Tests of interspousal contingency and gender role hypotheses. *Journal of Marriage and the Family, 58,* 945–957.

Klonoff, E.A., & Landrine, H. (1995). The Schedule of Sexist Events: A measure of lifetime and recent sexist discrimination in women's lives. *Psychology of Women Quarterly, 19,* 439–472.

Knapp, D.E., Faley, R.H., Ekeberg, S.E., & DuBois, C.L.Z. (1997). Determinants of target responses to sexual harassment: A conceptual framework. *Academy of Management Review, 22,* 687–729.

Koblinsky, S.A., & Sugawara, A.I. (1984). Nonsexist curricula, sex of teacher, and children's sex-role learning. *Sex Roles, 10,* 357–367.

Koch, R., Lewis, M.Y., & Quinones, W. (1998). Homeless: Mothering at rock bottom. In C. Garcia Coll, J.L. Surrey, & K. Weingarten (Eds.), *Mothering against the odds: Diverse voices of contemporary mothers*. New York: Guilford Press.

Kohlberg, L. (1966). A cognitive-developmental analysis of children's sex-role concepts and attitudes. In E.E. Maccoby (Ed.), *The development of sex differences* (pp. 82–173). Stanford, CA: Stanford University Press.

Komdeur, J., Daan, S., Tinbergen, J., & Mateman, C. (1997). Extreme adaptive modification in sex ratios of the Seychelle's warbler's eggs. *Nature, 385,* 522–525.

Komiya, N., Good, G.E., & Sherrod, N. (2000). Emotional openness as a contributing factor to reluctance to seek counseling among college students. *Journal of Counseling Psychology, 47,* 138–143.

Konrad, A.M., & Gutek, B.A. (1986). Impact of work experiences on attitudes toward sexual harassment. *Administrative Science Quarterly, 31,* 422–438.

Koss, M.P. (1993). Detecting the scope of rape: A review of prevalence research methods. *Journal of Interpersonal Violence, 8,* 198–222.

Koss, M.P. (1994). The negative impact of crime victimization on women's health and medical use. In A.J. Dan (Ed.), *Reframing women's health: Multidisciplinary research and practice* (pp. 189–200). Thousand Oaks, CA: Sage.

Koss, M.P. (1996). The measurement of rape victimization in crime surveys. *Criminal Justice and Behavior, 23,* 55–69.

Koss, M.P. (1998). Hidden rape: Sexual aggression and victimization in a national sample of students in higher education. In M.E. Odem & J. Clay-Warner (Eds.), *Confronting rape and sexual assault* (pp. 51–69). Wilmington, DE: SR Books/Scholarly Resources.

Koss, M.P., & Gaines, J.A. (1993). The prediction of sexual aggression by alcohol use, athletic participation, and fraternity affiliation. *Journal of Interpersonal Violence, 8,* 94–108.

Koss, M.P., Gidycz, C.A., & Wisniewski, N. (1987). The scope of rape: Incidence and prevalence of sexual aggression and victimization in a national sample of higher education students. *Journal of Consulting and Clinical Psychology, 55*(2), 162–170.

Koss, M.P., Goodman, L.A., Browne, A., Fitzgerald, L.F., Keita, G.P., & Russo, N.F. (1994a). *Male violence against women at home, at work, and in the community.* Washington, DC: American Psychological Association.

Koss, M.P., Goodman, L.A., Browne, A., Fitzgerald, L.F., Keita, G.P., & Russo, N.F. (1994b). *No safe haven: Violence against women at home, work, and in the community.* Washington, DC: American Psychological Association Press.

Koss, M.P., Woodruff, W.J., & Koss, P.G. (1991). Criminal victimization among primary care medical patients: Prevalence, incidence, and physician usage. *Behavioral Sciences and the Law, 9,* 85–96.

Kosson, D.S., Kelly, J.C., & White, J.W. (1997). Psychopathy-related traits predict self-reported sexual aggression among college men. *Journal of Interpersonal Violence, 12,* 241–254.

Kottler, A. (1996). Voices in the winds of change. *Feminism and Psychology, 6,* 61–68.

Kovacs, D.M., Parker, J.G., & Hoffman, L.W. (1996). Behavioral, affective, and social correlates of involvement in cross-sex friendship in elementary school. *Child Development, 67,* 2269–2286.

Koven, S., & Michel, S. (1993). Introduction: Mother worlds. In S. Koven & S. Michel (Eds.), *Mothers in a new world: Maternalist politics and the origins of welfare states* (pp. 1–41). New York: Routledge.

Krafft-Ebing, R. (1965). *Psychpathia sexualis* (M.E. Wedneck, Trans.). New York: Putnam. (Original work published 1882)

Krafka, C. (1985). *The effects of violent pornography on the sexual responsiveness and attitudes of women.* Unpublished doctoral dissertation, University of Wisconsin–Madison.

Krahe, B. (1988). Victim and observer characteristics as determinants of responsibility attributions to victims of rape. *Journal of Applied Social Psychology, 18,* 50–58.

Kramarae, C., & Treichler, P. (1985). *A feminist dictionary.* London: Pandora Press.

Kravetz, D. (1978). Consciousness-raising groups in the 1970's. *Psychology of Women Quarterly, 3,* 168–186.

Kravetz, D. (1980). Consciousness-raising and self-help. In A.M. Brodsky & R.T. Hare-Mustin (Eds.), *Women and psychotherapy: An assessment of research and practice* (pp. 267–284). New York: Guilford Press.

Kravetz, D., Marecek, J., & Finn, S.E. (1983). Factors influencing women's participation in consciousness-raising groups. *Psychology of Women Quarterly, 7,* 257–271.

Krebs, J.R., & Dawkins, R. (1984). Animal signals: Mindreading and manipulation. In J.R. Krebs & N.B. Davies (Eds.), *Behavioral ecology* (pp. 380–402). Sunderland, MA: Sinauer.

Kristof, N.D. (1996, September 22). Aging world, new wrinkles. *New York Times,* pp. E1, E5.

Kuchner, J.F., & Porcino, J. (1988). Delayed motherhood. In B. Birns & D.F. Hay (Eds.), *The different faces of motherhood.* New York: Plenum Press.

Kuhn, D., Nash, S., & Brucken, L. (1978). Sex role concepts of two- and three-year-olds. *Child Development, 49,* 445–451.

Kurdek, L.A., & Schmitt, J.P. (1986). Relationship quality of partners in heterosexual married, heterosexual cohabiting and gay and lesbian relationships. *Journal of Personality and Social Psychology, 51,* 711–720.

Kurien, P. (1999). Gendered ethnicity: Creating a Hindu Indian identity in the United States. *American Behavioral Scientist, 42,* 648–670.

Kurz, D. (1993). Physical assaults by husbands: A major social problem. In R.J. Gelles & D.L. Loseke (Eds.), *Current controversies in domestic violence* (pp. 88–103). Newbury Park, CA: Sage.

Kutchins, H., & Kirk, S.A. (1997). *Making us crazy:* DSM *the psychiatric bible and the creation of mental disorders.* New York: Free Press.

Kvale, S. (1996). *InterViews: An introduction to qualitative research interviewing.* Thousand Oaks, CA: Sage.

Lack, D.Z. (1982). Women and pain: Another feminist issue. *Women and Therapy, 1*(1), 55–64.

Lackey, P.N. (1989). Adults' attitudes about assignments of household chores to male and female children. *Sex Roles, 20,* 271–281.

LaFontaine, E., & Tredeau, L. (1986). The frequency, sources, and correlates of sexual harassment among women in traditional male occupations. *Sex Roles, 15,* 433–441.

LaFrance, M. (1991). School for scandal: Different educational experiences for females and males. *Gender and Education, 3,* 3–13.

LaFrance, M. (1992). Gender and interruptions: Individual infraction or violations of the social order? *Psychology of Women Quarterly, 16,* 497–512.

LaFrance, M. (1998). Pressure to be pleasant: Effects of sex and power on reactions to not smiling. *International Review of Social Psychology, 2,* 95–108.

LaFrance, M., & Hecht, M. (1999). Smiling and gender: A meta-analysis. In A. Fischer (Ed.), *Gender and emotion* (pp. 118–142). New York: Cambridge University Press.

LaFree, G. (1989). *Rape and criminal justice: The social construction of sexual assault.* Belmont, CA: Wadsworth.

LaFreniere, P., & Charlesworth, W.R. (1987). Preschool peer status, behavior and resource utilization in a cooperative/competitive situation. *International Journal of Behavioral Development, 10,* 345–358.

LaFromboise, T.D., Heyle, A.M., & Ozer, E.J. (1999). Changing and diverse roles of women in American Indian cultures. In L.A. Peplau, S.C. DeBro, R.C. Veniegas, & P.L. Taylor (Eds.), *Gender, culture, and ethnicity* (pp. 48–61). Mountain View, CA: Mayfield.

Lagerspetz, K.M.J., Bjorkqvist, K., & Peltonen, T. (1988). Is indirect aggression typical of females? Gender differences in 11- to 12-year old children. *Aggressive Behavior, 14,* 403–414.

Lakoff, R. (1975). *Language and woman's place.* New York: Harper & Row.

Lakoff, R. (1990). *Talking power: The politics of language.* New York: Basic Books.

Lalumière, M.L., Blanchard, R., & Zucker, K.J. (2000). Sexual orientation and handedness in men and women: A meta-analysis. *Psychological Bulletin, 126,* 575–592.

LaMar, L., & Kite, M. (1998). Sex differences in attitudes toward gay men and lesbians: A multi-dimensional perspective. *Journal of Sex Research, 35,* 189–196.

Lamb, M.E., Easterbrooks, M.A., & Holden, G.W. (1980). Reinforcement and punishment among preschoolers: Characteristics, effects and correlates. *Child Development, 51,* 1230–1236.

Lamb, M.E., & Roopnarine, J.L. (1979). Peer influences on sex-role development in preschoolers. *Child Development, 50,* 1219–1222.

Lamb, S. (1991). Acts without agents: An analysis of linguistic avoidance in journal articles on men who batter women. *American Journal of Orthopsychiatry, 61,* 250–257.

Lamb, S. (1996). *The trouble with blame: Victims, perpetrators, and responsibility.* Cambridge, MA: Harvard University Press.

Lamb, S., & Keon, S. (1995). Blaming the perpetrator: Language that distorts reality in newspaper articles on men battering women. *Psychology of Women Quarterly, 19,* 209–220.

Lamborn, S.D., Dornbusch, S.M., & Steinberg, L. (1996). Ethnicity and community context as moderators of the relations between family decision making and adolescent adjustment. *Child Development, 67,* 283–301.

Lamphere, L., Ragone, H., & Zavella, P. (Eds.). (1997). *Situated lives: Gender and culture in everyday life.* New York: Routledge.

Lancaster, R.N., & di Leonardo, M. (Eds.). (1997). *The gender sexuality reader.* New York: Routledge.

Landrine, H. (1985). Race X class stereotypes of women. *Sex Roles, 13,* 65–75.

Landrine, H. (Ed.). (1995). *Bringing cultural diversity to feminist psychology: Theory, research, and practice.* Washington, DC: American Psychological Association.

Landrine, H. (1999). Race X class stereotypes of women. In L.A. Peplau, S.C. DeBro, R.C. Veniegas, & P.L. Taylor (Eds.), *Gender, culture, and ethnicity: Current research about women and men* (pp. 38–47). Mountain View, CA: Mayfield.

Landrine, H., & Klonoff, E.A. (1996). The Schedule of Racist Events: A measure of racial discrimination and a study of its negative physical and mental health consequences. *Journal of Black Psychology, 22,* 144–168.

Landrine, H., Klonoff, E.A., & Brown-Collins, A. (1992). Cultural diversity and methodology in feminist psychology: Critique, proposal, and empirical example. *Psychology of Women Quarterly, 16,* 145–163.

Landrine, H., Klonoff, E.A., Gibbs, J., Manning, V., & Lund, M. (1995). Physical and psychiatric correlates of gender discrimination: An application of the Schedule of Sexist Events. *Psychology of Women Quarterly, 19,* 473–492.

Landsman, G.H. (1998). Reconstructing motherhood in the age of "perfect" babies: Mothers of infants and toddlers with disabilities. *Signs, 24,* 69–99.

Laner, M.R., & Laner, R.H. (1979). Personal style or sexual preference? Why gay men are disliked. *International Review of Modern Sociology, 9*, 215–228.

Laner, M.R., & Laner, R.H. (1980). Sexual preference or personal style? Why lesbians are disliked. *Journal of Homosexuality, 3*, 339–356.

Lanza, A.F., & Revenson, T.A. (1993, August). *Rheumatic diseases, social roles, and the social support matching hypothesis.* Paper presented at the meeting of the American Psychological Association, Toronto, Canada.

Lapsley, H., & Paulin, K. (1994). Lesbians in psychology. *Bulletin of the New Zealand Psychological Society, 80,* 24–26.

Lapsley, H., & Ritchie, J. (1997). Women and psychology in New Zealand: A retrospective and prospective. *Bulletin of the New Zealand Psychological Society, 92,* 26–29.

Laqueur, T. (1992). *Making sex: Body and gender from the Greeks to Freud.* Cambridge, MA: Harvard University Press.

Larkin, J. (1994). *Sexual harassment.* Toronto, Canada: Second Story Press.

Larkin, J., & Populeailk, K. (1994). Heterosexual courtship violence and sexual harassment: The private and public control of young women. *Feminism and Psychology, 4*(2), 213–227.

Larsen, K., Reed, M., & Hoffman, S. (1980). Sexual preference or personal style? Why lesbians are disliked. *Journal of Homosexuality, 5*, 339–356.

Larson, C.L. (1997). Re-presenting the subject: Problems in personal narrative inquiry. *Qualitative Studies in Education, 10*(4), 455–470.

Larson, R.W., Richards, M.H., & Perry-Jenkins, M. (1994). Divergent worlds: The daily emotional experience of mothers and fathers in domestic and public spheres. *Journal of Personality and Social Psychology, 67*(6), 1034–1046.

Lather, P. (1991). *Getting smart: Feminist research and pedagogy with/in the postmodern.* New York: Routledge.

Latteier, C. (1998). *Breasts: The women's perspective on an American obsession.* New York: Harrington Park Press.

Laumann, E.O., Gagnon, J.H., Michael, R.T., & Michaels, S. (1994). *The social organization of sexuality: Sexual practices in the United States.* Chicago: University of Chicago Press.

Lauver, D.R., Karon, S.L., Egan, J., Jacobson, M., Nugent, J., Settersten, L., & Shaw, V. (1999). Understanding lesbians' mammography utilization. *Women's Health Issues, 9,* 264–274.

Lea, M., & Spears, R. (1995). Love at first byte? Building personal relationships over computer networks. In J.T. Wood & S. Duck (Eds.), *Under-studied relationships: Off the beaten track* (pp. 197–233). Thousand Oaks, CA: Sage.

Leaper, C. (1995). The use of *masculine* and *feminine* to describe women's and men's behavior. *Journal of Social Psychology, 135,* 359–369.

Leary, M.R. (1989). Self presentational processes in leadership. In R.A. Giacalone & P. Rosenfeld (Eds.), *Impression management in the organization.* Hillsdale, NJ: Erlbaum.

Leary, M.R., Tchividjian, L.R., & Kraxberger, B.E. (1994). Self-presentation can be hazardous to your health: Impression management and health risk. *Health Psychology, 13,* 461–470.

Lee, C. (1997). Social context, depression and the transition to motherhood. *British Journal of Health Psychology, 2,* 93–108.

Lee, C. (1998). *Women's health: Psychological and social perspectives.* London: Sage.

Lee, D.B., & Saul, T.T. (1987). Counseling Asian men. In M. Scher, M. Stevens, G. Good, & G. Eichenfield (Eds.), *Handbook of counseling and psychotherapy with men* (pp. 180–191). Newbury Park, CA: Sage.

Lee, F., & Peterson, C. (1997). Content analysis of archival data. *Journal of Consulting and Clinical Psychology, 65,* 959–969.

Lee, J. (1996). The empowerment approach to social work practice. In F.J. Turner (Ed.), *Social work treatment: Interlocking theoretical approaches* (pp. 218–249). New York: Free Press.

Lee, J.A. (1998). Ideologies of lovestyle and sexstyle. In V.C. de Munck (Ed.), *Romantic love and sexual behavior* (pp. 33–76). Westport, CT: Praeger.

Lee, S.E., & Kite, M.E. (1998, May). *Comparison of three theoretical explanations for the derogation of gender role violators.* Paper presented at the meeting of the Midwestern Psychological Association, Chicago.

Lee, V.E., Croninger, R.G., Linn, E., & Chen, X. (1996). The culture of sexual harassment in secondary schools. *American Educational Research Journal, 33*(2), 383–417.

Lees, S. (1993). *Sugar and spice: Sexuality and adolescent girls.* London: Penguin Books.

Le Espiritu, Y. (1997). *Asian American women and men: Labor, laws, and love.* Thousand Oaks, CA: Sage.

Leet-Pellegrini, H.M. (1980). Conversational dominance as a function of gender and expertise. In H. Giles, P.R. Robinson, & P. Smith (Eds.), *Language: Social psychological perspectives* (pp. 79–104). Oxford, England: Pergamon Press.

Lefkowitz, V. (1997). *Our guys: The Glen Ridge rape and the secret life of the perfect suburb.* Berkeley: University of California Press.

Legato, M.J., Padus, E., & Slaughter, E. (1997). Women's perceptions of their general health, with special reference to their risk of coronary artery disease: Results of a national telephone survey. *Journal of Women's Health, 6,* 189–198.

LeGrange, D., Stone, A., & Brownell, K. (1998). Eating disturbances in White and minority female dieters. *International Journal of Eating Disorders, 24,* 395–403.

Lehne, G.K. (1976). Homophobia among men. In D. Davis & R. Brannon (Eds.), *The forty-nine percent majority.* Reading, MA: Addison-Wesley.

Leinbach, M.D., & Fagot, B.I. (1986). Acquisition of gender labels: A test for toddlers. *Sex Roles, 15,* 655–667.

Leinbach, M.D., & Fagot, B.I. (1993). Categorical habituation to male and female faces: Gender schematic processing in infancy. *Infant Behavior and Development, 16,* 317–332.

Leinbach, M.D., Hort, B.E., & Fagot, B.I. (1997). Bears are for boys: Metaphorical associations in young children's gender stereotypes. *Cognitive Development, 12,* 107–130.

Leitenberg, H., & Henning, K. (1995). Sexual fantasy. *Psychological Bulletin, 117,* 469–496.

Leland, J., & Miller, M. (1998, August 17). Can gays "convert"? *Newsweek,* 47–50.

Lemle, R., & Mishkind, M.E. (1989). Alcohol and masculinity. *Journal of Substance Abuse Treatment, 6,* 213–222.

Lengnick-Hall, M.L. (1995). Sexual harassment research: A methodological critique. *Personnel Psychology, 48,* 841–864.

Leonardo, C., & Chrisler, J.C. (1992). Women and sexually transmitted diseases. *Women and Health, 18*(4), 1–15.

Lepowsky, M. (1994). Women, men, and aggression in an egalitarian society. *Sex Roles, 30,* 199–211.

Lerman, H. (1986). *A mote in Freud's eye: From psychoanalysis to the psychology of women.* New York: Springer.

Lerman, H. (1987). Introduction. In C.M. Brody (Ed.), *Women's therapy groups: Paradigms of feminist treatment* (pp. xxiii–xxviii). New York: Springer.

Lerner, M., & West, C. (1995). *Jews and Blacks: Let the healing begin.* New York: Putnam.

Lerner, R.M., & Knapp, J.R. (1975). Actual and perceived intrafamilial attitudes of late adolescents and their parents. *Journal of Youth and Adolescence, 4,* 17–36.

Lesko, N. (1988). The curriculum of the body. In L. Roman, L. Christian-Smith, & E. Ellsworth (Eds.), *Becoming feminine* (pp. 124–142). Philadelphia: Falmer Press.

Letellier, P. (1996). Gay and bisexual male domestic violence victimization: Challenges to feminist theory and responses to violence. In L.K. Hamberger & C. Renzetti (Eds.), *Domestic partner abuse* (pp. 1–21). Springer.

Letourneau, E.J., Holmes, M., & Chasedunn-Roark, J. (1999). Gynecologic health consequences to victims of interpersonal violence. *Women's Health Issues, 9,* 115–120.

Levant, R.F. (1992). Toward the reconstruction of masculinity. *Journal of Family Psychology, 5*(3/4), 379–402.

Levant, R.F. (1995). Toward the reconstruction of masculinity. In R.F. Levant & W.S. Pollack (Eds.), *A new psychology of men* (pp. 229–251). New York: Basic Books.

Levant, R.F. (1997). Nonrelational sexuality in men. In R. Levant & G. Brooks (Eds.), *Men and sex: New psychological perspectives* (pp. 9–27). New York: Wiley.

Levant, R.F., Majors, R.G., & Kelley, M.L. (1998). Masculinity ideology among young African American and European American women and men in different regions of the United States. *Cultural Diversity and Ethnic Minority Psychology, 4,* 227–236.

Levant, R.F., & Pollack, W.S. (Eds.). (1995). *A new psychology of men.* New York: Basic Books.

LeVay, S. (1991). A difference in hypothalamic structure between heterosexual and homosexual men. *Science, 253,* 1034–1037.

LeVay, S. (1993). *The sexual brain.* Cambridge, MA: MIT Press.

Leventhal, H., Nerenz, D., & Strauss, A. (1982). Self-regulation and the mechanism for symptom appraisal. In D. Mechanic (Ed.), *Symptoms, illness behavior, and help-seeking* (pp. 55–86). New York: Neale Watson.

Leveroni, C.L., & Berenbaum, S.A. (1998). Early androgen effects on interest in infants: Evidence from children with congenital adrenal hyperplasia. *Developmental Neuropsychology, 14,* 321–340.

Levine, J.A., & Pittinsky, T.L. (1997). *Working fathers: New strategies for balancing work and family.* San Diego, CA: Harcourt Brace.

Levine, M.P., & Leonard, R. (1984). Discrimination against lesbians in the workforce. *Signs, 9*(4), 700–710.

Levinson, D.J., Darrow, C.N., Klein, E.B., Levinson, M.H., & McKee, B. (1978). *The seasons of a man's life.* New York: Knopf.

Levy, B., & Lobel, K. (1991). In B. Levy (Ed.), *Dating violence: Young women in danger* (pp. 203–208). Seattle, WA: Seal Press.

Levy, G.D. (1989). Relations among aspects of children's social environments, gender schematization, gender role knowledge, and flexibility. *Sex Roles, 21,* 803–823.

Levy, G.D. (1994). High and low gender schematic children's release from proactive interference. *Sex Roles, 30,* 93–108.

Levy, G.D. (1999). Gender-typed and non-gender-typed category awareness in toddlers. *Sex Roles, 41,* 851–873.

Levy, G.D., & Boston, M.B. (1994). Preschoolers' recall of own-sex and other-sex gender scripts. *Journal of Genetic Psychology, 155,* 369–371.

Levy, G.D., & Carter, D.B. (1989). Gender schema, gender constancy, and gender-role knowledge: The roles of cognitive factors in preschoolers' gender-role stereotype attributions. *Developmental Psychology, 25,* 444–449.

Levy, G.D., & Fivush, R. (1993). Scripts and gender: A new approach for examining gender-role development. *Developmental Review, 13,* 126–146.

Levy, G.D., & Haaf, R.A. (1994). Detection of gender-related categories by 10-month-old infants. *Infant Behavior and Development, 17,* 457–459.

Levy, G.D., Taylor, M.G., & Gelman, S.A. (1995). Traditional and evaluative aspects of flexibility in gender roles, social conventions, moral rules, and physical laws. *Child Development, 66,* 515–531.

Lewin, M. (Ed.). (1984). *In the shadow of the past: Psychology portrays the sexes.* New York: Columbia University Press.

Lewin, M., & Wild, C.L. (1991). The impact of the feminist critique on tests, assessment, and methodology. *Psychology of Women Quarterly, 15,* 591–596.

Lewis, L.J., Ritenbaugh, C., & Aickin, M. (1995). Breast cancer incidence and screening practices among university faculty women. *Women's Health Issues, 5,* 118–122.

Lewis, S. (1991). Motherhood and employment: The impact of social and organisational values. In A. Phoenix, A. Woollett, & E. Lloyd (Eds.), *Motherhood: Meanings, practices and ideologies* (pp. 195–215). London: Sage.

Lewis, S.E., & Nicolson, P. (1998). Talking about early motherhood: Recognizing loss and reconstructing depression. *Journal of Reproductive and Infant Psychology, 16,* 177–198.

Lewis, S.Y. (1994). Cognitive-behavioral therapy. In L. Comas-Diaz & B. Greene (Eds.), *Women of color: Integrating ethnic and gender identities in psychotherapy* (pp. 223–238). New York: Guilford Press.

Lewontin, R.C., Rose, S., & Kamin, L.J. (1984). *Not in our genes.* New York: Pantheon Books.

Li, G. (1995). The interaction effect of bereavement and sex on the risk of suicide in the elderly: An historical cohort study. *Social Science and Medicine, 40,* 825–828.

Li, G. (1998). Are female drivers safer? An application of the decomposition method. *Epidemiology, 9,* 379–384.

Liang, M., Partridge, A., Daltroy, L., Straaton, K., Galper, S., & Holman, H. (1991). Strategies for reducing excess morbidity and mortality in Blacks with systemic lupus erythematosus. *Arthritis and Rheumatism, 34,* 1187–1196.

Liao, Y., Cooper, R.S., Ghali, J.K., & Szocka, A. (1992). Survival rates with coronary artery disease for Black women compared with Black men. *Journal of the American Medical Association, 268,* 1867–1871.

Lie, G., Schilit, R., Bush, J., Montague, M., & Reyes, L. (1991). Lesbians in currently aggressive relationships: How frequently do they report aggressive past relationships? *Violence and Victims, 6,* 121–135.

Lieblich, A., & Josselson, R. (Eds.). (1994). *Exploring identity and gender: The narrative study of lives.* Thousand Oaks, CA: Sage.

Lillie-Blanton, M., Bowie, J., & Ro, M. (1996). African American women: Social factors and the use of preventive health services. In M.M. Falik & K.S. Collins (Eds.), *Women's health: The Commonwealth Fund survey* (pp. 99–122). Baltimore: Johns Hopkins University Press.

Lincoln, Y.S., & Guba, E.G. (1985). *Naturalistic inquiry.* Beverly Hills, CA: Sage.

Lips, H. (1997). *Sex and gender: An introduction* (3rd ed.). Mountain View, CA: Mayfield.

Lisak, D., & Luster, L. (1994). Educational, and occupational, and relationship histories of men who were sexually and/or physically abused as children. *Journal of Traumatic Stress, 7,* 507–523.

List, J.A., Collins, W.A., & Westby, S.D. (1983). Comprehension and inferences from traditional and nontraditional sex-role portrayals on television. *Child Development, 54,* 1579–1587.

Livesley, W.J., & Bromley, D.B. (1973). *Person perception in childhood and adolescence.* London: Wiley.

Livia, A. (1996). Daring to presume. *Feminism and Psychology, 6,* 31–41.

Livia, A., & Hall, K. (Eds.). (1996). *Queerly phrased: Language, gender, and sexuality.* New York: Oxford University Press.

Lloyd, S.A. (1991). The dark side of courtship. *Family Relations, 40,* 14–20.

Lobel, T.E. (1994). Sex typing and the social perception of gender stereotypic and nonstereotypic behavior: The uniqueness of feminine males. *Journal of Personality and Social Psychology, 66,* 379–385.

Lobel, T.E., Bempechat, J., Gewirtz, J., Shoken-Topaz, T., & Bashe, E. (1993). The role of gender-related information and self endorsement of traits in preadolescents' inferences and judgments. *Child Development, 64,* 1285–1294.

Lobel, T.E., & Menashri, J. (1993). The relations of conceptions of gender-role transgressions and gender constancy to gender-typed toy preferences. *Developmental Psychology, 29,* 150–155.

Lockhart, L.K., Ditto, P.H., Danks, J.H., Coppola, K.M., & Smucker, W.D. (in press). *The stability of older adult's judgments of fates better and worse than death.*

Lockhart, L.L., White, B.W., Causby, V., & Isaac, A. (1994). Letting out the secret: Violence in lesbian relationships. *Journal of Interpersonal Violence, 9,* 469–492.

Lockheed, M.E. (1985). Sex and social influence: A meta-analysis guided by theory. In J. Berger & M. Zelditch (Eds.), *Status, rewards, and influence.* San Francisco: Jossey-Bass.

Lockheed, M.E., & Hall, K.P. (1976). Conceptualizing sex as a status characteristic: Applications to leadership training strategies. *Journal of Social Issues, 32,* 111–124.

Loftus, E. (1993). The reality of repressed memories. *American Psychologist, 48,* 518–537.

Longino, H. (1994). Pornography, oppression, and freedom: A closer look. In A.M. Jaggar (Ed.), *Living with contradictions: Controversies in feminist social ethics* (pp. 154–160). Boulder, CO: Westview Press.

Lorber, J. (1997). *Gender and the social construction of illness.* Thousand Oaks, CA: Sage.

Lorber, J. (1999). Embattled terrain: Gender and sexuality. In M.M. Ferree, J. Lorber, & B.B. Hess (Eds.), *Revisioning gender: The gender lens* (pp. 416–448). Thousand Oaks, CA: Sage.

Lorde, A. (1980). *The cancer journals.* New York: Spinsters Ink.

Lorde, A. (1984a). Sexism: An American disease in Blackface. In *Sister outsider.* Freedom, CA: Crossing Press.

Lorde, A. (1984b). *Sister outsider.* New York: Crossing Press.

Lorde, A. (1990). Living with cancer. In E.C. White (Ed.), *The Black women's health book: Speaking for ourselves* (pp. 27–37). Seattle, WA: Seal Press.

Lott, B. (1981). *Becoming a woman: The socialization of gender.* Springfield, IL: Thomas.

Lott, B. (1991). Social psychology: Humanistic roots and feminist future. *Psychology of Women Quarterly, 15,* 505–519.

Lott, B. (1995a). Distancing from women: Interpersonal sexist discrimination. In B. Lott & D. Maluso (Eds.), *The social psychology of interpersonal discrimination* (pp. 12–49). New York: Guilford Press.

Lott, B. (1995b). "Who ever thought I'd grow up to be a feminist foremother?" In P. Chesler, E.D. Rothblum, & E. Cole (Eds.), *Feminist foremothers in women's studies, psychology, and mental health.* New York: Haworth Press.

Lott, B., Reilly, M.E., & Howard, D. (1982). Sexual assault and harassment: A campus community case study. *Signs, 8,* 296–318.

Love, S. (with Lindsey, K.). (1995). *Dr. Susan Love's breast book* (2nd ed.). Reading, MA: Addison-Wesley.

Lubkin, I.M. (1995). *Chronic illness: Impact and interventions* (3rd ed.). Sudbury, MA: Jones & Bartlett.

Luepnitz, D.A. (1988). *The family interpreted.* New York: Basic Books.

Lueptow, L.B., Garovich, L., & Lueptow, M.B. (1995). The persistence of gender stereotypes in the face of changing sex roles: Evidence contrary to the sociocultural model. *Ethology and Sociobiology, 16,* 509–530.

Luft, T.M., & Cairns, K.V. (1999). Responding to sexual harassment: Implications for counselling adolescent girls. *Canadian Journal of Counselling, 33,* 112–126.

Luker, K. (1984). *Abortion and the politics of motherhood.* Berkeley: University of California Press.

Lum, D. (1996). *Social work practice and people of color: A process stage model.* Pacific Grove, CA: Brooks/Cole.

Lutsky, S.M., & Knight, B.G. (1994). Explaining gender differences in caregiver distress: The roles of emotional attentiveness and coping styles. *Psychology and Aging, 9,* 513–519.

Luttrell, W. (1993). "The teachers, they all had their pets": Concepts of gender, knowledge, and power. *Signs, 18*(3), 505–546.

Lykes, M.B. (1989). Dialogue with Guatemalan Indian women: Critical perspectives on constructing collaborative research. In R.K. Unger (Ed.), *Representations: Social constructions of gender* (pp. 167–185). Amityville, NY: Baywood.

Lykes, M.B. (1994). Speaking against the silence: One Maya woman's exile and return. In C.E. Franz & A.V. Stewart (Eds.), *Women creating lives: Identities, resilience, and resistance* (pp. 97–114). Boulder, CO: Westview Press.

Lykes, M.B., & Stewart, A.S. (1986). Evaluating the feminist challenge to research in personality and social psychology: 1963–1983. *Psychology of Women Quarterly, 10,* 393–412.

Lynch, E., & Hanson, M. (1998). *Developing cross-cultural competence: A guide for working with children and their families.* Baltimore: Brookes.

Lyson, T.A. (1986). Race and sex differences in sex role attitudes of southern college students. *Psychology of Women Quarterly, 10,* 421–427.

Lytton, H., & Romney, D.M. (1991). Parents' differential socialization of boys and girls: A meta-analysis. *Psychological Bulletin, 109,* 267–296.

Mabry, E. (1985). The effects of gender composition and task structure on small group interaction. *Small Group Behavior, 16,* 75–96.

Maccoby, E.E. (1988). Gender as a social category. *Developmental Psychology, 24,* 755–765.

Maccoby, E.E. (1998). *The two sexes: Growing up apart, coming together.* Cambridge, MA: Harvard University Press.

Maccoby, E.E., & Jacklin, C.N. (1974). *The psychology of sex differences*. Palo Alto, CA: Stanford University Press.

MacDonald, A.P. (1976). Homophobia: Its roots and meanings. *Homosexual Counseling Journal, 3,* 23–33.

MacDonald, J. (1990). We'll deconstruct when they deconstruct [Special issue]. *Resources for Feminist Research, 19*(3/4), 89–90.

MacKinnon, C.A. (1979). *Sexual harassment of working women: A case of sexual discrimination*. New Haven, CT: Yale University Press.

MacKinnon, C.A. (1987). *Feminism unmodified: Discourses on life and law*. Cambridge, MA: Harvard University Press.

MacLachlan, M. (1997). *Culture and health: Psychological perspectives on problems and practice*. Chichester, England: Wiley.

MacMahon, B., & Pugh, T.F. (1965). Suicide in the widowed. *American Journal of Epidemiology, 81,* 23–31.

Macpherson, P., & Fine, M. (1995). Hungry for an us: Adolescent girls and adult women negotiating territories of race, gender, class, and difference. *Feminism and Psychology, 5,* 181–200.

Maggard, S.W. (1990). Gender contested: Women's participation in the Brookside coal strike. In G. West & R.L. Blumberg (Eds.), *Women and social protest* (pp. 75–98). New York: Oxford University Press.

Magley, V.J., Hulin, C.L., Fitzgerald, L.F., & DeNardo, M. (1999). Outcomes of self-labeling sexual harassment. *Journal of Applied Psychology, 84,* 390–402.

Magnusson, E. (1998). [Review of *Feminist visions of gender similarities and differences* by M. Kimball]. *Feminism & Psychology, 8,* 212–215.

Mahalik, J.R. (2000). Gender role conflict in men as a predictor of self-ratings of behavior on the interpersonal circle. *Journal of Social and Clinical Psychology, 19,* 276–292.

Mahalik, J.R., Cournoyer, R.J., DeFranc, W., Cherry, M., & Napolitano, J.M. (1988). Men's gender role conflict and use of psychological defenses. *Journal of Counseling Psychology, 45,* 247–255.

Major, B. (1989). Gender differences in comparisons and entitlement: Implications for comparable worth. *Journal of Social Issues, 45*(4), 99–115.

Major, B. (1993). Gender, entitlement, and the distribution of family labor. *Journal of Social Issues, 49*(3), 141–159.

Major, B., & Forcey, B. (1985). Social comparisons and pay evaluations: Preferences for same-sex and same-job wage comparisons. *Journal of Experimental Social Psychology, 21,* 393–405.

Majors, R., & Billson, J.M. (1992). *Coolpose: The dilemmas of Black manhood in America*. New York: Lexington Books.

Makepeace, J. (1986). Gender differences in courtship violence victimization. *Family Relations, 35,* 383–388.

Malamuth, N.M. (1998). The confluence model as an organizing framework for research on sexually aggressive men: Risk moderators, imagined aggression, and pornography consumption. In R.G. Geen & E. Donnerstein (Eds.), *Human aggression: Theories, research, and implications for social policy* (pp. 229–245). San Diego, CA: Academic Press.

Malamuth, N.M., Linz, D., Heavey, C.L., & Barnes, G. (1995). Using the confluence model of sexual aggression to predict men's conflict with women: A 10-year follow-up study. *Journal of Personality and Social Psychology, 69,* 353–369.

Malamuth, N.M., Sockloskie, R., Koss, M.P., & Tanaka, J. (1991). The characteristics of aggressors against women: Testing a model using a national sample of college students. *Journal of Counsulting and Clinical Psychology, 59,* 670–681.

Malamuth, N.M., & Thornhill, N.W. (1994). Hostile masculinity, sexual aggression, and gender-biased domineeringness in conversations. *Aggressive Behavior, 20,* 185–194.

Malaney, G.D., Williams, E.A., & Geller, W.W. (1997). Asessing campus climate for gays, lesbians, and bisexuals at two institutions. *Journal of College Student Development, 38*(4), 365–375.

Malgady, R.L., & Rogler, G.C. (1987). Ethnoculutral and linguistic bias in mental health evaluation of Hispanics. *American Psychologist, 42,* 228–234.

Malheux, B., Pineault, R., Lambert, J., Beland, F., & Berthiaume, M. (1989). Factors influencing physicians' preventive practices. *American Journal of Preventive Medicine, 5,* 201–206.

Malson, H. (1998). *The thin woman*. London: Routledge.

Maltz, D.N., & Borker, R.A. (1982). A cultural approach to male-female miscommunicaiton. In J.J. Gumperz (Ed.), *Language and social identity* (pp. 195–217). Cambridge, England: Cambridge University Press.

Mama, A. (1995). *Beyond the masks: Race, gender and subjectivity*. London: Routledge.

Mann, P. (1998). Toward a post-patriarchal society. In J. Haber & M. Halfon (Eds.), *Norms and values: Essays on the work of Virginia Held*. Lanham, MD: Rowman and Littlefield.

Mannheim, K. (1972). The problem of generations. In P.G. Altbach & R.S. Laufer (Eds.), *The new pilgrims: Youth protest in transition* (pp. 276–322). New York: David McKay. (Original work published 1928)

Manning, J.T., Scott, D., Wilson, J., & Lewis-Jones, D.I. (1998). The ratio of the 2nd to 4th digit length: A predictor of sperm numbers and levels of testosterone, LH, and oestrogen. *Human Reproduction, 13,* 3000–3004.

Mansfield, P.K., Koch, P.B., Henderson, J., & Vicary, J.R. (1991). The job climate for women in traditionally male blue-collar occupations. *Sex Roles, 25*(1/2), 63–79.

Marano, H.E. (1997, November/December). Gottman and Gray: The two Johns. *Psychology Today,* p. 28.

Marantz, S.A., & Mansfield, A.F. (1977). Maternal employment and the development of sex-role stereotyping in five- to eleven-year-old girls. *Child Development, 48,* 668–673.

Marchbanks, P.A., Lui, K.J., & Mercy, J.A. (1990). Risk of injury from resisting rape. *American Journal of Epidemiology, 132,* 540–549.

Marcia, J.E. (1966). Development and validation of ego identity status. *Journal of Personality and Social Psychology, 3,* 551–558.

Marcia, J.E. (1994). The empirical study of ego identity. In H.A. Bosma (Ed.), *Identity and development: An interdisciplinary approach* (pp. 67–80). Thousand Oaks, CA: Sage.

Marecek, J. (1995a). Gender, politics, and psychology's ways of knowing. *American Psychologist, 50,* 162–163.

Marecek, J. (1995b). Psychology and feminism: Can this relationship be saved? In D. Stanton & A.J. Stewart (Eds.), *Feminisms in the academy* (pp. 101–132). Ann Arbor: University of Michigan Press.

Marecek, J. (1999a). Comments on "subject to romance." *Psychology of Women Quarterly, 23,* 369–374.

Marecek, J. (1999b). *Feminist identities in the '90s: Necessity is the mother of (re-)invention.* Paper presented at the Seventh International interdisciplinary Congress on Women, Troms, Norway.

Marecek, J., Fine, M., & Kidder, L. (1997). Working between worlds: Qualitative and quantitative methods and social psychology. *Journal of Social Issues, 53,* 631–644.

Marecek, J., & Hare-Mustin, R.T. (1991). A short history of the future: Feminism and clinical psychology. *Psychology of Women Quarterly, 15,* 521–536.

Marecek, J., & Kravetz, D. (1998a). Power and agency in feminist therapy. In I.B. Seu & M.C. Heenan (Eds.), *Feminism and psychotherapy: Reflections on contemporary theories and practices* (pp. 13–29). London: Sage.

Marecek, J., & Kravetz, D. (1998b). Putting politics into practice: Feminist therapy as feminist praxis. *Women and Therapy, 21,* 17–36.

Marecek, J., Kravetz, D.F., & Finn, S.E. (1979). Comparison of women who enter feminist therapy and women who enter traditional therapy. *Journal of Consulting and Clinical Psychology, 47,* 734–742.

Margolies, L., Becker, M., & Jackson-Brewer, K. (1987). Internalized homophobia: Identifying and treating the oppressor within. In Boston Lesbian Psychologies Collective (Ed.), *Lesbian psychologies.* Urbana: University of Illinois Press.

Marin, G., & Marin, V.M. (1991). *Research with Hispanic populations.* Newbury Park, CA: Sage.

Markowitz, J. (1984). The impact of the sexist language controversy and regulation on language in university documents. *Psychology of Women Quarterly, 8,* 337–47.

Marks, D. (1996). Able-bodied dilemmas in teaching disability studies. *Feminism and Psychology, 6,* 69–73.

Marks, S.R., & MacDermid, S.M. (1996). Multiple roles and the self: A theory of role balance. *Journal of Marriage and the Family, 58,* 417–432.

Marris, V. (1996). *Lives worth living: Women's experiences of chronic illness.* San Francisco: HarperCollins.

Marshall, H. (1991). The social construction of motherhood: An analysis of childcare and parenting manuals. In A. Phoenix, A. Woollett, & E. Lloyd (Eds.), *Motherhood: Meanings, practices and ideologies* (pp. 66–85). London: Sage.

Marsiglio, W. (1993). Attitudes towards homosexual activity and gays as friends: A national survey of 15- to 19-year old males. *Journal of Sex Research, 30,* 12–17.

Martell, R.F. (1991). Sex bias at work: The effects of attentional and memory demands on performance ratings of men and women. *Journal of Applied Social Psychology, 21*(23), 1939–1960.

Martell, R.F., Lane, D.M., & Emrich, C. (1996). Male-female differences: A computer simulation. *American Psychologist, 51,* 157–158.

Martin, C.L. (1987). A ratio measure of sex stereotyping. *Journal of Personality and Social Psychology, 52,* 489–499.

Martin, C.L. (1989). Children's use of gender-related information in making social judgments. *Developmental Psychology, 25,* 80–88.

Martin, C.L. (1990). Attitudes and expectations about children with nontraditional and traditional gender roles. *Sex Roles, 22,* 151–165.

Martin, C.L. (1993). New directions for investigating children's gender knowledge. *Developmental Review, 13,* 184–204.

Martin, C.L. (1999). A developmental perspective on gender effects and gender concepts. In W.B. Swann, Jr., J.H. Langlois, & L.A. Gilbert (Eds.), *Sexism and stereotypes in modern society: The gender science of Janet Taylor Spence* (pp. 45–73). Washington, DC: American Psychological Association.

Martin, C.L., Eisenbud, L., & Rose, H. (1995). Children's gender-based reasoning about toys. *Child Development, 66,* 1453–1471.

Martin, C.L., & Halverson, C.F., Jr. (1981). A schematic processing model of sex typing and stereotyping in children. *Child Development, 52,* 1119–1134.

Martin, C.L., & Halverson, C.F., Jr. (1983a). The effects of sex-typing schemas on young children's memory. *Child Development, 54,* 563–574.

Martin, C.L., & Halverson, C.F., Jr. (1983b). Gender constancy: A methodological and theoretical analysis. *Sex Roles, 9,* 775–790.

Martin, C.L., & Little, J.K. (1990). The relation of gender understanding to children's sex-typed preferences and gender stereotypes. *Child Development, 61,* 1427–1439.

Martin, C.L., Wood, C.H., & Little, J.K. (1990). The development of gender stereotype components. *Child Development, 61,* 1891–1904.

Martin, E. (1987). *The woman in the body.* Boston: Beacon Press.

Martin, E. (1989). *The woman in the body: A cultural analysis of reproduction.* Milton Keynes, England: Open University Press.

Martin, J.R. (1994). Methodological essentialism, false difference, and other dangerous traps. *Signs, 19,* 630–657.

Martin, K.A. (1996). *Puberty, sexuality, and the self: Girls and boys at adolescence.* New York: Routledge.

Martin, K.A. (1998). Becoming a gendered body: Practices of preschools. *American Sociological Review, 63,* 494–511.

Martin, M., & Humphries, B. (1996). Representation and difference in cross-cultural research: The impact of institutional structures. *Feminism and Psychology, 6,* 210–215.

Martindale, M. (1991). *Sexual harassment in the military: 1988 Report.* Arlington, VA: Defense Manpower Data Center.

Mason, A., & Blankenship, V. (1987). Power and affiliation motivation, stress, and abuse in intimate relationships. *Journal of Personality and Social Psychology, 52,* 203–210.

Mason, C.A., Cauce, A.M., Gonzales, N., & Hiraga, Y. (1996). Neither too sweet nor too sour: Problem peers, maternal control, and problem behavior in African American adolescents. *Child Development, 67,* 2115–2130.

Mason, K.O., & Lu, Y. (1988). Attitudes toward women's familial roles: Changes in the United States, 1977–1985. *Gender and Society, 2,* 39–57.

Masser, B., & Abrams, D. (1999). Contemporary sexism: The relationships among hostility, benevolence, and neosexism. *Psychology of Women Quarterly, 23*(3), 503–517.

Masters, W.H., & Johnson, V.E. (1966). *Human sexual: Response.* Boston: Little, Brown.

Matsuda, M. (1995). Looking to the bottom: Critical legal studies and reparations. In K. Crenshaw, N. Gotanda, G. Peller, & K. Thomas (Eds.), *Critical race theory: Key writings that formed the movement.* New York: New Press.

Matsuda, M. (1996). *Where is your body?* Boston: Beacon Press.

Mauriello, L.M., & Chrisler, J.C. (1999). *The impact of chronic illness on women's friendships.* Manuscript submitted for publication.

Mauthner, N. (1998). "Its a woman's cry for help": A relational perspective on postnatal depression. *Feminism and Psychology, 8,* 325–355.

Mauthner, N., & Doucet, A. (1998). Reflections on a voice-centred relational method: Analysing maternal and domestic voices. In J. Ribbens & R. Edwards (Eds.), *Feminist dilemmas in qualitative research: Public knowledge and private lives* (pp. 119–146). London: Sage.

Mayfield, W. (1999). *Relationship among narcissistic vulnerability gay identity, masculinity ideology, and psychological adjustment in gay men.* Unpublished doctoral dissertation, University of Missouri, Columbia.

Maynard, M., & Purvis, J. (1994). *Researching women's lives from a feminist perspective.* London: Taylor & Francis.

Maynard Smith, J. (1997). Commentary on feminism and evolutionary biology. In P.A. Gowaty (Ed.), *Feminism and evolutionary biology: Boundaries, intersections, and frontiers* (pp. 522–526). New York: Chapman & Hall.

Mazer, D.B., & Percival, E.F. (1989). Students' experiences of sexual harassment in a small university. *Sex Roles, 20,* 1–22.

McAdam, D. (1992). Gender as a mediator of the activist experience: The case of freedom summer. *American Journal of Sociology, 97,* 1211–1240.

McAdoo, H.P. (Ed.). (1999). *Family ethnicity: Strength in diversity* (2nd ed.). Thousand Oaks, CA: Sage.

McCaul, K.D., Branstetter, A.D., Schroeder, D.M., & Glasgow, R.E. (1996). What is the relationship between breast cancer risk and mammography screening? A meta-analytic review. *Health Psychology, 15,* 423–429.

McCauley, J., Kern, D.E., Kolodner, K., Dill, L., & Schroeder, A.F. (1997). Clinical characteristics of women with a history of childhood abuse: Unhealed wounds. *AMA: Journal of the American Medical Association, 277,* 1362–1368.

McCloskey, D.N. (1999). *Crossing: A memoir.* Chicago: University of Chicago Press.

McClosky, K.A., & Fraser, J.S. (1997). Using feminist MRI brief therapy during initial contact with victims of domestic violence. *Psychotherapy, 34*, 433–446.

McConahay, J.B. (1983). Modern racism and modern discrimination: The effects of race, racial attitudes, and context on simulated hiring decisions. *Personality and Social Psychology Bulletin, 9*(4), 551–558.

McConahay, J.B. (1986). Modern racism, ambivalence, and the Modern Racism Scale. In J.F. Dovidio & S.L. Gaertner (Eds.), *Prejudice, discrimination, and racism* (pp. 91–125). Orlando, FL: Academic Press.

McConnell, J. (1992). Incest as conundrum: Judicial discourse on private wrong and public harm. *Texas Journal of Women and the Law, 1*, 143–172.

McCreary, D.R. (1994). The male role and avoiding femininity. *Sex Roles, 31*, 517–531.

McDonald, J.J., & Lees-Haley, P. (1995). Avoiding "junk science" in sexual harassment litigation. *Employee Relations Law Journal, 21*, 51–71.

McFadden, D. (1993). A masculinizing effect on the auditory systems of human females having male co-twins. *Proceedings of the National Academy of Sciences USA, 90*, 11900–11904.

McFadden, D. (1998). Sex differences in the auditory system. *Developmental Neuropsychology, 14*, 261–298.

McFadden, D., & Pasanen, E. (1998). Comparison of the auditory systems of heterosexuals and homosexuals: Click-evoked otoacoustic emissions. *Proceedings of the National Academy of Sciences USA, 95*, 2709–2713.

McFadden, D., & Pasanen, E. (1999). Spontaneous otoacoustic emissions in heterosexuals, homosexuals, and bisexuals. *Journal of the Acoustical Society of America, 105*, 2403–2413.

McGann, P.J. (1995). *The ballfields of our hearts.* Doctoral dissertation, Brandeis University, Waltham, MA.

McGann, P.J. (1999). Skirting the gender normal divide: A tomboy life story. In M. Romero & A.J. Stewart (Eds.), *Women's untold stories: Breaking silence, talking back, voicing complexity* (pp. 105–124). New York: Routledge.

McGinnis, A.L. (1997). *The balanced life: Achieving success in work and love.* Minneapolis, MN: Augsburg Fortress.

McGoldrick, M., Anderson, C.M., & Walsh, F. (Eds.). (1989). *Women in families: A framework for family therapy.* New York: Norton.

McGrath, E., Keita, G.P., Strickland, B.R., & Russo, N.F. (1990). *Women and depression.* Washington, DC: American Psychological Association.

McHugh, M.C., Koeske, R., & Frieze, I.H. (1986). Issues to consider in conducting nonsexist psychological research: A guide for researchers. *American Psychologist, 41*, 879–890.

McIntosh, J.L., & Santos, J.F. (1986). Methods of soucide by age: Sex and age differences among the young and old. *International Journal of Aging and Human Development, 22*, 123–139.

McIntosh, M. (1968). The homosexual role. *Social Problems, 16*(2), 182–192.

McIntosh, P. (1983). *Interactive phases of curricular revision: A feminist perspective.* Wellesley, MA: Wellesley College Center for Research on Women.

McIntosh, P. (1998). White privilege: Unpacking the invisible knapsack. In M. McGoldrick (Ed.), *Re-visioning family therapy: Race, culture, and gender in clinical practice* (pp. 147–152). New York: Guilford Press.

McKeachie, W.J. (1997). Student ratings: The validity of use. *American Psychologist, 52*, 1218–1225.

McKee, J.P., & Sheriffs, A.C. (1957). The differential evaluation of males and females. *Journal of Personality, 25*, 356–371.

McKenna, W., & Kessler, S.J. (1977). Experimental design as a source of sex bias in social psychology. *Sex Roles, 3*, 117–128.

McKenzie-Mohr, D., & Zanna, M.P. (1990). Treating women as sex objects: Look to the (gender schematic) male who has viewed pornography. *Personality and Social Psychology Bulletin, 16*, 296–308.

McKinney, K. (1992). Contrapower sexual harassment: The effects of student sex and type of behavior on faculty perceptions. *Sex Roles, 27*, 627–644.

McLean, C., Carey, M., & White, C. (1996). *Men's ways of being.* Boulder, CO: Westview Press.

McLeod, A., & Crawford, I. (1998). The postmodern family: An examination of the psychosocial and legal perspectives of gay and lesbian parenting. In G.M. Herek (Ed.), *Stigma and sexual orientation: Understanding prejudice against lesbians, gay men, and bisexuals.* London: Sage.

McPhatter, A.R. (1991). Assessment revisited: Comprehensive approach to understanding family dynamics. *Families in Society, 72*, 11–21.

Mecca, S.J., & Rubin, L.J. (1999). Definitional research on African American students and sexual harassment. *Psychology of Women Quarterly, 23*, 813–817.

Mednick, M.T.S. (1978). Now we are four: What should we be when we grow up? *Psychology of Women Quarterly, 3*, 123–138.

Mednick, M.T.S. (1989). On the politics of psychological constructs: Stop the bandwagon, I want to get off. *American Psychologist, 44*, 1118–1123.

Mednick, M.T.S., & Tangri, S.S. (Eds.). (1972). New perspectives on women [Special issue]. *Journal of Social Issues, 28*(2).

Mednick, M.T.S., & Urbanski, L.L. (1991). The origins and activities of APA's Division of the Psychology of Women. *Psychology of Women Quarterly, 15,* 651–663.

Meltzoff, J., & Kornreich, M. (1970). *Research in psychotherapy.* New York: Atherton.

Men's Health. (1998). *Men's Health/CNN National Men's Health Week survey–1998.* Men's Health Magazine.

Merck Research Laboratories. (1992). *The Merck manual of diagnosis and therapy* (16th ed.). Rahway, NJ: Merck.

Meritor Savings Bank v. Vinson, 477 U.S. 57 (1986).

Merrick, E. (1999). "Like chewing gravel": On the experience of analyzing qualitative research findings using a feminist epistemology. *Psychology of Women Quarterly, 23,* 47–57.

Messick, S. (1995). Validity of psychological assessment: Validation of inferences from persons' responses and performances as scientific inquiry into score meaning. *American Psychologist, 50*(9), 741–749,

Metts, S. (1997). Introduction. *Personal Relationships, 4,* 201–202.

Meyer, I.H. (1995). Minority stress and mental health in gay men. *Journal of Health and Social Behavior, 36,* 38–56.

Meyer, S., & Schwitzer, A.M. (1999). Stages of identity development among college students with minority sexual orientations. *Journal of College Student Psychotherapy, 13*(4), 41–65.

Meyer-Bahlburg, H.F.L. (1977). Sex hormones and male homosexuality in comparative perspective. *Archives of Sexual Behavior, 6,* 297–325.

Meyer-Bahlburg, H.F.L. (1979). Sex hormones and female homosexuality: A critical examination. *Archives of Sexual Behavior, 8,* 101–119.

Meyer-Bahlburg, H.F.L. (1984). Psychoendocrine research on sexual orientation: Current status and future options. *Progress in Brain Research, 61,* 375–398.

Meyer-Bahlburg, H.F.L. (1999). Gender assignment and reassignment in 46,XY pseudohermaphroditism and related conditions. *Journal of Clinical Endocrinology and Megabolism, 84,* 3455–3458.

Meyer-Bahlburg, H.F.L., Dolezal, C., Baker, S.W., Carlson, A., Obeid, J., Vogiatzi, M., & New, M.I. (1999, June). *Differences in behavioral masculinization between subtypes of classical congenital adrenal hyperplasia in girls.* Poster presented at the meeting of the International Academy of Sex Research, Stony Brook, NY.

Meyer-Bahlburg, H.F.L., Gruen, R.S., New, M.I., Bell, J.J., Morishima, A., Shimshi, M., Bueno, Y., Vargas, I., & Baker, S.W. (1996). Gender change from female to male in classical congenital adrenal hyperplasia. *Hormones and Behavior, 30,* 319–332.

Meyerowitz, B.E., & Hart, S. (1995). Women and cancer: Have assumptions about women limited our research agenda? In A.L. Stanton & S.J. Gallant (Eds.), *Psychology of women's health: Progress and challenges in research and applications* (pp. 51–84). Washington, DC: American Psychological Association.

Micceri, T. (1989). The unicorn, the normal curve, and other improbably creatures. *Psychological Bulletin, 105,* 156–166.

Middlebrook, D. (1998). *Suits me: The double life of Billy Tipton.* Boston: Houghton Mifflin.

Midgley, A. (1997). We respected our elders. In M. Miedzian & A. Malinovich (Eds.), *Generations: A century of women speak about their lives* (pp. 29–30). New York: Atlantic Monthly Press.

Miedzian, M., & Malinovich, A. (1997). *Generations: A century of women speak about their lives.* New York: Atlantic Monthly Press.

Migeon, C.J., & Wisniewski, A.B. (1998). Sexual differentiation: From genes to gender. *Hormone Research, 50,* 245–251.

Mikula, G., Petri, B., & Tanzer, N. (1990). What people regard as unjust: Types and structures of everyday experiences of injustice. *European Journal of Social Psychology, 20,* 133–149.

Miles, S.H., & August, A. (1990). Courts, gender and the "right to die." *Law, Medicine, and Health Care, 18,* 85–95.

Milkie, M.A., & Peltol, P. (1999). Playing all the roles: Gender and work-family balancing act. *Journal of Marriage and the Family, 61,* 467–490.

Miller, A. (1984). A transitional phase in gender constancy and its relationship to cognitive level and sex identification. *Child Study Journal, 13,* 259–275.

Miller, C. (1983). Developmental changes in male/female voice classification by infants. *Infant Behavior and Development, 6,* 313–330.

Miller, J. (1987). *Democracy is in the streets: From Port Huron to the seize of Chicago.* New York: Simon & Schuster.

Miller, J. (1998). The enemy inside: An exploration of the defensive processes of introjecting and identifying with the aggressor. *Psychodynamic Counselling, 4*(1), 55–70.

Miller, J.B. (1976). *Toward a new psychology of women.* Boston: Beacon Press.

Miller, J.B., & Stiver, I.P. (1997). *The healing connection: How women form relationships in therapy and in life.* Boston: Beacon Press.

Miller, M., Moen, P., & Dempster-McClain, D. (1991). Motherhood, multiple roles, and maternal well-being: Women of the 1950s. *Gender and Society, 5,* 565–582.

Miller, S.M. (1975). Effects of maternal employment on sex role perception, interests, and self-esteem in kindergarten girls. *Developmental Psychology, 11,* 405–406.

Mills, C.S., & Granoff, B.J. (1992). Date and acquaintance rape among a sample of college students. *Social Work, 37,* 504–509.

Milton, M., & Coyle, A. (1998). Psychotherapy with lesbian and gay clients. *Psychologist, 11,* 73–76.

Mindel, C.H., Habenstein, R.W., & Wright, R., Jr. (Eds.). (1988a). *Ethnic families in America: Patterns and variations.* New York: Elsevier.

Mindel, C.H., Habenstein, R.W., & Wright, R., Jr. (1988b). Family lifestyles of America's ethnic minorities: An introduction. In C.H. Mindel, R.W. Habenstein, & R. Wright Jr. (Eds.), *Ethnic families in America: Patterns and variations* (pp. 1–14). New York: Elsevier.

Mink, G. (1998). The lady and the trap. *Feminist Studies, 24,* 55–64.

Mintz, L.B., & O'Neill, J.M. (1990). Gender roles, sex, and the process of' psychotherapy: Many questions and few answers. *Journal of Counseling and Development, 68,* 381–387.

Mischel, W. (1966). A social-learning view of sex differences in behavior. In E.E. Maccoby (Ed.), *The development of sex differences* (pp. 56–81). Stanford, CA: Stanford University Press.

Mischel, W. (1979). On the interface of cognition and personality: Beyond the person-situation debate. *American Psychologist, 34,* 740–754.

Mishara, B.L. (1999). Synthesis of research and evidence on factors affecting the desire of terminally ill or seriously chronically ill persons to hasten death. *Omega: Journal of Death and Dying, 39,* 1–70.

Mishler, E.G. (1990). Validation in inquiry-guided research: The role of examples in narrative studies. *Harvard Educational Review, 60,* 415–441.

Mitchell, J.N., & Zucker, K.J. (1991, August). *The Recalled Childhood Gender Identity Scale: Psychometric properties.* Poster presented at the meeting of the International Academy of Sex Research, Barrie, Canada.

Mizrahi, K., & Rabinowitz, V.C. (1996, September 19–21). *NIH Policy for testing sex differences: Implications for women's health.* Poster presented at the conference on psychological and behavioral factors in women's health: Research, prevention, treatment, and service delivery in clinical and community settings, American Psychological Association, Washington, DC.

Mkhonza, S. (1995). Life histories as social texts of personal experiences in sociolinguistic studies: A look at the lives of domestic workers in Swaziland. In R. Josselson & A. Lieblich (Eds.), *The narrative study of lives: Interpreting experience* (Vol. 3, pp. 173–204). Thousand Oaks, CA: Sage.

Mo, B. (1992). Modesty, sexuality, and breast health in Chinese American women. *Western Journal of Medicine, 157,* 260–264.

Mohanty, C.T. (1988). Under Western eyes: Feminist scholarship and colonial discourse. *Feminist Review, 30,* 61–88.

Mohanty, C.T., Russo, A., & Torres, L. (Eds.). (1991). *Third world women and the politics of feminism.* Bloomington: Indiana University Press.

Moir, A., & Jessel, D. (1989). *Brainsex: The real difference between men and women.* London: Mandarin/Octopus.

Mom gets jail in abuse case. (1993, January 21). *The Times Picayune,* Metro Section.

Money, J. (1955). Hermaphroditism, gender and precocity in hyperadrenocorticism: Psychologic findings. *Bulletin of the Johns Hopkins Hospital, 96,* 253–264.

Money, J. (1975). Ablatio penis: Normal male infant sex-reassigned as a gir. *Archives of Sexual Behavior, 4,* 65–71.

Money, J. (1985). The conceptual neutering of gender and the criminalization of sex. *Archives of Sexual Behavior, 14,* 279–290.

Money, J., & Ehrhardt, A.A. (1972). *Man and woman, boy and girl: The differentiation and dimorphism of gender identity from conception to maturity.* Baltimore: Johns Hopkins Press.

Money, J., Hampson, J.G., & Hampson, J.L. (1957). Imprinting and the establishment of gender role. *Archives of Neurology and Psychiatry, 77,* 333–336.

Money, J., Schwartz, M., & Lewis, V.G. (1984). Adult erotosexual status and fetal hormonal masculinization and demasculinization: 46,XX congenital virilizing adrenal hyperplasia and 46,XY androgen-insensitivity syndrome compared. *Psychoneuroendocrinology, 9,* 405–414.

Monsour, M., Harris, B., Kurzweil, N., & Beard, C. (1994). Challenges confronting cross-sex friendships: "Much ado about nothing?" *Sex Roles, 31,* 55–77.

Monteith, M.J., Zuwerink, J.R., & Devine, P.G. (1994). Prejudice and prejudice reduction: Classic challenges, contemporary approaches. In P.G. Devine, D.L. Hamilton, & T.M. Ostrom (Eds.), *Social cognition: Impact on social psychology* (pp. 323–346). San Diego, CA: Academic Press.

Montemayor, R. (1974). Children's performance in a game and their attraction to it as a function of sex-typed labels. *Child Development, 45,* 152–156.

Moore, K.L., & Barr, M.L. (1955). Smears from the oral mucosa in the detection of chromosomal sex. *Lancet, 2,* 57–58.

Moore, M., Sixsmith, J., & Knowles, K. (1996). *Children's reflections on family life.* London: Falmer Press.

Moradi, B., Tokar, D.M., Schaub, M., Jome, L.M., & Serna, G.S. (2000). Revisiting the structural validity of the Gender Role Conflict Scale. *Psychology of Men and Masculinity, 1*(1), 62–69.

Morales, E.S. (1990). Ethnic minority families and minority gays and lesbians. In F.W. Bozett & M.B. Sussman (Eds.), *Homosexuality and family relations* (pp. 217–239). New York: Harrington Park Press.

Morawski, J. (1988). Impossible experiments and practical constructions: The social bases of psychologists' work. In J. Morawski (Ed.), *The rise of experimentation in American psychology* (pp. 72–93). New Haven, CT: Yale University Press.

Morawski, J. (1994). *Practicing feminisms, reconstructing psychology: Notes on a liminal science.* Ann Arbor: University of Michigan Press.

Morawski, J. (1997). The science behind feminist research methods. *Journal of Social Issues, 53,* 667–682.

Morawski, J.G., & Agronick, G. (1991). A restive legacy: The history of feminist work in experimental and cognitive psychology. *Psychology of Women Quarterly, 15,* 567–579.

Morell, C. (2000). Saying no: Women's experiences with reproductive refusal. *Feminism and Psychology, 20,* 313–322.

Morell, C.M. (1994). *Unwomanly conduct: The challenges of intentional childlessness.* New York: Routledge.

Morgan, D.L. (1997). *Focus groups as qualitative research* (2nd ed.). Thousand oaks, CA: Sage.

Morgan, M. (1999). Discourse, health and illness. In M. Murray & K. Chamberlain (Eds.), *Qualitative health psychology: Theories and methods* (pp. 64–97). London: Sage.

Morgan, R. (1970). *Sisterhood is powerful.* New York: Random House.

Morin, S.F. (1977). Heterosexual bias in psychological research on lesbianism and male homosexuality. *American Psychologist, 32,* 629–637.

Morin, S.F., & Rothblum, E.D. (1991). Removing the stigma: Fifteen years of progress. *American Psychologist, 46,* 947–949.

Moritz, S.E., & Watson, C.B. (1998). Levels of analysis issues in group psychology: Using efficacy as an example of a multilevel model. *Group Dynamics: Theory, Research, and Practice, 4,* 285–298.

Morris, A.D. (1984). *The origins of the civil rights movement: Black communities organizing for change.* New York: Free Press.

Morris, J. (1974). *Conundrum.* New York: Harcourt Brace Jovanovich.

Morrison, T. (1992a). *Playing in the dark: Whiteness and the literary imagination.* Cambridge, MA: Harvard University Press.

Morrison, T. (Ed.). (1992b). *Race-ing justice, en-gendering power: Essays on Anita Hill, Clarence Thomas, and the construction of social reality.* New York: Pantheon Books.

Moscovici, S. (1988). Notes towards a description of social representations. *European Journal of Social Psychology, 18,* 211–250.

Mulac, A. (1989). Men's and women's talk in same-gender and mixed-gender dyads: Power or polemic? *Journal of Language and Social Psychology, 8,* 249–270.

Mulaikal, R.M., Migeon, C.J., & Rock, J.A. (1987). Fertility rates in female patients with congenital adrenal hyperplasia due to 21-hydroxylase deficiency. *New England Journal of Medicine, 316,* 178–182.

Mulkay, M. (1988). *On humor.* New York: Basil Blackwell.

Munn, P. (1991). Mothering more than one child. In A. Phoenix, A. Woollett, & E. Lloyd (Eds.), *Motherhood: Meanings, practices and ideologies.* London: Sage.

Muñoz, V. (1995). *"Where something catches": Work, love, and identity in youth.* Albany: State University of New York Press.

Muñoz, V. (1997). The passion that absorbs you: Latina/Latino identity development through community development. *Education and Urban Society, 30*(1), 41–57.

Muram, D., Miller, K., & Cutler, A. (1992). Sexual assault of the elderly victim. *Journal of Interpersonal Violence, 7,* 70–76.

Murphy, M.L. (1997). The elusive bisexual: Social categorization and lexico-semantic change. In A. Livia & K. Hall (Eds.), *Queerly phrased: Language, gender, and sexuality* (pp. 35–57). Oxford, England: Oxford University Press.

Murray, S.B. (1988). The unhappy marriage of theory and practice: An analysis of a battered women's shelter. *NWSA Journal, 1,* 75–92.

Murrell, A.J. (1996). Sexual harassment and women of color. In M.S. Stockdale (Ed.), *Sexual harassment in the workplace: Perspectives, frontiers, and response strategies* (pp. 241–271). Newbury Park, CA: Sage.

Murrell, A.J., Olson, J.E., & Frieze, I.H. (1995). Sexual harassment and gender discrimination: A longitudinal study of women managers. *Journal of Social Issues, 51,* 139–150.

Murzynski, J., & Degelman, D. (1996). Body language of women and judgments of vulnerability to sexual assault. *Journal of Applied Social Psychology, 26,* 1617–1626.

Musick, J.S. (1993). *Young, poor, and pregnant.* New Haven, CT: Yale University Press.

Nadelman, L. (1974). Sex identity in American children: Memory, knowledge and preference tests. *Developmental Psychology, 10,* 413–417.

Nagata, D.K. (1999). Expanding the internment narrative: Multiple layers of Japanese American women's experiences. In M. Romero & A.J. Stewart (Eds.), *Women's untold stories: Breaking silence, talking back, voicing complexity* (pp. 71–82). New York: Routledge.

Nahmias, R., & Froehlich, J. (1993). Women's mental health: Implications for occupational therapy. *American Journal of Occupational Therapy, 47,* 35–41.

Naifeh, J., & Smith, G.W. (1984). *Why can't men open up?* New York: Warner.

Nataf, Z.I. (1996). *Lesbians talk transgender.* London: Scarlett Press.

National Alliance for Caregiving/AARP. (1997). *Family caregiving in the U.S.: Findings from a national survey.* Washington, DC: Author.

National Center for Health Statistics. (1991). Mortality. In *Vital statistics in the U.S.* Washington, DC: U.S. Government Printing Office.

National Center for Health Statistics. (1992). *Advance report on final mortality statistics.* Hyattsville, MD: U.S. Department of Health and Human Services.

National Center for Health Statistics. (1998, October 16). Men's health, FASTATS: A to Z. Available: http://www.cdc.gov

National Public Radio. (1998, June 22). *All things considered* [Radio program]. Washington, DC: Author.

National Report on Work and Family. (1996). *News on legislation, litigation, and employer policies, 9*(21), 171.

National Report on Work and Family. (1998). *National study on the changing workforce, 11*(8), 81–83.

Neal, M.B., Ingersoll-Dayton, B., & Starrels, M.E. (1997). Gender and relationship differences in care-giving patterns and consequences among employed caregivers. *The Gerontologist, 37,* 804–816.

Neal-Barnett, A., & Smith, J. (1997). African Americans. In S. Friedman (Ed.), *Cultural issues in the treatment of anxiety* (pp. 154–174). New York: Guilford Press.

Neft, N., & Levine, A.D. (1997). *Where women stand: An international report on the status of women in 140 countries.* New York: Random House.

Neisser, U. (1994). Self-narratives: True and false. In U. Neisser & R. Fivush (Eds.), *The remembering self: Construction and accuracy in the self-narrative* (pp. 1–18). Cambridge, England: Cambridge University Press.

Nestle, J. (1983). My mother liked to fuck. In A. Snitow, C. Stansell, & S. Thompson (Eds.), *Powers of desire: The politics of sexuality* (pp. 468–470). New York: Monthly Review Press.

New, M.I., Ghizzoni, L., & Speiser, P.W. (1996). Update on congenital adrenal hyperplasia. In F. Lifshitz (Ed.), *Pediatric endocrinology* (3rd ed., pp. 305–320). New York: Marcel Dekker.

New, M.I., & Josso, N. (1988). Disorders of gonadal differentiation and congenital adrenal hyperplasia. *Endocrinology and Metabolism Clinics of North America, 17,* 339–366.

Newell-Morris, L.L., Fahrenbruch, C.E., & Sackett, G.P. (1989). Prenatal psychological stress, dermatoglyphic asymmetry and pregnancy outcome in the pigtailed macaque (*Macaca nemestrina*). *Biology of the Neonate, 56,* 61–75.

Newson, J., & Newson, E. (1968). *Four years old in an urban community.* Harmondsworth, England: Penguin.

Newson, J., & Newson, E. (1976). *Seven year olds in the home environment.* Harmondsworth, England: Penguin.

Newtson, R.L., & Keith, P.M. (1997). Single women in later life. In J.M. Coyle (Ed.), *Handbook on women and aging* (pp. 385–399). Westport, CT: Greenwood Press.

Nichols, M. (1987). Lesbian sexuality: Issues and developing theory. In Boston Lesbian Psychologies Collective (Ed.), *Lesbian psychologies.* Urbana: University of Illinois Press.

Nichols, M. (1994). Therapy with bisexual women: Working on the edge of emerging cultural and personal identities. In M.P. Mirkin (Ed.), *Women in context: Toward a feminist reconstruction of psychotherapy* (pp. 149–169). New York: Guilford Press.

Nichols, P.C. (1980). Women in their speech communities. In S. McConnell-Ginet, R. Borker, & N. Furman (Eds.), *Women and language in literature and society* (pp. 140–149). New York: Praeger.

Nichols, P.C. (1983). Linguistic options and choices for Black women in the rural South. In B. Thorne, C. Kramarae, & N. Henley (Eds.), *Language, gender and society* (pp. 54–68). Rowley, MA: Newbury House.

Nicola, J.S., & Hawkes, G.R. (1986). Marital satisfaction of dual-career couples: Does sharing increase happiness? *Journal of Social Behavior and Personality, 1*(1), 47–60.

Nicolson, P. (1998). *Post natal depression: Psychology, science and the transition to motherhood.* London: Routledge.

Niemann, Y.F., Jennings, L., Rozelle, R.M., Baxter, J.C., & Sullivan, E. (1994). Use of free responses and cluster analysis to determine stereotypes of eight groups. *Personality and Social Psychology Bulletin, 20,* 379–390.

Nisbett, R.E. (1993). Violence and U.S. regional culture. *American Psychologist, 48,* 441–449.

Niven, C. (1992). *Psychological care for families: Before, during and after birth.* Oxford, England: Butterworth-Heinemann.

Nobles, W. (1978). Toward an empirical and theoretical framework for defining Black families. *Journal of Marriage and the Family, 40,* 679–688.

Nofsinger, R. (1991). *Everyday conversation.* Newbury Park: Sage.

Nollen, N.L., & Whitley, B.E., Jr. (1998, August). *A preliminary investigation of heterosexuals' attitudes toward bisexuality.* Paper presented at the meeting of the American Psychological Association, San Francisco.

Noller, R. (1993). Communication in marriage: Different culture or differential social power. *Journal of Language and Social Psychology, 12,* 132–152.

Norton, R. (1997). *The myth of the modern homosexual: Queer history and the search for cultural unity.* London: Cassell.

Nosek, B., & Banaji, M.R. (2000). Unpublished data. New Haven, CT: Yale University.

Nur, N. (1989). The sociobiology of human mate preference: On testing evolutionary hypotheses. *Behavioral and Brain Sciences, 12,* 28–29.

Nurcombe, B., & Gallagher, R. (1986). *The clinical process in psychiatry.* New York: Cambridge University Press.

Nutt, R., & Gottlieb, N.C. (1993). Gender diversity in clinical psychology: Research, practice and training. *Clinical Psychologist, 46,* 64–73.

Oakley, A. (1979). *Becoming a mother (also called From here to maternity).* Harmondsworth, England: Penguin.

O'Barr, W., & Atkins, B. (1980). "Women's language" or "powerless language?" In S. McConnell-Ginet, R. Borker, & N. Furman (Eds.), *Women and language in literature and society* (pp. 93–110). New York: Praeger.

Obermann, Y., & Josselson, R. (1996). Matrix of tensions: A model of mothering. *Psychology of Women Quarterly, 20,* 341–359.

O'Brien, M., & Huston, A.C. (1985). Development of sex-typed play behavior in toddlers. *Developmental Psychology, 21,* 866–871.

O'Brien, S.J., & Vertinsky, P.A. (1991). Unfit survivors: Exercise as a resource for aging women. *The Gerontologist, 31,* 347–357.

O'Campo, P., Gielen, A.C., Faden, R.R., & Kass, N. (1994). Verbal abuse and physical violence among a cohort of low-income pregnant women. *Women's Health Issues, 4,* 29–37.

O'Connell, A.N., & Rotter, N.G. (1979). The influence of stimulus age and sex on person perception. *Journal of Gerontology, 34,* 220–228.

O'Connell, A.N., & Russo, N.F. (Eds.). (1983). *Models of achievement: Reflections of eminent women in psychology.* New York: Columbia University Press.

O'Connell, A.N., & Russo, N.F. (Eds.). (1991). Women's heritage in psychology: Origins, development, and future directions. *Psychology of Women Quarterly, 15*(Whole).

O'Connor, J. (1996). Dependence, independence, and interdependence. *Current Sociology, 44,* 30–47.

O'Connor, M. (1998). Gender and the definition of sexual harassment: A meta-analysis of the empirical literature. Unpublished doctoral dissertation, University of Arizona, Tucson.

O'Connor, M., Stockdale, M.S., Gutek, B.A., Melançon, R., & Geer, T. (2000). *How subjective is sexual harassment? The effects of gender, the work environment, target response, and harasser status, on psychological and legal judgments of sexual harassment.* Manuscript in preparation.

O'Donohue, W. (Ed.). (1997). *Sexual harassment: Theory, research, and treatment.* Boston: Allyn & Bacon.

Offen, K. (1996). Was Mary Wollstonecraft a feminist? A contextual re-reading of *A Vindication of the Rights of Woman, 1792–1992.* In U. Parameswaran (Ed.), *Quilting a new canon: Stitching women's words* (pp. 3–24). Toronto, Canada: Sister Vision.

Ogbu, J. (1981). Origins of human competence: A cultural ecological perspective. *Child Development, 52,* 413–429.

Ogbu, J. (1989a). Class stratification, racial stratification, and schooling. In L. Weiss (Ed.), *Class, race, and gender in American education* (pp. 163–182). Albany: State University of New York Press.

Ogbu, J. (1989b). The individual in collective adaptation: A framework for focusing on academic underperformance and dropping out among involuntary minorities. In L. Weis, E. Farrar, & H.G. Petrie (Eds.), *Dropouts from school: Issues, dilemmas, and solutions.* Albany: State University of New York Press.

Oguntokun, R. (1998). A lesson in the seductive power of sameness: Representing Black African refugee women. *Feminism and Psychology, 8,* 525–529.

Ogur, B. (1986). Long day's journey into night: Women and prescription drug abuse. *Women and Health, 11*(1), 99–115.

O'Hare, E.A., & O'Donohue, W. (1998). Sexual harassment: Identifying risk factors. *Archives of Sexual Behavior, 27,* 561–580.

O'Heron, C.A., & Orlofsky, J.L. (1990). Stereotypic and nonstereotypic sex role trait and behavior orientations, gender identity, and psychological adjustment. *Journal of Personality and Social Psychology, 58,* 134–143.

Ohlson, E., & Wilson, M. (1974). Differentiating female homosexuals from female heterosexuals by the use of the MMPI. *Journal of Sex Research, 10*(4), 308–315.

Ohye, B., & Daniel, J.H. (1999). The "other" adolescent girls: Who are they? In N. Johnson, M. Roberts, & J. Worell (Eds.), *Beyond appearance: A new look at adolescent girls.* Washington, DC: American Psychological Association.

Okazake, S. (1998). Psychological assessment of Asian Americans: Research agenda for cultural competency. *Journal of Personality Assessment, 70,* 54–70.

O'Keefe, E.S., & Hyde, J.S. (1983). The development of occupational sex-role stereotypes: The effects of gender stability and age. *Sex Roles, 9,* 481–492.

O'Keeffe, N.K., Brockopp, K., & Chew, E. (1986). Teen dating violence. *Social Work, 31,* 465–468.

Okin, S.M. (1989). *Justice, gender, and the family.* New York: Basic Books.

Okun, B.F. (1987). *Effective helping in interviewing and counseling techniques.* Pacific Grove, CA: Brooks/Cole.

O'Leary, V.E., & Donoghue, J.M. (1978). Latitudes of masculinity: Reactions to sex-role deviance in men. *Journal of Social Issues, 34,* 17–28.

Oliver, M.B., & Hyde, J.S. (1993). Gender differences in sexuality: A meta-analysis. *Psychological Bulletin, 114,* 29–51.

Ollier, W., & Symmons, D.P.M. (1992). *Autoimmunity.* Oxford, England: BIOS Scientific.

Olweus, D. (1993). Victimization by peers: Antecedents and long-term outcomes. In K.H. Rubin & J.B. Asendorpf (Eds.), *Social withdrawal, inhibition, and shyness in childhood* (pp. 315–341). Hillsdale, NJ: Erlbaum.

Omatsu, G. (1993). The "four prisons" and the movements of liberation: Asian American activism from the 1960s to the 1990s. In K. Aguilar-San Juan (Ed.), *The state of Asian America: Activism and resistance in the 1990s* (pp. 19–69). Boston: South End Press.

Oncale v. Sundowner Offshore Services, Inc., 118 S.Ct. 998 (1998).

O'Neil, J.M. (1981). Male sex role conflicts, sexism, and masculinity: Psychological implications for men, women, and the counseling psychologist. *Counseling Psychologist, 9*(2), 61–79.

O'Neil, J.M., Good, G.E., & Holmes, S. (1995). Fifteen years of theory and research on men's gender role conflict: New paradigms for empirical research. In R.F. Levant & W.S. Pollack (Eds.), *A new psychology of men* (pp. 164–206). New York: Basic Books.

O'Neil, J.M., Helms, B.J., Gable, R.K., David, L., & Wrightsman, L.S. (1986). Gender role conflict scale: College men's fear of femininity. *Sex Roles, 14,* 335–350.

Ong, B.N. (1985). Understanding child abuse: Ideologies of motherhood. *Women's Studies International Forum, 8,* 411–419.

Orenstein, P. (1994). *Schoolgirls: Young women, self-esteem and the confidence gap.* New York: Doubleday.

Ormel, J., Kempen, G.I.J.M., Deeg, D.J.H., Brilman, E.I., van Sonderen, E., & Relyveld, J. (1998). Functioning, well-being, and health perception in middle-aged and older people: Comparing the effects of depressive symptoms and chronic medical conditions. *Journal of the American Geriatric Society, 46,* 39–48.

Ortner, S. (1996). *Making gender: The politics and erotics of culture.* Boston: Beacon Press.

Ory, M.G., & Warner, H.R. (1990). Introduction: Gender, health, and aging: Not just a women's issue. In M.G. Ory & H.R. Warner (Eds.), *Gender, health, and longevity* (pp. xxiii–xxix). New York: Springer.

Osgood, N.J., & Eisenhandler, S.A. (1995). By her own hand: The acquiescent suicide of older women. In S.S. Canetto & D. Lester (Eds.), *Women and suicidal behavior* (pp. 205–214). New York: Springer.

Osgood, N.J., & Malkin, M.J. (1997). Suicidal behavior in middle-aged and older women. In J.M. Coyle (Ed.), *Handbook on women and aging* (pp. 191–209). Westport, CT: Greenwood Press.

Ozer, E.M. (1995). The impact of childcare responsibility and self-efficacy on the psychological health of professional working mothers. *Psychology of Women Quarterly, 19,* 315–335.

Paetzold, R.L., & O'Leary-Kelly, A. (1996). The implications of U.S. Supreme Court and Circuit Court decisions for hostile environment sexual harassment cases. In M.S. Stockdale (Ed.), *Sexual harassment in the workplace* (pp. 85–104). Thousand Oaks, CA: Sage.

Pamuk, E., Makuc, D., Heck, K., Reuben, C., & Lochner, K. (1998). *Socioeconomic status and health chartbook: Health, United States.* Hyattsville, MD: National Center for Health Statistics.

Pang, S. (1997). Congenital adrenal hyperplasia. *Endocrinology and Metabolism Clinics of North America, 26,* 853–891.

Pang, S., Pollack, M.S., Loo, M., Green, O., Nussbaum, R., Clayton, G., Dupont, B., & New, M.I. (1985). Pitfalls of prenatal diagnosis of 21-hydroxylase deficiency congenital adrenal hyperplasia. *Journal of Clinical Endocrinology and Metabolism, 61,* 89–97.

Papalia, D.E., & Tennent, S.S. (1975). Vocational aspirations in preschoolers: A manifestation of early sex role stereotyping. *Sex Roles, 1,* 197–199.

Pardo, M. (1997). Mexican American women grassroots activists: "Mothers of East Los Angeles." In F.C. Garcia (Ed.), *Purusing power: Latinos and the political system* (pp. 151–168). Notre Dame, IN: University of Notre Dame Press.

Pardo, M. (1998). Creating community: Mexican American women in eastside Los Angeles. In N.A. Naples (Ed.), *Community activism and feminist politics: Organizing across race, class, and gender* (pp. 275–300). New York: Routledge.

Parker, I. (1997). Discursive psychology. In D. Fox & I. Prilleltensky (Eds.), *Critical psychology: An introduction* (pp. 284–298). London: Sage.

Parker, I., & Burman, E. (1993). Against discursive imperialism, empiricism, and constructionism: Thirty-two problems with discourse analysis. In E. Burman & I. Parker (Eds.), *Discourse analysis research: Repertoires and readings of texts in action* (pp. 155–172). London: Routledge.

Parker, L. (1998). The unequal bargain: Power issues in couples therapy. *Journal of Feminist Family Therapy, 10,* 17–37.

Parker, R. (1995). *Torn in two: The experience of maternal ambivalence.* London: Virago.

Parker, S., Nichter, M., Nichter, M., Vuckovic, N., Sims, C., & Ritenbaugh, C. (1995). Body image and weight concerns among African American and White adolescent females: Differences that make a difference. *Human Organization, 54*(2), 103–114.

Parks, C.A. (1998). Lesbian parenthood: A review of the literature. *American Journal of Orthopsychiatry, 68,* 376–389.

Parks, E.E., Carter, R.T., & Gushue, G.V. (1996). At the crossroads: Racial and womanist identity development in Black and White women. *Journal of Counseling and Development, 74,* 624–631.

Parlee, M.B. (1973). The premenstrual syndrome. *Psychological Bulletin, 80,* 454–465.

Parlee, M.B. (1979). Review essay: Psychology and women. *Signs, 5,* 121–129.

Parlee, M.B. (1981). Appropriate control groups in feminist research. *Psychology of Women Quarterly, 5,* 637–644.

Parlee, M.B. (1989, March). *The science and politics of PMS research.* Paper presented at the meeting of the Association for Women in Psychology, Newport, RI.

Parlee, M.B. (1993, June). *Contestation and consolidation in scientific discourse about premenstrual syndrome.* Paper presented at the Berkshire Conference on the History of Women, Poughkeepsie, NY.

Parsons, D. (1998, June 24). A mother's best judgment. The verdict: Michiko Kamiyama's decision to leave her 8-year-old home alone was hardly a crime. *Los Angeles Times.*

Pasco, J. (1998, June 20). Case highlights problem of children left home alone. Parenting: Mother's conviction, recently reversed on appeal, was unusual, but child v. work dilemma is not. *Los Angeles Times.*

Pastor, J., McCormick, J., & Fine, M. (1996). Makin' homes: An urban girl thing. In B.J.R. Leadbeater & N. Way (Eds.), *Urban girls: Resisting stereotypes, creating identities* (pp. 15–34). New York: New York University Press.

Patterson, C.J. (1992). Children of lesbian and gay parents. *Child Development, 63,* 1025–1042.

Patterson, C.J. (1994). Children of the lesbian baby boom: Behavioral adjustment, self-concepts and sex role identity. In B. Greene & G.M. Herek (Eds.), *Psychological perspectives on lesbian and gay issues.* London: Sage.

Patterson, C.J. (1995). Lesbian and gay parenthood. In M. Bornstein (Ed.), *Handbook of parenting: Status and social conditions of parenting* (Vol. 3, pp. 225–276). Hillsdale, NJ: Erlbaum.

Patterson, L.A., Cameron, J.E., & Lalonde, R.N. (1996). The intersection of race and gender: Examining the politics of identity in women's studies. *Canadian Journal of Behavioural Science, 28,* 229–239.

Paulsen, R. (1991). Education, social class, and participation in collective action. *Sociology of Education, 64,* 96–110.

Pauwels, A. (1998). *Women changing language.* New York: Addison Wesley Longman.

Payne, C. (1990). "Men led, but women organized": Movement participation of women in the Mississippi Delta. In G. West & R.L. Blumberg (Eds.), *Women and social protest* (pp. 156–165). New York: Oxford University Press.

Payne, S. (1990). Lay representations of breast cancer. *Psychology and Health, 5,* 1–11.

Payton, C. (1984). Who must do the hard things? *American Psychologist, 39,* 391–397.

Peacock, P. (1998). Marital rape. In R.K. Bergen (Ed.), *Issues in intimate violence* (pp. 225–235). Thousand Oaks, CA: Sage.

Pearson, P. (1997). *When she was bad: Violent women and the myth of innocence.* Newark, NJ: Penguin Putnam.

Pedersen, P., & Thomas, C.D. (1992). Prevalence and correlates of dating violence in a Canadian university sample. *Canadian Journal of Behavioural Science, 24,* 490–501.

Peel, E. (1999). Violence against lesbians and gay men: Decision-making in reporting and not reporting crime. *Feminism and Psychology, 9*(2), 161–167.

Pellegrini, A.D., & Perlmutter, J.C. (1989). Classroom contextual effects on children's play. *Developmental Psychology, 25,* 289–296.

Peplau, L.A., & Cochran, S.D. (1981). Value orientations in intimate relationships of gay men. *Journal of Homosexuality, 6,* 1–19.

Peplau, L.A., Cochran, S.D., Rook, K., & Padesky, C. (1978). Loving women: Attachment and autonomy in lesbian relationships. *Journal of Social Issues, 34*(3), 7–27.

Peplau, L.A., & Conrad, E. (1989). Beyond nonsexist research: The perils of feminist methods in psychology. *Psychology of Women Quarterly, 13,* 379–400.

Peplau, L.A., & Gordon, S.L. (1985). Women and men in love: Gender differences in close heterosexual relationships. In T.A. Roberts (Ed.), *The Lanahan readings in the psychology of women* (pp. 246–268). Baltimore: Lanahan.

Peplau, L.A., Spalding, L.R., Conley, T.D., & Veniegas, R.C. (1999). The development of sexual orientation in women. *Annual Review of Sex Research, 10,* 70–00.

Peplau, L.A., Veniegas, R.C., Taylor, P.L., & DeBro, S.C. (1999). Sociocultural perspectives on the lives of women and men. In L.A. Peplau, S.C. DeBro, R.C. Veniegas, & P.L. Taylor (Eds.), *Gender, culture, and ethnicity* (pp. 23–37). Mountain View, CA: Mayfield.

Perales, C.A., & Young, L.S. (Eds.). (1988). *Too little, too late: Dealing with the health needs of women in poverty.* New York: Harrington Park Press.

Perelle, I.B., & Ehrman, L. (1994). An international study of human handedness: The data. *Behavior Genetics, 24,* 217–227.

Perez-Foster, R. (1996). What is a multicultural perspective for psychoanalysis? In R.P. Foster, M. Moskowitz, & R. Javier (Eds.), *Reaching across boundaries of culture and class: Widening the scope of psychotherapy* (pp. 3–20). Northvale, NJ: Aronson.

Perkins, R.E. (1996). Rejecting therapy: Using our communities. In E.D. Rothblum & L.A. Bond (Eds.), *Preventing heterosexism and homophobia: Primary prevention of psychopathology* (pp. 71–83). Thousand Oaks, CA: Sage.

Perls, T.T. (1995, January). The oldest old. *Scientific American,* 70–75.

Perry, D.G., & Bussey, K. (1979). Social learning theory of sex differences: Imitation is alive and well. *Journal of Personality and Social Psychology, 37,* 1699–1712.

Perry, D.G., Perry, L.C., & Weiss, R.J. (1989). Sex differences in the consequences that children anticipate for aggression. *Developmental Psychology, 25,* 312–319.

Perry, D.G., White, A.J., & Perry, L.C. (1984). Does early sex typing result from children's attempts to match their behavior to sex role stereotypes? *Child Development, 55,* 2114–2121.

Perry, E.L., Schmidtke, J.M., & Kulik, C.T. (1998). Propensities to sexually harass: An exploration of gender differences. *Sex Roles, 38,* 443–460.

Perry, W.G., Jr. (1970). *Forms of intellectual and ethical development in the college years: A scheme.* New York: Holt, Rinehart and Winston.

Pessar, P.R. (1999). The role of gender, households, and social networks in the migration process: A review and appraisal. In C. Hirschman, P. Kasinitz, & J. DeWind (Eds.), *Handbook of international migration* (pp. 53–70). New York: Russell Sage Foundation.

Peters, J.K. (1998). *When mothers work: Loving our children without sacrificing ourselves.* Reading, MA: Perseus Books.

Peterson, B.E., & Duncan, L.E. (1999). Authoritarianism of parents and offspring: Intergenerational politics and adjustment to college. *Journal of Research in Personality, 33,* 494–513.

Peterson, B.E., & Stewart, A.J. (1990). Using personal and fictional documents to assess psychosocial development: A case study of Vera Brittain's generativity. *Psychology and Aging, 5*(3), 400–411.

Peterson, K.J. (1996). *Health care for lesbians and gay men: Confronting homophobia and heterosexism.* New York: Harrington Park Press.

Peterson, R.E., Imperato-McGinley, J., Gautier, T., & Sturla, E. (1977). Male pseudohermaphrodism due to steroid 5 alpha-reductase deficiency. *American Journal of Medicine, 62,* 170–191.

Petty, M.M., & Miles, R.H. (1976). Leader sex-role stereotyping in a female dominated work culture. *Personnel Psychology, 29,* 393–404.

Peyser, M. (1998, August 17). Battling backlash. *Newsweek,* 50–52.

Philliber, W., & Hiller, D. (1983). Relative occupational attainments of spouses and later changes in marriage and wife's work experience. *Journal of Marriage and the Family, 45,* 161–170.

Phillips, D., & Henderson, D. (1999). "Patient was hit in the face by a fist . . .": A discourse analysis of male violence against women. *American Journal of Orthopsychiatry, 69,* 116–121.

Phillips, L. (2000). *Flirting with danger: Sexuality and violence in young women's hetero-relations.* New York: New York University Press.

Phillipson, I.J. (1993). *On the shoulders of women: The feminization of psychotherapy.* New York: Guilford Press.

Phinney, J.S. (1989). Stages of ethnic identity in minority group adolescents. *Journal of Early Adolescence, 9,* 34–49.

Phinney, J.S., & Rotheram, M.J. (1989). *Children's ethnic socialization.* Newbury Park, CA: Sage.

Phoenix, A. (1991a). Mothers under twenty: Outsider and insider views. In A. Phoenix, A. Woollett, & E. Lloyd (Eds.), *Motherhood: Meanings, practices and ideologies* (pp. 86–102). London: Sage.

Phoenix, A. (1991b). *Young mothers?* Cambridge, England: Polity.

Phoenix, A. (1996). Social constructions of lone motherhood: A case of competing discourses. In E.B. Silva (Ed.), *Good enough mothering? Feminist perspectives on lone motherhood.* London: Routledge.

Phoenix, A. (1997). The place of "race" and ethnicity in the lives of children and young people. *Educational and Child Psychology, 14,* 5–24.

Phoenix, A., & Woollett, A. (1991). Motherhood: Social construction, politics and psychology. In A. Phoenix, A. Woollett, & E. Lloyd (Eds.), *Motherhood: Meanings, practices and ideologies* (pp.13–27). London: Sage.

Phoenix, A., Woollett, A., & Lloyd, E. (Eds.). (1991). *Motherhood: Meanings, practices and ideologies.* London: Sage.

Pierce, C.A., & Aguinis, H. (1997). Bridging the gap between romantic relationships and sexual harassment in organizations. *Journal of Organizational Behavior, 18,* 197–200.

Piliavin, J.A., & Martin, R.R. (1978). The effects of sex composition of groups on style of social interaction. *Sex Roles, 4,* 281–96.

Pilkington, J. (1992). "Don't try to make out that I'm nice!" The different strategies women and men use when gossiping. *Wellington Working Papers in Linguistics, 5,* 37–60.

Pilkington, N.W., & D'Augelli, A.R. (1995). Victimization of lesbian, gay and bisexual youth in community settings. *Journal of Community Psychology, 23,* 33–56.

Pill, R., & Stott, N.C. (1982). Concepts of illness causation and responsibility: Some preliminary data from a sample of working class mothers. *Social Science and Medicine, 16,* 43–52.

Pillemer, K., & Finkelhor, D. (1988). The prevalence of elder abuse: A random sample survey. *The Gerontologist, 28,* 51–57.

Pinderhughes, E. (1983). Empowerment for our clients and for ourselves. *Social Casework, 64,* 331–338.

Pinderhughes, H. (1997). *Race in the hood: Conflict and violence among urban youth.* Minneapolis: University of Minnesota Press.

Piotrkowski, C.S. (1998). Gender harassment, job satisfaction, and distress among employed white and minority women. *Journal of Occupational Health Psychology, 3,* 33–43.

Piran, N. (1995). Prevention: Can early lessons lead to a delineation of an alternative model? A critical look at prevention with schoolchildren. *Eating Disorders: The Journal of Treatment and Prevention, 3,* 28–37.

Piran, N. (1997). Prevention of eating disorders: Directions for future research. *Psychopharmacology Bulletin, 33*(3), 419–423.

Piran, N. (1999, August). *The Feminist Frame Scale.* Paper presented at the annual meeting of the American Psychological Association as part of a symposium titled: Measuring process and outcomes in short- and long-term feminist therapy, J. Worell (Chair), Boston.

Piran, N. (2001). Re-inhabiting the body from the inside out: Girls transform their school environment. In D. Tolman & M. Brydon-Miller (Eds.), *From subjects to subjectivities: A handbook of interpretive and participatory methods.* New York: New York University Press.

Pizan, C. de (1982). *The book of the city of ladies* (E.J. Richards, Trans.). New York: Persea Books. (Original work published 1405)

Pleck, J.H. (1981). *The myth of masculinity.* Boston: MIT Press.

Pleck, J.H. (1987). The contemporary man. In M. Scher, M. Stevens, G. Good, & G. Eichenfield (Eds.), *Handbook of counseling and psychotherapy with men* (pp. 16–27). Newbury Park, CA: Sage.

Pleck, J.H. (1988). Fathers and infant care leave. In E.F. Zigler & M. Frank (Eds.), *The parental leave crisis: Toward a national policy* (pp. 177–191). New Haven, CT: Yale University Press.

Pleck, J.H. (1993). Are "family supportive" employer policies relevant to men? In J.C. Hood (Ed.), *Men, work, and family* (pp. 217–237). Newbury Park, CA: Sage.

Pleck, J.H. (1995). The gender role strain paradigm: An update. In R.F. Levant & W.S. Pollack (Eds.), *A new psychology of men* (pp. 11–32). New York: Basic Books.

Pleck, J.H. (1996, June). *Paternal involvement: Levels, sources, and consequences.* Paper presented at the Co Parenting Roundtable of the Fathers and Families Roundtable, Boston.

Pleck, J.H., Sonenstein, F.L., & Ku, L.C. (1993a). Masculinity ideology: Its impact on adolescent males' heterosexual relationships. *Journal of Social Issues, 49,* 11–29.

Pleck, J.H., Sonenstein, F.L., & Ku, L.C. (1993b). Masculinity ideology and its correlates. In S. Oskamp & M. Costanzo (Eds.), *Gender issues in contemporary society* (pp. 85–110). Newbury Park, CA: Sage.

Pleck, J.H., Sonenstein, F.L., & Ku, L.C. (1994). Attitudes toward male roles among adolescent males: A discriminant validity analysis. *Sex Roles, 30,* 481–501.

Pliner, P., Chaiken, S., & Flett, G.L. (1990). Gender differences in concern with body weight and physical appearance over the life span. *Personality and Social Psychology Bulletin, 16,* 263–273.

Plitcha, S.B. (1996). Violence and abuse: Implications for women's health. In M.M. Falik & K.S. Collins (Eds.), *Women's health: The Commonwealth Fund survey* (pp. 237–272). Baltimore: Johns Hopkins University Press.

Plummer, K. (Ed.). (1981). *The making of the modern homosexual.* London: Hutchinson.

Plummer, K. (Ed.). (1992). *Modern homosexualities.* London: Routledge.

Polakow, V. (1993). *Lives on the edge: Single mothers and their children in the other America.* Chicago: University of Chicago Press.

Polier, N. (1998). True transgressions: Refusal and recolonization in the narrative of a Papuan migrant "bighead." *Feminist Studies, 24,* 511–533.

Pollack, W.S. (1995). No man is an island: Toward a new psychoanalytic psychology of men. In R.F. Levant & W.S. Pollack (Eds.), *A new psychology of men* (pp. 33–67). New York: Basic Books.

Pollack, W.S. (1998). *Real boys: Rescuing our sons from the myths of boyhood.* New York: Random House.

Pollack, W.S. (in press). "Masked men": New psychoanalytically-oriented treatment models for adult and young adult males. In G. Brooks & G. Good (Eds.), *The new handbook of psychotherapy and counseling with men.* San Francisco: Jossey-Bass.

Pollock, N.L. (1988). Sexual assault of older women. *Annals of Sex Research, 1,* 523–532.

Popay, J. (1992). "My health is all right, but I'm just tired all the time": Women's experiences of ill-health. In H. Roberts (Ed.), *Women's health matters.* London: Routledge.

Popkin, A. (1990). Social experience of bread and roses: Building a community and creating a culture. In K.V. Hansen & I.J. Philipson (Eds.), *Women, class and the feminist imagination* (pp. 182–212). Philadelphia: Temple University Press.

Popper, K.R. (1959). *The logic of scientific discovery.* New York: Basic Books.

Poran, M. (1998). *Body image, race and ethnicity.* Doctoral dissertation, Columbia University Graduate Center, New York.

Porter, M.J., Good, G.E., & Dillon, M. (1999, April). *Levels of self-disclosure of male characters on prime-time situation comedies.* Paper presented at the 1999 Joint Central States Communication Association and Southern States Communication Association Convention, St. Louis, MO.

Porter, N. (1999). Commentary: Reconstructing mountains from gravel: Remembering context in feminist research. *Psychology of Women Quarterly, 23,* 59–64.

Potter, J. (1996). *Representing reality: Discourse, rhetoric and social construction.* London: Sage.

Potter, J., & Wetherell, M. (1987). *Discourse and social psychology: Beyond attitudes and behaviour.* London: Sage.

Poulin-Dubois, D., Serbin, L.A., & Derbyshire, A. (1998). Toddlers' intermodal and verbal knowledge. *Merrill-Palmer Quarterly, 44,* 339–354.

Poulin-Dubois, D., Serbin, L.A., Eichstedt, J.A., & Sen, M.G. (2000). *Men don't put on make-up: Toddlers' knowledge of the gender stereotyping of household activities.* Manuscript in preparation.

Poulin-Dubois, D., Serbin, L.A., Kenyon, B., & Derbyshire, A. (1994). Infants' intermodal knowledge about gender. *Developmental Psychology, 30,* 436–442.

Poussiant, A. (1990). The mental health status of Black Americans. In D.S. Ruiz (Ed.), *Handbook of mental health and mental disorder among Black Americans* (pp. 97–119). New York: Greenwood Press.

Powlishta, K.K. (1994, April). *The salience of gender in person-perception.* Poster presented at the Conference on Human Development, Pittsburgh, PA.

Powlishta, K.K. (1995a). Gender bias in children's perception of personality traits. *Sex Roles, 32,* 17–28.

Powlishta, K.K. (1995b). Intergroup processes in childhood: Social categorization and sex role development. *Developmental Psychology, 31,* 781–788.

Powlishta, K.K., & Maccoby, E.E. (1990). Resource utilization in mixed-sex dyads: The influence of adult presence and task type. *Sex Roles, 29,* 723–737.

Powlishta, K.K., Serbin, L.A., Doyle, A., & White, D.C. (1994). Gender, ethnic, and body type biases: The generality of prejudice in childhood. *Developmental Psychology, 30,* 526–536.

Powlishta, K.K., Serbin, L.A., & Moller, L.C. (1993). The stability of individual differences in gender typing: Implications for understanding gender segregation. *Sex Roles, 29,* 723–737.

Pratto, F., Stallworth, L.M., Sidanius, J., & Siers, B. (1997). The gender gap in occupational role attainment: A social dominance approach. *Journal of Personality and Social Psychology, 72*(1), 37–53.

Prentice, D.A., & Miller, D.T. (1992). When small effects are impressive. *Psychological Bulletin, 112,* 160–164.

Preston, D.B. (1995). Marital status, gender roles, stress, and health in the elderly. *Health Care for Women International, 16,* 149–165.

Preston, K., & Stanley, K. (1987). "What's the worst thing . . . ?" Gender-directed insults. *Sex Roles, 17,* 209–219.

Price, S.J., & McKenry, P.C. (1988). *Divorce.* Beverly Hills, CA: Sage.

Prilleltensky, I., & Nelson, G. (1997). Community psychology: Reclaiming social justice. In D. Fox & I. Prilleltensky (Eds.), *Critical psychology: An introduction* (pp. 166–184). London: Sage.

Prilleltensky, O. (1996). Women with disabilities and feminist therapy. *Women and Therapy, 18,* 87–97.

Procter, E.K., & Davis, L.E. (1994). The challenge of racial difference: Skills for clinical practice. *Social Work, 39,* 314–321.

Prosser, J. (1998). *Second skins: The body narratives of transsexuality.* New York: Columbia University Press.

Pryor, J.B. (1987). Sexual harassment proclivities in men. *Sex Roles, 17,* 269–290.

Pryor, J.B., LaVite, C., & Stoller, L.M. (1993). A social psychological analysis of sexual harassment: The person/situation interaction. *Journal of Vocational Behavior, 2,* 68–83.

Pryor, J.B., & Stoller, L.M. (1994). Sexual cognition processes in men high in the likelihood to sexually harass. *Personality and Social Psychology Bulletin, 20,* 163–169.

Pryor, J.B., & Whalen, N.J. (1997). A typology of sexual harassment: Characteristics of harassers and the social circumstances under which sexual harassment occurs. In W. O'Donohue (Ed.), *Sexual harassment: Theory, research, and treatment* (pp. 129–151). Boston: Allyn & Bacon.

Psychology, Public Policy, and Law. (1999). 5 (3).

Purcell, D.W., Blanchard, R., & Zucker, K.J. (2000). Birth order in a contemporary sample of gay men. *Archives of Sexual Behavior, 29*, 349–356.

Purcell, P., & Stewart, L. (1990). Dick and Jane in 1989. *Sex Roles, 22*, 177–185.

Puri, J. (1997). Reading romance novels in post-colonial India. *Gender and Society, 11*(4), 434–452.

Pyke, S., & Greenglass, E. (1997). Women and organizational structures: An avenue to influence. *Newsletter of the CPA/SCP Section on Women and Psychology, 23*, 5–8.

Pyke, S., & Stark-Adamec, C. (1981). Canadian feminism and psychology: The first decade. *Canadian Psychology, 22*, 38–54.

Qazi, Q.H., & Thompson, M.W. (1972). Genital changes in congenital virilizing adrenal hyperplasia. *Journal of Pediatrics, 80*, 653–654.

Quadagno, D.M., Briscoe, R., & Quadagno, J.S. (1977). Effects of perinatal gonadal hormones on selected nonsexual behavior patterns: A critical assessment of the nonhuman and human literature. *Psychological Bulletin, 84*, 62–80.

Quinn, P.C., & Eimas, P.D. (1996). Perceptual organization and categorization in young children. In C. Rovee-Collier & L.P. Lipsitt (Eds.), *Advances in infancy research* (Vol. 10, pp. 1–36). Norwood, NJ: Ablex.

Raag, T., & Rackliff, C.L. (1998). Preschoolers' awareness of social expectations of gender: Relationships to toy choices. *Sex Roles, 38*, 685–700.

Rabinowitz, V.C., & Sechzer, J.A. (1993). Feminist perspectives on research methods. In F.L. Denmark & M.A. Paludi (Eds.), *Psychology of women: A handbook of issues and theories* (pp. 23–66). Westport, CT: Greenwood Press.

Rabinowitz, V.C., & Weseen, S. (1997). Elu(ci)d(at)ing epistemological impasses: Re-viewing the qualitative/quantitative debates in psychology. *Journal of Social Issues, 53*, 605–630.

Rabinowitz, V.C., & Weseen, S. (in press). Power, politics, and the qualitative/quantitative debates in psychology. In D.L. Tolman & M. Brydon-Miller (Eds.), *From subjects to subjectivities: A handbook of interpretive and participatory methods.* New York: New York University Press.

Radecic, P.J. (1993). *Lesbian health issues and recommendations.* Washington, DC: National Gay and Lesbian Task Force.

Radway, J. (1984). *Reading the romance: Women, patriarchy and popular literature.* Chapel Hill: University of North Carolina Press.

Rahman, Q. (1999). Psychology of human sexual orientation: What it is and why bother. *British Psychological Society Lesbian and Gay Psychology Section Newsletter, 2*, 6–10.

Raja, S. (1998). Culturally sensitive therapy for women of color. *Women and Therapy, 21*, 67–84.

Rajecki, D.W., De Graaf-Kaser, R., & Rasmussen, J.L. (1992). New impressions and more discrimination: Effects of individuation on gender-label stereotypes. *Sex Roles, 27*, 171–185.

Ralston, P.A. (1997). Midlife and older Black women. In J.M. Coyle (Ed.), *Handbook on women and aging* (pp. 273–289). Westport, CT: Greenwood Press

Ramirez de Arellano, A.B. (1996). Latino women: Health status and access to health care. In M.M. Falik & K.S. Collins (Eds.), *Women's health: The Commonwealth Fund survey* (pp. 123–144). Baltimore: Johns Hopkins University Press.

Rampage, C. (1998). Feminist couple therapy. In F.M. Dattilio (Ed.), *Case studies in couple and family therapy: Systemic and cognitive perspectives* (pp. 353–370). New York: Guilford Press.

Randall, C.E. (1989). Lesbian phobia among BSN educators: A survey. *Journal of Nursing Education, 28*, 302–306.

Randall, T. (1990). Domestic violence intervention calls for more than treating injuries. *Journal of the American Medical Association, 264*, 939–944.

Rankow, E.J. (1995). Breast and cervical cancer among lesbians. *Women's Health Issues, 5*, 123–129.

Rao, V. (1998). Wife beating in rural South India: A qualitative and econometric analysis. *Social Science and Medicine, 44*, 1169–1179.

Rapoport, R., & Rapoport, R.N. (1969). The dual-career family. *Human Relations, 22*, 3–30.

Rasmussen, J.L., & Moely, B.E. (1986). Impression formation as a function of the sex role appropriateness of linguistic behavior. *Sex Roles, 14*, 149–161.

Rave, E.J., & Larson, C.C. (1995). *Ethical decision making in therapy: Feminist perspectives.* New York: Guilford Press.

Rawlings, E.I., & Carter, D.K. (1977). *Psychotherapy for women: Treatment toward equality.* Springfield, IL: Thomas.

Ray, J. (1990). Interactional patterns and marital satisfaction among dual-career couples. *Journal of Independent Social Work, 4*(3), 61–73.

Reagan, P. (1981). The interaction of health care professionals and their lesbian clients. *Patient Counseling and Health Education, 3*, 21–25.

Reay, D. (1995). A silent majority: Mothers in parental involvement. *Women's Studies International Forum, 18,* 337–348.

Reay, D. (1996). Dealing with difficult differences: Reflexivity and social class in feminist research. *Feminism and Psychology, 6,* 443–456.

Reay, D. (1998). Classifying feminist research: Exploring the psychological impact of social class on mother's involvement in children's schooling. *Feminism and Psychology, 8,* 155–171.

Rees, K.B. (1996). A feminist therapy application of the boundary model with obese female binge eaters. *Applied and Preventive Psychology, 5,* 111–116.

Reeve, H.K., & Sherman, P.W. (1993). Adaptation and the goals of evolutionary research. *Quarterly Review of Biology, 68,* 1–31.

Reichardt, C.S., & Rallis, S.F. (Eds.) (1994a). *The qualitative/quantitative debate: New perspectives.* San-Francisco: Jossey-Bass.

Reichardt, C.S., & Rallis, S.F. (1994b). Qualitative and quantitative inquiries are not incompatible: A call for a new partnership. In C.S. Reichardt & S.F. Rallis (Eds.), *The qualitative/quantitative debate: New perspectives* (pp. 5–12). San-Francisco: Jossey-Bass.

Reid, A., & Deaux, K. (1996). Relationship between personal and social identities: Segregation or integration? *Journal of Personality and Social Psychology, 71,* 1084–1091.

Reid, P.T. (1993). Poor women in psychological research: Shut up and shut out. *Psychology of Women Quarterly, 17,* 133–150.

Reid, P.T., & Kelly, E. (1994). Research on women of color: From ignorance to awareness. *Psychology of Women Quarterly, 18,* 477–486.

Reid, P.T., & Trotter, K.H. (1993). Children's self-presentations with infants: Gender and ethnic comparisons. *Sex Roles, 29,* 171–181.

Reilly, M.E., Lott, B., & Gallogly, S.M. (1986). Sexual harassment of college students. *Sex Roles, 15,* 333–358.

Reinharz, S. (1983). Experiential analysis: A contribution to feminist research. In G. Bowles & R.D. Klein (Eds.), *Theories of women's studies* (pp. 162–191). London: Routledge & Kegan Paul.

Reinharz, S. (1992). *Feminist methods in social research.* New York: Oxford University Press.

Reis, H.T., & Wright, S. (1982). Knowledge of sex-role stereotypes in children aged 3 to 5. *Sex Roles, 8,* 1049–1056.

Reisine, S.T., Goodenow, C., & Grady, K.E. (1987). The impact of rheumatoid arthritis on the homemaker. *Social Science and Medicine, 25,* 89–95.

Reissman, C.K. (1993). *Narrative analysis.* Newbury Park, CA: Sage.

Reitz, R.R. (1999). Batterers' experiences of being violent: A phenomenological study. *Psychology of Women Quarterly, 23,* 143–165.

Remafedi, G., Farrow, J.A., & Deisher, R.W. (1991). Risk factors for attempted suicide in gay and bisexual youth. *Pediatrics, 87,* 869–875.

Remafedi, G., Resnick, M., Blum, R., & Harris, L. (1992). Demography of sexual orientation in adolescents. *Pediatrics, 89,* 714–721.

Renzetti, C.M. (1992). *Violent betrayal: Partner abuse in lesbian relationships.* Newbury Park, CA: Sage.

Renzetti, C.M. (1997). Violence in lesbian and gay relationships. In L. O'Toole & J.R. Schiffman (Eds.), *Gender violence: Interdisciplinary perspectives* (pp. 285–293). New York: New York University Press.

Renzetti, C.M., & Curran, D.J. (1995). *Women, men and society* (3rd ed.). Boston: Allyn & Bacon.

Repetti, R.L. (1984). Determinants of children's sex stereotyping: Parental sex-role traits and television viewing. *Personality and Social Psychology Bulletin, 10,* 457–468.

Resick, P.A. (1993). The psychological impact of rape. *Journal of Interpersonal Violence, 8*(2), 223–255.

Resick, P.A., & Schnicke, M.K. (1996). *Cognitive processing therapy for rape victims: A treatment manual.* Newbury Park, CA: Sage.

Reskin, B.F., & Roos, P.A. (1990). *Job queues, gender queues: Explaining women's inroads into male occupations.* Philadelphia: Temple University Press.

Reuterman, N.A., & Burcky, W.D. (1989). Dating violence in high school: A profile of the victims. *Psychology: A Journal of Human Behavior, 26,* 1–9.

Ribbens, J. (1994). *Mothers and their children: A feminist sociology of child rearing.* London: Sage.

Rice, F.P. (1984). *The adolescent: Development, relations, and culture.* Boston: Allyn & Bacon.

Rice, G., Anderson, C., Risch, N., & Ebers, G. (1999). Male homosexuality: Absence of linkage to microsatellite markers at Xq28. *Science, 284,* 665–667.

Rice, J.D., & Rice, J.K. (1973). Implications of the women's liberation movement for psychotherapy. *American Journal of Psychiatry, 130,* 1911–196.

Rice, J.K. (1994). Reconsidering research on divorce, family life cycle, and the meaning of family. *Psychology of Women Quarterly, 18,* 559–584.

Rich, A. (1977). *Of women born: Motherhood as experience and institution.* London: Virago.

Rich, A. (1983). Compulsory heterosexuality and lesbian existence. In A. Snitow, C. Stansell, & S. Thompson (Eds.), *Powers of desire: The politics of sexuality* (pp. 177–205). New York: Monthly Review Press.

Rich, A. (1989). Foreword to "Compulsory heterosexuality and lesbian existence." In L. Richardson & V. Taylor (Eds.), *Feminist frontiers II: Rethinking sex, gender, and society* (2nd ed.). New York: Random House.

Richardson, D. (1996a). Representing other feminists. *Feminism and Psychology, 6,* 192–196.

Richardson, D. (Ed.). (1996b). *Theorizing heterosexuality.* Philadelphia: Open University Press.

Richie, B. (1996). *Compelled to crime: The gender entrapment of battered Black women.* New York: Routledge.

Richman, J.A., Flaherty, J.A., & Rospenda, K.M. (1996). Perceived workplace harassment experiences and problem drinking among physicians: Broadening the stress/alienation paradigm. *Addiction, 91,* 391–403.

Ridgeway, C.L. (1981). Nonconformity, competence, and influence in groups: A test of two theories. *American Sociological Review, 46,* 333–347.

Ridgeway, C.L. (1987). Nonverbal behavior, dominance, and the basis of status in task groups. *American Sociological Review, 52,* 683–694.

Rieker, P.P., & Jankowski, M.K. (1995). Sexism and women's psychological status. In C. Willie, P. Rieker, B. Kramer, & B. Brown (Eds.), *Mental health, racism, and sexism* (pp. 27–50). New York: Taylor & Francis.

Riger, S. (1992). Epistemological debates, feminist voices: Science, social values, and the study of women. *American Psychologist, 47,* 730–740.

Riggs, D. (1993). Relationship problems and dating aggression. *Journal of Interpersonal Violence, 8,* 18–35.

Riggs, D.S., & Caulfield, M.B. (1997). Expected consequences of male violence against their female dating partners. *Journal of Interpersonal Violence, 12,* 229–240.

Rimer, B.K., & King, E. (1992). Why aren't older women getting mammograms and clinical breast exams? *Women's Health Issues, 2,* 94–101.

Rinfret-Raynor, M., & Cantin, S. (1997). Feminist therapy for battered women: An assessment. In G.K. Kantor & J.L. Jasinski (Eds.), *Out of darkness: Contemporary perspectives on family violence* (pp. 219–234). Thousand Oaks, CA: Sage.

Rix, S.E. (Ed.). (1987). *The American woman in 1987–88: A report in depth.* New York: Norton.

Robb, N.D., & Smith, B.G.N. (1996). Anorexia and bulimia nervosa (the eating disorders): Conditions of interest to the dental practitioner. *Journal of Dentistry, 24,* 7–16.

Roberts, D. (1997). Punishing drug addicts who have babies: Women of color, equality, and the right of privacy. In A. Wing (Ed.), *Critical race feminism: A reader* (pp. 127–135). New York: New York University Press.

Robin, R.W., Chester, B., Rasmussen, J.K., Jaranson, J.M., & Goldman, D. (1997). Prevalence and characteristics of trauma and posttraumatic stress disorder in a southwestern American Indian community. *American Journal of Psychiatry, 154,* 1582–1588.

Robinson, D. (1994). *Therapy with women: Empirical validation of a clinical expertise.* Unpublished doctoral dissertation, University of Kentucky, Lexington.

Robinson, D., & Worell, J. (1991). *The Therapy with Women Scale (TWS).* Unpublished manuscript, University of Kentucky, Lexington.

Robinson, S.J., & Manning, J.T. (in press). The ratio of 2nd to 4th digit length and male homosexuality. *Evolution and Human Behavior.*

Robinson, T., & Ward, J. (1991). "A belief far greater than anyone's disbelief": Cultivating resistance among African-American female adolescents. In C. Gilligan, A.G. Rogers, & D.L. Tolman (Eds.), *Women, girls and psychotherapy: Reframing resistance* (pp. 87–104). Binghamton, NY: Haworth Press.

Robinson, T.L., & Howard-Hamilton, M.F. (2000). *The convergence of race, ethnicity, and gender: Multiple identities in counseling.* Upper Saddle River, NJ: Merrill.

Rodin, J., & Ickovics, J.R. (1990). Women's health: Review and research agenda as we approach the 21st century. *American Psychologist, 45,* 1018–1034.

Rodriguez, E.M., & Ouellette, S.C. (2000). Religion and masculinity in Latino gay lives. In P. Nardi (Ed.), *Gay masculinities* (pp. 101–129). Thousand Oaks, CA: Sage.

Roediger, D.R. (1991). *The wages of whiteness.* New York: Verso.

Roediger, D.R. (1994). *Towards the abolition of whiteness.* New York: Verso.

Rogers, A., Brown, L.M., & Tappan, M. (1993). Interpreting loss of ego development in girls: Regression or resistance? In R. Josselson & A. Lieblich (Eds.), *Narrative study of lives.* Newbury Park, CA: Sage.

Rogers, L., & Walsh, J. (1982). Shortcomings of the psychomedical research of John Money and co-workers into sex differences in behavior: Social and political implications. *Sex Roles, 8,* 269–281.

Rogers, M.F., & Lott, P.B. (1997). Backlash, the matrix of domination, and Log Cabin Republicans. *Sociological Quarterly, 38,* 497–512.

Rogers, S.J. (1999). Wives' income and marital quality: Are there reciprocal effects? *Journal of Marriage and the Family, 61,* 123–132.

Rohrbaugh, J.B. (1988). Choosing children: Psychological issues in lesbian parenting. *Women and Therapy, 8,* 51–63.

Roiphe, K. (1993). *The morning after: Sex, fear, and feminism on campus.* Boston: Little, Brown.

Rollins, J. (1985). *Between women: Domestics and their employers.* Philadelphia: Temple University Press.

Romero, M. (1999). One of the family, or just the Mexican maid's daughter?: Belonging, identity, and social mobility. In M. Romero & A.J. Stewart (Eds.), *Women's untold stories: Breaking silence, talking back, voicing complexity.* New York: Routledge.

Romero, M., & Stewart, A. (Eds.). (1999a). *Outside the master narratives: Women's untold stories.* New York: Routledge.

Romero, M., & Stewart, A. (Eds.). (1999b). *Women's untold stories: Breaking silence, talking back, voicing complexity.* New York: Routledge.

Romito, P. (1997). Studying work, motherhood and women's well-being: A few notes about the construction of knowledge. *Journal of Reproductive and Infant Psychology, 15,* 209–220.

Roopnarine, J.L. (1986). Mothers' and fathers' behaviors toward the toy play of their infant sons and daughters. *Sex Roles, 14,* 59–68.

Rosario, V. (Ed.). (1997). *Science and homosexualities.* London: Routledge.

Roscoe, B., & Kelsey, T. (1986). Dating violence among high school students. *Psychology, 23,* 53–59.

Rosen, L.N., & Martin, L. (1998). Psychological effects of sexual harassment, appraisal of harassment, and organizational climate among U.S. Army soldiers. *Military Medicine, 163,* 63–67.

Rosen, R.C., & Beck, J.G. (1988). *Patterns of sexual arousal: Psychophysiological processes and clinical applications.* New York: Guilford Press.

Rosenberg, J., Perlstadt, H., & Phillips, W.R. (1993). Now that we are here: Discrimination, disparagement, and harassment at work and the experience of women lawyers. *Gender and Society, 7*(3), 415–433.

Rosenberg, R. (1982). *Beyond separate spheres: Intellectual roots of modern feminism.* New Haven, CT: Yale University Press.

Rosenberg, S., & Gara, M. (1985). The multiplicity of personal identity. *Review of Personality and Social Psychology, 6,* 87–113.

Rosenblatt, P.C., Karis, T.A., & Powell, R.D. (1995). *Multiracial couples: Black and White voices.* Thousand Oaks, CA: Sage.

Rosenfeld, P., Culbertson, A.L., Booth-Kewley, S., & Magnusson, P. (1992). *The Navy Equal Opportunity/Sexual Harassment Survey: Part I. Assessment of equal opportunity climate* (NPRDC TR 92–17). San Diego, CA: Navy Personnel Research and Development Center.

Rosenfeld, P., Newell, C.E., & Le, S. (1998). Equal opportunity climate of women and minorities in the Navy: Results from the Navy Equal Opportunity/Sexual Harassment (NEOSH) Survey. *Military Psychology, 10,* 69–85.

Rosenkrantz, P.S., Vogel, S.R., Bee, H., Broverman, I.K., & Broverman, D.M. (1968). Sex-role stereotypes and self-concepts in college students. *Journal of Consulting and Clinical Psychology, 32,* 287–295.

Rosenman, R.H., Brand, R.J., Jenkins, D., Friedman, M., Straus, R., & Wurm, M. (1975). Coronary heart disease in Western Collaborative Group study: Final follow-up experience of $8\frac{1}{2}$ years. *Journal of the American Medical Association, 233,* 872–877.

Rosenthal, N.B. (1984). Consciousness raising: From revolution to re-evaluation. *Psychology of Women Quarterly, 8,* 309–326.

Rospenda, K.M., Richman, J.A., & Nawyn, S.J. (1998). Doing power: The confluence of gender, race, and class in contrapower sexual harassment. *Gender and Society, 12,* 40–60.

Ross, M.W. (1983). *The married homosexual man: A psychological study.* Boston: Routledge & Kegan Paul.

Rossi, P.H., Wright, J.D., & Anderson, A.B. (Eds.). (1983). *Handbook of survey research.* Orlando, FL: Academic Press.

Rossiter, M.W. (1982). *Women scientists in America: Struggles and strategies till 1940.* Baltimore: Johns Hopkins University Press.

Rothbaum, F., & Tsang, B.Y-P. (1998). Lovesongs in the United States and China. *Journal of Cross-Cultural Psychology, 29,* 306–319.

Rothblum, E.D., & Bond, L.A. (Eds.). (1996). *Preventing heterosexism and homophobia.* London: Sage.

Rothblum, E.D., & Weinstock, J. (Eds.). (1996). *Lesbian friendships.* New York: New York University Press.

Rotheram-Borus, M.J., & Wyche, K.F. (1994). Ethnic differences in identity development in the United States. In S. Archer (Ed.), *Interventions for adolescent identity development* (pp. 62–83). Thousand Oaks, CA: Sage.

Rothman, B.K. (1989). *Recreating motherhood, ideology and technology in a patriarchal society.* New York: Norton.

Rowe, M. (1996). Dealing with harassment: A systems approach. In M.S. Stockdale (Ed.), *Sexual harassment in the workplace: Perspectives, frontiers, and response strategies* (pp. 241–271). Newbury Park, CA: Sage.

Rowland, R. (1987). Technology and motherhood: Reproductive choice reconsidered. *Signs: Journal of Women in Culture and Society, 12,* 512–528.

Rowland, R., & Thomas, A. (1996). Mothering sons: A crucial feminist challenge. *Feminism and Psychology, 6,* 93–99.

Rozee, P.D. (1993). Forbidden or forgiven? Rape in cross-cultural perspective. *Psychology of Women Quarterly, 17*, 499–514.

Rozee, P.D. (1996). Freedom from fear of rape: The missing link in women's freedom. In J.C. Chrisler, C. Golden, & P.D. Rozee (Eds.), *Lectures on the psychology of women* (pp. 309–324). New York: McGraw-Hill.

Rubin, G. (1984). Thinking sex: Notes for a radical theory of the politics of sexuality. In C.S. Vance (Ed.), *Pleasure and danger: Exploring female sexuality* (pp. 267–319). London: Pandora Press.

Rubin, J., Provenzano, F., & Luria, Z. (1974). The eye of the beholder: Parents' views on sex of newborns. *American Journal of Orthopsychiatry, 44*, 512–519.

Rubin, R.M. (1997). The economic status of older women. In J.M. Coyle (Ed.), *Handbook on women and aging* (pp. 75–92). Westport, CT: Greenwood Press.

Rubin, R.T., Reinish, J.M., & Haskett, R.F. (1981). Postnatal gonadal steroid effects on human behavior. *Science, 211*, 1318–1324.

Ruble, D., Fleming, A., Hackel, L., & Stangor, C. (1988). Changes in the marital relationship during the transition to first time motherhood: Effects of violated expectations concerning division of household labor. *Journal of Personality and Social Psychology, 55*, 78–87.

Ruble, D.N., & Goodnow, J.J. (1998). Social development in childhood and adulthood. In D.T. Gilbert, S.T. Fiske, & G. Lindzey (Eds.), *Handbook of social psychology* (4th ed., Vol. 1, pp. 741–787). Boston: McGraw-Hill.

Ruble, D.N., & Martin, C.L. (1998). Gender development. In W. Damon (Series Ed.) & N. Eisenberg (Ed.), *Handbook of child psychology: Vol. 3. Social, emotional, and personality development* (5th ed., pp. 933–1016). New York: Wiley.

Ruddick, S. (1989). *Maternal thinking: Toward a politics of peace.* Boston: Beacon Press.

Ruddick, S., & Daniels, P. (1977). *Working it out.* New York: Pantheon Books.

Rudman, L.A. (1998). Self-promotion as a risk factor for women: The costs and benefits of counterstereotypical impression management. *Journal of Personality and Social Psychology, 74*(3), 629–645.

Rudman, L.A. (1999). Feminized management and backlash toward agentic women: The hidden costs to women of a kinder, gentler image of middle managers. *Journal of Personality and Social Psychology, 77*, 1004–1010.

Rudman, L.A., & Borgida, E. (1995). The afterglow of construct accessibility: The behavioral consequences of priming men to view women as sexual objects. *Journal of Experimental Social Psychology, 31*, 493–517.

Rudman, L.A., Borgida, E., & Robertson, B.A. (1995). Suffering in silence: Procedural injustice versus gender socialization issues in university sexual harassment grievance procedures. *Basic and Applied Social Psychology, 17*, 519–541.

Rudman, L.A., & Glick, P. (1999). Feminized management and backlash toward agentic women: The hidden costs to women of a kinder, gentler image of middle managers. *Journal of Personality and Social Psychology, 77*, 1004–1010.

Ruggiero, K.M., & Major, B.N. (1998). Group status and attributions to discrimination: Are low- or high-status group members more likely to blame their failure on discrimination? *Personality and Social Psychology Bulletin, 24*(8), 821–837.

Ruggiero, K.M., & Taylor, D.M. (1995). Coping with discrimination: How disadvantaged group members perceive the discrimination that confronts them. *Journal of Personality and Social Psychology, 68*(5), 826–838.

Runquist, P. (1992a, May 7). Clark County: Child neglect trial for Vickie Gray delayed. *Courier Journal.*

Runquist, P. (1992b, April 9). Clark County: Friend describes affection Gray showed stepdaughter. *Courier Journal.*

Runquist, P. (1992c, April 2). Clark County: Mother, not stepfather, hurt child, defense says. *Courier Journal.*

Runquist, P. (1992d, April 7). Clark County: Wife of child abuse defendant describes her terror of him. *Courier Journal.*

Rusbult, C.E. (1980). Commitment and satisfaction in romantic associations: A test of the investment model. *Journal of Experimental Social Psychology, 16*, 172–186.

Rusbult, C.E. (1983). A longitudinal test of the investment model: The development (and deterioration) of satisfaction and commitment in heterosexual involvements. *Journal of Personality and Social Psychology, 45*, 101–117.

Rusbult, C.E., & Martz, J.M. (1995). Remaining in an abusive relationship: An investment model analysis of nonvoluntary dependence. *Personality and Social Psychology Bulletin, 21*, 558–571.

Rusbult, C.E., Martz, J.M., & Agnew, C.R. (1998). The investment model scale: Measuring commitment level, satisfaction level, quality of alternatives, and investment size. *Personal Relationships, 5*, 357–391.

Russ, C.R., & Winett, R.A. (1996). Adoption of breast self-examination among socioeconoically disadvantaged women: The importance of frequent caregiver contact. *Journal of Gender, Culture, and Health, 1*, 309–317.

Russell, D.E.H. (1990). *Rape in marriage.* Bloomington: Indiana University Press.

Russell, G.M., & Bohan, J.S. (1999a). Hearing voices: The uses of research and the politics of change. *Psychology of Women Quarterly, 23,* 403–418.

Russell, G.M., & Bohan, J.S. (1999b). Introduction: The conversation begins. In J.S. Bohan & G.M. Russell (with V. Cass, D.C. Haldeman, S. Iasenza, F. Klein, A.M. Omoto, & L. Tiefer) (Eds.), *Conversations about psychology and sexual orientation.* New York: New York University Press.

Russell, M., Lipov, E., Phillips, N., & White, B. (1989, Spring). Psychological profiles of violent and nonviolent maritally distressed couples. *Psychotherapy, 26,* 81–87.

Russell, S. (1989). From disability to handicap: An inevitable response to social constraints? *Canadian Review of Sociology and Anthropology, 26,* 276–293.

Russo, N.F. (1979). Overview: Sex roles, fertility and the motherhood mandate. *Psychology of Women Quarterly, 4,* 7–15.

Russo, N.F. (1995a). PWQ: A scientific voice in feminist psychology. *Psychology of Women Quarterly, 19,* 1–3.

Russo, N.F. (1995b). Women's mental health: A research agenda for the twenty-first century. In C. Willie, P. Rieker, B., Kramer, & B. Brown (Eds.), *Mental health, racism and sexism* (pp. 373–397). New York: Taylor & Francis.

Russo, N.F., & Dumont, A. (1997). Division 35: Origins, activities, future. In D. Dewsbury (Ed.), *A history of the divisions in the American Psychological Association* (pp. 211–237). Washington, DC: American Psychological Association.

Rutledge, R. (1997, February 22). Mother pleads not guilty in abuse. Kenosha woman accused of watching boyfriend beat son: Faces four counts. *Milwaukee Journal Sentinel.*

Ryan, J., & Sackrey, C. (1984). *Strangers in paradise: Academics from the working class.* Boston: South End Press.

Sable, M.R., & Libbus, M.K. (1998). Gender and contraception: A proposed conceptual model for research and practice. *Journal of Gender, Culture, and Health, 3,* 67–83.

Sabo, D., & Gordon, D.F. (1995). *Men's health and illness: Gender, power, and the body.* Thousand Oaks, CA: Sage.

Sacks, H. (1992). *Lectures on conversation* (G. Jefferson, Ed., 2 vols.). Oxford, England: Blackwell.

Sadik, N. (1997, Winter/Spring). What was said. *Ageing International,* 5–7.

Sadker, M., & Sadker, D. (1994). *Failing at fairness: How America's schools cheat girls.* New York: Charles Scribner's Sons.

Safir, M.P. (1986). The effects of nature or of nurture on sex differences in intellectual functioning: Israeli findings. *Sex Roles, 14,* 581–590.

Safran, C. (1976, November). What men do to women on the job. *Redbook, 149,* 217–223.

Sagrestano, L.M. (1992). The use of power and influence in a gendered world: Women and power [Special issue]. *Psychology of Women Quarterly, 16,* 439–447.

Sagrestano, L.M., Heavey, C.L., & Christensen, A. (1993). Theoretical approaches to understanding sex differences and similarities in conflict behaviors. In D.J. Canary & K. Dindia (Eds.), *Sex differences and similarities in communication* (pp. 287–302). Mahwah, NJ: Erlbaum.

Salisbury, J., Ginorio, A.B., Remick, H., & Stringer, D.M. (1986). Counseling victims of sexual harassment. *Psychotherapy, 23,* 316–324.

Saltzberg, E.A., & Chrisler, J.C. (1995). Beauty is the beast: Psychological effects of the pursuit of the perfect female body. In J. Freeman (Ed.), *Women: A feminist perspective* (5th ed., pp. 306–315). Mountain View, CA: Mayfield.

Samuel, R.S., Hausdorff, J.M., & Wei, J.Y. (1999). Congestive heart failure with preserved systolic function: Is it a woman's disease? *Women's Health Issues, 9,* 219–222.

Sanchez, L. (1994). Gender, labor allocations and the psychology of entitlement in the home. *Social Forces, 73,* 533–553.

Sanchez, L., & Kane, E.W. (1996). Women's and men's constructions of perceptions of housework fairness. *Journal of Family Issues, 17,* 385–387.

Sanday, P.R. (1981). The socio-cultural context of rape: A cross-cultural study. *Journal of Social Issues, 37,* 5–27.

Sandelowski, M. (1993). *With child in mind: Studies of the personal encounter with infertility.* Philadelphia: University of Pennsylvania Press.

Sandfort, J.D., & Hill, M.S. (1996). Assisting young, unmarried mothers to become self-sufficient: The effects of different types of early economic support. *Journal of Marriage and the Family, 58,* 311–326.

Sandler, B.R. (1991). Women faculty at work in the classroom: Or why it still hurts to be a woman in labor. *Communication Education, 40,* 6–15.

Sandler, B.R., & Hall, R.M. (1986). *The campus climate revisited: Chilly for women faculty, administrators, and graduate students.* Washington, DC: Project on the Status and Education of Women, Association of American Colleges.

Sandmaier, M. (1980). *The invisible alcoholics.* New York: McGraw-Hill.

Sang, B. (1977). Psychotherapy with lesbians: Some observations and tentative generalizations. In E.I. Rawlings & D.K. Carter (Eds.), *Psychotherapy for women: Treatment toward equality* (pp. 266–295). Springfield, IL: Thomas.

Saphira, M., & Glover, M. (1999). *National Lesbian Health Survey.* Auckland, New Zealand.

Sappington, A.A., Pharr, R., Tunstall, A., & Rickert, E. (1997). Relationships among child abuse, date abuse, and psychological problems. *Journal of Clincial Psychology, 53,* 319–329.

Satterfield, A.T., & Muehlenhard, C.L. (1997). The effects of an authority figure's flirtatiousness on women's and men's self-rated creativity. *Psychology of Women Quarterly, 21,* 395–416.

Savidge, C.J., Slade, P., Stewart, P., & Li, T.C. (1998). Women's perspectives on their experiences of chronic pelvic pain and medical care. *Journal of Health Psychology, 3,* 103–116.

Savin-Williams, R. (1994). Verbal and physical abuse as stressors in the lives of lesbian, gay male, and bisexual youths: Associations with school problems, running away, substance abuse, prostitution and suicide. *Journal of Consulting and Clinical Psychology, 62,* 261–269.

Sawyer, R.G., Pinciaro, P.J., & Jessell, J.K. (1998). Effects of coercion and verbal consent on university students' perception of date rape. *American Journal of Health Behavior, 22,* 46–53.

Sayers, S.L., Baucom, D.H., & Tierney, A.M. (1993). Sex roles, interpersonal control and depression: Who can get their way? *Journal of Research in Personality, 27,* 377–395.

Scarborough, E., & Furumoto, L. (1987). *Untold lives: The first generation of American women psychologists.* New York: Columbia University Press.

Scarr, S., & Eisenberg, M. (1993). Child care research: Issues, perspectives, and results. *Annual Review of Psychology, 44,* 613–44.

Schaie, K.W., & Willis, S.L. (1996). *Adult development and aging* (4th ed.). New York: HarperCollins.

Scharfe, E., & Bartholomew, K. (1994). Reliability and stability of adult attachment patterns. *Personal Relationships, 1,* 23–43.

Schechter, S. (1982). *Women and male violence: The visions and struggles of the battered women's movement.* Boston: South End Press.

Schegloff, E.A. (1997). Whose text? Whose context? *Discourse and Society, 8,* 165–187.

Schegloff, E.A. (1999a). Naivete vs. sophistication or discipline vs. self-indulgence: A rejoinder to Billig. *Discourse and Society, 10*(4), 577–582.

Schegloff, E.A. (1999b). Schegloff's texts as Billig's data: A critical reply. *Discourse and Society, 10*(4), 558–572.

Schellenberg, E.G., Hirt, J., & Sears, A. (1999). Attitudes towards homosexuals among students at a Canadian university. *Sex Roles, 40,* 139–152.

Scheper-Hughes, N. (1997). Lifeboat ethics: Mother love and child death in northeast Brazil. In R.N. Lancaster & M. di. Leonardo (Eds.), *The gender sexuality reader* (pp. 82–88). New York: Routledge.

Schilit, R., Lie, G., & Montagne, M. (1990). Substance use as a correlate of violence in intimate lesbian relationships. *Journal of Homosexuality, 19,* 51–65.

Schlozman, K.L., Burns, N., & Verba, S. (1994). Gender and pathways to participation: The role of resources. *Journal of Politics, 56,* 963–990.

Schmidt, D.F., & Boland, S.M. (1986). Structure of perceptions of older adults: Evidence for multiple stereotypes. *Psychology and Aging, 1,* 255–260.

Schneer, J.A., & Reitman, F. (1994). The importance of gender in mid-career: A longitudinal study of MBAs. *Journal of Organizational Behavior, 15*(3), 199–207.

Schneider, B.E. (1982). Consciousness about sexual harassment among heterosexual and lesbian women workers. *Journal of Social Issues, 38,* 75–98.

Schneider, B.E., & Gould, M. (1987). Female sexuality: Looking back into the future. In B.B. Hess & M.M. Ferree (Eds.), *Analyzing gender: A handbook of social science research.* Newbury Park, CA: Sage.

Schneider, J., & Hacker, S. (1973). Sex role imagery and the use of the generic "man" in introductory texts. *American Sociologist, 8,* 12–18.

Schneider, K.T., Swan, S., & Fitzgerald, L.F. (1997). Job-related and psychological effects of sexual harassment in the workplace: Empirical evidence from two organizations. *Journal of Applied Psychology, 82,* 401–415.

Schnitzer, P.K. (1998). He needs his father: The clinical discourse and politics of single mothering. In C. Garcia Coll, J.L. Surrey, & K. Weingarten (Eds.), *Mothering against the odds: Diverse voices of contemporary mothers* (pp. 151–172). London: Guilford Press.

Schoenberger, K. (1989, May 18). Korea's "Henyo" divers: Masters of the sea–but second class on land. *Los Angeles Times,* pp. 1, 12–13.

Schoenfeld, T.A. (1991). Biology and homosexuality [Letter]. *Science, 254,* 630.

Schone, B.S., & Weinick, R.M. (1998). Health-related behaviors and the benefits of marriage for elderly persons. *The Gerontologist, 38,* 618–627.

Schonert-Reichl, K. (1994). Gender differences in depressive symptomatology and egocentrism in adolescence. *Journal of Early Adolescence, 14*, 49–65.

Schuler, S.R., Hashemi, S.M., Riley, A.P., & Akhter, S. (1996). Credit programs, patriarchy and men's violence against women in rural Bangladesh. *Social Science Medicine, 43*, 1729–1742.

Schultz, V. (1998). Reconceptualizing sexual harassment. *Yale Law Journal, 107*, 1683–1805.

Schulz, M. (1975). The semantic derogation of women. In B. Thorne & N. Henley (Eds.), *Language and sex: Difference and dominance* (pp. 64–75). Rowley, MA: Newbury House.

Schulz, R., O'Brien, A.T., Bookwala, J., & Fleissner, K. (1995). Psychiatric and physical morbidity effects of dementia caregiving: Prevalence, correlates and causes. *The Gerontologist, 35*, 771–791.

Schuman, H., & Scott, J. (1989). Generations and collective memories. *American Sociological Review, 54*, 351–381.

Schwanberg, S.L. (1993). Attitudes towards gay men and lesbian women: Instrumentation issues. *Journal of Homosexuality, 26*, 99–136.

Schwartz, M.D. (1989). Asking the right questions: Battered wives are not all passive. *Sociological Viewpoints, 5*, 46–61.

Schwartz, P. (1994). *Peer marriage*. New York: Free Press.

Schwarz, N., Groves, R.M., & Schuman, H. (1998). Survey methods. In D.T. Gilbert, S.T. Fiske, & G. Lindzey (Eds.), *Handbook of social psychology* (4th ed., Vol. 1, pp. 143–179). Boston: McGraw-Hill.

Scott, B.A. (2000). Women and pornography: What we don't know can hurt us. In J.C. Chrisler, C. Golden, & P.D. Rozee (Eds.), *Lectures on the psychology of women* (pp. 271–287). Boston: McGraw-Hill.

Scott, J.W. (1982). The mechanization of women's work. *Scientific American, 247*, 167–185.

Scully, D. (1990). *Understanding sexual violence: A study of convicted rapists*. Boston: Unwin Hyman.

Seal, W.D., Bogart, L.M., & Ehrhardt, A.A. (1998). Small group dynamics: The utility of focus group discussions as a research method. *Group Dynamics: Theory, Research, and Practice, 2*, 253–266.

Seccombe, K., & Ishii-Kuntz, M. (1991). Perceptions of problems associated with aging: Comparisons among four older age cohorts. *The Gerontologist, 31*, 527–533.

Seccombe, K., James, D., & Walters, K.B. (1998). The social construction of the welfare mother. *Journal of Marriage and the Family, 60*, 849–865.

Sechrest, L., & Sidani, S. (1995). Quantitative and qualitative methods: Is there an alternative? *Evaluation and Program Planning, 18*, 77–87.

Secord, P. (1983). Imbalanced sex ratios: The social consequences. *Personality and Social Psychology Bulletin, 9*, 525–543.

Sedgwick, E.K. (1990). *Epistemology of the closet*. Berkeley: University of California Press.

Sedgwick, E.K. (1994). *Tendencies*. London: Routledge.

Seen, C.Y., & Radtke, H.L. (1990). Women's evaluations of and affective reactions to mainstream violent pornography. *Violence and Victims, 5*, 143–155.

Segal, E. (1996). Common medical problems in geriatric patients. In L. Carstensen, B. Edelstein, & L. Dornbrand (Eds.), *Practical handbook of clinical gerontology* (pp. 451–467). Thousand Oaks, CA: Sage.

Segal, L. (1994). *Straight sex: The politics of pleasure*. London: Virago.

Segura, D.A. (1992). Chicanos in white collar jobs: "You have to prove yourself more." *Sociological Perspectives, 35*, 163–182.

Sellers, N., Satcher, J., & Comas, R. (1999). Children's occupational aspirations: Comparisons by gender, gender role identity, and socioeconomic status. *Professional School Counseling, 2*, 314–317.

Sen, M.G., & Bauer, P.J. (2000). *Cognitive correlates of two-year-old children's differential memory for own-gender-stereotyped information*. Manuscript in preparation.

Serbin, L.A., Connor, J.M., Burchardt, C.J., & Citron, C.C. (1979). Effects of peer presence on sex-typing of children's play behavior. *Journal of Experimental Child Psychology, 27*, 303–309.

Serbin, L.A., Moller, L.C., Gulko, J., Powlishta, K.K., & Colburne, K.A. (1994). The emergence of gender segregation in toddler playgroups. In C. Leaper (Ed.), *Childhood gender segregation: Causes and consequences. New directions for child development* (Vol. 65, pp. 7–17). San Francisco: Jossey-Bass.

Serbin, L.A., Poulin-Dubois, D., Colburne, K.A., Sen, M.G., & Eichstedt, J.A. (in press). Gender stereotyping in infancy: Visual preferences for and knowledge of gender-stereotyped toys in the second year. *International Journal of Behavioral Development*.

Serbin, L.A., Powlishta, K.K., & Gulko, J. (1993). The development of sex-typing in middle childhood. *Monographs of the Society for Research in Child Development, 58*(Serial No. 232).

Serbin, L.A., & Sprafkin, C. (1982). Measurement of sex-typed play: A comparison between laboratory and naturalistic observation procedures. *Behavioral Assessment, 4*, 225–235.

Serbin, L.A., & Sprafkin, C. (1986). The salience of gender and the process of sex-typing in three- to seven-year-old children. *Child Development, 57*, 1188–1199.

Serbin, L.A., Tonick, I.J., & Sternglanz, S.H. (1977). Shaping cooperative cross-sex play. *Child Development, 48,* 924–929.

Sesan, R., & Katzman, M. (1998). Empowerment and the eating disordered client. In I.B. Seu & M.C. Heenan (Eds.), *Feminism and psychotherapy: Reflections on contemporary theories and practices* (pp. 78–95). Thousand Oaks, CA: Sage.

Seward, G.H. (1946). *Sex and the social order.* New York: McGraw-Hill.

Seward, G.H., & Clark, K.B. (1945). Race, sex, and democratic living. In G. Murphy (Ed.), *Human nature and enduring peace.* Boston: Houghton Mifflin.

Seward, J.P., & Seward, G.H. (1980). *Sex differences: Mental and temperamental.* Lexington, MA: Lexington Books.

Shadish, W.R. (1995). The quantitative/qualitative debates: "DeKuhnifying" the conceptual context. *Evaluation and Program Planning, 18,* 47–49.

Shah, S. (1993). Presenting the blue goddess: Toward a national, pan-Asian feminist agenda. In K. Aguilar-San Juan (Ed.), *The state of Asian America: Activism and resistance in the 1990s* (pp. 147–158). Boston: South End Press.

Shalit, W. (1999). *A return to modesty: Discovering the lost virtue.* New York: Free Press.

Shandler, S. (Ed.). (1999). *Ophelia speaks.* New York: Harper Perennial.

Sharp, C.E. (1997). Lesbianism and later life in an Australian sample: How does development of one affect anticipation of the other? *Journal of Gay, Lesbian and Bisexual Identity, 2*(3/4), 247–263.

Sharpe, P.A., Clark, N.M., & Janz, N.K. (1991). Differences in the impact and management of heart disease between older women and men. *Women and Health, 17*(2), 21–37.

Shaver, K. (1985). *Attribution of blame: Causality, responsibility, and blameworthiness.* New York: Springer-Verlag.

Sheahan, S.L., Coons, S.J., Seabolt, J.P., Churchill, L., & Dale, T. (1994). Sexual behavior, communication, and chlamydial infections among college women. *Health Care for Women International, 15,* 275–286.

Sheffey, S., & Tindale, R.S. (1992). Perceptions of sexual harassment in the workplace. *Journal of Applied Social Psychology, 22,* 1502–1520.

Shelly, R.R., &. Munroe, P.T. (1999). Do women engage in less task behavior than men? *Sociological Perspectives, 42,* 49–64.

Shepard, D.S. (1994). *Male gender role conflict and expression of depression.* Paper presented at the American Psychological Association, Los Angeles.

Shepard, W.O., & Hess, D.T. (1975). Attitudes in four age groups toward sex role division in adult occupations and activities. *Journal of Vocational Behavior, 6,* 27–39.

Sherif, C. (1979). Bias in psychology. In J.A. Sherman & E.T. Beck (Eds.), *The prism of sex: Essays in the sociology of knowledge* (pp. 93–133). Madison: University of Wisconsin Press.

Sherif, C. (1982). Needed concepts in the study of gender identity. *Psychology of Women Quarterly, 6,* 375–398.

Sherif, C.W. (1987). Bias in psychology. In S. Harding (Ed.), *Feminism and methodology: Social science issues* (2nd ed., pp. 37–56). Bloomington: Indiana University Press.

Sherif, M. (1962). The self and reference groups: Meeting ground of individual and group approaches. *Annals of the New York Academy of Sciences, 96,* 797–813.

Sherman, J.A. (1971). *On the psychology of women: A survey of empirical studies.* Springfield, IL: Thomas.

Sherman, J.A. (1980). Therapist attitudes and sex-role stereotyping. In A.M. Brodsky & R.T. Hare-Mustin (Eds.), *Women and psychotherapy: An assessment of research and practice* (pp. 35–66). New York: Guilford Press.

Sherman, P., & Reeve, K. (1997). Forward and backward: Alternative approaches to studying human social evolution. In L. Beitzig (Ed.), *Human nature: A critical reader* (pp. 147–158). New York: Oxford University Press.

Sherriffs, A.C., & McKee, J.P. (1957). Qualitative aspects of beliefs about men and women. *Journal of Personality, 25,* 451–464.

Sherrod, N.B., & Good, G.E. (2000). *A few good men: Exploring the development of college men's beliefs about rape.* Unpublished master's thesis, University of Missouri-Columbia.

Shidlo, A. (1994). Internalized homophobia: Conceptual and empirical issues in measurement. In B. Greene & G.M. Herek (Eds.), *Lesbian and gay psychology: Theory, research and clinical applications.* London: Sage.

Shields, C. (1994). *The stone diaries.* New York: Penguin Books.

Shields, S.A. (1975a). Functionalism, Darwinism, and the psychology of women: A study in social myth. *American Psychologist, 30,* 739–754.

Shields, S.A. (1975b). Ms. Pilgrim's progress: The contribution of Leta Stetter Hollingworth to the psychology of women. *American Psychologist, 30,* 852–857.

Shields, S.A. (1982). The variability hypothesis: The history of a biological model of sex differences in intelligence. *Signs, 7,* 769–797.

Shields, S.A., & Crowley, J.J. (1996). Appropriating questionnaires and rating scales for a feminist psychology: A multi-method approach to gender and emotion. In S. Wilkinson (Ed.), *Feminist social psychologies: International perspectives* (pp. 218–232). Buckingham, England: Open University Press.

Shields, S.A., & Koster, B.A. (1989). Emotional stereotyping of parents in child rearing manuals, 1915–1980. *Social Psychology Quarterly, 52*(1), 44–55.

Shih, M., Pittinsky, T.L., & Ambady, N. (1999). Stereotype susceptibility: Identity salience and shifts in quantitative performance. *Psychological Science, 10*(1), 80–83.

Shotland, R.L., & Craig, J.M. (1988). Can men and women differentiate between friendly and sexually interested behavior? *Social Psychology Quarterly, 51*, 66–73.

Shotland, R.L., & Goodstein, L. (1983). Just because she doesn't want to doesn't mean it's rape: An experimentally based causal model of the perception of rape in a dating situation. *Social Psychology Quarterly, 46*, 220–232.

Shotland, R.L., & Goodstein, L. (1992). Sexual precedence reduces the perceived legitimacy of sexual refusal: An examination of attributions concerning date rape and consensual sex. *Personality and Social Psychology Bulletin, 18*, 756–764.

Showalter, E. (1985). *The female malady.* New York: Viking Penguin.

Shrage, L. (1999). Do lesbian prostitutes have sex with their clients? *Sexualities, 2*(2), 259–260.

Shumaker, S.A., Brooks, M.M., Schron, E.B., Hale, C., Kellen, J.C., Inkster, M., Wimbush, F.B., Wiklund, I., & Morris, M. (1997). Gender differences in health-related quality of life among post-myocardial infarction patients: Brief report. *Women's Health: Research on Gender, Behavior, and Policy, 3*, 53–60.

Sidel, R. (1996). The enemy within: A commentary on the demonization of difference. *American Journal of Orthopsychiatry, 66*, 490–495.

Siegel, J.M., & Kuykendall, D.H. (1990). Loss, widowhood, and psychological distress among the elderly. *Journal of Consulting and Clinical Psychology, 58*, 519–524.

Siegelman, M. (1972). Adjustment of homosexual and heterosexual women. *British Journal of Psychiatry, 120*, 477–481.

Siever, M.D. (1994). Sexual orientation and gender as factors in sociocultural acquired vulnerability to body dissatisfaction and eating disorders. *Journal of Counseling and Clinical Psychology, 62*, 252–260.

Sigel, R. (1996). *Ambition and accommodation: How women view gender relations.* Chicago: University of Chicago Press.

Signorella, M.L. (1987). Gender schemata: Individual differences and context effects. In L.S. Liben & M.L. Signorella (Eds.), *Children's gender schemata* (pp.23–37). London: Jossey-Bass.

Signorella, M.L., Bigler, R.S., & Liben, L.S. (1993). Developmental differences in children's gender schemata about others: A meta-analytic review. *Developmental Review, 13*, 147–183.

Signorella, M.L., & Liben, L.S. (1984). Recall and reconstruction of gender-related pictures: Effects of attitude, task difficulty, and age. *Child Development, 55*, 393–405.

Silva, E.B. (1996). *Good enough mothering? Feminist perspectives on lone motherhood.* London: Routledge.

Silverstein, L.B. (1996). Fathering is a feminist issue. *Psychology of Women Quarterly, 20*, 3–37.

Silverstein, L.B., & Auerbach, C.F. (1999). Deconstructing the essential father. *American Psychologist, 54*, 397–407.

Silverstein, L.B., & Phares, V. (1996). Expanding the mother-child paradigm: An examination of dissertation research 1986–1994. *Psychology of Women Quarterly, 20*, 39–54.

Simon, A. (1998). The relationship between stereotypes of and attitudes toward lesbians and gays. In G.M. Herek (Ed.), *Stigma and sexual orientation.* London: Sage.

Simon, B.L. (1990). Rethinking empowerment. *Journal of Progressive Human Services, 1*, 27–37.

Simon, R.I. (1996). The credible forensic psychiatric evaluation in sexual harassment litigation. *Psychiatric Annals, 26*, 139–148.

Simoni, J.M. (1996). Confronting heterosexism in the teaching of psychology. *Teaching of Psychology, 23*(4), 220–226.

Simon-Roper, L. (1996). Victim's response cycle: A model for understanding the incestuous victim-offender relationship. *Journal of Child Sexual Abuse, 5*, 59–79.

Simpson, J.A., Campbell, B., & Berscheid, E. (1986). The association between romantic love and marriage: Kephart (1967) twice revisited. *Personality and Social Psychology Bulletin, 12*, 363–372.

Sinclair, A. (1995). Sex and the MBA. *Organization, 2*, 295–317.

Sinclair, H.C., & Bourne, L. (1998). Cycle of blame or just world: Effects of legal verdicts on gender patterns in rape-myth acceptance and victim empathy. *Psychology of Women Quarterly, 22*, 575–588.

Singh, J., & Verma, I.C. (1987). Influence of major histo (in) compatibility complex on reproduction. *American Journal of Reproductive Immunology and Microbiology, 15*, 150–152.

Six, B., & Eckes, T. (1991). A closer look at the complex structure of gender stereotypes. *Sex Roles, 24*, 57–71.

Skerrett, K. (1996). From isolation to mutuality: A feminist collaborative model of couples therapy. In M. Hill & E.D. Rothblum (Eds.), *Couples therapy: Feminist perspectives* (pp. 93–105). New York: Harrington Park Press.

Skevington, S., & Baker, D. (Eds.). (1989). *The social identity of women.* London: Sage.

Skitka, L., & Tetlock, P. (1992). Allocating scarce resources: A contingency model of distributive justice. *Journal of Experimental Social Psychology, 28,* 491–522.

Slabbekoorn, D., van Goozen, S.H.M., Sanders, G., Gooren, L.J.G., & Cohen-Kettenis, P.T. (2000). The dermatoglyphic characteristics of transsexuals: Is there evidence for an organizing effect of sex hormones? *Psychoneuroendocrinology, 25,* 365–375.

Slaby, R.G., & Frey, K.S. (1975). Development of gender constancy and selective attention to same-sex models. *Child Development, 52,* 849–856.

Slater, E. (1958). The sibs and children of homosexuals. In D.R. Smith & W.M. Davidson (Eds.), *Symposium on nuclear sex* (pp. 79–83). London: Heinemann Medical Books.

Slife, B.D., & Williams, R.N. (1997). Toward a theoretical psychology: Should a subdiscipline be formally recognized? *American Psychologist, 52,* 117–129.

Slijper, F.M.E. (1984). Androgens and gender role behaviour in girls with congenital adrenal hyperplasia (CAH). *Progress in Brain Research, 61,* 417–422.

Slijper, F.M.E., Drop, S.L.S., Molenaar, J.C., & de Muinck Keizer-Schrama, S.M.P.F. (1998). Long-term psychological evaluation of intersex children. *Archives of Sexual Behavior, 27,* 125–144.

Smith, B. (1991). Raising a resister. In C. Gilligan, A.G. Rogers, & D. Tolman (Ed.), *Women, girls and psychotherapy: Reframing resistance* (pp. 137–148). Binghamton, NY: Haworth Press.

Smith, B. (1992a, February 25). Home visits found no risk to child agency says . . . but malnutrition suspected in death of newborn. *St. Louis Post Dispatch.*

Smith, B. (1992b, February 22). State was warned of newborn's peril. *St. Louis Post Dispatch.*

Smith, B., Surrey, J.L., & Watkins, M. (1998). "Real" mothers: Adoptive mothers resisting marginalization and re-creating motherhood. In C. Garcia Coll, J.L. Surrey, & K. Weingarten (Eds.), *Mothering against the odds: Diverse voices of contemporary mothers* (pp. 194–214). New York: Guilford Press.

Smith, D. (1987). *The everyday world as problematic: A feminist sociology.* Boston: Northeastern University Press.

Smith, D., Marcus, M., Lewis, C., Fitzgibbon, M., & Schreiner, P. (1998). Eating disorders in women and men. *Annals of Behavioral Medicine, 20,* 227–232.

Smith, D.E. (1990). The biology of gender and aging. *Generations, 14,* 7–11.

Smith, E.A., Mulder, M.B., & Hill, K. (in press). Evolutionary analysis of human behaviour: Commentary on Daly and Wilson. *Animal Behaviour.*

Smith, J. (1991). Conceiving selves: A case study of changing identities during the transition to motherhood. *Journal of Language and Social Psychology, 10,* 225–243.

Smith, J., & Baltes, M.M. (1998). The role of gender in very old age: Profiles of functioning and everyday life patterns. *Psychology and Aging, 13,* 676–695.

Smith, J.A. (1999). Towards a relational self: Social engagement during pregnancy and psychological preparation for motherhood. *British Journal of Social Psychology, 38,* 409–426.

Smith, L.T. (1999). *Decolonizing methodologies: Research and indigenous peoples.* London: Zed Books.

Smith, M.D., & Self, G.D. (1980). The congruence between mothers' and daughters' sex-role attitudes: A research note. *Journal of Marriage and the Family, 42,* 105–109.

Smith, P.H., Earp, J.L., & DeVellis, R. (1995). Measuring battering: Development of the Women's Experiences with Battering (WEB) scale. *Women's Health: Research on Gender, Behavior & Piolicy, 1,* 273–288.

Smith, P.H., Edwards, G., & DeVellis, R. (1998, November). *Prevalence and health consequences of battering.* Washington, DC: American Public Health Association.

Smith, P.H., Smith, J.B., & Earp, J.L. (1999). Beyond the measurement trap: A reconstructed conceptualization and measurement of woman battering. *Psychology of Women Quarterly, 23,* 177–193.

Smith, P.H., White, J.W., & Humphrey, J.A. (1999, July). *Co-occurrence of physical and sexual victimization in the lives of women.* Paper presented at symposium on Developmental Antecedents of Violence against Women: A longitudinal approach at the 6th International Family Violence Research conference, Durham, NH.

Smith, V.L., & Clark, H.H. (1993). On the course of answering questions. *Journal of Memory and Language, 32*(1), 25–38.

Smith-Lovin, L., & Brody, C. (1989). Interruptions in group discussions: The effects of gender and group composition. *American Sociological Review, 54,* 424–435.

Smuts, B., & Smuts, R.W. (1993). Male aggression and sexual coercion of females in nonhuman primates and other mammals: Evidence and theoretical implications. *Advances in the Study of Behavior, 22,* 1–63.

Smuts, R.W. (1989). Behavior depends on context. *Behavioral and Brain Sciences, 12,* 33–34.

Snelling, S.J. (1999). Women's perspectives on feminism: A Q-methodological study. *Psychology of Women quarterly, 23*(2), 247–266.

Snodgrass, S.E. (1985). Women's intuition: The effect of subordinate role on interpersonal sensitivity. *Journal of Personality and Social Psychology, 49,* 146–155.

Snodgrass, S.E. (1992). Further effects of role versus gender on interpersonal sensitivity. *Journal of Personality and Social Psychology, 62,* 154–158.

Snowdon, C.C. (1997). The "nature" of sex differences: Myths of male and female. In P.A. Gowaty (Ed.), *Feminism and evolutionary biology: Boundaries, intersections, and frontiers* (pp. 276–293). New York: Chapman & Hall.

Snyder, C.R., & McCullough, M.R. (2000). A positive psychology field of dreams: "If you build it they will come. . . . " *Journal of Social and Clinical Psychology, 19,* 151–160.

Snyder, M., Tanke, E.D., & Berscheid, E. (1977). Social perception and interpersonal behavior: On the self-fulfilling nature of social stereotypes. *Journal of Personality and Social Psychology, 35*(9), 656–666.

Sofaer, S., & Abel, E. (1990). Older women's health and financial vulnerability: Implications of the Medicare benefit structure. *Women and Health, 16*(3/4), 47–67.

Sommer, B. (1992). Menstruation and performance. In J.T.E. Richardson (Ed.), *Cognition and the menstrual cycle* (pp. 39–66). London: Erlbaum.

Sorenson, S.B., & Siegel, J.M. (1992). Gender, ethnicity, and sexual assault: Findings from the Los Angeles epidemiological catchment area study. *Journal of Social Issues, 48,* 93–104.

Sorenson, S.B., Upchurch, D.M., & Shen, H. (1996). Violence and injury in marital arguments: Risk patterns and gender differences. *American Journal of Public Health, 86,* 35–40.

Spain, D. (1988, November). *Women's demographic past, present, and future.* Paper presented at the Radcliffe College on Women in the 21st Century, Cambridge, MA.

Sparks, E.E. (1996). Overcoming stereotypes of mothers in the African American context. In K.F. Wyche & F.J. Crosby (Eds.), *Women's ethnicities: Journeys through psychology* (pp. 67–85). Boulder CO: Westview Press.

Speer, S. (2001). Reconsidering the concept of hegemonic masculinity. *Feminism & Psychology, 11*(1), 83–111.

Spelman, E.V. (1988). *Inessential women: Problems of exclusion in feminist thought.* Boston: Beacon Press.

Spence, J.T. (1984). Masculinity, feminity, and gender-related traits: A conceptual analysis and critique of current research. In B.A. Maher & W.B. Maher (Eds.), *Progress in Experimental Research, 3,* 1–97.

Spence, J.T. (1985). Gender identification and its implications for masculinity and femininity. In T.B. Sonderegger (Ed.), *Nebraska symposium on motivation and achievement: Psychology and gender* (Vol. 32, pp. 59–95). Lincoln: University of Nebraska Press.

Spence, J.T. (1991). Do the BSRI and PAQ measure the same or different concepts? *Psychology of Women Quarterly, 15,* 141–165.

Spence, J.T. (1993). Gender-related traits and gender ideology: Evidence for a multifactorial theory. *Journal of Personality and Social Psychology, 64,* 624–635.

Spence, J.T., & Buckner, C.E. (2000). Instrumental and expressive traits, trait stereotypes, and sexist attitudes. *Psychology of Women Quarterly, 24,* 44–62.

Spence, J.T., & Hahn, E.D. (1997). The attitudes toward Women Scale and attitude change in college students. *Psychology of Women Quarterly, 21*(1), 17–34.

Spence, J.T., & Hall, S.K. (1996). Children's gender-related self-perceptions, activity preferences, and occupational stereotypes: A test of three models of gender constructs. *Sex Roles, 35,* 659–692.

Spence, J.T., & Helmreich, R.L. (1972a). The attitudes toward Women Scale: An objective instrument to measure the attitudes toward the rights and roles of women in contemporary society. *JSAS Catalog of Selected Documents in Psychology, 2*(66/67), 153.

Spence, J.T., & Helmreich, R.L. (1972b). Who likes competent women? Competence, sex-role congruence of interests, and subjects' attitudes toward women as determinants of interpersonal attraction. *Journal of Applied Social Psychology, 2*(3), 197–213.

Spence, J.T., & Helmreich, R.L. (1978). *Masculinity and femininity: The psychological dimensions, correlates, and antecedents.* Austin: University of Texas Press.

Spence, J.T., Helmreich, R.L., & Stapp, J. (1974). The personal attributes questionnaire: A measure of sex-role stereotypes and masculinity/femininity. *JSAS Catalog of Selected Documents in Psychology, 4,* 43.

Spence, J.T., Helmreich, R.L., & Stapp, J. (1975). Ratings of self and peers on sex role attributes and their relation to self-esteem and conceptions of masculinity and femininity. *Journal of Personality and Social Psychology, 32,* 29–39.

Spence, J.T., Losoff, M., & Robbins, A.S. (1991). Sexually aggressive tactics in dating relationships: Personality and attitudinal correlates. *Journal of Social and Clinical Psychology, 10,* 289–304.

Spencer, S.J., Steele, C.M., & Quinn, D.M. (1999). Stereotype threat and women's math performance. *Journal of Experimental Social Psychology, 35*(1), 4–28.

Spender, D. (1980). *Man made language.* London: Routledge & Kegan Paul.

Spivak, G.C. (1987). *In other worlds: Essays in cultural politics.* New York: Methuen.

Sprecher, S., Aron, A., Hatfield, E., Cortese, A., Potapova, E., & Levitskaya, A. (1994). Love: American style, Russian style, and Japanese style. *Personal Relationships, 1,* 349–369.

Sprecher, S., & Metts, S. (1989). Development of the Rromantic Beliefs Scale and examination of the effects of gender and gender-role orientation. *Journal of Social and Personal Relationships, 6,* 387–411.

Sprei, J.E. (1987). Group treatment of adult women incest survivors. In C.M. Brody (Ed.), *Women's therapy groups: Paradigms of feminist treatment* (pp. 198–216). New York: Springer.

Squire, C. (1989). *Significant differences: Feminism in psychology.* London: Routledge.

Stagner, R. (1986). Reminiscences about the founding of SPSSI. *Journal of Social Issues, 42,* 35–42.

Stahly, G.B. (1992). Cancer and stigma: Problems of seriously ill women. In J.C. Chrisler & D. Howard (Eds.), *New directions in feminist psychology: Practice, theory, and research* (pp. 141–153). New York: Springer.

Staines, G., & Pleck, J. (1986). Work flexibility and family life. *Journal of Occupational Behavior, 7,* 147–153.

Stake, J.E., Roades, L., Rose, S., & Ellis, L. (1994). The women's studies experience: Impetus for feminist activism. *Psychology of Women Quarterly, 18,* 17–24.

Stake, J.E., & Rose, S. (1994). The long-term impact of women's studies on students' personal lives and political activism. *Psychology of Women Quarterly, 18,* 403–412.

Stangor, C., & Ruble, D.N. (1987). Development of gender role knowledge and gender constancy. In L.S. Liben & M.L. Signorella (Eds.), *Children's gender schemata* (pp. 5–22). London: Jossey-Bass.

Stannard, U. (1977). *Mrs. man.* San Francisco: Germainbooks.

Stanton, A.L., & Dunkel-Schetter, C. (1991). *Infertility: Perspectives from stress and coping research.* New York: Plenum Press.

Stanton, A.L., & Gallant, S.J. (1995). *Psychology of women's health: Progress and challenges in research and application.* Washington, DC: American Psychological Association.

Stanton, D., & Stewart, A.J. (Eds.). (1995). *Feminisms in the academy.* Ann Arbor: University of Michigan Press.

Stanworth, M. (1987). *Reproductive technologies: Gender, motherhood and medicine.* Cambridge, England: Polity.

Stanworth, M. (1990). Birth pangs: Conceptive technologies and the threat to motherhood. In M. Hirsch & E.F. Keller (Eds.), *Conflicts in feminism* (pp. 288–304). New York: Routledge.

Staples, R., & Johnson, L.B. (1993). Black families at the crossroads. New York: Jossey-Bass.

Stark, E., & Flitcraft, A. (1988). Violence among intimates. In V.B. van Hasselt, R.L. Morrison, A.S. Bellack, & M. Herson (Eds.), *Handbook of family violence* (pp. 293–217). New York: Plenum Press.

Stark, E., & Flitcraft, A. (1996). *Women at risk: Domestic violence and women's health.* Thousand Oaks, CA: Sage.

Starrett, S.N. (1997). Gender identity: Unity through diversity. In L.L. Naylor (Ed.), *Cultural diversity in the United States* (pp. 215–228). Westport, CT: Gergin & Garvey.

Statham, A., Miller, E.M., & Mauksch, H.O. (Eds.). (1988). *The worth of women's work: A qualitative synthesis.* Albany: State University of New York Press.

Statham, A., Richardson, L., & Cook, J.A. (1991). *Gender and university teaching: A negotiated difference.* Albany: State University of New York Press.

Steele, C.M. (1997). A threat in the air: How stereotypes shape intellectual identity and performance. *American Psychologist, 52,* 613–629.

Steele, C.M., & Aronson, J. (1995). Stereotype threat and the intellectual test performance of African Americans. *Journal of Personality and Social Psychology, 69*(5), 797–811.

Stefani, G., & Dumont, T. (1995). Just a girl [Recorded by No Doubt]. On *Tragic Kindgom* [CD]. Los Angeles: Trauma Records.

Stegelin, D.A., & Frankel, J. (1993). Families of lower-income employed mothers. In J. Frankel (Ed.), *The employed mother and the family context* (pp. 115–131). New York: Springer.

Steil, J.M. (1997). *Marital equality: Its relationship to the well-being of husbands and wives.* Thousand Oaks, CA: Sage.

Steil, J.M. (1999). *Marital equality.* Thousand Oaks, CA: Sage.

Steil, J.M., & Weltman, K. (1991). Marital inequality: The importance of resources, personal attributes, and social norms on career valuing and the allocation of domestic responsibilities. *Sex Roles, 24,* 161–179.

Stein, A. (1997). *Sex and sensibility: Stories of a lesbian generation.* Berkeley: University of California Press.

Stein, E. (Ed.). (1992). *Forms of desire: Sexual orientation and the social constructionist controversy.* New York: Routledge.

Stein, J.A., Fox, S.A., & Murata, P.J. (1997). The influence of ethnicity, socioeconomic status, and psychological barriers on use of mammography. *Journal of Health and Social Behavior, 32,* 101–113.

Stein, N. (1981). *Sexual harassment of high school students: Preliminary research results.* Massachusetts Department of Education.

Stein, N. (1991). It happens here, too: Sexual harassment in the school. *Education Week, 11*(13), 32.

Stein, N. (1995). Sexual harassment in K–12 schools: The public performance of gendered violence. *Harvard Educational Review, 65,* 145–162.

Stein, N. (1999). *Classrooms and courtrooms: Facing sexual harassment in K–12 schools.* New York: Teachers College Press.

Stein, N., Marshall, N., & Tropp, L. (1993). *Secrets in public: Sexual harassment in our schools. A report on the results of the* Seventeen *magazine survey.* Wellesley, MA: Wellesley College Center for Research on Women.

Steinem, G. (1978, October). If men could menstruate: A political fantasy. *Ms, 7,* 110.

Steiner-Adair, C. (1986). The body-politic: Normal female adolescent development and the development of eating disorders. *Journal of the American Academy of Psychoanalysis, 14,* 95–114.

Steiner-Adair, C. (1990). The body politic: Normal female adolescent development and the development of eating disorders. In C. Gilligan, N. Lyons, & T. Hanmer (Eds.), *Making connections: The relational worlds of adolescent girls at Emma Willard School* (pp. 162–182). Cambridge, MA: Harvard University Press.

Steiner-Adair, C. (1991). When the body speaks: Girls, eating disorders, and psychotherapy. In C. Gilligan, A.G. Rogers, & D. Tolman (Eds.), *Women, girls and psychotherapy: Reframing resistance* (pp. 253–266). Binghamton, NY: Haworth Press.

Steingart, R.M., Packer, M., Hamm, P., Coglianese, M.E., Gersh, B., Geltman, E.M., Sollano, J., Katz, S., & Moye, L. (1991). Sex differences in the management of coronary artery disease. *New England Journal of Medicine, 325,* 226–230.

Steinitz, V., & Solomon, E. (1986). *Starting out: Class and community in the lives of working class youth.* Philadelphia: Temple University Press.

Stellman, J.M. (1988). The working environment of the working poor: An analysis based on workers' compensation claims, census data, and known risk factors. In C.A. Perales & L.S. Young (Eds.), *Too little, too late: Dealing with the health needs of women in poverty* (pp. 83–101). New York: Harrington Park Press.

Stermac, L., Du Mont, J., & Dunn, S. (1998). Violence in known-assailant sexual assaults. *Journal of Interpersonal Violence, 13,* 398–412.

Stern, M., & Karraker, K.H. (1989). Sex stereotyping of infants: A review of gender labeling studies. *Sex Roles, 20,* 501–522.

Stevens, M. (1985). Rape domain. In M. Stevens & R. Gebhardt's (Eds.), *Rape education for men curriculum guide* [Diagram 1]. Columbus: Ohio State University Rape Education and Prevention Program.

Stevens, P.E. (1992). Lesbian health care research: A review of the literature from 1970 to 1990. *Health Care for Women International, 13,* 91–120.

Stevens, P.E. (1998). The experience of lesbians of color in healthcare encounters: Narrative insights for improving access and quality. *Journal of Lesbian Studies, 2*(1), 77–94.

Stevenson, R.B., & Ellsworth, J. (1993). Dropouts and the silencing of critical voices. In L. Weis & M. Fine (Eds.), *Beyond silenced voices: Class, race, and gender in United States schools* (pp. 259–271). New York: State University of New York Press.

Stewart, A.J. (1994a). Toward a feminist strategy for studying women's lives. In C.E. Franz & A.J. Stewart (Eds.), *Women creating lives: Identities, resilience, and resistance* (pp. 11–36). Boulder, CO: Westview Press.

Stewart, A.J. (1994b). The women's movement and women's lives: Linking individual development and social events. In A. Lieblich & R. Josselson (Eds.), *Narrative study of lives: Exploring identity and gender* (Vol. 2, pp. 230–250). Thousand Oaks, CA: Sage.

Stewart, A.J., Franz, C.E., & Layton, L. (1988). The changing self: Using personal documents to study lives. *Journal of Personality, 56,* 41–74.

Stewart, A.J., & Gold-Steinberg, S. (1990). Midlife women's political consciousness. *Psychology of Women Quarterly, 14,* 543–566.

Stewart, A.J., & Healy, J.M., Jr. (1986). The role of personality development and experience in shaping political commitment: An illustrative case. *Journal of Social Issues, 42*(2), 11–31.

Stewart, A.J., & Healy, J.M., Jr. (1989). Linking individual development and social change. *American Psychologist, 44,* 30–42.

Stewart, A.J., & Maddren, K. (1997). Police officer's judgments of blame in family violence: The impact of gender and alcohol. *Sex Roles, 37,* 921–932.

Stewart, A.J., & Vandewater, E.A. (1993). The Radcliffe class of 1964: Career and family social clock projects in a transitional cohort. In K.D. Hulbert & D.T. Schuster (Eds.), *Women's lives through time* (pp. 235–258). San Francisco: Jossey-Bass.

Stewart, A.J., & Zucker, A.N. (1999). Comments on "feminist research process." *Psychology of Women Quarterly, 23,* 137–141.

Stewart, R.B. (1990). *The second child: Family transition and adjustment.* Thousand Oaks, CA: Sage.

Stillson, R.W., O'Neil, J.M., & Owen, S.V. (1991). Predictors of adult men's gender-role conflict: Race, class, unemployment, age, instrumentality-expressiveness, and personal strain. *Journal of Counseling Psychology, 38,* 458–464.

Stockdale, J.E. (1991). Sexual harassment at work. In J. Firth-Cozens & M.A. West (Eds.), *Women at work: Psychological and organizational perspectives* (pp. 54–65). Buckingham, England: Open University Press.

Stockdale, M.S. (Ed.). (1996). *Sexual harassment in the workplace: Perspectives, frontiers, and response strategies.* Newbury Park, CA: Sage.

Stockdale, M.S., & Hope, K.G. (1997). Confirmatory factory analysis of U.S. Merit Systems Protection Board's survey of sexual harassment: The fit of a three-factor model. *Journal of Vocational Behavior, 51,* 338–357.

Stockdale, M.S., & Vaux, A. (1993). What sexual harassment experiences lead respondents to acknowledge being sexually harassed? A secondary analysis of a university survey. *Journal of Vocational Behavior, 43,* 221–234.

Stockdale, M.S., Vaux, A., & Cashin, J. (1995). Acknowledging sexual harassment: A test of alternative models. *Basic and Applied Social Psychology, 17,* 469–496.

Stockdale, M.S., Visio, M., & Batra, L. (1999). The sexual harassment of men: Evidence for a broader theory of sexual harassment and sex discrimination. *Psychology, Public Policy and Law, 5,* 630–664.

Stokoe, E.H. (1998). Talking about gender: The conversational construction of gender categories in academic discourse. *Discourse and Society, 9*(2), 217–240.

Stoller, R.J. (1964). The hermaphroditic identity of hermaphrodites. *Journal of Nervous and Mental Disease, 139,* 453–457.

Stoppard, J.M., & Gunn Gruchy, C.D. (1993). Gender, context and expression of positive emotion. *Personality and Social Psychology Bulletin, 19,* 143–150.

Stoppard, J.M., & McMullen, L.M. (Eds.). (1999). Women and depression: Qualitative research approaches [Special issue]. *Canadian Psychology, 40,* 75–219.

Storer, J.H. (1992). Gender and kin role transposition as an accommodation to father-daughter incest. In T.L. Whitehead & B.V. Reid (Eds.), *Gender constructs and social issues* (pp. 70–102). Urbana: University of Illinois Press.

Strassberg, Z., Dodge, K.A., Pettit, G.S., & Bates, J.E. (1994). Spanking in the home and children's subsequent aggression toward kindergarten peers. *Development and Psychopathology, 6,* 445–461.

Straus, M.A. (1983). Ordinary violence, child abuse, and wife-beating: What do they have in common? In D. Finkelhor, R.J. Gelles, G.T. Hotaling, & M.A. Straus (Eds.), *The dark side of families: Current family violence research* (pp. 213–234). Beverly Hills, CA: Sage.

Straus, M.A. (1993). Physical assaults by wives: A major social problem. In R.J. Gelles & D.L. Loseke (Eds.), *Current controversies in domestic violence* (pp. 67–87). Newbury Park, CA: Sage.

Straus, M.A., & Gelles, R.J. (1990). *Physical violence in American families: Risk factors and adaptations to violence in 8,145 families.* New Brunswick, NJ: Transaction.

Straus, M.A., & Gelles, R.J. (1998). How violent are American families?: Estimates from the National Family Violence Resurvey and other studies. In G. Hotaling & D. Finkelhor (Eds.), *Family abuse and its consequences: New directions in research* (pp. 14–36). Newbury Park, CA: Sage.

Straus, M.A., Gelles, R., & Steinmetz, S. (Eds.). (1980). *Behind closed doors: Violence in the American family.* Garden City, NY: Anchor Press/Doubleday.

Straus, M.A., Kantor, G., & Moore, D.W. (1997). Change in cultural norms approving marital violence from 1968 to 1994. In G. Kantor & J.L. Jasinski (Eds.), *Out of darkness: Contemproary perspectives on family violence* (pp. 3–16). Thousand Oaks, CA: Sage.

Strauss, A., & Corbin, J. (1994). Grounded theory methodology: An overview. In N.K. Denzin & Y.S. Lincoln (Eds.), *Handbook of qualitative research* (pp. 273–285). Thousand Oaks, CA: Sage.

Strickland, B. (1997). Leaving the confederate closet. In B. Greene (Ed.), *Ethnic and cultural diversity among lesbians and gay men* (pp. 39–62). Thousand Oaks, CA: Sage.

Strodtbeck, F.L., & Mann, R.D. (1956). Sex role differentiation in jury deliberations. *Sociometry, 9,* 3–11.

Stryker, S. (1980). *Symbolic interactionism: A social structural version.* Menlo Park, CA: Benjamin/Cummings.

Stryker, S. (1986). Identity theory: Developments and extensions. In K. Yardley & T. Honess (Eds.), *Self and identity: Psychosocial perspectives* (pp. 89–103). London: Wiley.

Stryker, S., & Statham, A. (1985). Symbolic interaction and role theory. In G. Lindzey & E. Aronson (Eds.), *Handbook of social psychology* (3rd ed., Vol. 1, pp. 311–378). New York: Random House.

Stuart, E.P., & Campbell, J.C. (1989). Assessment of patterns of dangerousness with battered women. *Issues in Mental Health Nursing, 10,* 245–260.

Studd, M.V., & Gattiker, U. (1991). The evolutionary psychology of sexual harassment. *Etiology and Sociobiology, 12,* 249–290.

Sturgeon, N. (1997). *Ecofeminist natures: Race, gender, feminist theory, and political action.* New York: Routledge.

Sue, D.W. (1998). *Multicultural counseling competencies. Multicultural aspects of counseling series II.* Thousand Oaks, CA: Sage.

Sue, D.W. (in press). Treating Asian American men. In G. Brooks & G. Good (Eds.), *The new handbook of psychotherapy and counseling for men.* San Francisco: Jossey-Bass.

Sue, D.W., & Sue, S. (1999). *Counseling the culturally different: Theory and practice.* New York: Wiley.

Sue, S. (1999). Science, ethnicity, and bias: Where have we gone wrong? *American Psychologist, 54,* 1070–1077.

Sugarman, D.B., & Hotaling, G.T. (1989). Dating violence: Prevalence, context, and risk markers. In M.A. Pirog-Good & J.E. Stets (Eds.), *Violence in dating relationships.* New York: Praeger.

Suh, M. (1990). Lesbian battery. *Ms.: The World of Women, 1,* 48.

Surrey, J.L. (1991). The self-in-relation: A theory of women's development. In J.V. Jordan, A.G. Kaplan, J.B. Miller, I.P. Stiver, & J.L. Surrey (Eds.), *Women's growth in connection: Writings from the Stone Center* (pp. 51–66). New York: Guilford Press.

Sutkin, L.C., & Good, G.E. (1987). Therapy with men in health care settings. In M. Scher, M. Stevens, G. Good, & G.E. Eichenfield (Eds.), *Handbook of counseling and psychotherapy with men* (pp. 372–387). Newbury Park, CA: Sage.

Swaab, D.F., Gooren, L.J.G., & Hofman, M.A. (1992). Gender and sexual orientation in relation to hypothalamic structures. *Hormone Research, 38*(Suppl. 2), 51–61.

Swaab, D.F., & Hofman, M.A. (1990). An enlarged suprachiasmatic nucleus in homosexual men. *Brain Research, 537,* 141–148.

Swim, J.K., Aikin, K.J., Hall, W.S., & Hunter, B.A. (1995). Sexism and racism: Old-fashioned and modern prejudices. *Journal of Personality and Social Psychology, 68*(2), 199–214.

Swim, J.K., & Campbell, B. (2000). Sexism: Attitudes, beliefs, and behaviors. In R. Brown & S. Gaertner (Eds.), *Handbook of social psychology: Intergroup relations* (Vol. 4). Cambridge, MA: Blackwell.

Swim, J.K., & Cohen, L.L. (1997). Overt, covert, and subtle sexism: A comparison between the Attitudes toward Women and Modern Sexism Scales. *Psychology of Women Quarterly, 21,* 103–118.

Tajfel, H. (1982). Social psychology of intergroup relations. *Annual Review of Psychology, 33,* 1–39.

Tajfel, H. (1984). Intergroup relations, social myths and social justice in social psychology. In H. Tajfel (Ed.), *The social dimension: European developments in social psychology* (Vol. 2, pp. 695–715). Cambridge, England: Cambridge University Press.

Talbot, J., Bibace, R., Bokhour, B., & Bamberg, M. (1996). Affirmation and resistance of dominant discourses: The rhetorical construction of pregnancy. *Journal of Narrative and Life History, 6,* 225–251.

Tamminen, J.M. (1994). *Sexual harassment in the workplace: Managing corporate policy.* New York: Wiley.

Tangri, S.S., Burt, M., & Johnson, L. (1982). Sexual harassment at work: Three explanatory models. *Journal of Social Issues, 38,* 33–54.

Tangri, S.S., & Hayes, S.M. (1997). Theories of sexual harassment. In W. O'Donohue (Ed.), *Sexual harassment: Theory, research, and treatment* (pp. 112–128). Boston: Allyn & Bacon.

Tangri, S.S., & Jenkins, S.R. (1986). Stability and change in role innovation and life plans. *Sex Roles, 14,* 647–662.

Tangri, S.S., & Jenkins, S.R. (1997). Why expecting conflict is good. *Sex Roles, 37,* 921–932.

Tannen, D. (1990). *You just don't understand: Women and men in conversation.* New York: Morrow.

Tannen, D. (1993). *Framing in discourse.* New York: Oxford University Press.

Tannen, D. (1994). *Talking from 9 to 5: How women's and men's conversational styles: Who gets heard, who gets credit and what gets done at work:* New York: Morrow.

Tashakkori, A., & Teddlie, C. (1998). *Mixed methodology: Combining qualitative and quantitative approaches.* Thousand Oaks, CA: Sage.

Tasker, F.L., & Golombok, S. (1997). *Growing up in a lesbian family: Effects on child development.* New York: Guilford Press.

Task Force on Outcomes in Feminist Therapy. (1999, August). *Report to the executive committee of Division 35, The Psychology of Women.* Presented at the annual meeting of the American Psychological Association, Boston.

Tavris, C. (1992). *The mismeasure of woman.* New York: Simon & Schuster.

Tavris, C. (1993). The mismeasure of woman. *Feminism and Psychology, 3*(2), 149–168.

Tax, M. (1999, May 24–28). World culture war. *The Nation.*

Taylor, D.M., Ruggiero, K.M., & Louis, W.R. (1996). Personal/group discrimination discrepancy: Towards a two-factor explanation. *Canadian Journal of Behavioural Science, 28*(3), 193–202.

Taylor, J.M. (1996). Cultural stories: Latina and Portuguese daughters and mothers. In B.J.R. Leadbeater & N. Way (Eds.), *Urban girls: Resisting stereotypes, creating identities* (pp. 117–131). New York: New York University Press.

Taylor, J.M., Gilligan, C., & Sullivan, A.M. (1995). *Between voice and silence: Women and girls, race and relationship.* Cambridge, MA: Harvard University Press.

Taylor, M. (1996). The development of children's beliefs about the social and biological aspects of gender differences. *Child Development, 67,* 1555–1571.

Taylor, R.J., Jackson, J.S., & Chatters, L.M. (Eds.). (1997). *Family life in Black America.* Thousand Oaks, CA: Sage.

Taylor, S.E. (1995). *Health psychology* (3rd ed.). New York: McGraw-Hill.

Taylor, S.E., Fiske, S.T., Etcoff, N.L., & Ruderman, A.J. (1978). Categorical and contextual bases of person memory and stereotyping. *Journal of Personality and Social Psychology, 37,* 778–793.

Terborg-Penn, R. (1998). *African American women in the struggle for the vote, 1850–1920.* Bloomington: Indiana University Press.

Terpstra, D.E. (1996). The effects of diversity on sexual harassment: Some recommendations for research. *Employee Responsibilities and Rights Journal, 9,* 303–313.

Terpstra, D.E., & Baker, D. (1986). Psychological and demographic correlates of perception of sexual harassment. *Genetic, Social and General Psychology Monographs, 112,* 459–478.

Tetlock, P.E. (1999). Accountability theory: Mixing properties of human agents with properties of social systems. In L.L. Thompson, J.M. Levine, & D.M. Messick (Eds.), *Shared cognition in organizations: The management of knowledge. LEA's organization and management series* (pp. 117–137). Mahwah, NJ: Erlbaum.

Tetlock, P.E., Skitka, L., & Boettger, R. (1989). Social and cognitive strategies for coping with accountability: Conformity, complexity, and bolstering. *Journal of Personality and Social Psychology, 57*(4), 632–640.

Thacker, R.A., & Gohmann, S.F. (1996). Emotional and psychological consequences of sexual harassment: A descriptive study. *Journal of Psychology, 130,* 429–446.

Theodore, A. (1986). *The campus troublemakers: Academic women in protest.* Houston, TX: Cap and Crown Press.

Thibaut, J.W., & Kelley, H.H. (1959). *The social psychology of groups.* New York: Wiley.

Thoits, P.A., & Virshup, L.K. (1997). Me's and we's: Forms and functions of social identities. In R.D. Ashmore & L. Jussim (Eds.), *Self and identity: Fundamental issues* (pp. 106–133). New York: Oxford University Press.

Thomas, C. (1997). The baby and the bath water: Disabled women and motherhood in social context. *Sociology of Health and Illness, 19,* 622–643.

Thompson, B.W. (1995). *A hunger so wide and deep.* Minneapolis: University of Minnesota Press.

Thompson, E.H., & Pleck, J.H. (1986). The structure of male role norms. *American Behavioral Scientist, 29,* 531–543.

Thompson, E.H., & Pleck, J.H. (1995). Masculinity ideologies: A review of research and instrumentation of men and masculinities. In R.F. Levant & W.S. Pollack (Eds.), *A new psychology of men* (pp. 129–163). New York: Basic Books.

Thompson, E.H., Pleck, J.H., & Ferrera, D.L. (1992). Men and masculinities: Scales for masculinity ideology and masculinity-related constructs. *Sex Roles, 27,* 573–607.

Thompson, L. (1991). Family work: Women's sense of fairness. *Journal of Family Issues, 12,* 181–196.

Thompson, L., & Walker, A.J. (1989). Gender in families: Women and men in marriage, work and parenthood. *Journal of Marriage and the Family, 51,* 845–871.

Thompson, L., & Walker, A.J. (1995). The place of feminism in family studies. *Journal of Marriage and the Family, 57,* 847–865.

Thompson, S. (1990). Putting a big thing into a little hole: Teenage girls' accounts of sexual initiation. *Journal of Sex Research, 27*(3), 341–361.

Thompson, S. (1992). Search for tomorrow: On feminism and the reconstruction of teen romance. In C.S. Vance (Ed.), *Pleasure and danger: Exploring female sexuality* (pp. 350–384). London: Pandora Press.

Thompson, S. (1995). *Going all the way: Teenage girls' tales of sex, romance and pregnancy.* New York: Hill and Wang.

Thompson, S.K. (1975). Gender labels and early sex role development. *Child Development, 46,* 339–347.

Thomsen, C.J., Basu, A.M., & Reinitz, M.T. (1995). Effects of women's studies courses on gender-related attitudes of women and men. *Psychology of Women Quarterly, 19,* 419–426.

Thomson, R., & Holland, J. (1994). Young women and safer (hetero) sex: Context, constraints and strategies. In C. Kitzinger & S. Wilkinson (Eds.), *Women and health: Feminist perspectives* (pp. 13–32). London: Falmer Press.

Thorne, B. (1993). *Gender play: Girls and boys in school.* New Brunswick, NJ: Rutgers University Press.

Thorne, B., & Gilbert, L.A. (1998). Antecedents of work and family role expectations of college men. *Journal of Family Psychology, 12*(2), 259–267.

Thorne, B., & Henley, N. (Eds.). (1975). *Language and sex: Differences and dominance.* Rowley, MA: Newbury House.

Thorne, B., Kramarae, C., & Henley, N. (Eds.). (1983). *Language, gender and society.* Rowley, MA: Newbury House.

Thornhill, R., & Moller, A.P. (1997). Developmental stability, disease and medicine. *Biological Review, 72,* 497–548.

Thornton, H.B., & Lea, S.J. (1992). An investigation into the needs of people living with multiple sclerosis and their families. *Disability, Handicap, & Society, 7,* 321–338.

Tiefer, L. (1978). The context and consequences of contemporary sex research: A feminist perspective. In T.E. McGill, D.A. Dewsbury, & B.D. Sachs (Ed.), *Sex and behavior: Status and prospectus.* New York: Plenum Press.

Tiefer, L. (1987). Social constructionism and the study of human sexuality. *Review of Personality and Social Psychology, 7,* 77–94.

Tiefer, L. (1991). A brief history of the Association for Women in Psychology: 1969–1991. *Psychology of Women Quarterly, 15,* 635–649.

Tiefer, L. (1992). Critique of the *DSM-III-R* nosology of sexual dysfunctions. *Psychiatric Medicine, 10,* 227–246.

Tiefer, L. (1995). *Sex is not a natural act and other essays.* Boulder, CO: Westview Press.

Tiefer, L. (1996). Towards a feminist sex therapy. *Women and Therapy, 19,* 53–64.

Tiefer, L. (2000, March). *Beyond the biomedical model, despite the seductions of Viagramania.* Paper presented at the conference of the Association for Women in Psychology, Salt Lake City, UT.

Tilby, P.J., & Kalin, R. (1980). Effects of sex-role deviant lifestyles in otherwise normal persons on the perception of maladjustment. *Sex Roles, 6,* 581–592.

Till, F. (1980). *Sexual harassment: A report on the sexual harassment of students.* Washington, DC: National Advisory Council on Women's Educational Program.

Timmer, S.G., Eccles, J., & O'Brien, K. (1985). How children use time. In J.T. Juster & F.P. Stafford (Eds.), *Time, goods, and well-being* (pp. 353–382). Ann Arbor, MI: Institute for Social Research.

Ting-Toomey, S. (1991). Intimacy expression in three cultures: France, Japan, and the U.S. *International Journal of Intercultural Relations, 15,* 29–46.

Tizard, B. (1991). Employed mothers and the care of young children. In A. Phoenix, A. Woollett, & E. Lloyd (Eds.), *Motherhood: Meanings, practices and ideologies* (pp. 178–194). London: Sage.

Tizard, B., & Hughes, M. (1984). *Young children learning: Talking and thinking at home and school.* London: Fontana.

Tjaden, P., & Thoennes, N. (1998). *Stalking in American: Findings from the national violence against women survey.* Denver, CO: Center for Policy Research.

Tobin, J.N., Wassertheil-Smoller, S., Wexler, J.P., Steingart, R.M., Budner, N., Lense, L., & Wachpress, J. (1987). Sex bias in considering coronary bypass surgery. *Annals of Internal Medicine, 107,* 19–25.

Tolman, D.L. (1994a). Daring to desire: Culture and the bodies of adolescent girls. In J. Irvine (Ed.), *Sexual cultures: Adolescents, communities and the construction of identity.* Philadelphia: Temple University Press.

Tolman, D.L. (1994b). Doing desire: Adolescent girls' struggles for/with sexuality. *Gender and Society, 8*(3), 324–342.

Tolman, D.L. (1996). Adolescent girls' sexuality: Debunking the myth of the urban girl. In B.J.R. Leadbeater & N. Way (Eds.), *Urban girls: Resisting stereotypes, creating identities* (pp. 255–271). New York: New York University Press.

Tolman, D.L. (1999a). Female adolescent sexuality in relational context: Beyond sexual decision making. In N.G. Johnson, M.C. Roberts, & J. Worell (Eds.), *Beyond appearance: A new look at adolescent girls* (pp. 227–246). Washington, DC: American Psychological Association.

Tolman, D.L. (1999b). Femininity as a barrier to positive sexual health for adolescent girls. *Journal of the American Medical Women's Association, 54*(3), 133–138.

Tolman, D.L. (2000). Object lessons: Romance, violation and female adolescent sexual desire. *Journal of Sex Education and Therapy, 25*(1), 70–79.

Tolman, D.L., & Debold, E. (1993). Conflicts of body and image: Female adolescents, desire, and the no-body body. In P. Fallon, M. Katzman, & S. Wooley (Eds.), *Feminist perspectives on eating disorders* (pp. 301–317). New York: Guilford Press.

Tolman, D.L., & Higgins, T. (1996). How being a good girl can be bad for girls. In N.B. Maglin & D. Perry (Eds.), *Good girls/bad girls: Women, sex, violence and power in the 1990s* (pp. 205–225). New Brunswick, NJ: Rutgers University Press.

Tolman, D.L., & Porche, M.V. (2000). The Adolescent Femininity Ideology Scale: Development and validation of a new measure of gender. *Psychology of Women Quarterly, 24*(3), 365–376.

Tolman, D.L., & Szalacha, L.A. (1999). Dimensions of desire: Bridging qualitative and quantitative methods in a study of female adolescent sexuality. *Psychology of Women Quarterly, 23*(2), 7–39.

Toner, B.B., Segal, Z.V., Emmott, S., & Myran, D. (2000). *Chronic gut response: A cognitive-behavioral perspective on irritable bowel syndrome.* New York: Guilford Press.

Tong, R. (1998). *Feminist thought: A more comprehensive introduction* (2nd ed.). Boulder CO: Westview.

Tontodonato, P., & Crew, B.K. (1992). Dating violence, social learning theory, and gender: A multivariate analysis. *Violence and Victims, 7,* 3–14.

Toro, P.A., Trickett, E.F., Wall, D.D., & Salem, D.A. (1991). Homelessness in the United States: An ecological perspective. *American Psychologist, 46,* 1208–1218.

Torres, L. (1992). Women and language: From sex differences to power dynamics. In C. Kramarae & D. Spender (Eds.), *The knowledge explosion: Generations of feminist scholarship* (pp. 281–290). New York: Teachers College Press.

Torrez, D.J. (1997). The health of older women: A diverse experience. In J.M. Coyle (Ed.), *Handbook on women and aging* (pp. 131–148). Westport, CT: Greenwood Press.

Tougas, F., Brown, R., Beaton, A.M., & Joly, S. (1995). Neosexism: Plus ça change, plus c'est pareil. *Personality and Social Psychology Bulletin, 21*(8), 842–849.

Toupin, E. (1980). Counseling Asians: Psychotherapy in the context of racism and Asian American history. *American Journal of Orthopsychiatry, 50,* 76–86.

Towson, S.M.J., & Zanna, M.P. (1982). Toward a situational analysis of gender differences in aggression. *Sex Roles, 8,* 903–914.

Trautner, H.M., Helbing, N., Sahm, W.B., & Lohaus, A. (1989, April). *Beginning awareness-rigidity-flexibility: A Longitudinal analysis of sex-role stereotyping in 4- to 10-year-old children.* Paper presented at the meeting of the Society for Research in Child Development, Kansas City.

Travis, C.B. (1988). *Women and health psychology: Biomedical issues.* Hillsdale, NJ: Erlbaum.

Travis, C.B., Gressley, D.L., & Phillippi, R.H. (1993). Medical decision making, gender, and coronary heart disease. *Journal of Women's Health, 3,* 269–279.

Treirweiler, S.J., Neighbors, H.W., Munday, C., Thompson, E.E., Binion, V.J., & Gomez, J.P. (2000). Clinicians' attributions associated with the diagnosis of schizophrenia in African American and non-African American patients. *Journal of Consulting and Clinical Psychology, 68,* 171–175.

Trimboli, C., & Walker, M.B. (1984). Switching pauses in cooperative and competitive conversations. *Journal of Experimental Social Psychology, 20,* 297–311.

Trinh, T. Minh-ha. (1989). *Woman, native, other: Writing postcoloniality and feminism.* Bloomington: Indiana University Press.

Trippet, S.E., & Bain, J. (1992). Reasons American lesbians fail to seek traditional health care. *Health Care for Women International, 13,* 145–154.

Trivers, R.L. (1972). Parental investment and sexual selection. In B. Campbell (Ed.), *Sexual selection and the descent of man* (pp. 136–179). Chicago: Aldine.

Trivers, R.L. (1985). *Social evolution.* Menlo Park, CA: Benjamin/Cummings.

Trivers, R.L. (1991). Deceit and self-deception: The relationship between communication and consciousness. In M. Robinson & L. Tiger (Eds.), *Man and beast revisited* (pp. 175–191). Washington, DC: Smithsonian.

Trivers, R.L. (in press). The elements of a scientific theory of self-deception. *Annals of the New York Academy of Sciences.*

Trivers, R.L., & Williard, E.E. (1973). Natural selection to vary the sex ratio of offspring. *Science, 179,* 90–92.

Tronto, J. (1993). *Moral boundaries: A political argument for an ethic of care.* New York: Routledge.

Trotta, P. (1980). Breat self-examination: Factors influencing compliance. *Oncology Nursing Forum, 7*(3), 13–17.

True, H.R., Greene, B., Lopez, S., & Trimble, J. (1993). Ethnocultural diversity in clinical psychology. *Clinical Psychologist, 46*(2), 50–63.

Turk-Charles, S., Rose, T., & Gatz, M. (1996). The significance of gender in the treatment of older adults. In L.L. Carstensen, B.A. Edelstein, & L. Dornbrand (Eds.), *Practical handbook of clinical gerontology* (pp. 107–128). Thousand Oaks, CA: Sage.

Turner, M.J., & Shapiro, C.M. (1992). The biochemistry of anorexia nervosa. *International Journal of Eating Disorders, 12,* 179–193.

Turner, P.J., & Gervai, J. (1995). A multidimensional study of gender typing in preschool children and their parents: Personality, attitudes, preferences, behavior, and cultural differences. *Developmental Psychology, 31,* 759–772.

Turner, S. (1999). Intersex identities. *Gender and Socitey, 13*(4), 457–479.

Turner-Bowker, D.M. (1996). Gender stereotyped descriptors in children's picture books: Does "Curious Jane" exist in the literature? *Sex Roles, 35,* 461–488.

Tversky, A. (1977). Features of similarity. *Psychological Review, 84,* 327–352.

Twenge, J.M. (1997a). Attitudes toward women, 1970–1995: A meta-analysis. *Psychology of Women Quarterly, 21*(1), 35–51.

Twenge, J.M. (1997b). Changes in masculine and feminine traits over time: A meta-analysis. *Sex Roles, 36,* 305–325.

Twenge, J.M. (1998). Assertiveness, sociability and anxiety: A cross-temporal meta-analysis, 1928–1993. Unpublished doctoral dissertation, University of Michigan, Ann Arbor.

Twenge, J.M. (1999). Mapping gender: The multifactorial approach and the organization of gender-related attributes. *Psychology of Women Quarterly, 23*, 485–502.

Ullman, S. (1997). Review and critique of empirical studies of rape avoidance. *Criminal Justice and Behavior, 24*, 177–204.

Umbertson, D., Wortman, C.B., & Kessler, R.C. (1992). Widowhood and depression: Explaining long-term gender differences in vulnerability. *Journal of Health and Social Behavior, 33*, 10–24.

Unger, R.K. (1976). Male is greater than female: The socialization of status inequality. *Counseling Psychologist, 6*(2), 2–9.

Unger, R.K. (1979a). *Female and male: Psychological perspectives.* New York: Harper & Row.

Unger, R.K. (1979b). Toward a redefinition of sex and gender. *American Psychologist, 34*, 1085–1094.

Unger, R.K. (1982). Advocacy versus scholarship revisited: Issues in the psychology of women. *Psychology of Women Quarterly, 7*, 5–17.

Unger, R.K. (1983). Through the looking glass: No Wonderland yet! (The reciprocal relationship between methodology and models of reality.) *Psychology of Women Quarterly, 8*, 9–32.

Unger, R.K. (1984–1985). Explorations in feminist ideology: Surprising consistencies and unexamined conflicts. *Imagination, Cognition and Personality, 4*(4), 397–405.

Unger, R.K. (1986). SPSSI Council: A collective biography. *Journal of Social Issues, 42*(4), 81–88.

Unger, R.K. (1988). Psychological, feminist, and personal epistemology: Transcending contradiction. In M. Gergen (Ed.), *Feminist thought and the structure of knowledge* (pp. 124–141). New York: New York University Press.

Unger, R.K. (1989a). Explorations in feminist ideology: Surprising consistencies and unexamined conflicts. In R. Unger (Ed.), *Representations: Social constructions of gender* (pp. 203–211). New York: Baywood.

Unger, R.K. (Ed.). (1989b). *Representations: Social constructions of gender.* Amityville, NY: Baywood.

Unger, R.K. (1989c). Sex, gender and epistemology. In M. Crawford & M. Gentry (Eds.), *Gender and thought* (pp. 17–35). New York: Springer-Verlag.

Unger, R.K. (1990). Imperfect reflections of reality: Psychology constructs gender. In R.T. Hare-Mustin & J. Marecek (Eds.), *Making a difference: Psychology and the construction of gender* (pp. 102–149). New Haven, CT: Yale University Press.

Unger, R.K. (1992). Will the real sex difference please stand up? *Feminism and Psychology, 2*, 231–238.

Unger, R.K. (1995). Conclusion: Cultural diversity and the future of feminist psychology. In H. Landrine (Ed.), *Bringing cultural diversity to feminist psychology: Theory, research, and practice* (pp. 413–431). Washington, DC: American Psychological Association.

Unger, R.K. (1996). Using the master's tools: Epistemology and empiricism. In S. Wilkinson (Ed.), *Feminist social psychologies: International perspectives* (pp. 165–181). Buckingham, England: Open University Press.

Unger, R.K. (1998). *Resisting gender: Twenty-five years of feminist psychology.* London: Sage.

Unger, R.K. (1999). Comment on "focus groups." *Psychology of Women Quarterly, 23*, 245–246.

Unger, R., & Crawford, M. (1992). *Women and gender: A feminist psychology.* New York: McGraw-Hill.

Unger, R.K., & Crawford, M. (1993). Commentary: The troubled relationship between terms and concepts. *Psychological Science, 4*, 122–124.

Unger, R., & Crawford, M. (1996). *Women and gender: A feminist psychology* (2nd ed.). New York: McGraw-Hill.

Unger, R.K., & Denmark, F.L. (1975). *Woman: Dependent or independent variable?* New York: Psychological Dimensions.

Unger, R.K., Draper, R.D., & Pendergrass, M.L. (1986). Personal epistemology and personal experience. *Journal of Social Issues, 42*(2), 67–79.

Unger, R.K., Hilderbrand, M., & Madar, T. (1982). Physical attractiveness and assumptions about social deviance: Some sex-by-sex comparisons. *Personality and Social Psychology Bulletin, 8*, 293–301.

Unger, R.K., & Kahn, A.S. (1998). Carolyn Wood Sherif: A prescient wisdom. *Feminism and Psychology, 8*, 51–57.

Unger, R.K., O'Leary, V.E., & Fabian, S. (1977). *Membership characteristics of the Division of the Psychology of Women of the American Psychological Association.* Unpublished report to Division 35 executive committee.

Unger, R.K., Raymond, B.J., & Levine, S. (1974). Are women discriminated against? Sometimes! *International Journal of Group Tensions, 4*, 71–81.

Uniform crime report. (1985). Washington, DC: U.S. Federal Bureau of Investigations, U.S. Department of Justice.

United Nations. (1995). *The world's women 1995: Trends and statistics.* New York: Author.

United Nations Development Programme. (1998). *Human development report.* New York: Oxford University Press.

United States Department of Labor. (1999). *Highlights of women's earnings in 1998*(928). Washington, DC: Bureau of Labor Statistics.

United States Merit Systems Protection Board. (1981). *Sexual harassment in the federal workplace: Is it a problem?* Washington, DC: U.S. Government Printing Office.

United States Merit Systems Protection Board. (1988). *Sexual harassment in the federal government: An update.* Washington, DC: U.S. Government Printing Office.

United States Merit Systems Protection Board. (1995). *Sexual harassment in the federal workplace: Trends, progress, continuing challenges.* Washington, DC: U.S. Government Printing Office.

Updegraff, K.A., McHale, S.M., & Crouter, A.C. (1996). Gender roles in marriage: What do they mean for girls' and boys' school achievement? *Journal of Youth and Adolescence, 25,* 73–88.

Urberg, K.A. (1982). The development of the concepts of masculinity and femininity in young children. *Sex Roles, 8,* 659–668.

Urlich, M., & Weatherell, A. (2000). Motherhood and infertility: Viewing motherhood through the lens of infertility. *Feminism and Psychology, 20,* 323–336.

U.S. Bureau of the Census. (1997). *Statistical abstract of the United States* (117th ed.). Washington, DC: U.S. Government Printing Office.

U.S. Bureau of Labor Statistics. (1997, September). *Monthly Labor Review Online, 120*(9). Available: http://stats.bls.gov/opub/mlr/1997/09/contents.htm

U.S. Bureau of Labor Statistics. (1999). *Labor force statistics derived from the current population survey.* Washington, DC: U.S. Government Printing Office.

Ussher, J., & Nicolson, P. (1992). *Gender issues in clinical psychology.* London: Routledge.

Ussher, J.M. (1989). *Psychology of the female body.* London: Routledge.

Ussher, J.M. (Ed.). (1997). *Body talk: The material and discursive regulation of sexuality, madness and reproduction.* London: Routledge.

Ussher, J.M. (1999). Eclecticism and methodological pluralism. *Psychology of Women Quarterly, 23,* 41–46.

Valdes, L.F., Baron, A., & Ponce, F.Q. (1987). Counseling Hispanic men. In M. Scher, M. Stevens, G. Good, & G. Eichenfield (Eds.), *Handbook of counseling and psychotherapy with men* (pp. 203–217). Newbury Park, CA: Sage.s

Valian, V. (1998). *Why so slow? The advancement of women.* Cambridge, MA: MIT Press.

Vandello, J.A., & Cohen, D. (1999). Patterns of individualism and collectivism across the United States. *Journal of Personality and Social Psychology, 77,* 279–292.

Van Den Bergh, N. (1987). Renaming: Vehicle for empowerment. In J. Penfield (Ed.), *Women and language in transition* (pp. 130–136). Albany: State University of New York Press.

van den Brink-Muinen, A., Bensing, J.M., & Kerssens, J.J. (1998). Gender and communication style in general practice: Differences between women's health care and regular health care. *Medical Care, 36,* 100–106.

van den Wijngaard, M. (1997). *Reinventing the sexes: The biomedical construction of femininity and masculinity.* Bloomington: Indiana University Press.

Vandewater, E.A., Ostrove, J.M., & Stewart, A.J. (1997). Predicting women's well-being in midlife: The importance of personality development and social role involvements. *Journal of Personality and Social Psychology, 72,* 1147–1160.

van Dijk, T.A. (1993). Principles of critical discourse analysis. *Discourse and Society, 4*(2), 249–283.

Vangelisti, A.L., & Daly, J.A. (1997). Gender differences in standards for romantic relationships. *Personal Relationships, 4,* 203–219.

Van Horn, K.R., Arnone, A., Nesbitt, K., Desilets, L., Sears, T., Giffin, M., & Brudi, R. (1997). Physical distance and interpersonal characteristics in college students' romantic relationships. *Personal Relationships, 4,* 25–34.

VanHyning, M. (1993). *Crossed signals: How to say NO to sexual harassment.* Los Angeles: Infotrends Press.

Van Vollenhoven, R.E., & McGuire, J.L. (1994). Estrogen, progesterone, and testosterone: Can they be used to treat autoimmune diseases? *Cleveland Clinic Journal of Medicine, 61,* 276–284.

Varvaro, F.F., Sereika, S.M., Zullo, T.G., & Robertson, R.J. (1996). Fatigue in women with myocardial infarction. *Health Care for Women International, 17,* 593–602.

Vaux, A. (1993). Paradigmatic assumptions in sexual harassment research: Being guided without being misled. *Journal of Vocational Behavior, 42,* 116–135.

Vaz, K.M. (Ed.). (1995). *Black women in America.* Thousand Oaks, CA: Sage.

Vener, A.M., & Snyder, C.A. (1966). The preschool child's awareness and anticipation of adult sex-roles. *Sociometry, 29,* 159–168.

Veniegas, R.C., Taylor, P.L., & Peplau, L.A. (1999). Guide to resources about gender, culture, and ethnicity. In L.A. Peplau, S.C. DeBro, R.C. Veniegas, & P.L. Taylor (Eds.), *Gender, culture, and ethnicity* (pp. 1–14). Mountain View, CA: Mayfield.

Verbrugge, L.M. (1979). Female illness rates and illness behavior: Testing hypothese about sex differences in health. *Women and Health, 4,* 61–79.

Verbrugge, L.M. (1980). Sex differences in complaints and diagnoses. *Journal of Behavioral Medicine, 3,* 327–356.

Verbrugge, L.M. (1990). The twain meet: Empirical explanations for sex differences in health and mortality. In M.G. Ory & H.R. Warner (Eds.), *Gender, health, and longevity* (pp. 159–199). New York: Springer.

Verkauf, B.S., & Jones, H.W. (1970). Masculinization of the female genitalia in congenital adrenal hyperplasia: Relationship to the salt losing variety of the disease. *Southern Medical Journal, 63,* 634–638.

Vicary, J.R., Klingman, L.R., & Harkness, W.L. (1995). Risk factors associated with date rape and sexual assault of adolescent girls. *Journal of Adolescence, 18,* 289–306.

Vieth, I. (1965). *Hysteria: The history of a disease.* Chicago: University of Chicago Press.

Vilain, E., & McCabe, E.R.B. (1998). Mammalian sex determination: From gonads to brain. *Molecular Genetics and Metabolism, 65,* 74–84.

Vogel, L.C.M. (1999). Predictors of posttraumatic stress disorder in a community sample of women: Examination of the role of violence and ethnicity. *Dissertation Abstracts International: The Sciences and Engineering, 59*(7–B), 3776.

Vroman, G.M. (1983). The health of older women in our society. In M. Fooden, S. Gordon, & B. Hughley (Eds.), *Genes and gender IV: The second X and women's health* (pp. 185–204). New York: Gordian Press.

Vukovich, M.C. (1996). The prevalence of sexual harassment among female family practice residents in the United States. *Violence and Victims, 11,* 175–180.

Wade, C., & Tavris, C. (1999). Gender and culture. In L. Peplau, S. DeBro, R. Veniegas, & P. Taylor (Eds.), *Gender, culture, and ethnicity: Current research about women and men* (pp. 15–22). Mountain View, CA: Mayfield.

Wade, J.C. (1998). Male reference group identity dependence: A theory of male identity. *Counseling Psychologist, 26,* 349–383.

Wade, S. (1993, January 20). Clark County: Mother gets 10 years for neglect. *Courier Journal.*

Wager, M. (2000). Childless by choice? Ambivalence and the female identity. *Feminism and Psychology, 20,* 389–395.

Waitzkin, H.B., & Waterman, B. (1974). *The exploitation of illness in capitalist society.* Indianapolis, IN: Bobbs-Merrill.

Waldo, C.R., Berdahl, J.L., & Fitzgerald, L.F. (1998). Are men sexually harassed? If so, by whom? *Law and Human Behavior, 22,* 59–79.

Walker, A.J. (1992). Conceptual perspectives on gender and caregiving. In J.W. Dwyer & R.T. Coward (Eds.), *Gender, families and elder care* (pp. 34–46). Newbury Park, CA: Sage.

Walker, L. (1999). Psychology and domestic violence around the world. *American Psychologist, 54,* 21–29.

Walker, L.E. (1994). *Abused women and survivor therapy: A practical guide for the psychotherapist.* Washington, DC: American Psychological Association.

Walker-Andrews, A.S., Bahrick, L.E., Raglioni, S.S., & Diaz, I. (1991). Infants' bimodal perception of gender. *Ecological Psychology, 3,* 55–75.

Walkerdine, V. (1990). *Schoolgirl fictions.* New York: Verso.

Walkerdine, V. (1996a). Special issue on social class. *Feminism and Psychology* 6(3).

Walkerdine, V. (1996b). Working-class women: Psychological and social aspects of survival. In S. Wilkinson (Ed.), *Feminist social psychologies: International perspectives* (pp. 145–162). Buckingham, England: Open University Press.

Walkerdine, V., & Lucey, H. (1989). *Democracy in the kitchen: Regulating mothers and socializing daughters.* London: Virago.

Wallen, J., Waitzkin, H., & Stoekle, J. (1979). Physician stereotypes about female health and illness: A study of patient's sex and the informative process during medical interviews. *Women and Health, 4*(2), 135–146.

Wallen, K. (1996). Nature needs nurture: The interaction of hormonal and social influences on the development of behavioral sex differences in rhesus monkeys. *Hormones and Behavior, 30,* 364–378.

Waller, K. (1998). Women doctors for women patients? *British Journal of Medical Psychology, 61,* 125–135.

Wallis, L.A. (1992). Women's health: A specialty? Pros and cons. *Journal of Women's Health, 1,* 107–108.

Wallston, B.S. (1981). What are the questions in the psychology of women? A feminist approach to research. *Psychology of Women Quarterly, 5,* 597–617.

Wallston, B.S., & Grady, K.E. (1985). Integrating the feminist critique and the crisis in social psychology: Another look at research methods. In V.E. O'Leary, R.K. Unger, & B.S. Wallston (Eds.), *Women, gender, and social psychology* (pp. 7–33). Hillsdale, NJ: Erlbaum.

Walsh, F. (1993). *Normal family processes.* New York: Guildford Press.

Walsh, M., Hickey, C., & Duffy, J. (1999). Influence of item content and stereotype situation on gender differences in mathematical problem solving. *Sex Roles, 41,* 219–240.

Walsh, M.R. (1985). Academic professional women organizing for change: The struggle in psychology. *Journal of Social Issues, 41*, 17–28.

Walzer, S. (1996). Thinking about the baby: Gender and divisions of infant care. *Social Problems, 43*(2), 219–234.

Ward, J.V. (1990). Racial identity formation and transformation. In C. Gilligan, N. Lyons, & T. Hanmer (Eds.), *Making connections: The relational worlds of adolescent girls at Emma Willard School* (pp. 215–232). Cambridge, MA: Harvard University Press.

Ward, J.V. (1996). Raising resisters: The role of truth telling in the psychological development of African American girls. In B.J.R. Leadbeater & N. Way (Eds.), *Urban girls: Resisting stereotypes, creating identities* (pp. 85–99). New York: New York University Press.

Ward, J.V. (2000). *The skin we're in.* New York: Free Press.

Ward, J.V., & Taylor, J.M. (1992). Sexuality education for immigrant and minority students: Developing a culturally appropriate program. In J.T. Sears (Ed.), *Sexuality and the curriculum: The politics and practices of sexuality education* (pp. 183–202). New York: Teachers College Press.

Washington, C.S. (1987). Counseling Black men. In M. Scher, M. Stevens, G. Good, & G. Eichenfield (Eds.), *Handbook of counseling and psychotherapy with men* (pp. 192–202). Newbury Park, CA: Sage.

Waterman, C., Dawson, L., & Bologna, M. (1989). Sexual coercion in gay and lesbian relationships: Predictors and implications for support services. *Journal of Sex Research, 26*, 118–124.

Waters, M.C. (1996). The intersection of gender, race, and ethnicity in identity development in Caribbean American teens. In B.J.R. Leadbeater & N. Way (Eds.), *Urban girls: Resisting stereotypes, creating identities.* New York: New York University Press.

Watkins, P.L., Cartiglia, M.C., & Champion, J. (1998). Are Type A tendencies in women associated with eating disorder pathology? *Journal of Gender, Culture, and Health, 3*, 101–109.

Watkins, P.L., Eisler, R.M., Carpenter, L., Schechtman, K.B., & Fischer, E.B. (1991). Psychosocial and physiological correlates of male gender role stress among employed adults. *Behavioral Medicine, 17*, 86–90.

Way, N. (1996). Between experiences of betrayal and desire: Close friendships among urban adolescents. In B.J.R.Leadbeater & N. Way (Eds.), *Urban girls: Resisting stereotypes, creating identities* (pp. 173–192). New York: New York University Press.

Way, N. (1998). *Everyday courage: The lives and stories of urban teenagers.* New York: New York University Press.

Way, N., & Pahl, K. (1999). Friendship patterns among urban adolescent boys: A qualitative account. In M. Kopala & L.A. Suzuki (Eds.), *Using qualitative methods in psychology* (pp. 145–161). Thousand Oaks, CA: Sage.

Weakland, M.A., & Kite, M.E. (1999, August). *Sexual orientation and the implicit inversion model.* Paper presented at the meeting of the American Psychological Association, Boston.

Wearing, B. (1984). *The ideology of motherhood.* Sydney, Australia: Allen & Unwin.

Weaver, J.J., & Ussher, J. (1997). How motherhood changes life: A discourse analytic study with mothers of young children. *Journal of Reproductive and Infant Psychology, 15*, 51–68.

Webb, M. (1997). *The good death: The new American search to reshape the end of life.* New York: Bantam Books.

Weber, L., & Higginbotham, E. (1997). Black and White professional-managerial women's perceptions of racism and sexism in the workplace. In E. Higginbotham & M. Romero (Eds.), *Women and work: Exploring race, ethnicity, and class* (pp. 153–175). Thousand Oaks, CA: Sage.

Weeks, J. (1977). *Coming out: Homosexual politics in Britain from the nineteenth century to the present.* London: Quartet.

Weeks, J. (1981). Discourse, desire and sexual deviance. In K. Plummer (Ed.), *The making of the modern homosexual.* London: Hutchinson.

Weeks, J. (1991). *Against nature: Essays on history, sexuality, and identity.* London: Rivers Oram Press.

Weeks, J. (1998). The "homosexual role" after 30 years: An appreciation of the work of Mary McIntosh. *Sexualities, 1*(2), 131–153.

Weiner, B. (1995). *Judgments of responsibility.* New York: Guilford Press.

Weiner, H. (1991). Social and psychobiological factors in autoimmune disease. In R. Ader, D. Felton, & N. Cohen (Eds.), *Psychoneuroimmunology* (pp. 955–1011). New York: Academic Press.

Weinfeld, N.S., Sroufe, L.A., Egeland, B., & Carlson, E.A. (1999). The nature of individual differences in infant-caregiver attachment. In J. Cassidy & P.R. Shaver (Eds.), *Handbook of attachment: Theory, research, and clinical applications* (pp. 68–88). New York: Guilford Press.

Weinraub, M., Clemens, L.P., Sockloff, A., Ethridge, T., Gracely, E., & Meyers, B. (1984). The development of sex role stereotypes in the third year: Relationship to gender labeling, identity, sex-typed toy preference, and family characteristics. *Child Development, 55*, 1493–1503.

Weinstein, C.S., & Reeves, P. (1995). Gender differences in referral for neuropsychological evaluations. *Journal of Women's Health, 4*, 495–503.

Weintraub, M., & Grisglas, M.B. (1995). Single parenthood. In M. Bornstein (Ed.), *Handbook of parenting: Status and social conditions of parenting* (Vol. 3). Hillsdale, NJ: Erlbaum.

Weis, L. (1993). White male working-class youth: An exploration of relative privilege and loss. In L. Weis & M. Fine (Eds.), *Beyond silenced voices: Class, race, and gender in United States schools* (pp. 237–257). New York: State University of New York Press.

Weisman, C.S., & Teitelbaum, M.A. (1985). Physician gender and the physician-patient relationship: Recent evidence and relevant questions. *Social Science and Medicine, 20,* 1119–1127.

Weisner, T.S., Garnier, H., & Loucky, J. (1994). Domestic tasks, gender egalitarian values and children's gender typing in conventional and nonconventional families. *Sex Roles, 30,* 23–54.

Weiss, G.L., & Larson, D.L. (1990). Health value, health locus of control, and the prediction of health protective behaviors. *Social Behavior and Personality, 18,* 121–136.

Weisstein, N. (1968a). *Kinder, Küche, Kirche as scientific law: Psychology constructs the female.* Boston: New England Free Press.

Weisstein, N. (1968b). *Psychology constructs the female.* Boston: New England Free Press.

Weisstein, N. (1977). "How can a little girl like you teach a great big class of men?" the chairman said, and other adventures of a woman in science. In S. Ruddick & P. Daniels (Eds.), *Working it out* (pp. 241–250). New York: Pantheon Books.

Weisstein, N. (1993a). Power, resistance, and science: A call for a revitalized feminist psychology. *Feminism and Psychology, 3,* 239–245.

Weisstein, N. (1993b). Psychology constructs the female, *or* the fantasy life of the male psychologist. *Feminism and Psychology, 3*(2), 195–210.

Welsh, S. (1999). Gender and sexual harassment. *Annual Review of Sociology, 25,* 169–190.

Werner, P.B., & LaRussa, G.W. (1985). Persistence and change in sex-role stereotypes. *Sex Roles, 12,* 1089–1100.

Wertz, D.C. (1983). What birth has done for doctors: A historical view. *Women and Health, 8*(1), 7–24.

Wesson, M. (1992). Myths of violence and self defense: Myths for men, cautionary tales for women. *Texas Journal of Women and the Law, 1,* 1–57.

West, C. (1979). Against our will: Male interruptions of females in cross-sex conversation. *Annals of the New York Academy of Sciences, 327,* 81–97.

West, C. (1982). Why can't a woman be more like a man? An interactional note on organizational game playing for managerial women. *Work and Organizations, 9,* 5–29.

West, C. (1984). When the doctor is a lady: Power, status and gender in physician-patient encounters. *Symbolic Interaction, 7,* 87–105.

West, C., Lazar, M., & Kramarae, C. (1997). Gender in discourse. In T.A. Van Dijk (Ed.), *Discourse as social interaction* (pp. 119–143). London: Sage.

West, C., & Zimmerman, D.H. (1983). Small insults: A study of interruptions in cross-sex conversations between unacquainted persons. In B. Thorne, C. Kramarae, & N. Henley (Eds.), *Language, gender and society* (pp. 102–117). Rowley, MA: Newbury House.

West, C., & Zimmerman, D.H. (1987). Doing gender. *Gender and Society, 1,* 125–151.

Wetherell, M. (1995). Social structure, ideology and family dynamics: The case of parenting. In J. Muncie, M. Wetherell, R. Dallos, & A. Cochrane (Eds.), *Understanding the family* (pp. 213–256). London: Sage.

Wetherell, M. (1998). Positioning and interpretative repertoires: Conversation analysis and post-structuralism in dialogue. *Discourse and Society, 9*(3), 387–412.

Wetherell, M., & Edley, N. (1999). Negotiating hegemonic masculinity: Imaginary positions and psycho-discursive practices. *Feminism and Psychology, 9*(3), 335–356.

Wetherell, M., & Potter, J. (1992). *Mapping the language of racism: Discourse and the legitimation of exploitation.* London: Harvester/Wheatsheaf.

Whalen, M. (1996). *Counseling to end violence against women: A subversive model.* Thousand Oaks, CA: Sage.

Wharton, C.S. (1987). Establishing shelters for battered women: Local manifestations of a social movement. *Qualitative Sociology, 10,* 146–163.

Whelehan, I. (1995). *Modern feminist thought: From the second wave to post-feminism.* Washington Square: New York University Press.

White, C. (1988). Liberating laughter: An inquiry into the nature, content, and functions of feminist humor. In B. Bate & A. Taylor (Eds.), *Women communicating: Studies of women's talk* (pp. 75–90). Norwood, NJ: Ablex.

White, D., & Woollett, A. (1992). *Families: A context for development.* London: Falmer Press.

White, E.C. (1991). The abused Black woman: Challenging a legacy of pain. In B. Levy (Ed.), *Dating violence: Young women in danger* (pp. 84–93). Seattle, WA: Seal Press.

White, J.W., & Bondurant, B. (1996). Gendered violence. In J.T. Wood (Ed.), *Gendered relationships* (pp. 197–210). Mountain View, CA: Mayfield.

White, J.W., Bondurant, B., & Donat, P.L.N. (2000). Violence against women. In M. Crawford & R. Unger (Eds.), *Women and gender: A feminist psychology* (3rd ed., pp. 481–520). New York: McGraw-Hill.

White, J.W., Holland, L., Mazurek, C., & Lyndon, A. (1998, October). *Sexual assault experiences among community college students.* Paper presented at annual meeting of North Carolina Coalition against Sexual Assault, Asheville, NC.

White, J.W., & Humphrey, J.A. (1993, August 20). *Sexual revictimization: A longitudinal perspective.* Paper presented at American Psychological Association, Toronto, Canada.

White, J.W., & Humphrey, J.A. (1994). Female aggression in heterosexual relationships. *Aggressive Behavior, 20,* 195–202.

White, J.W., & Humphrey, J.A. (1999, March). *The social context of violence against women.* Paper presented at Southeastern Women's Studies Conference, Raleigh, NC.

White, J.W., & Koss, M.P. (1991). Courtship violence: Incidence in a national sample of higher education students. *Violence and Victims, 6,* 247–257.

White, J.W., & Koss, M.P. (1993). Adolescent sexual aggression within heterosexual relationships: Prevalence, characteristics and causes. In H.G. Barbabee, W.L. Marshall, & D.R. Laws (Eds.), *The juvenile sex offender* (pp. 182–202). New York: Guilford Press.

White, J.W., Koss, M.P., & Kissling, G. (1991, June 15). *An empirical test of a theoretical model of courtship violence.* Paper presented at the American Psychological Society, Washington, DC.

White, J.W., & Kowalski, R.M. (1994). Deconstructing the myth of the nonaggressive woman: A feminist analysis. *Psychology of Women Quarterly, 18,* 487–508.

White, J.W., & Kowalski, R.M. (1998). Violence against women: An integrative perspective. In R.G. Geen & E. Donnerstein (Eds.), *Perspectives on human aggression.* New York: Academic Press.

White, J.W., Merrill, L., & Koss, M.P. (1999). *Predictors of premilitary courtship violence in a Navy recruit sample* (Tech. Rep. No. 99–19). San Diego, CA: Naval Health Research Center, Bureau of Medicine and Surgery.

White, J.W., Smith, P.H., Koss, M.P., & Figueredo, A.J. (2000). Intimate partner aggression: What have we learned? Commentary on Archer's meta-analysis. *Psychological Bulletin.*

Whitley, B.E. (1984). Sex-role orientation and psychological well-being: Two meta-analyses. *Sex Roles, 12,* 207–225.

Whitley, B.E., & Kite, M.E. (1995). Sex differences in attitudes toward homosexuality: A comment on *Oliver and Hyde* (1993). *Psychological Bulletin, 117,* 146–154.

Whittaker, T. (1997). Violence, gender, and elder abuse: Toward a feminist analysis and practice. In L.L. O'Toole & J.R. Schiffman (Eds.), *Gender violence: Interdisciplinary perspectives* (pp. 294–303). New York: New York University Press.

Widdicombe, S. (1995). Identity, politics and talk: A case for the mundane and the everyday. In S. Wilkinson & C. Kitzinger (Eds.), *Feminism and discourse: Psychological perspectives* (pp. 106–127). London: Sage.

Wiener, R.L., Hurt, L., Russell, B., Mannen, K., & Gasper, C. (1997). Perceptions of sexual harassment: The effects of gender, legal standard, and ambivalent sexism. *Law and Human Behavior, 21,* 71–93.

Wilkie, J.R., Ferree, M.M., & Ratcliff, K.S. (1998). Gender and families: Marital satisfaction in two earner couples. *Journal of Marriage and the Family, 60,* 577–594.

Wilkinson, D. (1999). Reframing family ethnicity in America. In H.P. McAdoo (Ed.), *Family ethnicity: Strength in diversity* (2nd ed., pp. 15–60). Thousand Oaks, CA: Sage.

Wilkinson, S. (1990a). Women's organisations in psychology: Institutional constraints on social change. *Australian Psychologist, 25,* 256–269.

Wilkinson, S. (1990b). Women organizing within psychology. In E. Burman (Ed.), *Feminists and psychological practice* (pp. 140–151). London: Sage.

Wilkinson, S. (1991). Institutional power and historical hegemony: A reply to Williams (1991). *Australian Psychologist, 26,* 206–208.

Wilkinson, S. (Ed.). (1996a). *Feminist social psychologies: International perspectives.* Buckingham, England: Open University Press.

Wilkinson, S. (1996b). Representing the other: I. Editor's introduction. *Feminism and Psychology, 6,* 43–44.

Wilkinson, S. (1997a). Feminist psychology. In D. Fox & I. Prilleltensky (Eds.), *Critical psychology: An introduction* (pp. 247–264). London: Sage.

Wilkinson, S. (1997b). Prioritizing the political: Feminist psychology. In T. Ibanez & L. Inguez (Eds.), *Critical social psychology* (pp. 178–194). London: Sage.

Wilkinson, S. (1998a). Focus groups in health research: Exploring the meanings of health and illness. *Journal of Health Psychology, 3*(3), 329–348.

Wilkinson, S. (1998b). Focus group methodology: A review. *International Journal of Social Research Methodology, 1*(3), 181–203.

Wilkinson, S. (1999). Focus groups: A feminist method. *Psychology of Women Quarterly, 23,* 221–244.

Wilkinson, S. (2000a). Breast cancer: A feminist perspective. In J.M. Ussher (Ed.), *Women's health: An International reader.* Leicester, England: British Psychological Society.

Wilkinson, S. (2000b). Feminist research traditions in health psychology: Breast cancer research. *Journal of Health Psychology, 5*(3).

Wilkinson, S. (2000c). Women with breast cancer talking causes: Comparing content, biographical and discursive analyses. *Journal of Health Psychology.*

Wilkinson, S., & Kitzinger, C.C., (Eds.). (1993a). *Heterosexuality: A feminism and psychology reader.* London: Sage.

Wilkinson, S., & Kitzinger, C. (1993b). Whose breast is it anyway? A feminist consideration of advice and treatment for breast cancer. *Women's Studies International Forum, 16,* 229–238.

Wilkinson, S., & Kitzinger, C. (Eds.). (1995). *Feminism and discourse: Psychological perspectives.* London: Sage.

Wilkinson, S., & Kitzinger, C. (Eds.). (1996). *Representing the other: A feminism and psychology reader.* London: Sage.

Wilkinson, S., & Kitzinger, C. (2000). Thinking differently about thinking positive: A discursive approach to cancer patients' talk. *Social Science and Medicine.*

Wille, D.E. (1995). The 1990s: Gender differences in parenting roles. *Sex Roles, 33,* 803–817.

Williams, C.L., Giuffre, P.A., & Dellinger, K. (1999). Sexuality in the workplace: Organizational control, sexual harassment, and the pursuit of pleasure. *Annual Review of Sociology, 25,* 73–93.

Williams, G.C. (1966). *Adaptation and natural selection: A critique of some current evolutionary thought.* Princeton, NJ: Princeton University Press.

Williams, J.E., & Best, D.L. (1990a). *Measuring sex stereotypes: A multination study.* Newbury Park, CA: Sage.

Williams, J.E., & Best, D.L. (1990b). *Sex and psyche: Gender and self viewed cross-culturally.* Newbury Park, CA: Sage.

Williams, J.E., Bennett, S.M., & Best, D.L. (1975). Awareness and expression of sex stereotypes in young children. *Developmental Psychology, 11,* 635–642.

Williams, J.H. (1987). *Psychology of women: Behavior in a biosocial context.* New York: Norton.

Williams, O.J. (1992). Ethnically sensitive practice to enhance treatment participation of African American men who batter. *Families in Society, 10,* 588–595.

Williams, R., & Wittig, M.A. (1997). "I'm not a feminist but . . .": Factors contributing to the discrepancy between pro-feminist orientation and feminist social identity. *Sex Roles, 37,* 885–904.

Williams, T.J., Pepitone, M.E., Christensen, S.E., Cooke, B.M., Huberman, A.D., Breedlove, N.J., Breedlove, T.J., Jordan, C.L., & Breedlove, S.M. (2000). Finger-length ratios and sexual orientation. *Nature, 404,* 455–456.

Willig, C. (Ed.). (1999). *Applied discourse analysis: Social and psychological interventions.* Buckingham, England: Open University Press.

Wilmot, W.M., Carbaugh, D.A., & Baxter, L.A. (1985). Communicative strategies used to terminate romantic relationships. *Western Journal of Speech Communication, 49,* 204–216.

Wilmott, J. (2000). The experience of women with polycystic ovarian syndrome. *Feminism and Psychology, 10*(1), 107–116.

Wilson, J.D. (1999). The role of androgens in male gender role behavior. *Endocrine Reviews, 20,* 726–737.

Wilson, J.Q. (1993). *The moral sense.* New York: Free Press.

Wilson, M., & Daly, M. (1994). Spousal homicide. *Juristat, 14,* 1–15.

Wilson, M., & Green, R. (1971). Personality characteristics of female homosexuals. *Psychological Reports, 28,* 407–412.

Winkleby, M.A., Kraemer, H.C., Ahn, D.K., & Varady, A.N. (1998). Ethnic and socioeconomic differences in cardiovascular disease risk factors: Findings for women from the Third National Health and Nutrition Examination Survey, 1988–1994. *Journal of the American Medical Association, 280,* 356–362.

Winkler, A.E. (1998). Earnings of husbands and wives in dual-earner families. *Monthly Labor Review Online, 121*(4), 42–48. Available: http://stats.bls.gov/opub/mlr/1998/04/contents.htm

Winocur, S., Schoen, L.G., & Sirowatka, A.H. (1989). Perceptions of male and female academics within a teaching context. *Research in Higher Education, 30,* 317–329.

Winter, L. (1988). The role of sexual self-concept in the use of contraceptives. *Family Planning Perspectives, 20,* 123–127.

Wittig, M.A. (1985). Metatheoretical dilemmas in the psychology of gender. *American Psychologist, 40,* 800–811.

Wolf, D.A. (1995). Changes in the living arrangements of older women: An international study. *The Gerontologist, 35,* 724–731.

Wolf, S. (1985). A multi-factor model of deviant sexuality. *Victimology: An International Journal, 10,* 359–374.

Wolfe, J., Sharkansky, E.J., Read, J.P., Dawson, R., Martin, J.A., & Ouimette, P.C. (1998). Sexual harassment and assault as predictors of PTSD symptomatology among U.S. female Persian Gulf War military person-nel. *Journal of Interpersonal Violence, 13,* 40–57.

Wolfe, R., Morrow, J., & Fredrickson, B.L. (1996). Mood disorders in older adults. In L.L. Carstensen, B.A. Edelstein, & L. Dornbrand (Eds.), *Practical handbook of clinical gerontology* (pp. 274–303). Thousand Oaks, CA: Sage.

Wolkenstein, B.H., & Sterman, L. (1998). Unmet needs of older women in a clinic population: The discovery of possible long-term sequelae of domestic violence. *Professional Psychology: Research and Practice, 29,* 341–348.

Wollstonecraft, M. (1988). *A vindication of the rights of woman: An authoritative text, backgrounds, the Woll-stonecraft debate, criticism* (2nd ed.) [Carol H. Poston, Ed.]. New York: Norton. (Original work published 1792)

Women's Program Office. (1991). *Graduate faculty interested in the psychology of women.* Washington, DC: American Psychological Association.

Women's Program Office. (1993). *Women in the American Psychological Association.* Washington, DC: American Psychological Association.

Wood, A.D., & McHugh, M.C. (1994). Woman battering: The response of clergy. *Pastoral Psychology, 42,* 185–196.

Wood, J.T. (1997). Clarifying the issues. *Personal Relationships, 4,* 221–228.

Wood, W. (1987). Meta-analytic review of sex differences in group performance. *Psychological Bulletin, 102,* 53–71.

Wood, W., & Karten, S.J. (1986). Sex differences in interaction style as a product of perceived sex differences in competence. *Journal of Personality and Social Psychology, 50,* 341–47.

Woodward, K. (1997). Motherhood: Identities, meanings and myths. In K. Woodward (Ed.), *Identity and dif-ference: Culture, media and identities.* London: Sage.

Wooley, H.T. (1910). Psychological literature: A review of the recent literature on the psychology of sex. *Psy-chological Bulletin, 7,* 355–342.

Woolf, V. (1957). *A room of one's own.* New York: Harcourt, Brace & Jovanovich. (Original work published 1929)

Woolhandler, S., & Himmelstein, D.U. (1988). Reverse targeting of preventive services due to lack of health insurance. *Journal of the American Medical Association, 259,* 2872–2874.

Woollett, A. (1991). Having children: Accounts of childless women and women with reproductive problems. In A. Phoenix, A. Woollett, & E. Lloyd (Eds.), *Motherhood: Meanings, practices and ideologies* (pp. 47–65). London: Sage.

Woollett, A. (1996a). Infertility: From "inside/out" to "outside/in." *Feminism and Psychology, 6,* 74–78.

Woollett, A. (1996b). Reproductive decisions. In A. Walker & K. Niven (Eds.), *Psychology of reproduction: Con-ception, pregnancy and birth* (Vol. 2, pp. 1–13). Oxford, England: Butterworth-Heinemann.

Woollett, A. (1999). Families and their role in children's lives and development. In D. Messer & S. Millar (Eds.), *Exploring developmental psychology from infancy to adolescence* (pp. 323–340). London: Arnold.

Woollett, A., Dosanjh-Matwala, N., & Hadlow, J. (1991). Reproductive decision making: Asian and non-Asian women's ideas about family size, gender and spacing of children. *Journal of Reproductive and Infant Psy-chology, 9,* 237–252.

Woollett, A., & Marshall, H. (1997). Accounts of pregnancy and childbirth. In L. Yardley (Ed.), *Material dis-courses of health and illness* (pp. 176–198). London: Routledge.

Woollett, A., & Nicolson, P. (1998). The social construction of motherhood and fatherhood. In A. Walker & C. Niven (Eds.), *Psychology of reproduction: Infancy and parenthood* (Vol. 3, pp. 1–14). Oxford, England: But-terworth-Heinemann.

Woollett, A., & Parr, M. (1997). Psychological tasks for women and men in the post partum. *Journal of Repro-ductive and Infant Psychology, 15,* 159–183.

Woollett, A., & Phoenix, A. (1991). Psychological views of motherhood. In A. Phoenix, A. Woollett, & E. Lloyd (Eds.), *Motherhood: Meanings, practices and ideologies* (pp. 28–46). London: Sage.

Woollett, A., & Phoenix, A. (1996). Motherhood as pedagogy: Developmental psychology and the accounts of mothers of young children. In C. Luke (Ed.), *Feminisms and pedagogies of everyday life* (pp. 80–102). New York: State University of New York Press.

Woollett, A., & Phoenix, A. (1997). Deconstructing developmental psychology accounts of mothering. *Femi-nism and Psychology, 7*(2), 275–282.

Wooten, B.H. (1997). Gender differences in occupational employment. *Monthly Labor Review Online, 120*(4), 15–24. Available: http://stats.bls.gov/opub/mlr/1997/04/contents.htm

Worell, J. (1978). Sex roles and psychological well-being: Perspectives on methodology. *Journal of Consulting and Clinical Psychology, 46,* 777–791.

Worell, J. (1993a). Gender in close relationships: Public policy vs. personal prerogative. *Journal of Social Issues, 49*(3), 203–218.

Worell, J. (1993b, November). *What do we really know about feminist therapists? Approaches to research on process and outcomes.* Invited presentation, Texas Psychological Association.

Worell, J. (1996). Opening doors to feminist research. *Psychology of Women Quarterly, 20,* 469–485.

Worell, J. (2000). Feminist interventions: Life beyond symptom reduction. *Psychology of Women Quarterly, 24.*

Worell, J. (in press). Feminist therapies. In A. Kazdin (Ed.), *Encyclopedia of psychology.* Washington, DC: American Psychological Association.

Worell, J., & Chandler, R. (1996). *Personal Progress Scale.* Unpublished manuscript, University of Kentucky, Lexington.

Worell, J., Chandler, R., & Robinson, D. (1996). *Client Therapy with Women Scale.* Unpublished manuscript, University of Kentucky, Lexington.

Worell, J., Chandler, R., Robinson, D., & Cobulius, A. (1996, August). *Measuring beliefs and behaviors of feminist therapists.* Paper presented at the annual meeting of the American Psychological Association as part of a symposium titled: Evaluating process and outcomes in feminist therapy and counseling, J. Worell (Chair), Toronto.

Worell, J., & Etaugh, C. (1994). Transforming theory and research with women: Themes and variations. *Psychology of Women Quarterly, 18,* 433–450.

Worell, J., & Remer, P. (1992). *Feminist perspectives in therapy: An empowerment model for women.* New York: Wiley.

Worell, J., & Remer, P. (2000). *Empowerment therapy for women: Integrating diversity with feminist psychological practice.* New York: Wiley.

Worell, J., Stilwell, D., Robinson, D., & Oakley, D. (1999). Educating about women and gender: Cognitive, personal, and professional outcomes. *Psychology of Women Quarterly, 23.*

Work/life today. (1999). [Report]. (Available from the National Institute of Business Management, 1750 Old Meadow Road, McLean, VA 22102)

Worth, D. (1989). Sexual decision-making and AIDS: Why condom promotion among vulnerable women is likely to fail. *Studies in Family Planning, 20,* 297–307.

Worth, D.M., Matthews, P.A., & Coleman, W.R. (1990). Sex role, group affiliation, family background, and courtship violence in college students. *Journal of College Student Development, 31,* 250–254.

Wright, A.L., & Morgan, W.J. (1990). On the creation of "problem" patients. *Social Science and Medicine, 30,* 951–959.

Wright, C.I., & Fish, L.S. (1997). Feminist family therapy: The battle against subtle sexism. In N.V. Benokraitis (Ed.), *Subtle sexism: Current practice and prospects for change* (pp. 201–215). Thousand Oaks, CA: Sage.

Wright, R. (1996). The occupational masculinity of computing. In C. Cheng (Ed.), *Masculinities in organizations* (pp. 77–96). Thousand Oaks, CA: Sage.

Wyatt, G. (1985). The sexual abuse of Afro-American and White-American women in childhood. *Child Abuse and Neglect, 9,* 507–519.

Wyatt, G. (1991). Sociocultural context of African American and White American women's rape. *Journal of Social Issues, 48,* 77–91.

Wyatt, G.E., Guthrie, D., & Notgrass, C.M. (1992). Differential effects of women's child sexual abuse and subsequent sexual revictimization. *Journal of Consulting and Clinical Psychology, 60,* 167–173.

Wyche, K.F. (1995). Psychology and African-American women: Findings from applied research. *Applied and Preventive Psychology, 2,* 115–121.

Wyche, K.F. (1996). Conceptualizations of social class in African American women: Congruence of client and therapist definition. *Women and Therapy, 16*(3/4), 35–44.

Wyche, K.F. (1998). Let me suffer so my kids won't: African American mothers living with HIV/AIDS. In C. Garcia Coll, J. Surrey, & K. Weingarten (Eds.), *Mothering against the odds: Diverse voices of contemporary mothers.* New York: Guilford Press.

Wyche, K.F., & Crosby, F.J. (Eds.). (1996). *Women's ethnicities: Journeys through psychology.* Boulder, CO: Westview Press.

Wyche, K.F., & Rice, J.K. (1997). Feminist therapy: From dialogue to tenets. In J. Worell & N.G. Johnson (Eds.), *Shaping the future of feminist psychology: Education, research, and practice* (pp. 57–71). Washington, DC: American Psychological Association.

Wylie, M.S. (1995, May/June). Diagnosing for dollars. *Networker, 23–34,* 65–69.

Xiong, T., & Tatum, B.D. (1999). "In my heart I will always be Hmong": One Hmong American woman's pioneering journey toward activism. In M. Romero & A.J. Stewart (Eds.), *Women's untold stories: Breaking silence, talking back, voicing complexity.* New York: Routledge.

Yama, M.F., Tovey, S.L., & Fogas, B.S. (1993). Childhood family environment and sexual abuse as predictors of anxiety and depression in adult women. *American Journal of Orthopsychiatry, 63,* 136–141.

Yamada, E.M., Tjosvold, D., & Draguns, J.G. (1983). Effects of sex-linked situations and sex compositions on cooperation and style of interaction. *Sex Roles, 4,* 541–53.

Yang, K-S. (1996). Psychological transformation of the Chinese people as a result of societal modernization. In M. Bond (Ed.), *Handbook of Chinese psychology* (pp. 479–498). Hong Kong: Oxford University Press.

Yardley, L. (Ed.). (1997). *Material discourses of health and illness.* London: Routledge.

Yee, D. (1997). Issues and trends afecting Asian Americans, women and aging. In J.M. Coyle (Ed.), *Handbook on women and aging* (pp. 316–334). Westport, CT: Greenwood Press.

Yee, J.L., & Schulz, R. (2000). Gender differences in psychiatric morbidity among family caregivers: A review and analysis. *The Gerontologist, 40,* 147–164.

Yee, M., & Brown, R. (1994). The development of gender differentiation in young children. *British Journal of Social Psychology, 33,* 183–196.

Yeo, E.J. (1997). Some contradictions of social motherhood. In E.J. Yeo (Ed.), *Mary Wollstonecraft and 200 years of feminisms* (pp. 121–133). New York: Rivers Oram.

Yoder, J., & Aniakudo, P. (1997). "Outsider within" the firehouse: Subordination and difference in the social interactions of African American women firefighters. *Gender and Society, 11,* 324–341.

Yoder, J.D. (1985). An academic woman as a token: A case study. *Journal of Social Issues, 41,* 61–72.

Yoder, J.D. (1991). Rethinking tokenism: Looking beyond the numbers. *Gender and Society, 5,* 178–192.

Yoder, J.D., Schleicher, T.L., & McDonald, T.W. (1998). Empowering token women leaders: The importance of organizationally legitimated credibility. *Psychology of Women Quarterly, 22,* 209–222.

Yohalem, A.M. (1993). Columbia University graduate students, 1945–1951: The vanguard of professional women. In K.D. Hulbert & D.T. Schuster (Eds.), *Women's lives through time* (pp. 140–157). San Francisco: Jossey-Bass.

Yoshihama, M. (1991). In B. Levy (Ed.), *Dating violence: Young women in danger* (pp. 84–93). Seattle, WA: Seal Press.

Yoshihama, M., Parekh, A.L., & Boyington, D. (1991) Dating violence in Asian/Pacific communities. In B. Levy (Ed.), *Dating violence: Young women in danger* (pp. 84–93). Seattle, WA: Seal Press.

Young, E.W. (1988). Nurses' attitudes toward homosexuality: Analysis of change in AIDS workshops. *Journal of Continuing Education in Nursing, 19*(1), 9–12.

Young, R.F., & Kahana, E. (1993). Gender, recovery from late life heart attack, and medical care. *Women and Health, 20*(1), 11–31.

Yount, K. (1991). Ladies, flirts, and tomboys: Strategies for managing sexual harassment in an underground coal mine. *Journal of Contemporary Ethnography, 19,* 396–422.

Yu, D.W., & Shepard, G.H. (1998). Is beauty in the eye of the beholder? *Nature, 396,* 321–322.

Yuval-Davis, N. (1997). *Gender and nation.* Thousand Oaks, CA: Sage.

Zayas, L., Torres, L., Malcolm, J., & DesRosiers, F. (1996). Clinician's definitions of ethnically sensitive therapy. *Professional Psychology: Research and Practice, 27,* 78–82.

Zemore, S.E., Fiske, S.T., & Kim, H.J. (2000). Gender stereotypes and the dynamics of social interaction. In T. Eckes & H.M. Trautner (Eds.), *Developmental social psychology of gender* (pp. 207–241). Mahwah, NJ: Earlbaum.

Zillman, D., & Weaver, J.B. (1989). Pornography and men's sexual callousness toward women. In D. Zillman & J. Bryant (Eds.), *Pornography: Research advances and policy considerations* (pp. 95–125). Hillsdale, NJ: Earlbaum.

Zimmerman, D., & West, C. (1975). Sex roles, interruptions and silence in conversation. In B. Thorne & N. Henley (Eds.), *Language and sex: Difference and dominance* (pp. 105–129). Rowley, MA: Newbury House.

Zucker, A.N. (1998). *Understanding feminist identity in three generations of college-educated women.* Unpublished doctoral dissertation, University of Michigan, Ann Arbor.

Zucker, K.J. (1999). Intersexuality and gender identity differentiation. *Annual Review of Sex Research, 10,* 1–69.

Zucker, K.J., & Bradley, S.J. (1995). *Gender identity disorder and psychosexual problems in children and adolescents.* New York: Guilford Press.

Zucker, K.J., Bradley, S.J., Oliver, G., Blake, J., Fleming, S., & Hood, J. (1996). Psychosexual development of women with congenital adrenal hyperplasia. *Hormones and Behavior, 30,* 300–318.

Zucker, K.J., Wilson-Smith, D.N., Kurita, J.A., & Stern, A. (1995). Children's appraisals of sex-typed behavior in their peers. *Sex Roles, 33,* 703–725.

Zuckerman, H., Cole, J.R., & Bruer, J.T. (Eds.). (1991). *The outer circle: Women in the scientific community.* New York: Norton.

Zweig, J.M., Barber, B.L., & Eccles, J.S. (1997). *Journal of Interpersonal Violence, 12,* 291–30.

Zwicky, A. (1997). Two lavendar issues for linguists. In A. Livia & K. Hall (Eds.), *Queerly phrased: Language, gender, and sexuality* (pp. 21–34). Oxford, England: Oxford University Press.

Author Index

Gramsci, A., 409

Granfield, R., 94

Granoff, B.J., 350

Grauerholz, E., 370, 374, 378

Gray, J., 229, 232, 255

Gready, M., 194

Green, J., 251

Green, R., 112, 236, 278

Greenberg, D.J., 117

Greene, B.A., 15, 167, 284, 318, 322, 328, 331, 332, 333, 334, 335

Greene, J.C, 49

Greenfield, P.M., 178, 345

Greenglass, E.R., 10, 414

Greenspan, M., 317

Greenstein, T.N., 163

Greenwald, A.G., 216, 364

Gremmen, I., 76, 78

Griffin, C., 277, 312, 355, 424

Griscom, J.L., 4

Grisglas, M.B., 175

Groneman, C., 305

Grossman, A.H, 187

Grossman, F.K., 76, 79

Gruber, J.E., 161, 162, 162, 370, 374, 378, 382

Guba, E.G., 36, 48

Guldner, G.T., 261

Gulick, E.E., 294

Guralnik, J.M., 190

Gurin, P., 407, 421

Gutek, B.A., 45, 158, 368, 369, 370, 371, 372, 373, 374, 375, 376, 377, 378, 379, 381, 382, 383, 384, 385, 386

Gutierrez, L.M., 322

Guy-Sheftall, B., 23

Haaf, S., 117

Haag, P., 148, 151, 154

Haaken, J., 315, 316

Hackel, L.S., 181

Hacker, H.M., 411

Hacker, S., 239

Hacking, I., 315

Haddock, G., 219, 220, 275

Hahn, S., 217, 227

Haj-Yahla, M.M., 353

Hale, G., 352

Hall, J.A., 112, 251

Hall, K., 235, 246, 248, 249

Hall, L.S., 112

Hall, M., 311

Halpern, D.F., 69

Halverson, C.F., Jr., 116, 119, 120, 125, 126

Hamburger, A.C., 301

Hamer, D.H., 111, 281, 282

Hamilton, V., 275

Hamilton, W.D., 53

Hamlet, S., 374

Hammock, G.C., 349, 350

Hanisch, C., 311

Hansen, G.L., 275

Hansen, T.F., 57

Haqq, C.M., 101

Haraway, D.J., 62

Harding, S., 21, 37, 69

Harding, V., 422

Hardy-Fanta, C., 416

Hare-Mustin, R.T., 4, 7, 21, 23, 24, 30, 31, 40, 74, 97, 229, 304, 306, 316

Harnett, O., 15

Harris, B., 5

Harris, F.C., 318

Harris, J.R., 179

Harris, L., 137

Harris, M., 360

Harris, M.B., 184

Harrison, J., 202, 206, 213

Harrison, M., 290

Harry, J., 276

Hart, B., 80, 81

Hart, J., 281, 299, 353

Hartman, A., 338

Hartmann, H., 390

Hartsock, N., 21, 133

Harvey, K., 246

Haslett, B.B., 163

Haste, H., 22

Hatala, M.N., 209

Hatch, L.R., 185

Hatchett, S.J., 270

Haug, F., 47, 389, 390, 392

Haugh, S.S., 118

Hawkes, K., 57, 169

Hay, D.F., 171, 173, 174, 177

Hayes, S.M., 375, 376, 378, 380

Hazan, C., 258, 259

Healy, J.M., 90, 91, 94, 411, 412, 413

Heaton, T.B., 173

Heaven, P., 345

Heilman, M.E., 158, 160, 226, 383

Heise, L.L., 319

Helgeson, V.S., 223, 261, 262

Helleday, J., 108

Heller, K.A., 119, 120

Helmreich, R.L., 203, 217, 224, 359

Helms, J., 204, 335

Helwig, A.A., 118, 123

Hemstreet, A.H., 291, 292

Henderson, D., 306

Henderson-King, D.H., 95, 408, 421

Hendin, H., 196

Hendrick, C., 259, 260

Hendrick, S.S., 259, 260

Hendricks, J., 197

Hendrix, W.H., 384

Henle, M., 7

Henley, N.M., 12, 14, 73, 75, 77, 224, 228, 230, 139, 246, 321

Henning, K., 41

Henwood, K., 15, 21

Hepper, P.G., 113

Heppner, M.J., 213

Herdt, G., 103

Herek, G.M., 223, 273, 274, 275, 276

Heritage, J., 231

Herman, D., 274

Herman, J., 305, 311

Herzog, W.W.,126

Hess, B.H., 120, 186, 187, 189, 194

Hesson-McInnis, M.S., 158, 162, 377

Heywood, L., 411

Hibbard, D.R., 221

Higginbotham, E., 163

Higgins, T., 149

Hill, M., 311, 312

Hill, M.S., 158, 168

Hiller, J.E., 297, 391

Hillier, L., 82, 352

Himmelstein, G., 293

Hines, M., 108, 109, 111

Hirschl, T., 380

Hochschild, A., 247, 251, 391

Hoffman, C., 118, 123, 126

Hofland, S.L., 301

Hofstede, G., 266

Hogg, M.A., 88

Holland, D.C., 346, 347

Holland, J., 153, 154

Hollander, J., 216

Hollander, N., 237

Hollenshead, J., 194, 195, 354

Subject Index

Media. *See also* Communication
    advertisements about women's bodies
        (*Continued*)
    men, portrayal of, 205
    parental attitudes about math, effect of, 71
    and sexual harassment, high profile case in,
        368
Memory, 82, 119, 121, 126, 373
Men. *See also* Masculinity
    blame for violence, shifting from, 399–400
    cultural similarities between, 325
    as generic in language, 239–240
    and homophobia, 275
    midlife issues of, 211
    resources for study of, 214
    sexual harassment of, 374–375, 378
    sexually aggressive, perceptions of, 350
Menopause, 279. *See also* Midlife
Menstruation, 143–144
Mental health. *See also* Psychotherapy; Well
        being
    critique of issues in, 303–316
    of lesbians, 278–279
    services, racist biases in, 332
    of women of color, effect of stress on, 276
Mentoring, 15
Meta-analysis. *See also* Research
    of attitudes about gender roles, 91
    of conversational interruptions, 250
    feminist positions on, 15, 71–72
    of handedness and sexual orientation, 113
    of interpersonal orientation, 253
    of leadership, 226, 361
    of memory of gender-typed play in
        childhood, 104
    of parental socialization of girls and boys,
        130, 220
    of perceptions of sexual harassment, 385
    of television and children's gender typing,
        129
Methodology. *See also* Research
    analogue studies of therapist judgments,
        critique of, 304
    feminist critique of, 14, 29–52
    innovative, need for, 315
    and multiple forms of analysis, 78
    and sampling issues, 314
    sexual harassment research, concerns about,
        386–387
Midlife, 90. 211, 279, 282–283, 296, 412, 422
Miscommunication. *See* Communication
Mother(s). *See also* Fathers; Motherhood;
        Parenting
    abuse of, 355
    changes in, as children grow up, 179

characteristics that define "good" and
        "bad," 171–174, 177
    child relationship, effect on children, 129,
        177–179
    cultural context of, 178–179
    daughter relationship, 308, 322, 408, 419
    employment of, social class issues, in, 168
    feminist, effect on daughters, 150, 420
    first-time, and identity change, 95
    legal consequences to, of failure to protect
        children, 400–403
    as political activists among Latinas, 416–417
    single, 168, 174–175, 389
    study of, in own right, 170
Motherhood, 170–182. *See also* Mothers
    and blame for children's problems, 305–306
    changes in practices of, 309
    humor about, 236
    lesbians and, 284, 396
    social context and judgments about, 401
    women's inherent suitability for, 159
Ms, 241. *See also* Language
Multicultural perspective. *See also* Racism
    on counseling women of color, 330–340
    on psychotherapy, 304, 322
    on relationships, 269–270

Naming. *See* Labeling
Narrative, 21–23, 46, 90, 336. *See also* Feminist
        experiential theory; Voice
Neosexism Scale, 217–218, 359
Nepotism, 4–5
Nonsexist:
    curriculum and children's gender-typing,
        129
    language guidelines, 240–241
    psychotherapy, 319–320
Nontraditional women, 361–363, 371, 377. *See
        also* Sexism
Nonverbal behavior, 249–251, 254–255, 364. *See
        also* Dominance; Power
Norms:
    archival research and, 47
    about entitlement, 163
    gendered, 89–90, 250–251, 304, 379
    about gender roles, 150
    about homosexuality, 276
    internalization of, 6–7
    about mate preferences, 60
    about mental health, 331
    sex differences, effect of, 41
    about violence, and legitimization of, 349,
        352
    White middle class as, 135
Nurturance, 110, 159, 185, 265–266